IISS

THE
MILITARY
BALANCE
2015

published by

Routledge
Taylor & Francis Group

for

The International Institute for Strategic Studies
ARUNDEL HOUSE | 13–15 ARUNDEL STREET | TEMPLE PLACE | LONDON | WC2R 3DX | UK

THE **MILITARY BALANCE** 2015

The International Institute for Strategic Studies
ARUNDEL HOUSE | 13–15 ARUNDEL STREET | TEMPLE PLACE | LONDON | WC2R 3DX | UK

DIRECTOR-GENERAL AND CHIEF EXECUTIVE **Dr John Chipman**
DIRECTORS FOR DEFENCE AND MILITARY ANALYSIS **Adam Ward, Alexander Nicoll**
EDITOR **James Hackett**
ASSISTANT EDITOR **Nicholas Payne**

DEFENCE AND MILITARY ANALYSIS
LAND WARFARE **Brigadier (Retd) Benjamin Barry**
MILITARY AEROSPACE **Douglas Barrie**
NAVAL FORCES AND MARITIME SECURITY **Christian Le Mière**
DEFENCE AND MILITARY RESEARCH AND ANALYSIS **Henry Boyd, Joseph Dempsey, Ian Keddie, Tom Waldwyn**
DEFENCE ECONOMICS **Giri Rajendran**

EDITORIAL **Dr Ayse Abdullah, Anna Ashton, Annabel Corser, Jessica Delaney, Sarah Johnstone, Jill Lally, Chris Raggett, Carolyn West**
DESIGN, PRODUCTION, INFORMATION GRAPHICS **John Buck, Kelly Verity**
CARTOGRAPHY **John Buck, Kelly Verity**
RESEARCH SUPPORT **Noora AlSindi, Jack Baker, Maxime Humeau**

This publication has been prepared by the Director-General and Chief Executive of the Institute and his Staff, who accept full responsibility for its contents. The views expressed herein do not, and indeed cannot, represent a consensus of views among the worldwide membership of the Institute as a whole.

FIRST PUBLISHED February 2015

© The International Institute for Strategic Studies 2015
All rights reserved. No part of this publication may be reproduced, stored, transmitted, or disseminated, in any form, or by any means, without prior written permission from Taylor & Francis, to whom all requests to reproduce copyright material should be directed, in writing.

ISBN 978-1-85743-766-9
ISSN 0459-7222

Cover images: US Navy/Lockheed Martin/Andy Wolfe; AP/Darko Vojinovic; Xinhua/Landov/PA; AP/Raqqa Media Center; US Air Force/United Launch Alliance.

The *Military Balance* (ISSN 0459-7222) is published annually by Routledge Journals, an imprint of Taylor & Francis, 4 Park Square, Milton Park, Abingdon, Oxfordshire OX14 4RN, UK.

A subscription to the institution print edition, ISSN 0459-7222, includes free access for any number of concurrent users across a local area network to the online edition, ISSN 1479-9022.

All subscriptions are payable in advance and all rates include postage. Journals are sent by air to the USA, Canada, Mexico, India, Japan and Australasia. Subscriptions are entered on an annual basis, i.e. January to December. Payment may be made by sterling cheque, dollar cheque, international money order, National Giro, or credit card (Amex, Visa, Mastercard).

Please send subscription orders to: USA/Canada: Taylor & Francis Inc., Journals Department, 325 Chestnut Street, 8th Floor, Philadelphia, PA 19106, USA. UK/Europe/Rest of World: Routledge Journals, T&F Customer Services, T&F Informa UK Ltd., Sheepen Place, Colchester, Essex, CO3 3LP, UK.

The print edition of this journal is printed on ANSI conforming acid-free paper by Bell & Bain, Glasgow, UK.

Contents

Indexes of Tables, Figures and Maps 4
Editor's Introduction 5

Part One Capabilities, Trends and Economics

Chapter 1 Defence-policy trends and analysis 9
Directed energy weapons: finally coming of age? 9; Military space systems: US ambitions to secure space 13; Hybrid warfare: challenge and response 17

Chapter 2 Comparative defence statistics 21
Defence budgets and expenditure 21; Changes in the global submarine market since 1990 23; Key defence statistics 24; Precision attack by guided artillery 26; US rebalance to the Asia-Pacific: vessel deployments 2014–20 27; Latin American fixed-wing aircraft fleets, 1994–2014 28

Chapter 3 North America 29
United States: defence policy and economics 29;
Canada: defence policy 36;
Armed forces data section 37;
Selected arms procurements and deliveries 55

Chapter 4 Europe 57
Regional defence policy and economics overviews 61;
France: defence policy and economics 64;
UK: defence policy and economics 68;
Armed forces data section 72;
Selected arms procurements and deliveries 154

Chapter 5 Russia and Eurasia 159
Russia: defence policy and economics 159;
Central Asia: defence policy 167;
Ukraine: defence policy 168;
Armed forces data section 174;
Selected arms procurements and deliveries 205

Chapter 6 Asia 207
Regional defence policy and economics overviews 207;
China: defence policy and economics 212;
India: defence policy and economics 217;
Japan: defence policy and economics 221;
Myanmar: defence policy 225
North Korea: defence policy 226;
Armed forces data section 228;
Selected arms procurements and deliveries 296

Chapter 7 Middle East and North Africa 303
Regional defence policy and economics overviews 303;
Libya: defence policy 306;
Israel: defence policy 310;
UAE: defence policy and economics 314;
Armed forces data section 319;
Selected arms procurements and deliveries 360

Chapter 8 Latin America and the Caribbean 363
Regional defence policy and economics overviews 365;
Brazil: defence policy 369;
Colombia: defence policy and economics 370;
Armed forces data section 375;
Selected arms procurements and deliveries 418

Chapter 9 Sub-Saharan Africa 421
Regional defence policy and economics overviews 423;
Kenya: defence policy and economics 425;
The Somali National Army 427;
Armed forces data section 430;
Selected arms procurements and deliveries 480

Chapter 10 Country comparisons – commitments, force levels and economics 481
Selected Training Activity 2014 482;
International Comparisons of Defence Expenditure and Military Personnel 484;
Selected Non-State Armed Groups: Observed Equipment Holdings 491

Part Two Reference

Explanatory Notes 493
Principal Land Definitions 497; Principal Naval Definitions 498; Principal Aviation Definitions 499
List of Abbreviations for Data Sections 501
Index of Country/Territory Abbreviations 503
Index of Countries and Territories 504

Index of **TABLES**

1. US National Defense Budget Function and Other Selected Budgets 1995, 2006–15 34
2. Selected Arms Procurements and Deliveries, North America 55
3. Selected Arms Procurements and Deliveries, Europe 154
4. Russian Arms Procurement 2011–13 & Approximate State Armaments Programme 2020 Objectives 167
5. Selected Arms Procurements and Deliveries, Russia and Eurasia . 205
6. Selected Arms Procurements and Deliveries, Asia 296
7. Timeline: ISIS gains and coalition responses in 2014 304
8. Selected Arms Procurements and Deliveries, Middle East and North Africa 360
9. Selected Arms Procurements and Deliveries, Latin America and the Caribbean 418
10. Selected Arms Procurements and Deliveries, Sub-Saharan Africa 480
11. Selected Training Activity 2014 482
12. International Comparisons of Defence Expenditure and Military Personnel 484
13. List of Abbreviations for Data Sections 501
14. Index of Country/Territory Abbreviations 503
15. Index of Countries and Territories 504

Index of **FIGURES**

North America
1. Equipment Analysis: US Navy DDG 1000 *Zumwalt*-class Destroyer 31
2. US Defence Expenditure as % of GDP 35

Europe
3. Europe Real Defence Spending Changes 2010–14 by Sub-Region (%) 61
4. Europe Defence Spending by Country and Sub-Region 2014 61
5. Europe Regional Defence Expenditure as % of GDP 63
6. Europe: Selected Procurement & Upgrade Priorities Since 2010 ... 63

Russia and Eurasia
7. Equipment Analysis: Russian *Flanker* Combat Aircraft Development 162
8. Estimated Russian Defence Expenditure as % of GDP 164
9. Russia Defence Expenditure Trends (2005–17) 166

Asia
10. Composition of Real Defence Spending Increases 2013–14 211
11. Asia Regional Defence Expenditure as % of GDP 211
12. Asia: Selected Procurement & Upgrade Priorities Since 2010 212
13. Official PLA Budget 2001–14 217

Middle East and North Africa
14. Estimated MENA Defence Expenditure 2014: Sub-Regional Breakdown 309
15. Middle East and North Africa Regional Defence Expenditure as % of GDP 309
16. Middle East & North Africa: Selected Procurement & Upgrade Priorities Since 2010 310
17. Equipment Analysis: Israel's *Merkava* IV Main Battle Tank 312

Latin America and the Caribbean
18. Latin America and the Caribbean Regional Defence Expenditure as % of GDP 365
19. Latin America & the Caribbean Defence Spending by Country & Sub-Region 368
20. Latin America & the Caribbean: Selected Procurement & Upgrade Priorities Since 2010 369
21. Colombia Defence Budget Breakdown 2014 (%) 373
22. COTECMAR Defence Exports 2001–13 (COP bn) 373

Sub-Saharan Africa
23. Sub-Saharan Africa Regional Defence Expenditure as % of GDP 424

Index of **MAPS**

1. Europe Regional Defence Spending 62
2. France: Selected Deployments in Africa – 2014 65
3. Russia and Eurasia Regional Defence Spending 165
4. Russia Seizes Crimea 169
5. Conflict in Eastern Ukraine 171
6. Asia Regional Defence Spending 210
7. Middle East and North Africa Regional Defence Spending 308
8. Latin America and the Caribbean Regional Defence Spending 367
9. Sub-Saharan Africa Regional Defence Spending 423
10. AMISOM's *Operation Indian Ocean* 428

Editor's Introduction
Complex crises call for adaptable and durable capabilities

At the beginning of 2015, defence and security planners were reflecting on a preceding year that added extra crises to an already increasingly complex and fractured global security environment. European security faced its most significant challenge since the end of the Cold War with Russia's annexation of Crimea and fomenting of instability in eastern Ukraine. In the Middle East, meanwhile, rapid advances by ISIS in Syria and Iraq threatened the Iraqi state and led to greater military extroversion by regional states. The year ended with the US again committing to deploy troops on a training mission to Iraq; at the same time it was also leading a broad multinational coalition in offensive operations against ISIS.

The broader, long-term strategic trend of China and other Asian states' growing economic and military power, and the parallel US rebalance to the Asia-Pacific, continued. While the US and, to a limited extent, some other Western states still possessed dominant military capabilities, there was growing awareness that in some respects the West was not only at risk of losing its military-technological edge but could also, with continuing budgetary reductions, see some military capabilities further eroded or excised altogether.

Russia's assertiveness, notably its actions in Ukraine, refocused attention not just on Moscow's policy objectives and military capabilities, but also on the impact of financial constraints on Europe's armed forces. In real terms, European defence spending continued the downward trajectory seen since the 2008 economic crisis. Real European defence spending in 2014 was cumulatively 7.7% lower than in 2010. However, there were signs that the more challenging strategic environment in Europe had shifted budgetary priorities in some places, particularly in Northern and Eastern Europe. One way that European states had previously thought of boosting capability amid budgetary pressure was to do more together; NATO was at the forefront of such initiatives.

Many had expected NATO's September 2014 Wales Summit to be largely administrative and preordained – the Alliance would mark the end of its combat operations in Afghanistan and agree measures to improve cooperation – but instead NATO's Eastern European members pressed the Alliance for reassurance amid concern over Russia's actions in Ukraine and more widely. Any earlier hopes that some NATO leaders might have had of a post-Afghanistan 'strategic holiday' evaporated. At the same time, Russia's assertiveness reinvigorated the Alliance's core purpose of collective defence. The effectiveness of Russia's actions led some member states to question whether NATO would be able to defend them, should they be the target of actions similar to those in Ukraine. The Alliance realised this, reaffirming the Article V commitment to collective self-defence and embarking on a range of reassurance initiatives, including exercises and rotational deployments that will essentially lead to a permanent, though small, US presence in Eastern Europe.

Rediscovering 'hybrid warfare'

The politico-military methods employed by Russia gave NATO and its members pause for thought. Moscow successfully employed a broad range of traditional and non-traditional instruments to achieve its goals in Crimea, and to some degree in eastern Ukraine. The first problem for NATO was to define the nature of the challenge, and there was some concern in the West about possible gaps in its ability to counter Russia's employment of what was generally labelled 'hybrid' warfare. The methods applied included the use of military and non-military tools in an integrated campaign designed to achieve surprise, seize the initiative and gain psychological as well as physical advantages utilising diplomatic means; sophisticated and rapid information, electronic and cyber operations; covert and occasionally overt military and intelligence action; and economic pressure.

Although this problem is not new, some of the means used by Russia, and potentially others, to support proxies and subvert governments are innovative. Indeed, operations in Crimea in early 2014 showed that Russian thinking and capacity in these areas has matured. Russian forces demonstrated integrated use of rapid deployment, electronic warfare, information operations (IO), locally based naval infantry, airborne assault and special-forces capabilities, as well as wider use of cyberspace and strategic communications. The latter was used to shape a multifaceted and overall effective information campaign targeted as much at domestic as foreign audiences; one where continual denials and rebuttals from Moscow that it was militarily involved, even if increasingly implausible, had the potential to create a sense of cognitive dissonance in foreign decision-making circles. These operations demonstrated some of the fruits of Russia's military-reform process, although too much focus on the new personal equipment, weapons, vehicles, electronic-warfare (EW) and tactical-communications equipment seen in Crimea could be misleading when assessing the effects of military reform on the wider force.

Western responses

For the West (and, indeed, other states seeking to preserve the rule of law and the existing international order), improving the ability to defend against these threats applies beyond the challenges posed by Russia. Policymakers may anticipate that some current or potential state or non-state adversaries, possibly including states such as China and Iran, will learn from Russia's recent employment of hybrid warfare. Potential adversaries might discern what tactics worked and what capabilities are required to effect results; other lessons might derive from perceptions of how Western governments and armed forces react and adapt, politically as well as militarily. These lessons might not necessarily be applied in conflicts with Western states, but their potential to rapidly destabilise the existing order could, if applied in other zones of political and military competition, mean they have global ramifications.

Coping with the threat of hybrid warfare will require Western and other governments to invest in relevant capabilities. Investment could be made to bolster long-term strategic-intelligence capabilities, such that the de-prioritisation of, for instance, broad language skills that can result from a focus on current operational requirements is minimised. Some armed forces are looking to address this problem by regionally aligning selected units, but it is also an issue that could be considered by other government departments with international interests. Other capabilities include cyberspace, law-enforcement, information and financial tools as well as precision-strike and persistent ISR; but they still include deployable and adaptable sea, air and land forces. Meanwhile, the deterrent effect of high-readiness armed forces and pre-positioned forces and capabilities should not be underestimated.

Additionally, Western states and indeed NATO might perceive that better coordination of the informational efforts of member nations and international organisations, such as strategic communications, might improve speed of action while amplifying a common position. However, in many Western countries these capacities have been reduced since the Cold War; rebuilding and updating them will take time and political commitment.

This aspect of hybrid warfare was also evident in the media operations of ISIS in the Middle East. Fusing modern social-media savviness with sharp broadcasting techniques and even computer gaming to recruit, inspire and intimidate in equal measure, the actions of ISIS in this regard demonstrated some thematic similarities with the application of hybrid warfare in Ukraine, even if in another geographical area and a different operational environment. These similarities required an understanding that, while traditional military capabilities such as mobility, firepower and protection remain relevant and important, the application of force must also be effective on the 'battleground' of perception, particularly against enemies that can operate in and among populations and extend operations beyond physical battlegrounds to the realms of perception and subversion.

Indeed, this hybrid, adaptable nature of ISIS proved key to its advances: it has been part insurgency; part light-infantry; and part terrorist group. In the areas it captured, it relied on a minimal bureaucratic structure at the same time as repressive rule, enforcing strict codes and ruthlessly eliminating dissent. It adopted a decentralised structure to create greater flexibility on the ground and strengthen internal security, and has a core of highly motivated commanders, some of whom are former al-Qaeda or Sunni insurgents, while in Iraq some are former Saddam-era military officers. While ISIS's advance in Iraq led to a military collapse in that country's north, in Syria it combined with other factors, like the US decision to call off air-strikes in September 2013 in exchange for Damascus relinquishing its chemical arsenal, as well as continuing Western reluctance to back the armed rebellion. This created a situation by late 2014 where the position of President Bashar al-Assad seemed stronger than at any time since 2012.

The actual and potential threat to international security posed by ISIS triggered a degree of military engagement and political alignment by regional and international states that had not been seen for some time. Indeed, some Arab states, particularly in the Gulf, demonstrated their increasing strategic extroversion. The actions of both the United Arab Emirates and Egypt over their reported activity in Libya in 2014 marked something of a watershed in regional politics, illustrating a potential to use force and the capacity to operate independent of Washington. For all that, the US remained the strategic guarantor for most regional states, and still brought to bear unique military and political capabilities. The US was successful in enlisting the political and military support of key Arab states to join the coalition to defeat ISIS. Some Gulf states calculated that ISIS was becoming an ideological and security threat; they also believed that their involvement was essential to shape US strategy in Syria and to ensure that Iran would not be a principal beneficiary of the campaign. Bahrain, Jordan, Qatar, Saudi Arabia and the UAE all contributed aircraft and other military capabilities.

Wider concerns

The potential for 'hybrid' incidents also worried states in other parts of the world. In Japan, the government expressed unease at possible 'grey-zone' contingencies, short of actual conflict and possibly not involving regular armed forces, with the Senkaku/Diaoyu Islands a likely area of concern. For all that, and despite some Asian defence establishments' continuing concerns with internal security and a growing interest in improving capacity to deal with HA/DR and other human-security challenges, most regional defence programmes were driven by state-on-state threats and conventional capability procurements. Attempts to strengthen capabilities in the Asia-Pacific have focused particularly (though not exclusively) on the maritime domain, reflecting worries about conventional naval threats, as well as concerns over the need to defend natural resources, territorial claims and freedom of navigation.

Defence budgets in Asia have continued to rise, by an estimated 27% between 2010 and 2014. The biggest spender remained China. By 2014, China's share of Asian spending had risen to around 38%, up from 28% in 2010. This increased spending has provided for growing military procurement, the most newsworthy being in the maritime and air domains, while China and some other Asian states have increased their investment in defence science, and research and development. These states are making greater efforts to acquire and absorb foreign technologies and they are overhauling their existing defence-innovation systems.

China's technical advances in the defence sphere are legion, and are leveraging the resources of the defence as well as, in some cases, the national commercial sector – even if gaps remain, such as in advanced turbofan engines for high-performance combat aircraft. This rapid progress has led some in the US defence establishment to claim that the technology gap that hitherto allowed the US armed forces technological dominance is closing. Mindful of the differing trajectories in the two countries' defence budgets, US officials emphasise the need for continued innovation and the Pentagon is attempting to minimise potential vulnerabilities in its weapons systems arising from other states' technical developments. For instance, Washington is assessing its dependence on space, including GPS, and there has been greater attention to developing more resilient space systems and satellite constellations, as well as scrutiny of established technologies (such as inertial navigation) that could minimise the effects of these vulnerabilities on weapons systems.

While many countries will only have been affected tangentially by events in Ukraine, Syria and Iraq, even if there might have been incidents inspired by events in the Middle East, the lessons that potential adversaries could draw from these might be of greater long-term relevance. As such, their military planners will study these lessons in detail; but there will be as much interest in how the defence and security establishments of key states – in the West and the Gulf, as well as in Russia and Eurasia – react and adapt. For the US, unanticipated events like these were among the possible 'risks' to the country's armed forces highlighted in the 2014 Quadrennial Defense Review. Though the QDR, according to the US Chairman of the Joint Chiefs of Staff, largely protected certain capabilities, it also 'takes risk in the capacity of each service, but particularly in land forces'.

On current trajectories, cuts to land forces will continue in many states – and US Army chiefs are reported as saying that personnel strength might drop to around 450,000. That total, of course, dwarfs many other armed forces, but calculations change when the numbers are teased apart. According to

General Raymond Odierno, 55,000 are deployed troops, and 80,000 are stationed abroad in 150 countries; others will doubtless be forming part of the deployment cycle. Previous strategies had assumed that the demand for land forces would decline, but 2014 has seen additional – even if small-scale – Western land forces deploy to Eastern Europe and Iraq, and Russian ground forces played a key role in shaping operations in eastern Ukraine. The complex nature of some of these tasks might also lead to further questions about whether armed forces are even best suited for some of these complex crises, certainly those that require security attention short of war fighting; in some cases this might lead to a reassessment of the relative utility of paramilitary forces like gendarmeries.

It is unlikely that budget realities in the West will see forces grow once more, but that places a premium on policymakers and defence planners providing a suitable force mix and spectrum of capabilities, and generating adaptive military and security capacities able to deploy rapidly and operate across all domains. States also have to ensure nimble EW, IO, cyber and strategic-communications capacities so that they can operate in the information realm as well as in military theatres.

Chapter One
Directed energy weapons: finally coming of age?

Directed energy (DE) systems have been something of a chimera for defence planners. From their first appearances in science fiction, to the ambitious 1980s United States' Strategic Defense Initiative (SDI), they have been touted by advocates of the technology as a means of engaging military targets with, in the case of lasers, speed-of-light delivery and the possibility of near-unlimited magazines compared with kinetic-effect weapons, such as missiles or guns.

The US, several European countries, including the United Kingdom, Germany and France, as well as Russia, China and Israel, have all been engaged in long-standing research and development (R&D) into DE systems. While there has been limited transition from the laboratory and related test environments into weapons systems suitable and ready for operational exploitation, in spite of considerable levels of investment since the 1970s, the practical military employment of DE systems is drawing closer.

There is now the potential for DE to be adopted far more widely than in the niche applications in which it has been utilised so far, such as vehicle immobilisation. This is in part because technology has matured, but also because near-term ambitions have been reviewed by defence planners. DE is now seen as a disruptive technology that can potentially provide substantial military benefit at the tactical rather than strategic level – with the proviso that such systems must be brought to an appropriate level of maturity for deployment. Two areas, in particular, have long interested armed forces: laser systems and radio frequency (RF). These offer the most promise in terms of tactical application.

Laser weapons

The development of laser weaponry has had several expensive false starts. One of the most public was the US Airborne Laser (ABL) programme. This exemplified much that was wrong with DE weapons projects. Irrespective of the technical progress made during the programme, the project suffered from over-reach with regard to the maturity of the technology then available, and came in over budget. Today, the level of ambition, projected target set and power requirements for the laser systems most likely to be fielded in the near-to-medium term are more modest than systems such as ABL. While the ABL programme predates the 1980s Strategic Defence Initiative it received a major fillip from the Reagan-era initiative.

Laser systems are currently viewed, in the near term at least, as an adjunct or complement to existing weapons, rather than as direct replacements. In the maritime role, for instance, a laser could provide the ability to engage particular target sets – such as fast-attack craft or unmanned aerial vehicles (UAVs) – without having to expend a costlier weapon such as a missile, of which vessels will have limited stocks. Air-defence missiles could then be saved to engage more demanding targets, such as high-speed anti-ship cruise missiles, that remain beyond the power-output abilities of the lasers most likely to enter operational service by 2020. There is also interest in using laser weaponry to counter subsonic cruise missiles – both at sea and on land – either by degrading the performance of or damaging electro-optical (EO) seekers, or by causing structural damage to the missile airframe. Power requirements in the hundreds of kilowatts would likely be required for this role.

US naval laser research
Even though substantial funds have been invested into laser research, and the results have so far been mixed, the projected benefits in cost terms remain a significant motivation for continued military interest in the technology. The US Navy's (USN) Office of Naval Research has suggested that a typical 110kW high-energy laser (HEL) for a multi-second shot would cost less than US$1 per round. Firing a missile to fulfil a similar role costs substantially more, with most of this related to the round itself. With lasers, the costs lie with the engineering architecture required to generate, point and steer a beam of the required power for the requisite period of time; so far these costs have generally been prohibitively high. For instance, although Israel pursued a counter-rocket laser system with the US (the cancelled Mobile Tactical High Energy Laser), it still relies on a kinetic

approach to defeat rockets with its *Iron Dome* missile system.

Recent tests by the USN have been illustrative of the increasing likelihood that DE weaponry will soon be integrated into military platforms. In April 2014, the USN announced that the landing platform dock USS *Ponce* would carry out trials, during a year-long operational deployment to the Persian Gulf, with a Laser Weapon System (LaWS) demonstrator in order to examine its utility against a range of air and surface targets. These tests followed others in US home waters on board USS *Dewey*, an *Arleigh Burke*-class destroyer, where LaWS was used to engage a small UAV.

LaWS is a comparatively low-powered 30kW 'solid-state' laser. This modest power level has limited its notional target set to UAVs and fast inshore attack craft (usually by targeting the engine block to disable the craft), particularly when engaged in swarm attacks. Anticipating questions about the compatibility of LaWS with existing ship systems, the USN has said that the system could be directed onto targets from the radar track obtained from a Mk 15 *Phalanx* Close-In Weapon system or other targeting source. Indeed, integration with a relatively low-tier tracking and targeting system such as that used in *Phalanx* could, when allied with its relatively modest power requirement, increase the possibilities of LaWS being integrated more broadly across fleet platforms of varying sizes.

This deployment forms part of the USN's Solid-State Laser Quick Reaction Capability work strand, which it hopes will help inform the Solid-State Laser Technology Maturation programme (SSL-TM), which grew originally from the 2011 Maritime Laser Demonstration. In May 2014, Rear Admiral Matthew Klunder, the USN's chief of naval research, told the Senate Appropriations Defense Subcommittee: 'SSL-TM will help determine the load capacity and most effective means to integrate a HEL ... on surface ships such as DDG-51 [USS *Arleigh Burke*] and the Littoral Combat Ship. The SSL-TM goal is to demonstrate a 100–150 kilowatt Advanced Development Model ... by 2016. The programme will address technical challenges in rugged laser subsystems, optics suitable for maritime environments, and capability to propagate lethal power levels in the maritime atmosphere.'

However, while the USN might have ambitions to increase the power output of its laser systems, these are incremental steps towards realising fairly limited objectives. For instance, the power output of LaWS is dwarfed by the near-megawatt-level power output required for ABL to damage a ballistic missile at an operationally valid range. While ABL, housed in a Boeing 747-400 airframe, was first used in 2010 to successfully engage a ballistic-missile target at such a range, the project was some distance from providing a system suitable for introduction into general service.

Other defence-related laser research

Naval laser-damage or 'dazzle' weapons have already been developed by various states, including the former Soviet Union and the UK, with several other countries – including France, Germany and China – pursuing long-term R&D into laser dazzle or damage systems. The UK deployed a naval laser weapon, the Laser Dazzle Sight, during the Falklands campaign in 1982, although previously classified documents suggest it was not used in action.

As well as examining the utility of medium-power lasers for applications such as air defence, the UK has also pursued – since at least the late 1970s – projects to defend sensors and personnel against lasers. The original code name for this activity was *Raker*, while development projects arising from the research fell under the *Shingle* programme. These included coatings for EO sensors and attempts to develop eye-safe visors for aircrew. Conversely, the blinding effect of lasers has also been considered by some nations for both defensive and offensive anti-satellite purposes, including China, Russia and the US. Lasers can be used to degrade or disrupt the performance of space-based EO reconnaissance sensors.

A number of European countries, including the UK and Germany, also support R&D work into laser systems for maritime and land-based air defence. In the UK, there has been ongoing naval interest in laser systems with work streams examining effects, and pointing and tracking requirements. In Germany, MBDA Deutschland has been working under contract to the German defence ministry to develop and test a solid-state laser for the Counter-Rocket, Artillery and Mortar role and against UAVs, either to defeat sensors at extended ranges or to shoot down the air vehicle. A number of increasingly demanding trials were carried out in 2012 and 2013 to verify elements of the system, including the ability to engage a mortar round and to automatically acquire and track a high-speed target. Several possible applications are now being considered including land and naval roles. One option for the former might be to install a 10–20kW laser on an armoured vehicle to provide a counter-

UAV capability as a complement to existing missile systems.

The types of EO sensors used by UAVs in the intelligence, surveillance and reconnaissance (ISR) role are vulnerable to laser damage or blinding. The USN's Ground-Based Air Defense Directed Energy On-The-Move programme is being developed to address the threat to deployed forces presented by enemy UAV sensors. The programme is a result of the need to counter ISR surveillance of ground forces, as outlined in the US Marine Corps' Science and Technology Strategic Plan. While a 10kW laser was due to be tested before the end of 2014, the aim is to have a 30kW laser ready for field-testing during 2016. But again, there is no monopoly on this technology. EO sensor countermeasures were examined by the Soviet Union: the 1K11 *Stiletto* and 1K17 *Szhatie* were vehicle-mounted systems intended for battlefield use against NATO EO systems, and during the 1980s work was also carried out on a land-based tactical air-defence laser system.

Radio-frequency weapons
While lasers have garnered much attention, RF weapons have also seen both defensive and offensive research activity. RF systems are more commonly referred to as high-power microwave (HPM), and have possible applications across the air, land and sea domains. They provide the potential ability to temporarily or permanently disable systems that rely on computers or electronics by emitting very high-output, short-duration, electromagnetic bursts. Initial work into HPM or RF ordnance conducted in the 1990s by the UK utilised explosive-driven flux compression generators to produce the required energy, although this limited output to single shots. This led researchers to investigate other technologies, such as Marx Generators, which allow for the voltage of the output discharge to be far higher than the input, to deliver multiple bursts of RF energy.

Like laser systems, there have been some niche applications in terms of counter-personnel (such as the US Active Denial System, which relies on the sensation of skin heating), counter-vehicle and counter-improvised-explosive-device systems, but the development of 'stand-off' HPM or RF payloads to provide weapons effects has proved more challenging. Efforts to develop HPM warheads have been under way for at least three decades, and while systems have been tested in the laboratory and in the field, it remains unclear whether any have been operationally deployed (although there may be some applications in the classified realm). In common with lasers, though, the possibility is growing that an air-delivered RF weapon might soon be fielded.

In 2012, Boeing carried out flight tests of the Counter-electronics High-Powered Microwave Advanced Missile Project (CHAMP) on behalf of the US Air Force Research Laboratory. The CHAMP concept, housed within a cruise-missile airframe, used a compact pulsed-power system to provide a 'narrowband' HPM, with the system capable of generating multiple pulses to engage multiple targets. Narrowband sources provide high energy output over specific frequencies tailored to the systems they are intended to counter. ('Broadband', as the name suggests, is a less discriminate output of RF energy.)

The US is not alone in trying to exploit the potential of air-delivered HPM devices. For well over a decade, the UK has been developing and testing HPM payloads capable of cruise-missile delivery, while Russia has also considered an RF warhead for future air-to-air missile applications. The UK has carried out trials of an HPM payload against a variety of simulated targets in order to better understand the effects of this technology. The UK Ministry of Defence's *Black Shadow* Novel Air Vehicle project was believed to be related to the delivery of DE payloads, including HPM.

Challenges to and ramifications of RF weapon use
There are, arguably, three basic challenges to the use of an RF warhead: repeatability, battle damage assessment (BDA), and second- and third-order effects. One issue with early HPM systems was that the burst of energy could differ from one shot to the next, with this output variation meaning there was no guarantee the desired effect could be achieved. Much R&D activity has been devoted to this issue. BDA during operational use is another problem area for HPM payloads, particularly if the objective is to permanently or temporarily disable a surface-to-air missile system radar or a command-and-control node. Monitoring these may enable the detection of any degradation in capability, but generating such analysis may take time and serve only to generate additional intelligence requirements. A conventional cruise-missile strike, meanwhile – even against hardened structures – will show a penetration point, and post-detonation indicators may also be available to provide additional BDA data.

While a multiple-shot HPM payload has the

obvious advantage of providing the ability to engage more than one target, as opposed to a conventional one-hit warhead, it also gives rise to challenges. For instance, did the HPM payload work as intended or did the target simply shut down operation coincidentally at around the time of the planned engagement? Furthermore, what should be done with the cruise-missile airframe once the mission is completed? The airframe will likely house sensitive HPM technology – should the weapon be recovered like a UAV, or should it be fitted with an explosive warhead to try and ensure the RF elements of the payload are destroyed? Another option would be to fit a multi-shot HPM as part of an unmanned combat aerial vehicle (UCAV) payload, though this would require such levels of electromagnetic shielding to ensure the UCAV itself would not be affected by the HPM.

A further consideration is that of second-order effects, not least of all in terms of the laws of armed conflict. Legal issues surrounding previous and current RF and laser weaponry have to be taken into account in development and integration plans. In the case of the latter, a protocol on blinding laser weapons was adopted in 1995, which might need to be revisited as more powerful laser systems enter service.

For HPM systems, meanwhile, there are potential issues related to unanticipated, follow-on collateral effects, as opposed to collateral damage. In both technology areas, a key challenge for policymakers and legal experts is the speed of developments, which are, in many cases, outpacing current conceptual and legal frameworks. These concerns will need to be addressed as DE systems finally move out of the test environment and into broader operational service, instead of the niche applications that have typified their roles so far.

In the near term, DE systems will be drawn first into the wider inventory as complements to, rather than as replacements for, kinetic weapons. This level of ambition means that the capabilities deployed initially will be considerably more modest than some of the systems envisaged in the 1980s and 1990s. The defence-technology base was at that time incapable of delivering systems that provided robust and reusable operational utility, and was hampered by power-output and beam-steering demands it could not meet. This lowering of ambitions – at least initially – means that DE weapons are finding a path into active service, and it is only in the course of their fielding and use that the true operational and transformational aspects of these technologies will become clear.

Military space systems: US ambitions to secure space

Once the exclusive domain of the Cold War superpowers, national space capabilities are now maintained by a growing number of countries. Eleven states have an indigenous capacity to launch satellites, while 170 operate satellites or have a financial interest in a satellite constellation. Along with the established space-operating nations of the United States, Russia, France, the United Kingdom, Germany and Israel, nations such as China and India now possess significant, and in some cases growing, space capabilities.

While its early uses were dominated by national-security tasks, space is now of far broader economic, commercial and military importance. For example, the US Global Positioning System (GPS) provides precision timing and navigation data, among other information. Russia's *Glonass* offers a similar capability, and Europe has successfully launched four of its *Galileo* timing and navigation spacecraft into orbit. Recent commercial uses of space include the earth-observation collections from DigitalGlobe and others that drive imagery products such as Google Maps. Satellites providing these services are in low-Earth orbit (LEO); spacecraft in geosynchronous orbit (GEO) provide television and communications services.

However, the vulnerability of space systems to deliberate or inadvertent damage or interference is an increasing concern, not least in Washington, as the US seeks to sustain and protect those satellite systems that are not only central to its commercial and economic security, but also at the core of its military infrastructure.

Military uses of space have grown substantially in the years since the first satellite, *Sputnik*, orbited the Earth. Over the years, armed forces have increasingly relied on space-based systems for navigation, targeting, surveillance and communications. Reconnaissance satellites, for instance, typically operate in LEO – often within 400km of Earth – while critical ballistic-missile warning and communications payloads operate in GEO, roughly 35,000km away from the surface of the planet. However, both orbital regimes are under threat. There is particular concern about intentional and inadvertent radio-frequency jamming, as well as anti-satellite (ASAT) or kinetic kill mechanisms, and environmental hazards, including orbiting debris.

For the US armed forces, the perceived vulnerability of space-based systems is of increasing concern. In February 2014, referring to a satellite constellation under construction (the Advanced Extremely High Frequency satellite, or AEHF), then-Space Command chief Air Force General William Shelton said: 'if an adversary wanted to go after one of our satellites, [an AEHF satellite] might be the one you'd choose … If that happened, and one of the four gets knocked out, we're left with a big geographic hole in our ability to transmit data around the world and [help] the president give the direction that he needs to give.' Shelton also highlighted the potential of high-powered lasers to affect payload operation. Some lasers have the potential to blind electro-optical reconnaissance satellites (see p. 10).

China's ASAT test in January 2007 caused alarm in Washington. Beijing destroyed its own *Fengyun 1C* polar-orbiting weather satellite with what was thought to be an SC-19 missile, based on the DF-21 (CSS-5) intermediate-range ballistic missile. This resulted in a large debris field, much of which remains in orbit and has prompted numerous 'manoeuvres' by satellite operators in order to avoid secondary collisions in space.

China has continued to refine its capabilities since then, and is believed to have executed an attempted engagement of a ballistic missile in 2010. Another test, in 2014, was labelled by US officials as an ASAT operation. In August, Frank Rose, US deputy assistant secretary of state for space and defence policy, told the 2014 US Strategic Command Deterrence Symposium that, 'despite China's claims that this was not an ASAT test … the United States has high confidence in its assessment, that the event was indeed an ASAT test'. In contrast, China's state-run news agency claimed the test was a missile intercept. Western analysts believe that Beijing is investing significant resources in technologies and techniques to influence operations in space. If anything, these discussions are only illustrative of the concern expressed by the US government and its allies that space services are vulnerable.

Dealing with space debris

Space debris is a recognised issue affecting space-faring nations, but dealing with it remains a singular concern. 2015 could see the culmination of several years of work to address this problem, if the European Union-sponsored International Code of Conduct (ICOC) for Outer Space Activities gains traction. Multilateral consultation on the ICOC drew to a close in 2014, with EU member states then discussing how best to proceed.

In addressing the debris issue, the language of the draft ICOC called for nations to 'refrain from any action which brings about, directly or indirectly, damage or destruction of space objects unless such action is justified: by imperative safety considerations ... or in order to reduce the creation of space debris' or 'by the Charter of the United Nations'.

Signatories would in effect be foregoing carrying out any trials of anti-satellite systems that involved the kinetic kill of a target, such as the 2007 test by the Chinese of a weapon that resulted in the creation of a large debris field that still remains a cause for concern. There have been occasions where satellites have had to take avoiding action because of the danger of collision with debris. While China has not replicated this test, it has continued to trial the interceptor, including a test in July 2014, according to the US State Department.

Along with avoiding, or at least minimising, the creation of additional debris, there remains the challenge of dealing with the debris that is already in low-Earth orbit. One option remains the use of orbital systems to 'collect' the larger and more threatening pieces. Such technology, however, is problematic in that it is inherently dual use, and could be perceived as posing a threat to other satellites were such a capability to be operated on a national basis.

Classified efforts

As a consequence of perceived threats, greater resources are being directed towards securing access to, and operations in, space. One public US initiative aims to better characterise objects in space, including debris and spacecraft. Indeed, US officials have admitted that for decades their armed forces had operated nearly blind in space, relying only on 'dots and streaks' of data on objects in orbit provided by ageing terrestrial radars. In the last few years, however, there have been advances in hardware specifically designed to improve space situational awareness (SSA).

It is thought that most activity related to space security remains classified. For instance, Shelton revealed a previously secret satellite project with Orbital Sciences Corporation called the Geosynchronous Space Situational Awareness Program (GSSAP). Under this programme, two satellites were launched on 28 July 2014. These would 'drift' in GEO, collecting intelligence on other objects. Details remain classified, although US Air Force (USAF) officials have revealed that they employ electro-optical sensors. Pentagon sources have stated that GSSAP is expected to begin delivering information early in 2015; first light (the first instance of data gathering) has already been achieved. GSSAP satellites are the first acknowledged by Washington as designed to collect close-up imagery of objects in GEO. According to senior US officials, these satellites were in part crafted as a deterrent to would-be rivals in space, who once enjoyed the benefit of anonymity when acting in a hostile manner.

The influx of data from GSSAP is only one piece of Washington's maturing SSA architecture, which is increasingly focused on new electro-optical sensors. As a result of a 2012 agreement with Australia, the Space Surveillance Telescope (SST) – a highly advanced instrument developed by the Defense Advanced Research Projects Agency (DARPA) – has been delivered to Naval Communications Station Harold E. Holt in Exmouth, Western Australia. Slated to begin operating in 2016, the SST will, according to DARPA, provide 'much faster discovery and tracking of previously unseen, hard-to-find small objects in geosynchronous orbits'. Its advanced electro-optical sensor is specifically designed to collect imagery of small satellites; threats posed by highly manoeuvrable small and micro satellites are of concern to the US and its allies. DARPA has stated that the SST will be ten times more sensitive than today's terrestrial electro-optical sensors, and much more agile.

The USAF is also developing plans to fund a follow-on project to its *Pathfinder* Space-Based Space Surveillance (SBSS) satellite, which was launched in September 2010. Although this system is projected to come out of service in 2017, the follow-on programme is unlikely to achieve first launch before FY2022. Air Force Space Command (AFSPC) anticipates the purchase of three satellites – monitoring GEO from LEO – and US$251.7 million has been requested in the next budget to select a contractor by the end of FY2017. For the next SBSS satellite, officials are targeting a less complex design than that of *Pathfinder*, which featured a two-axis, gimballed sensor and cost US$823m.

Ground-based support

Washington is also improving the terrestrial radars used for SSA. A new *Space Fence* S-band active electronically scanned array is due to begin operating in 2018. The system, developed by Lockheed Martin, is intended to be installed at Kwajalein Atoll in the Pacific Ocean. A possible follow-on site could be in Western Australia, but that option on the US$914m contract has not yet been exercised. A C-band radar formerly in Antigua has already been relocated to Western Australia, the site of DARPA's SST. These radar assets are sited to provide intelligence on Chinese launches, specifically those from the Taiyuan Satellite Launch Centre. Until recently, the US lacked the ability to conduct continuous tracking of Chinese payloads launched into certain orbits.

US government officials have long held that SSA is only one aspect of the United States' posture in space. These radar upgrades will improve Washington's understanding of activity in space, making it easier to attribute actions there. Diplomatic agreements with space operators to deter irresponsible or hostile behaviour are known to exist, but only attribution can allow the US and its allies to properly apply diplomatic pressure and, if needed, military force in reaction to hostile acts against space assets. At an Air Force Association conference in 2014, AFSPC chief General John Hyten said: 'we have to be prepared to do all those things the president has told us to do and if deterrence fails, defeat efforts to attack us.'

Responses to perceived vulnerabilities

Absent from the public dialogue are technologies fielded to respond to threats. One is the United States' Counter Communications System, designed to deny an adversary the ability to access friendly military-satellite communications. Little has been revealed about the technology, but since 2006 it has been operated by the 4th Space Control Squadron at Peterson Air Force Base, Colorado. Another is the Rapid Attack, Identification, Detection and Reporting System, the prototype of which began operations in the Middle East in 2005. This system was designed to 'detect, characterize, geolocate and report' sources of interference to allied communications systems in the region and, according to the USAF, consists of a 'central operating location and a variety of transportable antennas'. During operations, data was relayed to teams that would physically locate, identify and nullify the interference.

A so-called Counter Surveillance and Reconnaissance System, which was conceived of more than ten years ago to impede an adversary's access to space-based reconnaissance assets, disappeared from US budget documents in 2004, suggesting that it was either terminated or classified so that funding accounts for continued work could be hidden.

The US has also been exploring alternative propulsion systems for its workhorse *Atlas* V two-stage expendable launch vehicle. Now operated by the United Launch Alliance (ULA), a joint venture between Lockheed Martin and Boeing, *Atlas* V relies on the Russian RD-180 engine, sold to ULA exclusively by a US–Russian joint venture. In 2014 increased tensions between Washington and Moscow prompted Dmitry Rogozin, Russia's deputy prime minister, to state that he would cut off the supply of engines used for military purposes. Although the threat had not been fulfilled by October 2014, it caused concern in Washington and, after months of wrangling, Congress was assessing whether to fund an alternative *Atlas* V engine.

Headway is also being made by Space Exploration Technologies (SpaceX). The private company's *Falcon* 9 v1.1 rocket, first flown in September 2013, has edged closer to USAF certification, expanding its potential market beyond NASA and commercial operators. Once certified, SpaceX can compete against ULA, which currently has a monopoly on large national-security launches in the US with its *Delta* IV and *Atlas* V rocket families. In the meantime, a lawsuit regarding the USAF's deal with ULA, filed by SpaceX in April 2014, is still pending. Rogozin made his threat around the same time that the lawsuit was filed, calling into question the USAF's future launch strategy.

The various challenges to US space security, which range from the increasing congestion of space to offensive actions by other states, have led Washington to see its space-based systems as increasingly vulnerable. This has prompted the development of a range of monitoring capacities, both earthbound and space-based, in a bid to improve SSA. But the US has also taken other steps. For instance, there has been some focus on increasing resilience by considering different constellation architectures. This might result in a move away from 'the multiple payload, big satellite construct into a less complex satellite architecture with multiple components', as Shelton said in 2014. It could mean that payloads are distributed across multiple platforms. Perceived vulnerabilities are also leading Washington to assess its level of military dependence on space, including its ability to operate in degraded information environments, such as one in which access to GPS is reduced. As a result, there has been some scrutiny of established technologies that could minimise the effects of vulnerabilities on weapons systems. For example, inertial guidance is being revisited, including technologies such as terrain mapping and the miniaturisation of atomic clocks. There is also a focus on hardening existing technology to minimise the risk of electromagnetic attack, and of GPS degradation or spoofing, in which false readings – perhaps imperceptible to the operator – may be generated by an adversary seeking to degrade satellite capabilities.

Hybrid warfare: challenge and response

Russia's actions in Ukraine in 2014 have given defence planners in the West, and beyond, much to consider. The sophisticated combinations of conventional and unconventional means of warfare deployed by Russia, seen by many analysts as a form of 'hybrid warfare', have demonstrated that policymakers need to take these activities into account when crafting new concepts and re-examining existing strategies.

Concerns over hybrid warfare are manifest for states in the West – particularly those in NATO, whose Eastern members feel threatened by the combination of an assertive Russia and its capacity to rapidly seize territory. Meanwhile, Alliance members are again engaged on military operations in the Middle East, where additional anxieties have been prompted by the blend of conventional light infantry, part-insurgent and part-terrorist tactics employed by the Islamic State of Iraq and al-Sham (ISIS), fuelled by illicit oil sales and criminal activity. Furthermore, in some areas, such as the employment of coercive information operations, the 2014 versions of hybrid warfare employed in these very different theatres, by very different actors, display some similarities. As part of a cohesive response to these challenges, and in order to deter or defend against state or non-state actors employing hybrid warfare, NATO, its members, and partner states must be able to develop, implement and adapt strategies combining diplomatic, military, informational, economic and law-enforcement efforts.

The lessons are broader, however. Western policymakers may anticipate that some current or potential state or non-state adversaries will also learn from these hybrid-warfare activities, potentially including states in East Asia or the Middle East. They might discern, simply, what tactics worked and what capabilities are required to effect results; other lessons might derive from perceptions of how Western governments and armed forces have reacted and adapted, politically as well as militarily. These lessons might not necessarily be applied in conflicts with Western states, but their potential to rapidly destabilise could, if applied in other zones of political and military competition, mean they have global ramifications.

A challenge to NATO

In the years immediately following the collapse of the Soviet Union and the end of the Cold War, NATO faced a crisis of confidence over its future role and its capabilities – capabilities weakened by reduced defence budgets and uncertain policy ambitions. NATO forces, trained to fight against a conventional threat, faced questions of relevance as conflicts emerged outside Alliance borders, leading to a debate about 'out of area' missions. With Russia's annexation of Crimea in March 2014 and its subsequent actions in Eastern Ukraine, collective defence under Article V of the NATO Charter has once again become the primary focus of the Alliance. However, the Alliance, and its member states, cannot return to Cold War concepts.

There is particular concern about gaps in the West's ability to counter Russia's employment of what has been labelled variously as 'hybrid', 'ambiguous' or 'non-linear' warfare: the use of military and non-military tools in an integrated campaign designed to achieve surprise, seize the initiative and gain psychological as well as physical advantages.

Although this problem is not new, some of the means available to Russia and others to support proxies and subvert governments are innovative. During the 4–5 September 2014 NATO Summit in Wales, much of the discussion centred on what to do about new threats that test the Alliance's ability to deter and, if necessary, respond to hostile actions against member states. In particular, the Alliance identified the need to counter hostile non-military as well as military actions while defending member states against campaigns that combine conventional and unconventional operations.

NATO has identified the threat of hybrid warfare as particularly dangerous because such an approach operates in grey areas that exploit seams in the Alliance. While NATO may be militarily prepared for traditional territorial conflict, it is less prepared for sophisticated campaigns that combine low-level conventional and special operations; offensive cyber and space actions; and psychological operations that use social and traditional media to influence popular perception and international opinion. States employing hybrid warfare might evade a response through ambiguity deliberately calculated to avoid an early declaration of Article V.

Perhaps most dangerous to NATO, adversaries might attack Alliance cohesiveness and magnify possible political divisions. Campaigns against NATO states could begin with efforts to shape the political, economic and social landscape through subversion, espionage and propaganda. An example of this tactic could be an appeal for the protection of ethnic minorities, similar to concerns expressed by Moscow over elements of the population in Eastern Ukraine, and the rapid formation of pressure groups that might be locally staffed, but externally directed and supported. The urgency for NATO to develop responses to these threats has been heightened due to Russia's aggressive application of hybrid warfare, particularly because of the fear, among those newer NATO members who might feel more vulnerable to Russian actions, that they could be directed against them.

Broader responses

In developing responses to hybrid warfare, policymakers might first look to the past, and to the history of the Cold War in particular. Russian conduct of hybrid warfare is grounded in *maskirovka*, the Soviet doctrine of denial and deception, featuring deniability, concealment, deception and disinformation, to accomplish political objectives. The current incarnation of *maskirovka* has received modern updates. Today, Russia has developed an ability to shape political, economic and social environments through division, subversion, espionage, information operations and social tension. As Russia's Chief of the General Staff General Valery Gerasimov observed in 2013, 'the means of achieving political and strategic goals has grown, and, in many cases, they have exceeded the power of force of weapons in their effectiveness'. These new means include the use of cyber warfare, entertainment television, business groups and social media to influence popular will and perception. There was evidence of cyber attacks on Ukrainian systems in 2014, including the reported insertion of an espionage tool called 'Snake', although as an example of cyber warfare the Ukraine crisis appeared muted in comparison with previous attacks, such as that by Russia on Estonia in 2007.

To prevail in what is a psychological and political contest supported by military operations, states – and international organisations like NATO – must consider how to counter three fundamental elements of hybrid warfare:

- the use of conventional and unconventional forces in combination with information operations to intimidate, coerce and foment ethnic conflict;
- the use of conventional and unconventional forces to strike rapidly in combination with cyber attacks;
- the establishment of new political structures, economic relationships and social structures to consolidate gains and prevent reverses.

Deterring and countering hybrid warfare will require states to improve capabilities in the information domain as well as strengthening military readiness and forward defence. For NATO, this should also involve building upon recent work on the 'comprehensive approach', its recognition that effective response to crises must combine civilian and military instruments. To that end, clause 89 in the Wales Summit Declaration – referring to NATO's 'Defence and Related Security Capacity Building Initiative' – was instructive, as it reflected awareness of broader capacity-building requirements.

Hybrid warfare entails the pursuit of psychological effects both on the target nation and internationally, and so Western states and NATO might improve their ability to clarify intentions; counter enemy disinformation and propaganda; bolster the resolve and cohesion of the nation or nations under attack; and expose the actions and duplicity of the enemy. For instance, quick action to counter Russia's narrative of its right to protect pro-Russian and Russian-speaking populations seems particularly important. Because deception has been employed to foster confusion and achieve deniability, it will be important for intelligence efforts to establish the foundation for information campaigns. Compelling intelligence products will help deny the enemy's ability to use ambiguity to avoid sanction. Intelligence will also be a critical component of countering efforts to sow dissension, doubt and division within and among nations. Influence agents working on behalf of adversaries could be systematically and publically exposed. For NATO, better coordination of the informational efforts of member nations, as well as those of international organisations such as the European Union, might improve speed of action while magnifying the Alliance's voice, but in many Western countries these capacities have been reduced since the Cold War; rebuilding and updating them will take time and political commitment.

Military aspects

The most important focus for NATO, to deter Russia in particular, might lie in strengthening the readiness of its military forces. That is because the Russian application of hybrid warfare in Ukraine is essentially an effort to wage limited war for limited objectives. Moscow believes that those limited objectives are attainable at an acceptable cost. If the cost of potential offensive action against a NATO member is high due to capable military forces ranged in opposition, Russia may well conclude that it cannot rapidly achieve its objectives in this way. While the development of the NATO Very High Readiness Joint Task Force is an important initiative, strengthening military forces on NATO's periphery and the forward-positioning of US or European forces may be more important to deterring future aggression. That is due, in part, to the often slow response by Western policymakers, particularly when aggressors are successful in preserving ambiguity. Conflicts in Georgia, Crimea and Eastern Ukraine demonstrated that Russia was able to act more quickly than international organisations could react. Hybrid warfare, like all warfare, is a contest of wills; the positioning of capable forces forward along a frontier remains a compelling way to communicate the determination to confront aggression.

Deterring and defending against a sophisticated campaign demands a comprehensive approach and the integration of military, diplomatic, informational, economic, cyber and law-enforcement activities. NATO has a well-developed focus on interoperability and integration across these and other domains, which could be applied to the problem of hybrid warfare. Contingency planning and training could be orientated to the hybrid model, and lessons could be applied from experiences in Afghanistan against networked insurgent and criminal organisations. Defence planners might look for asymmetrical advantages that could be applied to this problem. A potential advantage, often under-utilised, is the ability to take law-enforcement and financial action against enemy organisations so that their sources of strength and support are exposed and prohibited. International and non-governmental organisations may be mobilised to expose illicit financial flows and to sanction individuals and companies that aid and abet adversaries. The French, Italian and Dutch models of blending military and law-enforcement actions overseas might be applied at the operational and strategic levels. All of these efforts should add the dimension of cyberspace as a critical element in understanding hybrid warfare, defending against it and, if necessary, taking offensive action.

As NATO and many Western states look beyond the long war in Afghanistan, there has been a tendency to return to the orthodoxy of the 1990s Revolution in Military Affairs, and especially the belief that complex land-based problems can be effectively addressed by technology and precision-strike operations conducted at stand-off range. In hybrid warfare, exclusive use of stand-off capabilities leaves decisions in the hands of enemies who operate in and among populations and extend operations beyond physical battlegrounds to realms of perception and subversion. A significant aspect of Russia's hybrid warfare is the use of conventional forces, capable of mobilising quickly and massing to intimidate the target nation while shielding and supporting (directly and indirectly) unconventional forces employed inside that nation. The combination of tactics and capabilities employed in Ukraine, and the deniability professed by Moscow, even saw the insertion of conventional forces into Eastern Ukraine in mid-2014.

States wishing to respond effectively to hybrid-warfare threats are likely to have to apply greater investment in special operations and conventional land forces, irrespective of whether the threat manifests itself in the Baltic States, Eastern Europe, the greater Middle East or the broader Sahel. In particular, land forces should have the ability to deploy rapidly and transition to both offensive and security operations. Combinations of conventional and special-operations forces must have the ability not just to take direct action but to defeat hybrid enemy organisations, secure territory and isolate populations from enemy subversion as well. Traditional army capabilities such as mobility, protection and firepower will remain relevant and important, but forces must also be effective on the 'battleground' of perception while integrating military operations with broader efforts, including in the areas of counter-threat finance and law enforcement.

Hybrid warfare represents a grave threat to NATO's collective security. However, improving the ability to defend the Alliance and its member states from hybrid-warfare threats applies beyond those challenges posed by Russia. Other adversary or potential adversary states, as well as non-state actors like ISIS and various Taliban groups, will attempt to magnify possible divisions within the Alliance, and across Western states more broadly, in an attempt to prevent consensus-based responses. Furthermore, the rapid flow of people, money, weapons, illegal drugs and information through the global commons allows enemy organisations to mobilise and employ resources for hybrid warfare, while continuing to evade detection and test the threshold for response. Perhaps most important, coping with the threat of hybrid warfare will require Western states and NATO to invest in capabilities relevant to the problem. These include cyberspace, law enforcement, information and financial tools. More broadly, however, it is important for defence policymakers to remember that all wars are fundamentally political and human endeavours that demand a comprehensive approach consistent with the character of that conflict. Hybrid warfare, especially in its initial stages, manifests itself in what Nadia Schadlow of the Smith Richardson Foundation described as 'the space between' war and peace, 'a landscape churning with political, economic and security competitions that require constant attention'. Western states, their partners and NATO have, as a consequence, to operate effectively within that landscape.

Chapter Two
Comparative defence statistics

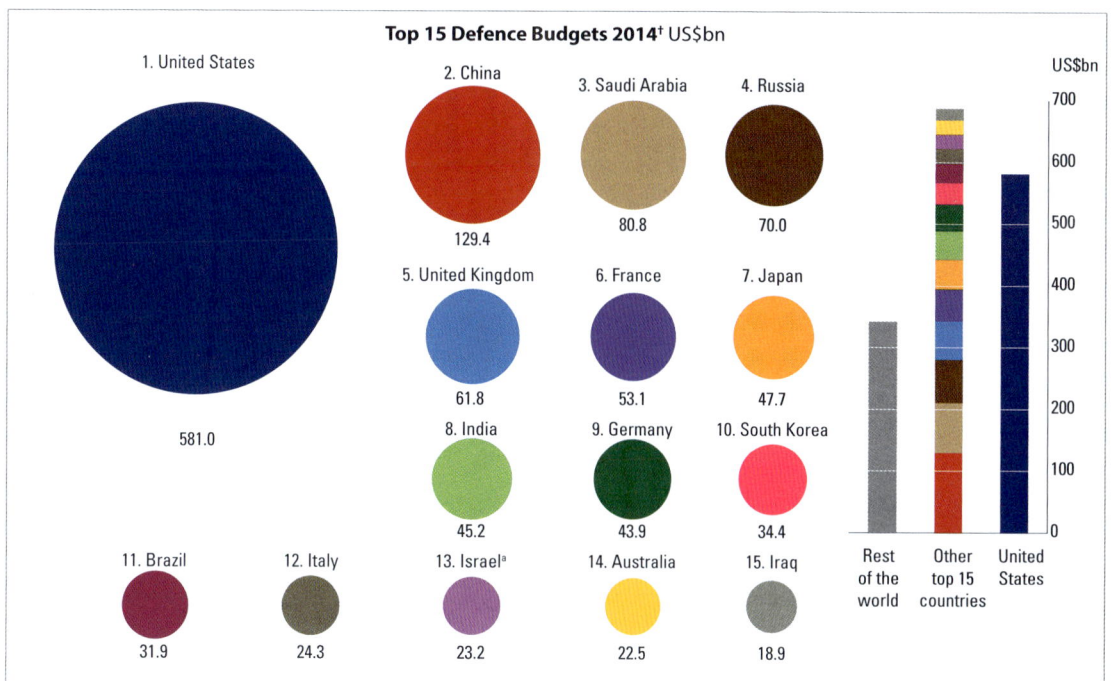

Top 15 Defence Budgets 2014† US$bn

1. United States — 581.0
2. China — 129.4
3. Saudi Arabia — 80.8
4. Russia — 70.0
5. United Kingdom — 61.8
6. France — 53.1
7. Japan — 47.7
8. India — 45.2
9. Germany — 43.9
10. South Korea — 34.4
11. Brazil — 31.9
12. Italy — 24.3
13. Israel[a] — 23.2
14. Australia — 22.5
15. Iraq — 18.9

Rest of the world | Other top 15 countries | United States

[a] Includes US Foreign Military Assistance

Note: US dollar totals are calculated using average market exchange rates for 2014, derived using IMF data. The relative position of countries will vary not only as a result of actual adjustments in defence spending levels, but also due to exchange-rate fluctuations between domestic currencies and the US dollar. The use of average exchange rates reduces these fluctuations, but the effects of such movements can be significant in a small number of cases.

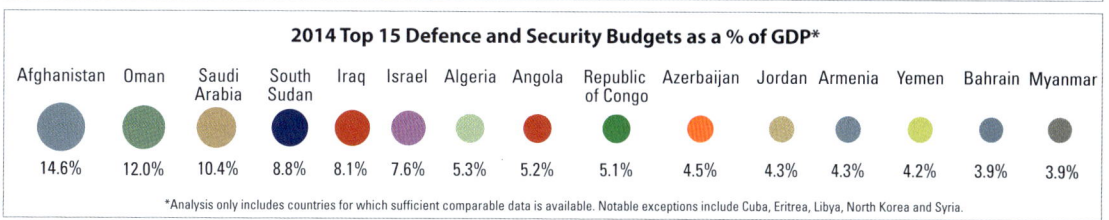

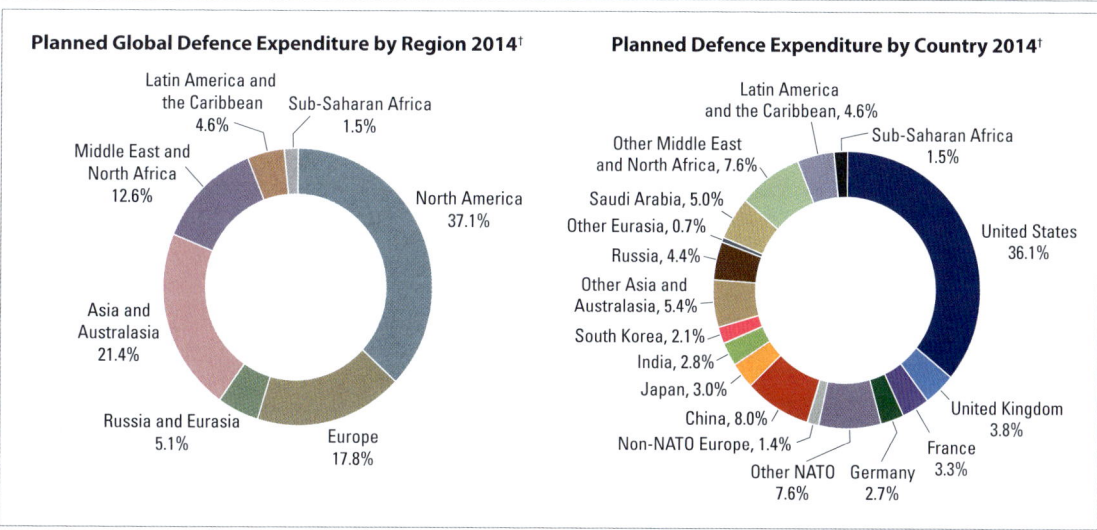

2014 Top 15 Defence and Security Budgets as a % of GDP*

Country	%
Afghanistan	14.6%
Oman	12.0%
Saudi Arabia	10.4%
South Sudan	8.8%
Iraq	8.1%
Israel	7.6%
Algeria	5.3%
Angola	5.2%
Republic of Congo	5.1%
Azerbaijan	4.5%
Jordan	4.3%
Armenia	4.3%
Yemen	4.2%
Bahrain	3.9%
Myanmar	3.9%

*Analysis only includes countries for which sufficient comparable data is available. Notable exceptions include Cuba, Eritrea, Libya, North Korea and Syria.

Planned Global Defence Expenditure by Region 2014†

- North America 37.1%
- Asia and Australasia 21.4%
- Europe 17.8%
- Middle East and North Africa 12.6%
- Russia and Eurasia 5.1%
- Latin America and the Caribbean 4.6%
- Sub-Saharan Africa 1.5%

Planned Defence Expenditure by Country 2014†

- United States 36.1%
- China 8.0%
- Other NATO 7.6%
- Other Middle East and North Africa 7.6%
- Other Asia and Australasia 5.4%
- Saudi Arabia 5.0%
- Latin America and the Caribbean 4.6%
- Russia 4.4%
- United Kingdom 3.8%
- France 3.3%
- Japan 3.0%
- India 2.8%
- Germany 2.7%
- South Korea 2.1%
- Sub-Saharan Africa 1.5%
- Non-NATO Europe 1.4%
- Other Eurasia 0.7%

† At current prices and exchange rates.

22 THE MILITARY BALANCE 2015

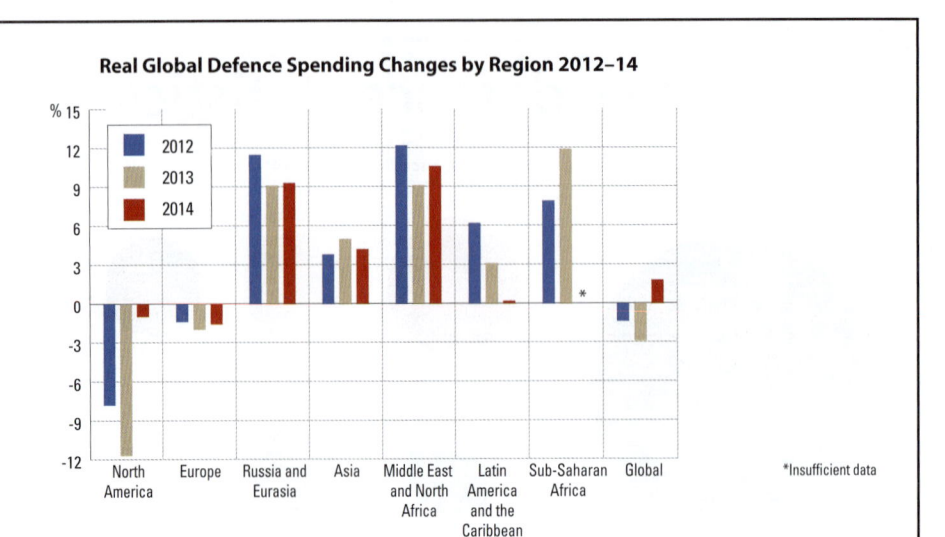

Real Global Defence Spending Changes by Region 2012–14

*Insufficient data

Planned Global Defence Expenditure by Country 2014 at PPP Exchange Rates

Purchasing Power Parity (PPP) rates can better enable international comparisons of the portion of military outlays allocated to goods and services that do not generally trade internationally, such as military personnel and infrastructure expenditure. It is a conceptual approach that, unlike average annual market exchange rates, simultaneously undertakes currency conversions as well as adjusts for domestic price differences between countries, although it should be used with a degree of caution as no military-specific PPP rates exist. Using PPP rates tends to shrink the proportion of global defence outlays accounted for by advanced economies, while expanding the proportion of outlays accounted for by emerging economies (compare figures in this graphic with those contained in the 'Planned Defence Expenditure by Country 2014' graphic on p. 21). The theoretically accurate composition of global military spending is likely to lie in between these two estimates.

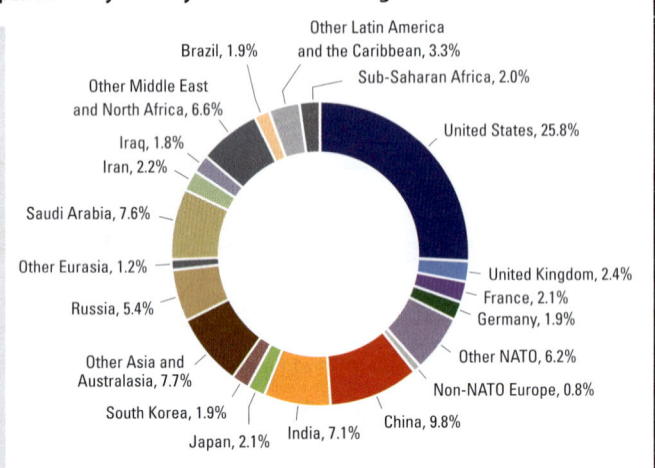

Brazil, 1.9%
Other Latin America and the Caribbean, 3.3%
Other Middle East and North Africa, 6.6%
Sub-Saharan Africa, 2.0%
Iraq, 1.8%
United States, 25.8%
Iran, 2.2%
Saudi Arabia, 7.6%
Other Eurasia, 1.2%
United Kingdom, 2.4%
Russia, 5.4%
France, 2.1%
Germany, 1.9%
Other NATO, 6.2%
Other Asia and Australasia, 7.7%
Non-NATO Europe, 0.8%
South Korea, 1.9%
China, 9.8%
Japan, 2.1%
India, 7.1%

Composition of Real Defence Spending Increases 2013–14†

Latin America and the Caribbean, 3.5%
Other Eurasia, 0.3%
Sub-Saharan Africa, 3.5%
Ukraine, 3.8%
China, 20.8%
Russia, 10.1%
Other Europe and Canada, 4.3%
India, 4.6%
Poland, 2.5%
Other Middle East and North Africa, 4.8%
Other Asia, 7.3%
Israel, 2.0%
Iraq, 2.2%
Algeria, 2.3%
Saudi Arabia, 27.8%

Total increases† 2013–14: US$43.1bn

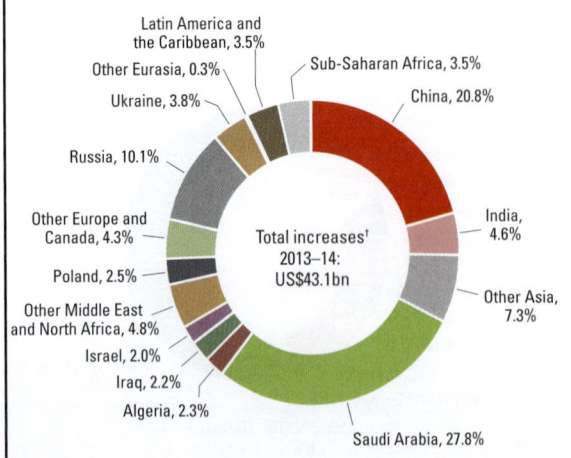

Composition of Real Defence Spending Reductions 2013–14†

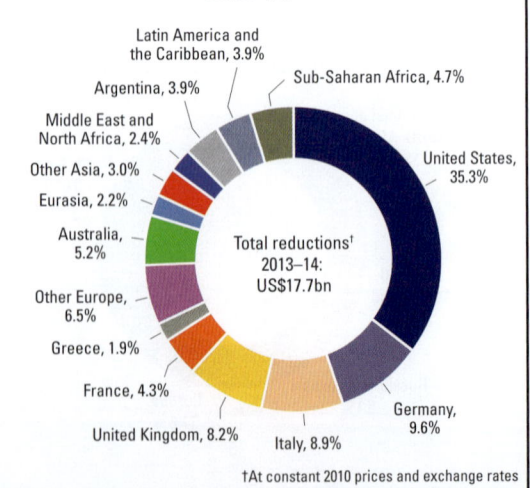

Latin America and the Caribbean, 3.9%
Argentina, 3.9%
Sub-Saharan Africa, 4.7%
Middle East and North Africa, 2.4%
Other Asia, 3.0%
United States, 35.3%
Eurasia, 2.2%
Australia, 5.2%
Other Europe, 6.5%
Greece, 1.9%
France, 4.3%
United Kingdom, 8.2%
Italy, 8.9%
Germany, 9.6%

Total reductions† 2013–14: US$17.7bn

†At constant 2010 prices and exchange rates

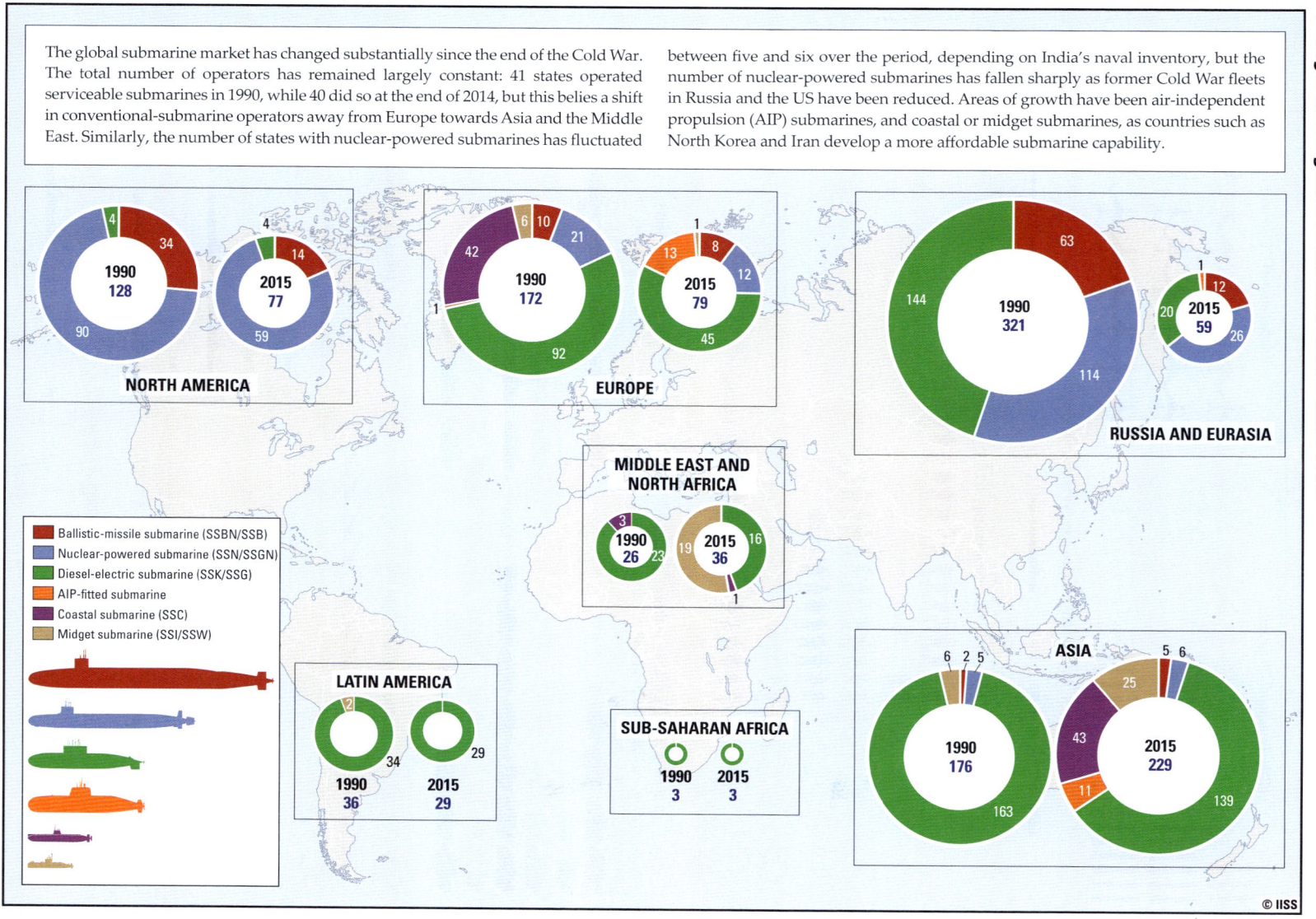

Comparative defence statistics

Changes in the global submarine market since 1990

The global submarine market has changed substantially since the end of the Cold War. The total number of operators has remained largely constant: 41 states operated serviceable submarines in 1990, while 40 did so at the end of 2014, but this belies a shift in conventional-submarine operators away from Europe towards Asia and the Middle East. Similarly, the number of states with nuclear-powered submarines has fluctuated between five and six over the period, depending on India's naval inventory, but the number of nuclear-powered submarines has fallen sharply as former Cold War fleets in Russia and the US have been reduced. Areas of growth have been air-independent propulsion (AIP) submarines, and coastal or midget submarines, as countries such as North Korea and Iran develop a more affordable submarine capability.

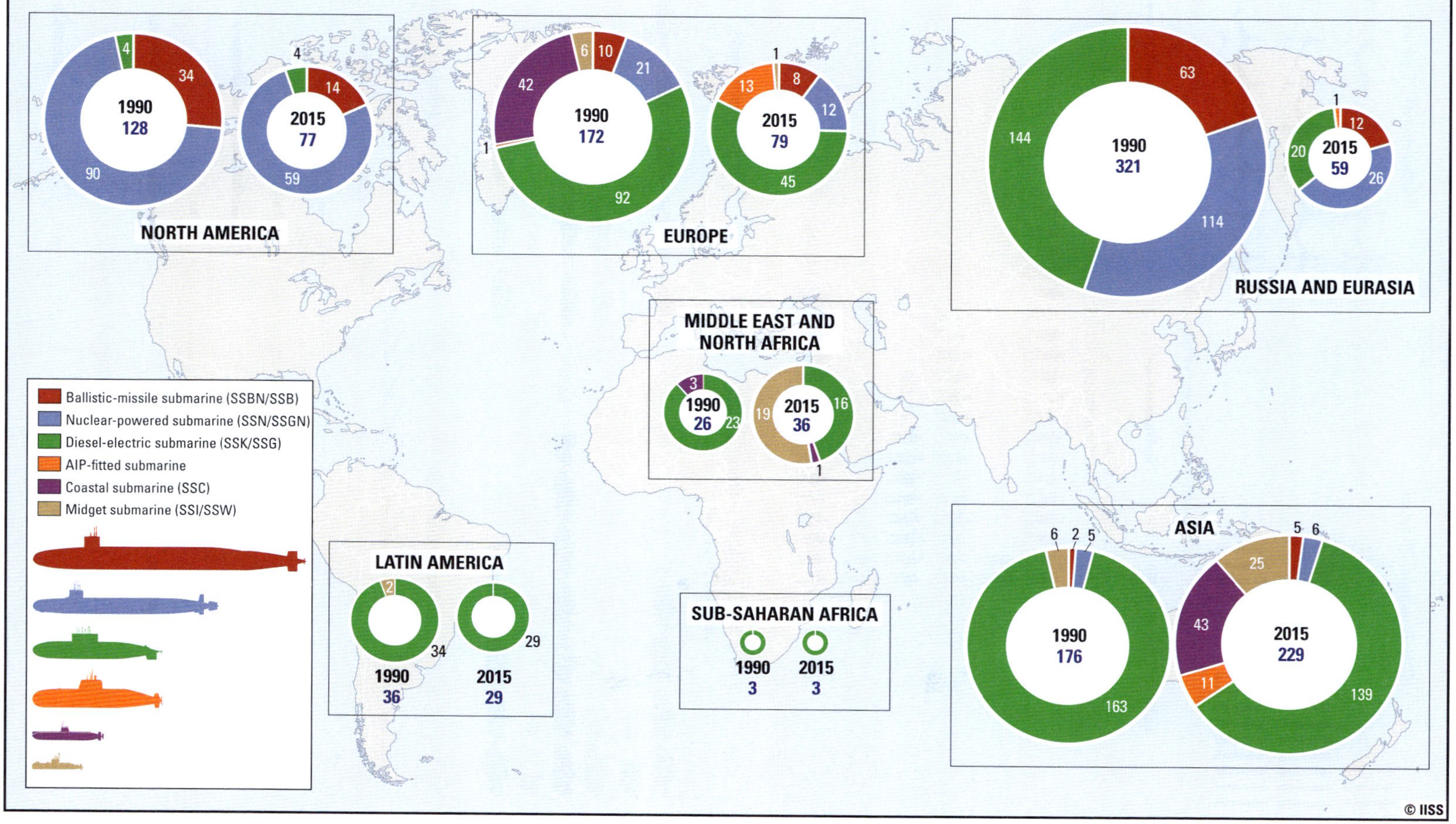

RUSSIA AND EURASIA

1990: 321 — 144, 63, 114
2015: 59 — 20, 1, 12, 26

ASIA

1990: 176 — 163, 6, 2, 5
2015: 229 — 139, 11, 25, 43, 5, 6

EUROPE

1990: 172 — 92, 21, 10, 6, 42, 1
2015: 79 — 45, 1, 8, 12, 13

MIDDLE EAST AND NORTH AFRICA

1990: 26 — 23, 3
2015: 36 — 19, 16, 1

SUB-SAHARAN AFRICA

1990: 3
2015: 3

NORTH AMERICA

1990: 128 — 90, 34, 4
2015: 77 — 59, 14, 4

LATIN AMERICA

1990: 36 — 34, 2
2015: 29 — 29

Legend:
- Ballistic-missile submarine (SSBN/SSB)
- Nuclear-powered submarine (SSN/SSGN)
- Diesel-electric submarine (SSK/SSG)
- AIP-fitted submarine
- Coastal submarine (SSC)
- Midget submarine (SSI/SSW)

© IISS

THE MILITARY BALANCE 2015

Key defence statistics

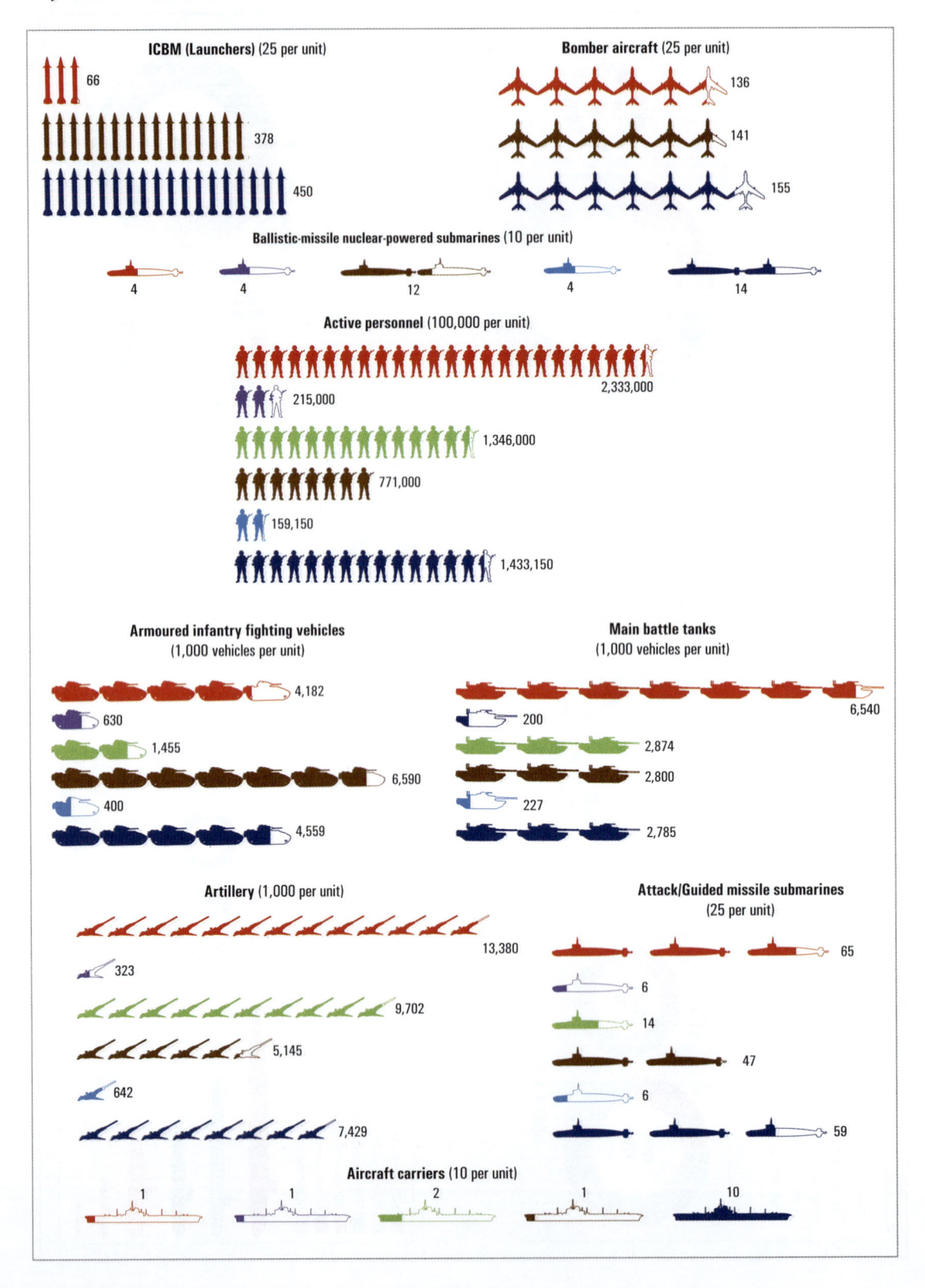

ICBM (Launchers) (25 per unit)
66
378
450

Bomber aircraft (25 per unit)
136
141
155

Ballistic-missile nuclear-powered submarines (10 per unit)
4
4
12
4
14

Active personnel (100,000 per unit)
2,333,000
215,000
1,346,000
771,000
159,150
1,433,150

Armoured infantry fighting vehicles (1,000 vehicles per unit)
4,182
630
1,455
6,590
400
4,559

Main battle tanks (1,000 vehicles per unit)
6,540
200
2,874
2,800
227
2,785

Artillery (1,000 per unit)
13,380
323
9,702
5,145
642
7,429

Attack/Guided missile submarines (25 per unit)
65
6
14
47
6
59

Aircraft carriers (10 per unit)
1
1
2
1
10

Comparative defence statistics

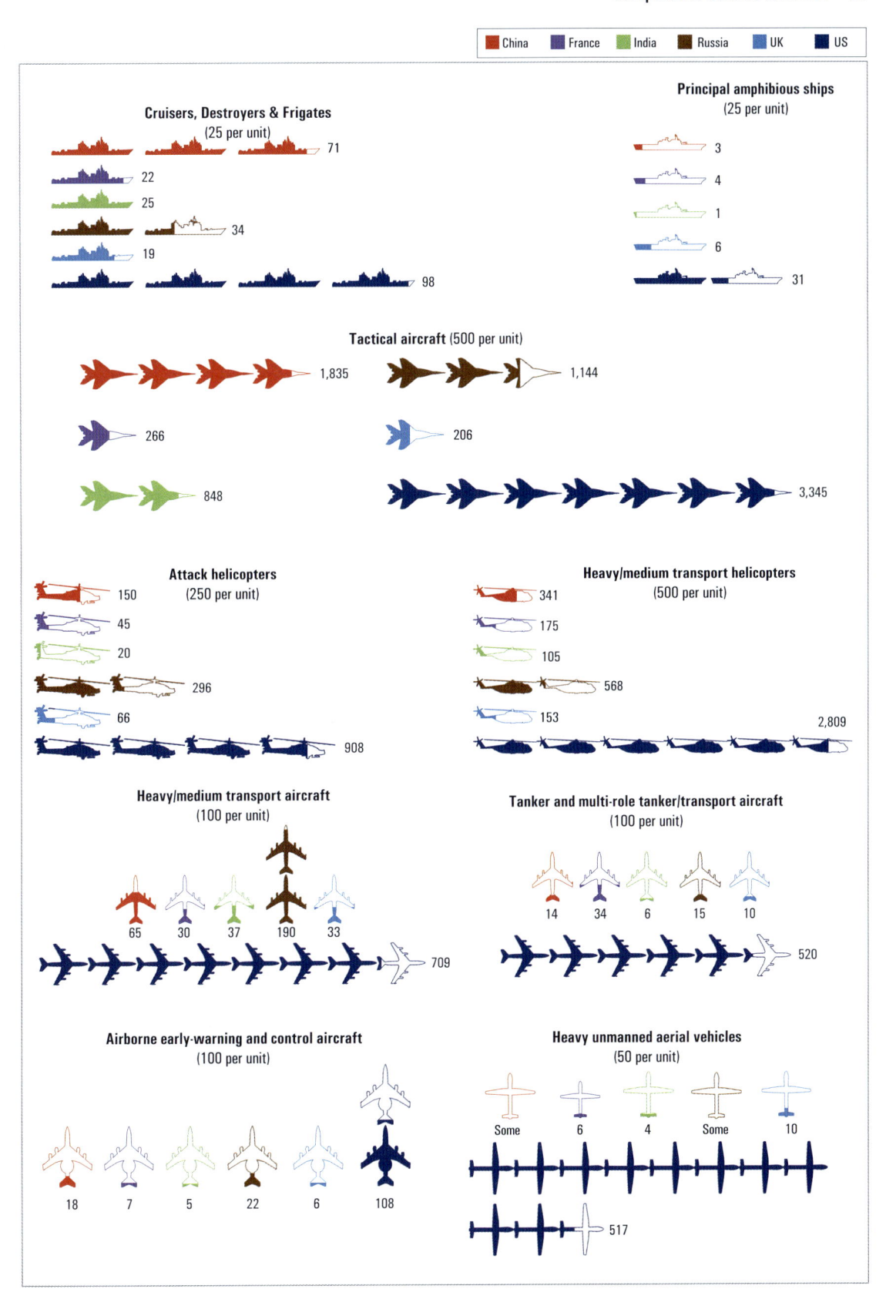

■ China ■ France ■ India ■ Russia ■ UK ■ US

Cruisers, Destroyers & Frigates
(25 per unit)

- China: 71
- France: 22
- India: 25
- Russia: 34
- UK: 19
- US: 98

Principal amphibious ships
(25 per unit)

- China: 3
- France: 4
- India: 1
- Russia: 0
- UK: 6
- US: 31

Tactical aircraft (500 per unit)

- China: 1,835
- France: 266
- India: 848
- Russia: 1,144
- UK: 206
- US: 3,345

Attack helicopters
(250 per unit)

- China: 150
- France: 45
- India: 20
- Russia: 296
- UK: 66
- US: 908

Heavy/medium transport helicopters
(500 per unit)

- China: 341
- France: 175
- India: 105
- Russia: 568
- UK: 153
- US: 2,809

Heavy/medium transport aircraft
(100 per unit)

- China: 65
- France: 30
- India: 37
- Russia: 190
- UK: 33
- US: 709

Tanker and multi-role tanker/transport aircraft
(100 per unit)

- China: 14
- France: 34
- India: 6
- Russia: 15
- UK: 10
- US: 520

Airborne early-warning and control aircraft
(100 per unit)

- China: 18
- France: 7
- India: 5
- Russia: 22
- UK: 6
- US: 108

Heavy unmanned aerial vehicles
(50 per unit)

- China: Some
- France: 6
- India: 4
- Russia: Some
- UK: 10
- US: 517

Precision attack by guided artillery

Land forces have long conducted indirect fire with mortars, artillery and unguided rockets. These have traditionally been 'area' weapons, the accuracy of which decreased with range. Over recent years these systems have had GPS guidance systems applied, which gives them greatly increased accuracy, independent of range. Hoped-for benefits of their increased accuracy include a reduction in the chances of civilian casualties and collateral damage. It also reduces numbers of rounds required, with logistic benefits.

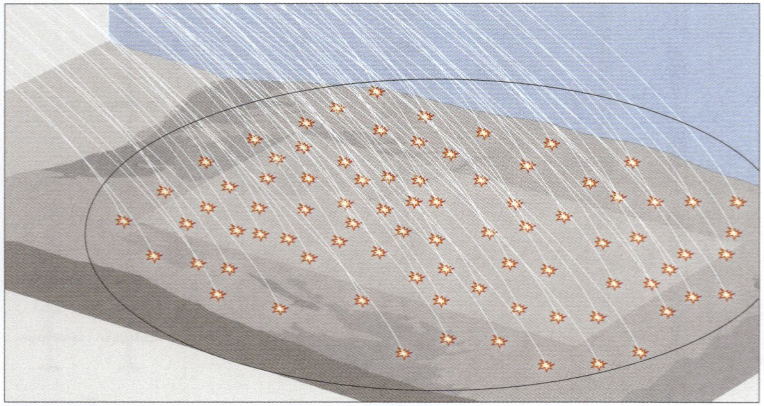

Unlike direct-fire weapons, such as tank guns, indirect-fire weapons such as unguided mortars, artillery and rockets are area weapons. Their accuracy decreases with range. It is further reduced by weather effects, especially wind. This means that large numbers of rounds are required to suppress, rather than destroy area targets. A typical unguided artillery shell has a Circular Error Probable (CEP)* of 50m at short range and 300m at long range.

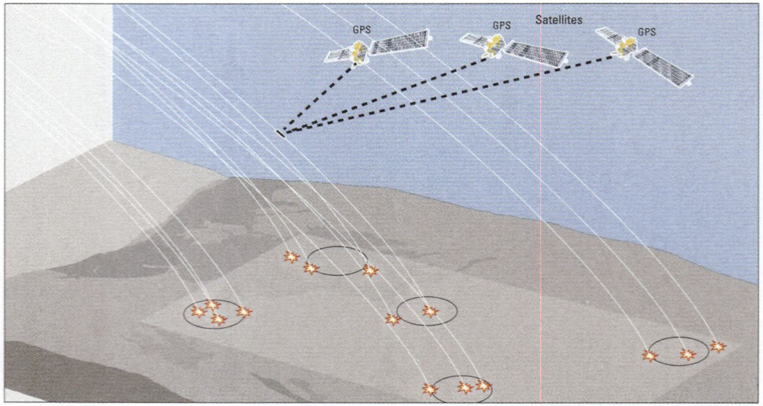

Adding GPS guidance means that accuracy becomes independent of range. Suppression of area targets therefore requires far fewer rounds, often 90% less. Guided artillery is also able to engage point targets. It also allows fire to be brought closer to friendly troops. This new capability has been used by US and allied forces in Iraq and Afghanistan. Claimed CEP for these weapons ranges from 1m to 10m.

GPS guided artillery in service with US forces

M31 Guided Unitary Rocket
Fired from US-designed Multiple Land Rocket System (MLRS) and High Mobility Artillery System (HIMARS)
Entered service 2007 **Calibre** 227mm **Range** 70km
CEP classified but claimed to be 1m **Operators** US, UK, France, Qatar
Ordered by Singapore, UAE

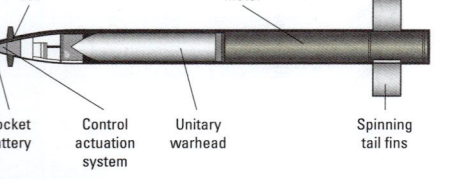

Labels: Guidance set, Rocket battery, Control actuation system, Rocket motor, Unitary warhead, Spinning tail fins

XM395 Precision Guided Mortar Munition
Fired by 120mm mortar
Entered service 2011 **Calibre** 120mm **Range** 7km
CEP 10m required, 1m claimed **Operator** US

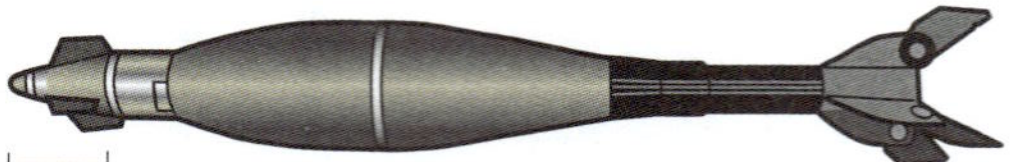

Labels: Precision guidance kit, Standard M9933/4 mortar warhead and body

M982 Excalibur Precision Guided Artillery Projectile
Fired by M109 and M777 howitzers
Entered service 2012 **Calibre** 155mm **Range** 40km **CEP** 4m
Operators US, Canada **Ordered by** Australia (army and navy)

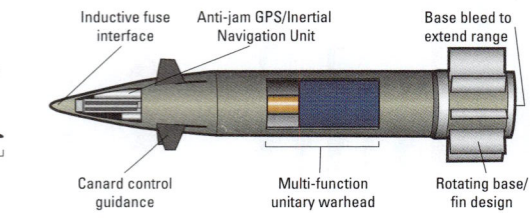

Labels: Inductive fuse interface, Canard control guidance, Anti-jam GPS/Inertial Navigation Unit, Multi-function unitary warhead, Base bleed to extend range, Rotating base/fin design

*Commonly understood as the radius within which 50% of all rounds will fall

Comparative defence statistics

US rebalance to the Asia-Pacific: vessel deployments 2014–20

The US rebalance to the Asia-Pacific was first announced in late 2011, but the detail of the naval rebalance is only now becoming clearer. Figures released in March 2014 suggest that the US remains dedicated to its goal of deploying 60% of US Navy vessels to the region by 2020, a plan revealed by then-defense secretary Leon Panetta at the 2012 Shangri-La Dialogue. However, this statistic includes those deployed in Hawaii and on the west coast of the US, particularly in San Diego. The number of vessels deployed to 7th Fleet, while increasing, will not approach the 60% figure. Further, continuing commitments elsewhere also reflect the fact that the rebalance to the Asia-Pacific is matched by similar moves elsewhere: the Middle East will also see an increase in deployed vessels.

Europe
Despite the numerical drawdown in hull numbers the navy will still play a part in safeguarding European security, particularly through the planned permanent deployment of four BMD-capable guided-missile destroyers to Spain beginning in 2014. This replaces the current arrangement whereby ten deploy from the US on a rotational basis. The six that are freed up will be deployed to the Asia-Pacific. The operational gap left will be filled by new Littoral Combat Ships and Joint High-Speed Vessels.

Asia-Pacific
Not all the vessels included in the rebalance are major assets; some will be smaller combatants or logistics vessels. The current plan is to base ten of the planned 32 Littoral Combat Ships in the region, four of which will be in Singapore on a rotational basis. A fourth nuclear-powered attack submarine will deploy to Guam in FY15. Also expected in 2015 is the deployment of amphibious-assault ship USS *Wasp* with a squadron of F-35Bs. Navy forces in Japan will also be reinforced by two BMD-capable destroyers by FY17, while the Pacific Fleet will also receive the first *Zumwalt*-class destroyer, expected to commission in FY16.

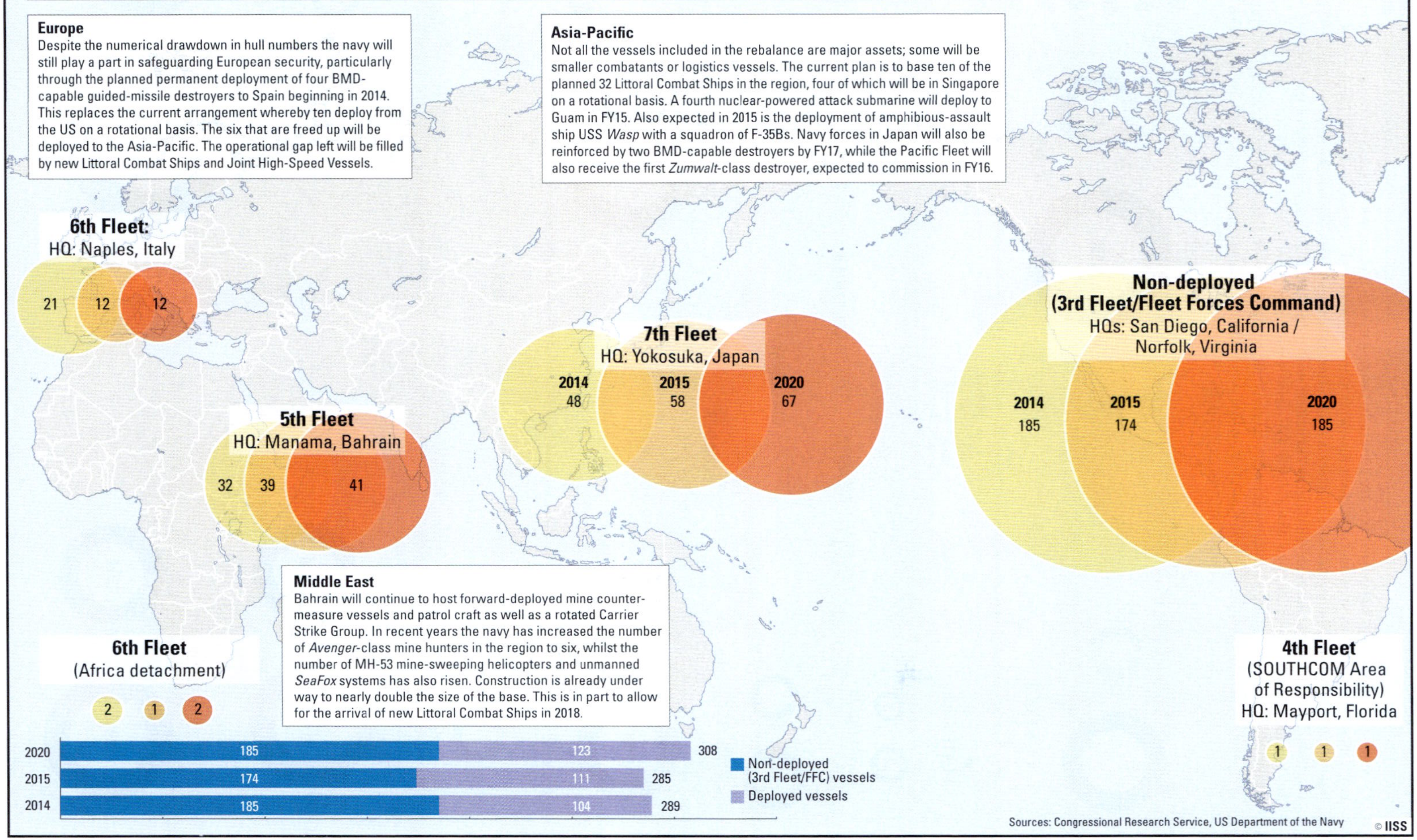

Middle East
Bahrain will continue to host forward-deployed mine counter-measure vessels and patrol craft as well as a rotated Carrier Strike Group. In recent years the navy has increased the number of *Avenger*-class mine hunters in the region to six, whilst the number of MH-53 mine-sweeping helicopters and unmanned SeaFox systems has also risen. Construction is already under way to nearly double the size of the base. This is in part to allow for the arrival of new Littoral Combat Ships in 2018.

6th Fleet: HQ: Naples, Italy
2014: 21 / 12 / 2
2015: 12 / 1 / 1
2020: 12 / — / 2

6th Fleet (Africa detachment)
2014: 185
2015: 174
2020: 185

5th Fleet HQ: Manama, Bahrain
2014: 32
2015: 39
2020: 41

7th Fleet HQ: Yokosuka, Japan
2014: 48
2015: 58
2020: 67

Non-deployed (3rd Fleet/Fleet Forces Command) HQs: San Diego, California / Norfolk, Virginia
2014: 185
2015: 174
2020: 185

4th Fleet (SOUTHCOM Area of Responsibility) HQ: Mayport, Florida
2014: 1
2015: 1
2020: 1

Deployed vessels / Non-deployed (3rd Fleet/FFC) vessels:
2014: 104 / 185 (total 289)
2015: 111 / 174 (total 285)
2020: 123 / 185 (total 308)

Sources: Congressional Research Service, US Department of the Navy

© IISS

Latin American fixed-wing aircraft fleets, 1994–2014

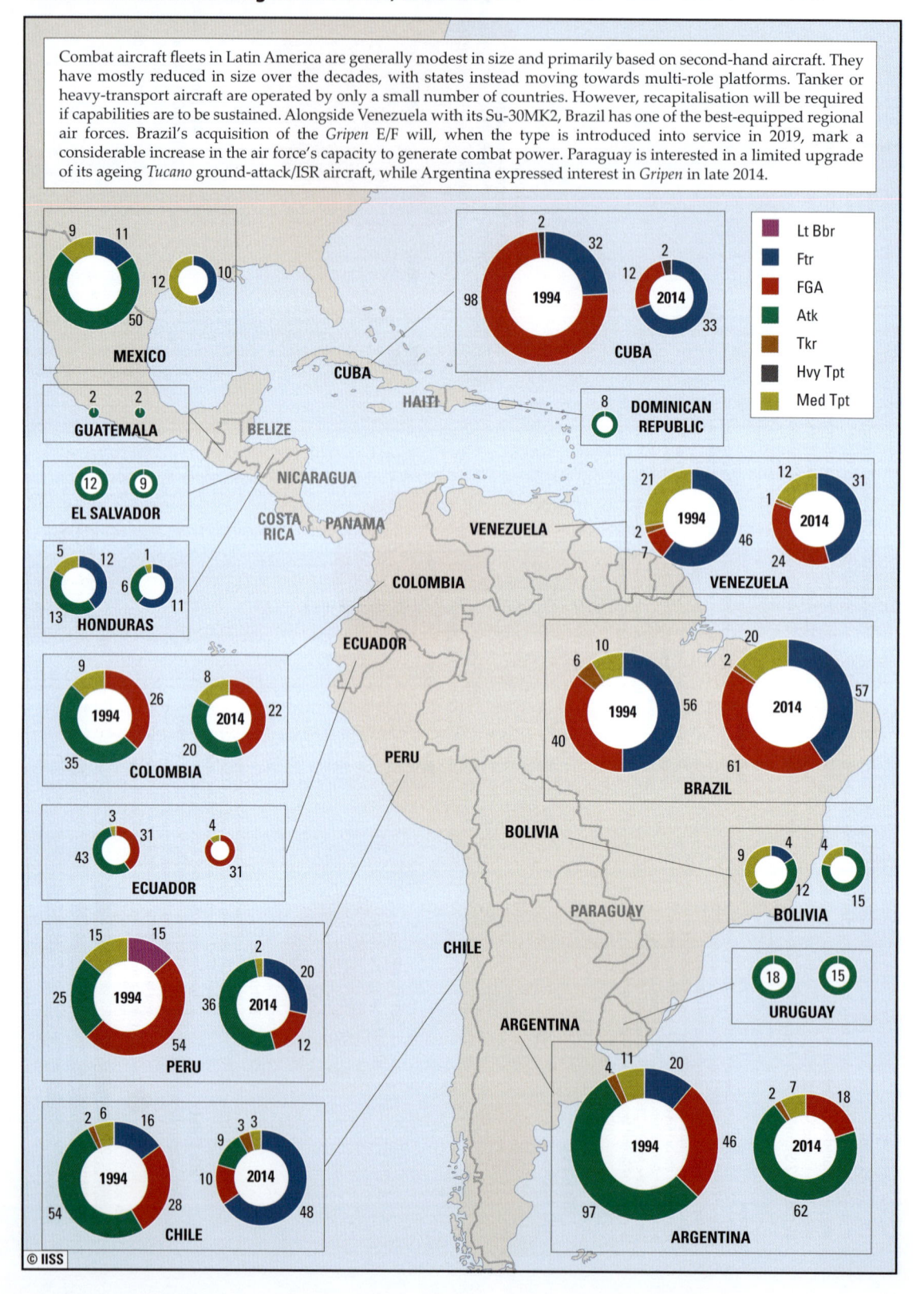

Combat aircraft fleets in Latin America are generally modest in size and primarily based on second-hand aircraft. They have mostly reduced in size over the decades, with states instead moving towards multi-role platforms. Tanker or heavy-transport aircraft are operated by only a small number of countries. However, recapitalisation will be required if capabilities are to be sustained. Alongside Venezuela with its Su-30MK2, Brazil has one of the best-equipped regional air forces. Brazil's acquisition of the *Gripen* E/F will, when the type is introduced into service in 2019, mark a considerable increase in the air force's capacity to generate combat power. Paraguay is interested in a limited upgrade of its ageing *Tucano* ground-attack/ISR aircraft, while Argentina expressed interest in *Gripen* in late 2014.

Legend:
- Lt Bbr
- Ftr
- FGA
- Atk
- Tkr
- Hvy Tpt
- Med Tpt

MEXICO: 9, 11, 50, 12 / 10, 12

CUBA 1994: 2, 32, 98
CUBA 2014: 2, 12, 33

GUATEMALA: 2, 2

DOMINICAN REPUBLIC: 8

EL SALVADOR: 12 / 9

HONDURAS: 5, 12, 1, 6, 11, 13

VENEZUELA 1994: 21, 7, 2, 46
VENEZUELA 2014: 12, 31, 24, 1

COLOMBIA 1994: 9, 26, 20, 35
COLOMBIA 2014: 8, 22

BRAZIL 1994: 10, 6, 56, 40
BRAZIL 2014: 20, 2, 57, 61

ECUADOR 1994: 3, 31, 43
ECUADOR 2014: 4, 31

BOLIVIA: 9, 4, 12 / 4, 15

PERU 1994: 15, 15, 25, 54
PERU 2014: 2, 20, 12, 36

URUGUAY: 18 / 15

CHILE 1994: 2, 6, 16, 28, 54
CHILE 2014: 3, 3, 9, 10, 48

ARGENTINA 1994: 11, 20, 46, 97, 4
ARGENTINA 2014: 2, 7, 18, 62

© IISS

Chapter Three
North America

UNITED STATES

At the start of 2014, US defence planners were facing complex security and policy preoccupations, including managing the drawdown in Afghanistan, China's continuing rise, the state of negotiations over the Iranian nuclear programme, the continuing campaign against terrorism, as well as dealing with the effects of defence-budget cuts. From early in the year, this defence agenda became more crowded and by October included the possible return of sequestration in FY2016; the Ukraine crisis and its effect on relations with Russia as well as on broader European security; the Ebola outbreak in Africa; and the increase in violence in Syria and Iraq – particularly the territorial gains made by the Islamic State of Iraq and al-Sham (ISIS).

However, on matters of military reform, budgetary reallocation, the downsizing of the army, the rebalance to the Asia-Pacific and overall defence-modernisation strategy, there was more continuity than change in both policy and budget debates. Indeed, the Obama administration continued the basic contours of the essentially realist foreign policy established during its first term: a preference for active diplomacy, emphasis on building counter-terrorism partnerships and avoiding protracted military deployments.

Quadrennial Defense Review

In this context, there was heightened interest in the findings of the 2014 Quadrennial Defense Review (QDR), released in March along with the FY2015 budget proposals. Among other conclusions, the QDR stated that US forces had to themselves rebalance 'for a broad spectrum of conflict', reflecting the range of threats and adversaries that could require attention. In common with recent years, US forces would not 'be sized to conduct long-scale protracted stability operations [though] we will preserve the expertise gained during the past ten years of counterinsurgency and stability operations'. 'Rebalance' was a much-used word. The QDR identified that while US presence and posture should be rebalanced, so should capability, capacity and readiness within the joint force.

While the Pentagon could carry out its strategy at current funding levels, there was concern about readiness and, in the long term, 'a lot of uncertainty in a security environment as dynamic as the one we face with a smaller force'. It was widely acknowledged that readiness had suffered due to the effects of sequestration on top of a decade of continuous operations. Further sequestration in FY2016 was an additional risk. For the services, this could mean, the QDR said: the air force retiring 80 more aircraft; active-duty army strength declining to 420,000 (the current target is 440,000–450,000); the navy retiring one aircraft carrier, reducing total carrier strike groups to ten; and the marines reducing further to 175,000. At the same time, some capability areas would be protected, including cyber, missile defence, precision strike, ISR, space and special operations forces (slated to grow to an end strength of nearly 70,000). Under the current allocated resources, the Pentagon could meet the strategy detailed in the QDR, though there would be 'increased risk in some areas', as Defense Undersecretary for Strategy, Plans and Force Development Christine Wormuth put it in March. However, should sequestration return in 2016 and beyond, Wormuth said, it would create capacity challenges that would make it 'harder to build security globally' and 'we would have a harder time generating sufficient forward presence to do all of the partnership activities that we think are necessary around the world'.

While the document was clear in stressing the threat to strategy and forces from continued sequestration, it also stressed the risks – particularly in the final assessment by Chairman of the Joint Chiefs of Staff General Martin Dempsey – posed by unanticipated events, evolving security dynamics and the erosion in the technological edge long enjoyed by US forces. In the next ten years, Dempsey expected 'interstate conflict in East Asia to rise, the vulnerability of our platforms and basing to increase, our technology edge to erode, instability to persist in the Middle East, and threats posed by violent extremist organizations to endure'. Though the QDR had largely protected certain capabilities, he noted that the force outlined in the QDR 'takes risk in the capacity of each Service but most notably in land forces. While a U.S. military response to aggression most often begins in the air or maritime domains – and in the future could begin with confrontations in the cyber and space domains – they typically include and end with some commitment of forces in the land domain.'

The rise of possible peer competitors required new investments in technology and tactics, but balanced, joint forces were also required. The services must be balanced in terms of mass as well as readiness. Problems with readiness were acknowledged, but the size of the joint force, although acknowledged as an issue, continued to reduce. Reflective of this trend, and of awareness that personnel numbers were unlikely to increase, the aspiration was for a joint force capable of rapidly adapting to threats, with flexible capabilities at its disposal. However, as army chief General Raymond Odierno said in October, 'as we continue to lose end-strength, our flexibility deteriorates, as does our ability to react to strategic surprise'.

At the end of 2014, the increasingly demanding strategic environment had led US forces to deploy additional resources to Eastern Europe as part of *Operation Atlantic Resolve* and, three years after leaving, to return on combat missions to Iraq, and then Syria, on *Operation Inherent Resolve*, targeting ISIS and also engaging in humanitarian-assistance missions. In early November, the president announced that 1,500 extra US personnel would deploy to Iraq to help train the Iraqi armed forces. In addition, the long-term, though incremental, rebalance to the Asia-Pacific continued; thousands of troops were mandated to remain in Afghanistan after the signing of a bilateral security agreement; and global counter-terrorism tasks, involving all forces, continued. The armed forces were also called on to help tackle the Ebola health crisis in West Africa, at the same time as maintaining myriad deployments and capacity-building operations.

These tasks reinforced the understanding that conflict and security crises are difficult to predict, and that, should stability unravel and fighting ensue, conflicts are uncertain endeavours with, ultimately, political objectives. However, 'the smaller and less capable military outlined in the QDR' means that meeting its obligations will be more difficult, said Dempsey. 'Most of our platforms will be older, and our advantages in some domains will have eroded. Our loss of depth across the force could reduce our ability to intimidate opponents from escalating conflict. Moreover, many of our most capable allies will lose key capabilities.' These concerns, and the emphasis placed in the QDR on risks to US armed forces, could be seen as applying pressure to the legislature over sequestration, certainly in light of the further identified cuts should sequestration go ahead. There was also pressure on Pentagon planners, equipment specialists and defence industry, as well as service chiefs, to design and equip future forces capable of working together effectively, and rapidly adapting and deploying; in essence, still being able to bring to bear current full-spectrum capabilities, but with reduced forces.

The armed services

In June 2014, the **US Army** published its latest Army Operating Concept, titled 'Win in a Complex World'. This was designed to provide the foundation for future force modernisation. It derived from the Army Capstone Concept, and in turn will drive combat-arm developments within the army. The document stressed both the continuities in and the changing nature of conflict, and how the army can deliver 'sustainable outcomes' on operations – perhaps reflective of the drive to leverage the lessons of recent conflicts for future operating environments. More complex security environments and more challenging and adaptable adversaries require well-trained and adaptable US troops, operating in a joint and cooperative fashion with other services, partner-nation forces and non-military organisations to accomplish tasks including preventing conflict, shaping security outcomes and winning in combat.

During the year the army continued its Brigade Combat Team (BCT) 2020 project, the structural-transition programme begun a year before. The plan is to reduce the overall number of BCTs and redistribute their assets to increase the remaining brigades to a level of three manoeuvre battalions each. BCT reorganisation began in earnest with the deactivation of the 4th BCT, 1st Cavalry Division in October 2013 and the redistribution of the component parts to its other brigades. Another five brigade combat teams were subsequently deactivated, with four more due to follow suit in FY2015.

New Brigade Engineer Battalions (BEBs) would also, by a combination of conversions and transfers, replace the previous Brigade Special Troops Battalions in all remaining brigades and regiments. Some divisions, such as the 1st Cavalry Division

Figure 1 Equipment Analysis: US Navy DDG 1000 *Zumwalt*-class Destroyer

Although labelled a destroyer, the *Zumwalt*-class will be among the largest surface warships in the world. With a full load displacement of more than 15,000 tonnes, it is roughly 50% heavier than the *Ticonderoga*-class cruisers currently in service. The sheer size of the vessel may have counted against it during the procurement process: an initial requirement for 32 was later cut to 24, then just seven and finally only three. In an era of predominantly land-based asymmetric warfare, the *Zumwalt* seemed expensive (with a unit cost of more than US$4bn) and misplaced. Nonetheless, the class brings various technological innovations, most notably its stealthy, tumblehome hull. The Advanced Gun System will fire the US Navy's first precision-guided, gun-loaded munitions, the Long-Range Land Attack Projectile, with a range of up to 100km and a rate of fire of ten rounds per minute. The primary armament will, though, remain an 80-cell vertical launch system for land-attack, air-defence and anti-ship missiles. The *Zumwalt*-class might better be seen as a technology demonstrator for future designs, and a way to maintain shipbuilding capacity, than a major ship class in its own right.

Specifications	Zumwalt	Type-45 (UK)	Type-52D (China)
Length (m)	182	152.4	157
Draft (m)	8.4	7.4	6
Displacement (t)	15,610	8,000	7,500
Power output (mW)	78	49.7	48.3
Speed (kts)	30	31	30
Range (nm)	4,500	6,500	4,500
Crew	142	191	280

Sources: US Navy, Raytheon, FY2015 Defense Budget, Congressional Research Service

Destroyer	Commissioned date
DDG 1000 USS *Zumwalt*	2016
DDG 1001 USS *Michael Monsoor*	2017
DDG 1002 USS *Lyndon B. Johnson*	2018

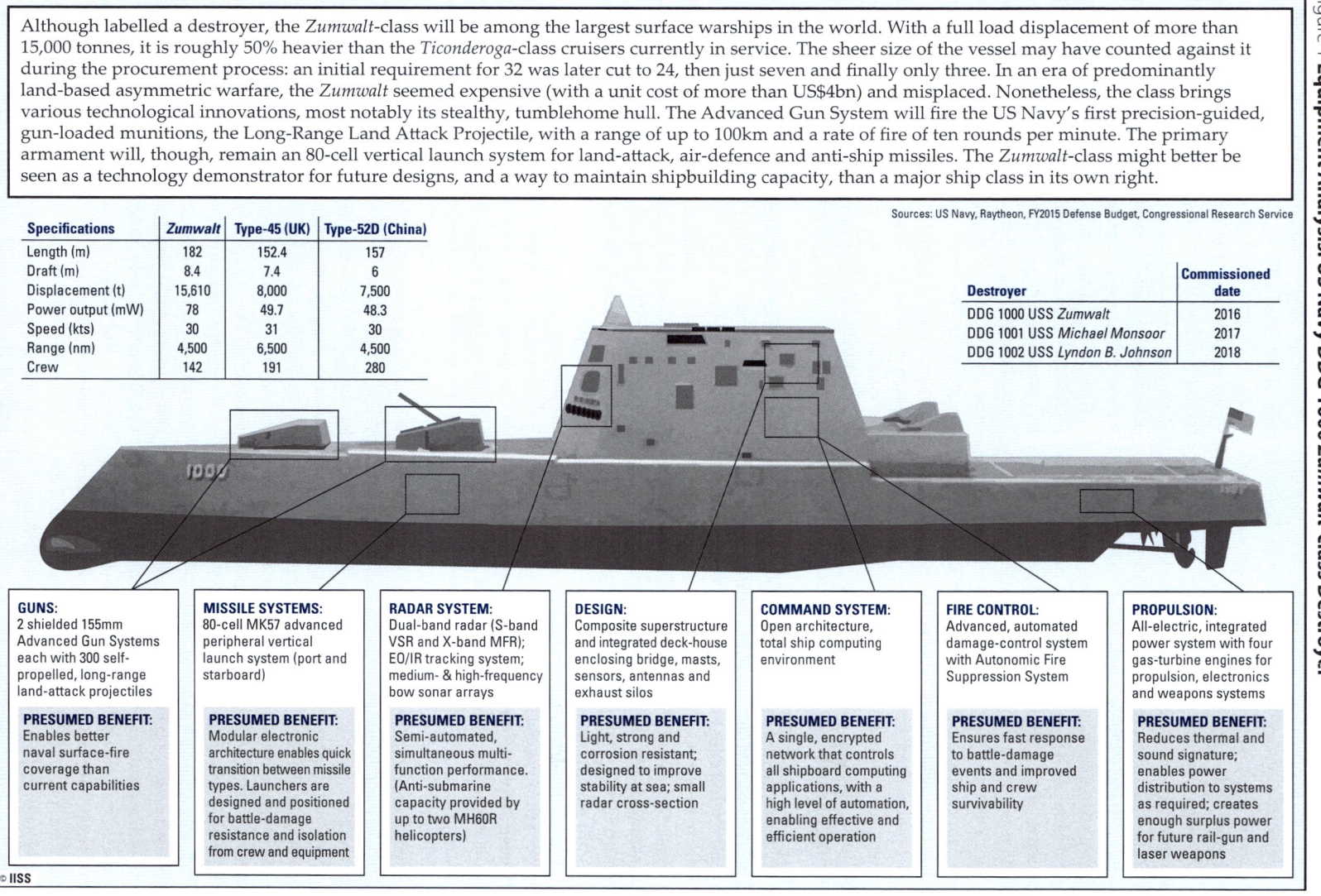

GUNS: 2 shielded 155mm Advanced Gun Systems each with 300 self-propelled, long-range land-attack projectiles

PRESUMED BENEFIT: Enables better naval surface-fire coverage than current capabilities

MISSILE SYSTEMS: 80-cell MK57 advanced peripheral vertical launch system (port and starboard)

PRESUMED BENEFIT: Modular electronic architecture enables quick transition between missile types. Launchers are designed and positioned for battle-damage resistance and isolation from crew and equipment

RADAR SYSTEM: Dual-band radar (S-band VSR and X-band MFR); EO/IR tracking system; medium- & high-frequency bow sonar arrays

PRESUMED BENEFIT: Semi-automated, simultaneous multi-function performance. (Anti-submarine capacity provided by up to two MH60R helicopters)

DESIGN: Composite superstructure and integrated deck-house enclosing bridge, masts, sensors, antennas and exhaust silos

PRESUMED BENEFIT: Light, strong and corrosion resistant; designed to improve stability at sea; small radar cross-section

COMMAND SYSTEM: Open architecture, total ship computing environment

PRESUMED BENEFIT: A single, encrypted network that controls all shipboard computing applications, with a high level of automation, enabling effective and efficient operation

FIRE CONTROL: Advanced, automated damage-control system with Autonomic Fire Suppression System

PRESUMED BENEFIT: Ensures fast response to battle-damage events and improved ship and crew survivability

PROPULSION: All-electric, integrated power system with four gas-turbine engines for propulsion, electronics and weapons systems

PRESUMED BENEFIT: Reduces thermal and sound signature; enables power distribution to systems as required; creates enough surplus power for future rail-gun and laser weapons

© IISS

and 82nd Airborne Division, had completed the transfer to new organisations, whilst others, like the 3rd Infantry Division, had only just started. The first tranche of Army National Guard brigades had begun to activate BEBs.

In 2014, the army announced an Aviation Restructuring Initiative, which proposed to cut three of the existing 13 active combat-aviation brigades by 2019. It also proposed retiring all the remaining *Kiowa* reconnaissance and TH-67 training helicopters, centralising all AH-64 *Apache* attack helicopters in the active army fleet and replacing National Guard *Apache*s with more *Blackhawk*s and *Lakota*s.

In October 2013 two new **US Navy** (USN) ships were launched in quick succession: USS *Zumwalt*, the first of three DDG-1000 multi-mission destroyers, and USS *Gerald R. Ford*, the first of the new-class aircraft carriers. Amphibious capabilities were boosted with the commissioning of the ninth *San Antonio*-class landing platform dock, USS *Somerset*, in March 2014 and the first *America*-class amphibious-assault ship in October. The fourth Littoral Combat Ship (LCS), USS *Coronado*, was also commissioned in March, and the eleventh *Virginia*-class nuclear-powered attack submarine in October.

While the navy maintained its long-running procurement and posture plans, significant new research was being undertaken, particularly into unmanned vessels and aircraft. The Office of Naval Research demonstrated synchronised, unmanned, autonomous vessels in October 2014, allowing multiple unmanned surface vessels to communicate and coordinate. However, the intended role requirements for some future programmes, including the Unmanned Carrier-Launched Airborne Surveillance and Strike project, the Small Surface Combatant and the LX(R) amphibious ship, have not been well defined.

The navy continued to consider paramount its 'rebalance' to the Asia-Pacific, but assurances that 60% of the navy would be transferred to the region belied the fact that many of the assets would be LCSs or Joint High-Speed Vessels. Additionally, the Pacific Fleet also is able to provide assets to the Persian Gulf, so the proposed 60:40 split does not necessarily mean that 60% of USN assets would deploy exclusively to the Pacific in the years ahead. Furthermore, the changes were happening at a gradual pace; for example, only one of the four LCS vessels was in Singapore, and the largest marine corps contingent to yet reach Australia numbered about 1,100 personnel.

Meanwhile, instability in the Middle East ensured a constant rotation of forces through the Fifth fleet's area of responsibility. In 2014, aircraft from the USS *George H.W. Bush* carried out air-strikes in Iraq and Syria, emphasising the navy's continuing role in the region. The new four-ship deployment to Rota, Spain and regular deployments of a guided-missile destroyer to the Black Sea since early 2014 underlined the navy's European presence.

The **US Air Force** (USAF) turned once again to traditional force development, focusing on current and projected high-end threats in contested airspace. This followed over a decade of air–ground-focused work in Iraq and Afghanistan, in a permissive air environment. The stress given to airlift and counter-insurgency combat operations during these campaigns resulted in the neglect or suspension of other capabilities core to the service's mission. Sequestration also required the USAF to make contentious cuts to some of the types in its equipment inventory.

For the first time in over two decades the USAF was considering the potential erosion of its technical edge, as other nations developed and fielded increasingly capable air-combat and air-defence systems. It was also contemplating an air-combat platform to follow the F-22 *Raptor*, with seed funding allocated in FY2015 for air dominance beyond 2030. Future equipment priorities centred on recapitalising ageing fighter, bomber and tanker fleets. The average airframe age within the fighter fleet, excluding the F-22, was 25 years; in the bomber fleet it was 32 years.

The Long-Range Strike Bomber (LRS-B), which will form part of the USAF's nuclear capability, has an anticipated initial operational capability of 2024–26. Given this compressed development timescale, it was perhaps surprising that a prime contractor was yet to be selected as of the end of 2014. However, the funding profile led some, including the Congressional Research Service, to suggest that some elements of the aircraft's research and development, and perhaps the aircraft itself, have existed as classified projects for some time.

Budgetary pressures resulted in the planned withdrawal from service of the A-10 *Thunderbolt* II close-air-support aircraft during FY2015, while the U-2 ISR aircraft was slated to be withdrawn from FY2016. The capability provided by the U-2 was planned to be met partly by the RQ-4 *Global Hawk* UAV, while the low-observable RQ-180 ISR UAV, developed as a classified project, was as of late 2014 likely nearing entry into service.

DEFENCE ECONOMICS

Three themes characterised the US defence budgetary process in 2014. Firstly, near-term US defence-spending plans seemed to stabilise in 2014 after several years of budgetary uncertainty, with the base budget avoiding sequestration and settling at real-terms levels higher than those seen during previous defence drawdowns. Secondly, the Pentagon seemed to have brought its plans in line with statutory spending caps, despite considerable political rhetoric in Congress about the dangers of lower defence-spending levels. Thirdly, the war-related budget looked set to remain in place to fund overseas operational requirements (despite the downscaling in Afghanistan operations for which it was initially created), but with a broader and more flexible interpretation than had been used in previous years. This could potentially open up a second, semi-permanent budget line to channel defence funding, which may in future be used to offset statutory pressures on the base budget. However, these developments remained unconfirmed at the start of FY2015, which began in October 2014: in common with recent years, final legislative action on the proposed 2015 defence budget had not been undertaken, as Congress adjourned in mid-September for the November mid-term elections. In order to prevent an electorally damaging repeat of the October 2013 federal government shutdown, a 'Continuing Resolution' was passed in mid-September to maintain defence funding at FY2014 levels until December 2014.

Overall, the proposed FY2015 defence budget (from October 2014 to September 2015) continued the gradual decline in total US defence-spending levels seen during the late Bush and early Obama administrations. After peaking at US$720 billion in 2010, the overall national defence-budget function declined to about US$580bn in 2015. (The national defence-budget function includes the Pentagon's base budget, war-related spending on overseas contingency operations (OCO), as well as Department of Energy nuclear-weapons-related costs.) Once inflation is factored in, this 2010–15 nominal reduction of 20% (or US$140bn) was closer to a 30% real-term reduction in the national defence-budget function over five years – although actual spending or outlays will have declined by less, since these generally lag cuts in budget-authority levels. Most of the US$140bn nominal reduction – around US$100bn – was accounted for by a decline in Iraq and Afghanistan OCO costs, which fell from US$160bn in 2010 to around US$60bn in 2015. By contrast, the decline in the base defence budget was relatively modest in nominal terms, at around US$40bn over five years. Nonetheless, once inflation is factored in, real cuts to the base budget exceeded 15% between 2010 and 2015.

Base defence budget stabilises in 2014

The year began with a reprieve for US defence spending. On 26 December 2013, the president signed the Bipartisan Budget Act of 2013 (BBA 2013), which amended for FY2014 and FY2015 the statutory caps limiting defence spending. This cleared the way for a full-year appropriations bill for FY2014, signed into law in mid-January 2014. The amended caps meant that nominal base defence spending would stay essentially flat until 2016 at FY2013 levels. Without the BBA 2013's reprieve, base defence spending in 2014 would have faced an additional US$20bn cut – a 6% drop relative to 2013. By amending the caps, the bill provided steady nominal-spending levels from 2013 through to 2016; a degree of stability after the steep 8% nominal drop that occurred between FY2012 and FY2013, caused by the automatic sequester of funds required by the 2011 Budget Control Act (BCA 2011). In real terms, the actual value of US defence spending was set to decline slightly each year from 2013 to 2016, but at less than 2% per annum. In FY2016 and beyond, the provisions of the BBA 2013 will expire, and spending levels will again be determined by the original statutory caps legislated in the BCA 2011.

These statutory funding levels have become known in Washington as 'sequester-level funding' or simply 'sequestration', though this incorrectly describes the true mechanism that achieves lower spending. With the exception of FY2013, the BCA 2011 law set annual spending levels by caps, which provide for an upper limit on total defence-spending levels. As long as the caps are not exceeded, funding below those levels can be allocated as the normal budget process determines. Only if the caps are exceeded does the automatic mechanism that cuts across the board, sequestration, come into effect. From FY2016 onwards, these caps increase at the expected rate of inflation. As long as inflation remains close to forecast levels, the base defence budget will remain constant in real terms through the expiration of the caps in 2021.

Political manoeuvrings continue

Framing statutory caps as 'sequester-level funding' has shaped the idea that these funding levels

Table 1 **US National Defense Budget Function[1] and Other Selected Budgets[2] 1995, 2006–15**

(US$bn)	National Defense Budget Function		Department of Defense		Atomic Energy Defense Activities	Department of Homeland Security	Veterans Administration	Total Federal Government Outlays	Total Federal Budget Surplus/Deficit
FY	BA	Outlay	BA	Outlay	BA	BA	BA		
1995	295.1	298.3	282.1	286.9	10.6	n.a.	33.9	1,516	-164
2006	617.1	521.8	593.7	499.3	17.4	40.4	71.0	2,655	-248
2007	625.8	551.2	602.9	528.6	17.2	43.0	79.6	2,729	-161
2008	696.3	616.1	674.7	594.6	16.6	47.3	88.5	2,983	-459
2009	697.8	661.0	667.5	631.9	22.9	52.7	97.0	3,518	-1,413
2010	721.3	693.6	695.6	666.7	18.2	56.0	124.4	3,457	-1,294
2011	717.4	705.6	691.5	678.1	18.5	54.8	122.8	3,603	-1,300
2012	706.8	677.9	655.4	650.9	18.3	60.0	124.2	3,537	-1,087
2013	610.1	633.4	585.2	607.8	17.4	59.2	136.1	3,455	-680
2014 est	613.6	620.6	586.9	593.3	18.6	60.7	151.0	3,651	-649
2015 est	636.6	631.3	581.3	584.3	19.3	60.9	160.9	3,901	-564

Notes

FY = Fiscal Year (1 October–30 September)

[1] The National Defense Budget Function subsumes funding for the DoD, the Department of Energy Atomic Energy Defense Activities and some smaller support agencies (including Federal Emergency Management and Selective Service System). It does not include funding for International Security Assistance (under International Affairs), the Veterans Administration, the US Coast Guard (Department of Homeland Security), nor for the National Aeronautics and Space Administration (NASA). Funding for civil projects administered by the DoD is excluded from the figures cited here.

[2] Early in each calendar year, the US government presents its defence budget to Congress for the next fiscal year, which begins on 1 October. The government also presents its Future Years Defense Program (FYDP), which covers the next fiscal year plus the following five. Until approved by Congress, the Budget is called the Budget Request; after approval, it becomes the Budget Authority.

represent draconian cuts. This has fuelled political rhetoric that defence spending must increase, despite the underlying stability in funding levels. The president's proposed budget for FY2015 respected the levels agreed to in the BBA 2013, though it also included an additional request for a US$28bn fund above the caps – a request that was largely ignored during the congressional budget process. The administration also proposed an average of US$34bn more than the statutory caps each year for FY2016 to FY2019. In response, the Republican-controlled House of Representatives endorsed a plan for those years that included an additional US$22bn average annual increase over and above the administration's request.

These proposed additional amounts were further complicated when Secretary of Defense Chuck Hagel testified in spring 2014 that if Congress signalled it was willing to further revise the caps, the US Department of Defense (DoD) would keep an additional aircraft carrier in operation and the army at a higher personnel level. Yet these plans were not included in the administration's proposed budget even with the additional funds. They would require yet more funding over not just the capped levels, but over the additional requested funds, or else require cuts to other programmes funded in the proposal.

DoD plans for statutory spending limits

Beneath the rhetoric calling for more spending, the DoD – in contrast to past years – apparently programmed its future force at the statutory caps. A month after the proposed defence budget was released, the department released a 36-page report – entitled 'Estimated Impacts of Sequestration-Level Funding – FY 2015 Defense Budget' – on how its five-year spending plan might be adjusted if the spending caps were not raised. Unlike previous official complaints about the effects of lower defence spending, this report detailed effects down to line-item accounts. This detail indicated that the DoD had built a complete budget at the capped spending levels, and therefore had determined how to allocate its funding even if the spending caps were not raised. In practice, it appeared to have accepted the statutory limits.

However, there was a degree of variation between the president's budget request and the DoD report. For example, while the FY2015 budget request included cuts to spending on military personnel (largely from reducing the size of the force), under the DoD report, personnel spending would remain nearly unaltered if the caps remained, falling only by an additional 1.5%. These DoD projections, however, were adjusted later in the year when the department proposed shifting 2014 funds to bolster procurement,

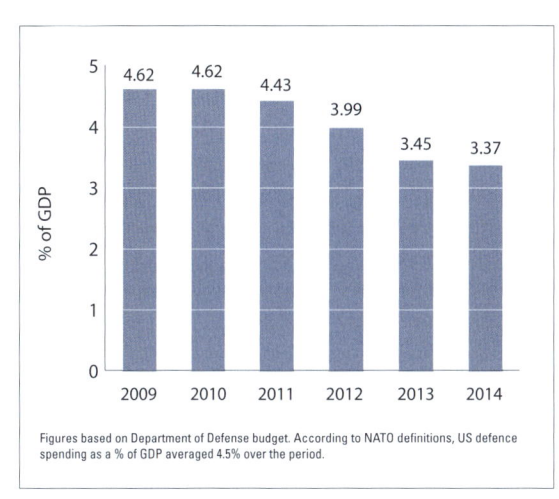

Figure 2 **US Defence Expenditure** as % of GDP

[Bar chart showing % of GDP: 2009: 4.62, 2010: 4.62, 2011: 4.43, 2012: 3.99, 2013: 3.45, 2014: 3.37. Figures based on Department of Defense budget. According to NATO definitions, US defence spending as a % of GDP averaged 4.5% over the period.]

and revised its estimate of how much would be spent on procurement in 2015.

OCO funding purpose redefined

US war-related funding also achieved a newfound degree of stability in 2014, even as the spending itself declined. OCO funding levels remained flat between FY2013 and FY2014, but the US$59bn 2015 OCO request, released in June – four months after the base-budget request – was significantly less than the US$85bn provided in FY2014. This 29% real-terms fall followed earlier reductions of 21% in FY2012 and 25% in FY2013.

The newfound stability came partly from a new rationale for war-related spending, one less tied to operations in Iraq and Afghanistan. While the DoD had always held that OCO was not limited strictly to operations in those countries, and included funding for other operations as well as for equipment repair and replacement, in reality the bulk of the justification had previously come from *Operation Iraqi Freedom* and ISAF. However, with US troop numbers in Afghanistan set to fall below 10,000 by the end of 2014, that justification looked increasingly outdated. For example, between FY2005 and FY2013, the cost per troop in Afghanistan averaged US$1.3 million per year. By contrast, in FY2014, the cost per troop rose to US$2.3m, and the full FY2015 request would carry a per troop cost of US$4.5m. Given the downscaling in US operational tempo in Afghanistan, these increases were clearly implausible under the existing OCO definition.

This apparent paradox was explained by a change in how the DoD justified its war-related funding request. Instead of aggregating all costs to Afghanistan expenses, the 2015 request split it into three separate categories: Afghanistan-related, in-theatre and other support costs. Afghanistan force-related costs were pegged at only US$11bn, or less than 19% of the total OCO request. That put cost-per-soldier at under US$1m and in line with previous funding levels. However, it also meant that other support elements represented more than 50% of the requested costs, costs now decoupled from Afghanistan operations. That separation changed the rationale for much of the OCO funding, tying it to broader operational needs.

This approach was most fully defended by Vice Chairman of the Joint Chiefs of Staff Sandy Winnefeld, who in testimony to the House Armed Services Committee argued that OCO funding was appropriate for 'anything that we do while we're deployed, or that supports our deployments that is over and above what we would normally do in a tabula rasa peaceful world'. This justification is referred to as the 'retainer model' because it assumes the base defence budget does not actually fund the DoD to do these things, implying that the DoD requires new funding for any new missions it takes on. It is unclear whether the administration fully endorses this 'retainer model', as Winnefeld's civilian colleagues have never justified the OCO request in quite the same way.

The 2015 OCO request also included two new funding mechanisms, reinforcing the new, broader interpretation of the OCO budget line's functions. The administration proposed a Counterterrorism Partnership Fund, costing US$5bn government-wide (meaning that the funds go to various departments, not just the DoD), as well as a European Reassurance Initiative, costing US$1bn government-wide. The administration provided few details on how the funding would be spent, and the Senate Appropriations Committee responded by halving the defence portion of the Counterterrorism Partnership Fund to US$1.9bn. However, the situation in Syria and Iraq led more members of Congress to express support for the open-ended request despite their earlier concerns.

Now that it is untethered from the wars in Iraq and Afghanistan, OCO funding is likely to persist, as global events will likely offer ample justification for contingency-related funding in future. This marks a significant step change in the US budgetary picture from previous years, when it was generally expected that OCO funding would end when the wars of 9/11 concluded.

CANADA

Canada ended 2014 by engaging in air-strikes in Iraq to degrade the capability of ISIS. Assets and personnel including six CF-18 *Hornet*s, CC-150T *Polaris* refuelling aircraft and two CP-140 *Aurora* surveillance aircraft were despatched on *Operation Impact* in October, and were based in Kuwait. It was reported that Canada intended to again upgrade its CF-18 *Hornet*s in order to keep the aircraft flying until 2025. This move was significant not just in the context of the operational capability of Canada's fixed-wing combat airpower, but also in relation to the ongoing discussions over Canada's participation in the F-35 Joint Strike Fighter programme.

The National Shipbuilding Procurement Strategy, designed to strengthen Canada's maritime capabilities and replace the surface fleet of the coast guard and navy, was proceeding, although some elements had come under scrutiny. An October report by the Parliamentary Budget Office on the Arctic/Offshore Patrol Ship (A/OPS) project said that 'the current budget will be insufficient to procure six to eight A/OPS as planned' and 'schedule slips, therefore, may have a significant impact on the government's purchasing power and on other projects down the pipeline, such as the Canadian Surface Combatant'. Nonetheless, it was announced that the patrol ships would be the *Harry DeWolf*-class, with the lead ship bearing the name of the late naval officer, who served until 1960 and whose last posting was as chief of naval staff.

Meanwhile, Canada announced in September that it was decommissioning two of its remaining *Iroquois*-class destroyers (one was left in service) and both *Protecteur*-class oilers, though the precise timeline was unclear; the vessels were all effectively non-operational and were beginning to be stripped. This raised some issues for naval deployments, as unless another vessel was introduced in the interim, it could leave the navy without a refuelling capability until the arrival of the replacement *Queenston*-class, based on the German *Berlin*-class and also part of the National Shipbuilding Procurement Strategy. The *Queenston*-class programme is the successor to the Joint Support Ship project and the class is not due to enter service until 2019.

Maritime security and counter-terrorism deployments continued in the Gulf region under Combined Task Force 150 (CTF-150). Canada was to assume command of CTF-150 from December 2014 to April 2015, leading the mission alongside Australia, which was to deploy seven naval personnel along with Canada's 24 to the headquarters contingent. Deployments also continued in the High North, where Canada has for some years conducted sovereignty operations in challenging environments. In 2014 *Operation Nunalivut* took place from 2 April to 3 May, involving army, navy and air force elements deploying to Resolute Bay to practise interoperability skills as well as cold-weather environment training.

Canada CAN

Canadian Dollar $		2013	2014	2015
GDP	C$	1.88tr	1.96tr	
	US$	1.83tr	1.79tr	
per capita	US$	52,037	50,577	
Growth	%	2.0	2.3	
Inflation	%	1.0	1.9	
Def bdgt	C$	16.6bn	17.4bn	
	US$	16.2bn	15.9bn	
US$1= C$			1.0	1.1

Population 34,834,841

Age	0 – 14	15 – 19	20 – 24	25 – 29	30 – 64	65 plus
Male	7.9%	3.0%	3.5%	3.4%	24.1%	7.7%
Female	7.5%	2.9%	3.3%	3.2%	23.8%	9.6%

Capabilities

Defence policy is based on three pillars: national defence, supporting the defence of North America and contributing to international operations within an alliance or partnership framework. Canada provided combat forces for operations in Afghanistan, and its remaining training personnel withdrew in March 2014. Retaining the lessons from the deployment will preoccupy defence planners in the near term. The 20-year Canada First Defence Strategy, published in 2008, is being updated, the outcome of which may affect operational readiness and some procurement ambitions; these – particularly shipbuilding programmes – are also subject to scrutiny within Canada. The P-3 *Orion* maritime-patrol aircraft is to be retained until 2030, in lieu of funds for a new fleet. The announced retirement of Canada's fleet tankers might, unless an interim capacity is identified, lead to a gap until the projected in-service date of its two new supply vessels, based on the German navy's *Berlin*-class, due tentatively for 2019. Discussions over the intended F-35 Joint Strike Fighter purchase continued. At the end of 2014 the air force participated in air-strikes – including the deployment of surveillance and refuelling capabilities – as part of the anti-ISIS coalition. (See p. 36.)

ACTIVE 66,000 (Army 34,800 Navy 11,300 Air Force 19,900)

CIVILIAN 4,500 (Coast Guard 4,500)

RESERVE 30,950 (Army 23,150, Navy 5,450, Air 2,350)

ORGANISATIONS BY SERVICE

Space
SATELLITES • SPACE SURVEILLANCE 1 *Sapphire*

Army 34,800
FORCES BY ROLE
COMMAND
  1 (1st div) Task Force HQ
MANOEUVRE
  Mechanised
  1 (1st) mech bde gp (1 armd regt, 2 mech inf bn, 1 lt inf bn, 1 arty regt, 1 cbt engr regt)
  2 (2nd & 5th) mech bde gp (1 armd recce regt, 2 mech inf bn, 1 lt inf bn, 1 arty regt, 1 cbt engr regt)
COMBAT SUPPORT
  1 AD regt
  1 engr/cbt spt regt
  3 int coy
  3 MP pl
COMBAT SERVICE SUPPORT
  3 log bn
  3 med bn
EQUIPMENT BY TYPE
MBT 120: 40 *Leopard* 2A6M; 80 *Leopard* 2A4; (61 *Leopard* 1C2 in store)
RECCE 194 LAV-25 *Coyote*
APC 1,212
  APC (T) 332: 64 Bv-206; 235 M113; 33 M577
  APC (W) 810: 635 LAV-III *Kodiak* (incl 33 RWS); 175 LAV *Bison* (incl 10 EW, 32 amb, 32 repair, 64 recovery)
PPV 70: 60 RG-31 *Nyala*; 5 *Cougar*; 5 *Buffalo*
ARTY 314
  TOWED 190 **105mm** 153: 27 C2 (M101); 98 C3 (M101); 28 LG1 MkII; **155mm** 37 M777
  MOR **81mm** 100
    SP **81mm** 24 LAV *Bison*
AT
  MSL
    SP 33 LAV-TOW
    MANPATS *Eryx*; TOW-2A/ITAS
  RCL **84mm** 1,075 *Carl Gustav*; M2/M3
AD • SAM • MANPAD *Starburst*
ARV 2 BPz-3 *Büffel*
UAV • ISR • Light *Skylark*

Reserve Organisations 23,150

Canadian Rangers 4,300 Reservists
Provide a limited military presence in Canada's northern, coastal and isolated areas. Sovereignty, public-safety and surveillance roles.
FORCES BY ROLE
MANOEUVRE
  Other
  5 (patrol) ranger gp (165 patrols)

Army Reserves
Most units have only coy sized establishments.
FORCES BY ROLE
COMMAND
  10 bde gp HQ
MANOEUVRE
  Reconnaissance
  18 armd recce regt
  Light
  51 inf regt
COMBAT SUPPORT
  14 fd arty regt
  2 indep fd arty bty

1 cbt engr regt
7 engr regt
3 indep engr sqn
1 EW sqn
4 int coy
6 sigs regt
16 indep sigs sqn
COMBAT SERVICE SUPPORT
10 log bn
14 med coy
4 med det
4 MP coy

Royal Canadian Navy 11,300
EQUIPMENT BY TYPE
SUBMARINES • SSK 4:
4 *Victoria* (ex-UK *Upholder*) with 6 single 533mm TT with Mk48 *Sea Arrow* HWT (2 currently operational)
PRINCIPAL SURFACE COMBATANTS 13
DESTROYERS • DDHM 1 mod *Iroquois* with 1 Mk41 29-cell VLS with SM-2MR SAM, 2 triple 324mm ASTT with Mk46 LWT, 1 *Phalanx* CIWS, 1 76mm gun (capacity 2 SH-3 (CH-124) *Sea King* ASW hel) (2 more awaiting decommissioning)
FRIGATES • FFGHM 12 *Halifax* with 2 quad lnchr with RGM-84 Block II *Harpoon* AShM, 2 octuple Mk48 VLS with RIM-7P *Sea Sparrow* SAM/RIM-162 ESSM SAM, 2 twin 324mm ASTT with Mk46 LWT, 1 *Phalanx* CIWS, 1 57mm gun (capacity 1 SH-3 (CH-124) *Sea King* ASW hel) (rolling modernisation programme until 2017)
MINE WARFARE • MINE COUNTERMEASURES • MCO 12 *Kingston*
LOGISTICS AND SUPPORT 24
AORH (2 *Protecteur* awaiting decommissioning)
AGOR 1 *Quest*
AX 9: **AXL** 8 *Orca*; **AXS** 1 *Oriole*
YDT 6 (2 *Granby* MCM spt; 4 *Sechelt* diving tender/spt)
YTB 6
YTL 2

Reserves 5,430 reservists
FORCES BY ROLE
MANOEUVRE
Other
24 navy div (tasked with crewing 10 of the 12 MCO, harbour defence & naval control of shipping)

Royal Canadian Air Force (RCAF) 19,900 (plus 2,350 Primary Reservists integrated within total Air Force structure)
FORCES BY ROLE
FIGHTER/GROUND ATTACK
3 sqn with F/A-18A/B *Hornet* (CF-18AM/BM)
ANTI-SUBMARINE WARFARE
3 sqn with SH-3 *Sea King* (CH-124)
MARITIME PATROL
3 sqn with P-3 *Orion* (CP-140 *Aurora*)
SEARCH & RESCUE/TRANSPORT
4 sqn with AW101 *Merlin* (CH-149 *Cormorant*); C-130E/H/H-30/J-30 (CC-130) *Hercules*
1 sqn with DHC-5 (CC-115) *Buffalo*
TANKER/TRANSPORT
1 sqn with A310/A310 MRTT (CC-150/CC-150T)
1 sqn with KC-130H
TRANSPORT
1 sqn with C-17A (CC-177)
1 sqn with CL-600 (CC-144B)
1 (utl) sqn with DHC-6 (CC-138) *Twin Otter*
TRANSPORT HELICOPTER
5 sqn with Bell 412 (CH-146 *Griffon*)
3 (cbt spt) sqn with Bell 412 (CH-146 *Griffon*)
1 (Spec Ops) sqn with Bell 412 (CH-146 *Griffon* – OPCON Canadian Special Operations Command)
1 sqn with CH-47F (CH-147F)
RADAR
1 (NORAD Regional) HQ located at Winnipeg;
1 Sector HQ at North Bay with 11 North Warning System Long Range Radar; 36 North Warning System Short Range Radar; 4 Coastal Radar; 2 Transportable Radar
EQUIPMENT BY TYPE
AIRCRAFT 95 combat capable
FGA 77: 59 F/A-18A (CF-18AM) *Hornet*; 18 F/A-18B (CF-18BM) *Hornet*
ASW 18 P-3 *Orion* (CP-140 *Aurora*)
TKR/TPT 7: 2 A310 MRTT (CC-150T); 5 KC-130H
TPT 58: **Heavy** 4 C-17A (CC-177) *Globemaster*; **Medium** 35: 10 C-130E (CC-130) *Hercules*; 6 C-130H (CC-130) *Hercules*; 2 C-130H-30 (CC-130) *Hercules*; 17 C-130J-30 (CC-130) *Hercules*; **Light** 10: 6 DHC-5 (CC-115) *Buffalo*; 4 DHC-6 (CC-138) *Twin Otter*; **PAX** 9: 3 A310 (CC-150 *Polaris*); 6 CL-600 (CC-144B/C)
TRG 4 DHC-8 (CT-142)
HELICOPTERS
ASW 28 SH-3 (CH-124) *Sea King*
MRH 68 Bell 412 (CH-146 *Griffon*)
TPT 29: **Heavy** 15 CH-47F (CH-147F) *Chinook*; **Medium** 14 AW101 *Merlin* (CH-149 *Cormorant*)
RADARS 53
AD RADAR • NORTH WARNING SYSTEM 47: 11 Long Range; 36 Short Range
STRATEGIC 6: 4 Coastal; 2 Transportable
MSL
ASM AGM-65 *Maverick*
AAM • IR AIM-9L *Sidewinder* **SARH** AIM-7M *Sparrow* **ARH** AIM-120C AMRAAM
BOMBS
Conventional: Mk82; Mk83; Mk84
Laser-Guided: GBU-10/GBU-12/GBU-16 *Paveway* II; GBU-24 *Paveway* III

NATO Flight Training Canada
EQUIPMENT BY TYPE
AIRCRAFT
TRG 45: 26 T-6A *Texan* II (CT-156 *Harvard* II); 19 *Hawk* 115 (CT-155) (advanced wpns/tactics trg)

Contracted Flying Services – Southport
EQUIPMENT BY TYPE
AIRCRAFT
TPT • Light 7 Beech C90B *King Air*
TRG 11 G-120A

HELICOPTERS
 MRH 9 Bell 412 (CH-146)
 TPT • Light 7 Bell 206 *Jet Ranger* (CH-139)

Canadian Special Operations Forces Command 1,500

FORCES BY ROLE
SPECIAL FORCES
 1 SF regt (Canadian Special Operations Regiment)
 1 SF unit (JTF2)
MANOEUVRE
 Aviation
 1 sqn, with Bell 412 (CH-146 *Griffon* – from the RCAF)
COMBAT SERVICE SUPPORT
 1 CBRN unit (Canadian Joint Incidence Response Unit – CJIRU)

EQUIPMENT BY TYPE
RECCE 4 LAV *Bison* NBC
HEL • MRH 10 Bell 412 (CH-146 *Griffon*)

Canadian Forces Joint Operational Support Group

FORCES BY ROLE
COMBAT SUPPORT
 1 engr spt coy
 1 (joint) sigs regt
COMBAT SERVICE SUPPORT
 1 (spt) log unit
 1 (movement) log unit
 1 med bn
 1 (close protection) MP coy

Canadian Coast Guard 4,500 (civilian)

Incl Department of Fisheries and Oceans; all platforms are designated as non-combatant.

EQUIPMENT BY TYPE
PATROL AND COASTAL COMBATANTS 68
 PSOH 1 *Leonard J Cowley*
 PSO 1 *Sir Wilfred Grenfell* (with hel landing platform)
 PCO 13: 2 *Cape Roger*; 1 *Gordon Reid*; 9 *Hero*; 1 *Tanu*
 PCC 3: 1 *Arrow Post*; 1 *Harp*; 1 *Louisbourg*
 PB 50: 3 *Post*; 1 *Quebecois*; 1 *Vakta*; 3 Type-100; 10 Type-300A; 31 Type-300B; 1 *Simmonds* (on loan from RCMP)
AMPHIBIOUS • LANDING CRAFT • LCAC 4 Type-400
LOGISTICS AND SUPPORT 41
 ABU 6
 AG 6
 AGB 15
 AGOR 5 (coastal and offshore fishery vessels)
 AGOS 9
HELICOPTERS • TPT 22: **Medium** 1 S-61; **Light** 21: 3 Bell 206L *Long Ranger*; 4 Bell 212; 14 Bo-105

Royal Canadian Mounted Police

In addition to the below, the RCMP also operates more than 370 small boats under 10 tonnes.

EQUIPMENT BY TYPE
PATROL AND COASTAL COMBATANTS • PB 5: 2 *Inkster*; 3 *Nadon*

Cyber

Canada published its Cyber Security Strategy in October 2010. The document said that the Communications Security Establishment Canada, the Canadian Security Intelligence Service and the Royal Canadian Mounted Police will investigate incidents according to their relevant mandates. Meanwhile, the armed forces will strengthen capacity to defend their networks. The Canadian Forces Network Operation Centre is the 'national operational Cyber Defence unit', permanently assigned tasks to support Canadian Forces operations.

DEPLOYMENT

ALBANIA
OSCE • Albania 2

CYPRUS
UN • UNFICYP (*Operation Snowgoose*) 1

DEMOCRATIC REPUBLIC OF THE CONGO
UN • MONUSCO (*Operation Crocodile*) 8

EGYPT
MFO (*Operation Calumet*) 28

GERMANY
NATO (ACO) 287

HAITI
UN • MINUSTAH (*Operation Hamlet*) 7

IRAQ
Operation Impact 70 (trg team)

KUWAIT
Operation Impact 530; 6 F/A-18A *Hornet* (CF-18AM); 2 P-3 *Orion* (CP-140); 1 A310 MRTT (C-150T)

LITHUANIA
NATO • Baltic Air Policing 4 F/A-18A *Hornet* (CF-18AM)

MEDITERRANEAN SEA
NATO • SNMG 2: 1 FFGHM

MIDDLE EAST
UN • UNTSO (*Operation Jade*) 8 obs

SERBIA
NATO • KFOR • *Joint Enterprise* (*Operation Kobold*) 4
OSCE • Kosovo 7

SOUTH SUDAN
UN • UNMISS (*Operation Soprano*) 5; 5 obs

UKRAINE
OSCE • Ukraine 5

UNITED STATES
US CENTCOM (*Operation Foundation*) 12
US NORTHCOM/NORAD/NATO (ACT) 300

FOREIGN FORCES

United Kingdom 420; 2 trg unit; 1 hel flt with SA341 *Gazelle*
United States 130

United States US

United States Dollar $		2013	2014	2015
GDP	US$	16.8tr	17.4tr	
per capita	US$	53,001	54,678	
Growth	%	2.2	2.2	
Inflation	%	1.5	2.0	
Def bdgt [a]	US$	578bn	581bn	580bn
Def Exp [b]	US$	754bn		

[a] Department of Defense budget
[b] NATO definition

Population 318,892,103

Age	0 – 14	15 – 19	20 – 24	25 – 29	30 – 64	65 plus
Male	9.9%	3.4%	3.7%	3.5%	22.5%	6.4%
Female	9.5%	3.2%	3.5%	3.4%	23.1%	8.1%

Capabilities

The US is the world's most capable military power. Its forces are well trained and designed for power projection and intervention on a global scale across the full spectrum of operations. It is actively developing its cyber capabilities and retains a nuclear triad with a substantial arsenal of warheads. The Pentagon continues to develop the plans for its 'rebalance' to the Asia-Pacific, and there will be a continuing deployment of personnel in Afghanistan in support roles as part of a bilateral security agreement beyond the December 2014 departure of combat troops. The armed forces are preoccupied with retaining and institutionalising capabilities and skills learnt in the Iraq and Afghan theatres whilst also dealing with budget cuts, force downsizing and the modernisation of much-used equipment. Added to this are concerns about continuing global instability in the form of transnational, hybrid and regional insurgencies; the rise of China; increasing Russian assertiveness; and the success of ISIS in Iraq and Syria, whilst attempting to avoid new, protracted military deployments. The March 2014 Quadrennial Defense Review highlighted concerns regarding force readiness and peer competitors, as well as 'risks' to forces. The possibility of continued sequestration forced planners to develop different scenarios for deeper force reductions, although in 2014 the base budget stabilised making further sequestration perhaps more dependent on adherence to inflation-pegged caps. Overseas Contingency Operations funding is also likely to continue, irrespective of the end of the ISAF mission. (See pp. 29–35.)

ACTIVE 1,433,150 (Army 539,450 Navy 326,800 Air Force 334,550 US Marine Corps 191,150 US Coast Guard 41,200)

CIVILIAN 14,000 (US Special Operations Command 6,400 US Coast Guard 7,600)

RESERVE 854,900 (Army 539,750 Navy 98,650 Air Force 168,850 Marine Corps Reserve 38,650 US Coast Guard 9,000)

ORGANISATIONS BY SERVICE

US Strategic Command

HQ at Offutt AFB (NE). Five missions: US nuclear deterrent; missile defence; global strike; info ops; ISR

US Navy

EQUIPMENT BY TYPE
SUBMARINES • STRATEGIC • SSBN 14 *Ohio* (mod) SSBN with up to 24 UGM-133A *Trident* D-5 strategic SLBM, 4 single 533mm TT with Mk48 *Sea Arrow* HWT

US Air Force • Global Strike Command

FORCES BY ROLE
MISSILE
  9 sqn with LGM-30G *Minuteman* III
BOMBER
  6 sqn (incl 1 AFRC) with B-52H *Stratofortress* (+1 AFRC sqn personnel only)
  2 sqn with B-2A *Spirit* (+1 ANG sqn personnel only)
EQUIPMENT BY TYPE
BBR 92: 20 B-2A *Spirit*; 72 B-52H *Stratofortress*
MSL • STRATEGIC
ICBM 450 LGM-30G *Minuteman* III (capacity 1-3 MIRV Mk12/Mk12A per missile)
LACM AGM-86B

Strategic Defenses – Early Warning

North American Aerospace Defense Command (NORAD) – a combined US–CAN org.
EQUIPMENT BY TYPE
SATELLITES (see Space)
RADAR
  NORTH WARNING SYSTEM 15 North Warning System Long Range (range 200nm); 40 North Warning System Short Range (range 80nm)
  OVER-THE-HORIZON-BACKSCATTER RADAR (OTH-B) 2: 1 AN/FPS-118 OTH-B (500–3,000nm) located at Mountain Home AFB (ID); 1 non-operational located at Maine (ME)
  STRATEGIC 2 Ballistic Missile Early Warning System (BMEWS) located at Thule, GL and Fylingdales Moor, UK; 1 (primary mission to track ICBM and SLBM; also used to track satellites) located at Clear (AK)
  SPACETRACK SYSTEM 11: 8 Spacetrack Radar located at Incirlik (TUR), Eglin (FL), Cavalier AFS (ND), Clear (AK), Thule (GL), Fylingdales Moor (UK), Beale AFB (CA), Cape Cod (MA); 3 Spacetrack Optical Trackers located at Socorro (NM), Maui (HI), Diego Garcia (BIOT)
  USN SPACE SURVEILLANCE SYSTEM (NAVSPASUR) 3 strategic transmitting stations; 6 strategic receiving sites in southeast US
  PERIMETER ACQUISITION RADAR ATTACK CHARACTERISATION SYSTEM (PARCS) 1 at Cavalier AFS (ND)
  PAVE PAWS 3 at Beale AFB (CA), Cape Cod AFS (MA), Clear AFS (AK); 1 (phased array radar 5,500km range) located at Otis AFB (MA)
  DETECTION AND TRACKING RADARS Kwajalein Atoll, Ascension Island, Australia, Kaena Point (HI), MIT Lincoln Laboratory (MA)

GROUND BASED ELECTRO OPTICAL DEEP SPACE SURVEILLANCE SYSTEM (GEODSS)
Socorro (NM), Maui (HI), Diego Garcia (BIOT)
STRATEGIC DEFENCES – MISSILE DEFENCES
SEA-BASED: *Aegis* engagement cruisers and destroyers
LAND-BASED: 26 ground-based interceptors at Fort Greely (AK); 4 ground-based interceptors at Vandenburg (CA)

Space
SATELLITES 123
COMMUNICATIONS 37: 3 AEHF; 8 DSCS-III; 2 *Milstar*-I; 3 *Milstar*-II; 2 MUOS; 1 PAN-1 (P360); 5 SDS-III; 7 UFO; 6 WGS SV2
NAVIGATION/POSITIONING/TIMING 34: 9 NAVSTAR Block II/IIA; 6 NAVSTAR Block IIF; 19 NAVSTAR Block IIR/IIRM
METEOROLOGY/OCEANOGRAPHY 7 DMSP-5
ISR 12: 2 FIA *Radar*; 5 *Evolved Enhanced/Improved Crystal* (visible and infrared imagery); 2 *Lacrosse* (*Onyx* radar imaging satellite); 1 ORS-1; 1 *TacSat*-4; 1 *TacSat*-6
ELINT/SIGINT 24: 2 *Mentor* (advanced *Orion*); 3 Advanced *Mentor*; 3 *Mercury*; 1 *Trumpet*; 3 *Trumpet*-2; 12 SBWASS (Space Based Wide Area Surveillance System); Naval Ocean Surveillance System
SPACE SURVEILLANCE 3: 2 GSSAP; 1 SBSS (Space Based Surveillance System)
EARLY WARNING 6: 4 DSP; 2 SBIRS *Geo*-1

US Army 520,000; 9,450 active ARNG; 10,000 active AR (total 539,450)
FORCES BY ROLE
Sqn are generally bn sized and tp are generally coy sized
COMMAND
3 (I, III & XVIII AB) corps HQ
SPECIAL FORCES
(see USSOCOM)
MANOEUVRE
Reconnaissance
1 (2nd CR) cav regt (1 recce sqn, 3 mech sqn, 1 arty sqn, 1 AT tp, 1 cbt engr sqn, 1 int tp, 1 sigs tp, 1 CSS sqn)
1 (3rd CR) cav regt (1 recce sqn, 3 mech sqn, 1 arty sqn, 1 AT tp, 1 cbt engr tp, 1 int tp, 1 sigs tp, 1 CSS sqn)
2 (BfSB) surv bde
Armoured
1 (1st) armd div (2 (2nd & 4th ABCT) armd bde (1 armd recce sqn, 2 armd/armd inf bn, 1 SP arty bn, 1 cbt spt bn, 1 CSS bn); 1 (1st SBCT) mech bde (1 armd recce sqn, 3 mech inf bn, 1 arty bn, 1 cbt engr bn, 1 CSS bn); 1 (3rd IBCT) lt inf bde (1 recce sqn, 2 inf bn, 1 arty bn, 1 cbt spt bn, 1 CSS bn); 1 (hy cbt avn) hel bde; 1 log bde)
1 (1st) cav div (3 (1st–3rd ABCT) armd bde (1 armd recce sqn, 3 armd/armd inf bn, 1 SP arty bn, 1 cbt engr bn, 1 CSS bn); 1 (hy cbt avn) hel bde; 1 log bde)
1 (1st) inf div (2 (1st & 2nd ABCT) armd bde (1 armd recce sqn, 2 armd/armd inf bn, 1 SP arty bn, 1 cbt engr bn, 1 CSS bn); 1 (4th IBCT) lt inf bde (1 recce sqn, 2 inf bn, 1 arty bn, 1 cbt spt bn, 1 CSS bn); 1 (cbt avn) hel bde; 1 log bde)
1 (3rd) inf div (3 (1st–3rd ABCT) armd bde (1 armd recce sqn, 2 armd/armd inf bn, 1 SP arty bn, 1 cbt spt bn, 1 CSS bn); 1 (4th IBCT) lt inf bde; (1 recce sqn, 2 inf bn, 1 arty bn, 1 cbt spt bn, 1 CSS bn); 1 (cbt avn) hel bde; 1 log bde)
1 (4th) inf div (1 (3rd ABCT) armd bde (1 armd recce sqn, 3 armd/armd inf bn, 1 SP arty bn, 1 cbt engr bn, 1 CSS bn); 1 (2nd ABCT) armd bde (1 armd recce sqn, 2 armd/armd inf bn, 1 SP arty bn, 1 cbt spt bn, 1 CSS bn); 1 (1st SBCT) mech bde (1 armd recce sqn, 3 mech inf bn, 1 arty bn, 1 AT coy, 1 cbt engr bn, 1 int coy, 1 sigs coy, 1 CSS bn); 1 (4th IBCT) lt inf bde (1 recce sqn, 2 inf bn, 1 arty bn, 1 cbt spt bn, 1 CSS bn); 1 (hvy cbt avn) hel bde; 1 log bde)
Mechanised
1 (2nd) inf div (1 (1st ABCT) armd bde (1 armd recce sqn, 2 armd/armd inf bn, 1 SP arty bn, 1 cbt spt bn, 1 NBC bn, 1 CSS bn); 1 (2nd SBCT) mech bde (1 armd recce sqn, 3 mech inf bn, 1 arty bn, 1 AT coy, 1 cbt engr bn, 1 int coy, 1 sigs coy, 1 CSS bn); 3 (3rd SBCT) mech bde (1 armd recce sqn, 3 mech inf bn, 1 arty bn, 1 AT coy, 1 cbt engr coy, 1 int coy, 1 sigs coy, 1 CSS bn); 1 (cbt avn) hel bde; 1 log bde)
1 (25th) inf div (1 (1st SBCT) mech bde (1 armd recce sqn, 3 mech inf bn, 1 arty bn, 1 AT coy, 1 cbt engr bn, 1 int coy, 1 sigs coy, 1 CSS bn); 1 (2nd SBCT) mech bde (1 armd recce sqn, 3 mech inf bn, 1 arty bn, 1 AT coy, 1 engr coy, 1 int coy, 1 sigs coy, 1 CSS bn); 1 (3rd IBCT) inf bde (1 recce sqn, 2 inf bn, 1 arty bn, 1 cbt engr bn, 1 CSS bn); 1 (4th AB BCT) AB bde (1 recce bn, 2 para bn, 1 arty bn, 1 cbt engr bn, 1 CSS bn); 1 (cbt avn) hel bde; 1 log bde)
Light
1 (10th Mtn) inf div (2 (1st & 2nd IBCT) lt inf bde (1 recce sqn, 3 inf bn, 1 arty bn, 1 cbt engr bn, 1 CSS bn); 1 (3rd IBCT) lt inf bde (1 recce sqn, 2 inf bn, 1 arty bn, 1 cbt spt bn, 1 CSS bn); 1 (cbt avn) hel bde; 1 log bde)
Air Manoeuvre
1 (82nd) AB div (3 (1st–3rd AB BCT) AB bde (1 recce bn, 3 para bn, 1 arty bn, 1 cbt engr bn, 1 CSS bn); 1 (cbt avn) hel bde; 1 log bde)
1 (101st) air aslt div (2 (1st & 3rd AB BCT) AB bde (1 recce bn, 3 para bn, 1 arty bn, 1 cbt engr bn, 1 CSS bn); 1 (2nd AB BCT) AB bde (1 recce bn, 2 para bn, 1 arty bn, 1 cbt spt bn, 1 CSS bn); 2 (cbt avn) hel bde; 1 log bde)
1 (173rd AB BCT) AB bde (1 recce bn, 2 para bn, 1 arty bn, 1 cbt spt bn, 1 CSS bn)
Aviation
1 indep (hy cbt avn) hel bde
1 indep (cbt avn) hel bde
Other
1 (11th ACR) trg armd cav regt (OPFOR) (2 armd cav sqn, 1 CSS bn)
COMBAT SUPPORT
8 arty bde
1 civil affairs bde
5 engr bde
2 EOD gp (2 EOD bn)
5 AD bde
8 int bde
2 int gp

4 MP bde
1 NBC bde
3 (strat) sigs bde
4 (tac) sigs bde
2 (Mnv Enh) cbt spt bde
COMBAT SERVICE SUPPORT
1 log bde
3 med bde
1 tpt bde

Reserve Organisations

Army National Guard 354,200 reservists (incl 9,500 active)
Normally dual funded by DoD and states. Civil-emergency responses can be mobilised by state governors. Federal government can mobilise ARNG for major domestic emergencies and for overseas operations.
FORCES BY ROLE
COMMAND
  8 div HQ
SPECIAL FORCES
  (see USSOCOM)
MANOEUVRE
  Reconnaissance
  2 recce sqn
  7 (BfSB) surv bde
  Armoured
  1 (ABCT) armd bde (1 armd recce sqn, 3 armd/armd inf bn, 1 SP arty bn, 1 cbt engr bn, 1 CSS bn)
  6 (ABCT) armd bde (1 armd recce sqn, 2 armd/armd inf bn, 1 SP arty bn, 1 cbt spt bn, 1 CSS bn)
  2 armd/armd inf bn
  Mechanised
  1 (SBCT) mech bde (1 armd recce sqn, 3 mech inf bn, 1 arty bn, 1 AT coy, 1 engr coy, 1 int coy, 1 sigs coy, 1 CSS bn)
  Light
  3 (IBCT) lt inf bde (1 recce sqn, 2 inf bn, 1 arty bn, 1 cbt engr bn, 1 CSS bn)
  17 (IBCT) lt inf bde (1 recce sqn, 2 inf bn, 1 arty bn, 1 cbt spt bn, 1 CSS bn)
  11 lt inf bn
  Aviation
  2 (hy cbt avn) hel bde
  6 (National Guard cbt avn) hel bde
  5 (theatre avn) hel bde
COMBAT SUPPORT
  7 arty bde
  2 AD bde
  7 engr bde
  1 EOD regt
  1 int bde
  3 MP bde
  1 NBC bde
  2 (tac) sigs bde
  16 (Mnv Enh) cbt spt bde
COMBAT SERVICE SUPPORT
  10 log bde
  17 (regional) log spt gp

Army Reserve 205,000 reservists (incl 10,000 active)
Reserve under full command of US Army. Does not have state-emergency liability of Army National Guard.
FORCES BY ROLE
SPECIAL FORCES
  (see USSOCOM)
MANOEUVRE
  Aviation
  1 (theatre avn) hel bde
COMBAT SUPPORT
  4 engr bde
  4 MP bde
  2 NBC bde
  2 sigs bde
  3 (Mnv Enh) cbt spt bde
COMBAT SERVICE SUPPORT
  9 log bde
  11 med bde

Army Standby Reserve 700 reservists
Trained individuals for mobilisation

EQUIPMENT BY TYPE
MBT 2,338 M1A1/A2 *Abrams* (ε3,500 more in store)
RECCE 1,900: 334 M7A3/SA BFIST; 545 M1127 *Stryker* RV; 134 M1128 *Stryker* MGS; 188 M1131 *Stryker* FSV; 234 M1135 *Stryker* NBCRV; 465 M1200 *Armored Knight*
AIFV 4,559 M2A2/A3 *Bradley*/M3A2/A3 *Bradley* (ε2,000 more in store)
APC 25,209
  APC (T) ε5,000 M113A2/A3 (ε8,000 more in store)
  APC (W) 2,792: 1,972 M1126 *Stryker* ICV; 348 M1130 *Stryker* CV; 168 M1132 *Stryker* ESV; 304 M1133 *Stryker* MEV
PPV 17,417: 11,658 MRAP (all models); 5,759 M-ATV
ARTY 5,923
  SP 155mm 969 M109A6 (ε500 more in store)
  TOWED 1,242: **105mm** 821 M119A2/3; **155mm** 421 M777A1/A2
  MRL 227mm 1,205: 375 M142 HIMARS; 830 M270/M270A1 MLRS (all ATACMS-capable)
  MOR 2,507: **81mm** 990 M252; **120mm** 1,517: 1,076 M120/M121; 441 M1129 *Stryker* MC
AT • MSL
  SP 1,512: 1,379 HMMWV TOW; 133 M1134 *Stryker* ATGM
  MANPATS *Javelin*
AMPHIBIOUS 126
  LCU 45: 11 LCU-1600 (capacity either 2 MBT or 350 troops); 34 LCU-2000
  LC 81: 8 *Frank Besson* (capacity 15 *Abrams* MBT); 73 LCM-8 (capacity either 1 MBT or 200 troops)
AIRCRAFT
  ISR 52: 11 RC-12D *Guardrail*; 6 RC-12H *Guardrail*; 9 RC-12K *Guardrail*; 13 RC-2N *Guardrail*; 4 RC-12P *Guardrail*; 9 RC-12X *Guardrail*
  ELINT 9: 7 *Dash-7* ARL-M (COMINT/ELINT); 2 *Dash-7* ARL-C (COMINT)
  TPT 157: **Light** 152: 113 Beech A200 *King Air* (C-12 *Huron*); 28 Cessna 560 *Citation* (UC-35A/B/C); 11 SA-227 *Metro* (C-26B/E); **PAX** 5: 1 Gulfstream III (C-20E); 1 Gulfstream IV (C-20F); 3 Gulfstream V (C-37A)

HELICOPTERS
  ATK 741: 650 AH-64D *Apache*; 91 AH-64E *Apache*
  MRH 356 OH-58D *Kiowa Warrior*
  ISR 72 OH-58A/C *Kiowa*
  SAR 168: 18 HH-60L *Black Hawk*; 150 HH-60M *Black Hawk* (medevac)
  TPT 2,854: **Heavy** 400: 100 CH-47D *Chinook*; 300 CH-47F *Chinook*; **Medium** 2,082: 885 UH-60A *Black Hawk*; 747 UH-60L *Black Hawk*; 450 UH-60M *Black Hawk*; **Light** 372: 307 EC145 (UH-72A *Lakota*); 65 UH-1H/V *Iroquois*
  TRG 154 TH-67 *Creek*
UAV 312
  CISR • Heavy 56 MQ-1C *Gray Eagle*
  ISR 256: **Heavy** 20 RQ-5A *Hunter*; **Medium** 236 RQ-7A *Shadow*
AD • SAM 1,207+
  SP 727: 703 M998/M1097 *Avenger*; 24 THAAD
  TOWED 480 MIM-104 *Patriot*/PAC-2/PAC-3
  MANPAD FIM-92 *Stinger*
RADAR • LAND 251: 98 AN/TPQ-36 *Firefinder* (arty); 56 AN/TPQ-37 *Firefinder* (arty); 60 AN/TRQ-32 *Teammate* (COMINT); 32 AN/TSQ-138 *Trailblazer* (COMINT); 5 AN/TSQ-138A *Trailblazer*
AEV 250 M9 ACE
ARV 1,108+: 1,096 M88A1/2 (ε1,000 more in store); 12 *Pandur*; some M578
VLB 60: 20 REBS; 40 *Wolverine* HAB
MW *Aardvark* JSFU Mk4; Hydrema 910 MCV-2; M58/M59 MICLIC; M139; *Rhino*

US Navy 323,600; 3,200 active reservists (total 326,800)

Comprises 2 Fleet Areas, Atlantic and Pacific. 5 Fleets: 3rd – Pacific; 4th – Caribbean, Central and South America; 5th – Indian Ocean, Persian Gulf, Red Sea; 6th – Mediterranean; 7th – W. Pacific; plus Military Sealift Command (MSC); Naval Reserve Force (NRF). For Naval Special Warfare Command, see US Special Operations Command.

EQUIPMENT BY TYPE
SUBMARINES 73
  STRATEGIC • SSBN 14 *Ohio* (mod) opcon USSTRATCOM with up to 24 UGM-133A *Trident* D-5 strategic SLBM, 4 single 533mm TT with Mk48 *Sea Arrow* HWT
  TACTICAL 59
    SSGN 45:
      4 *Ohio* (mod) with total of 154 *Tomahawk* LACM, 4 single 533mm TT with Mk48 *Sea Arrow* HWT
      8 *Los Angeles* with 1 12-cell VLS with *Tomahawk* LACM; 4 single 533mm TT with Mk48 *Sea Arrow* HWT/UGM-84 *Harpoon* AShM
      22 *Los Angeles* (Imp) with 1 12-cell VLS with *Tomahawk* LACM, 4 single 533mm TT with Mk48 *Sea Arrow* HWT/UGM-84 *Harpoon* AShM
      10 *Virginia* Flight I/II with 1 12-cell VLS with *Tomahawk* LACM, 4 single 533mm TT with Mk48 ADCAP mod 6 HWT
      1 *Virginia* Flight III with 2 6-cell VLS with *Tomahawk* LACM, 4 single 533mm TT with Mk48 ADCAP mod 6 HWT (additional vessels in build)
    SSN 14:
      11 *Los Angeles* with 4 single 533mm TT with Mk48 *Sea Arrow* HWT/UGM-84 *Harpoon* AShM
      3 *Seawolf* with 8 single 660mm TT with up to 45 *Tomahawk* LACM/UGM-84C *Harpoon* AShM, Mk48 *Sea Arrow* HWT
PRINCIPAL SURFACE COMBATANTS 105
  AIRCRAFT CARRIERS • CVN 10 *Nimitz* with 2–3 octuple Mk29 lnchr with RIM-7M/P *Sea Sparrow* SAM, 2 Mk49 GMLS with RIM-116 SAM, 2 *Phalanx* Mk15 CIWS (typical capacity 55 F/A-18 *Hornet* FGA ac; 4 EA-6B *Prowler*/EA-18G *Growler* EW ac; 4 E-2C/D *Hawkeye* AEW ac; 4 SH-60F *Seahawk* ASW hel; 2 HH-60H *Seahawk* SAR hel)
  CRUISERS • CGHM 22 *Ticonderoga* (*Aegis* Baseline 2/3/4) with *Aegis* C2, 2 quad lnchr with RGM-84 *Harpoon* AShM, 2 61-cell Mk41 VLS with SM-2ER SAM/*Tomahawk* LACM, 2 triple 324mm ASTT with Mk46 LWT, 2 *Phalanx* Block 1B CIWS, 2 127mm gun (capacity 2 SH-60B *Seahawk* ASW hel); (extensive upgrade programme scheduled from 2006–20 to include sensors and fire control systems; major weapons upgrade to include *Evolved Sea Sparrow* (ESSM), SM-3/SM-2 capability and 2 Mk45 Mod 2 127mm gun)
  DESTROYERS 62
    DDGHM 34 *Arleigh Burke* Flight IIA with *Aegis* C2, 1 29-cell Mk41 VLS with ASROC/SM-2ER SAM/*Tomahawk* (TLAM) LACM, 1 61-cell Mk41 VLS with ASROC ASsW/SM-2 ER SAM/*Tomahawk* LACM, 2 triple 324mm ASTT with Mk46 LWT, 2 *Phalanx* Block 1B CIWS, 1 127mm gun (capacity 2 SH-60B *Seahawk* ASW hel) (additional ships in build)
    DDGM 28 *Arleigh Burke* Flight I/II with *Aegis* C2, 2 quad lnchr with RGM-84 *Harpoon* AShM, 1 32-cell Mk41 VLS with ASROC/SM-2ER SAM/*Tomahawk* LACM, 1 64-cell Mk41 VLS with ASROC/SM-2 ER SAM/*Tomahawk* LACM, 2 Mk49 RAM with RIM-116 RAM SAM, 2 triple 324mm ASTT with Mk46 LWT, 2 *Phalanx* Block 1B CIWS, 1 127mm gun, 1 hel landing platform
  FRIGATES 11
    FFHM 4:
      2 *Freedom* with 1 21-cell Mk99 lnchr with RIM-116 SAM, 1 57mm gun (capacity 2 MH-60R/S *Seahawk* hel or 1 MH-60 with 3 MQ-8 *Firescout* UAV)
      2 *Independence* with 1 11-cell SeaRAM lnchr with RIM-116 SAM, 1 57mm gun (capacity 1 MH-60R/S *Seahawk* hel and 3 MQ-8 *Firescout* UAV)
    FFH 7 *Oliver Hazard Perry* with 2 triple 324mm ASTT with Mk46 LWT, 1 76mm gun, 1 *Phalanx* Block 1B CIWS (capacity 2 SH-60B *Seahawk* ASW hel)
PATROL AND COASTAL COMBATANTS 55
  PCF 13 *Cyclone*
  PBR 42
MINE WARFARE • MINE COUNTERMEASURES 11
  MCO 11 *Avenger* with 1 SLQ-48 MCM system; 1 SQQ-32(V)3 Sonar (mine hunting)
COMMAND SHIPS • LCC 2 *Blue Ridge* with 2 *Phalanx* Mk15 CIWS (capacity 3 LCPL; 2 LCVP; 700 troops; 1

med hel) (of which 1 vessel partially crewed by Military Sealift Command personnel)

AMPHIBIOUS
  PRINCIPAL AMPHIBIOUS SHIPS 31
    LHD 8 *Wasp* with 2 octuple Mk29 GMLS with RIM-7M/RIM-7P *Sea Sparrow* SAM, 2 Mk49 GMLS with RIM-116 RAM SAM, 2 *Phalanx* Mk15 CIWS (capacity: 6 AV-8B *Harrier* II FGA; 4 CH-53E *Sea Stallion* hel; 12 CH-46E *Sea Knight* hel; 4 AH-1W/Z hel; 3 UH-1Y hel; 3 LCAC(L); 60 tanks; 1,687 troops)
    LHA 2:
      1 *America* with 2 octuple Mk29 GMLS with RIM-162D ESSM SAM; 2 Mk49 GMLS with RIM-116 RAM SAM, 2 *Phalanx* Mk15 CIWS (capacity 6 F-35B *Lightning* II FGA ac; 12 MV-22B *Osprey* tpt ac; 4 CH-53E *Sea Stallion* hel; 7 AH-1Z *Viper*/UH-1Y *Iroquois* hel; 2 MH-60 hel)
      1 *Tarawa* with 2 Mk49 GMLS with RIM-116 RAM SAM, 2 *Phalanx* Mk15 CIWS (capacity 6 AV-8B *Harrier* II FGA ac; 12 MV-22B *Osprey* ac/CH-46E *Sea Knight* hel; 4 CH-53 *Sea Stallion* hel; 4 AH-1W/Z hel; 3 UH-1Y hel; 4 LCU; 100 tanks; 1,900 troops)
    LPD 9 *San Antonio* with 2 21-cell Mk49 GMLS with RIM-116 SAM (capacity 2 CH-53E *Sea Stallion* hel or 4 CH-46 *Sea Knight* or 2 MV-22 *Osprey*; 2 LCAC(L); 14 AAAV; 720 troops) (2 additional vessels in build)
    LSD 12:
      4 *Harpers Ferry* with 2 Mk 49 GMLS with RIM-116 SAM, 2 *Phalanx* Mk15 CIWS, 1 hel landing platform (capacity 2 LCAC(L); 40 tanks; 500 troops)
      8 *Whidbey Island* with 2 Mk49 GMLS with RIM-116 SAM, 2 *Phalanx* Mk15 CIWS, 1 hel landing platform (capacity 4 LCAC(L); 40 tanks; 500 troops)
  LANDING CRAFT 245
    LCU 32 LCU-1600 (capacity either 2 M1 *Abrams* MBT or 350 troops)
    LCP 108: 75 LCPL; 33 Utility Boat
    LCM 25: 10 LCM-6; 15 LCM-8
    LCAC 80 LCAC(L) (capacity either 1 MBT or 60 troops (undergoing upgrade programme))
  LOGISTICS AND SUPPORT 71
    AFDL 1 *Dynamic*
    AGE 4: 1 MARSS; 1 *Sea Fighter*; 1 *Sea Jet*; 1 *Stiletto* (all for testing)
    AGOR 6 (all leased out): 2 *Melville*; 3 *Thomas G Thompson*; 1 *Kilo Moana*
    APB 3
    ARD 3
    AX 1 *Prevail*
    AXS 1 *Constitution*
    SSA 2 (for testing)
    SSAN 1 (for propulsion plant training)
    UUV 1 *Cutthroat* (for testing)
    YDT 2
    YFRT 2 *Athena* (at Naval Surface Warfare Center)
    YP 25 (based at Naval Academy)
    YTB 17
    YTT 2 *Cape*
  SF 6 DDS opcon USSOCOM

Navy Reserve Surface Forces

EQUIPMENT BY TYPE
PRINCIPAL SURFACE COMBATANTS 3
  FFH 3 *Oliver Hazard Perry* with 2 triple 324mm ASTT with Mk46 LWT, 36 SM-1 MR SAM, 1 76mm gun (capacity 2 SH-60B *Seahawk* ASW hel)

Naval Reserve Forces 101,850 (incl 3,200 active)

Selected Reserve 59,100

Individual Ready Reserve 42,750

Naval Inactive Fleet

Under a minimum of 60–90 days notice for reactivation; still on naval vessel register.
EQUIPMENT BY TYPE
PRINCIPAL SURFACE COMBATANTS 1
  AIRCRAFT CARRIERS • CV 1 *Kitty Hawk*
AMPHIBIOUS 12
  2 LHA
  5 LPD
  5 LKA
LOGISTICS AND SUPPORT • ATF 1 *Mohawk*

Military Sealift Command (MSC)

Combat Logistics Force
EQUIPMENT BY TYPE
LOGISTICS AND SUPPORT 30
  AO 15 *Henry J. Kaiser*
  AOE 3 *Supply*
  AKEH 12 *Lewis and Clark*

Maritime Prepositioning Program
EQUIPMENT BY TYPE
LOGISTICS AND SUPPORT 26
  AG 2: 1 *V Adm K.R. Wheeler*; 1 *Fast Tempo*
  AK 4: 2 *LTC John U.D. Page*; 1 *Maj Bernard F. Fisher*; 1 *TSGT John A. Chapman*
  AKEH 2 *Lewis and Clark*
  AKR 13: 2 *Bob Hope*; 2 *Montford Point*; 1 *Stockham*; 8 *Watson*
  AKRH 5 *2nd Lt John P. Bobo*

Strategic Sealift Force
(At a minimum of 4 days readiness)
EQUIPMENT BY TYPE
LOGISTICS AND SUPPORT 28
  AOT 4: 1 *Champion*; 3 (long-term chartered, of which 1 *Peary*, 2 *State*)
  AK 6: 3 *Sgt Matej Kocak*; 3 (long-term chartered, of which 1 *Mohegan*, 1 *Sea Eagle*, 1 *BBC Seattle*)
  AKR 11: 5 *Bob Hope*; 2 *Gordon*; 2 *Shughart*; 1 *1st Lt Harry L Martin*; 1 *LCpl Roy M Wheat*
  AP 7: 2 *Guam*; 4 *Spearhead*; 1 *Westpac Express* (chartered until Aug 2015)

Special Mission Ships
EQUIPMENT BY TYPE
LOGISTICS AND SUPPORT 24

AGM 3: 1 *Howard O. Lorenzen*; 1 *Invincible*; 1 Sea-based X-band Radar
AGOS 5: 1 *Impeccable*; 4 *Victorious*
AGS 7: 6 *Pathfinder*; 1 *Waters*
AS 9 (long-term chartered, of which 1 *C-Champion*, 1 *C-Commando*, 1 *Malama*, 1 *Dolores Chouest*, 1 *Dominator*, 4 *Arrowhead*)

Service Support Ships
EQUIPMENT BY TYPE
LOGISTICS AND SUPPORT 14
  ARS 4 *Safeguard*
  AFSB 1 *Ponce* (modified *Austin*-class LPD)
  AH 2 *Mercy*, with 1 hel landing platform
  ARC 1 *Zeus*
  AS 2 *Emory S Land*
  ATF 4 *Powhatan*

US Maritime Administration (MARAD)

National Defense Reserve Fleet
EQUIPMENT BY TYPE
LOGISTICS AND SUPPORT 36
  AOT 4
  ACS 3 *Keystone State*
  AG 3
  AGOS 3
  AGS 3
  AK 16: 5; 1 T-AK (breakbulk)
  AP 4

Ready Reserve Force
Ships at readiness up to a maximum of 30 days
EQUIPMENT BY TYPE
LOGISTICS AND SUPPORT 47
  ACS 6 *Keystone State*
  AK 4: 2 *Wright* (breakbulk); 2 *Cape May* (heavy lift)
  AKR 36: 1 *Adm WM M Callaghan*; 8 *Algol*; 27 *Cape Island*
  AOT 1 *Petersburg*

Augmentation Force
EQUIPMENT BY TYPE
COMBAT SERVICE SUPPORT
  1 (active) Cargo Handling log bn
  12 (reserve) Cargo Handling log bn

Naval Aviation 98,600
10 air wg. Average air wing comprises 8 sqns: 4 with F/A-18 (2 with F/A-18C, 1 with F/A-18E, 1 with F/A-18F); 1 with MH-60R; 1 with EA-18G; 1 with E-2C/D; 1 with MH-60S

FORCES BY ROLE
FIGHTER/GROUND ATTACK
  10 sqn with F/A-18C *Hornet*
  15 sqn with F/A-18E *Super Hornet*
  10 sqn with F/A-18F *Super Hornet*
ANTI-SUBMARINE WARFARE
  11 sqn with MH-60R *Seahawk*
  1 sqn with SH-60B *Seahawk*
  1 ASW/CSAR sqn with HH-60H *Seahawk*; SH-60F *Seahawk*
  2 ASW/ISR sqn with MH-60R *Seahawk*; MQ-8B *Fire Scout*

ELINT
  1 sqn with EP-3E *Aries* II
ELINT/ELECTRONIC WARFARE
  1 sqn with EA-6B *Prowler*
  10 sqn with EA-18G *Growler*
  2 sqn (forming) with EA-18G *Growler*
MARITIME PATROL
  9 sqn with P-3C *Orion*
  1 sqn with P-8A *Poseidon*
  2 sqn (forming) with P-8A *Poseidon*
AIRBORNE EARLY WARNING & CONTROL
  9 sqn with E-2C *Hawkeye*
  1 sqn with E-2D *Hawkeye*
COMMAND & CONTROL
  2 sqn with E-6B *Mercury*
MINE COUNTERMEASURES
  2 sqn with MH-53E *Sea Dragon*
TRANSPORT
  2 sqn with C-2A *Greyhound*
TRAINING
  1 (FRS) sqn with EA-18G *Growler*
  1 (FRS) sqn with C-2A *Greyhound*; E-2C/D *Hawkeye*; TE-2C *Hawkeye*
  1 sqn with E-6B *Mercury*
  2 (FRS) sqn with F/A-18A/A+/B/C/D *Hornet*; F/A-18E/F *Super Hornet*
  1 (FRS) sqn (forming) with F-35C *Lightning* II
  2 (FRS) sqn with MH-60S *Knight Hawk*; HH-60H/SH-60F *Seahawk*
  1 (FRS) sqn with MH-60R *Seahawk*
  1 (FRS) sqn with MH-60R/SH-60B *Seahawk*
  1 sqn with P-3C *Orion*
  1 (FRS) sqn with P-3C *Orion*; P-8A *Poseidon*
  5 sqn with T-6A/B *Texan* II
  1 sqn with T-39G/N *Sabreliner*; T-45C *Goshawk*
  1 sqn T-34C *Turbo Mentor*
  1 sqn with T-44A/C *Pegasus*
  4 sqn with T-45A/C *Goshawk*
  1 sqn with TC-12B *Huron*
  3 hel sqn with TH-57B/C *Sea Ranger*
  1 (FRS) UAV sqn with MQ-8B *Fire Scout*; MQ-8C *Fire Scout*
TRANSPORT HELICOPTER
  14 sqn with MH-60S *Knight Hawk*
  1 tpt hel/ISR sqn with MH-60S *Knight Hawk*; MQ-8B *Fire Scout*
ISR UAV
  1 sqn (forming) with MQ-4C *Triton*
EQUIPMENT BY TYPE
AIRCRAFT 1,150 combat capable
  FGA 871: 12 F-35C *Lightning* II; 10 F/A-18A/A+ *Hornet*; 9 F/A-18B *Hornet*; 268 F/A-18C *Hornet*; 41 F/A-18D *Hornet*; 260 F/A-18E *Super Hornet*; 271 F/A-18F *Super Hornet*
  ASW 158: 140 P-3C *Orion*; 18 P-8A *Poseidon*
  EW 121: 15 EA-6B *Prowler**; 106 EA-18G *Growler**
  ELINT 11 EP-3E *Aries* II
  ISR 2: 1 RC-12F *Huron*; 1 RC-12M *Huron*
  AEW&C 76: 61 E-2C/TE-2C *Hawkeye*; 15 E-2D *Hawkeye*
  C2 16 E-6B *Mercury*
  TPT • **Light** 68: 4 Beech A200 *King Air* (C-12C *Huron*); 20 Beech A200 *King Air* (UC-12F/M *Huron*); 35 C-2A

Greyhound; 2 DHC-2 *Beaver* (U-6A); 7 SA-227-BC *Metro III* (C-26D)
TRG 640: 44 T-6A *Texan II*; 144 T-6B *Texan II*; 100 T-34C *Turbo Mentor*; 7 T-38C *Talon*; 5 T-39G *Sabreliner*; 13 T-39N *Sabreliner*; 55 T-44A/C *Pegasus*; 74 T-45A *Goshawk*; 171 T-45C *Goshawk*; 25 TC-12B *Huron*; 2 TE-2C *Hawkeye*
HELICOPTERS
ASW 255: 200 MH-60R *Seahawk*; 35 SH-60B *Seahawk*; 20 SH-60F *Seahawk*
MRH 255 MH-60S *Knight Hawk* (Multi Mission Support)
MCM 28 MH-53E *Sea Dragon*
ISR 3 OH-58C *Kiowa*
CSAR 11 HH-60H *Seahawk*
TPT 13: **Heavy** 2 CH-53E *Sea Stallion*; **Medium** 3 UH-60L *Black Hawk*; **Light** 8: 5 EC145 (UH-72A *Lakota*); 2 UH-1N *Iroquois*; 1 UH-1Y *Iroquois*
TRG 120: 44 TH-57B *Sea Ranger*; 76 TH-57C *Sea Ranger*
UAV • ISR 61
Heavy 26: 20 MQ-8B *Fire Scout*; 2 MQ-8C *Fire Scout*; 4 RQ-4A *Global Hawk* (under evaluation and trials)
Medium 35 RQ-2B *Pioneer*
MSL
AAM • IR AIM-9 *Sidewinder*; **IIR** AIM-9X *Sidewinder II*, **SARH** AIM-7 *Sparrow*; **ARH** AIM-120 AMRAAM
ASM AGM-65A/F *Maverick*; AGM-114B/K/M *Hellfire*; AGM-84E SLAM/SLAM-ER LACM; AGM-154A JSOW; **AShM** AGM-84D *Harpoon*; AGM-119A *Penguin 3*; **ARM** AGM-88B/C/E HARM
BOMBS
Laser-Guided: *Paveway* II (GBU-10/12/16); *Paveway* III (GBU-24)
INS/GPS guided: JDAM (GBU-31/32/38); Enhanced *Paveway* II; Laser JDAM (GBU-54)

Naval Aviation Reserve
FORCES BY ROLE
FIGHTER/GROUND ATTACK
  1 sqn with F/A-18A+ *Hornet*
ANTI-SUBMARINE WARFARE
  1 sqn with SH-60B *Seahawk*
ELECTRONIC WARFARE
  1 sqn with EA-18G *Growler*
MARITIME PATROL
  2 sqn with P-3C *Orion*
TRANSPORT
  5 log spt sqn with B-737-700 (C-40A *Clipper*)
  2 log spt sqn with Gulfstream III/IV (C-20A/D/G); Gulfstream V/G550 (C-37A/C-37B)
  5 sqn with C-130T *Hercules*
TRAINING
  2 (aggressor) sqn with F-5F/N *Tiger II*
  1 (aggressor) sqn with F/A-18A+ *Hornet*
TRANSPORT HELICOPTER
  2 sqn with HH-60H *Seahawk*
EQUIPMENT BY TYPE
AIRCRAFT 69 combat capable
  FTR 32: 2 F-5F *Tiger* II; 30 F-5N *Tiger* II
  FGA 20 F/A-18A+ *Hornet*
  ASW 12 P-3C *Orion*
  EW 5 EA-18G *Growler**

TPT 44: **Medium** 19 C-130T *Hercules*; **PAX** 25: 14 B-737-700 (C-40A *Clipper*); 3 Gulfstream III (C-20A/D); 4 Gulfstream IV (C-20G); 1 Gulfstream V (C-37A); 3 Gulfstream G550 (C-37B)
HELICOPTERS
ASW 6 SH-60B *Seahawk*
MCM 8 MH-53E *Sea Stallion*
CSAR 24 HH-60H *Seahawk*

US Marine Corps 190,200; 950 active reservists (total 191,150)
3 Marine Expeditionary Forces (MEF), 3 Marine Expeditionary Brigades (MEB), 7 Marine Expeditionary Units (MEU) drawn from 3 div. An MEU usually consists of a battalion landing team (1 SF coy, 1 lt armd recce coy, 1 recce pl, 1 armd pl, 1 amph aslt pl, 1 inf bn, 1 arty bty, 1 cbt engr pl), an aviation combat element (1 medium lift sqn with attached atk hel, FGA ac and AD assets) and a composite log bn, with a combined total of about 2,200 personnel. Composition varies with mission requirements.
FORCES BY ROLE
SPECIAL FORCES
  (see USSOCOM)
MANOEUVRE
Reconnaissance
  3 (MEF) recce coy
Amphibious
  1 (1st) mne div (2 armd recce bn, 1 recce bn, 1 armd bn, 3 inf regt (4 inf bn), 1 amph aslt bn, 1 arty regt (4 arty bn), 1 cbt engr bn, 1 EW bn, 1 int bn, 1 sigs bn)
  1 (2nd) mne div (1 armd recce bn, 1 recce bn, 1 armd bn, 1 inf regt (4 inf bn), 2 inf regt (3 inf bn), 1 amph aslt bn, 1 arty regt (2 arty bn), 1 cbt engr bn, 1 EW bn, 1 int bn, 1 sigs bn)
  1 (3rd) mne div (1 recce bn, 1 inf regt (3 inf bn), 1 arty regt (2 arty bn), 1 cbt spt bn (1 armd recce coy, 1 amph aslt coy, 1 cbt engr coy), 1 EW bn, 1 int bn, 1 sigs bn)
COMBAT SERVICE SUPPORT
  3 log gp
EQUIPMENT BY TYPE
MBT 447 M1A1 *Abrams*
RECCE 252 LAV-25 (25mm gun, plus 189 variants)
AAV 1,311 AAV-7A1 (all roles)
APC • PPV 4,059: 2,380 MRAP; 1,679 M-ATV
ARTY 1,506
  TOWED 832: **105mm:** 331 M101A1; **155mm** 501 M777A2
  MRL 227mm: 40 M142 HIMARS
  MOR 634: **81mm** 585: 50 LAV-M; 535 M252 **120mm** 49 EFSS
AT • MSL
  SP 95 LAV-TOW
  MANPATS *Predator*; TOW
AD • SAM • MANPAD FIM-92A *Stinger*
UAV • Light 100 BQM-147 *Exdrone*
RADAR • LAND 23 AN/TPQ-36 *Firefinder* (arty)
AEV 42 M1 ABV
ARV 185: 60 AAVRA1; 45 LAV-R; 80 M88A1/2
VLB 6 Joint Aslt Bridge

Marine Corps Aviation 34,700
3 active Marine Aircraft Wings (MAW) and 1 MCR MAW
Flying hours   365 hrs/year on tpt ac; 248 hrs/year on ac; 277 hrs/year on hel

FORCES BY ROLE
FIGHTER
1 sqn with F/A-18A/A+ *Hornet*
6 sqn with F/A-18C *Hornet*
4 sqn with F/A-18D *Hornet*
FIGHTER/GROUND ATTACK
6 sqn with AV-8B *Harrier* II
ELECTRONIC WARFARE
3 sqn with EA-6B *Prowler*
COMBAT SEARCH & RESCUE/TRANSPORT
1 sqn with Beech A200/B200 *King Air* (UC-12B/F *Huron*); Cessna 560 *Citation Ultra/Encore* (UC-35C/D); DC-9 *Skytrain* (C-9B *Nightingale*); Gulfstream IV (C-20G); HH-1N *Iroquois*; HH-46E *Sea Knight*
TANKER
3 sqn with KC-130J *Hercules*
TRANSPORT
14 sqn with MV-22B/C *Osprey*
TRAINING
1 sqn with AV-8B *Harrier* II; TAV-8B *Harrier*
1 sqn with EA-6B *Prowler*
1 sqn with F/A-18B/C/D *Hornet*
1 sqn with F-35B *Lightning* II
1 sqn with MV-22B *Osprey*
1 hel sqn with AH-1W *Cobra*; AH-1Z *Viper*; HH-1N *Iroquois*; UH-1Y *Venom*
1 hel sqn with CH-46E *Sea Knight*
1 hel sqn with CH-53E *Sea Stallion*
ATTACK HELICOPTER
6 sqn with AH-1W *Cobra*; UH-1Y *Venom*
3 sqn with AH-1Z *Viper*; UH-1Y *Venom*
TRANSPORT HELICOPTER
1 sqn with CH-46E *Sea Knight*
8 sqn with CH-53E *Sea Stallion*
1 (VIP) sqn with MV-22B *Osprey*; VH-3D *Sea King*; VH-60N *Presidential Hawk*
ISR UAV
3 sqn with RQ-7B *Shadow*
AIR DEFENCE
2 bn with M998/M1097 *Avenger*; FIM-92A *Stinger* (can provide additional heavy-calibre support weapons)
EQUIPMENT BY TYPE
AIRCRAFT 413 combat capable
   FGA 413: 33 F-35B *Lightning* II; 41 F/A-18A/A+ *Hornet*; 7 F/A-18B *Hornet*; 108 F/A-18C *Hornet*; 93 F/A-18D *Hornet*; 115 AV-8B *Harrier* II; 16 TAV-8B *Harrier*
   EW 27 EA-6B *Prowler*
   TKR 45 KC-130J *Hercules*
   TPT 20: **Light** 17: 10 Beech A200/B200 *King Air* (UC-12B/F *Huron*); 7 Cessna 560 *Citation Ultra/Encore* (UC-35C/D); **PAX** 3: 2 DC-9 *Skytrain* (C-9B *Nightingale*); 1 Gulfstream IV (C-20G)
   TRG 3 T-34C *Turbo Mentor*
TILTROTOR TPT • 208 MV-22B/C *Osprey*
HELICOPTERS
   ATK 151: 112 AH-1W *Cobra*; 39 AH-1Z *Viper*
   SAR 8: 4 HH-1N *Iroquois*; 4 HH-46E *Sea Knight*
   TPT 266: **Heavy** 139 CH-53E *Sea Stallion*; **Medium** 35: 16 CH-46E *Sea Knight*; 8 VH-60N *Presidential Hawk* (VIP tpt); 11 VH-3D *Sea King* (VIP tpt); **Light** 92 UH-1Y *Iroquois*
UAV • **ISR** • **Medium** 32 RQ-7B *Shadow*
AD
   SAM • **SP** some M998/M1097 *Avenger*
      MANPAD some FIM-92A *Stinger*
MSL
   AAM • **IR** AIM-9M *Sidewinder*; **IIR** AIM-9X; **SARH** AIM-7 *Sparrow*; **ARH** AIM-120 AMRAAM
   ASM AGM-65F IR *Maverick*/AGM-65E *Maverick*; AGM-114 *Hellfire*; AGM-176 *Griffin*; **AShM** AGM-84 *Harpoon*; **ARM** AGM-88 HARM
BOMBS
   Conventional CBU-59; CBU-99; Mk82 (500lb), Mk83 (1,000lb)
   Laser-Guided GBU 10/12/16 *Paveway* II (fits on Mk82, Mk83 or Mk84)
   INS/GPS Guided JDAM

Reserve Organisations

Marine Corps Reserve 39,600 (incl 950 active)
FORCES BY ROLE
MANOEUVRE
   Reconnaissance
   2 MEF recce coy
   Amphibious
   1 (4th) mne div (1 armd recce bn, 1 recce bn, 2 inf regt (3 inf bn), 1 amph aslt bn, 1 arty regt (3 arty bn), 1 cbt engr bn, 1 int bn, 1 sigs bn)
COMBAT SERVICE SUPPORT
   1 log gp

Marine Corps Aviation Reserve 11,600 reservists
FORCES BY ROLE
FIGHTER
   1 sqn with F/A-18A/A+ *Hornet*
TANKER
   2 sqn with KC-130J/T *Hercules*
TRANSPORT
   1 sqn with MV-22B *Osprey*
TRAINING
   1 sqn with F-5F/N *Tiger* II
ATTACK HELICOPTER
   1 sqn with AH-1W *Cobra*; UH-1Y *Iroquois*
TRANSPORT HELICOPTER
   1 sqn with CH-46E *Sea Knight*
   1 det with CH-53E *Sea Stallion*
ISR UAV
   1 sqn with RQ-7B *Shadow*
EQUIPMENT BY TYPE
AIRCRAFT 27 combat capable
   FTR 12: 1 F-5F *Tiger* II; 11 F-5N *Tiger* II
   FGA 15 F/A-18A/A+ *Hornet*
   TKR 25: 2 KC-130J *Hercules*; 23 KC-130T *Hercules*
   TPT • **Light** 7: 2 Beech 350 *King Air* (UC-12W *Huron*); 5 Cessna 560 *Citation Ultra/Encore* (UC-35C/D)
TILTROTOR • **TPT** 8 MV-22B *Osprey*
HELICOPTERS
   ATK 16 AH-1W *Cobra*

TPT 21: **Heavy** 6 CH-53E *Sea Stallion*; **Medium** 8 CH-46E *Sea Knight*; **Light** 7 UH-1Y *Iroquois*
UAV • **ISR** • **Medium** 8 RQ-7B *Shadow*

Marine Stand-by Reserve 700 reservists
Trained individuals available for mobilisation

US Coast Guard 41,200 (military); 7,600 (civilian)

9 districts (4 Pacific, 5 Atlantic)
PATROL AND COASTAL COMBATANTS 158
 PSOH 24: 1 *Alex Haley*; 13 *Famous*; 7 *Hamilton*; 3 *Legend*
 PCO 23: 14 *Reliance* (with 1 hel landing platform); 9 *Sentinel*
 PCC 38 *Island*
 PBI 73 *Marine Protector*
LOGISTICS AND SUPPORT 386
 AB 13: 1 *Cosmos*; 4 *Pamlico*; 8 *Anvil*
 ABU 52: 16 *Juniper*; 4 *WLI*; 14 *Keeper*; 18 *WLR*
 AGB 13: 9 *Bay*; 1 *Mackinaw*; 1 *Healy*; 2 *Polar* (of which one in reserve)
 AXS 1 *Eagle*
 YAG 179: 166 *Response*; 13 Utility Boat
 YP 117
 YTM 11

US Coast Guard Aviation

EQUIPMENT BY TYPE
AIRCRAFT
 SAR 27: 21 HC-130H *Hercules* (additional 4 in store); 6 HC-130J *Hercules*
 TPT 20: **Light** 18 CN-235-200 (HC-144A – MP role); **PAX** 2 Gulfstream V (C-37A)
HELICOPTERS
 SAR 125: 35 MH-60J/T *Jayhawk* (additional 7 in store); 90 AS366G1 (HH-65C/MH-65C/D) *Dauphin* II (additional 11 in store)

US Air Force (USAF) 327,600; 4,250 active ANG; 2,700 active AFR (total 334,550)

Flying hours Ftr 160, bbr 260, tkr 308, airlift 343
Almost the entire USAF (plus active force ANG and AFR) is divided into 10 Aerospace Expeditionary Forces (AEF), each on call for 120 days every 20 months. At least 2 of the 10 AEFs are on call at any one time, each with 10,000–15,000 personnel, 90 multi-role Ftr and bbr ac, 31 intra-theatre refuelling aircraft and 13 aircraft for ISR and EW missions.

Global Strike Command (GSC)

2 active air forces (8th & 20th); 6 wg
FORCES BY ROLE
MISSILE
 9 sqn with LGM-30G *Minuteman* III
BOMBER
 5 sqn (incl 1 trg) with B-52H *Stratofortress*
 2 sqn with B-2A *Spirit*
TRANSPORT HELICOPTER
 3 sqn with UH-1N *Iroquois*

Air Combat Command (ACC)

2 active air forces (9th & 12th); 15 wg. ACC numbered air forces provide the air component to CENTCOM, SOUTHCOM and NORTHCOM.

FORCES BY ROLE
BOMBER
 4 sqn with B-1B *Lancer*
FIGHTER
 3 sqn with F-22A *Raptor*
FIGHTER/GROUND ATTACK
 4 sqn with F-15E *Strike Eagle*
 5 sqn with F-16C/D *Fighting Falcon*
GROUND ATTACK
 3 sqn with A-10C *Thunderbolt* II
ELECTRONIC WARFARE
 1 sqn with EA-18G *Growler* (personnel only – USN aircraft)
 2 sqn with EC-130H *Compass Call*
ISR
 1 sqn with Beech 350ER *King Air* (MC-12W *Liberty*)
 5 sqn with OC-135/RC-135/WC-135
 2 sqn with U-2S
AIRBORNE EARLY WARNING & CONTROL
 4 sqn with E-3B/C *Sentry*
COMMAND & CONTROL
 1 sqn with E-4B
COMBAT SEARCH & RESCUE
 6 sqn with HC-130J/N/P *King*; HH-60G *Pave Hawk*
TRAINING
 2 sqn with A-10C *Thunderbolt* II
 1 sqn with Beech 350ER *King Air* (MC-12W *Liberty*)
 1 sqn with E-3B/C *Sentry*
 2 sqn with F-15E *Strike Eagle*
 1 sqn with F-22A *Raptor*
 1 sqn with RQ-4A *Global Hawk*; TU-2S
 2 UAV sqn with MQ-1B *Predator*
 3 UAV sqn with MQ-9A *Reaper*
COMBAT/ISR UAV
 4 sqn with MQ-1B *Predator*
 1 sqn with MQ-1B *Predator*/MQ-9A *Reaper*
 1 sqn with MQ-1B *Predator*/RQ-170 *Sentinel*
 2 sqn with MQ-9 *Reaper*
ISR UAV
 2 sqn with RQ-4B *Global Hawk*

Pacific Air Forces (PACAF)

Provides the air component of PACOM, and commands air units based in Alaska, Hawaii, Japan and South Korea. 3 active air forces (5th, 7th, & 11th); 8 wg
FORCES BY ROLE
FIGHTER
 2 sqn with F-15C/D *Eagle*
 2 sqn with F-22A *Raptor* (+1 sqn personnel only)
FIGHTER/GROUND ATTACK
 5 sqn with F-16C/D *Fighting Falcon*
GROUND ATTACK
 1 sqn with A-10C *Thunderbolt* II
AIRBORNE EARLY WARNING & CONTROL
 2 sqn with E-3B/C *Sentry*
COMBAT SEARCH & RESCUE
 1 sqn with HH-60G *Pave Hawk*
TANKER
 1 sqn with KC-135R (+1 sqn personnel only)
TRANSPORT
 1 sqn with B-737-200 (C-40B); Gulfstream V (C-37A)

2 sqn with C-17A *Globemaster*
1 sqn with C-130H *Hercules*
1 sqn with Beech 1900C (C-12J); UH-1N *Huey*
TRAINING
1 (aggressor) sqn with F-16C/D *Fighting Falcon*

United States Air Forces Europe (USAFE)

Provides the air component to both EUCOM and AFRICOM. 1 active air force (3rd); 5 wg
FORCES BY ROLE
FIGHTER
1 sqn with F-15C/D *Eagle*
FIGHTER/GROUND ATTACK
2 sqn with F-15E *Strike Eagle*
3 sqn with F-16C/D *Fighting Falcon*
COMBAT SEARCH & RESCUE
1 sqn with HH-60G *Pave Hawk*
TANKER
1 sqn with KC-135R *Stratotanker*
TRANSPORT
1 sqn with C-130J *Hercules*
2 sqn with Gulfstream III/IV (C-20); Gulfstream V (C-37); Learjet 35A (C-21)

Air Mobility Command (AMC)

Provides strategic and tactical airlift, air-to-air refuelling and aeromedical evacuation. 1 active air force (18th); 12 wg and 1 gp
FORCES BY ROLE
TANKER
4 sqn with KC-10A *Extender*
9 sqn with KC-135R/T *Stratotanker* (+2 sqn with personnel only)
TRANSPORT
1 VIP sqn with B-737-200 (C-40B); B-757-200 (C-32A)
1 VIP sqn with Gulfstream III/IV (C-20)
1 VIP sqn with VC-25 *Air Force One*
1 sqn with C-5M *Super Galaxy*
1 sqn with C-5B/C/M *Galaxy/Super Galaxy*
11 sqn with C-17A *Globemaster* III
4 sqn with C-130H *Hercules* (+1 sqn personnel only)
3 sqn with C-130J *Hercules* (+1 sqn personnel only)
1 sqn with Gulfstream V (C-37A)
2 sqn with Learjet 35A (C-21)

Air Education and Training Command

1 active air force (2nd), 10 active air wg and 1 gp
FORCES BY ROLE
TRAINING
1 sqn with C-17A *Globemaster* III
1 sqn with C-130H *Hercules*
1 sqn with C-130J *Hercules*
7 sqn with F-16C/D *Fighting Falcon*
2 sqn with F-35A *Lightning* II
1 sqn with KC-135R *Stratotanker*
5 (flying trg) sqn with T-1A *Jayhawk*
10 (flying trg) sqn with T-6A *Texan* II
10 (flying trg) sqn with T-38C *Talon*
1 UAV sqn with MQ-1B *Predator*

EQUIPMENT BY TYPE
AIRCRAFT 1,410 combat capable
BBR 137: 63 B-1B *Lancer* (2 more in test); 20 B-2A *Spirit* (1 more in test); 54 B-52H *Stratofortress* (2 more in test)
FTR 275: 106 F-15C *Eagle*; 10 F-15D *Eagle*; 159 F-22A *Raptor*
FGA 838: 211 F-15E *Strike Eagle*; 469 F-16C *Fighting Falcon*; 116 F-16D *Fighting Falcon*; 42 F-35A *Lightning* II
ATK 160 A-10C *Thunderbolt* II
EW 14 EC-130H *Compass Call*
ISR 82: 41 Beech 350ER *King Air* (MC-12W *Liberty*); 2 E-9A; 4 E-11A; 2 OC-135B *Open Skies*; 26 U-2S; 5 TU-2S; 2 WC-135 *Constant Phoenix*
ELINT 22: 8 RC-135V *Rivet Joint*; 9 RC-135W *Rivet Joint*; 3 RC-135S *Cobra Ball*; 2 RC-135U *Combat Sent*
AEW&C 32 E-3B/C *Sentry* (1 more in test)
C2 4 E-4B
TKR 167: 137 KC-135R *Stratotanker*; 30 KC-135T *Stratotanker*
TKR/TPT 59 KC-10A *Extender*
CSAR 22 HC-130J/N/P *Combat King/Combat King* II
TPT 390: **Heavy** 220: 14 C-5B *Galaxy*; 2 C-5C *Galaxy*; 22 C-5M *Super Galaxy*; 182 C-17A *Globemaster* III; **Medium** 107 C-130H/J-30 *Hercules*; **Light** 39: 4 Beech 1900C (C-12J); 35 Learjet 35A (C-21); **PAX** 24: 2 B-737-700 (C-40B); 4 B-757-200 (C-32A); 5 Gulfstream III (C-20B); 2 Gulfstream IV (C-20H); 9 Gulfstream V (C-37A); 2 VC-25A *Air Force One*
TRG 1,130: 179 T-1A *Jayhawk*; 405 T-6A *Texan* II; 546 T-38A *Talon*
HELICOPTERS
CSAR 81 HH-60G *Pave Hawk*
TPT • Light 62 UH-1N *Huey*
UAV 314
CISR • Heavy 279: 101 MQ-1B *Predator*; 178 MQ-9A/B *Reaper*
ISR • Heavy 35+: 3 EQ-4B; 31 RQ-4B *Global Hawk*; 1+ RQ-170 *Sentinel*
MSL
AAM • IR AIM-9 *Sidewinder*; **IIR** AIM-9X *Sidewinder* II; **SARH** AIM-7M *Sparrow* **ARH** AIM-120B/C AMRAAM
ASM AGM-65D/G *Maverick*; AGM-130A; AGM-176 *Griffin*
LACM AGM-86B (ALCM) (strategic); AGM-86C (CALCM) (tactical); AGM-86D (penetrator); AGM-158 JASSM; AGM-158B JASSM-ER
ARM AGM-88A/B HARM
EW MALD/MALD-J
MANPAD FIM-92 *Stinger*
BOMBS
Conventional: BLU-109/Mk84 (2,000lb); BLU-110/Mk83 (1,000lb); BLU-111/Mk82 (500lb)
Laser-guided: *Paveway* II, *Paveway* III (fits on Mk82, Mk83 or Mk84)
INS/GPS guided: JDAM (GBU 31/32/38); GBU-15 (with BLU-109 penetrating warhead or Mk84); GBU-39B Small Diameter Bomb (250lb); GBU-43B; GBU-57A/B; Enhanced *Paveway* III

Reserve Organisations

Air National Guard 105,400 reservists (incl 4,250 active)

FORCES BY ROLE
BOMBER
1 sqn with B-2A *Spirit* (personnel only)
FIGHTER
5 sqn with F-15C/D *Eagle*
1 sqn with F-22A *Raptor* (+1 sqn personnel only)
FIGHTER/GROUND ATTACK
11 sqn with F-16C/D *Fighting Falcon*
GROUND ATTACK
4 sqn with A-10C *Thunderbolt* II
ISR
3 sqn with E-8C J-STARS (mixed active force and ANG personnel)
COMBAT SEARCH & RESCUE
9 sqn with HC-130P/N *Hercules*; MC-130P *Combat Shadow*; HH-60G/M *Pave Hawk*
TANKER
16 sqn with KC-135R *Stratotanker* (+2 sqn personnel only)
3 sqn with KC-135T *Stratotanker*
TRANSPORT
1 sqn with B-737-700 (C-40C); Gulfstream G100 (C-38A)
3 sqn with C-17A *Globemaster* (+2 sqn personnel only)
1 sqn (forming) with C-17A *Globemaster*
14 sqn with C-130H *Hercules* (+1 sqn personnel only)
1 sqn with C-130H/LC-130H *Hercules*
2 sqn with C-130J-30 *Hercules*
1 sqn with Learjet 35A (C-21A)
1 sqn with WC-130H *Hercules*
TRAINING
1 sqn with C-130H *Hercules*
1 sqn with F-15C/D *Eagle*
4 sqn with F-16C/D *Fighting Falcon*
COMBAT/ISR UAV
5 sqn with MQ-1B *Predator*
1 sqn with MQ-9A/B *Reaper* (+4 sqn personnel only)
EQUIPMENT BY TYPE
AIRCRAFT 477 combat capable
 FTR 129: 92 F-15C *Eagle*; 19 F-15D *Eagle*; 18 F-22A *Raptor*
 FGA 276: 254 F-16C *Fighting Falcon*; 22 F-16D *Fighting Falcon*
 ATK 72 A-10C *Thunderbolt* II
 ISR 13 E-8C J-STARS
 ELINT 11 RC-26B *Metroliner* (being withdrawn)
 CSAR 7 HC-130P/N *Combat King*
 TKR 162: 138 KC-135R *Stratotanker*; 24 KC-135T *Stratotanker*
 TPT 209: **Heavy** 25 C-17A *Globemaster* III; **Medium** 177: 139 C-130H *Hercules*; 16 C-130J-30 *Hercules*; 10 LC-130H *Hercules*; 4 MC-130P *Combat Shadow*; 8 WC-130H *Hercules*; **Light** 2 Learjet 35A (C-21A); **PAX** 5: 3 B-737-700 (C-40C); 2 Gulfstream G100 (C-38A)
HELICOPTERS • CSAR 17: 10 HH-60G *Pave Hawk*; 7 HH-60M *Pave Hawk*
UAV • CISR • Heavy 48: 36 MQ-1B *Predator*; 12 MQ-9A *Reaper*

Air Force Reserve Command 70,400 reservists (incl 2,700 active)
FORCES BY ROLE
BOMBER
1 sqn with B-52H *Stratofortress* (personnel only)
FIGHTER
2 sqn with F-22A *Raptor* (personnel only)
FIGHTER/GROUND ATTACK
2 sqn with F-16C/D *Fighting Falcon* (+2 sqn personnel only)
GROUND ATTACK
1 sqn with A-10C *Thunderbolt* II (+2 sqn personnel only)
ISR
1 (Weather Recce) sqn with WC-130J *Hercules*
AIRBORNE EARLY WARNING & CONTROL
1 sqn with E-3B/C *Sentry* (personnel only)
COMBAT SEARCH & RESCUE
3 sqn with HC-130P/N *Hercules*; HH-60G *Pave Hawk*
TANKER
4 sqn with KC-10A *Extender* (personnel only)
6 sqn with KC-135R *Stratotanker* (+2 sqn personnel only)
TRANSPORT
1 (VIP) sqn with B-737-700 (C-40C)
2 sqn with C-5B *Galaxy* (+1 sqn personnel only)
1 sqn with C-5M *Super Galaxy* (personnel only)
2 sqn with C-17A *Globemaster* (+8 sqn personnel only)
8 sqn with C-130H *Hercules*
1 sqn with C-130J-30 *Hercules*
1 (Aerial Spray) sqn with C-130H *Hercules*
TRAINING
1 (aggressor) sqn with A-10C *Thunderbolt* II; F-15C/E *Eagle*; F-16 *Fighting Falcon*; F-22A *Raptor* (personnel only)
1 sqn with B-52H *Stratofortress*
1 sqn with C-5A *Galaxy*
1 sqn with F-16C/D *Fighting Falcon*
5 (flying training) sqn with T-1A *Jayhawk*; T-6A *Texan* II; T-38C *Talon* (personnel only)
COMBAT/ISR UAV
2 sqn with MQ-1B *Predator*/MQ-9A *Reaper* (personnel only)
ISR UAV
1 sqn with RQ-4B *Global Hawk* (personnel only)
EQUIPMENT BY TYPE
AIRCRAFT 97 combat capable
 BBR 18 B-52H *Stratofortress*
 FGA 52: 49 F-16C *Fighting Falcon*; 3 F-16D *Fighting Falcon*
 ATK 27 A-10C *Thunderbolt* II
 ISR 10 WC-130J *Hercules* (Weather Recce)
 CSAR 5 HC-130P/N *King*
 TKR 62 KC-135R *Stratotanker*
 TPT 110: **Heavy** 40: 8 C-5A *Galaxy*; 16 C-5B *Galaxy*; 16 C-17A *Globemaster* III; **Medium** 66: 56 C-130H *Hercules*; 10 C-130J-30 *Hercules*; **PAX** 4 B-737-700 (C-40C)
HELICOPTERS • CSAR 15 HH-60G *Pave Hawk*

Civil Reserve Air Fleet
Commercial ac numbers fluctuate
AIRCRAFT • TPT 517 international (391 long-range and 126 short-range); 36 national

Air Force Stand-by Reserve 16,858 reservists
Trained individuals for mobilisation

US Special Operations Command (USSOCOM) 60,200; 6,400 (civilian)
Commands all active, reserve and National Guard Special Operations Forces (SOF) of all services based in CONUS.

Joint Special Operations Command
Reported to comprise elite US SF including Special Forces Operations Detachment Delta ('Delta Force'), SEAL Team 6 and integral USAF support.

US Army Special Operations Command 32,400
FORCES BY ROLE
SPECIAL FORCES
  5 SF gp (3–4 SF bn, 1 spt bn)
  1 ranger regt (3 ranger bn; 1 cbt spt bn)
MANOEUVRE
  Aviation
  1 (160th SOAR) regt (4 avn bn)
COMBAT SUPPORT
  1 civil affairs bde (5 civil affairs bn)
  2 psyops gp (3 psyops bn)
COMBAT SERVICE SUPPORT
  1 (sustainment) log bde (1 sigs bn)
EQUIPMENT BY TYPE
APC • PPV 640 M-ATV
HELICOPTERS
  MRH 50 AH-6M/MH-6M *Little Bird*
  TPT 130: **Heavy** 68 MH-47G *Chinook*; **Medium** 62 MH-60K/L/M *Black Hawk*
UAV
  CISR • **Heavy** 12 MQ-1C *Gray Eagle*
  ISR • **Light** 29: 15 XPV-1 *Tern*; 14 XPV-2 *Mako*
  TPT • **Heavy** 28 CQ-10 *Snowgoose*

Reserve Organisations

Army National Guard
FORCES BY ROLE
SPECIAL FORCES
  2 SF gp (3 SF bn)

Army Reserve
FORCES BY ROLE
COMBAT SUPPORT
  2 psyops gp
  4 civil affairs comd HQ
  8 civil affairs bde HQ
  36 civil affairs bn (coy)

US Navy Special Warfare Command 9,500
FORCES BY ROLE
SPECIAL FORCES
  8 SEAL team (total: 48 SF pl)
  2 SEAL Delivery Vehicle team
EQUIPMENT BY TYPE
SF 6 DDS

Naval Reserve Force
SPECIAL FORCES
  8 SEAL det
  10 Naval Special Warfare det
  2 Special Boat sqn
  2 Special Boat unit
  1 SEAL Delivery Vehicle det

US Marine Special Operations Command (MARSOC) 3,000
FORCES BY ROLE
SPECIAL FORCES
  1 SF regt (3 SF bn)
COMBAT SUPPORT
  1 int bn
COMBAT SERVICE SUPPORT
  1 spt gp

Air Force Special Operations Command (AFSOC) 15,300
FORCES BY ROLE
GROUND ATTACK
  2 sqn with AC-130H/U *Spectre*
  1 sqn with AC-130W *Stinger* II
TRANSPORT
  1 sqn with An-26 *Curl*; DHC-6; M-28 *Skytruck* (C-145A); Mi-8 *Hip*; Mi-171
  2 sqn with CV-22B *Osprey*
  1 sqn with DHC-8; Do-328 (C-146A)
  2 sqn with MC-130H *Combat Talon*
  1 sqn with MC-130H *Combat Talon*; CV-22B *Osprey*
  1 sqn with MC-130J *Commando* II
  1 sqn with MC-130J *Commando* II; MC-130P *Combat Shadow*
  1 sqn with MC-130P *Combat Shadow*
  3 sqn with PC-12 (U-28A)
TRAINING
  1 sqn with CV-22A/B *Osprey*
  1 sqn with HC-130J *Combat King* II; MC-130J *Commando* II
  1 sqn with HC-130P/N *Combat King*; MC-130H *Combat Talon* II; MC-130P *Combat Shadow*
  1 sqn with Bell 205 (TH-1H *Iroquois*)
  1 sqn with HH-60G *Pave Hawk*; UH-1N *Huey*
COMBAT/ISR UAV
  1 sqn with MQ-1B *Predator*
  1 sqn with MQ-9 *Reaper*
EQUIPMENT BY TYPE
AIRCRAFT 37 combat capable
  ATK 37: 8 AC-130H *Spectre*; 17 AC-130U *Spectre*; 12 AC-130W *Stinger* II
  CSAR 4: 2 HC-130N *Combat King*; 1 HC-130P *Combat King*; 1 HC-130J *Combat King* II
  TPT 108: **Medium** 52: 3 C-27J *Spartan*; 20 MC-130H *Combat Talon* II; 7 MC-130J *Commando* II; 22 MC-130P *Combat Shadow*; **Light** 56: 1 An-26 *Curl*; 1 DHC-6; 5 DHC-8; 9 Do-328 (CC-146A); 4 M-28 *Skytruck* (C-145A); 36 PC-12 (U-28A)
TILT-ROTOR 35 CV-22A/B *Osprey* (3 more in test)

HELICOPTERS
CSAR 3 HH-60G *Pave Hawk*
TPT 38 **Medium** 4: 3 Mi-8 *Hip*; 1 Mi-171; **Light** 34: 24 Bell 205 (TH-1H *Iroquois*); 10 UH-1N *Huey*
UAV • CISR • **Heavy** 39: 29 MQ-1B *Predator*; 10 MQ-9 *Reaper*

Reserve Organisations

Air National Guard
FORCES BY ROLE
ELECTRONIC WARFARE
  1 sqn with C-130J *Hercules*/EC-130J *Commando Solo*
TRANSPORT
  1 flt with B-737-200 (C-32B)
EQUIPMENT BY TYPE
AIRCRAFT
  EW 3 EC-130J *Commando Solo*
  TPT 5: **Medium** 3 C-130J *Hercules*; **PAX** 2 B-757-200 (C-32B)

Air Force Reserve
FORCES BY ROLE
TRANSPORT
  1 sqn with M-28 *Skytruck* (C-145A)
TRAINING
  1 sqn with M-28 *Skytruck* (C-145A)
COMBAT/ISR UAV
  1 sqn with MQ-1B *Predator* (personnel only)
EQUIPMENT BY TYPE
AIRCRAFT
  TPT • **Light** 5 M-28 *Skytruck* (C-145A)

Cyber

US Army Cyber Command (ARCYBER), Fleet Cyber Command (the US 10th Fleet) and the 24th Air Force deliver cyber capability for land, sea and air forces. Marine Force Cyber Command was established in 2009. These service groups are commanded by US Cyber Command (itself under US Strategic Command, and co-located with the NSA). The NSA director also heads Cyber Command. DoD's November 2011 'Cyberspace Policy Report' said that 'if directed by the President, DoD will conduct offensive cyber operations in a manner consistent with the policy principles and legal regimes that the Department follows for kinetic capabilities, including the law of armed conflict'. In October 2012, President Barack Obama signed Presidential Policy Directive 20, the purpose of which was to establish clear standards for US federal agencies in confronting threats in cyberspace. The terms of the directive are secret but are thought to include an explicit distinction between network defence and offensive cyber operations. The 2014 QDR noted that the Pentagon will 'deter, and when approved by the President and directed by the Secretary of Defense, will disrupt and deny adversary cyberspace operations that threaten U.S. interests'. January 2014 saw the US stand up the Cyber National Mission Force – 'the US military's first joint tactical command with a dedicated mission focused on cyberspace operations'. There are plans to create 133 cyber mission teams by the end of FY2016, according to the Head of Cyber Command, General Keith Alexander.

DEPLOYMENT

AFGHANISTAN
NATO • ISAF 28,970; 1 corps HQ; 1 div HQ; 1 cav regt; 1 lt inf bde; 1 air aslt bde; 1 inf bn; 3 para bn; 2 cbt avn bde; 1 ARNG cav sqn; 2 ARNG inf bn
EQUIPMENT BY TYPE
F-16C/D *Fighting Falcon*; A-10 *Thunderbolt* II; EC-130H *Compass Call*; C-130 *Hercules*; AH-64 *Apache*; OH-58 *Kiowa*; CH-47 *Chinook*; UH-60 *Black Hawk*; HH-60 *Pave Hawk*; RQ-7B *Shadow*; MQ-1 *Predator*; MQ-9 *Reaper*

ALBANIA
OSCE • Albania 1

ARABIAN SEA
US Central Command • Navy • 5th Fleet: 1 DDGHM; 1 LHD; 1 LPD
Combined Maritime Forces • TF 53: 1 AE; 2 AKE; 1 AOH; 3 AO

ARUBA
US Southern Command • 1 Forward Operating Location at Aruba

ASCENSION ISLAND
US Strategic Command • 1 detection and tracking radar at Ascension Auxiliary Air Field

ATLANTIC OCEAN
US Northern Command • US Navy: 6 SSBN; 24 SSGN; 2 SSN; 3 CVN; 8 CGHM; 10 DDGHM; 11 DDGM; 4 FFH; 3 PCO; 4 LHD; 4 LPD; 6 LSD

AUSTRALIA
US Pacific Command • 180; 1 SEWS at Pine Gap; 1 comms facility at Pine Gap; 1 SIGINT stn at Pine Gap
US Strategic Command • 1 detection and tracking radar at Naval Communication Station Harold E Holt

BAHRAIN
US Central Command • 3,250; 1 HQ (5th Fleet)

BELGIUM
US European Command • 1,200

BOSNIA-HERZEGOVINA
OSCE • Bosnia and Herzegovina 5

BRITISH INDIAN OCEAN TERRITORY
US Strategic Command • 550; 1 Spacetrack Optical Tracker at Diego Garcia; 1 ground-based electro optical deep space surveillance system (*GEODSS*) at Diego Garcia
US Pacific Command • 1 MPS sqn (MPS-2 with equipment for one MEB) at Diego Garcia with 5 logistics and support ships; 1 naval air base at Diego Garcia, 1 support facility at Diego Garcia

CANADA
US Northern Command • 130

COLOMBIA
US Southern Command • 50

CUBA
US Southern Command • 750 (JTF-GTMO) at Guantánamo Bay

DEMOCRATIC REPUBLIC OF THE CONGO
UN • MONUSCO 3

DJIBOUTI
US Africa Command • 1,200; 1 tpt sqn with C-130H/J-30 *Hercules*; 1 spec ops sqn with MC-130H; PC-12 (U-28A); 1 CSAR sqn with HH-60G *Pave Hawk*; 1 naval air base

EGYPT
MFO 700; 1 ARNG inf bn; 1 spt bn

EL SALVADOR
US Southern Command • 1 Forward Operating Location (Military, DEA, USCG and Customs personnel)

ETHIOPIA
US Africa Command • some MQ-9 *Reaper*

GERMANY
US Africa Command • 1 HQ at Stuttgart
US European Command • 40,500; 1 Combined Service HQ (EUCOM) at Stuttgart–Vaihingen
  US Army 25,150
    FORCES BY ROLE
    1 HQ (US Army Europe (USAREUR)) at Heidelberg; 1 SF gp; 1 cav SBCT; 1 armd recce bn; 1 arty bn; 1 (hvy cbt avn) hel bde; 1 int bde; 1 MP bde; 1 sigs bde; 1 spt bde; 1 (APS) armd/armd inf bn eqpt set
    EQUIPMENT BY TYPE
    M1 *Abrams*; M2/M3 *Bradley*; *Stryker*; M109; M777; M270 MLRS; AH-64 *Apache*; CH-47 *Chinook*; UH-60 *Black Hawk*
  US Navy 500
  USAF 13,900
    FORCES BY ROLE
    1 HQ (US Air Force Europe (USAFE)) at Ramstein AB; 1 HQ (3rd Air Force) at Ramstein AB; 1 ftr wg at Spangdahlem AB with 1 ftr sqn with 24 F-16C/D *Fighting Falcon*; 1 tpt wg at Ramstein AB with 16 C-130J *Hercules*; 2 Gulfstream (C-20H); 9 Learjet (C-21A); 1 C-40B
  USMC 950

GREECE
US European Command • 380; 1 naval base at Makri; 1 naval base at Soudha Bay; 1 air base at Iraklion

GREENLAND (DNK)
US Strategic Command • 130; 1 ballistic missile early warning system (BMEWS) at Thule; 1 Spacetrack Radar at Thule

GUAM
US Pacific Command • 5,500; 2 SSGN; 1 SSN; 1 MPS sqn (MPS-3 with equipment for one MEB) with 4 Logistics and Support vessels; 1 tpt hel sqn with MH-60S; 1 AD bty with THAAD; 1 air base; 1 naval base

HAITI
UN • MINUSTAH 9

HONDURAS
US Southern Command • 370; 1 avn bn with CH-47F *Chinook*; UH-60 *Black Hawk*

INDIAN OCEAN
US European Command • US Navy • 6th Fleet: 1 DDGHM

IRAQ
US Central Command • *Operation Inherent Resolve* 1,400; 1 inf div HQ; 1 mne coy; 1 atk hel coy with AH-64D *Apache*; MQ-1B *Predator*

ISRAEL
US Strategic Command • 1 AN/TPY-2 X-band radar at Mount Keren

ITALY
US European Command • 11,360
  US Army 3,900; 1 AB IBCT(-)
  US Navy 3,600; 1 HQ (US Navy Europe (USNAVEUR)) at Naples; 1 HQ (6th Fleet) at Gaeta; 1 MP sqn with 9 P-3C *Orion* at Sigonella
  USAF 3,850; 1 ftr wg with 2 ftr sqn with 21 F-16C/D *Fighting Falcon* at Aviano
  USMC 10

JAPAN
US Pacific Command • 50,000
  US Army 2,300 1 SF gp; 1 avn bn; 1 SAM regt
  US Navy 19,600; 1 HQ (7th Fleet) at Yokosuka; 1 base at Sasebo; 1 base at Yokosuka
    EQUIPMENT BY TYPE
    1 CVN; 2 CGHM; 3 DDGHM; 4 DDGM; 1 LCC; 4 MCO; 1 LHD; 2 LSD
  USAF 12,400
    FORCES BY ROLE
    1 HQ (5th Air Force) at Okinawa – Kadena AB; 1 ftr wg at Okinawa – Kadena AB with 2 ftr sqn with 18 F-16C/D *Fighting Falcon* at Misawa AB; 1 ftr wg at Okinawa – Kadena AB with 1 AEW&C sqn with 2 E-3B *Sentry*, 1 CSAR sqn with 8 HH-60G *Pave Hawk*, 2 ftr sqn with 24 F-15C/D *Eagle*; 1 tpt wg at Yokota AB with 10 C-130H *Hercules*; 3 Beech 1900C (C-12J); 1 Special Ops gp at Okinawa – Kadena AB
  USMC 15,700
    FORCES BY ROLE
    1 Marine div (3rd); 1 ftr sqn with 12 F/A-18D *Hornet*; 1 tkr sqn with 12 KC-130J *Hercules*; 2 tpt sqn with 12 MV-22B *Osprey*
US Strategic Command • 1 AN/TPY-2 X-band radar at Shariki

JORDAN
US Central Command • *Operation Inherent Resolve* with 12 F-16C *Fighting Falcon*

KOREA, REPUBLIC OF
US Pacific Command • 28,500
  US Army 19,200
    FORCES BY ROLE
    1 HQ (8th Army) at Seoul; 1 div HQ (2nd Inf) located at Tongduchon; 1 armd bde; 1 armd BG; 1 (cbt avn) hel bde; 1 ISR hel bn; 1 arty bde; 1 AD bde
    EQUIPMENT BY TYPE
    M1 *Abrams*; M2/M3 *Bradley*; M109; M270 MLRS; AH-64 *Apache*; OH-58D *Kiowa Warrior*; CH-47 *Chinook*; UH-60 *Black Hawk*; MIM-104 *Patriot*/FIM-92A *Avenger*; 1 (APS) armd bde eqpt set
  US Navy 250
  USAF 8,800
    FORCES BY ROLE
    1 (AF) HQ (7th Air Force) at Osan AB; 1 ftr wg at Osan AB with 1 ftr sqn with 20 F-16C/D *Fighting Falcon*; 1 ftr

sqn with 24 A-10C *Thunderbolt* II; 1 ISR sqn at Osan AB with U-2S; 1 ftr wg at Kunsan AB with 1 ftr sqn with 20 F-16C /D *Fighting Falcon*; 1 Spec Ops sqn
USMC 250

KUWAIT
US Central Command • 13,000; 1 armd bde; 1 ARNG (cbt avn) hel bde; 1 ARNG spt bde; 2 AD bty with 16 PAC-3 *Patriot*; 1 (APS) armd bde set; 1 (APS) inf bde set

LIBERIA
Operation United Assistance 2,000; 1 air aslt div HQ; 1 mne recce coy; 1 engr bde
UN • UNMIL 5; 4 obs

MALI
UN • MINUSMA 10

MARSHALL ISLANDS
US Strategic Command • 1 detection and tracking radar at Kwajalein Atoll

MEDITERRANEAN SEA
US European Command • US Navy • 6th Fleet: 1 CVN; 1 CGHM; 3 DDGHM; 3 DDGM; 1 FFGH; 1 LCC
NATO • SNMG 2: 1 CGHM

MIDDLE EAST
UN • UNTSO 1 obs

MOLDOVA
OSCE • Moldova 3

NETHERLANDS
US European Command • 380

NORWAY
US European Command • 1 (APS) SP 155mm arty bn set

PACIFIC OCEAN
US Pacific Command • US Navy • 3rd Fleet: 8 SSBN; 19 SSGN; 11 SSN; 4 CVN; 8 CGHM; 13 DDGHM; 9 DDGM; 3 FFH; 4 FFHM; 1 MCO; 2 LHD; 1 LHA; 4 LPD; 2 LSD
US Pacific Command • US Navy • 7th Fleet: 1 CGHM; 2 DDGHM; 1 FFH; 1 LHA; 1 LSD
US Southern Command • US Navy • 4th Fleet: 1 FFH

PERSIAN GULF
US Central Command • Navy • 5th Fleet: 1 CVN; 1 CGHM; 2 DDGHM; 1 DDGM; 1 LSD; 1 AOE 10 PCO; 6 (Coast Guard) PCC
Combined Maritime Forces • CTF-152: 6 MCO; 1 AFSB

PHILIPPINES
US Pacific Command • 320 (JSOTF-P)

PORTUGAL
US European Command • 700; 1 spt facility at Lajes

QATAR
US Central Command • 8,000: 1 bbr sqn with 6 B-1B *Lancer*; 1 ISR sqn with 4 RC-135 *Rivet Joint*; 1 ISR sqn with 4 E-8C JSTARS; 1 tkr sqn with 24 KC-135R/T *Straotanker*; 1 tpt sqn with 4 C-17A *Globemaster*; 4 C-130H/J-30 *Hercules*
US Strategic Command • 1 AN/TPY-2 X-band radar

SAUDI ARABIA
US Central Command • 350

SERBIA
NATO • KFOR • *Joint Enterprise* 731; elm 1 AB bde HQ; 1 recce sqn
OSCE • Kosovo 5

SEYCHELLES
US Africa Command • some MQ-9 *Reaper* UAV

SINGAPORE
US Pacific Command • 180; 1 log spt sqn; 1 spt facility

SOUTH SUDAN
UN • UNMISS 5

SPAIN
US European Command • 2,100; 1 air base at Morón; 1 naval base at Rota

THAILAND
US Pacific Command • 300

TURKEY
US European Command • 1,550; MQ-1B *Predator* UAV at Incirlik; 1 air base at Incirlik; 1 support facility at Ankara; 1 support facility at Izmir
US Strategic Command • 1 Spacetrack Radar at Incirlik; 1 AN/TPY-2 X-band radar at Kürecik
NATO • *Active Fence*: 2 AD bty with MIM-104 *Patriot*

UKRAINE
OSCE • Ukraine 28

UNITED ARAB EMIRATES
US Central Command • 5,000: 1 ftr sqn with 6 F-22A *Raptor*; 1 ftr sqn with 12 F-15C *Eagle*; 1 FGA sqn with 12 F-15E *Strike Eagle*; 1 ISR sqn with 4 U-2; 1 AEW&C sqn with 4 E-3 *Sentry*; 1 tkr sqn with 12 KC-10A; 1 ISR UAV sqn with RQ-4 *Global Hawk*; 2 AD bty with MIM-104 *Patriot*

UNITED KINGDOM
US European Command • 9,500

FORCES BY ROLE
1 ftr wg at RAF Lakenheath with 1 ftr sqn with 24 F-15C/D *Eagle*, 2 ftr sqn with 23 F-15E *Strike Eagle*; 1 ISR sqn at RAF Mildenhall with OC-135/RC-135; 1 tkr wg at RAF Mildenhall with 15 KC-135R *Stratotanker*; 1 Spec Ops gp at RAF Mildenhall with 1 sqn with 5 MC-130H *Combat Talon* II; 5 CV-22B *Osprey*; 1 sqn with 1 MC-130J *Commando* II; 4 MC-130P *Combat Shadow*
US Strategic Command • 1 ballistic missile early warning system (BMEWS) and 1 Spacetrack Radar at Fylingdales Moor

FOREIGN FORCES
Canada 12 USCENTCOM; 303 NORTHCOM (NORAD)
Germany Air Force: trg units at Goodyear AFB (AZ)/Sheppard AFB (TX) with 40 T-38 *Talon* trg ac; 69 T-6A *Texan* II; 1 trg sqn Holloman AFB (NM) with 24 *Tornado* IDS; NAS Pensacola (FL); Fort Rucker (AL) • Missile trg located at Fort Bliss (TX)
Netherlands 1 hel trg sqn with AH-64D *Apache*; CH-47D *Chinook* at Fort Hood (TX)
United Kingdom Army, Navy, Air Force ε480

Table 2 Selected Arms Procurements and Deliveries, North America

Designation	Type	Quantity (Current)	Contract Value	Prime Nationality	Prime Contractor	Order Date	First Delivery Due	Notes
Canada (CAN)								
Commando	Recce	500	CAN$603m	US	Textron (Textron Marine & Land Systems)	2012	2014	Tactical Armoured Patrol Vehicle. Option for 100 more
Harry DeWolf-class	PSOH	8	See notes	CAN	Irving Shipyard	2013	2018	For navy. Arctic/Offshore Patrol Ship Project. Based on NOR Coast Guard *Svalbard*-class. Construction to begin Sep 2015
Queenston-class	AG	2	See notes	CAN	Vancouver Shipyards	2013	2019	For navy. TKMS design. Joint Support Ship. Option on a third vessel
CH-148 *Cyclone*	Med tpt hel	28	US$5bn	US	UTC (Sikorsky)	2004	n.k.	Programme has suffered delays. Amended contract signed early 2014
United States (US)								
GSSAP	Space Surv Sat	4	n.k.	US	Orbital Sciences	n.k.	2014	Geosynchronous Space Situational Awareness Program. First pair launched 2014. Second pair to be launched 2016
Space Fence	Radar	2	US$914m	US	Lockheed Martin	2014	2018	Two S-Band radars for tracking objects in orbit. IOC expected 2018
Stryker	APC (W)	4,507	US$14.8bn	US	General Dynamics (GDLS)	2001	2002	Includes multiple variants; includes Double V-Hull versions
Gerald R. Ford-class	CVN	2	US$16.9bn	US	Huntingdon Ingalls Industries	2008	2016	Keel of lead vessel laid in 2009. Total cost for both currently estimated at US$24.4bn
Virginia-class	SSN	20	US$56bn	US	General Dynamics (Electric Boat)	1998	2004	11 in service by late 2014
Zumwalt-class	CGHM	3	US$11.3bn	US	General Dynamics (BIW)/ Huntingdon Ingalls Industries	2008	2015	DDG 1000. First vessel launched 2013; ISD due 2015. Total cost currently estimated at US$12.4bn
Arleigh Burke-class	DDGHM	70	US$72.3bn	US	General Dynamics (BIW)/ Huntingdon Ingalls Industries	1985	1991	62 vessels in service by late 2014
Freedom/ Independence-class	FFHM	18	US$8.9bn	AUS/US	Austal (Austal USA)/Lockheed Martin	2005	2008	Littoral Combat Ship programme. At least 12 of each design to be built. Four in service as of late 2014
America-class	LHA	2	US$6.5bn	US	Huntingdon Ingalls Industries	2007	2014	First vessel commissioned Oct 2014. Third vessel planned
San Antonio-class	LPD	11	US$18.7bn	US	Huntingdon Ingalls Industries	1996	2002	Programme has suffered delays. Nine vessels in service by late 2014
F-35A *Lightning* II	FGA ac	103	US$18.9bn	US	Lockheed Martin	2007	2011	CTOL variant. 42 delivered as of late 2014
F-35B *Lightning* II	FGA ac	50	US$11.3bn	US	Lockheed Martin	2008	2011	STOVL variant. 33 delivered as of late 2014
F-35C *Lightning* II	FGA ac	26	US$6.7bn	US	Lockheed Martin	2010	2012	CV variant. 12 delivered as of late 2014
P-8A *Poseidon*	ASW ac	53	US$11.8bn	US	Boeing	2011	2012	18 delivered as of late 2014

Table 2 **Selected Arms Procurements and Deliveries, North America**

Designation	Type	Quantity (Current)	Contract Value	Prime Nationality	Prime Contractor	Order Date	First Delivery Due	Notes
EA-18G Growler	EW ac	135	US$13.5bn	US	Boeing	2003	2009	111 delivered as of late 2014
KC-46A Pegasus	Tkr ac	4	n.k.	US	Boeing	2011	2015	Test and evaluation ac. First flight delayed. FY15 would fund first seven production ac
C-130J-30 Hercules	Med tpt ac	94	US$7.4bn	US	Lockheed Martin	1995	1999	Deliveries ongoing
CV-22 Osprey	Tilt-Rotor ac	50	US$4.2bn	US	Textron (Bell)/Boeing	2002	2006	For USAF; 45 delivered as of late 2014
MV-22 Osprey	Tilt-Rotor ac	282	US$24.2bn	US	Textron (Bell)/Boeing	1997	1999	For USMC; 216 delivered as of late 2014
AH-1Z Viper	Atk hel	76	US$2.6bn	US	Textron (Bell)	2010	2013	First 37 remanufactured models delivered; remainder are new build
AH-64E Apache	Atk hel	141	US$3.3bn	US	Boeing	2010	2011	16 new build and 125 remanufactured
CH-47F/MH-47G Chinook	Hvy tpt hel	448	εUS$11.3bn	US	Boeing	2000	2004	242 new build and 206 remanufactured. 300 CH-47F delivered to army as of late 2014
UH-60M/HH-60M Black Hawk	Med tpt hel	679	US$11.9bn	US	UTC (Sikorsky)	2004	2006	Deliveries ongoing
EC145 (UH-72A Lakota)	Lt tpt hel	335	US$2.1bn	Int'l	Airbus Group (Airbus Group Inc)	2006	2006	300 delivered as of Jun 2014
MH-60R Seahawk	ASW hel	220	US$8.9bn	US	UTC (Sikorsky)	2000	2006	200 delivered as of late 2014
MH-60S Knight Hawk	MRH hel	267	US$6.6bn	US	UTC (Sikorsky)	1999	2002	Deliveries ongoing
MQ-1C Gray Eagle	Hvy CISR UAV	114	US$2.3bn	US	General Atomics/ASI	2010	2011	For army
MQ-8C Fire Scout	Hvy ISR UAV	17	εUS$374m	US	Northrop Grumman	2012	2013	Two in test as of mid-2014
MQ-9 Reaper	Hvy CISR UAV	260	US$4.2bn	US	General Atomics	2001	2002	Deliveries ongoing
RQ-4A/B Global Hawk	Hvy ISR UAV	45	US$4.3bn	US	Northrop Grumman	1995	1997	Deliveries ongoing
Terminal High Altitude Area Defense (THAAD)	SAM	30	US$2.7bn	US	Lockheed Martin	2010	2012	Four batteries delivered (including two RDT&E-funded batteries)

Chapter Four
Europe

Risks and threats to European security were in 2014 thrown into sharp relief by events in the region's eastern and southern periphery. To the southeast, the three-year-old civil war in Syria engulfed northern Iraq, with the Sunni jihadist organisation Islamic State of Iraq and al-Sham (ISIS) proclaiming in the summer a caliphate spanning parts of both countries. Conditions in Libya, which experienced NATO intervention in 2011, deteriorated further, with the attendant risk of comprehensive state failure. Insecurity and conflict continued on Europe's southern flank, with some member states' armed forces remaining on active, advisory or peacekeeping service in parts of Africa. In the east, Russia's illegal annexation of Crimea in March and continuous action to destabilise eastern Ukraine, including alleged direct Russian military support for separatist militias in the Donbass region, generated a fundamental test for Europe's security architecture with the potential to change the post-Cold War paradigm of European security.

Russia's challenge to European order

Throughout the first half of 2014, Western governments struggled to recognise that the two-decade policy of courting Russia as a partner in building Euro-Atlantic security had failed, and that a shift back to a more adversarial relationship was under way. Speaking in Estonia in May 2014, outgoing NATO Secretary-General Anders Fogh Rasmussen argued that 'by demonstrating a willingness to use force to intimidate and invade its neighbours, and by declaring a doctrine of protecting Russian speakers everywhere, Russia has created uncertainty, instability and insecurity across the continent'. A week later, he told delegates to a security-policy conference in Slovakia that Russian behaviour amounted to 'a blatant breach of the fundamentals of European security. It is a dangerous attempt to turn back the clock ... Russia is trying to establish a new sphere of influence.'

Most policymakers and analysts in Europe had subscribed, before 2014, to a security narrative that saw Europe as a zone of stability, built on cooperation and civilian conflict-resolution. Challenges to that order in recent years seemed limited to transnational risks and the indirect effects of state failure and fragility in other regions of the world. Defence reviews focused on how the weaknesses of other states contributed to international insecurity and instability, and armed forces were remodelled to support overseas deployments to mitigate the effects of these. Such challenges continued to exist, but decision-makers in Europe were forced to recognise that to the east of NATO and the EU a powerful actor was willing to employ military force in a way associated with the great-power conflicts of the past. Former German foreign minister Joschka Fischer wrote in August that Europe was 'being thrown back in time by the return of power politics at its borders'.

Russian actions may have looked anachronistic to European citizens and leaders, but that did not make the challenge less immediate. All three of the key multinational security organisations in the Euro-Atlantic space – NATO, the EU and the Organisation for Security and Cooperation in Europe (OSCE) – were tested in different but equally fundamental ways. The EU slowly increased both pressure on Moscow and support for Kiev, agreeing limited sanctions against Russia and signing an Association Agreement with Ukraine in June. Maintaining a united front was no small political feat given the varied levels of economic and energy interests that tie many EU governments to Russia. On 22 July, the EU established a civilian advisory mission for security-sector reform in Ukraine (EUAM Ukraine) with a two-year mandate. The European Council also repeatedly called on Russia to end any support to actors in the conflict, and to refrain from activities that might further destabilise the region.

However, while the EU was a crucial economic and diplomatic actor during the Ukraine crisis, its security and defence policy was, in common with recent years, influenced by and developed outside Europe, in places such as Africa, where the EU launched further military missions. For example, on 1 April, the EUFOR RCA operation was launched in Central African Republic, which assumed responsibility for Bangui M'Poko International Airport and certain areas in the capital city. Two weeks later, on 15 April, EUCAP Sahel Mali began a civilian mission to advise and train internal security forces.

The OSCE, recently preoccupied with tasks including election monitoring, found rediscovered purpose amid the hope by some governments that its more established track record of confidence-building and strategic transparency in such fields as arms control would prove to be helpful in the crisis situation. Monitoring missions indeed proved helpful, but the core question that the organisation will need to tackle in the wake of the chill in relations with Russia is whether its core assumption – that its member states share a common conception of the Euro-Atlantic space as being one of indivisible security – still has a future.

NATO Summit to reassure and deter

In the wake of the Ukraine crisis, NATO adopted a raft of measures designed to reassure allies who felt threatened by Russia's assertiveness. Starting in April 2014, these included increased air-policing and training activities in the Baltic; Airborne Early-warning and Control (AWACS) flights over Poland and Romania; maritime patrols in the Baltic Sea and the Mediterranean; and the augmentation of the military-planning functions of NATO headquarters.

For NATO, Russian assertiveness, on the one hand, reinvigorated the Alliance's core purpose of collective defence. On the other, the effectiveness of Russia's challenge led some member states to question whether the Alliance would be able to defend them, should they be the target of attacks similar to those in Ukraine. In particular, the methods employed by Russia gave pause for thought. Moscow's use of a broad array of traditional and non-traditional instruments to achieve its goals, combined effectively in Crimea and eastern Ukraine, was deemed successful by NATO. These methods included diplomatic means; sophisticated and rapid information, electronic and cyber operations; covert military and intelligence operations; and economic pressure.

The first challenge for NATO was defining the problem: what to call these actions? Was it subversion, invasion, incursion, 'ambiguous warfare'? 'Hybrid warfare' was used by most, though this term was not new. The second question that Alliance members had to consider was what this type of warfare meant for NATO planning, organisation, capability and responses. The third challenge was more fundamental and remained unacknowledged: determining how this kind of action could be deterred, not least when Western governments generally remained reluctant to consider the use of force, in particular deploying ground combat forces. That these offensive actions could produce outcomes – including the adjustment of internationally recognised borders – before those on the receiving end could even agree that they were under attack was a lesson not lost on NATO members in the Baltic and elsewhere in Central and Eastern Europe.

The 2014 NATO Summit, held 4–5 September in Wales, the United Kingdom, provided the platform to debate the effects of the Ukraine crisis. Until February 2014, the summit had been expected to be largely administrative and to follow a script – the Alliance would mark the end of its combat operations in Afghanistan and agree measures to improve cooperation both among allies and with partners, so as to maintain NATO's ability to respond to future crises. The slogan was in place: NATO would move from being deployed to being prepared.

Instead, NATO's eastern members pressed the Alliance for reassurance amid concern over Russia's actions. The United States, which since 2011 had focused much security attention on its 'rebalance' to the Asia-Pacific, now had to commit extra (though limited) personnel and resources to Europe. Any hope that NATO leaders might have had of a post-Afghanistan strategic holiday evaporated. But while the agenda grew longer, with Libya and Iraq again added, this did not alter the focus of discussions – European security was back centre stage.

As a consequence, a principal goal of the summit was to reassure members – and remind Russia – of the mutual-defence pledge at the heart of the Alliance. Germany's foreign minister, Frank-Walter Steinmeier, declared that it was 'a special summit at a particular time'. The Wales Summit Declaration cited Russia's 'aggressive actions against Ukraine' as the main reason for new measures to strengthen NATO's posture and capabilities decided in Wales.

The most important document endorsed by NATO leaders at the summit was the Readiness Action Plan. Under this, NATO forces would establish a deployment schedule to ensure 'continuous air, land and maritime presence and meaningful military activity in the eastern part of the Alliance', to be achieved by frequent force rotations. In addition, NATO's ability to respond quickly to events would be increased with the formation of a Very High Readiness Joint Task Force (VJTF) of 4,000–6,000 troops, available for deployment at two to five days' notice to move (NTM), which is more rapid than the existing NATO Response Force (NRF). While some command elements of the NRF are on a 48-hour NTM, the Immediate Response Force – the core of the NRF – is on 5–30 days' notice. The VJTF will effectively become the spearhead of the NRF. Its precise size, composition and command arrangements are due to be agreed by early 2015, and the force will bring together land, air and maritime elements, as well as special-operations units. NATO will also pre-position equipment and invest in infrastructure so that the VJTF will have host-nation support if deployed.

Denmark, Germany and Poland also jointly announced they would provide additional staff to the Multinational Corps Northeast, in Szczecin, Poland – the only NATO headquarters in a post-Cold War member state – in order to raise its status from lower readiness (180 days' notice) to high readiness (30 days' notice). NATO indicated that it would regularly test forces through exercises that might be announced at short notice – just as Russia has instituted a series of snap exercises.

On the theme of collective defence, leaders expanded the scope of the Article V mutual-defence commitment to include cyber attacks. The declaration stated: 'Cyber defence is part of NATO's core task of collective defence. A decision as to when a cyber attack would lead to the invocation of Article V would be taken by the North Atlantic Council on a case-by-case basis.' It was still unclear, however, what a cyber-attack response would actually mean in military terms.

The Alliance has since the 2012 NATO Summit in Chicago attempted to foster closer cooperation among member states through its Smart Defence programme and the Connected Forces Initiative. The purpose of such efforts has been to achieve greater military effectiveness in spite of budget cuts. A further step in this direction was agreed in 2014 in Wales, with endorsement of the Framework Nations Concept (FNC), a German idea in which groups of allies would work together to develop capabilities, making use of the experience of one 'framework' nation, an approach already employed by NATO nations on overseas operations.

In light of events in Ukraine, the Wales Declaration also discussed 'hybrid warfare', describing this as an approach in which a 'wide range of overt or covert military, paramilitary and civilian measures are employed in a highly integrated design'. In Wales, leaders discussed the need both to deter such tactics and to improve the agility of Alliance forces. The creation of higher-readiness forces, in addition to more frequent exercises and a sharper focus on improved information-sharing and strategic communication, is an important part of the Alliance's response (see pp. 8–11).

The summit marked a turning point for NATO, with the combat operation in Afghanistan almost over, although the nature and size of the follow-on mission was at that point unclear. Following the inauguration of Ashraf Ghani as president of Afghanistan, the signing on 30 September of a bilateral security agreement between Afghanistan and the US, and a status-of-forces agreement between Afghanistan and NATO, the up-to-12,000-strong *Operation Resolute Support* finally received the green light and was due to begin on 1 January 2015. The summit declaration signalled a significant change of direction, re-sharpening the Alliance's focus on collective defence.

European defence: changing trajectories

The deterioration in Europe's security environment is likely to have an effect on those trends that in recent years have shaped European defence policy. Firstly, most Western European countries have cut defence spending amid low threat perceptions and a focus on general budget consolidation after the 2008 financial crisis. Secondly, the sense prevailed that Europe's armed forces were more likely to be used in international crisis-management missions than tasks related to national and collective defence. Related to this, most countries concentrated on developing small, agile, professional and deployable armed forces. Lastly, governments have grown used to operating in multinational constellations, with established alliance structures serving as a toolbox to enable 'coalitions of the willing'. Taken together, the result has been that NATO member states' armed forces have only partial capacity for large-scale, conventional manoeuvres and rapid response, and – in some cases – have limited readiness.

Addressing the defence-spending issue has been a priority for NATO. Between 2011 and 2013, defence expenditure rose in every region of the world except Europe and North America. Among the European member states of NATO, Poland has been a notable exception, and the spectre of an assertive Russia has led the Baltic States and others in Central Europe to announce increased spending.

At the Wales Summit, an effort was made to begin reducing the steady decline in European defence spending. For the first time, leaders made explicit reference to the NATO goal that defence budgets should constitute 2% of GDP, with 20% of defence expenditure directed towards equipment purchases and research and development. However, the language used was not robust: the 24 allies currently below this level would 'aim to move towards the 2% guideline within a decade'. Before the summit, some NATO governments sought a binding commitment to 2%. That did not happen, but there was at least an undertaking from each nation to halt any decline in spending. This was cast as an important change of direction – one which Rasmussen had been seeking throughout his five-year term.

Non-NATO countries like Finland and Sweden are adopting positions which connect them more closely to the Alliance, and both have announced that they will provide host-nation support for NATO troops exercising or conducting missions in the region. One practical example is Sweden's decision to open its airspace to surveillance flights conducted by NATO AWACS aircraft. NATO member the Czech Republic announced in August 2014 that it will seek additional funding in order to expand its active reserve forces. Defence Minister Martin Stropnicky argued 'the current situation in eastern Ukraine confirms the need for several thousand trained and well-motivated reservists'. Later, in September, Czech government-coalition parties signed an agreement to raise spending to 1.4% of GDP by 2020. Poland, meanwhile, decided in May 2014 to accelerate important procurement efforts, including air-to-surface stand-off missiles for Poland's F-16 fighters, unmanned aerial vehicles and multiple-rocket launchers. Deputy Defence Minister Czesław Mroczek explained that these adjustments were designed to 'increase the Polish armed forces deterrent potential'.

The unifying theme behind these decisions is Russia's assertiveness and its actions in Ukraine. For the time being it remains unclear how profound any policy adjustments will be, and whether they will ultimately lead to a strategic reversal of the trends that have shaped European defence policy in recent years. Much will depend on Europe's biggest nations. The UK is likely to continue its push to get other European allies to spend more on defence and invest more in high-readiness expeditionary capability, not least because both would bolster NATO's deterrence in the east. In this context, analysts are awaiting the content of the UK's next Strategic Defence and Security Review (SDSR), planned for 2015, given that the 2010 SDSR reduced the UK's operational ambition and deployable capability.

Germany is reluctantly coming to grips with the shifting strategic focus, but is unlikely to increase spending significantly in the coming years. For the time being, the government continues to prioritise overall budget consolidation. However, Berlin's decision in August 2014 to supply arms to help counter the threat posed by ISIS indicates a gradual change in Germany's security policy. France, still engaged in numerous operations in Africa, was placed under pressure due to its arrangement to sell two *Mistral*-class amphibious-assault ships to Russia. The French government suspended delivery of the first vessel just before the NATO Summit. The variety of responses from governments across Europe indicated that – at that stage – Russia's assertiveness had not yet produced a united view on security-policy priorities, notwithstanding the decisions of the NATO Summit.

The crisis in Eastern Europe also raised the question of how the United States would respond. While the Obama administration was always aware of European concerns about a reduced US commitment to European security in the wake of the rebalance to the Asia-Pacific, it was now faced with a wish by several European allies for a clear signal that NATO's most powerful nation would support them. In the first half of 2014, the US initiated a series of measures to indicate it was ready to act in response to increased insecurity: a contingent from the 173th Airborne Brigade exercised in the Baltic States and in Poland; several US vessels sailed into the Black Sea to conduct exercises and port visits; and an air-force training detachment to Poland was augmented.

A more visible effort was announced on 3 June, when the president asked Congress to fund the so-called European Reassurance Initiative to the tune of US$1 billion, as part of the Pentagon's overseas-contingency-operations request for FY2015. Most of the activities encompassed by this relate to increased exercise and training activities, increased rotational presence in the territory of Eastern European allies, pre-positioning equipment and supporting capacity-building programmes. However, the initiative stops short of the permanent basing of US troops. So, while it is a highly visible indication that the US remains committed to safeguarding European security, its rather limited nature also suggests that Washington is not willing to let Europeans 'off the hook' in doing more to underpin the credibility of NATO's collective defence. Nevertheless, amid the realisation that there may still be conventional military threats to European security, the US contribution to NATO is likely to remain decisive.

DEFENCE ECONOMICS

Regional macroeconomics

Although financial-market turmoil in Europe has generally abated since 2012, growth remains subdued in much of the region. After two years of economic contraction, the eurozone was forecast for moderate growth in 2014 (0.8%), while some northern-European states displayed signs of accelerating economic activity, including the United Kingdom, Ireland, Sweden and Poland. However, output and investment in many states remained well below pre-crisis levels, with wide output gaps (the estimated percentage difference between actual and potential output) persisting in several countries – these were estimated by the International Monetary Fund (IMF) at between 3% and 5% of GDP in Spain, Italy, Portugal, Slovenia, Cyprus and the Netherlands, and close to 10% of GDP in Greece. Overall, aggregate demand was still constrained by high household debt and weak credit conditions, partly reflecting larger-than-expected bank-recapitalisation requirements. Consequently, fiscal deficits remained the norm in 2014, with only Norway, Germany, Switzerland, Luxembourg and Iceland projected to run budgetary surpluses. However, weakened public balance sheets have meant that, despite running fiscal deficits, most states were able to provide only limited demand support: average gross government debt as a proportion of GDP was forecast by the IMF to continue rising until at least 2015 before declining slightly, peaking at 68.9% of GDP in 2015, up from 41.7% of GDP in 2007. (In some states, including Greece, Portugal and Italy, government debt exceeds 100% of GDP.) Meanwhile, the absence of meaningful structural reforms to address underlying competition and productivity issues meant unemployment rates remain raised across Europe, estimated at above 8% in close to two-thirds of countries in the region (23 out of 37), and above 20% in Spain, Greece, Serbia, Bosnia-Herzegovina and FYR Macedonia.

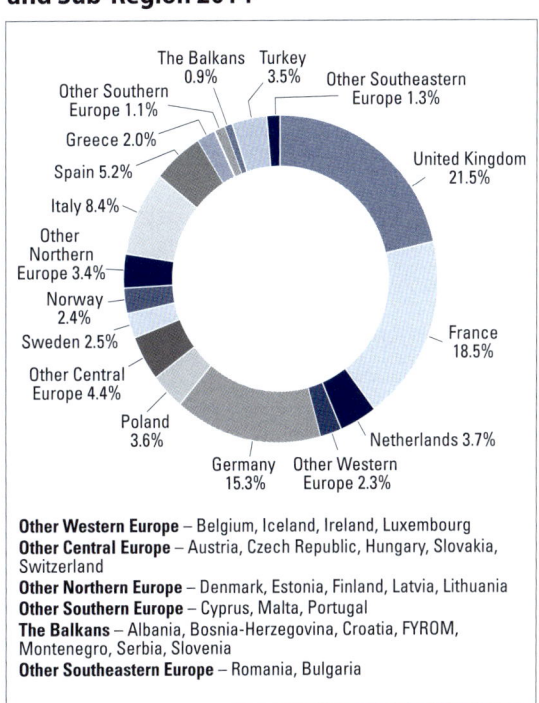

Regional defence spending

Nominal European defence spending saw a 1.9% annual increase in 2014, from US$281.5 billion to US$286.9bn. This was the highest level of nominal outlays in US-dollar terms since 2011. However, this increase was mainly the product of exchange-rate appreciation relative to the US dollar in 2014, in comparison to 2013 rates. After accounting for such fluctuations, as well as for inflationary effects, in real terms European defence outlays continued the downward trajectory seen since the 2008 crisis, though the year-on-year decline of 1.75% was slightly less than the 2% per annum average decline in real European spending seen since 2010. However, 2014 real reduc-

Figure 3 **Europe Real Defence Spending Changes 2010–14 by Sub-Region (%)**

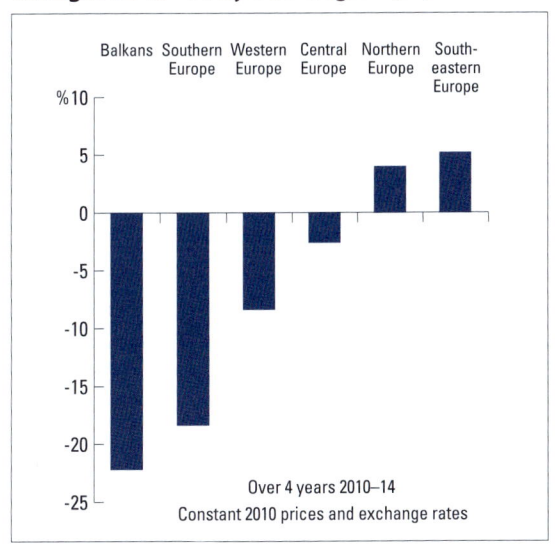

Figure 4 **Europe Defence Spending by Country and Sub-Region 2014**

Other Western Europe – Belgium, Iceland, Ireland, Luxembourg
Other Central Europe – Austria, Czech Republic, Hungary, Slovakia, Switzerland
Other Northern Europe – Denmark, Estonia, Finland, Latvia, Lithuania
Other Southern Europe – Cyprus, Malta, Portugal
The Balkans – Albania, Bosnia-Herzegovina, Croatia, FYROM, Montenegro, Serbia, Slovenia
Other Southeastern Europe – Romania, Bulgaria

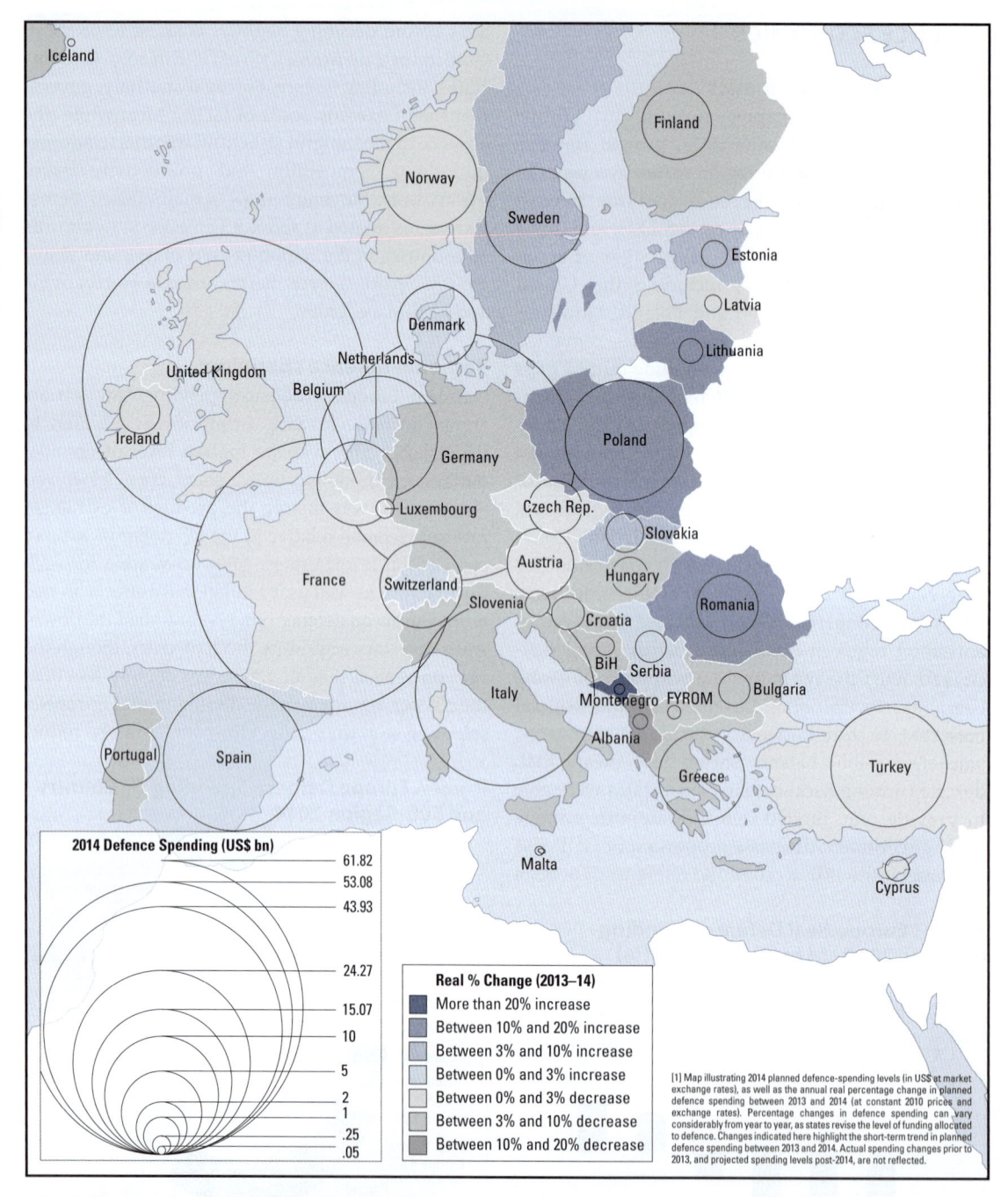

Map 1 Europe Regional Defence Spending[1]

Sub-regional groupings referred to in defence economics text: Central Europe (Austria, Czech Republic, Germany, Hungary, Poland, Slovakia and Switzerland), Northern Europe (Denmark, Estonia, Finland, Latvia, Lithuania, Norway and Sweden), Southern Europe (Cyprus, Greece, Italy, Malta, Portugal and Spain), Southeastern Europe (Bulgaria, Romania and Turkey), the Balkans (Albania, Bosnia-Herzegovina, Croatia, FYROM, Montenegro, Serbia and Slovenia) and Western Europe (Belgium, France, Iceland, Ireland, Luxembourg, the Netherlands and the United Kingdom).

[1] Map illustrating 2014 planned defence-spending levels (in US$ at market exchange rates), as well as the annual real percentage change in planned defence spending between 2013 and 2014 (at constant 2010 prices and exchange rates). Percentage changes in defence spending can vary considerably from year to year, as states revise the level of funding allocated to defence. Changes indicated here highlight the short-term trend in planned defence spending between 2013 and 2014. Actual spending changes prior to 2013, and projected spending levels post-2014, are not reflected.

tions were more widely distributed than in recent years: whereas real spending declined in just under half of European countries in 2013 (18 out of 37), in 2014 real cuts in outlays occurred in just over two-thirds of states (25 out of 37). Overall, real European spending levels in 2014 were cumulatively 7.7% lower than in 2010.

The extent of defence cuts has varied between sub-regions. As shown in Figure 3, between 2010 and 2014 the largest cumulative real reductions were in

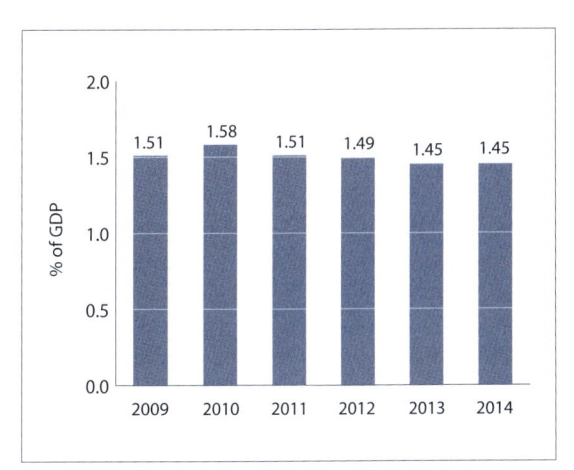

Figure 5 **Europe Regional Defence Expenditure** as % of GDP

Southern Europe and the Balkans, where spending levels have declined by around one-fifth. The most dramatic decreases have occurred in Greece and Slovenia, where real reductions of more than 10% have occurred each year since 2010 (the compound annual growth rate for both states is around 13%). Annual real reductions in excess of 5% have also been seen in Italy, Portugal and Serbia. Significant cuts have also occurred in Western Europe, with aggregate real outlays down 8.4% over four years – although Western Europe remains the continent's highest-spending sub-region, accounting for almost half of regional outlays (46%). A smaller cumulative decrease has been seen in Central Europe (-2.6%), although reductions in many parts of this sub-region (for example, in Austria, Hungry and the Czech Republic) have been offset somewhat by significant real increases in Poland (which has increased spending at a compound annual growth rate of 4% since 2010). Northern Europe and Southeastern Europe were the only sub-regions to register positive cumulative real adjustments in funding levels, with spending up by around 4–5% in both areas.

Changing budgetary priorities?

Despite continued real decreases in defence spending in 2014, the crisis in Ukraine has led to stronger calls for increased defence budgets, or at least for limiting cuts. For example, in April 2014, NATO Deputy Secretary-General Alexander Vershbow stated: 'If there was ever any doubt, the [Ukraine] crisis now makes clear why we must invest sufficiently in defence and security, and why we cannot just keep cutting our defence budgets every year while others around the world continue to boost theirs.'

There have been signs that the changing strategic landscape has shifted budgetary priorities in some areas, particularly Northern and Eastern Europe. For example, after several years of reductions, the Czech Republic announced in September 2014 it was planning to raise defence spending to 1.4% of GDP by 2020 (up from the 1% of GDP it currently allocates). Earlier, in March 2014, Lithuania's prime minister announced the intent to raise spending to 2% of GDP, also by 2020; while Latvia's defence minister stated he would

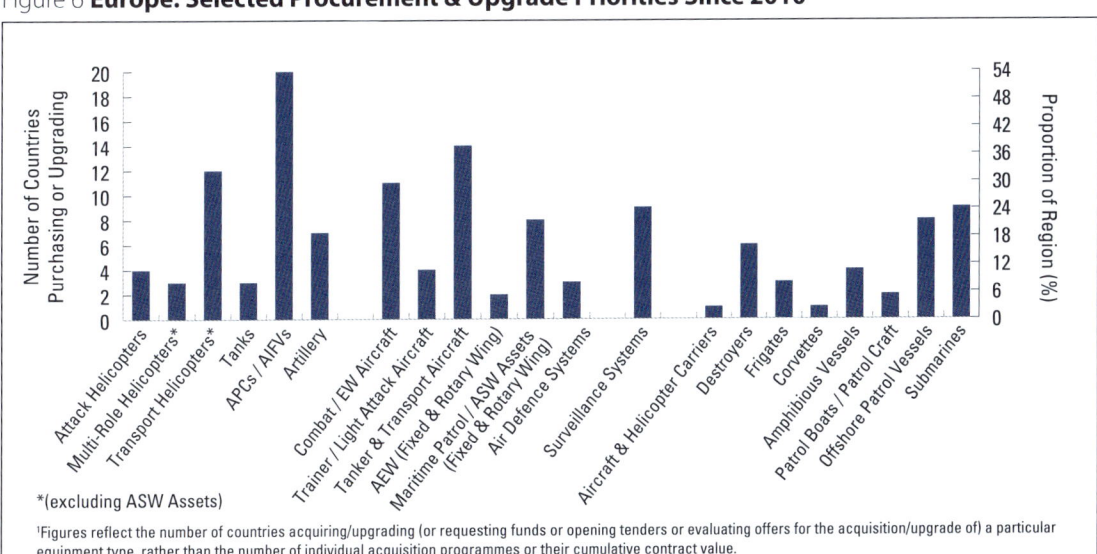

Figure 6 **Europe: Selected Procurement & Upgrade Priorities Since 2010**[1]

*(excluding ASW Assets)

[1] Figures reflect the number of countries acquiring/upgrading (or requesting funds or opening tenders or evaluating offers for the acquisition/upgrade of) a particular equipment type, rather than the number of individual acquisition programmes or their cumulative contract value.

make similar proposals in a new defence-funding law. In April 2014, Romania's prime minster called for parliament to consider increasing defence outlays from the current 1.4% of GDP to 2% of GDP between 2015 and 2017; four months later, in August 2014, Bulgaria's main political parties agreed to augment the proportion of defence funding channelled towards equipment. Elsewhere, the Netherlands announced in September 2014 an increase to its 2015 and 2016 proposed defence budgets, reversing more than 20 years of nominal spending reductions; while Norway further increased its 2014 defence funding above initially proposed levels, to support greater engagement on international operations. Sweden announced plans in April 2014 to increase defence outlays over ten years, while Poland stated it was accelerating procurement timetables. Additionally, at the September 2014 NATO Summit in Wales, states which did not currently allocate 2% of GDP towards defence agreed to halt current spending reductions and aim to move towards this NATO guideline threshold, as well as to aim to increase real-terms defence outlays as their economies grow.

FRANCE

French defence planners faced a series of pressing and interconnected problems in 2014. The backdrop was the poor state of the French economy and President François Hollande's determination to reduce the public-spending deficit by imposing, in February 2014, austerity measures to the tune of €50 billion (US$67.7bn). It was reported in May that finance-ministry proposals to further cut the defence budget led some service chiefs to threaten resignation; at the same time, amid concern over the future of defence spending, CEOs of seven key defence industries requested a crisis meeting with Hollande. Debate within government over the measures to tackle austerity came to a head in August 2014 with a revolt in government, the resignation of Prime Minister Manuel Valls, and his reappointment to a team purged of dissenters. Coming after a bruising result in the European elections in May, this intensified political problems for the ruling Socialist Party. Amid all this, France's defence establishment continued to implement the recommendations of the 2013 *Loi de Programmation Militaire* (LPM), resulting in further unit and base closures.

Nonetheless, France continued its energetic role in defence and foreign affairs. Operations persisted in the Sahel, where France consolidated and relocated its regional counter-terrorism effort as *Opération Barkhane*, and forces also remained deployed in the Central African Republic. Meanwhile, a new military mission was undertaken in the skies over Iraq. Aside from difficulties such as the contract with Russia for *Mistral*-class amphibious-assault ships, France's forward-leaning posture reinforced its position as a principal ally of the United States in a range of foreign-policy issues – notably those in Africa and the Middle East that required active military engagement.

Intervention and operations

France continued to undertake the majority of European intervention operations in Africa. Efforts to stabilise northern Mali (*Opération Serval*) proved to be only partial and temporary. Although official military communiqués released in the summer of 2014 stated that most rebel strongholds had been located and that France's remaining troops had effectively neutralised several hundred fighters, French fighter and transport aircraft continued to carry out dozens of sorties per week.

French Defence Minister Jean-Yves Le Drian indicated some frustration with the lack of progress in Mali. In the wake of an exchange of fire in late May between rebel forces and Malian troops during a visit to Kidal by Mali's prime minister, Moussa Mara, Le Drian cancelled a planned visit that was to have seen the conclusion of a bilateral defence agreement. Although *Serval*'s operations log could boast some 7,500 aircraft sorties and the seizure of 200 tons of weapons and a quantity of ammonium nitrate (a bomb-making component), the defence ministry recognised that the threat of terrorism in Mali had not been eliminated.

French policymakers were aware that the threat to Mali was really transnational in nature. As a consequence, *Serval* formally came to an end on 1 August and was replaced by *Opération Barkhane*. This amounted to a merger of the Mali mission with France's *Opération Épervier* in Chad, ongoing since 1986. *Barkhane* was presented as a strategic joint venture between France and five countries of the Sahel – Mauritania, Mali, Niger, Chad and Burkina-Faso. They had in February 2014 established the 'G5 Sahel' to boost cooperation on regional security. The French contingent assigned to *Barkhane* amounted to 3,000 troops with two main bases at Gao in Mali and N'Djamena in Chad, and a set of forward-based staging points in the Sahara (Atar in Mauritania,

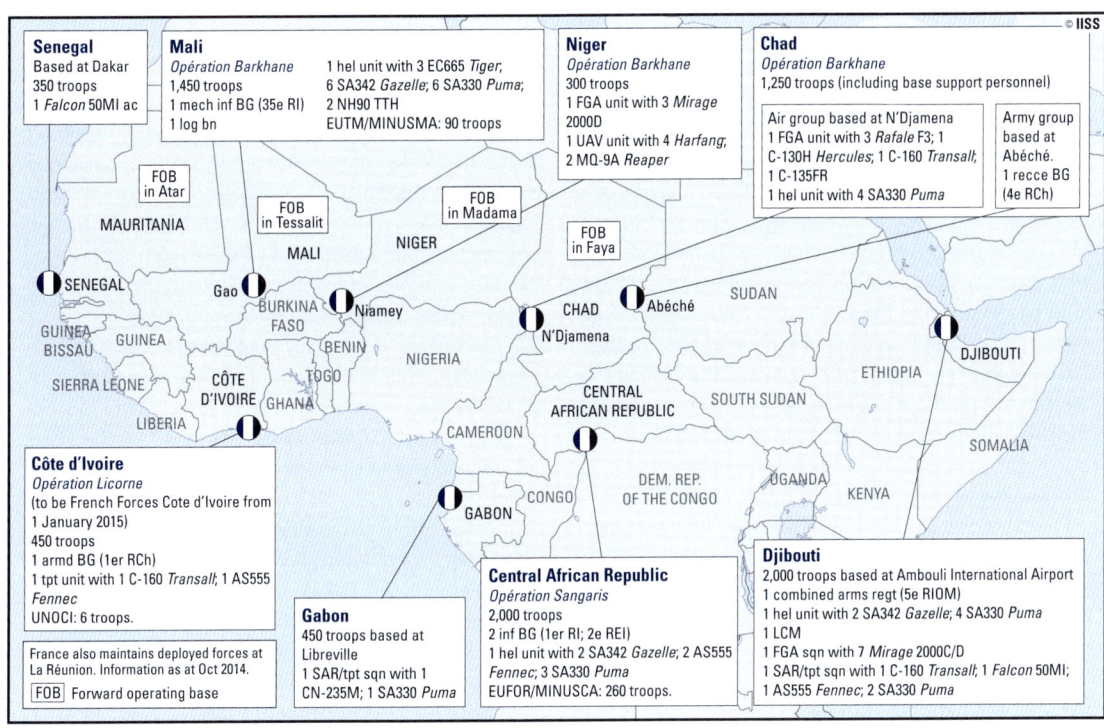

Map 2 **France: Selected Deployments in Africa – 2014**

Tessalit in Mali, Madama in Niger and Faya in Chad). It is supported by a range of armoured vehicles, rotary- and fixed-wing aircraft, and three unmanned aerial vehicles (UAVs). France's recently arrived *Reaper* UAVs were quickly deployed on operations over the Sahel. Any hopes of a swift exit from the region, such as were expressed by Foreign Minister Laurent Fabius in February 2013, were dashed, and France appears committed for the long haul. While this commitment could be undermined by ongoing budget squabbles in Paris, the rising operational costs accruing from France's recent military activities will not improve balance sheets.

Operations continued in Central African Republic (CAR) in 2014, where increasing inter-communal violence in late 2013 had led to the deployment of a French humanitarian mission. *Opération Sangaris* was launched on 5 December 2013 following the adoption of UN Security Council Resolution 2127, which called on both the UN and France to support the African Union mission in CAR (MISCA). MISCA eventually peaked at 6,000 troops but struggled to restore order, and in September 2014 was taken over directly by the UN. *Sangaris* involves some 2,000 French troops based principally in Bangui and Boda in the Christian southwest of the country, offering protection to several thousand Muslims who had not fled either to the north and east, or over the border into Cameroon. Initially intended to last no longer than six months, *Sangaris* was increasingly immersed in the chaotic situation that has led to the de facto partitioning of CAR. A French-dominated EU mission, EUFOR CAR, centred on Bangui, was struggling in mid-2014 to reach its full complement of troops. Neither the African Union/UN, nor the French or EU missions, have been able to do more than establish basic security in key urban centres – mainly Bangui – amid continuing inter-communal violence. Operations are not helped by the sheer size of the country – the equivalent of France and Belgium combined – and the mobility and communication problems arising from poor infrastructure.

Further north, Le Drian's visit to Algeria in May 2014 opened a new chapter both in France's relations with its former colony and its commitment to the stabilisation of the Maghreb and the Sahel regions. A defence agreement between France and Algeria was signed in 2008 and entered into force in 2013. The political symbolism of Le Drian's visit was enhanced by high-profile meetings with the president, the prime minister, the foreign and defence ministers and the military chief, and also by the statement that

Anglo-French defence cooperation persists

Efforts to advance Franco-British defence collaboration continued during 2014. London and Paris approved the next study phase of the Future Combat Air Capability (FCAC) project, examining the potential to jointly develop an unmanned combat air vehicle (UCAV) for entry into service in the 2030s. Not surprisingly, aligning national funding profiles has proved a challenging area for FCAC, with France in 2014 in a position to commit to a longer funding period than the UK. In the latter, the defence ministry was likely constrained by the upcoming 2015 Strategic Defence and Security Review and perhaps by the possibility of a change in government. In parallel, the two nations continued flight trials of their respective UCAV demonstrators, the French-led multinational *nEUROn* and the UK-only *Taranis*.

Paris also gave the long-awaited green light for development of the Anti-Navair Leger (ANL) anti-ship missile, known in the UK as the Future Anti-Surface Guided Weapon (FASGW), intended to arm their respective naval helicopters. The missile is now anticipated to enter service in 2020 with the Royal Navy and will be the principal anti-surface system for the Fleet Air Arm's *Wildcat* helicopter.

The French navy's NH90 helicopter, and potentially the AS565 *Panther*, will also carry the weapon. A £500 million (US$838m) development-and-production contract for the missile was signed with prime contractor MBDA in March 2014. Approval was also given for a long-mooted upgrade package for the joint SCALP EG/*Storm Shadow* air-launched land-attack cruise missile, with both countries also carrying out design trade options that could provide a replacement weapon beyond 2030.

In the guided-weapons sphere the two countries began in 2014 to explore the use of an extended-range variant of the *Aster* missile as the basis for a theatre missile-defence system. Shorter-range members of the *Aster* missile family are in service with both countries' armed forces.

The two nations also continued to work toward a Combined Joint Expeditionary Force (CJEF), which is due to be stood up in 2016. A Franco-British military headquarters was set up during exercise *Rochambeau* in May 2014 as part of a wider 14-nation exercise, and the first exercise trial of a CJEF headquarters took place at the end of the December 2013 exercise *Iron Triangle*.

France and Algeria 'have a common enemy'. Algeria has opened its airspace to French military aircraft and is ensuring supplies of fuel. There is growing cooperation in intelligence and there have been some joint missions against jihadi groups in northern Mali, born of France's frustrations with *Opération Serval*. Plans are being considered for direct general-staff contacts and permanent communications between headquarters. This degree of cooperation is remarkable, given the political differences that exist between Paris and Algiers over the long-term future of the region. Although Algeria still sees Russia as its principal military-equipment supplier, it has reportedly indicated a willingness to open up procurements to France.

By the end of October 2014, France's most recent deployment of military force had been to the Middle East. In June, when US President Barack Obama first announced the dispatch of military advisers to Iraq after the advance of fighters from the Islamic State of Iraq and al-Sham (ISIS), Paris expressed reluctance to get involved, arguing that Baghdad – together with neighbouring states – should assume responsibility for managing the crisis. However, by September, as the situation worsened, Hollande reignited the French military activism seen in 2013 when the Assad regime used chemical weapons in Syria.

After a lightning visit to Baghdad for talks on 14 September, Hollande authorised French reconnaissance flights over Iraq, the delivery of weapons to the Kurds fighting ISIS in Iraq's north and, in coordination with the US, air-strikes against ISIS. France was the first European state to engage in military action in Iraq, flying intelligence, surveillance and reconnaissance (ISR) and strike missions with nine *Rafale* combat aircraft, plus in-flight refuelling tankers from the permanent French base in the United Arab Emirates. The president announced on 19 September France's decision to join the US in supplying arms to the 'moderate Syrian opposition', but explicitly ruled out air-strikes inside Syria.

US–French defence cooperation is at a high point not seen in the last decade. Le Drian has visited the Pentagon four times since taking office in 2012. During his most recent visit in October 2014, US Secretary of Defense Chuck Hagel highlighted the relative alignment of interests on both sides, saying, 'American and French forces will continue to work side by side to support Iraqi forces on the ground', and noting that 'France's leadership in confronting extremist threats in the Sahel is particularly important as the United States continues to provide support to French operations in Mali'.

Closer to home, France has also been active in NATO measures to reassure Eastern European members concerned by Russia's actions in Ukraine. Le Drian spoke on 21 March in Estonia in support of NATO's reassurance initiative. France deployed four *Rafale* fighters to reinforce the NATO air-policing mission over the Baltic and dispatched an airborne early-warning and control aircraft to boost surveillance over Poland and Romania. Even before the Ukraine crisis, France, in November 2013, played a key role in NATO's *Steadfast Jazz* exercise in Poland and the Baltic States, sending the largest contingent, of 1,200 troops.

DEFENCE ECONOMICS

Implementing the *Loi de Programmation Militaire*

Further unit disbandments resulting from the *Loi de Programmation Militaire* (LPM) (see *The Military Balance 2014*, p. 69, for details of the first tranche) were announced in October 2014; they included the closure of the 1st Marine artillery regiment and the headquarters of the 1st Mechanised Brigade, the naval base at Anglet, and, for the air force, the start of the process of closing the air base at Dijon-Longvic. Some analysts posited that budget-related uncertainties, coming as they did on top of the closures detailed in the LPM, had exacerbated broader issues around service morale. Le Drian tried to place the situation in a positive light, saying on 3 October that the process 'was not about blind cuts' and that he 'understood that some units were tired of cuts'; but it remained an uphill battle. In addition, a new software program introduced to streamline military salaries hit problems, resulting in some personnel being under or overpaid. The main crisis, however, came in the form of the defence budget.

The five-year 2014–19 budget was announced in 2013, and set out €31.38 billion (US$42.5bn) for 2014 to 2016, rising to €32.51bn (US$44bn) by 2019. France's defence spending stood at 3% of GDP at the end of the Cold War; in 2013, it was 1.9%, but risks falling further, particularly if projected exceptional receipts are not realised. In May 2014, following February's austerity measures, finance-ministry projections envisaged an additional €1.5b–2bn (US$2b–2.7bn) in defence cuts per year until 2019. The apparent logic behind these numbers was that, since the defence budget accounted for 20% of overall state spending, the defence ministry should absorb 20% of overall state spending cuts. The situation became tense, with several analysts concluding that these bleak numbers were worse than the 'Z Scenario' calculations pressed by the finance ministry at the outset of LPM discussions in late 2012; these envisaged the cull of entire procurement programmes. Le Drian informed President François Hollande that, under the agreed figures for the LPM, his ministry was already looking likely to have lost 82,000 jobs since 2009. The defence ministry was also under pressure to accelerate job cuts of 7,200 in 2015, instead of the 6,700 initially agreed. Of the 11,500 public-sector jobs to be cut in 2015, 65% are mandated to be from the armed forces.

The head of the Council of French Defence Industries, Airbus's Marwan Lahoud, said that any further budget reductions could lead to as many as 165,000 job losses in the industry. On 16 May, the heads of the army, navy and air force, as well as the chief of the general staff, General Pierre de Villiers, all threatened resignation. To make matters worse, the projected €6bn (US$8.1bn) income in 'exceptional receipts' from the sale of state-owned assets, in particular the €3bn (US$4.06bn) windfall projected from the marketing of telecommunications frequencies, appeared in some doubt.

Political figures and some media outlets rallied to support defence in the face of possible further cuts. The 2013 *Livre Blanc* had outlined four main strategic priorities: territorial protection; collective guarantees for the security of Europe and the North Atlantic area; the stabilisation of Europe's neighbourhood; and a French (and European) contribution to stability in the Middle East and the Gulf. The opposition UMP party took up the cause of the LPM, which they had earlier criticised, with François Fillon and Alain Juppé denouncing any prospect of further cuts. The chairs of both the Senate and the National Assembly defence committees made a high-profile trip to the finance ministry to exercise their right to inspect the nation's accounts, demanding, in particular, evidence that the monies raised from the sale of defence-owned real estate (the 'exceptional receipts') were indeed being credited to the defence budget. Under the previous LPM, according to analysts, the finance ministry had siphoned them off elsewhere. Prime Minister Valls responded by saying that the government would not apply crude accountancy calculations to the defence sector.

Defence industry

Four key projects dominated during 2014. In mid-September, France received its fifth A400M *Atlas* transport aircraft in a year. The first was deployed to Mali three months after arriving in-service; the fifth was deployed to support *Opération Barkhane* in early October. However, with only 174 firm orders, the aircraft programme is at risk of substantial financial losses. Malaysia has ordered four aircraft, but otherwise the export book remains empty so far. Airbus expressed confidence that, once some teething problems were overcome, the aircraft would secure 400 sales for export. Despite the crisis in Ukraine, Hollande maintained – until 3 September 2014 – France's commitment to deliver two *Mistral*-class amphibious-assault ships to Russia; the first, *Vladivostok*, was due for transfer in October 2014, but as of early November remained at Saint-Nazaire. The second vessel was coincidentally named *Sevastopol*. Despite pressure from Washington and European capitals to reconsider the deal, Paris insisted that the contracts would be honoured. Hundreds of jobs were at stake at the Saint-Nazaire shipyard, where 400 Russian naval staff began training in June 2014. The construction of two further vessels was also being considered. However, when pro-Russian forces in eastern Ukraine began turning the military tide against the Ukrainian armed forces in late August – with what was widely believed to be direct and decisive Russian military assistance – Hollande finally ceded to international pressure and 'suspended' delivery of the *Vladivostok*.

Amid debate over the nature of US bilateral ties with some Gulf states, France was quick to reinforce its position in this potentially lucrative arms market, and there were discussions about the sale of air- and maritime-defence systems to Saudi Arabia, *Rafale* fighter aircraft to Qatar and Earth-observation satellites to the UAE. India's order for 126 *Rafales* required confirmation by the new Modi government, and as of September 2014 the contract had yet to be signed. This *Rafale* contract, in particular, was seen by French defence industry as vital. Qatar is phasing out its *Mirage* 2000 aircraft, with the *Rafale* a strong contender as a replacement. This is a critical situation for Dassault, which has not sold a single combat aircraft outside France for almost 15 years. Prospects for *Rafale* sales in European countries (with Belgium and Finland due to replace their F-16 and F-18 fleets respectively) remain uncertain.

UNITED KINGDOM

The target of an 8% real reduction in defence spending triggered by the 2010 Strategic Defence and Security Review (SDSR) has led to a 20–30% reduction in the UK's conventional military combat capability. Readiness was reduced, with more time allowed for mobilisation and deployment of troops and equipment, while front-line, conventional combat strength was also reduced by 20–30% (see *The Military Balance 2013*, p. 107). In 2014, the organisational changes required by the SDSR were almost complete, as was the UK's withdrawal from combat operations in Afghanistan. Against a difficult public-expenditure environment, the Ministry of Defence (MoD) began preparing for the 2015 SDSR. However, growing insecurity in and near to Europe has seen British forces deploying on a number of unanticipated operations. The operational demand on some capabilities has exceeded that anticipated in the SDSR, resulting in stress on strategic transport aircraft and fast-jet fleets, as well as intelligence, surveillance and reconnaissance (ISR) platforms and personnel. Consequently, the planned recuperation of military capability after withdrawal from the combat role in Afghanistan has been disrupted.

Operations

UK personnel in Afghanistan had been reduced to 2,000 by November 2014. The UK contribution to NATO's follow-on mission, *Operation Resolute Support*, is planned to comprise up to 450 personnel in Kabul on an advise-and-assist mission, particularly at the Afghan National Army Officer Academy.

A range of new missions also arose in 2014. Aircraft were committed to assist Nigerian authorities in the search for abducted schoolgirls in the country's north, while further west, in October, a logistics-brigade headquarters, engineers, medics, *Merlin* helicopters and the Royal Fleet Auxiliary ship *Argus* were committed to help Sierra Leone counter the Ebola-virus outbreak. Nearly a thousand troops were committed to this operation, which was likely to replace Afghanistan as the UK's largest overseas operation.

The Ukraine crisis saw deployments from all three services to the Baltic States and Poland as part of measures to reassure NATO allies. At the September 2014 NATO Summit in Wales, Prime Minister David Cameron subsequently reaffirmed the UK's strategic commitment to NATO and announced that a British brigade headquarters and a battle group would be assigned to the new NATO Very High Readiness Joint Task Force.

The unexpected defeat of Iraqi forces by the Islamic State of Iraq and al-Sham (ISIS) in 2014 (see pp. 304–06) resulted in humanitarian supply drops in August and the delivery of arms to Kurdish Peshmerga forces in Northern Iraq by RAF *Hercules* transport aircraft, as well as RC-135 *Rivet Joint* electronic intelligence and *Tornado* reconnaissance missions. UK air-strikes against ISIS in Iraq, by RAF *Tornado*s flying from Cyprus, began after the murder of British and US hostages, a formal request for assistance by the Iraqi government and British parliamentary assent. Any UK strikes in Syria would, the prime minister announced, require another parliamentary vote, although in October it was announced that *Reaper* UAVs and *Rivet Joint* aircraft would fly over Syria.

Military capability
Implementation of the '**Army** 2020' restructuring programme continued, including reductions in regular troop numbers. Barring the withdrawal from Germany, these were to be largely complete by early 2015. The new Force Troops Command, containing most of the army's combat support and combat service support units, and roughly one-third of army strength, was established on 1 April 2014. It also contains a number of new formations, including an intelligence and surveillance brigade and a security-assistance group.

Funding has been allocated to take into wider service equipment specifically procured as 'urgent operational requirements' for Afghanistan. This included *Warthog*, *Mastiff* and *Husky* armoured vehicles, as well as the Israeli *Spike* NLOS precision-attack missile. Meanwhile, a £3.5 billion (US$5.8bn) contract was signed in September to replace the ageing CVR (T) family of reconnaissance vehicles with the new *Scout* family of specialist vehicles.

The SDSR mandated that much greater use be made of the Army Reserve (formerly the 'Territorial Army'), requiring the army to more than double the reserve's trained strength to 30,000 personnel. This target has yet to be reached. Although the SDSR allocated an additional £1.5bn (US$2.3bn) to rebuilding reserve capability, employers, the reserves themselves and the regular army will have to undergo significant cultural change to meet the SDSR target. This challenge presents one of the greatest risks to the Army 2020 project.

The last aircraft carrier in the **Royal Navy** (RN), HMS *Illustrious*, was decommissioned in August 2014 after serving three years as a helicopter carrier. The prime minister confirmed at the NATO Summit that HMS *Prince of Wales* – the second *Queen Elizabeth*-class aircraft carrier, currently under construction – would be taken into service by the RN. This will enable the UK to maintain a carrier at sea at all times.

UK Chief of the Defence Staff General Sir Nicholas Houghton stated publicly that he 'would identify the Royal Navy as being perilously close to its critical mass in man-power terms'. US Coast Guard (USCG) personnel were from October 2014 due to fill some posts in the RN's engineering staff left by SDSR 2010 cuts, which made 500 engineers redundant. USCG personnel are due to serve on 36-month tours from 2014–19.

The **Royal Air Force** (RAF) continued a period of recapitalisation. The RC-135 *Rivet Joint* electronic-intelligence aircraft entered service; initial delivery of the A400M *Atlas* airlifter was due to be made in the fourth quarter of 2014; and the A330 MRTT *Voyager* replaced *Tristar* and VC10 tankers. *Predator* UAVs and *Sentinel* R1 ISR aircraft procured for Afghanistan were to be retained in service; the *Sentinel* R1 will also now remain in service at least until 2018. The combination of operations in Afghanistan, Iraq and Nigeria placed unprecedented strain on the RAF's small fleet of ISR platforms and on the remaining three *Tornado* squadrons. To alleviate this, and to provide time for the *Brimstone* and *Storm Shadow* missiles to be integrated onto *Typhoon*, the planned disbandment of a *Tornado* squadron was deferred for a year.

At the end of October 2014, the MoD announced an agreement in principle to order its first production batch of four F-35B *Lightning* II aircraft, the first of an assumed purchase of 48 aircraft to meet its carrier requirement. In the near term, however, the weight of RAF air-to-surface capability will be borne increasingly by the *Typhoon*, since the *Tornado* GR4 is to be withdrawn from service by 2018/19. The *Typhoon* Tranche 1 aircraft is also presently planned to be taken out of service by this date, although the air force will almost certainly extend the remainder of the *Typhoon* fleet's service beyond the present, and notional, 2030 out-of-service date. The third potential element of the air force's air-combat capability, alongside the F-35B and the *Typhoon*, is an unmanned combat aerial vehicle, with a decision on whether to move beyond the present phase of the Anglo-French Future Combat Air System likely in 2016.

Prospects
Rejection of independence by Scottish voters in the September 2014 referendum was welcomed by the MoD and armed forces. This removed the risk posed

to British military capability and credibility. While the UK armed forces field a wide range of capabilities and have the military culture, logistics and strategic lift to use them, the majority are close to critical mass. This affects all the services and joint capabilities such as ISR.

David Cameron has said that the UK has 'a massive investment programme of £160bn in our defence industries, in our equipment', but with much future spending already committed to programmes, there is little cushion against a rise in platform costs. General Houghton said in late 2013 that 'unattended, our current course leads to a strategically incoherent force structure: exquisite equipment, but insufficient resources to man that equipment or train on it ... what the Americans call the spectre of the hollow-force'.

The MoD has already begun an effort to study the key defence issues in advance of the 2015 SDSR. Much of this work involves re-examining familiar issues including NATO, European defence and regional dynamics. Former defence secretary Philip Hammond identified that key capability issues would include the size of the F-35 buy, rebuilding maritime-patrol capability, and future military-cyber capabilities.

However, the key strategic issue facing the UK is the deterioration in Europe's security since publication of the 2010 SDSR, including increased instability in Africa and the Middle East and the accompanying concern about the possible return of UK citizens from jihadi ranks. Meanwhile, if the UK is to honour its NATO Article V commitments in Eastern Europe by deploying credible forces, it will have to rebuild combat capabilities that have atrophied in the last decade. These include the ability to conduct maritime and air operations in contested battlespace, as well as armoured warfare and countering heavy indirect fire.

DEFENCE ECONOMICS

Macroeconomics
The UK economy began to recover in 2014, after six years of economic stagnation following the 2008 financial crisis. The International Monetary Fund (IMF) forecast in 2014 that the economy would expand by a robust 3.2%, on the back of improved business confidence, credit conditions and consumer spending. However, the effects of post-crisis economic stagnation continued to weigh on the country's public finances. The government planned to eliminate the budget deficit by FY2015/16, but the slower-than-expected economic recovery meant that this was pushed back to 2018 at the earliest. Consequently, public debt continues to rise as a proportion of GDP – exceeding 90% of GDP in 2013 – and is likely to continue to do so until at least 2015.

Defence spending
Since 2010, the Ministry of Defence (MoD) has taken extensive measures to achieve an 8% real reduction in defence spending by 2015, as well as plugging the £38 billion (US$59bn) 'unfunded liabilities' gap in its long-term equipment-acquisition plan.

However, in FY2013/14 the overall amount needed to finance the fiscal deficit stood at £108bn (US$169bn). This meant that additional government-wide budgetary consolidation was needed in 2014 and 2015 in order to eliminate this by the 2018 target. As a result, and like previous years, the chancellor announced in his December 2013 Autumn Statement that the MoD resource budget would see additional cuts, of £277 million (or US$464m) in 2014 and £272m (US$460m) in 2015. This equated to just over 1% of the resource budget for both years, though it could be offset by a newly created 'carry-forward' facility, which allows the MoD to use any unspent funds from previous years to contribute towards required reductions. These reductions apply only to the MoD resource budget – which funds current expenditure such as personnel and training costs – and not to the MoD capital budget, which funds defence investment spending in longer-term assets such as infrastructure and military equipment. The equipment-acquisition and -support budget, for example, is set to receive a 1% real-terms increase in its allocations after 2015.

Despite this commitment to increase funding for equipment procurement and support after 2015, the near-term trajectory of the overall defence budget depends heavily on the outcome of the comprehensive spending review scheduled to take place immediately after parliamentary elections in May 2015. With the IMF forecasting average economic growth of 2.5% between 2015 and 2019, it would appear that this return to growth might permit a corresponding increase in the overall defence budget, so as to maintain current levels of defence spending as a proportion of GDP (of around 2.4%). However, with the budget deficit still around 4.5% of GDP in 2014 and with current political commitments to eliminate this completely by 2018, it is likely that several years of steady economic growth will be required before real-terms increases in defence funding are possible. Therefore, without a change in current deficit-reduction plans and spending priorities, it is possible that real-terms reductions to the MoD resource budget will continue into the next parliament. Overall, continued cuts to the resource budget and the winding down of the operation in Afghanistan (which in the past has accounted for some 10% of total MoD outlays), when combined with rising GDP, raises the prospect that defence spending as a proportion of GDP could within the next parliament fall below the 2% NATO threshold.

Increased spending efficiency

Aware that tighter funding conditions post-2010 are likely to persist into the medium term, the MoD has attempted to improve the effectiveness of its resources. Perhaps most notable have been attempts to outsource defence services to the private sector, where it is hoped that competition will drive down costs, thereby increasing the efficiency of defence outlays. A key initiative has been the MoD's Materiel Strategy programme, intended to restructure Defence Equipment & Support (DE&S) – the agency responsible for equipment acquisition and through-life support – into a 'government-owned, contractor-operated' (Go-Co) entity (see *The Military Balance 2014*, pp. 73–4). Two of the three private-sector consortia bidding for the contract dropped out of contention during the assessment phase, and the MoD was eventually forced to abandon the process in December 2013 due to the lack of competition. Instead, DE&S was retained within the public sector, but from April 2014 was transformed into a central government trading entity operating within, but at arm's length from, the MoD. The new entity would have a separate governance and oversight structure, greater freedom to hire specialist staff from the private sector at rates above public-sector pay scales, and a chief executive directly accountable to Parliament. As part of this 'DE&S Plus' option, traditional areas of MoD weakness – such as programme management, financial control and commercial negotiations – will be delivered through a number of private-sector support contracts with 'managed service providers'. Other areas of private-sector service provision included human resources and information-management systems.

A more successful attempt at outsourcing in 2014 was the selection of a long-term strategic business partner for the Defence Infrastructure Organisation (DIO), which manages the MoD's entire 930-square-kilometre military estate. In June 2014, the MoD entered into a £400m (US$670m), ten-year contract with Capita to provide management and infrastructure-support services for substantial elements of the MoD's 4,000 sites, including airfields and training areas, among others. It would also handle the sale of prime property and surplus sites, raising additional funds. It was projected that the outsourcing contract would save in excess of £300m (around US$500m) per annum.

The MoD has also exerted greater financial discipline over its resources in recent years. For example, in its Major Projects Report 2013, released in February 2014, the National Audit Office (NAO) concluded that, except for long-running cost escalation in aircraft-carrier acquisition, none of the MoD's 11 largest defence-procurement projects displayed significant cost increases or delays over the preceding year. The ten remaining projects together demonstrated a net cost decrease of £46m (US$77m) overall, with six displaying cost reductions and only three registering increases. Similarly, the MoD has targeted efficiencies in equipment-support costs, with DE&S undertaking contract renegotiations with major suppliers. For example, in 2013 the MoD revised a large naval contract with BAE Systems, tightening terms and requiring BAE to bear a larger proportion of cost overruns.

Challenges remain

The MoD has undoubtedly made progress in strengthening its control over resources, as well as in improving the efficiency of defence outlays. However, challenges remain: both the NAO and the parliamentary Public Accounts Committee (PAC) raised concerns over the course of 2014 that the MoD did not yet fully understand the underlying drivers of the equipment-support costs that make up around half of its Defence Equipment Plan 2013–23. The PAC also reiterated its previous concern that the centrally held contingency contained within the plan could be insufficient, leading to future cost increases. Additionally, the PAC criticised the outsourcing in 2012 of army recruitment to private-sector firm Capita, which did not achieve the regular and reserve recruitment levels to fulfil the MoD's Army 2020 plan requirements. Addressing these shortcomings will be important to ensure the MoD remains on a stable financial footing in an environment of potential sustained budgetary consolidation after 2015.

Albania ALB

Albanian Lek		2013	2014	2015
GDP	lek	1.34tr	1.4tr	
	US$	12.7bn	13.6bn	
per capita	US$	4,565	4,900	
Growth	%	0.4	2.1	
Inflation	%	1.9	1.8	
Def exp [a]	lek	19.3bn		
	US$	182m		
Def bdgt	lek	19.3bn	16.8bn	17.1bn
	US$	182m	163m	
FMA (US)	US$	3m	2.6m	2.4m
US$1=lek		105.67	102.72	

[a] NATO definition

Population 3,020,209

Age	0–14	15–19	20–24	25–29	30–64	65 plus
Male	10.2%	4.9%	5.0%	4.4%	19.8%	5.2%
Female	9.1%	4.5%	4.8%	4.6%	21.7%	5.8%

Capabilities

Albania has limited military capability predicated on internal security and disaster-relief tasks. Efforts to reform its armed forces and upgrade equipment continue, though these are constrained by limited funding. Much defence activity is concerned with meeting NATO standards, including training, planning and the generation of strategy documents. The 2013 Defence Directive listed full integration into NATO as a prime objective; this was achieved in October. The army, the largest of the three services, has provided troops to ISAF, for duties including surveillance and force protection, and an EOD team to *Operation Althea*, in Bosnia. The small air brigade operates only rotary-wing and light liaison aircraft, and the country depends on NATO allies for air defence. The naval element has only littoral capabilities and relies on vessels of questionable serviceability.

ACTIVE 8,000 (Land Force 3,000, Naval Force 650 Air Force 550 Other 3,800) **Paramilitary 500**

ORGANISATIONS BY SERVICE

Land Force 3,000
FORCES BY ROLE
SPECIAL FORCES
  1 SF bn
  1 cdo bn
MANOEUVRE
  Light
  3 lt inf bn
COMBAT SUPPORT
  1 mor bty
  1 NBC coy

EQUIPMENT BY TYPE
ARTY • MOR 93: 82mm 81; 120mm 12

Naval Force 650
EQUIPMENT BY TYPE
PATROL AND COASTAL COMBATANTS • PB 4: 2 *Nyryat* I; 2 *Shanghai* II† (PRC) with two single 533mm TT
MINE WARFARE • MINE COUNTERMEASURES • MSO 1 T-43† (FSU Project 254)
LOGISTICS AND SUPPORT • ARL 1; YPT 1 *Poluchat*

Coast Guard
EQUIPMENT BY TYPE
PATROL AND COASTAL COMBATANTS 35
  PBF 13: 8 V-4000; 5 *Archangel*
  PB 9: 4 *Iluria* (Damen Stan 4207); 3 Mk3 *Sea Spectre*; 2 (other)
  PBR 13: 4 Type-227; 1 Type-246; 1 Type-303; 7 Type-2010

Air Force 550
Flying hours at least 10–15 hrs/year.
EQUIPMENT BY TYPE
HELICOPTERS
  TPT 28: **Medium** 5 AS532AL *Cougar;* **Light** 23: 1 AW109; 5 Bell 205 (AB-205); 7 Bell 206C (AB-206C); 8 Bo-105; 2 EC145

Regional Support Brigade 700
FORCES BY ROLE
COMBAT SUPPORT
  1 cbt spt bde (1 engr bn, 1 (rescue) engr bn, 1 CIMIC det)

Military Police
FORCES BY ROLE
COMBAT SUPPORT
  1 MP bn

Logistics Brigade 1,200
FORCES BY ROLE
COMBAT SERVICE SUPPORT
  1 log bde (1 tpt bn, 2 log bn)

Paramilitary ε500

DEPLOYMENT

Legal provisions for foreign deployment:
Constitution: Codified constitution (1998)
Decision on deployment of troops abroad: By the parliament upon proposal by the president (Art.171 II)

AFGHANISTAN
NATO • ISAF 22

BOSNIA-HERZEGOVINA
EU • EUFOR • *Operation Althea* 1

SERBIA
NATO • KFOR 12

UKRAINE
OSCE • Ukraine 2

FOREIGN FORCES
Austria OSCE 3
Canada OSCE 2
Germany OSCE 2
Italy OSCE 3
Macedonia (FYROM) OSCE 1
Montenegro OSCE 2
Slovenia OSCE 1
Spain OSCE 2
Switzerland OSCE 1
United Kingdom OSCE 3
United States OSCE 1

Austria AUT

Euro €		2013	2014	2015
GDP	€	313bn	322bn	
	US$	416bn	436bn	
per capita	US$	49,039	51,183	
Growth	%	0.3	1.0	
Inflation	%	2.1	1.7	
Def exp [a]	€	2.59bn		
	US$	3.43bn		
Def bdgt [a]	€	2.43bn	2.45bn	2.29bn
	US$	3.23bn	3.32bn	
US$1=€		0.75	0.74	

[a] Includes military pensions

Population   8,223,062

Age	0 – 14	15 – 19	20 – 24	25 – 29	30 – 64	65 plus
Male	7.0%	2.8%	3.1%	3.1%	24.7%	8.2%
Female	6.6%	2.7%	3.0%	3.0%	24.8%	11.0%

Capabilities

Territorial defence remains the key task for Austria's armed forces, despite the conclusion of the 2013 National Security Strategy that this is an unlikely contingency. The provision of a crisis-response capacity and taking part in peacekeeping operations are additional tasks. Funding pressures forced the ministry to look at further savings in 2014, including reportedly considering a reduction in the number of aircrew allocated to its Eurofighter *Typhoon* squadron, as well as cutting back on spares support for army vehicles. There were also suggestions that additional funding cuts might be required in 2015. Battalion- or company-sized contributions to multinational peacekeeping missions are the armed forces' primary operational activity, although some high-readiness units, comprising career soldiers, have been formed for potential crisis-management tasks. The services remain well trained, regularly participating in multinational exercises as well as EUFOR in Bosnia-Herzegovina, KFOR in Kosovo and the UNIFIL mission in Lebanon.

ACTIVE 22,500 (Army 12,000 Air 2,750 Support 7,750)
Conscript liability 6 months recruit trg, 30 days reservist refresher trg for volunteers; 120–150 days additional for officers, NCOs and specialists. Authorised maximum wartime strength of 55,000

RESERVE 161,800 (Joint structured 24,400; Joint unstructured 137,400)
Some 12,000 reservists a year undergo refresher trg in tranches

ORGANISATIONS BY SERVICE

Joint Command – Land Forces 12,000
FORCES BY ROLE
MANOEUVRE
  Mechanised
  1 (3rd) bde (1 recce/SP arty bn, 1 armd bn, 1 mech inf bn, 1 inf bn, 1 cbt engr bn, 1 CBRN defence coy, 1 spt bn)
  1 (4th) bde (1 recce/SP arty bn, 1 armd bn, 1 mech inf bn, 1 inf bn, 1 CBRN defence coy, 1 spt bn)
  Light
  1 (6th) bde (3 inf bn, 1 cbt engr bn, 1 CBRN defence coy, 1 spt bn)
  1 (7th) bde (1 recce/arty bn, 3 inf bn, 1 cbt engr bn, 1 CBRN defence coy, 1 spt bn)
EQUIPMENT BY TYPE
MBT 56 *Leopard* 2A4
RECCE 12 CBRN *Dingo*
AIFV 112 *Ulan*
APC 94
  APC (W) 71 *Pandur*
  PPV 23 *Dingo* II
ARTY 148
  SP • 155mm 58 M109A5ÖE
  MOR • 120mm 90 sGrW 86 (10 more in store)
AT • MSL • MANPATS PAL 2000 BILL
ARV 40: 30 4KH7FA-SB; 10 M88A1
MW 6 AID2000 Trailer

Joint Command - Air Force 2,750
The Air Force is part of Joint Forces Comd and consists of 2 bde; Air Support Comd and Airspace Surveillance Comd
Flying hours   160 hrs/year on hel/tpt ac; 110 hrs/year on ftr
FORCES BY ROLE
FIGHTER
  2 sqn with *Typhoon*
ISR
  1 sqn with PC-6B *Turbo Porter*
TRANSPORT
  1 sqn with C-130K *Hercules*
TRAINING
  1 trg sqn with Saab 105Oe*
  1 trg sqn with PC-7 *Turbo Trainer*
TRANSPORT HELICOPTER
  2 sqn with Bell 212 (AB-212)
  1 sqn with OH-58B *Kiowa*

1 sqn with S-70A *Black Hawk*
2 sqn with SA316/SA319 *Alouette* III
AIR DEFENCE
2 bn
1 radar bn
EQUIPMENT BY TYPE
AIRCRAFT 37 combat capable
  FTR 15 Eurofighter *Typhoon* Tranche 1
  TPT 11: **Medium** 3 C-130K *Hercules*; **Light** 8 PC-6B *Turbo Porter*
  TRG 34: 12 PC-7 *Turbo Trainer*; 22 Saab 105Oe*
HELICOPTERS
  MRH 24 SA316/SA319 *Alouette* III
  ISR 10 OH-58B *Kiowa*
  TPT 32: **Medium** 9 S-70A *Black Hawk*; **Light** 23 Bell 212 (AB-212)
AD
  SAM 24 *Mistral* (6 more in store)
  GUNS • **35mm** 24 Z-FIAK system (6 more in store)
MSL • AAM • IIR IRIS-T

Joint Command – Special Operations Forces
FORCES BY ROLE
SPECIAL FORCES
2 SF gp
1 SF gp (reserve)

Support 7,750
Support forces comprise Joint Services Support Command and several agencies, academies and schools.

Cyber
The Austrian Cyber Security Strategy was approved in March 2013. A Cyber Security Steering Group to coordinate on government level has been established. The MoD's primary goal is cyber defence by ensuring national defence in cyberspace as well as securing the information and communications technology of the MoDs and the Austrian Armed Forces. The Military Cyber Emergency Readiness Team (milCERT) will be expanded to further improve situational awareness.

DEPLOYMENT
Legal provisions for foreign deployment:
Constitution: incl 'Federal Constitutional Law' (1/1930)
Specific legislation: 'Bundesverfassungsgesetz über Kooperation und Solidarität bei der Entsendung von Einheiten und Einzelpersonen in das Ausland' (KSE-BVG, 1997)
Decision on deployment of troops abroad: By government on authorisation of the National Council's Main Committee; simplified procedure for humanitarian and rescue tasks (Art. 23j of the 'Federal Constitutional Law'; § 2 of the KSE-BVG)
AFGHANISTAN
NATO • ISAF 3
ALBANIA
OSCE • Albania 3
BOSNIA-HERZEGOVINA
EU • EUFOR • *Operation Althea* 314; 1 inf bn HQ; 1 inf coy
CENTRAL AFRICAN REPUBLIC
EU • EUFOR RCA 6
CYPRUS
UN • UNFICYP 4
LEBANON
UN • UNIFIL 171; 1 log coy
MALI
EU • EUTM Mali 8
MIDDLE EAST
UN • UNTSO 5 obs
SERBIA
NATO • KFOR 505; 1 mech inf coy
OSCE • Kosovo 5
UKRAINE
OSCE • Ukraine 7
WESTERN SAHARA
UN • MINURSO 3 obs

Belgium BEL

Euro €		2013	2014	2015
GDP	€	383bn	390bn	
	US$	508bn	528bn	
per capita	US$	45,538	47,164	
Growth	%	0.2	1.0	
Inflation	%	1.2	0.7	
Def exp [a]	€	3.96bn		
	US$	5.26bn		
Def bdgt [b]	€	3.75bn	3.72bn	3.94bn
	US$	4.99bn	5.04bn	
US$1=€		0.75	0.74	

[a] NATO definition
[b] Includes military pensions

Population 10,449,361

Age	0–14	15–19	20–24	25–29	30–64	65 plus
Male	8.0%	2.9%	3.1%	3.1%	23.9%	8.0%
Female	7.6%	2.7%	3.0%	2.9%	23.8%	11.0%

Capabilities

Despite financial constraints, Belgium continues to pursue more deployable forces, with orders placed for A400M *Atlas* transport aircraft and NH90 NFH/TTH anti-submarine warfare/transport helicopters. A quick-reaction force is maintained, but there is a limited ability for power projection, and only as part of a multinational deployment. The armed forces are well trained and exercise jointly on a regular basis; they also participate in a broad range of multinational training exercises. Belgian forces have deployed to ISAF since 2003. They also provided air transport and force-protection support for French operations in Mali in 2013, and Belgian troops were part of the EU training mission to Mali during the second part of 2013. The land component has been reshaped as a wheeled medium brigade and an airborne-capable light brigade, retiring its *Leopard* 1 tanks. The naval component focuses on escort and mine countermeasures for littoral and blue-water operations. The air component faces a significant change in inventory around the end of this decade, when it will need to replace its F-16 combat aircraft.

ACTIVE 30,700 (Army 11,300 Navy 1,500 Air 6,000 Medical Service 1,400 Joint Service 10,500)

RESERVE 6,800

1,450 assigned to units and headquarters in peacetime; others on ORBAT but only assigned in time of crisis.

ORGANISATIONS BY SERVICE

Land Component 11,300
FORCES BY ROLE
SPECIAL FORCES
  1 SF gp
MANOEUVRE
  Reconnaissance
    1 ISR gp (2 ISR coy, 1 surv coy)
  Mechanised
    1 (med) bde (4 mech bn)
  Light
    1 (lt) bde (1 cdo bn, 1 lt inf bn, 1 para bn)
COMBAT SUPPORT
  1 arty gp (1 arty bty, 1 mor bty, 1 AD bty)
  2 engr bn (1 cbt engr coy, 1 lt engr coy, 1 construction coy)
  1 EOD unit
  1 CBRN coy
  1 MP coy (with 1 pl dedicated to EUROCORPS)
  3 CIS sigs gp
COMBAT SERVICE SUPPORT
  3 log bn
EQUIPMENT BY TYPE
AIFV 37: 19 *Piranha* III-C DF30; 18 *Piranha* III-C DF90
APC 331
  APC (W) 123: 45 *Pandur*; 64 *Piranha* III-C; 14 *Piranha* III-PC
  PPV 208 *Dingo* 2 (inc 52 CP)
ARTY 105
  TOWED 105mm 14 LG1 MkII
  MOR 91: 81mm 39; **120mm** 52
AD • SAM 45 *Mistral*
AEV 11: 3 *Leopard* 1; 8 *Piranha* III-C
ARV 16: 3 *Leopard* 1; 4 *Pandur*; 9 *Piranha* III-C
VLB 4 *Leguan*

Naval Component 1,500
EQUIPMENT BY TYPE
PRINCIPAL SURFACE COMBATANTS 2
  FRIGATES • FFGHM 2 *Leopold* I (ex-NLD *Karel Doorman*) with 2 quad lnchr with *Harpoon* AShM, 1 16-cell Mk48 VLS with RIM-7P *Sea Sparrow* SAM, 4 single Mk32 324mm ASTT with Mk46 LWT, 1 *Goalkeeper* CIWS, 1 76mm gun (capacity 1 med hel)
PATROL AND COASTAL COMBATANTS
  PCC 1 *Castor*
MINE WARFARE • MINE COUNTERMEASURES
  MHC 6 *Flower* (*Tripartite*) (1 in drydock)
LOGISTICS AND SUPPORT 8
  AGFH 1 *Godetia* (log spt/comd) (capacity 1 *Alouette* III)
  AGOR 1 *Belgica*
  AXS 1 *Zenobe Gramme*
  YTL 3 *Wesp*
  YTM 2

Naval Aviation
(part of the Air Component)
EQUIPMENT BY TYPE
HELICOPTERS
  ASW 1 NH90 NFH
  MRH 3 SA316B *Alouette* III (to be replaced by NH90 NFH)

Air Component 6,000
Flying hours 165 hrs/yr on cbt ac. 300 hrs/yr on tpt ac. 150 hrs/yr on hel; 250 hrs/yr on ERJ

FORCES BY ROLE
FIGHTER/GROUND ATTACK/ISR
  4 sqn with F-16AM/BM *Fighting Falcon*
SEARCH & RESCUE
  1 sqn with *Sea King* Mk48
TRANSPORT
  1 sqn with A330; ERJ-135 LR; ERJ-145 LR; *Falcon* 20 (VIP); *Falcon* 900B
  1 sqn with C-130H *Hercules*
TRAINING
  1 OCU sqn with F-16AM/BM *Fighting Falcon*
  1 sqn with SF-260D/MB
  1 BEL/FRA unit with *Alpha Jet**
  1 OCU unit with AW109
TRANSPORT HELICOPTER
  2 sqn with AW109 (ISR)
ISR UAV
  1 sqn with RQ-5A *Hunter* (B-*Hunter*)
EQUIPMENT BY TYPE
AIRCRAFT 88 combat capable
  FTR 59: 49 F-16AM *Fighting Falcon*; 10 F-16BM *Fighting Falcon*
  TPT 19: **Medium** 11 C-130H *Hercules*; **Light** 4: 2 ERJ-135 LR; 2 ERJ-145 LR; **PAX** 4: 1 A321; 2 *Falcon* 20 (VIP); 1 *Falcon* 900B
  TRG 61: 29 *Alpha Jet**; 9 SF-260D; 23 SF-260MB
HELICOPTERS
  ASW 1 NH90 NFH opcon Navy
  MRH 3 SA316B *Alouette* III opcon Navy
  SAR 3 *Sea King* Mk48 (to be replaced by NH90 NFH)
  TPT 22: **Medium** 2 NH90 TTH; **Light** 20 AW109 (ISR)
UAV • ISR • Heavy 12 RQ-5A *Hunter* (B-*Hunter*)
MSL
  AAM • IR AIM-9M/N *Sidewinder*; **ARH** AIM-120B AMRAAM

BOMBS
INS/GPS guided: GBU-31 JDAM; GBU-38 JDAM; GBU-54 (dual-mode)
Laser-Guided: GBU-10/GBU-12 *Paveway* II; GBU-24 *Paveway* III
PODS Infrared/TV: 12 *Sniper*

Cyber

The MoD is actively participating in the development of the national Cyber Security Strategy and is following and supporting the initiatives by NATO and the EU on cyber security.

DEPLOYMENT

Legal provisions for foreign deployment:
Constitution: Codified constitution (1831)
Specific legislation: 'Loi relatif à la mise en oeuvre des forces armées, à la mise en condition, ainsi qu'aux périodes et positions dans lesquelles le militaire peut se trouver' (1994)
Decision on deployment of troops abroad: By the government (Federal Council of Ministers) and the minister of defence (1994 law, Art. 88, 106, 167 of constitution)

AFGHANISTAN
NATO • ISAF 160

DEMOCRATIC REPUBLIC OF THE CONGO
UN • MONUSCO 2

FRANCE
NATO • Air Component 28 *Alpha Jet* located at Cazeaux/Tours

GULF OF ADEN & INDIAN OCEAN
EU • Operation Atalanta 1 FFGHM

JORDAN
6 F-16AM *Fighting Falcon*

LEBANON
UN • UNIFIL 99; 1 engr coy

MALI
EU • EUTM Mali 82

MIDDLE EAST
UN • UNTSO 2 obs

NORTH SEA
NATO • SNMCMG 1: 1 MHC

UGANDA
EU • EUTM Somalia 5

UKRAINE
OSCE • Ukraine 3

FOREIGN FORCES

United States US European Command: 1,200

Bosnia-Herzegovina BIH

Convertible Mark		2013	2014	2015
GDP	mark	26.4bn	27.1bn	
	US$	17.9bn	19bn	
per capita	US$	4,620	4,905	
Growth	%	2.1	0.7	
Inflation	%	-0.1	1.1	
Def exp [a]	mark	326m		
	US$	221m		
Def bdgt	mark	336m	325m	331m
	US$	228m	227m	
FMA (US)	US$	4.5m	4.5m	4m
US$1=mark		1.47	1.43	

[a] Includes military pensions

Population 3,871,643

Age	0 – 14	15 – 19	20 – 24	25 – 29	30 – 64	65 plus
Male	7.0%	3.2%	3.4%	3.8%	26.2%	5.2%
Female	6.6%	3.0%	3.2%	3.7%	26.7%	8.1%

Capabilities

Bosnia's armed forces are an uneasy amalgam of troops from all three formerly warring entities. Negotiations on NATO membership were opened in 2009, and while there has been limited progress towards this ambition defence reforms have proceeded with this objective in mind. The aim is to field small and mobile forces, including reserves, that are interoperable and compatible with NATO forces. Despite only rotary-wing airlift capabilities, Bosnian forces are capable of making modest contributions to international operations, particularly peacekeeping, and have identified an infantry company, a military police platoon and an EOD platoon as possible contributions. Bosnia has deployed forces to Iraq, Afghanistan, Serbia and the DRC.

ACTIVE 10,500 (Armed Forces 10,500)

ORGANISATIONS BY SERVICE

Armed Forces 10,500

1 ops comd; 1 spt comd
FORCES BY ROLE
MANOUEVRE
  Light
  3 inf bde (1 recce coy, 3 inf bn, 1 arty bn)
COMBAT SUPPORT
  1 cbt spt bde (1 tk bn, 1 engr bn, 1 EOD bn, 1 int bn, 1 MP bn, 1 CBRN coy, 1 sigs bn)
COMBAT SERVICE SUPPORT
  1 log comd (5 log bn)
EQUIPMENT BY TYPE
MBT 45 M60A3
APC • APC (T) 20 M113A2
ARTY 224
  TOWED 122mm 100 D-30

MRL 122mm 24 APRA 40
MOR 120mm 100 M-75
AT
 MSL
  SP 60: 8 9P122 *Malyutka*; 9 9P133 *Malyutka*; 32 BOV-1; 11 M-92
  MANPATS 9K11 *Malyutka* (AT-3 *Sagger*); 9K111 *Fagot* (AT-4 *Spigot*); 9K115 *Metis* (AT-7 *Saxhorn*); HJ-8; *Milan*
VLB MTU
MW Bozena

Air Force and Air Defence Brigade 800
FORCES BY ROLE
HELICOPTER
 1 sqn with Bell 205; Mi-8MTV *Hip*; Mi-17 *Hip* H
 1 sqn with Mi-8 *Hip*; SA342H/L *Gazelle* (HN-42/45M)
AIR DEFENCE
 1 AD bn
EQUIPMENT BY TYPE
AIRCRAFT
 FGA (7 J-22 *Orao* in store)
 ATK (6 J-1 (J-21) *Jastreb*; 3 TJ-1(NJ-21) *Jastreb* all in store)
 ISR (2 RJ-1 (IJ-21) *Jastreb** in store)
 TRG (1 G-4 *Super Galeb* (N-62)* in store)
HELICOPTERS
 MRH 13: 4 Mi-8MTV *Hip*; 1 Mi-17 *Hip* H; 1 SA-341H *Gazelle* (HN-42); 7 SA-342L *Gazelle* (HN-45M)
 TPT 21: **Medium** 8 Mi-8 *Hip* **Light** 13 Bell 205 (UH-1H *Iroquois*)
 TRG 1 Mi-34 *Hermit*
AD
 SAM
  SP 27: 1 *Strela*-10M3 (SA-13 *Gopher*); 20 2K12 *Kub* (SA-6 *Gainful*); 6 *Strela*-1 (SA-9 *Gaskin*)
  MANPAD 9K34 *Strela*-3 (SA-14 *Gremlin*); 9K310 (SA-16 *Gimlet*)
 GUNS 764
  SP 169: **20mm** 9 BOV-3 SPAAG; **30mm** 154: 38 M53; 116 M-53-59; **57mm** 6 ZSU 57/2
  TOWED 595: **20mm** 468: 32 M-55A2, 4 M38, 1 M55 A2B1, 293 M55 A3/A4, 138 M75; **23mm** 38: 29 ZU-23, 9 GSh-23; **30mm** 33 M-53; **37mm** 7 Type-55; **40mm** 49: 31 L60, 16 L70, 2 M-12

DEPLOYMENT
Legal provisions for foreign deployment:
Constitution: Codified constitution within Dayton Peace Agreement (1995)
Specific legislation: 'Law on participation of military, police, state and other employees in peacekeeping operations and other activities conducted abroad'
Decision on deployment of troops abroad: By the members of the Presidency (2003 'Defence Law' Art. 9, 13)

AFGHANISTAN
NATO • ISAF 8

DEMOCRATIC REPUBLIC OF THE CONGO
UN • MONUSCO 5 obs

SERBIA
OSCE • Kosovo 14

FOREIGN FORCES
Part of EUFOR – *Operation Althea* unless otherwise stated.
Albania 1
Austria 314; 1 inf bn HQ; 1 inf coy
Bulgaria 10
Chile 15
Czech Republic 2 • OSCE 1
Finland 8 • OSCE 1
France 2
Germany OSCE 3
Greece 3
Ireland 7 • OSCE 6
Italy OSCE 7
Macedonia (FYORM) 11
Netherlands 3
Poland 34 • OSCE 1
Portugal OSCE 1
Romania 37
Russia OSCE 2
Slovakia 35 • OSCE 1
Slovenia 13
Spain 10 • OSCE 1
Sweden 2
Switzerland 20
Turkey 239; 1 inf coy
United Kingdom 95; 1 inf coy • OSCE 3
United States OSCE 5

Bulgaria BLG

Bulgarian Lev L		2013	2014	2015
GDP	L	78.1bn	78.3bn	
	US$	53bn	55.1bn	
per capita	US$	7,328	7,648	
Growth	%	0.9	1.4	
Inflation	%	0.4	-1.2	
Def exp [a]	L	1.11bn		
	US$	750m		
Def bdgt [b]	L	1.1bn	1.05bn	1.05bn
	US$	750m	736m	
FMA (US)	US$	8.6m	7m	5m
US$1=L		1.47	1.42	

[a] NATO definition
[b] Excludes military pensions

Population 6,924,716

Age	0–14	15–19	20–24	25–29	30–64	65 plus
Male	7.3%	2.3%	2.9%	3.5%	24.0%	7.8%
Female	6.9%	2.2%	2.7%	3.3%	25.5%	11.6%

Capabilities

The armed forces' main tasks are territorial defence, peacetime domestic security and international peacekeeping and security missions. An Armed Forces Development Plan in 2010 and a new defence white paper in 2011 outlined the intent to replace Soviet-era equipment. The armed forces are also due to transition to a modified force structure by the end of 2014, although it is unclear whether this will occur on time. The aim is to achieve smaller, more balanced armed forces capable of multiple tasks. Funding shortages have curtailed or delayed some procurement, and the ambition to acquire a more modern fighter type for the air force has yet to be fulfilled. As a NATO member, Bulgarian armed forces have contributed to ISAF, exercise regularly at the national level and also participate in NATO exercises.

ACTIVE 31,300 (Army 16,300 Navy 3,450 Air 6,700 Central Staff 4,850) **Paramilitary 16,000**

RESERVE 303,000 (Army 250,500 Navy 7,500 Air 45,000)

ORGANISATIONS BY SERVICE

Army 16,300
Forces are being reduced in number.
FORCES BY ROLE
SPECIAL FORCES
  1 SF bde
MANOEUVRE
  Reconnaissance
    1 recce bn
  Mechanised
    2 mech bde
COMBAT SUPPORT
  1 arty regt
  1 engr regt
  1 NBC bn
COMBAT SERVICE SUPPORT
  1 log regt
EQUIPMENT BY TYPE
MBT 80 T-72
RECCE *Maritza* NBC
AIFV 160: 90 BMP-1; 70 BMP-2/3
APC 127
  APC (T) 100 MT-LB
  APC (W) 27: 20 BTR-60; 7 M1117 ASV
ARTY 311
  SP • **122mm** 48 2S1
  TOWED • **152mm** 24 D-20
  MRL 122mm 24 BM-21
  MOR 120mm 215 2S11 SP *Tundzha*
AT
  MSL
    SP 24 9P148 *Konkurs* (AT-5 *Spandrel*)
    MANPATS 9K111 *Fagot* (AT-4 *Spigot*); 9K113 *Konkurs* (AT-5 *Spandrel*); (9K11 *Malyutka* (AT-3 *Sagger*) in store)
  GUNS 126: **85mm** (150 D-44 in store); **100mm** 126 MT-12

AD
  SAM
    SP 24 9K33 *Osa* (SA-8 *Gecko*)
    MANPAD 9K32 *Strela* (SA-7 *Grail*)‡
  GUNS 400 **100mm** KS-19 towed/**57mm** S-60 towed/**23mm** ZSU-23-4 SP/ZU-23 towed
RADARS • **LAND** GS-13 *Long Eye* (veh); SNAR-1 *Long Trough* (arty); SNAR-10 *Big Fred* (veh, arty); SNAR-2/-6 *Pork Trough* (arty); *Small Fred/Small Yawn* (veh, arty)
AEV MT-LB
ARV T-54/T-55; MTP-1; MT-LB
VLB BLG67; TMM

Navy 3,450
EQUIPMENT BY TYPE
PRINCIPAL SURFACE COMBATANTS 4
  FRIGATES 4
    FFGM 3 *Drazki* (ex-BEL *Wielingen*) with 2 twin lnchr with MM-38 *Exocet* AShM, 1 octuple Mk29 GMLS with RIM-7P *Sea Sparrow* SAM, 2 single 533mm ASTT with L5 HWT, 1 sextuple 375mm MLE 54 Creusot-Loire A/S mor, 1 100mm gun
    FFM 1 *Smeli* (ex-FSU *Koni*) with 1 twin lnchr with 2 *Osa-M* (SA-N-4 *Gecko*) SAM, 2 RBU 6000 *Smerch* 2, 2 twin 76mm gun
PATROL AND COASTAL COMBATANTS 3
  PCFGM 1 *Mulnaya* (ex-FSU *Tarantul* II) with 2 twin lnchr with P-15M *Termit-M* (SS-N-2C *Styx*) AShM, 2 quad lnchr (manual aiming) with *Strela-2* (SA-N-5 *Grail*) SAM, 1 76mm gun
  PCM 2 *Reshitelni* (ex-FSU *Pauk* I) with 1 *Strela-2* (SA-N-5 *Grail*) SAM (manual aiming), 4 single 406mm TT, 2 RBU 1200, 1 76mm gun
MINE COUNTERMEASURES 6
  MHC 1 *Tsibar* (Tripartite – ex-BEL *Flower*)
  MSC 3 *Briz* (ex-FSU *Sonya*)
  MSI 2 *Olya* (ex-FSU)
AMPHIBIOUS 1
  LCU 1 *Vydra*
LOGISTICS AND SUPPORT 14: 1 **ADG**; 2 **AGS**; 2 **AOL**; 1 **ARS**; 2 **AT**; 1 **AX**; 2 **YDT**; 1 **YPT**; 2 **YTR**

Naval Aviation
HELICOPTERS • **ASW** 3 AS565MB *Panther*

Air Force 6,700
Flying hours 30–40 hrs/yr
FORCES BY ROLE
FIGHTER/ISR
  1 sqn with MiG-21bis/UM *Fishbed*
  1 sqn with MiG-29A/UB *Fulcrum*
FIGHTER/GROUND ATTACK
  1 sqn with Su-25K/UBK *Frogfoot*
TRANSPORT
  1 sqn with An-30 *Clank*; C-27J *Spartan*; L-410UVP-E; PC-12M
TRAINING
  1 sqn with L-39ZA *Albatros*
  1 sqn with PC-9M

ATTACK HELICOPTER
  1 sqn with Mi-24D/V *Hind* D/E
TRANSPORT HELICOPTER
  1 sqn with AS532AL *Cougar*; Bell 206 *Jet Ranger*; Mi-17 *Hip* H
EQUIPMENT BY TYPE
AIRCRAFT 42 combat capable
  FTR 16: 12 MiG-29A *Fulcrum*; 4 MiG-29UB *Fulcrum*
  FGA 12: 10 MiG-21bis *Fishbed*; 2 MiG-21UM *Mongol* B (to be withdrawn by end-2014)
  ATK 14: 10 Su-25K *Frogfoot*; 4 Su-25UBK *Frogfoot* (to be withdrawn by end-2014)
  ISR 1 An-30 *Clank*
  TPT 7: **Medium** 3 C-27J *Spartan*; **Light** 4: 1 An-2T *Colt*; 2 L-410UVP-E; 1 PC-12M
  TRG 12: 6 L-39ZA *Albatros*; 6 PC-9M (basic)
HELICOPTERS
  ATK 6 Mi-24D/V *Hind* D/E
  MRH 6 Mi-17 *Hip* H
  TPT 18: **Medium** 12 AS532AL *Cougar*; **Light** 6 Bell 206 *Jet Ranger*
UAV • EW *Yastreb*-2S
AD
  SAM S-300 (SA-10 *Grumble*); S-75 *Dvina* (SA-2 *Guideline* towed); S-125 *Pechora* (SA-3 *Goa*); S-200 (SA-5 *Gammon*); 2K12 *Kub* (SA-6 *Gainful*)
MSL
  AAM • IR R-3 (AA-2 *Atoll*)‡ R-73 (AA-11 *Archer*) **SARH** R-27R (AA-10 *Alamo* A)
  ASM Kh-29 (AS-14 *Kedge*); Kh-23 (AS-7 *Kerry*)‡; Kh-25 (AS-10 *Karen*)

Paramilitary 16,000

Border Guards 12,000
Ministry of Interior
FORCES BY ROLE
MANOEUVRE
  Other
    12 paramilitary regt
EQUIPMENT BY TYPE
PATROL AND COASTAL COMBATANTS 26
  PB 18: 1 Obzor (NLD Damen Stan 4207); 9 *Grif* (FSU *Zhuk*); 3 *Nesebar* (ex-GER *Neustadt*); 5 *Burgas* (GER Lurssen 21)
  PBF 8 Emine (EST Baltic 130)

Security Police 4,000

DEPLOYMENT

Legal provisions for foreign deployment:
Constitution: Codified constitution (1991)
Decision on deployment of troops abroad: By the president upon request from the Council of Ministers and upon approval by the National Assembly (Art. 84 XI)

AFGHANISTAN
NATO • ISAF 320

ARMENIA/AZERBAIJAN
OSCE • Minsk Conference 1

BOSNIA-HERZEGOVINA
EU • EUFOR • *Operation Althea* 10

LIBERIA
UN • UNMIL 1 obs

SERBIA
NATO • KFOR 11
OSCE • Kosovo 2

UKRAINE
OSCE • Ukraine 8

Croatia CRO

Croatian Kuna k		2013	2014	2015
GDP	k	327bn	322bn	
	US$	57.4bn	58.3bn	
per capita	US$	13,401	13,624	
Growth	%	-0.9	-0.8	
Inflation	%	2.2	-0.3	
Def exp [a]	k	4.85bn		
	US$	850m		
Def bdgt	k	4.55bn	4.28bn	4.56bn
	US$	799m	774m	
FMA (US)	US$	2.5m	2.5m	2.5m
US$1=k		5.70	5.53	

[a] NATO definition

Population 4,470,534

Age	0 – 14	15 – 19	20 – 24	25 – 29	30 – 64	65 plus
Male	7.4%	3.1%	3.1%	3.3%	24.1%	7.2%
Female	7.0%	2.9%	3.0%	3.2%	25.0%	10.6%

Capabilities

Croatia continues to work towards the long-term goals laid out in its 2005 defence review and the associated 2006–15 long-term development plan, as well as the National Security Strategy, Defence Strategy and Military Strategy. The latter details the armed forces' development and modernisation plans. Military tasks cover national sovereignty, the defence of Croatia and its allies, the ability to participate in crisis-response operations overseas and support to civil institutions. Croatia joined NATO in 2009 and defence-policy focus is directed at further integration into NATO structures and planning processes. In October 2012, its armed forces were formally integrated into NATO. The country contributed to ISAF and also provides support to UN missions. It has declared reaction forces to NATO and EU missions; these can deploy within Europe. Force modernisation and re-equipment plans have been hampered by the economic downturn, but in 2014 began to recommence with programmes involving the acquisition of second-hand artillery systems and excess US MRAP vehicles.

ACTIVE 16,550 (Army 11,250 Navy 1,600 Air 1,850 Joint 1,850) Paramilitary 3,000
Conscript liability Voluntary conscription, 8 weeks

ORGANISATIONS BY SERVICE

Joint 1,850 (General Staff)
FORCES BY ROLE
SPECIAL FORCES
  1 SF bn

Army 11,250
FORCES BY ROLE
MANOEUVRE
  Armoured
    1 armd bde
  Light
    1 mot inf bde
  Other
    1 inf trg regt
COMBAT SUPPORT
  1 arty/MRL regt
  1 AT regt
  1 ADA regt
  1 engr regt
  1 int bn
  1 MP regt
  1 NBC bn
  1 sigs regt
COMBAT SERVICE SUPPORT
  1 log regt
EQUIPMENT BY TYPE
MBT 75 M-84
AIFV 102 M-80
APC 139
  APC (T) 15 BTR-50
  APC (W) 108: 1 BOV-VP; 23 LOV OP; 84 Patria AMV
  PPV 16: 4 Cougar HE; 12 Maxxpro
ARTY 215
  SP 122mm 8 2S1
  TOWED 64: **122mm** 27 D-30; **130mm** 19 M-46H1; **155mm** 18 M-1H1
  MRL 39: **122mm** 37: 6 M91 Vulkan 31 BM-21 Grad; **128mm** 2 LOV RAK M91 R24
  MOR 104: **82mm** 29 LMB M96; **120mm** 75: 70 M-75; 5 UBM 52
AT • MSL
  SP 28 POLO BOV 83
  MANPATS 9K11 Malyutka (AT-3 Sagger); 9K111 Fagot (AT-4 Spigot); 9K115 Metis (AT-7 Saxhorn); 9K113 Konkurs (AT-5 Spandrel); Milan (reported)
AD
  SP 9 Strijela-10 CRO
  GUNS 96
    SP 20mm 39 BOV-3 SP
    TOWED 20mm 57 M55A4
ARV M84A1; WZT-3
VLB 3 MT-55A
MW Bozena; 1 Rhino

Navy 1,600
Navy HQ at Split
EQUIPMENT BY TYPE
PATROL AND COASTAL COMBATANTS 5
  PCGF 1 Koncar with 2 twin lnchr with RBS-15B AShM, 1 AK630 CIWS, 1 57mm gun
  PCG 4:
    2 Kralj with 2–4 twin lnchr with RBS-15B AShM, 1 AK630 CIWS, 1 57mm gun
    2 Vukovar (ex-FIN Helsinki) with 4 twin lnchr with RBS-15M AShM, 1 57mm gun
MINE WARFARE • MINE COUNTERMEASURES •
MHI 1 Korcula
AMPHIBIOUS
  LCT 2 Cetina with 1 quad lnchr with Strela-2‡ (SA-N-5 Grail) SAM
  LCVP 3: 2 Type-21; 1 Type-22
LOGISTICS AND SUPPORT 11: **AKL** 1; **YDT** 2; **YFL** 1; **YFU** 5; **YTM** 2
MSL • TACTICAL • AShM 3 RBS-15K

Marines
FORCES BY ROLE
MANOEUVRE
  Amphibious
    2 indep mne coy

Coast Guard
FORCES BY ROLE
Two divisions, headquartered in Split (1st div) and Pula (2nd div).
EQUIPMENT BY TYPE
PATROL AND COASTAL COMBATANTS • PB 4 Mirna
LOGISTICS AND SUPPORT • AX 5

Air Force and Air Defence 1,850
Flying hours 50 hrs/year

FORCES BY ROLE
FIGHTER/GROUND ATTACK
  1 (mixed) sqn with MiG-21bis/UMD Fishbed
TRANSPORT
  1 sqn with An-32 Cline
TRAINING
  1 sqn with PC-9M; Z-242L
  1 hel sqn with Bell 206B Jet Ranger II
FIRE FIGHTING
  1 sqn with AT-802FA Fire Boss; CL-415
TRANSPORT HELICOPTER
  2 sqn with Mi-8MTV Hip H; Mi-8T Hip C; Mi-171Sh
EQUIPMENT BY TYPE
AIRCRAFT 9 combat capable
  FGA 9: 5 MiG-21bis Fishbed; 4 MiG-21UMD Fishbed
  TPT • Light 2 An-32 Cline
  TRG 25: 20 PC-9M; 5 Z-242L
  FF 11: 5 AT-802FA Fire Boss; 6 CL-415
HELICOPTERS
  MRH 11 Mi-8MTV Hip H
  TPT 21: **Medium** 13: 3 Mi-8T Hip C; 10 Mi-171Sh; **Light** 8 Bell 206B Jet Ranger II

UAV • ISR • **Medium** *Hermes* 450
AD • SAM
  SP S-300 (SA-10 *Grumble*); 9K31 *Strela*-1 (SA-9 *Gaskin*)
  MANPAD 9K34 *Strela*-3 (SA-14 *Gremlin*); 9K310 *Igla*-1 (SA-16 *Gimlet*)
RADAR 11: 5 FPS-117; 3 S-600; 3 PRV-11
MSL • AAM • IR R-3S (AA-2 *Atoll*)‡; R-60 (AA-8 *Aphid*)

Paramilitary 3,000

  Police 3,000 armed

DEPLOYMENT

Legal provisions for foreign deployment:
Constitution: Codified constitution (2004)
Decision on deployment of troops abroad: By the parliament (Art. 7 II); simplified procedure for humanitarian aid and military exercises

AFGHANISTAN
NATO • ISAF 153

INDIA/PAKISTAN
UN • UNMOGIP 7 obs

LEBANON
UN • UNIFIL 1

LIBERIA
UN • UNMIL 2

SERBIA
NATO • KFOR 23
OSCE • Kosovo 5

UKRAINE
OSCE • Ukraine 4

WESTERN SAHARA
UN • MINURSO 3 obs

Cyprus CYP

Cypriot Pound C£		2013	2014	2015
GDP	C£	16.5bn	15.8bn	
	US$	21.9bn	21.3bn	
per capita	US$	24,867	23,955	
Growth	%	-5.4	-3.2	
Inflation	%	0.4	0.0	
Def exp	C£	290m		
	US$	385m		
Def bdgt	C£	347m	319m	310m
	US$	460m	432m	
US$1=C£		0.75	0.74	

Population 1,172,458

Age	0 – 14	15 – 19	20 – 24	25 – 29	30 – 64	65 plus
Male	8.1%	3.6%	4.8%	4.9%	24.9%	4.9%
Female	7.6%	3.1%	3.9%	4.0%	24.0%	6.4%

Capabilities

The country's national guard is predominantly a land force supplemented by small air and maritime units. It is intended to act as a deterrent to any possible Turkish incursion, and to provide enough opposition until military support can be provided by Greece, its primary ally. The air wing has a small number of rotary- and fixed-wing utility platforms, including Mi-35 attack helicopters, while the maritime wing is essentially a constabulary force. Key procurements include SAR helicopters, offshore-patrol vessels and T-80U MBTs. Expeditionary deployments have been limited, with some officers joining UN and EU missions. Recent economic difficulties may have hampered procurement ambitions, but there is the possibility that revenues from potential natural-gas finds could help overcome the temporary hiatus.

ACTIVE 12,000 (National Guard 12,000)
Paramilitary 750
Conscript liability 24 months

RESERVE 50,000 (National Guard 50,000)
Reserve service to age 50 (officers dependent on rank; military doctors to age 60)

ORGANISATIONS BY SERVICE

National Guard 1,300 regular; 10,700 conscript (total 12,000)

FORCES BY ROLE
SPECIAL FORCES
  1 comd (regt) (1 SF bn)
MANOEUVRE
  Armoured
  1 lt armd bde (2 armd bn, 1 armd inf bn)
  Mechanised
  1 (1st) mech inf div (1 armd recce bn, 2 mech inf bn)
  1 (2nd) mech inf div (1 armd recce bn, 2 armd bn, 2 mech inf bn)
  Light
  3 (4th, 7th & 8th) lt inf bde (2 lt inf regt)
COMBAT SUPPORT
  1 arty comd (8 arty bn)
COMBAT SERVICE SUPPORT
  1 (3rd) spt bde
EQUIPMENT BY TYPE
MBT 134: 82 T-80U; 52 AMX-30B2
RECCE 67 EE-9 *Cascavel*
AIFV 43 BMP-3
APC 294
  APC (T) 168 *Leonidas*
  APC (W) 126 VAB (incl variants)
ARTY 452
  SP 155mm 24: 12 Mk F3; 12 *Zuzana*
  TOWED 104: **100mm** 20 M-1944; **105mm** 72 M-56; **155mm** 12 TR-F-1
  MRL 22: **122mm** 4 BM-21; **128mm** 18 M-63 *Plamen*
  MOR 302: **81mm** 170 E-44; (70+ M1/M9 in store); **107mm** 20 M2/M30; **120mm** 112 RT61

AT
  MSL
    SP 33: 15 EE-3 *Jararaca* with *Milan*; 18 VAB with HOT
    MANPATS HOT; *Milan*
  RCL 106mm 144 M40A1
  RL 112mm 1,000 APILAS
AD
  SAM
    SP 6 9K322 *Tor* (SA-15 *Gauntlet*); *Mistral*
    STATIC 12 *Aspide*
    MANPAD *Mistral*
  GUNS • TOWED 60: **20mm** 36 M-55; **35mm** 24 GDF-003 (with *Skyguard*)
ARV 2 AMX-30D; 1 BREM-1

Maritime Wing
FORCES BY ROLE
COMBAT SUPPORT
  1 (coastal defence) AShM bty with MM-40 *Exocet* AShM
EQUIPMENT BY TYPE
PATROL AND COASTAL COMBATANTS 4
  PBF 4: 2 *Rodman 55*; 2 *Vittoria*
MSL • AShM 3 MM-40 *Exocet*

Air Wing
AIRCRAFT
  TPT • Light 1 BN-2B *Islander*
  TRG 1 PC-9
HELICOPTERS
  ATK 11 Mi-35P *Hind*
  MRH 7: 3 AW139 (SAR); 4 SA342L1 *Gazelle* (with HOT for anti-armour role)
  TPT • Light 2 Bell 206L-3 *Long Ranger*

Paramilitary 750+

Armed Police 500+
FORCES BY ROLE
MANOEUVRE
  Other
    1 (rapid-reaction) paramilitary unit
EQUIPMENT BY TYPE
APC (W) 2 VAB VTT
HELICOPTERS • MRH 2 Bell 412 SP

Maritime Police 250
PATROL AND COASTAL COMBATANTS 10
  PBF 5: 2 *Poseidon*; 1 *Shaldag*; 2 *Vittoria*
  PB 5 SAB-12

DEPLOYMENT
Legal provisions for foreign deployment:
Constitution: Codified constitution (1960)
Decision on deployment of troops abroad: By parliament, but president has the right of final veto (Art. 50)

LEBANON
UN • UNIFIL 2

FOREIGN FORCES
Argentina UNFICYP 268; 2 inf coy; 1 hel flt
Austria UNFICYP 4
Brazil UNFICYP 1
Canada UNFICYP 1
Chile UNFICYP 13
Greece Army: 950; ε200 (officers/NCO seconded to Greek-Cypriot National Guard)
Hungary UNFICYP 76; 1 inf pl
Norway UNFICYP 2
Paraguay UNFICYP 14
Serbia UNFICYP 46; elm 1 inf coy
Slovakia UNFICYP 159; elm 1 inf coy; 1 engr pl
United Kingdom 2,600; 2 inf bn; 1 hel sqn with 4 Bell 412 *Twin Huey* • Operation Shader 1 FGA sqn with 8 *Tornado* GR4; 1 A330 MRTT *Voyager* KC3; 1 C-130J *Hercules*; 4 CH-47D *Chinook* HC4 • UNFICYP 268: 1 inf coy

TERRITORY WHERE THE GOVERNMENT DOES NOT EXERCISE EFFECTIVE CONTROL

Data here represents the de facto situation on the northern half of the island. This does not imply international recognition as a sovereign state.

Capabilities

ACTIVE 3,500 (Army 3,500) **Paramilitary 150**
Conscript liability 24 months

RESERVE 26,000 (first line 11,000 second line 10,000 third line 5,000)
Reserve liability to age 50.

ORGANISATIONS BY SERVICE

Army ε3,500
FORCES BY ROLE
MANOEUVRE
  Light
    7 inf bn
EQUIPMENT BY TYPE
ARTY • MOR • 120mm 73
AT
  MSL • MANPATS 6 *Milan*
  RCL • 106mm 36

Paramilitary

Armed Police ε150
FORCES BY ROLE
SPECIAL FORCES
  1 (police) SF unit

Coast Guard
PATROL AND COASTAL COMBATANTS 6
  PCC 5: 2 SG45/SG46; 1 *Rauf Denktash*; 2 US Mk 5
  PB 1

FOREIGN FORCES

TURKEY
Army ε43,000
1 army corps HQ, 1 armd bde, 2 mech inf div, 1 avn comd

EQUIPMENT BY TYPE
MBT 348: 8 M48A2 (trg); 340 M48A5T1/2
APC (T) 627: 361 AAPC (incl variants); 266 M113 (incl variants)
ARTY
  SP 155mm 90 M-44T
  TOWED 102: **105mm** 72 M101A1; **155mm** 18 M114A2; **203mm** 12 M115
  MRL 122mm 6 T-122
  MOR 450: **81mm** 175; **107mm** 148 M-30; **120mm** 127 HY-12
AT
  MSL • MANPATS *Milan*; TOW
  RCL 106mm 192 M40A1
AD • GUNS
  TOWED 20mm Rh 202; **35mm** 16 GDF-003; **40mm** 48 M1
AIRCRAFT • TPT • Light 3 Cessna 185 (U-17)
HELICOPTER • TPT 4 Medium 1 AS532UL *Cougar* **Light** 3 Bell 205 (UH-1H *Iroquois*)
PATROL AND COASTAL COMBATANTS 1 PB

Czech Republic CZE

Czech Koruna Kc		2013	2014	2015
GDP	Kc	3.88tr	4.02tr	
	US$	198bn	200bn	
per capita	US$	18,871	18,985	
Growth	%	-0.9	2.5	
Inflation	%	1.4	0.6	
Def exp [a]	Kc	42bn		
	US$	2.15bn		
Def bdgt [b]	Kc	42.1bn	41.9bn	43.5bn
	US$	2.15bn	2.09bn	
FMA (US)	US$	5m	3m	1m
US$1=Kc		19.57	20.08	

[a] NATO definition
[b] Includes military pensions

Population   10,627,448

Age	0–14	15–19	20–24	25–29	30–64	65 plus
Male	7.6%	2.3%	3.1%	3.5%	25.3%	7.2%
Female	7.2%	2.2%	3.0%	3.3%	24.9%	10.3%

Capabilities

Defence-policy priorities are protecting the security of the Czech Republic and contributing to the security of the Euro-Atlantic area by maintaining and developing multilateral security and defence institutions; membership of NATO is at the heart of defence policy. Political-military ambitions are to provide a brigade-sized task force for Article V operations; to participate in international crisis-management tasks with units assigned to high-readiness standby arrangements; and contributing to additional operations with specialised forces or expert teams. The 4th Brigade Task Force will be part of the NATO Response Force in 2015. The lease of *Gripen* combat aircraft was extended in May 2014 for 12 more years, while the air force supported the Multinational Force and Observers mission in Sinai with a C-295M during the year. The forces are well trained and equipped. However, defence expenditure declined markedly over the past half-dozen years, a trend the government in 2014 stated it hoped to reverse as concerns over events in Ukraine began to influence the defence debate. In September 2014, Czech political parties signed an agreement to stabilise defence expenditures. Falling defence-budget allocations had 'severely impacted the Czech Republic's national defence capability and … collective security commitments'. The defence budget would, the document projected, rise to 1.4% of GDP by 2020.

ACTIVE 21,000 (Army 12,200, Air 5,100, Other 3,700) **Paramilitary 3,100**

ORGANISATIONS BY SERVICE

Army 12,200
FORCES BY ROLE
MANOEUVRE
  Reconnaissance
  1 ISR/EW regt (1 recce bn, 1 EW bn)
  Armoured
  1 (7th) mech bde (1 armd bn, 2 armd inf bn, 1 mot inf bn)
  Mechanised
  1 (4th) rapid reaction bde (2 mech bn, 1 mot inf bn, 1 AB bn)
COMBAT SUPPORT
  1 (13th) arty regt (2 arty bn)
  1 engr regt (3 engr bn, 1 EOD bn)
  1 CBRN regt (2 CBRN bn)
  1 sigs bn
  1 CIMIC pl
COMBAT SERVICE SUPPORT
  1 log regt

Active Reserve
FORCES BY ROLE
COMMAND
  14 (territorial defence) comd
MANOEUVRE
  Armoured
  1 armd coy
  Light
  14 inf coy (1 per territorial comd) (3 inf pl, 1 cbt spt pl, 1 log pl)

EQUIPMENT BY TYPE
MBT 30 T-72M4CZ; (93 T-72 in store)
AIFV 206: 103 BMP-2; 103 *Pandur* II (inc variants); (98 BMP-1; 82 BMP-2; 34 BPzV all in store)
APC 21:
  APC (T) (17 OT-90 in store)

APC (W) (5 OT-64 in store)
PPV 21 *Dingo 2*
ARTY 146:
  SP 152mm 95 M-77 *Dana* (inc 6 trg); (35 more in store)
  MOR 120mm 51: 43 M-1982 (inc 3 trg); 8 SPM-85; (42 M-1982 in store);
AT • MSL • MANPATS 9K113 *Konkurs* (AT-5 *Spandrel*)
RADAR • LAND 3 ARTHUR
ARV 4+: MT-72; VT-72M4CZ; VPV-ARV; WPT-TOPAS; 4 *Pandur* II
VLB AM-50; MT-55A
MW UOS-155 *Belarty*

Air Force 5,100

Principal task is to secure Czech airspace. This mission is fulfilled within NATO Integrated Extended Air Defence System (NATINADS) and, if necessary, by means of the Czech national reinforced air-defence system. The air force also provides CAS for army SAR, and performs a tpt role.

Flying hours 120hrs/yr cbt ac; 150 for tpt ac

FORCES BY ROLE
FIGHTER/GROUND ATTACK
  1 sqn with *Gripen* C/D
  1 sqn with L-159 ALCA/L-159T
TRANSPORT
  2 sqn with A319CJ; C-295M; CL-601 *Challenger*; L-410 *Turbolet*; Yak-40 *Codling*
TRAINING
  1 sqn with L-39ZA*
ATTACK HELICOPTER
  1 sqn with Mi-24/Mi-35 *Hind*
TRANSPORT HELICOPTER
  1 sqn with Mi-17 *Hip* H; Mi-171Sh
  1 sqn with Mi-8 *Hip*; Mi-17 *Hip* H; PZL W-3A *Sokol*
AIR DEFENCE
  1 (25th) SAM bde (2 AD gp)

EQUIPMENT BY TYPE
AIRCRAFT 47 combat capable
  FGA 14: 12 *Gripen* C (JAS 39C); 2 *Gripen* D (JAS 39D)
  ATK 24: 19 L-159 ALCA; 5 L-159T
  TPT 15: Light 12: 4 C-295M; 6 L-410 *Turbolet*; 2 Yak-40 *Codling*; PAX 3: 2 A319CJ; 1 CL-601 *Challenger*
  TRG 9 L-39ZA*
HELICOPTERS
  ATK 24: 6 Mi-24 *Hind* D; 18 Mi-35 *Hind* E
  MRH 8 Mi-17 *Hip* H
  TPT 26: Medium 20: 4 Mi-8 *Hip*; 16 Mi-171Sh (med tpt); Light 6 PZL W3A *Sokol*
AD
  SAM RBS-70; 9K32 *Strela*-2‡ (SA-7 *Grail*) (available for trg RBS-70 gunners)
MSL
  AAM • IR AIM-9M *Sidewinder*; ARH AIM-120C-5 AMRAAM
BOMBS
  Laser-guided: GBU *Paveway*

Other Forces

FORCES BY ROLE
SPECIAL FORCES
  1 SF gp
MANOEUVRE
Other
  1 (presidential) gd bde (2 bn)
  1 (honour guard) gd bn (2 coy)
COMBAT SUPPORT
  1 int gp
  1 (central) MP comd
  3 (regional) MP comd
  1 (protection service) MP comd

Paramilitary 3,100

Border Guards 3,000

Internal Security Forces 100

Cyber

In 2011, a National Security Authority was established to supervise the protection of classified information and perform tasks related to communications and information-systems security. A Cyber Security Strategy was published in 2011 to coordinate government approaches to network security and create a framework for legislative developments, international cooperative activity and the development of technical means, as well as promoting network security. It also announced the creation of a national CERT agency.

DEPLOYMENT

Legal provisions for foreign deployment:
Constitution: Codified constitution (1992), Art. 39, 43
Decision on deployment of troops abroad: External deployments require approval by parliament. As an exception, such as in urgent cases, the government can decide on such a deployment for up to 60 days with the aim of fulfilling international treaty obligations concerning collective defence.

AFGHANISTAN
NATO • ISAF 227
UN • UNAMA 2 obs

ARMENIA/AZERBAIJAN
OSCE • Minsk Conference 1

BOSNIA-HERZEGOVINA
EU • EUFOR • *Operation Althea* 2
OSCE • Bosnia and Herzegovina 1

CENTRAL AFRICAN REPUBLIC
UN • MINUSCA 2 obs

DEMOCRATIC REPUBLIC OF THE CONGO
UN • MONUSCO 3 obs

EGYPT
MFO 13; 1 C-295M

MALI
EU • EUTM Mali 38

MOLDOVA
OSCE • Moldova 1

SERBIA
NATO • KFOR 9
OSCE • Kosovo 1
UN • UNMIK 2 obs

UKRAINE
OSCE • Ukraine 9

Denmark DNK

Danish Krone kr		2013	2014	2015
GDP	kr	1.86tr	1.9tr	
	US$	331bn	347bn	
per capita	US$	59,129	61,885	
Growth	%	0.4	1.5	
Inflation	%	0.8	0.6	
Def exp [a]	kr	25.6bn		
	US$	4.55bn		
Def bdgt [b]	kr	25.6bn	26.3bn	
	US$	4.55bn	4.81bn	
US$1=kr		5.62	5.46	

[a] NATO definition
[b] Includes military pensions

Population 5,569,077

Age	0–14	15–19	20–24	25–29	30–64	65 plus
Male	8.7%	3.4%	3.3%	2.9%	22.8%	8.2%
Female	8.3%	3.2%	3.2%	2.9%	23.0%	10.2%

Capabilities

Danish defence policy is predicated on supporting national sovereignty, and its security and foreign policies. Membership of NATO is viewed as a cornerstone of military policy. While Denmark's forces are small they are comparatively well trained and equipped, and are regular participants in international operations. Danish security interests in the High North, exemplified by organisational and procurement decisions in recent years, were sharpened during the course of 2014 by tensions stemming from Russia's annexation of Crimea. The air force participates in NATO's Baltic Air Policing mission, and was part of an increased deployment from May 2014. It faces a key procurement decision, anticipated by mid-2015, on whether to pursue its involvement in the F-35 or to buy an alternative type to replace the F-16 combat aircraft. The latter will likely need to be withdrawn from service by the early 2020s. Defence structures are being revised as part of ongoing savings efforts: Defence Command will be replaced by a Joint Defence Command that will include the operational service commands and Arctic Command. A Special Operations Command will also be set up within the Joint Defence Command. Denmark is also part of the Nordic defence cooperation group, NORDEFCO.

ACTIVE 17,200 (Army 7,950 Navy 3,000 Air 3,150 Joint 3,100)
Conscript liability 4–12 months, most voluntary

RESERVES 53,500 (Army 40,800 Navy 4,500 Air Force 5,300 Service Corps 2,900)

ORGANISATIONS BY SERVICE

Army 6,950; 1,000 conscript (total 7,950)

Div and bde HQ are responsible for trg only; if necessary, can be transformed into operational formations

FORCES BY ROLE
COMMAND
  1 div HQ
  2 bde HQ
SPECIAL FORCES
  1 SF unit
MANOEUVRE
  Reconnaissance
  1 recce bn
  1 ISR bn
  Armoured
  1 tk bn
  Mechanised
  5 armd inf bn
COMBAT SUPPORT
  1 SP arty bn
  1 cbt engr bn
  1 EOD bn
  1 MP bn
  1 sigs regt (1 sigs bn, 1 EW coy)
COMBAT SERVICE SUPPORT
  1 construction bn
  1 log regt (1 spt bn, 1 log bn, 1 maint bn, 1 med bn)

EQUIPMENT BY TYPE
MBT 55 *Leopard* 2A4/5
RECCE 113: 22 *Eagle* 1; 91 *Eagle* IV
AIFV 45 CV9030 Mk II
APC 494
  APC (T) 343 M113 (incl variants); (196 more in store awaiting disposal)
  APC (W) 111 *Piranha* III (incl variants)
  PPV 40 *Cougar*
ARTY 44
  SP 155mm 24 M109
  MRL 227mm (12 MLRS in store awaiting disposal)
  MOR • TOWED 120mm 20 Soltam K6B1
AT
  MSL • MANPATS TOW
  RCL 84mm 349 *Carl Gustav*
AD • SAM • MANPAD FIM-92A *Stinger*
RADAR • LAND ARTHUR
ARV 11 *Bergepanzer* 2
VLB 10 *Biber*
MW 14 910-MCV-2

Navy 2,850; 150 conscript (total 3,000)

EQUIPMENT BY TYPE
PRINCIPAL SURFACE COMBATANTS 7
  DESTROYERS • DDGHM 3 *Iver Huitfeldt* with 4 quad lnchr with RGM-84 *Harpoon* Block II AShM, 1 32-cell Mk41 VLS with SM-2 IIIA SAM, 2 12-cell Mk56 VLS with RIM-162 SAM, 2 twin 324mm TT with MU90 LWT, 2 76mm guns (capacity 1 med hel)
  FRIGATES • FFH 4 *Thetis* with 2 twin lnchr with *Stinger* SAM, 1 76mm gun (capacity 1 *Super Lynx* Mk90B)

PATROL AND COASTAL COMBATANTS 9
  PSO 2 *Knud Rasmussen* with 1 76mm gun, 1 hel landing platform
  PCC 7: 1 *Agdlek*; 6 *Diana*
MINE WARFARE • MINE COUNTERMEASURES 6
  MCI 4 MSF MK-I
  MSD 2 *Holm*
LOGISTICS AND SUPPORT 23
  ABU 2 (primarily used for MARPOL duties)
  AE 1 *Sleipner*
  AG 2 *Absalon* (flexible support ships) with 2 octuple VLS with RGM-84 Block 2 *Harpoon* 2 AShM, 4 twin lnchr with *Stinger* SAM, 3 12-cell Mk 56 VLS with RIM-162B *Sea Sparrow* SAM, 2 twin 324mm TT, 2 *Millenium* CIWS, 1 127mm gun (capacity 2 LCP, 7 MBT or 40 vehicles; 130 troops)
  AGE 1 *Dana*
  AGS 3 Ska 11
  AGSC 2 *Holm*
  AKL 2 *Seatruck*
  AX 1 *Søløven* (used as diving trainer)
  AXL 2 *Holm*
  AXS 2 *Svanen*
  YPL 3
  YTL 2

Air Force 3,050; 100 conscript (total 3,150)

Flying hours   165 hrs/yr

Tactical Air Comd

FORCES BY ROLE
FIGHTER/GROUND ATTACK
  2 sqn with F-16AM/BM *Fighting Falcon*
ANTI-SUBMARINE WARFARE
  1 sqn with *Super Lynx* Mk90B
SEARCH & RESCUE/TRANSPORT HELICOPTER
  1 sqn with AW101 *Merlin*
  1 sqn with AS550 *Fennec* (ISR)
TRANSPORT
  1 sqn with C-130J-30 *Hercules*; CL-604 *Challenger* (MP/VIP)
TRAINING
  1 unit with MFI-17 *Supporter* (T-17)
EQUIPMENT BY TYPE
AIRCRAFT 45 combat capable
  FTR 45: 35 F-16AM *Fighting Falcon*; 10 F-16BM *Fighting Falcon* (30 operational)
  TPT 7: **Medium** 4 C-130J-30 *Hercules*; **PAX** 3 CL-604 *Challenger* (MP/VIP)
  TRG 27 MFI-17 *Supporter* (T-17)
HELICOPTERS
  ASW 7 *Super Lynx* Mk90B
  MRH 8 AS550 *Fennec* (ISR) (4 more non-operational)
  TPT • Medium 14 AW101 *Merlin* (8 SAR; 6 Tpt)
MSL
  AAM • IR AIM-9L; **IIR** AIM-9X; **ARH** AIM-120 AMRAAM
  ASM AGM-65 *Maverick*

BOMBS
  LGB/INS/GPS-guided: GBU-31 JDAM; EGBU-12/GBU-24 *Paveway* LGB

Control and Air Defence Group

1 Control and Reporting Centre, 1 Mobile Control and Reporting Centre. 4 Radar sites.

Reserves

Home Guard (Army) 40,800 reservists (to age 50)
FORCES BY ROLE
MANOEUVRE
  Light
  2 regt cbt gp (3 mot inf bn, 1 arty bn)
  5 (local) def region (up to 2 mot inf bn)

Home Guard (Navy) 4,500 reservists (to age 50) organised into 30 Home Guard units
EQUIPMENT BY TYPE
PATROL AND COASTAL COMBATANTS 31
  PB 31: 18 MHV800; 1 MHV850; 12 MHV900

Home Guard (Air Force) 5,300 reservists (to age 50)

Home Guard (Service Corps) 2,900 reservists

Cyber

Denmark has a national CERT. Within the army, the 3rd Electronic Warfare Company is in charge of exploiting and disrupting enemy communications. A cyber-warfare unit within the Defence Intelligence Service is planned, with the aim of protecting military technology.

DEPLOYMENT

Legal provisions for foreign deployment:
Constitution: Codified constitution (1849)
Decision on deployment of troops abroad: On approval by the parliament (Art. 19 II)

AFGHANISTAN
NATO • ISAF 145

GULF OF ADEN & SOMALI BASIN
NATO • *Operation Ocean Shield* 1 AG; 1 CL-604 (MP)

KUWAIT
140; 7 F-16AM *Fighting Falcon*

LIBERIA
UN • UNMIL 2; 3 obs

MALI
UN • MINUSCA 10 obs

MIDDLE EAST
UN • UNTSO 11 obs

POLAND
NATO • Baltic Air Policing 4 F-16AM *Fighting Falcon*

SERBIA
NATO • KFOR 43

OSCE • Kosovo 1

SOUTH SUDAN
UN • UNMISS 13; 2 obs

UKRAINE
OSCE • Ukraine 9

Estonia EST

Euro € [a]		2013	2014	2015
GDP	€	18.7bn	19.5bn	
	US$	24.9bn	26.4bn	
per capita	US$	18,852	19,777	
Growth	%	1.6	1.2	
Inflation	%	3.2	0.8	
Def Exp [a]	€	361m		
	US$	480m		
Def bdgt [b]	€	361m	384m	402m
	US$	480m	520m	
FMA (US)	US$	2.4m	2.4m	1.5m
US$1=€		0.75	0.74	

[a] NATO definition
[b] Includes military pensions

Population 1,257,921

Age	0–14	15–19	20–24	25–29	30–64	65 plus
Male	8.0%	2.5%	3.2%	3.9%	21.7%	6.2%
Female	7.6%	2.3%	3.1%	3.9%	25.1%	12.4%

Capabilities

Estonia's defence concerns were highlighted in 2014 by Russia's annexation of Crimea and the conflict in Ukraine. The country has small, land-focused armed forces and is wholly dependent on NATO for defence from state-level external threats. Strongly supportive of the Alliance, the government provided an additional air base, at Amari, for NATO's Baltic Air Policing mission, which enabled an increase in the number of aircraft allocated to this task. The Estonian air unit, however, has no air-defence-capable aircraft. Estonian defence officials also suggested that, in response to the Russian intervention in Ukraine, NATO could consider permanently stationing NATO ground forces in the Baltic region. Estonian personnel have participated in ISAF and UN peacekeeping missions, and the armed forces are also part of the EU's Nordic Battlegroup. As part of its 2013–22 defence-development plan, the defence ministry began discussions in mid-2014 to buy the *Javelin* anti-armour missile for both infantry and the Defence League's territorial defence units. The cabinet in March 2014 stated it intended to maintain defence expenditure at 2% of GDP, in line with NATO's target. Alliance partner states conducted military exercises in Estonia in 2014, including bolstered air-policing activity, while US troops and armour deployed as part of the US *Operation Atlantic Resolve*.

ACTIVE 5,750 (Army 5,300 Navy 200 Air 250)
Defence League 12,000

Conscript liability 8 months, officers and some specialists 11 months. (Conscripts cannot be deployed.)

RESERVE 30,000 (Joint 30,000)

ORGANISATIONS BY SERVICE

Army 2,800; 2,500 conscript (total 5,300)
4 def region. All units except one inf bn are reserve based

FORCES BY ROLE
MANOEUVRE
　Reconnaissance
　1 recce bn
　Light
　1 (1st) bde (2 inf bn, 1 CSS bn)
　3 indep inf bn
COMBAT SUPPORT
　1 arty bn
　1 AD bn
　1 engr bn
　1 sigs bn
COMBAT SERVICE SUPPORT
　1 log bn

Defence League 12,000
15 Districts

EQUIPMENT BY TYPE
APC 144
　APC (W) 137: 56 XA-180 *Sisu*; 66 XA-188 *Sisu*; 15 BTR-80
　PPV 7 *Mamba*
ARTY 376
　TOWED 66: **122mm** 42 D-30 (H 63); **155mm** 24 FH-70
　MOR 310: **81mm** 131: 41 B455; 10 NM 95; 80 M252; **120mm** 179: 14 2B11; 165 41D
AT
　MSL • MANPAT Milan; IMI MAPATS
　RCL 160+; **106mm**: 30 M40A1; **84mm** *Carl Gustav*; **90mm** 130 PV-1110
AD • SAM • MANPAD *Mistral*

Navy 200
EQUIPMENT BY TYPE
PATROL AND COASTAL COMBATANTS • PB 1 *Ristna* (FIN *Rihtniemi*) with 2 RBU 1200
MINE WARFARE • MINE COUNTERMEASURES 4
　MCD 1 *Tasuja* (DNK *Lindormen*)
　MHC 3 *Admiral Cowan* (UK *Sandown*)

Air Force 250
Flying hours 120 hrs/year

FORCES BY ROLE
TRANSPORT
　1 sqn with An-2 *Colt*
TRANSPORT HELICOPTER
　1 sqn with R-44 *Raven* II
EQUIPMENT BY TYPE
AIRCRAFT • TPT • Light 2 An-2 *Colt*
HELICOPTERS • TPT • Light 4 R-44 *Raven* II

Paramilitary

Border Guard
The Estonian Border Guard is subordinate to the Ministry of the Interior. Air support is provided by the Estonian Border Guard Aviation Corps.

EQUIPMENT BY TYPE
PATROL AND COASTAL COMBATANTS 22
  PCO 1 *Kindral Kurvits*
  PCC 1 *Kou* (FIN *Silma*)
  PB 9: 1 *Maru* (FIN *Viima*); 8 (other)
  PBR 11
AMPHIBIOUS • LANDING CRAFT • LCU 2
LOGISTICS & SUPPORT • AGF 1 *Balsam*
AIRCRAFT • TPT • Light 2 L-410
HELICOPTERS • TPT • 3 AW139

Cyber
Estonia established CERT-ee in 2006 and has further developed its cyber-security infrastructure after the cyber attacks of 2007. It adopted a national Cyber Security Strategy in 2008. As well as domestic capacities, Tallinn hosts the NATO Cooperative Cyber Security Centre of Excellence, established in 2008 to enhance NATO's cyber-defence capability.

DEPLOYMENT

Legal provisions for foreign deployment:
Constitution: Codified constitution (1992)
Decision on deployment of troops abroad: By parliament (Art. 128). Also, International Military Cooperation Act stipulates conditions for deployment abroad. For collective defence purposes, ratification of the North Atlantic Treaty is considered a parliamentary decision that would allow cabinet to deploy troops. The president, chairman of the parliament and chairman of the parliament's State Defence Commission shall be immediately informed of such a decision. For other international operations, a separate parliamentary decision is necessary: the Ministry of Defence prepares a draft legal act and coordinates this with the Ministry of Foreign Affairs and the Ministry of Justice. It also asks the opinion of the chief of defence. The draft is then proposed to cabinet for approval and submission for parliamentary consideration.

AFGHANISTAN
NATO • ISAF 4

MALI
EU • EUTM Mali 8
UN • MINUSMA 2

MIDDLE EAST
UN • UNTSO 3 obs

MOLDOVA
OSCE • Moldova 1

NORTH SEA
NATO • SNMCMG 1: 1 MHC

SERBIA
NATO • KFOR 2

UKRAINE
OSCE • Ukraine 7

FOREIGN FORCES
Germany NATO Baltic Air Policing 6 Eurofighter *Typhoon*

Finland FIN

Euro €		2013	2014	2015
GDP	€	201bn	204bn	
	US$	267bn	276bn	
per capita	US$	49,055	50,451	
Growth	%	-1.2	-0.2	
Inflation	%	2.2	1.2	
Def exp [a]	€	2.82bn		
	US$	3.75bn		
Def bdgt	€	2.87bn	2.75bn	2.69bn
	US$	3.81bn	3.72bn	
US$1=€		0.75	0.74	

[a] Excludes military pensions

Population 5,268,799

Age	0 – 14	15 – 19	20 – 24	25 – 29	30 – 64	65 plus
Male	8.0%	3.0%	3.2%	3.1%	23.3%	8.3%
Female	7.8%	2.9%	3.1%	2.9%	22.9%	11.5%

Capabilities

Finland's security and defence policy is based on national territorial defence, bilateral and multilateral cooperation, and general conscription. A debate as to whether Helsinki should apply for NATO membership was rekindled by the crisis in Ukraine during 2014. A reform process begun in 2011, including structural cuts, was due to conclude by 2015, though it was not known by late 2014 whether elements of the plan might be reconsidered. Senior military officials have expressed concern about pressure on resources, and about the ability of the armed forces to effectively meet all of their allocated tasks. Increased defence cooperation with Sweden is being pursued as a means of increasing defence efficiency. All three services exercise routinely, with the air force and navy also increasingly involved in multilateral exercises. The armed forces have an intra-theatre transport capacity, but much beyond national boundaries this would be dependent on international partners. Finland is a participant in NORDEFCO, an EU member and a NATO partner state.

ACTIVE 22,200 (Army 16,000 Navy 3,500 Air 2,700)
Paramilitary 2,800
Conscript liability 6–9–12 months (12 months for officers NCOs and soldiers with special duties.) Conscript service was reduced by 15 days in early 2013.

RESERVE 354,000 (Army 285,000 Navy 31,000 Air 38,000) **Paramilitary 11,500**
25,000 reservists a year do refresher training: total obligation 40 days (75 for NCOs, 100 for officers) between conscript service and age 50 (NCOs and officers to age 60).

ORGANISATIONS BY SERVICE

Army 5,000; 11,000 conscript (total 16,000)
FORCES BY ROLE
Finland's army maintains a mobilisation strength of about 285,000. In support of this requirement, two conscription cycles, each for about 15,000 conscripts, take place each year. After conscript training, reservist commitment is to the age of 60. Reservists are usually assigned to units within their local geographical area. All service appointments or deployments outside Finnish borders are voluntary for all members of the armed services. All brigades are reserve based.

Reserve Organisations
60,000 in manoeuvre forces and 225,000 in territorial forces
FORCES BY ROLE
SPECIAL FORCES
  1 SF bn
MANOEUVRE
  Armoured
    2 armd BG (regt)
  Mechanised
    2 (Karelia & Pori Jaeger) mech bde
  Light
    3 (Jaeger) bde
    6 lt inf bde
  Aviation
    1 hel bn
COMBAT SUPPORT
  1 arty bde
  1 AD regt
  7 engr regt
  3 sigs bn
COMBAT SERVICE SUPPORT
  Some log unit
EQUIPMENT BY TYPE
MBT 100 *Leopard* 2A4
AIFV 212: 110 BMP-2; 102 CV90
APC 613
  APC (T) 142: 40 MT-LBu; 102 MT-LBV
  APC (W) 471: 260 XA-180/185 *Sisu*; 101 XA-202 *Sisu*; 48 XA-203 *Sisu*; 62 AMV (XA-360)
ARTY 647
  SP 122mm 36 2S1 (PsH 74)
  TOWED 324: **122mm** 234 D-30 (H 63); **130mm** 36 K 54; **155mm** 54 K 83/K 98
  MRL 227mm 22 M270 MLRS
  MOR 120mm 265: 261 KRH 92; 4 XA-361 AMOS
AT • MSL • MANPATS *Spike*; TOW 2
HELICOPTERS
  MRH 7: 5 Hughes 500D; 2 Hughes 500E
  TPT • Medium 16 NH90 TTH
UAV • ISR • Medium 11 ADS-95 *Ranger*
AD
  SAM
    SP 60+: 16 ASRAD (ITO 05); 20 *Crotale* NG (ITO 90); 24 NASAMS II FIN (ITO 12); 9K37 *Buk*-M1 (ITO 96)
    MANPAD FIM-92A *Stinger* (ITO 15); RBS 70 (ITO 05/05M)
  GUNS 400+: **23mm; 35mm**
AEV 6 *Leopard* 2R CEV
ARV 27: 15 MTP-LB; 12 VT-55A
VLB 15+: BLG-60M2; 6 *Leopard* 2L; 9 SISU *Leguan*
MW *Aardvark* Mk 2; KMT T-55; RA-140 DS

Navy 1,600; 1,900 conscript (total 3,500)
FORCES BY ROLE
Naval Command HQ located at Turku; with two subordinate Naval Commands (Gulf of Finland and Archipelago Sea); 1 Naval bde; 3 spt elm (Naval Materiel Cmd, Naval Academy, Naval Research Institute)
EQUIPMENT BY TYPE
PATROL AND COASTAL COMBATANTS 8
  PBG 4 *Rauma* with 6 RBS-15SF3 (15SF) AShM
  PCG 4 *Hamina* with 4 RBS-15 (15SF) AShM, 1 octuple VLS with *Umkhonto* SAM, 1 57mm gun
MINE WARFARE 19
  MINE COUNTERMEASURES 10
    MHSO 3 *Katanpää* (expected FOC 2016/17)
    MSI 7: 4 *Kiiski*; 3 *Kuha*
  MINELAYERS • ML 6:
    2 *Hameenmaa* with 1 octuple VLS with *Umkhonto* SAM, 2 RBU 1200, up to 100–120 mines, 1 57mm gun
    3 *Pansio* with 50 mines
AMPHIBIOUS • LANDING CRAFT 51
  LCU 1 *Kampela*
  LCP 50
LOGISTICS AND SUPPORT 29
  AG 3: 1 *Louhi*; 2 *Hylje*
  AGB 7 (Board of Navigation control)
  AKSL 6: 4 *Hila*; 2 *Valas*
  AX 4: 3 *Fabian Wrede*; 1 *Lokki*
  YFB 6
  YTM 1 *Haukipaa*

Coastal Defence
ARTY • COASTAL • 130mm 30 K-53tk (static)
MSL • TACTICAL • 4 RBS-15K AShM

Air Force 1,950; 750 conscript (total 2,700)
3 Air Comds: Satakunta (West), Karelia (East), Lapland (North)

Flying hours 90–140 hrs/year

FORCES BY ROLE
FIGHTER/GROUND ATTACK
  3 sqn with F/A-18C/D *Hornet*
ISR
  1 (survey) sqn with Learjet 35A
TRANSPORT
  1 flt with C-295M
  4 (liaison) flt with PC-12NG
TRAINING
  1 sqn with *Hawk* Mk50/51A/66* (air defence and ground attack trg)
  1 unit with L-70 *Vinka*
EQUIPMENT BY TYPE
AIRCRAFT 107 combat capable
  FGA 62: 55 F/A-18C *Hornet*; 7 F/A-18D *Hornet*
  MP 1 F-27-400M

ELINT 1 C-295M
TPT • Light 11: 2 C-295M; 3 Learjet 35A (survey; ECM trg; tgt-tow); 6 PC-12NG
TRG 73: 29 *Hawk* Mk50/51A*; 16 *Hawk* Mk66*; 28 L-70 *Vinka*
MSL • AAM • IR AIM-9 *Sidewinder*; IIR AIM-9X *Sidewinder*; ARH AIM-120 AMRAAM

Paramilitary

Border Guard 2,800
Ministry of Interior. 4 Border Guard Districts and 2 Coast Guard Districts
FORCES BY ROLE
MARITIME PATROL
  1 sqn with Do-228 (maritime surv); AS332 *Super Puma*; Bell 412 (AB-412) *Twin Huey*; Bell 412EP (AB-412EP) *Twin Huey*; AW119KE *Koala*
EQUIPMENT BY TYPE
PATROL AND COASTAL COMBATANTS 52
  PCO 1 *Turva*
  PCC 3: 2 *Tursas*; 1 *Merikarhu*
  PB 48
AMPHIBIOUS • LANDING CRAFT • LCAC 7
AIRCRAFT • TPT • Light 2 Do-228
HELICOPTERS
  MRH 5: 4 Bell 412 (AB-412) *Twin Huey*; 1 Bell 412EP (AB-412EP) *Twin Huey*
  TPT 7: Medium 3 AS332 *Super Puma*; Light 4 AW119KE *Koala*

Reserve 11,500 reservists on mobilisation

Cyber

Finland published a national cyber-security strategy in 2013 and published an implementation programme for this in 2014. In accordance with the strategy the FDF will create a comprehensive cyber-defence capacity for their statutory tasks. A military cyber-defence capacity encompasses intelligence as well as cyber-attack and cyber-defence capabilities.

DEPLOYMENT

Legal provisions for foreign deployment:
Specific legislation: 'Act on Military Crisis Management (211/2006).
Decision on deployment of troops abroad: The President of the Republic upon proposal by the Council of State (Act on Military Crisis Management (211/2006), paragraph 2). Before making the proposal the Council of State must consult the Parliament (Act on Military Crisis Management (211/2006), paragraph 3).

AFGHANISTAN
NATO • ISAF 88

BOSNIA-HERZEGOVINA
EU • EUFOR • *Operation Althea* 8
OSCE • Bosnia and Herzegovina 1

CENTRAL AFRICAN REPUBLIC
EU • EUFOR RCA 30; 1 CIMIC unit; 1 EOD unit

INDIA/PAKISTAN
UN • UNMOGIP 6 obs

LEBANON
UN • UNIFIL 344; elm 1 mech inf bn

LIBERIA
UN • UNMIL 3; 1 obs

MALI
EU • EUTM Mali 12
UN • MINUSMA 6

MIDDLE EAST
UN • UNTSO 18 obs

SERBIA
NATO • KFOR 22
OSCE • Kosovo 2

UGANDA
EU • EUTM Somalia 10

UKRAINE
OSCE • Ukraine 21

France FRA

Euro €		2013	2014	2015
GDP	€	2.11tr	2.14tr	
	US$	2.81tr	2.9tr	
per capita	US$	44,099	45,384	
Growth	%	0.3	0.4	
Inflation	%	1.0	0.7	
Def exp [a]	€	39.4bn		
	US$	52.3bn		
Def bdgt [b]	€	39.4bn	39.2bn	
	US$	52.3bn	53.1bn	
US$1=€		0.75	0.74	

[a] NATO definition
[b] Includes pensions

Population 66,259,012

Age	0–14	15–19	20–24	25–29	30–64	65 plus
Male	9.6%	3.0%	3.0%	3.1%	22.4%	7.8%
Female	9.1%	2.9%	2.9%	3.0%	22.7%	10.5%

Capabilities

The 2013 *Livre Blanc* attempts to sustain France's ambition to retain the full spectrum of military capabilities, but with reductions in personnel and equipment. Despite cuts, France remains one of the two pre-eminent defence powers in Europe, maintaining rapidly deployable armed forces, capable of self-sustainment and operation. This capacity was evident during *Opération Serval* in Mali and *Sangaris* in CAR. Also apparent were weaknesses, such as strategic lift and ISR. The latter capability gap was rapidly addressed by the purchase of *Reaper* UAVs, with associated systems. The size of the forces for such tasks, however, is being reduced. The 2008 *Livre Blanc* identified a ground-force deployment of up to 30,000; the 2013 document reduced this to 15,000. One of the army's medium brigades is to be disbanded, but the ambitious *Scorpion* army-modernisation plan continues. Similarly, combat aircraft earmarked for rapid deployment are to be cut from 70 to 45. Funding plans for 2014–19 reduced the number of *Rafale* aircraft to be purchased over the period to 26 (from 66). Strategic airlift will be strengthened with the delivery of the A400M *Atlas*, the first of which was accepted by the air force in August 2013. There are also plans to acquire 12 A330-based tankers to replace the KC-135. These platforms will support France's ability to project power on a global scale. Substantial overseas deployments are maintained, and all the services exercise regularly and jointly at the national level, while also participating in a broad range of international exercises. A particular focus has been France–UK exercises to develop mutual interoperability. (See pp. 64–68.)

ACTIVE 215,000 (Army 115,000 Navy 36,750 Air 45,500, Other Staffs 17,750) Paramilitary 103,400

RESERVE 27,650 (Army 15,400, Navy 4,850, Air 4,350, Other Staffs 3,050) Paramilitary 40,000

ORGANISATIONS BY SERVICE

Strategic Nuclear Forces

Navy 2,200
SUBMARINES • STRATEGIC • SSBN 4
  2 *Le Triomphant* with 16 M45 SLBM with 6 TN-75 nuclear warheads, 4 single 533mm TT with F17 Mod 2 HWT/SM-39 *Exocet* AShM
  2 *Le Triomphant* with 16 M51 SLBM with 6 TN-75 nuclear warheads, 4 single 533mm TT with F17 Mod 2 HWT/SM-39 *Exocet* AShM
AIRCRAFT • FGA 20 *Rafale* M F3 with ASMP-A msl

Air Force 1,800

Air Strategic Forces Command
FORCES BY ROLE
STRIKE
  1 sqn with *Mirage* 2000N with ASMP/ASMP-A msl
  1 sqn with *Rafale* B F3 with ASMP/ASMP-A msl
TANKER
  1 sqn with C-135FR; KC-135 *Stratotanker*

EQUIPMENT BY TYPE
AIRCRAFT 43 combat capable
  FGA 43: 23 *Mirage* 2000N; 20 *Rafale* B F3
  TKR/TPT 11 C-135FR
  TKR 3 KC-135 *Stratotanker*

Paramilitary

Gendarmerie 40

Space
SATELLITES 8
  COMMUNICATIONS 2 *Syracuse*-3 (designed to integrate with UK *Skynet* & ITA *Sicral*)
  ISR 4: 2 *Helios* (2A/2B); 2 *Pleiades*
  EARLY WARNING 2 *Spirale*

Army 115,000 (incl 7,300 Foreign Legion; 12,800 Marines)
Regt and BG normally bn size
FORCES BY ROLE
COMMAND
  2 (task force) HQ
MANOEUVRE
  Reconnaissance
  1 ISR bde (1 recce regt, 1 UAV regt, 2 EW regt, 1 int bn)
  Armoured
  1 armd bde (1 armd regt, 2 armd inf regt, 1 MLRS regt, 1 AD regt, 1 engr regt)
  1 armd bde (2 armd regt, 2 armd inf regt, 1 SP arty regt, 1 engr regt)
  Mechanised
  1 lt armd bde (1 armd cav regt, 2 mech inf regt, 1 SP arty regt, 1 engr regt)
  1 (FRA/GER) mech bde (1 armd cav regt, 1 mech inf regt)
  1 mech inf bde (1 armd cav regt, 1 armd inf regt, 1 mech inf regt, 1 SP arty regt, 1 engr regt)
  1 mech inf bde (1 armd cav regt, 1 armd inf regt, 1 SP arty regt, 1 engr regt)
  1 mech BG (UAE)
  1 mech regt (Djibouti)
  Light
  2 regt (French Guiana)
  1 regt (New Caledonia)
  1 coy (Mayotte)
  Air Manoeuvre
  1 AB bde (1 armd cav regt, 4 para regt, 1 arty regt, 1 engr regt, 1 spt regt)
  1 AB regt (Réunion)
  1 AB bn (Gabon)
  Amphibious
  1 lt armd bde (1 armd cav regt, 2 mech inf regt, 1 SP arty regt, 1 engr regt)
  Mountain
  1 mtn bde (1 armd cav regt, 3 mech inf regt, 1 arty regt, 1 engr regt)
  Aviation
  3 avn regt
  Other
  4 SMA regt (French Guiana, French West Indies & Indian Ocean)
  3 SMA coy (French Polynesia, Indian Ocean & New Caledonia)
COMBAT SUPPORT
  1 CBRN regt
  1 sigs bde (5 sigs regt)
COMBAT SERVICE SUPPORT
  1 log bde (5 tpt regt, 1 log regt, 1 med regt)
  3 trg regt

Special Operation Forces 2,200
FORCES BY ROLE
SPECIAL FORCES
  2 SF regt
MANOEUVRE
  Aviation
  1 avn regt

Reserves 16,000 reservists
Reservists form 79 UIR (Reserve Intervention Units) of about 75 to 152 troops, for 'Proterre' – combined land projection forces bn, and 23 USR (Reserve Specialised Units) of about 160 troops, in specialised regt.

EQUIPMENT BY TYPE
MBT 200 *Leclerc*
RECCE 1,868: 248 AMX-10RC; 110 ERC-90F4 *Sagaie*; 40 VAB Reco NBC; 1,470 VBL M-ll
AIFV 630 VBCI (inc 110 VCP)
APC 3,157
  APC (T) 53 BvS-10
  APC (W) 3,086: 3,000 VAB; 60 VAB BOA; 26 VAB NBC
  PPV 18: 14 *Aravis*; 4 *Buffalo*
ARTY 323
  SP 155mm 114: 37 AU-F-1; 77 CAESAR
  TOWED 155mm 43 TR-F-1
  MRL 227mm 26 MLRS
  MOR 140+: **81mm** LRR 81mm; **120mm** 140 RT-F1
AT • MSL
  SP 325: 30 VAB HOT; 110 VAB *Milan*; 185 VAB *Eryx*
  MANPATS *Javelin*; *Milan*
AIRCRAFT • TPT • Light 16: 5 PC-6B *Turbo Porter*; 8 TBM-700; 3 TBM-700B
HELICOPTERS
  ATK 45: 39 EC665 *Tiger* HAP; 6 EC665 *Tiger* HAD
  MRH 127 SA341F/342M *Gazelle* (all variants)
  TPT 132: **Heavy** 8 EC725AP *Caracal* (CSAR); **Medium** 124: 23 AS532UL *Cougar*; 13 NH90 TTH; 88 SA330 *Puma*; **Light** 35 EC120B *Colibri*
UAV • ISR • Medium 20 SDTI (*Sperwer*)
AD • SAM • MANPAD *Mistral*
RADAR • LAND 66: 10 *Cobra*; 56 RASIT/RATAC
AEV 56 AMX-30EBG
ARV 76+: 58 AMX-30D; 18 *Leclerc* DNG; VAB-EHC
VLB 67: 39 EFA; 18 PTA; 10 SPRAT
MW 20+: AMX-30B/B2; 20 *Minotaur*

Navy 37,850 (incl 2,200 opcon Strategic Nuclear Forces)

EQUIPMENT BY TYPE
SUBMARINES 10
  STRATEGIC • SSBN 4:
    2 *Le Triomphant* opcon Strategic Nuclear Forces with 16 M45 SLBM with 6 TN-75 nuclear warheads, 4 single 533mm TT with F17 Mod 2 HWT/SM-39 *Exocet* AShM (currently undergoing modernisation programme to install M51 SLBM; expected completion 2018)
    2 *Le Triomphant* opcon Strategic Nuclear Forces with 16 M51 SLBM with 6 TN-75 nuclear warheads, 4 single 533mm TT with F17 Mod 2 HWT/SM-39 *Exocet* AShM

  TACTICAL • SSN 6:
    6 *Rubis* with 4 single 533mm TT with F-17 HWT/SM-39 *Exocet* AShM
PRINCIPAL SURFACE COMBATANTS 23
  AIRCRAFT CARRIERS 1
    CVN 1 *Charles de Gaulle* with 4 octuple VLS with *Aster* 15 SAM, 2 sextuple *Sadral* lnchr with *Mistral* SAM (capacity 35–40 *Super Etendard/Rafale* M/E-2C *Hawkeye*/AS365 *Dauphin*)
  DESTROYERS • DDGHM 11:
    2 *Cassard* with 2 quad lnchr with MM-40 *Exocet* Block 2 AShM, 1 Mk13 GMLS with SM-1MR SAM, 2 sextuple *Sadral* lnchr with *Mistral* SAM, 2 single 533mm ASTT with L5 HWT, 1 100mm gun (capacity 1 AS565SA *Panther* ASW hel)
    2 *Forbin* with 2 quad lnchr with MM-40 *Exocet* Block 3 AShM, 1 48-cell VLS with *Aster* 15/*Aster* 30 SAM, 2 twin 324mm ASTT with MU-90, 2 76mm gun (capacity 1 NH90 TTH hel)
    1 *Georges Leygues* with 2 twin lnchr with MM-38 *Exocet* AShM, 1 octuple lnchr with *Crotale* SAM, 2 sextuple *Sadral* lnchr with *Mistral* SAM, 2 single 533mm ASTT with L5 HWT, 1 100mm gun (capacity 2 *Lynx* hel)
    2 *Georges Leygues* with 2 quad lnchr with MM-40 *Exocet* AShM, 1 octuple lnchr with *Crotale* SAM, , 2 sextuple *Sadral* lnchr with *Mistral* SAM, 2 single 533mm ASTT with L5 HWT, 1 100mm gun (capacity 2 *Lynx* hel)
    3 *Georges Leygues* (mod) with 2 quad lnchr with MM-40 *Exocet* AShM, 1 octuple lnchr with *Crotale* SAM, 2 twin *Simbad* lnchr with *Mistral* SAM, 2 single 324mm ASTT with MU90 LWT, 1 100mm gun (capacity 2 *Lynx* hel)
    1 *Aquitaine* with 2 octuple *Sylver* A70 VLS with MdCN (SCALP Naval) LACM, 2 quad lnchr with MM-40 *Exocet* Block 3 AShM, 2 octuple *Sylver* A43 VLS with *Aster* 15 SAM, 2 twin B515 324mm ASTT with MU90 LWT, 1 76mm gun (capacity 1 NH90 NFH hel)
  FRIGATES • FFGHM 11:
    6 *Floreal* with 2 single lnchr with MM-38 *Exocet* AShM, 1 twin *Simbad* lnchr with *Mistral* SAM, 1 100mm gun (capacity 1 AS565SA *Panther* hel)
    5 *La Fayette* with 2 quad lnchr with MM-40 *Exocet* Block 3 AShM, 1 octuple lnchr with *Crotale* SAM, (space for fitting 2 octuple VLS lnchr for *Aster* 15/30), 1 100mm gun (capacity 1 AS565SA *Panther*/SA321 *Super Frelon* hel)
PATROL AND COASTAL COMBATANTS 21
  FSM 9 *D'Estienne d'Orves* with 1 twin *Simbad* lnchr with *Mistral* SAM, 4 single ASTT, 1 100mm gun
  PCC 7: 4 *L'Audacieuse* (all deployed in the Pacific or Caribbean); 3 *Flamant*
  PCO 4: 1 *Lapérouse*; 1 *Le Malin*; 1 *Fulmar*; 1 *Gowind* (owned by private company DCNS; currently operated by French Navy)
  PSO 1 *Albatros*
MINE WARFARE • MINE COUNTERMEASURES 18
  MCS 7: 3 *Antares* (used as route survey vessels); 4 *Vulcain* (used as mine diving tenders)
  MHO 11 *Éridan*

AMPHIBIOUS
  PRINCIPAL AMPHIBIOUS SHIPS 4
    LHD 3 *Mistral* with 2 twin *Simbad* lnchr with *Mistral* SAM, (capacity up to 16 NH90/SA330 *Puma*/AS532 *Cougar*/EC665 *Tiger* hel; 2 LCAC or 4 LCM; 60 AFVs; 450 troops)
    LPD 1 *Foudre* with 2 twin *Simbad* lnchr with *Mistral* SAM, (capacity 4 AS532 *Cougar*; either 2 LCT or 10 LCM; 22 tanks; 470 troops)
    LANDING SHIPS • LST 2 *Batral* (capacity 12 trucks; 140 troops)
    LANDING CRAFT 41
      LCT 5: 1 CDIC; 4 EDA-R
      LCM 11 CTM
      LCVP 25
  LOGISTICS AND SUPPORT 145
    ABU 1 *Telenn Mor*
    AE 1 *Denti*
    AFS 1 *Revi*
    AG 4: 1 *Lapérouse* (used as trials ships for mines and divers); 3 *Chamois*
    AGE 1 *Corraline*
    AGI 1 *Dupuy de Lome*
    AGM 1 *Monge*
    AGOR 2: 1 *Pourquoi pas?* (used 150 days per year by Ministry of Defence; operated by Ministry of Research and Education otherwise); 1 *Beautemps-beaupré*
    AGS 3 *Lapérouse*
    AORH 4 *Durance* with 1-3 twin *Simbad* lnchr with *Mistral* SAM (capacity 1 SA319 *Alouette* III/AS365 *Dauphin*/*Lynx*)
    ATA 2 *Malabar*
    AXL 12: 8 *Léopard*; 2 *Glycine*; 2 *Engageante*
    AXS 4: 2 *La Belle Poule*; 2 other
    YAG 2 *Phaéton* (towed array tenders)
    YD 5
    YDT 10: 1 *Alize*; 9 VIP 21
    YFB 2 VTP
    YFL 9 V14
    YFRT 2 *Athos*
    YFU 8
    YGS 7 VH8
    YTB 3 *Bélier*
    YTL 34: 4 RP10; 4 PSS10; 26 PS4
    YTM 21: 3 *Maïto*; 16 *Fréhel*; 2 *Esterel*
    YTR 5: 3 *Avel Aber*; 2 *Las*

Naval Aviation 6,500

Flying hours 180–220 hrs/yr on strike/FGA ac

FORCES BY ROLE
STRIKE/FIGHTER/GROUND ATTACK
  2 sqn with *Rafale* M F3
FIGHTER/GROUND ATTACK
  1 sqn with *Super Etendard Modernisé*
ANTI-SURFACE WARFARE
  1 sqn with AS565SA *Panther*
ANTI-SUBMARINE WARFARE
  2 sqn (forming) with NH90 NFH
  1 sqn with *Lynx* Mk4
MARITIME PATROL
  2 sqn with *Atlantique* 2
  1 sqn with *Falcon* 20H *Gardian*
  1 sqn with *Falcon* 50MI
AIRBORNE EARLY WARNING & CONTROL
  1 sqn with E-2C *Hawkeye*
SEARCH & RESCUE
  1 sqn with AS365N/F *Dauphin* 2
  1 sqn with EC225
TRAINING
  1 sqn with SA319B *Alouette* III
  1 unit with *Falcon* 10 M
  1 unit with CAP 10; EMB 121 *Xingu*; MS-880 *Rallye*

EQUIPMENT BY TYPE
AIRCRAFT 74 combat capable
  FGA 55: 34 *Rafale* M F3; 21 *Super Etendard Modernisé*
  ASW 12 *Atlantique* 2 (10 more in store)
  AEW&C 3 E-2C *Hawkeye*
  SAR 1 *Falcon* 50MS
  TPT 26: **Light** 11 EMB-121 *Xingu*; **PAX** 15: 6 *Falcon* 10MER; 5 *Falcon* 20H *Gardian*; 4 *Falcon* 50MI
  TRG 14: 7 CAP 10; 7 MS-880 *Rallye**
HELICOPTERS
  ASW 31: 20 *Lynx* Mk4; 11 NH90 NFH
  MRH 49: 9 AS365N/F/SP *Dauphin* 2; 2 AS365N3; 16 AS565SA *Panther*; 22 SA319B *Alouette* III
  TPT • **Medium** 2 EC225 *Super Puma*
MSL
  AAM • **IR** R-550 *Magic* 2; **IIR** *Mica* IR; **ARH** *Mica* RF
  AShM AM-39 *Exocet*
  ASM ASMP-A; AS-30 *Laser*; AASM

Marines 2,000

Commando Units 550
FORCES BY ROLE
MANOEUVRE
  Reconnaissance
  1 recce gp
  Amphibious
  2 aslt gp
  1 atk swimmer gp
  1 raiding gp
  COMBAT SUPPORT
  1 cbt spt gp

Fusiliers-Marin 1,450
FORCES BY ROLE
MANOEUVRE
  Other
  2 sy gp
  7 sy coy

Public Service Force

Naval personnel performing general coast-guard, fishery-protection, SAR, anti-pollution and traffic surveillance duties. Command exercised through Maritime Prefectures (Premar): Manche (Cherbourg), Atlantique (Brest), Méditerranée (Toulon).

FORCES BY ROLE
MARITIME PATROL
  1 sqn with *Falcon* 50M; *Falcon* 200 *Gardian*

EQUIPMENT BY TYPE
PATROL AND COASTAL COMBATANTS 6
  PSO 1 *Albatros*
  PCO 1 *Arago*
  PCC 4: 3 *Flamant*; 1 *Grèbe*
AIRCRAFT • MP 9: 4 *Falcon* 50M; 5 *Falcon* 200 *Gardian*
HELICOPTERS • MRH 4 AS365 *Dauphin* 2

Reserves 5,500 reservists

Air Force 47,550

Flying hours 180 hrs/year

Strategic Forces
FORCES BY ROLE
STRIKE
  1 sqn with *Mirage* 2000N with ASMP/ASMP-A msl
  1 sqn with *Rafale* B F3 with ASMP/ASMP-A msl
TANKER
  1 sqn with C-135FR; KC-135 *Stratotanker*
EQUIPMENT BY TYPE
AIRCRAFT 43 combat capable
  FGA 43: 23 *Mirage* 2000N; 20 *Rafale* B F3
  TKR/TPT 11 C-135FR
  TKR 3 KC-135 *Stratotanker*

Combat Brigade
FORCES BY ROLE
FIGHTER
  1 sqn with *Mirage* 2000-5
  1 sqn with *Mirage* 2000B/C
FIGHTER/GROUND ATTACK
  3 sqn with *Mirage* 2000D
  1 (composite) sqn with *Mirage* 2000C/D (Djibouti)
  2 sqn with *Rafale* B/C F3
  1 sqn with *Rafale* B/C F3 (UAE)
ELECTRONIC WARFARE
  1 flt with C-160G *Gabriel* (ESM)
TRAINING
  1 OCU sqn with *Mirage* 2000D
  1 OCU sqn with *Rafale* B/C F3
  1 (aggressor) sqn with *Alpha Jet**
  4 sqn with *Alpha Jet**
ISR UAV
  1 sqn with *Harfang*
EQUIPMENT BY TYPE
AIRCRAFT 235 combat capable
  FTR 40: 34 *Mirage* 2000-5/2000C; 6 *Mirage* 2000B
  FGA 128: 60 *Mirage* 2000D; 25 *Rafale* B F3; 43 *Rafale* C F3
  ELINT 2 C-160G *Gabriel* (ESM)
  TRG 67 *Alpha Jet**
  UAV • ISR • Heavy 6: 4 *Harfang*; 2 MQ-9A *Reaper*
  MSL
    AAM • IR R-550 *Magic* 2; **IIR** *Mica* IR; **SARH** *Super* 530D; **ARH** *Mica* RF
    ASM ASMP-A; AS-30L; *Apache*; AASM
    LACM SCALP EG
  BOMBS
    Laser-guided: GBU-12 *Paveway* II

Air Mobility Brigade
FORCES BY ROLE
SEARCH & RESCUE/TRANSPORT
  5 sqn with C-160R *Transall*; CN-235M; DHC-6-300 *Twin Otter*; SA330 *Puma*; AS555 *Fennec* (Djibouti, French Guiana, Gabon, Indian Ocean & New Caledonia)
TANKER/TRANSPORT
  2 sqn with C-160R *Transall*
TRANSPORT
  1 sqn with A310-300; A330; A340-200 (on lease)
  3 sqn with A400M *Atlas*; C-130H/H-30 *Hercules*; C-160R *Transall*
  2 sqn with CN-235M
  1 sqn with EMB-121
  1 sqn with *Falcon* 7X (VIP); *Falcon* 900 (VIP); *Falcon* 2000
  3 flt with TBM-700A
  1 (mixed) gp with AS532 *Cougar*; C-160 *Transall*; DHC-6-300 *Twin Otter*
TRAINING
  1 OCU sqn with SA330 *Puma*; AS555 *Fennec*
  1 OCU unit with C-160 *Transall*
TRANSPORT HELICOPTER
  2 sqn with AS555 *Fennec*
  2 sqn with AS332C/L *Super Puma*; SA330 *Puma*; EC725 *Caracal*
EQUIPMENT BY TYPE
AIRCRAFT
  TKR/TPT 20 C-160R *Transall*
  TPT 112: Heavy 5 A400M *Atlas*; Medium 25: 5 C-130H *Hercules*; 9 C-130H-30 *Hercules*; 11 C-160R *Transall*; Light 70: 19 CN-235M-100; 8 CN-235M-300; 5 DHC-6-300 *Twin Otter*; 23 EMB-121 *Xingu*; 15 TBM-700; PAX 12: 3 A310-300; 1 A330; 2 A340-200 (on lease); 2 *Falcon* 7X; 2 *Falcon* 900 (VIP); 2 *Falcon* 2000
HELICOPTERS
  MRH 37 AS555 *Fennec*
  TPT 43: Heavy 11 EC725 *Caracal*; Medium 32: 3 AS332C *Super Puma*; 4 AS332L *Super Puma*; 3 AS532UL *Cougar* (tpt/VIP); 22 SA330B *Puma*

Air Space Control Brigade
FORCES BY ROLE
SPACE
  1 (satellite obs) sqn with *Helios*
AIRBORNE EARLY WARNING & CONTROL
  1 (Surveillance & Control) sqn with E-3F *Sentry*
AIR DEFENCE
  3 sqn with *Crotale* NG; SAMP/T
  1 sqn with SAMP/T
EQUIPMENT BY TYPE
SATELLITES see Space
AIRCRAFT • AEW&C 4 E-3F *Sentry*
AD
  SAM 20: 12 *Crotale* NG; 8 SAMP/T
  GUNS 20mm 76T2
  SYSTEMS STRIDA (Control)

Security and Intervention Brigade
FORCES BY ROLE
SPECIAL FORCES
3 SF gp
MANOEUVRE
Other
24 protection units
30 fire fighting and rescue scn

Air Training Command
FORCES BY ROLE
TRAINING
3 sqn with CAP 10; Grob G120A-F; TB-30 *Epsilon*
EQUIPMENT BY TYPE
AIRCRAFT
TRG 48: 5 CAP 10; 18 Grob G120A-F; 25 TB-30 *Epsilon* (incl many in storage)

Reserves 4,750 reservists

Paramilitary 103,400

Gendarmerie 103,400; 40,000 reservists
EQUIPMENT BY TYPE
LT TK 28 VBC-90
APC (W) 153 VBRG-170
ARTY • MOR 81mm some
PATROL AND COASTAL COMBATANTS 39
PB 39: 4 *Géranium*; 1 *Glaive*; 2 VSC 14; 24 VSCM; 8 EBSLP
HELICOPTERS • TPT • Light 35: 20 EC135; 15 EC145

Customs (Direction Générale des Douanes et Droits Indirects)
EQUIPMENT BY TYPE
PATROL AND COASTAL COMBATANTS 30
PCO 2: 1 *Jacques Oudart Fourmentin*; 1 *Kermovan*
PB 28: 7 *Plascoa* 2100; 7 *Haize Hegoa*; 2 *Avel Gwalarn*; 1 *Rafenua*; 1 *Arafenua*; 1 *Vent d'Amont*; 1 *La Rance*; 8 others

Coast Guard (Direction des Affaires Maritimes)
EQUIPMENT BY TYPE
PATROL AND COASTAL COMBATANTS 25
PCO 1 *Themis*
PCC 1 *Iris*
PB 23: 4 *Callisto*; 19 others
LOGISTICS AND SUPPORT • AG 7

Cyber

The French Network and Information Security Agency (ANSSI) was established in 2009 to conduct surveillance on sensitive government networks and respond to cyber attacks. The 2008 French Defence White Paper placed emphasis on cyber threats, calling for programmes in offensive and defensive cyber-war capabilities. In July 2011, the MoD produced a classified Joint Cyber Defence Concept. Ahead of the new *Livre Blanc*, the general secretariat on defence and national security (SGDSN) released a preparatory document stressing the strategic dimension of cyber threats and confirming the development of technical capabilities to control access to cyberspace. The 2013 white paper marked 'a crucial new stage in recognition of cyber threats and development of cyber defence capabilities'. Cyber featured throughout the document and, 'for the first time, the armed forces model includes military cyber defence capabilities, in close liaison with intelligence and defensive and offensive planning, in preparation for or support of military operations'.

DEPLOYMENT

Legal provisions for foreign deployment:
Constitution: Codified constitution (1958)
Specific legislation: 'Order of 7 January 1959'
Decision on deployment of troops abroad: De jure: by the minister of defence, under authority of the PM and on agreement in council of ministers ('Order of 7 January 1959', Art. 16, Art. 20-1 of constitution)

AFGHANISTAN
NATO • ISAF 88

ARABIAN SEA & GULF OF ADEN
Combined Maritime Forces • *Operation Chammal* 1 DDGHM

BOSNIA-HERZEGOVINA
EU • EUFOR • *Operation Althea* 2

CENTRAL AFRICAN REPUBLIC
Operation Sangaris 2,000; 2 inf BG; 1 spt det; 1 hel det with 2 SA342 *Gazelle*; 1 hel det with 2 AS555 *Fennec*; 1 SAR/tpt det with 3 SA300 *Puma*
EU • EUFOR RCA 250; 1 inf coy
UN • MINUSCA 8

CHAD
Operation Barkhane 1,250; 1 recce BG; 1 air unit with 3 *Rafale* F3; 1 C-130H *Hercules*; 1 C-160 *Transall*; 1 C-135FR; 1 hel det with 4 SA330 *Puma*

CÔTE D'IVOIRE
Operation Licorne 450; 1 armd BG; 1 C-160 *Transall*; 1 AS555 *Fennec*
UN • UNOCI 6

DEMOCRATIC REPUBLIC OF THE CONGO
UN • MONUSCO 4

DJIBOUTI
2,000; 1 (Marine) combined arms regt with (2 recce sqn, 2 inf coy, 1 arty bty, 1 engr coy); 1 hel det with 4 SA330 *Puma*; 2 SA342 *Gazelle*; 1 LCM; 1 FGA sqn with 7 *Mirage* 2000C/D; 1 SAR/tpt sqn with 1 C-160 *Transall*; 1 *Falcon* 50MI; 1 AS555 *Fennec*; 2 SA330 *Puma*

EGYPT
MFO 2

FRENCH GUIANA
2,150: 1 (Foreign Legion) inf regt; 1 (Marine) inf regt; 1 SMA regt; 2 PCC; 1 tpt sqn with 1 CN-235M; 6 SA330 *Puma*; 3 AS555 *Fennec*; 3 gendarmerie coy; 1 AS350 *Ecureuil*

FRENCH POLYNESIA
950: (incl Centre d'Expérimentation du Pacifique); 1 SMA coy; 1 naval HQ at Papeete; 1 FFGHM; 1 LST; 1 AFS; 3 Falcon 200 *Gardian*; 1 SAR/tpt sqn with 3 CN-235M; 1 AS332 *Super Puma*; 1 AS555 *Fennec*

FRENCH WEST INDIES
1,200; 1 (Marine) inf coy; 2 SMA regt; 2 FFGHM; 1 LST; 1 naval base at Fort de France (Martinique); 4 gendarmerie coy; 2 AS350 *Ecureuil*

GABON
450; 1 SAR/tpt sqn with 1 CN-235M; 1 SA330 *Puma*

GERMANY
2,000 (incl elm Eurocorps and FRA/GER bde); 1 (FRA/GER) mech bde (1 armd cav regt, 1 mech inf regt)

GULF OF GUINEA
Operation Corymbe 1 FSM

HAITI
UN • MINUSTAH 2

INDIAN OCEAN
1,850 (incl La Réunion and TAAF); 1 (Marine) para regt; 1 (Foreign Legion) inf coy; 1 SMA regt ; 1 SMA coy; 2 FFGHM; 1 PSO; 1 PCO; 1 LST; 1 LCM; 1 naval HQ at Port-des-Galets (La Réunion); 1 naval base at Dzaoudzi (Mayotte); 1 SAR/tpt sqn with 2 C-160 *Transall*; 2 AS555 *Fennec*; 5 gendarmerie coy; 1 SA319 *Alouette* III

LEBANON
UN • UNIFIL 845; 1 inf BG; *Leclerc*; AMX-10P; VBCI; PVP; VAB; CAESAR; AU-F1 155mm; *Mistral*

LIBERIA
UN • UNMIL 1

MALI
Operation Barkhane 1,450; 1 mech inf BG; 1 log bn; 1 hel unit with 3 EC665 *Tiger*; 2 NH90 TTH; 6 SA330 *Puma*; 6 SA342 *Gazelle*
EU • EUTM Mali 70
UN • MINUSMA 20

MIDDLE EAST
UN • UNTSO 1 obs

MOLDOVA
OSCE • Moldova 1

NEW CALEDONIA
1,450; 1 (Marine) mech inf regt; 1 SMA coy; 6 ERC-90F1 *Lynx*; 1 FFGHM; 2 PCC; 1 base with 2 *Falcon* 200 *Gardian* at Nouméa; 1 tpt unit with 3 CN-235 MPA; 4 SA330 *Puma*; 1 AS555 *Fennec*; 4 gendarmerie coy; 2 AS350 *Ecureuil*

NIGER
Operation Barkhane 300; 1 FGA det with 3 *Mirage* 2000D; 1 UAV det with 4 *Harfang*; 2 MQ-9A *Reaper*

SENEGAL
350; 1 *Falcon* 50MI; 1 C-160 *Transall*

SERBIA
NATO • KFOR 9
OSCE • Kosovo 5

UKRAINE
OSCE • Ukraine 12

UNITED ARAB EMIRATES
750: 1 (Foreign Legion) BG (2 recce coy, 2 inf coy, 1 arty bty, 1 engr coy); 1 FGA sqn with 9 *Rafale* F3; 1 *Atlantique* 2; 1 KC-135F

WESTERN SAHARA
UN • MINURSO 11 obs

FOREIGN FORCES
Belgium 28 *Alpha Jet* trg ac located at Cazaux/Tours
Germany 400 (GER elm Eurocorps)
Singapore 200; 1 trg sqn with 12 M-346 *Master*

Germany GER

Euro €		2013	2014	2015
GDP	€	2.74tr	2.82tr	
	US$	3.64tr	3.82tr	
per capita	US$	44,999	47,201	
Growth	%	0.5	1.4	
Inflation	%	1.6	0.9	
Def exp [a]	€	36.7bn		
	US$	48.8bn		
Def bdgt [b]	€	33.3bn	32.4bn	
	US$	44.2bn	43.9bn	
US$1=€		0.75	0.74	

[a] NATO definition
[b] Includes military pensions

Population   80,996,685

Age	0–14	15–19	20–24	25–29	30–64	65 plus
Male	6.7%	2.5%	2.9%	3.1%	24.7%	9.2%
Female	6.3%	2.4%	2.8%	3.0%	24.4%	11.9%

Capabilities

Germany's armed services are continuing to undergo a period of restructuring, as reductions and reforms from 2010 and 2011 are worked through. There have been moves to improve pay and conditions, and the defence minister has called for a new defence white paper to analyse security policy and the future of the Bundeswehr. Additionally, the government is trying to improve the defence-procurement process. In March 2014, military contacts with Russia were halted as a result of the Ukraine crisis. Airlift capability will be bolstered with the entry into service of the A400M *Atlas* transport aircraft; the first of 53 was due to be delivered in November 2014. Germany in the latter half of 2014 was also considering a future medium-range air-defence requirement that was intended to be met by the tri-national MEADS programme. US withdrawal from the production phase of the project in 2011, however, left the future of the programme in considerable doubt. The second of two army divisional headquarters to be disbanded as part of cuts was closed in June 2014, with the two airborne brigades expected to be consolidated into one during the course of 2015.

ACTIVE 181,550 (Army 63,450 Navy 15,850 Air 31,400 Joint Support Service 44,850 Joint Medical Service 19,500 Other 6,500)

Conscript liability Voluntary conscription only. Voluntary conscripts can serve up to 23 months.

RESERVE 45,000 (Army 14,800 Navy 1,800 Air 6,050 Joint Support Service 15,650 Joint Medical Service 6,100 Other 600)

ORGANISATIONS BY SERVICE

Space
EQUIPMENT BY TYPE
SATELLITES 7
  COMMUNICATIONS 2 COMSATBw (1 & 2)
  ISR 5 SAR-*Lupe*

Army 63,450
FORCES BY ROLE
MANOEUVRE
  Armoured
  1 (1st) armd div (1 armd recce bn; 1 armd bde (1 armd recce coy, 2 armd bn, 1 armd inf bn, 1 SP arty bn, 1 engr coy, 1 log bn); 1 armd bde (1 recce coy, 1 armd bn, 1 armd inf bn, 1 air mob inf regt, 1 SP arty bn, 1 engr coy, 1 log bn); 1 mech bde (1 recce bn, 1 armd bn, 2 armd inf bn, 1 engr bn, 1 sigs bn, 1 log bn) 1 arty regt; 1 engr regt; 1 sigs regt; 1 sigs bn; 1 log bn)
  1 (Süd) armd div (1 armd bde (1 recce bn, 1 armd bn, 2 armd inf bn, 1 engr bn, 1 sigs bn, 1 log bn); 1 mech bde (1 recce bn, 1 armd bn, 2 armd inf bn, 1 engr bn, 1 sigs bn, 1 log bn); 1 mtn inf bde (1 recce bn, 3 mtn inf bn, 1 engr bn, 1 sigs bn, 1 log bn); 1 arty bn; 1 arty trg bn; 1 engr bn; 1 sy bn)
  Light
  2 bn (GER/FRA bde)
  Air Manoeuvre
  1 rapid reaction div (1 SF bde; 2 AB bde (1 recce coy, 2 para bn, 1 engr coy, 1 log bn); 1 atk hel regt; 2 tpt hel regt; 1 sigs bn)
COMBAT SUPPORT
  1 arty bn (GER/FRA bde)
  1 cbt engr coy (GER/FRA bde)
COMBAT SERVICE SUPPORT
  1 log bn (GER/FRA bde)
EQUIPMENT BY TYPE
MBT 410 *Leopard* 2A6
RECCE 339: 220 *Fennek* (incl 24 engr recce, 19 fires spt); 94 Tpz-1 *Fuchs* CBRN; 25 *Wiesel* (16 recce; 9 engr)
AIFV 529: 421 *Marder* 1A2/A3; 5 *Puma* (test); 103 *Wiesel* (with 20mm gun)
APC 1,576
  APC (T) 418: 177 Bv-206D/S; 241 M113 (inc variants)
  APC (W) 868: 132 *Boxer* (inc variants); 736 TPz-1 *Fuchs* (inc variants)
PPV 290 APV-2 *Dingo* 2

ARTY 298
  SP 155mm 138 PzH 2000
  MRL 227mm 56 MLRS
  MOR 120mm 104 *Tampella*
AT • MSL
  SP 86 *Wiesel* (TOW)
  MANPATS *Milan*
AMPHIBIOUS 30 LCM (river engr)
HELICOPTERS
  ATK 21 EC665 *Tiger*
  MRH/ISR 99 Bo-105M/Bo-105P PAH-1 (with HOT)
  TPT 91: **Medium** 22 NH90; **Light** 69: 55 Bell 205 (UH-1D *Iroquois*); 14 EC135
UAV • ISR 15: **Medium** 6 KZO; **Light** 9 LUNA
RADARS 101: 8 *Cobra*; 76 RASIT (veh, arty); 17 RATAC (veh, arty)
AEV 77: 53 *Dachs*; 24 *Leopard* A1
ARV 63: 61 *Büffel*; 2 M88A1
VLB 78: 32 *Biber*; 30 M3; 16 Panzerschnellbrücke 2
MW 124+: 100 Area Clearing System; 24 *Keiler*; Minelayer 5821; *Skorpion* Minelauncher

Navy 15,850
EQUIPMENT BY TYPE
SUBMARINES • TACTICAL • SSK 5:
  5 Type-212A with 6 single 533mm TT with 12 A4 *Seehecht* DM2 HWT (1 further vessel ISD 2015)
PRINCIPAL SURFACE COMBATANTS 16
  DESTROYERS • DDGHM 7:
    4 *Brandenburg* with 2 twin lnchr with MM-38 *Exocet* AShM, 1 16-cell Mk41 VLS with RIM-7M/P, 2 Mk49 GMLS with RIM-116 RAM SAM, 2 twin 324mm ASTT with Mk46 LWT, 1 76mm gun (capacity 2 *Sea Lynx* Mk88A hel)
    3 *Sachsen* with 2 quad Mk141 lnchr with RGM-84F *Harpoon* AShM, 1 32-cell Mk41 VLS with SM-2MR/RIM-162B *Sea Sparrow* SAM, 2 21-cell Mk49 GMLS with RIM-116 RAM SAM, 2 triple Mk32 324mm ASTT with MU90 LWT, 1 76mm gun (capacity 2 *Sea Lynx* Mk88A hel)
  FRIGATES 9
    FFGHM 4 *Bremen* with 2 quad Mk141 lnchr with RGM-84A/C *Harpoon* AShM, 1 octuple Mk29 GMLS with RIM-7M/P *Sea Sparrow* SAM, 2 Mk49 GMLS with RIM-116 RAM SAM, 2 twin 324mm ASTT with Mk46 LWT, 1 76mm gun (capacity 2 *Sea Lynx* Mk88A hel)
    FFGM 5 *Braunschweig* (K130) with 2 twin lnchr with RBS-15 AShM, 2 Mk49 GMLS each with RIM-116 RAM SAM, 1 76mm gun, 1 hel landing platform
PATROL AND COASTAL COMBATANTS • PCGM 8
  8 *Gepard* with 2 twin lnchr with MM-38 *Exocet* AShM, 1 Mk49 GMLS with RIM-116 RAM SAM, 1 76mm gun
MINE WARFARE • MINE COUNTERMEASURES 34
  MHO 12: 10 *Frankenthal* (2 used as diving support); 2 *Kulmbach*
  MSO 4 *Ensdorf*
  MSD 18 *Seehund*

AMPHIBIOUS 2
  LCU 2 Type-520
LOGISTICS AND SUPPORT 52
  AFH 3 *Berlin* Type-702 (capacity 2 *Sea King* Mk41 hel; 2 RAMs)
  AG 5: 2 *Schwedeneck* Type-748; 3 *Stollergrund* Type-745
  AGI 3 *Oste* Type-423
  AGOR 1 *Planet* Type-751
  AO 2 *Walchensee* Type-703
  AOR 6 *Elbe* Type-404 (2 specified for PFM support; 1 specified for SSK support; 3 specified for MHC/MSC support)
  AOT 2 *Spessart* Type-704
  APB 3: 1 *Knurrhahn*; 2 *Ohre*
  ATR 1 *Helgoland*
  AXS 1 *Gorch Fock*
  YAG 2 (used as trials ships)
  YDT 4 *Wangerooge*
  YFD 5
  YFRT 4 *Todendorf* Type-905
  YPC 2 *Bottsand*
  YTM 8 *Vogelsand*

Naval Aviation 2,200
EQUIPMENT BY TYPE
AIRCRAFT 8 combat capable
  ASW 8 AP-3C *Orion*
  TPT • Light 2 Do-228 (pollution control)
HELICOPTERS
  ASW 22 *Lynx* Mk88A with *Sea Skua*
  SAR 21 *Sea King* Mk41
MSL AShM *Sea Skua*

Air Force 31,400
Flying hours   140 hrs/year (plus 40 hrs high-fidelity simulator)

FORCES BY ROLE
FIGHTER
  2 wg (2 sqn with Eurofighter *Typhoon*)
FIGHTER/GROUND ATTACK
  1 wg (2 sqn with *Tornado* IDS)
  1 wg (2 sqn with Eurofighter *Typhoon*)
ISR
  1 wg (1 ISR sqn with *Tornado* ECR/IDS; 1 UAV sqn (ISAF only) with *Heron*)
TANKER/TRANSPORT
  1 (special air mission) wg (3 sqn with A310 MRTT; A340; AS532U2 *Cougar* II; Global 5000)
TRANSPORT
  2 wg (2 sqn with C-160D *Transall*)
  1 wg (1 sqn with C-160D *Transall*)
TRAINING
  1 sqn located at Holloman AFB (US) with *Tornado* IDS
  1 unit (ENJJPT) located at Sheppard AFB (US) with T-6 *Texan* II; T-38A
  1 hel unit located at Fassberg
TRANSPORT HELICOPTER
  1 wg (total: 2 sqn with CH-53G/GA/GE/GS *Stallion*)
AIR DEFENCE
  1 wg (3 SAM gp) with *Patriot*
  1 AD gp with ASRAD *Ozelot*; C-RAM MANTIS
  1 AD trg unit located at Fort Bliss (US) with ASRAD *Ozelot*; C-RAM MANTIS; *Patriot*
  3 (tac air ctrl) radar gp

EQUIPMENT BY TYPE
AIRCRAFT 237 combat capable
  FTR 101 Eurofighter *Typhoon*
  FGA 114 *Tornado* IDS
  EW/FGA 23 *Tornado* ECR*
  TKR/TPT 4 A310 MRTT
  TPT 66: **Medium** 58 C-160D *Transall*; **PAX** 8: 2 A340 (VIP); 2 A319; 4 Global 5000
  TRG 109: 69 T-6 *Texan* TII, 40 T-38A
HELICOPTERS
  CSAR 18 CH-53GS/GE *Stallion*
  TPT 67: **Heavy** 64 CH-53G/GA *Stallion*; **Medium** 3 AS532U2 *Cougar* II (VIP)
UAV • ISR • Heavy 1 *Heron*
AD • SAM
  SP 12 ASRAD *Ozelot* (with FIM-92A *Stinger*)
  TOWED 14: 12 *Patriot* PAC-3, 2 C-RAM MANTIS
MSL
  AAM • IR AIM-9L/Li *Sidewinder*; **IIR** IRIS-T; **ARH** AIM 120A/B AMRAAM
  LACM KEPD 350 *Taurus*
  ARM AGM-88B HARM
BOMBS • LGB: GBU-24 *Paveway* III, GBU-54 JDAM

Joint Support Services 44,850
FORCES BY ROLE
COMBAT SUPPORT
  4 EW bn
  3 MP regt
  1 NBC regt
  1 NBC bn
  2 sigs regt
COMBAT SERVICE SUPPORT
  6 log bn

Joint Medical Services 19,500
FORCES BY ROLE
COMBAT SERVICE SUPPORT
  8 med regt
  5 fd hospital

Paramilitary

Coast Guard 500
EQUIPMENT BY TYPE
PATROL AND COASTAL COMBATANTS 12
  PCO 6: 3 *Bad Bramstedt*; 1 *Bredstedt*; 2 *Sassnitz*
  PB 6: 5 *Prignitz*; 1 *Rettin*

Cyber
Germany issued a Cyber Security Strategy in February 2011. The National Cyber Security Council, an inter-ministerial body at state secretary level, analyses cyber-related issues. A National Cyber Response Centre was set up at the Federal Office for Information Security on 1 April 2011. It serves as an information platform for administrative cooperation

between several federal offices including Federal Office for Information Security, the Federal Intelligence Service, the Federal Criminal Police Office and the Bundeswehr, all of whom participate within the framework of their constitutional and statutory requirements. The Bundeswehr with its CERT team (CERTBw) maintains an updated picture of the IT security situation and continually analyses and assesses the threats and risks posed to the Bundeswehr IT system. The Bundeswehr IT System Centre, the central management facility for the entire Bundeswehr IT system, maintains an overall situation picture of the IT system that also monitors risks and hazards in order to identify operating anomalies possibly caused by cyber attacks. A Computer Network Operation (CNO) unit has been formed within the Strategic Reconnaissance Command and achieved an initial capability in late December 2011.

DEPLOYMENT

Legal provisions for foreign deployment:
Constitution: Codified constitution ('Basic Law', 1949)
Specific legislation: 'Parlamentsbeteiligungsgesetz' (2005)
Decision on deployment of troops abroad: a) By parliament: prior consent for anticipated military involvement; simplified consent procedure for deployments of limited intensity or extension; subsequent consent admitted in cases requiring immediate action or deployments aimed at rescuing persons from danger, provided parliamentary discussion would have endangered life; b) by government: preparation, planning and humanitarian aid and assistance provided by the armed forces where weapons are carried for self-defence, provided it is not expected that military personnel will be involved in armed engagements; other deployments short of an involvement or anticipated involvement in armed engagements.

AFGHANISTAN
NATO • ISAF 1,599; 1 bde HQ; 1 inf BG; C-160; CH-53 Stallion; *Heron* UAV
UN • UNAMA 2 obs

ALBANIA
OSCE • Albania 2

BOSNIA-HERZEGOVINA
OSCE • Bosnia and Herzegovina 3

CENTRAL AFRICAN REPUBLIC
EU • EUFOR RCA 4

DJIBOUTI
EU • *Operation Atalanta* 1 AP-3C *Orion*

ESTONIA
NATO • Baltic Air Policing 6 Eurofighter *Typhoon*

FRANCE
400 (incl GER elm Eurocorps)

GULF OF ADEN & INDIAN OCEAN
EU • *Operation Atalanta* 1 FFGHM

LEBANON
UN • UNIFIL 144; 1 FFGM

MALI
EU • EUTM Mali 146
UN • MINUSMA 6

MEDITERRANEAN SEA
NATO • SNMG 2: 1 FFGHM
NATO • SNMCMG 2: 1 MHO

MOLDOVA
OSCE • Moldova 1

NORTH SEA
NATO • SNMCMG 1: 1 MHO

POLAND
67 (GER elm Corps HQ (multinational))

SERBIA
NATO • KFOR 674
OSCE • Kosovo 5

SOUTH SUDAN
UN • UNMISS 7; 7 obs

SUDAN
UN • UNAMID 10

TURKEY
NATO • *Active Fence*: 2 AD bty with *Patriot* PAC-3

UGANDA
EU • EUTM Somalia 6

UKRAINE
OSCE • Ukraine 21

UNITED STATES
Trg units with 40 T-38 *Talon*; 69 T-6A *Texan* II at Goodyear AFB (AZ)/Sheppard AFB (TX); 1 trg sqn with 14 *Tornado* IDS at Holloman AFB (NM); NAS Pensacola (FL); Fort Rucker (AL); Missile trg at Fort Bliss (TX)

UZBEKISTAN
NATO • ISAF 100

WESTERN SAHARA
UN • MINURSO 3 obs

FOREIGN FORCES

Canada NATO 226
France 2,000; 1 (FRA/GER) mech bde (1 armd cav rgt, 1 mech inf regt)
United Kingdom 12,300; 1 div with (1 armd bde; 1 inf bde; 1 log bde)
United States
US Africa Command: **Army**; 1 HQ at Stuttgart
US European Command: 40,500; 1 combined service HQ (EUCOM) at Stuttgart-Vaihingen
    Army 25,150; 1 HQ (US Army Europe (USAREUR) at Heidelberg; 1 SF gp; 1 cav SBCT; 1 armd recce bn; 1 arty bn; 1 (hvy cbt avn) hel bde; 1 int bde; 1 MP bde; 1 sigs bde; 1 spt bde; 1 (APS) armd/armd inf bn eqpt set; M1 *Abrams*; M2/M3 *Bradley*; *Stryker*; M109; M119A2; M777;

M270 MLRS; AH-64 *Apache*; CH-47 *Chinook*; UH-60 *Black Hawk*
Navy 500
USAF 13,900; 1 HQ (US Airforce Europe (USAFE)) at Ramstein AB; 1 HQ (3rd Air Force) at Ramstein AB; 1 ftr wg at Spangdahlem AB with 1 ftr sqn with 24 F-16CJ *Fighting Falcon*; 1 airlift wg at Ramstein AB with 16 C-130E/J *Hercules*; 2 C-20 *Gulfstream*; 9 C-21 *Learjet*; 1 C-40B
USMC 950

Greece GRC

Euro €		2013	2014	2015
GDP	€	182bn	182bn	
	US$	242bn	246bn	
per capita	US$	21,857	22,318	
Growth	%	-3.9	0.6	
Inflation	%	-0.9	-0.8	
Def exp [a]	€	4.28bn		
	US$	5.68bn		
Def bdgt [b]	€	4.44bn	4.16bn	
	US$	5.9bn	5.64bn	
US$1=€		0.75	0.74	

[a] NATO definition

[b] Includes military pensions and peacekeeping operations allocations

Population 10,775,557

Age	0–14	15–19	20–24	25–29	30–64	65 plus
Male	7.2%	2.4%	2.6%	2.9%	24.9%	8.9%
Female	6.8%	2.3%	2.5%	2.9%	25.2%	11.4%

Capabilities

Greece's armed forces have traditionally been well funded, given territorial defence tasks and a requirement to support Cyprus. However, recent economic difficulties have hampered the country's ability to procure new equipment and fund defence programmes. At the same time, forces have undergone cuts to military salaries, and significant reductions in training and exercises as a result of the financial crisis. This situation is now beginning to ease, with a US$1bn package for defence upgrades approved in mid-2014. A National Defence Policy was adopted in 2011 which emphasised deterrence, internal cooperation and enhanced situational awareness, as well as primary security tasks. Conscription remains in place, and is particularly important for the army.

ACTIVE 144,950 (Army 93,500, Navy 18,450 Air 21,400, Joint 11,600) **Paramilitary 4,000**

Conscript liability Up to 9 months in all services

RESERVE 216,650 (Army 177,650 Navy 5,000, Air 34,000)

ORGANISATIONS BY SERVICE

Army 48,500; 45,000 conscripts (total 93,500)

Units are manned at 3 different levels – Cat A 85% fully ready, Cat B 60% ready in 24 hours, Cat C 20% ready in 48 hours (requiring reserve mobilisation). 3 military regions.

FORCES BY ROLE
COMMAND
  3 corps HQ (incl NDC-GR)
  1 armd div HQ
  3 mech inf div HQ
  1 inf div HQ
SPECIAL FORCES
  1 SF comd
  1 cdo/para bde
MANOEUVRE
  Reconnaissance
  4 recce bn
  Armoured
  4 armd bde (2 armd bn, 1 mech inf bn, 1 SP arty bn)
  Mechanised
  9 mech inf bde (1 armd bn, 2 mech inf bn, 1 SP arty bn)
  Light
  1 inf div
  3 inf bde (1 armd bn, 3 inf regt, 1 arty regt)
  Air Manoeuvre
  1 air mob bde
  1 air aslt bde
  Amphibious
  1 mne bde
  Aviation
  1 avn bde (1 hel regt with (2 atk hel bn), 2 tpt hel bn, 4 hel bn)
COMBAT SUPPORT
  1 arty regt (1 arty bn, 2 MRL bn)
  3 AD bn (2 with I-HAWK, 1 with *Tor* M1)
  3 engr regt
  2 engr bn
  1 EW regt
  10 sigs bn
COMBAT SERVICE SUPPORT
  1 log corps HQ
  1 log div (3 log bde)
EQUIPMENT BY TYPE
MBT 1,354: 170 *Leopard* 2A6HEL; 183 *Leopard* 2A4; 526 *Leopard* 1A4/5; 100 M60A1/A3; 375 M48A5
RECCE 229 VBL
AIFV 398 BMP-1
APC 2,374
  APC (T) 2,363: 86 *Leonidas* Mk1/2; 2,064 M113A1/A2; 213 M577
  PPV 11 *Maxxpro*
ARTY 3,353
  SP 547: **155mm** 442: 418 M109A1B/A2/A3GEA1/A5; 24 PzH 2000; **203mm** 105 M110A2
  TOWED 410: **105mm** 281: 263 M101; 18 M-56; **155mm** 129 M114
  MRL 147: **122mm** 111 RM-70 *Dana*; **227mm** 36 MLRS (incl ATACMS)
  MOR 2,249: **81mm** 1,629; **107mm** 620 M-30 (incl 231 SP)

AT
  MSL 1,108
    SP 528: 196 HMMWV with 9K135 *Kornet*-E (AT-14 *Spriggan*); 42 HMMWV with *Milan*; 290 M901
    MANPATS 9K111 *Fagot* (AT-4 *Spigot*); *Milan*; TOW
  RCL 3,927:
    SP 106mm 581 M40A1
    MANPATS 84mm *Carl Gustav*; **90mm** EM-67
AIRCRAFT • **TPT** • **Light** 20: 1 Beech 200 *King Air* (C-12C) 2 Beech 200 *King Air* (C-12R/AP *Huron*); 17 Cessna 185 (U-17A/B)
HELICOPTERS
  ATK 29: 19 AH-64A *Apache*; 10 AH-64D *Apache*
  TPT 132: **Heavy** 15: 9 CH-47D *Chinook*; 6 CH-47SD *Chinook*; **Medium** 8 NH90 TTH; **Light** 108: 95 Bell 205 (UH-1H *Iroquois*); 13 Bell 206 (AB-206) *Jet Ranger*
UAV • **ISR** • **Medium** 2 *Sperwer*
AD
  SAM 614
    SP 113: 21 9K331 *Tor*-M1 (SA-15 *Gauntlet*); 38 9K33 *Osa*-M (SA-8B *Gecko*); 54 ASRAD HMMWV
    TOWED 42 MIM-23B I-HAWK
    MANPAD FIM-92A *Stinger*
  GUNS • **TOWED** 727: **20mm** 204 Rh 202; **23mm** 523 ZU-23-2
RADAR • **LAND** 76: 3 ARTHUR, 5 AN/TPQ-36 *Firefinder* (arty, mor); 8 AN/TPQ-37(V)3; 40 BOR-A; 20 MARGOT
ARV 262: 12 *Büffel*; 43 Leopard 1; 94 M88A1; 112 M578
VLB 12+: 12 Leopard 1; *Leguan*
MW *Giant Viper*

National Guard 33,000 reservists
Internal security role
FORCES BY ROLE
MANOEUVRE
  Light
    1 inf div
  Air Manoeuvre
    1 para regt
  Aviation
    1 avn bn
COMBAT SUPPORT
  8 arty bn
  4 AD bn

Navy 16,850; 1,600 conscript; (total 18,450)
EQUIPMENT BY TYPE
SUBMARINES • **TACTICAL** • **SSK** 8:
  4 *Poseidon* (GER Type-209/1200) (of which 1 modernised with AIP technology) with 8 single 533mm TT with SUT HWT
  3 *Glavkos* (GER Type-209/1100) with 8 single 533mm TT with UGM-84C *Harpoon* AShM/SUT HWT
  1 *Papanikolis* (GER Type-214) with 8 single 533mm TT with UGM-84C *Harpoon* AShM/SUT HWT (5 additional vessels expected)
PRINCIPAL SURFACE COMBATANTS 13
  FRIGATES • **FFGHM** 13:
    4 *Elli* Batch I (NLD *Kortenaer* Batch 2) with 2 quad Mk141 lnchr with RGM-84A/C *Harpoon* AShM, 1 octuple Mk29 GMLS with RIM-7M/P *Sea Sparrow* SAM, 2 twin 324mm ASTT with Mk46 LWT, 1 *Phalanx* CIWS, 1 76mm gun (capacity 2 Bell 212 (AB-212) hel)
    2 *Elli* Batch II (NLD *Kortenaer* Batch 2) with 2 quad Mk141 lnchr with RGM-84A/C *Harpoon* AShM, 1 octuple Mk29 GMLS with RIM-7M/P *Sea Sparrow* SAM, 2 twin 324mm ASTT with Mk46 LWT, 1 *Phalanx* CIWS, 2 76mm gun (capacity 2 Bell 212 (AB-212) hel)
    3 *Elli* Batch III (NLD *Kortenaer* Batch 2) with 2 quad Mk141 lnchr with RGM-84A/C *Harpoon* AShM, 1 octuple Mk29 lnchr with RIM-7M/P *Sea Sparrow* SAM, 2 twin 324mm ASTT with Mk46 LWT, 1 *Phalanx* CIWS, 1 76mm gun (capacity 2 Bell 212 (AB-212) hel)
    4 *Hydra* (GER MEKO 200) with 2 quad lnchr with RGM-84G *Harpoon* AShM, 1 16-cell Mk48 Mod 5 VLS with RIM-162 ESSM SAM, 2 triple 324mm ASTT each with Mk46 LWT, 2 *Phalanx* CIWS, 1 127mm gun (capacity 1 S-70B *Seahawk* ASW hel)
PATROL AND COASTAL COMBATANTS 32
  CORVETTES • **FSGM** 4 *Roussen* (*Super Vita*) with 2 quad lnchr with MM-40 *Exocet* Block 2 AShM, 1 21-cell Mk49 GMLS with RIM-116 RAM SAM, 1 76mm gun (3 additional vessels in build)
  PCFG 12:
    5 *Kavaloudis* (FRA *La Combattante* II, III, IIIB) with 6 RB 12 *Penguin* AShM, 2 single 533mm TT with SST-4 HWT, 2 76mm gun
    4 *Laskos* (FRA *La Combattante* II, III, IIIB) with 4 MM-38 *Exocet* AShM, 2 single 533mm TT with SST-4 HWT, 2 76mm gun
    1 *Votsis* (FRA *La Combattante*) with 2 twin Mk-141 lnchr with RGM-84C *Harpoon* AShM, 1 76mm gun
    2 *Votsis* (FRA *La Combattante* IIA) with 2 twin MM-38 *Exocet* AShM, 1 76mm gun
  PCO 8:
    2 *Armatolos* (DNK *Osprey*) with 1 76mm gun
    2 *Kasos* with 1 76mm gun
    4 *Machitis* with 1 76mm gun
  PB 8: 4 *Andromeda* (NOR *Nasty*); 2 *Stamou*; 2 *Tolmi*
MINE COUNTERMEASURES 4
  MHO 4: 2 *Evropi* (UK *Hunt*); 2 *Evniki* (US *Osprey*)
AMPHIBIOUS
  LANDING SHIPS • **LST** 5:
    5 *Chios* (capacity 4 LCVP; 300 troops) with 1 76mm gun, 1 hel landing platform (for med hel)
  LANDING CRAFT 13
    LCU 3
    LCA 7
    LCAC 3 *Kefallinia* (*Zubr*) with 2 AK630 CIWS, (capacity either 3 MBT or 10 APC (T); 230 troops)
LOGISTICS AND SUPPORT 50
  ABU 2
  AG 2 *Pandora*
  AGOR 1 *Pytheas*
  AGS 2: 1 *Stravon*; 1 *Naftilos*
  AOR 2 *Axios* (ex-GER *Luneburg*)
  AORH 1 *Prometheus* (ITA *Etna*) with 1 *Phalanx* CIWS
  AOT 4 *Ouranos*
  AWT 6 *Kerkini*
  AXL 1

AXS 5
YFU 4
YNT 1 *Thetis*
YPT 3 *Evrotas*
YTM 16

Naval Aviation
FORCES BY ROLE
ANTI-SUBMARINE WARFARE
1 div with S-70B *Seahawk*; Bell 212 (AB-212) ASW
EQUIPMENT BY TYPE
AIRCRAFT • ASW (5 P-3B *Orion* in store undergoing modernisation)
HELICOPTERS
ASW 19: 8 Bell 212 (AB-212) ASW; 11 S-70B *Seahawk*
MSL
ASM AGM-119 *Penguin*, AGM-114 *Hellfire*

Air Force 19,650; 1,750 conscripts (total 21,400)
Tactical Air Force
FORCES BY ROLE
FIGHTER/GROUND ATTACK
2 sqn with F-4E *Phantom* II
3 sqn with F-16CG/DG Block 30/50 *Fighting Falcon*
3 sqn with F-16CG/DG Block 52+ *Fighting Falcon*
1 sqn with F-16C/D Block 52+ ADV *Fighting Falcon*
1 sqn with *Mirage* 2000-5EG/BG Mk2
1 sqn with *Mirage* 2000EG/BG
ISR
1 sqn with RF-4E *Phantom* II
AIRBORNE EARLY WARNING
1 sqn with EMB-145H *Erieye*
EQUIPMENT BY TYPE
AIRCRAFT 244 combat capable
FGA 234: 34 F-4E *Phantom* II; 70 F-16CG/DG Block 30/50 *Fighting Falcon*; 56 F-16CG/DG Block 52+; 30 F-16C/D Block 52+ ADV *Fighting Falcon*; 20 *Mirage* 2000-5EG Mk2; 5 *Mirage* 2000-5BG Mk2; 17 *Mirage* 2000EG; 2 *Mirage* 2000BG
ISR 10 RF-4E *Phantom* II*
AEW 4 EMB-145AEW (EMB-145H) *Erieye*
MSL
AAM • IR AIM-9L/P *Sidewinder*; R-550 *Magic* 2 IIR IRIS-T; *Mica* IR; SARH Super 530; ARH AIM-120B/C AMRAAM; *Mica* RF
ASM AGM-65A/B/G *Maverick*; AGM-154C JSOW
LACM SCALP EG
AShM AM 39 *Exocet*
ARM AGM-88 HARM
BOMBS
Conventional Mk81; Mk82; Mk83; Mk84
Electro-optical guided: GBU-8B HOBOS
Laser-guided: GBU-12/GBU-16 *Paveway* II; GBU-24 *Paveway* III
INS/GPS-guided GBU-31 JDAM

Air Defence
FORCES BY ROLE
AIR DEFENCE
6 sqn/bty with PAC-3 *Patriot* (MIM-104 A/B SOJC/D GEM)
2 sqn/bty with S-300PMU-1 (SA-10C *Grumble*)
12 bty with *Skyguard*/RIM-7 *Sparrow*/guns; *Crotale* NG/GR; *Tor*-M1 (SA-15 *Gauntlet*)
EQUIPMENT BY TYPE
AD
SAM • TOWED 61+: 36 PAC-3 *Patriot*; 12 S-300 PMU-1 (SA-10C *Grumble*); 9 *Crotale* NG/GR; 4 9K331 *Tor*-M1 (SA-15 *Gauntlet*); some *Skyguard*/*Sparrow*
GUNS 35+ 35mm

Air Support Command
FORCES BY ROLE
SEARCH & RESCUE/TRANSPORT HELICOPTER
1 sqn with AS332C *Super Puma* (SAR/CSAR)
1 sqn with AW109; Bell 205A (AB-205A) (SAR); Bell 212 (AB-212 - VIP, tpt)
TRANSPORT
1 sqn with C-27J *Spartan*
1 sqn with C-130B/H *Hercules*
1 sqn with EMB-135BJ *Legacy*; ERJ-135LR; Gulfstream V
FIRE FIGHTING
2 sqn with CL-215; CL-415
1 sqn with M-18 *Dromader*
EQUIPMENT BY TYPE
AIRCRAFT
TPT 26: Medium 23: 8 C-27J *Spartan*; 5 C-130B *Hercules*; 10 C-130H *Hercules*; Light 2: 1 EMB-135BJ *Legacy*; 1 ERJ-135LR; PAX 1 Gulfstream V
FF 42: 13 CL-215; 8 CL-415; 21 M-18 *Dromader*
HELICOPTERS
TPT 31: Medium 11 AS332C *Super Puma*; Light 20: 13 Bell 205A (AB-205A) (SAR); 4 Bell 212 (AB-212) (VIP, Tpt); 3 AW109

Air Training Command
FORCES BY ROLE
TRAINING
2 sqn with T-2C/E *Buckeye*
2 sqn with T-6A/B *Texan* II
1 sqn with T-41D
EQUIPMENT BY TYPE
AIRCRAFT • TRG 94: 30 T-2C/E *Buckeye*; 20 T-6A *Texan* II; 25 T-6B *Texan* II; 19 T-41D

Paramilitary • Coast Guard and Customs 4,000
EQUIPMENT BY TYPE
PATROL AND COASTAL COMBATANTS 122: PCC 3; PBF 54; PB 65
LOGISTICS AND SUPPORT • YPC 4
AIRCRAFT • TPT • Light 4: 2 Cessna 172RG *Cutlass*; 2 TB-20 *Trinidad*

Cyber

A new Joint Cyber Command in the Hellenic National Defence General Staff (HNDGS) was established in 2014, replacing the existing Cyber Defence Directorate. New and revised documents on Military Cyber Defence Doctrine, Policy and Strategy were published in 2013–14.

DEPLOYMENT

Legal provisions for foreign deployment:
Constitution: Codified constitution (1975/1986/2001)
Specific legislation: 'Law 2295/95' (1995)
Decision on deployment of troops abroad: By the Government Council on Foreign Affairs and Defence

AFGHANISTAN
NATO • ISAF 9

BOSNIA-HERZEGOVINA
EU • EUFOR • *Operation Althea* 3

CYPRUS
Army 950 (ELDYK army); ε200 (officers/NCO seconded to Greek-Cypriot National Guard) (total 1,150);
1 mech bde (1 armd bn, 2 mech inf bn, 1 arty bn); 61 M48A5 MOLF MBT; 80 *Leonidas* APC; 12 M114 arty; 6 M110A2 arty

LEBANON
UN • UNIFIL 48; 1 PB

MALI
EU • EUTM Mali 4

SERBIA
NATO • KFOR 117; 1 mech inf coy
OSCE • Kosovo 4

UKRAINE
OSCE • Ukraine 1

FOREIGN FORCES
United States US European Command: 380; 1 naval base at Makri; 1 naval base at Soudha Bay; 1 air base at Iraklion

Hungary HUN

Hungarian Forint f		2013	2014	2015
GDP	f	29.1tr	30.3tr	
	US$	132bn	130bn	
per capita	US$	13,388	13,154	
Growth	%	1.1	2.8	
Inflation	%	1.7	0.3	
Def exp [a]	f	271bn		
	US$	1.23bn		
Def bdgt [b]	f	242bn	234bn	
	US$	1.1bn	1bn	
FMA (US)	US$	1m	1m	0.0
US$1=f		219.85	233.49	

[a] NATO definition
[b] Excludes military pensions

Population 9,919,128

Age	0–14	15–19	20–24	25–29	30–64	65 plus
Male	7.6%	2.8%	3.2%	3.2%	24.1%	6.7%
Female	7.2%	2.6%	3.0%	3.1%	25.3%	11.2%

Capabilities

Defence of national territory and the ability to participate in NATO and other international operations were central tenets of the country's 2012 National Military Strategy. This included the medium-term aim of having forces capable of taking part in high-intensity operations, however the defence ministry continues to struggle with funding issues. While the air force operates the *Gripen* combat aircraft under lease, and the country is also host to the multinational C-17 strategic-airlift unit, elements of its land-systems inventory remain centred on ageing Soviet-era equipment. Though defence budgets have fallen in recent years, and efforts to improve the rotary-lift capability through the acquisition of additional helicopters failed to progress by mid-2014, Hungary was reported to have signed a deal to upgrade elements of its air-defence system. In late 2014, US personnel arrived for a joint exercise with Hungarian troops. The country is a participant in the Visegrad Group.

ACTIVE 26,500 (Army 10,300, Air 5,900 Joint 10,300) **Paramilitary 12,000**

RESERVE 44,000 (Army 35,200 Air 8,800)

ORGANISATIONS BY SERVICE
Hungary's armed forces have reorganised into a joint force.

Land Component 10,300 (incl riverine element)
FORCES BY ROLE
SPECIAL FORCES
  1 SF bn
MANOEUVRE
  Mechanised
  1 (5th) mech inf bde (1 armd recce bn; 3 mech inf bn, 1 cbt engr coy, 1 sigs coy, 1 log bn)
  1 (25th) mech inf bde (1 tk bn; 1 mech inf bn, 1 AB bn, 1 arty bn, 1 AT bn, 1 log bn)
COMBAT SUPPORT
  1 engr regt
  1 EOD/rvn regt
  1 CBRN bn
  1 sigs regt
COMBAT SERVICE SUPPORT
  1 log regt
EQUIPMENT BY TYPE
MBT 30 T-72
RECCE 24+: 24 K90 CBRN Recce; PSZH-IV CBRN Recce
AIFV 120 BTR-80A
APC (W) 260 BTR-80
ARTY 68
  TOWED 152mm 18 D-20
  MOR 82mm 50
AT • MSL • MANPATS 9K111 *Fagot* (AT-4 *Spigot*); 9K113 *Konkurs* (AT-5 *Spandrel*)
PATROL AND COASTAL COMBATANTS • PBR 2
AEV BAT-2
ARV BMP-1 VPV; T-54/T-55; VT-55A
VLB BLG-60; MTU; TMM

Air Component 5,900

Flying hours   50 hrs/yr

FORCES BY ROLE
FIGHTER/GROUND ATTACK
  1 sqn with *Gripen* C/D
TRANSPORT
  1 sqn with An-26 *Curl*
TRAINING
  1 sqn with Yak-52
ATTACK HELICOPTER
  1 sqn with Mi-24 *Hind*
TRANSPORT HELICOPTER
  1 sqn with Mi-8 *Hip*; Mi-17 *Hip* H
AIR DEFENCE
  1 regt (9 bty with *Mistral*; 3 bty with 2K12 *Kub* (SA-6 *Gainful*))
  1 radar regt
EQUIPMENT BY TYPE
AIRCRAFT 14 combat capable
  FGA 14: 12 *Gripen* C; 2 *Gripen* D
  TPT • Light 4 An-26 *Curl*
  TRG 8 Yak-52
HELICOPTERS
  ATK 11: 3 Mi-24D *Hind* D; 6 Mi-24V *Hind* E; 2 Mi-24P *Hind* F
  MRH 7 Mi-17 *Hip* H
  TPT • Medium 13 Mi-8 *Hip*
AD • SAM 61
  SP 16 2K12 *Kub* (SA-6 *Gainful*)
  MANPAD *Mistral*
  RADAR: 3 RAT-31DL, 6 P-18: 6 SZT-68U; 14 P-37
MSL
  AAM • IR AIM-9 *Sidewinder*; R-73 (AA-11 *Archer*)
  SARH R-27 (AA-10 *Alamo* A); **ARH** AIM-120C AMRAAM
  ASM AGM-65 *Maverick*; 3M11 *Falanga* (AT-2 *Swatter*); 9K114 *Shturm*-V (AT-6 *Spiral*)

Paramilitary 12,000

Border Guards 12,000 (to reduce)
Ministry of Interior
FORCES BY ROLE
MANOEUVRE
  Other
    1 (Budapest) paramilitary district (7 rapid reaction coy)
    11 (regt/district) paramilitary regt
EQUIPMENT BY TYPE
  APC (W) 68 BTR-80

Cyber

There is no dedicated cyber organisation, but IT network management contains INFOSEC and cyber-defence elements. In February 2012, the government adopted a National Security Strategy, noting an intent to prevent and avert cyber attacks. The MoD has also developed a Military Cyber Defence concept.

DEPLOYMENT

Legal provisions for foreign deployment:
Legislation: Fundamental Law (2011)

Decision on deployment of troops abroad: Government decides on cross-border troop movements or employment, in the case of NATO (Paragraph 2.) For operations not based on NATO or EU decisions, the Fundamental Law gives parliament the prerogative to decide on the employment of Hungarian armed forces or foreign forces in, or from, Hungarian territory.

AFGHANISTAN
NATO • ISAF 101

CYPRUS
UN • UNFICYP 76; 1 inf pl

EGYPT
MFO 26; 1 MP unit

LEBANON
UN • UNIFIL 4

MALI
EU • EUTM Mali 13

SERBIA
NATO • KFOR 336; 1 inf coy (KTM)
OSCE • Kosovo 4

UGANDA
EU • EUTM Somalia 4

UKRAINE
OSCE • Ukraine 18

WESTERN SAHARA
UN • MINURSO 7 obs

Iceland ISL

Icelandic Krona K		2013	2014	2015
GDP	Kr	1.79tr	1.88tr	
	US$	14.6bn	16.2bn	
per capita	US$	45,416	50,006	
Growth	%	3.3	2.9	
Inflation	%	3.9	2.5	
Sy Bdgt [a]	Kr	4.64bn	4.51bn	
	US$	38m	39m	
US$1=K		122.20	116.10	

[a] Coast Guard budget

Population   317,351

Age	0–14	15–19	20–24	25–29	30–64	65 plus
Male	10.0%	3.5%	3.8%	3.4%	23.0%	6.2%
Female	9.7%	3.5%	3.7%	3.4%	22.6%	7.3%

Capabilities

While a NATO member, Iceland has only a coast guard and no armed forces. Alliance partners provide air policing and defence, and there are occasional air-defence and air-surveillance exercises with Nordic states and other NATO members.

ACTIVE NIL **Paramilitary** 200

ORGANISATIONS BY SERVICE

Paramilitary

Iceland Coast Guard 200
EQUIPMENT BY TYPE
PATROL AND COASTAL COMBATANTS 3
  PSOH: 2 *Aegir*
  PSO 1 *Thor*
LOGISTICS AND SUPPORT • AGS 1 *Baldur*
AIRCRAFT • TPT • Light 1 DHC-8-300
HELICOPTERS
  TPT • Medium 3 AS332L1 *Super Puma*

FOREIGN FORCES

NATO • Iceland Air Policing: Aircraft and personnel from various NATO members on a rotating basis.

Ireland IRL

Euro €		2013	2014	2015
GDP	€	175bn	181bn	
	US$	232bn	246bn	
per capita	US$	45,888	51,159	
Growth	%	0.17	3.618	
Inflation	%	0.51	0.586	
Def Exp [a]	€	899m		
	US$	1.19bn		
Def bdgt [a]	€	905m	899m	885m
	US$	1.2bn	1.22bn	
US$1=€		0.75	0.74	

[a] Includes military pensions and capital expenditure

Population 4,832,765

Age	0 – 14	15 – 19	20 – 24	25 – 29	30 – 64	65 plus
Male	10.9%	3.1%	3.0%	3.4%	23.9%	5.7%
Female	10.5%	2.9%	2.9%	3.5%	23.5%	6.7%

Capabilities

The armed forces' primary task is to defend the state against armed aggression. They are also routinely called upon to conduct EOD operations within Ireland due to paramilitary activity, and conduct a range of security and support services such as maritime patrols and fishery protection. Irish forces also participate in UN peace-support, crisis-management and humanitarian-relief operations, most significantly in Lebanon and the Golan Heights. The army is the largest service, supported by a small air corps and naval service. During 2013, army units were consolidated within a new two-brigade structure and personnel were redeployed from support functions to operational units. Ireland's armed forces have been trimmed as a result of economic difficulties, with further defence-budget reductions planned for 2013–14, while some procurement programmes are being extended over a longer period to spread costs. Nevertheless, maritime recapitalisation continues, with the defence department exercising an option on a third PSO on top of the two already purchased to replace two older vessels. An initial draft of the new white paper was expected to be submitted to the defence minister by the end of 2014.

ACTIVE 9,350 (Army 7,500 Navy 1,050 Air 800)

RESERVE 4,630 (Army 4,350 Navy 260 Air 20)

ORGANISATIONS BY SERVICE

Army 7,500
FORCES BY ROLE
SPECIAL FORCES
  1 ranger coy
MANOEUVRE
  Reconnaissance
  1 armd recce sqn
  Mechanised
  1 mech inf coy
  Light
  1 inf bde (1 cav recce sqn, 4 inf bn, 1 arty regt (3 fd arty bty, 1 AD bty), 1 fd engr coy, 1 sigs coy, 1 MP coy, 1 tpt coy)
  1 inf bde (1 cav recce sqn, 3 inf bn, 1 arty regt (3 fd arty bty, 1 AD bty), 1 fd engr coy, 1 sigs coy, 1 MP coy, l tpt coy)
EQUIPMENT BY TYPE
LT TK 14 *Scorpion*
RECCE 15 *Piranha* IIIH
APC 94
  APC (W) 67: 65 *Piranha* III; 2 XA-180 *Sisu*
  PPV 27 RG-32M
ARTY 519
  TOWED 24: **105mm** 24 L-118 Light Gun
  MOR 495: **81mm** 400; **120mm** 95
AT
  MSL • MANPATS *Javelin*
  RCL 84mm *Carl Gustav*
AD
  SAM • MANPAD 7 RBS-70
  GUNS • TOWED 40mm 32 L/70 each with 8 *Flycatcher*
MW *Aardvark* Mk 2

Reserves 4,350 reservists (to reduce to 3,800)
FORCES BY ROLE
MANOEUVRE
  Reconnaissance
  1 (integrated) armd recce sqn
  4 (integrated) cav tp
  Mechanised
  1 (integrated) mech inf coy
  Light
  23 (integrated) inf coy
COMBAT SUPPORT
  4 (integrated) arty bty
  2 engr pl
  2 MP pl

COMBAT SERVICE SUPPORT
2 med det
4 tpt pl

Naval Service 1,050
EQUIPMENT BY TYPE
PATROL AND COASTAL COMBATANTS 8
  PSOH 1 *Eithne* with 1 57mm gun
  PSO 3: 2 *Roisin* with 1 76mm gun; 1 *Samuel Beckett* with 1 76mm gun
  PCO 4: 2 *Emer*; 2 *Orla* (ex-UK *Peacock*) with 1 76mm gun
LOGISTICS AND SUPPORT 6
  AXS 2
  YFL 3
  YTM 1

Air Corps 800
2 ops wg; 2 spt wg; 1 trg wg; 1 comms and info sqn
EQUIPMENT BY TYPE
AIRCRAFT
  MP 2 CN-235 MPA
  TPT 7: **Light** 6: 5 Cessna FR-172H; 1 Learjet 45 (VIP); **PAX** 1 Gulfstream GIV
  TRG 7 PC-9M
HELICOPTERS:
  MRH 6 AW139
  TPT • **Light** 2 EC135 P2 (incl trg/medevac; 1 non-operational)

DEPLOYMENT

Legal provisions for foreign deployment:
Constitution: Codified constitution (1937)
Specific legislation: 'Defence (Amendment) Act' 2006
Decision on deployment of troops abroad: requires (a) the authorisation of the operation by the UNSC or UNGA; (b) the approval of the Irish government; and (c) the approval of parliament, in accordance with Irish law. There is no requirement for parliament approval for dispatch as part of an international force where that force is unarmed or where the contingent does not exceed twelve members. Government approval is necessary for the deployment of Irish personnel for training, participation in exercises abroad; monitoring, observation, advisory or reconnaissance missions; and humanitarian operations in response to actual or potential disasters or emergencies.

AFGHANISTAN
NATO • ISAF 7

BOSNIA-HERZEGOVINA
EU • EUFOR • *Operation Althea* 7
OSCE • Bosnia and Herzegovina 6

CÔTE D'IVOIRE
UN • UNOCI 2 obs

DEMOCRATIC REPUBLIC OF THE CONGO
UN • MONUSCO 4

LEBANON
UN • UNIFIL 195; elm 1 mech inf bn

MALI
EU • EUTM Mali 8

MIDDLE EAST
UN • UNTSO 12 obs

SERBIA
NATO • KFOR 12
OSCE • Kosovo 7

SYRIA/ISRAEL
UN • UNDOF 135; 1 inf coy

UGANDA
EU • EUTM Somalia 10

UKRAINE
OSCE • Ukraine 4

WESTERN SAHARA
UN • MINURSO 3 obs

Italy ITA

Euro €		2013	2014	2015
GDP	€	1.56tr	1.57tr	
	US$	2.07tr	2.13tr	
per capita	US$	34,715	35,512	
Growth	%	-1.9	-0.2	
Inflation	%	1.3	0.1	
Def exp [a]	€	19bn		
	US$	25.2bn		
Def bdgt [b]	€	19bn	17.9bn	17bn
	US$	25.2bn	24.3bn	
US$1=€		0.75	0.74	

[a] NATO definition
[b] Includes military pensions

Population 61,680,122

Age	0-14	15-19	20-24	25-29	30-64	65 plus
Male	7.0%	2.4%	2.6%	2.7%	24.5%	9.0%
Female	6.7%	2.3%	2.6%	2.8%	25.4%	12.0%

Capabilities

The armed forces' primary role is territorial defence and participation in NATO operations, with the ability for extended deployment as part of a multinational force. The armed forces have been undergoing a process of reform involving force reductions and platform modernisation for over a decade. Defence expenditure remains under pressure, with major budget and capability cuts made in 2012. The defence ministry has dealt with budget reductions by focusing resources on units deployed abroad on operations; by postponing and/or downsizing some procurement programmes; and by cutting training and exercise expenditures. The government is also engaged in a review of defence ambitions, organisation, doctrine and equipment, with the outcome of this process expected in a white paper by the end of 2014. While the overall number of F-35 combat aircraft on order has been cut, the senate voted to support the programme in July 2013, approving the purchase of 60 F-35A and 30 F-35B models. The air force's ability to support long-range deployment has been boosted by the belated entry into service of four KC-767 tanker-transports. It lacks, however, a dedicated strategic-airlift platform. The forces train regularly at the national and NATO levels, and support a number of overseas deployments, including leading the UN Mission in Lebanon and the EU Training Mission in Somalia. Italy intends to commit a substantial contingent to NATO's follow-on mission in Afghanistan from 2015.

ACTIVE 176,000 (Army 103,100 Navy 31,000 Air 41,900) Paramilitary 183,500

RESERVES 18,300 (Army 13,400 Navy 4,900)

ORGANISATIONS BY SERVICE

Space
SATELLITES 6
  COMMUNICATIONS 2 *Sicral*
  IMAGERY 4 *Cosmo* (*Skymed*)

Army 103,100
Regt are bn sized
FORCES BY ROLE
COMMAND
  1 (NRDC-IT) corps HQ (1 sigs bde, 1 spt regt)
MANOEUVRE
  Mechanised
  1 (*Friuli*) div (1 (*Ariete*) armd bde (1 cav regt, 2 tk regt, 1 mech inf regt, 1 arty regt, 1 engr regt, 1 log regt); 1 (*Pozzuolo del Friuli*) cav bde (2 cav regt, 1 air mob regt, 1 amph regt, 1 arty regt, 1 cbt engr regt, 1 log regt, 2 avn regt)
  1 (*Acqui*) div (1 (*Pinerolo*) mech bde (3 mech inf regt, 1 SP arty regt, 1 cbt engr regt); 1 (*Granatieri*) mech bde (1 cav regt, 1 mech inf regt); 1 (*Garibaldi Bersaglieri*) mech bde (1 cav regt, 1 tk regt, 2 mech inf regt, 1 SP arty regt, 1 cbt engr regt); 1 (*Aosta*) mech bde (1 cav regt, 3 mech inf regt, 1 SP arty regt, 1 cbt engr regt); 1 (*Sassari*) lt mech bde (3 mech inf regt, 1 cbt engr regt))
  Mountain
  1 (*Tridentina*) mtn div (1 (*Taurinense*) mtn bde (1 cav regt, 3 mtn inf regt, 1 arty regt, 1 mtn cbt engr regt, 1 spt bn); 1 (*Julia*) mtn bde (3 mtn inf regt, 1 arty regt, 1 mtn cbt engr regt, 1 spt bn))
  Air Manoeuvre
  1 (*Folgore*) AB bde (1 cav regt, 3 para regt, 1 arty regt, 1 cbt engr regt)
  Aviation
  1 avn bde (3 avn regt)
COMBAT SUPPORT
  1 arty comd (3 arty regt, 1 NBC regt)
  1 AD comd (2 SAM regt, 1 ADA regt)
  1 engr comd (2 engr regt, 1 ptn br regt, 1 CIMIC regt)
  1 EW/sigs comd (1 EW/ISR bde (1 EW regt, 1 int regt, 1 UAV regt); 1 sigs bde with (7 sigs regt))

COMBAT SERVICE SUPPORT
  1 log comd (4 (manoeuvre) log regt, 4 tpt regt)
  1 spt regt
EQUIPMENT BY TYPE
MBT 160 C1 *Ariete*
RECCE 314: 300 B-1 *Centauro*; 14 VAB-RECO NBC
AIFV 346: 200 VCC-80 *Dardo*; 146 VBM 8×8 *Freccia*
APC 911
  APC (T) 361: 246 Bv-206; 115 M113 (incl variants)
  APC (W) 533 *Puma*
  PPV 17: 6 *Buffalo*; 11 *Cougar*
AAV 16: 14 AAVP-7; 1 AAVC-7; 1 AAVR-7
ARTY 915
  SP 155mm 192: 124 M109L; 68 PzH 2000
  TOWED 155mm 164 FH-70
  MRL 227mm 22 MLRS
  MOR 537: 81mm 212; 120mm 325: 183 Brandt; 142 RT-F1
AT
  MSL • MANPATS *Spike*; *Milan*
  RCL 80mm *Folgore*
AIRCRAFT • TPT • Light 6: 3 Do-228 (ACTL-1); 3 P-180 *Avanti*
HELICOPTERS
  ATK 50 AW129CBT *Mangusta*
  MRH 21 Bell 412 (AB-412) *Twin Huey*
  TPT 147: Heavy 17 CH-47C *Chinook*; Medium 26 NH90 TTH; Light 104: 8 AW109; 48 Bell 205 (AB-205); 31 Bell 206 *Jet Ranger* (AB-206); 17 Bell 212 (AB-212)
AD
  SAM
    TOWED 48: 16 SAMP-T; 32 *Skyguard/Aspide*
    MANPAD FIM-92A *Stinger*
  GUNS • SP 25mm 64 SIDAM
AEV 40 *Leopard* 1; M113
ARV 137 *Leopard* 1
VLB 64 *Biber*
MW 3 *Miniflail*

Navy 31,000
EQUIPMENT BY TYPE
SUBMARINES • TACTICAL • SSK 6:
  4 *Pelosi* (imp *Sauro*, 3rd and 4th series) with 6 single 533mm TT with Type-A-184 HWT
  2 *Salvatore Todaro* (Type-U212A) with 6 single 533mm TT with Type-A-184 HWT/DM2A4 HWT (2 additional vessels under construction)
PRINCIPAL SURFACE COMBATANTS 19
  AIRCRAFT CARRIERS • CVS 2:
    1 *G. Garibaldi* with 2 octuple *Albatros* lnchr with *Aspide* SAM, 2 triple 324mm ASTT with Mk46 LWT (capacity mixed air group of either 12–18 AV-8B *Harrier* II; 17 SH-3D *Sea King* or AW101 *Merlin*)
    1 *Cavour* with 4 octuple VLS with *Aster* 15 SAM, 2 76mm guns (capacity mixed air group of 18–20 AV-8B *Harrier* II; 12 AW101 *Merlin*)
  DESTROYERS • DDGHM 7:
    2 *Andrea Doria* with 2 quad lnchr with *Otomat* Mk2A AShM, 1 48-cell VLS with *Aster* 15/*Aster* 30 SAM, 2 single 324mm ASTT with MU90 LWT, 3 76mm guns (capacity 1 AW101 *Merlin*/NH90 hel)

2 *Luigi Durand de la Penne* (ex-*Animoso*) with 2 quad lnchr with *Milas* AS/*Otomat* Mk 2A AShM, 1 Mk13 GMLS with SM-1MR SAM, 1 octuple *Albatros* lnchr with *Aspide* SAM, 2 triple 324mm ASTT with Mk46 LWT, 1 127mm gun, 3 76mm guns (capacity 2 Bell 212 (AB-212) hel)

3 *Bergamini* with 2 quad lnchr with *Otomat* Mk2A AShM, 1 16-cell VLS with *Aster* 15/*Aster* 30 SAM, 2 triple 324mm ASTT with MU90 LWT, 1 127mm gun, 1 76mm gun (capacity 2 AW101/NH90 hel)

FRIGATES • FFGHM 10:

2 *Artigliere* with 8 single lnchr with *Otomat* Mk 2 AShM, 1 octuple *Albatros* lnchr with *Aspide* SAM, 1 127mm gun, (capacity 1 Bell 212 (AB-212) hel)

8 *Maestrale* with 4 single lnchr with *Otomat* Mk2 AShM, 1 octuple *Albatros* lnchr with *Aspide* SAM, 2 triple 324mm ASTT with Mk46 LWT, 1 127mm gun (capacity 2 Bell 212 (AB-212) hel)

PATROL AND COASTAL COMBATANTS 19

CORVETTES 5

FSM 4 *Minerva* with 1 octuple *Albatros* lnchr with *Aspide* SAM, 1 76mm gun

FS 1 *Minerva* with 1 76mm gun

PSOH 6:

4 *Comandante Cigala Fuligosi* with 1 76mm gun (capacity 1 Bell 212 (AB-212)/NH90 hel)

2 *Comandante Cigala Fuligosi* (capacity 1 Bell 212 (AB-212)/NH-90 hel)

PCO 4 *Cassiopea* with 1 76mm gun (capacity 1 Bell 212 (AB-212) hel)

PB 4 *Esploratore*

MINE WARFARE • MINE COUNTERMEASURES 10

MHO 10: 8 *Gaeta*; 2 *Lerici*

AMPHIBIOUS

PRINCIPAL AMPHIBIOUS SHIPS • LPD 3:

2 *San Giorgio* with 1 76mm gun (capacity 3-5 AW101/NH90/SH3-D/Bell 212; 1 CH-47 *Chinook* tpt hel; 3 LCM 2 LCVP; 30 trucks; 36 APC (T); 350 troops)

1 *San Giusto* with 1 76mm gun (capacity 4 AW101 *Merlin*; 1 CH-47 *Chinook* tpt hel; 3 LCM 2 LCVP; 30 trucks; 36 APC (T); 350 troops)

LANDING CRAFT 30: 17 **LCVP**; 13 **LCM**

LOGISTICS AND SUPPORT 125

ABU 5 *Ponza*

AFD 19

AGE 2: 1 *Vincenzo Martellota*; 1 *Raffaele Rosseti*

AGI 1 *Elettra*

AGOR 1 *Leonardo* (coastal)

AGS 3: 1 *Ammiraglio Magnaghi* with 1 hel landing platform; 2 *Aretusa* (coastal)

AKSL 6 *Gorgona*

AORH 3: 1 *Etna* with 1 76mm gun (capacity 1 AW101/NH90 hel); 2 *Stromboli* with 1 76mm gun (capacity 1 AW101/NH90 hel)

AOT 7 *Depoli*

ARSH 1 *Anteo* (capacity 1 Bell 212 (AB-212) hel)

ATS 3 *Ciclope*

AT 9 (coastal)

AWT 7: 1 *Bormida*; 2 *Simeto*; 4 *Panarea*

AXL 3 *Aragosta*

AXS 8: 1 *Amerigo Vespucci*; 1 *Palinuro*; 1 *Italia*; 5 *Caroly*

YDT 2 *Pedretti*

YFT 1 *Aragosta*

YFU 2 Men 215

YPT 1 Men 212

YTB 9 *Porto*

YTM 32

Naval Aviation 2,200

FORCES BY ROLE

FIGHTER/GROUND ATTACK

1 sqn with AV-8B *Harrier* II; TAV-8B *Harrier*

ANTI-SUBMARINE WARFARE/TRANSPORT

5 sqn with AW101 ASW *Merlin*; Bell 212 ASW (AB-212AS); Bell 212 (AB-212); NH90 NFH

MARITIME PATROL

1 flt with P-180

AIRBORNE EARLY WANRING & CONTROL

1 flt with AW101 *Merlin* AEW

EQUIPMENT BY TYPE

AIRCRAFT 16 combat capable

FGA 16: 14 AV-8B *Harrier* II; 2 TAV-8B *Harrier*

MP 3 P-180

HELICOPTERS

ASW 33: 10 AW101 ASW *Merlin*; 12 Bell 212 ASW; 11 NH90 NFH

AEW 4 AW101 *Merlin* AEW

TPT 14: **Medium** 8 AW101 *Merlin*; **Light** 6 Bell 212 (AB-212)

MSL

AAM • IR AIM-9L *Sidewinder*; ARH AIM-120 AMRAAM

ASM AGM-65 *Maverick*

AShM *Marte* Mk 2/S

Marines 2,000

FORCES BY ROLE

MANOEUVRE

Amphibious

1 mne regt (1 SF coy, 2 mne bn, 1 cbt engr coy, 1 log bn)

1 landing craft gp

COMBAT SERVICE SUPPORT

1 log regt (1 log bn)

EQUIPMENT BY TYPE

APC (T) 24 VCC-2

AAV 28: 15 AAVP-7; 12 AAVC-7; 1 AAVR-7

ARTY • MOR 12: **81mm** 8 Brandt; **120mm** 4 Brandt

AT • MSL • MANPATS Milan; Spike

AD • SAM • MANPAD FIM-92A *Stinger*

ARV 1 AAV-7RAI

Air Force 41,900

FORCES BY ROLE

FIGHTER

4 sqn with Eurofighter *Typhoon*

FIGHTER/GROUND ATTACK

2 sqn with AMX *Ghibli*

1 (SEAD/EW) sqn with *Tornado* ECR

2 sqn with *Tornado* IDS

FIGHTER/GROUND ATTACK/ISR

1 sqn with AMX *Ghibli*

MARITIME PATROL
  1 sqn (opcon Navy) with BR1150 *Atlantic*
TANKER/TRANSPORT
  1 sqn with KC-767A
COMBAT SEARCH & RESCUE
  1 sqn with AB-212 ICO
SEARCH & RESCUE
  1 wg with AW139 (HH-139A); Bell 212 (HH-212); HH-3F *Pelican*
TRANSPORT
  2 (VIP) sqn with A319CJ; AW139 (VH-139A); *Falcon* 50; *Falcon* 900 *Easy*; *Falcon* 900EX; SH-3D *Sea King*
  2 sqn with C-130J/C-130J-30/KC-130J *Hercules*
  1 sqn with C-27J *Spartan*
  1 (calibration) sqn with P-180 *Avanti*
TRAINING
  1 sqn with Eurofighter *Typhoon*
  1 sqn with MB-339PAN (aerobatic team)
  1 sqn with MD-500D/E (NH-500D/E)
  1 sqn with *Tornado*
  1 sqn with AMX-T *Ghibli*
  1 sqn with MB-339A
  1 sqn with MB-339CD*
  1 sqn with SF-260EA
ISR UAV
  1 sqn with MQ-9A *Reaper*; RQ-1B *Predator*
AIR DEFENCE
  2 bty with *Spada*
EQUIPMENT BY TYPE
  AIRCRAFT 242 combat capable
    FTR 69 Eurofighter *Typhoon*
    FGA 124: 53 *Tornado* IDS; 63 AMX *Ghibli*; 8 AMX-T *Ghibli*
    FGA/EW 15 *Tornado* ECR*
    ASW 6 BR1150 *Atlantic*
    SIGINT 1 AML Gulfstream III
    TKR/TPT 6: 4 KC-767A; 2 KC-130J *Hercules*
    TPT 66: **Medium** 31: 9 C-130J *Hercules*; 10 C-130J-30 *Hercules*; 12 C-27J *Spartan*; **Light** 25: 15 P-180 *Avanti*; 10 S-208 (liaison); **PAX** 10: 3 A319CJ; 2 *Falcon* 50 (VIP); 2 *Falcon* 900 *Easy*; 3 *Falcon* 900EX (VIP)
    TRG 103: 3 M-346; 21 MB-339A; 28 MB-339CD*; 21 MB-339PAN (aerobatics); 30 SF-260EA
  HELICOPTERS
    MRH 58: 10 AW139 (HH-139A/VH-139A); 2 MD-500D (NH-500D); 46 MD-500E (NH-500E)
    SAR 12 HH-3F *Pelican*
    TPT 31: **Medium** 2 SH-3D *Sea King* (liaison/VIP); **Light** 29 Bell 212 (HH-212)/AB-212 ICO
  UAV • ISR • Heavy 11: 6 MQ-9A *Reaper*; 5 RQ-1B *Predator*
  AD • SAM • TOWED *Spada*
  MSL
    AAM • IR AIM-9L *Sidewinder*; **IIR** IRIS-T; **ARH** AIM-120 AMRAAM
    ARM AGM-88 HARM
    LACM SCALP EG/*Storm Shadow*
  BOMBS
    Laser-guided/GPS: Enhanced *Paveway* II; Enhanced *Paveway* III

Joint Special Forces Command (COFS)
Army
FORCES BY ROLE
SPECIAL FORCES
  1 SF regt (9th *Assalto paracadutisti*)
  1 STA regt (185th RAO)
  1 ranger regt (4th *Alpini paracadutisti*)
COMBAT SUPPORT
  1 psyops regt
TRANSPORT HELICOPTER
  1 spec ops hel regt

Navy (COMSUBIN)
FORCES BY ROLE
SPECIAL FORCES
  1 SF gp (GOI)
  1 diving gp (GOS)

Air Force
FORCES BY ROLE
SPECIAL FORCES
  1 sqn (17th *Stormo Incursori*)

Paramilitary
Carabinieri
FORCES BY ROLE
SPECIAL FORCES
  1 spec ops gp (GIS)

Paramilitary 184,250

Carabinieri 104,950
The Carabinieri are organisationally under the MoD. They are a separate service in the Italian Armed Forces as well as a police force with judicial competence.

Mobile and Specialised Branch
FORCES BY ROLE
MANOEUVRE
  Aviation
  1 hel gp
  Other
  1 (mobile) paramilitary div (1 bde (1st) with (1 horsed cav regt, 11 mobile bn); 1 bde (2nd) with (1 (1st) AB regt, 2 (7th & 13th) mobile regt))
EQUIPMENT BY TYPE
APC • APC (T) 3 VCC-2
AIRCRAFT • TPT • Light: 1 P-180 *Avanti*
HELICOPTERS
  MRH 24 Bell 412 (AB-412)
TPT • Light 19 AW109
PATROL AND COASTAL COMBATANTS • PB 69

Customs 68,100
(Servizio Navale Guardia Di Finanza)
EQUIPMENT BY TYPE
PATROL AND COASTAL COMBATANTS 179
  PCF 1 *Antonio Zara*

PBF 146: 19 *Bigliani*; 24 *Corrubia*; 9 *Mazzei*; 62 V-2000; 32 V-5000/V-6000
PB 32: 24 *Buratti*; 8 *Meatini*
LOGISTICS AND SUPPORT • AX 1 *Giorgio Cini*

Coast Guard 11,200
(Guardia Costiera – Capitanerie Di Porto)
EQUIPMENT BY TYPE
PATROL AND COASTAL COMBATANTS 328
   PCO 3: 2 *Dattilo*; 1 *Gregoretti*
   PCC 43: 5 *Diciotti*; 1 *Saettia*; 28 200-class; 9 400-class
   PB 282: 19 300-class; 3 454-class; 72 500-class; 12 600-class; 33 700-class; 94 800-class; 49 2000-class
   AIRCRAFT MP 9: 6 ATR-42 MP *Surveyor*, 1 P-180GC; 2 PL-166-DL3
   HELICOPTERS • MRH 13: 4 AW139; 9 Bell 412SP (AB-412SP *Griffin*)

Cyber

Overall responsibility for cyber security rests with the presidency of the Council of Ministers and the Inter-Ministerial Situation and Planning Group, which includes, among others, representatives from the defence, interior and foreign-affairs ministries. A Joint Integrated Concept on Computer Network Operations was approved in 2009. In 2011, an Inter-Forces Committee on Cyberspace (CIAC) was established to advise the chief of defence staff. In January 2012, an Inter-Forces Policy Directive was approved to provide a vision for both operational management (under the C4 Defence Command, the Inter-Forces Intelligence Centre and individual armed forces) and strategic direction (under the chief of defence staff (CDS) and CIAC). CDS established the Computer and Emergency Response Team (CERT-Defence) to promote the security of IT networks and share knowledge on cyber threats and cyber defence including through the collaboration with national and international CERTs.

DEPLOYMENT

Legal provisions for foreign deployment:
Constitution: Codified constitution (1949)
Decision on deployment of troops abroad: By the government upon approval by the parliament.

AFGHANISTAN
NATO • ISAF 1,411; 1 mech inf bde HQ; 1 mech inf regt; 1 avn det; AW129 *Mangusta*; CH-47; NH90; *Tornado*; C-130
UN • UNAMA 2 obs

ALBANIA
OSCE • Albania 3

BOSNIA-HERZEGOVINA
OSCE • Bosnia and Herzegovina 7

CENTRAL AFRICAN REPUBLIC
EU • EUFOR RCA 49; 1 engr pl

EGYPT
MFO 79; 3 coastal patrol unit

GULF OF ADEN & INDIAN OCEAN
EU • *Operation Atalanta* 1 DDGHM

INDIA/PAKISTAN
UN • UNMOGIP 4 obs

KUWAIT
1 KC-767A

LEBANON
UN • UNIFIL 1,200; 1 mech bde HQ; 1 mech inf bn; 1 hel flt; 1 engr coy; 1 sigs coy; 1 CIMIC coy(-)

MALI
EU • EUTM Mali 15
UN • MINUSMA 2

MALTA
25; 2 Bell 212 (HH-212)

MEDITERRANEAN SEA
NATO • SNMCMG 2: 1 FFGHM

MIDDLE EAST
UN • UNTSO 6 obs

SERBIA
NATO • KFOR 575; 1 recce BG HQ; 1 Carabinieri unit
OSCE • Kosovo 10

SOUTH SUDAN
UN • UNMISS 1 obs

UGANDA
EU • EUTM Somalia 78

UKRAINE
OSCE • Ukraine 13

WESTERN SAHARA
UN • MINURSO 4 obs

FOREIGN FORCES

United States US European Command: 11,360
   Army 3,900; 1 AB IBCT(-)
   Navy 3,600; 1 HQ (US Navy Europe (USNAVEUR)) at Naples; 1 HQ (6th Fleet) at Gaeta; 1 MP Sqn with 9 P-3C *Orion* at Sigonella
   USAF 3,850; 1 ftr wg with 2 ftr sqn with 21 F-16C/D *Fighting Falcon* at Aviano
   USMC 10

Latvia LVA

Latvian Lat L		2013	2014	2015
GDP	L	23.3bn	24.2bn	
	US$	31bn	32.8bn	
per capita	US$	15,187	16,145	
Growth	%	4.1	2.7	
Inflation	%	0.0	0.7	
Def exp [a]	L	154m		
	US$	205m		
Def bdgt [b]	L	158m		
	US$	210m		
FMA (US)	US$	2.2m	2.25m	1.5m
US$1=L		0.75	0.74	

[a] NATO definition
[b] Includes military pensions

Population 2,165,165

Age	0–14	15–19	20–24	25–29	30–64	65 plus
Male	7.2%	2.2%	3.4%	4.3%	23.6%	5.6%
Female	6.9%	2.1%	3.3%	4.2%	25.5%	11.6%

Capabilities

Latvia's small armed forces mainly comprise ground forces, and the country is dependent on NATO membership as a security guarantor against external state-level threats. As of mid-2014, a small reduction planned for the 2015 budget was expected to be reversed in response to Russia's intervention in Ukraine, with the spending figure rising from 0.87% to 1% of GDP. In July, the defence ministry announced that spending would rise to 2% of GDP by 2020. The Latvian Armed Forces Development Plan 2012–24 includes airspace surveillance capacities among its priorities. Plans to mechanise its single infantry brigade appeared to be progressing in mid-2014, with the proposed purchase of ex-British Army CVR (T) armoured vehicles, including *Scimitar* and *Spartan*, and also, reportedly, *Spike* missiles. National Guard combat capabilities were also intended to develop, with reports indicating that rapid-reaction task groups would be formed. Latvia participates in NATO and EU missions and its forces train regularly with NATO partners, as well as taking part in other multilateral exercises. NATO partner states conducted military exercises in Latvia in 2014, including bolstered air policing, while US troops and armour deployed as part of Washington's *Operation Atlantic Resolve*.

ACTIVE 5,310 (Army 1,250 Navy 550 Air 310 Joint Staff 2,600 National Guard 600)

RESERVE 7,850 (National Guard 7,850)

ORGANISATIONS BY SERVICE

Joint 2,600

FORCES BY ROLE
SPECIAL FORCES
 1 SF unit
COMBAT SUPPORT
 1 MP bn

Army 1,250
FORCES BY ROLE
MANOEUVRE
 Light
 1 inf bde (2 inf bn, 1 cbt spt bn HQ, 1 CSS bn HQ)

National Guard 600; 7,850 part-time (8,450 total)
FORCES BY ROLE
MANOEUVRE
 Light
 11 inf bn
COMBAT SUPPORT
 1 arty bn
 1 AD bn
 1 engr bn
 1 NBC bn
COMBAT SERVICE SUPPORT
 3 spt bn
EQUIPMENT BY TYPE
MBT 3 T-55 (trg)
APC • PPV 8 *Cougar* (on loan from US)
ARTY 76
 TOWED 100mm 23 K-53
 MOR 53: **81mm** 28 L16; **120mm** 25 M120
AT
 MANPATS *Spike*-LR
 RCL **84mm** *Carl Gustav*
 GUNS **90mm** 130
AD
 SAM • MANPAD RBS-70
 GUNS • TOWED **40mm** 24 L/70

Navy 550 (incl Coast Guard)
Naval Forces Flotilla separated into an MCM squadron and a patrol boat squadron. LVA, EST and LTU have set up a joint naval unit, BALTRON, with bases at Liepaja, Riga, Ventspils (LVA), Tallinn (EST), Klaipeda (LTU). Each nation contributes 1–2 MCMVs
EQUIPMENT BY TYPE
PATROL AND COASTAL COMBATANTS 5
 PB 5 *Skrunda* (GER *Swath*)
MINE WARFARE • MINE COUNTERMEASURES 6
 MHO 5 *Imanta* (ex-NLD *Alkmaar/Tripartite*)
 MCCS 1 *Vidar* (NOR)
LOGISTICS AND SUPPORT 2
 AXL 2: 1 *Storm* (NOR) with 1 76mm gun; 1 *Varonis* (comd and spt ship, ex-*Buyskes*, NLD)

Coast Guard
Under command of the Latvian Naval Forces.
PATROL AND COASTAL COMBATANTS
 PB 6: 1 *Astra*; 5 KBV 236 (ex-SWE)

Air Force 310

Main tasks are airspace control and defence, maritime and land SAR and air transportation.

FORCES BY ROLE
TRANSPORT
1 (mixed) tpt sqn with An-2 *Colt*; Mi-17 *Hip* H; PZL Mi-2 *Hoplite*
AIR DEFENCE
1 AD bn
1 radar sqn (radar/air ctrl)
AIRCRAFT • TPT • Light 4 An-2 *Colt*
HELICOPTERS
MRH 4 Mi-17 *Hip* H
TPT • Light 2 PZL Mi-2 *Hoplite*

Paramilitary

State Border Guard
PATROL AND COASTAL COMBATANTS
PB 3: 1 *Valpas* (ex-FIN); 1 *Lokki* (ex-FIN); 1 *Randa*

Cyber

A Cyber Defence Unit is under development within the National Guard. A National Cyber Security Strategy is also under development. Cyber-defence capabilities are under development, and technical capabilities are provided according to NATO standards.

DEPLOYMENT

Legal provisions for foreign deployment:
Constitution: Codified constitution (1922)
Specific legislation: 'Law on Participation of the National Armed Forces of Latvia in International Operations' (1995) (Annex of 21 Jan 2009 allows Latvian armed forces to take part in quick response units formed by NATO/EU).
Decision on deployment of troops abroad: a) By parliament (Section 5 I of the 1995 'Law on Participation', in combination with Art. 73 of constitution); b) by cabinet, for rescue or humanitarian operations (Section 5 II of the 1995 law) or military exercises in non-NATO states (Section 9 of the 1995 law); c) by defence minister for rescue and humanitarian-aid operations in NATO/EU states. Latvian units can be transferred under the control of an international organisation or another country to conduct international operations for a limited time frame only in compliance with and under conditions defined by a parliamentary decree.

AFGHANISTAN
NATO • ISAF 11

CENTRAL AFRICAN REPUBLIC
EU • EUFOR RCA 40

MALI
EU • EUTM Mali 7

NORTH SEA
NATO • SNMCMG 1: 1 MHO

SERBIA
OSCE • Kosovo 1

UKRAINE
OSCE • Ukraine 5

Lithuania LTU

Lithuanian Litas L		2013	2014	2015
GDP	L	119bn	124bn	
	US$	46.5bn	48.7bn	
per capita	US$	15,649	16,476	
Growth	%	3.3	3.0	
Inflation	%	1.2	0.3	
Def exp [a]	L	921m		
	US$	359m		
Def bdgt [b]	L	923m	1.11bn	1.5bn
	US$	359m	436m	
FMA (US)	US$	2.55m	2.55m	1.5m
US$1=L		2.57	2.55	

[a] NATO definition
[b] Includes military pensions

Population 3,505,738

Age	0–14	15–19	20–24	25–29	30–64	65 plus
Male	6.9%	2.8%	3.6%	4.0%	23.8%	5.9%
Female	6.6%	2.6%	3.5%	3.9%	25.2%	11.1%

Capabilities

The country fields small, land-focused armed forces with NATO membership the basis of its defence policy. Like its Baltic partners, Lithuania was concerned by Russia's intervention in Ukraine and also by what it saw as Russia bolstering military capacity in Kaliningrad. As of mid-2014, final preparations were under way for the formation of a Lithuania–Poland–Ukraine army brigade, which had originally been intended to be set up by the third quarter of 2011. Developing further the combat capacity of its single mechanised infantry brigade continues as a priority, if in a constrained funding environment. Under the National Defence System Development Programme 2014–23, Riga aims to procure more modern wheeled APCs for two of the mechanised infantry units to replace their M113s. NATO partner states conducted military exercises in Lithuania in 2014, including bolstered air policing, while US troops and armour have deployed as part of Washington's *Operation Atlantic Resolve*.

ACTIVE 10,950 (Army 7,500 Navy 500 Air 900 Joint 2,050) **Paramilitary 11,000**
Conscript liability 12 months

RESERVE 6,700 (Army 6,700)

ORGANISATIONS BY SERVICE

Army 3,200; 4,300 active reserves (total 7,500)
FORCES BY ROLE
MANOEUVRE
    Mechanised
    1 mech bde (3 mech inf bn, 1 arty bn)

Light
3 mot inf bn
COMBAT SUPPORT
1 engr bn
COMBAT SERVICE SUPPORT
1 trg regt
EQUIPMENT BY TYPE
APC (T) 126 M113A1
ARTY 48
  TOWED 105mm 18 M101
  MOR 120mm 30: 5 2B11; 10 M/41D; 15 M113 with Tampella
AT • MSL
  SP 10 M1025A2 HMMWV with *Javelin*
  MANPATS *Javelin*
  RCL 84mm *Carl Gustav*
AD • SAM • MANPAD *Stinger*
AEV 8 MT-LB
ARV 4 M113

Reserves
National Defence Voluntary Forces 4,300 active reservists
FORCES BY ROLE
MANOEUVRE
  Other
    6 (territorial) def unit

Navy 500
LVA, EST and LTU established a joint naval unit, BALTRON, with bases at Liepaja, Riga, Ventpils (LVA), Tallinn (EST), Klaipeda (LTU)
EQUIPMENT BY TYPE
PATROL AND COASTAL COMBATANTS 4
  PCC 3 *Zematis* (ex-DNK *Flyvefisken*) with 1 76mm gun
  PB 1 *Storm* (ex-NOR) with 1 76mm gun
MINE WARFARE • MINE COUNTERMEASURES 4
  MHC 3: 1 *Sūduvis* (ex-GER *Lindau*); 2 *Skulvis* (ex-UK *Hunt*)
  MCCS 1 *Jotvingis* (ex-NOR *Vidar*)
LOGISTICS AND SUPPORT 4
  AAR 1 *Sakiai*
  YAG 1 *Lokys* (ex-DNK)
  YGS 1
  YTL 1 (ex-SWE)

Air Force 950
Flying hours 120 hrs/year
FORCES BY ROLE
AIR DEFENCE
  1 AD bn
EQUIPMENT BY TYPE
AIRCRAFT
  TPT 5: **Medium** 3 C-27J *Spartan*; **Light** 2 L-410 *Turbolet*
  TRG 1 L-39ZA *Albatros*
HELICOPTERS • TPT • **Medium** 8 Mi-8 *Hip* (tpt/SAR)
AD • SAM • MANPAD FIM-92A *Stinger*; RBS-70

Special Operation Force
FORCES BY ROLE
SPECIAL FORCES
  1 SF gp (1 CT unit; 1 Jaeger bn, 1 cbt diver unit)

Joint Logistics Support Command 900
FORCES BY ROLE
COMBAT SERVICE SUPPORT
  1 log bn

Joint Training and Doctrine Command (TRADOC) 500
FORCES BY ROLE
COMBAT SERVICE SUPPORT
  1 trg regt

Other Units 650
FORCES BY ROLE
COMBAT SUPPORT
  1 MP bn

Paramilitary 11,000

Riflemen Union 7,000

State Border Guard Service 4,000
Ministry of Internal Affairs

Coast Guard 530
EQUIPMENT BY TYPE
PATROL AND COASTAL COMBATANTS • PB 3: 1 *Lokki* (ex-FIN); 1 KBV 041 (ex-SWE); 1 KBV 101 (ex-SWE)
AMPHIBIOUS • LANDING CRAFT • UCAC 2 *Christina* (*Griffon* 2000)

Cyber
In April 2013, a Cyber Security Strategy was adopted, defining ways and means to strengthen cyber security in defence organisations. A strategy-implementation plan was adopted in 2014. Critical information infrastructure will be identified in 2015, to be followed by a Cyber Defence Plan for this infrastructure. A Law on Cyber Security was expected to be approved by parliament in late 2014 and come into force in 2015.

DEPLOYMENT
Legal provisions for foreign deployment:
Constitution: Codified constitution (1992)
Decision on deployment of troops abroad: By parliament (Art. 67, 138, 142) According to legislation, the defence minister has the authority to establish the exact amount or size of contingent to be deployed, and the duration of the deployment, not exceeding the limits set out by the parliament.

AFGHANISTAN
NATO • ISAF 84
UN • UNAMA 1 obs

CENTRAL AFRICAN REPUBLIC
EU • EUFOR RCA 1

MALI
EU • EUTM Mali 3

NORTH SEA
NATO • SNMCMG 1: 1 MCCS

SERBIA
NATO • KFOR 1

UKRAINE
OSCE • Ukraine 2

FOREIGN FORCES

Canada NATO Baltic Air Policing 4 F/A-18A *Hornet* (CF-18AM)

Portugal NATO Baltic Air Policing 6 F-16AM *Fighting Falcon*

Luxembourg LUX

Euro €		2013	2014	2015
GDP	€	45.5bn	47.2bn	
	US$	60.4bn	63.9bn	
per capita	US$	112,473	116,752	
Growth	%	2.1	2.7	
Inflation	%	1.7	1.1	
Def exp [a]	€	187m		
	US$	248m		
Def bdgt	€	188m	189m	
	US$	249m	255m	
US$1=€		0.75	0.74	

[a] NATO definition

Population 520,672

Foreign citizens: ε124,000

Age	0-14	15-19	20-24	25-29	30-64	65 plus
Male	9.2%	3.2%	3.3%	3.2%	23.8%	6.5%
Female	8.7%	3.0%	3.2%	3.3%	23.8%	8.9%

Capabilities

Luxembourg maintains a small army, with no air or naval capacity. It continues to support EU anti-piracy operations by funding the Luxembourg Maritime Patrol and Reconnaissance programme. This uses contractor-operated *Merlin* IIIC maritime-patrol aircraft as part of the counter-piracy *Operation Atalanta*. It has joined the European Defence Agency's programme for a European air-tanker pool.

ACTIVE 900 (Army 900) **Paramilitary 610**

ORGANISATIONS BY SERVICE

Army 900

FORCES BY ROLE
MANOEUVRE
Reconnaissance
2 recce coy (1 to Eurocorps/BEL div, 1 to NATO pool of deployable forces)
Light
1 lt inf bn

EQUIPMENT BY TYPE
APC • PPV 48 *Dingo* II
ARTY • MOR 81mm 6
AT • MSL• MANPATS 6 TOW

Paramilitary 610

Gendarmerie 610

DEPLOYMENT

Legal provisions for foreign deployment:
Constitution: Codified constitution (1868)
Specific legislation: 'Loi du 27 juillet 1992 relatif à la participation du Grand-Duché de Luxembourg à des opérations pour le maintien de la paix (OMP) dans le cadre d'organisations internationales'.
Decision on deployment of troops abroad: By government after formal consultation of relevant parliamentary committees and the Council of State (Art. 1–2 of the 1992 law).

CENTRAL AFRICAN REPUBLIC
EU • EUFOR RCA 1

LEBANON
UN • UNIFIL 2

MALI
EU • EUTM Mali 1

SERBIA
NATO • KFOR 23

Macedonia, Former Yugoslav Republic FYROM

Macedonian Denar d		2013	2014	2015
GDP	d	473bn	491bn	
	US$	10.2bn	10.9bn	
per capita	US$	4,931	5,262	
Growth	%	2.9	3.4	
Inflation	%	2.8	1.0	
Def bdgt	d	n.k.	5.87bn	
	US$	n.k.	131m	
FMA (US)	US$	3.6m	3.6m	4m
US$1=d		46.32	44.94	

Population 2,091,719

Age	0–14	15–19	20–24	25–29	30–64	65 plus
Male	9.2%	3.6%	3.6%	3.9%	24.2%	5.3%
Female	8.5%	3.4%	3.4%	3.7%	24.0%	7.1%

Capabilities

Macedonia maintains a small, joint force focused on the army, with a minimal maritime wing and modest air wing. Ambitious reform plans spelt out in the 2003 Defence Concept, and reiterated in the 2005 Defence White Paper, have so far only partly been realised, though the armed forces have been reorganised. The 2003 Defence Concept called for armed forces to support territorial integrity, regional stability, peace-support missions and deployed operations. The country continues to aspire to NATO membership, having joined the NATO Membership Action Plan in 1999, but is hindered by a number of factors including an impasse with Greece over the state's name. The air arm consists mainly of transport and armed support helicopters, but there is no organic fixed-wing airlift.

ACTIVE 8,000 (Joint 8,000)

RESERVE 4,850

ORGANISATIONS BY SERVICE

Joint Operational Command 8,000

Army
FORCES BY ROLE
SPECIAL FORCES
  1 (Special Purpose) SF regt (1 SF bn, 1 Ranger bn)
MANOEUVRE
  Armoured
   1 tk bn
  Mechanised
   1 mech inf bde
COMBAT SUPPORT
  1 (mixed) arty regt
  1 AD coy
  1 engr bn
  1 MP bn
  1 NBC coy
  1 sigs bn

Logistic Support Command
FORCES BY ROLE
COMBAT SUPPORT
  1 engr bn (1 active coy)
COMBAT SERVICE SUPPORT
  3 log bn

Reserves
FORCES BY ROLE
MANOEUVRE
  Light
   1 inf bde
EQUIPMENT BY TYPE
MBT 31 T-72A
RECCE 51: 10 BRDM-2; 41 M1114 HMMWV
AIFV 11: 10 BMP-2; 1 BMP-2K
APC 200
  APC (T) 47: 9 *Leonidas*; 28 M113A; 10 MT-LB
  APC (W) 153: 57 BTR-70; 12 BTR-80; 84 TM-170 *Hermelin*

ARTY 126
  TOWED 70: **105mm** 14 M-56; **122mm** 56 M-30 M-1938
  MRL 17: **122mm** 6 BM-21; **128mm** 11
  MOR 39: **120mm** 39
AT
  MSL • MANPATS *Milan*
  RCL 57mm; **82mm** M60A
AD
  SAM
   SP 8 9K35 *Strela*-10 (SA-13 *Gopher*)
   MANPAD 9K310 *Igla*-1 (SA-16 *Gimlet*)
  GUNS 40mm 36 L20

Marine Wing
EQUIPMENT BY TYPE
PATROL AND COASTAL COMBATANTS • PB 2 *Botica*

Air Wing
Air Wg is directly under Joint Operational Cmd
FORCES BY ROLE
TRANSPORT
  1 (VIP) sqn with An-2 *Colt*
TRAINING
  1 sqn with Bell 205 (UH-1H *Iroquois*)
  1 sqn with Z-242
ATTACK HELICOPTER
  1 sqn with Mi-24K *Hind* G2; Mi-24V *Hind* E
TRANSPORT HELICOPTER
  1 sqn with Mi-8MTV *Hip*; Mi-17 *Hip* H
EQUIPMENT BY TYPE
AIRCRAFT
  TPT • Light 1 An-2 *Colt*
  TRG 5 Z-242
HELICOPTERS
  ATK 4 Mi-24V *Hind* E (10: 2 Mi-24K *Hind* G2; 8 Mi-24V *Hind* E in store)
  MRH 6: 4 Mi-8MTV *Hip*; 2 Mi-17 *Hip* H
  TPT • Light 2 Bell 205 (UH-1H *Iroquois*)

Paramilitary

Police 7,600 (some 5,000 armed)
incl 2 SF units
EQUIPMENT BY TYPE
APC BTR APC (W)/M113A APC (T)
HELICOPTERS 3
  MRH 1 Bell 412EP *Twin Huey*
  TPT • Light 2: 1 Bell 206B (AB-206B) *Jet Ranger* II; 1 Bell 212 (AB-212)

DEPLOYMENT

Legal provisions for foreign deployment of armed forces:
Constitution: Codified constitution (1991)
Specific legislation: 'Defence Law' (2005)
Decision on deployment of troops abroad: a) by the government if deployment is for humanitarian missions or military exercises; b) by the parliament if for peacekeeping operations ('Defence Law', Art. 41).

AFGHANISTAN
NATO • ISAF 152

ALBANIA
OSCE • Albania 1

BOSNIA-HERZEGOVINA
EU • EUFOR • *Operation Althea* 11

LEBANON
UN • UNIFIL 1

SERBIA
OSCE • Kosovo 22

UKRAINE
OSCE • Ukraine 1

Malta MLT

Maltese Lira ML		2013	2014	2015
GDP	ML	7.26bn	7.58bn	
	US$	9.65bn	10.3bn	
per capita	US$	22,892	24,314	
Growth	%	2.9	2.2	
Inflation	%	1.0	1.0	
Def exp [a]	ML	41m		
	US$	54m		
Def bdgt [a]	ML	45m	45m	
	US$	60m	61m	
US$1=ML		0.75	0.74	

[a] Excludes military pensions

Population 412,655

Age	0–14	15–19	20–24	25–29	30–64	65 plus
Male	7.8%	3.0%	3.4%	3.5%	24.0%	8.0%
Female	7.4%	2.9%	3.2%	3.3%	23.5%	9.9%

Capabilities

The armed forces consist of a limited number of army personnel supported by small naval and air units. Recently there have been efforts to improve maritime surveillance with the acquisition of *King Air* maritime-patrol aircraft, while two AW139s were to enter service in a search-and-rescue role. Malta also intends to procure a *King Air* B200 in the future for border control. Consideration is being given to procuring a new coastal patrol craft and upgrading the existing PCC.

ACTIVE 1,950 (Armed Forces 1,950)

RESERVE 180 (Emergency Volunteer Reserve Force 120 Individual Reserve 60)

ORGANISATIONS BY SERVICE

Armed Forces of Malta 1,950

FORCES BY ROLE
MANOEUVRE
  Light
    1 (1st) inf regt (3 inf coy, 1 AD/cbt spt coy)
COMBAT SUPPORT
    1 (3rd) cbt spt regt (1 cbt engr sqn, 1 EOD sqn, 1 maint sqn)
    1 (4th) cbt spt regt (1 CIS coy, 1 sy coy (Revenue Security Corps))

Maritime Squadron

Organised into 5 divisions: offshore patrol; inshore patrol; rapid deployment and training; marine engineering; and logistics.

EQUIPMENT BY TYPE
PATROL AND COASTAL COMBATANTS 7
  PCC 1 *Diciotti*
  PB 6: 4 Austal 21m; 2 *Marine Protector*
LOGISTICS AND SUPPORT 2
  AAR 2 *Cantieri Vittoria*

Air Wing

1 base party. 1 flt ops div; 1 maint div; 1 integrated log div; 1 rescue section

EQUIPMENT BY TYPE
AIRCRAFT
  TPT • Light 4: 2 Beech 200 *King Air* (maritime patrol); 2 BN-2B *Islander*
  TRG 3 *Bulldog* T MK1
HELICOPTERS
  MRH 4: 1 AW139 (SAR); 3 SA316B *Alouette* III

DEPLOYMENT

Legal provisions for foreign deployment:
Constitution: Codified constitution (1964)
Decision on deployment of troops abroad: The government decides on a case-by-case basis on the deployment of Maltese military personnel abroad (Malta Armed Forces Act, Chapter 220 of the Laws of Malta).

SERBIA
OSCE • Kosovo 1

FOREIGN FORCES

Italy 25; 2 Bell 212 (HH-212) hel

Montenegro MNE

Euro €		2013	2014	2015
GDP	€	3.34bn	3.41bn	
	US$	4.43bn	4.66bn	
per capita	US$	7,112	7,466	
Growth	%	3.5	2.3	
Inflation	%	2.2	-0.6	
Def exp [a]	€	49m		
	US$	65m		
Def bdgt [a]	€	49m	59m	60m
	US$	65m	80m	
FMA (US)	US$	1.2m	1.2m	1.2m
US$1=€		0.75	0.74	

[a] Includes military pensions

Population 650,036

Age	0 – 14	15 – 19	20 – 24	25 – 29	30 – 64	65 plus
Male	7.4%	2.1%	3.0%	4.2%	27.5%	5.6%
Female	7.8%	2.7%	3.0%	3.6%	24.6%	8.5%

Capabilities

Force and organisational changes are under way that will likely see a further reduction in numbers, mainly in the army. The country participates in NATO's Membership Action Plan, with the aim of becoming a member of the Alliance, but its capability is limited to relatively undemanding internal security missions. Under the MAP, Montenegro has worked towards addressing sets of 'partnership goals', such as developing international defence-cooperation and training contacts. This process of integration with NATO was emphasised in the country's June 2013 Strategic Defence Review, which also highlighted the requirement for medium, multi-role helicopters; maritime-domain awareness; air-surveillance radar; and patrol boats. Maintenance issues have affected operational availability of equipment.

ACTIVE 2,080 (Army 1,500 Navy 350 Air Force 230)
Paramilitary 10,100

ORGANISATIONS BY SERVICE

Army 1,500
FORCES BY ROLE
SPECIAL FORCES
  1 SF bde
MANOEUVRE
  Reconnaissance
  1 recce coy
  Light
  1 mot inf bde (1 SF coy, 2 inf regt (1 inf bn, 1 mtn bn), 1 arty bty, 1 cbt spt coy, 1 CBRN pl, 1 sig pl)
COMBAT SUPPORT
  1 engr coy
  3 sigs pl
  1 MP coy

EQUIPMENT BY TYPE
APC (W) 8 BOV-VP M-86
ARTY 149
  TOWED 122mm 12 D-30
  MRL 128mm 18 M63/M94 *Plamen*
  MOR 119: **82mm** 76; **120mm** 43
AT
  SP 8 BOV-1
  MSL • MANPATS 9K111 *Fagot* (AT-4 *Spigot*); 9K113 *Konkurs* (AT-5 *Spandrel*); 9K114 *Shturm* (AT-6 *Spiral*)

Navy 350
1 Naval Cmd HQ with 4 operational naval units (patrol boat; coastal surveillance; maritime detachment; and SAR) with additional sigs, log and trg units with a separate Coast Guard element. Some listed units are in the process of decommissioning.

EQUIPMENT BY TYPE
PATROL AND COASTAL COMBATANTS 5
  PSO 1 *Kotor* with 1 twin 76mm gun (1 further vessel in reserve)
  PCFG 2 *Rade Končar* with 2 single lnchr with P-15 *Termit* (SS-N-2B *Styx*) AShM (missiles disarmed)
  PB 2 *Mirna* (Type-140) (Police units)
AMPHIBIOUS • LANDING CRAFT 5
  LCU 5: 3 (Type-21); 2 (Type-22)
LOGISTICS AND SUPPORT 3
  AOTL 1 *Drina*; **AET** 1 *Lubin*; **AXS** 1 *Jadran*

Air Force 230
Golubovci (Podgorica) air base under army command.
FORCES BY ROLE
TRAINING
  1 (mixed) sqn with G-4 *Super Galeb*; Utva-75 (none operational)
TRANSPORT HELICOPTER
  1 sqn with SA341/SA342L *Gazelle*
EQUIPMENT BY TYPE
AIRCRAFT • TRG (4 G-4 *Super Galeb* non-operational; 4 Utva-75 non-operational)
HELICOPTERS
  MRH 7 SA341/SA342L *Gazelle* (8 more non-operational)
  TPT • Medium (1 Mi-8T awaiting museum storage)

Paramilitary ε10,100

Montenegrin Ministry of Interior Personnel ε6,000

Special Police Units ε4,100

DEPLOYMENT
Legal provisions for foreign deployment:
Constitution: Constitution (2007)
Decision on deployment of troops abroad: The Assembly, on the proposal of the Council for Defence and Security, decide on the use of Montenegrin armed forces in international forces (Article 82, item 8).

AFGHANISTAN
NATO • ISAF 25

ALBANIA
OSCE • Albania 2

SERBIA
OSCE • Kosovo 1

UKRAINE
OSCE • Ukraine 1

Multinational Organisations

Capabilities

The following represent shared capabilities held by contributors collectively rather than as part of national inventories.

ORGANISATIONS BY SERVICE

NATO AEW&C Force
Based at Geilenkirchen (GER). 12 original participating countries (BEL, CAN, DNK, GER, GRC, ITA, NLD, NOR, PRT, TUR, USA) have been subsequently joined by 5 more (CZE, ESP, HUN, POL, ROM).

FORCES BY ROLE
AIRBORNE EARLY WARNING & CONTROL
1 sqn with B-757 (trg); E-3A *Sentry* (NATO standard)
EQUIPMENT BY TYPE
AIRCRAFT
AEW&C 17 E-3A *Sentry* (NATO standard)
TPT • PAX 1 B-757 (trg)

Strategic Airlift Capability
Heavy Airlift Wing based at Papa airbase (HUN). 12 participating countries (BLG, EST, FIN, HUN, LTU, NLD, NOR, POL, ROM, SVN, SWE, USA).
EQUIPMENT BY TYPE
AIRCRAFT
TPT • Heavy 3 C-17A *Globemaster*

Strategic Airlift Interim Solution
Intended to provide strategic airlift capacity pending the delivery of A400M aircraft by leasing An-124s. 14 participating countries (BEL, CAN, CZE, DNK, FIN, FRA, GER, HUN, LUX, NOR, POL, ROM, SVK, SVN, SWE, UK)
EQUIPMENT BY TYPE
AIRCRAFT
TPT • Heavy 2 An-124-100 (4 more available on 6–9 days notice)

Netherlands NLD

Euro €		2013	2014	2015
GDP	€	643bn	650bn	
	US$	854bn	880bn	
per capita	US$	50,816	52,249	
Growth	%	-0.7	0.6	
Inflation	%	2.6	0.5	
Def exp [a]	€	7.78bn		
	US$	10.3bn		
Def bdgt [b]	€	7.79bn	7.89bn	8bn
	US$	10.3bn	10.7bn	
US$1=€		0.75	0.74	

[a] NATO definition
[b] Includes military pensions

Population 16,877,351

Age	0–14	15–19	20–24	25–29	30–64	65 plus
Male	8.7%	3.0%	3.2%	3.1%	23.6%	7.9%
Female	8.3%	2.9%	3.1%	3.1%	23.5%	9.7%

Capabilities

The Netherlands is looking to meet broad security needs through its relationships with key allies, following the implementation of 2011 spending cuts and subsequent force reductions. Power projection and combat readiness have been affected by these reductions. The intent remains to be able to field a brigade-size contribution on international operations and to provide battalion-level support for long-term stabilisation operations. The armed forces also maintain a commitment to the NATO rapid-response force, including a mine-hunter, mechanised infantry and F-16 combat aircraft. Even though the financial climate informed thinking in the 'In the Interest of the Netherlands' 2013 policy paper, there was also focus on innovation and new investments, including the replacement of the F-16 with the F-35, and the accelerated formation of a cyber command. The marines are rebuilding their links with the UK Royal Marines and the army has close cooperation with the German Army, including integration of ground-based air- and missile-defence units, and fire-support units. Its air-mobile brigade is being integrated into the German *Schnelle Kraft* (rapid forces) division. The Germany–Netherlands Corps headquarters in Münster will develop further into a rapidly deployable joint headquarters, capable of directing combined land-based and air-based operations. Irrespective of recent challenges, the armed forces remain a motivated and professional force, capable of participating in demanding joint operations in a NATO Alliance context.

ACTIVE 37,400 (Army 20,850; Navy 8,500; Air 8,050)
Military Constabulary 5,900

RESERVE 3,200 (Army 2,700; Navy 80; Air 420)
Military Constabulary 80
Reserve liability to age 35 for soldiers/sailors, 40 for NCOs, 45 for officers

ORGANISATIONS BY SERVICE

Army 20,850
FORCES BY ROLE
COMMAND
  elm 1 (GER/NLD) Corps HQ
SPECIAL FORCES
  4 SF coy
MANOEUVRE
  Reconnaissance
  1 ISR bn (2 armd recce sqn, 1 EW coy, 2 int sqn, 1 UAV bty)
  Mechanised
  2 (13th & 43rd) mech bde (1 armd recce sqn, 2 armd inf bn, 1 engr bn, 1 maint coy, 1 medical coy)
  Air Manoeuvre
  1 (11th) air mob bde (3 air mob inf bn, 1 mor coy, 1 AD coy, 1 engr coy, 1 med coy, 1 supply coy, 1 maint coy)
COMBAT SUPPORT
  1 arty bn (3 arty bty)
  1 AD comd (1 AD sqn; 3 AD bty)
  1 CIMIC bn
  1 engr bn
  2 EOD coy
  1 (CIS) sigs bn
  1 CBRN coy
COMBAT SERVICE SUPPORT
  1 med bn
  5 fd hospital
  3 maint coy
  2 tpt bn

Reserves 2,700 reservists

National Command
Cadre bde and corps tps completed by call-up of reservists (incl Territorial Comd)
FORCES BY ROLE
MANOEUVRE
  Light
  3 inf bn (could be mobilised for territorial def)
EQUIPMENT BY TYPE
RECCE 305: 296 *Fennek*; 9 *Tpz-1 Fuchs* CBRN
AIFV 184 CV9035N
APC 229
  APC (W) 144: 60 *Boxer* (8 driver trg; 52 ambulance being delivered); 14 M577A1; 70 XA-188
  PPV 85 *Bushmaster* IMV
ARTY 61:
  SP 155mm 18 PzH 2000
  MOR 43: **81mm** 27 L16/M1; **120mm** 16 Brandt
AT
  MSL
    SP 40 *Fennek* MRAT
    MANPATS *Spike*-MR (*Gil*)
AD • SAM
  SP 36: 18 *Fennek* with FIM-92A *Stinger*; 18 MB with FIM-92A *Stinger*
  TOWED 20 MIM-104 *Patriot* (TMD Capable/PAC-3 msl)
  MANPAD FIM-92A *Stinger*

RADAR • LAND 6+: 6 AN/TPQ-36 *Firefinder* (arty, mor); WALS; *Squire*
AEV 30: 10 *Kodiak*; 20 *Leopard* 1
ARV 77: 25 *Büffel*; 52 *Leopard* 1
VLB 8 *Leopard* 1
MW Bozena

Navy 8,500 (incl Marines)
EQUIPMENT BY TYPE
SUBMARINES • TACTICAL • SSK 4:
  4 *Walrus* with 4 single 533mm TT with Mk48 *Sea Arrow* HWT (equipped for UGM-84C *Harpoon* AShM, but none embarked)
PRINCIPAL SURFACE COMBATANTS 6
  DESTROYERS • DDGHM 4:
    3 *Zeven Provinciën* with 2 quad Mk141 lnchr with RGM-84F *Harpoon* AShM, 1 40-cell Mk41 VLS with SM-2MR/ESSM SAM, 2 twin 324mm ASTT with Mk46 LWT, 1 *Goalkeeper* CIWS, 1 127mm gun, (capacity 1 NH90 hel)
    1 *Zeven Provinciën* with 2 quad Mk141 lnchr with RGM-84F *Harpoon* AShM, 1 40-cell Mk41 VLS with SM-2MR/ESSM SAM, 2 twin 324mm ASTT with Mk46 LWT, 2 *Goalkeeper* CIWS, 1 127mm gun, (capacity 1 NH90 hel)
  FRIGATES • FFGHM 2:
    2 *Karel Doorman* with 2 quad Mk141 lnchr with RGM-84A/C *Harpoon* AShM, 1 Mk48 VLS with RIM-7P *Sea Sparrow* SAM, 2 twin 324mm ASTT with Mk46 LWT, 1 *Goalkeeper* CIWS, 1 76mm gun, (capacity 1 NH90 hel)
PATROL AND COASTAL COMBATANTS
  PSOH 4 *Holland* with 1 76mm gun (capacity 1 NH90 hel)
MINE WARFARE • MINE COUNTERMEASURES
  MHO 6 *Alkmaar* (*tripartite*)
AMPHIBIOUS
  PRINCIPAL AMPHIBIOUS SHIPS • LPD 2:
    1 *Rotterdam* with 2 *Goalkeeper* CIWS, (capacity 4 NH90/AS532 *Cougar* hel; either 6 LCVP or 2 LCU and 3 LCVP; either 170 APC or 33 MBT; 538 troops)
    1 *Johan de Witt* with 2 *Goalkeeper* CIWS, (capacity 6 NH90 hel or 4 AS532 *Cougar* hel; either 6 LCVP or 2 LCU and 3 LCVP; either 170 APC or 33 MBT; 700 troops)
  LANDING CRAFT 17
    LCU 5 Mk9
    LCVP 12 Mk5
LOGISTICS AND SUPPORT 31
  AGS 2 *Snellius*
  AK 1 *Pelikaan*
  AOT 1 *Patria*
  ASL 1 *Mercuur*
  AXL 2: 1 *Thetis* (diving trg); 1 *Van Kingsbergen*
  AXS 1 *Urania*
  YDT 5: 4 *Cerberus*; 1 *Soemba*
  YFL 6
  YTM 5 *Linge*
  YTL 7 *Breezand*

Marines 2,650
FORCES BY ROLE
SPECIAL FORCES
1 SF gp (1 SF sqn, 1 CT sqn)
MANOEUVRE
  Amphibious
  2 mne bn
  1 amph aslt gp
COMBAT SERVICE SUPPORT
1 spt gp (coy)
EQUIPMENT BY TYPE
APC (T) 160: 87 Bv-206D; 73 BvS-10 *Viking*
ARTY • MOR 81mm 12 L16/M1
AT • MSL • MANPATS *Spike*-MR (*Gil*)
  RL 84mm *Pantserfaust* III *Dynarange* 2000
AD • SAM • MANPAD FIM-92A *Stinger*
ARV 4 BvS-10; 4 *Leopard* 1
MED 4 BvS-10

Air Force 8,050
Flying hours 180 hrs/year
FORCES BY ROLE
FIGHTER/GROUND ATTACK
  3 sqn with F-16AM/BM *Fighting Falcon*
ANTI-SUBMARINE WARFARE/SEARCH & RESCUE
  1 sqn with NH90 NFH
SEARCH & RESCUE
  1 sqn with Bell 412SP (AB-412SP *Griffin*)
TANKER/TRANSPORT
  1 sqn with C-130H/H-30 *Hercules*
  1 sqn with KDC-10; Gulfstream IV
TRAINING
  1 OEU sqn with F-35A *Lightning* II
  1 sqn with PC-7 *Turbo Trainer*
  1 hel sqn with AH-64D *Apache*; CH-47D *Chinook* (based at Fort Hood, TX)
ATTACK HELICOPTER
  1 sqn with AH-64D *Apache*
TRANSPORT HELICOPTER
  1 sqn with AS532U2 *Cougar* II
  1 sqn with CH-47D/F *Chinook*
EQUIPMENT BY TYPE
AIRCRAFT 74 combat capable
  FTR 72 F-16AM/BM *Fighting Falcon*
  FGA 2 F-35A *Lightning* II (in test)
  TKR 2 KDC-10
  TPT 5: **Medium** 4: 2 C-130H *Hercules*; 2 C-130H-30 *Hercules*; **PAX** 1 Gulfstream IV
  TRG 13 PC-7 *Turbo Trainer*
HELICOPTERS
  ATK 29 AH-64D *Apache*
  ASW 12 NH90 NFH
  MRH 7: 3 Bell 412 (AB-412SP *Griffin*); 4 SA316 *Alouette* III
  TPT 25: **Heavy** 17: 11 CH-47D *Chinook*; 6 CH-47F *Chinook*; **Medium** 8 AS532U2 *Cougar* II
MSL
  AAM • IR AIM-9L/M/N *Sidewinder*; **ARH** AIM-120B AMRAAM
  ASM AGM-114K *Hellfire*; AGM-65D/G *Maverick*

BOMBS
  Conventional Mk 82; Mk 84
  Laser-guided GBU-10/GBU-12 *Paveway* II; GBU-24 *Paveway* III (all supported by LANTIRN)

Paramilitary

Royal Military Constabulary 5,900
Subordinate to the Ministry of Defence, but performs most of its work under the authority of other ministries.
FORCES BY ROLE
MANOEUVRE
  Other
  6 paramilitary district (total: 25 paramilitary 'bde')
EQUIPMENT BY TYPE
AIFV 24 YPR-765

Cyber
Six areas were prioritised in the 2012 Defence Cyber Strategy: Digital security; resilience; capacity to mount cyber operations; strengthening intelligence capacities; increasing the knowledge base; and more international cooperation. A Defence Cyber Command (DCC) is being established as part of the army but comprising personnel from all the armed services. DCC will be responsible for the cyber security of the defence organisation and its partners. DCC will consist of three segments: Defence Cyber Expertise Centre, serving as a MOD cyber-knowledge gathering, assurance and dissemination institute; the Cyber Operations Division, providing cyber specialists to military operational units; and a Technology Division, capable of preparing and performing actual cyber attacks, if and when decided by the appropriate authority. There is also a Defence Computer Emergency Response Team working within the Joint Information Technology Command (JITC) of the Defence Materiel Organisation. JTIC will cooperate with the Dutch intelligence and security service. A Defence Cyber Doctrine is currently being drafted and is expected to be formalised in 2015.

DEPLOYMENT
Legal provisions for foreign deployment:
Constitution: Codified constitution (1815)
Decision on deployment of troops abroad: By the government (Art. 98)

AFGHANISTAN
NATO • ISAF 30

BOSNIA-HERZEGOVINA
EU • EUFOR • *Operation Althea* 3

CENTRAL AFRICAN REPUBLIC
EU • EUFOR RCA 1

EGYPT
MFO 4

GULF OF ADEN & INDIAN OCEAN
EU • *Operation Atalanta* 1 FFGHM

JORDAN
8 F-16AM *Fighting Falcon*

MALI
EU • EUTM Mali 1
UN • MINUSMA 544; 1 SF coy; 1 atk hel sqn; 1 engr coy

MIDDLE EAST
UN • UNTSO 12 obs

NORTH SEA
NATO • SNMCMG 1: 1 MHO

SERBIA
NATO • KFOR 5

SOUTH SUDAN
UN • UNMISS 6; 2 obs

SYRIA/ISRAEL
UN • UNDOF 2

TURKEY
NATO • *Active Fence*: 2 AD bty with MIM-104 *Patriot*

UGANDA
EU • EUTM Somalia 8

UKRAINE
OSCE • Ukraine 6

UNITED STATES
1 hel trg sqn with AH-64D *Apache*; CH-47D *Chinook* based at Fort Hood (TX)

FOREIGN FORCES
United Kingdom Air Force 90
United States US European Command: 380

Norway NOR

Norwegian Kroner kr		2013	2014	2015
GDP	kr	3.01tr	3.13tr	
	US$	513bn	512bn	
per capita	US$	100,579	99,295	
Growth	%	0.6	1.8	
Inflation	%	2.1	2.0	
Def exp [a]	kr	43.4bn		
	US$	7.39bn		
Def bdgt	kr	42.5bn	42.7bn	
	US$	7.24bn	6.98bn	
US$1=kr		5.87	6.12	

[a] NATO definition

Population 5,147,792

Age	0–14	15–19	20–24	25–29	30–64	65 plus
Male	9.3%	3.3%	3.5%	3.5%	23.4%	7.3%
Female	8.9%	3.1%	3.3%	3.3%	22.3%	8.8%

Capabilities

Norway's continuing focus on the High North was brought into even sharper focus in 2014 as a result of the more challenging relationship with Russia. It sustains small but well-equipped and trained armed forces – around a third of whom are conscripts at any one time – with territorial defence at the core of its security policy. In late 2013, Norwegian conscription became gender neutral, and women will be conscripted from January 2015. Recapitalisation of the equipment inventory is ongoing, reflecting Norway's comparatively high level of defence expenditure. The first of 16 AW101 search-and-rescue helicopters will enter service in 2017, and the *Sea King* Mk43B is to be withdrawn from service by 2020. The first of the 52 F-35As it intends to buy will also arrive in-country in 2017, with an initial service capability pencilled in for 2019. The navy, meanwhile, will take delivery of a new ELINT ship to replace the *Marjata* in 2016. Oslo is a strong supporter of NATO, and former prime minister Jens Stoltenberg took over as the Alliance's Secretary-General in October 2014.

ACTIVE 25,800 (Army 9,350, Navy 4,500, Air 3,950, Central Support 7,500, Home Guard 500)
Conscript liability 18 months maximum. Conscripts first serve 12 months from 19–21, and then up to 4–5 refresher training periods until age 35, 44, 55 or 60 depending on rank and function. Active numbers include conscripts on initial service. Conscription extended to women in 2015.

RESERVE 45,940 (Army 270, Navy 320, Central Support 350, Home Guard 45,000)

Readiness varies from a few hours to several days

ORGANISATIONS BY SERVICE

Army 4,500; 4,850 conscript (total 9,350)

The mechanised brigade – Brigade North – trains new personnel of all categories and provides units for international operations. At any time around one-third of the brigade will be trained and ready to conduct operations. The brigade includes one high-readiness mechanised battalion (Telemark Battalion) with combat support and combat service support units on high readiness.

FORCES BY ROLE
MANOEUVRE
  Reconnaissance
  1 (Border Guard) lt bn (3 coy (HQ/garrison, border control & trg))
  Mechanised
  1 mech inf bde (1 ISR bn, 2 mech inf bn, 1 lt inf bn, 1 arty bn, 1 engr bn, 1 MP coy, 1 CIS bn, 1 spt bn, 1 med bn)
  Light
  1 lt inf bn (His Majesty The King's Guards)
EQUIPMENT BY TYPE
MBT 52 *Leopard* 2A4
RECCE TPz-1 *Fuchs* NBC
AIFV 104 CV9030N
APC 410

APC (T) 315 M113 (incl variants)
APC (W) 75 XA-186 *Sisu*/XA-200 *Sisu*
PPV 20 *Dingo* II
ARTY 204
  SP 155mm 18 M109A3GN
  MOR 186:
    SP 81mm 36: 24 M106A1; 12 M125A2
    81mm 150 L-16
AT
  MANPATS *Javelin*
  RCL 84mm *Carl Gustav*
RADAR • LAND 12 ARTHUR
AEV 22 *Alvis*
ARV 9+: 3 M88A1; M578; 6 *Leopard* 1
VLB 35: 26 *Leguan*; 9 *Leopard* 1
MW 9 910 MCV-2

Navy 2,450; 2,050 conscripts (total 4,500)

Joint Command – Norwegian National Joint Headquarters. The Royal Norwegian Navy is organised into four elements under the command of the chief of staff of the Navy: the naval units '*Kysteskadren*', the schools '*Sjoforsvarets Skoler*', the naval bases and the coast guard '*Kystvakten*'.

FORCES BY ROLE
MANOEUVRE
  Reconnaissance
  1 ISR coy (Coastal Rangers)
COMBAT SUPPORT
  1 EOD pl

EQUIPMENT BY TYPE
SUBMARINES • TACTICAL • SSK 6 *Ula* with 8 single 533mm TT with A3 *Seal* DM2 HWT
PRINCIPAL SURFACE COMBATANTS 5
  DESTROYERS • DDGHM 5 *Fridtjof Nansen* with 2 quad lnchr with NSM AShM, 1 8-cell Mk41 VLS with ESSM SAM, 2 twin 324mm ASTT with *Sting Ray* LWT, 1 76mm gun, (capacity 1 NH90 hel)
PATROL AND COASTAL COMBATANTS • PCFGM 6 *Skjold* with 8 single lnchr with NSM AShM, 1 twin *Simbad* lnchr with *Mistral* SAM, 1 76mm gun
MINE WARFARE • MINE COUNTERMEASURES 6:
  MSC 3 *Alta* with 1 twin *Simbad* lnchr with *Mistral* SAM
  MHC 3 *Oksoy* with 1 twin *Simbad* lnchr with *Mistral* SAM
AMPHIBIOUS • LANDING CRAFT • LCP 16 S90N
LOGISTICS AND SUPPORT 20
  AGI 1 *Marjata* with 1 hel landing platform
  AGDS 1 *Tyr*
  AGS 6: 1 *HU Sverdrup II*; 4 *Oljevern*; 1 *Geofjord*
  ATS 1 *Valkyrien*
  AXL 5: 2 *Hessa*; 2 *Kvarnen*; 1 *Reine*
  YAC 1 *Norge*
  YDT 5

Coast Guard
PATROL AND COASTAL COMBATANTS 15
  PSO 8: 3 *Barentshav*; 1 *Svalbard* with 1 57mm gun, 1 hel landing platform; 1 *Harstad*; 3 *Nordkapp* with 1 57mm gun, 1 hel landing platform
  PCO 7: 1 *Aalesund*; 5 *Nornen*; 1 *Reine*

Air Force 2,800; 1150 conscript (total 3,950)

Joint Command – Norwegian National HQ
Flying hours 180 hrs/year

FORCES BY ROLE
FIGHTER/GROUND ATTACK
  3 sqn with F-16AM/BM *Fighting Falcon*
MARITIME PATROL
  1 sqn with P-3C *Orion*; P-3N *Orion* (pilot trg)
ELECTRONIC WARFARE
  1 sqn with *Falcon* 20C (EW, Flight Inspection Service)
SEARCH & RESCUE
  1 sqn with *Sea King* Mk43B
TRANSPORT
  1 sqn with C-130J-30 *Hercules*
TRAINING
  1 sqn with MFI-15 SAAB *Safari*
TRANSPORT HELICOPTER
  2 sqn with Bell 412SP *Twin Huey*
  1 sqn with *Lynx* Mk86
  1 sqn with NH90 (forming)
AIR DEFENCE
  1 bty(+) with NASAMS II

EQUIPMENT BY TYPE
AIRCRAFT 63 combat capable
  FTR 57: 47 F-16AM *Fighting Falcon*; 10 F-16BM *Fighting Falcon*
  ASW 6: 4 P-3C *Orion*; 2 P-3N *Orion* (pilot trg)
  EW 3 *Falcon* 20C
  TPT • Medium 4 C-130J-30 *Hercules*
  TRG 16 MFI-15 *Safari*
HELICOPTERS
  ASW 8: 5 *Lynx* Mk86 ; 3 NH90 NFH (delivery schedule of all 14 revised to an FOC of 2017)
  SAR 12 *Sea King* Mk43B
  MRH 18: 6 Bell 412HP; 12 Bell 412SP
AD
  SAM • TOWED NASAMS II
MSL
  AAM • IR AIM-9L *Sidewinder*; IIR IRIS-T; ARH AIM-120B AMRAAM
BOMBS
  Laser-guided EGBU-12 *Paveway* II
  INS/GPS guided JDAM

Special Operations Command (NORSOCOM)
FORCES BY ROLE
SPECIAL FORCES
  1 (army) SF comd (2 SF gp)
  1 (navy) SF comd (1 SF gp)

Central Support, Administration and Command 6,500; 1,000 conscripts (total 6,500)

Central Support, Administration and Command includes military personnel in all joint elements and they are responsible for logistics and CIS in support of all forces in Norway and abroad.

Home Guard 550 (45,000 reserves)

The Home Guard is a separate organisation, but closely cooperates with all services. The Home Guard can be mobilised on very short notice for local security operations.

Land Home Guard 41,150 with reserves

11 Home Guard Districts with mobile Rapid Reaction Forces (3,000 troops in total) as well as reinforcements and follow-on forces (38,150 troops in total).

Naval Home Guard 1,900 with reserves

Consisting of Rapid Reaction Forces (500 troops), and 17 'Naval Home Guard Areas'. A number of civilian vessels can be requisitioned as required.

EQUIPMENT BY TYPE
PATROL AND COASTAL COMBATANTS • PB 11: 4 *Harek*; 2 *Gyda*; 5 Alusafe 1290

Air Home Guard 1,450 with reserves

Provides force protection and security detachments for air bases.

Cyber

The Ministry of Defence is responsible for defending military networks and national coordination in armed conflict. The 2012 Cyber Security Strategy for Norway contains cross-governmental guidelines for cyber defence. Nor-CERT, part of the National Security Authority, is responsible for information exchange and cooperation at the operational level. Norwegian Armed Forces Cyber Defence supports the armed forces with establishing, operating and protecting networks. It is responsible for defending military networks against cyber attack. It also supports the Norwegian Armed Forces at home and abroad with the establishment, operation, development and protection of their communications systems, and is responsible for defending the military networks against cyber attacks as well as the development of Network Based Defence.

DEPLOYMENT

Legal provisions for foreign deployment: Constitution: Codified constitution (1814)
Decision on deployment of troops abroad: By royal prerogative exercised by the government (Art. 25, 26).

AFGHANISTAN
NATO • ISAF 57
UN • UNAMA 1 obs

CYPRUS
UN • UNFICYP 2

EGYPT
MFO 3

MALI
UN • MINUSMA 19

MIDDLE EAST
UN • UNTSO 12 obs

NORTH SEA
NATO • SNMCMG 1: 1 MHC

SERBIA
NATO • KFOR 2

SOUTH SUDAN
UN • UNMISS 10; 3 obs

UKRAINE
OSCE • Ukraine 7

FOREIGN FORCES

United States US European Command: 1 (APS) 155mm SP Arty bn eqpt set

Poland POL

Polish Zloty z		2013	2014	2015
GDP	z	1.64tr	1.7tr	
	US$	518bn	552bn	
per capita	US$	13,435	14,330	
Growth	%	1.6	3.2	
Inflation	%	0.9	0.1	
Def exp [a]	z	28.7bn		
	US$	9.09bn		
Def bdgt [b]	z	28.3bn	32bn	38.5bn
	US$	8.94bn	10.4bn	
FMA (US)	US$	24m	14m	9m
US$1=z		3.16	3.09	

[a] NATO definition
[b] Includes military pensions

Population   38,346,279

Age	0–14	15–19	20–24	25–29	30–64	65 plus
Male	7.5%	2.7%	3.4%	3.9%	25.1%	5.8%
Female	7.1%	2.6%	3.2%	3.8%	25.8%	9.2%

Capabilities

The two central pillars of Poland's defence policy are defending territorial integrity and membership of the NATO Alliance. The armed forces are recapitalising equipment inventories, a process that has been leant more urgency by concern over events in Ukraine. In September 2014, a plan was approved to raise defence spending to 2% of GDP, with this process due to start in 2016. Later that month, agreement was signed to create a joint Lithuania–Poland–Ukraine brigade with an HQ in Lublin, though discussions had been ongoing for some time. Air-related procurements include the purchase of up to 70 medium-lift helicopters and up to 32 attack helicopters to replace ageing Soviet-era types still in service. These procurements are part of the 2013–22 modernisation programme. The US JASSM land-attack cruise missile for the F-16 combat aircraft and an additional coastal-defence missile battery are also planned acquisitions while new UAV capacities were discussed in late 2014. A limited upgrade to its MiG-29 *Fulcrum* aircraft was due for completion at the end of the year, while its Su-22M are to remain in service until the mid-2020s. A new patrol vessel, the *Slazak*, is due to be finished by the end of 2016, with the navy also aiming to introduce three new *Miecznik*-class coastal-patrol vessels later in the decade. Poland is a participant in the Visegrad Group.

ACTIVE 99,300 (Army 48,200, Navy 7,700, Air Force 16,600, Special Forces 3,000, Joint 23,800) Paramilitary 73,400

ORGANISATIONS BY SERVICE

Army 48,200

Transition to lighter forces is continuing but is hampered by lack of funds.

FORCES BY ROLE
COMMAND
  1 (2nd) mech corps HQ
  elm 1 (MNC NE) corps HQ
MANOEUVRE
  Reconnaissance
  3 recce regt
  Armoured
  1 (11th) armd cav div (2 armd bde, 1 mech bde, 1 arty regt)
  Mechanised
  1 (12th) div (2 mech bde, 1 (coastal) mech bde, 1 arty regt)
  1 (16th) div (2 armd bde, 2 mech bde, 1 arty regt)
  1 (21st) mech bde (1 armd bn, 3 mech bn, 1 arty bn, 1 AD bn, 1 engr bn)
  Air Manoeuvre
  1 (6th) air aslt bde (3 air aslt bn)
  1 (25th) air cav bde (3 air cav bn, 2 tpt hel bn, 1 (casevac) med unit)
  Aviation
  1 (1st) avn bde (2 atk hel sqn with Mi-24D/V *Hind* D/E, 1 CSAR sqn with Mi-24V *Hind* E; PZL W-3PL *Gluszec*; 2 ISR hel sqn with Mi-2URP; 2 hel sqn with Mi-2)
COMBAT SUPPORT
  2 engr regt
  1 ptn br regt
  2 chem regt
  3 AD regt

EQUIPMENT BY TYPE
MBT 926: 128 *Leopard* 2A4; 49 *Leopard* 2A5; 232 PT-91 *Twardy*; 517 T-72/T-72M1D/T-72M1
RECCE 366: 237 BRDM-2; 37 BWR; 92 WD R-5
AIFV 1,838: 1,268 BMP-1; 570 *Rosomak*
APC • PPV 70: 40 *Cougar* (on loan from US); 30 *Maxxpro*
ARTY 767
  SP 403: **122mm** 292 2S1; **152mm** 111 M-77 *Dana*
  MRL 122mm 180: 75 BM-21; 30 RM-70; 75 WR-40 *Langusta*
  MOR 184: **98mm** 89 M-98; **120mm** 95 M120
AT • MSL • MANPATS 9K11 *Malyutka* (AT-3 *Sagger*); 9K111 *Fagot* (AT-4 *Spigot*); *Spike*-LR
AD
  SAM
    SP 84: 20 2K12 *Kub* (SA-6 *Gainful*); 64 9K33 *Osa*-AK (SA-8 *Gecko*)
    MANPAD 9K32 *Strela*-2‡ (SA-7 *Grail*); GROM
  GUNS 352
    SP 23mm 28: 8 ZSU-23-4; 20 ZSU-23-4MP *Biala*
    TOWED 23mm 324; 252 ZU-23-2; 72 ZUR-23-2KG/PG
RADAR • LAND 3 LIWIEC (veh, arty)
HELICOPTERS
  ATK 25 Mi-24D/V *Hind* D/E
  MRH 60: 7 Mi-8MT *Hip*; 3 Mi-17 *Hip* H; 1 Mi-17AE *Hip* (aeromedical); 5 Mi-17-1V *Hip*; 16 PZL Mi-2URP *Hoplite*; 24 PZL W-3W/WA *Sokol*; 4 PZL W-3PL *Gluszec* (CSAR)
  TPT 34: **Medium** 7 Mi-8T *Hip*; **Light** 27: 25 PZL Mi-2 *Hoplite*; 2 PZL W-3AE *Sokol* (aeromedical)
AEV IWT; MT-LB
ARV 65+: 10 *Leopard* 1; 15 MT-LB; TRI; WPT-TOPAS; 40 WZT-3
VLB 52: 4 *Biber*; 48 BLG67M2
MW 18: 14 Bozena; 4 *Kalina* SUM

Navy 7,700

EQUIPMENT BY TYPE
SUBMARINES • TACTICAL 5
  SSK 5:
    4 *Sokol* (ex-NOR Type-207) with 8 single 533mm TT
    1 *Orzel* (ex-FSU *Kilo*) with 6 single 533mm TT each with T-53/T-65 HWT
PRINCIPAL SURFACE COMBATANTS 2
  FRIGATES • FFGHM 2 *Pulaski* (ex-US *Oliver Hazard Perry*) with 1 Mk13 GMLS with RGM-84D/F *Harpoon* AShM/SM-1MR SAM, 2 triple 324mm ASTT with MU90 LWT, 1 *Phalanx* Block 1B CIWS, 1 76mm gun (capacity 2 SH-2G *Super Seasprite* ASW hel) (1 vessel used as training ship)
PATROL AND COASTAL COMBATANTS 4
  CORVETTES • FSM 1 *Kaszub* with 2 quad lnchr with 9K32 *Strela*-2 (SA-N-5 *Grail*) SAM, 2 twin 533mm ASTT with SET-53 HWT, 2 RBU 6000 *Smerch* 2, 1 76mm gun
  PCFGM 3:
    3 *Orkan* (ex-GDR *Sassnitz*) with 1 quad lnchr with RBS-15 Mk3 AShM, 1 quad lnchr (manual aiming) with *Strela*-2 (SA-N-5 *Grail*) SAM, 1 AK630 CIWS, 1 76mm gun
MINE WARFARE • MINE COUNTERMEASURES 21
  MCCS 1 Project 890
  MHI 4 *Mamry*
  MHO 3 *Krogulec*
  MSI 13 *Goplo*
AMPHIBIOUS 8
  LANDING SHIPS • LSM 5 *Lublin* (capacity 9 tanks; 135 troops)
  LANDING CRAFT • LCU 3 *Deba* (capacity 50 troops)
LOGISTICS AND SUPPORT 38
  AGI 2 *Moma*
  AGS 8: 2 *Heweliusz*; 6 (coastal)
  AORL 1 *Baltyk*
  AOL 1 *Moskit*
  ARS 4: 2 *Piast*; 2 *Zbyszko*
  ATF 2
  AX 1 *Wodnik* with 1 twin AK230 CIWS
  AXS 1 *Iskra*
  YDG 2 *Mrowka*
  YDT 3
  YFB 7

YPT 1 *Kormoran*
YTM 5

Naval Aviation 1,300
FORCES BY ROLE
ANTI SUBMARINE WARFARE/SEARCH & RESCUE
  1 sqn with MI-14PL *Haze* A; MI-14PS *Haze* C
  1 sqn with PZL W-3RM *Anakonda*; SH-2G *Super Seasprite*
TRANSPORT
  1 sqn with An-28B1R; An-28E
  1 sqn with An-28TD; Mi-17 *Hip* H; PZL Mi-2 *Hoplite*; PZL W-3RM
EQUIPMENT BY TYPE
AIRCRAFT
  MP 10: 8 An-28B1R *Bryza*; 2 An-28E *Bryza* (ecological monitoring)
  TPT • **Light** 4 An-28TD *Bryza*
HELICOPTERS
  ASW 11: 7 Mi-14PL *Haze*; 4 SH-2G *Super Seasprite*
  MRH 2 Mi-17 *Hip* H
  SAR 8: 2 Mi-14PS *Haze* C; 6 PZL W-3RM *Anakonda*
  TPT • **Light** 4 PZL Mi-2 *Hoplite*

Air Force 16,600
Flying hours 160 to 200 hrs/year

FORCES BY ROLE
FIGHTER
  2 sqn with MiG-29A/UB *Fulcrum*
FIGHTER/GROUND ATTACK
  3 sqn with F-16C/D Block 52+ *Fighting Falcon*
FIGHTER/GROUND ATTACK/ISR
  2 sqn with Su-22M-4 *Fitter*
SEARCH AND RESCUE
  1 sqn with Mi-2; PZL W-3 *Sokol*
TRANSPORT
  1 sqn with C-130E; PZL M-28 *Bryza*
  1 sqn with C-295M; PZL M-28 *Bryza*
TRAINING
  1 sqn with PZL-130 *Orlik*
  1 sqn with TS-11 *Iskra*
  1 hel sqn with SW-4 *Puszczyk*
TRANSPORT HELICOPTER
  1 (Spec Ops) sqn with Mi-17 *Hip* H
  1 (VIP) sqn with Mi-8; W-3WA *Sokol*
AIR DEFENCE
  1 bde with S-125 *Neva* SC (SA-3 *Goa*); S-200C *Vega* (SA-5 *Gammon*)
EQUIPMENT BY TYPE
AIRCRAFT 113 combat capable
  FTR 32: 26 MiG-29A *Fulcrum*; 6 MiG-29UB *Fulcrum*
  FGA 81: 36 F-16C Block 52+ *Fighting Falcon*; 12 F-16D Block 52+ *Fighting Falcon*; 27 Su-22M-4 *Fitter*; 6 Su-22UM3K *Fitter*
  TPT 44: **Medium** 5 C-130E *Hercules*; **Light** 39: 16 C-295M; 23 M-28 *Bryza* TD
  TRG 60: 28 PZL-130 *Orlik*; 32 TS-11 *Iskra*
HELICOPTERS
  MRH 8 Mi-17 *Hip* H
  TPT 70: **Medium** 30: 9 Mi-8 *Hip*; 11 PZL W-3 *Sokol*; 10 PZL W-3WA *Sokol* (VIP); **Light** 40: 16 PZL Mi-2 *Hoplite*; 24 SW-4 *Puszczyk* (trg)

AD • SAM
  SP 17 S-125 *Neva* SC (SA-3 *Goa*)
  STATIC 1 S-200C *Vega* (SA-5 *Gammon*)
MSL
  AAM • IR R-60 (AA-8 *Aphid*); R-73 (AA-11 *Archer*); AIM-9 *Sidewinder*; R-27T (AA-10B *Alamo*); ARH AIM-120C AMRAAM
  ASM AGM-65J/G *Maverick*; Kh-25 (AS-10 *Karen*); Kh-29 (AS-14 *Kedge*)

Special Forces 3,000
FORCES BY ROLE
SPECIAL FORCES
  3 SF units (GROM, FORMOZA & cdo)
COMBAT SUPPORT/
  1 cbt spt unit (AGAT)
COMBAT SERVICE SUPPORT
  1 spt unit (NIL)

Paramilitary 73,400

Border Guards 14,300
Ministry of Interior

Maritime Border Guard 3,700
PATROL AND COASTAL COMBATANTS 18
  PCC 2 *Kaper*
  PBF 6: 2 *Straznik*; 4 IC16M
  PB 10: 2 *Wisloka*; 2 *Baltic* 24; 6 others
  AMPHIBIOUS • LANDING CRAFT • LCAC 2 *Griffon* 2000TDX

Prevention Units (Police) 59,100
Anti-terrorist Operations Bureau n.k.
Ministry of Interior

Cyber
Poland has both national and government CERTs and is involved in informal CERT communities. A national cyber strategy is in the process of being drafted and Poland is an active participant in international cyber exercises.

DEPLOYMENT
Legal provisions for foreign deployment:
Constitution: Codified constitution (1997); Act on Principles of Use or External Deployment of the Polish Armed Forces (17/12/1998)
Decision on deployment of troops abroad:
a) By president on request of prime minister in cases of direct threat (Art. 136);
b) in general, specified by ratified international agreement or statute (both must be passed by parliament, Art. 117)

AFGHANISTAN
NATO • ISAF 304
UN • UNAMA 1 obs

ARMENIA/AZERBAIJAN
OSCE • Minsk Conference 1

BOSNIA-HERZEGOVINA
EU • EUFOR • *Operation Althea* 34
OSCE • Bosnia and Herzegovina 1

CENTRAL AFRICAN REPUBLIC
EU • EUFOR RCA 50

CÔTE D'IVOIRE
UN • UNOCI 2 obs

DEMOCRATIC REPUBLIC OF THE CONGO
UN • MONUSCO 3 obs

LIBERIA
UN • UNMIL 1 obs

MALI
EU • EUTM Mali 20

MOLDOVA
OSCE • Moldova 1

NORTH SEA
NATO • SNMCMG 1: 1 MHO

SERBIA
NATO • KFOR 254; 1 inf coy
OSCE • Kosovo 3
UN • UNMIK 2 obs

SOUTH SUDAN
UN • UNMISS 2 obs

UKRAINE
OSCE • Ukraine 12

WESTERN SAHARA
UN • MINURSO 2 obs

FOREIGN FORCES
Denmark NATO Baltic Air Policing 4 F-16AM *Fighting Falcon*
Germany 67 (elm Corps HQ (multinational))

Portugal PRT

Euro €		2013	2014	2015
GDP	€	166bn	168bn	
	US$	220bn	228bn	
per capita	US$	20,995	21,748	
Growth	%	-1.4	1.0	
Inflation	%	0.4	0.0	
Def exp [a]	€	2.5bn		
	US$	3.32bn		
Def bdgt	€	2.09bn	1.94bn	
	US$	2.77bn	2.63bn	
US$1=€		0.75	0.74	

[a] NATO definition

Population 10,813,834

Age	0–14	15–19	20–24	25–29	30–64	65 plus
Male	8.3%	3.0%	3.1%	3.2%	23.6%	7.6%
Female	7.6%	2.6%	2.7%	2.9%	24.3%	11.0%

Capabilities

Homeland defence, supporting NATO Article V and UN-, EU- and NATO-led operations are core roles for the country's armed forces, along with maritime security. As with several southern European states, Portugal has been badly affected by Europe's economic crisis. This is apparent partly in the number of procurement projects that have been cut or shelved. Armoured-vehicle and rotary-wing projects have all been downscaled. An offshore-patrol-vessel programme was shelved after the delivery of the first of its class. Overseas operations were also reduced. In April 2013, a new *Defesa 2020* document was published, setting out defence roles as well as an aspiration to allocate 1.5% of GDP to defence. This considered personnel numbers, the development of integrated civil-military capabilities, moving ahead with cyber-defence capacities and restructuring the armed forces. Ambitions revolve around an immediate-response force, permanent sovereignty forces and a deployable modular force. The aim remains to be able to deploy a battalion-size force in a high-intensity conflict as part of NATO operations, while also being able to support similar-sized peace-support or humanitarian missions.

ACTIVE 34,600 (Army 17,900 Navy 9,850 Air 6,850)
Paramilitary 45,250

RESERVE 211,950 (Army 210,000 Navy 1,250, Air Force 700)
Reserve obligation to age 35

ORGANISATIONS BY SERVICE

Army 17,900
5 territorial comd (2 mil region, 1 mil district, 2 mil zone)
FORCES BY ROLE
SPECIAL FORCES
  1 SF unit
MANOEUVRE
  Reconnaissance
  1 ISR bn
  Mechanised
  1 mech bde (1 cav tp, 1 tk regt, 2 mech inf bn, 1 arty bn. 1 AD bty, 1 engr coy, 1 sigs coy, 1 spt bn)
  1 (intervention) bde (1 cav tp, 1 recce regt, 2 mech inf bn, 1 arty bn, 1 AD bty, 1 engr coy, 1 sigs coy, 1 spt bn)
  Air Manoeuvre
  1 (rapid reaction) bde (1 cav tp, 1 cdo bn, 2 para bn, 1 arty bn, 1 AD bty, 1 engr coy, 1 sigs coy, 1 spt bn)
  Other
  1 (Madeira) inf gp (2 inf bn, 1 AD bty)
  1 (Azores) inf gp (1 inf bn, 1 AD bty)
COMBAT SUPPORT
  1 STA bty
  1 AD bn
  1 engr bn
  1 EOD unit
  1 ptn br coy
  1 EW coy

2 MP coy
1 CBRN coy
1 psyops unit
1 CIMIC coy (joint)
1 sigs bn
COMBAT SERVICE SUPPORT
1 construction coy
1 maint coy
1 log coy
1 tpt coy
1 med unit

Reserves 210,000

FORCES BY ROLE
MANOEUVRE
Light
3 (territorial) def bde (on mobilisation)
EQUIPMENT BY TYPE
MBT 56: 37 *Leopard* 2A6; 19 M60A3
RECCE 46: 14 V-150 *Chaimite*; 32 ULTRAV M-11
APC 435
 APC (T) 260: 180 M113A1; 30 M113A2; 50 M577A2
 APC (W) 175: 31 V-200 *Chaimite*; 144 *Pandur* II (all variants)
ARTY 364
 SP 155mm 23: 6 M109A2; 17 M109A5
 TOWED 58: **105mm** 33: 18 L-119; 8 M101A1; 5 M-56 **155mm** 25 M114A1
 MOR 283: **81mm** 182 (incl 21 SP); **107mm** 52 M30 (incl 20 SP); **120mm** 49 *Tampella*
AT
 MSL
  SP 18: 14 M113 with TOW; 4 M901 with TOW
  MANPATS *Milan*; *Spike* LR; *Spike* MR; TOW
 RCL 237: **106mm** 51 M40; **84mm** 152 *Carl Gustav*; **90mm** 34 M67
AD • SAM
 SP 29 MIM-72 *Chaparral*
 MANPAD FIM-92A *Stinger*
AEV M728
ARV 6 M88A1, 7 *Pandur*
VLB M48

Navy 9,850 (incl 1,450 Marines)

EQUIPMENT BY TYPE
SUBMARINES • TACTICAL • SSK 2 *Tridente* (GER Type-214) with 8 533mm TT with *Black Shark* HWT
PRINCIPAL SURFACE COMBATANTS 5
 FRIGATES • FFGHM 5:
  3 *Vasco Da Gama* with 2 Mk141 quad lnchr with RGM-84C *Harpoon* AShM, 1 octuple Mk 29 GMLS with RIM-7M *Sea Sparrow* SAM, 2 Mk32 triple 324mm ASTT with Mk46 LWT, 1 *Phalanx* Block 1B CIWS, 1 100mm gun (capacity 2 *Lynx* Mk95 (*Super Lynx*) hel)
  2 *Bartolomeu Dias* (ex-NLD *Karel Doorman*) with 2 quad Mk141 lnchr with RGM-84C *Harpoon* AShM, 1 Mk48 VLS with RIM-7M *Sea Sparrow* SAM, 2 Mk32 twin 324mm ASTT with Mk46 LWT, 1 *Goalkeeper* CIWS, 1 76mm gun (capacity: 1 *Lynx* Mk95 (*Super Lynx*) hel)

PATROL AND COASTAL COMBATANTS 22
 CORVETTES • FS 5:
  3 *Baptista de Andrade* with 1 100mm gun, 1 hel landing platform
  2 *Joao Coutinho* with 1 twin 76mm gun, 1 hel landing platform
 PSO 2 *Viana do Castelo* with 1 hel landing platform
 PCC 3 *Cacine*
 PBR 12: 2 *Albatroz*; 5 *Argos*; 4 *Centauro*; 1 *Rio Minho*
AMPHIBIOUS • LANDING CRAFT • LCU 1 *Bombarda*
LOGISTICS AND SUPPORT 21
 ABU 2: 1 *Schultz Xavier*; 1 *Guia*
 AGS 4: 2 *D Carlos* I (ex-US *Stalwart*); 2 *Andromeda*
 AORL 1 *Bérrio* (ex-UK *Rover*) with 1 hel landing platform (for medium hel)
 AXS 3: 1 *Sagres*; 1 *Creoula*; 1 *Polar*
 YGS 3
 YP 8

Marines 1,450

FORCES BY ROLE
SPECIAL FORCES
 1 SF det
MANOEUVRE
 Light
  2 lt inf bn
COMBAT SUPPORT
 1 mor coy
 1 MP det
EQUIPMENT BY TYPE
ARTY • MOR 120mm 30

Naval Aviation

HELICOPTERS • ASW 5 *Lynx* Mk95 (*Super Lynx*)

Air Force 6,850

Flying hours 180 hrs/year on F-16 *Fighting Falcon*
FORCES BY ROLE
FIGHTER/GROUND ATTACK
 2 sqn with F-16AM/BM *Fighting Falcon*
MARITIME PATROL
 1 sqn with P-3C *Orion*
ISR/TRANSPORT
 1 sqn with C-295M
COMBAT SEARCH & RESCUE
 1 sqn with with AW101 *Merlin*
TRANSPORT
 1 sqn with C-130H/C-130H-30 *Hercules*
 1 sqn with *Falcon* 50
TRAINING
 1 sqn with *Alpha Jet**
 1 sqn with SA316 *Alouette* III
 1 sqn with TB-30 *Epsilon*
EQUIPMENT BY TYPE
AIRCRAFT 42 combat capable
 FTR 30: 26 F-16AM *Fighting Falcon*; 4 F-16BM *Fighting Falcon*
 ASW 5 P-3C *Orion*
 ISR: 7: 5 C-295M (maritime surveillance), 2 C-295M (photo recce)

TPT 14: **Medium** 6: 3 C-130H *Hercules*; 3 C-130H-30 *Hercules* (tpt/SAR); **Light** 5 C-295M; **PAX** 3 *Falcon* 50 (tpt/VIP)
TRG 20: 6 *Alpha Jet**; 14 TB-30 *Epsilon*
HELICOPTERS
MRH 6 SA316 *Alouette* III (trg, utl)
TPT • **Medium** 12 AW101 *Merlin* (6 SAR, 4 CSAR, 2 fishery protection)
MSL
AAM • **IR** AIM-9L/I *Sidewinder*; **ARH** AIM-120 AMRAAM
ASM AGM-65A *Maverick*
AShM AGM-84A *Harpoon*
BOMBS
Enhanced Paveway II; GBU-49; GBU-31 JDAM

Paramilitary 45,250

National Republican Guard 22,650
APC (W): some *Commando* Mk III (*Bravia*)
PATROL AND COASTAL COMBATANTS • PB 16
 PBF 12
 PB 4
HELICOPTERS • MRH 7 SA315 *Lama*

Public Security Police 22,600

Cyber

A Cyberdefence Centre is being established, under the command of the Portuguese CHOD.

DEPLOYMENT

Legal provisions for foreign deployment:
Constitution: Codified constitution (1976) (revised in 2005)
Decision on deployment of troops abroad: By government

AFGHANISTAN
NATO • ISAF 37
UN • UNAMA 1 obs

LITHUANIA
NATO • Baltic Air Policing 6 F-16AM *Fighting Falcon*

MALI
EU • EUTM Mali 7
UN • MINUSMA 47

SERBIA
NATO • KFOR 186; 1 AB coy (KTM)
OSCE • Kosovo 2

UGANDA
EU • EUTM Somalia 5

FOREIGN FORCES

United States US European Command: 700; 1 spt facility at Lajes

Romania ROM

New Lei		2013	2014	2015
GDP	lei	629bn	660bn	
	US$	189bn	202bn	
per capita	US$	8,874	10,161	
Growth	%	3.5	2.4	
Inflation	%	4.0	1.5	
Def exp [a]	lei	8.67bn		
	US$	2.6bn		
Def bdgt [b]	lei	8.06bn	9.38bn	9.21bn
	US$	2.42bn	2.88bn	
FMA (US)	US$	14m	8m	5.4m
US$1=lei		3.33	3.26	

[a] NATO definition
[b] Includes military pensions

Population 21,729,871

Age	0–14	15–19	20–24	25–29	30–64	65 plus
Male	7.5%	2.7%	3.1%	4.0%	25.2%	6.2%
Female	7.1%	2.6%	3.0%	3.9%	25.7%	9.2%

Capabilities

Romania has sizeable armed forces that, despite a modernisation process, are hampered by ageing Soviet-era equipment. NATO membership is at the heart of the country's defence posture, a factor enhanced since the Ukraine crisis of 2014, which saw six Canadian CF-18s deployed to Romania. The army has been restructured to support deployed operations, with Romanian contingents joining NATO, EU and UN missions. Thirteen years of deployment to Afghanistan in combat operations ended in June 2014. An ageing fighter fleet undermines air-force combat capability, with the replacement programme constrained by budget shortfalls. There are a small number of tactical airlifters and Romania is a member of the Strategic Airlift Capability's C-17 unit. The armed forces exercise regularly on a national and multinational basis. Romania's Deveselu base is to be the site of a new US Naval Support Facility, as well as the site for the land-based ballistic-missile defence system's missile-interceptor silos.

ACTIVE 71,400 (Army 42,600, Navy 6,900, Air 8,400, Joint 13,500) **Paramilitary 79,900**

RESERVE 45,000 (Joint 45,000)

ORGANISATIONS BY SERVICE

Army 42,600
Readiness is reported as 70–90% for NATO-designated forces (1 div HQ, 1 mech bde, 1 inf bde & 1 mtn inf bde) and 40–70% for other forces

FORCES BY ROLE
COMMAND
 3 div HQ

SPECIAL FORCES
1 SF bde (2 SF bn, 1 para bn, 1 log bn)
MANOEUVRE
  Reconnaissance
  3 recce bn
  Mechanised
  5 mech bde (1 tk bn, 2 mech inf bn, 1 arty bn, 1 AD bn, 1 log bn)
  Light
  1 inf bde (2 inf bn, 1 arty bn, 1 AD bn, 1 log bn)
  1 inf bde (2 inf bn, 1 mtn inf bn, 1 arty bn, 1 AD bn, 1 log bn)
  Mountain
  2 mtn inf bde (3 mtn inf bn, 1 arty bn, 1 AD bn, 1 log bn)
COMBAT SUPPORT
  1 arty bde (3 MRL bn, 1 log bn)
  3 arty regt
  3 AD regt
  1 engr bde (1 engr bn, 2 ptn br bn, 1 log bn)
  3 engr bn
  3 sigs bn
  1 CIMIC bn
  1 MP bn
  3 CBRN bn
COMBAT SERVICE SUPPORT
  4 spt bn
EQUIPMENT BY TYPE
MBT 437: 250 T-55; 42 TR-580; 91 TR-85; 54 TR-85 M1
AIFV 124: 23 MLI-84; 101 MLI-84 JDER
APC 1,609
  APC (T) 75 MLVM
  APC (W) 969: 69 B33 TAB *Zimbru*; 31 *Piranha* III; 367 TAB-71; 140 TAB-77; 362 TABC-79
  TYPE VARIANTS 505 APC
  PPV 60 *Maxxpro*
ARTY 899
  SP 122mm 24: 6 2S1; 18 Model 89
  TOWED 422: **122mm** 72 (M-30) M-1938 (A-19); **152mm** 350: 247 M-1981 Model 81; 103 M-1985
  MRL 122mm 187: 133 APR-40; 54 LAROM
  MOR 120mm 266 M-1982
AT
  MSL • SP 134: 12 9P122 *Malyutka* (AT-3 *Sagger*); 74 9P133 *Malyutka* (AT-3 *Sagger*); 48 9P148 *Konkurs* (AT-5 *Spandrel*)
  GUNS 100mm 232: 209 M1977 Gun 77; 23 SU-100 SP
AD • GUNS 66
  SP 35mm 42 *Gepard*
  TOWED • 35mm 24 GDF-203
RADARS • LAND 8 SNAR-10 *Big Fred*
ARV 3 BPz-2

Navy 6,900

EQUIPMENT BY TYPE
PRINCIPAL SURFACE COMBATANTS 3
  DESTROYERS 3:
    DDGH 1 *Marasesti* with 4 twin lnchr with P-15M *Termit*-M (SS-N-2C *Styx*) AShM, 2 triple 533mm ASTT with RUS 53–65 ASW, 2 RBU 6000 *Smerch* 2, 2 twin 76mm guns (capacity 2 SA-316 (IAR-316) *Alouette* III hel)
    DDH 2 *Regele Ferdinand* (ex-UK Type-22), with 2 triple 324mm TT, 1 76mm gun (capacity 1 SA330 (IAR-330) *Puma*)
PATROL AND COASTAL COMBATANTS 21
  CORVETTES 4
    FSH 2 *Tetal* II with 2 twin 533mm ASTT, 2 RBU 6000 *Smerch* 2, 2 AK630 CIWS, 1 76mm gun (capacity 1 SA316 (IAR-316) *Alouette* III hel)
    FS 2 *Tetal* I with 2 twin 533mm ASTT with RUS 53-65 ASW, 2 RBU 2500 *Smerch* 1, 2 twin 76mm guns
  PCFG 3 *Zborul* with 2 twin lnchr with P-15M *Termit*-M (SS-N-2C *Styx*) AShM, 2 AK630 CIWS, 1 76mm gun
  PCR 8:
    1 *Brutar* I with 2 BM-21 MRL, 1 100mm gun
    4 *Brutar* II with 2 BM-21 MRL, 1 100mm gun
    3 *Kogalniceanu* with 2 BM-21 MRL, 2 100mm guns
  PBR 6 VD 141 (ex MSI now used for river patrol)
MINE WARFARE 11
  MINE COUNTERMEASURES 10
    MSO 4 *Musca* with 2 quad lnchr with *Strela* 2M (SA-N-5 *Grail*) SAM, 2 RBU 1200, 2 AK230 CIWS
    MSI 6 VD141 (used for river MCM)
  MINELAYERS • ML 1 *Corsar* with up to 100 mines, 2 RBU 1200, 2 AK630 CIWS, 1 57mm gun
LOGISTICS AND SUPPORT 12
  ADG 1 *Magnetica*
  AETL 2 *Constanta* with 2 RBU 1200, 2 twin 57mm guns
  AGOR 1 *Corsar*
  AGS 2: 1 *Emil Racovita*; 1 *Catuneanu*
  AOL 1 *Tulcea*
  ATF 1 *Grozavu*
  AXS 1 *Mircea*
  YTL 3

Naval Infantry

FORCES BY ROLE
MANOEUVRE
  Light
  1 naval inf bn
EQUIPMENT BY TYPE
APC (W) 14: 11 ABC-79M; 3 TABC-79M

Air Force 8,400

Flying hours 120 hrs/year

FORCES BY ROLE
FIGHTER
  2 sqn with MiG-21 *Lancer* C
FIGHTER/GROUND ATTACK
  1 sqn with MiG-21 *Lancer* A/B
TRANSPORT
  1 sqn with An-26 *Curl*; An-30 *Clank*; C-27J *Spartan*
  1 sqn with C-130B/H *Hercules*
TRAINING
  1 sqn with IAR-99 *Soim**
  1 sqn with SA316B *Alouette* III (IAR-316B); Yak-52 (Iak-52)
TRANSPORT HELICOPTER
  2 (multirole) sqn with IAR-330 SOCAT *Puma*
  3 sqn with SA330 *Puma* (IAR-330)
AIR DEFENCE
  1 AD bde

COMBAT SERVICE SUPPORT
1 engr regt

EQUIPMENT BY TYPE
AIRCRAFT 69 combat capable
FGA 36: 10 MiG-21 *Lancer* A; 6 MiG-21 *Lancer* B; 20 MiG-21 *Lancer* C
ISR 2 An-30 *Clank*
TPT 14: **Medium** 11: 6 C-27J *Spartan*; 4 C-130B *Hercules*; 1 C-130H *Hercules*; **Light** 3 An-26 *Curl*
TRG 32: 10 IAR-99 *Soim**; 10 IAR-99C *Soim**; 12 Yak-52 (Iak-52)
HELICOPTERS
MRH 30: 23 IAR-330 SOCAT *Puma*; 7 SA316B *Alouette* III (IAR-316B)
TPT • **Medium** 37: 21 SA330L *Puma* (IAR-330L); 16 SA330M *Puma* (IAR-330M)
AD • **SAM** 14: 6 S-75M3 *Volkhov* (SA-2 *Guideline*); 8 MIM-23 HAWK PIP III
MSL
AAM • IR R-73 (AA-11 *Archer*); R-550 *Magic* 2; Python 3
ASM *Spike*-ER

Paramilitary 79,900

Border Guards 22,900 (incl conscripts)
Ministry of Interior

EQUIPMENT BY TYPE
PATROL AND COASTAL COMBATANTS 14
PCO 1 *Stefan cel Mare* (Damen OPV 900)
PBF 1 *Bigliani*
PB 12: 4 *Neustadt*; 3 *Mai*; 5 SNR-17

Gendarmerie ε57,000
Ministry of Interior

Cyber
In 2013, Romania adopted its first Cyber Security Strategy, at national level, which defines the conceptual framework, aim, objectives, priorities and courses of action to provide cyber security. A military CERT (CERTMIL) exists within the Ministry of National Defence, having responsibility for cyber-incident management in the defence realm.

DEPLOYMENT

Legal provisions for foreign deployment:
Constitution: Codified constitution (1991)
Decision on deployment of troops abroad: By parliament (Art. 62); or b) by president upon parliamentary approval (Art. 92).

AFGHANISTAN
NATO • ISAF 327
UN • UNAMA 2 obs

BOSNIA-HERZEGOVINA
EU • EUFOR • *Operation Althea* 37

COTE D'IVOIRE
UN • UNOCI 6 obs

DEMOCRATIC REPUBLIC OF THE CONGO
UN • MONUSCO 21 obs

LIBERIA
UN • UNMIL 2 obs

MALI
NATO • EUTM Mali 1

SERBIA
NATO • KFOR 67
OSCE • Kosovo 1
UN • UNMIK 1 obs

SOUTH SUDAN
UN • UNMISS 2; 5 obs

UKRAINE
OSCE • Ukraine 14

Serbia SER

Serbian Dinar d		2013	2014	2015
GDP	d	3.62tr	3.69tr	
	US$	42.5bn	42.6bn	
per capita	US$	5,902	5,924	
Growth	%	2.5	-0.5	
Inflation	%	7.7	2.3	
Def bdgt	d	58.7bn	61.4bn	64.2bn
	US$	689m	711m	
FMA (US)	US$	1.8m	1.8m	1.8m
US$1=d		85.15	86.42	

Population 7,209,764

Age	0–14	15–19	20–24	25–29	30–64	65 plus
Male	7.6%	2.9%	3.1%	3.4%	24.7%	7.1%
Female	7.2%	2.7%	3.0%	3.3%	25.0%	10.2%

Capabilities

Serbia's land- and air-focused forces are undergoing a restructuring process to enable better ties with NATO. Following the conflicts of the 1990s and the political turmoil of the turn of the century, the armed forces have reduced in size, but with the long-term aim of crafting a capable and modern force. Primary goals of Serbia's defence policy are the armed forces' transformation and professionalisation, and capability development. The land forces are built around four combined-arms brigades, supported by an army-aviation unit run by the air force. The latter has a small number of combat aircraft in service, and aims to procure one or two squadrons of a modern multi-role type. Funding constraints have meant that this project has been delayed. Serviceability and platform availability are likely to be a problem for the air force.

ACTIVE 28,150 (Army 13,250, Air Force and Air Defence 5,100, Training Command 3,000, Guards 1,600; Other MoD 5,200)
Conscript liability 6 months (voluntary)

RESERVE 50,150

ORGANISATIONS BY SERVICE

Army 13,250
FORCES BY ROLE
SPECIAL FORCES
1 SF bde (1 CT bn, 1 cdo bn, 1 para bn, 1 log bn)
MANOEUVRE
Mechanised
1 (1st) bde (1 tk bn, 2 mech inf bn, 1 inf bn, 1 SP arty bn, 1 MRL bn, 1 AD bn, 1 engr bn, 1 log bn)
3 (2nd, 3rd & 4th) bde (1 tk bn, 2 mech inf bn, 2 inf bn, 1 SP arty bn, 1 MRL bn, 1 AD bn, 1 engr bn, 1 log bn)
COMBAT SUPPORT
1 (mixed) arty bde (4 arty bn, 1 MRL bn, 1 spt bn)
2 ptn bridging bn
1 NBC bn
1 sigs bn
2 MP bn

Reserve Organisations
FORCES BY ROLE
MANOEUVRE
　Light
　　8 (territorial) inf bde
EQUIPMENT BY TYPE
MBT 212: 199 M-84; 13 T-72
RECCE 46 BRDM-2
AIFV 323 M-80
APC 39 BOV VP M-86
ARTY 515
　SP 122mm 67 2S1
　TOWED 204: **122mm** 78 D-30; **130mm** 18 M-46; **152mm** 36 M-84; **155mm** 72: 66 M-1; 6 M-65
　MRL 81: **128mm** 78: 18 M-63 *Plamen*; 60 M-77 *Organj*; **262mm** 3 *Orkan*
　MOR 163: **82mm** 106 M-69; **120mm** 57 M-74/M-75
AT
　MSL
　　SP 48 BOV-1 (M-83) with 9K11 *Malyutka* (AT-3 *Sagger*)
　　MANPATS 9K11 *Malyutka* (AT-3 *Sagger*); 9K111 *Fagot* (AT-4 *Spigot*)
　RCL 90mm 6 M-79
AD • SAM 156
　SP 94: 77 2K12 *Kub* (SA-6 *Gainful*); 12 S-1M (SA-9 *Gaskin*); 5 SAVA S10M
　MANPADS S-2M (SA-7 *Grail*)‡; *Šilo* (SA-16 *Gimlet*)
GUNS 36
　TOWED 40mm 36 Bofors L70
AEV IWT
ARV M84A1; T-54/T-55
VLB MT-55; TMM

River Flotilla
The Serbian-Montenegrin navy was transferred to Montenegro upon independence in 2006, but the Danube flotilla remained in Serbian control. The flotilla is subordinate to the Land Forces.

EQUIPMENT BY TYPE
PATROL AND COASTAL COMBATANTS 5
　PBR 5: 3 Type-20; 2 others

MINE WARFARE • MINE COUNTERMEASURES 4
　MSI 4 *Nestin*
AMPHIBOUS • LANDING CRAFT • LCU 5 Type-22
LOGISTICS AND SUPPORT 5
　ADG 1 *Šabac*
　AGF 1 *Kozara*
　AOL 1
　YFD 1
　YTL 1

Air Force and Air Defence 5,100
Flying hours: Ftr – 40 per yr
FORCES BY ROLE
FIGHTER
　1 sqn with MiG-21bis *Fishbed*; MiG-29 *Fulcrum*
FIGHTER/GROUND ATTACK
　1 sqn with G-4 *Super Galeb**; J-22 *Orao*
ISR
　2 flt with IJ-22 *Orao* 1*; MiG-21R *Fishbed* H*
TRANSPORT
　1 sqn with An-2; An-26; Do-28; Yak-40 (Jak-40); 1 PA-34 *Seneca* V
TRAINING
　1 sqn with G-4 *Super Galeb** (adv trg/light atk); SA341/342 *Gazelle*; Utva-75 (basic trg)
ATTACK HELICOPTER
　1 sqn with SA341H/342L *Gazelle*; (HN-42/45); Mi-24 *Hind*
TRANSPORT HELICOPTER
　2 sqn with Mi-8 *Hip*; Mi-17 *Hip* H
AIR DEFENCE
　1 bde (5 bn (2 msl, 3 SP msl) with S-125 *Neva* (SA-3 *Goa*); 2K12 *Kub* (SA-6 *Gainful*); 9K32 *Strela*-2 (SA-7 *Grail*); 9K310 *Igla*-1 (SA-16 *Gimlet*))
　2 radar bn (for early warning and reporting)
COMBAT SUPPORT
　1 sigs bn
COMBAT SERVICE SUPPORT
　1 maint bn
EQUIPMENT BY TYPE
AIRCRAFT 83 combat capable
　FTR 30: 20 MiG-21bis *Fishbed* L & N; 6 MiG-21UM *Mongol* B; 3 MiG-29 *Fulcrum*; 1 MiG-29UB *Fulcrum*
　FGA 17 J-22 *Orao* 1
　ISR 12: 10 IJ-22R *Orao* 1*; 2 MiG-21R *Fishbed* H*
　TPT • Light 10: 1 An-2 *Colt*; 4 An-26 *Curl*; 2 Do-28 *Skyservant*; 2 Yak-40 (Jak-40); 1 PA-34 *Seneca* V
　TRG 45: 24 G-4 *Super Galeb**; 11 Utva-75; 10 *Lasta* 95
HELICOPTERS
　ATK 2 Mi-24 *Hind*
　MRH 51: 2 Mi-17 *Hip* H; 2 SA341H *Gazelle* (HI-42); 34 SA341H *Gazelle* (HN-42)/SA342L *Gazelle* (HN-45); 13 SA341H *Gazelle* (HO-42)/SA342L1 *Gazelle* (HO-45)
　TPT • Medium 7 Mi-8T *Hip* (HT-40)
AD
　SAM 15: 6 S-125 *Pechora* (SA-3 *Goa*); 9 2K12 *Kub* (SA-6 *Gainful*)
　MANPAD 9K32 *Strela*-2 (SA-7 *Grail*)‡; 9K310 *Igla*-1 (SA-16 *Gimlet*)

GUNS • **40mm** 24 Bofors L-70
MSL
  AAM • IR R-60 (AA-8 *Aphid*)
  ASM AGM-65 *Maverick*; A-77 *Thunder*

Guards 1,600
MANOEUVRE
  Other
  1 (ceremonial) gd bde (1 gd bn, 1 MP bn, 1 spt bn)

DEPLOYMENT
Legal provisions for foreign deployment:
Constitution: Codified constitution (2006)
Decision on deployment of troops abroad: By parliament (Art. 140)

CENTRAL AFRICAN REPUBLIC
EU • EUFOR RCA 6

CÔTE D'IVOIRE
UN • UNOCI 3 obs

CYPRUS
UN • UNFICYP 46; elm 1 inf coy

DEMOCRATIC REPUBLIC OF THE CONGO
UN • MONUSCO 8

LEBANON
UN • UNIFIL 143; 1 inf coy

LIBERIA
UN • UNMIL 4 obs

MIDDLE EAST
UN • UNTSO 1 obs

UGANDA
EU • EUTM Somalia 5

TERRITORY WHERE THE GOVERNMENT DOES NOT EXERCISE EFFECTIVE CONTROL
Data here represent the de facto situation in Kosovo. This does not imply international recognition as a sovereign state. In February 2008, Kosovo declared itself independent. Serbia remains opposed to this, and while Kosovo has not been admitted to the United Nations, a number of states have recognised Kosovo's self-declared status.

Kosovo Security Force 2,500; reserves 800
The Kosovo Security Force was formed, in January 2009, as a non-military organisation with responsibility for crisis response, civil protection and EOD. The force is armed with small arms and light vehicles only. A July 2010 law created a reserve force.

FOREIGN FORCES
All under Kosovo Force (KFOR) comd. unless otherwise specified.
Albania 12
Armenia 36
Austria 505; 1 mech inf coy • OSCE 5
Bosnia-Herzegovina OSCE 14
Bulgaria 11 • OSCE 2
Canada 4 • OSCE 7
Croatia 23 • OSCE 5
Czech Republic 9 • OSCE 1 • UNMIK 2 obs
Denmark 43 • OSCE 1
Estonia 2
Finland 22 • OSCE 2
France 9 • OSCE 5
Georgia OSCE 4
Germany 674 • OSCE 5
Greece 117; 1 mech inf coy • OSCE 4
Hungary 336; 1 inf coy (KTM) • OSCE 4
Ireland 12 • OSCE 7
Italy 575; 1 recce BG HQ; 1 Carabinieri unit • OSCE 10
Kyrgyzstan OSCE 1
Latvia OSCE 1
Lithuania 1
Luxembourg 23
Macedonia (FYROM) OSCE 22
Malta OSCE 1
Moldova 41
Montenegro OSCE 1
Netherlands 5
Norway 2
Poland 254; 1 inf coy • OSCE 3 • UNMIK 2 obs
Portugal 186; 1 AB coy (KTM) • OSCE 2
Romania 67 • OSCE 1 • UNMIK 1 obs
Russia OSCE 1
Slovakia OSCE 1
Slovenia 314; 2 mot inf coy
Spain OSCE 1
Sweden 7 • OSCE 2
Switzerland 177; 1 inf coy • OSCE 1
Turkey 353; 1 inf coy • OSCE 4 • UNMIK 1 obs
Ukraine 25 • OSCE 1 • UNMIK 2 obs
United Kingdom 1 • OSCE 15
United States 731; elm 1 AB bde HQ; 1 recce sqn • OSCE 5

Slovakia SVK

Euro €		2013	2014	2015
GDP	€	72.1bn	73.9bn	
	US$	95.8bn	100bn	
per capita	US$	17,706	18,480	
Growth	%	0.9	2.4	
Inflation	%	1.5	0.1	
Def exp [a]	€	752m		
	US$	999m		
Def bdgt [b]	€	748m	785m	831m
	US$	994m	1.06bn	
FMA (US)	US$	1m	0.45m	
US$1=€		0.75	0.74	

[a] NATO definition
[b] Includes military pensions

Population 5,492,677

Age	0–14	15–19	20–24	25–29	30–64	65 plus
Male	7.9%	2.8%	3.5%	3.9%	25.2%	5.3%
Female	7.6%	2.6%	3.3%	3.7%	25.7%	8.6%

Capabilities

Faced with ageing Soviet-era equipment, Slovakia is planning to replace its small fighter and rotary–wing transport fleets in the latter half of this decade. There are also ambitions to replace army equipment with more modern technology, however it remains to be seen whether such procurement ambitions can be reconciled with the comparatively low level of defence spending. Following a defence accord signed with the Czech Republic in 2013 there have been moves toward some joint procurement that could include a new jet trainer.

ACTIVE 15,850 (Army 6,250, Air 3,950, Central Staff 2,550, Support and Training 3,100)
Conscript liability 6 months

ORGANISATIONS BY SERVICE

Central Staff 2,550
SPECIAL FORCES
1 (5th Special) recce regt

Army 6,250
FORCES BY ROLE
MANOEUVRE
Mechanised
1 (1st) mech bde (3 mech inf bn, 1 engr coy, 1 spt bn)
1 (2nd) mech bde (1 ISR coy, 1 tk bn, 2 mech inf bn, 1 mixed SP arty bn, 1 engr coy, 1 spt bn)
COMBAT SUPPORT
1 MRL bn
1 engr bn
1 MP bn
1 NBC bn

EQUIPMENT BY TYPE
MBT 30 T-72M
AIFV 239: 148 BMP-1; 91 BMP-2
APC 101+
  APC (T) 72 OT-90
  APC (W) 22: 7 OT-64; 15 *Tatrapan* (6×6)
  PPV 7+ RG-32M
ARTY 68
  SP 19: **152mm** 3 M-77 *Dana*; **155mm** 16 M-2000 *Zuzana*
  TOWED 122mm 19 D-30
  MRL 30: **122mm** 4 RM-70; **122/227mm** 26 RM-70/85 MODULAR
AT
  SP 9S428 with *Malyutka* (AT-3 *Sagger*) on BMP-1; 9P135 *Fagot* (AT-4 *Spigot*) on BMP-2; 9P148 (AT-5 *Spandrel*) on BRDM-2
  MANPATS 9K11 *Malyutka* (AT-3 *Sagger*); 9K113 *Konkurs* (AT-5 *Spandrel*)
AD
  SAM
    SP 48 9K35 *Strela*-10 (SA-13 *Gopher*)
    MANPADS 9K32 *Strela*-2 (SA-7 *Grail*); 9K310 *Igla*-1 (SA-16 *Gimlet*)
RADAR • LAND SNAR-10 *Big Fred* (veh, arty)
ARV MT-55; VT-55A; VT-72B; WPT-TOPAS
VLB AM-50; MT-55A
MW Bozena; UOS-155 *Belarty*

Air Force 3,950

Flying hours 90 hrs/yr for MiG-29 pilots (NATO Integrated AD System); 90 hrs/yr for Mi-8/17 crews (reserved for EU & NATO)

FORCES BY ROLE
FIGHTER
1 sqn with MiG-29AS/UBS *Fulcrum*
TRANSPORT
1 flt with An-26 *Curl*
1 flt with L-410FG/T/UVP *Turbolet*
TRANSPORT HELICOPTER
1 sqn with Mi-8 *Hip*; Mi-17 *Hip* H
1 sqn with PZL MI-2 *Hoplite*
TRAINING
1 sqn with L-39CM/ZA/ZAM *Albatros*
AIR DEFENCE
1 bde with 2K12 *Kub* (SA-6 *Gainful*); 9K32 *Strela*-2 (SA-7 *Grail*); S-300 (SA-10 *Grumble*)

EQUIPMENT BY TYPE
AIRCRAFT 20 combat capable
  FTR 20: 10 MiG-29AS *Fulcrum*; 2 MiG-29UBS *Fulcrum*; 8 MiG-29A/UB *Fulcrum*
  TPT • Light 9: 1 An-26 *Curl*; 2 L-410FG *Turbolet*; 2 L-410T *Turbolet*; 4 L-410UVP *Turbolet*
  TRG 13: 6 L-39CM *Albatros*; 5 L-39ZA *Albatros*; 2 L-39ZAM *Albatros*
HELICOPTERS
  ATK (15: 5 Mi-24D *Hind* D; 10 Mi-24V *Hind* E all in store)
  MRH 14 Mi-17 *Hip* H
  TPT 7: **Medium** 1 Mi-8 *Hip*; **Light** 6 PZL MI-2 *Hoplite*
AD • SAM
  SP S-300 (SA-10B *Grumble*); 2K12 *Kub* (SA-6 *Gainful*)
  MANPAD 9K32 *Strela*-2 (SA-7 *Grail*)‡

MSL
AAM • IR R-60 (AA-8 *Aphid*); R-73 (AA-11 *Archer*);
SARH R-27R (AA-10A *Alamo*)
ASM S5K/S5KO (57mm rockets); S8KP/S8KOM (80mm rockets)

DEPLOYMENT

Legal provisions for foreign deployment:
Constitution: Codified constitution (1992)
Decision on deployment of troops abroad: By the parliament (Art. 86)

AFGHANISTAN
NATO • ISAF 277

BOSNIA-HERZEGOVINA
EU • EUFOR • *Operation Althea* 35
OSCE • Bosnia and Herzegovina 1

CYPRUS
UN • UNFICYP 159; elm 1 inf coy; 1 engr pl

MIDDLE EAST
UN • UNTSO 2 obs

SERBIA
OSCE • Kosovo 1

UKRAINE
OSCE • Ukraine 4

Slovenia SVN

Euro €		2013	2014	2015
GDP	€	36.1bn	36.9bn	
	US$	48bn	49.9bn	
per capita	US$	23,317	24,211	
Growth	%	-1.0	1.4	
Inflation	%	1.8	0.5	
Def exp [a]	€	391m		
	US$	519m		
Def bdgt [b]	€	351m	336m	332m
	US$	466m	455m	
FMA (US)	US$	0.45m	0.45m	
US$1=€		0.75	0.74	

[a] NATO definition
[b] Excludes military pensions

Population   1,988,292

Age	0–14	15–19	20–24	25–29	30–64	65 plus
Male	6.9%	2.4%	2.7%	3.3%	26.2%	7.2%
Female	6.5%	2.3%	2.6%	3.2%	26.1%	10.7%

Capabilities

Territorial defence and the ability to take part in peace-support operations are central to the defence strategy of Slovenia. The country joined NATO in March 2004 and has contributed regularly to Alliance operations in Kosovo and Afghanistan. It is also a participant in the EU Training Mission in Mali. Development of Slovenia's armed forces is constrained by the amount of available funding. Its small air wing is not equipped to provide air defence; Hungary took over from Italy in 2014 in providing this capability.

ACTIVE 7,600 (Army 7,600) **Paramilitary** 5,950

RESERVE 1,500 (Army 1,500) **Paramilitary** 260

ORGANISATIONS BY SERVICE

Army 7,600
FORCES BY ROLE
Regt are bn sized
SPECIAL FORCES
1 SF unit (1 spec ops coy, 1 CSS coy)
MANOEUVRE
Reconnaissance
1 ISR bn (2 coy)
Mechanised
1 mech inf bde (1st) (1 mech inf regt, 1 mtn inf regt, 1 cbt spt bn)
1 mech inf bde (72nd) (2 mech inf regt, 1 cbt spt bn)
Other
1 armd trg bn (1 armd coy)
COMBAT SUPPORT
1 arty bn (2 arty bty)
1 engr bn (2 engr coy)
1 EW coy
1 MP bn (3 MP coy)
1 CBRN bn (3 CBRN coy)
1 sigs bn (3 sigs coy)
COMBAT SERVICE SUPPORT
1 log bde (1 log regt, 1 maint regt, 1 med regt)

Reserves
FORCES BY ROLE
MANOEUVRE
Mountain
2 inf regt (territorial - 1 allocated to each inf bde)
EQUIPMENT BY TYPE
MBT 46 M-84 (trg role)
RECCE 10 *Cobra* CBRN
APC (W) 115: 85 *Pandur* 6×6 (*Valuk*); 30 *Patria* 8×8 (*Svarun*)
ARTY 63
TOWED • 155mm 18 TN-90
MOR 120mm 45 MN-9
AT • MSL
SP 24: 12 BOV-3 with 9K11 *Malyutka* (AT-3 *Sagger*); 12 BOV-3 with 9K111 *Fagot* (AT-4 *Spigot*)
MANPATS 9K11 *Malyutka* (AT-3 *Sagger*); 9K111 *Fagot* (AT-4 *Spigot*)
ARV VT-55A
VLB MTU

Army Maritime Element 170
FORCES BY ROLE
MANOEUVRE
Amphibious
1 maritime det

EQUIPMENT BY TYPE
PATROL AND COASTAL COMBATANTS 2
    PBF 1 *Super Dvora* MkII
    PCC 1 *Triglav* III (RUS *Svetlyak*)

Air Element 650
FORCES BY ROLE
TRANSPORT
    1 sqn with L-410 *Turbolet*; PC-6B *Turbo Porter*
TRAINING
    1 unit with Bell 206 *Jet Ranger* (AB-206); PC-9; PC-9M*; Z-143L; Z-242L
TRANSPORT HELICOPTER
    1 sqn with AS532AL *Cougar*; Bell 412 *Twin Huey* (some armed)
AIR DEFENCE
    1 AD bn (2 AD bty)
COMBAT SERVICE SUPPORT
    1 maint sqn
EQUIPMENT BY TYPE
AIRCRAFT 9 combat capable
    TPT • **Light** 3: 1 L-410 *Turbolet*; 2 PC-6B *Turbo Porter*
    TRG 21: 2 PC-9; 9 PC-9M*; 2 Z-143L; 8 Z-242L
HELICOPTERS
    MRH 8: 5 Bell 412EP *Twin Huey*; 2 Bell 412HP *Twin Huey*; 1 Bell 412SP *Twin Huey* (some armed)
    TPT 8: **Medium** 4 AS532AL *Cougar*; **Light** 4 Bell 206 *Jet Ranger* (AB-206)
AD • SAM 138
    SP 6 *Roland* II
    MANPAD 132: 36 9K310 *Igla*-1 (SA-16 *Gimlet*); 96 9K38 *Igla* (SA-18 *Grouse*)

Paramilitary 5,950

Police 5,950; 260 reservists
Ministry of Interior (civilian; limited elements could be prequalified to cooperate in military defence with the armed forces during state of emergency or war)
PATROL AND COASTAL COMBATANTS • PBF 1 *Ladse*
HELICOPTERS
    MRH 1 Bell 412 *Twin Huey*,
    TPT • **Light** 5: 1 AW109; 2 Bell 206 (AB-206) *Jet Ranger*; 1 Bell 212 (AB-212); 1 EC135

Cyber
A National Cyber Strategy was expected by the end of 2014.

DEPLOYMENT
Legal provisions for foreign deployment:
Constitution: Codified constitution (1991)
Decision on deployment of troops abroad: By government (Art. 84 of Defence Act)

AFGHANISTAN
NATO • ISAF 2

ALBANIA
OSCE • Albania 1

BOSNIA-HERZEGOVINA
EU • EUFOR • *Operation Althea* 13

LEBANON
UN • UNIFIL 14

MALI
EU • EUTM Mali 3

MIDDLE EAST
UN • UNTSO 3 obs

SERBIA
NATO • KFOR 314; 2 mot inf coy

UKRAINE
OSCE • Ukraine 1

Spain ESP

Euro €		2013	2014	2015
GDP	€	1.02tr	1.03tr	
	US$	1.36tr	1.4tr	
per capita	US$	29,150	30,113	
Growth	%	-1.2	1.3	
Inflation	%	1.5	-0.03	
Def exp [a]	€	9.61bn		
	US$	12.8bn		
Def bdgt [b]	€	11bn	11.1bn	
	US$	14.6bn	15.1bn	
US$1=€		0.75	0.74	

[a] NATO definition
[b] Includes military pensions

Population   47,737,941

Age	0–14	15–19	20–24	25–29	30–64	65 plus
Male	7.9%	2.4%	2.6%	3.1%	25.9%	7.5%
Female	7.5%	2.2%	2.4%	2.8%	25.6%	10.1%

Capabilities

Budgetary pressures continue to affect Spain's military capacity. The country's only aircraft carrier, the *Principe de Asturias*, was withdrawn from service in February 2013, while some newly delivered *Typhoon* combat aircraft were placed in storage. The *Mirage* F-1 was also withdrawn from service during the course of 2013. The 2013–16 defence plan sets out defence requirements against the backdrop of continuing austerity. Spain intends to join the European Air Transport Command, which will provide access to additional airlift. Although the country is a partner in the A400M *Atlas* airlifter, and home to the aircraft's final assembly line, Madrid is reportedly also looking to sell 13 of the 27 A400Ms it has on its order book. The number of *Pizarro* AFVs is also reduced. The armed forces are well versed in combined operations with other countries. Spain has been a long-term contributor to ISAF, and intends to play a major role in NATO's follow-on support mission.

ACTIVE 133,250 (Army 69,350 Navy 22,200, Air 20,400 Joint 21,300) **Paramilitary 80,700**

RESERVE 13,900 (Army 2,700 Navy 9,000 Air 2,200)

ORGANISATIONS BY SERVICE

Space
EQUIPMENT BY TYPE
SATELLITES • COMMUNICATIONS 2: 1 *Spainsat*; 1 *Xtar-Eur*

Army 69,350
The Land Forces High Readiness HQ Spain provides one NATO Rapid Deployment Corps HQ (NRDC-SP).
FORCES BY ROLE
Infantry regiments usually comprise 2 bn. Spain deploys its main battle tanks within its armd/mech inf formations, and its armd cav regt
COMMAND
1 corps HQ (CGTAD) (1 int regt, 1 MP bn)
2 div HQ
SPECIAL FORCES
1 comd (3 spec ops bn, 1 int coy, 1 sigs coy, 1 log bn)
MANOEUVRE
Reconnaissance
1 (2nd) bde (3 lt armd cav regt, 1 fd arty regt, 1 AD coy, 1 engr bn, 1 int coy, 1 NBC coy, 1 sigs coy, 1 log bn)
Armoured
1 (12th) bde (1 recce sqn, 1 armd inf regt, 1 mech inf regt, 1 SP arty bn, 1 AD coy, 1 engr bn, 1 int coy, 1 NBC coy, 1 sigs coy, 1 log bn)
Mechanised
2 (10th & 11th) bde (1 recce sqn, 1 armd inf bn, 1 mech inf regt, 1 SP arty bn, 1 AT coy, 1 AD coy, 1 engr bn, 1 int coy, 1 NBC coy, 1 sigs coy, 1 log bn)
Light
2 (2nd/La Legion & 7th) bde (1 recce bn, 2 inf regt, 1 fd arty bn, 1 AT coy, 1 AD coy, 1 engr bn, 1 int coy, 1 NBC coy, 1 sigs coy, 1 log bn)
1 (5th) bde (2 lt inf regt)
Air Manoeuvre
1 (6th) bde (2 para bn, 1 air mob bn, 1 fd arty bn, 1 AT coy, 1 AD coy, 1 engr bn, 1 int coy, 1 NBC coy, 1 sigs coy, 1 log bn)
Mountain
1 (1st) comd (3 mtn inf regt)
Other
1 (Canary Islands) comd (1 lt inf bde (3 lt inf regt, 1 fd arty regt, 1 AT coy, 1 engr bn, 1 int coy, 1 NBC coy, 1 sigs coy, 1 log bn); 1 spt hel bn; 1 AD regt)
1 (Balearic Islands) comd (1 inf regt)
2 (Ceuta and Melilla) comd (1 cav regt, 2 inf regt, 1 arty regt, 1 engr bn, 1 sigs coy, 1 log bn)
Aviation
1 (FAMET) avn comd (1 atk hel bn, 2 spt hel bn, 1 tpt hel bn, 1 sigs bn, 1 log unit (1 spt coy, 1 supply coy))
COMBAT SUPPORT
1 arty comd (3 arty regt; 1 coastal arty regt)
1 AD comd (5 ADA regt, 1 sigs unit)
1 engr comd (2 engr regt, 1 bridging regt)
1 EW/sigs bde with (1 EW regt, 3 sigs regt)
1 EW regt
1 NBC regt
1 railway regt
1 sigs regt
1 CIMIC bn
COMBAT SERVICE SUPPORT
1 log bde (5 log regt)
1 med bde (1 log unit, 2 med regt, 1 fd hospital unit)
EQUIPMENT BY TYPE
MBT 327: 108 *Leopard* 2A4; 219 *Leopard* 2A5E
RECCE 286: 84 B-1 *Centauro*; 202 VEC-3562 BMR-VEC
AIFV 144 *Pizarro* (incl 21 comd)
APC 875
  APC (T) 453 M113 (incl variants)
  APC (W) 312 BMR-600/BMR-600M1
PPV 110 RG-31
ARTY 1,894
  SP 155mm 96 M109A5
  TOWED 329: **105mm** 224: 56 L118 light gun; 168 Model 56 pack howitzer; **155mm** 64 SBT 155/52 SIAC
  COASTAL 155mm 19 SBT 155/52 APU SBT V07
  MOR 1,450: **81mm** 989; **120mm** 461
AT • MSL
  SP 116 *Milan*
  MANPATS *Spike*-LR; *Milan*; TOW
HELICOPTERS
  ATK 6 EC665 *Tiger* HAP-E (18 HAD-E on order)
  MRH 21 Bo-105 HOT
  TPT 89: **Heavy** 17 CH-47D *Chinook* (HT-17D); **Medium** 34: 16 AS332B *Super Puma* (HU-21); 12 AS532UL *Cougar*; 6 AS532AL *Cougar*; **Light** 38: 15 Bell-205 (HU-10B *Iroquois*); 5 Bell 212 (HU.18); 14 EC135T2 (HE.26) (trg); 4 EC-135P2 (HU.26)
UAV • ISR • Medium 4: 2 *Searcher* Mk II-J (PASI); 2 *Searcher* Mk-III (PASI)
AD 370
  SAM 279
    SP 18 *Roland*
    TOWED 81: 52 MIM-23B I-HAWK Phase III; 13 *Skyguard/Aspide*; 8 NASAMS; 8 PAC-2 *Patriot*
    MANPAD *Mistral*
  GUNS • TOWED 35mm 91 GDF-005
RADAR • LAND 6: 4 ARTHUR; 2 AN/TPQ-36 *Firefinder*
AEV 37 CZ-10/25E
ARV 57: 16 *Büffel*; 1 AMX-30; 1 BMR 3560.55; 4 *Centauro* REC; 22 M47-VR; 1 M578; 12 M113
VLB 13: 1 M47; 12 M60

Navy 22,200 (incl Naval Aviation and Marines)
EQUIPMENT BY TYPE
SUBMARINES • TACTICAL • SSK 3:
  3 *Galerna* with 4 single 533mm TT with F17 Mod 2/L5 HWT
PRINCIPAL SURFACE COMBATANTS 11
  DESTROYERS • DDGHM 5:
    5 *Alvaro de Bazan* with Baseline 5 *Aegis* C2, 2 quad Mk141 lnchr with RGM-84F *Harpoon* AShM, 1 48-cell Mk41 VLS (LAM capable) with SM-2MR/RIM-162B *Sea*

Sparrow SAM, 2 twin 324mm ASTT with Mk46 LWT, 1 127mm gun (capacity 1 SH-60B *Seahawk* ASW hel)
FRIGATES • FFGHM 6:
6 *Santa Maria* with 1 Mk13 GMLS with RGM-84C *Harpoon* AShM/SM-1MR SAM, 2 Mk32 triple 324mm ASTT with Mk46 LWT, 1 76mm gun (capacity 2 SH-60B *Seahawk* ASW hel)
AMPHIBIOUS
PRINCIPAL AMPHIBIOUS SHIPS 3:
LHD 1 *Juan Carlos I* (capacity 4 LCM; 42 APC; 46 MBT; 700 troops; able to operate as platform for aviation group)
LPD 2 *Galicia* (capacity 6 Bell 212 or 4 SH-3D *Sea King* hel; 4 LCM; 130 APC or 33 MBT; 450 troops)
LANDING CRAFT 14
LCM 14 LCM 1E
LOGISTICS AND SUPPORT 2
AORH 2: 1 *Patino* (capacity 3 Bell 212 or 2 SH-3D *Sea King* hel); 1 *Cantabria* (capacity 3 Bell 212 or 2 SH-3D *Sea King* hel)

Navy – Maritime Action Force
PATROL AND COASTAL COMBATANTS 23
PSO 7:
3 *Alboran* each with 1 hel landing platform
4 *Descubierta* with 1 76mm gun
PSOH 4 *Meteoro* (*Buques de Accion Maritima*) with 1 76mm gun (additional vessels on order)
PCO 4 *Serviola* with 1 76mm gun
PCC 3 *Anaga* with 1 76mm gun
PB 2 *Toralla* with 1 76mm gun
PBR 3 P-101/114/201
MINE WARFARE • MINE COUNTERMEASURES 6
MHO 6 *Segura*
LOGISTICS AND SUPPORT 76
AGDS 1 *Neptuno*
AGI 1 *Alerta*
AGOR 2 (with ice-strengthened hull, for polar research duties in Antarctica)
AGS 3: 2 *Malaspina*; 1 *Castor*
AK 2: 1 *Martin Posadillo* (with 1 hel landing platform); 1 *El Camino Español*
AP 1 *Contramaestre* (with 1 hel landing platform)
ATF 3: 1 *Mar Caribe*; 1 *Mahon*; 1 *La Grana*
AXL 8: 4 *Contramaestre*; 4 *Guardiamarina*
AXS 8
YO 22
YTM 25

Naval Aviation 800
Flying hours 150 hrs/year on AV-8B *Harrier* II FGA ac; 200 hrs/year on hel

FORCES BY ROLE
FIGHTER/GROUND ATTACK
1 sqn with AV-8B *Harrier* II; AV-8B *Harrier* II Plus
ANTI-SUBMARINE WARFARE
1 sqn with SH-60B *Seahawk*
AIRBORNE EARLY WARNING
1 sqn with SH-3H AEW *Sea King*
TRANSPORT
1 (liaison) sqn with Cessna 550 *Citation* II; Cessna 650 *Citation* VII
TRAINING
1 sqn with Hughes 500MD8
1 flt with TAV-8B *Harrier*
TRANSPORT HELICOPTER
1 sqn with Bell 212 (HU-18)
1 sqn with SH-3D *Sea King*
EQUIPMENT BY TYPE
AIRCRAFT 17 combat capable
FGA 17: 4 AV-8B *Harrier* II; 12 AV-8B *Harrier* II Plus; 1 TAV-8B *Harrier* (on lease from USMC)
TPT • Light 4: 3 Cessna 550 *Citation* II; 1 Cessna 650 *Citation* VII
HELICOPTERS
ASW 19: 7 SH-3D *Sea King* (tpt); 12 SH-60B *Seahawk*
MRH 9 Hughes 500MD
AEW 3 SH-3H AEW *Sea King*
TPT • Light 7 Bell 212 (HA-18)
MSL
AAM • IR AIM-9L *Sidewinder*; ARH AIM-120 AMRAAM
ASM AGM-65G *Maverick*
AShM AGM-119 *Penguin*

Marines 5,300
FORCES BY ROLE
SPECIAL FORCES
1 spec ops unit
MANOEUVRE
Amphibious
1 mne bde (1 recce unit, 1 mech inf bn, 2 inf bn, 1 arty bn, 1 log bn)
5 mne garrison gp
EQUIPMENT BY TYPE
MBT 16 M60A3TTS
APC (W) 39 *Piranha* IIIC
AAV 18: 16 AAV-7A1/AAVP-7A1; 2 AAVC-7A1
ARTY 18
SP 155mm 6 M109A2
TOWED 105mm 12 M-56 (pack)
AT
MSL • MANPATS 24 TOW-2
RL 90mm C-90C
AD • SAM • MANPAD 12 *Mistral*
ARV 1 AAVR-7A1

Air Force 20,400
The Spanish Air Force is organised in 3 commands – General Air Command, Combat Air Command and Canary Islands Air Command

Flying hours 120 hrs/year on hel/tpt ac; 180 hrs/year on FGA/ftr

FORCES BY ROLE
FIGHTER
2 sqn with Eurofighter *Typhoon*
FIGHTER/GROUND ATTACK
5 sqn with F/A-18A/B MLU *Hornet* (EF-18A/B MLU)

MARITIME PATROL
  1 sqn with P-3A/M *Orion*
ISR
  1 sqn with Beech C90 *King Air*
  1 sqn with Cessna 550 *Citation* V; CN-235 (TR-19A)
ELECTRONIC WARFARE
  1 sqn with B-707 *Santiago*; C-212 *Aviocar*; *Falcon* 20D/E
SEARCH & RESCUE
  1 sqn with AS332B/B1 *Super Puma*; CN-235 VIGMA
  1 sqn with AS332B *Super Puma*; CN-235 VIGMA
  1 sqn with C-212 *Aviocar*; CN-235 VIGMA; SA330J/L *Puma* (AS330)
TANKER/TRANSPORT
  1 sqn with B-707/B-707 tkr
  1 sqn with KC-130H *Hercules*
TRANSPORT
  1 VIP sqn with A310; *Falcon* 900
  1 sqn with C-130H/H-30 *Hercules*
  1 sqn with C-212 *Aviocar*
  2 sqn with C-295
  1 sqn with CN-235
TRAINING
  1 OCU sqn with Eurofighter *Typhoon*
  1 OCU sqn with F/A-18A/B (EF-18A/B MLU) *Hornet*
  1 sqn with Beech F33C *Bonanza*
  2 sqn with C-101 *Aviojet*
  1 sqn with C-212 *Aviocar*
  1 sqn with T-35 *Pillan* (E-26)
  2 (LIFT) sqn with F-5B *Freedom Fighter*
  1 hel sqn with EC120 *Colibri*
  1 hel sqn with S-76C
FIRE FIGHTING
  1 sqn with CL-215; CL-415
TRANSPORT HELICOPTER
  1 sqn with AS332M1 *Super Puma*; AS532UL *Cougar* (VIP)
EQUIPMENT BY TYPE
AIRCRAFT 149 combat capable
  FTR 58: 39 Eurofighter *Typhoon*; 19 F-5B *Freedom Fighter*
  FGA 86: 20 F/A-18A *Hornet* (EF-18A); 54 EF-18A MLU; 12 EF-18B MLU
  ASW 5: 2 P-3A *Orion*; 3 P-3M *Orion*
  MP 8 CN-235 VIGMA
  ISR 2 CN-235 (TR-19A)
  EW 6: 1 B-707 *Santiago* (TM.17); 1 C-212 *Aviocar* (TM.12D); 2 *Falcon* 20D; 2 *Falcon* 20E
  TKR 7: 5 KC-130H *Hercules*, 2 B-707 Tkr
  TPT 82: **Medium** 7: 6 C-130H *Hercules*; 1 C-130H-30 *Hercules*; **Light** 67: 3 Beech C90 *King Air*; 22 Beech F33C *Bonanza*; 18 C-212 *Aviocar* (incl 8 trg); 13 C-295; 8 CN-235; 3 Cessna 550 *Citation* V (ISR); **PAX** 8: 2 A310; 1 B-707; 5 *Falcon* 900 (VIP)
  TRG 101: 64 C-101 *Aviojet*; 37 T-35 *Pillan* (E-26)
  FF 17: 14 CL-215; 3 CL-415
HELICOPTERS
  TPT 45: **Medium** 22: 10 AS332B/B1 *Super Puma*; 4 AS332M1 *Super Puma*; 2 AS532UL *Cougar* (VIP); 4 SA330J *Puma* (AS330); 2 SA330L *Puma* (AS330); **Light** 23: 15 EC120 *Colibri*; 8 S-76C

AD
  SAM *Mistral*
  TOWED *Skyguard/Aspide*
MSL
  AAM • IR AIM-9L/JULI *Sidewinder*; **IIR** IRIS-T; **SARH** AIM-7P *Sparrow*; **ARH** AIM-120B/C AMRAAM
  ARM AGM-88B HARM
  ASM AGM-65G *Maverick*
  AShM AGM-84D *Harpoon*
  LACM *Taurus* KEPD 350
BOMBS
  Conventional: Mk 82; Mk 83; Mk 84; BR-250; BR-500; BRP-250
  Laser-guided: GBU-10/12/16 *Paveway* II; GBU-24 *Paveway* III; EGBU-16 *Paveway* II; BPG-2000

Emergencies Military Unit (UME)
FORCES BY ROLE
COMMAND
  1 div HQ
FIRE FIGHTING
  1 sqn with CL-215; CL-415 opcon Air Force
MANOEUVRE
  Aviation
  1 hel bn opcon Army
  Other
  5 Emergency Intervention bn

Paramilitary 80,700

Guardia Civil 79,950
9 regions, 56 Rural Comds
FORCES BY ROLE
SPECIAL FORCES
  10 (rural) gp
MANOEUVRE
  Other
  17 (Tercios) paramilitary regt
  6 (traffic) sy gp
  1 (Special) sy bn
EQUIPMENT BY TYPE
APC (W) 18 BLR
HELICOPTERS
  MRH 26 Bo-105ATH
  TPT • Light 12: 8 BK-117; 4 EC-135P2

Guardia Civil Del Mar 750
EQUIPMENT BY TYPE
PATROL AND COASTAL COMBATANTS 72
  PSO 1 with 1 hel landing platform
  PCC 2
  PBF 40
  PB 29

Cyber
Spain has established a cyber command. It has a national CERT and is a member of the European CERT group. The national intelligence CERT (CCN–CERT) is responsible for coordinating CERT activities.

DEPLOYMENT

Legal provisions for foreign deployment:
Constitution: Codified constitution (1978)
Specific legislation: 'Ley Orgánica de la Defensa Nacional' (2005)
Decision on deployment of troops abroad: a) By the government (Art. 6 of the 'Defence Law'); b) parliamentary approval is required for military operations 'which are not directly related to the defence of Spain or national interests' (Art. 17 of the 'Defence Law')

AFGHANISTAN
NATO • ISAF 181

ALBANIA
OSCE • Albania 2

BOSNIA-HERZEGOVINA
EU • EUFOR • *Operation Althea* 10
OSCE • Bosnia and Herzegovina 1

CENTRAL AFRICAN REPUBLIC
EU • EUFOR RCA 99; 1 SF unit

COTE D'IVOIRE
UN • UNOCI 1

DJIBOUTI
EU • *Operation Atalanta* 1 P-3A Orion

GULF OF ADEN & INDIAN OCEAN
EU • *Operation Atalanta* 1 FFGHM

LEBANON
UN • UNIFIL 589; 1 cav bde HQ; 1 lt armd cav BG

MALI
EU • EUTM Mali 114

MEDITERRANEAN SEA
NATO • SNMG 2: 1 DDGHM

MOLDOVA
OSCE • Moldova 1

SERBIA
OSCE • Kosovo 1

UGANDA
EU • EUTM Somalia 14

UKRAINE
OSCE • Ukraine 8

FOREIGN FORCES
United States US European Command: 2,100; 1 air base at Morón; 1 naval base at Rota

Sweden SWE

Swedish Krona Skr		2013	2014	2015
GDP	Skr	3.64tr	3.74tr	
	US$	559bn	559bn	
per capita	US$	58,014	57,557	
Growth	%	1.6	2.1	
Inflation	%	-0.04	0.1	
Def bdgt [a]	Skr	42.3bn	47.2bn	
	US$	6.49bn	7.05bn	
US$1=Skr		6.51	6.69	

[a] Excludes military pensions and peacekeeping expenditure

Population 9,723,809

Age	0 – 14	15 – 19	20 – 24	25 – 29	30 – 64	65 plus
Male	8.7%	2.8%	3.5%	3.5%	22.3%	9.1%
Female	8.2%	2.6%	3.4%	3.3%	21.8%	10.7%

Capabilities

The Swedish armed forces remain configured mainly for the defence of national territory, with all three services equipped and trained to meet this task. A period of defence cuts and restructuring, however, coupled with a more assertive Russia, has resulted in some analysts questioning whether reductions have proceeded too quickly. The tension in relations with Russia in 2014, evidenced by Russian air-force sorties and the possible submarine sighting near Stockholm in October, has also seen renewed debate over Sweden's relationship with NATO. The country has taken part in NATO-led operations and there is support for closer involvement with the Alliance, though not for full membership. The key procurement project for the air force is the JAS-39E fighter aircraft; a mid-2014 revision to the acquisition approach will mean these are new-build airframes rather than reworked JAS-39Cs. The first E-model is expected to be delivered to the air force in 2018. An increase in the order from 60 to 70 aircraft is also being considered. In June 2014, the government awarded an initial contract to Saab for the development of a new submarine class for the navy; the company was as of mid-2014 in the process of purchasing the former Kockums shipyard from German firm ThyssenKrupp. Meanwhile, a proposal for Swedish vehicle manufacturer Volvo's French subsidiary and Russia's Uralvagonzavod to build an AIFV was put on hold in April 2014 as a result of the Ukraine crisis.

ACTIVE 15,300 (Army 5,550 Navy 3,000 Air 3,300 Staff 3,450) **Paramilitary 800 Voluntary Auxiliary Organisations 22,000**

ORGANISATIONS BY SERVICE

Army 5,550
The army has been transformed to provide brigade-sized task forces depending on the operational requirement.

FORCES BY ROLE
COMMAND
  1 div HQ (on mobilisation)
  2 bde HQ
MANOEUVRE
  Reconnaissance
  1 recce bn
  Armoured
  3 armd coy
  Mechanised
  4 mech bn
  Light
  2 mot inf bn
  1 lt inf bn
  Air Manoeuvre
  1 AB bn
  Other
  1 sy bn
COMBAT SUPPORT
  2 arty bn
  2 AD bn
  2 engr bn
  2 MP coy
COMBAT SERVICE SUPPORT
  2 log bn

Reserves
FORCES BY ROLE
MANOEUVRE
  Other
    40 Home Guard bn
EQUIPMENT BY TYPE
MBT 132: 12 *Leopard* 2A4 (Strv-121); 120 *Leopard* 2A5 (Strv 122)
AIFV 354 CV9040 (Strf 9040)
APC 665+
  APC (T) 244+: 194 Pbv 302; 50+ BvS10 MkII
  APC (W) 161+: 23 XA-180 *Sisu* (Patgb 180); 1 XA-202 *Sisu* (Patgb 202); 136 XA-203 *Sisu* (Patgb 203); 1+ XA-360 (Patgb 360)
  PPV 260 RG-32M
ARTY 195
  SP 155mm 4 *Archer*
  MOR 120mm 191
AT
  MSL • MANPATS RB-55; RB-56 *Bill*
  RCL 84mm *Carl Gustav*
AD
  SAM
    SP 16 RBS-70
    TOWED RBS-90
    MANPAD RBS-70
  GUNS • SP 40mm 30 Strv 90LV
RADAR • LAND ARTHUR (arty); M113A1GE *Green Archer* (mor)
UAV • ISR • Medium 3 *Sperwer*
AEV *Kodiak*
ARV 40: 14 Bgbv 120; 26 CV90
MW *Aardvark* Mk2; 33 Area Clearing System

Navy 2,150; 850 Amphibious; (total 3,000)
EQUIPMENT BY TYPE
SUBMARINES 6
  TACTICAL • SSK 5:
    3 *Gotland* (AIP fitted) with 2 single 400mm TT with Tp432/Tp 451, 4 single 533mm TT with Tp613/Tp62
    2 *Sodermanland* (AIP fitted) with 6 single 533mm TT with Tp432/Tp451/Tp613/Tp62
  SSW 1 *Spiggen* II
PATROL AND COASTAL COMBATANTS 22
  CORVETTES • FSG 5 *Visby* with 8 RBS-15 AShM, 4 single 400mm ASTT with Tp45 LWT, 1 57mm gun, 1 hel landing plaform
  PCG 4:
    2 *Göteborg* with 4 twin lnchr with RBS-15 Mk2 AShM, 4 single 400mm ASTT with Tp431 LWT, 4 Saab 601 A/S mor, 1 57mm gun
    2 *Stockholm* with 4 twin lnchr with RBS-15 Mk2 AShM, 4 Saab 601 mortars, 4 single ASTT with Tp431 LWT, 1 57mm gun
  PB 2
  PBR 11 *Tapper*
MINE WARFARE • MINE COUNTERMEASURES 13
  MCC 5 *Koster*
  MCD 2 *Spårö*
  MSD 6: 5 *Sam*; 1 *Sokaren*
AMPHIBIOUS • LANDING CRAFT 159
  LCM 9 *Trossbat*
  LCPL 147 Combatboat 90E/H/HS
  LCAC 3 Griffon 8100TD
LOGISTICS AND SUPPORT 46
  AG 2: 1 *Carlskrona* with 2 57mm gun, 1 hel landing platform (former ML); 1 *Trosso* (spt ship for corvettes and patrol vessels but can also be used as HQ ship)
  AGF 2 Combatboat 450
  AGI 1 *Orion*
  AGS 2 (Government Maritime Forces)
  AK 1 *Loke*
  ARS 2: 1 *Belos* III; 1 *Furusund* (former ML)
  AX 5 *Altair*
  AXS 2: 1 *Falkan*; 1 *Gladan*
  YAG 16 *Trossbat*
  YDT 1 *Agir*
  YPT 1 *Pelikanen*
  YTM 11

Amphibious 850
FORCES BY ROLE
MANOEUVRE
  Amphibious
  1 amph bn
EQUIPMENT BY TYPE
ARTY • MOR 81mm 12
MSL • AShM 8 RBS-17 *Hellfire*

Air Force 3,300
Flying hours 100–150 hrs/year

FORCES BY ROLE
FIGHTER/GROUND ATTACK/ISR
  4 sqn with JAS 39C/D *Gripen*

SIGINT
1 sqn with Gulfstream IV SRA-4 (S-102B)
AIRBORNE EARLY WARNING & CONTROL
1 sqn with S-100B/D *Argus*
TRANSPORT
1 sqn with C-130E/H *Hercules* (Tp-84); KC-130H *Hercules* (Tp-84)
TRAINING
1 sqn with JAS-39A/B *Gripen*
1 OCU sqn with JAS-39A/B/C/D *Gripen*
1 unit with Sk-60
AIR DEFENCE
1 (fighter control and air surv) bn
EQUIPMENT BY TYPE
AIRCRAFT 134 combat capable
  FGA 134 JAS39A/B/C/D *Gripen*
  ELINT 2 Gulfstream IV SRA-4 (S-102B)
  AEW&C 3: 1 S-100B *Argus*; 2 S-100D *Argus*
  TKR 1 KC-130H *Hercules* (Tp-84)
  TPT 10: **Medium** 7 C-130E/H *Hercules* (Tp-84); **Light** 2 Saab 340 (OS-100A/Tp-100C); **PAX** 1 Gulfstream 550 (Tp-102D)
  TRG 80 Sk-60W
UAV • **ISR** • **Medium** 8 RQ-7 *Shadow* (AUV 3 *Örnen*)
MSL
  ASM AGM-65 *Maverick* (RB-75)
  AShM RB-15F
  AAM • **IR** AIM-9L *Sidewinder* (RB-74); **IIR** IRIS-T (RB-98); **ARH** AIM-120B AMRAAM (RB-99)

Armed Forces Hel Wing

FORCES BY ROLE
TRANSPORT HELICOPTER
  3 sqn with AS332 *Super Puma* (Hkp-10A/B/D); AW109 (Hkp 15A); AW109M (Hkp-15B); NH90 TTH (Hkp-14); UH-60M *Black Hawk* (Hkp-16)

EQUIPMENT BY TYPE
HELICOPTERS
  TPT 54: **Medium** 34: 9 AS332 *Super Puma* (Hkp-10A/B/D - SAR); 15 UH-60M *Black Hawk* (Hkp-16); 10 NH90 TTH (Hkp-14); **Light** 20: 12 AW109 (Hkp-15A); 8 AW109M (Hkp-15B)

Paramilitary 800

Coast Guard 800

EQUIPMENT BY TYPE
PATROL AND COASTAL COMBATANTS 30
  PSO 3 KBV-001
  PCO 1 KBV-181 (fishery protection)
  PCC 2 KBV-201
  PB 24: 1 KBV-101; 4 KBV-281; 3 KBV-288; 11 KBV-301; 5 KBV-312
AMPHIBIOUS • **LANDING CRAFT** • **LCAC** 2 Griffon 2000 TDX (KBV-591)
LOGISTICS AND SUPPORT • **AG** 12: 8 MARPOL-CRAFT; 4 KBV-031

Air Arm

EQUIPMENT BY TYPE
AIRCRAFT • **TPT** • **Light** 3 DHC-8Q-300

Cyber

Sweden has a national CERT, is involved in informal CERT communities and is a member of the European Government CERTs group (EGC). A national cyber-security strategy has also been adopted. Four ministries have a cyber remit: defence, foreign affairs, justice, and enterprise and industry. The Swedish Civil Contingencies Agency (AMS), which reports to the MoD, is in charge of supporting and coordinating security across society.

DEPLOYMENT

Legal provisions for foreign deployment:
Constitution: Constitution consists of four fundamental laws; the most important is 'The Instrument of Government' (1974)
Decision on deployment of troops abroad: By the government upon parliamentary approval (Ch. 10, Art. 9)

AFGHANISTAN
NATO • ISAF 13
UN • UNAMA 1 obs

ARMENIA/AZERBAIJAN
OSCE • Minsk Conference 1

BOSNIA-HERZEGOVINA
EU • EUFOR • *Operation Althea* 2

DEMOCRATIC REPUBLIC OF THE CONGO
UN • MONUSCO 5 obs

INDIA/PAKISTAN
UN • UNMOGIP 5 obs

KOREA, REPUBLIC OF
NNSC • 5 obs

MALI
EU • EUTM Mali 10
UN • MINUSMA 26

MIDDLE EAST
UN • UNTSO 7 obs

MOLDOVA
OSCE • Moldova 1

SERBIA
NATO • KFOR 7
OSCE • Kosovo 2

SOUTH SUDAN
UN • UNMISS 2; 3 obs

UGANDA
EU • EUTM Somalia 8

UKRAINE
OSCE • Ukraine 9

Switzerland CHE

Swiss Franc fr		2013	2014	2015
GDP	fr	603bn	611bn	
	US$	650bn	679bn	
per capita	US$	81,276	84,344	
Growth	%	1.9	1.3	
Inflation	%	-0.2	0.1	
Def exp [a]	fr	4.5bn		
	US$	4.86bn		
Def bdgt [a]	fr	4.69bn	4.73bn	4.93bn
	US$	5.05bn	5.26bn	
US$1=fr		0.93	0.90	

[a] Includes military pensions

Population 8,061,516

Age	0–14	15–19	20–24	25–29	30–64	65 plus
Male	7.8%	2.8%	3.0%	3.3%	24.8%	7.6%
Female	7.3%	2.7%	2.9%	3.3%	24.6%	9.9%

Capabilities

Overwhelmingly conscript based, the armed forces are geared for territorial defence and limited participation in international peace-support operations. Plans to replace the ageing F-5 with the *Gripen* had to be scrapped after a national referendum in May 2014 rejected the proposal. The withdrawal of the F-5 was planned for 2016 and if implemented would cut the air force's combat-aircraft inventory by more than half. A hijacked Ethiopian Airlines Boeing 767 that was flown to Geneva in February was escorted by Italian and French fighter aircraft since the Swiss air force did not operate a 24-hour quick-reaction alert. Implementation of a round-the-clock capability has been mooted for almost a decade. The *Hermes* 900 UAV was chosen in June 2014 as the successor to the *Ranger* UAV, with the intent that the latter type be withdrawn fully from service by 2020.

ACTIVE 21,250 (Joint 21,250)

Conscript liability Recruit trg of 18, 21 or 25 weeks (depending on military branch) at age 19–20, followed by 7, 6 or 5 refresher trg courses (3 weeks each) over a 10-year period between ages 20–30

RESERVE 155,050 (Army 102,250, Air 23,900, Armed Forces Logistic Organisation 13,600, Command Support Organisation 15,300)

Civil Defence 72,000

ORGANISATIONS BY SERVICE

Joint 3,350 active; 17,900 conscript (21,250 total)

Land Forces (Army) 102,250 on mobilisation
4 Territorial Regions. With the exception of military security all units are non-active.

FORCES BY ROLE
COMMAND
4 regional comd (2 engr bn, 1 sigs bn)
MANOEUVRE
  Armoured
   1 (1st) bde (1 recce bn, 2 armd bn, 2 armd inf bn, 1 sp arty bn, 2 engr bn, 1 sigs bn)
   1 (11th) bde (1 recce bn, 2 armd bn, 2 armd inf bn, 1 inf bn, 2 SP arty bn, 1 engr bn, 1 sigs bn)
  Light
   1 (2nd) bde (1 recce bn, 4 inf bn, 2 SP arty bn, 1 engr bn, 1 sigs bn)
   1 (5th) bde (1 recce bn, 3 inf bn, 2 SP arty bn, 1 engr bn, 1 sigs bn)
   1 (7th) reserve bde (3 recce bn, 3 inf bn, 2 mtn inf bn, 1 sigs bn)
  Mountain
   1 (9th) bde (5 mtn inf bn, 1 SP Arty bn, 1 sigs bn)
   1 (12th) bde (2 inf bn, 3 mtn inf bn, 1 (fortress) arty bn, 1 sigs bn)
   1 (10th) reserve bde (1 recce bn, 2 armd bn, 3 inf bn, 2 mtn inf bn, 2 SP arty bn, 2 sigs bn)
  Other
   1 sy bde
COMBAT SERVICE SUPPORT
  1 armd/arty trg unit
  1 inf trg unit
  1 engr rescue trg unit
  1 log trg unit
EQUIPMENT BY TYPE
MBT 134 *Leopard* 2 (Pz-87 *Leo*)
RECCE 455: 443 *Eagle* II; 12 *Piranha* IIIC CBRN
AIFV 186: 154 CV9030; 32 CV9030 CP
APC 914
  APC (T) 238 M113A2 (incl variants)
  APC (W) 676: 346 *Piranha* II; 330 *Piranha* I/II/IIIC CP
ARTY 383
  SP 155mm 133 M109
  MOR • SP 81mm 250 M113 with M72/91
AT • MSL • SP 110 *Piranha* I TOW-2
AD • SAM • MANPAD FIM-92A *Stinger*
AEV 12 *Kodiak*
ARV 25 *Büffel*
MW 46: 26 Area Clearing System; 20 M113A2
PATROL AND COASTAL COMBATANTS • PBR 11 *Aquarius*

Air Force 23,900 (incl air defence units and military airfield guard units)

Flying hours 200–250 hrs/year

FORCES BY ROLE
FIGHTER
  3 sqn with F-5E/F *Tiger* II
  3 sqn with F/A-18C/D *Hornet*
TRANSPORT
  1 sqn with Beech 350 *King Air*; DHC-6 *Twin Otter*; PC-6 *Turbo Porter*; PC-12
  1 VIP Flt with Beech 1900D; Cessna 560XL *Citation*; Falcon 900EX

TRAINING
1 sqn with PC-7CH *Turbo Trainer*; PC-21
1 sqn with PC-9 (tgt towing)
1 OCU Sqn with F-5E/F *Tiger* II
TRANSPORT HELICOPTER
6 sqn with AS332M *Super Puma*; AS532UL *Cougar*; EC635
ISR UAV
1 sqn with ADS 95 *Ranger*
EQUIPMENT BY TYPE
AIRCRAFT 86 combat capable
FTR 54: 42 F-5E *Tiger* II; 12 F-5F *Tiger* II
FGA 32: 26 F/A-18C *Hornet*; 6 F/A-18D *Hornet*
TPT 22: **Light** 21: 1 Beech 350 *King Air*; 1 Beech 1900D; 1 Cessna 560XL *Citation*; 1 DHC-6 *Twin Otter*; 15 PC-6 *Turbo Porter*; 1 PC-6 (owned by armasuisse, civil registration); 1 PC-12 (owned by armasuisse, civil registration); **PAX** 1 *Falcon* 900EX
TRG 44: 28 PC-7CH *Turbo Trainer*; 8 PC-9; 8 PC-21
HELICOPTERS
TPT 46: **Medium** 26: 15 AS332M *Super Puma*; 11 AS532UL *Cougar*; **Light** 20 EC635
UAV • ISR • **Medium** 16 ADS 95 *Ranger* (4 systems)
MSL • AAM • IR AIM-9P *Sidewinder*; IIR AIM-9X *Sidewinder*; ARH AIM-120B AMRAAM

Ground Based Air Defence (GBAD)

GBAD assets can be used to form AD clusters to be deployed independently as task forces within Swiss territory.

EQUIPMENT BY TYPE
AD
  SAM
    TOWED *Rapier*
    MANPAD FIM-92A *Stinger*
  GUNS 35mm
  RADARS • AD RADARS *Skyguard*

Armed Forces Logistic Organisation 13,600 on mobilisation

FORCES BY ROLE
COMBAT SERVICE SUPPORT
  1 log bde

Command Support Organisation 15,950 on mobilisation

FORCES BY ROLE
COMBAT SERVICE SUPPORT
  1 spt bde

Civil Defence 72,000

(not part of armed forces)

Cyber

Five major Swiss government organisations maintain an overview of elements of cyber threats and responses: the Federal Intelligence Service; the Military Intelligence Service; the Command Support Organisation; Information Security and Facility Protection; and the Federal Office for Civil Protection. A National Cyber Defence Strategy was published in 2012.

DEPLOYMENT

Legal provisions for foreign deployment:
Constitution: Codified constitution (1999)
Decision on deployment of troops abroad:
Peace promotion (66, 66a, 66b Swiss Mil Law): UN.OSCE mandate. Decision by govt; if over 100 tps deployed or op over 3 weeks Fed Assembly must agree first, except in emergency.
Support service abroad (69, 60 Swiss Mil Law): Decision by govt; if over 2,000 tps or op over 3 weeks Fed Assembly must agree in next official session

ALBANIA
OSCE • Albania 1

BOSNIA-HERZEGOVINA
EU • EUFOR • *Operation Althea* 20

DEMOCRATIC REPUBLIC OF THE CONGO
UN • MONUSCO 4

INDIA/PAKISTAN
UN • UNMOGIP 2 obs

KOREA, REPUBLIC OF
NNSC • 5 officers

MALI
UN • MINUSMA 1

MIDDLE EAST
UN • UNTSO 14 obs

MOLDOVA
OSCE • Moldova 1

SERBIA
NATO • KFOR 177 (military volunteers); 1 inf coy
OSCE • Kosovo 1

SOUTH SUDAN
UN • UNMISS 1; 2 obs

UKRAINE
OSCE • Ukraine 9

WESTERN SAHARA
UN • MINURSO 1 obs

Turkey TUR

New Turkish Lira L		2013	2014	2015
GDP	L	1.56tr	1.77tr	
	US$	820bn	813bn	
per capita	US$	10,721	10,518	
Growth	%	4.1	3.0	
Inflation	%	7.5	9.0	
Def exp [a]	L	27.3bn		
	US$	14.3bn		
Def bdgt [b]	L	20.4bn	21.8bn	22.9bn
	US$	10.7bn	10bn	
US$1=L		1.90	2.17	

[a] NATO definition

[b] Includes funding for Undersecretariat of Defence Industries. Excludes military procurement allocations.

Population 81,619,392

Age	0–14	15–19	20–24	25–29	30–64	65 plus
Male	13.1%	4.3%	4.2%	4.2%	21.4%	3.1%
Female	12.5%	4.1%	4.1%	4.1%	21.2%	3.6%

Capabilities

Turkey has capable armed forces intended to meet national defence requirements and its NATO obligations. The role of the armed forces has been recast since the end of the Cold War, with internal security and regional instability providing challenges. The army is becoming smaller but more capable, with the aim of improving its ability to meet a full range of NATO missions while providing a highly mobile force able to fight across the spectrum of conflict. The air force is well equipped and well trained, and is introducing airborne early-warning aircraft. It already operates tanker aircraft and will bolster its transport fleet with the A400M *Atlas* airlifter; the first arrived in mid-2014. The armed forces have ambitious procurement plans, which will require a significant increase in funding over the period to 2016. Single and inter-service training is carried out regularly, as is mobilisation training, and the armed forces participate in multinational exercises with NATO partners. Under NATO auspices, the US, the Netherlands and Germany deployed *Patriot* missile batteries to southern Turkey in 2013, in light of perceived threats from the conflict in Syria.

ACTIVE 510,600 (Army 402,000 Navy 48,600 Air 60,000) **Paramilitary 102,200**

Conscript liability 15 months. Active figure reducing.

RESERVE 378,700 (Army 258,700 Navy 55,000 Air 65,000) **Paramilitary 50,000**

Reserve service to age of 41 for all services.

ORGANISATIONS BY SERVICE

Space

SATELLITES • ISR 1 *Gokturk*-2

Army ε77,000; ε325,000 conscript (total 402,000)

FORCES BY ROLE
COMMAND
 4 army HQ
 9 corps HQ
SPECIAL FORCES
 4 cdo bde
 1 mtn cdo bde
 1 cdo regt
MANOEUVRE
 Armoured
 1 (52nd) armd div (2 armd bde, 1 mech bde)
 7 armd bde
 Mechanised
 2 (28th & 29th) mech div
 14 mech inf bde
 Light
 1 (23rd) mot inf div (3 mot inf regt)
 11 mot inf bde
 Aviation
 4 avn regt
 4 avn bn
COMBAT SUPPORT
 2 arty bde
 1 trg arty bde
 6 arty regt
 2 engr regt

EQUIPMENT BY TYPE
MBT 2,504: 325 *Leopard* 2A4; 170 *Leopard* 1A4; 227 *Leopard* 1A3; 274 M60A1; 658 M60A3; 850 M48A5 T1/T2 (2,000 more in store)
RECCE 320+: ε250 *Akrep*; 70+ ARSV *Cobra*
AIFV 650 AIFV
APC 3,943
 APC (T) 3,643: 830 AAPC; 2,813 M113/M113A1/M113A2
 PPV 300+ *Kirpi*
ARTY 7,837+
 SP 1,118: **105mm** 391: 26 M108T; 365 M-52T; **155mm** 472: 222 M-44T1; ε250 T-155 *Firtina* (K-9 *Thunder*); **175mm** 36 M107; **203mm** 219 M110A2
 TOWED 760+: **105mm** 75+ M101A1; **155mm** 523: 517 M114A1/M114A2; 6 *Panter*; **203mm** 162 M115
 MRL 146+: **107mm** 48; **122mm** ε36 T-122; **227mm** 12 MLRS (incl ATACMS); **302mm** 50+ TR-300 *Kasirga* (WS-1)
 MOR 5,813+
  SP 1,443+: **81mm**; **107mm** 1,264 M-30; **120mm** 179
  TOWED 4,370: **81mm** 3,792; **120mm** 578
AT
 MSL 1,363
  SP 365 TOW
  MANPATS 9K135 *Kornet*-E (AT-14 *Spriggan*); *Cobra*; *Eryx*; *Milan*
 RCL 3,869: **57mm** 923 M18; **75mm** 617; **106mm** 2,329 M40A1
AIRCRAFT
 TPT • **Light** 38: 5 Beech 200 *King Air*; 30 Cessna 185 (U-17B); 3 Cessna 421

TRG 74: 45 Cessna T182; 25 T-41D *Mescalero*; 4 T-42A *Cochise*
HELICOPTERS
ATK 43: 18 AH-1P *Cobra*; 12 AH-1S *Cobra*; 6 AH-1W *Cobra*; 4 TAH-1P *Cobra*; 3 T129A
MRH 28 Hughes 300C
ISR 3 OH-58B *Kiowa*
TPT 221+: **Medium** 80+: 30 AS532UL *Cougar*; 50+ S-70A *Black Hawk*; **Light** 141: 12 Bell 204B (AB-204B); ε45 Bell 205 (UH-1H *Iroquois*); 64 Bell 205A (AB-205A); 20 Bell 206 *Jet Ranger*
UAV • ISR **Heavy** *Falcon* 600/*Firebee*; **Medium** CL-89; *Gnat*; **Light** *Harpy*
AD
SAM
SP 148: 70 *Altigan* PMADS octuple *Stinger* lnchr, 78 *Zipkin* PMADS quad *Stinger* lnchr
MANPAD 935: 789 FIM-43 *Redeye* (being withdrawn); 146 FIM-92A *Stinger*
GUNS 1,664
SP **40mm** 262 M42A1
TOWED 1,402: **20mm** 439 GAI-D01; **35mm** 120 GDF-001/GDF-003; **40mm** 843: 803 L/60/L/70; 40 T-1
RADAR • LAND AN/TPQ-36 *Firefinder*
AEV 12+: 12 M48; M113A2T2
ARV 150: 12 *Leopard* 1; 105 M48T5; 33 M88A2
VLB 52 Mobile Floating Assault Bridge
MW *Tamkar*

Navy 14,100; 34,500 conscript (total 48,600 including 2,200 Coast Guard and 3,100 Marines)

EQUIPMENT BY TYPE
SUBMARINES • TACTICAL • SSK 14:
6 *Atilay* (GER Type-209/1200) with 8 single 533mm ASTT with SST-4 HWT
8 *Preveze/Gür* (GER Type-209/1400) with 8 single 533mm ASTT with UGM-84 *Harpoon* AShM/*Tigerfish* Mk2 HWT
PRINCIPAL SURFACE COMBATANTS 18
FRIGATES • FFGHM 18:
2 *Barbaros* (mod GER MEKO 200 F244 & F245) with 2 quad Mk141 lnchr with RGM-84C *Harpoon* AShM, 1 octuple Mk29 lnchr with *Aspide* SAM, 2 Mk32 triple 324mm ASTT with Mk46 LWT, 3 *Sea Zenith* CIWS, 1 127mm gun (capacity: 1 Bell 212 (AB-212) hel)
2 *Barbaros* (mod GER MEKO 200 F246 & F247) with 2 quad Mk141 lnchr with RGM-84C *Harpoon* AShM, 1 8-cell Mk41 VLS with *Aspide* SAM, 2 Mk32 triple 324mm ASTT with Mk46 LWT, 3 *Sea Zenith* CIWS, 1 127mm gun (capacity: 1 Bell 212 (AB-212) hel)
3 *Gaziantep* (ex-US *Oliver Hazard Perry*-class) with 1 Mk13 GMLS with RGM-84C *Harpoon* AShM/SM-1MR SAM, 1 8-cell Mk41 VLS with RIM-162 SAM, 2 Mk32 triple 324mm ASTT with Mk46 LWT, 1 *Phalanx* Block 1B CIWS, 1 76mm gun (capacity: 1 S-70B *Seahawk* ASW hel)
5 *Gaziantep* (ex-US *Oliver Hazard Perry*-class) with 1 Mk13 GMLS with RGM-84C *Harpoon* AShM/SM-1MR SAM, 2 Mk32 triple 324mm ASTT with Mk46 LWT, 1 *Phalanx* Block 1B CIWS, 1 76mm gun (capacity: 1 S-70B *Seahawk* ASW hel)
4 *Yavuz* (GER MEKO 200TN) with 2 quad Mk141 lnchr with RGM-84C *Harpoon* AShM, 1 octuple Mk29 GMLS with *Aspide* SAM, 2 Mk32 triple 324mm ASTT with Mk46 LWT, 3 *Sea Zenith* CIWS, 1 127mm gun (capacity: 1 Bell 212 (AB-212) hel)
2 *Ada* with 2 quad lnchr with RCM-84C *Harpoon* AShM, 1 Mk49 21-cell lnchr with RIM-116 SAM, 2 Mk32 twin 324mm ASTT with Mk46 LWT, 1 76mm gun (capacity: 1 S-70B *Seahawk* hel)
PATROL AND COASTAL COMBATANTS 61
CORVETTES • FSGM 6:
6 *Burak* (ex-FRA *d'Estienne d'Orves*) with 2 single lnchr with MM-38 *Exocet* AShM, 4 single 324mm ASTT with Mk46 LWT, 1 Mk54 A/S mor, 1 100mm gun
PCFG 19:
8 *Dogan* (GER Lurssen-57) with 2 quad lnchr with RGM-84A/C *Harpoon* AShM, 1 76mm gun
9 *Kilic* with 2 quad Mk 141 lnchr with RGM-84C *Harpoon* AShM, 1 76mm gun
2 *Yildiz* with 2 quad lnchr with RGM-84A/C *Harpoon* AShM, 1 76mm gun
PCC 19: 12 *Tuzla*; 6 *Karamursel* (GER *Vegesack*); 1 *Trabzon*;
PBFG 6 *Kartal* (GER *Jaguar*) with 4 single lnchr with RB 12 *Penguin* AShM, 2 single 533mm TT
PBF 4: 2 *Kaan* 20; 2 MRTP22
PB 7:
4 PGM-71 with 1 Mk22 *Mousetrap* A/S mor
3 *Turk* with 1 Mk20 *Mousetrap* A/S mor
MINE WARFARE • MINE COUNTERMEASURES 28:
MCM SPT 8 (tenders)
MHO 11: 5 *Edineik* (FRA *Circe*); 6 *Aydin*
MSC 5 *Silifke* (US *Adjutant*)
MSI 4 *Foca* (US *Cape*)
AMPHIBIOUS
LANDING SHIPS • LST 4:
1 *Ertugrul* (US *Terrebonne Parish*) with 3 76mm gun, (capacity 18 tanks; 400 troops) (with 1 hel landing platform)
1 *Osman Gazi* with 1 *Phalanx* CIWS, (capacity 4 LCVP; 17 tanks; 980 troops) (with 1 hel landing platform)
2 *Sarucabey* with 1 *Phalanx* CIWS (capacity 11 tanks; 600 troops) (with 1 hel landing platform)
LANDING CRAFT 49
LCT 33: 8 C-151; 12 C-117; 13 C-130
LCM 16 C-302
LOGISTICS AND SUPPORT 79
ABU 2: 1 AG5; 1 AG6 with 1 76mm gun
AGS 3: 2 *Cesme* (US *Silas Bent*); 1 *Cubuklu*
AKL 1 *Eregli*
AOR 2 *Akar* with 1 twin 76mm gun, 1 *Phalanx* CIWS, 1 hel landing platform
AORL 1 *Taskizak*
AOT 2 *Burak*
AOL 1 *Gurcan*
AO 4 (harbour)
AP 1 *Iskenderun*

ARS 1 *Isin*
ASR 1 *Akin*
ATA 1 *Tenace*
ATR 1 *Inebolu*
ATS 3: 1 *Akbas*; 1 *Gazal*; 1 *Darica*
AWT 9: 5; 4 (harbour)
AXL 8
AX 2 *Pasa* (GER *Rhein*)
YAG 2 *Mesaha*
YFD 13
YPB 2
YPT 3
YTM 16

Marines 3,100
FORCES BY ROLE
MANOEUVRE
Amphibious
1 mne bde (3 mne bn; 1 arty bn)

Naval Aviation
FORCES BY ROLE
ANTI-SUBMARINE WARFARE
2 sqn with Bell 212 ASW (AB-212 ASW); S-70B *Seahawk*
1 sqn with ATR-72-600; CN-235M-100; TB-20 *Trinidad*
EQUIPMENT BY TYPE
AIRCRAFT
MP 6 CN-235M-100
TPT • **Light** 6: 1 ATR-72-600; 5 TB-20 *Trinidad*
HELICOPTERS
ASW 29: 11 Bell 212 ASW (AB-212 ASW); 18 S-70B *Seahawk*

Air Force 60,000
2 tac air forces (divided between east and west)
Flying hours 180 hrs/year
FORCES BY ROLE
FIGHTER
1 sqn with F-4E *Phantom* II
2 sqn with F-16C/D *Fighting Falcon*
FIGHTER/GROUND ATTACK
2 sqn with F-4E *Phantom* II
8 sqn with F-16C/D *Fighting Falcon*
ISR
2 sqn with RF-4E/ETM *Phantom* II
1 unit with *King Air* 350
AIRBORNE EARLY WARNING & CONTROL
1 sqn (forming) with B-737 AEW&C
EW
1 unit with CN-235M EW
SEARCH & RESCUE
1 sqn with AS532AL/UL *Cougar*
TANKER
1 sqn with KC-135R *Stratotanker*
TRANSPORT
1 sqn with A400M *Atlas*; C-160D *Transall*
1 sqn with C-130B/E/H *Hercules*
1 (VIP) sqn with Cessna 550 *Citation* II (UC-35); Cessna 650 *Citation* VII; CN-235M; Gulfstream 550
3 sqn with CN-235M
10 (liaison) flt with Bell 205 (UH-1H *Iroquois*); CN-235M
TRAINING
1 sqn with F-4E *Phantom* II; F-16C/D *Fighting Falcon*
1 sqn with F-5A/B *Freedom Fighter*; NF-5A/B *Freedom Fighter*
1 OCU sqn with F-16C/D *Fighting Falcon*
1 sqn with SF-260D
1 sqn with KT-IT
1 sqn with T-38A/M *Talon*
1 sqn with T-41D *Mescalero*
AIR DEFENCE
4 sqn with MIM-14 *Nike Hercules*
2 sqn with *Rapier*
8 (firing) unit with MIM-23 HAWK
MANOEUVRE
Air Manoeuvre
1 AB bde
EQUIPMENT BY TYPE
AIRCRAFT 335 combat capable
FTR 53: 18 F-5A *Freedom Fighter*; 8 F-5B *Freedom Fighter*; 17 NF-5A *Freedom Fighter*; 10 NF-5B *Freedom Fighter* (48 F-5s being upgraded as LIFT)
FGA 282: 52 F-4E *Phantom* 2020; 212 F-16C/D *Fighting Falcon* (all being upgraded to Block 50 standard); 9 F-16C Block 50 *Fighting Falcon*; 9 F-16D Block 50 *Fighting Falcon*
ISR 38: 33 RF-4E/ETM *Phantom* II; 5 Beech 350 *King Air*
EW 2+ CN-235M EW
AEW&C 3 B-737 AEW&C (1 more on order)
TKR 7 KC-135R *Stratotanker*
TPT 87: **Heavy** 1 A400M *Atlas*; **Medium** 35: 6 C-130B *Hercules*; 12 C-130E *Hercules*; 1 C-130H *Hercules*; 16 C-160D *Transall*; **Light** 50: 2 Cessna 550 *Citation* II (UC-35 - VIP); 2 Cessna 650 *Citation* VII; 46 CN-235M; **PAX** 1 Gulfstream 550
TRG 172: 34 SF-260D; 70 T-38A/M *Talon*; 28 T-41D *Mescalero*; 40 KT-IT
HELICOPTERS
TPT 40: **Medium** 20: 6 AS532AL *Cougar* (CSAR); 14 AS532UL *Cougar* (SAR); **Light** 20 Bell 205 (UH-1H *Iroquois*)
UAV • **ISR** 27: **Heavy** 9 *Heron*; **Medium** 18 *Gnat* 750
AD
SAM *Rapier*
TOWED MIM-23 HAWK
STATIC MIM-14 *Nike Hercules*
MSL
AAM • **IR** AIM-9S *Sidewinder*; *Shafrir* 2(‡); **SARH** AIM-7E *Sparrow*; **ARH** AIM-120A/B AMRAAM
ARM AGM-88A HARM
ASM AGM-65A/G *Maverick*; *Popeye* I
BOMBS
Conventional BLU-107;
Electro-optical guided GBU-8B HOBOS (GBU-15)
Laser-guided *Paveway* I; *Paveway* II
PODS

Infrared 80: 40 AN/AAQ-14 LANTIRN; 40 AN/AAQ-13 LANTIRN

Paramilitary

Gendarmerie/National Guard 100,000; 50,000 reservists (total 150,000)
Ministry of Interior; Ministry of Defence in war
FORCES BY ROLE
SPECIAL FORCES
 1 cdo bde
MANOEUVRE
 Other
 1 (border) paramilitary div
 2 paramilitary bde
EQUIPMENT BY TYPE
RECCE *Akrep*
APC (W) 560: 535 BTR-60/BTR-80; 25 *Condor*
AIRCRAFT
 ISR Some O-1E *Bird Dog*
 TPT • **Light** 2 Do-28D
HELICOPTERS
 MRH 19 Mi-17 *Hip* H
 TPT 36: **Medium** 13 S-70A *Black Hawk*; **Light** 23: 8 Bell 204B (AB-204B); 6 Bell 205A (AB-205A); 8 Bell 206A (AB-206A) *Jet Ranger*; 1 Bell 212 (AB-212)

Coast Guard 800 (Coast Guard Regular element); 1,050 (from Navy); 1,400 conscript (total 3,250)
EQUIPMENT BY TYPE
PATROL AND COASTAL COMBATANTS 115
 PSOH 4 *Dost* with 1 76mm gun
 PBF 54
 PB 57
AIRCRAFT • **MP** 1 CN-235 MPA (2 more to be delivered)
HELICOPTERS • **MRH** 8 Bell 412EP (AB-412EP – SAR)

DEPLOYMENT

Legal provisions for foreign deployment:
Constitution: Codified constitution (1985)
Decision on deployment of troops abroad: a) In general, by parliament (Art. 92); b) in cases of sudden aggression and if parliament is unable to convene, by president (Art. 92, 104b)

AFGHANISTAN
NATO • ISAF 393
UN • UNAMA 1 obs

ARABIAN SEA & GULF OF ADEN
Combined Maritime Forces • CTF-151: 1 FFGHM

BOSNIA-HERZEGOVINA
EU • EUFOR • *Operation Althea* 239; 1 inf coy

CYPRUS (NORTHERN)
ε43,000; 1 army corps HQ; 1 armd bde; 2 mech inf div; 1 avn comd; 8 M48A2 (trg;) 340 M48A5T1/T2; 361 AAPC (incl variants); 266 M113 (incl variants); 72 M101A1; 18 M114A2; 12 M115; 90 M-44T; 6 T-122; 175 81mm mor; 148 M-30; 127 HY-12; 66 *Milan*; 48 TOW; 192 M40A1; Rh 202; 16 GDF-003; 48 M1; 3 Cessna 185 (U-17); 1 AS532UL *Cougar*; 3 UH-1H *Iroquois*; 1 PB

LEBANON
UN • UNIFIL 53; 1 FSGM

MEDITERRANEAN SEA
NATO • SNMG 2: 1 FFGHM
NATO • SNMCMG 2: 1 MHO

SERBIA
NATO • KFOR 353; 1 inf coy
OSCE • Kosovo 4
UN • UNMIK 1 obs

UKRAINE
OSCE • Ukraine 6

FOREIGN FORCES

Germany *Active Fence*: 2 bty with *Patriot* PAC-3
Netherlands *Active Fence*: 2 bty with MIM-104 *Patriot*
United States US European Command: 1,550; 4 MQ-1B *Predator* UAV at Incirlik; 1 spt facility at Izmir; 1 spt facility at Ankara; 1 air base at Incirlik • US Strategic Command: 1 Spacetrack Radar at Incirlik; 1 AN/TPY-2 X-band radar at Kürecik • *Active Fence*: 2 bty with MIM-104 *Patriot*

United Kingdom UK

British Pound £		2013	2014	2015
GDP	£	1.61tr	1.7tr	
	US$	2.52tr	2.85tr	
per capita	US$	39,372	44,141	
Growth	%	1.7	3.2	
Inflation	%	2.6	1.6	
Def exp [a]	£	38.6bn		
	US$	60.4bn		
Def bdgt [b]	£	37.1bn	36.9bn	
	US$	58.1bn	61.8bn	
US$1=£		0.64	0.60	

[a] NATO definition
[b] Net Cash Requirement figures. These will differ from official figures based on Resource Accounting & Budgeting. Excludes military pensions covered by the Armed Forces Pension Scheme (AFPS) and the Armed Forces Compensation Scheme (AFCS).

Population	63,742,977					
Age	0–14	15–19	20–24	25–29	30–64	65 plus
Male	8.9%	3.0%	3.4%	3.5%	23.0%	7.8%
Female	8.4%	2.9%	3.3%	3.4%	22.5%	9.7%

Capabilities

The UK remains, along with France, Europe's pre-eminent military force, albeit one now close to critical mass in

148 THE MILITARY BALANCE 2015

many key areas. The 2010 Strategic Defence and Security Review (SDSR) aimed to provide a balanced and affordable path to Future Force 2020. Defence funding is secure for 2015, when it is assumed that a new SDSR will reassess defence strategy, funding and capability. The Ministry of Defence has greatly reduced in size and budget, and responsibility has been devolved to the three services and a new Joint Forces Command. The Army 2020 restructuring programme requires a cut of 20,000 regular troops by 2017. This process is almost complete, and unit disbandment and reorganisation, as well as withdrawal from Germany, have begun. A major uplift in the army's reserves has become politically controversial, particularly as recruitment has proved more difficult than envisaged. The navy received the last of its six Type-45 destroyers in September 2013, while the air force continued to receive *Voyager* tanker/transport aircraft based on the A330. Numbers of British troops in Afghanistan have greatly reduced, with the UK planning for a much smaller military role and footprint after 2014. (See pp. 68–71.)

ACTIVE 159,150 (Army 91,600 Navy 32,900 Air 34,650)

RESERVE 79,100 (Regular Reserve ε51,000 (incl 4,850 RAF); Volunteer Reserve 28,100 (Army 24,100; Navy 2,650; Air 1,350)
Includes both trained and those currently under training within the Regular Forces, excluding university cadet units.

ORGANISATIONS BY SERVICE

Strategic Forces 1,000

Royal Navy
EQUIPMENT BY TYPE
SUBMARINES • STRATEGIC • SSBN 4:
4 *Vanguard* with 1 16-celll VLS with UGM-133A *Trident* D-5 SLBM, 4 533mm TT with *Spearfish* HWT (Each boat will not deploy with more than 48 warheads, but each missile could carry up to 12 MIRV; some *Trident* D-5 capable of being configured for sub-strategic role)
MSL • STRATEGIC 48 UGM-133A *Trident* D-5 SLBM (Fewer than 160 declared operational warheads)

Royal Air Force
EQUIPMENT BY TYPE
RADAR • STRATEGIC 1 Ballistic Missile Early Warning System (BMEWS) at Fylingdales Moor

Space
EQUIPMENT BY TYPE
SATELLITES • COMMUNICATIONS 7: 1 NATO-4B; 3 *Skynet*-4; 3 *Skynet*-5

Army 88,800; 2,800 Gurkhas (total: 91,600)
Transitioning to a new Army 2020 structure, which is to be complete by the beginning of 2016. Force Troops Command was activated in 2014 to control the non-divisional cbt spt/CSS bdes. Regt normally bn size

FORCES BY ROLE
COMMAND
1 (ARRC) corps HQ
MANOEUVRE
  Armoured
  1 (3rd) div (2 (1st & 12th) armd inf bde (1 armd recce regt, 1 armd regt, 2 armd inf bn, 1 inf bn); 1 log bde (5 log regt; 3 maint regt; 2 med regt))
  Light
  1 (1st) div (1 (7th Armd) inf bde (1 recce regt, 1 armd recce regt, 1 inf bn; 1 SP arty regt; 1 cbt engr regt; 1 maint regt; 1 med regt); 1 (20th Armd) armd bde (1 armd recce regt, 1 armd regt, 1 armd inf bn, 3 inf bn; 1 SP arty regt; 1 cbt engr regt; 1 sigs regt; 1 maint regt; 1 med regt); 1 (4th) inf bde (1 recce regt, 1 armd regt, 3 inf bn, 1 (Gurkha) lt inf bn); 1 (11th) inf bde (2 inf bn; 1 (Gurkha) lt inf bn); 3 (38th, 42nd & 51st) inf bde (2 inf bn); 1 (160th Inf) inf bde (1 inf bn) 1 MP regt, 2 sigs regt; 1 log bde (3 log regt))
  5 inf bn (inc 2 in Cyprus and 2 in London)
  Other
  1 trg BG (based on 1 armd inf bn)
COMBAT SUPPORT
1 arty bde (2 SP arty regt, 1 arty regt, 1 MRL regt)
2 AD regt
1 engr bde (1 engr regt, 3 EOD regt, 1 air spt regt,1 log regt)
1 (geographic) engr regt
1 ISR bde (1 STA regt, 1 EW regt, 3 int regt, 2 UAV regt)
1 MP bde (2 MP bn)
1 sigs bde (5 sigs regt)
1 sigs bde (2 sigs regt; 1 (ARRC) sigs bn)
COMBAT SERVICE SUPPORT
1 log bde (3 log regt)
1 med bde (3 fd hospital; 10 fd hospital (AR))
1 (Security Assistance) spt gp (1 (Stabilisation) spt gp; 1 psyops gp; 1 (media ops) spt gp (AR))

Reserves

Army Reserve 24,100 reservists
The Army Reserve (AR) generates individuals, sub-units and some full units. Army 2020 will subordinate the majority of units to regular formation headquarters and pair them with one or more regular units.
FORCES BY ROLE
MANOEUVRE
  Reconnaissance
  3 recce regt
  Armoured
  1 armd regt
  Light
  13 lt inf bn
  Aviation
  1 UAV regt
COMBAT SUPPORT
2 arty regt
1 STA regt

1 MRL regt
1 AD regt
5 engr regt
3 engr sqn
3 EOD sqn
4 int bn
5 sigs regt
COMBAT SERVICE SUPPORT
11 log regt
6 maint regt
3 med regt
EQUIPMENT BY TYPE
MBT 227 *Challenger* 2
RECCE 648: 200 *Jackal*; 110 *Jackal* 2; 130 *Jackal* 2A; 200 *Scimitar*; 8 Tpz-1 *Fuchs* NBC
AIFV 400 *Warrior*
APC 2,250
  APC (T) 1,260: 880 *Bulldog* Mk3; 275 FV103 *Spartan*; 105 *Warthog*
  PPV 990: 400 *Foxhound*; 420 *Mastiff* (6×6); 170 *Ridgback*
ARTY 574
  SP 155mm 89 AS90 *Braveheart*
  TOWED 105mm 90 L118 Light Gun
  MRL 227mm 35 M270 MLRS
  MOR 81mm 360
AT • MSL
  SP ε14 *Exactor* (*Spike* NLOS)
  MANPATS *Javelin*
AD • SAM
  SP 60 FV4333 *Stormer*
  TOWED 14 *Rapier* FSC
  MANPAD *Starstreak* (LML)
AEV 93: 60 *Terrier*; 33 *Trojan*
ARV 155: 80 CRARRV; 35 *Samson*; 40 *Warrior* ARRV
MW 94: 64 *Aardvark*; 30 M139
VLB 71: 38 M3; 33 *Titan*
RADAR • LAND 144: 5 *Mamba*; 139 MSTAR
UAV • ISR • Medium 18: 8 *Hermes* 450; 10+ *Watchkeeper*
AMPHIBIOUS 6 LCVP
LOGISTICS AND SUPPORT 5 RCL

Joint Helicopter Command

Tri-service joint organisation including Royal Navy, Army and RAF units.

Army
FORCES BY ROLE
MANOEUVRE
  Air Manoeuvre
  1 (16th) air aslt bde (1 recce pl, 2 para bn, 1 atk hel regt (3 sqn with AH-64D *Apache*), 1 atk hel regt (2 sqn with AH-64D *Apache*), 1 hel regt (3 sqn with *Lynx* AH7/9A), 1 arty regt, 1 engr regt, 1 MP coy, 1 log regt, 1 maint regt, 1 med regt)
  Aviation
  1 avn regt (1 sqn with BN-2 *Defender/Islander*; 1 sqn with SA341B *Gazelle* AH1)
  1 hel regt (1 sqn with AW159 *Wildcat* AH1; 1 sqn with *Lynx* AH7/9A)

1 hel sqn with *Lynx* AH7//9A
1 hel sqn with AS365N3; SA341B *Gazelle* AH1
1 (test) hel sqn with *Lynx* AH7/9A
1 trg hel regt (1 sqn with AH-64D *Apache*; 1 sqn with AS350B *Ecureuil*; 1 sqn with Bell 212; *Lynx* AH7; SA341B *Gazelle* AH1)
1 hel flt with Bell 212 (Brunei)
1 hel flt with SA341B *Gazelle* AH1 (Canada)

Army Reserve
FORCES BY ROLE
MANOEUVRE
  Air Manoeuvre
  1 para bn
  Aviation
  1 hel regt (4 sqn)

Royal Navy
FORCES BY ROLE
ATTACK HELICOPTER
  1 lt sqn with *Lynx* AH9A
TRANSPORT HELICOPTER
  1 sqn with AW101 *Merlin* HC3/3A
  1 sqn with *Sea King* HC4

Royal Air Force
FORCES BY ROLE
TRANSPORT HELICOPTER
  3 sqn with CH-47D/SD/F *Chinook* HC2/2A/4/6
  1 sqn with AW101 *Merlin* HC3/3A
  2 sqn with SA330 *Puma* HC2
EQUIPMENT BY TYPE
ARTY • TOWED 105mm 18 L-118 Light Gun
AIRCRAFT • TPT • Light 15: 9 BN-2T-4S *Defender*; 6 BN-2 *Islander*
HELICOPTERS
ATK 66 AH-64D *Apache*
MRH 109 : 5 AS365N3; 22 AW159 *Wildcat* AH1; 27 *Lynx* AH7; 21 *Lynx* AH9A; 34 SA341B *Gazelle* AH1
TPT 129: **Heavy** 52: 8 CH-47D *Chinook* HC2; 6 CH-47D *Chinook* HC2A; 24 CH-47D *Chinook* HC4; 8 CH-47SD *Chinook* (HC3); 6 CH-47F *Chinook* HC6; **Medium** 60: 25 AW101 *Merlin* (HC3/3A); 24 SA330 *Puma* (HC2); 11 *Sea King* (HC4); **Light** 17: 9 AS350B *Ecureuil*; 8 Bell 212

Royal Navy 32,900
EQUIPMENT BY TYPE
SUBMARINES 10
  STRATEGIC • SSBN 4:
  4 *Vanguard*, opcon Strategic Forces with 1 16-cell VLS with UGM-133A *Trident* D-5 SLBM, 4 single 533mm TT with *Spearfish* HWT (each boat will not deploy with more than 40 warheads, but each missile could carry up to 12 MIRV; some *Trident* D-5 capable of being configured for sub strategic role)
  TACTICAL • SSN 6:
  4 *Trafalgar* with 5 single 533mm TT with *Spearfish* HWT/UGM 84 *Harpoon* AShM/*Tomahawk* tactical LACM

2 *Astute* with 6 single 533mm TT with *Spearfish* HWT/ UGM-84 *Harpoon* AShM/*Tomahawk* tactical LACM (5 additional vessels on order)

PRINCIPAL SURFACE COMBATANTS 19
  DESTROYERS • DDHM 6:
    6 *Daring* (Type-45) with 1 48-cell VLS with *Sea Viper* SAM, 2 *Phalanx* Block 1B CIWS, 1 114mm gun (capacity 1 *Lynx*/AW101 *Merlin* hel) (4 being fitted with RGM-84C *Harpoon* AShM)
  FRIGATES • FFGHM 13:
    13 *Norfolk* (Type-23) with 2 quad Mk141 lnchr with RGM-84C *Harpoon* AShM, 1 32-cell VLS with *Sea Wolf* SAM, 2 twin 324mm ASTT with *Sting Ray* LWT, 1 114mm gun (capacity either 2 *Lynx* or 1 AW101 *Merlin* hel)

PATROL AND COASTAL COMBATANTS 22
  PSO 4: 3 *River*; 1 *River* (mod) with 1 hel landing platform
  PB 18: 16 *Archer* (trg); 2 *Scimitar*

MINE WARFARE • MINE COUNTERMEASURES 16
  MCO 8 *Hunt* (incl 4 mod *Hunt*)
  MHC 8 *Sandown* (1 decommissioned and used in trg role)

AMPHIBIOUS
  PRINCIPAL AMPHIBIOUS SHIPS 3
    LPD 2 *Albion* with 2 *Goalkeeper* CIWS (capacity 2 med hel; 4 LCVP; 6 MBT; 300 troops) (1 at extended readiness)
    LPH 1 *Ocean* with 3 *Phalanx* Block 1B CIWS (capacity 18 hel; 4 LCU or 2 LCAC; 4 LCVP; 800 troops)

LOGISTICS AND SUPPORT 10
  AGB 1 *Protector* with 1 hel landing platform
  AGS 3: 1 *Scott*; 2 *Echo* (all with 1 hel landing platform)
  YGS 6: 1 *Gleaner*; 5 *Nesbitt*

Royal Fleet Auxiliary

Support and Miscellaneous vessels are mostly manned and maintained by the Royal Fleet Auxiliary (RFA), a civilian fleet owned by the UK MoD, which has approximately 2,500 personnel with type comd under CINCFLEET.

AMPHIBIOUS • PRINCIPAL AMPHIBIOUS SHIPS 3
  LSD 3 *Bay* (capacity 4 LCU; 2 LCVP; 24 CR2 *Challenger* 2 MBT; 350 troops)

LOGISTICS AND SUPPORT 16
  AORH 3: 2 *Wave*; 1 *Fort Victoria*
  AOR 1 *Leaf*
  AORLH 2 *Rover*
  AFSH 2 *Fort Rosalie*
  ARH 1 *Diligence*
  AG 1 *Argus* (aviation trg ship with secondary role as primarily casualty receiving ship)
  AKR 6 *Point* (not RFA manned)

Naval Aviation (Fleet Air Arm) 5,000

FORCES BY ROLE
ANTI-SUBMARINE WARFARE
  1 sqn with AW101 ASW *Merlin* HM1
  2 sqn with AW101 ASW *Merlin* HM2
  1 sqn with *Lynx* HAS3/HMA8
  1 flt with *Lynx* HAS3

AIRBORNE EARLY WARNING
  3 sqn with *Sea King* AEW7
SEARCH & RESCUE
  1 sqn (and detached flt) with *Sea King* HU5
TRAINING
  1 sqn with Beech 350ER *King Air*
  1 sqn with G-115 (op under contract)
  1 sqn with *Hawk* T1
  1 OCU sqn with AW101 ASW *Merlin* HM2
  1 OCU sqn with AW159 *Wildcat* HMA2

EQUIPMENT BY TYPE
AIRCRAFT 12 combat capable
  TPT • Light 4 Beech 350ER *King Air*
  TRG 17: 5 G-115 (op under contract); 12 *Hawk* T1*
HELICOPTERS
  ASW 89: 7 AW159 *Wildcat* HMA2; 7 *Lynx* HAS3; 33 *Lynx* HMA8; 18 AW101 ASW *Merlin* HM1; 24 AW101 ASW *Merlin* HM2
  AEW 13 *Sea King* AEW7
  TPT • Medium 16 *Sea King* HU5
MSL • AShM *Sea Skua*

Royal Marines 7,050

FORCES BY ROLE
MANOEUVRE
  Amphibious
    1 (3rd Cdo) mne bde (3 mne bn; 1 amph aslt sqn; 1 (army) arty regt; 1 (army) engr regt; 1 ISR gp (1 EW sqn; 1 cbt spt sqn; 1 sigs sqn; 1 log sqn),1 log regt)
    3 landing craft sqn opcon Royal Navy
  Other
    1 (Fleet Protection) sy gp

EQUIPMENT BY TYPE
APC (T) 142: 118 BvS-10 *Viking*; 24 BvS-10 Mk2 *Viking*
ARTY 50
  TOWED 105mm 18 L-118 Light Gun
  MOR 81mm 32
AT • MSL • MANPATS *Javelin*
PATROL AND COASTAL COMBATANTS • PB 2 *Island*
AMPHIBIOUS • LANDING CRAFT 37
  LCU 10
  LCVP 23
  LCAC 4 Griffon 2400TD
AD • SAM • HVM
RADAR • LAND 4 MAMBA (*Arthur*)

Royal Air Force 34,650

Flying hours 210/yr on fast jets; 290 on tpt ac; 240 on support hels; 90 on *Sea King*

FORCES BY ROLE
FIGHTER
  2 sqn with *Typhoon* FGR4/T3
FIGHTER/GROUND ATTACK
  3 sqn with *Tornado* GR4/4A
  2 sqn with *Typhoon* FGR4/T3
ISR
  1 sqn with *Sentinel* R1
  1 sqn with *Shadow* R1

AIRBORNE EARLY WARNING & CONTROL
  1 sqn with E-3D *Sentry*
SEARCH & RESCUE
  2 sqn with *Sea King* HAR-3A
  1 sqn with Bell 412EP *Griffin* HAR-2
TANKER/TRANSPORT
  2 sqn with A330 MRTT *Voyager* KC2/3
TRANSPORT
  1 (comms) sqn with AW109E; BAe-125; BAe-146; BN-2A *Islander* CC2
  1 sqn with C-17A *Globemaster*
  3 sqn with C-130J/J-30 *Hercules*
TRAINING
  1 OCU sqn with *Tornado*
  1 OCU sqn with *Typhoon*
  1 OEU sqn with *Typhoon, Tornado*
  1 OCU sqn with E-3D *Sentry*; *Sentinel* R1
  1 OEU sqn with E-3D *Sentry*; *Sentinel* R1
  1 OCU sqn with *Sea King* HAR-3A
  1 sqn with Beech 200 *King Air*
  1 sqn with EMB-312 *Tucano* T1
  2 sqn with *Hawk* T1/1A/1W
  1 sqn with *Hawk* T2
  3 sqn with *Tutor*
COMBAT/ISR UAV
  2 sqn with MQ-9A *Reaper*
EQUIPMENT BY TYPE
AIRCRAFT 266 combat capable
  FGA 206: 3 F-35B *Lightning* II (in test); 90 *Tornado* GR4/GR4A; 113 *Typhoon* FGR4/T3
  ISR 11: 5 *Sentinel* R1; 6 *Shadow* R1
  ELINT 1 RC-135V *Rivet Joint* (IOC)
  AEW&C 6 E-3D *Sentry*
  TKR/TPT 10 A330 MRTT *Voyager* KC2/3
  TPT 52: **Heavy** 9: 1 A400M *Atlas*; 8 C-17A *Globemaster*; **Medium** 24: 10 C-130J *Hercules*; 14 C-130J-30 *Hercules*; **Light** 10: 5 Beech 200 *King Air* (on lease); 2 Beech 200GT *King Air* (on lease); 3 BN-2A *Islander* CC2; **PAX** 9: 5 BAe-125 CC-3; 4 BAe-146 CC2/C3
  TRG 202: 41 EMB-312 *Tucano* T1 (50 more in store); 101 G-115E *Tutor*; 28 *Hawk* T2*; 32 *Hawk* T1/1A/1W* (ε40 more in store)
HELICOPTERS
  MRH 5: 1 AW139; 4 Bell 412EP *Griffin* HAR-2
  TPT 28: **Medium** 25 *Sea King* HAR-3A; **Light** 3 AW109E
UAV • **CISR** • **Heavy** 10 MQ-9A *Reaper*
MSL
  AAM • **IR** AIM-9L/9L/I *Sidewinder*; **IIR** ASRAAM; **ARH** AIM-120B/C5 AMRAAM
  ASM *Brimstone*; *Dual-Mode Brimstone*; AGM-65G2 *Maverick*
  LACM *Storm Shadow*
BOMBS
  Laser-Guided/GPS: *Paveway* II; GBU-10 *Paveway* III; Enhanced *Paveway* II/III; GBU-24 *Paveway* IV

Royal Air Force Regiment
FORCES BY ROLE
COMMAND
  3 (tactical Survive To Operate (STO)) sqn
MANOEUVRE
  Other
  7 sy sqn
COMBAT SUPPORT
  1 CBRN sqn

Tri-Service Defence Helicopter School
FORCES BY ROLE
TRAINING
  1 hel sqn with Bell 412EP *Griffin* HT1
  2 hel sqn with AS350B *Ecureuil*
EQUIPMENT BY TYPE
HELICOPTERS
  MRH 11 Bell 412EP *Griffin* HT1
  TPT • **Light** 27: 25 AS350B *Ecureuil*; 2 AW109E

Volunteer Reserve Air Forces
(Royal Auxiliary Air Force/RAF Reserve)
MANOEUVRE
  Other
  5 sy sqn
COMBAT SUPPORT
  2 int sqn
COMBAT SERVICE SUPPORT
  1 med sqn
  1 (air movements) sqn
  1 (HQ augmentation) sqn
  1 (C-130 Reserve Aircrew) flt

UK Special Forces
Includes Royal Navy, Army and RAF units
FORCES BY ROLE
SPECIAL FORCES
  1 (SAS) SF regt
  1 (SBS) SF regt
  1 (Special Reconnaissance) SF regt
  1 SF BG (based on 1 para bn)
MANOEUVRE
  Aviation
  1 wg (includes assets drawn from 3 army avn sqn, 1 RAF tpt sqn and 1 RAF hel sqn)
COMBAT SUPPORT
  1 sigs regt

Reserve
FORCES BY ROLE
SPECIAL FORCES
  2 (SAS) SF regt

Cyber

Defence Cyber Operations Group
FORCES BY ROLE
COMBAT SUPPORT
  2 cyber unit

The Office of Cyber Security & Information Assurance (OSCIA) works with the Cyber Security Operations Centre and ministries and agencies to implement cyber-security programmes. CSOC is hosted by GCHQ. A Cyber Security Strategy was published in November 2011. The Defence Cyber Operations Group was set up in 2011 to place 'cyber at the heart of defence operations, doctrine and training'. This group was transferred to Joint Forces Command on this formation's establishment in April 2012. A Joint Forces Cyber Group was set up in 2013, including a Joint Cyber Reserve, providing support to two Joint Cyber Units and other information-assurance units across the defence establishment.

DEPLOYMENT

Legal provisions for foreign deployment:
Constitution: Uncodified constitution which includes constitutional statutes, case law, international treaties and unwritten conventions
Decision on deployment of troops abroad: By the government

AFGHANISTAN
NATO • ISAF 300; *Hermes* 450; *Watchkeeper*; *Shadow* R1; MQ-9A *Reaper*

ALBANIA
OSCE • Albania 3

ARABIAN SEA & GULF OF ADEN
Combined Maritime Forces • CTF-150: 1 FFGHM

ASCENSION ISLAND
20

ATLANTIC (NORTH)/CARIBBEAN
1 FFGHM

ATLANTIC (SOUTH)
1 FFGHM

BAHRAIN
20; 1 BAe-125; 1 BAe-146

BELIZE
10

BOSNIA-HERZEGOVINA
EU • EUFOR • *Operation Althea* 95; 1 inf coy
OSCE • Bosnia and Herzegovina 3

BRITISH INDIAN OCEAN TERRITORY
40; 1 Navy/Marine det

BRUNEI
550; 1 (Gurkha) lt inf bn; 1 jungle trg centre; 1 hel flt with 3 Bell 212

CANADA
430; 2 trg units; 1 hel flt with SA341 *Gazelle* AH1

CYPRUS
2,600; 2 inf bn; ; 1 SAR sqn with 4 Bell 412 *Twin Huey*; 1 radar (on det)

Operation Shader 1 FGA sqn with 8 *Tornado* GR4; 1 A330 MRTT *Voyager* KC3; 1 C-130J *Hercules*; 4 CH-47D *Chinook* HC4
UN • UNFICYP 268; 1 inf coy

DEMOCRATIC REPUBLIC OF THE CONGO
UN • MONUSCO 6

FALKLAND ISLANDS
1,500; 1 inf coy(+); 1 AD det with *Rapier*; 1 PSO; 1 ftr flt with 4 *Typhoon* FGR4; 1 SAR sqn with *Sea King* HAR-3/3A; 1 tkr/tpt flt with C-130J *Hercules*

GERMANY
12,300; 1 div with (1 armd bde; 1 inf bde; 1 log bde)

GIBRALTAR
410 (incl 175 pers of Gibraltar regt); 2 PB

GULF OF ADEN & INDIAN OCEAN
EU • *Operation Atalanta* 1 LSD

IRAQ
Operation Shader 12 (trg team)

KENYA
210 (trg team)

KUWAIT
40 (trg team)
Operation Shader MQ-9A *Reaper*

MALI
EU • EUTM Mali 37
UN • MINUSMA 2

MEDITERRANEAN SEA
NATO • SNMCMG 2: 1 MHC

MOLDOVA
OSCE • Moldova 1

NEPAL
280 (Gurkha trg org)

NETHERLANDS
120

OMAN
70; 1 *Sentinel* R1

PERSIAN GULF
Combined Maritime Forces • CTF-151: 1 DDGHM
Combined Maritime Forces • CTF-152: 2 MCO; 2 MHC

QATAR
Operation Shader 1 RC-135V *Rivet Joint*

SERBIA
NATO • KFOR 1
OSCE • Kosovo 15

SIERRA LEONE
Operation Gritlock 750: 1 AG; 3 AW101 ASW *Merlin* HM2

SOUTH SUDAN
UN • UNMISS 4

UGANDA
EU • EUTM Somalia 5

UKRAINE
OSCE • Ukraine 15

UNITED ARAB EMIRATES
1 tpt flt with C-17A *Globemaster*; C-130J *Hercules*

UNITED STATES
600

FOREIGN FORCES

United States
US European Command: 9,550; 1 ftr wg at RAF Lakenheath with (1 ftr sqn with 24 F-15C/D *Eagle*, 2 ftr sqn with 23 F-15E *Strike Eagle*); 1 ISR sqn at RAF Mildenhall with OC-135/RC-135; 1 tkr wg at RAF Mildenhall with 15 KC-135R *Stratotanker*; 1 Special Ops gp at RAF Mildenhall with (1 sqn with 5 MC-130H *Combat Talon* II; 5 CV-22B *Osprey*; 1 sqn with 1 MC-130J *Commando* II; 4 MC-130P *Combat Shadow*)
US Strategic Command: 1 Ballistic Missile Early Warning System (BMEWS) at Fylingdales Moor; 1 *Spacetrack* radar at Fylingdales Moor

Table 3 Selected Arms Procurements and Deliveries, Europe

Designation	Type	Quantity (Current)	Contract Value	Prime Nationality	Prime Contractor	Order Date	First Delivery Due	Notes
Belgium (BEL)								
A400M *Atlas*	Hvy tpt ac	7	n.k.	Int'l	Airbus Group (Airbus Defence & Space)	2003	2018	Delivery expected 2018/19
NH90 NFH/TTH	ASW/Med tpt hel	8	€293m (US$400m)	FRA/GER/ITA/NLD	NH Industries	2007	2012	Three TTH and two NFH delivered
Denmark (DNK)								
MH-60R *Seahawk*	ASW hel	9	DKK4bn (US$686m)	US	UTC (Sikorsky)	2012	2016	To replace *Lynx*. First delivery due mid-2016
Estonia (EST)								
XA-188	APC (W)	80	€20m (US$27m)	NLD	Government surplus	2010	2010	Second-hand Dutch veh. Delivery to be completed in 2015
CV9035	AIFV	44	n.k.	NLD	Government surplus	2014	n.k.	Ex-Dutch army surplus veh. Contract to be finalised by end of 2014
Finland (FIN)								
NH90 TTH	Med tpt hel	20	€370m (US$331m)	FRA/GER/ITA/NLD	NH Industries	2001	2008	16 delivered by late 2013
France (FRA)								
Barracuda	SSN	6	€8bn (US$10.5bn)	FRA	DCNS	2006	2016	First to enter service 2017. One SSN to be delivered every two years until 2027
Aquitaine-class	DDGHM	11	US$23.6bn	FRA	DCNS	2002	2012	Fourth vessel in sea trials as of Oct 2014
Missile de Croisière Naval (SCALP Naval)	LACM	150	See notes	FRA/GER/ITA/UK	MBDA	2007	2015	Original contract value €910m (US$1.2bn) for 250 msl. IOC with *Aquitaine*-class DDGHM now due 2015, with *Barracuda*-class SSN in 2018
Rafale F3	FGA ac	180	n.k.	FRA	Dassault	1984	2006	127 delivered as of late 2014
A400M *Atlas*	Hvy tpt ac	50	n.k.	Int'l	Airbus Group (Airbus Defence & Space)	2003	2013	Five delivered as of late 2014
EC665 *Tiger*	Atk hel	80	n.k.	Int'l	Airbus Group (Airbus Helicopters)	1999	2005	40 HAP, 40 HAD variant. All HAP delivered. First HAD variant delivered Apr 2013
NH90 NFH	ASW hel	27	n.k.	FRA/GER/ITA/NLD	NH Industries	2000	2010	For navy; 12 delivered as of late 2014. Final delivery due 2019
NH90 TTH	Med tpt hel	68	n.k.	FRA/GER/ITA/NLD	NH Industries	2007	2012	For army; deliveries ongoing
MQ-9 *Reaper*	ISR UAV	16	US$1.5bn	US	General Atomics	2013	2014	Two delivered and deployed to Niger in 2014
Meteor	AAM	200	n.k.	FRA/GER/ITA/UK	MBDA	2011	2018	For integration with *Rafale* F3Rs
Germany (GER)								
Puma	AIFV	350	n.k.	GER	PSM	2007	n.k.	To replace *Marder* 1A3/A4/A5 AIFVs. Order reduced from 450. ISD moved to post-2014
Boxer (8x8)	APC (W)	272	€1.5bn (US$2.1bn)	GER/NLD	ARTEC GmbH	2006	2009	135 APC, 65 CP, 72 armoured ambulance variants

Table 3 **Selected Arms Procurements and Deliveries, Europe**

Designation	Type	Quantity (Current)	Contract Value	Prime Nationality	Prime Contractor	Order Date	First Delivery Due	Notes
Type-212A	SSK	2	n.k.	GER	TKMS (HDW)	2006	2014	U-35 in service 2014. U-36 ISD 2015
Baden-Württemberg-class	DDGHM	4	€2bn (US$2.7bn)	GER	TKMS	2007	2016	First to be delivered end of 2016. Final delivery due late 2018
Eurofighter Typhoon	FGA ac	143	n.k.	GER/ITA/ESP/UK	Eurofighter GmbH (Airbus Defence & Space)	1998	2003	101 delivered as of late 2014
A400M *Atlas*	Hvy tpt ac	53	n.k.	Int'l	Airbus Group (Airbus Defence & Space)	2003	2014	First flight Oct 2014
EC665 *Tiger* (UHT variant)	Atk hel	57	US$2.6bn	Int'l	Airbus Group (Airbus Helicopters)	1984	2005	Order cut from 80 to 57 in early 2013. 21 delivered as of late 2014
NH90 *Sea Lion*	ASW hel	18	n.k.	FRA/GER/ITA/NLD	NH Industries	2013	2017	Modified NH90 NFH with GER-specific equipment
NH90 TTH	Med tpt hel	82	n.k.	FRA/GER/ITA/NLD	NH Industries	2000	2007	50 for army, 32 for air force. 22 delivered as of late 2014
Greece (GRC)								
Katsonis-class	SSK	6	€1.67bn (US$1.54bn)	GER	TKMS	2000	2010	Second boat launched Oct 2014
NH90 TTH	Med tpt hel	20	€657m (US$620m)	FRA/GER/ITA/NLD	NH Industries	2002	2011	16 tac tpt variants and four spec ops variants. Option on further 14. Nine delivered as of late 2014
Ireland (IRL)								
Samuel Beckett-class	PSO	2	US$136m	UK	Babcock International	2010	2014	First vessel commissioned May 2014. Option for a third vessel
Italy (ITA)								
Todaro-class	SSK	2	€915m (US$1.34bn)	ITA	Fincantieri	2008	2015	Second batch; option exercised from 1996 contract. With AIP. First boat launched Oct 2014
Bergamini-class	DDGHM	6	€1.6bn (US$2.3bn)	FRA/ITA	Orizzonte Sistemi Navali	2002	2013	Fourth vessel launched Mar 2014
Eurofighter Typhoon	FGA ac	96	n.k.	GER/ITA/ESP/UK	Eurofighter GmbH (Finmeccanica)	1998	2004	70 delivered as of late 2014
F-35A *Lightning* II	FGA ac	8	n.k.	US	Lockheed Martin	2013	2015	Planned procurement cut from 131 to 90
Gulfstream G550 CAEW	AEW&C ac	2	US$750m	ISR	IAI	2012	2015	Linked to ISR purchase of 30 M-346 trg ac
ATR-72MP	MP ac	4	€360–400m (US$501–557m)	ITA	Finmeccanica (Alenia Aermacchi)	2009	2012	To be fitted with long-range surv suite. Deliveries ongoing
NH90 NFH/TTH	ASW/Med tpt hel	116	n.k.	FRA/GER/ITA/NLD	NH Industries	2000	2007	60 TTH for army; 46 NFH and ten TTH for navy
CH-47F *Chinook*	Hvy tpt hel	16	€900m (US$1.25bn)	US	Boeing	2009	2014	First two delivered Oct 2014
Latvia (LVA)								
Scimitar CVR (T)	Recce	123	€48m (US$67.5m)	UK	Government surplus	2014	2016	Total to include four variants

Table 3 **Selected Arms Procurements and Deliveries, Europe**

Designation	Type	Quantity (Current)	Contract Value	Prime Nationality	Prime Contractor	Order Date	First Delivery Due	Notes
Luxembourg (LUX)								
A400M *Atlas*	Hvy tpt ac	1	n.k.	Int'l	Airbus Group (Airbus Defence & Space)	2003	2018	First delivery now expected 2018
NATO								
RQ-4 *Global Hawk* Block 40	ISR UAV	5	€1.3bn (US$1.7bn)	US	Northrop Grumman	2012	2015	Part of NATO's Alliance Ground Surveillance programme. Fuselage of first ac completed Aug 2014
Netherlands (NLD)								
Boxer (8x8)	APC (W)	200	€595m (US$747m)	GER/NLD	ARTEC GmbH	2006	2013	To replace YPR 765. Deliveries began 2013
Karel Doorman-class	AFSH	1	€364m (US$545m)	NLD	Damen Schelde	2009	2014	Expected to commission in 2015
F-35A *Lightning* II	FGA ac	2	n.k.	US	Lockheed Martin	2013	2014	Two delivered so far. Test sqn has been formed
NH90 NFH/TTH	ASW/Med tpt hel	14	n.k.	FRA/GER/ITA/NLD	NH Industries	2001	2011	Six for ASW, eight for coast guard. FOC expected 2017. Five delivered by 2014
Norway (NOR)								
CV90	AIFV/AIFV upgrade	144	GB£500m (US$750m)	UK	BAE Systems (BAE Land & Armaments)	2012	2014	41 new build CV90s and 103 existing CV9030s to be ugraded. Two pre-series upgraded CV9030s in trials. Series production will begin in 2015
Poland (POL)								
Leopard 2A4/5	MBT	119	€180m (US$243m)	GER	Government surplus	2013	2014	105 *Leopard* 2A5 and 14 *Leopard* 2A4. Final delivery due in 2015
Rosomak	AIFV	997	US$2.2bn	FIN	Patria	2003	2004	Includes 2013 follow-on order for 307
Romania (ROM)								
F-16AM/BM *Fighting Falcon*	FGA ac	12	US$250m	PRT	Government surplus	2013	2016	Nine ex-PRT F-16 MLUs and three ex-USAF ac upgraded to MLU status by PRT
Slovakia (SVK)								
C-27J *Spartan*	Med tpt ac	2	n.k.	ITA	Finmeccanica (Alenia Aermacchi)	2014	n.k.	Procurement originally suspended due to funding constraints. New contract signed in Oct 2014
Spain (ESP)								
S-80A	SSK	4	n.k.	ESP	Navantia	2003	2017	Delivery delayed by redesign. Construction awaiting approval from MoD

Table 3 Selected Arms Procurements and Deliveries, Europe

Designation	Type	Quantity (Current)	Contract Value	Prime Nationality	Prime Contractor	Order Date	First Delivery Due	Notes
Eurofighter Typhoon	FGA ac	74	n.k.	GER/ITA/ESP/UK	Eurofighter GmbH (Airbus Defence & Space)	1998	2003	Deliveries since 2012 have gone into storage
A400M Atlas	Hvy tpt ac	27	n.k.	Int'l	Airbus Group (Airbus Defence & Space)	2003	2018	First delivery now scheduled for 2018. Current plans envisage an operational fleet of only 14 ac
EC665 Tiger (HAP/HAD)	Atk hel	24	€1.4bn (US$1.6bn)	Int'l	Airbus Group (Airbus Helicopters)	2003	2007	Six HAP-E delivered 2007/08. HAD variant is in test
NH90 TTH	Med tpt hel	45	n.k.	FRA/GER/ITA/NLD	NH Industries	2007	2012	Discussions over proposed order reduction to 22 hel. First ESP assembeled hel due for delivery by end of 2014

Sweden (SWE)

Designation	Type	Quantity (Current)	Contract Value	Prime Nationality	Prime Contractor	Order Date	First Delivery Due	Notes
Patgb 360	APC (W)	113	€240m (US$338m)	FIN	Patria	2009	2013	79 APC and 34 other variants. Deliveries ongoing
BvS10	APC (T)	102	SEK800m (US$120m)	UK	BAE Systems (BAE Land & Armaments)	2013	2014	Exercised option from previous contract. Final delivery due in 2015
FH-77 BW L52 Archer 6x6	Arty (155mm SP)	24	n.k.	UK	BAE Systems (BAE Land & Armaments)	2010	2013	Four delivered Sep 2013; series production deliveries from 2016
NH90 NFH/TTH	ASW/Med tpt hel	18	n.k.	FRA/GER/ITA/NLD	NH Industries	2001	2007	13 TTT/SAR and five ASW variants. Option for seven more. Seven delivered by mid-2012
JAS-39E Gripen	FGA ac	60	US$2.5bn	SWE	Saab	2013	2018	Proposal for additional ten under discussion in 2014

Turkey (TUR)

Designation	Type	Quantity (Current)	Contract Value	Prime Nationality	Prime Contractor	Order Date	First Delivery Due	Notes
Gokturk-1	Sat	1	€270m (US$380m)	ITA/FRA	Telespazio/Thales	2009	2015	Launch delayed until 2015
Altay	MBT	4	US$500m	TUR	Otokar	2007	2014	Prototypes. Plans to order up to 250 more after testing
Firtina 155mm/52-cal	Arty (155mm SP)	350	n.k.	ROK	Samsung Techwin	2001	2003	ROK Techwin K9 Thunder. Total requirement of 350. Deliveries ongoing
Kirpi	PPV	468	n.k.	TUR	BMC	2009	2010	Delivery resumed after 2011 suspension
Type-214	SSK	6	€1.96bn (US$2.9bn)	GER	MFI/TKMS (HDW)	2011	2015	To be built at Golcuk shipyard
Ada-class	FFGHM	4	n.k.	TUR	Istanbul Naval Shipyard/RMK Marine	1996	2011	Two in service by late 2014
Tuzla-class	PCC	16	€402m (US$545m)	TUR	Dearsan Shipyard	2007	2010	Twelfth vessel commissioned Jul 2014
ATR-72MP/ATR-72	MP ac/Lt tpt ac	8	€260m (US$324m)	ITA	Finmeccanica (Alenia Aermacchi)	2005	2013	Programme delayed; order revised in 2013 to six MPA and two utility ac. First utl ac del Jul 2013. First MPA due Feb 2017
B-737 AEW	AEW&C ac	4	US$1bn	US	Boeing	2002	2014	Peace Eagle programme. Three delivered as of late 2014
A400M Atlas	Hvy tpt ac	10	n.k.	Int'l	Airbus Group (Airbus Defence & Space)	2003	2014	First ac accepted Apr 2014
T129A	Atk hel	9	€150m (US$208m)	TUR/ITA	TAI/Aselsan/Finmeccanica (Agusta Westland)	2010	2014	Interim procurement until large-scale production of T129B begins. First three delivered Jun 2014

Table 3 Selected Arms Procurements and Deliveries, Europe

Designation	Type	Quantity (Current)	Contract Value	Prime Nationality	Prime Contractor	Order Date	First Delivery Due	Notes
T-129B	Atk hel	50	US$3bn	TUR/ITA	TAI/Aselsan/Finmeccanica (Agusta Westland)	2007	2015	Option on further 41
CH-47F *Chinook*	Hvy tpt hel	6	n.k.	US	Boeing	2011	2014	Original aim to acquire 14 for US$1.2bn, but order cut to six; five for the army and one for SF Comd

United Kingdom (UK)

Designation	Type	Quantity (Current)	Contract Value	Prime Nationality	Prime Contractor	Order Date	First Delivery Due	Notes
Scout	Recce	589	GB£3.5bn (US$5.9bn)	US	General Dynamics (General Dynamics UK)	2014	2017	First delivery due in 2017
Astute-class	SSN	6	n.k.	UK	BAE Systems (BAE Maritime)	1994	2010	Second vessel commissioned in 2013. Third in sea trials late 2014. To be fitted with *Tomahawk* Block IV SLCM
Queen Elizabeth-class	CV	2	GB£3.9bn (US$8bn)	UK	BAE Systems (BAE Maritime)	2007	2016	Both vessels now to be brought into service
Tide-class	AOT	4	GB£452m (US$757m)	ROK	Daewoo Shipbuilding and Marine Engineering (DSME)	2012	2016	MARS programme
Eurofighter *Typhoon*	FGA ac	160	n.k.	GER/ITA/ESP/UK	Eurofighter GmbH (BAE Systems)	1998	2004	113 delivered as of late 2014
F-35B *Lightning II*	FGA ac	8	n.k.	US	Lockheed Martin	2008	2012	Three delivered and in test in US
Voyager (A330-200 MRTT)	Tkr/Tpt ac	14	GB£13bn (US$26bn)	Int'l	AirTanker Consortium	2008	2011	Tenth delivered 2014
RC-135 *Rivet Joint*	ELINT ac	3	εGB£700m (US$1bn)	US	Boeing	2010	2013	First ac in service 2014
A400M *Atlas*	Hvy tpt ac	22	n.k.	Int'l	Airbus Group (Airbus Defence & Space)	2003	2014	First delivered Nov 2014
AW159 *Wildcat*	MRH hel	62	GB£1bn (US$1.8bn)	ITA	Finmeccanica	2006	2012	34 for army, 28 for navy. Option for a further four hel. Final delivery due in 2015
Watchkeeper WK450	ISR UAV	54	GB£800m (US$1.2bn)	FRA	Thales	2005	2014	In service 2014

Chapter Five
Russia and Eurasia

RUSSIA

Modernisation of the Russian armed forces, begun in 2008 under Defence Minister Anatoly Serdyukov and merely adjusted under his successor Sergei Shoigu, continued in 2014. The appointment in May of a new Ground Forces Commander-in-Chief, Colonel-General Oleg Salyukov, ended a period with no commander in office, but this was the only major personnel change during the year. It was also a year of relative organisational stability, although preparations began for the creation of a new Joint Strategic Command (OSK) North, based around the navy's Northern Fleet. Shoigu announced in October that, as part of the expansion of Russia's military presence in the Arctic, units would be stationed 'along the entire Arctic Circle' by the end of the year; Russia has, however, aspired to revive its Arctic presence for some years, as noted in recent issues of *The Military Balance*. However, much international attention focused on Russian activity in Ukraine, and the performance there, and actions, of its troops.

The practice of 'snap inspections' continued, although on a reduced scale. The inspections were first carried out in 2013. Analysis of shortcomings in that year's inspections led to changes in 2014; in particular, the assessment that there was inadequate training of equipment crews – especially in those crews comprising soldiers serving their one-year conscription term – was addressed by intensifying the combat-training programme. Deficiencies in live-firing routines were dealt with by increasing, by a factor of five to six, munitions allocated for exercises and problems with vehicle handling were addressed by boosting, by a factor of two to three, the training hours allocated for combat-vehicle driving.

Exercises also revealed that the serviceability levels of military equipment were generally unsatisfactory. Serviceability in the air force and the navy was assessed at less than 55%, and in the land forces at less than 65%. This deficiency also led to remedial action. The Oboronservis state corporation, which repairs equipment and provides support functions for military units – and was the subject of corruption allegations linked to the resignation of Serdyukov (see *The Military Balance 2013*, p. 199) – was radically restructured. Its repair plants and bases became state-industrial corporations, reducing staff numbers from 130,000 to 30,000 in the process. At the same time, first-line equipment-repair and maintenance units were strengthened; some of these had been cut during previous reforms.

Experience in the large-scale redeployment of troops and equipment, which the Russian armed forces had acquired during strategic exercises and large-scale, snap combat-readiness inspections, was put to use in 2014 during the annexation of Crimea. Snap inspections simultaneously mounted in two military districts from 26 February to 3 March provided cover for the covert concentration of incursion forces, as well as providing diversionary political effect. In the fast-paced operation that followed, a mobile group of army special forces, airborne troops and Crimea-based naval infantry, plus motor-rifle and artillery units, was able to concentrate in a peninsula that has no land bridge to Russia. Resupply lines were also successfully established. (The Russian Black Sea Fleet had remained in Crimea under a 1997 agreement with Ukraine; fleet headquarters remain at Sevastopol.)

In comparison with their performance in the 2008 conflict in Georgia, Russian forces in Crimea benefited from improvements in personal equipment, logistics, personnel discipline, electronic-warfare capability and junior-commander training. The military capabilities, tactics, escalation control and integration of state instruments of power with information-warfare tools that the Crimea operation demonstrated – and, seen later, to some degree in eastern Ukraine – were linked by commentators with the earlier public explanation by Chief of the General Staff Valeriy Gerasimov of the new nature of war, described as 'non-linear', 'hybrid' or 'ambiguous' warfare, among other terms (see pp. 17–20).

Nonetheless, too much focus on the new personal equipment, weapons, vehicles and tactical-communications equipment in evidence during the Crimea mission can be misleading. The troops involved in the operation mainly comprised elite special-operations groups from the Southern Military District and the Airborne Assault Troops (VDV), which have long been given priority over regular ground forces in terms of training, equipment and funding. Therefore, lessons from the Crimea operation do not reflect the overall state of the Russian armed forces, for which change in these areas has been positive but less striking. Due to the chronic under-manning and conscription issues now characteristic of the Russian Army (see textbox, p. 163), even these elite formations could not be used in their entirety. On the whole, the operation was a test of elite units and special forces, and they performed well.

The annexation of Crimea and the conflict in eastern Ukraine led to the worst political confrontation between Russia and the West since the Cold War. Inside Russia, it initiated an examination of existing defence doctrines. This officially began in August 2014 with the establishment of a working group to revise the Military Doctrine of the Russian Federation, last published in 2010. The new doctrine is expected to be more overtly inimical to NATO and the United States, and will inevitably also lead to changes in the classified State Defence Plan, which was adopted in 2013.

There was no announcement of a further increase in defence spending, not even on rearmament. Russia is facing a general economic slowdown as well as dealing with the effects of international sanctions imposed after its annexation of Crimea; under these conditions, even its current military plans present economic difficulties. By mid-2014, some individuals and sectors had been sanctioned, including sanctions revoking and denying licences for the export of defence and dual-use equipment to Russia, a move implemented by a number of states including the US, the UK and Germany, as well as the EU. Financially driven amendments were announced that affect long-term plans to re-equip Russia's conventional forces, including the postponement of some programmes into the next funding period (2016–25), and there was a new emphasis on import substitution stemming from sanctions, as well as the loss of component and engine supplies from Ukraine (see textbox, p. 166).

Land forces

Last year's *Military Balance* highlighted the latest changes to the structural reform of Russian ground forces, when two divisions were restored in the Western Military District and the 68th Army Corps was formed in the Russian Far East. The initial results of these changes forced broader revisions to earlier plans. Transitioning from 'permanent-readiness' brigades to full divisions with regimental structures proved difficult, primarily because divisions have a much larger establishment. This led Russian defence planners to consider a compromise structure, in which newly established divisional commands would combine two or three current brigades.

These apparently counter-intuitive reversals of earlier reform achievements have been interpreted as a concession to opponents of transformation within the armed forces. However, they have little relevance to the ad hoc battalion task groups that were formed and concentrated near the Ukrainian border during peaks in the confrontation in eastern Ukraine.

Experiments to subdivide ground-force brigades into 'light', 'medium' and 'heavy' were suspended, as implementation proved too difficult. In particular, planners found that the light brigades had to be further subdivided into 'motor-rifle', 'mountain' and 'air-mobile' units, failing to deliver the standardisation originally intended. Subsequently, a large proportion of the brigades intended to be 'light' were reassigned en masse from the land forces to the VDV. (These were the three army air-assault brigades – the 11th, 56th and 83rd Brigades.) Nor has the formal subdivision into 'medium' and 'heavy' brigades taken place. Differentiation will instead continue on the basis of the type of armoured vehicles used – whether tracked or wheeled – in effect retaining the distinction between armoured and motor-rifle formations. At present it is intended that motor-rifle units will remain largely wheeled, and will be equipped with new infantry fighting vehicles (IFVs) based on the *Bumerang* platform.

In anticipation of the new-design wheeled and tracked vehicle platforms that are due to be introduced in the next few years, re-equipment of the ground forces with newly manufactured armoured vehicles, including the T-90 main battle tank (MBT) or BMP-3 armoured IFV, slowed significantly. However, large-scale deliveries of the wheeled BTR-82A continued. This vehicle has an enhanced weapons fit, including the TKN-04GA day/night-sight. Meanwhile, mass modernisation of the T-72B MBT fleet to the T-72B3 standard is also under way. Considerable effort is going into re-equipping the missile brigades, with *Iskander* replacing the *Tochka-U* tactical missile, bringing increased strike capability through improvements to range and accuracy.

The first public presentation of the new vehicle platforms is due to take place during the Victory Day Parade on 9 May 2015 in Moscow. The first models should start to be delivered to the troops for trials in the same year. Due to be unveiled at the parade are a tank and a self-propelled gun based on the *Armata* platform; a tracked armoured personnel carrier (APC) and a tracked IFV based on the *Kurganets*-25 platform; and the *Bumerang*-based wheeled combat vehicles intended to replace the BTR APC. Combined with the *Typhoon* wheeled logistics vehicle platform, which formed the basis for vehicles shown at the 2014 parade, these platforms are intended to shape the capabilities of Russia's land forces in the coming decades.

Despite the impressive quantity of new equipment due to take part in the 2015 parade (the plan is, analysts believe, for 24 vehicles on the *Kurganets*-25 platform alone to be shown), all of the platforms will be prototypes and as such not fully representative of technical configuration or even final appearance. The complexity of parallel development and testing of whole new families of combat equipment has led to inevitable delays in their production timetables (see pp. 164–67).

Air force

Structural reform of the air force has been the most controversial of the service reforms. The air force has undergone three waves of major change: reorganisation into the 'air base' system (see *The Military Balance 2012*, p. 186) and two successive regroupings of these bases into increasingly larger formations. It was discovered during snap inspections, and a review of the Serdyukov–Makarov 'new look' reforms, that the resulting class-one 'mega air bases', dispersed over four to seven airfields and combining different fixed- and rotary-wing aircraft types, were ineffective. The overly cumbersome structure, compounded by a weakened staff component in comparison to the pre-reform aviation divisions and corps, failed to provide sufficient command-and-control and combat readiness. As a result, the reform was abandoned and the original division–regiment structure reinstated.

Aerospace-defence brigades, however, retain their post-2008 structure and army-aviation reform remains incomplete, with 'air bases' retained alongside new army-aviation brigades, which are continuing to be formed. At present, army-aviation units report to the Air and Air-Defence Forces Command in each Operational Strategic Command.

Progress in delivering new equipment to the air force has been far more successful. In 2013, 56 new and upgraded fixed-wing aircraft, 122 helicopters and two regiments' worth of S-400 surface-to-air missile systems were delivered. By the end of 2014, the air force was due to receive another 220 fixed- and rotary-wing aircraft. Research work on the development of the *PAK DA* future strategic bomber also started in 2014. This new long-range aircraft will reportedly be subsonic and of a 'flying wing' design reminiscent of the US B-2 *Spirit* bomber. The current target is to begin testing prototypes in 2019, for entry into service in 2025.

Air-force testing of Russia's fifth-generation *PAK FA* combat aircraft is officially scheduled to begin in 2016, though 'captive carry' trials of air-to-air and air-to-surface weapons on external hardpoints have already begun. Despite intense lobbying by the military-industrial complex, the defence ministry has not yet expressed interest in developing or procuring a lighter fifth-generation fighter based on concepts proposed by the MiG design bureau. This project is at an early stage and is being led by the bureau on its own initiative, though efforts could be stepped up if a foreign customer emerges.

The delivery of new, modern aircraft has exacerbated problems with the pace of delivery of precision-guided air weapons. At present, new non-nuclear munitions for long-range aviation, such as the Kh-101 and Kh-32 cruise missiles, have still not entered service. The Kh-555 (AS-15C *Kent*) programme, however, has been successful, allowing Shoigu to announce a radical increase in long-range cruise missile purchases. Analysts estimate that the number of Kh-555s is projected to increase, by 2020, by a factor of 30 from the current undisclosed figure.

The air force still lacks its own fleet of unmanned aerial vehicles (UAVs). A number of domestically produced UAV models are now in service, but the vast majority of the more than 500 systems available to the Russian armed forces are concentrated in the land forces and the airborne troops. These are light models for tactical reconnaissance, none of which have strike capabilities. This situation should change with the launch of development work on a family of three strike UAVs (with a take-off weight of one tonne, five tonnes and 20 tonnes) commissioned by the defence ministry for the air force. MiG's *Skat* unmanned combat aerial vehicle (UCAV) concept was superseded by a 20-tonne UCAV being developed by Sukhoi with MiG as a subcontractor, which is planned to fly by 2018. UCAVs of this class have a range and combat payload comparable to manned strike aircraft.

Figure 7 Equipment Analysis: Russian *Flanker* Combat Aircraft Development

The Sukhoi Su-27 *Flanker* family has become a centrepiece of Russian tactical aviation. This comes after a difficult start; the prototype aircraft underwent complete redesign in the late 1970s to address performance shortcomings. The aircraft has developed from a single-role to a multi-role fighter with greatly improved combat performance including in the detection and engagement ranges of potential targets. Originally intended for the export arena, the Russian air force ordered 48 Su-35S in 2009, and deliveries should be completed during 2015. An additional order for a further 48 is widely anticipated. The Su-35S will see service likely well into the 2030s as a complement to the air force's fifth-generation fighter, being developed under the Sukhoi T-50 programme.

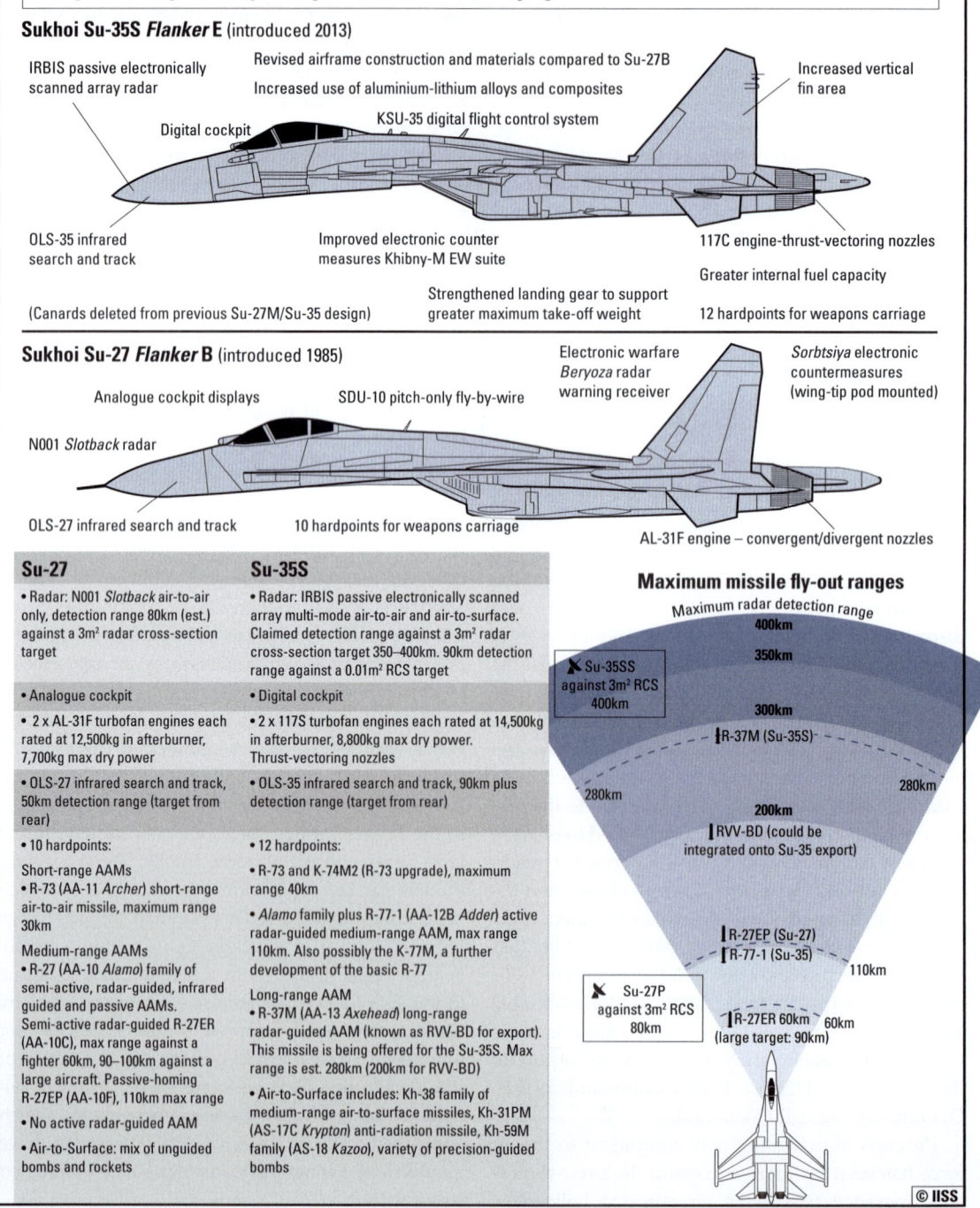

Sukhoi Su-35S *Flanker* E (introduced 2013)

- IRBIS passive electronically scanned array radar
- Revised airframe construction and materials compared to Su-27B
- Increased use of aluminium-lithium alloys and composites
- Increased vertical fin area
- Digital cockpit
- KSU-35 digital flight control system
- OLS-35 infrared search and track
- Improved electronic counter measures Khibny-M EW suite
- 117C engine-thrust-vectoring nozzles
- Greater internal fuel capacity
- (Canards deleted from previous Su-27M/Su-35 design)
- Strengthened landing gear to support greater maximum take-off weight
- 12 hardpoints for weapons carriage

Sukhoi Su-27 *Flanker* B (introduced 1985)

- Analogue cockpit displays
- SDU-10 pitch-only fly-by-wire
- Electronic warfare *Beryoza* radar warning receiver
- *Sorbtsiya* electronic countermeasures (wing-tip pod mounted)
- N001 *Slotback* radar
- OLS-27 infrared search and track
- 10 hardpoints for weapons carriage
- AL-31F engine – convergent/divergent nozzles

Su-27

- Radar: N001 *Slotback* air-to-air only, detection range 80km (est.) against a 3m² radar cross-section target
- Analogue cockpit
- 2 x AL-31F turbofan engines each rated at 12,500kg in afterburner, 7,700kg max dry power
- OLS-27 infrared search and track, 50km detection range (target from rear)
- 10 hardpoints:
  Short-range AAMs
- R-73 (AA-11 *Archer*) short-range air-to-air missile, maximum range 30km
  Medium-range AAMs
- R-27 (AA-10 *Alamo*) family of semi-active, radar-guided, infrared guided and passive AAMs. Semi-active radar-guided R-27ER (AA-10C), max range against a fighter 60km, 90–100km against a large aircraft. Passive-homing R-27EP (AA-10F), 110km max range
- No active radar-guided AAM
- Air-to-Surface: mix of unguided bombs and rockets

Su-35S

- Radar: IRBIS passive electronically scanned array multi-mode air-to-air and air-to-surface. Claimed detection range against a 3m² radar cross-section target 350–400km. 90km detection range against a 0.01m² RCS target
- Digital cockpit
- 2 x 117S turbofan engines each rated at 14,500kg in afterburner, 8,800kg max dry power. Thrust-vectoring nozzles
- OLS-35 infrared search and track, 90km plus detection range (target from rear)
- 12 hardpoints:
- R-73 and K-74M2 (R-73 upgrade), maximum range 40km
- *Alamo* family plus R-77-1 (AA-12B *Adder*) active radar-guided medium-range AAM, max range 110km. Also possibly the K-77M, a further development of the basic R-77
  Long-range AAM
- R-37M (AA-13 *Axehead*) long-range radar-guided AAM (known as RVV-BD for export). This missile is being offered for the Su-35S. Max range is est. 280km (200km for RVV-BD)
- Air-to-Surface includes: Kh-38 family of medium-range air-to-surface missiles, Kh-31PM (AS-17C *Krypton*) anti-radiation missile, Kh-59M family (AS-18 *Kazoo*), variety of precision-guided bombs

Maximum missile fly-out ranges

Maximum radar detection range
- 400km
- 350km
- Su-35SS against 3m² RCS 400km
- 300km
- R-37M (Su-35S)
- 280km — 280km
- 200km
- RVV-BD (could be integrated onto Su-35 export)
- R-27EP (Su-27)
- R-77-1 (Su-35) 110km
- Su-27P against 3m² RCS 80km
- R-27ER 60km — 60km (large target: 90km)

© IISS

Navy

According to the State Armaments Programme to 2020, the navy will focus on nuclear-submarine construction in the medium term. This primarily concerns two projects: eight *Borey*-class nuclear-powered ballistic-missile submarines equipped with the *Bulava* (SS-N-X-32) ballistic missile, and seven *Yasen*-class multi-purpose, nuclear-powered attack submarines equipped with cruise missiles. In addition, construction of several 'special-purpose' nuclear submarines is planned. These highly classified programmes include the Project 210 *Losharik* and Project 09851 *Khabarovsk*, which will be crewed entirely by officers and used for special operations of an undisclosed nature. It seems unlikely that these ambitious plans will be implemented on schedule, given the difficulties already experienced in building 50 or so major surface warships, and the time it has taken to complete those submarines that have gone into service in recent years. Nor is the main armament ready for the *Borey*-class boats, as demonstrated by the failure of the *Bulava* test launch in September

Personnel issues

The Russian armed forces continue to suffer the effects of personnel problems noted in *The Military Balance 2013*. Demographic pressure combined with the reduction in the conscript service term to one year, as well as ongoing challenges in recruiting professional servicemen and women, meant that at the beginning of 2014 the services were only 82% manned – a shortage of nearly 200,000 personnel. Despite exceeding contract-service recruitment targets for 2013, this problem persisted throughout 2014, leading to a reduction in 2014 recruitment plans.

The total number of contract-service soldiers was intended to reach 240,000 by the end of 2014. These mainly staff the combat sub-units of the Airborne Assault Troops (VDV) and other special-operations forces, although they also work on submarines and other complex or costly equipment. Support and artillery sub-units, however, remain largely conscript-manned, including those in VDV divisions. As a consequence, even elite formations are suffering from the introduction of the one-year conscription term. Special-forces units, for example, could not be deployed in full to Crimea in 2014, as they included a contingent of conscripts only drafted the previous autumn. These troops had been in the armed forces for less than six months at that point and had to remain behind. As a result, these units could field no more than two-thirds of their official strength.

Plans to increase the number of contract-service personnel to 350,000 by 2015 have been announced. This would require a recruitment campaign of unprecedented scale, bringing in 150,000 new contract-service personnel for the army within a year – significantly higher than both the 2013 and 2014 recruitment figures. The intention is to fill contract posts in the VDV, increase numbers in the land forces more broadly and put contract-service personnel in 75% of semi-skilled posts, such as combat-vehicle drivers and maintenance staff.

Strong Russian public support for operations in Crimea has boosted the armed forces' popularity, adding to the prestige of military service, and contributed to much-improved morale and a renewed sense of purpose within the services. Furthermore, salary improvements have helped recruitment by providing highly competitive remuneration. Nevertheless, it remains unlikely that the ambitious recruitment plan can be fulfilled within one year. Analysts suggest that the long-established pattern of failing to meet unrealistic contract-recruitment targets will persist.

Meanwhile, improved results have been reported for conscription. The spring 2014 draft brought in 154,000 personnel, with an apparent 20% reduction in evasion. From autumn 2014, recruits with a higher level of education have the option of serving on superior contract terms for two years instead of completing the mandatory one-year conscription period.

Increased attention to training reserves was a major new initiative. A special Reserves Command was formed at the end of 2013 in each of the four military districts. These are responsible for the training and mobilisation of reservists as well as the maintenance of equipment at storage depots; and for using these reserves and equipment to deploy full-strength combat units during mobilisation. They are a major departure from the previous practice, whereby call-up offices and the commanders of active brigades and divisions were responsible for mobilisation. The new system should relieve these commanders of a number of associated tasks. It can also be seen as a response to changes in armed forces' staffing in recent years, which has led to fewer trained reservists being available after conscript service, and therefore more care required in their management.

In addition, the new commands will be responsible for new types of reserves, such as a voluntary high-readiness reserve made up of those who have recently completed military service. In the first phase, in 2015, the defence ministry plans to recruit 8,600 of this type of reservist, primarily in specialist trades.

2013. This has forced a series of at least five further tests, to be carried out between 2014 and 2016.

The most significant modernisation projects in naval aviation are the replacement of the Su-24 *Fencer* ground-attack aircraft with the multi-role Su-30SM and the delivery of MiG-29K/KUB fighters to the Northern Fleet's shipborne-aviation regiment. However, the planned delivery of several dozen helicopters for the new *Mistral*-class amphibious-assault ships' air wings, including 32 navalised Ka-52K *Hokum*s, is in doubt following the French decision to suspend the warship's delivery amid pressure after the annexation of Crimea.

Strategic Rocket Forces

The Strategic Rocket Forces (SRF) remain the service least affected by Russia's military transformation programme. Most of the changes experienced by the service have related to rearmament. Deputy Defence Minister Yurii Borisov confirmed in 2014 that research-and-development work was under way for the *Sarmat*, a new heavy, liquid-fuel, silo-based intercontinental ballistic missile (ICBM). This missile is viewed in Russia as a response to the deployment of foreign missile-defence systems. Its increased thrust-to-weight ratio should allow the use of different strike trajectories, making it harder and more expensive to intercept. However, such ICBMs are a distant prospect, with analysts assessing little progress likely before 2020. The SRF's current focus is deploying the light, solid-fuel RS-24 *Yars* missile, in road-mobile and silo-based versions. Problems with serial production have been resolved, with three regiments at once scheduled to be re-equipped with *Yars* in 2014. The RS-26, a newer ICBM, is planned to enter service from 2015.

DEFENCE ECONOMICS

Defence Spending

As noted in *The Military Balance 2014*, the percentage of Russian GDP devoted to defence spending has been steadily increasing, and in 2014 it rose to almost 3.5% of GDP from 3.15% the previous year. According to the draft federal budget sent to the State Duma at the end of September, in 2015 there will be a large increase to more than 4.2% of GDP, falling to 3.7% in 2016 and 3.6% in 2017. The elevated level of military spending in 2015, an increase in real terms of more than 25%, is explained in part by a decision to dispense with state-guaranteed credits as a means of funding the state defence order, likely because economic sanctions

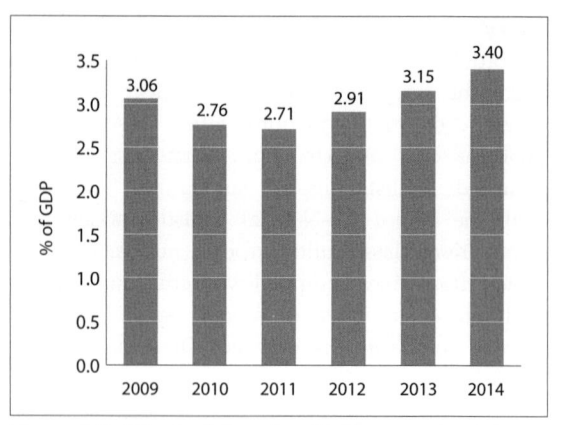

Figure 8 **Estimated Russian Defence Expenditure** as % of GDP

have made external borrowing more difficult. The projected defence budget in 2015 will be R3.3 trillion (US$88.3bn), compared with R2.5tr (US$70bn) in 2014 and R2.1tr (US$66.1bn) in 2013.

State Armaments Programme

The current high spending levels can be explained almost entirely by Russia's commitment to fund as fully as possible the ambitious State Armaments Programme to 2020, at least during the first five years (2011–15). From the outset it was envisaged that almost one-third of total funding (of more than R20tr, or around US$436.5bn) would be allocated during those five years; available evidence indicates that this will be achieved, notwithstanding the faltering Russian economy. It is possible that the Ukraine conflict and economic sanctions have reinforced the spending commitment for 2015, however some planned procurement for 2016 and 2017 has been postponed until a later date. The reason given was the inability of Russia's defence industry to cope with the large volume of orders. While this is a plausible explanation, it is likely that there may also have been concerns that defence was becoming too heavy a burden on the state budget. Nonetheless, with such a large budgetary increase planned for 2015, the problem of limited defence-industrial capacity will likely be encountered during the year.

According to the armaments programme, by the end of 2020 at least 70% of equipment will be 'modern', although the precise definition of this remains unclear. To date, implementation has been uneven (see Table 4, p. 167). While the procurement of new intercontinental ballistic missiles (ICBMs) has generally been successful, this has not been the case

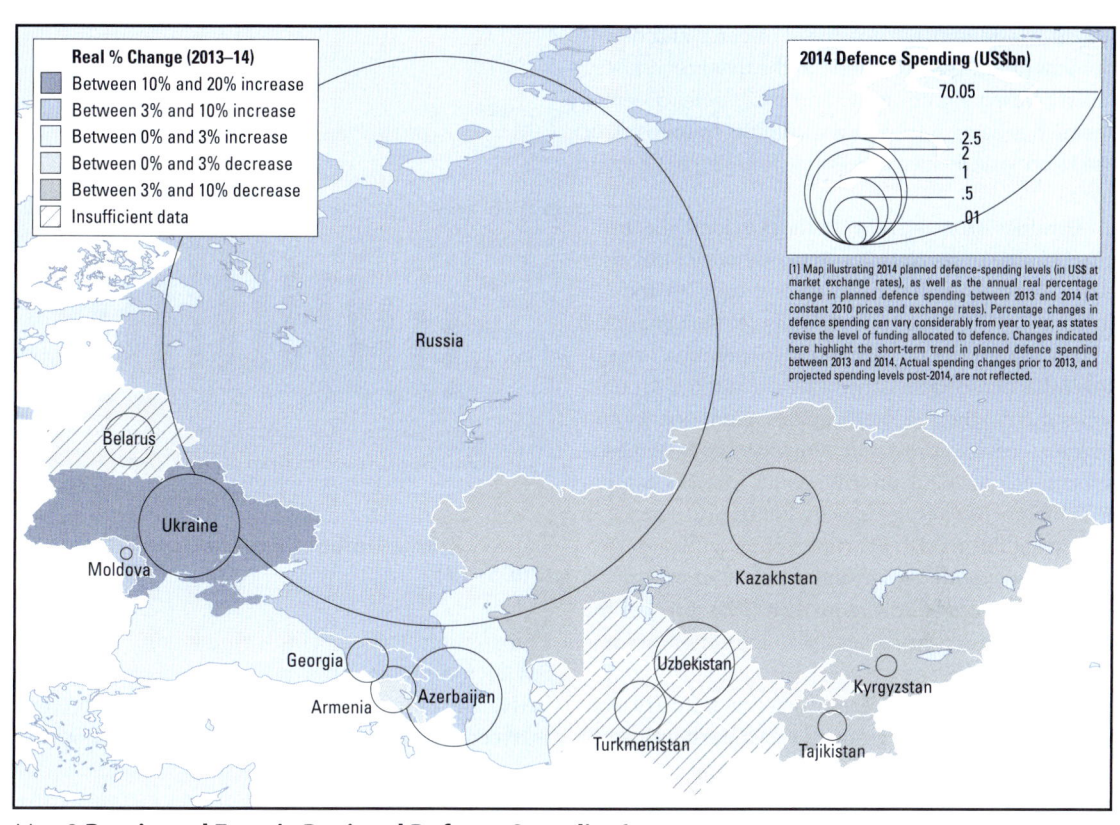

Map 3 **Russia and Eurasia Regional Defence Spending**[1]

[1] Map illustrating 2014 planned defence-spending levels (in US$ at market exchange rates), as well as the annual real percentage change in planned defence spending between 2013 and 2014 (at constant 2010 prices and exchange rates). Percentage changes in defence spending can vary considerably from year to year, as states revise the level of funding allocated to defence. Changes indicated here highlight the short-term trend in planned defence spending between 2013 and 2014. Actual spending changes prior to 2013, and projected spending levels post-2014, are not reflected.

for submarine-launched ballistic-missile development, due to problems with the *Bulava* missile and delays in building and commissioning new ballistic-missile submarines. In addition, the construction of attack submarines and large surface naval vessels has lagged behind schedule. Progressively greater numbers of new combat aircraft and helicopters have been received, and the introduction of the S-400 air-defence system has been proceeding steadily, though there are doubts whether the level of development of the new S-500 system will allow significant procurement before 2020. The ground forces have received little new equipment and much now depends on development of the new *Armata*-class heavy armoured-vehicle platform and the *Kurganets* and *Bumerang* vehicle families, scheduled to enter production in 2015–16.

An update of the existing State Armaments Programme to 2025 is under way, with the schedule for 2016–25 due for presidential approval by the end of 2015. The lack of an approved long-term economic forecast and long-term budget strategy has hampered this update. Before the Ukraine conflict, and the deterioration of relations with Western states, there was a clearly stated intention to moderate the pace of armaments renewal after 2020, with discussion about reorientating the defence industry towards modernising the civilian economy. However, the new strategic landscape may lead to a reinforced commitment to military modernisation, albeit at a more moderate pace than the past five years.

Defence industry

Russia's defence industry is experiencing improved funding levels due to sustained increases in order volumes in recent years. Pay rates have been rising, permitting better retention and recruitment of new personnel. The workforce is once again expanding and the average age has been falling. Investment has increased sharply, boosted by both improved company earnings and funding under the classified programme entitled Development of the Defence-Industrial Complex to 2020, of which a new version is being drafted. Many industrial enterprises producing end-product armaments, especially those prioritised in the State Armaments Programme, are now undergoing major modernisation and re-equipment, mainly with imported machine tools and other capital goods. In addition, the volume of research and development funding within, and for, the defence industry has increased significantly, and basic defence-sector research is being introduced within the framework of the Fund for Advanced Research, founded in October 2012.

Earnings from arms exports provided the principal source of funding for many defence industries until recently, with Russia second only to the US in terms of sales volume. In 2013, Russia reported US$15.7bn in 'military-technical cooperation', but of this total, end-product arms sales accounted for only around 60%, the rest being spares, components and military-services provision. However, with domestic procurement taking priority, some Russian companies are encountering capacity constraints, and it is likely that the growth of arms exports will moderate. Rosoboronexport, responsible for 85% of exports, is forecasting sales of little more than US$13bn over the next two to three years, similar to the export volume achieved in 2013.

In 2006, oversight of the defence industry was handed to the government's Military-Industrial Commission (MIC). This commission, unlike its Soviet forerunner, was principally a coordinating body, with limited authority to resolve differences between the defence ministry and industry, or within

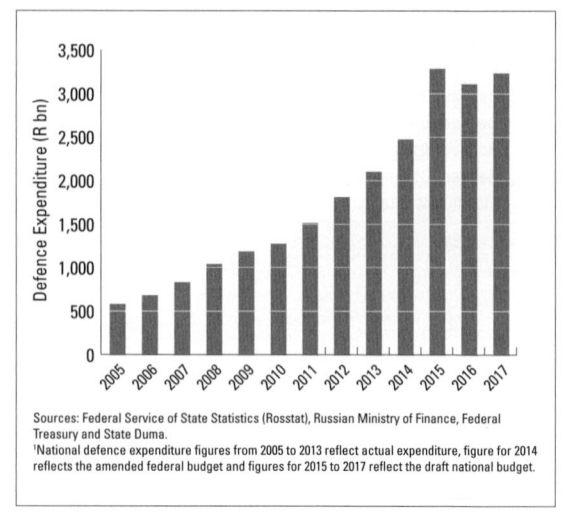

Sources: Federal Service of State Statistics (Rosstat), Russian Ministry of Finance, Federal Treasury and State Duma.
[1] National defence expenditure figures from 2005 to 2013 reflect actual expenditure, figure for 2014 reflects the amended federal budget and figures for 2015 to 2017 reflect the draft national budget.

Figure 9 **Russia Defence Expenditure Trends (2005–17)**[1]

The Ukraine crisis & Russia's defence industry in 2014

The conflict in Ukraine posed new problems for Russia's defence industry, in particular the decision by Ukraine's new president, Petro Poroshenko, to prohibit all military cooperation with Russia. While the overall volume of Ukrainian military deliveries to Russia has been relatively modest, there are several major dependencies that could create difficulties. The most significant are Ukraine's significant role as a supplier of engines for some Russian-built helicopters and fixed-wing aircraft, the supply of power units for ships (including some of the new surface vessels now being built under the State Armaments Programme) and the role of Ukrainian enterprises in keeping Russia's RS-20 (SS-18 *Satan*) heavy ICBMs in operational use. The Russian government has either adopted an import substitution programme to secure domestic production of military materiel currently supplied by Ukraine, or it has turned to Belarus to augment supply chains. Additionally, some Ukrainian aircraft- and shipbuilding-sector workers are reported to have transferred to Russia following the loss of their jobs, although the extent and impact that this influx of skilled labour will have on Russian defence production is unclear. Deputy Prime Minister Dmitry Rogozin stated that Russia will need two to three years to achieve independence from Ukrainian inputs, but this is probably overly optimistic. Full import substitution will require billions of dollars' worth of investment, and will likely take at least five to ten years to achieve.

Sanctions imposed by the United States and the European Union on the defence sector – including measures against specific Russian companies – are unlikely to have a significant impact on the implementation of the State Armaments Programme, principally because there has been no far-reaching defence-industrial integration with Western states. More significant threats to Russia's military-modernisation efforts are moves by the West to restrict its access to dual-use technologies. Russia's defence industry will likely be hard hit by a cessation of European electronic-component imports, and may come to rely more heavily on China and other Asian producers for substitutes. Russia's ambitious programme to modernise its defence-industrial production base will also be affected. With few exceptions, the domestic machine-tool industry is unable to produce the advanced equipment required. Consequently, Russian defence-industrial plants have been buying advanced machine tools and other production equipment in significant quantities from leading European, Japanese and US firms, and the state-owned arms manufacturer Rostec Corporation has been organising joint enterprises with some of these companies in Russia.

Table 4 **Russian Arms Procurement 2011–13 & Approximate State Armaments Programme 2020 Objectives**

	2011	2012	2013	2014 State Defence Order	Total to 2020
ICBMs	7	9	15*	15*	400+
SLBMs	20*	15*	15*		
Military Satellites[a]	9	6	15		100+
Fixed-wing aircraft	28	35	67	100	850*
of which combat aircraft	16*	30*	45*		450*
Helicopters	82	118	100	90*	1,120
of which combat helicopters	22	35	31		350*
UAVs			15		4,000+
S-400 air-defence systems (divisions)	2	2	2	2	56
Strategic nuclear submarines	0	0	2	1	8
Multi-role nuclear submarines	0	0	0	1	7
Diesel-electric submarines	0	0	0	1	8 to 10
Surface combat ships[b]	1	1	1	4	50
Tanks					2,300+
Iskander missile systems (brigades)			2	2	10

*Estimates
[a]Total number, excluding failed launches; [b]Mainly frigates and corvettes

the defence sector itself. From 10 September 2014, responsibility for the MIC passed to the Presidential Administration, with President Vladimir Putin as chairperson, Deputy Prime Minister Dmitry Rogozin (previously chair) as deputy chair and Yurii Borisov, deputy defence minister for armaments, as secretary. It is likely that this move will lead to the MIC having powers similar to those enjoyed by its Soviet forerunner. Before this decision, two specialist agencies involved in arms acquisition – Rosoboronpostavka, which procures about a third of all military hardware for the defence ministry, and Rosoboronzakaz, which monitors all procurement activity – were dissolved and their powers transferred to the defence and industry ministries, and to other government departments. In effect, these measures restored key features of the Soviet system of arms procurement.

The previous defence minister, Anatoly Serdyukov, had attempted to change the arms acquisition system to enhance the power of the defence ministry as a customer, weakening the dominance of defence-industry suppliers – a legacy of the Soviet Union. He also began opening up the arms market to foreign participation, challenging the Soviet-era autarkic orientation. This new policy was symbolised by the 2011 contract to buy two *Mistral*-class amphibious-assault ships from France. Under the current minister, Sergei Shoigu, this partial internationalisation has been halted, with no new foreign deals, although some contracts that had been agreed were continued, such as the domestic manufacture under licence of Israeli unmanned aerial vehicles. Recent political and strategic developments have served to reinforce this reversion to self-reliance.

CENTRAL ASIA

The trend continues of growing Russian interest in Central Asian security. In May 2014, the Kazakh Parliament ratified the Joint Air-Defence Agreement with Russia. This had been signed in 2013, and headquarters are due to be located at Almaty. In October 2013, and after considerable delay, Tajikistan's president Emomalii Rahmon signed a decree confirming a 30-year extension to the basing rights for Russia's 201st Motor-rifle Division. The division, with some 7,000 troops, is Russia's largest foreign deployment, mainly at Dushanbe, though Russia maintains additional facilities in Tajikistan at Kulob and Qurghonteppa. Meanwhile, Moscow promised to assist in the modernisation of the Tajik armed forces by providing military-technical assistance. In February, Russia announced the reinforcement of Kant Air Base in Kyrgyzstan with four additional Su-25 *Frogfoot* ground-attack aircraft, to join the eight already there. Russia has also tried to professionalise the deployment, by shifting its staffing structure away from conscripts towards contract soldiers. Kyrgyzstan did not offer the United States an extension for its Air Transit Center at Manas, and the base closed on 3

June 2014 after providing support to US operations in Afghanistan for more than 12 years. There is speculation as to whether the US is seeking alternative basing rights in Uzbekistan, but for the time being a facility at Romania's Mihail Kogalniceanu Air Base has replaced those offered at Manas.

Central Asian states have not publicly expressed strong views on Russian intervention in Ukraine. Kazakhstan, with a 6,800km border with Russia and a 25% ethnic-Russian population, is probably the most uneasy; however it is in a very different geopolitical situation to Ukraine and has a close economic relationship with Russia through the emerging Eurasian Economic Union. Kazakhstan's concerns are partly economic – sanctions that weaken the Russian economy indirectly weaken its own. The Tenge was devalued in February 2014 and additional delays to production in the Kashagan oil field, in the Kazakh zone of the Caspian Sea, could affect confidence in the economy. Downturns in the Russian economy also particularly affect Tajikistan, where approximately 50% of GDP consists of remittances provided by migrant labour in Russia.

The impact of the end of NATO's combat operations in Afghanistan and the drawdown of personnel and equipment continue to be discussed in Central Asia. Turkmenistan and Uzbekistan, bordering Afghanistan, may feel the effect of any ongoing instability more than Kazakhstan; though the greatest impact will be felt in Tajikistan, where a porous 1,400km border with Afghanistan makes combating narcotics trafficking a particular challenge. In June 2014 there was further unrest in Gorno-Badakhshan Autonomous Province, with disturbances related to the narcotics trade, prompting fears of action by Tajik security forces, as happened in 2013.

Russia continues to promote the Collective Security Treaty Organization (CSTO) as a means of reaching low-level security agreements in Central Asia. However, the disparity in economic wealth between the five Central Asian states has led to differing national military capabilities, and the programme of CSTO summits, meetings and exercises places demands on the limited resources of Kazakhstan, Kyrgyzstan and Tajikistan. (Uzbekistan suspended membership in 2013 and Turkmenistan has never been a member.) Exercise scenarios are generally anti-terrorist-related, though it remains unlikely, analysts assess, that KSOR (the CSTO Collective Rapid Reaction Force) will assist Tajikistan with Afghan border control. In September 2014 President Vladimir Putin submitted to the Duma for ratification a 2009 agreement to create, according to Moscow, 'a secure command system for the forces and resources of the Collective Security Treaty Organisation collective security system'.

In autumn 2014, Kazakhstan's Peacekeeping Brigade (KAZBRIG) exercised for the first time in Europe. A company-level deployment was rehearsed, using Kazakh C-295 transport aircraft, and interoperability training with NATO units took place during the *Steppe Eagle* exercise at Joint Multinational Command Training Centre Hohenfels, Germany. Late in 2013, Kazakhstan passed a law to enable the deployment of Kazakh personnel on UN missions, and, with ambitions for non-permanent UN Security Council membership in 2017, the country retains a desire to improve capability through engagement with NATO.

The third biennial Kazakhstan Defence Equipment Exhibition took place in May 2014, with representatives of 208 companies from 28 countries participating. The defence ministry demonstrated Kazakhstan's land and air capabilities, which are still based on Russian-built equipment, and made clear an ambition to improve the armed forces' equipment. The goal to develop joint ventures between state-owned Kazakhstan Engineering and Western companies to enable technology transfer continues, but excessive levels of bureaucracy and a number of high-profile corruption cases, most noticeably with the conviction of a deputy minister of defence, have resulted in companies from outside the Commonwealth of Independent States exercising caution.

UKRAINE

The crisis in Ukraine during 2014 altered the European security landscape, bringing to the fore antagonism between Russia and the West not seen since the Cold War. The broader political and economic factors that had for some years fed this growing distrust on the geopolitical level are analysed in *Strategic Survey 2014* (pp. 151–64), but the crisis began as a domestic political dispute in Ukraine in response to the government's failure to sign an expected Association Agreement with the EU and culminated in a cycle of escalatory violence that led on 19–20 February to some 70 anti-government protesters being killed.

As state authority collapsed, President Viktor Yanukovych fled Kiev, even though a 21 February agreement brokered by the EU and Russia, designed to return Ukraine to the 2004 constitution, meant he

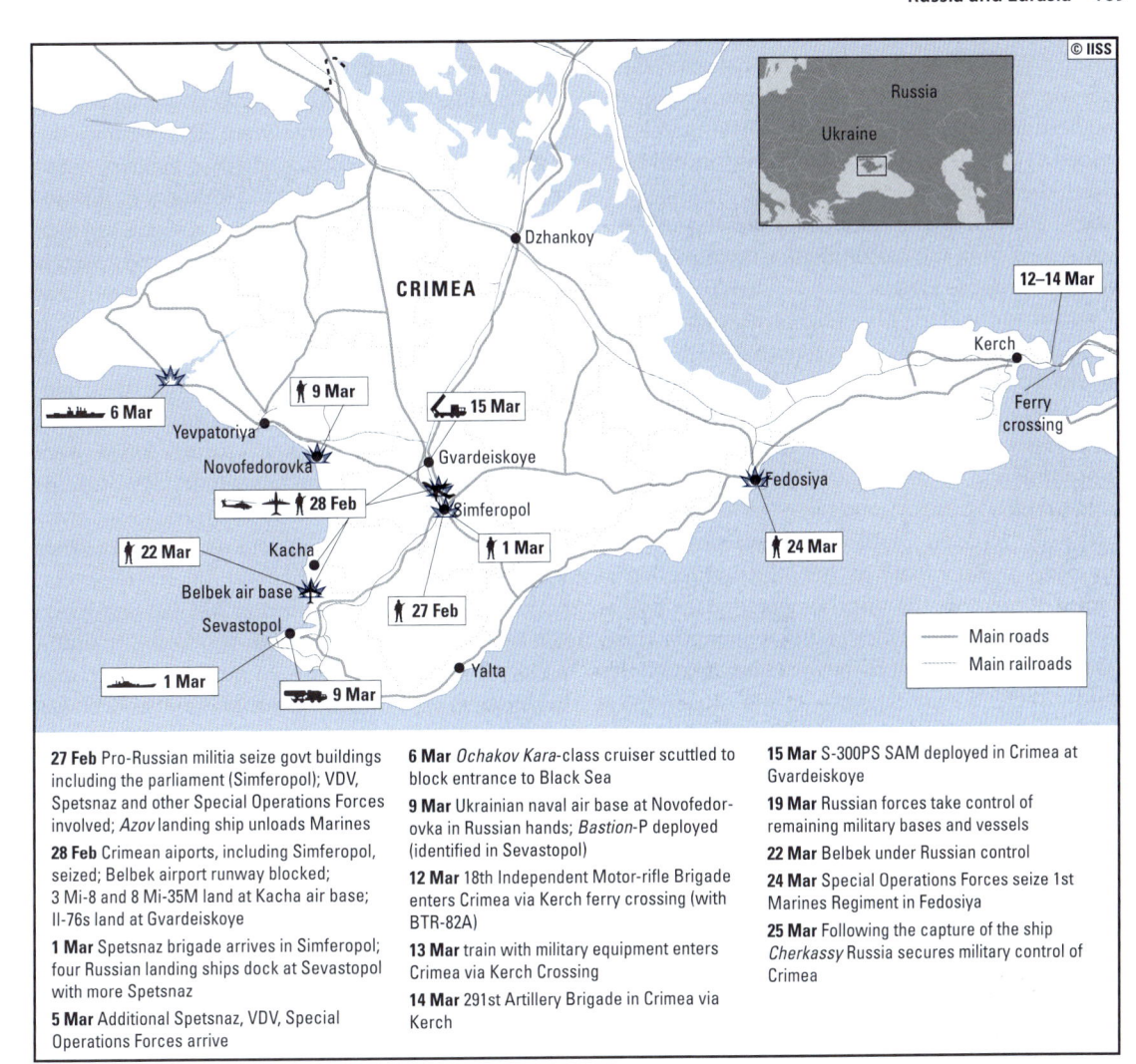

Map 4 **Russia Seizes Crimea**

27 Feb Pro-Russian militia seize govt buildings including the parliament (Simferopol); VDV, Spetsnaz and other Special Operations Forces involved; *Azov* landing ship unloads Marines

28 Feb Crimean aiports, including Simferopol, seized; Belbek airport runway blocked; 3 Mi-8 and 8 Mi-35M land at Kacha air base; Il-76s land at Gvardeiskoye

1 Mar Spetsnaz brigade arrives in Simferopol; four Russian landing ships dock at Sevastopol with more Spetsnaz

5 Mar Additional Spetsnaz, VDV, Special Operations Forces arrive

6 Mar *Ochakov Kara*-class cruiser scuttled to block entrance to Black Sea

9 Mar Ukrainian naval air base at Novofedorovka in Russian hands; *Bastion*-P deployed (identified in Sevastopol)

12 Mar 18th Independent Motor-rifle Brigade enters Crimea via Kerch ferry crossing (with BTR-82A)

13 Mar train with military equipment enters Crimea via Kerch Crossing

14 Mar 291st Artillery Brigade in Crimea via Kerch

15 Mar S-300PS SAM deployed in Crimea at Gvardeiskoye

19 Mar Russian forces take control of remaining military bases and vessels

22 Mar Belbek under Russian control

24 Mar Special Operations Forces seize 1st Marines Regiment in Fedosiya

25 Mar Following the capture of the ship *Cherkassy* Russia secures military control of Crimea

could have stayed in power until at least December. In a constitutionally controversial move, parliament voted on 22 February to remove him from office and change the government, but this new administration significantly shifted the balance of internal Ukrainian regional representation. Two-thirds of Yanukovych's administration hailed from Ukraine's south and east. By contrast, 60% of the new administration came from the west of Ukraine.

Russia's leadership regarded events in Kiev as a coup, and feared that this new administration would move Ukraine rapidly towards EU and NATO membership. Moscow was also concerned for the future of Russia's Black Sea Fleet, headquartered at Sevastopol in Crimea. For President Vladimir Putin, the 'interests of the Russian nation and the Russian state' were at stake.

The seizure of Crimea

The Russian decision to deploy force to Crimea was driven by fear of losing its Black Sea Fleet base, but it was also an attempt to coerce Kiev into accommodating broader Russian demands. On 27–28 February, ostensibly pro-Russia militiamen, described as 'local self-defence forces', seized the parliament building in Simferopol. However, 'it was obvious that the operation to seize the Crimean parliament was carried out by an unidentified but very professional special task force', according to analysts at Moscow's Centre for Analysis of Strategies and Technologies. Larger groups of unidentified troops in unmarked uniforms, who took up posts outside Ukrainian military bases and key infrastructure locations, were also clearly well equipped, organised and highly trained; these were also Russian troops, a presence that was denied by Moscow until April. Nearly all, analysts believe, were from elite special-operations groups from the Southern Military District and the Airborne Assault Troops (VDV), some inserted covertly in advance, with others subsequently deployed in waves of rotary- and fixed-wing airlift. Personnel were also despatched from the naval infantry units co-located with the Black Sea Fleet.

Ukrainian military personnel at bases in Crimea were instructed by the Russian troops to defect, disarm or surrender but, though warning shots were fired, neither side engaged in combat. Russian troops were evidently under instruction to exercise fire-control and, as far as possible, secure objectives without bloodshed. Meanwhile, Ukrainian troops reportedly received conflicting or no orders from a ministry in Kiev that was doubtless struggling to come to terms with the surprise operation, as well as working to unpick details about the strength, objectives and broader intent of the invading force; all this amid a revolutionary situation in the capital and a newly installed cabinet. Internationally, Ukrainian defence officials had to contend with the cognitive dissonance created by the continual, if increasingly unconvincing, denials from Moscow that the so-called 'little green men' were in fact Russian troops.

Under intense pressure, some Ukrainian troops defected while others disarmed and eventually left Crimea. Some Ukrainian helicopters had managed to leave Belbek air base, but other aircraft could not because the runway had been blocked. These included MiG-29 combat aircraft; over half of Ukraine's MiG-29 fleet had been stationed at Belbek. The Russians later allowed some of these aircraft to leave by road convoy, while other military supplies, including armoured vehicles and naval vessels, were also returned to Ukraine. The Ukrainian Coast Guard was able to withdraw most of its fleet from Crimea, but naval vessels were blockaded, and most seized by Russia. A number of Ukrainian installations held out for nearly a month, but, hemmed in by tight Russian (and pro-Russia militia) blockades, they had all fallen by 25 March, when the last naval vessel, the *Cherkassy*, was seized by Russian commandos.

Ukraine's armed forces

By 2014, Ukraine's armed forces were a shadow of those the country had inherited after the collapse of the Soviet Union. They operated mainly Soviet-era equipment, with much of this in need of upgrade or replacement. Defence spending remained stubbornly low, consistently at around 1% of GDP in recent years. While the services suffered from inadequate financing, defence reforms were also significantly underfunded. The Ukrainian defence ministry noted in a 2012 white paper that the weakness in defence legislation and insufficient budget affected training, readiness and combat capability. Procurement targets were routinely missed and plans to end conscription by 2011 were not achieved. This plan was revived in 2013, and it was declared that the autumn draft would be the last. Unsurprisingly, conscription was reinstated in May 2014, after fighting broke out in the east.

As of early 2014, Ukraine's armed forces were showing the effects of cumulative funding reductions and changes in government priorities away from defence. Aircraft availability and serviceability levels were low, as were flying hours. While there was on paper an impressive number of MiG-29 and Su-27 combat aircraft, problems with serviceability and a policy of keeping a significant number of airframes in storage meant the total available combat fleet was much smaller; this was laid bare by the situation at Belbek, where only a limited proportion of the fixed-wing combat-aircraft fleet was operational at any one time.

Conflict in Ukraine's east

A contentious plebiscite on 16 March, in which a reported 97% of voters backed union with Russia, was 'held under the watchful eye of Russian servicemen in unmarked uniforms'. It was followed five days later by Russia's annexation of the Crimean peninsula. Growing diplomatic and economic pressure on Russia after this, coupled with intensified Western overtures to Ukraine, led Moscow to ratchet up pressure on Kiev. Snap military inspections were launched just over the border at the end of March, where Russian forces remained encamped, in strength, for some time.

In early April, an insurrection began to gather steam in the east, and armed separatists and pro-Russian activists seized government buildings in cities in Donetsk and Luhansk regions. Kiev launched an 'anti-terrorist' operation in response, deploying the regular armed forces and the newly created (and poorly trained) national guard, supported by paramilitary groups. *Strategic Survey 2014* notes that 'the decision to designate [the insurgency] a terrorist movement was likely to deepen the civil conflict', given that many in the east reportedly viewed the Kiev government as illegitimate or at least unrepresentative

The emergence of a pro-Russian separatist movement in eastern Ukraine in 2014, centred in the Donetsk and Luhansk oblasts, and supported by armed militia, has led to bitter military confrontation with forces loyal to Kiev. Slovyansk, some 150km west of Luhansk, marked the most westerly extent of separatist gains by April. The city was retaken in early July 2014 as the government's initially faltering counter-offensive gained strength. By the first week in August, state forces had effectively surrounded Luhansk, while there was heavy fighting between government and separatist forces in Donetsk. Now under heavy pressure themselves, the separatists were able to launch an offensive in the far south of the Dontesk region at the end of August, seizing Novoazovsk and advancing toward Mariupol on the coast. This was part of a broader effort – with significant Russian support – to push back the Ukrainian armed forces and to regain as much territory as possible. Government forces pulled back from Luhansk airport at the beginning of September while fighting continued throughout October despite a 5 September truce, including around Donetsk and its airport. In early November both NATO and the OSCE reported new sightings of unmarked military columns with heavy weaponry inside separatist-held areas.

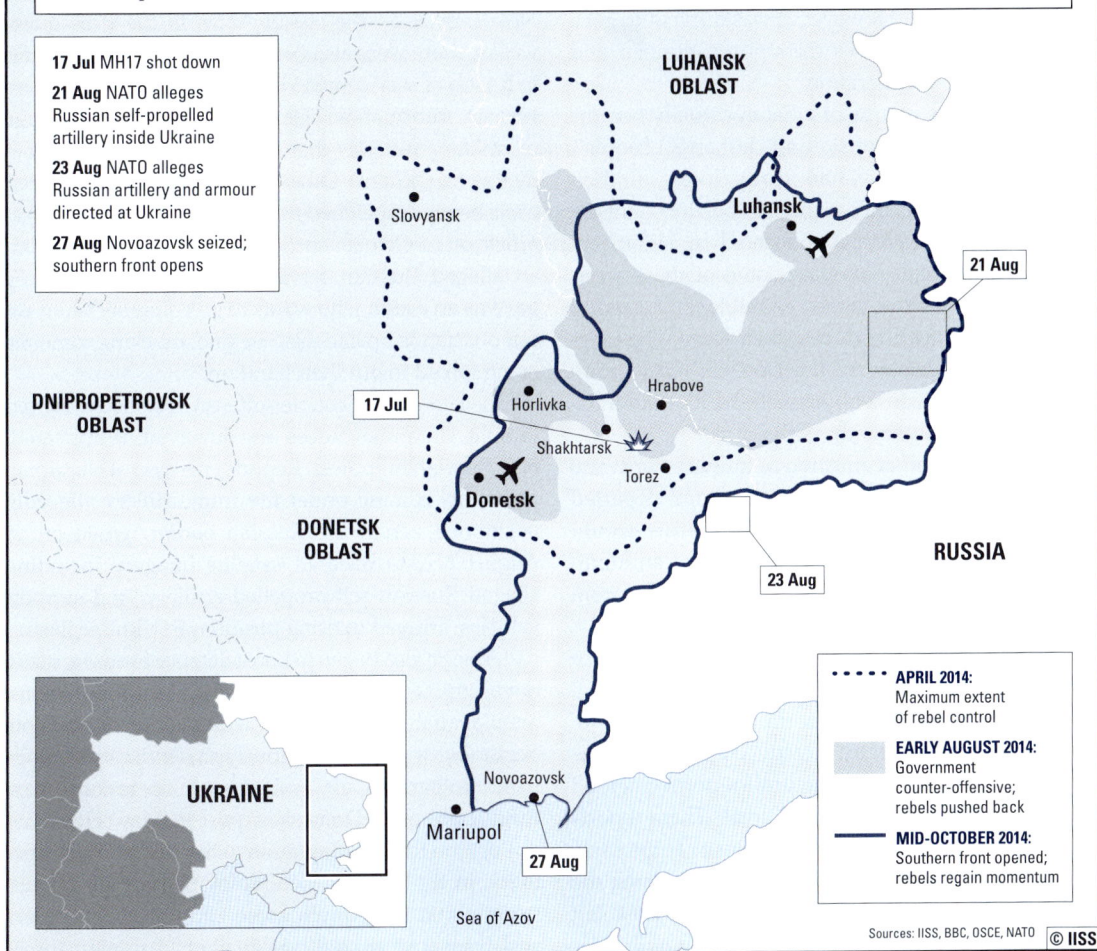

17 Jul MH17 shot down
21 Aug NATO alleges Russian self-propelled artillery inside Ukraine
23 Aug NATO alleges Russian artillery and armour directed at Ukraine
27 Aug Novoazovsk seized; southern front opens

APRIL 2014: Maximum extent of rebel control
EARLY AUGUST 2014: Government counter-offensive; rebels pushed back
MID-OCTOBER 2014: Southern front opened; rebels regain momentum

Sources: IISS, BBC, OSCE, NATO © IISS

Map 5 **Conflict in Eastern Ukraine**

of the country as a whole. This problem was exacerbated by Ukrainian tactics of engaging urban areas with long-range unguided munitions before sending in troops. During the conflict, they employed long-range artillery, mortars and multiple-barrel rocket launchers. However, the tactics used on both sides had negative consequences. Indeed, both government and rebel forces made much use of artillery before ground assaults; a reflection, perhaps, of their shared Soviet military heritage. Human Rights Watch (HRW) also alleged the use of cluster munitions by Ukrainian forces, though HRW later said that 'there are also serious allegations that pro-Russian rebel forces, and possibly Russia itself, have used cluster munitions in eastern Ukraine. All parties to the conflict in eastern Ukraine have access to similar weapons, so it is not always possible to draw definitive conclusions with respect to specific attacks.'

Negative consequences also arose from the relative lack of training and professional discipline on the part of irregular forces. Amnesty International chronicled human-rights abuses perpetrated by the volunteer battalions in areas formerly held by separatists, while it also said there was 'no doubt that summary killings and atrocities are being committed by both pro-Russian separatists and pro-Kyiv forces in Eastern Ukraine'. However, it was difficult to get a sense of the scale of abuses, the report continued, and there was much exaggeration.

The insurgent groups of what eventually became the self-declared Donetsk and Luhansk People's Republics undoubtedly had many locals in their ranks, including former regional Interior Ministry troops, but they were also bolstered by significant numbers of Russian nationals; some of these were, according to Moscow, either ex-military or serving personnel volunteering during their leave. The long-time 'defence minister' of the Donetsk rebel group was a Russian citizen who had left the Russian intelligence service only months earlier.

The rebels' rapid acquisition of military hardware raised interest. Once government troops departed from military bases in the east, separatists would have had access to remaining weapons, ammunition and armour, but weapons were also seized from government troops and volunteer fighters.

Reports of Russian military-intelligence presence among the rebels continued throughout the spring, but, initially, there was little in the way of hard, open-source evidence to directly connect Moscow to operations in east Ukraine until reports emerged of Russian armour in rebel-held areas. These reports had increased in frequency by mid-year, at the same time as government forces seemed to be gaining the upper hand in parts of the east. On 5 July rebels left a command centre at Slovyansk and a month later fighting broke out in Donetsk, Luhansk having been encircled two days before. On 17 July Malaysian Airlines flight MH17 was shot down, coming down near the town of Hrabove in Donetsk Oblast and killing nearly 300 people onboard. The aircraft was widely believed to have been brought down by an advanced surface-to-air missile system, possibly a *Buk*, and allegations persisted that the engagement was conducted from within rebel-held areas.

As Ukrainian forces continued to advance on the rebels, evidence of direct Russian involvement grew. Alleged Russian servicemen were shown, as prisoners, on Ukrainian television on 26 August (Moscow said they crossed the border by mistake), while IISS analysis of imagery at the same time assessed that some main battle tanks seen in separatist hands were likely to be Russian. The variant shown, the T-72BM, was only operated by Russian ground forces. Government gains seemed to force Moscow's hand, and reports of direct involvement grew dramatically after 27 August, when a new front opened up in the south, near Novoazovsk on the Sea of Azov. In the subsequent weeks, there were also press reports of 'secret' burials in Russia of servicemen killed on operations and there was an information clampdown there on coverage of military funerals that might be linked to combat deaths in Ukraine. Other reports pointed to formed units being despatched from Russia. A *Financial Times* article on 22 October carried the following quote from an alleged Russian serviceman in Luhansk: '"They gave us an order: who wants to go volunteer? And we put our hands up like this," he said, mocking someone being forced to put their hand up.'

The late-August counter-offensive seemed designed to split Ukrainian forces and involved, it appeared, new Russian firepower. Reports emerged of Ukrainian personnel coming under fire from artillery allegedly positioned across the Russian border, while on 28 August NATO released satellite imagery including alleged Russian self-propelled artillery, and support vehicles, arrayed in firing positions in Ukraine itself.

Ukraine also began to boost defence funding, using novel crowd-funding methods (see p. 173), and equipment availability improved, with maintenance plants beginning to repair previously unserviceable equipment. Integrated air and ground operations were conducted, as at Donetsk airport in May. However, opposition forces' adaptation to this developing capability, in the form of the employment of air-defence screens that shot down some Ukrainian helicopters and transport aircraft, meant that Ukrainian forces also had to keep changing tactics.

The ebb and flow of conflict in Ukraine's east was restrained, but not halted, by a ceasefire signed on 5 September. The period of conflict from February 2014 will have given Ukraine's armed forces pointers for the future: tactics and doctrines that had dominated since the 1990s, mainly inherited from the Soviet-era, have generally been unsuited to the current fighting amid urban areas and among populations. As time progressed, many of Kiev's ground operations were conducted either by special forces or by limited numbers of combat-ready general forces, but most prominently by irregular forces formed as volunteer battalions – some of these from rightist groups and others financed by the country's tycoons. Conventional army and interior-ministry structures were often employed to carry out combat support or combat service support tasks. Volunteer battalions were nominally subordinated to either the defence or interior ministries, but this seemed a formality, as many operated with little coordination with, or support from, formal government forces. Regularising these groups and their tactics will be a significant challenge for a government struggling with a multi-faceted crisis.

Future training and force development could focus on more flexible regular formations, able to conduct coordinated operations with the national guard and volunteer battalions. Although some older equipment is being brought out of store to replace attrition losses, Kiev will likely, in the long run, look to procure equipment suitable for modern requirements. This could include mine-resistant ambush-protected vehicles and equipment that has demonstrated its effectiveness during 2014, such as precision artillery rockets.

Defence economics

Even before the Crimea crisis erupted, Ukraine's economy was faltering due to a combination of high levels of state intervention in markets, a challenging business climate and poor domestic macroeconomic policymaking. Declining investment levels, weak external demand and tight monetary policy – employed to defend the Ukrainian Hryvnia exchange-rate peg – combined to draw the economy into recession in mid-2012, where it remained as the crisis began in March 2014. As the year progressed, growing political uncertainty slowed domestic consumption and industrial production levels; overall economic contraction in 2014 was projected to be -6.5%. Capital flight placed downward pressure on the pegged exchange rate, which was abandoned in February 2014 as the international reserves required to defend it were depleted. Despite a US$17 billion IMF loan facility agreed in April, the collapsing currency reached record lows over the course of the year, placing strain on the banking sector and raising the possibility that the government might default on its external-debt obligations.

Ukraine prioritised its defence budget amid this broader economic pressure, and reduced health, agriculture and welfare budgets in order to augment defence spending. The existing budget law for 2014 was revised in March to allocate around UAH40.53bn (US$3.59bn) towards defence and security (including funding for the interior ministry), which the government claimed as a 15.6% nominal increase over 2013 levels. This was supplemented by a UAH6.9bn (US$611 million) general budget reserve fund and a UAH5bn (US$442m) special defence and security reserve fund, bringing total defence and security outlays in 2014 to UAH52.4bn (US$4.64bn). Separately, in March, the defence ministry established a 'Support the Ukrainian Army' fund for private citizens and business to contribute donations via text messages or bank transfers, which would fund medical and logistics support. By November 2014, this had raised UAH151m (US$13.4m). In addition, there were numerous reported instances of small-scale, non-governmental assistance provided by local residents or business groups to supply their local battalions with equipment (e.g. ammunition, bullet-proof vests), although much of this remains undocumented, and there were also international initiatives to supply non-lethal equipment to Ukraine. Overall, most of these funding increments are estimated to have been channelled towards the land, air and joint forces; expenditure on land and air forces more than doubled in 2014, and spending on joint forces increased by around 77%. By contrast, allocations to the navy fell by more than a fifth. Despite these efforts, in July the finance minister stated that high operational and maintenance spending had meant that the government was running out of funds to pay salaries, and in response proposed new tax measures and subsidy reforms to expand the fiscal space available in the national budget.

Longer-term funding increases were announced later in 2014: in August the president announced that some US$3bn (around UAH34bn) would be assigned to re-equip the army, while in September the finance minister proposed an allocation of UAH63bn (US$4.88bn) for defence and security in the draft 2015 budget. Then, in October, the government announced – as part of its 'Strategy 2020' programme – that it was planning a fivefold increase in the defence budget by 2020, to 5% of GDP, financed by new taxes on salaries, goods and housing. However, Ukraine has in the past underspent its initially planned budgetary allocations, and in the current climate it is difficult to estimate the degree to which these aspirations reflect realistic budgetary projections.

Armenia ARM

Armenian Dram d		2013	2014	2015
GDP	d	4.27tr	4.59tr	
	US$	10.4bn	11.1bn	
per capita	US$	3,173	3,373	
Growth	%	3.5	3.2	
Inflation	%	5.8	1.8	
Def bdgt [a]	d	188bn	194bn	
	US$	458m	470m	
FMA (US)	US$	2.7m	2.7m	1.7m
US$1=d		409.63	412.81	

[a] Includes imported military equipment, excludes military pensions

Population 3,060,927

Age	0–14	15–19	20–24	25–29	30–64	65 plus
Male	9.8%	3.4%	4.2%	4.7%	21.4%	4.2%
Female	9.3%	3.3%	4.3%	4.8%	24.2%	6.3%

Capabilities

Given continuing tensions with neighbouring Azerbaijan over Nagorno-Karabakh, the armed forces' main focus is territorial defence. Armenia is a CSTO member, and Russia provides national air defence from a leased base. Conscription continues, but there is also a growing cohort of professional officers. Equipment is mainly of Russian origin, and serviceability and maintenance of mainly ageing aircraft has been a problem for the air force. While overall military doctrine remains influenced strongly by Russian thinking, overseas deployments, including to ISAF in Afghanistan, have enabled personnel to learn from international counterparts. The country aims to develop its peacekeeping contingent into one brigade with NATO standards, so that Armenia can deploy a battalion capable of self-sustainment and interoperability with NATO forces. However, defence ties with Russia continue on a broad range of issues, and both countries signed a cooperation agreement in 2014. Armenia completed a Strategic Defence Review in May 2011 and has also signed an Individual Partnership Action Plan with NATO.

ACTIVE 44,800 (Army 41,850 Air/AD Aviation Forces (Joint) 1,100 other Air Defence Forces 1,850) **Paramilitary 4,300**

Conscript liability 24 months.

RESERVES some mob reported, possibly 210,000 with military service within 15 years.

ORGANISATIONS BY SERVICE

Army 22,900; 18,950 conscripts (total 41,850)
FORCES BY ROLE
SPECIAL FORCES
  1 SF regt
MANOEUVRE
  Mechanised
  1 (1st) corps (1 recce bn, 1 tk bn, 2 MR regt, 1 maint bn)
  1 (2nd) corps (1 recce bn, 1 tk bn, 2 MR regt, 1 lt inf regt, 1 arty bn)
  1 (3rd) corps (1 recce bn, 1 tk bn, 4 MR regt, 1 lt inf regt, 1 arty bn, 1 MRL bn, 1 sigs bn, 1 maint bn)
  1 (4th) corps (4 MR regt; 1 SP arty bn; 1 sigs bn)
  1 (5th) corps (with 2 fortified areas) (1 MR regt)
  Other
  1 indep MR trg bde
COMBAT SUPPORT
  1 arty bde
  1 MRL bde
  1 AT regt
  1 AD bde
  2 AD regt
  1 (radiotech) AD regt
  1 engr regt
EQUIPMENT BY TYPE
MBT 109: 3 T-54; 5 T-55; 101 T-72
AIFV 98: 75 BMP-1; 6 BMP-1K; 5 BMP-2; 12 BRM-1K
APC (W) 130: 8 BTR-60; 100 look-a-like; 18 BTR-70; 4 BTR-80
ARTY 232
  SP 38: **122mm** 10 2S1; **152mm** 28 2S3
  TOWED 131: **122mm** 69 D-30; **152mm** 62: 26 2A36; 2 D-1; 34 D-20
  MRL 51: **122mm** 47 BM-21; **273mm** 4 WM-80
  MOR 120mm 12 M120
AT • MSL • SP 22: 9 9P148; 13 9P149
AD
  SAM
    SP 2K11 *Krug* (SA-4 *Ganef*); 2K12 *Kub* (SA-6 *Gainful*); 9K33 *Osa* (SA-8 *Gecko*)
    TOWED S-75 *Dvina* (SA-2 *Guideline*); S-125 *Pechora* (SA-3 *Goa*)
    MANPAD 9K310 *Igla-1* (SA-16 *Gimlet*); 9K38 *Igla* (SA-18 *Grouse*)
  GUNS
    SP ZSU-23-4
    TOWED 23mm ZU-23-2
UAV Light 15 *Krunk*
RADAR • LAND 6 SNAR-10
MSL • TACTICAL • SSM 12: 8 9K72 *Elbrus* (SS-1C *Scud B*); 4 9K79 *Tochka* (SS-21 *Scarab*)
AEV MT-LB
ARV BREhM-D; BREM-1

Air and Air Defence Aviation Forces 1,100

1 Air & AD Joint Command
FORCES BY ROLE
GROUND ATTACK
  1 sqn with Su-25/Su-25UBK *Frogfoot*
EQUIPMENT BY TYPE
AIRCRAFT 15 combat capable
  ATK 15: 13 Su-25 *Frogfoot*; 2 Su-25UBK *Frogfoot*
  TPT 3: **Heavy** 2 Il-76 *Candid*; **PAX** 1 A319CJ
  TRG 14: 4 L-39 *Albatros*; 10 Yak-52

HELICOPTERS
ATK 7 Mi-24P *Hind*
ISR 4: 2 Mi-24K *Hind*; 2 Mi-24R *Hind* (cbt spt)
MRH 10 Mi-8MT (cbt spt)
C2 2 Mi-9 *Hip* G (cbt spt)
TPT • Light 7 PZL Mi-2 *Hoplite*
SAM • SP S-300/S-300PM (SA-10/SA-20)

Paramilitary 4,300

Ministry of Internal Affairs
FORCES BY ROLE
MANOEUVRE
  Other
    4 paramilitary bn
EQUIPMENT BY TYPE
AIFV 55: 5 BMD-1; 44 BMP-1; 1 BMP-1K; 5 BRM-1K
APC (W) 24 BTR-60/BTR-70/BTR-152

Border Troops
Ministry of National Security
EQUIPMENT BY TYPE
AIFV 43: 5 BMD-1; 35 BMP-1; 3 BRM-1K
APC (W) 23: 5 BTR-60; 18 BTR-70

DEPLOYMENT
Legal provisions for foreign deployment:
Constitution: Codified constitution (1995, amended 2005)
Specific legislation: 'Law on Defence of the Republic of Armenia'
Decision on deployment of troops abroad: by the president, in accordance with 'Law on Defence of the Republic of Armenia' (Article 5 (2) (1)). Also, under Art. 55 (13) of constitution, president can call for use of armed forces (and National Assembly shall be convened). (Also Art. 81 (3) of constitution.)

AFGHANISTAN
NATO • ISAF 121

LEBANON
UN • UNIFIL 1

SERBIA
NATO • KFOR 36

UKRAINE
OSCE • Ukraine 2

FOREIGN FORCES
OSCE figures represent total Minsk Conference mission personnel in both Armenia and Azerbaijan
Bulgaria OSCE 1
Czech Republic OSCE 1
Poland OSCE 1
Russia 3,300: 1 mil base with (1 MR bde; 74 T-72; 80 BMP-1; 80 BMP-2; 12 2S1; 12 BM-21); 1 ftr sqn with 18 MiG-29 *Fulcrum*; 2 SAM bty with S-300V (SA-12 *Gladiator/Giant*); 1 SAM bty with 2K12 *Kub* (SA-6 *Gainful*)
Sweden OSCE 1
Ukraine OSCE 1

Azerbaijan AZE

Azerbaijani New Manat m		2013	2014	2015
GDP	m	57.7bn	60.5bn	
	US$	73.5bn	77.9bn	
per capita	US$	7,900	8,303	
Growth	%	5.8	4.5	
Inflation	%	2.4	2.8	
Def exp	m	2.75bn		
	US$	3.5bn		
Def bdgt [a]	m	1.53bn	1.64bn	
	US$	1.95bn	2.11bn	
FMA (US)	US$	2.7m	2.7m	1.7m
US$1=m		0.78	0.78	

[a] Official defence budget. Excludes a significant proportion of procurement outlays.

Population 9,686,210

Age	0 – 14	15 – 19	20 – 24	25 – 29	30 – 64	65 plus
Male	12.1%	4.2%	5.2%	4.8%	20.7%	2.4%
Female	10.5%	3.9%	5.0%	4.6%	22.7%	3.9%

Capabilities

Given continuing tensions with neighbouring Armenia over Nagorno-Karabakh, a major focus for the armed forces is territorial defence. While they have yet to successfully transition from a Soviet-era model, rising oil revenues have allowed an increase in defence expenditure, providing the opportunity to acquire additional platform capabilities, including the Russian S-300 SAM system. However, it is unclear whether the potential benefits brought by such modern systems have been felt in terms of operational capability. The armed forces still rely on conscription, and readiness within the services varies between units. The air force also suffers from training and maintenance problems, and the armed forces cannot organically support external deployments. Azerbaijan maintains defence relationships with NATO through an Individual Partnership Action Plan, and has a close military relationship with Turkey. US military assistance has included support to maritime-security operations in the Caspian Sea. Peacekeeping deployments have included a small number of personnel in Afghanistan.

ACTIVE 66,950 (Army 56,850 Navy 2,200 Air 7,900)
Paramilitary 15,000
Conscript liability 17 months, but can be extended for ground forces.

RESERVE 300,000
Some mobilisation reported; 300,000 with military service within 15 years

ORGANISATIONS BY SERVICE

Army 56,850

FORCES BY ROLE
COMMAND
5 corps HQ
MANEOEUVRE
Mechanised
4 MR bde
Light
19 MR bde
Other
1 sy bde
COMBAT SUPPORT
1 arty bde
1 arty trg bde
1 MRL bde
1 AT bde
1 engr bde
1 sigs bde
COMBAT SERVICE SUPPORT
1 log bde
EQUIPMENT BY TYPE
MBT 433: 95 T-55; 244 T-72; 94 T-90S
AIFV 218: 20 BMD-1; 43 BMP-1; 33 BMP-2; 100 BMP-3; 15 BRM-1; 7 BTR-80A
APC 568
 APC (T) 336 MT-LB
 APC (W) 142: 10 BTR-60; 132 BTR-70
 PPV 90: 45 *Marauder*; 45 *Matador*
ARTY 542
 SP 87: **122mm** 46 2S1; **152mm** 24: 6 2S3; 18 2S19 *Msta-S*; **155mm** 5 ATMOS-2000; **203mm** 12 2S7
 TOWED 207: **122mm** 129 D-30; **130mm** 36 M-46; **152mm** 42: 18 2A36; 24 D-20
 GUN/MOR 120mm 36: 18 2S9 NONA; 18 2S31 *Vena*
 MRL 100+: **122mm** 52+: 43 BM-21; 9+ IMI *Lynx*; **128mm** 12 RAK-12; **220mm** 6 TOS-1A; **300mm** 30 9A52 *Smerch*
 MOR 120mm 112: 5 CARDOM; 107 PM-38
AT • MSL • MANPATS 9K11 *Malyutka* (AT-3 *Sagger*); 9K111 *Fagot* (AT-4 *Spigot*); 9K113 *Konkurs* (AT-5 *Spandrel*); 9K115 *Metis* (AT-7 *Saxhorn*); *Spike*-LR
AD • SAM • SP 2K11 *Krug* (SA-4 *Ganef*); 9K33 *Osa* (SA-8 *Gecko*)‡; 9K35 *Strela*-10 (SA-13 *Gopher*); 9K37M *Buk*-M1 (SA-11 *Gadfly*)
MANPAD 9K32 *Strela* (SA-7 *Grail*;) 9K34 *Strela*-3; (SA-14 *Gremlin*); 9K310 *Igla*-1 (SA-16 *Gimlet*); 9K338 *Igla*-S (SA-24 *Grinch*)
MSL • SSM ε4 9M79 *Tochka* (SS-21 *Scarab*)
RADAR • LAND SNAR-1 *Long Trough*/SNAR-2/-6 *Pork Trough* (arty); *Small Fred*/*Small Yawn*/SNAR-10 *Big Fred* (veh, arty); GS-13 *Long Eye* (veh)
UAV • ISR • Medium 3 *Aerostar*
AEV MT-LB
MW *Bozena*

Navy 2,200
EQUIPMENT BY TYPE
PATROL AND COASTAL COMBATANTS 8
 CORVETTES • FS 1 *Kusar* (ex-FSU *Petya II*) with 2 RBU 6000 *Smerch* 2, 2 twin 76mm gun
 PSO 1 *Luga* (*Woodnik* 2 Class) (FSU Project 888; additional trg role)
 PCC 3: 2 *Petrushka* (FSU UK-3; additional trg role); 1 *Shelon* (ex-FSU Project 1388M)
 PB 3: 1 *Araz* (ex-TUR AB 25); 1 *Bryza* (ex-FSU Project 722); 1 *Poluchat* (ex-FSU Project 368)
MINE WARFARE • MINE COUNTERMEASURES 4
 MHC 4: 2 *Yevgenya* (FSU Project 1258); 2 *Yakhont* (FSU *Sonya*)
AMPHIBIOUS 6
 LSM 3: 1 *Polnochny A* (FSU Project 770) (capacity 6 MBT; 180 troops); 2 *Polnochny B* (FSU Project 771) (capacity 6 MBT; 180 troops)
 LCU 1 *Vydra*† (FSU) (capacity either 3 AMX-30 MBT or 200 troops)
 LCM 2 T-4 (FSU)
LOGISTICS AND SUPPORT 4
 AGS 1 (FSU Project 10470)
 YTB 2
 YTD 1

Air Force and Air Defence 7,900
FORCES BY ROLE
FIGHTER
 1 sqn with MiG-29 *Fulcrum*
FIGHTER/GROUND ATTACK
 1 regt with MiG-21 *Fishbed*; Su-17 *Fitter*; Su-24 *Fencer*; Su-25 *Frogfoot*; Su-25UB *Frogfoot* B
TRANSPORT
 1 sqn with An-12 *Cub*; Yak-40 *Codling*
ATTACK/TRANSPORT HELICOPTER
 1 regt with Mi-8 *Hip*; Mi-24 *Hind*; PZL Mi-2 *Hoplite*
EQUIPMENT BY TYPE
AIRCRAFT 44 combat capable
 FTR 14 MiG-29 *Fulcrum*
 FGA 11: 4 MiG-21 *Fishbed* (1 more in store); 4 Su-17 *Fitter*; 1 Su-17U *Fitter*; 2 Su-24 *Fencer*†
 ATK 19: 16 Su-25 *Frogfoot*; 3 Su-25UB *Frogfoot* B
 TPT 4: **Medium** 1 An-12 *Cub*; **Light** 3 Yak-40 *Codling*
 TRG 40: 28 L-29 *Delfin*; 12 L-39 *Albatros*
HELICOPTERS
 ATK 26 Mi-24 *Hind*
 MRH 20+ Mi-17-IV *Hip*
 TPT 20: **Medium** 13 Mi-8 *Hip*; **Light** 7 PZL Mi-2 *Hoplite*
UAV • ISR • Medium 4 *Aerostar*
AD • SAM S-75 *Dvina* (SA-2 *Guideline*); S-125 *Neva* (SA-3 *Goa*); /S-200 *Vega* (SA-5 *Gammon*) static; S-300PM/PMU2 (SA-20 *Gargoyle*)
MSL • AAM • IR R-60 (AA-8 *Aphid*); R-73 (AA-11 *Archer*)
IR/SARH R-27 (AA-10 *Alamo*)

Paramilitary ε15,000

Border Guard ε5,000
Ministry of Internal Affairs
EQUIPMENT BY TYPE
AIFV 168 BMP-1/2
APC (W) 19 BTR-60/70/80
ARTY • MRL 122mm 3 T-122
HELICOPTERS • ATK 24 Mi-35M *Hind*

Coast Guard
The Coast Guard was established in 2005 as part of the State Border Service.
EQUIPMENT BY TYPE
PATROL AND COASTAL COMBATANTS 12
  PBF 8: 1 *Osa* II (FSU Project 205); 2 *Shaldag* V; 2 Silver Ships 48ft; 3 *Stenka*
  PB 4: 2 Baltic 150; 1 *Point* (US); 1 *Grif* (FSU *Zhuk*)
LOGISTICS AND SUPPORT • **ARS** 1 *Iva* (FSU *Vikhr*)

Militia 10,000+
Ministry of Internal Affairs
EQUIPMENT BY TYPE
APC (W) 7 BTR-60/BTR-70/BTR-80

DEPLOYMENT
Legal provisions for foreign deployment:
Constitution: Codified constitution (1995)
Decision on deployment of troops abroad: By parliament upon proposal by president (Art. 109, No. 28)

AFGHANISTAN
NATO • ISAF 94

FOREIGN FORCES
OSCE figures represent total Minsk Conference mission personnel in both Armenia and Azerbaijan
Bulgaria OSCE 1
Czech Republic OSCE 1
Poland OSCE 1
Sweden OSCE 1
Ukraine OSCE 1

TERRITORY WHERE THE GOVERNMENT DOES NOT EXERCISE EFFECTIVE CONTROL

Data presented here represents an assessment of the de facto situation. Nagorno-Karabakh was part of the Azerbaijani Soviet Socialist Republic (SSR), but mostly populated by ethnic Armenians. In 1988, when inter-ethnic clashes between Armenians and Azeris erupted in Azerbaijan, the local authorities declared their intention to secede from Azerbaijan and join the Armenian SSR. Baku rejected this and armed conflict erupted. A ceasefire was brokered in 1994. All ethnic Azeris had been expelled from Nagorno-Karabakh and almost all ethnic Armenians were forced to leave Azerbaijan. Since 1994, Armenia has controlled most of Nagorno-Karabakh, and also seven adjacent regions of Azerbaijan, often called the 'occupied territories'. While Armenia provides political, economic and military support to Nagorno-Karabakh, the region has declared itself independent – although this has not been recognised by any other state, including Armenia. Azerbaijan claims, and the rest of the international community generally regards, Nagorno-Karabakh and the occupied territories as part of Azerbaijan. (See IISS Strategic Comment, *Medvedev momentum falters in Nagorno-Karabakh*, August 2011.)

Available estimates vary with reference to military holdings in Nagorno-Karabakh. Main battle tanks are usually placed at around 200–300 in number, with similar numbers for armoured combat vehicles and artillery pieces, with small numbers of fixed- and rotary-wing aviation. Available personnel number estimates are between 18,000–20,000. (See p. 491.)

Belarus BLR

Belarusian Ruble r		2013	2014	2015
GDP	r	637tr	820tr	
	US$	71.7bn	77.2bn	
per capita	US$	7,577	8,195	
Growth	%	0.9	0.9	
Inflation	%	18.3	18.6	
Def exp	r	ε6.05tr		
	US$	ε681m		
US$1=r		8,879.99	10,630.36	

Population 9,608,058

Age	0–14	15–19	20–24	25–29	30–64	65 plus
Male	7.9%	2.5%	3.4%	4.3%	23.9%	4.5%
Female	7.5%	2.4%	3.3%	4.1%	26.5%	9.7%

Capabilities

The primary role of the armed forces is to protect territorial integrity. The announcement that a Russian air base will be set up in Belarus in 2016, housing Su-27 combat aircraft, will provide additional air capability within the country. Much of the military inventory consists of ageing Soviet-era equipment. Air-combat capabilities could be bolstered by plans to upgrade its Su-27s and there are also plans to procure UAVs. The Belarusian defence relationship with Russia includes regular joint exercises, and Minsk could notionally support a regional joint operation with Moscow. However, with the exception of the 5th Spetsnaz Bde, ground-force capability is probably limited – although snap inspections began at the start of 2014 to try and improve readiness. In 2014 Moscow approved the donation of an unknown number of S-300PM SAM systems to Belarus. Minsk is exploring defence-industrial cooperation with Russia, but capacity limitations in the Belarusian defence industry will limit substantive cooperation. Belarus is currently under EU and US sanctions and an arms embargo is in place.

ACTIVE 48,000 (Army 16,500 Air 15,000 Special Operations Forces 6,000 Joint 10,500) **Paramilitary 110,000**

RESERVE 289,500 (Joint 289,500 with mil service within last 5 years)

ORGANISATIONS BY SERVICE

Army 16,500

FORCES BY ROLE
COMMAND
  2 comd HQ (West & North West)
MANOEUVRE
  Mechanised
  2 mech bde
  2 mech bde(-)
COMBAT SUPPORT
  2 arty bde
  2 MRL regt
  2 engr regt
  1 NBC regt
EQUIPMENT BY TYPE
MBT 515: 446 T-72; 69 T-80
AIFV 1,011: 875 BMP-2; 136 BRM-1
APC • APC (T) 50 MT-LB
ARTY 957
  SP 434: **122mm** 198 2S1; **152mm** 236: 108 2S3; 116 2S5; 12 2S19 *Farm*
  TOWED 152mm 180: 48 2A36; 132 2A65
  GUN/MOR 120mm 48 2S9 NONA
  MRL 234: **122mm** 126 BM-21; **220mm** 72 9P140 *Uragan*; **300mm** 36 9A52 *Smerch*
  MOR 120mm 61 2S12
AT • MSL
  SP 236: 126 9P148 *Konkurs*; 110 9P149 *Shturm*
  MANPATS 9K111 *Fagot* (AT-4 *Spigot*); 9K113 *Konkurs* (AT-5 *Spandrel*); 9K114 *Shturm* (AT-6 *Spiral*); 9K115 *Metis* (AT-7 *Saxhorn*)
RADAR • LAND GS-13 *Long Eye*/SNAR-1 *Long Trough*/SNAR-2/-6 *Pork Trough* (arty); some *Small Fred/Small Yawn*/SNAR-10 *Big Fred* (veh, arty)
MSL • TACTICAL • SSM 96: 36 FROG/9M79 *Tochka* (SS-21 *Scarab*); 60 *Scud*
AEV MT-LB
VLB MTU

Air Force and Air Defence Forces 15,000

Flying hours 15 hrs/year
FORCES BY ROLE
FIGHTER
  2 sqn with MiG-29S/UB *Fulcrum*
GROUND ATTACK
  2 sqn with Su-25K/UBK *Frogfoot* A/B
TRANSPORT
  1 base with An-12 *Cub*; An-24 *Coke*; An-26 *Curl*; Il-76 *Candid*; Tu-134 *Crusty*
TRAINING
  Some sqn with L-39 *Albatros*
ATTACK HELICOPTER
  Some sqn with Mi-24 *Hind*
TRANSPORT HELICOPTER
  Some (cbt spt) sqn with Mi-6 *Hook*; Mi-8 *Hip*; Mi-24K *Hind* G2; Mi-24R *Hind* G1; Mi-26 *Halo*
EQUIPMENT BY TYPE
AIRCRAFT 72 combat capable
  FTR 38 MiG-29S/UB *Fulcrum*
  FGA (21 Su-27P/UB *Flanker* B/C non-operational)
  ATK 34 Su-25K/UBK *Frogfoot* A/B
  TPT 13: **Heavy** 2 Il-76 *Candid* (+9 civ Il-76 available for mil use); **Medium** 3 An-12 *Cub*; **Light** 8: 1 An-24 *Coke*; 6 An-26 *Curl*; 1 Tu-134 *Crusty*
  TRG Some L-39 *Albatros*
HELICOPTERS
  ATK 49 Mi-24 *Hind*
  ISR 20: 8 Mi-24K *Hind* G2; 12 Mi-24R *Hind* G1
  TPT 168: **Heavy** 43: 29 Mi-6 *Hook*; 14 Mi-26 *Halo*; **Medium** 125 Mi-8 *Hip*
MSL
  ASM Kh-25 (AS-10 *Karen*); Kh-29 (AS-14 *Kedge*)
  ARM Kh-58 (AS-11 *Kilter*)
  AAM • IR R-60 (AA-8 *Aphid*); R-73 (AA-11 *Archer*)
  SARH R-27R (AA-10 *Alamo* A)

Air Defence

AD data from Uzal Baranovichi EW radar
FORCES BY ROLE
AIR DEFENCE
  1 bde with S-200 (SA-5 *Gammon*)
  1 bde with S-200 (SA-5 *Gammon*); S-300PS (SA-10B *Grumble*)
  1 bde with S-300V(SA-12A *Gladiator*/SA-12B *Giant*)
  1 bde with 9K37 *Buk* (SA-11 *Gadfly*)
  1 bde with 9K37 *Buk* (SA-11 *Gadfly*); 9K332 *Tor*-M2E (SA-15 *Gauntlet*)
  2 bde with 9K33 *Osa* (SA-8 *Gecko*)
  2 regt with S-300PS (SA-10B *Grumble*)
  1 regt with S-200 (SA-5 *Gammon*)
EQUIPMENT BY TYPE
AD • SAM
  SP 9K37 *Buk* (SA-11 *Gadfly*); S-300V(SA-12A *Gladiator*/SA-12B *Giant*); 9K35 *Strela*-10 (SA-13 *Gopher*); 9K33 *Osa* (SA-8 *Gecko*); S-300PS (SA-10B *Grumble*); 12 9K332 *Tor*-M2E (SA-15 *Gauntlet*)
  TOWED S-125 *Pechora* (SA-3 *Goa*)
  STATIC S-200 (SA-5 *Gammon*)

Special Operations Forces 6,000

FORCES BY ROLE
SPECIAL FORCES
  1 SF bde
MANOEUVRE
  Mechanised
  2 (mobile) mech bde
EQUIPMENT BY TYPE
APC • APC (W) 192: 39 BTR-70; 153 BTR-80
ARTY • TOWED 122mm 48 D-30
AT • MSL • MANPATS 9K111 *Fagot* (AT-4 *Spigot*); 9K113 *Konkurs* (AT-5 *Spandrel*); 9K114 *Shturm* (AT-6 *Spiral*); 9K115 *Metis* (AT-7 *Saxhorn*)

Joint 10,500 (Centrally controlled units and MoD staff)

FORCES BY ROLE
COMBAT SUPPORT
  1 arty gp
  1 MRL bde
  2 SSM bde
  2 engr bde
  1 EW unit

1 ptn bridging regt
2 sigs bde

EQUIPMENT BY TYPE
APC • **APC (T)** 20 MT-LB
ARTY 196
  SP 152mm 70 2S5
  TOWED 152mm 90 2A65
  300mm 36 9A52 *Smerch*
MSL • TACTICAL • SSM 96: 36 FROG/9M79 *Tochka* (SS-21 *Scarab*); 60 *Scud*

Paramilitary 110,000

Border Guards 12,000
Ministry of Interior

Militia 87,000
Ministry of Interior

Ministry of Interior Troops 11,000

DEPLOYMENT

LEBANON
UN • UNIFIL 2

SOUTH SUDAN
UN • UNMISS 4 obs

UKRAINE
OSCE • Ukraine 1

FOREIGN FORCES

Russia 1 ftr flt with 5 Su-27 *Flanker*; 1 A-50 *Mainstay*; 4 SAM units with S-300 (SA-10 *Grumble*)

Georgia GEO

Georgian Lari		2013	2014	2015
GDP	lari	26.8bn	29.2bn	
	US$	16.1bn	16.1bn	
per capita	US$	3,597	3,607	
Growth	%	3.2	5.0	
Inflation	%	-0.5	4.6	
Def bdgt	lari	660m	711m	750m
	US$	397m	393m	
FMA (US)	US$	14m	12m	10m
US$1=lari		1.66	1.81	
Population	4,935,880			

Age	0 – 14	15 – 19	20 – 24	25 – 29	30 – 64	65 plus
Male	9.3%	3.2%	4.1%	4.0%	21.2%	6.0%
Female	8.3%	2.8%	3.9%	4.0%	23.8%	9.3%

Capabilities

Georgia's armed forces continue to make efforts to address lessons from the conflict with Russia in 2008, which revealed significant shortcomings in key areas, including reservist organisation, communications, anti-armour and air-defence capabilities. A substantial amount of US-supplied equipment was destroyed or captured in the conflict, and Georgia lost a number of its Russian-origin T-72 MBTs. The Israeli short-range *Spyder* system was subsequently acquired to bolster the air-defence capability and rapid-reaction special forces have improved capabilities through training and exercising. A 2012 enhanced defence-cooperation agreement with the US will provide training in cyber defence, border security, military-education development and counter-insurgency operations. Moves are under way to generate a pool of four-year-contract servicemen to boost professionalisation. Current plans call for the small air force – comprising Soviet-era ground-attack aircraft, combat-support helicopters and transport and utility helicopters – to merge with the army. Georgia deployed personnel to ISAF in Afghanistan, and has aspirations for NATO membership. Training activity involves international forces, including the US.

ACTIVE 20,650 (Army 17,750 Air 1,300 National Guard 1,600) **Paramilitary 11,700**
Conscript liability 18 months

ORGANISATIONS BY SERVICE

Army 14,000; 3,750 conscript (total 17,750)
FORCES BY ROLE
SPECIAL FORCES
  1 SF bde
MANOEUVRE
  Light
  5 inf bde
  Amphibious
  2 mne bn (1 cadre)
COMBAT SUPPORT
  2 arty bde
  1 engr bde
  1 sigs bn
  1 SIGINT bn
  1 MP bn
COMBAT SERVICE SUPPORT
  1 med bn
EQUIPMENT BY TYPE
MBT 123: 23 T-55; 100 T-72
RECCE 4+ *Didgori*-2
AIFV 72: 25 BMP-1; 46 BMP-2; 1 BRM-1K
APC 199+
  APC (T) 69+: 3+ *Lazika*; 66 MT-LB
  APC (W) 120+: 25 BTR-70; 19 BTR-80; 8+ *Didgori*-1; 3+ *Didgori*-3; 65 *Ejder*
  PPV 10 *Cougar*
ARTY 240
  SP 67 **152mm** 66: 32 DANA; 20 2S1; 13 2S3; 1 2S19; **203mm** 1 2S7
  TOWED 71: **122mm** 58 D-30; **152mm** 13: 3 2A36; 10 2A65
  MRL 122mm 37: 13 BM-21; 6 GRADLAR; 18 RM-70
  MOR 120mm 65: 14 2S12; 33 M-75; 18 M120

AT ε50
  MSL ε10
  GUNS ε40
AD • SAM • SP 9K35 *Strela-10* (SA-13 *Gopher*); *Spyder*
  MANPAD *Grom*; 9K32 *Strela-2* (SA-7 *Grail*)‡; 9K36 *Strela-3* (SA-14 *Gremlin*); 9K310 *Igla-1* (SA-16 *Gimlet*)

Air Force 1,300 (incl 300 conscript)

1 avn base, 1 hel air base

EQUIPMENT BY TYPE
AIRCRAFT 12 combat capable
  ATK 12: 3 Su-25 *Frogfoot*; 7 Su-25K *Frogfoot* A; 2 Su-25UB *Frogfoot* B
  TPT • Light 9: 6 An-2 *Colt*; 1 Tu-134A *Crusty* (VIP); 2 Yak-40 *Codling*
  TRG 9 L-29 *Delfin*
HELICOPTERS
  ATK 6 Mi-24 *Hind*
  TPT 29 Medium 17 Mi-8T *Hip*; Light 12 Bell 205 (UH-1H *Iroquois*)
UAV • ISR • Medium 1+ *Hermes* 450
AD • SAM 1–2 bn 9K37 *Buk*-M1 (SA-11 *Gadfly*), 8 9K33 *Osa*-AK (SA-8B *Gecko*) (two bty), 6-10 9K33 *Osa*-AKM updated SAM systems.

National Guard 1,600 active reservists opcon Army

FORCES BY ROLE
MANOEUVRE
  Light
    1 inf bde

Paramilitary 11,700

Border Guard 5,400

Coast Guard

HQ at Poti. The Navy was merged with the Coast Guard in 2009 under the auspices of the Georgian Border Guard, within the Ministry of the Interior.

EQUIPMENT BY TYPE
PATROL AND COASTAL COMBATANTS 21
  PBF 6: 4 Ares 43m; 1 *Kaan* 33; 1 *Kaan* 20
  PB 15: 1 *Akhmeta*; 2 *Dauntless*; 2 *Dilos* (ex-GRC); 1 *Kutaisi* (ex-TUR AB 25); 2 *Point*; 7 *Zhuk* (3 ex-UKR) (up to 20 patrol launches also in service)
AMPHIBIOUS • LANDING CRAFT • LCU 1 *Vydra* (ex-BLG)
LOGISTIC AND SUPPORT • YTL 1

Ministry of Interior Troops 6,300

DEPLOYMENT

Legal provisions for foreign deployment of armed forces:
Constitution: Codified constitution (1995)
Decision on deployment of troops abroad: By the presidency upon parliamentary approval (Art. 100)

AFGHANISTAN
NATO • ISAF 755; 1 mtn inf bn

CENTRAL AFRICAN REPUBLCI
NATO • ISAF 140; 1 inf coy

SERBIA
OSCE • Kosovo 4

UKRAINE
OSCE • Ukraine 1

TERRITORY WHERE THE GOVERNMENT DOES NOT EXERCISE EFFECTIVE CONTROL

Following the August 2008 war between Russia and Georgia, the areas of Abkhazia and South Ossetia declared themselves independent. Data presented here represents the de facto situation and does not imply international recognition as sovereign states.

FOREIGN FORCES

Russia 7,000; 1 mil base at Gudauta (Abkhazia) with (1 MR bde; 40 T-90A; 120 BTR-82A; 18 2S3; 12 2S12; 18 BM-21; some S-300 SAM; some atk hel); 1 mil base at Djava/Tskhinvali (S. Ossetia) with (1 MR bde; 40 T-72; 120 BMP-2; 36 2S3; 12 2S12)

Kazakhstan KAZ

Kazakhstani Tenge t		2013	2014	2015
GDP	t	35.3tr	40.3tr	
	US$	232bn	226bn	
per capita	US$	13,509	12,950	
Growth	%	6.0	4.6	
Inflation	%	5.8	6.9	
Def bdgt	t	348bn	363bn	377bn
	US$	2.29bn	2.03bn	
FMA (US)	US$	1.8m	1.5m	0.8m
US$1=t		152.13	178.68	

Population 17,948,816

Ethnic groups: Kazakh 51%; Russian 32%; Ukrainian 5% ; German 2% ; Tatar 2% ; Uzbek 13%

Age	0 – 14	15 – 19	20 – 24	25 – 29	30 – 64	65 plus
Male	12.5%	3.7%	4.5%	4.7%	20.1%	2.4%
Female	12.6%	3.5%	4.4%	4.7%	22.4%	4.6%

Capabilities

Kazakhstan's armed forces are small and reliant on Soviet-era equipment. A 2011 Military Doctrine identified both internal and external security concerns, and risks from regional instability, but there were few force-structure changes detailed, with much focus on the development of Kazakhstan's defence industry. Kazakhstan maintains a close defence relationship with Russia, reinforced through its membership of the CSTO and SCO. Moscow operates a radar station at Balkash, and seeks to include Kazakhstan in a regional air-defence network for the CSTO. As such, Russia is aiming to provide S-300PS air-defence systems gratis from its own stocks and in May 2014 a Joint Air-Defence Agreement was ratified. In the army, air-mobile units are held at the highest level of readiness, with other units at lower levels. There are ongoing efforts to improve the navy and the air force, with modest procurement projects under way. Airlift is being improved, with joint ventures and production envisaged with European companies for rotary-wing and medium-lift fixed-wing aircraft and continued receipt of the C-295. However, airworthiness remains problematic. The navy, meanwhile, is seeking to procure its first corvette from overseas designs.

ACTIVE 39,000 (Army 20,000 Navy 3,000 Air 12,000 MoD 4,000) **Paramilitary 31,500**
Conscript liability 12 months

ORGANISATIONS BY SERVICE

Army 20,000
4 regional comd: Astana, East, West and Southern
FORCES BY ROLE
MANOEUVRE
  Armoured
  1 tk bde
  Mechanised
  4 mech bde
  Air Manoeuvre
  4 air aslt bde
COMBAT SUPPORT
  3 arty bde
  1 SSM unit
  3 cbt engr bde
EQUIPMENT BY TYPE
MBT 300 T-72
RECCE 100: 40 BRDM; 60 BRM
AIFV 652: 500 BMP-2; 107 BTR-80A; 43 BTR-82A; 2 BTR-3E
APC 357
  APC (T) 150 MT-LB
  APC (W) 207: 190 BTR-80; 17 *Cobra*
ARTY 602
  SP 246: **122mm** 126: 120 2S1; 6 *Semser*; **152mm** 120 2S3
  TOWED 150: **122mm** 100 D-30; **152mm** 50 2A65; (**122mm** up to 300 D-30 in store)
  GUN/MOR 120mm 25 2S9 *Anona*
  MRL 118: **122mm** 100 BM-21 *Grad*; **300mm** 18 *Lynx* (with 50 msl); (**122mm** 100 BM-21 *Grad*; **220mm** 180 9P140 *Uragan* all in store)
  MOR 63 **SP 120mm** 18 CARDOM **120mm** 45 2B11/M120
AT
  MSL
    SP 3 BMP-T
    MANPATS 9K111 *Fagot* (AT-4 *Spigot*); 9K113 *Konkurs* (AT-5 *Spandrel*); 9K115 *Metis* (AT-6 *Spiral*)
  GUNS 100mm 68 MT-12/T-12

MSL • SSM 12 9K79 *Tochka* (SS-21 *Scarab*)
AEV MT-LB

Navy 3,000
PATROL AND COASTAL COMBATANTS 17
  PCG 1 *Kazakhstan* with 2 quad lnchr with 3424 *Uran* (SS-N-25 *Switchblade*) AShM, 1 *Ghibka* lnchr with SA-N-10 *Gimlet* SAM
  PBF 5: 3 *Sea Dolphin*; 2 *Saygak*;
  PB 15: 4 *Almaty*; 3 *Archangel*; 1 *Dauntless*; 4 *Sardar*; 1 *Turk* (AB 25); 2 *Zhuk* (of which 1 may be operational)
LOGISTICS AND SUPPORT • AGS 1 *Zhaik*

Coastal Defence
MANOEUVRE
  Other
  1 coastal defence bde

Air Force 12,000 (incl Air Defence)
Flying hours 100 hrs/year
FORCES BY ROLE
FIGHTER
  1 sqn with MiG-29/MiG-29UB *Fulcrum*
  2 sqn with MiG-31/MiG-31BM *Foxhound*
FIGHTER/GROUND ATTACK
  2 sqn with MiG-27 *Flogger* D; MiG-23UB *Flogger* C
  2 sqn with Su-27/Su-27UB *Flanker*
GROUND ATTACK
  1 sqn with Su-25 *Frogfoot*
TRANSPORT
  1 unit with Tu-134 *Crusty*; Tu-154 *Careless*,
  1 sqn with An-12 *Cub*, An-26 *Curl*, An-30 *Clank*, An-72 *Coaler*
TRAINING
  1 sqn with L-39 *Albatros*
ATTACK HELICOPTER
  5 sqn with Mi-24V *Hind*
TRANSPORT HELICOPTER
  Some sqn with Bell 205 (UH-1H); EC145; Mi-8 *Hip*; Mi-17V-5 *Hip*; Mi-26 *Halo*
AIR DEFENCE
  Some regt with S-75M *Volkhov* (SA-2 *Guideline*); S-125 *Neva* (SA-3 *Goa*); S-300 (SA-10 *Grumble*); 2K11 *Krug* (SA-4 *Ganef*); S-200 *Angara* (SA-5 *Gammon*); 2K12 *Kub* (SA-6 *Gainful*)
EQUIPMENT BY TYPE
AIRCRAFT 122 combat capable
  FTR 55: 12 MiG-29 *Fulcrum*; 2 MiG-29UB *Fulcrum*; 41 MiG-31/MiG-31BM *Foxhound*
  FGA 53: 24 MiG-27 *Flogger* D; 4 MiG-23UB *Flogger* C; 21 Su-27 *Flanker*; 4 Su-27UB *Flanker*
  ATK 14: 12 Su-25 *Frogfoot*; 2 Su-25UB *Frogfoot*
  ISR 1 An-30 *Clank*
  TPT 15: **Medium** 2 An-12 *Cub*; **Light** 12; 6 An-26 *Curl*, 2 An-72 *Coaler*; 2 C-295; 2 Tu-134 *Crusty*; **PAX** 1 Tu-154 *Careless*
  TRG 17 L-39 *Albatros*
HELICOPTERS
  ATK 40+ Mi-24V *Hind* (first 9 upgraded)
  MRH 20 Mi-17V-5 *Hip*

TPT 64: **Heavy** 2 Mi-26 *Halo*; **Medium** 50 Mi-8 *Hip*;
Light 12: 6 Bell-205 (UH-1H); 6 EC145
AD • **SAM** 147+
SP 47+: 20 2K12 *Kub* (SA-6 *Gainful*); 27+ 2K11 *Krug* (SA-4 *Ganef*)/S-200 *Angara* (SA-5 *Gammon*); static; S-300 (SA-10 *Grumble*)
TOWED 100 S-75M *Volkhov* (SA-2 *Guideline*); S-125 *Neva* (SA-3 *Goa*)
MSL
ASM Kh-23 (AS-7 *Kerry*)‡; Kh-25 (AS-10 *Karen*); Kh-29 (AS-14 *Kedge*)
ARM Kh-28 (AS-9 *Kyle*); Kh-27 (AS-12 *Kegler*); Kh-58 (AS-11 *Kilter*)
AAM • IR R-60 (AA-8 *Aphid*); R-73 (AA-11 *Archer*); IR/SARH R-27 (AA-10 *Alamo*); SARH R-33 (AA-9 *Amos*); ARH R-77 (AA-12 *Adder* – on MiG-31BM)

Paramilitary 31,500

Government Guard 500

Internal Security Troops ε20,000
Ministry of Interior

Presidential Guard 2,000

State Border Protection Forces ε9,000
Ministry of Interior
PATROL AND COASTAL COMBATANTS
HEL • TPT • **Medium** 1 Mi-171

DEPLOYMENT

WESTERN SAHARA
UN • MINURSO 2 obs

Kyrgyzstan KGZ

Kyrgyzstani Som s		2013	2014	2015
GDP	s	350bn	391bn	
	US$	7.23bn	7.65bn	
per capita	US$	1,280	1,342	
Growth	%	10.5	4.1	
Inflation	%	6.6	8.0	
Def bdgt [a]	s	4.91bn	4.87bn	
	US$	101m	95m	
FMA (US)	US$	1.5m	1.5m	
US$1=s		48.45	51.16	

[a] Expenses on Ministry of Defence & Ministry of Interior.

Population 5,604,212

Ethnic groups: Kyrgyz 56%; Russian 17%; Uzbek 13%; Ukrainian 3%

Age	0–14	15–19	20–24	25–29	30–64	65 plus
Male	15.2%	4.7%	5.2%	4.8%	17.3%	1.9%
Female	14.5%	4.5%	5.1%	4.7%	19.1%	3.0%

Capabilities

Kyrgyzstan maintains one of the smaller armed forces in Central Asia, with ageing land equipment, limited air-combat capabilities and no navy. A new military doctrine was enacted in July 2013, setting out possible threats to the state and plans to reform the armed forces. The reform plans promise, among other things, modern armed forces with enhanced command-and-control, effective military logistics and a modern air-defence system, adding the term 'mobilisation readiness'. In general, combat readiness remains low with large numbers of poorly trained conscripts within the armed forces. For these reasons, Kyrgyzstan has a close strategic relationship with Russia, being a member of both the CSTO and the SCO. Moscow maintains a modest presence of strike and transport aircraft in Kant air base, which it has leased since 2003, and in February 2014 Russia announced that four additional Su-25 *Frogfoot* ground-attack aircraft would be based there. Kyrgyzstan did not offer the US an extension for its presence at Manas air base, which closed in June 2014.

ACTIVE 10,900 (Army 8,500 Air 2,400) **Paramilitary 9,500**
Conscript liability 18 months

ORGANISATIONS BY SERVICE

Army 8,500
FORCES BY ROLE
SPECIAL FORCES
  1 SF bde
MANOEUVRE
  Mechanised
  2 MR bde
  1 (mtn) MR bde
COMBAT SUPPORT
  1 arty bde
  1 AD bde
EQUIPMENT BY TYPE
MBT 150 T-72
RECCE 30 BRDM-2
AIFV 320: 230 BMP-1; 90 BMP-2
APC (W) 35: 25 BTR-70; 10 BTR-80
ARTY 246
  SP **122mm** 18 2S1
  TOWED 141: **100mm** 18 M-1944; **122mm** 107: 72 D-30; 35 M-30 (M-1938); **152mm** 16 D-1
  GUN/MOR **120mm** 12 2S9 *Anona*
  MRL 21: **122mm** 15 BM-21; **220mm** 6 9P140 *Uragan*
  MOR **120mm** 54: 6 2S12; 48 M-120
AT • MSL • MANPATS 9K11 (AT-3 *Sagger*); 9K111 (AT-4 *Spigot*); 9K113 (AT-5 *Spandrel*)
  RCL **73mm** SPG-9
  GUNS **100mm** 18 MT-12/T-12
AD • SAM • MANPAD 9K32 *Strela-2* (SA-7 *Grail*)‡
  GUNS 48
    SP **23mm** 24 ZSU-23-4
    TOWED **57mm** 24 S-60

Air Force 2,400
FORCES BY ROLE
FIGHTER
 1 regt with L-39 Albatros*
FIGHTER/TRANSPORT
 1 (comp avn) regt with MiG-21 Fishbed; An-2 Colt; An-26 Curl
ATTACK/TRANSPORT HELICOPTER
 1 regt with Mi-24 Hind; Mi-8 Hip
AIR DEFENCE
 Some regt with S-125 Pechora (SA-3 Goa); S-75 Dvina (SA-2 Guideline)
EQUIPMENT BY TYPE
AIRCRAFT 33 combat capable
 FGA 29 MiG-21 Fishbed
 TPT • Light 6: 4 An-2 Colt; 2 An-26 Curl
 TRG 4 L-39 Albatros*
HELICOPTERS
 ATK 2 Mi-24 Hind
 TPT • Medium 8 Mi-8 Hip
AD • SAM
 SP 2K11 Krug (SA-4 Ganef)
 TOWED S-75 Dvina (SA-2 Guideline); S-125 Pechora (SA-3 Goa)

Paramilitary 9,500

Border Guards 5,000 (KGZ conscript, RUS officers)

Interior Troops 3,500

National Guard 1,000

DEPLOYMENT

LIBERIA
UN • UNMIL 3 obs

MOLDOVA
OSCE • Moldova 1

SERBIA
OSCE • Kosovo 1

SOUTH SUDAN
UN • UNMISS 2 obs

SUDAN
UN • UNAMID 2 obs
UN • UNISFA 1 obs

UKRAINE
OSCE • Ukraine 4

FOREIGN FORCES

Russia ε500 Military Air Forces: 5 Su-25 Frogfoot; 2 Mi-8 Hip

Moldova MDA

Moldovan Leu L		2013	2014	2015
GDP	L	100bn	108bn	
	US$	7.97bn	7.74bn	
per capita	US$	2,239	2,176	
Growth	%	8.9	1.8	
Inflation	%	4.6	5.1	
Def exp	L	303m		
	US$	24m		
Def bdgt [a]	L	304m	355m	403m
	US$	24m	25m	
FMA (US)	US$	1.25m	1.25m	1.25m
US$1=L		12.59	13.95	

[a] Excludes military pensions

Population 3,583,288

Age	0 – 14	15 – 19	20 – 24	25 – 29	30 – 64	65 plus
Male	9.1%	3.3%	4.1%	4.7%	23.2%	4.2%
Female	8.6%	3.1%	3.8%	4.4%	24.6%	6.9%

Capabilities

Moldova has limited military capability and mainly Soviet-era equipment. Its conscript-based armed forces' primary focus remains the disputed territory of Transdniestr, though the country is also looking to develop further its capacity to contribute to peacekeeping and crisis-management missions in a multinational context. Moldovan forces are deployed in small numbers on UN operations and the country is developing units for interoperability with NATO. Implementing the recommendations of the 2011 Strategic Defence Review, carried out with UK support, is a priority, though funding problems mean this could prove a challenge. Russia continues to station an army garrison as well as a 'peacekeeping' contingent in Transdniestr, and in early 2014 conducted exercises in the territory. Following the annexation of Crimea and Moldova's developing ties with the West, this presence is additionally problematic. The strategic and military implications of the June 2014 signing of an association agreement with the EU are as yet unclear.

ACTIVE 5,350 (Army 3,250 Air 800 Logistic Support 1,300) **Paramilitary 2,400**

RESERVE 58,000 (Joint 58,000)

ORGANISATIONS BY SERVICE

Army 1,300; 1,950 conscript (total 3,250)
FORCES BY ROLE
SPECIAL FORCES
 1 SF bn
MANOEUVRE
 Light
 3 mot inf bde
 1 mot inf bn

Other
1 gd bn
COMBAT SUPPORT
1 arty bn
1 engr bn
1 NBC coy
1 sigs coy
EQUIPMENT BY TYPE
RECCE 5 BRDM-2
AIFV 44 BMD-1
APC 157
  APC (T) 62: 9 BTR-D; 53 MT-LB
  APC (W) 95: 11 BTR-80; 84 TAB-71
ARTY 148
  TOWED 69: **122mm** 17 (M-30) *M-1938*; **152mm** 52: 21 2A36; 31 D-20
  GUN/MOR • SP 120mm 9 2S9 *Anona*
  MRL 220mm 11 9P140 *Uragan*
  MOR 59: **82mm** 52; **120mm** 7 M-120
AT
  MSL • MANPATS 9K111 *Fagot* (AT-4 *Spigot*); 9K113 *Konkurs* (AT-5 *Spandrel*); 9K114 *Shturm* (AT-6 *Spiral*)
  RCL 73mm SPG-9
  GUNS 100mm 36 MT-12
AD • GUNS • TOWED 39: **23mm** 28 ZU-23; **57mm** 11 S-60
RADAR • LAND 4: 2 ARK-1; 2 SNAR-10

Air Force 800 (incl 250 conscripts)
FORCES BY ROLE
TRANSPORT
  2 sqn with An-2 *Colt*; An-26 *Curl*; An-72 *Coaler*; Mi-8PS *Hip*; Yak-18
AIR DEFENCE
  1 regt with S-125 *Neva* (SA-3 *Goa*)
EQUIPMENT BY TYPE
AIRCRAFT
  TPT • Light 6: 2 An-2 *Colt*; 1 An-26 *Curl*; 2 An-72 *Coaler*; 1 Yak-18
HELICOPTERS
  MRH 4 Mi-17-1V *Hip* H
  TPT • Medium 2 Mi-8PS *Hip*
AD • SAM 3 S-125 *Neva* (SA-3 *Goa*)

Paramilitary 2,400
Ministry of Interior

OPON 900 (riot police)
Ministry of Interior

DEPLOYMENT
Legal provisions for foreign deployment:
Constitution: Codified constitution (1994)
Decision on deployment of troops abroad: By the parliament (Art. 66)

CÔTE D'IVOIRE
UN • UNOCI 4 obs

LIBERIA
UN • UNMIL 2 obs

SERBIA
NATO • KFOR 41

SOUTH SUDAN
UN • UNMISS 1

UKRAINE
OSCE • Ukraine 9

FOREIGN FORCES
Czech Republic OSCE 1
Estonia OSCE 1
France OSCE 1
Germany OSCE 1
Kyrgyzstan OSCE 1
Poland OSCE 1
Russia ε1,500 (including 350 peacekeepers) Military Air Forces 7 Mi-24 *Hind*/Mi-8 *Hip*
Spain OSCE 1
Sweden OSCE 1
Switzerland OSCE 1
Ukraine 10 mil obs (Joint Peacekeeping Force)
United Kingdom OSCE 1
United States OSCE 3

Russia RUS

Russian Rouble r		2013	2014	2015
GDP	r	66.8tr	72.7tr	
	US$	2.1tr	2.06tr	
	US$ [a]	3.5tr	3.6tr	
per capita	US$	14,591	14,317	
Growth	%	1.3	0.2	
Inflation	%	6.8	7.4	
Def bdgt	r	2.1tr	2.47tr	3.29tr
	US$	66.1bn	70bn	
	US$ [a]	110bn	121bn	
US$1=r	MER	31.84	35.33	
	PPP	19.12	20.42	

[a] PPP estimate

Population 142,470,272

Ethnic groups: Tatar 4%; Ukrainian 3%; Chuvash 1%; Bashkir 1%; Belarussian 1%; Moldovan 1%; Other 8%

Age	0–14	15–19	20–24	25–29	30–64	65 plus
Male	8.2%	2.4%	3.5%	4.4%	23.7%	4.0%
Female	7.8%	2.3%	3.3%	4.4%	26.8%	9.1%

Capabilities

The various strands of Russian military modernisation described in previous editions of *The Military Balance* continue. Some of these measures were successfully tested during the Russian military seizure of Crimea in 2014. New infantry equipment, communications and *Tigr* light-armoured vehicles were observed during this operation, as was electronic-warfare equipment. But the operation did not reflect the effect of reform on the broader force; troops in Crimea were initially mainly VDV and special forces, reflective of the higher levels of training, command-and-control, equipment and funding that these forces have enjoyed. The tactics displayed showed an integrated use of special forces, rapid mobility and electronic-warfare tools, coupled with deniability and deception that demonstrated the 'non-linear' warfare discussed by a top Russian military official, described by some in the West as 'hybrid warfare'. The concurrent rapid mobilisation of the Western and Southern Military districts, which brought a reported 40,000 troops to assembly areas close to the Ukrainian border, also apparently proceeded smoothly. These 'snap inspections' in most Military Districts continued. Some were huge in scale, and Russia continues to use these to identify areas for improvement. Although most conventional combat capability was not tested in 2014, the standing and morale of the Russian armed forces will have been boosted by the Crimea operation. (See pp. 159–67.)

ACTIVE 771,000 (Army 230,000 Navy 130,000 Air 148,000 Strategic Deterrent Forces 80,000 Airborne 32,000 Special Operations Forces 1,000 Command and Support 150,000) **Paramilitary 489,000**
Conscript liability 12 months.

RESERVE 2,000,000 (all arms)
Some 2,000,000 with service within last 5 years; reserve obligation to age 50.

ORGANISATIONS BY SERVICE

Strategic Deterrent Forces ε80,000 (incl personnel assigned from the Navy and Air Force)

Navy
EQUIPMENT BY TYPE
SUBMARINES • STRATEGIC • SSBN 12:
3 *Kalmar* (*Delta* III) with 16 RSM-50 (SS-N-18 *Stingray*) strategic SLBM
6 *Delfin* (*Delta* IV) with 16 R-29RMU *Sineva* (SS-N-23 *Skiff*) strategic SLBM (of which 1 vessel in repair following a fire; expected return to service 2014)
1 *Akula* (*Typhoon*)† in reserve with capacity for 20 *Bulava* (SS-N-X-32) strategic SLBM (trials/testing)
2 *Borey* with capacity for 16 *Bulava* (SS-N-X-32) SLBM (missiles not yet operational), (1 additional unit with expected ISD 2014/15)

Strategic Rocket Force Troops
3 Rocket Armies operating silo and mobile launchers organised in 12 divs. Launcher gps normally with 10 silos (6 for RS-20/SS-18), or 9 mobile lnchr, and one control centre
EQUIPMENT BY TYPE
MSL • STRATEGIC 378

ICBM 378: 54 RS-20 (SS-18 *Satan*) (mostly mod 5, 10 MIRV per msl); 160 RS-12M (SS-25 *Sickle*) (mobile single warhead); 40 RS-18 (SS-19 *Stiletto*) (mostly mod 3, 6 MIRV per msl.); 60 RS-12M2 *Topol*-M (SS-27M1) silo-based (single warhead); 18 RS-12M2 *Topol*-M (SS-27M1) road mobile (single warhead); 42 RS-24 *Yars* (SS-27M2; ε3 MIRV per msl); 4 RS-24 *Yars* (SS-27M2; ε3 MIRV per msl) silo-based

Long-Range Aviation Command
FORCES BY ROLE
BOMBER
1 sqn with Tu-160 *Blackjack*
3 sqn with Tu-95MS *Bear*
EQUIPMENT BY TYPE
AIRCRAFT
BBR 78: 16 Tu-160 *Blackjack* each with up to 12 Kh-55 SM (AS-15A/B *Kent*) nuclear ALCM; 31 Tu-95MS6 (*Bear* H-6) each with up to 6 Kh-55/SM (AS-15A/B *Kent*) nuclear ALCM; 31 Tu-95MS16 (*Bear* H-16) each with up to 16 Kh-55 (AS-15A *Kent*) nuclear ALCM; (Kh-102 likely now in service on Tu-95MS)

Aerospace Defence Forces
Formations and units to detect missile attack on the RF and its allies, to implement BMD, and to be responsible for military/dual-use spacecraft launch and control

Space Command
EQUIPMENT BY TYPE
SATELLITES 74
COMMUNICATIONS 35: 3 Mod *Globus* (*Raduga*-1M); 9 *Strela*; 19 *Rodnik* (*Gonets*-M); 4 *Meridian*
NAVIGATION/POSITIONING/TIMING 33 GLONASS
ELINT/SIGINT 4: 1 *Kondor*; 1 *Liana* (*Lotos*-S); 1 *Persona*; 1 *Tselina*-2;
EARLY WARNING 2 *Oko*
RADAR 12; Russia leases ground-based radar stations in Baranovichi (Belarus) and Balkhash (Kazakhstan). It also has radars on its own territory at Lekhtusi, (St Petersburg); Armavir, (Krasnodar); Olenegorsk, (Murmansk); Mishelekvka, (Irkuts); Kaliningrad; Pechora, (Komi); Yeniseysk, (Krasnoyarsk); Baranul, (Altayskiy); Orsk, (Orenburg) and Gorodets/Kovylkino (OTH)

Aerospace Defence Command
FORCES BY ROLE
AIR DEFENCE
3 AD bde HQ
8 regt with S-300PS (SA-10 *Grumble*); S-300PM (SA-20 *Gargoyle*)
4 regt with S-400 (SA-21 *Growler*); 96K6 *Pantsir*-S1 (SA-22 *Greyhound*)
EQUIPMENT BY TYPE
AD • SAM • SP 222: 150 S-300PS/PM (SA-10 *Grumble*/SA-20 *Gargoyle*); 48 S-400 (SA-21 *Growler*); 24 96K6 *Pantsir*-S1 (SA-22 *Greyhound*)

MISSILE DEFENCE 68 53T6 (ABM-3 *Gazelle*); (32 51T6 (ABM-4 *Gorgon*) in store; possibly destroyed)
RADAR 1 ABM engagement system located at Sofrino (Moscow)

Army ε230,000; (incl conscripts)

Transformation process continues; 4 military districts (West (HQ St Petersburg), Centre (HQ Yekaterinburg), South (HQ Rostov-on-Don) & East (HQ Khabarovsk)), each with a unified Joint Strategic Command.

FORCES BY ROLE
COMMAND
10 army HQ
SPECIAL FORCES
7 (Spetsnaz) SF bde
MANOEUVRE
  Reconnaissance
  1 recce bde
  Armoured
  1 (4th) tk div (2 tk regt, 1 arty regt)
  3 tk bde (1 armd recce bn; 3 tk bn; 1 MR bn; 1 arty bn; 1 MRL bn; 2 AD bn; 1 engr bn; 1 EW coy; 1 NBC coy)
  Mechanised
  2 (2nd & 201st) MR div (2 MR regt, 1 arty regt)
  28 MR bde (1 recce bn; 1 tk bn; 3 MR bn; 2 arty bn; 1 MRL bn; 1 AT bn; 2 AD bn; 1 engr bn; 1 EW coy; 1 NBC coy)
  2 MR bde (4–5 MR bn; 1 arty bn; 1 AD bn; 1 engr bn)
  3 (lt/mtn) MR bde (1 recce bn; 2 MR bn; 1 arty bn)
  1 (18th) MGA div (2 MGA regt; 1 arty regt; 1 tk bn; 2 AD bn)
COMBAT SUPPORT
8 arty bde
4 MRL bde
1 MRL regt
4 SSM bde with 9K720 *Iskander*-M (SS-26 *Stone*)
5 SSM bde with 9K79 *Tochka* (SS-21 *Scarab* – to be replaced by *Iskander*-M)
9 AD bde
4 engr bde
1 MP bde
5 NBC bde
COMBAT SERVICE SUPPORT
10 log bde

EQUIPMENT BY TYPE
MBT 2,600: 1,300 T-72B/BA; 400 T-72B3; 550 T-80BV/U; 350 T-90/T-90A; (17,500 in store: 2,800 T-55; 2,500 T-62; 2,000 T-64A/B; 7,000 T-72/T-72A/B; 3,000 T-80B/BV/U; 200 T-90)
RECCE 1,200+: 100+ *Dozor*, 100+ *Tigr*, 1,000 BRDM-2/2A; (1,000+ BRDM-2 in store)
AIFV 5,125+: 500 BMP-1; 3,000 BMP-2; 500+ BMP-3; 700 BRM-1K; 275 BTR-80A/82A; 150 BTR-82AM; (8,500 in store: 7,000 BMP-1; 1,500 BMP-2)
APC 6,000+
  APC (T) 3,500+: some BMO-T; 3,500 MT-LB; (2,000 MT-LB in store)
  APC (W) 2,500: 800 BTR-60; 200 BTR-70; 1,500 BTR-80; (4,000 BTR-60/70 in store)
ARTY 4,180+
  SP 1,500: **122mm** 150 2S1; **152mm** 1,350: 800 2S3; 100 2S5; 450 2S19; (4,300 in store: **122mm** 2,000 2S1; **152mm** 1,950: 1,000 2S3; 850 2S5; 150 2S19; **203mm** 320 2S7)
  TOWED 150: **152mm** 150 2A65; (12,415 in store: **122mm** 8,150: 4,400 D-30; 3,750 M-30 (M-1938); **130mm** 650 M-46; **152mm** 3,575: 1,100 2A36; 600 2A65; 1,075 D-20; 700 D-1 M-1943; 100 ML-20 M-1937; **203mm** 40 B-4M)
  GUN/MOR 180+
    SP 120mm 80+: 30 2S23 NONA-SVK; 50+ 2S34
    TOWED 120mm 100 2B16 NONA-K
  MRL 850+ **122mm** 550 BM-21; **220mm** 200 9P140 *Uragan*; some TOS-1A; **300mm** 100 9A52 *Smerch*; (3,220 in store: **122mm** 2,420: 2,000 BM-21; 420 9P138; **132mm** 100 BM-13; **220mm** 700 9P140 *Uragan*)
  MOR 1,500
    SP (**240mm** 430 2S4 in store)
    TOWED 1,500: **82mm** 800 2B14; **120mm** 700 2S12; (2,200 in store: **120mm** 1,900: 1,000 2S12; 900 PM-38; **160mm** 300 M-160)
AT
  MSL
    SP BMP-T with 9K120 *Ataka* (AT-9 *Spiral* 2); 9P149 with 9K114 *Shturm* (AT-6 *Spiral*); 9P157-2 with 9K123 *Khrisantema* (AT-15 *Springer*)
    MANPATS 9K111 *Fagot* (AT-4 *Spigot*); 9K112 *Kobra* (AT-8 *Songster*); 9K113 *Konkurs* (AT-5 *Spandrel*); 9K114 *Shturm* (AT-6 *Spiral*); 9K115 *Metis* (AT-7 *Saxhorn*); 9K115-1 *Metis-M* (AT-13 *Saxhorn* 2); 9K116 *Bastion/Basnya* (AT-10 *Stabber*); 9K119 *Reflex/Svir* (AT-11 *Sniper*); 9K135 *Kornet* (AT-14 *Spriggan*)
  RCL 73mm SPG-9
  RL 105mm RPG-29
  GUNS • TOWED 100mm 526 MT-12; (**100mm** 2,000 T-12/MT-12 in store)
AD
  SAM 1,570+
    SP 1,570+: 350+ 9K37/9K317 *Buk* (SA-11 *Gadfly*/SA-17 *Grizzly*); 400 9K33M3 *Osa-AKM* (SA-8B *Gecko*); 400 9K35M3 *Strela*-10 (SA-13 *Gopher*); 120+ 9K330/9K331 *Tor* (SA-15 *Gauntlet*); 250+ 2K22 *Tunguska* (SA-19 *Grison*)
    MANPAD 9K310 *Igla*-1 (SA-16 *Gimlet*); 9K38 *Igla* (SA-18 *Grouse*); 9K333 *Verba*; 9K338 *Igla-S* (SA-24 *Grinch*); 9K34 *Strela*-3 (SA-14 *Gremlin*)
  GUNS
    SP 23mm ZSU-23-4
    TOWED 23mm ZU-23-2; **57mm** S-60
UAV • Heavy Tu-143 *Reys*; Tu-243 *Reys*/Tu-243 *Reys* D; Tu-300 *Korshun* **Light** BLA-07; *Pchela*-1; *Pchela*-2
MSL • SRBM 120: 70 9K79 *Tochka* (SS-21 *Scarab*); 50 9K720 *Iskander*-M (SS-26 *Stone*); (some *Scud* in store)
AEV BAT-2; IMR; IMR-2; IRM; MT-LB
ARV BMP-1; BREM-1/64/K/L; BTR-50PK(B); M1977; MTP-LB; RM-G; T-54/55; VT-72A
VLB KMM; MT-55A; MTU; MTU-20; MTU-72; PMM-2
MW BMR-3M; GMX-3; MCV-2 (reported); MTK; MTK-2

Reserves
Cadre formations
FORCES BY ROLE
MANOEUVRE
  Armoured
  1 tk bde
  Mechanised
  13 MR bde

Navy ε130,000; (incl conscripts)
4 major fleet organisations (Northern Fleet, Pacific Fleet, Baltic Fleet, Black Sea Fleet) and Caspian Sea Flotilla

EQUIPMENT BY TYPE
SUBMARINES 59
STRATEGIC • SSBN 12:

3 *Kalmar* (*Delta* III) with 16 R-29R *Volna* (SS-N-18 *Stingray*) strategic SLBM

6 *Delfin* (*Delta* IV) with 16 R-29RMU *Sineva* (SS-N-23 *Skiff*) strategic SLBM (1 expected to return to service by end-2014 following repair)

1 *Akula* (*Typhoon*)† in reserve for training with capacity for 20 *Bulava* (SS-N-X-32) strategic SLBM (trials/testing)

2 *Borey* with capacity for 16 *Bulava* (SS-N-X-32) SLBM (missiles not yet operational); (1 additional vessel with expected ISD 2014/15)

TACTICAL 47
SSGN 9:

8 *Antyey* (*Oscar* II) (of which 3 in reserve/repair) with 2 12-cell lnchr with 3M45 *Granit* (SS-N-19 *Shipwreck*) AShM, 2 single 650mm TT each with T-65 HWT, 4 single 553mm TT

1 *Yasen* (*Graney*) with 1 octuple VLS with 3M55 *Onyx* AShM; 3M14 *Kalibr* (SS-N-30) SLCM; 8 single 533mm TT

SSN 17:

2 *Schuka-B* (*Akula* II) with 4 single 533mm TT each with 3M10 *Granat* (SS-N-21 *Sampson*) SLCM, 4 single 650mm TT with T-65 HWT

8 *Schuka-B* (*Akula* I) (of which 2 in reserve) with 4 single 533mm TT with 3M10 *Granat* (SS-N-21 *Sampson*) SLCM, 4 single 650mm TT with T-65 HWT (one further boat leased to India for 10 years from 2012)

2 *Kondor* (*Sierra* II) with 4 single 533mm TT each with 3M10 *Granat* (SS-N-21 *Sampson*) SLCM, 4 single 650mm TT with T-65 HWT

1 *Barracuda* (*Sierra* I) (in reserve) with 4 single 533mm TT with 3M10 *Granat* (SS-N-21 *Sampson*) SLCM, RPK-2 (SS-N-15 *Starfish*) and T-53 HWT, 4 single 650mm TT with RPK-7 (SS-N-16 *Stallion*) AShM and T-65 HWT

4 *Schuka* (*Victor* III) (of which 1 in reserve) with 4 single 533mm TT each with 3M10 *Granat* (SS-N-21 *Sampson*) SLCM, 2 single 650mm TT with T-65 HWT

SSK 21:

15 *Paltus* (*Kilo*) with 6 single 533mm TT with T-53 HWT

5 *Varshavyanka* (*Kilo*) with 6 single 533mm TT (2 additional vessels under construction)

1 *Lada* (AIP fitted) with 6 single 533mm TT (2 additional vessels in build)

PRINCIPAL SURFACE COMBATANTS 35
AIRCRAFT CARRIERS • CV 1 *Orel* (*Kuznetsov*) with 1 12-cell VLS with 3M45 *Granit* (SS-N-19 *Shipwreck*) AShM, 4 sextuple VLS with 3K95 *Kindzhal* (SA-N-9 *Gauntlet*) SAM, 2 RBU 12000 *Udav* 1, 8 CADS-N-1 *Kortik* CIWS with 3M311 (SA-N-11 *Grison*) SAM, 6 AK630 CIWS (capacity 18-24 Su-33 *Flanker D* FGA ac; 15 Ka-27 *Helix* ASW hel, 2 Ka-31R *Helix* AEW hel)

CRUISERS 6
CGHMN 2:

2 *Orlan* (*Kirov*) with 10 twin VLS with 3M45 *Granit* (SS-N-19 *Shipwreck*) AShM, 2 twin lnchr with *Osa*-M (SA-N-4 *Gecko*) SAM, 12 octuple VLS with *Fort/Fort* M (SA-N-6 *Grumble*/SA-N-20 *Gargoyle*) SAM, 2 octuple VLS with 3K95 *Kindzhal* (SA-N-9 *Gauntlet*) SAM, 10 single 533mm ASTT, 1 RBU 12000 *Udav* 1, 2 RBU 1000 *Smerch* 3, 6 CADS-N-1 *Kortik* CIWS with 3M311 (SA-N-11 *Grison*) SAM, 1 twin 130mm gun (capacity 3 Ka-27 *Helix* ASW hel) (1 non-operational; undergoing extensive refit and expected return to service in 2017)

CGHM 4:

1 *Berkot-B* (*Kara*)† (scheduled to be decommissioned), with 2 quad lnchr with *Rastrub* (SS-N-14 *Silex*) AShM/ASW, 2 twin lnchr with 4K60 *Shtorm* (SA-N-3 *Goblet*) SAM, 2 twin lnchr with *Osa*-M (SA-N-4 *Gecko*) SAM, 2 quintuple 533mm ASTT, 2 RBU 6000, 2 twin 76mm guns (capacity 1 Ka-27 *Helix* ASW hel)

3 *Atlant* (*Slava*) with 8 twin lnchr with *Vulkan* (SS-N-12 mod 2 *Sandbox*) AShM, 8 octuple VLS with *Fort/Fort* M (SA-N-6 *Grumble*/SA-N-20 *Gargoyle*) SAM, 2 single lnchr with *Osa*-M (SA-N-4 *Gecko*) SAM, 2 quintuple 533mm ASTT, 2 RBU 6000 *Smerch* 2, 6 AK650 CIWS, 1 twin 130mm gun (capacity 1 Ka-27 *Helix* ASW hel) (1 currently non-operational; expected return to service in 2015)

DESTROYERS 18
DDGHM 17:

8 *Sarych* (*Sovremenny*) (of which 3 in reserve†) with 2 quad lnchr with 3M80 *Moskit* (SS-N-22 *Sunburn*) AShM, 2 twin lnchr with 3K90 *Uragan*/9K37 *Yezh* (SA-N-7 *Gadfly*/SA-N-12 *Grizzly*) SAM, 2 twin 533mm TT, 2 RBU 1000 *Smerch* 3, 4 AK630 CIWS, 2 twin 130mm guns (capacity 1 Ka-27 *Helix* ASW hel)

8 *Fregat* (*Udaloy* I) each with 2 quad lnchr with *Rastrub* (SS-N-14 *Silex*) AShM/ASW, 8 octuple VLS with 3K95 *Kindzhal* (SA-N-9 *Gauntlet* SAM), 2 quad 533mm ASTT, 2 RBU 6000 *Smerch* 2, 4 AK630 CIWS, 2 100mm guns (capacity 2 Ka-27 *Helix* ASW hel)

1 *Fregat* (*Udaloy* II) with 2 quad lnchr with 3M80 *Moskit* (SS-N-22 *Sunburn*) AShM, 8 octuple VLS with 3K95 *Kindzhal* (SA-N-9 *Gauntlet*) SAM, 2 CADS-N-1 *Kortik* CIWS with 3M311 (SA-N-11 *Grison*) SAM, 10 single 533mm ASTT, 2 RBU 6000 *Smerch* 2, 1 twin 130mm gun (capacity 2 Ka-27 *Helix* ASW hel)

DDGM 1:

1 *Komsomolets Ukrainy* (*Kashin* mod) with 2 quad lnchr with 3M24 *Uran* (SS-N-25 *Switchblade*) AShM, 2 twin lnchr with *Volnya* (SA-N-1 *Goa*) SAM, 5 single 533mm ASTT, 2 RBU 6000 *Smerch* 2, 1 twin 76mm gun

FRIGATES 10
  FFGHM 6:
    2 *Jastreb* (*Neustrashimy*) with 2 quad lnchr with 3M24 *Uran* (SS-N-25 *Switchblade*) AShM, 4 octuple VLS with 3K95 *Kindzhal* (SA-N-9 *Gauntlet*) SAM, 6 single 533mm ASTT, 1 RBU 12000, 2 CADS-N-1 *Kortik* CIWS with 3M311 (SA-N-11 *Grison*) SAM, 1 100mm gun (capacity 1 Ka-27 *Helix* ASW) (3rd vessel launched, but production halted in 1997; unclear status)
    1 *Steregushchiy* (Project 20380) with 2 quad lnchr with 3M24 *Uran* (SS-N-25 *Switchblade*) AShM, 2 quad 324mm ASTT, 1 CADS-N-1 *Kortik* CIWS with 3M311 (SA-N-11 *Grison*) SAM, 2 AK630 CIWS, 1 100mm gun
    3 *Steregushchiy* (Project 20381) with 2 quad lnchr with 3M24 *Uran* (SS-N-25 *Switchblade*) AShM, 1 12-cell VLS with 3K96 *Redut* SAM, 2 quad 324mm ASTT, 1 CADS-N-1 *Kortik* CIWS with 3M311 (SA-N-11 *Grison*) SAM, 2 AK630 CIWS, 1 100mm gun (4 additional vessels in build, of which two are improved *Steregushchiy* II)
  FFGM 4:
    1 *Gepard* with 2 quad lnchr with 3M24 *Uran* (SS-N-25 *Switchblade*) AShM, 1 twin lnchr with *Osa*-M (SA-N-4 *Gecko*) SAM, 2 AK630 CIWS, 1 76mm gun
    1 *Gepard* with 1 8-cell VLS with 3M14 *Kaliber* (SS-N-30) LACM, 2 quad lnchr with 3M24 *Uran* (SS-N-25 *Switchblade*) AShM, 1 twin lnchr with *Osa*-M (SA-N-4 *Gecko*) SAM, 1 AK630 CIWS, 1 76mm gun
    1 *Burevestnik* (*Krivak* I mod)† with 1 quad lnchr with *Rastrub* (SS-N-14 *Silex*) AShM/ASW, 1 twin lnchr with *Osa*-M (SA-N-4 *Gecko*) SAM, 2 quad 533mm ASTT, 2 RBU 6000 *Smerch* 2, 2 twin 76mm guns
    1 *Burevestnik* M (*Krivak* II) each with 1 quad lnchr with RPK-3 *Rastrub* (SS-N-14 *Silex*) AShM/ASW, 2 twin lnchr with 10 *Osa*-M (SA-N-4 *Gecko* SAM), 2 quad 533mm ASTT, 2 RBU 6000 *Smerch* 2, 2 100mm guns

PATROL AND COASTAL COMBATANTS 84
  CORVETTES 48
    FSGM 17:
      2 *Grad Sviyazhsk* (*Buyan*-M) with 1 octuple VLS with 3M55 *Onyx* AShM; 3M14 *Kalibr* (SS-N-30) LACM, 2 sextuple lnchr with 3M47 *Gibka* (SA-N-10 *Grouse*) SAM; 1 AK630-M2 CIWS, 1 100mm gun (6 additional vessels in build)
      2 *Sivuch* (*Dergach*) with 2 quad lnchr with 3M80 *Moskit* (SS-N-22 *Sunburn*) AShM, 1 twin lnchr with *Osa*-M (SA-N-4 *Gecko*) SAM, 2 AK630 CIWS, 1 76mm gun
      12 *Ovod* (*Nanuchka* III) with 2 triple lnchr with P-120 *Malakhit* (SS-N-9 *Siren*) AShM, 1 twin lnchr with *Osa*-M (SA-N-4 *Gecko*), 1 76mm gun
      1 *Ovod* (*Nanuchka* IV) with 2 triple lnchr with 3M55 *Onyx* (SS-N-26) AShM, 1 twin lnchr with *Osa*-M (SA-N-4 *Gecko*), 1 76mm gun
    FSM 31:
      3 *Albatros* (*Grisha* III) with 1 twin lnchr with *Osa*-M (SA-N-4 *Gecko*) SAM, 2 twin 533mm ASTT, 2 RBU 6000 *Smerch* 2. 1 twin 57mm gun
      18 *Albatros* (*Grisha* V) with 1 twin lnchr with *Osa*-M (SA-N-4 *Gecko*) SAM, 2 twin 533mm ASTT, 1 RBU 6000 *Smerch* 2, 1 76mm gun
      3 *Astrakhan* (*Buyan*) with 1 sextuple lnchr with 3M47 *Gibka* (SA-N-10 *Grouse*), 1 A-215 *Grad*-M 122mm MRL, 2 AK630 CIWS, 1 100mm gun
      7 *Parchim* II with 2 quad lnchr with *Strela*-2 (SA-N-5 *Grail*) SAM, 2 twin 533mm ASTT, 2 RBU 6000 *Smerch* 2, 1 AK630 CIWS, 1 76mm gun
  PCFG 25:
    6 *Molnya* (*Tarantul* II) with 2 twin lnchr with P-15M *Termit* (SS-N-2C/D *Styx*) AShM, 1 quad lnchr (manual aiming) with *Strela*-2 (SA-N-5 *Grail*) SAM, 2 AK630 CIWS, 1 76mm gun
    19 *Molnya* (*Tarantul* III) with 2 twin lnchr with 3M80 *Moskit* (SS-N-22 *Sunburn*) AShM, 1 quad lnchr (manual aiming) with *Strela*-2 (SA-N-5 *Grail*) SAM, 2 AK630 CIWS, 1 76mm gun
  PBM 7 *Grachonok* with 1 quad lnchr with 3M47 *Gibka* (SA-N-10 *Grouse*), (original design was as diving tender)
  PHG 3 *Vekhr* (*Matka*) with 2 single lnchr with P-15M *Termit* (SS-N-2C/D *Styx*) AShM, 1 AK630 CIWS, 1 76mm gun
  PHT 1 *Sokol* (*Mukha*) with 2 quad 406mm TT, 2 AK630 CIWS, 1 76mm gun

MINE WARFARE • MINE COUNTERMEASURES 53
  MHO 2 *Rubin* (*Gorya*) with 2 quad lnchr with *Strela*-2 (SA-N-5 *Grail*) SAM, 1 AK630 CIWS, 1 76mm gun
  MSO 11: 10 *Akvamaren* (*Natya*); 1 *Agat* (*Natya* II) (all with 2 quad lnchr (manual aiming) with *Strela*-2 (SA-N-5 *Grail*) SAM, 2 RBU1200 *Uragan*, 2 twin AK230 CIWS
  MSC 25: 23 *Yakhont* (*Sonya*) with 4 AK630 CIWS (some with 2 quad lnchr with *Strela*-2 (SA-N-5 *Grail*) SAM); 2 Project 1258 (*Yevgenya*)
  MHI 15: 9 *Sapfir* (*Lida*) with 1 AK630 CIWS; 3 Project 696 (*Tolya*); 3 *Malakhit* (*Olya*)

AMPHIBIOUS
  LANDING SHIPS • LST 20:
    4 *Tapir* (*Alligator*) with 2-3 twin lnchr with *Strela*-2 (SA-N-5 *Grail*) SAM, 2 twin 57mm guns (capacity 20 tanks; 300 troops)
    12 Project 775 (*Ropucha* I) with 2 twin 57mm guns (capacity either 10 MBT and 190 troops or 24 APC (T) and 170 troops)
    3 Project 775M (*Ropucha* II) with 2 AK630 CIWS, 1 76mm gun (capacity either 10 MBT and 190 troops or 24 APC (T) and 170 troops)
    1 *Tapir* (*Alligator* (mod)) with 2 AK630 CIWS, 1 76mm gun (capacity 1 Ka-29 *Helix* B; 13 MBT; 300 troops) (vessel launched in 2012; expected ISD end-2013))
  LANDING CRAFT 25
    LCU 11:
      2 *Dyugon* (3 more in build)
      9 Project 11770 (*Serna*) (capacity 100 troops)
    LCM 7 *Akula* (*Ondatra*) (capacity 1 MBT)
    LCAC 7:
      2 *Dzheryan* (*Aist*) with 2 twin AK630 CIWS (capacity 4 lt tk)
      2 *Pomornik* (*Zubr*) with 2 AK630 CIWS (capacity 230 troops; either 3 MBT or 10 APC (T)
      3 *Kalmar*† (*Lebed*) (capacity 2 lt tk)

LOGISTICS AND SUPPORT 626
SSAN 7: 1 *Orenburg* (*Delta III* Stretch); 1 *Losharik* (one further vessel under construction); 2 Project 1851 (*Paltus*); 3 *Kashalot* (*Uniform*)
SSA 1 *Sarov*
ABU 12: 8 *Kashtan*; 4 *Sura*
AE 2: 1 *Muna*; 1 *Dubnyak*
AEM 3: 2 *Amga*; 1 *Lama*
AG 3: 2 *Vytegrales*; 1 *Potok*
AGB 4 *Dobrynya Mikitich*
AGE 2: 1 *Tchusovoy*; 1 *Zvezdochka* (2 more vessels under construction)
AGI 11: 2 *Alpinist*; 1 *Balzam*; 3 *Moma*; 5 *Vishnya*
AGM 1 *Marshal Nedelin*
AGOR 6: 1 *Akademik Krylov*; 2 *Sibiriyakov*, 2 *Vinograd*; 1 *Seliger*
AGS 21: 3 BGK-797; 6 *Kamenka*; 9 *Onega*; 3 *Vaygach*
AGSH 1 *Samara*
AGSI 50: 8 *Biya*; 25 *Finik*; 7 *Moma*; 12 *Yug*
AH 3 *Ob* †
AK 2 *Bira*
AOL 13: 2 *Dubna*; 5 *Uda*; 6 *Altay* (mod)
AOR 5 *Boris Chilikin*
AORL 3: 1 *Kaliningradneft*; 2 *Olekma*
AOS 1 *Luza*
AR 13 *Amur*
ARC 7: 4 *Emba*; 3 *Klasma*
ARS 14: 4 *Mikhail Rudnitsky*; 10 *Goryn*
AS 1 Project 2020 (*Malina*)
ASR 2: 1 *Nepal*; 1 *Alagez*
ATF 62: 1 *Alexander Piskunov*; 2 *Baklazhan*; 5 *Katun*; 3 *Ingul*; 2 *Neftegaz*; 14 *Okhtensky*; 18 *Prometey*; 1 *Prut*; 3 *Sliva*, 13 *Sorum*
AWT 2 *Manych*
AXL 12: 10 *Petrushka*; 2 *Smolny* with 2 RBU 2500, 2 twin 76mm guns
YDG 28: 15 *Bereza*; 13 *Pelym*
YDT 91: 40 *Flamingo*; 20 *Nyryat 2*; 28 *Yelva*; 3 Project 11980
YGS 60 GPB-480
YO 36: 5 *Khobi*; 30 *Toplivo*; 1 *Konda*
YPB 30 *Bolva*
YPT 12 *Shelon*
YTB 60: 3 PE-65; 2 Project 745MB/S; 9 Project 16609; 11 *Stividor*; 35 *Sidehole*
YTR 42: 27 *Pozharny*; 15 *Morkov*

Naval Aviation ε28,000
4 Fleet Air Forces
Flying hours 60+ hrs/year
FORCES BY ROLE
FIGHTER
1 sqn with Su-33 *Flanker* D; Su-25UTG *Frogfoot*
1 sqn (forming) with MiG-29K/KUB *Fulcrum*
1 sqn with Su-27 *Flanker*
ANTI-SURFACE WARFARE/ISR
1 regt with Su-24M/MR *Fencer*
1 sqn with Su-24M/MR *Fencer*
ANTI-SUBMARINE WARFARE
2 sqn with Il-18D; Il-20RT *Coot* A; Il-22 *Coot* B; Il-38/Il-38N *May**
8 sqn with Ka-27/Ka-29 *Helix*
1 sqn with Mi-14 *Haze* A
2 sqn with Tu-142M/MR *Bear* F/J*
1 unit with Ka-31R *Helix*
MARITIME PATROL/TRANSPORT
1 sqn with An-26 *Curl*; Be-12 *Mail**; Mi-8 *Hip*
SEARCH & RESCUE/TRANSPORT
1 sqn with An-12PS *Cub*; An-26 *Curl*; Tu-134
TRANSPORT
1 sqn with An-12BK *Cub*; An-24RV *Coke*; An-26 *Curl*; An-72 *Coaler*; An-140
2 sqn with An-26 *Curl*; Tu-134
TRAINING
1 sqn with Su-30SM; L-39 *Albatros*
1 sqn with An-140; Tu-134; Tu-154
TRANSPORT HELICOPTER
1 sqn with Mi-8 *Hip*
EQUIPMENT BY TYPE
AIRCRAFT 136 combat capable
FTR 40: 2 MiG-29K *Fulcrum*; 2 MiG-29KUB *Fulcrum*; 18 Su-33 *Flanker* D; 18 Su-27/Su-27UB *Flanker*
FGA 31: 28 Su-24M *Fencer*; 3 Su-30SM
ATK 5 Su-25UTG *Frogfoot*
ASW 27 Tu-142M/MR *Bear* F/J
MP 26: 3 Be-12 *Mail**; 1 Il-18D; 22 Il-38/Il-38N *May**
ISR 8 Su-24MR *Fencer* E*
SAR 3 An-12PS *Cub*
EW • ELINT 4: 2 Il-20RT *Coot* A; 2 Il-22 *Coot* B
TPT 50: **Medium** 2 An-12BK *Cub*; **Light** 46: 1 An-24RV *Coke*; 27 An-26 *Curl*; 6 An-72 *Coaler*; 2 An-140; 10 Tu-134; **PAX** 2 Tu-154M *Careless*
TRG 4 L-39 *Albatros*
HELICOPTERS
ASW 83: 63 Ka-27 *Helix*; 20 Mi-14 *Haze* A
EW 8 Mi-8 *Hip* J
AEW 2 Ka-31R *Helix*
SAR 56: 16 Ka-27PS *Helix* D; 40 Mi-14PS *Haze* C
TPT • Medium 36: 28 Ka-29 *Helix*; 4 Mi-8T *Hip*; 4 Mi-8MT *Hip*
MSL
ASM Kh-25 (AS-10 *Karen*); Kh-59 (AS-13 *Kingbolt*)
ARM Kh-58 (AS-11 *Kilter*); Kh-25MP (AS-12 *Kegler*)
AAM • IR R-27T/ET (AA-10B/D *Alamo*); R-60 (AA-8 *Aphid*); R-73 (AA-11 *Archer*); **SARH** R-27R/ER (AA-10A/C *Alamo*)

Naval Infantry (Marines) ε20,000
FORCES BY ROLE
SPECIAL FORCES
1 (fleet) SF bde (1 para bn, 2–3 underwater bn, 1 spt unit)
2 (fleet) SF bde (cadre) (1 para bn, 2–3 underwater bn, 1 spt unit)
MANOEUVRE
Mechanised
2 MR bde
1 MR bde (forming)
1 MR regt
5 indep naval inf bde
1 indep naval inf regt

COMBAT SUPPORT
1 arty bde
1 arty regt
1 SSM bde with 9K79 Tochka (SS-21 Scarab)
AIR DEFENCE
2 SAM regt with 9K33 Osa (SA-8 Gecko); Strela-1/Strela-10 (SA-9 Gaskin/SA-13 Gopher)
1 SAM regt with S-300PS (SA-10 Grumble)
1 SAM regt with S-400 (SA-21 Growler)
EQUIPMENT BY TYPE
MBT 200 T-72/T-80
RECCE 60 BRDM-2 each with 9K11 Malyutka (AT-3 Sagger)
AIFV 300 BMP-2
APC 800
  APC (T) 300 MT-LB
  APC (W) 500 BTR-80
ARTY 365
  SP 263: **122mm** 113: 95 2S1; 18 2S19; **152mm** 150: 50 2A36; 50 2A65; 50 2S3
  GUN/MOR 66
    SP 120mm 42: 12 2S23 NONA-SVK; 30 2S9 NONA-S
    TOWED 120mm 24 2B16 NONA-K
  MRL 122mm 36 BM-21
AT
  MSL
    SP 9P149 with 9K114 Shturm (AT-6 Spiral); 9P157-2 with 9K123 Khrisantema (AT-15 Springer)
    MANPATS 9K11 Malyutka (AT-3 Sagger); 9K113 Konkurs (AT-5 Spandrel)
  GUNS 100mm T-12
AD
  SAM
    SP 86: 20 9K33 Osa (SA-8 Gecko); 50 Strela-1/Strela-10 (SA-9 Gaskin/SA-13 Gopher); 8 S-300PS (SA-10 Grumble); 8 S-400 (SA-21 Growler)
    MANPAD 9K32 Strela-2 (SA-7 Grail)
  GUNS 23mm 60 ZSU-23-4
MSL • SRBM 12 9K79 Tochka (SS-21 Scarab)

Coastal Missile and Artillery Troops 2,000
FORCES BY ROLE
COASTAL DEFENCE
3 AShM bde
2 AShM regt
1 indep AShM bn
EQUIPMENT BY TYPE
ARTY • SP 130mm ε36 A-222 Bereg
AShM 36+: 24 3K60 Bal (SS-C-6 Sennight); 12 K-300P Bastion (SS-C-5 Stooge); some 4K44 Redut (SS-C-1 Sepal); some 4K51 Rubezh (SS-C-3 Styx)

Military Air Forces ε148,000 (incl conscripts)
Flying hours 60 to 100 hrs/year (combat aircraft)
               120+ (transport aircraft)

HQ at Balashikha, near Moscow. A joint CIS Unified Air Defence System covers RUS, ARM, BLR, KAZ, KGZ, TJK, TKM, UKR and UZB. The Russian Air Force is currently undergoing a period of restructuring, both in terms of general organisation as well as air-base and unit structure.

FORCES BY ROLE
BOMBER
4 sqn with Tu-22M3/MR Backfire C
3 sqn with Tu-95MS Bear
1 sqn with Tu-160 Blackjack
FIGHTER
1 regt with MiG-29/MiG-29UB Fulcrum
1 regt with MiG-29SMT/UBT Fulcrum
1 regt with MiG-31BM Foxhound
1 regt with MiG-31 Foxhound; Su-27/Su-27UB Flanker
1 regt with MiG-31; Su-27SM2; Su-30M2
4 sqn with MiG-31 Foxhound
2 regt with Su-27/Su-27UB Flanker
FIGHTER/GROUND ATTACK
1 regt with MiG-31BM; Su-24M/M2/MR
1 regt with Su-27SM2 Flanker; Su-35S Flanker; Su-30M2
1 regt with Su-27SM3 Flanker; Su-30M2
1 regt with Su-25 Frogfoot; Su-30SM
GROUND ATTACK
1 regt with Su-24M/M2 Fencer
2 sqn with Su-24M/M2 Fencer
8 sqn with Su-25/Su-25SM Frogfoot
1 regt with Su-34 Fullback; Su-24M/M2 Fencer
GROUND ATTACK/ISR
1 regt with Su-34 Fullback; Su-24MR Fencer*
ELECTRONIC WARFARE
1 sqn with Mi-8PPA Hip
ISR
2 regt with Su-24MR Fencer*
1 sqn with Su-24MR Fencer*
1 flt with An-30 Clank
AIRBORNE EARLY WARNING & CONTROL
1 sqn with A-50/A-50U Mainstay
TANKER
1 sqn with Il-78/Il-78M Midas
TRANSPORT
6 regt/sqn with An-12BK Cub; An-26 Curl; Tu-134 Crusty; Tu-154 Careless; Mi-8 Hip
1 regt with An-124 Condor; Il-76MD Candid
1 regt with An-12BK Cub; Il-76MD Candid
1 sqn with An-22 Cock
3 regt with Il-76MD Candid
ATTACK HELICOPTER
1 bde with Ka-52A Hokum B; Mi-28N Havoc B; Mi-35 Hind; Mi-26 Halo; Mi-8MTV-5 Hip
2 sqn with Ka-52A Hokum B
4 sqn with Mi-24 Hind
3 sqn with Mi-28N Havoc B
1 sqn with Mi-35 Hind
TRANSPORT HELICOPTER
17 sqn with Mi-8 Hip/Mi-26 Halo
AIR DEFENCE
8 AD bde HQ
4 regt with 9K37/9K317 Buk (SA-11 Gadfly/SA-17 Grizzly); S-300V (SA-12 Gladiator/Giant)
17 regt with S-300PS (SA-10 Grumble); S-300PM (SA-20)
2 regt with S-400 (SA-21 Growler); 96K6 Pantsir-S1 (SA-22 Greyhound)

EQUIPMENT BY TYPE
AIRCRAFT 1,201 combat capable
  BBR 141: 63 Tu-22M3/MR *Backfire* C; 31 Tu-95MS6 *Bear*; 31 Tu-95MS16 *Bear*; 16 Tu-160 *Blackjack*
  FTR 420: 120 MiG-29 *Fulcrum*; 30 MiG-29UB *Fulcrum*; 100 MiG-31B/31BS *Foxhound*; 50 MiG-31BM *Foxhound*; 100 Su-27 *Flanker*; 20 Su-27UB *Flanker*
  FGA 345: 28 MiG-29SMT *Fulcrum*; 6 MiG-29UBT *Fulcrum*; 100 Su-24M *Fencer*; 50 Su-24M2 *Fencer*; 47 Su-27SM2 *Flanker*; 14 Su-27SM3 *Flanker*; 14 Su-30M2; 15 Su-30SM; 46 Su-34 *Fullback*; 25 Su-35S *Flanker*
  ATK 215: 150 Su-25 *Frogfoot*; 50 Su-25SM *Frogfoot*; 15 Su-25UB *Frogfoot*
  ISR 86: 4 An-30 *Clank*; 80 Su-24MR *Fencer**; 2 Tu-214ON
  ELINT 32: 15 Il-20M *Coot* A; 5 Il-22 *Coot* B; 12 Il-22M *Coot* B
  AEW&C 22: 15 A-50 *Mainstay*; 3 A-50U *Mainstay*; 4 Il-76SKIP (Be-976 – telemetry aircraft)
  C2 6: 2 Il-76VKP; 4 Il-86VKP *Maxdome*
  TKR 15: 5 Il-78 *Midas*; 10 Il-78M *Midas*
  TPT 432: **Heavy** 123: 9 An-124 *Condor*; 4 An-22 *Cock*; 110 Il-76MD/MF *Candid*; **Medium** 65 An-12BK *Cub*; **Light** 226: 115 An-26 *Curl*; 25 An-72 *Coaler*; 5 An-140; 27 L-410; 54 Tu-134 *Crusty*; **PAX** 18 Tu-154 *Careless*
  TRG 198: 150 L-39 *Albatros*; 48 Yak-130 *Mitten*
HELICOPTERS
  ATK 296+: 12 Ka-50 *Hokum*; 56+ Ka-52A *Hokum* B; 150 Mi-24D/V/P *Hind*; 54+ Mi-28N *Havoc* B; 24 Mi-35 *Hind*
  EW 54: 50 Mi-8PPA *Hip*; 4 Mi-8MTRP-1 *Hip*
  TPT 532: **Heavy** 32 Mi-26/Mi-26T *Halo*; **Medium** 500 Mi-8/Mi-8MT/Mi-8MTSh/Mi-8MTV-5 *Hip*
  TRG 30: 10 Ka-226; 20 Ansat-U
UAV • ISR Light some *Pchela*-1T
AD • SAM • SP 376: 80 9K37/9K317 *Buk* (SA-11 *Gadfly*/SA-17 *Grizzly*); 240 S-300PS/PM (SA-10 *Grumble*/SA-20 *Gargoyle*); 20 S-300V (SA-12 *Gladiator*/*Giant*); 24 S-400 (SA-21 *Growler*); 12 96K6 *Pantsir*-S1 (SA-22 *Greyhound*)
MSL
  AAM • IR R-27T/ET (AA-10B/D *Alamo*); R-73 (AA-11 *Archer*); R-60T (AA-8 *Aphid*); SARH R-27R/ER (AA-10A/C *Alamo*); R-33/33S (AA-9 *Amos* A/B); ARH R-77/R-77-1 (AA-12/AA-X-12B *Adder*); K-37M (AA-13 *Axehead*); PRH R-27P/EP (AA-10E/F *Alamo*)
  ARM Kh-58 (AS-11 *Kilter*); Kh-25MP (AS-12 *Kegler*); Kh-15P (AS-16 *Kickback*) Kh-31P/PM (PM entering production) (AS-17A *Krypton*)
  ASM Kh-25 (AS-10 *Karen*); Kh-59/Kh-59M (AS-13 *Kingbolt*/AS-18 *Kazoo*); Kh-29 (AS-14 *Kedge*); Kh-31A/AM (AM entering production) (AS-17B *Krypton*); Kh-38 (entering production)
  LACM Kh-22/32 (AS-4 *Kitchen*); Kh-55/55SM (AS-15A/B *Kent*); Kh-101; Kh-102; Kh-555 (AS-15C *Kent*)
BOMBS • **Laser-guided** KAB-500; KAB-1500L; **TV-guided** KAB-500KR; KAB-1500KR; KAB-500OD;UPAB 1500

Airborne Troops ε32,000
FORCES BY ROLE
SPECIAL FORCES
  1 (AB Recce) SF regt
MANOEUVRE
  Air Manoeuvre
  4 AB div (2 para/air aslt regt; 1 arty regt; 1 AD regt)
  1 indep AB bde
  3 air aslt bde
EQUIPMENT BY TYPE
RECCE *Tigr*
AIFV 1,165: 100 BMD-1; 1,000 BMD-2; 10 BMD-3; 30 BMD-4; 25 BTR-80A
APC • APC (T) 700 BTR-D
ARTY 600+
  TOWED 122mm 150 D-30
  GUN/MOR • SP 120mm 250 2S9 NONA-S (500 in store: 120mm 500 2S9 NONA-S)
  MOR • TOWED 200+ 82mm 150 2B14; 120mm 50+ 2B23
AT
  MSL
    SP 100 BTR-RD
    MANPATS 9K111 *Fagot* (AT-4 *Spigot*); 9K112 *Kobra* (AT-8 *Songster*); 9K113 *Konkurs* (AT-5 *Spandrel*); 9K114 *Shturm* (AT-6 *Spiral*); 9K115 *Metis* (AT-7 *Saxhorn*); 9K115-1 *Metis*-M (AT-13 *Saxhorn* 2); 9K116 *Bastion*/*Basnya* (AT-10 *Stabber*); 9K119 *Reflex*/*Svir* (AT-11 *Sniper*); 9K135 *Kornet* (AT-14 *Spriggan*)
  RCL 73mm SPG-9
  RL 105mm RPG-29
  GUNS • SP: 125mm 36+ 2S25
  AD • SAM
    SP 150 BTR-ZD
    MANPAD 9K310 *Igla*-1 (SA-16 *Gimlet*); 9K38 *Igla* (SA-18 *Grouse*); 9K333 *Verba*; 9K338 *Igla*-S (SA-24 *Grinch*); 9K34 *Strela*-3 (SA-14 *Gremlin*)
  ARV BREM-D; BREhM-D

Special Operations Forces ε1,000
FORCES BY ROLE
SPECIAL FORCES
  2 SF unit

Russian Military Districts

Western Military District
HQ at St Petersburg

Army
FORCES BY ROLE
COMMAND
  2 army HQ
SPECIAL FORCES
  2 (Spetsnaz) SF bde
MANOEUVRE
  Armoured
  1 tk div
  1 tk bde
  Mechanised
  1 MR div
  4 MR bde
COMBAT SUPPORT
  2 arty bde
  1 MRL bde

2 SSM bde with *Iskander*-M
1 SSM bde with *Tochka* (SS-21 *Scarab*)
2 AD bde
1 engr bde
1 MP bde
1 NBC bde
COMBAT SERVICE SUPPORT
2 log bde

Reserves
FORCES BY ROLE
MANOEUVRE
Armoured
1 tk bde
Mechanised
2 MR bde

Northern Fleet
EQUIPMENT BY TYPE
SUBMARINES 33
STRATEGIC 9 SSBN (one to transfer to PF)
TACTICAL 24: 4 SSGN; 13 SSN; 7 SSK
PRINCIPAL SURFACE COMBATANTS 11: 1 **CV**; 2 **CGHMN** (one non-operational); 1 **CGHM** (in repair); 7 **DDGHM**
PATROL AND COASTAL COMBATANTS 9: 3 **FSGM**; 6 **FSM**
MINE WARFARE 12: 1 **MHO** (in repair); 3 **MSO**; 8 **MSC**
AMPHIBIOUS 4 LST

Naval Aviation
FORCES BY ROLE
FIGHTER
2 sqn with Su-33 *Flanker* D; Su-25UTG *Frogfoot*
ANTI-SUBMARINE WARFARE
1 sqn with Il-20RT *Coot* A; Il-38 *May**; Tu-134
3 sqn with Ka-27/Ka-29 *Helix*
1 sqn with Tu-142M/MR *Bear* F/J
EQUIPMENT BY TYPE
AIRCRAFT
FTR 18 Su-33 *Flanker* D
ATK 5 Su-25UTG *Frogfoot*
ASW 13 Tu-142M/MR *Bear* F/J
EW • ELINT 3: 2 Il-20RT *Coot* A; 1 Il-22 *Coot* B
MP 14 Il-38 *May**
TPT 9: 8 An-26 *Curl*; 1 Tu-134
HELICOPTERS
ASW Ka-27 *Helix* A
TPT Ka-29 *Helix* B; Mi-8 *Hip*

Naval Infantry
FORCES BY ROLE
MANOEUVRE
Mechanised
1 MR bde
1 MR bde (forming)
1 naval inf bde
1 naval inf regt

Coastal Artillery and Missile Troops
FORCES BY ROLE
COASTAL DEFENCE
1 AShM bde

Baltic Fleet
EQUIPMENT BY TYPE
SUBMARINES • TACTICAL 3 SSK: 1 *Lada*; 2 *Paltus* (*Kilo*)
PRINCIPAL SURFACE COMBATANTS 8: 2 **DDGHM**; 6 **FFGHM**
PATROL AND COASTAL COMBATANTS 20: 4 **FSGM**; 7 **FSM**; 8 **PCFG**; 1 **PBM**
MINE WARFARE • MINE COUNTERMEASURES 15: 4 **MSC**; 11 **MHI**
AMPHIBIOUS 13: 4 **LST**; 2 **LCU**; 5 **LCM**; 2 **LCAC**

Naval Aviation
FORCES BY ROLE
FIGHTER
1 sqn with Su-27 *Flanker*
GROUND ATTACK/ISR
1 sqn with Su-24M/MR *Fencer*
ANTI-SUBMARINE WARFARE
1 sqn with Ka-27/Ka-29 *Helix*
TRANSPORT
1 sqn with An-26 *Curl*; Tu-134 *Crusty*
TRANSPORT HELICOPTER
1 sqn with Mi-8 *Hip*
EQUIPMENT BY TYPE
AIRCRAFT
FTR 18 Su-27/Su-27UB *Flanker*
FGA 10 Su-24M *Fencer*
ISR 4 Su-24MR *Fencer**
TPT 8: 6 An-26 *Curl*; 2 Tu-134 *Crusty*
HELICOPTERS
ASW Ka-27 *Helix*
TPT • Medium Ka-29 *Helix*; Mi-8 *Hip*

Naval Infantry
FORCES BY ROLE
MANOEUVRE
Mechanised
1 MR bde
1 MR regt
1 naval inf bde
COMBAT SUPPORT
1 arty bde
1 SSM bde with *Tochka* (SS-21 *Scarab*)
AIR DEFENCE
1 SAM regt

Coastal Artillery and Missile Troops
FORCES BY ROLE
COASTAL DEFENCE
1 AShM regt

Military Air Force

1st Air Force & Air Defence Command
FORCES BY ROLE
FIGHTER
1 regt with MiG-29SMT *Fulcrum*
1 regt with MiG-31 *Foxhound*; Su-27 *Flanker*
1 regt with Su-27 *Flanker*
FIGHTER/GROUND ATTACK/ISR
1 regt with MiG-31BM *Foxhound*; Su-24M/M2/MR *Fencer*
GROUND ATTACK/ISR
1 regt with Su-34 *Fullback*; Su-24MR *Fencer*
ISR
1 flt with A-30 *Clank*
ELECTRONIC WARFARE
1 sqn with Mi-8PPA *Hip*
TRANSPORT
1 regt with An-12 *Cub*; An-26 *Curl*; Tu-134 *Crusty*
ATTACK HELICOPTER
1 bde with Ka-52A *Hokum* B; Mi-28N *Havoc* B; Mi-35 *Hind*; Mi-26 *Halo*; Mi-8MTV-5 *Hip*
2 sqn with Mi-24 *Hind*
TRANSPORT HELICOPTER
3 sqn with Mi-8 *Hip*
AIR DEFENCE
1 regt with 9K37/9K317 *Buk* (SA-11 *Gadfly*/SA-17 *Grizzly*); S-300V (SA-12 *Gladiator/Giant*)
7 regt with S-300PS (SA-10 *Grumble*); S-300PM (SA-20 *Gargoyle*)
EQUIPMENT BY TYPE
AIRCRAFT
FTR 160: 51 MiG-31 *Foxhound*; 109 Su-27/Su-27UB *Flanker*
FGA 102: 28 MiG-29SMT *Fulcrum*; 6 MiG-29UBT *Fulcrum*; 44 Su-24M/M2 *Fencer*; 24 Su-34 *Fullback*
ISR 38: 4 An-30 *Clank*; 10 MiG-25RB *Foxbat** 24 Su-24MR *Fencer**
TPT 12 An-12/An-26/Tu-134
HELICOPTERS
ATK 58+: 12 Ka-52A *Hokum* B; 30 Mi-24 *Hind*; 12 Mi-28N *Havoc* B; 4+ Mi-35 *Hind*
EW 10 Mi-8PPA *Hip*
TPT • **Medium** 50 Mi-8 *Hip*
AD • **SAM** • **SP** 9K37/9K317 *Buk* (SA-11 *Gadfly/*SA-17 *Grizzly*); S-300PS/PM (SA-10 *Grumble*/SA-20 *Gargoyle*); S-300V (SA-12 *Gladiator/Giant*)

Airborne Troops
FORCES BY ROLE
SPECIAL FORCES
1 (AB Recce) SF regt
MANOEUVRE
Air Manoeuvre
3 AB div

Central Military District
HQ at Yekaterinburg

Army
FORCES BY ROLE
COMMAND
2 army HQ
SPECIAL FORCES
2 (Spetsnaz) SF bde
MANOEUVRE
Armoured
1 tk bde
Mechanised
1 (201st) MR div
7 MR bde
COMBAT SUPPORT
2 arty bde
1 MRL bde
2 SSM bde with *Tochka* (SS-21 *Scarab*)
2 AD bde
1 engr bde
2 NBC bde
COMBAT SERVICE SUPPORT
2 log bde

Reserves
FORCES BY ROLE
MANOEUVRE
Mechanised
3 MR bde

Military Air Force

2nd Air Force & Air Defence Command
FORCES BY ROLE
FIGHTER
1 regt with MiG-31BM *Foxhound*
2 sqn with MiG-31 *Foxhound*
GROUND ATTACK
2 sqn with Su-24 *Fencer*
ISR
1 sqn with Su-24MR *Fencer* E
TRANSPORT
1 regt with An-12 *Cub*; An-26 *Curl*; Tu-134 *Crusty*; Tu-154; Mi-8 *Hip*
ATTACK HELICOPTER
2 sqn with Mi-24 *Hind*
TRANSPORT HELICOPTER
2 sqn with Mi-8 *Hip*/Mi-26 *Halo*
AIR DEFENCE
6 regt with S-300PS (SA-10 *Grumble*)
EQUIPMENT BY TYPE
AIRCRAFT
FTR 73 MiG-31 *Foxhound*
FGA 26 Su-24M *Fencer*
ISR 13 Su-24MR *Fencer* E
TPT 36 An-12 *Cub*/An-26 *Curl*/Tu-134 *Crusty*/Tu-154 *Careless*
HELICOPTERS
ATK 24 Mi-24 *Hind*
TPT 46: 6 Mi-26 *Halo*; 40 Mi-8 *Hip*
AD • **SAM** • **SP** S-300PS (SA-10 *Grumble*)

Airborne Troops
FORCES BY ROLE
MANOEUVRE
 Air Manoeuvre
 1 AB bde

Southern Military District
HQ located at Rostov-on-Don

Army
FORCES BY ROLE
COMMAND
 2 army HQ
SPECIAL FORCES
 2 (Spetsnaz) SF bde
MANOEUVRE
 Reconnaissance
 1 recce bde
 Mechanised
 6 MR bde
 1 MR bde (Armenia)
 1 MR bde (Abkhazia)
 1 MR bde (South Ossetia)
 3 (lt/mtn) MR bde
COMBAT SUPPORT
 1 arty bde
 1 MRL bde
 1 MRL regt
 1 SSM bde with Iskander-M (SS-26 Stone)
 2 AD bde
 1 engr bde
 1 NBC bde
COMBAT SERVICE SUPPORT
 2 log bde

Black Sea Fleet
The Black Sea Fleet is primarily based in the Crimea, at Sevastopol, Karantinnaya Bay and Streletskaya Bay.
EQUIPMENT BY TYPE
SUBMARINES • TACTICAL 2 SSK (also 1 Som (Tango) in reserve)
PRINCIPAL SURFACE COMBATANTS 5: 2 CGHM; 1 DDGM; 2 FFGM
PATROL AND COASTAL COMBATANTS 20: 4 FSGM; 6 FSM; 1 PHM; 5 PCFG; 3 PBM; 1 PHT
MINE WARFARE • MINE COUNTERMEASURES 9: 1 MHO; 6 MSO; 2 MSC
AMPHIBIOUS 9: 8 LST; 1 LCU

Naval Aviation
FORCES BY ROLE
FIGHTER
 ANTI-SURFACE WARFARE/ISR
 1 regt with Su-24M/MR Fencer
 ANTI-SUBMARINE WARFARE
 1 sqn with Ka-27 Helix
 1 sqn with Mi-14 Haze
 MARITIME PATROL/TRANSPORT
 1 sqn with An-26 Curl; Be-12 Mail*; Mi-8

EQUIPMENT BY TYPE
AIRCRAFT
 FGA 18 Su-24M Fencer
 ISR 4 Su-24MR Fencer E
 MP 6 Be-12 Mail*
 TPT 6 An-26
HELICOPTERS
 ASW Ka-27 Helix
 TPT • Medium Mi-8 Hip (MP/EW/Tpt)

Naval Infantry
FORCES BY ROLE
MANOEUVRE
 Mechanised
 2 naval inf bde
COMBAT SUPPORT
 1 arty regt
AIR DEFENCE
 1 SAM regt

Coastal Artillery and Missile Troops
FORCES BY ROLE
COASTAL DEFENCE
 1 AShM bde
 1 indep AShM bn

Caspian Sea Flotilla
EQUIPMENT BY TYPE
PRINCIPAL SURFACE COMBATANTS 2 FFGM
PATROL AND COASTAL COMBATANTS 11: 2 FSGM; 3 FSM; 2 PCFG; 3 PHM; 1 PBM
MINE WARFARE • MINE COUNTERMEASURES 7: 5 MSC; 2 MHI
AMPHIBIOUS 11: 2 LCM; 4 LCU; 5 LCAC

Military Air Force

4th Air Force & Air Defence Command
FORCES BY ROLE
FIGHTER
 1 regt with MiG-29 Fulcrum
 1 sqn with MiG-29 Fulcrum (Armenia)
FIGHTER/GROUND ATTACK
 2 regt with Su-27 Flanker; Su-27SM3 Flanker; Su-30M2
GROUND ATTACK
 6 sqn with Su-25/Su-25SM Frogfoot
 1 regt with Su-34 Fullback; Su-24M Fencer
ISR
 1 regt with Su-24MR Fencer E
TRANSPORT
 1 sqn with An-12 Cub/Mi-8 Hip
ATTACK HELICOPTER
 1 sqn with Ka-52A Hokum B
 3 sqn with Mi-28N Havoc B
 1 sqn with Mi-35 Hind
TRANSPORT HELICOPTER
 6 sqn with Mi-8 Hip/Mi-26 Halo
AIR DEFENCE
 1 regt with 9K37/9K317 Buk (SA-11 Gadfly/SA-17 Grizzly)

2 regt with S-300PM (SA-20 *Gargoyle*)
1 regt with S-400 (SA-21 *Growler*); 96K6 *Pantsir*-S1 (SA-22 *Greyhound*)

EQUIPMENT BY TYPE
AIRCRAFT
FTR 121: 63 MiG-29 *Fulcrum*; 58 Su-27 *Flanker*
FGA 88: 62 Su-24M *Fencer*; 12 Su-27SM3 *Flanker*; 2 Su-30M2; 12 Su-34 *Fullback*
ATK 129 Su-25/Su-25SM *Frogfoot*
ISR 24 Su-24MR *Fencer**
TPT 12 An-12 *Cub*
HELICOPTERS
ATK 64: 16 Ka-52A *Hokum* B; 34 Mi-28N *Havoc* B; 14 Mi-35 *Hind*
TPT 72: **Heavy** 10 Mi-26 *Halo*; **Medium** 62 Mi-8 *Hip*
AD • SAM • SP 9K37/9K317 *Buk* (SA-11 *Gadfly*/SA-17 *Grizzly*); S-300PM (SA-20 *Gargoyle*); S-400 (SA-21 *Growler*); 96K6 *Pantsir*-S1 (SA-22 *Greyhound*)

Airborne Troops

FORCES BY ROLE
MANOEUVRE
  Air Manoeuvre
  1 AB div
  1 air aslt bde

Eastern Military District

HQ located at Khabarovsk

Army

FORCES BY ROLE
COMMAND
  4 army HQ
SPECIAL FORCES
  1 (Spetsnaz) SF bde
MANOEUVRE
  Armoured
  1 tk bde
  Mechanised
  10 MR bde
  1 MGA div
COMBAT SUPPORT
  3 arty bde
  1 MRL bde
  3 SSM bde with *Tochka* (SS-21 *Scarab*)
  3 AD bde
  1 engr bde
  1 NBC bde
COMBAT SERVICE SUPPORT
  4 log bde

Reserves

FORCES BY ROLE
MANOEUVRE
  Mechanised
  8 MR bde

Pacific Fleet

EQUIPMENT BY TYPE
SUBMARINES 22
  STRATEGIC 3 **SSBN**
  TACTICAL 19: 5 **SSGN**; 5 **SSN**; 9 **SSK**
PRINCIPAL SURFACE COMBATANTS 9: 1 **CGHM**; 8 **DDGHM** (of which three in reserve)
PATROL AND COASTAL COMBATANTS 23: 3 **FSGM**; 9 **FSM**; 10 **PCFG**; 1 **PBM**
MINE WARFARE 7: 2 **MSO**; 5 **MSC**
AMPHIBIOUS 6: 4 **LST**; **2 LCU**

Naval Aviation

FORCES BY ROLE
FIGHTER
  2 sqn with MiG-31 *Foxhound*
ANTI-SUBMARINE WARFARE
  3 sqn with Ka-27/Ka-29 *Helix*
  1 sqn with Il-18D; Il-22 *Coot* B; Il-38 *May**
  1 sqn with Tu-142M/MR *Bear* F/J*
TRANSPORT
  2 sqn with An-12BK *Cub*; An-26 *Curl*; Tu-134
EQUIPMENT BY TYPE
AIRCRAFT
  FTR 24 MiG-31 *Foxhound*
  ASW 14 Tu-142M/MR *Bear* F/J*
  MP 15 Il-38 *May**
  EW • ELINT 1 Il-22 *Coot* B
  TPT 6: 2 An-12BK *Cub*; 3 An-26 *Curl*; 1 Tu-134
HELICOPTERS
  ASW Ka-27 *Helix*
  TPT • **Medium** Ka-29 *Helix*; Mi-8 *Hip*

Naval Infantry

FORCES BY ROLE
MANOEUVRE
  Mechanised
  2 naval inf bde
AIR DEFENCE
  1 SAM regt

Coastal Artillery and Missile Troops

FORCES BY ROLE
COASTAL DEFENCE
  1 AShM bde
  1 AShM regt

Military Air Force

3rd Air Force & Air Defence Command

FORCES BY ROLE
FIGHTER
  1 regt with MiG-31 *Foxhound*; Su-27SM2 *Flanker*; Su-30M2
  1 regt with Su-27SM2 *Flanker*; Su-30M2; Su-35S *Flanker*
FIGHTER/GROUND ATTACK
  1 regt with Su-25 *Frogfoot*; Su-30SM
GROUND ATTACK
  1 regt with Su-24M/M2 *Fencer*
  2 sqn with Su-25 *Frogfoot*
ISR
  1 regt with Su-24MR *Fencer* E

TRANSPORT
  2 sqn with An-12 *Cub*/An-26 *Curl*/Tu-134 *Crusty*/Tu-154 *Careless*
ATTACK HELICOPTER
  2 sqn with Mi-24 *Hind*
  1 sqn with Ka-52A *Hokum* B
TRANSPORT HELICOPTER
  6 sqn with Mi-8 *Hind*/Mi-26 *Halo*
AIR DEFENCE
  2 regt with 9K37/9K317 *Buk* (SA-11 *Gadfly*/SA-17 *Grizzly*); S-300V (SA-12 *Gladiator/Giant*)
  3 regt with S-300PS (SA-10 *Grumble*); S-300PM (SA-20 *Gargoyle*)
  1 regt with S-400 (SA-21 *Growler*); 96K6 *Pantsir*-S1 (SA-22 *Greyhound*)
EQUIPMENT BY TYPE
AIRCRAFT
  FTR 20 MiG-31 *Foxhound*
  FGA 103: 44 Su-24M *Fencer*; 10 Su-24M2 *Fencer*; 47 Su-27SM2 *Flanker*; 2 Su-30M2
  ATK 72 Su-25 *Frogfoot*
  ISR 28 Su-24MR *Fencer* E
  TPT 22 An-12 *Cub*/An-26 *Curl*; 1 Tu-134 *Crusty*; 1 Tu-154 *Careless*
HELICOPTERS
  ATK 44: 20 Ka-52A *Hokum* B; 24 Mi-24 *Hind*
  TPT 60: **Heavy** 4 Mi-26 *Halo*; **Medium** 56 Mi-8 *Hip*
  AD • SAM • SP 9K37/9K317 *Buk* (SA-11 *Gadfly*/SA-17 *Grizzly*); S-300PS/PM (SA-10 *Grumble*/SA-20 *Gargoyle*); S-300V (SA-12 *Gladiator/Giant*); S-400 (SA-21 *Growler*); 96K6 *Pantsir*-S1 (SA-22 *Greyhound*)

Airborne Troops

FORCES BY ROLE
MANOEUVRE
  Air Manoeuvre
  2 air aslt bde

Paramilitary 489,000

Federal Border Guard Service ε160,000

Directly subordinate to the president; now reportedly all contract-based personnel
FORCES BY ROLE
10 regional directorates
MANOEUVRE
  Other
  7 frontier gp
EQUIPMENT BY TYPE
AIFV/APC (W) 1,000 BMP/BTR
ARTY • SP 90: **122mm** 2S1; **120mm** 2S12; **120mm** 2S9 *Anona*
PRINCIPAL SURFACE COMBATANTS
  FRIGATES • FFHM 3 *Nerey* (*Krivak* III) with 1 twin lnchr with *Osa*-M (SA-N-4 *Gecko*) SAM, 2 quad 533mm TT lnchr, 2 RBU 6000 *Smerch* 2 lnchr, 1 100mm gun (capacity 1 Ka-27 *Helix* A ASW hel)

PATROL AND COASTAL COMBATANTS 233
  PCM 46:
    2 *Molnya* II (*Pauk* II) with 1 quad lnchr with *Strela*-2 (SA-N-5 *Grail* SAM), 2 twin 533mm TT lnchr, 2 RBU 1200 lnchr, 1 AK630 CIWS, 1 76mm gun
    27 *Svetljak* (*Svetlyak*) with 1 quad lnchr with *Strela*-2 (SA-N-5 *Grail* SAM), 2 single 406mm TT, 1 AK630 CIWS, 1 76mm gun
    17 *Molnya* I (*Pauk* I) with 1 quad lnchr with *Strela*-2 (SA-N-5 *Grail* SAM), 4 single 406mm TT, 2 RBU 1200, 1 AK630 CIWS, 1 76mm gun
  PHT 2 *Antares* (*Muravey*)
  PCO 17: 8 Project 503 (*Alpinist*); 1 *Sprut*; 5 *Rubin* with 1 AK630 CIWS; 2 *Antur*; 1 *Purga*
  PSO 4 *Komandor*
  PCC 13 *Tarantul* (*Stenka*) with 4 406mm TT, 2 twin AK630 CIWS
  PB 45: 3 Project 14310 (*Mirazh*); 13 Type 1496; 12 *Grif* (*Zhuk*); 17 *Kulik*
  PBR 25: 3 *Ogonek* with 2 AK630 CIWS; 8 *Piyavka* with 1 AK630 CIWS; 5 *Shmel* with 1 76mm gun; 6 *Moskit* (*Vosh*) with 1 AK630 CIWS, 1 76mm gun; 2 *Slepen* (*Yaz*) with 2 115mm guns; 1 *Gornostay*
  PBF 81: 1 A-125; 2 *Bogomol* with 2 twin AK630 CIWS, 1 76mm gun; 17 *Mangust*; 4 *Mustang* (Project 18623); 15 *Saygak*; ε40 *Sobol*; 2 *Sokzhoi*
AMPHIBIOUS • LC • LCAC 7 *Tsaplya* (used for patrol duties)
LOGISTICS AND SUPPORT 41
  AGB 5 *Ivan Susanin* (primarily used as patrol ships)
  AGS 2 *Yug* (primarily used as patrol ships)
  AK 8 *Neon Antonov*
  AKSL 6 *Kanin*
  AO 2: 1 *Baskunchak*; 1 Project 1510
  ATF 18 *Sorum* (primarily used as patrol ships)
AIRCRAFT • TPT ε86: 70 An-24 *Coke*/An-26 *Curl*/An-72 *Coaler*/Il-76 *Candid*/Tu-134 *Crusty*/Yak-40 *Codling*; 16 SM-92
HELICOPTERS: ε200 Ka-28 (Ka-27) *Helix* ASW/Mi-24 *Hind* Atk/Mi-26 *Halo* Spt/Mi-8 *Hip* Spt

Federal Agency for Special Construction (MOD) ε50,000

Federal Communications and Information Agency ε55,000

FORCES BY ROLE
MANOEUVRE
  Other
  4 paramilitary corps
  28 paramilitary bde

Federal Protection Service ε10,000–30,000 active

Org include elm of ground forces (mech inf bde and AB regt)
FORCES BY ROLE
MANOEUVRE
  Mechanised
  1 mech inf regt

Air Manoeuvre
1 AB regt
Other
1 (Presidential) gd regt

Federal Security Service ε4,000 active (armed)
FORCES BY ROLE
MANOEUVRE
Other
Some cdo unit (including Alfa and Vympel units)

Interior Troops ε170,000
FORCES BY ROLE
7 Regional Commands: Central, Urals, North Caucasus, Volga, Eastern, North-Western and Siberian
MANOEUVRE
Other
3 (55th, 59th & ODON) paramiltiary div (2–5 paramilitary regt)
18 (OBRON) paramilitary bde (3 mech bn, 1 mor bn)
2 indep paramilitary bde (OBR/OSMBR)
102 paramilitary regt/bn (incl special motorised units)
11 (special) paramilitary unit
Aviation
8 sqn
COMBAT SUPPORT
1 arty regt
EQUIPMENT BY TYPE
MBT 9
AIFV/APC (W) 1,650 BMP-1/BMP-2/BTR-80
ARTY 35
  TOWED 122mm 20 D-30
  MOR 120mm 15 PM-38
AIRCRAFT TPT 23: **Heavy** 9 Il-76 *Candid*; **Medium** 2 An-12 *Cub*; **Light** 12 An-26 *Curl*; 6 An-72 *Coaler*
HELICOPTERS • TPT 70: **Heavy** 10 Mi-26 *Halo*; **Medium** 60 Mi-8 *Hip*

Railway Troops (MOD) ε20,000
4 regional commands
FORCES BY ROLE
COMBAT SERVICE SUPPORT
10 (railway) tpt bde

Cyber

Until 2003, activities within the cyber domain were the responsibility of the Russian SIGINT agency, FAPSI. In 2003, this agency was abolished and its responsibilities divided between the defence ministry and the internal security service (FSB). The first official doctrinal statement on the role of the Russian military in cyberspace, the 'Conceptual Views on the Activity of the Russian Federation Armed Forces in Information Space', was released at the end of 2011, and described cyber-force tasks with little correlation to those of equivalent commands in the West. In particular, the document contains no mention of the possibility of offensive cyber activity. It is also entirely defensive in tone, and focuses on force protection and prevention of information war, including allowing for a military role in negotiating international treaties governing information security. Following a mixed performance in the information aspects of the armed conflict with Georgia in 2008, there was discussion about creating 'Information Troops', whose role would include cyber capability; but this initiative was publicly scotched by the FSB. In January 2012, then-CGS Makarov gave a different picture of the three main tasks for any new command: 'disrupting adversary information systems, including by introducing harmful software; defending our own communications and command systems'; and 'working on domestic and foreign public opinion using the media, Internet and more'. The third task is a reminder that, unlike some other nations with advanced cyber capabilities, Russia deals in cyber warfare as an integral component of information warfare. Operations in Crimea in early 2014, and in the wider information space concerning the conflict in Ukraine, demonstrate that Russian thinking and capacity has matured in these areas. In Crimea, Russian troops demonstrated integrated use of EW and SOF capabilities, as well as wider use of cyberspace and strategic communications to shape an effective information campaign targeted as much at domestic as foreign audiences.

DEPLOYMENT

ARMENIA
3,300: 1 mil base with (1 MR bde; 74 T-72; 80 BMP-1; 80 BMP-2; 12 2S1; 12 BM-21); 1 sqn with 18 MiG-29 *Fulcrum*; 2 AD bty with S-300V (SA-12 *Gladiator/Giant*); 1 AD bty with 2K12 *Kub* (SA-6 *Gainful*)

BELARUS
1 ftr flt with 5 Su-27 *Flanker*; 1 A-50 *Mainstay*; 4 SAM units with S-300 (SA-10 Grumble); 1 radar station at Baranovichi (*Volga* system; leased); 1 naval comms site

BOSNIA-HERZEGOVINA
OSCE • Bosnia and Herzegovina 2

CÔTE D'IVOIRE
UN • UNOCI 11 obs

DEMOCRATIC REPUBLIC OF THE CONGO
UN • MONUSCO 28 obs

GEORGIA
7,000; Abkhazia 1 mil base with (1 MR bde; 40 T-90A; 120 BTR-82A; 18 2S3; 12 2S12; 18 BM-21; some S-300 SAM; some atk hel); South Ossetia 1 mil base with (1 MR bde; 40 T-72; 120 BMP-2; 36 2S3; 12 2S12)

KAZAKHSTAN
1 radar station at Balkash (*Dnepr* system; leased)

KYRGYZSTAN
ε500; 5 Su-25 *Frogfoot*; 2 Mi-8 *Hip* spt hel

LIBERIA
UN • UNMIL 3 obs

MIDDLE EAST
UN • UNTSO 4 obs

MOLDOVA/TRANSDNIESTR
ε1,500 (including 350 peacekeepers); 2 MR bn; 100 MBT/AIFV/APC; 7 Mi-24 *Hind*; some Mi-8 *Hip*

SERBIA
OSCE • Kosovo 1

SOUTH SUDAN
UN • UNMISS 3; 2 obs

SUDAN
UN • UNISFA 1 obs

SYRIA
1 naval facility at Tartus

TAJIKISTAN
5,000; 1 mil base with (1 (201st) MR div; 40 T-72B1; 60 BMP-2; 80 BTR-80; 40 MT-LB; 18 2S1; 36 2S3; 6 2S12/12 9P140 *Uragan*); 4 Mi-8 *Hip*

UKRAINE
Crimea: 20,000; 2 naval inf bde; 1 arty bde; 80 BMP-2 AIFV; 20 BTR-80 APC: 150 MT-LB; 18 2S1 arty; 12 BM-21 MRL; 1 SAM bn with S-300PM; 1 AShM unit with K-300P *Bastion*; 1 Fleet HQ located at Sevastopol; 2 radar stations located at Sevastopol (*Dnepr* system) and Mukachevo (*Dnepr* system)

Donetsk/Luhansk: 300+ (reported)

OSCE • Ukraine 16

WESTERN SAHARA
UN • MINURSO 11 obs

Tajikistan TJK

Tajikistani Somoni Tr		2013	2014	2015
GDP	Tr	40.5bn	46.6bn	
	US$	8.5bn	9.16bn	
per capita	US$	1,045	1,103	
Growth	%	7.4	6.0	
Inflation	%	5.0	6.6	
Def bdgt [a]	Tr	923m	ε946m	
	US$	194m	186m	
FMA (US)	US$	0.8m	1.5m	0.7m
US$1=Tr		4.8	5.1	

[a] Defence and law enforcement expenses

Population 8,051,512

Ethnic groups: Tajik 67%; Uzbek 25%; Russian 2%; Tatar 2%

Age	0–14	15–19	20–24	25–29	30–64	65 plus
Male	16.8%	5.0%	5.2%	5.1%	16.3%	1.3%
Female	16.2%	4.8%	5.1%	5.0%	17.3%	1.8%

Capabilities

The Tajik armed forces have little capacity to deploy other than token forces and most equipment is of Soviet origin, with no significant procurement plans in place. The paucity of military capability partially reflects that the primary security concern remains internal and border security, with the country sharing an extended border with Afghanistan. Tajikistan's membership of the CSTO provides a security guarantee and, along with Dushanbe's defence relationship with Moscow, this is reinforced by the presence in Tajikistan of Russia's largest overseas military base (since the annexation of Crimea brought Sevastopol under Russia's direct administration). Given the overall weaknesses of the Tajik armed and security forces – which include limited special-forces training and personnel issues revolving around high numbers of conscripts and low planning capacity – low-level militant activity linked to drug trafficking could continue to burden and challenge the armed forces.

ACTIVE 8,800 (Army 7,300, Air Force/Air Defence 1,500) **Paramilitary 7,500**
Conscript liability 24 months

ORGANISATIONS BY SERVICE

Army 7,300
FORCES BY ROLE
MANOEUVRE
  Mechanised
    3 MR bde
  Air Manoeuvre
    1 air aslt bde
COMBAT SUPPORT
  1 arty bde
  1 SAM regt

EQUIPMENT BY TYPE
MBT 37: 30 T-72; 7 T-62
AIFV 23: 8 BMP-1; 15 BMP-2
APC (W) 23 BTR-60/BTR-70/BTR-80
ARTY 23
  TOWED 122mm 10 D-30
  MRL 122mm 3 BM-21
  MOR 120mm 10
AD • SAM 20+
  TOWED 20 S-75 *Dvina* (SA-2 *Guideline*); S-125 *Pechora-2M* (SA-3 *Goa*)
  MANPAD 9K32 *Strela-2* (SA-7 *Grail*)‡

Air Force/Air Defence 1,500
FORCES BY ROLE
TRANSPORT
  1 sqn with Tu-134A *Crusty*
ATTACK/TRANSPORT HELICOPTER
  1 sqn with Mi-24 *Hind*; Mi-8 *Hip*; Mi-17TM *Hip H*

EQUIPMENT BY TYPE
AIRCRAFT
  TPT • Light 1 Tu-134A *Crusty*
  TRG 4+: 4 L-39 *Albatros*; some Yak-52
HELICOPTERS
  ATK 4 Mi-24 *Hind*
  TPT • Medium 11 Mi-8 *Hip*/Mi-17TM *Hip H*

Paramilitary 7,500

Interior Troops 3,800

National Guard 1,200

Emergencies Ministry 2,500

Border Guards

DEPLOYMENT

UKRAINE
OSCE • Ukraine 1

FOREIGN FORCES
Russia 5,000; 1 mil base with (1 (201st) MR div; 40 T-72B1; 60 BMP-2; 80 BTR-80; 40 MT-LB; 18 2S1; 36 2S3; 6 2S12/12 9P140 *Uragan*); 4 Mi-8 *Hip*

Turkmenistan TKM

Turkmen New Manat TMM		2013	2014	2015
GDP	TMM	116bn	135bn	
	US$	40.8bn	47.5bn	
per capita	US$	7,157	8,203	
Growth	%	10.2	10.1	
Inflation	%	6.8	5.0	
Def exp	TMM	ε1.75bn		
	US$	ε612m		
FMA (US)	US$		0.69m	0.1m
USD1=TMM		2.85	2.85	

Population 5,171,943

Ethnic groups: Turkmen 77%; Uzbek 9%; Russian 7%; Kazak 2%

Age	0–14	15–19	20–24	25–29	30–64	65 plus
Male	13.4%	4.9%	5.3%	5.1%	19.1%	1.8%
Female	13.0%	4.8%	5.2%	5.1%	19.9%	2.4%

Capabilities

Turkmenistan's largely conscript-based armed forces are poorly equipped and remain reliant on Soviet-era equipment and doctrine. The country declared neutrality in 1999 and enshrined this principle in its 2009 Military Doctrine. Delivery of around 30 T-90S MBTs, ordered from Russia in 2011, has yet to be finalised. The air force has a limited number of combat aircraft and helicopters, though availability is uncertain. Airlift is modest, and insufficient to deliver substantial military effect overseas, or even across the country. There are plans to strengthen coastal naval forces by 2015, and some assets have already been procured, leading to a moderate improvement in the Caspian Sea naval presence. Military capability is believed to be limited by low levels of training and availability of spare parts.

ACTIVE 22,000 (Army 18,500 Navy 500 Air 3,000)
Conscript liability 24 months

ORGANISATIONS BY SERVICE

Army 18,500
5 Mil Districts

FORCES BY ROLE
MANOEUVRE
  Mechanised
  3 MR div
  2 MR bde
  Air Manouvre
  1 air aslt bn
  Other
  1 MR trg div
COMBAT SUPPORT
  1 arty bde
  1 MRL regt
  1 AT regt
  1 SSM bde with *Scud*
  2 SAM bde
  1 engr regt

EQUIPMENT BY TYPE †
MBT 680: 10 T-90S; 670 T-72
RECCE 170 BRDM/BRDM-2
AIFV 942: 930 BMP-1/BMP-2; 12 BRM
APC (W) 829 BTR-60/BTR-70/BTR-80
ARTY 570
  SP 56: **122mm** 40 2S1; **152mm** 16 2S3
  TOWED 269: **122mm** 180 D-30; **152mm** 89: 17 D-1; 72 D-20
  GUN/MOR 120mm 17 2S9 *Anona*
  MRL 131: **122mm** 65: 9 9P138; 56 BM-21; **220mm** 60 9P140 *Uragan*; **300mm** 6 9A52 *Smerch*
  MOR 97: **82mm** 31; **120mm** 66 PM-38
AT
  MSL • **MANPATS** 9K11 (AT-3 *Sagger*); 9K111 (AT-4 *Spigot*); 9K113 (AT-5 *Spandrel*); 9K115 (AT-6 *Spiral*)
  GUNS 100mm 72 MT-12/T-12
AD • **SAM** 53+
  SP 53: 40 9K33 *Osa* (SA-8 *Gecko*); 13 9K35 *Strela*-10 (SA-13 *Gopher*)
  MANPAD 9K32 *Strela*-2 (SA-7 *Grail*)‡
  GUNS 70
  SP 23mm 48 ZSU-23-4
  TOWED 57mm 22 S-60
MSL • **SSM** 10 SS-1 *Scud*

Navy 500

EQUIPMENT BY TYPE
PATROL AND COASTAL COMBATANTS 19
  PCFG 2 *Edermen* (RUS *Molnya*) with 4 quad lnchr with 3M24E *Uran* AShM, 1 quad lnchr (manual aiming) with 9K32 *Strela*-2 (SA-N-5 *Grail*) SAM, 1 76mm gun
  PCC 4 *Arkadag*
  PBF 12: 5 *Grif*-T; 5 Dearsan 14: 2 *Sobol*
  PB 1 *Point*

Air Force 3,000

FORCES BY ROLE
FIGHTER/GROUND ATTACK
  2 sqn with MiG-29 *Fulcrum*; MiG-29UB *Fulcrum*; Su-17 *Fitter*; Su-25MK *Frogfoot*
TRANSPORT
  1 sqn with An-26 *Curl*; Mi-8 *Hip*; Mi-24 *Hind*

TRAINING
 1 unit with Su-7B *Fitter* A; L-39 *Albatros*
AIR DEFENCE
 Some sqn with S-75 *Dvina* (SA-2 *Guideline*); S-125 *Pechora* (SA-3 *Goa*); S-200 *Angara* (SA-5 *Gammon*)
EQUIPMENT BY TYPE
AIRCRAFT 94 combat capable
 FTR 24: 22 MiG-29 *Fulcrum*; 2 MiG-29UB *Fulcrum*
 FGA 68: 3 Su-7B *Fitter* A; 65 Su-17 *Fitter* B
 ATK 2 Su-25MK *Frogfoot* (41 more being refurbished)
 TPT • **Light** 1 An-26 *Curl*
 TRG 2 L-39 *Albatros*
HELICOPTERS
 ATK 10 Mi-24 *Hind*
 TPT • **Medium** 8 Mi-8 *Hip*
AD • SAM 50 S-75 *Dvina* (SA-2 *Guideline*)/S-125 *Pechora* (SA-3 *Goa*)/S-200 *Angara* (SA-5 *Gammon*)

Ukraine UKR

Ukrainian Hryvnia h		2013	2014	2015
GDP	h	1.45tr	1.52tr	
	US$	178bn	135bn	
per capita	US$	3,930	2,979	
Growth	%	-0.0	-6.5	
Inflation	%	-0.3	11.4	
Def bdgt [a]	h	19.7bn	40.5bn	63bn
	US$	2.41bn	3.59bn	
FMA (US)	US$	7m	4.2m	2m
US$1=h		8.16	11.30	

[a] Defence & security budget, includes funds for the Interior Ministry. 2014 figure excludes funding from general budget reserve fund and special defence and security reserve fund.

Population 44,291,413

Age	0–14	15–19	20–24	25–29	30–64	65 plus
Male	7.2%	2.6%	3.3%	4.2%	23.4%	5.2%
Female	6.8%	2.4%	3.2%	4.1%	26.9%	10.7%

Capabilities

In 2014, Ukrainian armed forces were evicted from Crimea by Russian VDV, Spetsnaz and other special-operations forces. Air-force and navy units based there lost the majority of their materiel, with a large number of vessels co-opted by Russian forces, although some equipment such as SU-27s was returned in various states of disrepair. Ukraine's subsequent mobilisation showed that combat capability had been greatly 'hollowed out' by inadequate resourcing and reduced training over many years. The country continues to operate mainly Soviet-era equipment, or derivatives of these designs, and only a small proportion of the army and air force are combat ready, with initial operations to evict pro-Russian rebels from eastern Ukraine reportedly dependent on a few soldiers and helicopters and a single airborne regiment with inadequate logistics. A new national guard and irregular volunteer militias formed in 2014, and took part in the fighting in the east. Meanwhile, conscription was reinstated in May; it had only been suspended for a short time, so much experience in conscript management and related infrastructure would have remained. Defence spending has remained low, with most areas underfunded. By the end of 2014, Ukraine's defence plants (a substantial defence industry remains) were returning to service the first aircraft recovered by road from Crimea. (See pp. 168–73.)

ACTIVE 121,500 (Army 64,000 Navy 7,000 Air 45,000 Airborne 5,500) **Paramilitary n.k.**
Conscript liability Army, Air Force 18 months, Navy 2 years. During the Autumn 2013 draft, authorities indicated that conscription could be suspended in 2014. Contract servicemen comprise just over 50% of the armed forces.

RESERVE 1,000,000 (Joint 1,000,000)
Military service within 5 years

ORGANISATIONS BY SERVICE

Army 64,000
Includes both Land Forces and 8th Army Corps. Ground combat in the east is conducted by a mixture of regular and national guard units, and irregular formations.

FORCES BY ROLE
COMMAND
 1 corps HQ
SPECIAL FORCES
 2 SF regt
MANOEUVRE
 Armoured
 2 tk bde
 Mechanised
 9 mech bde
 1 mtn bde
 Aviation
 2 avn bde
 1 avn regt
COMBAT SUPPORT
 2 arty bde
 3 MRL regt
 1 SSM bde
 3 AD regt
 4 engr regt
 1 EW regt
 1 CBRN regt
 4 sigs regt
EQUIPMENT BY TYPE
MBT 700 T-64BV/BM; (10 T-84 *Oplot*; 165 T-80; 600 T-72; 650 T-64; 20 T-55 all in store)
RECCE 450 BRDM-2
AIFV 1,249: 15 BMD-1, 15 BMD-2; 200 BMP-1; 900 BMP-2; 4 BMP-3; 115 BRM-1K
APC 490
 APC (T) 15 BTR-D
 APC (W) 360: up to 10 BTR-4; 5 BTR-60; 235 BTR-70; 110 BTR-80
ARTY 1,862
 SP 528+: **122mm** 240 2S1; **152mm** 288: 35 2S19 *Farm*; 235 2S3; 18 2S5; **203mm** 2S7 (up to 90 in store)

TOWED 515: **122mm** 75 D-30; **152mm** 440: 180 2A36; 130 2A65; 130 D-20
GUN/MOR • 120mm • TOWED 2 2B16 NONA-K
MRL 348: **122mm** 203: 18 9P138; 185 BM-21; **220mm** 70 9P140 *Uragan*; **300mm** 75 9A52 *Smerch*
MOR 120mm 220: 190 2S12; 30 PM-38
AT
  MSL • MANPATS 9K111 *Fagot* (AT-4 *Spigot*); 9K113 *Konkurs* (AT-5 *Spandrel*); 9K114 *Shturm* (AT-6 *Spiral*)
  GUNS 100mm ε500 MT-12/T-12
HELICOPTERS
  ATK 134 Mi-24 *Hind*
  TPT • Medium 30 Mi-8 *Hip*
AD
  SAM • SP 9K35 *Strela*-10 (SA-13 *Gopher*); 9K33 *Osa* (SA-8 *Gecko*); (Some S-300V (SA-12 *Gladiator*) in store)
  GUNS 470:
    SP 23mm ZU-23-2; **30mm** 70 2S6
    TOWED 57mm ε400 S-60
RADAR • LAND *Small Fred*/*Small Yawn*/SNAR-10 *Big Fred* (arty)
MSL • SSM 212: 50 FROG; 90 *Tochka* (SS-21 *Scarab*); 72 *Scud*-B
AEV 53 BAT-2; MT-LB
ARV BREM-2; BREM-64; T-54/T-55
VLB MTU-20

Navy 7,000 (incl Naval Aviation and Naval Infantry)

After Russia's annexation of Crimea, HQ shifted to Odessa. Several additional vessels remain in Russian possession in Crimea.

EQUIPMENT BY TYPE
PRINCIPAL SURFACE COMBATANTS 1
  FRIGATES • FFHM 1 *Hetman Sagaidachny* (RUS *Krivak* III) with 1 twin lnchr with *Osa-M* (SA-N-4 *Gecko*) SAM, 2 quad 533mm ASTT with T-53 HWT, 1 100mm gun, (capacity 1 Ka-27 *Helix* ASW hel)
PATROL AND COASTAL COMBATANTS 7
  CORVETTES • FSM 1 *Grisha* (II/V) with 1 twin lnchr with *Osa-M* (SA-N-4 *Gecko*) SAM, 2 twin 533mm ASTT with SAET-60 HWT, 1-2 RBU 6000 *Smerch* 2, 1 76mm gun
  PCFGM 2 *Tarantul* II (FSU *Molnya*) with 2 twin lnchr with P-15 Termit-R (SS-N-2D *Styx*) AShM; 1 quad lnchr (manual aiming) with 9K32 *Strela*-2 (SA-N-5 *Grail*); 1 76mm gun
  PHG 2 *Matka* (FSU *Vekhr*) with 2 single lnchr with P-15 Termit-M/R (SS-N-2C/D *Styx*) AShM, 1 76mm gun
  PCMT 1 *Pauk* I (FSU *Molnya* II) with 1 quad lnchr (manual aiming) with 9K32 Strela-2 (SA-N-5 *Grail*) SAM, 4 single 406mm TT, 2 RBU-1200, 1 76mm gun
  PB 1 *Zhuk* (FSU *Grif*)
MINE WARFARE • MINE COUNTERMEASURES 4
  MHI 1 *Yevgenya* (FSU *Korund*)
  MSO 1 *Natya* with 2 RBU 1200
  MSC 2 *Sonya* (FSU *Yakhont*)
AMPHIBIOUS
  LANDING SHIPS
    LSM 1 *Polnochny* C (capacity 6 MBT; 180 troops)

LANDING CRAFT 3
  LCAC 1 *Pomornik* (*Zubr*) with 2 quad lnchr with 9K32 *Strela*-2 (SA-N-5 *Grail*) SAM, 2 AK630 CIWS, (capacity 230 troops; either 3 MBT or 10 APC (T))
  LCU 2
LOGISTICS AND SUPPORT 30
  AG 2
  AGI 2 *Muna*
  AGS 1 *Biya*
  AKL 1
  AO 2 *Toplivo*
  AWT 1 *Sudak*
  AXL 3 *Petrushka*
  YDT 13: 1 *Yelva*; 12 other
  YTM 2
  YTR 2 *Pozharny*
  YY 1 *Sokal*

Naval Aviation ε1,000

EQUIPMENT BY TYPE
AIRCRAFT 1 combat capable
  ASW 1 Be-12 *Mail*
  TPT • Light 2 An-26 *Curl*
HELICOPTERS
  ASW 3 Mi-14 *Haze*
  TPT • Medium 1 Ka-29 *Helix*-B

Naval Infantry ε500

FORCES BY ROLE
MANOEUVRE
  Light
    1 inf bn

Air Forces 45,000

Flying hours 40 hrs/yr

FORCES BY ROLE
FIGHTER
  4 bde with MiG-29 *Fulcrum*; Su-27 *Flanker*
FIGHTER/GROUND ATTACK
  2 bde with Su-24M *Fencer*; Su-25 *Frogfoot*
ISR
  2 sqn with Su-24MR *Fencer* E*
TRANSPORT
  3 bde with An-24; An-26; An-30; Il-76 *Candid*; Tu-134 *Crusty*
TRAINING
  Some sqn with L-39 *Albatros*
TRANSPORT HELICOPTER
  Some sqn with Mi-8; Mi-9; PZL Mi-2 *Hoplite*
AIR DEFENCE
  11 bde/regt with 9K37M *Buk*-M1 (SA-11); S-300P/PS/PT (SA-10)
EQUIPMENT BY TYPE
AIRCRAFT 202 combat capable
  FTR 116: 80 MiG-29 *Fulcrum*; 36 Su-27 *Flanker*
  FGA 34 Su-24 *Fencer*
  ATK 29 Su-25 *Frogfoot*
  ISR 25: 2 An-30 *Clank*; 23 Su-24MR *Fencer* E*
  TPT 43: **Heavy** 18 Il-76 *Candid*; **Light** 25: 3 An-24 *Coke*; 20 An-26 *Curl*; 2 Tu-134 *Crusty*
  TRG 37 L-39 *Albatros*

HELICOPTERS
C2 4 Mi-9
TPT 33: **Medium** 30 Mi-8 *Hip*; **Light** 3 PZL Mi-2 *Hoplite*
AD • SAM • SP 322: 250 S-300P/PS/PT (SA-10 *Grumble*); 72 9K37M *Buk-M1* (SA-11 *Gadfly*)
MSL
ASM: Kh-25 (AS-10 *Karen*); Kh-59 (AS-13 *Kingbolt*); Kh-29 (AS-14 *Kedge*);
ARM: Kh-58 (AS-11 *Kilter*); Kh-25MP (AS-12 *Kegler*); Kh-28 (AS-9 *Kyle*)
AAM • IR R-60 (AA-8 *Aphid*); R-73 (AA-11 *Archer*)
SARH R-27 (AA-10A *Alamo*)

Airborne Forces ε5,500
FORCES BY ROLE:
MANOEUVRE
Air Manoeuvre
1 AB bde
3 air mob bde
EQUIPMENT BY TYPE
AIFV 75: 30 BMD-1; 45 BMD-2
APC 136
APC (T) 25 BTR-D
APC (W) 111: 1 BTR-60; 110 BTR-80
ARTY 118
TOWED • **122mm** 54 D-30
GUN/MOR • SP • **120mm** 40 2S9 *Anona*
MOR **120mm** 24 2S12

Paramilitary

National Guard ε33,000
Ministry of Internal Affairs; 6 territorial comd
FORCES BY ROLE
MANOEUVRE
Armoured
Some tk bn
Mechanised
Some mech bn
Light
Some lt inf bn
EQUIPMENT BY TYPE
MBT T-64; T-72 (reported)
AIFV BTR-3; ε50 BTR-4
APC
APC (W) BTR-70; BTR-80
PPV Streit *Cougar*; Streit *Spartan*

Border Guard n.k.

Maritime Border Guard
The Maritime Border Guard is an independent subdivision of the State Commission for Border Guards and is not part of the navy.
FORCES BY ROLE
PATROL
4 (cutter) bde
2 rvn bde
MINE WARFARE
1 MCM sqn

TRANSPORT
3 sqn
TRANSPORT HELICOPTER
1 sqn
COMBAT SERVICE SUPPORT
1 trg div
1 (aux ships) gp
EQUIPMENT BY TYPE
PATROL AND COASTAL COMBATANTS 26
PCFT 6 *Stenka* with 4 single 406mm TT
PCT 3 *Pauk* I with 4 single 406mm TT, 2 RBU-1200, 1 76mm gun
PHT 1 *Muravey* with 2 single 406mm TT, 1 76mm gun
PB 12: 11 *Zhuk*; 1 *Orlan* (seven additional vessels under construction)
PBR 4 *Shmel*
LOGISTICS AND SUPPORT • AGF 1
AIRCRAFT • **TPT Medium** An-8 *Camp*; **Light** An-24 *Coke*; An-26 *Curl*; An-72 *Coaler*
HELICOPTERS • ASW: Ka-27 *Helix* A

Civil Defence Troops n.k.
(Ministry of Emergency Situations)
FORCES BY ROLE
MANOEUVRE
Other
4 paramilitary bde
4 paramilitary regt

DEPLOYMENT
Legal provisions for foreign deployment:
Constitution: Codified constitution (1996)
Specific legislation: 'On the procedures to deploy Armed Forces of Ukraine units abroad' (1518-III, March 2000).
Decision on deployment of troops abroad: Parliament authorised to approve decision to provide military assistance, deploy troops abroad and allow foreign military presence in Ukraine (Art. 85, para 23); Also, in accordance with Art. 7 of the specific legislation (above), president is authorised to take a decision to deploy troops abroad and at the same time to submit a draft law to the Parliament of Ukraine for approval.

AFGHANISTAN
NATO • ISAF 10

ARMENIA/AZERBAIJAN
OSCE • Minsk Conference 1

CÔTE D'IVOIRE
UN • UNOCI 40; 1 hel flt

CYPRUS
UN • UNFICYP 2

DEMOCRATIC REPUBLIC OF THE CONGO
UN • MONUSCO 254; 10 obs; 2 atk hel sqn; 1 hel sqn

LIBERIA
UN • UNMIL 177; 2 obs; 1 hel sqn

MOLDOVA
10 obs

SERBIA
NATO • KFOR 25
OSCE • Kosovo 1
UN • UNMIK 2 obs

SOUTH SUDAN
UN • UNMISS 1; 3 obs

SUDAN
UN • UNISFA 2; 4 obs

FOREIGN FORCES

Albania OSCE 2
Armenia OSCE 2
Austria OSCE 7
Belarus OSCE 1
Belgium OSCE 3
Bosnia-Herzegovina OSCE 3
Bulgaria OSCE 8
Canada OSCE 5
Croatia OSCE 4
Czech Republic OSCE 9
Denmark OSCE 9
Estonia OSCE 7
Finland OSCE 21
France OSCE 12
Georgia OSCE 1
Germany OSCE 21
Greece OSCE 1
Hungary OSCE 18
Ireland OSCE 4
Italy OSCE 13
Kyrgyzstan OSCE 4
Latvia OSCE 5
Lithuania OSCE 2
Macedonia (FYROM) OSCE 1
Moldova OSCE 9
Montenegro OSCE 1
Netherlands OSCE 6
Norway OSCE 7
Poland OSCE 12
Romania OSCE 14
Russia OSCE 16
Slovakia 4
Slovenia 1
Spain OSCE 8
Sweden OSCE 9
Switzerland OSCE 9
Tajikistan OSCE 1
Turkey OSCE 6
United Kingdom OSCE 15
United States OSCE 28

TERRITORY WHERE THE GOVERNMENT DOES NOT EXERCISE EFFECTIVE CONTROL

Following the overthrow of Ukraine's President Yanukovich in February 2014, the region of Crimea requested to join the Russian Federation after a referendum regarded as unconstitutional by the new Ukrainian government. Data presented here represents the de facto situation and does not imply international recognition.

FOREIGN FORCES

Russia Crimea: 20,000; 2 naval inf bde; 1 arty bde; 80 BMP-2; 20 BTR-80; 150 MT-LB; 18 2S1 arty; 12 BM-21 MRL; 1 SAM bn with S-300PM; 1 AShM unit with K-300P *Bastion*; 1 Fleet HQ located at Sevastopol; 2 radar stations located at Sevastopol (*Dnepr* system) and Mukachevo (*Dnepr* system)

Donetsk/Luhansk: 300+ (reported)

Uzbekistan UZB

Uzbekistani Som s		2013	2014	2015
GDP	s	119tr	142tr	
	US$	56.8bn	63.1bn	
per capita	US$	1,878	2,061	
Growth	%	8.0	7.0	
Inflation	%	11.2	10.0	
Def exp	s	ε3.33tr		
	US$	ε1.59bn		
FMA (US)	US$	2.7m	1.2m	0.7m
US$1=s		2,094.66	2,249.76	

Population 28,929,716

Ethnic groups: Uzbek 73%; Russian 6%; Tajik 5%; Kazakh 4%; Karakalpak 2%; Tatar 2%; Korean <1%; Ukrainian <1%

Age	0–14	15–19	20–24	25–29	30–64	65 plus
Male	12.8%	5.0%	5.4%	5.3%	19.3%	2.0%
Female	12.1%	4.8%	5.4%	5.2%	20.0%	2.7%

Capabilities

Uzbekistan's conscript-based armed forces are the most capable in Central Asia, and better equipped than those of its immediate neighbours. In contrast to other Central Asian states, Uzbekistan maintains an ambivalent strategic relationship with Russia: although it uses mainly Soviet-era equipment, maintains bilateral defence ties and is a member of the SCO, it suspended its membership of the CSTO in mid-2012. The relationship with Russia may strengthen, though, after the withdrawal of international forces from Afghanistan leaves a potentially unstable country with multiple security concerns on Uzbekistan's border. As part of an agreement covering transit rights for US and UK military equipment returning from Afghanistan, the Uzbek armed forces will receive some military equipment, although the type and amount are unclear. Fixed-wing airlift is limited, but there is substantial rotary-wing lift, allowing for deployment across the country's challenging topography. Flying hours are reported to be low, with logistical and maintenance shortcomings affecting the availability of aircraft.

ACTIVE 48,000 (Army 24,500 Air 7,500 Joint 16,000)
Paramilitary 20,000
Conscript liability 12 months

ORGANISATIONS BY SERVICE

Army 24,500
4 Mil Districts; 2 op comd; 1 Tashkent Comd
FORCES BY ROLE
SPECIAL FORCES
  1 SF bde
MANOEUVRE
  Armoured
  1 tk bde
  Mechanised
  11 MR bde
  Air Manoeuvre
  1 air aslt bde
  1 AB bde
  Mountain
  1 lt mtn inf bde
COMBAT SUPPORT
  3 arty bde
  1 MRL bde
EQUIPMENT BY TYPE
MBT 340: 70 T-72; 100 T-64; 170 T-62
RECCE 19: 13 BRDM-2; 6 BRM
AIFV 399: 120 BMD-1; 9 BMD-2; 270 BMP-2
APC 309
  APC (T) 50 BTR-D
  APC (W) 259: 24 BTR-60; 25 BTR-70; 210 BTR-80
ARTY 487+
  SP 83+: **122mm** 18 2S1; **152mm** 17+: 17 2S3; 2S5 (reported); **203mm** 48 2S7
  TOWED 200: **122mm** 60 D-30; **152mm** 140 2A36
  GUN/MOR 120mm 54 2S9 *Anona*
  MRL 108: **122mm** 60: 24 9P138; 36 BM-21; **220mm** 48 9P140 *Uragan*
  MOR 120mm 42: 5 2B11; 19 2S12; 18 PM-120
AT • MSL • MANPATS 9K11 *Malyutka* (AT-3 *Sagger*); 9K111 *Fagot* (AT-4 *Spigot*)
  GUNS 100mm 36 MT-12/T-12

Air Force 7,500
FORCES BY ROLE
FIGHTER
  1 regt with MiG-29/MiG-29UB *Fulcrum*; Su-27/Su-27UB *Flanker*
FIGHTER/GROUND ATTACK
  1 regt with Su-24 *Fencer*; Su-24MP *Fencer* F*
GROUND ATTACK
  1 regt with Su-25/Su-25BM *Frogfoot*; Su-17M (Su-17MZ) *Fitter* C; Su-17UM-3 (Su-17UMZ) *Fitter* G
ELINT/TRANSPORT
  1 regt with An-12/An-12PP *Cub*; An-26/An-26RKR *Curl*
TRANSPORT
  Some sqn with An-24 *Coke*; Tu-134 *Crusty*
TRAINING
  Some sqn with L-39 *Albatros*
ATTACK/TRANSPORT HELICOPTER
  1 regt with Mi-24 *Hind*; Mi-26 *Halo*; Mi-8 *Hip*;
  1 regt with Mi-6 *Hook*; Mi-6AYa *Hook* C
EQUIPMENT BY TYPE
AIRCRAFT 135 combat capable
  FTR 30 MiG-29/MiG-29UB *Fulcrum*
  FGA 74: 26 Su-17M (Su-17MZ)/Su-17UM-3 (Su-17UMZ) *Fitter* C/G; 23 Su-24 *Fencer*; 25 Su-27/Su-27UB *Flanker*
  ATK 20 Su-25/Su-25BM *Frogfoot*
  EW/Tpt 26 An-12 *Cub* (med tpt)/An-12PP *Cub* (EW)
  ELINT 11 Su-24MP *Fencer* F*
  ELINT/Tpt 13 An-26 *Curl* (lt tpt)/An-26RKR *Curl* (ELINT)
  TPT • Light 2: 1 An-24 *Coke*; 1 Tu-134 *Crusty*
  TRG 5 L-39 *Albatros* (9 more in store)
HELICOPTERS
  ATK 29 Mi-24 *Hind*
  C2 2 Mi-6AYa *Hook* C
  TPT 79 **Heavy** 27: 26 Mi-6 *Hook*; 1 Mi-26 *Halo*; **Medium** 52 Mi-8 *Hip*
AD • SAM 45
  TOWED S-75 *Dvina* (SA-2 *Guideline*); S-125 *Pechora* (SA-3 *Goa*)
  STATIC S-200 *Angara* (SA-5 *Gammon*)
MSL
  ASM Kh-23 (AS-7 *Kerry*); Kh-25 (AS-10 *Karen*)
  ARM Kh-25P (AS-12 *Kegler*); Kh-28 (AS-9 *Kyle*); Kh-58 (AS-11 *Kilter*)
  AAM • IR R-60 (AA-8 *Aphid*); R-73 (AA-11 *Archer*); **IR/SARH** R-27 (AA-10 *Alamo*)

Paramilitary up to 20,000

Internal Security Troops up to 19,000
Ministry of Interior

National Guard 1,000
Ministry of Defence

FOREIGN FORCES
Germany 100; some C-160 *Transall*

Table 5 Selected Arms Procurements and Deliveries, Russia and Eurasia

Designation	Type	Quantity (Current)	Contract Value	Prime Nationality	Prime Contractor	Order Date	First Delivery Due	Notes
Azerbaijan (AZE)								
T-90S	MBT	100	n.k.	RUS	UKBTM	2013	2013	Deliveries ongoing
Sa'ar 62 OPV	PSO	6	n.k.	ISR	Israel Shipyards	2014	n.k.	For Coast Guard
Belarus (BLR)								
S-300PM	SAM	16	Free transfer	RUS	Government surplus	2014	n.k.	Donation of four batteries
Kazakhstan (KAZ)								
BTR-82A	AIFV	190	n.k.	RUS	VPK	2011	2011	Deliveries ongoing
C-295M	Lt tpt ac	2	n.k.	Int'l	Airbus Group (Airbus Defence & Space)	2013	2014	Follow-on to original 2012 order. Part of an eight ac MoU. First ac in test
Russia (RUS)								
Bulava (SS-N-X-32)	SLBM	n.k.	n.k.	RUS	MITT	n.k.	2009	In development. For Borey-class SSBNs
T-72B3	MBT upgrade	n.k.	n.k.	RUS	UKBTM	n.k.	2013	Upgrade of existing T-72 fleet. First delivered to Western Military District in 2013
Armata	AFV	n.k.	n.k.	RUS	UKBTM	2014	2015	Heavy tracked universal combat platform programme. Serial production scheduled to commence 2016
Kurganets-25	AFV	n.k.	n.k.	RUS	KMZ	2014	2015	Medium tracked universal combat platform programme. Serial production scheduled to commence 2016
Bumerang	AFV	n.k.	n.k.	RUS	VPK	2014	2015	Medium wheeled universal combat platform programme
BTR-82A	AIFV	n.k.	n.k.	RUS	VPK	n.k.	2011	Improved BTR-80A series; first production models delivered to Southern Military District in 2011
Borey-class	SSBN	3	n.k.	RUS	Sevmash Shipyard	1996	2012	Second vessel commissioned Dec 2013. Third in sea trials. 16 SLBM launch tubes
Borey-A-class	SSBN	5	n.k.	RUS	Sevmash Shipyard	2012	2015	Two vessels laid down so far. Pricing dispute continues and will be reviewed in 2015
Yasen-class	SSN	5	n.k.	RUS	Sevmash Shipyard	1993	2013	First vessel commissioned Dec 2013. Delayed for financial reasons. Fourth laid down May 2014
Varshavyanka-class (Kilo)	SSK	6	n.k.	RUS	Admiralty Shipyards	2010	2014	First vessel commissioned Aug 2014. Fifth and sixth laid down late Oct 2014
Lada-class	SSK	3	n.k.	RUS	Admiralty Shipyards	1997	2010	First vessel accepted in 2010. Construction on further two boats suspended in 2011 but resumed in 2012/13
Admiral Gorshkov-class	FFGHM	6	US$400m	RUS	Severnaya Verf Shipyard	2005	2014	First vessel in trials as of late 2014
Steregushchiy-class	FFGHM	6	n.k.	RUS	Severnaya Verf Shipyard/ Komosololsk Shipyard	2001	2008	Third vessel delivered to Baltic Fleet May 2013; fourth vessel delivered Jun 2014. Two more in build for Pacific Fleet

Table 5 Selected Arms Procurements and Deliveries, Russia and Eurasia

Designation	Type	Quantity (Current)	Contract Value	Prime Nationality	Prime Contractor	Order Date	First Delivery Due	Notes
Improved Steregushchiy-class	FFGHM	2	n.k.	RUS	Severnaya Verf Shipyard	2011	2015	First of class laid down Feb 2012. Second of class laid down Jul 2013
Admiral Grigorovich-class (*Krivak* IV)	FFGHM	6	n.k.	RUS	Yantar Shipyard	2010	2014	Six vessels in build for Black Sea Fleet. First vessel launched Mar 2014. ISD expected Nov 2014
Buyan-M-class	FSG	12	n.k.	RUS	Zelenodolsk Shipyard	2010	2014	Nine for Caspian Flotilla and three for Black Sea Fleet. First vessels commissioned Jul 2014
Vladivostok-class (*Mistral*)	LHD	2	US$1.2bn	FRA	DCNS/STX	2011	n.k.	Contract suspended by France Sep 2014 citing Russian actions in Ukraine
Tu-160 *Blackjack*	Bbr ac upgrade	15	n.k.	RUS	UAC	2007	2012	Upgrade of *Blackjack* fleet, programme lagging behind original schedule
MiG-29K *Fulcrum* D	Ftr ac	24	n.k.	RUS	UAC (MiG)	2012	2013	20 MiG-29K and four MiG-29KUB. For navy. Deliveries ongoing
MiG-29SMT *Fulcrum*	FGA ac	16	R17bn (US$470m)	RUS	UAC (MiG)	2014	2015	Eight to be delivered in 2015 and remainder in 2016
Su-30M2	FGA ac	16	n.k.	RUS	UAC (Sukhoi)	2012	2014	Deliveries ongoing
Su-30SM	FGA ac	72	n.k.	RUS	UAC (Sukhoi)	2012	2012	Twelve for navy and 60 for air force. Deliveries under way
Su-34 *Fullback*	FGA ac	60	n.k.	RUS	UAC (Sukhoi)	2012	2014	Deliveries ongoing
Su-35S *Flanker*	FGA ac	48	See notes	RUS	UAC (Sukhoi)	2009	2012	Part of combined order for 48 Su-35S, 12 Su-27SM3 and four Su-30 worth US$2.5bn. Deliveries ongoing
Il-76MD-90A	Hvy tpt ac	39	US$4bn	RUS	Aviastar-SP	2012	2014	First ac rolled out Jun 2014; delivery due by end of 2014
Ka-52 *Hokum* B	Atk hel	140	US$4bn	RUS	Russian Helicopters (Kamov)	2011	2011	Deliveries ongoing
Mi-28N *Havoc*	Atk hel	30	n.k.	RUS	Russian Helicopters (Rostvertol)	2010	2013	Follow-up to 2005 order for 67. Deliveries ongoing
Mi-8AMTSh *Hip*	Med tpt hel	172	n.k.	Rus	Russian Helicopters (Ulan-Ude)	2010	2010	Deliveries began in late 2010 and are ongoing
Mi-8MTV-5 *Hip*	Med tpt hel	140	n.k.	RUS	Russian Helicopters (Kazan)	2011	2014	First batch delivered Oct 2014
Tor-M2 (SA-15 *Gauntlet*)	SAM	n.k.	n.k.	RUS	Almaz-Antey	n.k.	n.k.	Deliveries ongoing
Buk-M2 (SA-17 *Grizzly*)	SAM	n.k.	n.k.	RUS	Almaz-Antey	n.k.	n.k.	One bde set delivered. May be succeeded by *Buk*-M3
S-400 *Triumf* (SA-21 *Growler*)	SAM	18	n.k.	RUS	Almaz-Antey	n.k.	2007	Seventh regt deployed 2014
S-300V4 (SA-23 *Gladiator/Giant*)	SAM	12	n.k.	RUS	Almaz-Antey	2012	n.k.	Three battalion sets
96K6 *Pantsir*-S1	AD	n.k.	n.k.	RUS	KBP Instrument Design Bureau	n.k.	2010	Delivery in progress to S-400 regiments
9K720 *Iskander*	SRBM/ LACM	n.k.	n.k.	RUS	KBM	2005	2006	Ballistic and cruise missile variants. In service with four brigades by late 2014
Ukraine (UKR)								
BTR-4	APC (W)	194	n.k.	UKR	KMDB	2014	2014	Being delivered to national-guard units

Chapter Six
Asia

Recent efforts throughout the Asia-Pacific to enhance military capabilities have focused on the maritime domain, reflecting growing disquiet over vulnerability to attack from the sea as well as concerns over natural resources, territorial claims and freedom of navigation. In some cases, these efforts have included bolstering sea-denial capacity, with the aim of complicating potential adversaries' naval deployments and operations. For instance, an important objective of China's growing maritime and air-warfare capabilities is the deterrence of United States naval deployments in its littoral waters. This is to be achieved, according to Western defence officials, by establishing an effective 'anti-access/area-denial' capacity that benefits from China's development of advanced anti-ship cruise missiles and over-the-horizon targeting.

Meanwhile, Asian states with ambitious naval programmes have prioritised the development of aviation-capable platforms and marinised fixed- and rotary-wing aircraft. In 2012, China's People's Liberation Army Navy (PLAN) conducted flight trials of J-15 combat aircraft on its first aircraft carrier, the *Liaoning*. The carrier sailed on exercises in December 2013, accompanied by escorts and support vessels, highlighting China's efforts to develop a carrier battle group. There are reports that China is building a second carrier. Alongside the continuing development and construction of other major surface combatants, notably the Type-052D destroyer and the reported Type-55 cruiser programme, these projects showcased China's growing investment in maritime power-projection capabilities (see pp. 213, 215).

Japan's December 2013 Mid-Term Defense Plan outlined procurement projects for the 2014–19 period, including new destroyers, additional submarines, unmanned aerial vehicles for long-range maritime surveillance, F-35A Joint Strike Fighters and tilt-rotor aircraft. The easing, from April 2014, of Tokyo's self-imposed ban on arms exports, following the new National Security Strategy announced in December 2013 and subsequent 'Three Principles on Defense Equipment Transfers', may help strengthen the country's military capabilities by allowing greater joint development of equipment (see pp. 221–25).

South Korea, engaged in a dispute with Japan over the Dokdo/Takeshima Islands and with China over Socotra Rock, is pursuing several ambitious maritime programmes. These encompass an eventual fleet of nine *Son Won-il*-class (German Type-214) submarines, new frigates under the FFX programme – the fourth of which was launched in August 2014 – and a second helicopter carrier. In March 2014, South Korea agreed to buy 40 F-35A Joint Strike Fighters as the third stage of its FX combat-aircraft programme. Under its 2013–17 Mid-Term Defense Plan, Seoul continues to strengthen its deterrent and defensive capabilities in response to North Korea's nuclear, missile, conventional and cyber capacity. Central to these emerging capabilities is the 'Kill Chain' programme, which, according to the 2012 defence white paper, could allow South Korea to mount pre-emptive strikes on North Korean missiles and their 'command and support force'. To provide some protection against the threat from North Korea's missiles, Seoul is developing the Korean Air and Missile Defense system, based on the US *Patriot* surface-to-air missile system, and locally built air-defence radars.

Vietnam's efforts to enhance its naval and air capabilities are intended to deter Chinese naval operations in contested areas of the South China Sea. The first two of six Project 636-class (*Kilo*-class) submarines ordered in 2009 from Russia were delivered by March 2014. The US government announced in October 2014 that it would further ease its long-standing arms embargo, to 'allow for the future transfer of maritime security related lethal defense articles to Vietnam'. Analysts believe this might open the way for Vietnam to acquire refurbished US Navy surplus P-3C *Orion* patrol and anti-submarine-warfare aircraft or even P-8A *Poseidon*s, both of which Hanoi is reported to have considered. In the medium to long term, Vietnam may also be interested in acquiring European combat aircraft such as the Swedish *Gripen* E.

The Philippines, another state directly facing China's assertiveness in the South China Sea, has traditionally been unwilling to devote resources to external defence on the same scale as Vietnam, relying primarily on a reinvigorated alliance with the US to bolster its security. In August 2013, the US and the Philippines began negotiations with the aim of boosting rotational deployments of US forces. In April 2014, these talks led to an Enhanced Defense Cooperation Agreement, under which US forces would be granted wider access to Philippine bases and allowed to pre-position equipment. However, a revived emphasis by the Armed Forces of the Philippines (AFP) on external defence is evident. In February 2014, there was agreement to buy 12 South Korean-built FA-50 armed advanced training aircraft. Although an earlier plan to purchase F-16 *Fighting Falcon*s from the US was abandoned, a medium-term requirement for high-performance combat aircraft remains. Despite an increasing emphasis on external defence, countering internal security challenges remained a significant AFP role, notably in Sulu Province, where operations continued against the 200-strong Abu Sayyaf Group.

Singapore also takes external defence seriously. Minister for Defence Dr Ng Eng Hen used the March 2014 parliamentary budget debate to outline the 'SAF 2030' plan that will guide the development of the Singapore Armed Forces (SAF) over the next decade and a half. According to the minister, Singapore needed to adopt a 'more robust and resilient approach' and develop the SAF into an even more highly connected force, in response to the prevailing regional security environment. The SAF would benefit from greater mobility deriving from further army mechanisation and possibly also larger, helicopter-equipped amphibious ships. In November 2013, Singapore announced a contract for two new Type-218SG submarines from Germany, which are due to come into service by 2020, alongside two *Archer*-class (modernised Swedish A-17-class) boats commissioned in 2011 and 2013. It was unclear whether the Type-218SG would be derived from the German Type-214 already exported to several other countries or the much larger, 4,000-tonne Type-216 that features a vertical-launch system allowing armament with anti-ship and land-attack cruise missiles. Singapore also maintained efforts to enhance its air capabilities. Additional batches of F-15SG long-range strike aircraft, delivered between 2012 and 2014, will bring the SAF's total inventory of the type to 40. The SAF is also widely expected to acquire F-35 Joint Strike Fighters to replace its F-16C/D *Fighting Falcon*s, although in December 2013 Defence Minister Ng said that Singapore was 'in no particularly hurry'.

In Indonesia, rapid economic growth has allowed the government to increase defence funding. In January 2013, Defence Minister Purnomo Yusgiantoro announced the acceleration of plans to establish a 'Minimum Essential Force' (MEF) to defend against external and domestic threats, the target date for which has moved forward from 2024 to 2019. Reflecting Jakarta's concern over rising tensions in the South China Sea, the MEF has a strong maritime emphasis. Indonesia's most important and likely most expensive defence-procurement programme involves submarines. Jakarta ordered an initial three German-designed Type 209-1400 submarines from South Korea in 2011; the first and second boats are scheduled for delivery by 2017. Reports indicate that Jakarta might be considering *Kilo*-class boats from Russia in future. New surface ships on order or entering service include two additional *Sigma*-class corvettes (to be partially built in Indonesia) and three British-built corvettes originally constructed for Brunei. Meanwhile, Indonesia's air force took delivery in July of the first three of 24 refurbished ex-US Air Force (USAF) F-16C/D fighters provided under the Peace Bima Sena III programme. In the middle of the year, it also began receiving a batch of nine ex-USAF C-130H *Hercules* transport aircraft.

Malaysia's government has continued incremental efforts to modernise its armed forces. However, domestic spending priorities have constrained defence-spending increases despite significant capability gaps, exposed by security-related crises in 2013–14. In February and March 2013, intruders from the southern Philippines provoked a battle with Malaysia's armed forces at Lahad Datu in Sabah State. This led to new demands on the defence and security budget. In October 2014, the government announced that its 2015 budget included RM660 million (US$211m) to bolster the Eastern Sabah Security Command, established in March 2013 following the Lahad Datu incident. This would include the construction of new camps for army and police battalions, the relocation of an air-force *Hawk* squadron to Labuan Island and the procurement of advanced monitoring radars. Though Malaysia's air force received a new air-defence sector operations centre, including a *Ground Master* 400 radar in early 2013, the disappearance of Malaysian Airlines flight MH370 in March 2014 revealed weaknesses in the country's air surveillance and command, control and communications network, suggesting further modernisation is necessary.

Thailand's armed forces, which seized power again in a May 2014 coup, have benefited from increased defence budgets and major procurement projects since an earlier coup in 2006. With completion of the air force's acquisition of *Gripen* combat aircraft and airborne early-warning platforms, and a programme to upgrade its F-16A/Bs under way, the procurement focus has shifted to the navy, which in August 2013 ordered from South Korea the first of two frigates to replace its *Knox*-class ships. In July 2014, the navy inaugurated its submarine headquarters and training school at Sattahip Naval Base, but there was no indication of when adequate funding for the purchase of boats would be available. Meanwhile, the insurgency in Thailand's southernmost Malay-majority provinces continued unabated, indicating that internal security would remain an important preoccupation for the armed forces, in particular the army.

Australia's commitment to enhancing its defence capabilities has been striking. Under the Labor administration, which lost power following the September 2013 general election, naval modernisation included acquisition of three *Hobart*-class air-warfare destroyers, which will enter service from 2016, and two *Canberra*-class amphibious ships, the first of which began sea trials in August 2014. The new conservative coalition led by Prime Minister Tony Abbott made electoral promises to increase defence spending to 2% of GDP and to review defence plans in a white paper due for publication in 2015. In April 2014, Abbott and Defence Minister David Johnston announced Australia's commitment to purchase 58 more F-35A Joint Strike Fighters in addition to the 14 aircraft ordered in 2009. The first two F-35As for Australia were rolled out in July 2014, and initial operational capability is scheduled for 2020. In addition, 12 EA-18G *Growler* electronic-warfare aircraft, optimised for the suppression of enemy air defences, will be delivered from 2017. In August 2014, Canberra ordered four P-8A maritime-patrol aircraft, from a planned total of eight approved in February 2014. The eventual replacement of the *Collins*-class submarines was the priority naval programme, and the Abbott government showed serious interest in the possibility of acquiring Japanese *Soryu*-class boats to fulfil this requirement. However, this idea was controversial in Japan as well as Australia, and there were major obstacles to its realisation.

New Zealand's defence programme has remained low-key, but defence planners have made considerable efforts to secure capability improvements, despite severe funding constraints. Equipment orders include ten ex-Australian SH-2G *Super Seasprite* naval helicopters, due to be delivered from late 2014, and 11 Beechcraft T-6C *Texan* IIs, which will revive the air force's high-performance pilot-training capability from mid-2015. The latest Defence Capability Plan, released in June 2014, outlined a 'more integrated defence force'. It also listed procurement ambitions for the next decade, including a new 'maritime sustainment capability' to replace the support ship HMNZS *Endeavour* and new 'littoral operations' ships. The document anticipated the need for 'special investment' to replace existing frigates and maritime-patrol aircraft after 2020.

DEFENCE ECONOMICS

Regional macroeconomics

Asian regional growth rose from 5.2% in 2013 to a projected 5.5% in 2014, supported by healthy domestic demand and tight labour markets in most states. In many cases these were augmented by a combination of supportive monetary policies, strong credit growth and improved exports. Although Chinese growth is down from the double-digit levels common between 2003 and 2010, it was at a steady 7.5% in 2014 – after 7.7% in the preceding two years – partly due to mini-stimulus measures enacted in support of moderating economic activity in the second half of 2013. Growth in India was projected to exceed 5% in 2014 (after two years of below 5% increases) on the back of higher investment spending, increased export competitiveness following the depreciation of the rupee and improved business sentiment after the BJP's electoral victory in April 2014. Political instability in Bangladesh in 2013 and in Thailand in 2014 affected growth, while fiscal consolidation in Japan (see textbox, p. 224) and the slowdown in mining-investment activity in Australia weighed on economic activity in these states. Nonetheless, with the exception of Japan, 2014 growth was projected by the International Monetary Fund (IMF) to exceed 2% in all 26 countries in the region, and more than half of these (15 states) were expected to surpass 5%, reflecting the generally strong fundamentals underlying regional economic activity.

Regional defence spending

Defence spending in Asia has risen by 27.2% since 2010, from US$270.6 billion to US$344.2bn in 2014. Although just under half this nominal increase occurred between 2010 and 2011 (partly the product of currency appreciation and elevated regional infla-

210 THE MILITARY BALANCE 2015

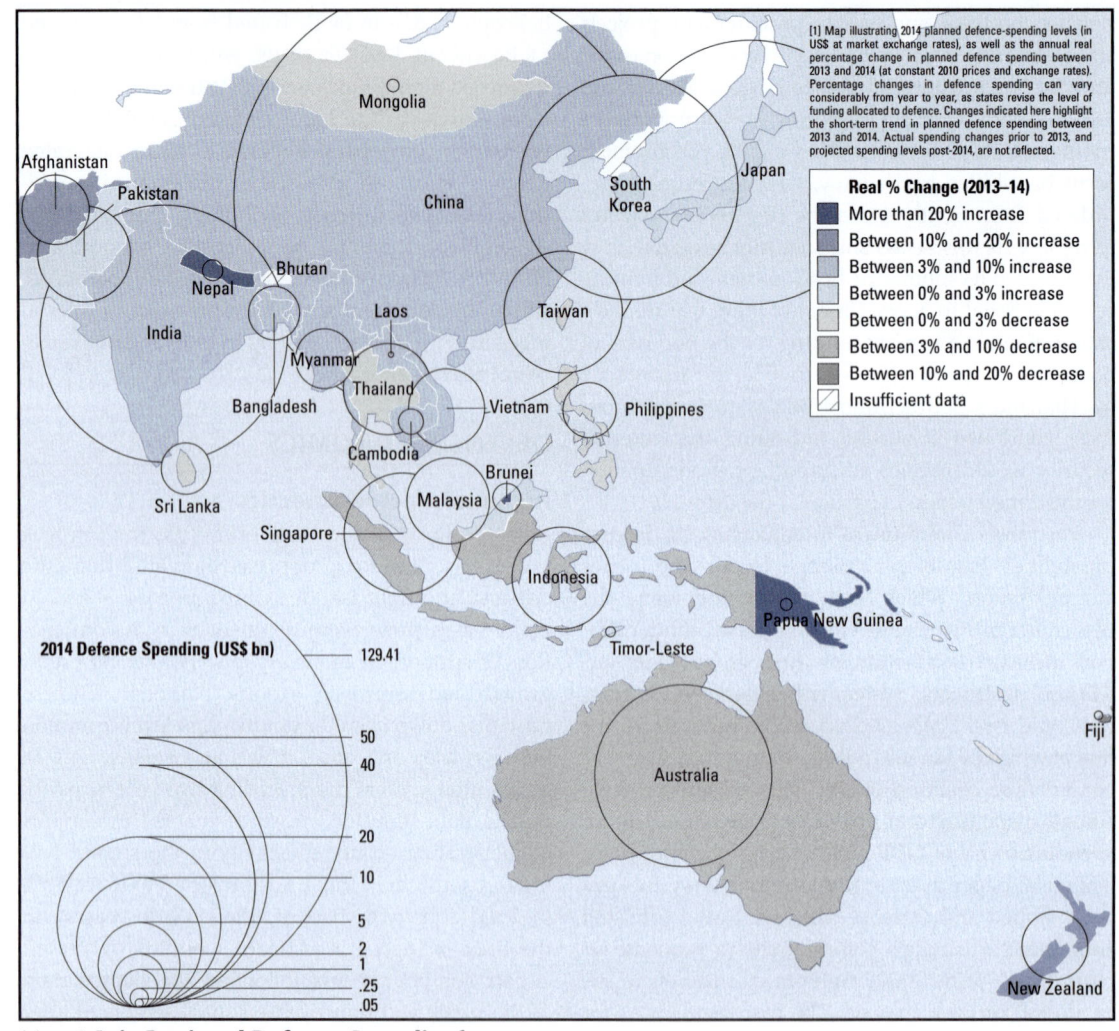

Map 6 **Asia Regional Defence Spending**[1]

tion), there were also strong, sustained increments in real defence spending between 2011 and 2014, averaging 4.3% over the period. In 2014, real regional defence outlays decelerated to 4.2%, from 5.0% in the previous year. Real defence spending rose most quickly in East Asia (5.4%) followed by South Asia (4.8%) and Southeast Asia (1.2%). The surprisingly low Southeast Asian increase was well below its recent trajectory – the sub-region has led Asian defence-spending growth since 2010, averaging 5.1% over the period – and may reflect an adjustment after a near 10% real increase in 2013. Overall, real Asian defence spending in 2014 was 16.1% higher than in 2010, equivalent to a real compound annual growth rate of 3.8%. However, a significant proportion of these increases reflects rapid growth in the Chinese defence budget, which, if excluded from the analysis, would cause average real Asian defence spending rises between 2010 and 2014 to fall to 2.4% per annum instead of 3.8%.

China dominates 2014 spending increases

Chinese defence-spending increases have outstripped those of other regional states in recent years. While China accounted for some 28% of the Asian total in 2010, by 2014 this had risen to around 38%. By contrast, Japan's share of regional outlays fell from 20.2% in 2010 to 13.9% in 2014, while that of India dropped from 15.4% to 13.1%. This medium-term reconfiguration of overall regional defence outlays towards China accelerated in 2014: China's 12.2% nominal defence-budget increase accounted for nearly two-thirds (63.4%) of total real Asian increases in 2014 (see Figure 10), dwarfing spending growth

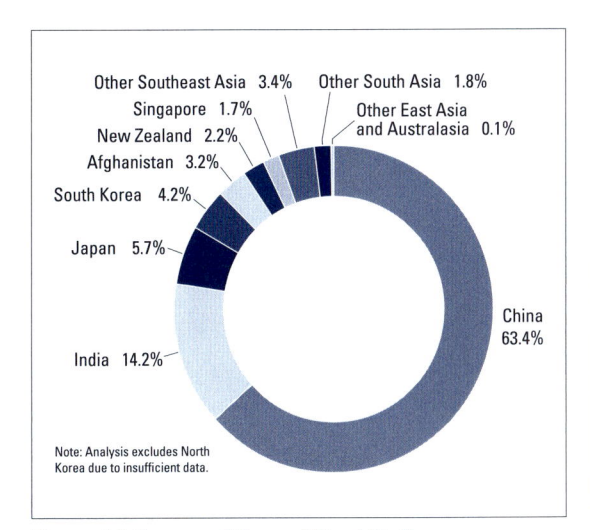

Figure 10 **Composition of Real Defence Spending Increases 2013–14**

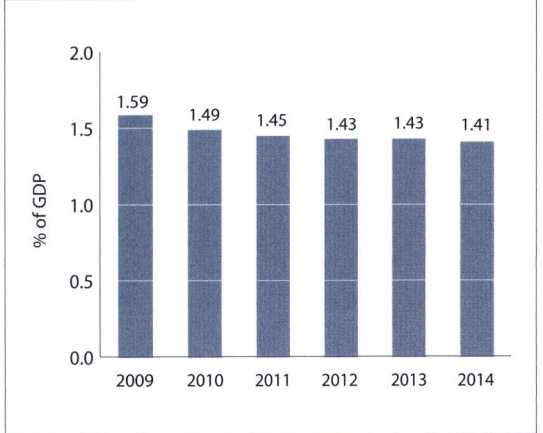

Figure 11 **Asia Regional Defence Expenditure** as % of GDP

elsewhere in the region, including India (14.2% of total increases), Japan (5.7%) and South Korea (4.2%). There are indications that this trend may continue into the latter half of the decade, with the IMF projecting that China will increase its share of total Asian GDP from 32% in 2010 to 46% by 2019. Even if rates of defence-spending increases in China only matched its broader GDP growth rates – as has generally been the case for the past ten years (see The Military Balance 2014, pp. 209–10) – China would still account for just over 41% of total regional defence outlays by the end of the decade.

GDP growth and real defence-budget increases
In contrast to the above-GDP growth increase seen in China, in general 2014 Asian real defence spending did not keep pace with GDP growth. Real defence-budget growth trailed economic growth rates in 17 out of 26 regional states. The gap between economic growth and defence-spending increases indicates that, in a majority of states, there might be fiscal space to expand defence outlays. It is also reflected in the general decline in defence spending as a proportion of regional GDP, which has gradually fallen from 1.59% of GDP in 2009 to 1.4% in 2014 (see Figure 11).

Analysis of defence spending and economic growth rates over a three-year period shows a degree of variation between Asian states over the extent to which strong economic growth rates have filtered through to defence-budget growth. Average real defence-spending growth between 2012 and 2014 exceeded average GDP growth in 13 out of 26 Asian states, including Indonesia, Vietnam, New Zealand and Brunei – although it should be noted that increases in the latter two were partly the product of budgetary reclassifications and changes to reporting methods. Over the same period, average real defence spending fell below average GDP growth in 12 countries, including in five of the largest spenders in the region: India, Japan, South Korea, Taiwan and Singapore.

Regional funding patterns in 2014
Increased funding was directed towards a variety of different priorities across the region in 2014. In Taiwan, personnel expenditure rose as the country continued its transition to an all-volunteer force, while in Papua New Guinea funding increases were principally directed towards management and support services, as well as a proposed expansion in personnel. Higher levels of equipment procurement were seen in Japan, Indonesia and the Philippines, with all three states in the midst of multi-year acquisition programmes. In all these states, defence-infrastructure investment also received increased budgetary priority, as facilities were built and upgraded to accommodate changes to force dispositions.

However, defence spending as a proportion of GDP in these three states remains among the lowest in the region, at or below 1% of GDP. In an attempt to reverse this trend, Japan has announced a series of progressively larger nominal increases to its defence budget (0.8% in 2013, 2.8% in 2014 and a proposed 5% in 2015), while the incoming Indonesian president, Joko Widodo, has pledged to maintain the country's plan to raise the defence budget to 1.5% of GDP over

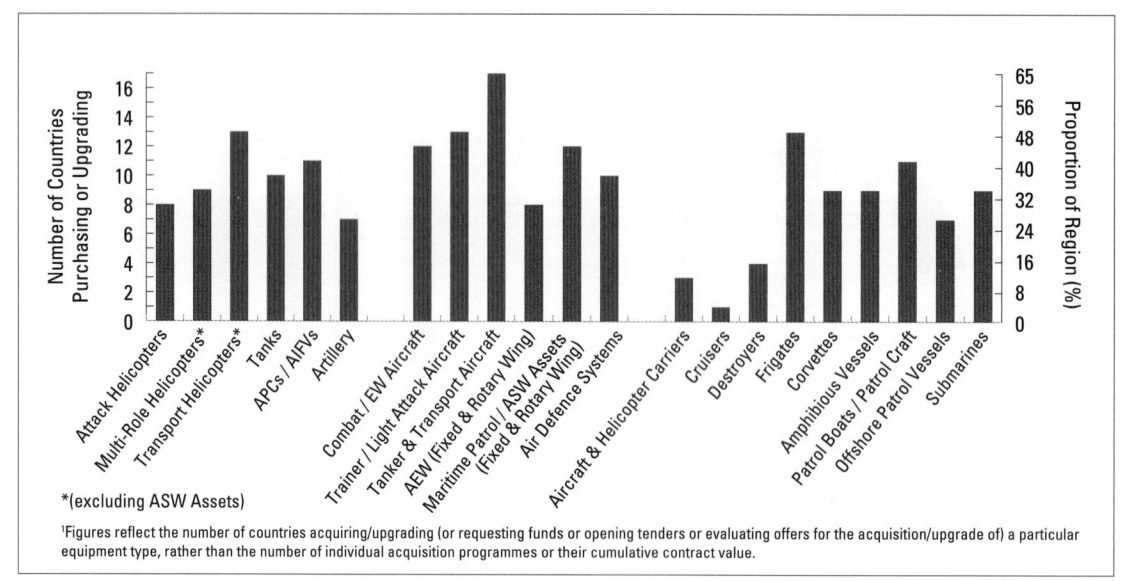

Figure 12 **Asia: Selected Procurement & Upgrade Priorities Since 2010**[1]

*(excluding ASW Assets)

[1] Figures reflect the number of countries acquiring/upgrading (or requesting funds or opening tenders or evaluating offers for the acquisition/upgrade of) a particular equipment type, rather than the number of individual acquisition programmes or their cumulative contract value.

the next five years. In August 2014, the Philippines Department of National Defense requested PHP10bn (US$227m) in supplemental funding for equipment procurement, on top of the 29% nominal increase (PHP26bn, or US$591m) in the 2015 defence budget it was due to receive.

Elsewhere in the region, defence-spending increases have prioritised local defence-industrial production facilities and supply chains. For example, in Pakistan – where state underfunding has meant that the domestic aerospace sector has had to rely on Chinese loans to maintain production lines – the national assembly announced in late June 2014 an additional PKR1.49bn (US$14m) for the Ministry of Defence Production. This was to support expenditures relating to overhaul of the production and repair machinery owned by the Karachi Shipyard and Engineering Works, and came on top of an earlier allocation of PKR937.3m (US$8.9m) in the national budget. Similarly, the new Australian government announced in December 2013 that the defence budget would be protected from further cuts, stating that this was partly due to concerns over the rapid loss of highly skilled jobs in the defence sector, particularly in naval manufacturing.

The rate of defence-spending growth in 2014 slowed in Bangladesh (a 5.1% real increase), where there had been – between 2012 and 2014 – spending increases that averaged 17% in nominal terms (10% in real terms), as the country undertook a military-modernisation programme. Defence spending growth also slowed in Malaysia (a real increase of 1%), and in Thailand (a decline of -0.6%), as financial constraints in the former and political turmoil in the latter restricted new equipment outlays in 2014, the dissolution of parliament in the case of Thailand leading to delays in budgetary approvals. Modest real-spending increases were seen in Singapore (2.8%), New Zealand (approximately 3%) and India (4.5%). Singapore maintained its policy of avoiding sharp spikes and troughs in its spending trends, while in December 2013 New Zealand abandoned its 2010 policy of achieving efficiency savings of NZ$400m (US$344m) per year. India, meanwhile, was constrained by broader economic pressures, leaving its non-pension defence budget at its lowest percentage of GDP in more than 50 years. This was despite the Modi administration's minor 2.18% increase in the final budget over the initial outlay proposed by the outgoing coalition.

CHINA

Despite a weaker economic environment in China in 2014, there has been no reduction in either the country's strategic or military ambitions. Defence spending has still increased at double-digit percentages, and substantial procurement programmes continue unabated across the services. Driven by leadership concerns about mounting challenges to the country's regional security and technological capabilities, more investment is being poured into research and development (R&D), greater effort is being made to acquire and absorb foreign technologies and the existing defence-innovation system is being overhauled.

Military development has taken on greater importance under the leadership of President Xi Jinping. Assertive security policies in the East and South China seas in 2014 led to continued tension with China's neighbours, notably during the deployment of an oil rig and associated fleet of civilian and paramilitary vessels south of the Paracel Islands between May and July. Meanwhile, overseas exercises have become more frequent and greater in ambition: in February 2014, the first Chinese exercise in the southeastern Indian Ocean took place, and in July the People's Liberation Army (PLA) made its debut in the annual, US-led RIMPAC naval exercise.

Reflecting a greater strategic confidence within China under the Xi administration, such activity affirms the president's strong position within the PLA more broadly. The president's career has been closely linked to the armed forces and security services: his first political and professional position was as a secretary in the Central Military Commission (CMC), and he was subsequently first political commissar for the People's Armed Police in Hebei, first secretary for the Nanjing Military Region, first political commissar for the PLA's Reserve Artillery Division in Fujian, and director of the National Defense Mobilisation Committee in Fujian and Zhejiang provinces.

This military pedigree in Xi's political positions, his ability to centralise power and his image as a strong leader afford the president significant influence over the PLA and security services. Xi has overseen a series of personnel reshuffles, including five army group commanders and four political commissars in 2014. These have further strengthened his hand in dealing with the PLA. This influence comes despite introducing potentially unpopular anti-corruption measures. The president undertook a comprehensive purge against key individuals, including Zhou Yongkang, the former secretary of the Central Political and Legal Committee who oversaw the country's security apparatus, as well as expelling Xu Caihou, former vice-chairman of the CMC, from the Chinese Communist Party in June 2014 during a bribery investigation.

He has also emphasised the importance to the PLA of R&D. Chairing an August 2014 study session of the Politburo devoted to examining trends in military innovation, Xi said that a global revolution in military science and technology was taking place 'at a speed so fast, in a scope so wide, at a level so deep, and with an impact so great that it has been rarely seen since the end of World War Two'. He added that this represented both a challenge and an opportunity, which required China's defence establishment 'to vigorously promote military innovation'.

However, even this area of the military is not immune to graft. At the PLA's annual conference on military-discipline inspection work in January 2014, CMC Vice-Chairman General Xu Qiliang pointed out that armament research, production and procurement was an area that required 'better oversight' to prevent corruption and malfeasance. The scale of corruption in the procurement system is difficult to gauge, due to an unwillingness to provide public information, although some corruption activities in non-sensitive areas such as military construction projects have been disclosed.

People's Liberation Army Navy

The PLAN appears to be entering a new era in its development. The 'leapfrog' development of platforms over the last 20 years – with just one or two vessels in a class being built – has now ended as China has become satisfied with the quality and technology level of its shipbuilding. In its place, the PLAN is undertaking mass production of destroyers (Type-052D), frigates (Type-054A) and corvettes (Type-056) to build a navy sufficient in numbers to patrol its near seas and project power into the Pacific and Indian oceans.

Counter-piracy patrols in the Indian Ocean continue, with the 18th PLAN task force dispatched in August 2014 including, for the first time, a submarine. The presence of the Type-039 boat, as well as the fact that piracy has been almost eliminated off the coast of Somalia, indicates that the counter-piracy patrols are no longer solely about maritime security. Rather, as indicated by a host of port visits and diplomatic events, they represent useful extra-regional forays, to build relationships, experience and presence. Such expeditions are not confined to the Indian Ocean; the PLAN sent a four-ship flotilla to the world's largest multinational naval exercise, the US-led RIMPAC, for the first time in 2014.

After a flurry of new equipment programmes in recent years, from the *Liaoning* aircraft carrier to destroyers and corvettes, more are under way. Perhaps the most significant is what analysts are calling the Type-055 cruiser, revealed in 2014 through

PLA ground forces: structural developments

The PLA's ground forces underwent two rounds of personnel and force-structure reductions, beginning in 1997 and 2003. Before that, main combat forces were organised into 24 'group armies' (corps-equivalents) and independent units numbering about 78 infantry and 12 tank divisions; two infantry and 13 tank brigades; six artillery divisions and 23 artillery brigades; and seven helicopter (army aviation) regiments, as well as numerous support units. No special-operations forces (SOF) units were acknowledged. Not all units were maintained at full strength, but those that were generally followed former-Soviet organisational principles. In the 17 years since 1997, this order of battle has undergone significant change in terms of structure and numbers. Further reforms are expected in coming years.

In its defence white papers, Beijing has provided a general outline of past force changes, summarised as 'reducing quantity and improving quality' and, in particular, accelerating development of 'new types of combat forces', such as army aviation, light mechanised, SOF and 'digitised' units. Some observers have called the changes a 'brigadisation' of the army, but that has not yet been totally realised: about 20 infantry divisions and one armoured division remain both in the 18 group armies and as independent units. (No artillery divisions currently exist.) These divisions, however, have been restructured from the former Soviet model; transitioning from four to three manoeuvre regiments plus associated support units.

In the years after these reductions began, many divisions were downsized into one brigade of the same type. However, since 2011 several divisions have been restructured into two brigades of different types. Among the first units to undergo this transformation was the showcase 196th Infantry Division in Yangcun, near Tianjin, which in 1998 had become the 196th Motorised Infantry Brigade. At the same time, the 6th Artillery Division, located nearby, downsized into a single brigade.

Recently, all armoured divisions – except the 6th Armoured Division in Beijing – have transformed into brigades. The last eight armoured divisions were restructured into an armoured brigade and a mechanised infantry brigade. Since 2012, several infantry divisions have also transformed into two brigades, and the last two artillery divisions assigned to the 1st and 42nd Group Armies were also broken into two brigades each. Of these four new artillery brigades, two are equipped with 300mm Type-03 (PHL-03) long-range multiple-rocket launchers (Type-03 is also found in the battalions of several other artillery brigades.)

Infantry and armoured brigades consist of six manoeuvre battalions supported by an artillery regiment (slightly smaller than a divisional artillery regiment), air-defence and engineer/chemical-defence battalions, plus reconnaissance and support elements. Currently, around 49 infantry brigades, 17 armoured brigades and 21 artillery brigades are found in the group armies and as independent units. Infantry brigades are classified as mechanised (with tracked AFV/IFVs), light mechanised (with wheeled AFV/IFVs), motorised or mountain. All former anti-aircraft artillery brigades have become air-defence brigades consisting of both surface-to-air missile and anti-aircraft artillery units. Some engineer, pontoon-bridging and electronic-countermeasures brigades have also been formed, often out of pre-existing regiments.

Since 1997, SOF and army aviation units have expanded in size and number. They have also been pushed down the chain of command, so that most are now commanded by group armies rather than reporting to military regions. From seven helicopter regiments in 1997, the force has grown to four operational regiments and seven brigades (including one subordinate to the General Staff Department). SOF units now number roughly two groups/regiments and ten brigades. Several of the new brigades were formed from infantry units. All SOF units include both young officers on their first assignments and conscripts, indicating that their structure and capabilities more resemble commando units than front-rank counter-terrorist forces. Army aviation and SOF units frequently train together, but PLA SOF units are not supported by dedicated, special-mission aircraft and other support elements often found in other armed forces.

Army aviation, SOF, electronic-countermeasures and long-range rocket units, along with a handful of cyber-warfare units in military regions, give the army the capability to reach deep into enemy territory. These units will become increasingly important as the army prepares to support campaigns beyond China's borders that feature naval, air and missile forces.

It is not clear if all army divisions will be eliminated in future reforms, leading to full brigadisation. A major objective of brigadisation is to streamline the chain of command by eliminating regimental headquarters. However, battalion headquarters on their own do not have adequate personnel for combined arms operations command and control, which likely is one reason for maintaining a small core of divisions retaining this higher command function. However, when this shortfall is resolved, battalions should be able to operate more effectively without the help of regimental staffs.

images of a land-based simulation structure taken outside a research institute in Wuhan and subsequently circulated online. This is a common means by which new Chinese procurement programmes are disclosed: anonymous images are publicised before further details are released through official press statements. A mock-up still in situ at the same institute was likely also employed for research and analysis into aircraft-carrier design and operations; it appeared some time before the *Liaoning* was commissioned.

The simulation structure at Wuhan gives some insight into future design. The visible superstructure includes an integrated mast that might house an X-band radar as well as multiple S-band Type-346 radars, while a 130mm main gun appears forward, along with a Type-1130 close-in weapon system. Analysts believe that space also currently exists for up to 128 vertical-launch tubes.

The vessel's size and armament, if it is produced at the scale of the mock-up, would represent a significant step forward for China's primary surface combatants, in particular the surface fleet's land-attack capabilities. Although several years from construction, the Type-055 would be the largest combatant in the region's naval fleets and a powerful symbol of PLAN modernisation.

People's Liberation Army Air Force

The PLAAF continued to recapitalise its fixed- and rotary-wing fleets during 2014, as well as developing and flight-testing next-generation aircraft designs and improved air-launched weapons.

The third, considerably modified prototype of the Chengdu J-20 fighter aircraft was flown for the first time in March 2014, with the fourth following in July. The airframe showed numerous refinements based on the flight-test programme of the first two aircraft, along with the addition of an electro-optical targeting system in a faceted fairing just aft of the nose. Several modifications appeared intended to reduce the aircraft's radar signature. Work also continued on the J-10B, an upgraded Chengdu J-10 variant, although no operational unit of the type had begun to form by late 2014. The emergence of an image believed to show senior figures from the original J-10 design team in front of an Israeli *Lavi* fighter prototype, apparently on a trip to Israel in the late 1980s or early 1990s, suggested a link between the two designs. Flight testing of the Shenyang J-31 (possibly J-21) combat aircraft also continued, though as of the fourth quarter of 2014 only one airframe was observed and the extent of state support for the programme remained a matter of debate.

Beijing and Moscow continued to negotiate the sale of 24 Su-35 *Flanker* aircraft and an associated weapons package during the latter half of 2014. While Russia was frustrated by China's 'copying' of the Su-33 naval aviation variant of the *Flanker* with the Chinese J-15, the Chinese defence-aerospace sector remained an attractive export market.

With additional Il-76 strategic airlifters currently providing Chinese transport and further tanker needs, the third prototype Y-20 airlifter entered the flight-test programme at the end of July. The aircraft is intended to provide the basis for the air force's future heavy-lift requirements. In all likelihood, it will also fulfil a range of special-mission needs, including tanker and airborne early-warning platforms.

The air force is also continuing to introduce into service and further develop a broad range of unmanned aerial vehicle (UAV) systems. During the 2014 *Peace Mission* exercise conducted with Russia, it appeared that the CH-4 medium UAV was demonstrated engaging a surface target, possibly with a semi-active laser-guided missile.

Naval aviation also continued to develop, with the first handful of production-standard J-15 carrier-borne combat aircraft likely handed over to the navy in 2014. Imagery also surfaced of a two-seat variant, which could fulfil both training and combat roles. Also in development for the navy is an anti-submarine-warfare (ASW) variant of the Y-8 transport aircraft, referred to as the Y-8FQ, at least two of which are in flight test. An ASW/surface-warfare helicopter based on the Z-18 transport helicopter was also identified during the course of 2014.

DEFENCE ECONOMICS

Defence budget

The rapid growth of China's defence budget (see Figure 13) has generally outpaced increases seen in the rest of Asia, as the country intensifies its efforts to build a globally competitive defence science, technology and industrial (DSTI) base. Despite its slowing economy, China's 12.2% official defence-budget increase in 2014 (to RMB805 billion, or US$129bn) was higher than the 10.7% and 8% increases seen in 2013 and 2012, and accounted for nearly two-thirds of the total rise in Asian defence outlays in 2014 (see pp. 210–11). The official budget, however, does not include disbursements on the People's Armed Police (PAP), which are instead included under the Public Security budget. It is also widely held to exclude some other military-related expenditure, such as science, technology and innovation funding. A useful proxy indicator of defence R&D growth is the change in the overall level of investment in national R&D. China's R&D expenditure in 2014 was set at RMB1.34 trillion (US$215bn). This was around 2.2% of GDP and a sizeable increase over the 2013 level of RMB1.19tr (US$192bn), although the proportion of this allocated to defence-related activities is uncertain. The government has set a target for science and technology spending to reach 2.5% of GDP by 2020, which indicates the potential for higher rates of defence-related R&D growth over the next few years. If estimates of these additional items are included, Chinese defence spending in 2013 rises by a factor of approximately 1.4 relative to officially published figures, to an estimated RMB1.13tr (US$181bn) using market exchange rates.

Commitment to reform efforts

As more investment is channelled into China's defence-innovation system, reform efforts are simultaneously being undertaken to overhaul the procurement, production and R&D apparatus, as well as to improve the country's capacity to acquire and absorb foreign technologies. This push is being led by China's top leadership, particularly by President Xi Jinping. China's current strategy for developing its innovation capabilities is set out in long-term science and technology development plans (both civilian and military) drawn up in the mid-2000s. These have been criticised for their poor track record in achieving domestic defence-industrial innovation; in response, Xi has paid particular attention to the development of China's technological capabilities. The Xi administration is considering whether to adopt a new long-term science and technology development strategy, at the same time as the military authorities are formulating the next Five-Year Plan (2016–20) for defence development.

As part of these top-down efforts to establish a more capable innovation system, a major overhaul of the DSTI base is under way. This restructuring is part of a broader initiative to revamp the Chinese economy, unveiled at the Chinese Communist Party (CCP) Central Committee's Third Plenum in November 2013. Key goals included the reform of the defence research, development and acquisition (RDA) system; the introduction of private-sector competition into a defence market currently dominated by large, state-owned corporations; the development of more effective coordination mechanisms within the defence-innovation system; and the forging of closer cooperation between the military and civilian components of the national economy. Some of these reforms have been implemented on a trial basis in selected parts of the People's Liberation Army (PLA) over the past few years, with mixed results – largely due to opposition from entrenched interests in the defence-industrial base and the PLA. The ten largest state corporations dominate the defence sector and see little need to open it up to private competition, while the procurement system remains tightly wedded to its central-planning legacy.

Acquisition reform
The PLA's General Armaments Department (GAD) announced in January 2014 that it would pursue structural reform of the procurement-management system to make it more accountable and less susceptible to anti-competitive malpractices, such as collusion, which have undermined efficiency and fuelled corruption. Formulation, negotiation and implementation of contracts have all traditionally been conducted by a single entity. This will be separated in favour of a system of checks and balances to better prevent contractual abuses. The PLA will also conduct pilot studies and reforms of equipment-pricing practices over the next few years. Another area set for an extensive shake-up is the military-representative system, the PLA's on-the-ground monitoring system for weapons projects in which military officers are embedded into defence research and production facilities to provide coordination and oversight. Conflicts of interest have compromised the integrity of this system because, for example, the defence enterprises cover the military representatives' salaries and housing costs. The military-procurement system has also been a target of anti-corruption investigations. PLA leaders have highlighted the RDA system as a high-risk area for malfeasance because of poor transparency and weak regulatory oversight.

Improving civil–military integration

The CCP's Third Plenum initiative also called for greater effort in fostering civil–military integration (CMI) – the harnessing of the civilian economy for military and dual-use purposes. While Chinese policymakers view CMI as a major potential source

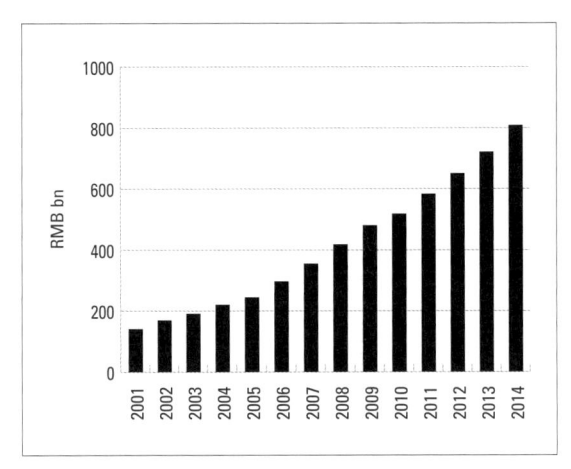

Figure 13 **Official PLA Budget 2001–14**

of defence-innovation creativity, the track record of more than a decade of CMI policies has been underwhelming. A high priority is the development of a tight-knit civilian–military R&D system between universities, academic research institutes, corporate research outfits and military organisations. In 2013, for example, Tsinghua University signed a strategic-cooperation agreement with the PLA's Second Artillery Corps for research cooperation and talent cultivation.

Another area of growing CMI activity is the competitive opening up of the RDA system to the private sector. Until a few years ago, the RDA system was the exclusive preserve of the ten state-owned conglomerates that dominated the defence-industrial base. More than 500 private firms have so far received licences that allow them to bid for contracts, although it is likely that the overwhelming flow of business will remain with the established state giants.

Increasing capital-markets financing

The use of capital markets to fund weapons projects could have the most significant impact on innovation. While defence companies have been allowed to list subsidiaries on stock markets since the 1990s, this was limited to their non-defence operations. This changed in 2013 when the State Administration for Science, Technology and Industry for National Defense permitted firms to issue share placements based on military assets. In September 2013, the China Shipbuilding Industry Corporation (CSIC) became the first defence firm to undertake such a placement, when it raised RMB8.5bn (US$940m) from ten unidentified Chinese parties. Dalian Shipyard is one of the CSIC facilities set to receive part of the proceeds from the private-share issue, and it is reportedly building China's first domestically designed aircraft carrier.

The aviation industry, in the form of monopoly Aviation Industries Corporation of China (AVIC), has been the most active in tapping financial markets, with several of the most important entities in its defence portfolio privately issuing shares over the past year, including Chengdu Aviation Corporation, AVIC Precision Machinery Corporation and AVIC's engine operations. After raising more than US$2bn for its engine business, AVIC is integrating all of its engine facilities into a single, consolidated entity in the hope that this will finally allow the company to build its own advanced turbofan engines.

Overall, only around 30–40% of Chinese defence-industry assets are estimated to have been floated on capital markets, a relatively low proportion when compared to figures of around 80% in the US and Europe. Access to financial markets offers a lucrative supplementary source of funding for defence firms as they seek to step up development of technological capabilities. Nonetheless, AVIC and CSIC's success in raising large amounts of funds reflects the strong economic position that defence companies enjoy, with ample order books and an extensive R&D pipeline of weapons programmes. Industry-wide revenues and profits continue to show robust annual growth, both reportedly increasing by an estimated 10% between 2012 and 2013.

The high level of state commitment to the defence economy shows few signs of weakening, despite economic growth slowing since 2010. As military policymakers prepare for the next Five-Year Plan, they will likely seek rates of growth in defence allocations similar to, or even higher than, current levels. The Third Plenum's decisions on reforming China's defence economy represent a potentially significant step forward in the country's long-term transition from a late technological follower to an advanced state at the global-innovation frontier. But overcoming existing barriers will not be easy. There is no shortage of funds or technology, but institutional systems and mechanisms are hurdles to developing the PLA's armaments.

INDIA

India's security concerns in 2014 were characterised by continuity. Close attention is still paid to the withdrawal of most United States and allied personnel from Afghanistan; the rise of China, in the context

Afghanistan

In 2014, Afghan forces assumed full security responsibility for their country, with ISAF correspondingly reduced to about 30,000 troops. A Taliban offensive in June failed to achieve its strategic aims. Although there was heavy fighting around Sangin in northern Helmand, none of the key areas cleared in the 2010–11 surge fell. Afghan forces' layered defences of Kabul eventually defeated most attempts to attack the capital city. However, there were heavy Afghan combat casualties during the year.

The Afghan security operation to protect the 2014 elections saw very few successful Taliban attempts to disrupt voting. A US-brokered political deal between presidential candidates allowed the October signing of the Bilateral Security Agreement and Status of Forces Agreement with the US and NATO. This finally allowed planning to move ahead for *Operation Resolute Support*, NATO's non-combat training, advice and assistance mission. The US announced that 9,800 US troops would remain in country, both in the NATO mission and in a separate counter-terrorist force. These forces would halve by 2016 and depart by 2017.

The Afghan Army is probably capable of holding the main cities and key rural areas. But isolated border areas, such as eastern Afghanistan and northern Helmand, are likely to remain insurgent strongholds, particularly if there is no significant improvement in security cooperation with Pakistan. A complicating military factor is that the Afghan Air Force is unlikely to achieve full capability before 2017. Afghan commanders have argued for continued external air support until the air force is fully operational.

of its increased strategic interests in South Asia and renewed attention to military dispositions on the de facto India–China land border; managing stalled diplomacy and renewed violence on the border with Pakistan; and internal security and terrorism. The national security adviser to new Prime Minister Narendra Modi, Ajit Doval, was particularly interested in counter-terrorism and counter-extremism, analysts believed, being the former chief of India's domestic-intelligence agency. New Delhi is yet to introduce defence-policy reforms that would affect its military modernisation, and while there have been significant changes to defence-industrial affairs, in terms of policy development the new Modi government has largely chosen to concentrate on better implementation of existing plans.

Strategic policy developments

Pakistan Prime Minister Nawaz Sharif's attendance at Modi's swearing-in ceremony in May 2014 was a positive, if short-lived, episode in the two countries' complex relationship. By mid-August, in a speech at Kargil (the scene of a 1999 conflict with Pakistan), Modi accused Islamabad of 'continuing to engage in the proxy war of terrorism' against India. Ceasefire violations across the Line of Control dividing the disputed Kashmir region also escalated in 2014. These were the worst exchanges of fire in a decade and reduced the chance of restarting dialogue, which stalled in early 2013. As a precondition for restarting dialogue, India says Pakistan should stop attacks and infiltration by militants.

The end of NATO's combat mission and the withdrawal of most of its combat forces from Afghanistan have led to Indian concern that terrorist groups might again settle there. Furthermore, New Delhi is concerned by what it perceives as Pakistan's efforts to force the withdrawal of Indian economic aid and personnel from Afghanistan. Former Afghan president Hamid Karzai said that the Pakistan-based terror group Lashkar-e-Taiba was involved in an attack on India's consulate-general building in Herat on 23 May. Islamabad rejected charges of complicity in terrorism and argued that after 2001 New Delhi had built up its influence and significant presence in Afghanistan for the sole purpose of preventing Pakistan from attaining 'strategic depth'.

China, however, is India's longer-term foreign- and defence-policy challenge. Perceived Chinese assertiveness on the undemarcated and disputed northern border with India led to a tense, two-week-long stand-off during President Xi Jinping's first visit to India. The stand-off occurred despite a border-management agreement signed in October 2013. India's concerns also contain a strong maritime dimension; in September, the first port visit to Sri Lanka by two People's Liberation Army Navy submarines was carefully watched by Indian defence circles.

Armed forces

Reflecting the ship's importance, Modi's first official engagement outside Delhi was to dedicate, in June, the **navy's** latest aircraft carrier, INS *Vikramaditya*, bringing to an end its ten-year procurement saga. By then, the ship had already deployed operationally with its complement of MiG-29K combat aircraft. To assist carrier-aviation development, the navy had commissioned a new shore-based facility at the naval station Hansa, near Goa, in January to test aircraft and train pilots, initially for the *Vikramaditya*.

The maiden ship in the *Kolkata*-class (Project 15A) was commissioned in August. This 6,800-tonne guided-missile destroyer, equipped with the navalised *Brahmos* supersonic cruise missile, was built by Mazagon Dock in Mumbai and launched in 2006. Follow-on ships *Kochi* and *Chennai* are expected to be commissioned at eight-month intervals. In the same month, the first of four *Kamorta*-class anti-submarine-warfare frigates were commissioned into the Eastern Naval Command (ENC).

The navy is also building a new base on the east coast to boost force levels in the Indian Ocean. Under the code name *Project Varsha*, it will be located at Rambilli, 50km southwest of ENC headquarters at Visakhapatnam, in Andhra Pradesh state. Scheduled for completion by 2021/22, analysts believe this could be the base for the indigenous carrier INS *Vikrant*, currently under construction, and five to six nuclear-powered ballistic-missile submarines (SSBNs), among other warships. In February, *Kilo*-class submarine INS *Sindhuratna* – sister ship of the ill-fated *Sindhurakshak*, which caught fire and sank in a Mumbai dockyard in 2013 – caught fire at sea, with the loss of two lives; the boat itself was saved. Following a string of fatal accidents on vessels, new naval chief Admiral R.K. Dhowan announced a 'safety audit' after taking charge in April, though the timescale for this was unclear.

General Dalbir Singh Suhag took over as **army** chief in August, saying that his priorities would be to 'enhance operational preparedness and effectiveness', adding that force modernisation, infrastructure development and personnel welfare were also important.

Platform-modernisation plans also proceeded. Defence Minister Arun Jaitley announced that a tender would be issued for a light utility helicopter requirement, after the defence ministry cancelled in August – for the second time since 2007 – the acquisition of 133 helicopters for army aviation and 64 for the air force. A new, local 'Make and Buy (Indian)' tender was expected by the end of the year, with analysts anticipating competition between state-run Hindustan Aeronautics Limited (HAL) and private Indian companies engaged in joint ventures with overseas firms. Other rotary-wing developments included the Defence Acquisition Council's approval in August of a possible purchase of 15 CH47F *Chinook* and 22 AH-64E *Apache* helicopters, associated with the army's new XVII Mountain Strike Corps. This unit could comprise two high-altitude infantry divisions, two independent infantry brigades and two armoured brigades across Ladakh, Uttarakhand and Sikkim.

The **air force** commissioned its seventh C-17 *Globemaster* III in July, with the remaining three of the ten C-17s it ordered in 2011 awaiting delivery. This brings substantial lift capability to the air force, although procurements remained dominated by combat aircraft. During the visit of its foreign minister in June, France continued to express confidence in the negotiations to sell 126 *Rafale* fighters to meet India's Medium Multi-role Combat Aircraft requirement. Since India and France's Dassault entered into exclusive negotiations in 2012, disagreements over costs and work-share with HAL have delayed the US$20bn deal. India continues to partner Russia in its PAK-FA fifth-generation-fighter requirement, however the relationship has been strained by technical and industrial issues.

Meanwhile, the first canister-launch-system test of India's *Agni*-V ballistic missile was expected by the end of 2014. The *Agni*-IV, a 4,000km-range nuclear-capable missile, was tested in January, and in March India conducted an underwater launch of a 3,000km-range K-4 nuclear-capable ballistic missile believed to be intended for the indigenous *Arihant*-class SSBN. To aid the missile-test regime, Defence Minister Jaitley informed parliament in July that the Defence Research and Development Organisation had identified Rutland Island in the Andaman and Nicobar Islands and Nagayalanka in Andhra Pradesh state as new test-range sites.

DEFENCE ECONOMICS

Macroeconomics

India's GDP was forecast to grow at 5.5% in FY 2014/15, after below-5% increases in the preceding two years. This marginal improvement in headline GDP growth came amid improving macroeconomic indicators. The current account deficit – which the Ministry of Finance said had reached a 'worryingly high level' of 4.7% of GDP in 2012/13 – had fallen to 1.7% in 2013/14. Over the same period, the government's fiscal deficit reduced from 4.9% of GDP to 4.5%, although much of this was accounted for by expenditure cuts rather than increased revenue inflows. New prime minister Modi set out plans to gradually reduce the fiscal deficit to 3% of GDP by 2016/17 (from an estimated 4.1% in 2014/15). Improvements were also observed in the rupee–dollar exchange rate, foreign-exchange reserves and the inflation rate. Modi's government has also undertaken reform initiatives to boost economic activity. Its first budget, presented in July 2014, proposed to raise the limit on foreign direct investment (FDI) in the defence-manufacturing sector from 26% to 49%. Measures were also proposed to overhaul India's tax-administration system, subsidy regime and public-expenditure management framework.

Defence spending

The FY2014/15 defence budget was, at INR2.29tr (US$36.4bn, excluding pensions), 2.2% higher than the interim budget presented by the previous government. It was also a 12.4% increase over both the original and revised FY2013/14 budgets. This means that there had been no mid-year downward revision of the 2013/14 allocation, a trend often seen in India's defence spending. Forty-one per cent of the defence budget (INR945.9bn, or US$15bn) was earmarked for capital expenditure, and of this sum 79% (INR751.5bn, or US$12bn) was allocated to the three services' capital acquisition. However, the army is the only service whose capital-acquisition budget has actually increased, from INR129bn (US$2.1bn) to INR204bn (US$3.2bn). Both the air force and navy have seen theirs decline: the navy's acquisition budget saw a year-on-year reduction from INR235bn (US$3.9bn) to INR229bn (US$3.6bn), while that of the air force was cut even further, from INR370bn (US$6.1bn) to INR318bn (US$5.1bn). Paradoxically, the decline in the air force's acquisition budget comes at a time when it is close to signing a series of multi-billion-dollar projects – including the 126-aircraft, US$15–20bn Medium Multi-role Combat Aircraft (MMRCA) requirement, under which the Dassault *Rafale* has been selected. Should the government sign the contract in FY2014/15, additional allocations seem inevitable. (For the MMRCA contract alone, the air force has already projected that the initial payment would be an extra INR150bn (US$2.4bn).)

India's defence procurements are still dominated by imports, with domestic industry still plagued by inefficiency and other constraints (see *The Military Balance 2014*, pp. 214–15). In 2013/14, nearly 43% of total capital-acquisition expenditure was on imports. India also spends substantial sums on indirect imports, sourcing from various countries the parts, components and raw materials used in domestic defence-industrial production. In recent years, the US has emerged as one of India's largest arms suppliers, signing deals worth nearly US$9bn since 2001. Between FY2011/12 and FY2013/14, it received 39% (INR326bn, or US$6bn) of the total funds spent by India on capital acquisition. Russia was second, with a 30% share (INR254bn, or US$4.7bn), followed by France with 14% (INR120bn, or US$2.2bn) and Israel with 4% (INR34bn, or US$626m).

Domestic defence industry

India's defence-industrial sector remains dominated by state-owned enterprises, comprising nine Defence Public Sector Undertakings and 41 Ordnance Factors, under the administrative control of the Department of Defence Production of the Ministry of Defence. In FY2013/14, these enterprises produced equipment valued at an estimated INR434bn (US$7.2bn), an increase of 2.4% over the previous year. However, this falls short of the armed forces' requirements. As an example, FY2012/13 saw a production gap of around INR380bn (US$7bn), a significant proportion of which was met through imports.

Indian private companies still have a limited role in defence production, although this is increasing annually. By June 2014, 121 private companies had obtained industrial licences – a prerequisite for entering the defence-manufacturing sector – and 28 had formed joint ventures with foreign equity. A noticeable development for the private sector has been the relatively short time now required to make a foreign sale. In 2013/14, total private-sector defence exports, based on 'no objection' certificates issued by the government, amounted to INR2.86bn (US$47.3m). The figure in FY2010/11 was INR290m (US$6.4m) and is likely to increase further, not least because several companies are undertaking sizeable work for the major global defence firms. For instance, Dynamatic Technologies has orders worth INR39bn (US$620m) from Boeing, Airbus and Bell Helicopter. Similarly, Tata – with 14 group companies active in the defence sector – had an order book of INR80bn (US$1.3bn) in 2013/14, including from Sikorsky and Lockheed Martin. To boost private-sector participation in domestic defence production, the Modi government approved the previous government's proposal for the private sector to manufacture 40 aircraft for the air force. Domestic production for the air force was previously the preserve of Hindustan Aeronautics Limited, the state-owned monopoly criticised for high levels of inefficiency.

Industrial licensing and FDI reforms
Within a few months of coming to power, the Modi government announced a series of reforms affecting the defence industry. On 26 June 2014, it issued a list (Ministry of Commerce and Industry Press Note No. 3, 2014 Series) identifying defence items that would need industrial licences. The list comprised four broad categories: tanks and other armoured fighting vehicles; military aircraft, spacecraft and parts thereof; warships of all kinds; arms, ammunition and associated items, and parts and accessories thereof. A further defence-ministry press note on 18 July said that items not covered by the list would not require a licence for defence purposes, and as a consequence some items that used to require a defence licence, e.g. parts/components of equipment, castings, forgings and test equipment, would no longer require an industrial licence. For dual-use items not mentioned in the list, this press note clarified that they would not be subject to licensing.

The new government took other measures related to licensing. In Press Note No. 5, announced on 2 July, the government extended the life of an industrial licence from two to three years. In a bid to speed up decision-making and improve accountability, the government also stipulated a maximum 12-week time period within which the Ministry of Home Affairs should grant security clearance on licence applications. Previously, an affidavit from a judicial magistrate was necessary to pre-comply with security and safety regulations; licence applicants can now self-certify.

The government formally announced a revision to India's defence FDI policy on 26 August 2014. This raised the foreign-investment cap from 26% to 49%, including a maximum of 24% in portfolio investments (such as investments by foreign institutional investors), which was banned under the previous policy. Portfolio investment is now allowed automatically, although non-portfolio investments are still subject to government approval. For FDI proposals over the new maximum, the Cabinet Committee on Security (CCS) chaired by the prime minister will decide on each proposal 'whenever it is likely to result in access to modern and state-of-the-art technology'. The revised FDI policy also removed an earlier provision related to the control of joint ventures, which required the single-largest resident Indian shareholder to have at least a 51% equity share. Under the new regulations, however, this shareholder now has the power to appoint a majority of the directors in a joint venture, thereby influencing the company's policy decisions.

The above changes notwithstanding, foreign companies have little to cheer about. The increase in the FDI cap to 49% still does not give them management control of the joint venture, which is vital for the transfer of proprietary technology. This is the main reason why the previous policy did not succeed in attracting large inward investments, prompting the commerce ministry to initiate a debate on increasing the cap beyond 49%. Meanwhile, for foreign companies wishing to establish joint ventures via the CCS route there remains a lack of clarity over what precisely constitutes 'modern and state-of-the-art technology', this being the basis on which decisions to increase the FDI threshold above 49% would be taken.

JAPAN

Japan continued on a path towards a more assertive security stance in 2014, motivated in particular by increasing Sino-Japanese military tensions. Under Prime Minister Shinzo Abe, Japan has also strengthened its defence posture. This has been enabled by a willingness to partially overcome, through reinterpretation, previous constitutional and anti-militaristic constraints; augment Japan Self-Defense Force (JSDF) doctrines and capabilities; as well as an apparent new budgetary resolve to fund defence aspirations.

Defence-policy drivers
Japan's defence policymakers have increasingly focused their energies on responding to China's military modernisation, although they remain troubled by North Korea's ongoing ballistic-missile development and nuclearisation. Japan's immediate security concerns about China centre on the perceived risk that the People's Liberation Army Navy (PLAN) or another Chinese force might, in a 'grey-zone' contingency short of warfare, attempt to forcibly seize the disputed Senkaku/Diaoyu Islands. Beyond the Senkaku/Diaoyu issue, Japanese anxieties revolve around China's military rise and its impact on maritime security in the East China Sea; Japan's sea lines

of communication; the US commitment to defending Japan; and shifts in the overall regional balance of power.

Japan's leaders strongly condemned China's unilateral declaration of an Air-Defence Identification Zone (ADIZ) over the East China Sea in November 2013. They view this and other displays of PLAN anti-access/area-denial capabilities – and China's growing military power in and around Japan's territorial waters – as part of a long-term intimidation campaign to neutralise Japanese control and effectively 'lever' the Japan Maritime Self-Defense Force (JMSDF), and eventually the US Navy, out of the region. During 2013, Japan Air Self-Defense Force (JASDF) scramble intercepts of Chinese airspace incursions increased by around 30%. In May 2014, Japan condemned PLA Air Force (PLAAF) fighter pilots' tactics of flying within 30m of JASDF and JMSDF aircraft; this followed the 'radar-lock' incident of February 2013, when a PLAN fire-control radar locked onto a JMSDF vessel. Consequently, Japan's new National Security Strategy (NSS) and revised National Defense Program Guidelines (NDPG) – both released in December 2013 – talked of China's attempt to change the territorial status quo by force and the possibility of its tactics precipitating an unexpected military contingency. Meanwhile, Japan, for its part, failed to quell political tensions with both China and South Korea that had been exacerbated by Abe's provocative visit in December 2013 to the controversial Yasukuni Shrine.

Breaking security constraints

Japan's response to this more volatile regional security environment centred on the promotion of a 'proactive contribution to peace' – a slogan attempting to emphasise continuities with past Japanese anti-militaristic traditions whilst actually breaking existing taboos and seeking a change in the direction of security policy. The release of Japan's first NSS in December was accompanied by the creation of the National Security Council (NSC), modelled on those of the United States and the United Kingdom and designed to serve as a 'control tower' to overcome previous inter-agency rivalries in the coordination of a more assertive security policy. The defence ministry's simultaneous release of the revised NDPG and the Mid-Term Defense Program (MTDP) – the documents that outline Japan's defence doctrine alongside necessary JSDF capabilities – meant that for the first time Japan had systematically aligned its grand security strategy, doctrines and military-force requirements. The NSS and NDPG advanced the concept of 'proactive contribution to peace', and stressed in particular the indivisibility of national security with that of the international system, pointing to the need to increase Japanese contributions to international security activities.

The Abe administration's first major step in realising its new security strategy came in April 2014 with the decision to overcome Japan's near-total ban on the export of defence technologies, in place since 1976, and to adopt instead the 'Three Principles of Defense Equipment Transfers'. The next objective was tackling the ban on the exercise of collective self-defence, active since the mid-1950s. After extensive intra-coalition negotiations during spring and early summer between Abe's governing Liberal Democratic Party (LDP) and its more dovish New Komeito (NK) partner, a Cabinet resolution was issued on 1 July, revising the prohibition on collective self-defence. The LDP and NK argued that collective self-defence could now be exercised because of the significant changes to the nature of the security environment around Japan. The Abe administration suggested that new types of threat and weaponry had presented new security contingencies that affected the US and other states; these could now, in turn, directly affect Japan. Therefore, to ensure its continued security, Japan should be able to come to the assistance of these states.

To preserve their coalition, the LDP and NK formulated a compromise on 'limited collective self-defense', meaning that the right can only be exercised to defend states with a 'very close relationship' to Japan and only under three conditions: an attack on another state posing a 'clear danger' to Japan's survival or fundamentally overturning Japanese citizens' constitutional right to life and well-being; there being no other way of repelling the attack and protecting Japan and its citizens without the use of force; and the use of force being limited to the minimum level necessary.

Although the Abe administration stressed that these changes were moderate, it nevertheless envisaged a range of unprecedented scenarios for the exercise of Japanese military power. The government outlined eight major scenarios, including the protection of US ships carrying Japanese nationals; defending and refuelling US warships under attack close to Japan; defending the US armed forces against ballistic-missile attacks; forceful interdiction of shipping; and protecting critical sea lanes. It is also proposed that Japan should be able to practise a form of collective security, rather than just collective self-defence, in the clearance of mines from sea lanes in situations such as Persian Gulf contingencies, so long as this was permitted by United Nations resolutions.

The Abe administration will look to guide 17 legislative bills through the Diet in early 2015 to amend laws to enable the JSDF to undertake collective self-defence. At the same time, Tokyo has investigated legal revisions to make more explicit the circumstances in which it can exercise individual self-defence and the use of force in grey-zone contingencies around the Senkaku/Diaoyu Islands.

The Abe's government's 'proactive contribution to peace' and emphasis on international security cooperation has led to attempts to strengthen the US–Japan alliance, as well as defence ties with other US allies and partners. In February 2013, both countries began a review of the US–Japan defence guidelines, with the expectation that it would be finished by the end of 2014. Within the framework of the 1960 US–Japan Security Treaty, these guidelines specify bilateral cooperation for contingencies that affect Japan's own security and the wider regional security environment. The revised guidelines are likely to focus on enhancing bilateral efforts in intelligence, surveillance and reconnaissance; maritime security; ballistic-missile defence (BMD); cyber security; Japanese logistical support for US forces in combat zones; and preventing the seizure of remote Japanese islands. Japan has also expanded strategic ties with Australia, signing a new Economic Partnership Agreement in April 2014 and pledging further cooperation on cyber security and defence-technology exchanges. Japan and India have made further strides in their security relationship, agreeing in September 2013 to strengthen director-level defence dialogue, to institute regular bilateral maritime exercises and to explore Japan joining US–India maritime exercises.

Capability procurements

The 2013 NDPG and MTDP continued to commit Japan's forces to transitioning to a more technologically advanced and mobile force, capable of defending Japan against new threats from China and North Korea and projecting power in the East Asia region and beyond. The earlier 2010 NDPG had already abandoned the previous Cold War concept of the 'Basic Defense Force', designed for the static defence of Japan itself against the Soviet Union, in favour of a 'Dynamic Defense Force', intended to move the most capable JSDF deployments southwards and to respond flexibly to contingencies around Japan's territory and periphery. The 2013 NDPG built on these changes by introducing the concept of a 'Dynamic Joint Defense Force' (DJDF) and highlighting the need for improved interoperability between the services.

The revised mid-term programme maintained the acquisition of 42 F-35A Joint Strike Fighter aircraft and research into an Advanced Technology Demonstrator-X combat aircraft – a potentially indigenously produced fighter to replace the F-2 or F-15J *Eagle*. The JASDF continued to procure the 6,500km-range Kawasaki C-2 transport aircraft, which will improve airlift capacity, and is set to procure unmanned aerial vehicles to help patrol Japan's extensive airspace, coastline and remote islands. The revised NDPG mandates the JMSDF to maintain a destroyer force of 54 vessels, an increase over the 48 originally designated in the 2010 document, including two additional *Atago*-class *Aegis* destroyers and new multi-mission 25DD *Akizuki*-class ships. The revised NDPG and MTDP continue the 2010 guidelines' decision to expand the submarine fleet from 16 to 22 boats, and introduce the *Soryu*-class submarine, which incorporates the *Stirling*-cycle air-independent propulsion system. The JMSDF will acquire the Kawasaki P-1 maritime-patrol aircraft to replace its P-3C *Orion* fleet, and the SH-60K *Seahawk* helicopter to boost anti-submarine-warfare capabilities. Meanwhile, in September 2014 the *Izumo*, the lead vessel in Japan's new class of helicopter carrier (also called a 'helicopter destroyer' or 'escort vessel') was photographed while reportedly on initial sea trials.

The revised NDPG also stated that the Japan Ground Self-Defense Force (JGSDF) would for the first time acquire a full amphibious capability to retake remote islands. The force is planned to consist of approximately 3,000 personnel, equipped with the force's first amphibious-assault vehicles. The first few vehicles were bought second-hand from the US Marine Corps for testing and evaluation; 52 are planned in all. Further, it was announced in mid-2014 that Japan would look to buy tilt-rotor aircraft.

Defence economics

Japan's military build-up is underpinned by a renewed determination to provide requisite budgetary resources. The administration announced a 0.8% increase in the defence budget in 2013 and a 2.2% increase in 2014, and has requested a 2.4% increase for 2015. The administration has arrested a decade-long period of essentially stagnant defence budgets and brought them back up to levels of ¥5tr (around US$55bn), commensurate with the high watermark of late 1990s spending. Japan will clearly struggle to match China's rapid increases in military expenditure, but Prime Minister Shinzo Abe's statement of intent for Japan to raise its defence profile is clear.

Japan's budgetary expansion is supported by attempts to further stretch resources by improving the efficiency of defence procurement. The defence ministry is to create a new Defense Procurement Agency, bringing together the Technical Research Development Institute, Equipment Procurement and Construction Office, Joint Staff and Internal Bureau. The new agency will look to coordinate procurement among the three services; involve defence industry in Integrated Project Teams to develop and monitor capabilities throughout their life cycle; acquire defence imports more cost effectively; and expand international cooperation on defence-technology transfers. Defence planners hold out increasing hopes that the new 'Three Principles of Defense Equipment Transfers' will help to maintain Japan's defence-industrial base; increase opportunities for the export and joint development of advanced technologies; and forge wider strategic cooperation with the US and other democracies.

Japan first imposed restrictions on arms exports in 1967, preventing transfers to communist states, states under UN sanctions and states involved in international conflicts. A total ban on all arms exports was then imposed in 1976. The only partial exemptions were those to enable, from 1983, cooperation with the US on bilateral projects such as the development of the F-2 combat aircraft, and then from 2004 for bilateral development of the SM-3 missile for ballistic-

Medium-term economic and defence-spending trends

For more than two decades Japan's economy has been caught in a 'liquidity trap', characterised by persistent low growth, deflationary pressures and rising public debt, despite close-to-zero nominal interest rates. The country's ageing population has also meant the workforce is shrinking by 0.5% per year, restricting economic expansion and limiting the extent to which defence outlays could be raised; between 1999 and 2013 the average nominal increase in annual defence spending was -0.25%. However, despite flat or declining nominal budgets, real defence spending in Japan has risen in recent years, due to the country's long-standing pattern of low inflation or deflation. For example, real Japanese defence spending in 2013 was 6.6% higher than its 2008 level.

In an attempt to revitalise the stagnant economy, Prime Minister Shinzo Abe launched a new economic policy ('Abenomics') in January 2013. This focuses on 'three arrows': monetary easing, flexible fiscal policies and structural reforms. On the first point, the Bank of Japan announced its 'Quantitative & Qualitative Monetary Easing' programme in April 2013, aiming to double the monetary base and achieve an inflation target of 2% within two years. Some progress was also made on the second 'arrow', with an additional US$110bn in government expenditure introduced in 2013, combined with a reduction in corporate taxes and an increase in consumption taxes. Both tax measures were aimed at increasing revenues to deal with persistently large budget deficits. These measures succeeded in creating a mild inflationary environment – core inflation had risen to 1.3% by April 2014 – although this was partly explained by higher imported inflation arising from raised energy costs after the 20% depreciation in the value of the yen.

However, 18 months after its announcement, Abe's plan had yet to stimulate a domestic credit cycle. More importantly, it had failed to adequately anchor strong expectations of higher future inflation. These are crucial to spurring the wage increases required to boost household incomes, and consequently strengthen domestic demand. Without strong demand signals, there were few signs of the reduction in high levels of corporate savings that analysts hoped would arise by channelling the savings towards business investment; this would raise the sustainable rate of economic growth, as well as help tackle the fiscal deficit. The piecemeal manner in which the third 'arrow' has been implemented has meant that Japan's growth outlook is unlikely to be as dynamic as initially portrayed under the original Abenomics plan. Structural challenges are likely to continue, limiting the fiscal space for defence allocations, particularly if successive administrations maintain their commitment to achieve fiscal surplus by 2020. Higher inflation levels will also have the opposite effect on real defence outlays as the outlined deflationary effects, serving to erode budgetary increases rather than augment them.

missile defence and cooperation with other states on anti-terrorism and anti-piracy technologies. In 2011, the ruling DPJ administration lifted the ban on exports for cases involving UN peacekeeping and the multilateral development of weapons systems.

The Abe administration's formal overhaul of the ban in 2014 in effect inverted the former system to make exports, with some restrictions, the norm in all cases – so returning to the spirit of the 1967 legislation. The principles prevent export only to states considered inimical to international peace and security, such as those transgressing international treaties or those under UN sanctions. Exports are encouraged to states contributing to international peace or Japan's security – such as the US, NATO members and those engaged in UN peacekeeping operations – and which can demonstrate controls to prevent re-export to other countries.

The Japanese government has subsequently looked to secure a variety of agreements and partners for defence exports. In July 2014, it signed an agreement with Australia on the transfer of defence equipment. In the same month, the NSC approved plans for the joint development by Japan and the UK of the *Meteor* air-to-air missile. The Abe administration has also been keen to export the ShinMaywa US-2 amphibious search-and-rescue aircraft to India, and Japan has agreed to export patrol boats to the Philippines and to investigate providing similar maritime-security support to Vietnam.

However, not all of Japan's efforts have yet paid off. The 2013 decision to form a working group with India regarding a possible sale of US-2 aircraft has not progressed, and some analysts consider India to be more interested in technology transfer than actual aircraft purchases. Meanwhile, many Japanese defence-equipment producers appear more interested in international cooperation as a means to showcase their technology to generate civil-sector exports than in large-scale defence collaboration. Nevertheless, Japan has in a relatively short period begun to demonstrate genuine intent to join the ranks of major weapons exporters.

MYANMAR

Myanmar remains one of Asia's poorest and least-developed countries, notwithstanding enthusiasm about its economic potential and political reforms since 2010. Although national elections are scheduled for 2015, for the time being the Tatmadaw (armed forces) dominate the nominally civilian government. Although the defence budget for FY2013/14 was slightly smaller than in the previous year, the government continued to provide lavish funding – amounting to more than 20% of the overall state budget – for the Tatmadaw. Moreover, the Law on Special Funds adopted in 2011 allows the armed forces to use income from the businesses they control and it is likely that this has increased through the further exploitation of natural gas and other natural resources.

The principal focus for Myanmar's large armed forces since independence in 1948 has been holding together the large, ethnically diverse state, particularly in the face of some of the world's longest-running insurgencies, conducted by ethnic-minority groups around the country's periphery. Ceasefires with many of the rebel groups over the last two decades have reduced the need for counter-insurgency operations. Talks aimed at establishing a 'nationwide ceasefire' began in 2011, and in August 2014 a government negotiator claimed there was a 95% chance of a ceasefire agreement before the end of October. However, a sixth round of talks in late September 2014 between the Nationwide Ceasefire Coordination Team, representing 16 rebel groups, and the government's Union Peace-making Work Committee apparently foundered.

Crucially, rebel groups have refused to disarm until the establishment of a 'federal army', which has been anathema to the armed forces since the defection in the late 1940s of Karen and other ethnic-minority units from the original Tatmadaw. Even though the largest and best-equipped rebel group, the United Wa State Army, continues to respect a 2011 truce, it remains outside the nationwide ceasefire negotiations. With 20,000–30,000 fighters and tacit support from China, it remains a potent force that could severely challenge the Tatmadaw in future.

Meanwhile, the army – sometimes supported by air-force ground-attack aircraft and helicopters – has remained heavily engaged in internal security operations, particularly against the Kachin Independence Army (KIA) and other groups such as the Shan State Army–North and the Democratic Karen Benevolent Army. Operations against the 10,000-strong KIA between mid-2011 and late 2012 were particularly costly for the Tatmadaw, which reportedly lost as many as 5,000 troops. Fighting escalated again in October 2014 following the impasse in September in the sixth round of peace talks. Both the Tatmadaw and rebel groups have acknowledged their use of child soldiers, and both have publicised their efforts to halt the practice. Human-rights groups have also accused the Tatmadaw of widespread abuses, including torture and sexual violence, against civilians.

Myanmar's continuing internal focus and relatively small defence budget has limited its procurement of major conventional military equipment. However, the international naval response to Cyclone Nargis in 2008 exacerbated the Tatmadaw's concerns regarding the weakness of its defences against potential foreign intervention, spurring efforts to improve naval and air capabilities. The Tatmadaw is also concerned about the possibility of conflict with neighbouring Bangladesh, following a 2009 border confrontation.

It seems likely that Myanmar has paid for much of its international defence procurement through barter trade. Important naval acquisitions since 2011 include two Type-053H1 *Jianghu* II-class frigates from China, and as many as six domestically built (though apparently Chinese-designed) *Aung Zeya*-class missile frigates. The second *Aung Zeya* frigate, the UMS *Kyansitthar*, commissioned in March 2014, supposedly possesses stealth characteristics and may belong to a second class; a third ship is under construction. Weapons and tactical systems on these frigates include Western as well as Chinese, Indian and Russian equipment. In mid-2014, the navy reportedly entered into talks with shipbuilder PAL Indonesia over Myanmar's possible purchase of ships based on the *Makassar*-class landing platform dock.

Significant air-force acquisitions include an additional 20 MiG-29 *Fulcrum* combat aircraft from Russia, delivered between 2011 and 2013, as well as Mi-35 attack helicopters and S-125 *Pechora*-2M (SA-3 *Goa*) surface-to-air missiles. In mid-2014 it was reported that Myanmar might buy JF-17 multi-role combat aircraft, produced jointly by China and Pakistan. What little is known of Myanmar's air operations suggests that the MiG-29s and other aircraft suffer from low serviceability, and that lack of pilot experience and inadequate command, control and communications systems have also undermined overall operational effectiveness.

Myanmar has an extensive defence industry consisting of an estimated 20 plants that mainly produce small arms, explosives and ammunition but also include the Sinmalike Naval Dockyard and the Air Force Production and Maintenance Base at Meiktila Air Base, which may be capable of assembling aircraft such as the K-8 *Karakorum* advanced jet trainer.

Western arms embargoes are likely to remain in place, along with a reluctance to become more than superficially engaged with the Tatmadaw, until Myanmar has made greater progress towards establishing democratic government, peacefully resolving its internal security problems, instituting civilian control of its armed forces and ending military abuses. In the meantime, there have been tentative contacts with Western armed forces. In February 2013 the Tatmadaw sent observers to the US-led, multinational *Cobra Gold* exercise in Thailand for the first time, and in June 2013 the UK's chief of defence staff offered security-sector reform assistance during a visit to Myanmar.

NORTH KOREA

Given the antiquated nature of much of its equipment, North Korea's conventional military capabilities are qualitatively inferior to South Korea's modern forces. In July 2014, after at least two 1950s-era MiG fighters had crashed while training in the previous three months, North Korea suspended flight drills. The nation's tanks, armoured personnel carriers and vessels are similarly around 50 years old. A propaganda photo in summer 2014 featured Kim Jong-un aboard a *Romeo*-class submarine – a type first produced in the 1950s. An SO-1 patrol boat sank during naval exercises in late 2013 and it was also reported, in June 2014, that a military helicopter had exploded in mid-air, a month after a new 23-story apartment building for officials in Pyongyang collapsed due to faulty construction.

In terms of rocket and non-conventional capabilities, however, North Korea has made significant advances. The eight months from February to September 2014 involved the most intense rocket and missile testing the nation has ever conducted. More than one hundred *Scud* and *Nodong* ballistic missiles and other rockets were launched during this period, all in breach of UN sanctions. The *Nodong* tests were the first since 2006. They appeared to be intended to demonstrate a boost in accuracy rather than range. North Korea said the missile launches in August were aimed at countering the annual *Ulchi Freedom Guardian* US–South Korea joint military exercise that month. North Korea also threatened a pre-emptive nuclear strike in response to the exercise. While the dramatic threat was unfulfilled, the week-long exercise ended a day earlier than scheduled, perhaps as part of a move to dampen tensions.

The series of test launches included an upgrade to the surface-to-surface missile designated KN-02 by the US. Based on the Russian-made 9K79 *Tochka* (SS-21 *Scarab*), it has an extended range of 220km, a sharp increase from the previous maximum range of 140km. Tests of this system in spring 2014 were previously thought to have been 300mm-calibre artillery rockets. North Korea obtained the *Tochka* system from Syria in the 1990s. The extended range can reach almost half of South Korea's territory; North Korean media referred to it being able to strike Republic of Korea military command centres in the middle of the country, near the city of Daejeon. Claims were also made about the improved accuracy of the KN-02, which was already the nation's most accurate ballistic missile, with a 100-metre circular error probability.

A previously unseen anti-ship cruise missile was also observed in 2014, albeit by means of a brief illustration in a propaganda film, which showed a missile similar to the Russian 3M24 *Uran* (SS-N-25 *Switchblade*). This is a sea-skimming, anti-ship cruise missile with features similar to the US *Harpoon*.

It is not clear whether North Korea obtained the 130km-range 3M24 directly from Russia or from a third party. The missile's ability to fly at an altitude of 10–15m could pose problems for the older *Pohang*-class corvettes and other patrol vessels that South Korea uses for coastal defence. In the naval realm, satellite imagery in 2014 identified two new helicopter-carrying corvettes, the largest surface ships constructed by North Korea in 25 years and apparently designed for anti-submarine operations. Satellite imagery of Singpo dockyard from July indicated an unidentified submarine type estimated to be at least twice as large as known indigenous DPRK submarine designs.

Of greatest international concern, however, were the continued advances in North Korea's apparent quest for an intercontinental ballistic missile. Work begun in 2013 to modify the launch pad at Sohae Satellite Launching Station appeared to be on track for completion by the end of 2014. The upgrade would allow the launch of rockets up to 50–55m tall, significantly larger than the 32m *Unha* space-launch vehicle tested in December 2012. In 2014, North Korea also appeared to have conducted four tests of an engine for the mobile intercontinental missile under development, known in the West as KN-08.

Meanwhile, with Six-Party Talks on the nuclear issue on hold since 2008, concerned nations continued to prioritise sanctions, adding the North Korean firm Ocean Maritime Management (which managed the vessel *Chong Chon Gang*, see *The Military Balance 2014*, p. 216) to the UN blacklist. It was also hoped that China's quiet pressure could help to dissuade North Korean provocations. Presidential visits between Beijing and Seoul and the absence of any interest in the same with Pyongyang demonstrated China's frustration with its ally.

Afghanistan AFG

New Afghan Afghani Afs		2013	2014	2015
GDP	Afs	1.15tr	1.25tr	
	US$	20.7bn	21.7bn	
per capita	US$	679	694	
Growth	%	3.60	3.24	
Inflation	%	7.39	6.11	
Def exp	Afs	153bn		
	US$	2.76bn		
Def bdgt [a]	Afs	152bn	189bn	
	US$	2.75bn	3.29bn	
US$1=Afs		55.37	57.53	

[a] Security expenditure. Includes expenditure on Ministry of Defence, Ministry of Interior, Ministry of Foreign Affairs, National Security Council and the General Directorate of National Security. Also includes donor funding.

Population 31,822,848

Ethnic groups: Pashtun 38%; Tajik 25%; Hazara 19%; Uzbek 12%; Aimaq 4%; Baluchi 0.5%

Age	0–14	15–19	20–24	25–29	30–64	65 plus
Male	21.3%	6.2%	5.1%	3.9%	13.0%	1.2%
Female	20.7%	6.0%	4.9%	3.8%	12.6%	1.3%

Capabilities

Afghanistan's armed forces are optimised for counter-insurgency. With the withdrawal of NATO forces from a combat role, Afghan forces lead all operations against the Taliban. US and NATO advisers have greatly reduced in number and are not deployed forward of Afghan Corps HQs. Afghan forces assumed the security lead across the country in 2014 and, while Taliban adversaries have still been able to mount attacks, these have eventually been neutralised by Afghan forces. The current priority is to develop combat support, logistic leadership and technical expertise. Although there are plans and funding to give the air force fixed- and rotary-wing lift capability, including ex-US C-130H *Hercules*, as well as ISR, multi-role and attack helicopters and *Super Tucano* turboprop light-strike fighters, corruption and a shortage of sufficiently educated personnel to undertake pilot training mean the air force is unlikely to reach full capability in 2015. NATO's training and advisory mission, *Operation Resolute Support*, which is focused on building medical, counter-IED and intelligence capabilities, was able to proceed following the signing of a Bilateral Security Agreement and SOFA in October 2014. (See pp. 218.)

ACTIVE 178,500 (Army 172,000 Air Force 6,500)
Paramilitary 152,150

ORGANISATIONS BY SERVICE

Afghan National Army (ANA) 172,000
5 regional comd.

FORCES BY ROLE
SPECIAL FORCES
1 spec ops div (1 SF gp; 1 mech inf bn (2 mech inf coy), 2 cdo bde (1 mech inf coy, 4 cdo bn))
MANOEUVRE
Mechanised
2 (1st MSF) mech bde (2 mech inf bn)
1 (2nd MSF) mech bde (3 mech inf bn)
Light
1 (201st) corps (3 inf bde (4 inf bn, 1 sy coy, 1 cbt spt bn, 1 CSS bn), 1 inf bde (3 inf bn, 1 sy coy, 1 cbt spt bn, 1 CSS bn), 1 engr bn, 1 int bn, 2 MP coy, 1 sigs bn)
1 (203rd) corps (2 inf bde (5 inf bn, 1 sy coy, 1 cbt spt bn, 1 CSS bn), 2 inf bde (4 inf bn, 1 sy coy, 1 cbt spt bn, 1 CSS bn), 1 engr bn, 1 int bn, 2 MP coy, 1 sigs bn)
1 (205th) corps (4 inf bde (4 inf bn, 1 sy coy, 1 cbt spt bn, 1 CSS bn), 1 engr bn, 1 int bn, 2 MP coy, 1 sigs bn)
2 (207th & 209th) corps (3 inf bde (4 inf bn, 1 sy coy, 1 cbt spt bn, 1 CSS bn), 1 engr bn, 1 int bn, 2 MP coy, 1 sigs bn)
1 (215th) corps (3 inf bde (4 inf bn, 1 sy coy, 1 cbt spt bn, 1 CSS bn), 1 inf bde (2 inf bn, 1 cbt spt bn, 1 CSS bn), 1 engr bn, 1 int bn, 2 MP coy, 1 sigs bn)
1 (111st Capital) div (1 inf bde (1 tk bn, 1 mech inf bn, 2 inf bn, 1 sy coy, 1 cbt spt bn, 1 CSS bn), 1 inf bde (4 inf bn, 1 sy coy, 1 cbt spt bn, 1 CSS bn), 1 int bn)

EQUIPMENT BY TYPE
MBT 20 T-55/T-62 (24 more in store†)
APC 796
  APC (T) 173 M113A2†
  APC (W) 623 MSFV (inc variants)
ARTY 214
  TOWED 109: **122mm** 85 D-30†; **155mm** 24 M114A1†
  MOR 82mm 105 M-69†
MW Bozena

Afghan Air Force (AAF) 6,500
Including Special Mission Wing
EQUIPMENT BY TYPE
AIRCRAFT
  TPT 37: **Medium** 2 C-130H *Hercules*; **Light** 35: 6 Cessna 182; 26 Cessna 208B; 3 PC-12 (Special Mission Wing)
HELICOPTERS
  ATK 5 Mi-35 *Hind*
  MRH 78: 6 MD-530F; 72 Mi-17 *Hip* H (incl 30 Special Mission Wing hel)

Paramilitary 152,150

Afghan National Police 152,150
Under control of Interior Ministry. Includes 113,400 Afghan Uniformed Police (AUP), 12,700 Afghan National Civil Order Police (ANCOP), 21,650 Afghan Border Police (ABP), Police Special Forces (GDPSU) and Afghan Anti-Crime Police (AACP).

FOREIGN FORCES

All under ISAF comd unless otherwise specified.
Albania 22

Armenia 121

Australia 273; 1 UAV det with RQ-7B *Shadow* 200; 1 UAV det with *Heron* • UNAMA 2 obs

Austria 3

Azerbaijan 94

Belgium 160

Bosnia-Herzegovina 8

Bulgaria 320

Croatia 153

Czech Republic 227 • UNAMA 2 obs

Denmark 145; 1 mech inf BG

Estonia 4

Finland 88

France 88

Georgia 755; 1 mtn inf bn

Germany 1,599; 1 bde HQ; 1 inf BG; CH-53G *Stallion*; C-160 *Transall*; *Heron* UAV • UNAMA 2 obs

Greece 9

Hungary 101

Ireland 7

Italy 1,411; 1 mech inf bde HQ; 1 mech inf regt; 1 avn det; AW129 *Mangusta*; CH-47 *Chinook*; NH90; RQ-1 *Predator*; C-27J *Spartan*; C-130 *Hercules*

Jordan 626; 1 mech inf bn

Korea, Republic of 50

Latvia 11

Lithuania 84 • UNAMA 1 obs

Macedonia (FYROM) 152

Malaysia 2

Mongolia 40

Montenegro 25

Netherlands 30

New Zealand 1

Norway 57 • UNAMA 1 obs

Poland 304 • UNAMA 1 obs

Portugal 37 • UNAMA 1 obs

Romania 327 • UNAMA 2 obs

Slovakia 277

Slovenia 2

Spain 181

Sweden 13 • UNAMA 1 obs

Turkey 393 • UNAMA 1 obs

Ukraine 10

United Arab Emirates 35

United Kingdom 300; *Hermes* 450; *Watchkeeper*; MQ-9 *Reaper*; *Shadow* R1

United States 28,970; 1 corps HQ; 1 div HQ; 1 cav regt; 1 lt inf bde; 1 air aslt bde; 1 inf bn; 3 para bn; 2 cbt avn bde; 1 ARNG cav sqn; 2 ARNG inf bn; F-16C/D *Fighting Falcon*; A-10 *Thunderbolt* II; EC-130H *Compass Call*, C-130 *Hercules*; AH-64 *Apache*; OH-58 *Kiowa*; CH-47 *Chinook*; UH-60 *Black Hawk*; HH-60 *Pave Hawk*; RQ-7B *Shadow*; MQ-1 *Predator*; MQ-9 *Reaper*

Australia AUS

Australian Dollar A$		2013	2014	2015
GDP	A$	1.56tr	1.61tr	
	US$	1.51tr	1.48tr	
per capita	US$	64,578	62,822	
Growth	%	2.3	2.8	
Inflation	%	2.5	2.7	
Def exp	A$	23.3bn		
	US$	22.6bn		
Def bdgt	A$	25.3bn	24.4bn	26.8bn
	US$	24.5bn	22.5bn	
US$1=A$		1.03	1.09	

Population 22,507,617

Age	0–14	15–19	20–24	25–29	30–64	65 plus
Male	9.2%	3.2%	3.6%	3.6%	23.5%	7.0%
Female	8.8%	3.1%	3.4%	3.5%	23.0%	8.1%

Capabilities

Australia has a strong military tradition and its armed forces' considerable operational experience, together with high levels of technological expertise, a defence-industrial base and international defence relationships (particularly with the US) contribute substantially to its military capabilities. Continuing modernisation of all three services seems likely to ensure that equipment at least matches, and in many cases continues to surpass, that of nations in its immediate region. Future procurement includes up to 100 F-35 Joint Strike Fighters, with two test F-35As rolled out in 2014, and new conventional submarines to replace the *Collins*-class. Two *Canberra*-class LHDs are also under construction. The armed forces have high training standards and participate frequently in joint-service exercises at the national, bilateral and multinational levels with a view to future operational deployments in Southeast Asia and possibly further afield. The drawdown from Afghanistan, the Solomon Islands and Timor-Leste has allowed Australia's forces to intensify engagement with those of neighbouring states, notably Indonesia. The May 2013 Defence White Paper considered in detail the implications of Asia's rapid economic growth, the US rebalance to the Asia-Pacific and enhanced US defence cooperation with Australia, as well as operational drawdowns by Australian forces. Though the paper emphasised commitment to earlier plans to boost capabilities, doubts remained over the capacity to fund these improvements. In April 2014, the government announced that it would issue a new white paper in 2015 to outline the tasks the government expects the armed forces to perform and 'how these can be achieved with the resources available'.

ACTIVE 56,750 (Army 29,000 Navy 13,550 Air 14,200)

RESERVE 23,100 (Army 14,100 Navy 4,700 Air 4,300)
Integrated units are formed from a mix of reserve and regular personnel. All ADF operations are now controlled by Headquarters Joint Operations Command (HQJOC).

ORGANISATIONS BY SERVICE

Space
EQUIPMENT BY TYPE
SATELLITES • COMMUNICATIONS 1 *Optus* C1 (dual use for civil/mil comms)

Army 29,000

Forces Command
FORCES BY ROLE
COMMAND
  1 (1st) div HQ
MANOEUVRE
  Mechanised
  3 (1st, 3rd & 7th) mech inf bde (1 armd cav regt, 2 mech inf bn, 1 arty regt, 1 cbt engr regt, 1 sigs regt, 1 CSS bn)
  Amphibious
  1 (2nd RAR) amph bn
  Aviation
  1 (16th) avn bde (1 regt (2 ISR hel sqn), 1 regt (3 tpt hel sqn), 1 regt (1 spec ops hel sqn, 1 avn sqn))
COMBAT SUPPORT
  1 (6th) cbt spt bde (1 STA regt (1 STA bty, 1 UAV bty, 1 CSS bty), 1 AD/FAC regt (integrated), 1 engr regt (2 (construction) engr sqn, 1 EOD sqn), 1 int bn)
  1 EW regt
COMBAT SERVICE SUPORT
  1 (17th) CSS bde (3 log bn, 3 med bn, 1 MP bn)

Special Operations Command
FORCES BY ROLE
SPECIAL FORCES
  1 (SAS) SF regt
  1 (SF Engr) SF regt
  2 cdo bn
COMBAT SUPPORT
  3 sigs sqn (incl 1 reserve sqn)
COMBAT SERVICE SUPPORT
  1 CSS sqn

Reserve Organisations

Force Command 16,200 reservists
FORCES BY ROLE
COMMAND
  1 (2nd) div HQ
MANOEUVRE
  Reconnaissance
  3 (regional force) surv unit (integrated)
  Light
  6 inf bde (total: 3 recce regt, 3 recce sqn, 12 inf bn, 6 arty bty)
COMBAT SUPPORT
  3 cbt engr regt
  3 cbt engr sqn 1 sigs regt
COMBAT SERVICE SUPPORT
  6 CSS bn

EQUIPMENT BY TYPE
MBT 59 M1A1 *Abrams*
AIFV 253 ASLAV-25 (all variants)
APC 1,431
  APC (T) 431 M113AS4
  PPV 1,000 *Bushmaster* IMV
ARTY 378
  TOWED 190: **105mm** 101 L-118 Light Gun; **155mm** 89: 35 M198; 54 M777A2
  MOR **81mm** 188
AT
  MSL • MANPATS *Javelin*
  RCL • **84mm** *Carl Gustav*
AMPHIBIOUS 15 LCM-8 (capacity either 1 MBT or 200 troops)
HELICOPTERS
  ATK 22 EC665 *Tiger*
  TPT 107: **Heavy** 6 CH-47D *Chinook*; **Medium** 60: 25 NH90 TTH (MRH90 TTH); 35 S-70A *Black Hawk*; **Light** 41 Bell 206B-1 *Kiowa*
UAV • ISR • **Medium** 10 RQ-7B *Shadow* 200
AD • SAM • MANPAD RBS-70
RADAR • LAND 34: 3 *Giraffe*; 31 LCMR
ARV 17: 9 ASLAV-F; 1 ASLAV-R; 7 M88A2
VLB 5 *Biber*
MW 11: 3 *Chubby*; 8 ST-AT/V

Navy 13,550
Fleet Comd HQ located at Stirling; Naval Strategic Comd HQ located at Canberra

EQUIPMENT BY TYPE
SUBMARINES • TACTICAL • SSK 6 *Collins* with 6 single 533mm TT with Mk48 *Sea Arrow* ADCAP HWT/UGM-84C *Harpoon* AShM
PRINCIPAL SURFACE COMBATANTS 12
  FRIGATES • FFGHM 12
    4 *Adelaide* (Mod) with 1 Mk13 GMLS with RGM-84C *Harpoon* AShM/SM-2 MR SAM, 1 8 cell Mk41 VLS with RIM-162 *Evolved Sea Sparrow* SAM, 2 triple Mk32 324mm ASTT with MU90 LWT, 1 *Phalanx* Block 1B CIWS, 1 76mm gun (capacity 2 S-70B *Seahawk* ASW hel)
    8 *Anzac* (GER MEKO 200) with 2 quad Mk141 lnchr with RGM-84C *Harpoon* AShM, 1 8 cell Mk41 VLS with RIM-162 *Evolved Sea Sparrow* SAM, 2 triple 324mm ASTT with MU90 LWT, 1 127mm gun (capacity 1 S-70B *Seahawk* ASW hel) (capability upgrades in progress)
PATROL AND COASTAL COMBATANTS • PHSC 14 *Armidale*
MINE WARFARE • MINE COUNTERMEASURES • MHO 6 *Huon*
AMPHIBIOUS
  PRINCIPAL AMPHIBIOUS SHIPS 3
    LHD 1 *Canberra* (capacity 8 hel; 4 LCM; 100 veh; 1,000 troops)
    LSD 1 *Choules* (UK *Bay*) (capacity 4 LCU; 2 LCVP; 24 MBT; 350 troops) with 1 hel landing platform
    LSL 1 *Tobruk* (capacity 2 LCM; 2 LCVP; 40 APC and 18 MBT; 500 troops) with 1 hel landing platform

LANDING CRAFT 9
   LCM 4 LCM-1E
   LCVP 5
LOGISTICS AND SUPPORT 37
   AGHS 2 *Leeuwin* with 1 hel landing platform
   AGS 4 *Paluma*
   AORH 1 *Success*
   AOR 1 *Sirius*
   The following vessels are operated by a private company, DMS Maritime:
   AE 3 *Wattle*
   AOL 4 *Warrigal*
   ASR 3
   AX 2: 1 **AXL**; 1 **AXS**
   YDT 4
   YPT 3
   YTL 4
   YTM 6

Naval Aviation 1,350
FORCES BY ROLE
ANTI SUBMARINE WARFARE
   1 sqn with NH90 (MRH90)
   1 sqn with S-70B-2 *Seahawk*
TRAINING
   1 sqn with AS350BA *Ecureuil*; Bell 429
EQUIPMENT BY TYPE
HELICOPTERS
   ASW 17: 4 MH-60R *Seahawk*; 13 S-70B-2 *Seahawk*
   TPT 22: **Medium** 6 NH90 (MRH90); **Light** 16: 13 AS350BA *Ecureuil*; 3 Bell 429

Air Force 14,050
Flying hours   175 hrs/year on F/A-18 *Hornet*

FORCES BY ROLE
FIGHTER/GROUND ATTACK
   3 sqn with F/A-18A/B *Hornet*
   2 sqn with F/A-18F *Super Hornet*
ANTI SUBMARINE WARFARE
   2 sqn with AP-3C *Orion*
AIRBORNE EARLY WARNING & CONTROL
   1 sqn with B-737-700 *Wedgetail* (E-7A)
TANKER/TRANSPORT
   1 sqn with A330 MRTT (KC-30A)
TRANSPORT
   1 VIP sqn with B-737BBJ; CL-604 *Challenger*
   1 sqn with Beech 350 *King Air*
   1 sqn with C-17A *Globemaster*
   1 sqn with C-130J-30 *Hercules*
TRAINING
   1 OCU with F/A-18A/B *Hornet*
   1 sqn with Beech 350 *King Air*
   2 (LIFT) sqn with *Hawk* MK127*
   1 sqn with PC-9/A(F)
ISR UAV
   1 flt with *Heron*
EQUIPMENT BY TYPE
AIRCRAFT 146 combat capable
   FGA 95: 55 F/A-18A *Hornet*; 16 F/A-18B *Hornet*; 24 F/A-18F *Super Hornet*
   ASW 18 AP-3C *Orion*
   AEW&C 6 B-737-700 *Wedgetail* (E-7A)
   TKR/TPT 5 A330 MRTT (KC-30A)
   TPT 39: **Heavy** 6 C-17A *Globemaster*; **Medium** 12 C-130J-30 *Hercules*; **Light** 16 Beech 300 *King Air*; **PAX** 5: 2 B-737BBJ (VIP); 3 CL-604 *Challenger* (VIP)
   TRG 96: 33 *Hawk* Mk127*; 63 PC-9/A (incl 4 PC-9/A(F) for tgt marking)
UAV • ISR • **Heavy** 4 *Heron*
RADAR • AD RADAR 7
   OTH-B 3 *Jindalee*
   Tactical 4 AN/TPS-77
MSL
   AAM • **IIR** AIM-9X *Sidewinder*; ASRAAM; **ARH** AIM-120B/C-5 AMRAAM
   ASM AGM-154 JSOW
   AShM AGM-84A *Harpoon*
   LACM AGM-158 JASSM
BOMBS
   Conventional Mk82; Mk83; Mk84; BLU-109/B
   Laser-guided *Paveway* II/IV; Laser JDAM (being delivered)
   INS/GPS guided JDAM; JDAM-ER (in development)

Paramilitary
Border Protection Command
Has responsibility for operational coordination and control of both civil and military maritime-enforcement activities within Australia's EEZ. At any one time, 7 *Armidale*-class patrol boats, 1 major fleet unit and 3 AP-3C *Orion* aircraft are assigned to BPC activities.
EQUIPMENT BY TYPE
PATROL AND COASTAL COMBATANTS 11
   PSO 1 *Ocean Protector* with 1 hel landing platform
   PCO 3: 1 *Triton* with 1 hel landing platform; 2 *Cape*
   PCC 7: 1 *Ashmore Guardian*; 6 *Bay*
AIRCRAFT
   TPT • **Light** 12: 10 DHC-8; 2 F-406 *Caravan* II
HELICOPTERS • TPT 2: **Medium** 1 Bell 214; **Light** 1 AS350

Cyber
The Cyber Security Operations Centre contributes to addressing the cyber security threat. Hosted at the Australian Signals Directorate, the centre continues to work closely within Defence and with other government agencies to ensure that Australia is both protected against emerging cyber threats and adequately positioned to meet the government's requirement to implement the Top 4 Strategies to Mitigate Targeted Cyber Intrusions — a mandatory requirement after 2013, under the Financial Management and Accountability Act 1997. Partial implementation of the Australian Signals Directorate's top four mitigations was achieved in 2014. Defence will continue to implement the remaining mitigation strategies in 2015.

DEPLOYMENT
Legal provisions for foreign deployment:
Constitution: Constitution (1900)

Decision on deployment of troops abroad: By government exercising its executive power under Section 61 of the Australian Constitution.

AFGHANISTAN
NATO • ISAF 273; 1 UAV det with RQ-7B *Shadow* 200; 1 UAV det with *Heron*
UN • UNAMA 2 obs

ARABIAN SEA
Combined Maritime Forces • CTF-150 1 FFGHM

EGYPT
MFO (*Operation Mazurka*) 25

MALAYSIA
130; 1 inf coy (on 3-month rotational tours); 1 AP-3C *Orion* (on occasion)

MIDDLE EAST
UN • UNTSO 12 obs

PAPUA NEW GUINEA
38; 1 trg unit; 1 LSD

SOUTH SUDAN
UN • UNMISS 18; 4 obs

UNITED ARAB EMIRATES
Operation Accordion 400: 1 tpt det with 3 C-130J *Hercules*; 1 MP det with 2 AP-3C *Orion*
Operation Okra 400; 1 FGA det with 8 F/A-18F *Super Hornet*; 1 B-737-700 *Wedgetail* (E-7A); 1 A330 MRTT (KC-30A)

FOREIGN FORCES

New Zealand 9 (air navigation trg)
Singapore 230: 1 trg sqn at Pearce with PC-21 trg ac; 1 trg sqn at Oakey with 12 AS332 *Super Puma*; AS532 *Cougar*
United States US Pacific Command: 180; 1 SEWS at Pine Gap; 1 comms facility at NW Cape; 1 SIGINT stn at Pine Gap • US Strategic Command: 1 detection and tracking radar at Naval Communication Station Harold E Holt

Bangladesh BGD

Bangladeshi Taka Tk		2013	2014	2015
GDP	Tk	12.7tr	14.5tr	
	US$	162bn	187bn	
per capita	US$	1,033	1,179	
Growth	%	6.1	6.2	
Inflation	%	7.5	7.2	
Def Exp	Tk	120bn		
	US$	1.53bn		
Def bdgt	Tk	135bn	152bn	165bn
	US$	1.72bn	1.96bn	
FMA (US)	US$	2.2m	2.5m	2m
US$1=Tk		78.81	77.60	

Population 166,280,712
Religious groups: Muslim 90%; Hindu 9%; Buddhist 1%

Age	0–14	15–19	20–24	25–29	30–64	65 plus
Male	16.4%	4.8%	4.0%	3.5%	17.4%	2.5%
Female	15.9%	5.2%	4.8%	4.3%	18.6%	2.5%

Capabilities

Bangladesh has a limited military capability, with minimal inter-service cooperation, and is optimised for border and domestic security. It has shown itself capable of mobilising and deploying quickly to counter internal threats, albeit with considerable use of lethal force. The armed forces reportedly retain extensive business interests, in real estate, banks and other businesses. There has been significant investment in naval capabilities, including new frigates, patrol craft, training aircraft and multi-role helicopters, as well as plans to acquire submarines; a requirement for maritime-domain awareness and security is inspiring further spending. Maritime disputes with Myanmar and India were settled in Bangladesh's favour in March 2012 and July 2014 respectively. Meanwhile, other services have seen more modest investments in capabilities. Bangladesh's long record of service in UN missions has brought considerable peacekeeping experience.

ACTIVE 157,050 (Army 126,150 Navy 16,900 Air 14,000) **Paramilitary 63,900**

ORGANISATIONS BY SERVICE

Army 126,150
FORCES BY ROLE
COMMAND
  7 inf div HQ
SPECIAL FORCES
  1 cdo bn
MANOEUVRE
  Armoured
  1 armd bde
  6 indep armd regt
  Light
  18 inf bde
  1 (composite) bde

Aviation
1 avn regt (1 avn sqn; 1 hel sqn)
COMBAT SUPPORT
20 arty regt
1 AD bde
1 engr bde
1 sigs bde
EQUIPMENT BY TYPE
MBT 276: 174 Type-59; 58 Type-69/Type-69G; 44 Type-90-II (MBT-2000)
LT TK 8 Type-62
RECCE 5+ BOV M11
AIFV 155 BTR-80A
APC 151
  APC (T) 134 MT-LB
  APC (W) 17 *Cobra*
ARTY 839+
  SP 155mm 4+ NORA B-52
  TOWED 363+: **105mm** 170: 56 Model 56A1; 114 Model 56/L 10A1 pack howitzer; **122mm** 131: 57 Type-54/54-1 (M-30); 20 Type-83; 54 Type-96 (D-30), **130mm** 62 Type-59-1 (M-46)
  MOR 472: **81mm** 11 M29A1; **82mm** 366 Type-53/87/M-31 (M-1937); **120mm** 95 MO-120-AM-50 M67/UBM 52
AT
  MSL • MANPATS 9K115-2 *Metis* M1 (AT-13 *Saxhorn*-2)
  RCL 106mm 238 M40A1
AMPHIBIOUS • LANDING CRAFT 3: 1 LCT; 2 LCVP
AIRCRAFT • TPT • Light 6: 5 Cessna 152; 1 PA-31T *Cheyenne*
HELICOPTERS
  MRH 2 AS365N3 *Dauphin*
  TPT • Light 3 Bell 206L-4 *Long Ranger*
AD • SAM
  SP FM-90
    MANPAD QW-2; HN-5A (being replaced by QW-2)
  GUNS • TOWED 166: **37mm** 132 Type-65/74; **57mm** 34 Type-59 (S-60)
AEV MT-LB
ARV 3+: T-54/T-55; Type-84; 3 Type-654
VLB MTU

Navy 16,900
EQUIPMENT BY TYPE
PRINCIPAL SURFACE COMBATANTS • FRIGATES 6
  FFGHM 1 *Bangabandhu* (ROK Modified *Ulsan*) with 2 twin lnchr with *Otomat* Mk2 AShM, 1 octuple HQ-7 SAM, 2 triple 324mm TT with A244 LWT, 1 76mm gun (capacity: 1 AW109E hel)
  FFG 3:
    2 *Abu Bakr* (ex-PRC *Jianghu* III) with 2 twin lnchr with C-802A AShM, 2 RBU 1200, 2 twin 100mm gun
    1 *Osman* (ex-PRC *Jianghu* I) with 2 quad lnchr with C-802 (CSS-N-8 *Saccade*) AShM, 2 RBU 1200, 2 twin 100mm gun
  FF 2:
    1 *Somudro Joy* (ex-USCG *Hero*) with 1 76mm gun, hel landing platform
    1 *Umar Farooq*† (UK *Salisbury* – trg role) with 3 *Squid*, 1 twin 115mm gun

PATROL AND COASTAL COMBATANTS 47
  CORVETTES • FSG 4:
    2 *Durjoy* with 2 twin lnchr with C-704 AShM, 1 76mm gun
    2 *Bijoy* (ex-UK *Castle*) with 2 twin lnchr with C-704 AShM, 1 76mm gun, 1 hel landing platform
  PCFG 4 *Durdarsha* (ex-PRC *Huangfeng*) with 4 single lnchr with HY-2 (CSS-N-2 *Safflower*) AShM
  PCO 6: 1 *Madhumati* (*Sea Dragon*) with 1 57mm gun; 5 *Kapatakhaya* (ex-UK *Island*)
  PCC 8:
    2 *Meghna* with 1 57mm gun (fishery protection)
    1 *Nirbhoy* (ex-PRC *Hainan*) with 4 RBU 1200; 2 twin 57mm gun
    5 *Padma*
  PBFG 5 *Durbar* (PRC *Hegu*) with 2 single lnchr with SY-1 AShM
  PBFT 4 *Huchuan* (PRC) with 2 single 533mm TT each with YU 1 Type-53 HWT
  PBF 4 *Titas* (ROK *Sea Dolphin*)
  PB 12: 1 *Barkat* (ex-PRC *Shanghai* III); 1 *Bishkali*; 2 *Karnaphuli*; 1 *Salam* (ex-PRC *Huangfen*); 7 *Shaheed Daulat* (PRC *Shanghai* II)
MINE WARFARE • MINE COUNTERMEASURES 5
  MSO 5: 1 *Sagar*; 4 *Shapla* (ex-UK *River*)
AMPHIBIOUS
  LANDING SHIPS • LSL 1
  LANDING CRAFT 10:
    LCU 2†
    LCVP 3†
    LCM 5 *Darshak* (*Yuchin*)
LOGISTICS AND SUPPORT 11
  AG 1
  AGHS 2: 1 *Agradoot*; 1 *Anushandhan*
  AOR 2 (coastal)
  AR 1†
  ATF 1†
  AX 1 *Shaheed Ruhul Amin*
  YTM 3

Naval Aviation
EQUIPMENT BY TYPE
AIRCRAFT • TPT • Light 2 Do-228NG (MP)
HELICOPTERS • TPT • Light 2 AW109E *Power*

Air Force 14,000
FORCES BY ROLE
FIGHTER
  1 sqn with MiG-29B/UB *Fulcrum*
FIGHTER/GROUND ATTACK
  1 sqn with F-7MB/FT-7B *Airguard*
  1 sqn with F-7BG/FT-7BG *Airguard*
  1 sqn with F-7BGI/FT-7BGI *Airguard*
GROUND ATTACK
  1 sqn with A-5C (Q-5III) *Fantan*; FT-6 (MiG-19UTI) *Farmer*
TRANSPORT
  1 sqn with An-32 *Cline*
  1 sqn with C-130B *Hercules*
TRAINING
  1 (OCU) sqn with K-8W *Karakorum**; L-39ZA *Albatros**
  1 sqn with PT-6

TRANSPORT HELICOPTER
2 sqn with Mi-17 *Hip* H; Mi-17-1V *Hip* H; Mi-171Sh
1 sqn with Bell 212
1 trg sqn with Bell 206L *Long Ranger*

EQUIPMENT BY TYPE†
AIRCRAFT 90 combat capable
FTR 61: 10 F-7MB *Airguard*; 11 F-7BG *Airguard*; 12 F-7BGI *Airguard*; 5 FT-7B *Airguard*; 4 FT-7BG *Airguard*; 4 FT-7BGI *Airguard*; 7 FT-6 *Farmer*; 6 MiG-29 *Fulcrum*; 2 MiG-29UB *Fulcrum*
ATK 18 A-5C *Fantan*
TPT 7: **Medium** 4 C-130B *Hercules*; **Light** 3 An-32 *Cline*†
TRG 21: 4 K-8W *Karakorum**; 7 L-39ZA *Albatros**; 10 PT-6
HELICOPTERS
MRH 14: 12 Mi-17 *Hip* H; 2 Mi-17-1V *Hip* H (VIP)
TPT 9: **Medium** 3 Mi-171Sh; **Light** 6: 2 Bell 206L *Long Ranger*; 4 Bell 212
MSL • AAM • IR R-3 (AA-2 *Atoll*)‡; R-73 (AA-11 *Archer*); PL-5; PL-7; **SARH** R-27R (AA-10A *Alamo*)

Paramilitary 63,900

Ansars 20,000+
Security Guards

Rapid Action Battalions 5,000
Ministry of Home Affairs
FORCES BY ROLE
MANOEUVRE
  Other
    14 paramilitary bn

Border Guard Bangladesh 38,000
FORCES BY ROLE
MANOEUVRE
  Amphibious
    1 rvn coy
  Other
    54 paramilitary bn

Coast Guard 900
EQUIPMENT BY TYPE
PATROL AND COASTAL COMBATANTS 9
  PB 4: 1 *Ruposhi Bangla*; 1 *Shaheed Daulat*; 2 *Shetgang*
  PBR 5 *Pabna*

DEPLOYMENT

CÔTE D'IVOIRE
UN • UNOCI 1,682; 12 obs; 2 mech inf bn; 1 avn coy; 1 engr coy; 1 sigs coy; 1 fd hospital

CENTRAL AFRICAN REPUBLIC
UN • MINUSCA 332; 1 inf bn(-)

DEMOCRATIC REPUBLIC OF THE CONGO
UN • MONUSCO 2,550; 20 obs; 2 mech inf bn; 2 engr coy; 1 avn coy; 2 hel coy

LEBANON
UN • UNIFIL 326; 1 FFG; 1 FSG

LIBERIA
UN • UNMIL 515; 12 obs; 2 engr coy; 1 log pl; 1 fd hospital

MALI
UN • MINUSMA 1,471; 1 inf bn; 1 engr coy; 1 rvn coy; 2 sigs coy; 1 tpt coy

SOUTH SUDAN
UN • UNMISS 275; 4 obs; 1 engr coy

SUDAN
UN • UNAMID 220; 15 obs; 1 inf coy

WESTERN SAHARA
UN • MINURSO 20; 7 obs; 1 fd hospital

Brunei BRN

Brunei Dollar B$		2013	2014	2015
GDP	B$	20.2bn	21.9bn	
	US$	16.1bn	17.4bn	
per capita	US$	39,659	42,239	
Growth	%	-1.8	5.3	
Inflation	%	0.4	0.4	
Def bdgt	B$	516m	719m	
	US$	413m	573m	
US$1=B$		1.25	1.25	

Population 422,675

Ethnic groups: Malay, Kedayan, Tutong, Belait, Bisaya, Dusun, Murut 66.3%; Chinese 11.2%; Iban, Dayak, Kelabit 6%; Other 11.8%

Age	0–14	15–19	20–24	25–29	30–64	65 plus
Male	12.5%	4.3%	4.3%	4.8%	21.9%	2.0%
Female	11.7%	4.2%	4.5%	5.1%	22.7%	2.1%

Capabilities

The Royal Brunei Armed Forces are an important source of employment in this oil-rich state. Despite these small, professional forces being well trained, they could offer little resistance on their own to a determined aggressor. However, the sultanate has long-established defence relations with the UK and Singapore, with which its forces train. It has deployed small peacekeeping contingents, under Malaysian command, to Lebanon (UNIFIL) and the southern Philippines (IMT).

ACTIVE 7,000 (Army 4,900 Navy 1,000 Air 1,100)
Paramilitary 2,250

RESERVE 700 (Army 700)

ORGANISATIONS BY SERVICE

Army 4,900
FORCES BY ROLE
MANOEUVRE
  Light
    3 inf bn

COMBAT SUPPORT
1 cbt spt bn (1 armd recce sqn, 1 engr sqn)

Reserves 700
FORCES BY ROLE
MANOEUVRE
  Light
  1 inf bn
EQUIPMENT BY TYPE
LT TK 20 *Scorpion* (16 to be upgraded)
APC (W) 45 VAB
ARTY • MOR 81mm 24
ARV 2 *Samson*

Navy 1,000
FORCES BY ROLE
SPECIAL FORCES
  1 SF sqn
EQUIPMENT BY TYPE
PATROL AND COASTAL COMBATANTS 12
  CORVETTES • FSG 4 *Darussalam* with 2 twin lnchr with MM-40 *Exocet* Block II AShM, 1 57mm gun, 1 hel landing platform
  PCC 4 *Ijtihad*
  PBF 1 *Mustaed*
  PB 3 *Perwira*
AMPHIBIOUS • LANDING CRAFT • LCU 4: 2 *Teraban*; 2 *Cheverton Loadmaster*

Air Force 1,100
FORCES BY ROLE
MARITIME PATROL
  1 sqn with CN-235M
TRAINING
  1 sqn with PC-7; Bell 206B *Jet Ranger* II
TRANSPORT HELICOPTER
  1 sqn with Bell 212; Bell 214 (SAR)
  1 sqn with Bo-105
  1 sqn with S-70i *Black Hawk*
AIR DEFENCE
  1 sqn with *Rapier*
  1 sqn with *Mistral*
EQUIPMENT BY TYPE
AIRCRAFT
  MP 1 CN-235M
  TRG 4 PC-7
HELICOPTERS
  TPT 23: **Medium** 5: 1 Bell 214 (SAR); 4 S-70i *Black Hawk*; **Light** 18: 2 Bell 206B *Jet Ranger* II; 10 Bell 212; 6 Bo-105 (armed, 81mm rockets)
AD • SAM 12+: *Rapier*; 12 *Mistral*

Paramilitary ε2,250

Gurkha Reserve Unit 400-500
FORCES BY ROLE
MANOEUVRE
  Light
  2 inf bn(-)

Royal Brunei Police 1,750
EQUIPMENT BY TYPE
PATROL AND COASTAL COMBATANTS • PB 10: 3 *Bendaharu*; 7 PDB-type

DEPLOYMENT

LEBANON
UN • UNIFIL 30

PHILIPPINES
IMT 9

FOREIGN FORCES

Singapore 1 trg camp with infantry units on rotation; 1 trg school; 1 hel det with AS332 *Super Puma*

United Kingdom 550; 1 Gurhka bn; 1 trg unit; 1 hel flt with 3 hel

Cambodia CAM

Cambodian Riel r		2013	2014	2015
GDP	r	62tr	68.4tr	
	US$	15.5bn	16.9bn	
per capita	US$	1,028	1,104	
Growth	%	7.4	7.2	
Inflation	%	3.0	4.5	
Def bdgt	r	1.59tr	1.8tr	
	US$	400m	446m	
FMA (US)	US$	0.8m	1m	
US$1=r		3,995.12	4,045.47	

Population 15,458,332

Ethnic groups: Khmer 90%; Vietnamese 5%; Chinese 1%

Age	0–14	15–19	20–24	25–29	30–64	65 plus
Male	15.9%	4.7%	5.4%	5.1%	15.9%	1.5%
Female	15.7%	4.8%	5.5%	5.2%	17.9%	2.5%

Capabilities

Despite their name, which reflects Cambodia's formal status as a constitutional monarchy, and their integration in the early 1990s of two non-communist resistance armies, the Royal Cambodian Armed Forces are essentially the modern manifestation of the armed forces of the former People's Republic of Kampuchea, established in 1979 following Vietnam's invasion. The army is organised into many under-strength 'divisions', and is top-heavy with senior officers. Minor skirmishes on the border with Thailand since 2008 provide little indication of a capacity for high-intensity combat, which is probably limited. Cambodian peacekeeping troops are deployed in Lebanon (UNIFIL) and South Sudan (UNMISS).

ACTIVE 124,300 (Army 75,000 Navy 2,800 Air 1,500 Provincial Forces 45,000) **Paramilitary 67,000**

Conscript liability Authorised but not implemented since 1993

ORGANISATIONS BY SERVICE

Army ε75,000
6 Military Regions (incl 1 special zone for capital)
FORCES BY ROLE
SPECIAL FORCES
  1 AB/SF regt
MANOEUVRE
  Reconnaissance
  Some indep recce bn
  Armoured
  3 armd bn
  Light
  12 inf div(-)
  3 indep inf bde
  9 indep inf regt
  Other
  1 (70th) sy bde (4 sy bn)
  17 (border) sy bn
COMBAT SUPPORT
  2 arty bn
  1 AD bn
  4 fd engr regt
COMBAT SERVICE SUPPORT
  1 (construction) engr regt
EQUIPMENT BY TYPE
MBT 200+: 50 Type-59; 150+ T-54/T-55
LT TK 20+: Type-62; 20 Type-63
RECCE 4+ BRDM-2
AIFV 70 BMP-1
APC 230+
  APC (T) M113
  APC (W) 230: 200 BTR-60/BTR-152; 30 OT-64
ARTY 433+
  TOWED 400+ **76mm** ZIS-3 (M-1942)/**122mm** D-30/**122mm** M-30 (M-1938)/**130mm** Type-59-I
  MRL 33+: **107mm** Type-63; **122mm** 13: 8 BM-21; 5 RM-70; **132mm** BM-13-16 (BM-13); **140mm** 20 BM-14-16 (BM-14)
  MOR 82mm M-37; **120mm** M-43; **160mm** M-160
AT • **RCL 82mm** B-10; **107mm** B-11
AD
  MSL • **MANPAD** 50 FN-6; FN-16 (reported)
  GUNS • **TOWED 14.5mm** ZPU-1/ZPU-2/ZPU-4; **37mm** M-1939; **57mm** S-60
ARV T-54/T-55
MW Bozena; RA-140 DS

Navy ε2,800 (incl 1,500 Naval Infantry)
EQUIPMENT BY TYPE
PATROL AND COASTAL COMBATANTS 15
  PBF 2 *Stenka*
  PB 11: 4 (PRC 46m); 3 (PRC 20m); 2 *Shershen*; 2 *Turya*
  PBR 2 *Kaoh Chhlam*
AMPHIBIOUS • **CRAFT**
  LCU 1

Naval Infantry 1,500
FORCES BY ROLE
MANOEUVRE
  Light
  7 inf bn

COMBAT SUPPORT
  1 arty bn

Air Force 1,500
FORCES BY ROLE
ISR/TRAINING
  1 sqn with P-92 *Echo*; L-39 *Albatros**
TRANSPORT
  1 VIP sqn (reporting to Council of Ministers) with An-24RV *Coke*; AS350 *Ecureuil*; AS355F2 *Ecureuil* II
  1 sqn with BN-2 *Islander*; Y-12 (II)
TRANSPORT HELICOPTER
  1 sqn with Mi-26 *Halo*; Mi-17 *Hip* H; Mi-8 *Hip*; Z-9
EQUIPMENT BY TYPE
AIRCRAFT 5 combat capable
  TPT • **Light** 10: 2 An-24RV *Coke*; 1 BN-2 *Islander*; 5 P-92 *Echo* (pilot trg/recce); 2 Y-12 (II)
  TRG 5 L-39 *Albatros**
HELICOPTERS
  MRH 14: 3 Mi-17 *Hip* H; 11 Z-9
  TPT 10: **Heavy** 2 Mi-26 *Halo*; **Medium** 4 Mi-8 *Hip*; **Light** 4: 2 AS350 *Ecureuil*; 2 AS355F2 *Ecureuil* II

Provincial Forces 45,000+
Reports of at least 1 inf regt per province, with varying numbers of inf bn (with lt wpn)

Paramilitary
Police 67,000 (including gendarmerie)

DEPLOYMENT
LEBANON
UN • UNIFIL 184; 1 engr coy
MALI
UN • MINUSMA 306; 1 engr coy; 1 EOD coy
SOUTH SUDAN
UN • UNMISS 145; 3 obs; 1 fd hospital
SUDAN
UN • UNAMID 3 obs
UN • UNISFA 3 obs

China, People's Republic of PRC

Chinese Yuan Renminbi Y		2013	2014	2015
GDP	Y	58.7tr	64.5tr	
	US$	9.47tr	10.4tr	
	US$ [a]			
per capita	US$	6,959	7,572	
Growth	%	7.7	7.4	
Inflation	%	2.6	2.3	
Def exp	Y	ε1.0tr		
	US$	ε162bn		
	US$ [a]	ε277bn		
Def bdgt [b]	Y	718bn	805bn	
	US$	116bn	129bn	
US$1=Y	MER	6.20	6.22	
	PPP	3.63	3.66	

[a] PPP estimate
[b] Includes central government expenditure only.

Population 1,362,805,264

Ethnic groups: Tibetan, Uighur and other non-Han 8%

Age	0–14	15–19	20–24	25–29	30–64	65 plus
Male	9.2%	3.6%	4.2%	4.4%	25.4%	4.6%
Female	7.9%	3.1%	3.8%	4.2%	24.5%	5.0%

Capabilities

China continues to develop and recapitalise its military capabilities, with a 12.2% increase in defence expenditure in 2014 reflecting the support of President Xi Jinping for the armed forces. Beijing's military ambition is aimed at providing at least regional power projection and a conventional deterrent capacity to discourage external intervention. It also aims to sustain a credible nuclear deterrent. A second conventional aircraft carrier is under construction, and the navy reportedly introduced the JL-2 submarine-launched ballistic missile into service in 2014. Territorial disputes continued to be reflected in Chinese defence policy with the declaration of an Air-Defence Identification Zone in the East China Sea region at the end of 2013. Combat, support, maritime and special-mission aircraft developments also continued: the third and fourth J-20 fighter development aircraft flew in 2014 as did the second Y-20 military airlifter. A dedicated anti-submarine-warfare variant of the Y-8 is now being tested. Construction of indigenous destroyers and frigates continued as China's shipbuilding capability matured further. ASW is one of a number of areas of weakness the PLA is attempting to address; another is integrated joint operations between two or more of the services. The forces exercise regularly and are increasingly training with international partners. Without evidence from active operations, however, the actual extent of improvements in China's equipment inventory and military doctrine remain difficult to assess. (See pp. 212–17.)

ACTIVE 2,333,000 (Army 1,600,000 Navy 235,000 Air Force 398,000 Strategic Missile Forces 100,000) **Paramilitary 660,000**

Conscript liability Selective conscription; all services 2 years

RESERVE ε510,000

Overall organisation: army leadership is exercised by the four general headquarters/departments. A military region exercises direct leadership over the army units under it. The navy, air force and Second Artillery Force each have a leading body consisting of the headquarters, political department, logistics department and armaments department. These direct the military, political, logistical and equipment work of their respective troops, and take part in the command of joint operations.

ORGANISATIONS BY SERVICE

Strategic Missile Forces (100,000+)

Offensive

The Second Artillery Force organises and commands its own troops to launch nuclear counter-attacks with strategic missiles and to conduct operations with conventional missiles. Org as launch bdes subordinate to 6 army-level msl bases (1 in Shenyang & Beijing MR, 1 in Jinan MR, 1 in Nanjing MR, 2 in Guangzhou MR and 1 in Lanzhou MR). Org varies by msl type. The DF-16 MRBM is reported to be in service, but it is not yet clear which formation it has been assigned to.

FORCES BY ROLE
MISSILE
  1 ICBM bde with DF-4
  3 ICBM bde with DF-5A
  1 ICBM bde with DF-31
  2 ICBM bde with DF-31A
  1 IRBM bde with DF-3A/DF-21
  1 MRBM bde with DF-16 (reported)
  1 MRBM bde with DF-21
  6 MRBM bde with DF-21A
  2 MRBM bde with DF-21C
  1 MRBM bde forming with DF-21D (reported)
  4 SRBM bde with DF-11A
  4 SRBM bde with DF-15
  2 SSM bde with DH-10
  2 SSM trg bde
MSL • STRATEGIC 458
  ICBM 66: ε10 DF-4 (CSS-3); ε20 DF-5A (CSS-4 Mod 2); ε12 DF-31 (CSS-10 Mod 1); ε24 DF-31A (CSS-10 Mod 2)
  IRBM ε6 DF-3A (CSS-2 Mod)
  MRBM 134: ε12 DF-16 (CSS-11); ε80 DF-21/DF-21A (CSS-5 Mod 1/2); ε36 DF-21C (CSS-5 Mod 3); ε6 DF-21D (CSS-5 Mod 5 - ASBM) reported
  SRBM 252: ε108 DF-11A/M-11A (CSS-7 Mod 2); ε144 DF-15/M-9 (CSS-6)
  LACM ε54 DH-10

Navy
EQUIPMENT BY TYPE
SUBMARINES • STRATEGIC • SSBN 4:
1 *Xia* with 12 JL-1 (CSS-N-3) strategic SLBM
3 *Jin* with up to 12 JL-2 (CSS-NX-14) strategic SLBM (operational status unknown)

Air Force
FORCES BY ROLE
BOMBER
2 regt with H-6K
EQUIPMENT BY TYPE
AIRCRAFT • BBR ε36 H-6K
LACM CJ-10/CJ-20 (reported)

Defensive
RADAR • STRATEGIC: some phased array radar; some detection and tracking radars (covering Central Asia and Shanxi on the northern border) located in Xinjiang province

Space
SATELLITES 68
COMMUNICATIONS 5 *Zhongxing* (dual use telecom satellites for civ/mil comms)
NAVIGATION/POSITIONING/TIMING 17: 2 *Beidou*-1; 5 *Beidou*-2(M); 5 *Beidou*-2(G); 5 *Beidou*-2 (IGSO)
ISR 31: 1 *Haiyang* 2A; 28 *Yaogan Weixing* (remote sensing); 2 *Zhangguo Ziyuan* (ZY-2 - remote sensing)
ELINT/SIGINT 15: 8 *Shijian* 6 (4 pairs - reported ELINT/SIGINT role); 7 *Shijian* 11 (reported ELINT/SIGINT role)

People's Liberation Army ε800,000; ε800,000 conscript (total ε1,600,000)
7 military region commands are subdivided into a total of 28 military districts.
FORCES BY ROLE
COMMAND
7 mil region
18 (Group) army HQ
SPECIAL FORCES
10 SF bde
2 SF gp (regt)
MANOEUVRE
Armoured
1 armd div (3 armd regt, 1 arty regt, 1 AD regt)
16 armd bde
Mechanised
6 mech inf div (1 armd regt, 2 mech inf regt, 1 arty regt, 1 AD regt)
2 (high alt) mech inf div (1 armd regt, 2 mech inf regt, 1 arty regt, 1 AD regt)
20 mech inf bde
1 (high alt) mech inf bde
2 indep mech inf regt
Light
1 mot inf div (1 armd regt, 3 mot inf regt, 1 arty regt, 1 AD regt)
6 mot inf div (1 armd regt, 2 mot inf regt, 1 arty regt, 1 AD regt)
3 (high alt) mot inf div (1 armd regt, 2 mot inf regt, 1 arty regt, 1 AD regt)
21 mot inf bde
2 (high alt) mot inf bde
Amphibious
1 amph armd bde
2 amph mech div (1 armd regt, 2 mech inf regt, 1 arty regt, 1 AD regt)
Mountain
5 mtn inf bde
Other
1 (OPFOR) mech inf bde
1 mech gd div (1 armd regt, 2 mech inf regt, 1 arty regt, 1 AD regt)
1 sy gd div (4 sy regt)
59 (border) sy regt
1 (border) sy gp
Aviation
7 avn bde
3 avn regt
4 trg avn regt
COMBAT SUPPORT
19 arty bde
2 MRL bde
19 (coastal defence) AShM regt
22 AD bde
2 engr bde
19 engr regt
10 EW regt
50 sigs regt

Reserves
FORCES BY ROLE
MANOEUVRE
Armoured
2 armd regt
Light
18 inf div
4 inf bde
3 indep inf regt
COMBAT SUPPORT
3 arty div
7 arty bde
17 AD div
8 AD bde
8 AD regt
15 engr regt
1 ptn br bde
3 ptn br regt
10 chem regt
10 sigs regt
COMBAT SERVICE SUPPORT
9 log bde
1 log regt
EQUIPMENT BY TYPE
MBT 6,540: 2,000 Type-59; 500 Type-59-II; 550 Type-59D; 300 Type-79; 500 Type-88A/B; 1,000 Type-96; 1,050 Type-96A; 40 Type-98A; 500 Type-99; 100 Type-99A
LT TK 750: 350 Type-05 AAAV (ZTD-05); 350 Type-62; 50 Type-63A

RECCE 200 Type-09 (ZTL-09)
AIFV 3,850: 500 Type-04 (ZBD-04); 250 Type-04A (ZBD-04A); 300 Type-05 AAAV (ZBD-05); 400 Type-09 (ZBL-09); 600 Type-86; 650 Type-86A; 550 Type-92; 600 Type-92B
APC 5,020
  APC (T) 4,150: 2,400 Type-63/Type-63C; 1,750 Type-89
  APC (W) 870: 700 Type-92A; 120 Type-09A (ZBL-09A); 50 Type-93
ARTY 13,178+
  SP 2,280: **122mm** 1,600: 700 Type-89; 300 Type-07 (PLZ-07); 150 Type-07B (PLZ-07B); 300 Type-09 (PLC-09); 150 Type-09 (PLL-09); **152mm** 390 Type-83A/B; **155mm** 290 Type-05 (PLZ-05)
  TOWED 6,140: **122mm** 3,800 Type-54-1 (M-1938)/Type-83/Type-60 (D-74)/Type-96 (D-30); **130mm** 234 Type-59 (M-46)/Type-59-I; **152mm** 2,106 Type-54 (D-1)/Type-66 (D-20)
  GUN/MOR 120mm 300: 200 Type-05 (PLL-05); 100 Type-05A (PLZ-05A)
  MRL 1,872+
    SP 1,818+: **107mm** some; **122mm** 1,643: 1,250 Type-81; 375 Type-89 (PHZ-89); 18 Type-10 (PHZ-10); **300mm** 175 Type-03 (PHL-03)
    TOWED • 107mm 54 Type-63
  MOR 2,586
    TOWED 82mm Type-53 (M-37)/Type-67/Type-82/Type-87; **100mm** Type-89
AT
  MSL
    SP 924: 450 HJ-8 (veh mounted); 24 HJ-10; 450 ZSL-02B
    MANPATS HJ-73A/B/C; HJ-8A/C/E
  RCL 3,966: **75mm** Type-56; **82mm** Type-65 (B-10)/Type-78; **105mm** Type-75; **120mm** Type-98
  GUNS 1,788
    SP 480 **100mm** 250 Type-02 (PTL-02); **120mm** 230 Type-89 (PLZ-89)
    TOWED • 100mm 1,308 Type-73 (T-12)/Type-86
AIRCRAFT • TPT 8 Medium 4 Y-8; Light 4 Y-7
HELICOPTERS
  ATK 150: 90 Z-10; 60 Z-19
  MRH 351: 22 Mi-17 *Hip* H; 3 Mi-17-1V *Hip* H; 38 Mi-17V-5 *Hip* H; 25 Mi-17V-7 *Hip* H; 8 SA342L *Gazelle*; 21 Z-9A; 31 Z-9W; 10 Z-9WA; 193 Z-9WZ
  TPT 338: **Heavy** 61: 4 Mi-26 *Halo*; 9 Z-8A; 48 Z-8B; **Medium** 209: 50 Mi-8T *Hip*; 140 Mi-171; 19 S-70C2 (S-70C) *Black Hawk*; **Light** 68: 53 AS350 *Ecureuil*; 15 EC120
UAV • ISR • Heavy BZK-005; BZK-009; WZ-5 **Medium** ASN-105; ASN-206; BZK-006; BZK-007; **Light** ASN-104; W-50
AD
  SAM
    SP 296: 24 9K331 *Tor*-M1 (SA-15 *Gauntlet*); 30 HQ-6D *Red Leader*; 200 HQ-7A; 24 HQ-16A; 18 HQ-17
    MANPAD HN-5A/HN-5B *Hong Nu*; FN-6/QW-1/QW-2
  GUNS 7,376+
    SP 376: **25mm** 270 Type-04A; **35mm** 100 Type-07; **37mm** 6 Type-88
    TOWED 7,000+: **25mm** Type-87; **35mm** Type-99 (GDF-002); **37mm** Type-55 (M-1939)/Type-65/Type-74; **57mm** Type-59 (S-60); **100mm** Type-59 (KS-19)
RADAR • LAND *Cheetah*; RASIT; Type-378

MSL
  AShM HY-1 (CSS-C-2 *Silkworm*); HY-2 (CSS-C-3 *Seersucker*); HY-4 (CSS-C-7 *Sadsack*)
  ASM AKD-8; AKD-9; AKD-10
ARV Type-73; Type-84; Type-85; Type-97; Type-654
VLB KMM; MTU; TMM; Type-84A
MW Type-74; Type-79; Type-81-II; Type-84

Navy ε200,000; 35,000 conscript (total 235,000)

The PLA Navy is organised into five service arms: submarine, surface, naval aviation, coastal defence and marine corps, as well as other specialised units. There are three fleets, the Beihai Fleet (North Sea), Donghai Fleet (East Sea) and Nanhai Fleet (South Sea).

EQUIPMENT BY TYPE
SUBMARINES 70
  STRATEGIC • SSBN 4:
    1 *Xia* (Type-092) with 12 JL-1 (CSS-N-3) strategic SLBM
    3 *Jin* (Type-094) with up to 12 JL-2 (CSS-NX-14) strategic SLBM (operational status unknown)
  TACTICAL 66
    SSN 5:
      3 *Han* (Type-091) with YJ-82 (CSS-N-7) AShM, 6 single 533mm TT
      2 *Shang* (Type-093) with 6 single 533mm TT
    SSK 60:
      12 *Kilo* (2 Project 877, 2 Project 636, 8 Project 636N) with 3M54 *Klub* (SS-N-27B *Sizzler*) ASCM; 6 single 533mm TT
      20 *Ming* (4 Type-035, 12 Type-035G, 4 Type-035B) with 8 single 533mm TT
      16 *Song* (Type-039/039G) with YJ-82 (CSS-N-7) ASCM, 6 single 533mm TT
      4 *Yuan* (Type-039A) with 6 533mm TT
      8 *Yuan* II (Type-039B) with 6 533mm TT
    SSB 1 *Qing* (Type-032) (SLBM trials)
PRINCIPAL SURFACE COMBATANTS 72
  AIRCRAFT CARRIERS • CV 1
    1 *Liaoning* with 4 18-cell GMLS with HQ-10 SAM, 2 RBU 6000 *Smerch* 2, 3 Type 1030 CIWS (capacity 18–24 J-15 ac; 17 Ka-28/Ka-31/Z-8S/Z-8JH/Z-8AEW hel)
  DESTROYERS 17
    DDGHM 15:
      2 *Hangzhou* (RUS *Sovremenny*) with 2 quad lnchr with 3M80/3M82 *Moskit* (SS-N-22 *Sunburn*) AShM, 2 3K90 *Uragan* (SA-N-7 *Gadfly*) SAM, 2 twin 533mm ASTT, 2 RBU 1000 *Smerch* 3, 2 CADS-N-1 *Kashtan* CIWS, 2 twin 130mm gun (capacity 1 Z-9C/Ka-28 *Helix* A hel)
      2 *Hangzhou* (RUS *Sovremenny*) with 2 quad lnchr with 3M80/3M82 *Moskit* (SS-N-22 *Sunburn*) AShM, 2 *Yezh* (SA-N-12 *Grizzly*) SAM, 2 twin 533mm ASTT, 2 RBU 1000 *Smerch* 3, 4 AK630 CIWS, 1 twin 130mm gun (capacity 1 Z-9C/Ka-28 *Helix* A hel)
      2 *Luyang* (Type-052B) with 4 quad lnchr with YJ-83 AShM, 2 single lnchr with *Yezh* (SA-N-12 *Grizzly*) SAM, 2 triple 324mm TT with Yu-7 LWT, 2 Type 730 CIWS, 1 100mm gun (capacity 1 Ka-28 *Helix* A hel)

5 *Luyang* II (Type-052C) with 2 quad lnchr with YJ-62 AShM, 8 sextuple VLS with HHQ-9 SAM, 2 triple 324mm TT with Yu-7 LWT, 2 Type 730 CIWS, 1 100mm gun (capacity 2 Ka-28 *Helix* A hel)

1 *Luyang* III (Type-052D) with 8 octuple VLS with HHQ-9 SAM, 1 24-cell GMLS with HQ-10 SAM, 2 triple 324mm TT with Yu-7 LWT, 1 Type 730 CIWS, 1 130mm gun (capacity 2 Ka-28 *Helix* A hel)

1 *Luhai* (Type-051B) with 4 quad lnchr with YJ-83 AShM, 1 octuple lnchr with HQ-7 SAM, 2 triple 324mm ASTT with Yu-7 LWT, 1 twin 100mm gun (capacity 2 Z-9C/Ka-28 *Helix* A hel)

2 *Luhu* (Type-052) with 4 quad lnchr with YJ-83 AShM, 1 octuple lnchr with HQ-7 SAM, 2 triple 324mm ASTT with Yu-7 LWT, 2 FQF 2500, 2 Type 730 CIWS, 1 twin 100mm gun (capacity 2 Z-9C hel)

DDGM 2:

2 *Luzhou* (Type-051C) with 2 quad lnchr with YJ-83 AShM; 6 sextuple VLS with SA-N-20 *Grumble* SAM, 2 Type 730 CIWS, 1 100mm gun, 1 hel landing platform

FRIGATES 54

FFGHM 32:

2 *Jiangkai* (Type-054) with 2 quad lnchr with YJ-83 AShM, 1 octuple lnchr with HQ-7 SAM, 2 triple 324mm TT with Yu-7 LWT, 2 RBU 1200, 4 AK630 CIWS, 1 100mm gun (capacity 1 Ka-28 *Helix* A/Z-9C hel)

16 *Jiangkai* II (Type-054A) with 2 quad lnchr with YJ-83 AShM, 1 32-cell VLS with HQ-16 SAM (reported), 2 triple 324mm TT with Yu-7 LWT, 2 RBU 1200, 2 Type 730 CIWS, 1 76mm gun (capacity 1 Ka-28 *Helix* A/Z-9C hel) (4 additional vessels launched)

4 *Jiangwei* I (Type-053H2G) with 2 triple lnchr with YJ-83 AShM, 1 sextuple lnchr with HQ-61 (CSA-N-2) SAM, 2 RBU 1200, 1 twin 100mm gun (capacity 2 Z-9C hel)

10 *Jiangwei* II (Type-053H3) with 2 quad lnchr with YJ-83 AShM, 1 octuple lnchr with HQ-7 SAM, 2 RBU 1200, 1 twin 100mm gun (capacity 2 Z-9C hel)

FFGH 1:

1 *Jianghu* IV (Type-053H1Q - trg role) with 1 triple lnchr with HY-2 (CSS-N-2) AShM, 4 RBU 1200, 1 100mm gun (capacity 1 Z-9C hel)

FFGM 4:

2 *Luda* III (Type-051DT) with 4 quad lnchr with YJ-83 AShM, 1 octuple lnchr with HQ-7 SAM, 2 FQF 2500, 2 130mm gun, 3 twin 57mm gun

2 *Luda* III (Type-051G) with 4 quad lnchr with YJ-83 AShM, 1 octuple lnchr with HQ-7 SAM, 2 FQF 2500, 2 triple 324mm ASTT, 2 twin 100mm gun

FFG 17:

2 *Jianghu* I (Type-053H) with 2 triple lnchr with SY-1 (CSS-N-1) AShM, 4 RBU 1200, 2 100mm gun

6 *Jianghu* II (Type-053H1) with 2 triple lnchr with HY-2 (CSS-N-2) AShM, 2 RBU 1200, 1 twin 100mm gun (capacity 1 Z-9C hel)

1 *Jianghu* III (Type-053H2) with 2 quad lnchr with YJ-83 AShM, 2 RBU 1200, 2 twin 100mm gun

6 *Jianghu* V (Type-053H1G) with 2 quad lnchr with YJ-83 AShM, 2 RBU 1200, 2 twin 100mm gun

2 *Luda* II (Type-051) with 2 triple lnchr with HY-2 (CSS-N-2) AShM, 2 triple 324mm ASTT, 2 FQF 2500, 2 twin 130mm gun, (mine-laying capability)

PATROL AND COASTAL COMBATANTS 223+

CORVETTES • FSGM 15:

15 *Jiangdao* (Type-056) with 2 twin lnchr with YJ-83 AShM, 1 8-cell GMLS with HQ-10 SAM, 2 triple ASTT, 1 76mm gun, 1 hel landing platform

PCFG 76+

65+ *Houbei* (Type-022) with 2 quad lnchr with YJ-83 AShM

11 *Huangfen* (Type-021) with 2 twin lnchr with HY-2 (CSS-N-2) AShM

PCG 26

6 *Houjian* (Type-037/II) with 2 triple lnchr with YJ-8 (CSS-N-4) AShM

20 *Houxin* (Type-037/IG) with 2 twin lnchr with YJ-8 (CSS-N-4) AShM

PCC 72

2 *Haijiu* (Type-037/I) with 4 RBU 1200, 1 twin 57mm gun

48 *Hainan* (Type-037) with ε4 RBU 1200, 2 twin 57mm gun

22 *Haiqing* (Type-037/IS) with 2 Type-87

PB 34+ *Haizui*/*Shanghai* III (Type-062/I)

MINE WARFARE 53

MINE COUNTERMEASURES 54

MCO 12: 4 *Wochi*; 6 *Wochi* mod; 2 *Wozang*

MSO 16 T-43

MSC 16 *Wosao*

MSD 10: 4 *Futi* (Type-312 - 42 more in reserve); 6 Type-529

MINELAYERS • ML 1 *Wolei* with 1 twin 57mm gun

AMPHIBIOUS

PRINCIPAL AMPHIBIOUS SHIPS • LPD 3 *Yuzhao* (Type-071) with 4 AK630 CIWS, 1 76mm gun (capacity 2 LCAC or 4 UCAC plus supporting vehicles; 500–800 troops; 2 hel)

LANDING SHIPS 85

LSM 59:

10 *Yubei* (Type-074A) (capacity 10 tanks or 150 troops)

1 *Yudeng* (Type-073) with 1 twin 57mm gun (capacity 6 tk; 180 troops)

10 *Yuhai* (Type-074) (capacity 2 tk; 250 troops)

28 *Yuliang* (Type-079) (capacity 5 tk; 250 troops)

10 *Yunshu* (Type-073A) (capacity 6 tk)

LST 26:

7 *Yukan* with 1 twin 57mm gun (capacity 10 tk; 200 troops)

9 *Yuting* (capacity 10 tk; 250 troops; 2 hel)

10 *Yuting* II (capacity 4 LCVP; 10 tk; 250 troops)

LANDING CRAFT 153

LCU 120 *Yunnan*

LCM 20 *Yuchin*

LCAC 3: 1 *Yuyi*; 2 *Zubr*

UCAC 10

LOGISTICS AND SUPPORT 211
  ABU 7 *Yannan*
  AG 4 *Qiongsha* (capacity 400 troops)
  AGI 1 *Dadie*
  AGM 5: 2 Type-815; 3 Yuan Wang (space and missile tracking)
  AGOR 8: 1 *Bin Hai*; 1 *Shuguang*; 2 *Dahua*; 2 *Kan*; 2 Type 636B
  AGS 5: 1 *Ganzhu*; 4 *Yenlai*
  AH 3: 1 *Daishan*; 2 *Qiongsha* (hospital conversion)
  AK 24: 7 *Dandao*; 6 *Danlin*; 1 *Danyao*; 2 *Dayun*; 6 *Hongqi*; 2 *Yantai*
  AOL 5 *Guangzhou*
  AORH 7: 2 *Fuchi* (Type-903); 2 *Fuchi* mod (Type-903A); 2 *Fuqing*; 1 *Nanyun*
  AOT 50: 7 *Danlin*; 20 *Fulin*; 18 *Fuzhou*; 3 *Jinyou*; 2 *Shengli*
  ARS 2: 1 *Dadao*; 1 *Dadong*
  AS 7: 4 *Dalang*; 2 *Dazhou*; 1 *Dongxiu*
  ASR 6: 3 *Dalao*; 3 *Dajiang* (capacity 2 Z-8)
  ATF 51: 1 *Daozha*; 17 *Gromovoy*; 10 *Hujiu*; 19 *Roslavl*; 4 *Tuzhong*
  AWT 18: **8** *Fuzhou*; 10 *Leizhou*
  AX 3: 1 *Daxin*; 1 *Shichang*; 1 *Xuxiake*
  YDG 5 *Yen Pai*
MSL • **AShM** 72 YJ-62 (coastal defence) (3 regt)

Naval Aviation 26,000
FORCES BY ROLE
BOMBER
  1 regt with H-6DU/G
  1 regt with H-6G
FIGHTER
  1 regt with J-8F
FIGHTER/GROUND ATTACK
  1 regt with J-10A/S
  2 regt with J-11B/BS
  1 regt (forming) with J-11B/BS
  1 regt with Su-30MK2
ATTACK
  2 regt with JH-7
  3 regt with JH-7A
ELINT/ISR/AEW
  1 regt with Y-8J/JB/W/X
TRANSPORT
  1 regt with Y-7; Y-7H; Y-8
  1 regt with Y-7; Y-8; Z-8; Z-9
TRAINING
  1 regt with CJ-6A
  2 regt with HY-7
  1 regt with JL-8
  1 regt with JL-9
  1 regt with Mi-8 *Hip*; Z-9C
  1 regt with Y-5
HELICOPTER
  1 regt with Mi-8; Ka-28; Ka-31
  1 regt with SH-5; AS365; Ka-28; Z-9; Z-8A/JH/S
EQUIPMENT BY TYPE
AIRCRAFT 332 combat capable
  BBR 30 H-6G
  FTR 24 J-8F *Finback*

  FGA 228: 120 JH-7/JH-7A; 16 J-10A; 8 J-10S; 60 J-11B/BS; 24 Su-30MK2 *Flanker*
  ASW 3 SH-5
  ELINT 7: 4 Y-8JB *High New* 2; 3 Y-8X
  AEW&C 10: 4 Y-8J; 6 Y-8W *High New* 5
  ISR 7 HZ-5
  TKR 3 H-6DU
  TPT 66: **Medium** 4 Y-8; **Light** 62: 50 Y-5; 4 Y-7; 6 Y-7H; 2 Yak-42
  TRG 106+: 38 CJ-6; 5 HJ-5*; 21 HY-7; 14 JJ-6*; 4 JJ-7*; 12 JL-8*; 12+ JL-9
HELICOPTERS
  ASW 44: 19 Ka-28 *Helix* A; 25 Z-9C
  AEW 10+: 9 Ka-31; 1+ Z-8 AEW
  SAR 6: 4 Z-8JH; 2 Z-8S
  TPT 43: **Heavy** 35: 15 SA321 *Super Frelon*; 20 Z-8/Z-8A; **Medium** 8 Mi-8 *Hip*
UAV • **ISR Heavy** BZK-005; **Medium** BZK-007
MSL
  AAM • **IR** PL-5; PL-8; PL-9; R-73 (AA-11 *Archer*); **SARH** PL-11; **IR/SARH** R-27 (AA-10 *Alamo*); **ARH** R-77 (AA-12 *Adder*); PL-12
  ASM Kh-31A (AS-17B *Krypton*); KD-88
  AShM YJ-61; YJ-8K; YJ-83K
  ARM YJ-91
BOMBS
  Conventional: Type-200-4/Type-200A
  Laser-Guided: LS-500J
  TV-Guided: KAB-500KR; KAB-1500KR

Marines ε10,000
FORCES BY ROLE
MANOEUVRE
  Amphibious
  2 mne bde (1 spec ops bn, 1 SF amph recce bn, 1 recce bn, 1 tk bn, 2 mech inf bn, 1 arty bn, 1 AT/AD bn, 1 engr bn, 1 sigs bn)
EQUIPMENT BY TYPE
LT TK 73 Type-05 AAAV (ZTD-05)
AIFV 152 Type-05 AAAV (ZBD-05)
ARTY 40+
  SP 122mm 40+: 20+ Type-07; 20+ Type-89
  MRL 107mm Type-63
  MOR 82mm
AT
  MSL • **MANPATS** HJ-73; HJ-8
  RCL 120mm Type-98
AD • **SAM** • **MANPAD** HN-5

Air Force 398,000
The PLAAF organises its command through seven military-region air forces (MRAF) – Shenyang, Beijing, Lanzhou, Jinan, Nanjing, Guangzhou and Chengdu – five corps deputy leader-grade command posts (Datong, Kunming, Wuhan, Xian and Fuzhou); four corps deputy leader-grade bases (Nanning, Urumqi, Shanghai and Dalian); and four division leader-grade command posts (Lhasa, Hetian, Zhangzhou and Changchun). Each MRAF, CP, and base is responsible for all subordinate combat organisations (aviation, SAM, AAA and radar) in its area of operations. The regiments of four air divisions have

been reorganised into new brigades, and MRAF training formations have been consolidated into three new flying academies.

Flying hours Ftr, ground attack and bbr pilots average 100–150 hrs/yr. Tpt pilots average 200+ per year. Each regt has two quotas to meet during the year – a total number of hours, and the percentage of flight time dedicated to tactics trg.

FORCES BY ROLE
BOMBER
  1 regt with H-6A/M
  3 regt with H-6H
  2 regt with H-6K
FIGHTER
  7 regt with J-7 *Fishbed*
  6 regt with J-7E *Fishbed*
  4 regt with J-7G *Fishbed*
  1 regt with J-8B *Finback*
  1 regt with J-8F *Finback*
  2 regt with J-8H *Finback*
  1 regt with Su-27SK/UBK *Flanker*
  6 regt with J-11/Su-27UBK *Flanker*
  2 regt with J-11B/BS
  2 bde with J-7/J-7G *Fishbed*
FIGHTER/GROUND ATTACK
  2 regt with Su-30MKK *Flanker*
  8 regt with J-10/J-10A/J-10S
  2 bde with J-7E *Fishbed*; J-11B/BS; Q-5D/E *Fantan*
  2 bde with J-8H *Finback*; J-11B/BS; JH-7A
FIGHTER/GROUND ATTACK/ISR
  2 bde with J-7E *Fishbed*; J-8H *Finback*; JZ-8F *Finback** Su-30MKK
GROUND ATTACK
  4 regt with JH-7A
  4 regt with Q-5C/D/E *Fantan*
ELECTRONIC WARFARE
  1 regt with Y-8CB/G/XZ
  1 regt with Y-8/Y-8CB/Y-8G
ISR
  1 regt with JZ-8F *Finback**
  1 regt with Y-8H1
AIRBORNE EARLY WARNING & CONTROL
  1 regt with KJ-200; KJ-2000; Y-8T
COMBAT SEARCH & RESCUE
  1 regt with Mi-171; Z-8
TANKER
  1 regt with H-6U
TRANSPORT
  1 (VIP) regt with B-737; CRJ-200/700
  1 (VIP) regt with B-737; Tu-154M; Tu-154M/D
  1 regt with Il-76MD/TD *Candid*
  1 regt with Il-76MD *Candid*; Il-78 *Midas*
  1 regt with Mi-17V-5; Y-7
  1 regt with Y-5/Y-7/Z-9
  1 regt with Y-5/Y-7
  2 regt with Y-7
  1 regt with Y-8
  1 regt with Y-8; Y-9

TRAINING
  2 regt with J-7; JJ-7
  5 bde with CJ-6/6A/6B; JL-8*; Y-5; Y-7; Z-9
TRANSPORT HELICOPTER
  1 regt with AS332 *Super Puma* (VIP)
ISR UAV
  1 regt with *Gongji*-1
AIR DEFENCE
  3 SAM div
  2 mixed SAM/ADA div
  9 SAM bde
  2 mixed SAM/ADA bde
  2 ADA bde
  9 indep SAM regt
  1 indep ADA regt
  4 indep SAM bn

EQUIPMENT BY TYPE
AIRCRAFT 2,239 combat capable
  BBR 106: ε70 H-6A/H/M; ε36 H-6K
  FTR 842: 216 J-7 *Fishbed*; 192 J-7E *Fishbed*; 120 J-7G *Fishbed*; 24 J-8B *Finback*; 24 J-8F *Finback*; 96 J-8H *Finback*; 95 J-11; 43 Su-27SK *Flanker*; 32 Su-27UBK *Flanker*
  FGA 573+: 78 J-10; 144+ J-10A; 48 J-10S; 110+ J-11B/BS; 120 JH-7A; 73 Su-30MKK *Flanker*
  ATK 120 Q-5C/D/E *Fantan*
  EW 13: 4 Y-8CB *High New 1*; 7 Y-8G *High New 3*; 2 Y-8XZ *High New 7*
  ELINT 4 Tu-154M/D *Careless*
  ISR 51: 24 JZ-8 *Finback**; 24 JZ-8F *Finback**; 3 Y-8H1
  AEW&C 8+: 4+ KJ-200; 4 KJ-2000
  C2 5: 2 B-737; 3 Y-8T *High New 4*
  TKR 11: 10 H-6U; 1 Il-78 *Midas*
  TPT 325+ **Heavy** 16+ Il-76MD/TD *Candid*; **Medium** 41+: 40 Y-8; 1+ Y-9; **Light** 239: 170 Y-5; 41 Y-7/Y-7H; 20 Y-11; 8 Y-12 **PAX** 29: 9 B-737 (VIP); 5 CRJ-200; 5 CRJ-700; 10 Tu-154M *Careless*
  TRG 950: 400 CJ-6/6A/6B; 200 JJ-7*; 350 JL-8*
HELICOPTERS
  MRH 22: 20 Z-9; 2 Mi-17V-5 *Hip H*
  TPT 28+: **Heavy** 18+ Z-8 (SA321) **Medium** 10+: 6+ AS332 *Super Puma* (VIP); 4+ Mi-171
UAV • ISR • Heavy CH-1 *Chang Hong*; *Chang Kong* 1; *Firebee*; 4+ *Gongji*-1; **Light** *Harpy*
AD
  SAM 600+
    SP 300+: 24 HD-6D; 60+ HQ-7; 32+ HQ-9; 24 HQ-12 (KS-1A); 32 S-300PMU (SA-10B *Grumble*); 64 S-300PMU1 (SA-20 *Gargoyle*); 64 S-300PMU2 (SA-20 *Gargoyle*)
    TOWED 300+ HQ-2 (SA-2) *Guideline* Towed/HQ-2A/HQ-2B(A)
  GUNS 16,000 100mm/85mm
MSL
  AAM • IR PL-2B‡; PL-5B/C; PL-8; R-73 (AA-11 *Archer*); **SARH** PL-11; **IR/SARH** R-27 (AA-10 *Alamo*); **ARH** PL-12; R-77 (AA-12 *Adder*)
  ASM KD-88; Kh-29 (AS-14 *Kedge*); Kh-31A/P (AS-17 *Krypton*); Kh-59 (AS-18 *Kazoo*); YJ-91 (Domestically produced Kh-31P variant)
  LACM YJ(KD)-63; CJ-10/CJ-20 (reported)

15th Airborne Corps
FORCES BY ROLE
SPECIAL FORCES
  1 SF unit
MANOEUVRE
  Reconnaissance
  1 recce regt
  Air Manoeuvre
  2 AB div (2 AB regt; 1 arty regt)
  1 AB div (1 AB regt; 1 arty regt)
  Aviation
  1 hel regt
COMBAT SUPPORT
  1 sigs gp
COMBAT SERVICE SUPPORT
  1 log gp
TRANSPORT
  1 regt with Y-7; Y-8
EQUIPMENT BY TYPE
AIFV 180 Type-03 (ZBD-03)
APC (T) 4 Type-03 (ZZZ-03)
ARTY 162+
  TOWED • 122mm ε54 Type-96 (D-30)
  MRL • TOWED • 107mm ε54 Type-63
  MOR • 82mm some 100mm 54
AT • SP some HJ-9 *Red Arrow 9*
AD
  SAM • MANPAD QW-1
  GUNS • TOWED 25mm 54 Type-87
AIRCRAFT • TPT • Light 8: 2 Y-7; 6 Y-8
HELICOPTERS
  CSAR 8 Z-8KA
  MRH 12 Z-9WZ

Military Regions
This represents the geographical disposition of the PLA's group armies, fleets and air divisions within China, as opposed to a joint-service command structure. Designated Rapid Reaction Units (RRU) are indicated.

Shenyang MR (North East)

Land Forces
(Heilongjiang, Jilin, Liaoning MD)
16th Group Army
(1 SF bde, 1 armd bde, 3 mech inf bde,1 mot inf div, 1 mot inf bde, 1 arty bde, 1 AD bde, 1 engr regt)
39th Group Army
(1 SF gp, 1 armd bde, 1 mech inf div, 2 mech inf bde, 2 mot inf bde; 1 avn regt, 1 arty bde, 1 AD bde, 1 engr regt, 1 EW regt)
40th Group Army
(1 armd bde, 1 mech inf bde, 2 mot inf bde, 1 arty bde, 1 AD bde, 1 engr regt)

North Sea Fleet Naval Aviation
Other Forces
(1 trg regt with CJ-6A; 1 trg regt with HY-7; 1 trg regt with Y-5)

Shenyang MRAF
1st Fighter Division
(1 ftr regt with J-11B; 1 FGA regt with J-10/J-10A/J-10S; 1 ftr regt with J-8F)
11th Attack Division
(1 atk regt with JH-7A; 1 atk regt with Q-5)
16th Special Mission Division
(1 EW regt with Y-8/Y-8CB/Y-8G; 1 ISR regt with JZ-8F; 1 tpt regt with Y-5/Y-7)
21st Fighter Division
(1 ftr regt with J-7E; 1 ftr regt with J-8H; 1 ftr regt with J-7H)
Dalian Base
(2 FGA bde with J-7E; J-11B; Q-5)
Harbin Flying Academy
(2 trg bde with CJ-6; JL-8; Y-5; Y-7)
Other Forces
(1 (mixed) SAM/ADA bde; 1 SAM bde)

Beijing MR (North)

Land Forces
(Beijing, Tianjin Garrison, Inner Mongolia, Hebei, Shanxi MD)
27th Group Army
(1 armd bde, 2 mech inf bde, 2 mot inf bde, 1 arty bde, 1 AD bde, 1 engr regt)
38th Group Army
(1 SF bde, 1 armd div, 2 mech inf div, 1 avn bde, 1 arty bde, 1 AD bde, 1 engr regt)
65th Group Army
(1 armd bde, 2 mech inf bde, 2 mot inf bde, 1 arty bde, 1 AD bde, 1 engr regt)
Other Forces
(1 (OPFOR) mech inf bde; 2 (Beijing) gd div; 1 avn bde)

North Sea Fleet Naval Aviation
2nd Naval Air Division
(1 tpt regt with Y-7/Y-8)
Other Forces
(1 trg regt with JL-9; 1 trg regt with HY-7; 1 trg regt with JL-8; 1 trg regt with Mi-8; Z-9)

Beijing MRAF
7th Fighter Division
(1 ftr regt with J-11; 1 ftr regt with J-7G; 1 ftr regt with J-7)
15th Fighter/Attack Division
(1 FGA regt with J-10A/S; 1 ftr regt with J-7; 1 atk regt with Q-5C)
24th Fighter Division
(1 ftr regt with J-7G; 1 FGA regt with J-10/J-10A/J-10S)
Shijiazhuang Flying Academy
(1 trg bde with CJ-6; JL-8; Y-5; Y-7) **Other Forces**
(1 Flight Test Centre; 3 SAM div; 1 (mixed) SAM/ADA div)

Other Forces
34th VIP Transport Division
(1 tpt regt with B-737; CRJ200/700; 1 tpt regt with B-737; Tu-154M; Tu-154M/D; 1 tpt regt with Y-7; 1 hel regt with AS332)

Lanzhou MR (West)

Land Forces
(Ningxia, Shaanxi, Gansu, Qing-hai, Xinjiang, South Xinjiang MD)
21st Group Army
(1 SF bde, 1 armd bde, 1 mech inf bde, 1 mot inf div (RRU), 1 arty bde, 1 AD bde, 1 engr regt, 1 EW regt)
47th Group Army
(1 armd bde, 1 mech inf bde, 2 (high alt) mot inf bde, 1 arty bde, 1 AD bde, 1 engr regt)
Xinjiang MD
(1 SF bde, 1 (high alt) mech div, 1 indep mech inf regt, 3 (high alt) mot div, 1 avn bde, 1 arty bde, 1 AD bde, 1 engr regt, 1 EW regt)

Lanzhou MRAF
6th Fighter Division
(1 ftr regt with J-11; 1 ftr regt with J-7E; 1 ftr regt with J-7)
36th Bomber Division
(1 surv regt with Y8H-1; 1 bbr regt with H-6M; 1 bbr regt with H-6H)
Urumqi Base
(2 FGA bde with J-8H; J-11B; JH-7A)
Xi'an Flying Academy
(2 trg bde with CJ-6; JL-8; Y-7; Z-9)
Other Forces
(1 (mixed) SAM/ADA div; 1 SAM bde; 4 indep SAM regt)

Jinan MR (Centre)

Land Forces
(Shandong, Henan MD)
20th Group Army
(1 armd bde, 2 mech inf bde, 1 arty bde, 1 AD bde, 1 engr regt)
26th Group Army
(1 SF bde, 1 armd bde, 1 mech inf bde, 3 mot inf bde, 1 avn regt, 1 arty bde, 1 AD bde, 1 engr regr, 1 EW rgt)
54th Group Army
(1 SF bde, 1 armd bde, 2 mech inf div (RRU), 1 mech bde, 1 avn regt, 1 arty bde, 1 AD bde, 1 engr regt)

North Sea Fleet
Coastal defence from DPRK border (Yalu River) to south of Lianyungang (approx 35°10′N); equates to Shenyang, Beijing and Jinan MR, and to seaward; HQ at Qingdao; support bases at Lushun, Qingdao. 9 coastal-defence districts
1 **SSBN**; 3 **SSN**; 20 **SSK**; 1 **CV**; 2 **DDGHM**; 2 **DDGM**; 8 **FFGHM**; 2 **FFGM**; 1 **FFGH**; 3 **FFG**; 4 **FSGM**; ε18 **PCFG/PCG**; ε28 **PCC**; 9 **LS**; 1 **ML**; ε9 **MCMV**

North Sea Fleet Naval Aviation
2nd Naval Air Division
(1 EW/ISR/AEW regt with Y-8J/JB/W/X; 1 MP/hel regt with SH-5; AS365; Ka-28; SA321; Z-8; Z-9)
5th Naval Air Division
(2 FGA regt with JH-7A; 1 ftr regt with J-8F)

Jinan MRAF
5th Attack Division
(1 atk regt with Q-5E; 1 atk regt with JH-7A)
12th Fighter Division
(1 ftr regt with J-10A/S; 1 ftr regt with J-8B; 1 ftr regt with J-7G)
19th Fighter Division
(1 ftr regt with Su-27SK; 1 ftr regt with J-7; 1 trg regt with J-7/JJ-7)
32nd Fighter Division
(1 ftr regt with J-11B; 1 tpt regt with Y-5/Y-7/Z-9; 1 trg regt with J-7/JJ-7)
Other Forces
(1 Flight Instructor Training Base with CJ-6; JL-8; 4 SAM bn)

Nanjing MR (East)

Land Forces
(Shanghai Garrison, Jiangsu, Zhejiang, Fujian, Jiangxi, Anhui MD)
1st Group Army
(1 armd bde, 1 amph mech div, 1 mech inf bde, 1 mot inf bde, 1 avn bde, 1 arty bde, 1 MRL bde, 1 AD bde, 1 engr regt, 1 EW regt)
12th Group Army
(1 SF bde, 1 armd bde, 2 mech inf bde, 1 mot inf bde, 1 arty bde, 1 AD bde, 1 engr regt)
31st Group Army
(1 SF bde, 1 (amph) armd bde, 2 mot inf div (incl 1 RRU), 1 mot inf bde, 1 avn regt, 1 arty bde, 1 AD bde, 1 engr regt, 1 EW regt)

East Sea Fleet
Coastal defence from south of Lianyungang to Dongshan (approx 35°10′N to 23°30′N); equates to Nanjing Military Region, and to seaward; HQ at Ningbo; support bases at Fujian, Zhoushan, Ningbo. 7 coastal defence districts
18 **SSK**; 7 **DDGHM**; 16 **FFGHM**; 4 **FFG**; 4 **FSGM**; ε34 **PCFG/PCG**; ε22 **PCC**; 24 **LS**; ε19 **MCMV**

East Sea Fleet Naval Aviation
4th Naval Aviation Division
(1 FGA regt with Su-30MK2; 1 FGA regt with J-10A)
6th Naval Aviation Division
(2 FGA regt with JH-7; 1 bbr regt with H-6G)
Other Forces
(1 hel regt with Mi-8; Ka-28; Ka-31)

Nanjing MRAF
3rd Fighter Division
(1 ftr regt with J-7G; 1 FGA regt with J-10/J-10A/J-10S; 1 FGA regt with Su-30MKK)
10th Bomber Division
(1 bbr regt with H-6H; 1 bbr regt with H-6K)
14th Fighter Division
(2 ftr regt with J-11; 1 ftr regt with J-7E)
26th Special Mission Division
(1 AEW&C regt with KJ-200/KJ-2000/Y-8T; 1 CSAR regt with M-171/Z-8)

28th Attack Division
(2 atk regt with JH-7A; 1 atk regt with Q-5D/E)
Shanghai Base
(2 FGA/ISR bde with J-7E; J-8H; JZ-8F; Su-30MKK)
Other Forces
(3 SAM bde; 1 ADA bde; 2 indep SAM regt)

Guangzhou MR (South)

Land Forces
(Hubei, Hunan, Guangdong, Guangxi, Hainan MD)
41st Group Army
(1 armd bde, 1 mech inf div (RRU), 1 mot inf bde, 1 mtn inf bde, 1 arty bde, 1 AD bde, 1 engr regt)
42nd Group Army
(1 SF bde, 1 armd bde, 1 amph mech div (RRU), 2 mot inf bde, 1 avn bde, 1 arty bde, 1 MRL bde, 1 AD bde, 1 engr regt, 1 EW regt)
Other Forces
(1 mot inf bde; 1 (composite) mot inf bde (Composed of units drawn from across the PLA and deployed to Hong Kong on a rotational basis); 1 hel sqn (Hong Kong), 1 AD bn (Hong Kong))

South Sea Fleet
Coastal defence from Dongshan (approx 23°30′N) to VNM border; equates to Guangzhou MR, and to seaward (including Paracel and Spratly Islands); HQ at Yulin, Guangzhou
3 **SSBN**; 2 **SSN**; 18 **SSK**; 6 **DDGHM**; 8 **FFGHM**; 12 **FFG**; 7 **FSGM**; ε42 **PCFG/PCG**; ε20 **PCC**; 3 **LPD**; 51 **LS**; ε16 **MCMV**

South Sea Fleet Naval Aviation
8th Naval Aviation Division
(2 FGA regt with J-11B; 1 bbr regt with H-6G)
9th Naval Aviation Division
(1 FGA regt with J-11B, 1 FGA regt with JH-7A; 1 tpt regt with Y-7; Y-8; Z-8; Z-8JH/S; Z-9)

Guangzhou MRAF
2nd Fighter Division
(1 ftr regt with J-8H; 1 FGA regt with J-10/J-10S; 1 ftr regt with J-11)
8th Bomber Division
(1 tkr regt with H-6U; 1 bbr regt with H-6H; 1 bbr regt with H-6K)
9th Fighter Division
(1 FGA regt with J-10A/S; 2 ftr regt with J-7E)
13th Transport Division
(1 tpt regt with Y-8; 1 tpt regt with Il-76MD/TD; 1 tpt regt with Il-76MD; Il-78)
18th Fighter Division
(1 ftr regt with J-7; 1 FGA regt with Su-30MKK)
Nanning Base
(2 ftr bde with J-7/J-7G *Fishbed*)
Other Forces
(4 SAM Bde, 1 ADA bde, 1 indep ADA regt)

Other Forces
Marines
(2 mne bde)

15th Airborne Corps
(3 AB div)

Chengdu MR (South-West)

Land Forces
(Chongqing Garrison, Sichuan, Guizhou, Yunnan, Tibet MD)
13th Group Army
(1 SF bde, 1 armd bde, 1 (high alt) mech inf div (RRU), 1 mot inf div, 1 avn bde, 1 arty bde, 1 AD bde, 1 engr regt, 1 EW regt)
14th Group Army
(1 armd bde, 2 mot inf bde, 2 mtn inf bde, 1 arty bde, 1 AD bde, 1 engr regt)
Xizang Military District
(1 SF gp; 1 (high alt) mech inf bde; 2 mtn inf bde; 1 arty regt, 1 AD bde, 1 engr bde, 1 EW regt)

Chengdu MRAF
4th Transport Division
(1 tpt regt with Y-8/Y-9; 1 tpt regt with Y-7; 1 tpt regt with Mi-17V-5/Y-7)
20th Special Mission Division
(1 tpt regt with Y-7; 1 EW regt with Y-8CB/G/XZ)
33rd Fighter Division
(1 ftr regt with J-7E; 1 ftr regt with J-11)
44th Fighter Division
(1 ftr regt with J-7; 1 FGA regt with J-10/J-10A/J-10S)
Other Forces
(1 (mixed) SAM/ADA bde; 3 indep SAM regt)

Paramilitary 660,000+ active

People's Armed Police ε660,000

Internal Security Forces ε400,000
FORCES BY ROLE
MANOEUVRE
  Other
  14 (mobile) paramilitary div
  22 (mobile) indep paramilitary regt
  Some (firefighting/garrison) unit

Border Defence Force ε260,000
FORCES BY ROLE
COMMAND
  30 div HQ
MANOEUVRE
  Other
  110 (border) paramilitary regt
  20 (marine) paramilitary regt

China Coast Guard
In March 2013, four of China's maritime law-enforcement agencies were unified under the State Oceanic Administration and renamed the China Coast Guard
EQUIPMENT BY TYPE
PATROL AND COASTAL COMBATANTS 394+
  PSOH 1
  PSO 32

PCO 57
PB/PBF 304+
AMPHIBIOUS • **LST** 1 *Yuting* II

Maritime Safety Administration (MSA)
Various tasks including aid to navigation
EQUIPMENT BY TYPE
PATROL AND COASTAL COMBATANTS 215+
PSO 5
PCO 10
PB 200+

Cyber

The PLA has devoted much attention to information warfare over the past decade, both in terms of battlefield EW and wider, cyber-warfare capabilities. The main doctrine is the 'Integrated Network Electronic Warfare' document, which guides PLA computer-network operations. PLA thinking appears to have moved beyond INEW towards a new concept of 'information confrontation' (*xinxi duikang*) which aims to integrate both electronic and non-electronic aspects of information warfare within a single command authority. PLA thinking sees warfare under informationised conditions as characterised by opposing sides using complete systems of ground, naval, air, space and electromagnetic forces. It aspires to link all service branches to create a system of systems to improve battlespace situational awareness. Three PLA departments – Informatisation, Strategic Planning and Training – have either been established or re-formatted to help enable this transformation. Since 2008, major PLA military exercises, including *Kuayue 2009* and *Lianhe 2011*, have all had cyber- and information-operations components that have been both offensive and defensive in nature. China's cyber assets fall under the command of two main departments of the General Staff Department. Computer-network attacks and EW would, in theory, come under the 4th Department (ECM), and computer-network defence and intelligence gathering come under the 3rd Department (SIGINT). The 3rd Department (3PLA) is supported by a variety of 'militia units' comprising both military cyber-warfare personnel and civilian hackers. In a February 2013 report, US security company Mandiant described a secret Chinese military unit, 'Unit 61398', subordinate to 3PLA that had, Mandiant alleged, systematically exfiltrated substantial amounts of data from 141 companies since its facility was built, in 2007, in Shanghai.

DEPLOYMENT

CÔTE D'IVOIRE
UN • UNOCI 4 obs

DEMOCRATIC REPUBLIC OF THE CONGO
UN • MONUSCO 221; 12 obs; 1 engr coy; 1 fd hospital

GULF OF ADEN
1 FFGHM; 1 LPD; 1 AORH

LEBANON
UN • UNIFIL 218; 1 engr coy; 1 fd hospital

LIBERIA
UN • UNMIL 563; 2 obs; 1 engr coy; 1 tpt coy; 1 fd hospital

MALI
UN • MINUSMA 402; 1 sy coy; 1 engr coy; 1 fd hospital

MIDDLE EAST
UN • UNTSO 5 obs

SOUTH SUDAN
UN • UNMISS 347; 3 obs; 1 engr coy; 1 fd hospital

SUDAN
UN • UNAMID 233; 1 engr coy

WESTERN SAHARA
UN • MINURSO 10 obs

Fiji FJI

Fijian Dollar F$		2013	2014	2015
GDP	F$	7.43bn	7.88bn	
	US$	4.03bn	4.17bn	
per capita	US$	4,578	4,712	
Growth	%	4.6	3.8	
Inflation	%	2.9	1.2	
Def bdgt	F$	107m	94m	86m
	US$	58m	50m	
US$1=F$		1.84	1.89	

Population   903,207

Ethnic groups: Fijian 51%; Indian 44%; European/Others 5%

Age	0–14	15–19	20–24	25–29	30–64	65 plus
Male	14.4%	4.4%	4.3%	4.2%	20.8%	2.7%
Female	13.8%	4.2%	4.1%	4.0%	19.9%	3.2%

Capabilities

The Fijian armed forces are small, but have substantial operational experience, having participated in international peacekeeping missions in Lebanon, Sinai and Iraq. Since the 1980s, however, they have also been heavily involved in domestic politics, mounting a coup for the third time in 2006. This intervention disrupted relations with Fiji's traditional military partners, Australia and New Zealand, leading the military-controlled government to emphasise the potential of defence ties with China, India and South Korea. In 2011, the Engineers Regiment received a gift of major civil-engineering equipment from China, allowing an expansion of its development role. The small naval unit operates patrol boats, primarily in EEZ-protection and search-and-rescue roles. Though it has operated helicopters in the past, the armed forces presently have no aircraft.

ACTIVE 3,500 (Army 3,200 Navy 300)

RESERVE ε6,000
(to age 45)

ORGANISATIONS BY SERVICE

Army 3,200 (incl 300 recalled reserves)
FORCES BY ROLE
SPECIAL FORCE
  1 spec ops coy
MANOEUVRE
  Light
  3 inf bn
COMBAT SUPPORT
  1 arty bty
  1 engr bn
COMBAT SUPPORT
  1 log bn

Reserves 6,000
FORCES BY ROLE
MANOEUVRE
  Light
  3 inf bn
EQUIPMENT BY TYPE
ARTY 16
  TOWED 85mm 4 25-pdr (ceremonial)
  MOR 81mm 12

Navy 300
EQUIPMENT BY TYPE
PATROL AND COASTAL COMBATANTS • PB 5: 3 *Kula* (AUS *Pacific*); 2 *Levuka*

DEPLOYMENT

EGYPT
MFO 338; 1 inf bn

IRAQ
UN • UNAMI 192; 2 sy unit

SOUTH SUDAN
UN • UNMISS 4: 2 obs

SYRIA/ISRAEL
UN • UNDOF 445; 1 inf bn

India IND

Indian Rupee Rs		2013	2014	2015
GDP	Rs	114tr	129tr	
	US$	1.88tr	2.05tr	
per capita	US$	1,509	1,626	
Growth	%	5.0	5.6	
Inflation	%	9.5	7.8	
Def bdgt [a]	Rs	2.53tr	2.84tr	
	US$	41.9bn	45.2bn	
US$1=Rs		60.50	62.86	

[a] Includes defence civil estimates, which include military pensions.

Population	1,236,344,631

Religious groups: Hindu 80%; Muslim 14%; Christian 2%; Sikh 2%

Age	0–14	15–19	20–24	25–29	30–64	65 plus
Male	15.1%	5.0%	4.6%	4.3%	20.1%	2.8%
Female	13.3%	4.4%	4.1%	4.0%	19.2%	3.1%

Capabilities

India has the third-largest armed forces in the world and is making serious efforts to improve their capabilities. They regularly carry out combined-arms and joint-service exercises, and have joined international exercises with France, Singapore, the UK and the US, among others. India is among the troop-contributing countries for UN peacekeeping operations. It has ambitious procurement programmes aimed at modernising inventories, and in recent years these have diversified from a legacy of Soviet and Russian equipment to include major contracts with US and European suppliers. However, procurement, particularly from the inefficient indigenous defence industry, has often been hampered by bureaucratic delays. In late 2014, the air force had still to conclude an agreement over the purchase of 126 French *Rafale*s to meet its MMRCA requirement. Current procurement programmes, including new aerial refuellers, destroyers and indigenous aircraft carriers, promise to improve India's power-projection capabilities over the next decade. India is in the process of developing the last element of its nuclear capabilities with a first-generation submarine-launched ballistic missile. The army is modernising one of the world's largest fleets of armoured vehicles, and is forming a new mountain corps specifically for operations along its land border with China. (See pp. 217–21.)

ACTIVE 1,346,000 (Army 1,150,900, Navy 58,350 Air 127,200, Coast Guard 9,550) **Paramilitary 1,403,700**

RESERVE 1,155,000 (Army 960,000 Navy 55,000 Air 140,000) **Paramilitary 987,800**

Army first-line reserves (300,000) within 5 years of full-time service, further 500,000 have commitment to the age of 50.

ORGANISATIONS BY SERVICE

Strategic Forces Command
Strategic Forces Command (SFC) is a tri-service command established in 2003. The commander-in-chief of SFC, a senior three-star military officer, manages and administers all strategic forces through separate army and air-force chains of command.

FORCES BY ROLE
MISSILE
  1 gp with *Agni* I
  1 gp with *Agni* II
  1 gp (reported forming) with *Agni* III
  2 gp with SS-150/250 *Prithvi* I/II

EQUIPMENT BY TYPE
MSL • STRATEGIC 54
  ICBM *Agni* V (in test)
  IRBM 24+: ε12 *Agni* I (80–100 msl); ε12 *Agni* II (20–25 msl); some *Agni* III (entering service); *Agni* IV (in test)
  SRBM 30+: ε30 SS-150 *Prithvi* I/SS-250 *Prithvi* II; some SS-350 *Dhanush* (naval testbed)
  LACM *Nirbhay* (likely nuclear capable; in development)
Some Indian Air Force assets (such as *Mirage* 2000H or Su-30MKI) may be tasked with a strategic role

Space
SATELLITES 5
  COMMUNICATIONS 2 GSAT
  ISR 3: 1 *Cartosat* 2A; 2 RISAT

Army 1,150,900
6 Regional Comd HQ (Northern, Western, Central, Southern, Eastern, South Western), 1 Training Comd (ARTRAC)

FORCES BY ROLE
COMMAND
  4 (strike) corps HQ
  10 (holding) corps HQ
MISSILE
  2 msl gp with *Agni* I/II
  2 msl gp with SS-150/250 *Prithvi* I/II
SPECIAL FORCES
  8 SF bn
MANOEUVRE
  Armoured
  3 armd div (2–3 armd bde, 1 SP arty bde (1 medium regt, 1 SP arty regt))
  8 indep armd bde
  Mechanised
  6 (RAPID) mech inf div (1 armd bde, 2 mech inf bde, 1 arty bde)
  2 indep mech bde
  Light
  15 inf div (2–5 inf bde, 1 arty bde)
  1 inf div (forming)
  7 indep inf bde
  Air Manoeuvre
  1 para bde
  Mountain
  12 mtn div (3-4 mtn inf bde, 3–4 art regt)
  2 indep mtn bde

Aviation
  14 hel sqn
COMBAT SUPPORT
  3 arty div (2 arty bde (3 med art regt, 1 STA/MRL regt))
  8 AD bde
  2 SSM regt with PJ-10 *Brahmos*
  4 engr bde

Reserve Organisations
Reserves 300,000 reservists (first-line reserve within 5 years full time service); 500,000 reservists (commitment until age of 50) (total 800,000)

Territorial Army 160,000 reservists (only 40,000 regular establishment)

FORCES BY ROLE
MANOEUVRE
  Light
  42 inf bn
COMBAT SUPPORT
  6 (Railway) engr regt
  2 engr regt
  1 sigs regt
COMBAT SERVICE SUPPORT
  6 ecological bn

EQUIPMENT BY TYPE
MBT 2,874+ 124 *Arjun*; 1,950 T-72M1; 800+ T-90S; (ε1,100 various models in store)
RECCE 110 BRDM-2 with 9K111 *Fagot* (AT-4 *Spigot*)/9K113 *Konkurs* (AT-5 *Spandrel*); *Ferret* (used for internal security duties along with some indigenously built armd cars)
AIFV 1,455+: 350+ BMP-1; 980 *Sarath* (BMP-2); 125 BMP-2K
APC 336+
  APC (W) 157+ OT-62/OT-64
PPV 179: 165 *Casspir*; 14 *Yukthirath* MPV (of 327 order)
ARTY 9,702+
  SP 20+: **130mm** 20 M-46 *Catapult*; **152mm** 2S19 *Farm* (reported)
  TOWED 2,970+: **105mm** 1,350+: 600+ IFG Mk1/Mk2/Mk3 (being replaced); up to 700 LFG; 50 M-56; **122mm** 520 D-30; **130mm** ε600 M-46; (500 in store) **155mm** 500: ε300 FH-77B; ε200 M-46 (mod)
  MRL 192: **122mm** ε150 BM-21/LRAR **214mm** 14 *Pinaka* (non operational) **300mm** 28 9A52 *Smerch*
  MOR 6,520+
    SP **120mm** E1
    TOWED 6,520+: **81mm** 5,000+ E1 **120mm** ε1,500 AM-50/E1 **160mm** 20 M-58 *Tampella*
AT • MSL
  SP 9K111 *Fagot* (AT-4 *Spigot*); 9K113 *Konkurs* (AT-5 *Spandrel*)
  MANPATS 9K11 *Malyutka* (AT-3 *Sagger*) (being phased out); 9K111 *Fagot* (AT-4 *Spigot*); 9K113 *Konkurs* (AT-5 *Spandrel*); *Milan* 2
RCL **84mm** *Carl Gustav*; **106mm** 3,000+ M40A1 (10 per inf bn)
HELICOPTERS
  MRH 275+: 80 *Dhruv*; 12 *Lancer*; 3+ *Rudra*; 120 SA315B *Lama* (*Cheetah*); 60 SA316B *Alouette* III (*Chetak*)
UAV • ISR • Medium 26: 14 *Nishant*; 12 *Searcher* Mk I/II

AD
  SAM 3,300+
    SP 680+: 180 2K12 *Kub* (SA-6 *Gainful*); 50+ 9K33 *Osa* (SA-8B *Gecko*); 200 9K31 *Strela*-1 (SA-9 *Gaskin*); 250 9K35 *Strela*-10 (SA-13 *Gopher*); *Akash*
    MANPAD 2,620+: 620 9K32 *Strela*-2 (SA-7 *Grail* – being phased out)‡; 2,000+ 9K31 *Igla*-1 (SA-16 *Gimlet*); 9K38 *Igla* (SA-18 *Grouse*)
  GUNS 2,395+
    SP 155+: **23mm** 75 ZSU-23-4; ZU-23-2 (truck-mounted); **30mm** 20-80 2S6 *Tunguska*
    TOWED 2,240+: **20mm** Oerlikon (reported); **23mm** 320 ZU-23-2; **40mm** 1,920 L40/70
RADAR • LAND 38+: 14 AN/TPQ-37 *Firefinder*; BSR Mk.2; 24 *Cymbeline*; EL/M-2140; M113 A1GE *Green Archer* (mor); MUFAR; *Stentor*
AMPHIBIOUS 2 LCVP
MSL
  IRBM 24+: ε12 *Agni*-I (80-100 msl); ε12 *Agni*-II (20-25 msl); some *Agni*-III (successfully tested)
  SRBM 30: ε30 SS-150 *Prithvi* I/SS-250 *Prithvi* II
  LACM 8–10 PJ-10 *Brahmos*
AEV BMP-2; FV180
ARV T-54/T-55; VT-72B; WZT-2; WZT-3
VLB AM-50; BLG-60; BLG T-72; *Kartik*; MTU-20; MT-55; *Sarvatra*
MW 910 MCV-2

Navy 58,350 (incl 7,000 Naval Avn and 1,200 Marines)

Fleet HQ New Delhi; Commands located at Mumbai, Vishakhapatnam, Kochi & Port Blair

EQUIPMENT BY TYPE
SUBMARINES • TACTICAL 14
  SSN 1 *Chakra* (ex-RUS *Nerpa*) with 4 single 533mm TT with 3M54 *Klub* (SS-N-27 *Sizzler*) SLCM, 4 single 650mm TT with T-65 HWT (RUS lease agreement)
  SSK 13:
    4 *Shishumar* (GER T-209/1500) with 8 single 533mm TT
    4 *Sindhughosh* (FSU *Kilo*) with 6 single 533mm TT (one undergoing refit with 3M54 *Klub* (SS-N-27 *Sizzler*) SLCM by 2015)
    5 *Sindhughosh* (FSU *Kilo*) with 6 single 533mm TT with 3M54 *Klub* (SS-N-27 *Sizzler*) SLCM
PRINCIPAL SURFACE COMBATANTS 27
  AIRCRAFT CARRIERS 2
    CV 1 *Vikramaditya* (ex-FSU *Kiev* mod) (capacity: 12 MiG-29K/KUB *Fulcrum* FGA ac; 6 Ka-28 *Helix* A ASW hel/Ka-31 *Helix* B AEW hel)
    CVS 1 *Viraat* (ex-UK *Hermes*) with 2 octuple VLS with *Barak*-1 SAM, 2 twin AK230 CIWS (capacity 30 *Sea Harrier* FRS 1 (*Sea Harrier* FRS MK51) FGA ac; 7 Ka-27 *Helix* ASW hel/*Sea King* Mk42B ASW hel)
  DESTROYERS 12
    DDGHM 7:
      3 *Delhi* with 4 quad lnchr with 3M24 *Uran* (SS-N-25 *Switchblade*) AShM, 2 single lnchr with 3K90 *Uragan* (SA-N-7 *Gadfly*) SAM, 4 octuple VLS with *Barak*-1 SAM, 5 single 533mm ASTT, 2 RBU 6000; 2 AK630 CIWS, 1 100mm gun (capacity either 2 *Dhruv* hel/*Sea King* Mk42A ASW hel)
      1 *Kolkata* with 2 octuple VLS with *Brahmos* AShM; 4 octuple VLS fitted for *Barak*-8 SAM; 2 twin 533mm TT with SET-65E HWT, 2 RBU 6000 *Smerch* 2, 2 AK630 CIWS, 1 76mm gun (capactiy 2 *Dhruv*/*Sea King* Mk42B hel)
      3 *Shivalik* with 1 octuple VLS with 3M54 *Klub* (SS-N-27 *Sizzler*) AScM, 4 octuple VLS with *Barak*-1 SAM, 1 single lnchr with 3K90 *Uragan* (SA-N-7 *Gadfly*) SAM, 2 triple 324mm ASTT, 2 RBU 6000 *Smerch* 2, 2 AK630 CIWS, 1 76mm gun (capacity 1 *Sea King* Mk42B ASW hel)
  DDGM 5:
    2 *Rajput* (FSU *Kashin*) with 2 twin lnchr with P-15M *Termit* (SS-N-2C *Styx*) AShM, 2 twin lnchr with M-1 *Volna* (SA-N-1 *Goa*) SAM, 5 single 533mm ASTT, 2 RBU 6000 *Smerch* 2, 2 AK630 CIWS, 1 76mm gun (capacity Ka-28 *Helix* A hel)
    1 *Rajput* (FSU *Kashin*) with 2 twin lnchr with *Brahmos* AShM, 2 single lnchr with P-15M *Termit* (SS-N-2C *Styx*) AShM, 2 twin lnchr with M-1 *Volna* (SA-N-1 *Goa*) SAM, 5 single 533mm ASTT, 2 RBU 6000 *Smerch* 2, 2 AK630 CIWS, 1 76mm gun (capacity 1 Ka-28 *Helix* A hel)
    2 *Rajput* (FSU *Kashin*) with 1 octuple VLS with *Brahmos* AShM, 2 twin lnchr with P-15M *Termit* (SS-N-2C *Styx*) AShM, 2 octuple VLS with *Barak* SAM. 1 twin lnchr with M-1 *Volna* (SA-N-1 *Goa*) SAM, 5 single 533mm ASTT, 2 RBU 6000 *Smerch* 2, 2 AK630 CIWS, 1 76mm gun (capacity 1 Ka-28 *Helix* A hel)
FRIGATES 13
  FFGHM 12:
    3 *Brahmaputra* with 4 quad lnchr with 3M24 *Uran* (SS-N-25 *Switchblade*) AShM, 3 octuple VLS with *Barak*-1 SAM, 2 triple 324mm ASTT with A244 LWT, 4 Ak630 CIWS, 1 76mm gun (capacity 2 SA316B *Alouette* III (*Chetak*)/*Sea King* Mk42 ASW hel)
    3 *Godavari* with 4 single lnchr with P-15M *Termit* (SS-N-2D *Styx*) AShM, 1 octuple VLS with *Barak*-1 SAM, 2 triple 324mm ASTT, with A244 LWT, 4 AK630 CIWS, 1 76mm gun (capacity 2 SA316B *Alouette* III (*Chetak*)/*Sea King* Mk42 ASW hel)
    3 *Talwar* I with 1 octuple VLS with 3M54 *Klub* (SS-N-27 *Sizzler*) AShM, 6 single lnchr with 3K90 *Uragan* (SA-N-7 *Gadfly*) SAM, 2 twin 533mm ASTT, 2 RBU 6000 *Smerch* 2, 2 CADS-N-1 *Kashtan* CIWS, 1 100mm gun (capacity 1 *Dhruv*/Ka-28 *Helix* A ASW hel)
    3 *Talwar* II with 1 octuple VLS with *Brahmos*/3M54 *Klub* (SS-N-27 *Sizzler*) AShM, 6 single lnchr with 3K90 *Uragan* (SA-N-7 *Gadfly*) SAM, 2 twin 533mm ASTT, 2 RBU 6000 *Smerch* 2, 2 AK630 CIWS, 1 100mm gun (capacity 1 *Dhruv*/Ka-28 *Helix* A ASW hel)
  FFH 1:
    1 *Kamorta* with 2 twin 533mm TT, 2 RBU 6000 *Smerch* 2, 2 AK630 CIWS, 1 76mm gun (capacity 1 *Dhruv*/Ka-28 *Helix* A ASW hel)

PATROL AND COASTAL COMBATANTS 96
  CORVETTES 24
    FSGM 20:
      4 *Khukri* with 2 twin lnchr with P-15M *Termit* (SS-N-2C *Styx*) AShM, 2 twin lnchr (manual aiming) with 9K32M *Strela*-2M (SA-N-5 *Grail*) SAM, 2 AK630 CIWS, 1 76mm gun, 1 hel landing platform (for *Dhruv*/SA316 *Alouette* III (*Chetak*))
      4 *Kora* with 4 quad lnchr with 3M24 *Uran* (SS-N-25 *Switchblade*) AShM, 1 quad lnchr (manual aiming) with 9K32M *Strela*-2M (SA-N-5 *Grail*) SAM, 2 AK630 CIWS, 1 76mm gun, 1 hel landing platform (for *Dhruv*/SA316 *Alouette* III (*Chetak*))
      10 *Veer* (FSU *Tarantul*) with 4 single lnchr with P-15M *Termit* (SS-N-2D *Styx*) AShM, 2 quad lnchr (manual aiming) with 9K32M *Strela*-2M (SA-N-5 *Grail*), 2 AK630 CIWS, 1 76mm gun
      2 *Prabal* (mod *Veer*) each with 4 quad lnchr with 3M24 *Uran* (SS-N-25 *Switchblade*) AShM, 1 quad lnchr (manual aiming) with 9K32M *Strela*-2M (SA-N-5 *Grail*) SAM, 2 AK630 CIWS, 1 76mm gun
    FSM 4:
      4 *Abhay* (FSU *Pauk* II) with 1 quad lnchr (manual aiming) with 9K32M *Strela*-2M (SA-N-5 *Grail*) SAM, 2 twin 533mm ASTT, 2 RBU 1200, 1 76mm gun
  PSOH 10: 4 *Saryu* with 2 AK630 CIWS, 1 76mm gun (capacity 1 *Dhruv*); 6 *Sukanya* with 4 RBU 2500 (capacity 1 SA316 *Alouette* III (*Chetak*))
  PCC 16: 10 *Car Nicobar*; 6 *Trinkat* (SDB Mk5)
  PBF 46: 10 Immediate Support Vessel; 15 Plascoa 1300 (SPB); 5 *Super Dvora*; 16 Solas Marine Interceptor (additional vessels in build)
MINE WARFARE • MINE COUNTERMEASURES 7
  MSO 7 *Pondicherry* (FSU *Natya*) with 2 RBU 1200
AMPHIBIOUS
  PRINCIPAL AMPHIBIOUS VESSELS 1
    LPD 1 *Jalashwa* (ex-US *Austin*) with 1 *Phalanx* CIWS, (capacity up to 6 med spt hel; either 9 LCM or 4 LCM and 2 LCAC; 4 LCVP; 930 troops)
  LANDING SHIPS 9
    LSM 4 *Kumbhir* (FSU *Polnocny* C) (capacity 5 MBT or 5 APC; 160 troops)
    LST 5:
      2 *Magar* (capacity 15 MBT or 8 APC or 10 trucks; 500 troops)
      3 *Magar* mod (capacity 11 MBT or 8 APC or 10 trucks; 500 troops)
  LANDING CRAFT 32
    LCM 4 LCM-8 (for use in *Jalashwa*)
    LCU 8: 2 LCU Mk4; 6 *Vasco de Gama* Mk2/3 LC (capacity 2 APC; 120 troops)
    LCVP 20 (for use in *Magar*)
LOGISTICS AND SUPPORT 56
  AGOR 1 *Sagardhwani* with 1 hel landing platform
  AGHS 8 *Sandhayak*
  AGS 2 *Makar*
  AH 1
  AOL 7: 6 *Poshak*; 1 *Ambika*
  AOR 1 *Jyoti* with 1 hel landing platform
  AORH 3: 1 *Aditya* (mod *Deepak*); 2 *Deepak* with 4 AK630 CIWS
  AP 3 *Nicobar* with 1 hel landing platform
  ASR 1
  ATF 1
  AWT 2
  AX 4: 1 *Tir*; 3 AXS
  YPT 2
  YDT 3
  YTB 2
  YTL/YTM 15

Naval Aviation 7,000

Flying hours 125–150 hrs/year on *Sea Harrier*

FORCES BY ROLE
FIGHTER/GROUND ATTACK
  1 sqn with MiG-29K/KUB *Fulcrum*
  1 sqn with *Sea Harrier* FRS 1 (Mk51); *Sea Harrier* T-4N (T-60)
ANTI SUBMARINE WARFARE
  4 sqn with Ka-28 *Helix* A; SA316B *Alouette* III (*Chetak*); *Sea King* Mk42A/B
MARITIME PATROL
  2 sqn with BN-2 *Islander*; Do-228-101; Il-38 *May*; Tu-142M *Bear* F
AIRBORNE EARLY WARNING & CONTROL
  1 sqn with Ka-31 *Helix* B
SEARCH & RESCUE
  1 sqn with SA316B *Alouette* III (*Chetak*); *Sea King* Mk42C
  1 sqn with *Dhruv*
TRANSPORT
  1 (comms) sqn with Do-228
  1 sqn with HS-748M (HAL-748M)
TRAINING
  1 sqn with HJT-16 *Kiran* MkI/II, *Hawk* Mk132
TRANSPORT HELICOPTER
  1 sqn with UH-3H *Sea King*
ISR UAV
  1 sqn with *Heron*; *Searcher* MkII
EQUIPMENT BY TYPE
AIRCRAFT 47 combat capable
  FTR 23 MiG-29K/KUB *Fulcrum*
  FGA 10: 8 *Sea Harrier* FRS 1 (Mk51); 2 *Sea Harrier* T-4N (T-60)
  ASW 14: 5 Il-38 *May*; 4 Tu-142M *Bear* F; 5 P-8I *Neptune*
  MP 14 Do-228-101
  TPT 37: **Light** 27: 17 BN-2 *Islander*; 10 Do-228; **PAX** 10 HS-748M (HAL-748M)
  TRG 16: 6 HJT-16 *Kiran* MkI; 6 HJT-16 *Kiran* MkII; 4 *Hawk* Mk132*
HELICOPTERS
  ASW 47: 12 Ka-28 *Helix* A; 21 *Sea King* Mk42A; 14 *Sea King* Mk42B
  MRH 58: 10 *Dhruv*; 25 SA316B *Alouette* III (*Chetak*); 23 SA319 *Alouette* III
  AEW 9 Ka-31 *Helix* B
  TPT • Medium 11: 5 *Sea King* Mk42C; up to 6 UH-3H *Sea King*

UAV • ISR 11: **Heavy** 4 *Heron;* **Medium** 7 *Searcher* Mk II
MSL
    AShM Kh-35 (*Bear* and *May* ac cleared to fire); *Sea Eagle* (service status unclear); *Sea Skua*
    ASCM PJ-10 *Brahmos*
    AAM • **IR** R-550 *Magic/Magic* 2; R-73 (AA-11 *Archer*)
    IR/SARH R-27 (AA-10 *Alamo*); **ARH** *Derby*; R-77 (AA-12 *Adder*)

Marines ε1,200 (Additional 1,000 for SPB duties)

After the Mumbai attacks, the Sagar Prahari Bal (SPB), with 80 PBF, was established to protect critical maritime infrastructure.

FORCES BY ROLE
SPECIAL FORCES
  1 (marine) cdo force
MANOEUVRE
  Amphibious
    1 amph bde

Air Force 127,200

5 regional air comds: Western (New Delhi), Southwestern (Gandhinagar), Eastern (Shillong), Central (Allahabad), Southern (Trivandrum). 2 support comds: Maintenance (Nagpur) and Training (Bangalore)

Flying hours   180 hrs/year

FORCES BY ROLE
FIGHTER
  3 sqn with MiG-29 *Fulcrum;* MiG-29UB *Fulcrum*
FIGHTER/GROUND ATTACK
  4 sqn with *Jaguar* IB/IS
  8 sqn with MiG-21bis/*Bison*
  3 sqn with MiG-21M/MF *Fishbed*
  6 sqn with MiG-27ML *Flogger*
  3 sqn with *Mirage* 2000E/ED (2000H/TH - secondary ECM role)
  9 sqn with Su-30MKI *Flanker*
ANTI SURFACE WARFARE
  1 sqn with *Jaguar* IM with *Sea Eagle* AShM
ISR
  1 unit with Gulfstream IV SRA-4
AIRBORNE EARLY WARNING & CONTROL
  1 sqn with Il-76TD *Phalcon*
TANKER
  1 sqn with Il-78 *Midas*
TRANSPORT
  1 sqn with C-130J-30 *Hercules*
  1 sqn with C-17A *Globemaster* III
  5 sqn with An-32/An-32RE *Cline*
  1 (comms) sqn with B-737; B-737BBJ; EMB-135BJ   4 sqn with Do-228; HS-748
  2 sqn with Il-76MD *Candid*
  1 flt with HS-748
TRAINING
  1 sqn with *Tejas*
  Some units with An-32; Do-228; *Hawk* Mk 132*; HJT-16 *Kiran* MkI/II; *Jaguar* IS/IM; MiG-21bis; MiG-21FL; MiG-21M/MF; MiG-27ML; PC-7 *Turbo Trainer* MkII; SA316B *Alouette* III (*Chetak*)

ATTACK HELICOPTER
  2 sqn with Mi-25 *Hind*; Mi-35 *Hind*
TRANSPORT HELICOPTER
  5 sqn with *Dhruv*
  7 sqn with Mi-8 *Hip*
  7 sqn with Mi-17/Mi-17-1V *Hip* H
  4 sqn with Mi-17V-5 *Hip* H
  2 sqn with SA316B *Alouette* III (*Chetak*)
  1 flt with Mi-8 *Hip*
  1 flt with Mi-26 *Halo*
  2 flt with SA315B *Lama* (*Cheetah*)
  2 flt with SA316B *Alouette* III (*Chetak*)
ISR UAV
  5 sqn with *Searcher* MkII
AIR DEFENCE
  25 sqn with S-125 *Pechora* (SA-3B *Goa*)
  6 sqn with 9K33 *Osa*-AK (SA-8B *Gecko*)
  2 sqn with *Akash*
  10 flt with 9K38 *Igla*-1 (SA-18 *Grouse*)

EQUIPMENT BY TYPE
AIRCRAFT 881 combat capable
  FTR 62: 55 MiG-29 *Fulcrum* (incl 12+ MiG-29UPG); 7 MiG-29UB *Fulcrum*
  FGA 753: 14 *Jaguar* IB; 81 *Jaguar* IS; 10 *Jaguar* IM; 31 MiG-21bis; 116 MiG-21 *Bison*; 54 MiG-21M *Fishbed*; 16 MiG-21MF *Fishbed*; 40 MiG-21U/UM *Mongol*; 126 MiG-27ML *Flogger* J2; 40 *Mirage* 2000E (2000H); 10 *Mirage* 2000ED (2000TH); ε215 Su-30MKI *Flanker*
  ISR 3 Gulfstream IV SRA-4
  AEW&C 5: 2 EMB-145AEW (in test; 1 more on order); 3 Il-76TD *Phalcon*
  TKR 6 Il-78 *Midas*
  TPT 243: **Heavy** 32: 8 C-17A *Globemaster* III; 24 Il-76MD *Candid;* **Medium** 5 C-130J-30 *Hercules*; **Light** 142: 69 An-32; 34 An-32RE *Cline*; 35 Do-228; 4 EMB-135BJ; **PAX** 64: 1 B-707; 4 B-737; 3 B-737BBJ; 56 HS-748
  TRG 290: 66 *Hawk* Mk132*; 120 HJT-16 *Kiran* MkI; 55 HJT-16 *Kiran* MkII; 49 PC-7 *Turbo Trainer* MkII
HELICOPTERS
  ATK 20 Mi-25/Mi-35 *Hind*
  MRH 319: 40 *Dhruv*; 80 Mi-17/Mi-17-1V *Hip* H; 99 Mi-17V-5 *Hip* H; 60 SA315B *Lama* (*Cheetah*); 40 SA316B *Alouette* III (*Chetak*)
  TPT 94: **Heavy** 4 Mi-26 *Halo*; **Medium** 90 Mi-8
UAV • **ISR** • **Medium** some *Searcher* MkII
AD • **SAM** S-125 *Pechora* (SA-3B *Goa*)
  SP 9K33 *Osa*-AK (SA-8B *Gecko*); *Akash*
  MANPAD 9K38 *Igla*-1 (SA-18 *Grouse*)
MSL
  AAM • **IR** R-60 (AA-8 *Aphid*); R-73 (AA-11 *Archer*) R-550 *Magic*; **IR/SARH** R-27 (AA-10 *Alamo*); **SARH** Super 530D **ARH** R-77 (AA-12 *Adder*)
  AShM AM-39 *Exocet*; *Sea Eagle*
  ASM AS-11; AS-11B (ATGW); Kh-29 (AS-14 *Kedge*); Kh-59 (AS-13 *Kingbolt*); Kh-59M (AS-18 *Kazoo*); Kh-31A (AS-17B *Krypton*); AS-30; Kh-23 (AS-7 *Kerry*)‡
  ARM Kh-25MP (AS-12 *Kegler*); Kh-31P (AS-17A *Krypton*)
  LACM *Nirbhay* (likely nuclear capable; in development)

Coast Guard 9,550
EQUIPMENT BY TYPE
PATROL AND COASTAL COMBATANTS 89
  PSOH 9: 2 *Sankalp (additional vessels in build)*; 4 *Samar* with 1 76mm gun; 3 *Vishwast*
  PSO 3 *Samudra* with 1 hel landing platform
  PCO 5 *Vikram*
  PCC 33: 6 *Aadesh*; 7 *Priyadarshini*; 8 *Rajshree*; 5 *Rani Abbakka*; 7 *Sarojini Naidu*
  PBF 25: 13 *Interceptor*; 12 (various)
  PB 14: 4 *Tara Bai*; 10 (various)
AMPHBIBIOUS • LCAC 18 Griffon 8000TD
AIRCRAFT • TPT • Light 24 Do-228
HELICOPTERS • MRH 17 SA316B *Alouette* III (*Chetak*)

Paramilitary 1,403,700

Rashtriya Rifles 65,000
Ministry of Defence. 15 sector HQ
FORCES BY ROLE
MANOEUVRE
  Other
    65 paramilitary bn

Assam Rifles 63,900
Ministry of Home Affairs. Security within northeastern states, mainly army-officered; better trained than BSF
FORCES BY ROLE
Equipped to roughly same standard as an army inf bn
COMMAND
  7 HQ
MANOEUVRE
  Other
    46 paramilitary bn
EQUIPMENT BY TYPE
ARTY • MOR 81mm 252

Border Security Force 230,000
Ministry of Home Affairs.
FORCES BY ROLE
MANOEUVRE
  Other
    175 paramilitary bn
EQUIPMENT BY TYPE
Small arms, lt arty, some anti-tank weapons
ARTY • MOR 81mm 942+
AIRCRAFT • TPT some (air spt)

Central Industrial Security Force 134,100 (lightly armed security guards)
Ministry of Home Affairs. Guards public-sector locations

Central Reserve Police Force 229,700
Ministry of Home Affairs. Internal security duties, only lightly armed, deployable throughout the country.
FORCES BY ROLE
MANOEUVRE
  Other
    198 paramilitary bn
    10 (rapid action force) paramilitary bn
    10 (CoBRA) paramilitary bn
    4 (Mahila) paramilitary bn (female)

Defence Security Corps 31,000
Provides security at Defence Ministry sites

Indo-Tibetan Border Police 36,300
Ministry of Home Affairs. Tibetan border security SF/guerrilla-warfare and high-altitude-warfare specialists; 49 bn.

National Security Guards 7,350
Anti-terrorism contingency deployment force, comprising elements of the armed forces, CRPF and Border Security Force.

Railway Protection Forces 70,000

Sashastra Seema Bal 73,350
Guards the borders with Nepal and Bhutan

Special Frontier Force 10,000
Mainly ethnic Tibetans

Special Protection Group 3,000
Protection of ministers and senior officials

State Armed Police 450,000
For duty primarily in home state only, but can be moved to other states. Some bn with GPMG and army standard infantry weapons and equipment.
FORCES BY ROLE
MANOEUVRE
  Other
    24 (India Reserve Police) paramilitary bn (cdo trained)

Reserve Organisations

Civil Defence 500,000 reservists
Operate in 225 categorised towns in 32 states. Some units for NBC defence

Home Guard 487,800 reservists (515,000 authorised str)
In all states except Arunachal Pradesh and Kerala; men on reserve lists, no trg. Not armed in peacetime. Used for civil defence, rescue and firefighting provision in wartime; 6 bn (created to protect tea plantations in Assam).

Cyber
National agencies include the Computer and Emergency Response Team (CERT-In), which has authorised designated individuals to carry out penetration tests against infrastructure. The Defence Information Assurance and Research Agency (DIARA) is mandated to deal with cyber-security-related issues of the armed services. All services have their own cyber-security policies and CERT teams, and headquarters maintain information-security policies. The Indian Army, in 2005, raised the Army Cyber Security Establishment and, in April 2010, set up the Cyber Security Laboratory at the Military College of Telecommunications Engineering (under the Corps of

Signals). There was reporting in 2013 and 2014 that India is considering setting up a Cyber Command.

DEPLOYMENT

AFGHANISTAN
300 (Indo-Tibetan Border Police paramilitary: facilities protection)

CÔTE D'IVOIRE
UN • UNOCI 9 obs

DEMOCRATIC REPUBLIC OF THE CONGO
UN • MONUSCO 3,720; 38 obs; 3 mech inf bn; 1 inf bn; 1 fd hospital; 1 hel coy

GULF OF ADEN
1 PSOH

IRAQ
UN • UNAMI 1 obs

LEBANON
UN • UNIFIL 890; 1 mech inf bn; 1 fd hospital

SOUTH SUDAN
UN • UNMISS 2,250; 5 obs; 2 inf bn; 1 engr coy; 1 fd hospital

SUDAN
UN • UNISFA 2

SYRIA/ISRAEL
UN • UNDOF 191; 1 log bn(-)

MINURSO
UN • MINURSO 3 obs

FOREIGN FORCES

Total numbers for UNMOGIP mission in India and Pakistan
Chile 2 obs
Croatia 7 obs
Finland 6 obs
Ghana 1 obs
Italy 4 obs
Korea, Republic of 7 obs
Philippines 4 obs
Sweden 5 obs
Switzerland 2 obs
Thailand 3 obs
Uruguay 1 obs

Indonesia IDN

Indonesian Rupiah Rp		2013	2014	2015
GDP	Rp	9,084tr	10,069tr	
	US$	870bn	856bn	
per capita	US$	3,510	3,404	
Growth	%	5.8	5.2	
Inflation	%	6.4	6.0	
Def exp	Rp	87.5tr		
	US$	8.38bn		
Def bdgt	Rp	81.8tr	83.2tr	94.9tr
	US$	7.85bn	7.09bn	
FMA (US)	US$	14m	14m	14m
US$1=Rp		10,438.05	11,761.43	

Population 253,609,643

Ethnic groups: Javanese 45%; Sundanese 14%; Madurese 8%; Malay 8%; Chinese 3%; other 22%

Age	0–14	15–19	20–24	25–29	30–64	65 plus
Male	13.3%	4.5%	4.2%	4.0%	21.1%	2.8%
Female	12.9%	4.4%	4.0%	3.9%	21.2%	3.7%

Capabilities

Indonesia's army remains the country's dominant armed force and its 'territorial' structure deploys personnel throughout the country down to village level. Within the army, the better-trained and -equipped Strategic Command (KOSTRAD) and Special Forces Command (KOPASSUS) units are trained for deployment nationwide. In West Papua, where resistance to Indonesian rule continues, the army still deploys operationally and has faced accusations of serious human-rights abuses. Efforts to improve capabilities are guided by the notion of establishing, by 2029, a Minimum Essential Force, including a substantially strengthened navy and air force. Rising defence spending has permitted improved pay and modest equipment purchases for all three services, and for the construction of new forward bases around the country's periphery, including on the Natuna Islands in the South China Sea. Indonesia buys equipment from diverse sources, while using technology-transfer agreements with foreign suppliers to develop the national defence industry. The armed forces lack the capacity for significant autonomous military deployments beyond national territory; however, they participate regularly in bilateral and multilateral military exercises with regional and international partners, including Australia and Singapore.

ACTIVE 395,500 (Army 300,400 Navy 65,000 Air 30,100) **Paramilitary 281,000**

Conscription liability 2 years selective conscription authorised

RESERVE 400,000

Army cadre units; numerical str n.k., obligation to age 45 for officers

ORGANISATIONS BY SERVICE

Army ε300,400

Mil Area Commands (KODAM)
13 comd (I, II, III, IV, V, VI, VII, IX, XII, XVI, XVII, Jaya & Iskandar Muda)
FORCES BY ROLE
MANOEUVRE
  Mechanised
  3 armd cav bn
  6 cav bn
  Light
  1 inf bde (1 cav bn, 3 inf bn)
  3 inf bde (1 cdo bn, 2 inf bn)
  4 inf bde (3 inf bn)
  45 indep inf bn
  8 cdo bn
  Aviation
  1 composite avn sqn
  1 hel sqn
COMBAT SUPPORT
  12 fd arty bn
  1 AD regt (2 ADA bn, 1 SAM unit)
  6 ADA bn
  3 SAM unit
  7 cbt engr bn
COMBAT SERVICE SUPPORT
  4 construction bn

Special Forces Command (KOPASSUS)
FORCES BY ROLE
SPECIAL FORCES 3 SF gp (total: 2 cdo/para unit, 1 CT unit, 1 int unit)

Strategic Reserve Command (KOSTRAD)
FORCES BY ROLE
COMMAND
  2 div HQ
MANOEUVRE
  Mechanised
  2 armd cav bn
  Light
  3 inf bde (total: 4 cdo bn; 4 inf bn)
  Air Manoeuvre
  3 AB bde (3 AB bn)
COMBAT SUPPORT
  2 fd arty regt (total: 6 arty bn)
  1 arty bn
  2 AD bn
  2 cbt engr bn

EQUIPMENT BY TYPE
MBT 26 *Leopard* 2A4
LT TK 350: 275 AMX-13 (partially upgraded); 15 PT-76; 60 *Scorpion* 90
RECCE 142: 55 *Ferret* (13 upgraded); 69 *Saladin* (16 upgraded); 18 VBL
AIFV 52: 22 *Black Fox*; 30 *Marder* 1A3
APC 533+
  APC (T) 93+: 75 AMX-VCI; 15 FV4333 *Stormer*; 3 M113A1-B
  APC (W) 437: 14 APR-1; ε150 *Anoa*; 40 BTR-40; 34 BTR-50PK; 22 *Commando Ranger*; 45 FV603 *Saracen* (14 upgraded); 100 LAV-150 *Commando*; 32 VAB-VTT
  PPV 3+: *Barracuda*; 3 *Bushmaster*; *Casspir*
ARTY 1,088+
  SP 155mm 4 CAESAR
  TOWED 133+: **105mm** 110+: some KH-178; 60 M101; 50 M-56; **155mm** 23: 5 FH-88; 18 KH-179
  MRL 127mm 13 *Astros* Mk6
  MOR 955: **81mm** 800; **120mm** 155: 75 Brandt; 80 UBM 52
AT
  MSL • MANPATS SS.11; *Milan*; 9K11 *Malyutka* (AT-3 *Sagger*)
  RCL 90mm M67; **106mm** M40A1
  RL 89mm LRAC
AIRCRAFT • TPT • Light 9: 1 BN-2A *Islander*; 6 C-212 *Aviocar* (NC-212); 2 *Turbo Commander* 680
HELICOPTERS
  ATK 6 Mi-35P *Hind*
  MRH 35: 18 Bell 412 *Twin Huey* (NB-412); 17 Mi-17V-5 *Hip* H
  TPT • Light 30: 8 Bell 205A; 20 Bo-105 (NBo-105); 2 EC120B *Colibri*
  TRG 12 Hughes 300C
AD
  SAM
    SP 2 *Kobra* (with 125 GROM-2 msl); TD-2000B (*Giant Bow II*)
    TOWED 93: 51 *Rapier*; 42 RBS-70
    MANPAD QW-3
  GUNS • TOWED 411: **20mm** 121 Rh 202; **23mm** *Giant Bow*; **40mm** 90 L/70; **57mm** 200 S-60
AEV 1 M113A1-B-GN
ARV 11+: 2 AMX-13; 6 AMX-VCI; 3 BREM-2; *Stormer*; T-54/T-55
VLB 12+: 10 AMX-13; *Leguan*; 2 *Stormer*

Navy ε65,000 (including Marines and Aviation)
Two fleets: East (Surabaya), West (Jakarta). It is currently planned to change to three commands: Riau (West); Papua (East); Makassar (Central). Two Forward Operating Bases at Kupang (West Timor) and Tahuna (North Sulawesi)
EQUIPMENT BY TYPE
SUBMARINES • TACTICAL • SSK 2 *Cakra*† (Type-209/1300) with 8 single 533mm TT with SUT HWT
PRINCIPAL SURFACE COMBATANTS 11
  FRIGATES 11
    FFGHM 7
      3 *Ahmad Yani* (ex-NLD *Van Speijk*) with 2 quad Mk 141 lnchr with RGM-84A *Harpoon* AShM, 2 SIMBAD twin lnchr (manual) with *Mistral* SAM, 2 triple 324mm ASTT with Mk46 LWT, 1 76mm gun (capacity 1 Bo-105 (NBo-105) hel)
      1 *Ahmad Yani* (ex-NLD *Van Speijk*) with 2 twin-cell VLS with 3M55 *Yakhont* (SS-N-26 *Strobile*) AShM, 2 SIMBAD twin lnchr (manual) with *Mistral* SAM, 2 triple 324mm ASTT with Mk46 LWT, 1 76mm gun (capacity 1 Bo-105 (NBo-105) hel)
      2 *Ahmad Yani* (ex-NLD *Van Speijk*) with 4 single lnchr with C-802 AShM, 2 SIMBAD twin lnchr (manual)

with *Mistral* SAM, 2 triple 324mm ASTT with Mk46 LWT, 1 76mm gun (capacity 1 Bo-105 (NBo-105) hel)

1 *Hajar Dewantara* (trg role) with 2 twin lnchr with MM-38 *Exocet* AShM, 2 single 533mm ASTT with SUT HWT, 1 57mm gun (capacity 1 Bo-105 (NBo-105) hel)

FFGM 4:

4 *Diponegoro* (NLD SIGMA 9113) with 2 twin lnchr with MM-40 *Exocet* Block II AShM, 2 quad *Tetral* lnchr with *Mistral* SAM, 2 triple 324mm ASTT with MU90 LWT, 1 76mm gun, 1 hel landing platform

PATROL AND COASTAL COMBATANTS 88

CORVETTES 18:

FSGH 1:

1 *Nala* with 2 twin lnchr with MM-38 *Exocet* AShM, 1 twin 375mm A/S mor, 1 120mm gun (capacity 1 lt hel)

FSG 2:

2 *Fatahillah* with 2 twin lnchr with MM-38 *Exocet* AShM, 2 triple B515 *ILAS*-3/Mk32 324mm ASTT with A244/Mk46 LWT, 1 twin 375mm A/S mor, 1 120mm gun

FSM 15 *Kapitan Patimura* (GDR *Parchim* I) with 2 quad lnchr with 9K32M *Strela*-2 (SA-N-5 *Grail*) SAM, 4 single 400mm ASTT, 2 RBU 6000 *Smerch* 2, 1 twin 57mm gun

PSOH 3 *Bung Tomo* with 1 76mm gun (capacity: 1 Bo-105 hel)

PCFG 4 *Mandau* with 4 single lnchr with MM-38 *Exocet* AShM, 1 57mm gun

PCT 4 *Singa* with 2 single 533mm TT, 1 57mm gun

PCC 16: 4 *Kakap*; 2 *Pandrong*; 3 *Pari*; 3 *Sampari* (KCR-60M) with 2 twin lnchr for C-705 AShM, 1 57mm gun; 4 *Todak* with 1 57mm gun

PBG 10:

2 *Clurit* with 2 twin lnchr with C-705 AShM, 1 AK630 CIWS

6 *Clurit* with 2 twin lnchr with C-705 AShM

2 *Badau* (ex-BRN *Waspada*) with 2 twin lnchr for MM-38 *Exocet* AShM

PB 33: 1 *Cucut* (ex-*SGP Jupiter*); 13 *Kobra*; 1 *Krait*; 8 *Sibarau*; 10 *Viper*

MINE WARFARE • MINE COUNTERMEASURES 11

MCO 2 *Pulau Rengat*

MSC 9 *Palau Rote*† (ex-GDR *Wolgast*)

AMPHIBIOUS

PRINCIPAL AMPHIBIOUS VESSELS • LPD 5:

1 *Dr Soeharso* (Ex-*Tanjung Dalpele*; capacity 2 LCU/LCVP; 13 tanks; 500 troops; 2 AS332L *Super Puma*)

4 *Makassar* (capacity 2 LCU/LCVP; 13 tanks; 500 troops; 2 AS332L *Super Puma*)

LANDING SHIPS • LST 21

1 *Teluk Amboina* (capacity 16 tanks; 200 troops);

1 *Teluk Bintuni* (capacity 10 MBT)

11 *Teluk Gilimanuk* (ex-GDR *Frosch*)

2 *Teluk Langsa* (capacity 16 tanks; 200 troops);

6 *Teluk Semangka* (capacity 17 tanks; 200 troops)

LANDING CRAFT 55

LCM 20

LCU 5

LCVP 30

LOGISTICS AND SUPPORT 32

AGF 1 *Multatuli* with 1 hel landing platform

AGOR 7: 5 *Baruna Jaya*; 1 *Jalanidhi*; 1 *Burujulasad* with 1 hel landing platform

AGSH 1

AKSL 4

AOL 1

AORLH 1 *Arun* (ex-UK *Rover*)

AOT 3: 2 *Khobi*; 1 *Sorong*

ATF 2

AXS 2

AP 7: 1 *Tanjung Kambani* (troop transport) with 1 hel landing platform; 2 *Tanjung Nusanive* (troop transport); 4 *Karang Pilang* (troop transport)

YTM 3

Naval Aviation ε1,000

EQUIPMENT BY TYPE

AIRCRAFT

MP 23: 3 CN-235 MPA; 14 N-22B *Searchmaster* B; 6 N-22SL *Searchmaster* L

TPT • Light 32: 4 Beech G36 Bonaza; 21 C-212-200 *Aviocar*; 2 DHC-5D *Buffalo*; 3 TB-9 *Tampico*; 2 TB-10 *Tobago*

HELICOPTERS

MRH 4 Bell 412 (NB-412) *Twin Huey*

TPT 15: **Medium** 3 AS332L *Super Puma* (NAS322L); **Light** 12: 3 EC120B *Colibri*; 9 Bo-105 (NBo-105)

Marines ε20,000

FORCES BY ROLE

SPECIAL FORCES

1 SF bn

MANOEUVRE

Amphibious

2 mne gp (1 cav regt, 3 mne bn, 1 arty regt, 1 cbt spt regt, 1 CSS regt)

1 mne bde (3 mne bn)

EQUIPMENT BY TYPE

LT TK 55 PT-76†

RECCE 21 BRDM

AIFV 122: 24 AMX-10P; 10 AMX-10 PAC 90; 22 BMP-2; 54 BMP-3F; 12 BTR-80A

AAV 10 LVTP-7A1

APC (W) 100 BTR-50P

ARTY 59+

TOWED 50: **105mm** 22 LG1 MK II; **122mm** 28 M-38

MRL 122mm 9 RM-70

MOR 81mm

AD • GUNS 150: **40mm** 5 L/60/L/70; **57mm** S-60

Air Force 30,100

2 operational comd (East and West) plus trg comd.

FORCES BY ROLE

FIGHTER

1 sqn with F-5E/F *Tiger* II

1 sqn with F-16A/B/C/D *Fighting Falcon*

FIGHTER/GROUND ATTACK

1 sqn with Su-27SK/SKM *Flanker*; Su-30MK/MK2 *Flanker*

2 sqn with *Hawk* Mk109*/Mk209*

1 sqn with T-50i *Golden Eagle**

GROUND ATTACK
  1 sqn with EMB-314 (A-29) *Super Tucano**
MARITIME PATROL
  1 sqn with B-737-200; CN-235M-220 MPA
TANKER/TRANSPORT
  1 sqn with C-130B/KC-130B *Hercules*
TRANSPORT
  1 VIP sqn with B-737-200; C-130H/H-30 *Hercules*; L-100-30; F-27-400M *Troopship*; F-28-1000/3000; AS332L *Super Puma* (NAS332L); SA330SM *Puma* (NAS300SM)
  1 sqn with C-130H/H-30 *Hercules*; L-100-30
  1 sqn with C-212 *Aviocar* (NC-212)
  1 sqn with CN-235M-110; C-295M
TRAINING
  1 sqn with Grob 120TP
  1 sqn with KT-1B; T-34C *Turbo Mentor*
  1 sqn with SF-260M; SF-260W *Warrior*
TRANSPORT HELICOPTER
  2 sqn with AS332L *Super Puma* (NAS332L); SA330J/L *Puma* (NAS330J/L); EC120B *Colibri*
EQUIPMENT BY TYPE
Only 45% of ac op
AIRCRAFT 97 combat capable
  FTR 22: 8 F-5E *Tiger II*; 4 F-5F *Tiger II*; 7 F-16A *Fighting Falcon*; 3 F-16B *Fighting Falcon*
  FGA 21: 3 F-16C *Fighting Falcon*; 2 F-16D *Fighting Falcon*; 2 Su-27SK *Flanker*; 3 Su-27SKM *Flanker*; 2 Su-30MK *Flanker*; 9 Su-30MK2 *Flanker*
  MP 5: 3 B-737-200; 2 CN-235M-220 MPA
  TKR 1 KC-130B *Hercules*
  TPT 41: **Medium** 15: 4 C-130B *Hercules*; 3 C-130H *Hercules*; 6 C-130H-30 *Hercules*; 2 L-100-30; **Light** 19: 7 C-295 (2 more on order); 6 C-212 *Aviocar* (NC-212); 5 CN-235-110; 1 F-27-400M *Troopship*; **PAX** 5: 1 B-737-200; 1 B-737-800BBJ; 1 F-28-1000; 2 F-28-3000
  TRG 115: 8 EMB-314 (A-29) *Super Tucano** (8 more on order); 18 Grob 120TP; 7 Hawk Mk109*; 23 *Hawk* Mk209*; 11 KT-1B; 10 SF-260M; 7 SF-260W *Warrior*; 15 T-34C *Turbo Mentor*; 16 T-50i *Golden Eagle**
HELICOPTERS
  TPT 31: **Medium** 19: 10 AS332 *Super Puma* (NAS332L) (VIP/CSAR); 1 SA330SM *Puma* (NAS330SM) (VIP); 4 SA330J *Puma* (NAS330J); 4 SA330L *Puma* (NAS330L); **Light** 12 EC120B *Colibri*
MSL
  ASM AGM-65G *Maverick*
  AAM • **IR** AIM-9P *Sidewinder*; R-73 (AA-11 *Archer*); **IR/SARH** R-27 (AA-10 *Alamo*)
  ARM Kh-31P (AS-17A *Krypton*)

Special Forces (Paskhasau)
FORCES BY ROLE
SPECIAL FORCES
  3 (PASKHASAU) SF wg (total: 6 spec ops sqn)
  4 indep SF coy
EQUIPMENT BY TYPE
AD
  SAM • **MANPAD** QW-3
  GUNS • **TOWED 35mm** 6 Oerlikon *Skyshield*

Paramilitary ε281,000 active

Customs
EQUIPMENT BY TYPE
PATROL AND COASTAL COMBATANTS 65
  PBF 15
  PB 50

Marine Police
EQUIPMENT BY TYPE
PATROL AND COASTAL COMBATANTS 37
  PSO 2 *Bisma*
  PCC 5
  PBF 3 *Gagak*
  PB 27: 14 *Bango*; 13 (various)
LOGISTICS AND SUPPORT • **AP** 1

Police ε280,000 (including 14,000 police 'mobile bde' (BRIMOB) org in 56 coy, incl CT unit (Gegana))
EQUIPMENT BY TYPE
APC (W) 34 *Tactica*
AIRCRAFT • **TPT** • **Light** 5: 2 Beech 18; 2 C-212 *Aviocar* (NC-212); 1 *Turbo Commander* 680
HELICOPTERS • **TPT** • **Light** 22: 3 Bell 206 *Jet Ranger*; 19 Bo-105 (NBo-105)

KPLP (Coast and Seaward Defence Command)
Responsible to Military Sea Communications Agency
EQUIPMENT BY TYPE
PATROL AND COASTAL COMBATANTS 28
  PCO 4: 2 *Arda Dedali*; 2 *Trisula*
  PB 24: 4 *Golok* (SAR); 5 *Kujang*; 15 (various)
LOGISTICS AND SUPPORT • **ABU** 1 *Jadayat*

Reserve Organisations

Kamra People's Security ε40,000 (report for 3 weeks' basic training each year; part-time police auxiliary)

DEPLOYMENT

CENTRAL AFRICAN REPUBLIC
UN • MONUSCO 168; 1 engr coy

DEMOCRATIC REPUBLIC OF THE CONGO
UN • MONUSCO 175; 14 obs; 1 engr coy

HAITI
UN • MINUSTAH 2

LEBANON
UN • UNIFIL 1,287; 1 mech inf bn; 1 log bn(-); 1 FFGM

LIBERIA
UN • UNMIL 1 obs

PHILIPPINES
IMT 9

SOUTH SUDAN
UN • UNMISS 3 obs

SUDAN
UN • UNAMID 1; 3 obs
UN • UNISFA 2; 2 obs

WESTERN SAHARA
UN • MINURSO 4 obs

Japan JPN

Japanese Yen ¥		2013	2014	2015
GDP	¥	478tr	489tr	
	US$	4.9tr	4.77tr	
per capita	US$	38,468	37,540	
Growth	%	1.5	0.9	
Inflation	%	0.4	2.7	
Def bdgt	¥	4.75tr	4.88tr	5.05tr
	US$	48.7bn	47.7bn	
US$1=¥		97.60	102.44	

Includes military pensions, excludes expenditure on US military realignment and SACO-related projects.

Population 127,103,388

Ethnic groups: Korean <1%

Age	0–14	15–19	20–24	25–29	30–64	65 plus
Male	6.8%	2.6%	2.4%	2.6%	22.8%	11.2%
Female	6.4%	2.3%	2.4%	2.7%	23.1%	14.6%

Capabilities

Relations with China and related territorial disputes, along with a territorial dispute with Russia and security concerns over North Korea, continue to be defence-policy drivers, as does Tokyo's relationship with Washington. Assets for power projection in the maritime and air domains were earmarked for acquisition in the latest (2014–17) five-year plan. These include tilt-rotors for its nascent amphibious force as well as additional tanker aircraft, and a growing emphasis on persistent maritime ISR. Heavy armour is planned to be substantially reduced, reflecting the growing emphasis on rapid mobility. In July 2014, the air force's ATD-X low-observable combat-aircraft demonstrator was rolled out, which will potentially complement the national development of transport and ASW aircraft. All three services are well equipped, predominately with US systems, and train regularly in a joint environment and with US forces. Japan is also trying to forge closer defence ties with other regional powers, including Australia. This partly reflects changes to its arms-export policy that will enable closer equipment cooperation with the US and partner nations. (See pp. 221–25.)

ACTIVE 247,150 (Ground Self-Defense Force 151,050; Maritime Self- Defense Force 45,500; Air Self-Defense Force 47,100; Central Staff 3,500) Paramilitary 12,650

RESERVE 56,100 (General Reserve Army (GSDF) 46,000; Ready Reserve Army (GSDF) 8,200; Navy 1,100; Air 800)

ORGANISATIONS BY SERVICE

Space
SATELLITES • ISR 4: IGS 1/3/4/5

Ground Self-Defense Force 151,050
FORCES BY ROLE
COMMAND
  5 army HQ (regional comd)
SPECIAL FORCES
  1 spec ops unit (bn)
MANOEUVRE
  Armoured
  1 (7th) armd div (1 armd recce sqn, 3 tk regt, 1 armd inf regt, 1 avn sqn, 1 SP arty regt, 1 AD regt, 1 cbt engr bn, 1 sigs bn, 1 NBC bn, 1 log regt)
  Mechanised
  1 (2nd) inf div (1 armd recce sqn, 1 tk regt, 1 mech inf regt, 2 inf regt, 1 avn sqn, 1 SP arty regt, 1 AT coy, 1 AD bn, 1 cbt engr bn, 1 sigs bn, 1 NBC bn, 1 log regt)
  1 (4th) inf div (1 armd recce sqn, 1 tk bn, 1 mech inf regt, 3 inf regt, 1 inf coy, 1 avn sqn, 1 arty regt, 1 AT coy, 1 AD bn, 1 cbt engr bn, 1 sigs bn, 1 NBC bn, 1 log regt)
  1 (9th) inf div (1 armd recce sqn, 1 tk bn, 2 mech inf regt, 1 inf regt, 1 avn sqn, 1 arty regt, 1 AD bn, 1 cbt engr bn, 1 sigs bn, 1 NBC bn, 1 log regt)
  2 (5th & 11th) inf bde (1 armd recce sqn, 1 tk bn, 3 mech inf regt, 1 avn sqn, 1 SP arty bn, 1 AD coy, 1 cbt engr coy, 1 sigs coy, 1 NBC coy, 1 log bn)
  Light
  1 (8th) inf div (1 recce sqn, 1 tk bn, 4 inf regt, 1 avn sqn, 1 arty regt, 1 AD bn, 1 cbt engr bn, 1 sigs bn, 1 NBC bn, 1 log regt)
  4 (1st, 3rd, 6th & 10th) inf div (1 recce sqn, 1 tk bn, 3 inf regt, 1 avn sqn, 1 arty regt, 1 AD bn, 1 cbt engr bn, 1 sigs bn, 1 NBC bn, 1 log regt)
  1 (13th) inf bde (1 recce sqn, 1 tk coy, 3 inf regt, 1 avn sqn, 1 arty bn, 1 AD coy, 1 cbt engr coy, 1 sigs coy, 1 log bn)
  1 (14th) inf bde (1 recce sqn, 1 tk coy, 2 inf regt, 1 avn sqn, 1 arty bn, 1 AD coy, 1 cbt engr coy, 1 sigs coy, 1 log bn)
  1 (15th) inf bde (1 recce sqn, 1 inf regt, 1 avn sqn, 1 AD bn, 1 cbt engr coy, 1 EOD coy, 1 sigs coy, 1 log bn)
  Air Manoeuvre
  1 (1st) AB bde (3 AB bn, 1 arty bn, 1 cbt engr coy, 1 sigs coy, 1 log bn)
  1 (12th) air mob inf bde (1 recce sqn, 4 inf regt, 1 avn sqn, 1 SP arty bn, 1 AD coy, 1 cbt engr coy, 1 sigs coy, 1 log bn)
  Aviation
  1 hel bde
  5 avn gp (1 atk hel bn, 1 hel bn)
COMBAT SUPPORT
  1 arty bde
  2 arty unit (bde)
  2 AD bde
  4 AD gp
  4 engr bde
  1 engr unit
  1 EW bn

5 int bn
1 MP bde
1 sigs bde
COMBAT SERVICE SUPPORT
5 log unit (bde)
5 trg bde
EQUIPMENT BY TYPE
MBT 688: 39 Type-10; 308 Type-74; 341 Type-90
RECCE 164: 109 Type-87; 55 Chemical Reconnaissance Vehicle
AIFV 68 Type-89
APC 790
  APC (T) 234 Type-73
  APC (W) 556: 210 Type-82; 346 Type-96
ARTY 1,777
  SP 160: **155mm** 93: 93 Type-99; **203mm** 67 M110A2
  TOWED 155mm 422 FH-70
  MRL 227mm 99 M270 MLRS
  MOR 1,096
    SP 120mm 24 Type-96
    TOWED 1,072: **81mm** 646 L16 **120mm** 426
AT
  MSL
    SP 34 Type-96 MPMS
    MANPATS Type-79 *Jyu*-MAT; Type-87 *Chu*-MAT; Type-01 LMAT
  RCL • 84mm Carl Gustav
  RL 89mm
AIRCRAFT
  TPT • Light 9: 2 MU-2 (LR-1); 7 Beech 350 *King Air* (LR-2)
HELICOPTERS
  ATK 114: 66 AH-1S *Cobra*; 10 AH-64D *Apache*; 38 OH-1
  ISR 71 OH-6D
  TPT 255: **Heavy** 57: 28 CH-47D *Chinook* (CH-47J); 29 CH-47JA *Chinook*; **Medium** 38: 2 EC225LP *Super Puma* MkII+ (VIP); 36 UH-60L *Black Hawk* (UH-60JA); **Light** 160: 130 Bell-205 (UH-1J); 30 Enstrom 480B (TH-480B)
AD
  SAM
    SP 203: 40 Type-03 *Chu*-SAM; 50 Type-81 *Tan*-SAM; 113 Type-93 *Kin*-SAM
    TOWED 126 MTM-23B I-HAWK
    MANPAD Type-91 *Kei*-SAM
  GUNS • SP 35mm 52 Type-87
MSL • AShM 86 Type-88
ARV 69: 2 Type-11; 37 Type-78; 30 Type-90
VLB 22 Type-91

Maritime Self-Defense Force 45,500

Surface units organised into 4 Escort Flotillas with a mix of 7–8 warships each. Bases at Yokosuka, Kure, Sasebo, Maizuru, Ominato. SSK organised into two flotillas with bases at Kure and Yokosuka. Remaining units assigned to five regional districts.

EQUIPMENT BY TYPE
SUBMARINES • TACTICAL • SSK 18:
  2 *Harushio* (trg role) with 6 single 533mm TT with T-89 HWT/UGM-84C *Harpoon* AShM
  11 *Oyashio* with 6 single 533mm TT with T-89 HWT/UGM-84C *Harpoon* AShM
  5 *Soryu* (AIP fitted) with 6 single 533mm TT with T-89 HWT/UGM-84C *Harpoon* AShM (additional vessels in build)
PRINCIPAL SURFACE COMBATANTS 47
  AIRCRAFT CARRIERS • CVH 2 *Hyuga* with 1 16-cell Mk41 VLS with ASROC/RIM-162/ESSM *Sea Sparrow*, 2 triple 324mm ASTT with Mk46 LWT, 2 *Phalanx* Block 1B CIWS, (normal ac capacity 3 SH-60 *Seahawk* ASW hel; plus additional ac embarkation up to 7 SH-60 *Seahawk* or 7 MCH-101)
  CRUISERS • CGHM 2 *Atago* (*Aegis* Base Line 7) with 2 quad lnchr with SSM-1B AShM, 1 64-cell Mk41 VLS with SM-2 MR SAM/ASROC, 1 32-cell Mk41 VLS with SM-2 MR SAM, 2 triple 324mm ASTT with Mk46 LWT, 2 *Phalanx* Block 1B CIWS, 1 127mm gun (capacity 1 SH-60 *Seahawk* ASW hel)
  DESTROYERS 34:
  DDGHM 26:
    8 *Asagiri* with 2 quad Mk141 lnchr with RGM-84C *Harpoon* AShM, 1 octuple Mk29 lnchr with *Sea Sparrow* SAM, 2 triple 324mm ASTT with Mk46 LWT, 1 octuple Mk112 lnchr with ASROC, 2 *Phalanx* CIWS, 1 76mm gun (capacity 1 SH-60 *Seahawk* ASW hel)
    4 *Akizuki* with 2 quad lnchr with SS-1B AShM, 1 32-cell Mk41 VLS with ASROC/ESSM *Sea Sparrow* SAM, 2 triple 324mm ASTT with Mk46 LWT, 2 *Phalanx* Block 1B CIWS, 1 127mm gun (capacity 1 SH-60 *Seahawk* ASW hel)
    9 *Murasame* with 2 quad lnchr with SSM-1B AShM, 1 16-cell Mk48 VLS with RIM-7M *Sea Sparrow* SAM, 2 triple 324mm TT with Mk46 LWT, 1 16-cell Mk41 VLS with ASROC, 2 *Phalanx* CIWS, 2 76mm gun (capacity 1 SH-60 *Seahawk* ASW hel)
    5 *Takanami* (improved *Murasame*) with 2 quad lnchr with SSM-1B AShM, 1 32-cell Mk41 VLS with ASROC/RIM-7M/ESSM *Sea Sparrow* SAM, 2 triple 324mm TT with Mk46 LWT, 2 *Phalanx* CIWS, 1 127mm gun (capacity 1 SH-60 *Seahawk* ASW hel)
  DDGM 6:
    2 *Hatakaze* with 2 quad Mk141 lnchr with RGM-84C *Harpoon* AShM, 1 Mk13 GMLS with SM-1 MR SAM, 2 triple 324mm ASTT with Mk46 LWT, 1 octuple Mk112 lnchr with ASROC, 2 *Phalanx* CIWS, 2 127mm gun, 1 hel landing platform
    4 *Kongou* (*Aegis* Baseline 4/5) with 2 quad Mk141 lnchr with RGM-84C *Harpoon* AShM, 1 29-cell Mk41 VLS with SM-2/3 SAM/ASROC, 1 61-cell Mk41 VLS with SM-2/3 SAM/ASROC, 2 triple 324mm ASTT, 2 *Phalanx* Block 1B CIWS, 1 127mm gun
  DDHM 2 *Shirane* with 1 octuple Mk112 lnchr with ASROC, 1 octuple Mk29 lnchr with RIM-7M *Sea Sparrow* SAM, 2 triple ASTT with Mk46 LWT, 2 *Phalanx* CIWS, 2 127mm gun (capacity 3 SH-60 *Seahawk* ASW hel)

FRIGATES 9:
  FFGHM 3 *Hatsuyuki* with 2 quad Mk141 lnchr with RGM-84C *Harpoon* AShM, 1 octuple Mk29 lnchr with RIM-7F/M *Sea Sparrow* SAM, 2 triple ASTT with Mk46 LWT, 1 octuple Mk112 lnchr with ASROC, 2 *Phalanx* CIWS, 1 76mm gun (capacity 1 SH-60 *Seahawk* ASW hel)
  FFGM 6 *Abukuma* with 2 quad Mk141 lnchr with RGM-84C *Harpoon* AShM, 2 triple ASTT with Mk 46 LWT, 1 Mk112 octuple lnchr with ASROC, 1 *Phalanx* CIWS, 1 76mm gun

PATROL AND COASTAL COMBATANTS 6
  PBFG 6 *Hayabusa* with 4 SSM-1B AShM, 1 76mm gun

MINE WARFARE • MINE COUNTERMEASURES 35
  MCM SPT 4:
    2 *Nijma*
    2 *Uraga* with 176mm gun, 1 hel landing platform (for MH-53E)
  MSO 25: 3 *Hirashima*; 12 *Sugashima*; 5 *Uwajima*; 3 *Yaeyama*; 2 *Enoshima*
  MSD 6

AMPHIBIOUS
  LANDING SHIPS • LST 3 *Osumi* with 2 *Phalanx* CIWS, 1 hel landing platform (for 2 CH-47 hel) (capacity 10 Type-90 MBT; 2 LCAC(L) ACV; 330 troops)
  LANDING CRAFT 20
    LCU 2 *Yusotei*
    LCM 12
    LCAC 6 LCAC(L) (capacity either 1 MBT or 60 troops)

LOGISTICS AND SUPPORT 82
  AGH 1 *Asuka* with 1 8-cell VLS (wpn trials) (capacity 1 SH-60B *Seahawk* hel)
  AGBH 1 *Shirase* (capacity 2 AW101 *Merlin* hel)
  AGOS 2 *Hibiki* with 1 hel landing platform
  AGS 4: 1 *Futami*; 1 *Nichinan*; 1 *Shonan*; 1 *Suma*
  AOE 5: 2 *Mashu* (capacity 2 med hel); 3 *Towada* with 1 hel landing platform
  ARC 1 *Muroto*
  ASR 2: 1 *Chihaya* with 1 hel landing platform; 1 *Chiyoda* with 1 hel landing platform
  ATF 28
  AX 8:
    1 *Kashima* with 2 triple 324mm ASTT, 1 76mm gun, 1 hel landing platform
    1 *Kurobe* with 1 76mm gun (trg spt ship)
    3 *Shimayuki* with 2 quad lnchr with RGM-84 *Harpoon* AShM, 1 octuple Mk29 lnchr with RIM-7M *Sea Sparrow* SAM, 1 octuple Mk112 lnchr with ASROC, 2 triple 324mm ASTT with Mk46 LWT, 2 *Phalanx* CIWS, 1 76mm gun
    1 *Tenryu* (trg spt ship); with 1 76mm gun (capacity: 1 med hel)
    2 (various)
  YAC 1 *Hashidate*
  YDT 6
  YG 5 *Hiuchi*
  YTM 16
  YTR 2

Naval Aviation ε9,800

7 Air Groups
FORCES BY ROLE
ANTI SUBMARINE/SURFACE WARFARE
  5 sqn with SH-60B (SH-60J)/SH-60K *Seahawk*
MARITIME PATROL
  4 sqn with P-3C *Orion*
ELECTRONIC WARFARE
  1 sqn with EP-3 *Orion*
MINE COUNTERMEASURES
  1 sqn with MH-53E *Sea Dragon*; MCH-101
SEARCH & RESCUE
  1 sqn with *Shin Meiwa* US-1A/US-2
  2 sqn with UH-60J *Black Hawk*
TRANSPORT
  1 sqn with AW101 *Merlin* (CH-101); Beech 90 *King Air* (LC-90); YS-11M
TRAINING
  1 sqn with Beech 90 *King Air* (TC-90)
  1 sqn with P-3C *Orion*
  1 sqn with T-5
  1 hel sqn with EC135 (TH-135); OH-6DA; SH-60B (SH-60J) *Seahawk*
EQUIPMENT BY TYPE
AIRCRAFT 78 combat capable
  ASW 80: 7 P-1; 73 P-3C *Orion*
  ELINT 5 EP-3C *Orion*
  SAR 7: 2 *Shin Meiwa* US-1A; 5 *Shin Meiwa* US-2
  TPT • Light 27: 3 YS-11M; 5 Beech 90 *King* Air (LC-90); 19 Beech 90 *King Air* (TC-90)
  TRG 31 T-5
HELICOPTERS
  ASW 86: 43 SH-60B *Seahawk* (SH-60J); 42 SH-60K *Seahawk*; 1 USH-60K *Seahawk*
  MCM 11: 6 MH-53E *Sea Dragon*; 5 MCH-101
  ISR 3 OH-6DA
  SAR 19 UH-60J *Black Hawk*
  TPT 12: **Medium** 2 AW101 *Merlin* (CH-101) (additional ac being delivered); **Light** 10 EC135 (TH-135)

Air Self-Defense Force 47,100

Flying hours   150 hrs/year
7 cbt wg
FORCES BY ROLE
FIGHTER
  7 sqn with F-15J *Eagle*
  2 sqn with F-4EJ (F-4E) *Phantom* II
  3 sqn with Mitsubishi F-2
ELECTRONIC WARFARE
  2 sqn with Kawasaki EC-1; YS-11E
ISR
  1 sqn with RF-4EJ (RF-4E) *Phantom II**
AIRBORNE EARLY WARNING & CONTROL
  2 sqn with E-2C *Hawkeye*
  1 sqn with E-767
SEARCH & RESCUE
  1 wg with U-125A *Peace Krypton*; MU-2 (LR-1); UH-60J *Black Hawk*

TANKER
  1 sqn with KC-767J
TRANSPORT
  1 (VIP) sqn with B-747-400
  3 sqn with C-1; C-130H *Hercules*; YS-11
  Some (liaison) sqn with Gulfstream IV (U-4); T-4*
TRAINING
  1 (aggressor) sqn with F-15J *Eagle*
TEST
  1 wg with F-15J *Eagle*; T-4*
TRANSPORT HELICOPTER
  4 flt with CH-47 *Chinook*
EQUIPMENT BY TYPE
AIRCRAFT 552 combat capable
  FTR 201 F-15J *Eagle*
  FGA 152: 92 F-2A/B; 60 F-4E *Phantom* II (F-4EJ)
  EW 3: 1 Kawasaki EC-1; 2 YS-11EA
  ISR 17: 13 RF-4E *Phantom* II* (RF-4J); 4 YS-11EB
  AEW&C 17: 13 E-2C *Hawkeye*; 4 E-767
  SAR 26 U-125A *Peace Krypton*
  TKR 4 KC-767J
  TPT 64: **Medium** 15 C-130H *Hercules*; **PAX** 49: 2 B-747-400; 13 Beech T-400; 25 C-1; 5 Gulfstream IV (U-4); 4 YS-11
  TRG 245: 196 T-4*; 49 T-7
HELICOPTERS
  SAR 36 UH-60J *Black Hawk*
  TPT • Heavy 15 CH-47 *Chinook*
MSL
  ASM ASM-1 (Type-80); ASM-2 (Type-93)
  AAM • IR AAM-3 (Type-90); AIM-9 *Sidewinder*; **IIR** AAM-5 (Type-04); **SARH** AIM-7 *Sparrow*; **ARH** AAM-4 (Type-99)

Air Defence
Ac control and warning. 4 wg; 28 radar sites
FORCES BY ROLE
AIR DEFENCE
  6 SAM gp (total: 24 SAM bty with MIM-104 *Patriot*)
  1 (Air Base Defence) AD gp with Type-81 *Tan*-SAM; M167 *Vulcan*
EQUIPMENT BY TYPE
AD
  SAM
    SP Type-81 *Tan*-SAM
    TOWED 120 MIM-104 *Patriot*
  GUNS • TOWED 20mm M167 *Vulcan*

Paramilitary 12,650

Coast Guard
Ministry of Land, Transport, Infrastructure and Tourism (no cbt role)
EQUIPMENT BY TYPE
PATROL AND COASTAL COMBATANTS 395+
  PSOH 14: 2 *Mizuho* (capacity 1 Bell 212); 2 *Shikishima* (capacity 2 Bell 212); 10 *Soya* (capacity 1 Bell 212)
  PSO 28:
    3 *Hida* with 1 hel landing platform
    1 *Izu* with 1 hel landing platform
    1 *Kojima* (trg) with 1 hel landing platform
    4 *Kunigami* with 1 hel landing platform
    1 *Miura* with 1 hel landing platform
    1 *Nojima* with 1 hel landing platform
    7 *Ojika* with 1 hel landing platform
    10 *Shiretoko*
  PCO 28: 3 *Aso*; 9 *Hateruma*; 3 *Iwami*; 2 *Takatori*; 11 *Teshio*
  PCC 26: 4 *Amami*; 22 *Tokara*
  PBF 47: 20 *Hayagumo*; 5 *Mihashi*; 14 *Raizan*; 2 *Takatsuki*; 6 *Tsuruugi*
  PB 252+: 8 *Akizuki*; 4 *Asogiri*; 200+ CL-Type; 15 *Hayanami*; 1 *Matsunami*; 7 *Murakumo*; 2 *Natsugiri*; 3 *Shimagiri*; 10 *Yodo*; 2 *Katonami*
LOGISTICS AND SUPPORT 37
  ABU 1 *Teshio*
  AGS 12
  AKSL 7
  YAG 5
  YPC 3
  YTR 9
AIRCRAFT
  MP 2 *Falcon* 900 MPA
  ISR 2 Beech 200T
  TPT 21: **Light** 12: 10 Beech 350 *King Air* (LR-2); 1 Cessna 206 *Stationair* (U-206G); 1 YS-11A; **PAX** 9: 3 CL-300; 2 Gulfstream V (MP); 4 Saab 340B
HELICOPTERS
  MRH 7 Bell 412 *Twin Huey*
  TPT 40: **Medium** 6: 4 AS332 *Super Puma*; 2 EC225 *Super Puma*; **Light** 34: 5 AW139; 4 Bell 206B *Jet Ranger II*; 20 Bell 212; 4 S-76C; 1 S-76D

Cyber

The Self-Defense Forces (SDF) established a Command Control Communication Computer (C4) Systems Command in 2008. In 2012, a 'Cyber Planning Office' was established in the C4 Systems Planning Division, Joint Staff Office (JSO) of the Ministry of Defense to consolidate the cyber-planning functions of the JSO and create a more systematic structure to respond to cyber attacks. The National Defense Program Guidelines for FY2014 and beyond stated that 'Japan will build up persistent ISR [intelligence, surveillance and reconnaissance] capabilities to prevent any acts that could impede efficient action by the SDF' and, in case of any incident, 'will identify the event without delay and swiftly repair any damage'. A Cyber Defense Group was launched in March 2014 to respond to cyber threats. The group monitors MOD and SDF networks and provides responses to cyber attacks.

DEPLOYMENT

DJIBOUTI
180; 2 P-3C *Orion*

GULF OF ADEN & INDIAN OCEAN
2 DDGHM

SOUTH SUDAN
UN • UNMISS 271; 1 engr coy

FOREIGN FORCES

United States
US Pacific Command: 50,000
Army 2,300; 1 SF gp; 1 avn bn; 1 SAM regt
Navy 19,600; 1 CVN; 2 CG; 8 DDG; 1 LCC; 2 MCM; 1 LHD; 2 LSD; 1 base at Sasebo; 1 base at Yokosuka
USAF: 12,400; 1 HQ (5th Air Force) at Okinawa–Kadena AB; 1 ftr wg at Okinawa–Kadena AB (2 ftr sqn with 18 F-16C/D *Fighting Falcon* at Misawa AB); 1 ftr wg at Okinawa–Kadena AB (1 SAR sqn with 8 HH-60G *Pave Hawk*, 1 AEW sqn with 2 E-3B *Sentry*, 2 ftr sqn with total of 24 F-15C/D *Eagle*); 1 airlift wg at Yokota AB with 10 C-130H *Hercules*; 2 C-12J; 1 spec ops gp at Okinawa–Kadena AB
USMC 15,700; 1 Marine div (3rd); 1 ftr sqn with 12 F/A-18D *Hornet*; 1 tkr sqn with 12 KC-130J *Hercules*; 2 tpt sqn with 12 MV-22B *Osprey*;
US Strategic Command: 1 AN/TPY-2 X-band radar at Shariki

Korea, Democratic People's Republic of DPRK

North Korean Won		2012	2013	2014
GDP	US$			
per capita	US$			
Def exp	won			
	US$			

US$1=won

*definitive economic data not available

Population	24,851,627					
Age	0–14	15–19	20–24	25–29	30–64	65 plus
Male	10.9%	4.0%	4.2%	3.8%	22.2%	3.3%
Female	10.6%	4.0%	4.1%	3.7%	22.8%	6.4%

Capabilities

North Korea remains reliant on a predominantly obsolescent equipment inventory across all three services, combined with significant capacity for infiltration and disruption operations, underpinned by its pursuit of a missile-delivered nuclear capability. In personnel terms its land forces are by far the largest of the services, with numerical strength in part intended to offset its ageing equipment inventory. Large-scale exercises are carried out, though these are mainly single service, and often appear staged. Maintaining ageing fleets of equipment while approaching anything resembling adequate training hours is likely an increasing difficulty. The air force reportedly ceased all flying for a short period in 2014 following the fatal crash of an obsolete MiG-17. The extent to which dependency on this equipment affects morale is difficult to assess, but it likely has an effect. As of mid-2014 there was no open-source evidence of *Hwasong*-13 (KN-08) road-mobile ICBM tests, mock-ups of which have been shown on at least two occasions. Imagery of a local anti-ship cruise missile similar in design to the Russian 3M24 (SS-N-25 *Switchblade*) did emerge in 2014, although the system may have been in service for some time. (See pp. 226–27.)

ACTIVE 1,190,000 (Army ε1,020,000 Navy 60,000 Air 110,000) **Paramilitary 189,000**

Conscript liability Army 5–12 years, Navy 5–10 years, Air Force 3–4 years, followed by compulsory part-time service to age 40. Thereafter service in the Worker/Peasant Red Guard to age 60.

RESERVE ε600,000 (Armed Forces ε600,000), **Paramilitary 5,700,000**

Reservists are assigned to units (see also Paramilitary)

ORGANISATIONS BY SERVICE

Strategic Forces

North Korea's *Nodong* missiles and H-5 (Il-28) bombers could in future be used to deliver nuclear warheads or bombs. At present, however, there is no conclusive evidence to suggest that North Korea has successfully produced a warhead or bomb capable of being delivered by either of these systems.

Army ε1,020,000

FORCES BY ROLE
COMMAND
  2 mech corps HQ
  9 inf corps HQ
  1 (Capital Defence) corps HQ
MANOEUVRE
  Armoured
  1 armd div
  15 armd bde
  Mechanised
  4 mech div
  Light
  27 inf div
  14 inf bde
COMBAT SUPPORT
  1 arty div
  21 arty bde
  9 MRL bde
  1 SSM bde with *Scud*
  1 SSM bde with FROG-7
  5–8 engr river crossing / amphibious regt
  1 engr river crossing bde

Special Purpose Forces Command 88,000

FORCES BY ROLE
SPECIAL FORCES
  8 (Reconnaissance General Bureau) SF bn
MANOEUVRE
  Reconnaissance
  17 recce bn
  Light
  9 lt inf bde
  6 sniper bde

Air Manoeuvre
3 AB bde
1 AB bn
2 sniper bde
Amphibious
2 sniper bde

Reserves 600,000
FORCES BY ROLE
MANOEUVRE
Light
40 inf div
18 inf bde
EQUIPMENT BY TYPE (ε)
MBT 3,500+ T-34/T-54/T-55/T-62/Type-59/*Chonma*/*Pokpoong*
LT TK 560+: 560 PT-76; M-1985
APC 2,500+
  APC (T) Type-531 (Type-63); VTT-323
  APC (W) 2,500 BTR-40/BTR-50/BTR-60/BTR-80A/BTR-152/BTR look-a-like
ARTY 21,100+
  SP/TOWED 8,500: **SP 122mm** M-1977/M-1981/M-1985/M-1991; **130mm** M-1975/M-1981/M-1991; **152mm** M-1974/M-1977; **170mm** M-1978/M-1989
  TOWED 122mm D-30/D-74/M-1931/37; **130mm** M-46; **152mm** M-1937/M-1938/M-1943
  GUN/MOR 120mm (reported)
  MRL 5,100: **107mm** Type-63; **122mm** BM-11/M-1977 (BM-21)/M-1985/M-1992/M-1993; **200mm** BMD-20; **240mm** BM-24/M-1985/M-1989/M-1991
  MOR 7,500: **82mm** M-37; **120mm** M-43; **160mm** M-43
AT • MSL
  SP 9K11 *Malyutka* (AT-3 *Sagger*)
  MANPATS 2K15 *Shmel* (AT-1 *Snapper*); 9K111 *Fagot* (AT-4 *Spigot*); 9K113 *Konkurs* (AT-5 *Spandrel*)
  RCL 82mm 1,700 B-10
AD
  SAM
    SP 9K35 *Strela*-10 (SA-13 *Gopher*)
    MANPAD 9K310 *Igla*-1 (SA-16 *Gimlet*); 9K32 *Strela*-2 (SA-7 *Grail*)‡
  GUNS 11,000
    SP 14.5mm M-1984; **23mm** M-1992; **37mm** M-1992; **57mm** M-1985
    TOWED 11,000: **14.5mm** ZPU-1/ZPU-2/ZPU-4; **23mm** ZU-23; **37mm** M-1939; **57mm** S-60; **85mm** M-1939 KS-12; **100mm** KS-19
MSL
  SSM 64+: 24 FROG-3/FROG-5/FROG-7; KN-08 (in development); some *Musudan*; ε10 *Nodong* (ε90+ msl); 30+ *Scud*-B/*Scud*-C (ε200+ msl)

Navy ε60,000
EQUIPMENT BY TYPE
SUBMARINES • TACTICAL 72
  SSK 20 PRC Type-031/FSU *Romeo*† with 8 single 533mm TT with 14 SAET-60 HWT
  SSC 32+:
    30 *Sang-O* with 2 single 533mm TT with Type-53–65 HWT;
    2+ *Sang-O* II with 4 single 533mm TT with Type-53–65 HWT;
  SSW 20† (some *Yugo* with 2 single 406mm TT; some *Yeono* with 2 single 533mm TT)
PRINCIPAL SURFACE COMBATANTS 3
  FRIGATES • FFG 3:
    2 *Najin* with 2 single lnchr with P-15 *Termit* (SS-N-2) AShM, 2 RBU 1200, 2 100mm gun , 2 twin 57mm gun
    1 *Soho* with 4 single lnchr with P-15 *Termit* (SS-N-2) AShM, 2 RBU 1200, 1 100mm gun, 1 hel landing platform (for med hel)
PATROL AND COASTAL COMBATANTS 382
  PCG 18:
    8 *Osa* I with 4 single lnchr with P-15 *Termit* (SS-N-2) AShM, 2 twin AK230 CIWS
    10 *Soju* with 4 single lnchr with P-15 *Termit* (SS-N-2) AShM
  PCO 5: 4 *Sariwon* with 2 twin 57mm gun; 1 *Tral* with 1 85mm gun
  PCC 18:
    6 *Hainan* with 4 RBU 1200, 2 twin 57mm gun
    7 *Taechong* I with 2 RBU 1200, 1 85mm gun, 1 twin 57mm gun
    5 *Taechong* II with 2 RBU 1200, 1 100mm gun, 1 twin 57mm gun
  PBFG 16:
    4 *Huangfen* with 4 single lnchr with P-15 *Termit* (SS-N-2) AShM, 2 twin AK230 CIWS
    6 *Komar* with 2 single lnchr with P-15 *Termit* (SS-N-2) AShM
    6 *Sohung* with 2 single lnchr with P-15 *Termit* (SS-N-2) AShM
  PBF 229: 54 *Chong-Jin* with 1 85mm gun; 142 *Ku Song/Sin Hung/Sin Hung (mod)*; 33 *Sinpo*
  PB 96:
    59 *Chaho*
    6 *Chong-Ju* with 2 RBU 1200, 1 85mm gun
    13 *Shanghai* II
    18 SO-1 with 4 RBU 1200, 2 twin 57mm gun
MINE WARFARE • MINE COUNTERMEASURES 24: 19 *Yukto* I; 5 *Yukto* II
AMPHIBIOUS
  LANDING SHIPS • LSM 10 *Hantae* (capacity 3 tanks; 350 troops)
  LANDING CRAFT 257
    LCPL 96 *Nampo* (capacity 35 troops)
    LCM 25
    LCVP 136 (capacity 50 troops)
LOGISTICS AND SUPPORT 23:
  AGI 14 (converted fishing vessels)
  AS 8 (converted cargo ships)
  ASR 1 *Kowan*

Coastal Defence
FORCES BY ROLE
COMBAT SUPPORT
  2 AShM regt with HY-1 (6 sites, and probably some mobile launchers)
EQUIPMENT BY TYPE
ARTY

TOWED 122mm M-1931/37; **152mm** M-1937
COASTAL **130mm** M-1992; SM-4-1
MSL • AShM HY-1; KN-01 (in development)

Air Force 110,000

4 air divs. 1st, 2nd and 3rd Air Divs (cbt) responsible for N, E and S air defence sectors respectively; 8th Air Div (trg) responsible for NE sector. The AF controls the national airline.

Flying hours   20 hrs/year on ac

FORCES BY ROLE
BOMBER
  3 lt regt with H-5
FIGHTER
  6 regt with J-5
  4 regt with J-6
  5 regt with J-7/MiG-21F-13 *Fishbed*/MiG-21PFM *Fishbed*
  1 regt with MiG-21bis *Fishbed*
  1 regt with MiG-23ML/P *Flogger*
  1 regt with MiG-29A/S/UB *Fulcrum*
FIGHTER/GROUND ATTACK
  1 regt with Su-7 *Fitter*
GROUND ATTACK
  1 regt with Su-25/Su-25UBK *Frogfoot*
TRANSPORT
  Some regt with Y-5 (to infiltrate 2 air-force sniper brigades deep into ROK rear areas), but possibly grounded; An-24 *Coke*; Il-18 *Coot*; Il-62M *Classic*; Tu-134 *Crusty*; Tu-154 *Careless*
TRAINING
  Some regt with CJ-6; FT-2; MiG-21 *Fishbed*
ATTACK HELICOPTER
  1 regt with Mi-24 *Hind*
TRANSPORT HELICOPTER
  Some regt with Hughes 500D; Mi-8 *Hip*; Mi-17 *Hip* H; PZL Mi-2 *Hoplite*; Z-5
AIR DEFENCE
  19 bde with S-125 *Pechora* (SA-3 *Goa*); S-75 *Dvina* (SA-2 *Guideline*); S-200 *Angara* (SA-5 *Gammon*); 9K36 *Strela*-3 (SA-14 *Gremlin*); 9K310 *Igla*-1 (SA-16 *Gimlet*); 9K32 *Strela*-2 (SA-7 *Grail*)‡; (KN-06 SAM system shown in 2010)

EQUIPMENT BY TYPE
AIRCRAFT 563 combat capable
  BBR 80 H-5†
  FTR 401+: 107 J-5; 100 J-6; 120 J-7/MiG-21F-13 *Fishbed*/MiG-21PFM *Fishbed*†; 46 MiG-23ML *Flogger*; 10 MiG-23P *Flogger*; 18+ MiG-29A/S/UB *Fulcrum*
  FGA 48: 30 MiG-21bis *Fishbed*†; 18 Su-7 *Fitter*
  ATK 34 Su-25/Su-25UBK *Frogfoot*
  TPT 217: **Light** 208: 6 An-24 *Coke*; 2 Tu-134 *Crusty*; ε200 Y-5; **PAX** 9: 2 Il-18 *Coot*; 2 Il-62M *Classic*; 4 Tu-154 *Careless*; 1 Tu-204-300
  TRG 215+: 180 CJ-6; 35 FT-2; some MiG-21U/UM
HELICOPTERS
  ATK 20 Mi-24 *Hind*
  MRH 80 Hughes 500D†
  TPT 202: **Medium** 63: 15 Mi-8 *Hip*/Mi-17 *Hip* H; 48 Z-5 **Light** 139 PZL Mi-2 *Hoplite*
UAV • ISR • **Light** Pchela-1 (*Shmel*)

AD • SAM
  TOWED 312+: 179+ S-75 *Dvina* (SA-2 *Guideline*); 133 S-125 *Pechora* (SA-3 *Goa*)
  STATIC/SHELTER 38 S-200 (SA-5 *Gammon*)
  MANPAD 9K32 *Strela*-2 (SA-7 *Grail*)‡; 9K36 *Strela*-3 (SA-14 *Gremlin*); 9K310 *Igla*-1 (SA-16 *Gimlet*)
MSL
  ASM Kh-23 (AS-7 *Kerry*); Kh-25 (AS-10 *Karen*)
  AShM KN-01
  AAM • IR R-3 (AA-2 *Atoll*)‡; R-60 (AA-8 *Aphid*); R-73 (AA-11 *Archer*); PL-5; PL-7; SARH R-23/24 (AA-7 *Apex*); R-27R/ER (AA-10 A/C *Alamo*)

Paramilitary 189,000 active

Security Troops 189,000 (incl border guards, public safety personnel)
Ministry of Public Security

Worker/Peasant Red Guard ε5,700,000 reservists
Org on a provincial/town/village basis; comd structure is bde–bn–coy–pl; small arms with some mor and AD guns (but many units unarmed)

Cyber

Since the 1970s, the North Korean military (the Korean People's Army – KPA) has maintained a modest electronic-warfare (EW) capability. As a result of strategic reviews following *Operation Desert Storm*, the KPA established an information-warfare (IW) capability under the concept of 'electronic intelligence warfare' (EIW). Complementing these EIW developments, the KPA is believed to have expanded its EW capabilities with the introduction of more modern ELINT equipment, jammers and radars. In 1998, Unit 121 was reportedly established within the Reconnaissance Bureau of the General Staff Department to undertake offensive cyber operations. Staff are trained in North Korea but some also receive training in Russia and China. In early 2012, activity attributed to Pyongyang included jamming the global positioning systems of aircraft using Seoul's main international airports, as well as those of vessels in nearby waters for two weeks. North Korea also continued to launch distributed denial-of-service attacks on South Korean institutions and pursue cyber infiltration against military and other government agencies.

Korea, Republic of ROK

South Korean Won		2013	2014	2015
GDP	won	1428tr	1503tr	
	US$	1.3tr	1.45tr	
per capita	US$	25,975	28,739	
Growth	%	3.0	3.7	
Inflation	%	1.3	1.6	
Def bdgt	won	34.5tr	35.7tr	
	US$	31.5bn	34.4bn	
US$1=won		1,094.93	1,036.81	

Population 49,039,986

Age	0–14	15–19	20–24	25–29	30–64	65 plus
Male	7.3%	3.5%	3.6%	3.4%	26.9%	5.2%
Female	6.8%	3.2%	3.2%	3.0%	26.4%	7.4%

Capabilities

South Korea's primary military concern remains its relationship with the North and its ability to deter or, if required, counter and defeat threats from Pyongyang. Its armed forces are well trained and equipped, exercising regularly, including with the US. The capacity to defend against North Korea's ballistic-missile arsenal is a priority, with defensive and offensive systems being purchased to address this. Seoul is acquiring or developing a number of stand-off precision-strike systems, including cruise and ballistic missiles, and in 2014 formally selected the F-35 to meet its latest combat-aircraft requirement. F-35 deliveries are hoped to begin in 2018, while the first of four additional tanker aircraft should enter the inventory in 2017. South Korea was also due to assume wartime operational control of its forces at the end of 2015, as agreed with the US in 2007 (an initial handover date of 2012 had been moved to allow additional time for planning). As of mid-2014, however, this had been further postponed by the US in response to the security situation in the peninsula and North Korea's ongoing nuclear and missile activities.

ACTIVE 655,000 (Army 522,000 Navy 68,000 Air 65,000) Paramilitary 4,500

Conscript liability Army, Navy and Air Force 26 months

RESERVE 4,500,000

Reserve obligation of three days per year. First Combat Forces (Mobilisation Reserve Forces) or Regional Combat Forces (Homeland Defence Forces) to age 33.

Reserve Paramilitary 3,000,000
Being reorganised

ORGANISATIONS BY SERVICE

Army 522,000

FORCES BY ROLE
COMMAND
  2 army HQ
  8 corps HQ
  1 (Capital Defence) comd HQ
SPECIAL FORCES
  1 (Special Warfare) SF comd
  7 SF bde
MANOEUVRE
  Armoured
  5 armd bde
  Mechanised
  6 mech inf div (1 recce bn, 1 armd bde, 2 mech inf bde, 1 fd arty bde, 1 engr bn)
  Light
  16 inf div (1 recce bn, 1 tk bn, 3 inf regt, 1 arty regt (4 arty bn), 1 engr bn)
  2 indep inf bde
  Air Manoeuvre
  1 air aslt bde
  Other
  3 (Counter Infiltration) bde
  Aviation
  1 (army avn) comd
COMBAT SUPPORT
  3 SSM bn
  1 ADA bde
  5 ADA bn
  6 engr bde
  5 engr gp
  1 CBRN defence bde
  8 sigs bde
COMBAT SERVICE SUPPORT
  4 log cpt cmd
  5 sy regt

Reserves

FORCES BY ROLE
COMMAND
  1 army HQ
MANOEUVRE
  Light
  24 inf div

EQUIPMENT BY TYPE
MBT 2,414: 1,000 K1; 484 K1A1; 253 M48; 597 M48A5; 80 T-80U; (400 M47 in store)
AIFV 340: 40 BMP-3; ε300 K21
APC 2,790
  APC (T) 2,560: 300 Bv 206; 1,700 KIFV; 420 M113; 140 M577
  APC (W) 220; 20 BTR-80; 200 KM-900/-901 (Fiat 6614)
PPV 10 *MaxxPro*
ARTY 11,038+
  SP 1,353+: **155mm** 1,340: ε300 K9 *Thunder*; 1,040 M109A2 (K55/K55A1); **175mm** some M107; **203mm** 13 M110
  TOWED 3,500+: **105mm** 1,700 M101/KH-178; **155mm** 1,800+ KH-179/M114/M115
  MRL 185: **130mm** 156 *Kooryong*; **227mm** 29 MLRS (all ATACMS capable)
  MOR 6,000: **81mm** KM-29 (M29); **107mm** M30
AT
  MSL • MANPATS 9K115 *Metis* (AT-7 *Saxhorn*); TOW-2A
  RCL **57mm**; **75mm**; **90mm** M67; **106mm** M40A2

GUNS 58
  SP 90mm 50 M36
  TOWED 76mm 8 M18 *Hellcat* (AT gun)
HELICOPTERS
  ATK 60 AH-1F/J *Cobra*
  MRH 175: 130 Hughes 500D; 45 MD-500
  TPT 246+ **Heavy** 37: 31 CH-47D *Chinook*; 6 MH-47E *Chinook*; **Medium** 97+: 10+ KUH-1 *Surion*; 87 UH-60P *Black Hawk*; **Light** 112: ε100 Bell-205 (UH-1H *Iroquois*); 12 Bo-105
AD
  SAM
    SP *Chun Ma* (*Pegasus*)
    MANPAD FIM-43 *Redeye*; FIM-92A *Stinger*; *Javelin*; *Mistral*; 9K31 Igla-1 (SA-16 *Gimlet*)
  GUNS 330+
    SP 170: **20mm** ε150 KIFV *Vulcan* SPAAG; **30mm** 20 BIHO *Flying Tiger*
    TOWED 160: **20mm** 60 M167 *Vulcan*; **35mm** 20 GDF-003; **40mm** 80 L/60/L/70; M1
RADAR • LAND AN/TPQ-36 *Firefinder* (arty, mor); AN/TPQ-37 *Firefinder* (arty); RASIT (veh, arty)
MSL
  SRBM 30 *Hyonmu* I/IIA/IIB
  LACM *Hyonmu* III
AEV 207 M9
ARV 238: 200 K1; K288A1; M47; 38 M88A1
VLB 56 K1

Navy 68,000 (incl marines)

Three separate fleet elements; 1st Fleet Donghae (East Sea/Sea of Japan); 2nd Fleet Pyeongtaek (West Sea/Yellow Sea); 3rd Fleet Busan (South Sea/Korea Strait); additional three flotillas (incl SF, mine warfare, amphibious and spt elements) and 1 Naval Air Wing (3 gp plus spt gp).

EQUIPMENT BY TYPE
SUBMARINES • TACTICAL 23
  SSK 12:
    6 *Chang Bogo* (GER Type-209/1200; KSS-1) with 8 single 533mm TT with SUT HWT
    3 *Chang Bogo* with 8 single 533mm TT with SUT HWT/UGM-84B *Harpoon* AShM
    3 *Son Won-il* (GER Type 214; KSS-2; AIP fitted) with 8 single 533mm TT with SUT HWT (additional vessels in build)
  SSC 11:
    9 *Cosmos*
    2 *Dolgorae* (KSS-1) with 2 single 406mm TT
PRINCIPAL SURFACE COMBATANTS 23
  CRUISERS • CGHM 3:
    3 *Sejong* (KDX-3) with 2 quad Mk141 lnchr with RGM-84 *Harpoon* AShM, 1 48-cell Mk41 VLS with SM-2MR SAM, 1 32-cell Mk41 VLS with SM-2MR SAM, 1 Mk49 GMLS with RIM-116 SAM, 2 triple Mk32 324mm ASTT with K745 LWT, 1 32-cell VLS with ASROC, 1 *Goalkeeper* CIWS, 1 127mm gun (capacity 2 *Lynx* Mk99 hel)
  DESTROYERS • DDGHM 6:
    6 *Chungmugong Yi Sun-Jhin* (KDX-2) with 2 quad Mk141 lnchr with RGM-84C *Harpoon* AShM (some may be fitted with *Hae Sung* AShM), 1 or 2 32-cell Mk41 VLS with SM-2 MR SAM/ASROC, 1 Mk49 GMLS with RIM-116 SAM, 2 triple Mk32 324mm ASTT with Mk46 LWT, 1 *Goalkeeper* CIWS, 1 127mm gun (capacity 1 *Lynx* Mk99 hel)
  FRIGATES 14
    FFGHM 5:
      3 *Gwanggaeto Daewang* (KDX-1) with 2 quad Mk141 lnchr with RGM-84 *Harpoon* AShM, 1 16 cell Mk48 VLS with *Sea Sparrow* SAM, 2 triple Mk32 324mm ASTT with Mk46 LWT, 1 *Goalkeeper* CIWS, 1 127mm gun (capacity 1 *Lynx* Mk99 hel)
      2 *Incheon* with 2 quad lnchr with *Hae Sung* AShM, 1 21-cell Mk49 lnchr with RIM-116 SAM, 2 triple 324mm ASTT with K745 *Blue Shark* LWT, 1 Mk15 1B *Phalanx* CIWS, 1 127 mm gun
    FFGM 9:
      9 *Ulsan* with 2 quad Mk141 lnchr with RGM-84C *Harpoon* AShM, 2 triple Mk32 324mm ASTT with Mk46 LWT, 2 76mm gun
PATROL AND COASTAL COMBATANTS 116
  CORVETTES • FSG 36:
    15 *Gumdoksuri* with 2 twin lnchr with *Hae Sung* AShM, 1 76mm gun
    2 *Po Hang* with 2 single lnchr with MM-38 *Exocet* AShM, 2 triple 324mm ASTT with Mk 46 LWT, 1 76mm gun
    19 *Po Hang* with 2 twin lnchr with RGM-84 *Harpoon* AShM, 2 triple 324mm ASTT with Mk46 LWT, 2 76mm gun
  PBF 80 *Sea Dolphin*
MINE WARFARE 10
  MINE COUNTERMEASURES 9
    MHO 6 *Kan Kyeong*
    MSO 3 *Yang Yang*
  MINELAYERS • ML 1 *Won San* with 2 triple Mk32 324mm ASTT, 1 76mm gun, 1 hel landing platform
AMPHIBIOUS
  PRINCIPAL AMPHIBIOUS SHIPS 1
    LPD 1 *Dokdo* with 1 Mk49 GMLS with RIM-116 SAM, 2 *Goalkeeper* CIWS (capacity 2 LCAC; 10 tanks; 700 troops; 10 UH-60 hel)
  LANDING SHIPS • LST 4 *Alligator* with 1 hel landing platform (capacity 20 tanks; 300 troops)
  LANDING CRAFT 41
    LCAC 5: 3 *Tsaplya* (capacity 1 MBT; 130 troops); 2 LSF-II
    LCM 10 LCM-8
    LCT 6
    LCVP 20
LOGISTICS AND SUPPORT 24
  AG 1 *Sunjin* (trials spt)
  AGOR 17 (civil manned, funded by the Ministry of Transport)
  AORH 3 *Chun Jee*
  ARS 1
  ATS 2

Naval Aviation

AIRCRAFT 16 combat capable
  ASW 16: 8 P-3C *Orion*; 8 P-3CK *Orion*
  TPT • **Light** 5 Cessna F406 *Caravan* II

HELICOPTERS
ASW 24: 11 *Lynx* Mk99; 13 *Lynx* Mk99-A
MRH 3 SA319B *Alouette* III
TPT 15: **Medium** 8 UH-60P *Black Hawk* **Light** 7 Bell 205 (UH-1H *Iroquois*)

Marines 27,000
FORCES BY ROLE
MANOEUVRE
Amphibious
2 mne div (1 recce bn, 1 tk bn, 3 mne regt, 1 amph bn, 1 arty regt, 1 engr bn)
1 mne bde
COMBAT SUPPORT
Some cbt spt unit
EQUIPMENT BY TYPE
MBT 100: 50 K1A1; 50 M48
AAV 166 AAV-7A1
ARTY • TOWED 105mm; 155mm
AT • MSL • SP 2 *Spike* NLOS
MSL • AShM RGM-84A *Harpoon* (truck mounted)

Air Force 65,000
4 Comd (Ops, Southern Combat, Logs, Trg)
FORCES BY ROLE
FIGHTER/GROUND ATTACK
3 sqn with F-4E *Phantom* II
10 sqn with F-5E/F *Tiger* II
3 sqn with F-15K *Eagle*
10 sqn with F-16C/D *Fighting Falcon* (KF-16C/D)
1 sqn with FA-50 *Fighting Eagle*
ISR
1 wg with KO-1
SIGINT
1 sqn with Hawker 800RA/XP
SEARCH & RESCUE
2 sqn with AS332L *Super Puma*; Bell 412EP; HH-47D *Chinook*; HH-60P *Black Hawk*; Ka-32 *Helix* C
TRANSPORT
1 VIP sqn with B-737-300; B-747; CN-235-220; S-92A *Superhawk*; VH-60P *Black Hawk* (VIP)
3 sqn (incl 1 Spec Ops) with C-130H/H-30/J-30 *Hercules*
2 sqn with CN-235M-100/220
TRAINING
2 sqn with F-5E/F *Tiger* II
1 sqn with F-16C/D *Fighting Falcon*
1 sqn with *Hawk* Mk67
4 sqn with KT-1
1 sqn with Il-103
3 sqn with T-50/TA-50 *Golden Eagle**
TRANSPORT HELICOPTER
1 sqn with UH-60P *Black Hawk* (Spec Ops)
AIR DEFENCE
3 AD bde (total: 3 SAM bn with I-HAWK; 2 SAM bn with *Patriot* PAC-2)
EQUIPMENT BY TYPE
AIRCRAFT 571 combat capable
FTR 174: 142 F-5E *Tiger* II; 32 F-5F *Tiger* II
FGA 314: 70 F-4E *Phantom* II; 60 F-15K *Eagle*; 118 F-16C *Fighting Falcon* (KF-16C); 46 F-16D *Fighting Falcon* (KF-16D); 20 FA-50 *Fighting Eagle*; (some F-4D *Phantom* II in store)
AEW&C 4 B-737 AEW
ISR 24: 4 Hawker 800RA; 20 KO-1
SIGINT 4 Hawker 800SIG
TPT 38: **Medium** 16: 8 C-130H *Hercules*; 4 C-130H-30 *Hercules*; 4 C-130J-30 *Hercules*; **Light** 20: 12 CN-235M-100; 8 CN-235M-220 (incl 2 VIP); **PAX** 2: 1 B-737-300; 1 B-747
TRG 189: 15 *Hawk* Mk67*; 23 Il-103; 83 KT-1; 49 T-50 *Golden Eagle**; 9 T-50B *Black Eagle** (aerobatics); 10 TA-50 *Golden Eagle**
HELICOPTERS
SAR 16: 5 HH-47D *Chinook*; 11 HH-60P *Black Hawk*
MRH 3 Bell 412EP
TPT • **Medium** 30: 2 AS332L *Super Puma*; 8 Ka-32 *Helix* C; 3 S-92A *Superhawk*; 7 UH-60P *Black Hawk*; 10 VH-60P *Black Hawk* (VIP)
UAV • ISR 103+ **Medium** 3+: some *Night Intruder*; 3 *Searcher* **Light** 100 *Harpy*
AD • SAM 206
SP 48 *Patriot* PAC-2
TOWED 158 MIM-23B I-HAWK
MSL
ASM AGM-65A *Maverick*; AGM-84H SLAM-ER
AShM AGM-84 *Harpoon*; AGM-130; AGM-142 *Popeye*
ARM AGM-88 HARM
AAM • IR AIM-9 *Sidewinder*; IIR AIM-9X *Sidewinder*; SARH AIM-7 *Sparrow*; ARH AIM-120B/C5 AMRAAM

Paramilitary ε4,500 active

Civilian Defence Corps 3,000,000 reservists (to age 50)

Coast Guard ε4,500
PATROL AND COASTAL COMBATANTS 50
PSOH 1 *Sambongho*
PSO 5: 1 *Sumjinkang*; 3 *Mazinger*
PCO 16: 1 *Han Kang* with 1 76mm gun; 15 *Tae Geuk*
PCC 24: 4 *Bukhansan*; 6 (430 tonne); 14 *Hae Uri*
PB 9: 5 Hyundai Type; ε4 (various)
LOGISTICS AND SUPPORT • ARS 30+
AIRCRAFT
MP 5: 1 C-212-400 MP; 4 CN-235-110 MPA
TPT • **PAX** 1 CL-604
HELICOPTERS
MRH 8: 6 AS365 *Dauphin* II; 1 AW139; 1 Bell 412SP
TPT • **Medium** 8 Ka-32 *Helix* C

Cyber
South Korea established a Cyber Warfare Command Centre in early 2010, with over 200 personnel, in the wake of a substantial distributed denial-of-service attack in 2009. The new centre responds to the attention given to cyber and information security by the National Intelligence Service and the Defense Security Command. In early 2014, the first meeting took place of a new Korea–US National Defense Cyber Cooperation Working Group, designed to share information and enhance cooperation in terms of policy, strategy, doctrine and training.

DEPLOYMENT

AFGHANISTAN
NATO • ISAF 50

ARABIAN SEA
Combined Maritime Forces • CTF-151: 1 DDGHM

CÔTE D'IVOIRE
UN • UNOCI 2 obs

HAITI
UN • MINUSTAH 2

INDIA/PAKISTAN
UN • UNMOGIP 7 obs

LEBANON
UN • UNIFIL 321; 1 mech inf bn

LIBERIA
UN • UNMIL 1; 1 obs

SOUTH SUDAN
UN • UNMISS 273; 2 obs; 1 engr coy

SUDAN
UN • UNAMID 2

UAE
150 (trg activities at UAE Spec Ops School)

WESTERN SAHARA
UN • MINURSO 4 obs

FOREIGN FORCES

Sweden NNSC: 5 obs
Switzerland NNSC: 5 obs
United States US Pacific Command: 28,500
  Army 19,200; 1 HQ (8th Army) at Seoul; 1 div HQ (2nd Inf) at Tongduchon; 1 armd bde with M1 *Abrams*; M2/M3 *Bradley*; M109; 1 armd BG; 1 (FS cbt avn) hel bde with AH-64 *Apache*; CH-47 *Chinook*; UH-60 *Black Hawk*; 1 ISR hel bn with OH-58D *Kiowa Warrior*; 1 arty (fires) bde with M270 MLRS; 1 AD bde with MIM 104 *Patriot*/FIM-92A *Avenger*; 1 (APS) armd bde eqpt set
  Navy 250
  USAF 8,800; 1 HQ (7th Air Force) at Osan AB; 1 ftr wg at Kunsan AB (1 ftr sqn with 20 F-16C/D *Fighting Falcon*); 1 ftr wg at Kunsan AB (1 ftr sqn with 20 F-16C/D *Fighting Falcon*, 1 ftr sqn with 24 A-10C *Thunderbolt* II at Osan AB)
  USMC 250

Laos LAO

New Lao Kip		2013	2014	2015
GDP	kip	84.6tr	95.5tr	
	US$	10.8bn	11.7bn	
per capita	US$	1,594	1,697	
Growth	%	8.0	7.4	
Inflation	%	6.4	5.5	
Def bdgt	kip	ε172bn	ε197bn	
	US$	ε22m	ε24m	
FMA	US$			0.2m
US$1=kip		7,839.45	8,158.49	

Population 6,803,699

Ethnic groups: Lao 55%; Khmou 11%; Hmong 8%

Age	0–14	15–19	20–24	25–29	30–64	65 plus
Male	17.6%	5.4%	5.1%	4.3%	15.5%	1.7%
Female	17.2%	5.5%	5.2%	4.4%	15.9%	2.1%

Capabilities

The Lao People's Armed Forces (LPAF) have considerable military experience from the Second Indo-China War and the 1988 border war with Thailand. However, Laos is one of the world's poorest countries and the defence budget and military procurement have been extremely limited for more than 20 years. The armed forces remain closely linked to the ruling Communist Party, and their primary role is internal security, with operations continuing against Hmong rebels. Contacts with the Chinese and Vietnamese armed forces continue, but the LPAF have made no international deployments and have little capacity for sustained high-intensity operations.

ACTIVE 29,100 (Army 25,600 Air 3,500) **Paramilitary 100,000**

Conscript liability 18 months minimum

ORGANISATIONS BY SERVICE

Army 25,600
FORCES BY ROLE
4 mil regions
MANOEUVRE
  Armoured
  1 armd bn
  Light
  5 inf div
  7 indep inf regt
  65 indep inf coy
  Aviation
  1 (liaison) flt
COMBAT SUPPORT
  5 arty bn
  9 ADA bn

1 engr regt
2 (construction) engr regt

EQUIPMENT BY TYPE
MBT 25: 15 T-54/T-55; 10 T-34/85
LT TK 10 PT-76
APC (W) 50: 30 BTR-40/BTR-60; 20 BTR-152
ARTY 62+
  TOWED 62: **105mm** 20 M101; **122mm** 20 D-30/M-30 M-1938; **130mm** 10 M-46; **155mm** 12 M114
  MOR **81mm**; **82mm**; **107mm** M-1938/M-2A1; **120mm** M-43
AT • RCL **57mm** M18/A1; **75mm** M20; **106mm** M40; **107mm** B-11
AD • SAM • MANPAD 9K32 *Strela*-2 (SA-7 *Grail*)‡; 25 9K310 *Igla*-1 (SA-16 *Gimlet*)
  GUNS
    SP **23mm** ZSU-23-4
    TOWED **14.5mm** ZPU-1/ZPU-4; **23mm** ZU-23; **37mm** M-1939; **57mm** S-60
ARV T-54/T-55
VLB MTU

Army Marine Section ε600
PATROL AND COASTAL COMBATANTS 52
  PBR 52†
AMPHIBIOUS LCM 4†

Air Force 3,500
FORCES BY ROLE
TRANSPORT
  1 sqn with An-2 *Colt*; An-26 *Curl*; An-74 *Coaler*; Y-7; Y-12; Yak-40 *Codling* (VIP)
TRAINING
  1 sqn with Yak-18 *Max*
TRANSPORT HELICOPTER
  1 sqn with Ka-32T *Helix* C; Mi-6 *Hook*; Mi-8 *Hip*; Mi-17 *Hip* H; Mi-26 *Halo*; SA360 *Dauphin*

EQUIPMENT BY TYPE
AIRCRAFT
TPT • **Light** 15: 4 An-2 *Colt*; 3 An-26 *Curl*; 1 An-74 *Coaler*; 5 Y-7; 1 Y-12; 1 Yak-40 *Codling* (VIP)
TRG 8 Yak-18 *Max*
HELICOPTERS
MRH 12 Mi-17 *Hip* H
TPT 15 **Heavy** 2: 1 Mi-6 *Hook*; 1 Mi-26 *Halo* **Medium** 10: 1 Ka-32T *Helix* C (5 more on order); 9 Mi-8 *Hip* **Light** 3 SA360 *Dauphin*
MSL • AAM • IR R-3 (AA-2 *Atoll*)†

Paramilitary

Militia Self-Defence Forces 100,000+
Village 'home guard' or local defence

Malaysia MYS

Malaysian Ringgit RM		2013	2014	2015
GDP	RM	987bn	1.08tr	
	US$	313bn	337bn	
per capita	US$	10,457	11,062	
Growth	%	4.7	5.9	
Inflation	%	2.1	2.9	
Def bdgt	RM	15.3bn	16.1bn	
	US$	4.84bn	5.03bn	
US$1=RM		3.15	3.20	

Population   30,073,353

Ethnic groups: Malay and other indigenous (Bunipatre) 64%; Chinese 27%; Indian 9%

Age	0–14	15–19	20–24	25–29	30–64	65 plus
Male	14.8%	4.4%	4.2%	4.0%	20.7%	2.6%
Female	14.0%	4.3%	4.1%	4.0%	20.1%	2.9%

Capabilities

Malaysia's armed forces have considerable experience of counter-insurgency, but substantial modernisation programmes over the last 30 years have helped to develop their capacity for external defence. Army units have deployed on UN peacekeeping operations, and the navy has achieved well-publicised successes with its anti-piracy patrols in the Gulf of Aden. There is also considerable emphasis on joint-service operations. Malaysian forces regularly participate in Five Power Defence Arrangements and other exercises with regional and international partners. However, the armed intrusion at Lahad Datu in Sabah state in February and March 2013 and the aftermath of the disappearance of Malaysian Airlines flight MH370 in March 2014 both revealed serious shortcomings in the armed forces' capacity to protect the country's borders. Although the government increased defence spending in the 2014 budget, gaps in maritime surveillance and air-defence coverage can probably only be resolved in the medium term with the procurement of modern maritime-patrol aircraft and the development of an airborne early-warning capability.

ACTIVE 109,000 (Army 80,000 Navy 14,000 Air 15,000) Paramilitary 24,600

RESERVE 51,600 (Army 50,000, Navy 1,000 Air Force 600) Paramilitary 244,700

ORGANISATIONS BY SERVICE

Army 80,000 (to be 60–70,000)
2 mil region, 4 area comd (div)

FORCES BY ROLE
SPECIAL FORCES
  1 SF bde (3 SF bn)
MANOEUVRE
  Armoured
    1 tk regt (5 armd bn)

Mechanised
5 armd regt
1 mech inf bde (3 mech bn, 1 cbt engr sqn)
Light
1 inf bde (4 inf bn, 1 arty regt)
5 inf bde (3 inf bn, 1 arty regt)
2 inf bde (2 inf bn)
1 inf bde (2 inf bn)
Air Manoeuvre
1 (Rapid Deployment Force) AB bde (1 lt tk sqn, 3 AB bn, 1 lt arty regt, 1 engr sqn)
Aviation
1 hel sqn
COMBAT SUPPORT
9 arty regt
1 arty locator regt
1 MRL regt
3 ADA regt
1 cbt engr sqn
3 fd engr regt (total: 7 cbt engr sqn, 3 engr spt sqn)
1 int unit
4 MP regt
1 sigs regt
COMBAT SERVICE SUPPORT
1 const regt

EQUIPMENT BY TYPE
MBT 48 PT-91M *Twardy*
LT TK 21 *Scorpion-90*
RECCE 296: 130 AML-60/90; 92 *Ferret* (60 mod); K216A1 (as CBRN recce); 74 SIBMAS (some †)
AIFV 44: 31 ACV300 *Adnan* (25mm *Bushmaster*); 13 ACV300 *Adnan* AGL
APC 787
  APC (T) 265: 149 ACV300 *Adnan* (incl 69 variants); 13 FV4333 *Stormer* (upgraded); 63 K-200A; 40 K-200A1
  APC (W) 522: 32 *Anoa*; 300 *Condor* (incl variants); 150 LAV-150 *Commando*; 30 M3 Panhard; 10 VBL
ARTY 424
  TOWED 134: **105mm** 100 Model 56 pack howitzer; **155mm** 34: 12 FH-70; 22 G-5
  MRL 36 ASTROS II (equipped with 127mm SS-30)
  MOR 254: **81mm SP** 14: 4 K281A1; 10 ACV300-S; **120mm SP** 8 ACV-S **81mm**: 232
AT • MSL
  SP 8 ACV300 *Baktar Shikan*; K263
  MANPATS 9K115 *Metis* (AT-7 *Saxhorn*); 9K115-2 *Metis-M* (AT-13 *Saxhorn* 2); *Eryx*; *Baktar Shihan* (HJ-8); C90-CRRB; SS.11
  RCL 260: **84mm** 236 *Carl Gustav*; **106mm** 24 M40
AMPHIBIOUS • LCA 165 Damen Assault Craft 540 (capacity 10 troops)
HELICOPTERS • TPT • Light 10 AW109
AD
  SAM 15 *Jernas* (*Rapier* 2000)
  MANPAD *Anza*; HY-6 (FN-6); 9K38 *Igla* (SA-18 *Grouse*); QW-1 *Vanguard*; *Starburst*
  GUNS • TOWED 52: **35mm** 16 GDF-005; **40mm** 36 L40/70
AEV 9: 3 MID-M; 6 WZT-4

ARV 41+: *Condor*; 15 ACV300; 4 K-288A1; 22 SIBMAS
VLB 5+: *Leguan*; 5 PMCz-90

Reserves
Territorial Army
Some paramilitary forces to be incorporated into a re-organised territorial organisation.
FORCES BY ROLE
MANOEUVRE
  Mechanised
  4 armd sqn
  Light
  16 inf regt (3 inf bn)
  Other
  1 (border) sy bde (5 bn)
  5 (highway) sy bn
COMBAT SUPPORT
  5 arty bty
  2 fd engr regt
  1 int unit
  3 sigs sqn
COMBAT SUPPORT
  4 med coy
  5 tpt coy

Navy 14,000
3 Regional Commands; Kuantan (East Coast); Kinabalu (Borneo) & Langkawi (West Coast)
EQUIPMENT BY TYPE
SUBMARINES • TACTICAL • SSK 2 *Tunku Abdul Rahman* (FRA *Scorpene*) with 6 single 533mm TT with WASS *Black Shark* HWT/SM-39 *Exocet* AShM
PRINCIPAL SURFACE COMBATANTS 10
  FRIGATES 10
    FFGHM 2:
      2 *Lekiu* with 2 quad lnchr with MM-40 *Exocet* Block II AShM, 1 16-cell VLS with *Sea Wolf* SAM, 2 B515 ILAS-3 triple 324mm ASTT with *Sting Ray* LWT, 1 57mm gun (capacity 1 *Super Lynx* hel)
    FFG 2:
      2 *Kasturi* with 2 quad lnchr with MM-40 *Exocet* Block II AShM, 1 twin 375mm A/S mor, 1 100mm gun, 1 57m gun, 1 hel landing platform
    FF 6:
      6 *Kedah* (GER MEKO) with 1 76mm gun, 1 hel landing platform, (fitted for MM-40 *Exocet* AShM & RAM CIWS)
PATROL AND COASTAL COMBATANTS 37
  CORVETTES • FSGM 4:
    4 *Laksamana* with 3 twin lnchr with Mk 2 *Otomat* AShM, 1 *Albatros* quad lnchr with *Aspide* SAM, 2 B515 ILAS-3 triple 324mm TT with A244 LWT, 1 76mm gun
  PCFG 4 *Perdana* (FRA *Combattante* II) with 2 single lnchr with MM-38 *Exocet* AShM, 1 57mm gun
  PBG 4 *Handalan* (SWE *Spica-M*) with 2 twin lnchr with MM-38 *Exocet* AShM , 1 57mm gun
  PBF 17 *Tempur* (SWE CB90)
  PB 8: 6 *Jerong* (Lurssen 45) with 1 57mm gun; 2 *Sri Perlis*
MINE WARFARE • MINE COUNTERMEASURES
  MCO 4 *Mahamiru* (ITA *Lerici*)

AMPHIBIOUS
  LANDING CRAFT 115 **LCM/LCU**
LOGISTICS AND SUPPORT 14
  AGH 2 *Bunga Mas Lima* (capacity 1 AS555 *Fennec*)
  AGS 2: 1 *Mutiara* with 1 hel landing platform; 1 *Perantau*
  AP 2 *Sri Gaya*
  AOR 2 with 1 or 2 57mm gun
  ASR 1 *Mega Bakti*
  ATF 2
  AX 1 *Hang Tuah* with 1 57mm gun, 1 hel landing platform
  AXS 1
  YTM 1

Naval Aviation 160
HELICOPTERS
  ASW 6 *Super Lynx* 300
  MRH 6 AS555 *Fennec*
MSL • AShM *Sea Skua*

Special Forces
FORCES BY ROLE
SPECIAL FORCES
  1 (mne cdo) SF unit

Air Force 15,000
1 air op HQ, 2 air div, 1 trg and log Cmd, 1 Intergrated Area Def Systems HQ

Flying hours   60 hrs/year

FORCES BY ROLE
FIGHTER
  2 sqn with MiG-29/MiG-29UB *Fulcrum*
FIGHTER/GROUND ATTACK
  1 sqn with F/A-18D *Hornet*
  1 sqn with Su-30MKM *Flanker*
  2 sqn with *Hawk* Mk108*/Mk208*
FIGHTER/GROUND ATTACK/ISR
  1 sqn with F-5E/F *Tiger* II; RF-5E *Tigereye*
MARITIME PATROL
  1 sqn with Beech 200T
TANKER/TRANSPORT
  2 sqn with KC-130H *Hercules*; C-130H *Hercules*; C-130H-30 *Hercules*; Cessna 402B
TRANSPORT
  1 (VIP) sqn with A319CT; AW109; B-737-700 BBJ; BD700 *Global Express*; F-28 *Fellowship*; *Falcon* 900
  1 sqn with CN-235
TRAINING
  1 unit with PC-7; SA316 *Alouette* III
TRANSPORT HELICOPTER
  4 (tpt/SAR) sqn with EC725 *Super Cougar*; S-61A-4 *Nuri*; S-61N; S-70A *Black Hawk*
AIR DEFENCE
  1 sqn with *Starburst*
SPECIAL FORCES
  1 (Air Force Commando) unit (airfield defence/SAR)
EQUIPMENT BY TYPE
AIRCRAFT 67 combat capable
  FTR 21: 8 F-5E *Tiger* II; 3 F-5F *Tiger* II; 8 MiG-29 *Fulcrum* (MiG-29N); 2 MiG-29UB *Fulcrum* (MIG-29NUB) (MiG-29 to be withdrawn from service)
  FGA 26: 8 F/A-18D *Hornet*; 18 Su-30MKM
  ISR 6: 4 Beech 200T; 2 RF-5E *Tigereye**
  TKR 4 KC-130H *Hercules*
  TPT 32: **Medium** 10: 2 C-130H *Hercules*; 8 C-130H-30 *Hercules*; **Light** 17: 8 CN-235M-220 (incl 2 VIP); 9 Cessna 402B (2 modified for aerial survey); **PAX** 5: 1 A319CT; 1 B-737-700 BBJ; 1 BD700 *Global Express*; 1 F-28 *Fellowship*; 1 *Falcon* 900
  TRG 80: 6 *Hawk* Mk108*; 12 *Hawk* Mk208*; 8 MB-339C; 7 MD3-160 *Aero Tiga*; 30 PC-7; 17 PC-7 Mk II *Turbo Trainer*
HELICOPTERS
  MRH 17 SA316 *Alouette* III
  TPT 45: **Heavy** 12 EC725 *Super Cougar*; **Medium** 32: 28 S-61A-4 *Nuri*; 2 S-61N; 2 S-70A *Black Hawk*; **Light** 1 AW109
UAV • ISR • Medium *Aludra*
AD • SAM •MANPAD *Starburst*
MSL
  AAM • IR AIM-9 *Sidewinder*; R-73 (AA-11 *Archer*) **IR/SARH** R-27 (AA-10 *Alamo*); **SARH** AIM-7 *Sparrow*; **ARH** AIM-120C AMRAAM; R-77 (AA-12 *Adder*)
  ASM AGM-65 *Maverick*
  AShM AGM-84D *Harpoon*

Paramilitary ε24,600

Police-General Ops Force 18,000
FORCES BY ROLE
COMMAND
  5 bde HQ
SPECIAL FORCES
  1 spec ops bn
MANOEUVRE
  Other
  19 paramilitary bn
  2 (Aboriginal) paramilitary bn
  4 indep paramilitary coy
EQUIPMENT BY TYPE
RECCE ε100 S52 *Shorland*
APC (W) 170: 140 AT105 *Saxon*; ε30 SB-301

Malaysian Maritime Enforcement Agency (MMEA) ε4,500
Controls 5 Maritime Regions (Northern Peninsula; Southern Peninsula; Eastern Peninsula; Sarawak; Sabah), subdivided into a further 18 Maritime Districts. Supported by one provisional MMEA Air Unit.
EQUIPMENT BY TYPE
PATROL AND COASTAL COMBATANTS 189
  PSO 2 *Langkawi* with 1 57mm gun, 1 hel landing platform
  PBF 57: 18 *Penggalang 17* (TUR MRTP 16); 2 *Penggalang 18*; 6 *Penyelamat 20*; 16 *Penggalang 16*; 15 *Tugau*
  PB 130: 15 *Gagah*; 4 *Malawali*; 2 *Nusa*; 3 *Nusa 28*; 1 *Peninjau*; 7 *Ramunia*; 2 *Rhu*; 4 *Semilang*; 15 *Sipadan* (ex-*Kris/Sabah*); 8 *Icarus 1650*; 10 *Pengawal*; 10 *Pengawal 13*; 27 *Pengawal 23*; 4 *Penyelamat*; 9 *Sipadan Steel*; 9 *Sipadan Kayu*
LOGISTICS AND SUPPORT • AX 1 *Marlin*
AIRCRAFT • MP 2 Bombardier 415MP

HELICOPTERS
    MRH 3 AS365 *Dauphin*

Marine Police 2,100
EQUIPMENT BY TYPE
PATROL AND COASTAL COMBATANTS 132
    PBF 12: 6 *Sangitan*; 6 Stan Patrol 1500
    PB/PBR 120

Police Air Unit
AIRCRAFT
    TPT • Light 17: 4 Cessna 206 *Stationair*; 6 Cessna 208 *Caravan*; 7 PC-6 *Turbo-Porter*
HELICOPTERS
    TPT • Light 3: 1 Bell 206L *Long Ranger*; 2 AS355F *Ecureuil* II

Area Security Units (R) 3,500
(Auxiliary General Ops Force)
FORCES BY ROLE
MANOEUVRE
    Other
    89 paramilitary unit

Border Scouts (R) 1,200
in Sabah, Sarawak

People's Volunteer Corps 240,000 reservists (some 17,500 armed)
RELA

Customs Service
PATROL AND COASTAL COMBATANTS 23
    PBF 10
    PB 13

DEPLOYMENT

AFGHANISTAN
NATO • ISAF 2

DEMOCRATIC REPUBLIC OF THE CONGO
UN • MONUSCO 9; 4 obs

LEBANON
UN • UNIFIL 828; 1 mech inf bn

LIBERIA
UN • UNMIL 4 obs

PHILIPPINES
IMT 14

SUDAN
UN • UNAMID 13; 3 obs
UN • UNISFA 1 obs

WESTERN SAHARA
UN • MINURSO 10 obs

FOREIGN FORCES
Australia 130; 1 inf coy (on 3-month rotational tours); 1 AP-3C *Orion* on occasion

Mongolia MNG

Mongolian Tugrik t		2013	2014	2015
GDP	t	17.6tr	21.1tr	
	US$	11.5bn	11.7bn	
per capita	US$	3,996	4,008	
Growth	%	11.7	9.1	
Inflation	%	8.6	14.1	
Def bdgt	t	173bn	190bn	
	US$	117m	108m	
FMA (US)	US$	3m	2.4m	2m
US$1=t		1,523.98	1,802.40	

Population 2,953,190
Ethnic groups: Khalka 80%; Kazakh 6%

Age	0–14	15–19	20–24	25–29	30–64	65 plus
Male	13.7%	4.4%	5.0%	5.1%	19.2%	1.7%
Female	13.2%	4.3%	5.0%	5.2%	20.9%	2.4%

Capabilities

Mongolia has looked at bolstering its ageing equipment inventory over the past few years, reportedly considering the acquisition of limited numbers of combat and transport aircraft. So far, however, these ambitions have not been fulfilled, leaving its small armed forces reliant on Soviet-era equipment. Despite limitations the army has been involved increasingly in peacekeeping operations, with this becoming a focus for the development of its ground forces. The country hosts an annual multilateral peacekeeping exercise, and participates in bilateral training.

ACTIVE 10,000 (Army 8,900 Air 800 Construction Troops 300) **Paramilitary 7,500**
Conscript liability One year for males aged 18–25

RESERVE 137,000 (Army 137,000)

ORGANISATIONS BY SERVICE

Army 5,600; 3,300 conscript (total 8,900)
FORCES BY ROLE
MANOEUVRE
    Mechanised
    1 MR bde
    Light
    1 (rapid deployment) lt inf bn (2nd bn to form)
    Air Manoeuvre
    1 AB bn
COMBAT SUPPORT
    1 arty regt
EQUIPMENT BY TYPE
MBT 420: 370 T-54/T-55; 50 T-72A
RECCE 120 BRDM-2
AIFV 310 BMP-1
APC (W) 210: 150 BTR-60; 40 BTR-70M; 20 BTR-80
ARTY 570

TOWED ε300: **122mm** D-30/M-30 (M-1938); **130mm** M-46; **152mm** ML-20 (M-1937)
MRL **122mm** 130 BM-21
MOR 140: **120mm**; **160mm**; **82mm**
AT • GUNS 200: **85mm** D-44/D-48; **100mm** M-1944/MT-12
AD • SAM 2+ S-125 *Pechora* 2M (SA-3B *Goa*)
ARV T-54/T-55

Air Force 800
FORCES BY ROLE
TRANSPORT
  1 sqn with An-24 *Coke*; An-26 *Curl*
ATTACK/TRANSPORT HELICOPTER
  1 sqn with Mi-8 *Hip*; Mi-171
AIR DEFENCE
  2 regt with S-60/ZPU-4/ZU-23
EQUIPMENT BY TYPE
AIRCRAFT • TPT • **Light** 3: 2 An-24 *Coke*; 1 An-26 *Curl*
HELICOPTERS
  TPT • **Medium** 13: 11 Mi-8 *Hip*; 2 Mi-171
AD • GUNS • TOWED 150: **14.5mm** ZPU-4; **23mm** ZU-23; **57mm** S-60

Paramilitary 7,500 active

Border Guard 1,300; 4,700 conscript (total 6,000)

Internal Security Troops 400; 800 conscript (total 1,200)
FORCES BY ROLE
MANOEUVRE
  Other
  4 gd unit

Construction Troops 300

DEPLOYMENT
AFGHANISTAN
NATO • ISAF 40
DEMOCRATIC REPUBLIC OF THE CONGO
UN • MONUSCO 2 obs
SOUTH SUDAN
UN • UNMISS 856; 2 obs; 1 inf bn
SUDAN
UN • UNAMID 70; 1 fd hospital
UN • UNISFA 2 obs
WESTERN SAHARA
UN • MINURSO 4 obs

Myanmar MMR

Myanmar Kyat K		2013	2014	2015
GDP	K	54.8tr	63.3tr	
	US$	56.8bn	65.3bn	
per capita	US$	1,113	1,270	
Growth	%	8.3	8.5	
Inflation	%	5.7	6.6	
Def bdgt	K	2.1tr	2.36tr	
	US$	2.18bn	2.43bn	
US$1=K		964.72	969.86	

Population 55,746,253

Ethnic groups: Burman 68%; Shan 9%; Karen 7%; Rakhine 4%; Chinese 3+%; Other Chin, Kachin, Kayan, Lahu, Mon, Palaung, Pao, Wa 9%

Age	0–14	15–19	20–24	25–29	30–64	65 plus
Male	13.5%	4.6%	4.7%	4.5%	20.2%	2.3%
Female	12.9%	4.5%	4.6%	4.5%	20.9%	3.0%

Capabilities

Myanmar's large, army-dominated armed forces have, since the country's independence struggle in the 1940s, been intimately involved in domestic politics, which they still dominate despite the advent of a nominally civilian government in March 2011. Their focus has always been on holding together this ethnically diverse state, particularly in the face of one of the world's longest-running insurgencies, conducted by the Karen, Kachin, Mon, Shan and other minority groups around the country's perimeter. However, ceasefires with most of the rebel groups have for the last two decades contributed to a decline in the army's operational experience. Morale among ordinary soldiers (mainly poorly paid conscripts) is reportedly low. While the army grew substantially after the military seized power in 1988, its counter-insurgency focus means that it has remained essentially a light-infantry force. Nevertheless, since the 1990s, large-scale military procurement has resulted in new armoured vehicles, air-defence weapons, artillery, combat aircraft and naval vessels from China, Russia and other diverse sources entering service. (See pp. 225–26.)

ACTIVE 406,000 (Army 375,000 Navy 16,000 Air 15,000) **Paramilitary 107,250**

ORGANISATIONS BY SERVICE

Army ε375,000
14 military regions, 7 regional op comd
FORCES BY ROLE
COMMAND
  20 div HQ (military op comd)
  10 inf div HQ
  34+ bde HQ (tactical op comd)
MANOEUVRE
  Armoured
  10 armd bn

Light
100 inf bn (coy)
337 inf bn (coy) (regional comd)
COMBAT SUPPORT
7 arty bn
37 indep arty coy
7 AD bn
6 cbt engr bn
54 fd engr bn
40 int coy
45 sigs bn

EQUIPMENT BY TYPE
MBT 185+: 10 T-55; 50 T-72S; 25+ Type-59D; 100 Type-69-II
LT TK 105 Type-63 (ε60 serviceable)
RECCE 127+: 12+ EE-9 *Cascavel*; 45 *Ferret*; 40 Humber *Pig*; 30 Mazda
AIFV 10+ BTR-3U
APC 391+
 APC (T) 331: 26 MT-LB; 250 Type-85; 55 Type-90
 APC (W) 50+: 20 Hino; 30+ Type-92
 PPV 10 MPV
ARTY 410+
 SP 155mm 36: 30 NORA B-52; 6 SH-1
 TOWED 264+: 105mm 132: 36 M-56; 96 M101; 122mm 100 D-30; 130mm 16 M-46; 140mm; 155mm 16 Soltam M-845P
 MRL 30+: 107mm 30 Type-63; 122mm BM-21 (reported); Type-81; 240mm M-1991 (reported)
 MOR 80+: 82mm Type-53 (M-37); 120mm 80+: 80 Soltam; Type-53 (M-1943)
AT
 RCL 1,000+: 106mm M40A1; 84mm ε1,000 *Carl Gustav*
 GUNS 84
  SP 105mm 24 PTL-02 mod
  TOWED 60: 57mm 6-pdr; 76.2mm 17-pdr
AD
 SAM
  TOWED S-125 *Pechora* (SA-3 *Goa*)
  SPAAGM Some 2K22 *Tunguska* (SA-19 *Grison*)
  MANPAD HN-5 *Hong Nu/Red Cherry* (reported); 9K310 *Igla*-1 (SA-16 *Gimlet*)
 GUNS 46
  SP 57mm 12 Type-80
  TOWED 34: 37mm 24 Type-74; 40mm 10 M1
MSL • SSM some *Hwasong*-6 (reported)
ARV Type-72

Navy ε16,000

EQUIPMENT BY TYPE
PRINCIPAL SURFACE COMBATANTS • FRIGATES 4
 FFGH 1 *Kyansitthar* with 2 twin lnchr with DPRK AShM (possibly KN-01), 4 AK630 CIWS, 1 76mm gun (capacity 1 med hel)
 FFG 3:
  1 *Aung Zeya* with 2 twin lnchr with DPRK AShM (possibly KN-01), 4 AK630 CIWS, 1 76mm gun, 1 hel landing platform
  2 *Mahar Bandoola* (PRC Type-053H1) with 2 quad lnchr with C-802 (CSS-N-8 *Saccade*) AShM, 2 RBU 1200, 2 twin 100mm gun

PATROL AND COASTAL COMBATANTS 113
 CORVETTES • FSG 2 *Anawrahta* with 2 twin lnchr with C-802 (CSS-N-8 *Saccade*) AShM; 1 76mm gun, 1 hel landing platform
 PCG 7: 6 *Houxin* with 2 twin lnchr with C-801 (CSS-N-4 *Sardine*) AShM; 1 Type-491 with 2 twin lnchr with C-802 (CSS-N-8 *Saccade*) AShM
 PCO 2 *Indaw*
 PCC 9 *Hainan* with 4 RBU 1200, 2 twin 57mm gun
 PBG 4 *Myanmar* with 2 twin lnchr with C-801 (CSS-N-4 *Sardine*) AShM
 PBF 1 Type-201
 PB 31: 3 PB-90; 6 PGM 401; 6 PGM 412; 13 *Myanmar*; 3 *Swift*
 PBR 57: 4 *Sagu*; 9 Y-301†; 1 Y-301 (Imp); 43 (various)
AMPHIBIOUS • CRAFT 18: 8 LCU 10 LCM
LOGISTICS AND SUPPORT 18
 ABU 1; AGS 1; AK 1; AKSL 5; AP 9; YAC 1

Naval Infantry 800
FORCES BY ROLE
MANOEUVRE
 Light
  1 inf bn

Air Force ε15,000
FORCES BY ROLE
FIGHTER
 4 sqn with F-7 *Airguard*; FT-7; MiG-29B *Fulcrum*; MiG-29UB *Fulcrum*
GROUND ATTACK
 2 sqn with A-5M *Fantan*
TRANSPORT
 1 sqn with An-12 *Cub*; F-27 *Friendship*; FH-227; PC-6A/B *Turbo Porter*
TRAINING
 2 sqn with G-4 *Super Galeb**; PC-7 Turbo Trainer*; PC-9*
 1 (trg/liaison) sqn with Cessna 550 *Citation* II; Cessna 180 *Skywagon*; K-8 *Karakorum**
TRANSPORT HELICOPTER
 4 sqn with Bell 205; Bell 206 *Jet Ranger*; Mi-17 *Hip* H; Mi-35P *Hind*; PZL Mi-2 *Hoplite*; PZL W-3 *Sokol*; SA316 *Alouette* III

EQUIPMENT BY TYPE
AIRCRAFT 155 combat capable
 FTR 88: 49 F-7 *Airguard*; 10 FT-7; 18 MiG-29 *Fulcrum*; 6 MiG-29SE *Fulcrum*; 5 MiG-29UB *Fulcrum*
 ATK 22 A-5M *Fantan*
 TPT 22: Medium 2 An-12 *Cub*; Light 16: 3 Beech 1900D; 4 Cessna 180 *Skywagon*; 1 Cessna 550 *Citation* II; 3 F-27 *Friendship*; 5 PC-6A/B *Turbo Porter*; PAX 4 FH-227
 TRG 45+: 12 G-4 *Super Galeb**; 12+ K-8 *Karakorum**; 12 PC-7 Turbo Trainer*; 9 PC-9*
HELICOPTERS
 ATK 7 Mi-35P *Hind*
 MRH 20: 11 Mi-17 *Hip* H; 9 SA316 *Alouette* III
 TPT 46: Medium 10 PZL W-3 *Sokol*; Light 36: 12 Bell 205; 6 Bell 206 *Jet Ranger*; 18 PZL Mi-2 *Hoplite*
MSL • AAM • IR PL-5; R-73 (AA-11 *Archer*) IR/SARH R-27 (AA-10 *Alamo*)

Paramilitary 107,250

People's Police Force 72,000

People's Militia 35,000

People's Pearl and Fishery Ministry ε250

EQUIPMENT BY TYPE
PATROL AND COASTAL COMBATANTS • PBR 6 *Carpentaria*

Nepal NPL

Nepalese Rupee NR		2013	2014	2015
GDP	NR	1.69tr	1.93tr	
	US$	19.2bn	19.6bn	
per capita	US$	692	699	
Growth	%	3.9	5.5	
Inflation	%	9.9	9.0	
Def exp	NR	20.8bn		
	US$	236m		
Def bdgt [a]	NR	20.5bn	30.5bn	28.7bn
	US$	234m	312m	
FMA (US)	US$	1.24m	1.3m	1m
US$1=NR		87.96	98.21	

Population 30,986,975

Religious groups: Hindu 90%; Buddhist 5%; Muslim 3%

Age	0–14	15–19	20–24	25–29	30–64	65 plus
Male	16.1%	6.0%	5.3%	4.2%	15.5%	2.1%
Female	15.5%	5.9%	5.4%	4.5%	17.0%	2.4%

Capabilities

Nepal's armed forces have traditionally focused on internal security. The army dominates, reflecting the country's history of counter-insurgency in the 1990s and 2000s. Following a 2006 peace accord with the Maoist People's Liberation Army, and the subsequent transition from monarchy to republic, Maoist personnel went through a process of demobilisation or integration into the regular forces. A 2011 draft national-security policy focused on territorial integrity. Mobility remains a challenge, due to limited transport assets and the country's challenging topography, and an order for multi-role helicopters is as yet unfulfilled. The military has no power-projection capability – though a small air wing provides transport and support capability – but is extensively involved in UN peace-support operations, particularly in Africa and the Middle East. Training support is provided by several countries, including the US, India and China.

ACTIVE 95,750 (Army 95,750) **Paramilitary** 62,000

ORGANISATIONS BY SERVICE

Army 95,750

FORCES BY ROLE
COMMAND
 6 inf div HQ
 1 (valley) comd
SPECIAL FORCES
 1 bde (1 SF bn, 1 AB bn, 1 cdo bn, 1 ranger bn, 1 mech inf bn)
MANOEUVRE
 Light
 16 inf bde (total: 63 inf bn)
 32 indep inf coy
COMBAT SUPPORT
 4 arty regt
 2 AD regt
 4 indep AD coy
 5 engr bn
EQUIPMENT BY TYPE
RECCE 40 *Ferret*
APC 253
 APC (W) 13: 8 OT-64C; 5 WZ-551
 PPV 240: 90 *Casspir*; 150 MPV
ARTY 92+
 TOWED 105mm 22: 8 L118 Lt Gun; 14 Pack Howitzer (6 non-operational)
 MOR 70+: 81mm; 120mm 70 M-43 (est 12 op)
AD • GUNS • TOWED 32+: 14.5mm 30 Type-56 (ZPU-4); 37mm (PRC); 40mm 2 L/60

Air Wing 320
AIRCRAFT • TPT 4: Light 3: 1 BN-2T *Islander*; 2 M-28 *Skytruck*; PAX 1 BAe-748
HELICOPTERS
 MRH 9: 1 *Dhruv*; 2 *Lancer*; 3 Mi-17-1V *Hip* H; 1 SA315B *Lama* (*Cheetah*); 2 SA316B *Alouette* III
 TPT 3: Medium 1 SA330J *Puma*; Light 2 AS350B2/B3 *Ecureuil*

Paramilitary 62,000

Armed Police Force 15,000
Ministry of Home Affairs

Police Force 47,000

DEPLOYMENT

CENTRAL AFRICAN REPUBLIC
UN • MINUSCA 1

CÔTE D'IVOIRE
UN • UNOCI 1; 3 obs

DEMOCRATIC REPUBLIC OF THE CONGO
UN • MONUSCO 1,031; 18 obs; 1 inf bn; 1 engr coy

HAITI
UN • MINUSTAH 13

IRAQ
UN • UNAMI 77; 1 sy unit

LEBANON
UN • UNIFIL 869; 1 inf bn

LIBERIA
UN • UNMIL 18; 2 obs

MALI
UN • MINUSMA 145; 1 EOD coy

MIDDLE EAST
UN • UNTSO 4 obs

SOUTH SUDAN
UN • UNMISS 1,701; 4 obs; 2 inf bn

SUDAN
UN • UNAMID 364; 15 obs; 1 SF coy; 1 inf coy

SYRIA/ISRAEL
UN • UNDOF 153; 1 HQ coy

WESTERN SAHARA
UN • MINURSO 4 obs

FOREIGN FORCES
United Kingdom 280 (Gurkha trg org)

New Zealand NZL

New Zealand Dollar NZ$		2013	2014	2015
GDP	NZ$	221bn	234bn	
	US$	182bn	201bn	
per capita	US$	40,516	44,294	
Growth	%	2.8	3.6	
Inflation	%	1.1	1.6	
Def exp	NZ$	3.16bn		
	US$	2.59bn		
Def bdgt	NZ$	3.18bn	3.71bn	
	US$	2.61bn	3.19bn	
US$1=NZ$		1.22	1.16	

Population 4,401,916

Ethnic groups: NZ European 58%; Maori 15%; Other European 13%; Other Polynesian 5% ; Chinese 2%; Indian 1%; Other 6%

Age	0–14	15–19	20–24	25–29	30–64	65 plus
Male	10.2%	3.5%	3.6%	3.3%	22.5%	6.6%
Female	9.7%	3.3%	3.5%	3.2%	22.8%	7.7%

Capabilities

The New Zealand Defence Force is small, but draws on a strong national military tradition. The country has contributed forces to almost every conflict in which its larger allies have been involved over the last century and minor contingents remain deployed overseas. The NZDF exercises regularly with regional and international counterparts, including its partners in the Five Power Defence Arrangements. Despite funding shortfalls and capability losses, including the withdrawal from service of combat aircraft in 2001, the NZDF is characterised by high training standards, professionalism and morale. The 2010 Defence White Paper promised to maintain and enhance existing capabilities, and to provide some additional elements. Two Defence Capability plans followed, the most recent in June 2014, which noted how the NZDF's Savings and Redistribution Programme has generated additional funding for front-line capabilities such as new maritime helicopters. A new Pilot Training Capability will use T-6C advanced trainers. Improved C4ISR will be an important element of the 'enhanced combat capability' planned for 2020.

ACTIVE 8,500 (Army 4,250 Navy 1,900 Air 2,350)

RESERVE 2,290 (Army 1,800 Navy 300 Air Force 190)

ORGANISATIONS BY SERVICE

Army 4,250
FORCES BY ROLE
SPECIAL FORCES
  1 SF gp
MANOEUVRE
  Light
  1 inf bde (1 armd recce regt, 2 lt inf bn, 1 arty regt (2 arty bty, 1 AD tp), 1 engr regt(-), 1 MI coy, 1 MP coy, 1 sigs regt, 2 log bn, 1 med bn)
COMBAT SUPPORT
  1 EOD sqn
EQUIPMENT BY TYPE
AIFV 95 NZLAV-25
ARTY 74
  TOWED 105mm 24 L-118 Light Gun
  MOR 81mm 50
AT • MSL • MANPATS 24 *Javelin*
  RCL 84mm 42 *Carl Gustav*
AEV 7 NZLAV
ARV 3 LAV-R

Reserves

Territorial Force 1,800 reservists
Responsible for providing trained individuals for augmenting deployed forces
FORCES BY ROLE
COMBAT SERVICE SUPPORT
  3 (Territorial Force Regional) trg regt

Navy 1,900
Fleet HQ at Auckland
EQUIPMENT BY TYPE
PRINCIPAL SURFACE COMBATANTS • FRIGATES • FFHM 2:
  2 *Anzac* (GER MEKO 200) with 1 octuple Mk41 VLS with RIM-7M *Sea Sparrow* SAM, 2 triple Mk32 324mm TT, 1 Mk15 *Phalanx* Block 1B CIWS, 1 127mm gun (capacity 1 SH-2G (NZ) *Super Seasprite* ASW hel)
PATROL AND COASTAL COMBATANTS 6
  PSOH 2 *Otago* (capacity 1 SH-2G *Super Seasprite* ASW hel)
  PCC 4 *Rotoiti*
AMPHIBIOUS • LANDING CRAFT • LCM 2

LOGISTICS AND SUPPORT 4
  AKRH 1 *Canterbury* (capacity 4 NH90 tpt hel; 1 SH-2G *Super Seasprite* ASW hel; 2 LCM; 16 NZLAV; 14 NZLOV; 20 trucks; 250 troops)
  AOR 1 *Endeavour* with 1 hel landing platform
  YDT 1 *Manawanui*

Air Force 2,350

Flying hours 190

FORCES BY ROLE
MARITIME PATROL
  1 sqn with P-3K2 *Orion*
TRANSPORT
  1 sqn with B-757-200 (upgraded); C-130H *Hercules* (upgraded)
ANTI-SUBMARINE/SURFACE WARFARE
  1 (RNZAF/RNZN) sqn with SH-2G *Super Seasprite* (SH-2G(NZ))
TRAINING
  1 sqn with CT-4E *Airtrainer* (leased); T-6C *Texan* II
  1 sqn with Beech 200 *King Air* (leased)
  1 (transition) hel unit with AW109; NH90
TRANSPORT HELICOPTER
  1 sqn with Bell 205 (UH-1H *Iroquois*) (to be replaced by NH90)
EQUIPMENT BY TYPE
AIRCRAFT 6 combat capable
  ASW 6 P-3K2 *Orion*
  TPT 12: **Medium** 5 C-130H *Hercules* (upgraded); **Light** 5 Beech 200 *King Air* (leased, to be replaced); **PAX** 2 B-757-200 (upgraded)
  TRG 17: 13 CT-4E *Airtrainer* (leased); 4 T-6C *Texan* II
HELICOPTERS
  ASW 5 SH-2G *Super Seasprite* (SH-2G(NZ))
  TPT 26: **Medium** 8 NH90; **Light** 18: 5 AW109; 13 Bell 205 (UH-1H *Iroquois*) (being replaced by NH90)
  MSL • ASM AGM-65B/G *Maverick*

DEPLOYMENT

AFGHANISTAN
NATO • ISAF 1

DJIBOUTI
Combined Maritime Forces • CTF-151: 1 P-3K2 *Orion*

EGYPT
MFO 28; 1 trg unit; 1 tpt unit

MIDDLE EAST
UN • UNTSO 7 obs

SOUTH SUDAN
UN • UNMISS 1; 2 obs

Pakistan PAK

Pakistani Rupee Rs		2013	2014	2015
GDP	Rs	22.5tr	25.4tr	
	US$	233bn	241bn	
per capita	US$	1,275	1,231	
Growth	%	3.7	4.1	
Inflation	%	7.4	8.6	
Def bdgt [a]	Rs	573bn	632bn	703bn
	US$	6.01bn	6.31bn	
FMA (US) [b]	US$	80m	300m	280m
US$1=Rs		96.62	105.22	

[a] Includes budget for Ministry of Defence Production
[b] FMA figure does not include US Overseas Contingency Operations funding, the FY2015 request for which amounted to US$280m.

Population   196,174,380
Religious groups: Hindu less than 3%

Age	0–14	15–19	20–24	25–29	30–64	65 plus
Male	17.1%	5.7%	5.4%	4.7%	16.4%	2.0%
Female	16.2%	5.4%	5.0%	4.4%	15.3%	2.3%

Capabilities

Pakistan's nuclear and conventional forces have traditionally been orientated and structured against a prospective threat from India. Since 2008, however, a priority for the army has been counter-insurgency operations, mainly against Islamist groups for which forces have been redeployed from the Indian border. These operations have usually been tactically successful but the Pakistani Taliban is a continued threat to the state and has demonstrated the ability to mount attacks and breach the security of military bases. The potential power vacuum left by the 2014 ISAF drawdown from Afghanistan, and use of the route through Pakistan for equipment transportation, is also of concern to senior officials. The air force is modernising its combat-aircraft inventory with procurements from China and the US, while also improving its precision-strike and ISR capabilities. However, the May 2011 US helicopter-borne attack on Osama bin Laden's compound outside Abbottabad called into question the effectiveness of Pakistan's air defences. The navy is currently too small to sustain a long campaign against a significant competitor, such as India, but recent and likely future investment in Chinese-supplied frigates, missile craft and submarines should improve sea-denial capabilities. The army continues to contribute to UN peacekeeping operations.

ACTIVE 643,800 (Army 550,000 Navy 23,800 Air 70,000) **Paramilitary 304,000**

ORGANISATIONS BY SERVICE

Strategic Forces

Operational control rests with the National Command Authority (NCA); army and air-force strategic forces are responsible for technical aspects, training and administrative control of the services' nuclear assets.

Army Strategic Forces Command 12,000-15,000

Commands all land-based strategic nuclear forces.

EQUIPMENT BY TYPE
MSL • STRATEGIC 60+
  MRBM ε30 *Ghauri/Ghauri* II (*Hatf*-5)/*Shaheen*-2 (*Hatf*-6 – in test)
  SRBM 30+: ε30 *Ghaznavi* (*Hatf*-3 - PRC M-11)/*Shaheen*-1 (*Hatf*-4); some *Abdali* (*Hatf*-2)
  LACM *Babur* (*Hatf*-7); *Ra'ad* (*Hatf*-8 – in test)
ARTY • MRL *Nasr* (*Hatf*-9 – likely nuclear capable; in development)

Air Force

1-2 sqn of F-16A/B or *Mirage* 5 may be assigned a nuclear strike role

Army 550,000

FORCES BY ROLE
COMMAND
  9 corps HQ
  1 (area) comd
SPECIAL FORCES
  2 SF gp (total: 4 SF bn)
MANOEUVRE
  Armoured
    2 armd div
    7 indep armd bde
  Mechanised
    2 mech inf div
    1 indep mech bde
  Light
    18 inf div
    5 indep inf bde
  Aviation
    1 VIP avn sqn
    4 avn sqn
    3 atk hel sqn
    2 ISR hel sqn
    2 SAR hel sqn
    2 tpt hel sqn
    1 spec ops hel sqn
COMBAT SUPPORT
  9 (corps) arty bde
  5 indep arty bde
  1 AD comd (3 AD gp (total: 8 AD bn))
  7 engr bde

EQUIPMENT BY TYPE
MBT 2,531+: 385 *Al-Khalid* (MBT 2000); 320 T-80UD; 51 T-54/T-55; 1,100 Type-59/*Al-Zarrar*; 400 Type-69; 275+ Type-85; (270 M48A5 in store)
APC 1,390
  APC (T) 1,260: 1,160 M113/*Talha*; ε100 Type-63
  APC (W) 120 BTR-70/BTR-80
  PPV 10 *Dingo* II
ARTY 4,472+
  SP 375: **155mm** 315: 200 M109A2; ε115 M109A5 **203mm** 60 M110/M110A2
  TOWED 1,659: **105mm** 329: 216 M101; 113 M-56; **122mm** 570: 80 D-30 (PRC); 490 Type-54 M-1938; **130mm** 410 Type-59-I; **155mm** 322: 144 M114; 148 M198; ε30 *Panter*; **203mm** 28 M115
  MRL 88+: **107mm** Type-81; **122mm** 52+: 52 *Azar* (Type-83); some KRL-122; **300mm** 36 A100
  MOR 2,350+: **81mm**; **120mm** AM-50
AT
  MSL
    SP M901 TOW
    MANPATS HJ-8/TOW; 9K119 *Refleks* (AT-11 *Sniper*)
  RCL 75mm Type-52; **106mm** M40A1
  RL 89mm M20
  GUNS 85mm 200 Type-56 (D-44)
AIRCRAFT
  TPT • Light 14: 1 Beech 200 *King Air*; 1 Beech 350 *King Air*; 3 Cessna 208B; 1 Cessna 421; 1 Cessna 550 *Citation*; 1 Cessna 560 *Citation*; 2 Turbo Commander 690; 4 Y-12(II)
  TRG 88 MFI-17B *Mushshak*
HELICOPTERS
  ATK 38 AH-1F/S *Cobra* with TOW (1 Mi-24 *Hind* in store)
  MRH 114+: 10 AS550C3 *Fennec*; 6 AW139; 26 Bell 412EP *Twin Huey*; 40+ Mi-17 *Hip* H; 12 SA315B *Lama*; 20 SA319 *Alouette* III
  TPT 76: **Medium** 36: 31 SA330 *Puma*; 4 Mi-171; 1 Mi-172; **Light** 40: 17 AS350B3 *Ecureuil* (SAR); 5 Bell 205 (UH-1H *Iroquois*); 5 Bell 205A-1 (AB-205A-1); 13 Bell 206B *Jet Ranger* II
  TRG 10 Hughes 300C
UAV • ISR • Light *Bravo*; *Jasoos*; *Vector*
AD
  SAM
    SP some M113 with RBS-70
    MANPAD Mk1/Mk2; FIM-92A *Stinger*; HN-5A; *Mistral*; RBS-70
  GUNS • TOWED 1,933: **14.5mm** 981; **35mm** 248 GDF-002/GDF-005 (with 134 *Skyguard* radar units); **37mm** 310 Type-55 (M-1939)/Type-65; **40mm** 50 L/60; **57mm** 144 Type-59 (S-60); **85mm** 200 Type-72 (M-1939) KS-12
RADAR • LAND AN/TPQ-36 *Firefinder* (arty, mor); RASIT (veh, arty); SLC-2
MSL
  STRATEGIC
    MRBM ε30 *Ghauri/Ghauri* II (*Hatf*-5); some *Shaheen*-2 (*Hatf*-6 - in test)
    SRBM ε30 *Ghaznavi* (*Hatf*-3 – PRC M-11)/*Shaheen*-1 (*Hatf*-4); some *Abdali* (*Hatf*-2)
    LACM some *Babur* (*Hatf*-7)
  TACTICAL • SRBM 105 *Hatf*-1
ARV 117+: 65 Type-653; *Al-Hadeed*; 52 M88A1; T-54/T-55
VLB M47M; M48/60
MW *Aardvark* Mk II

Navy 23,800 (incl ε3,200 Marines and ε2,000 Maritime Security Agency (see Paramilitary))

EQUIPMENT BY TYPE
SUBMARINES • TACTICAL 8
  SSK 5:
    2 *Hashmat* (FRA *Agosta* 70) with 4 single 533mm ASTT with F17P HWT/UGM-84 *Harpoon* AShM
    3 *Khalid* (FRA *Agosta* 90B – 1 with AIP) with 4 single 533mm ASTT with F17 Mod 2 HWT/SM-39 *Exocet* AShM
  SSI 3 MG110 (SF delivery) each with 2 single 533mm TT

PRINCIPAL SURFACE COMBATANTS • FRIGATES 10
FFGHM 4 *Sword* (F-22P) with 2 quad lnchr with C-802A AShM, 1 octuple lnchr with HQ-7 SAM, 2 triple 324mm ASTT with Mk 46 LWT, 2 sextuple Type 87 A/S mor, 1 Type 730B CIWS, 1 76mm gun (capacity 1 Z-9C *Haitun* hel)
FFGH 2:
  1 *Tariq* (UK *Amazon*) with 2 twin Mk141 lnchr with RGM-84D *Harpoon* AShM, 2 triple 324mm ASTT with Mk 46 LWT, 1 *Phalanx* Block 1B CIWS, 1 114mm gun (capacity 1 hel)
  1 *Tariq* (UK *Amazon*) with 2 quad Mk141 lnchr with RGM-84D *Harpoon* AShM, 2 single 400mm TT with TP 45 LWT, 1 *Phalanx* Block 1B CIWS, 1 114mm gun (capacity 1 hel)
FFHM 3 *Tariq* (UK *Amazon*) with 1 sextuple lnchr with LY-60 (*Aspide*) SAM, 2 single 400mm TT with TP 45 LWT, 1 *Phalanx* Block 1B CIWS, 1 114mm gun (capacity 1 hel)
FFH 1 *Alamgir* (US *Oliver Hazard Perry*) with 2 triple 324mm ASTT with Mk46 LWT, 1 *Phalanx* CIWS, 1 76mm gun
PATROL AND COASTAL COMBATANTS 18
PCG 2 *Azmat* (PRC *Houjian* mod) with 2 quad lnchr with C-802A AShM, 1 AK630 CIWS
PBFG 2 *Zarrar* (33) with 4 single each with RGM-84 *Harpoon* AShM
PBG 4:
  2 *Jalalat* with 2 twin lnchr with C-802 (CSS-N-8 *Saccade*) AShM
  2 *Jurrat* with 2 twin lnchr with C-802 (CSS-N-8 *Saccade*) AShM
PBF 2 *Kaan* 15
PB 6: 1 *Larkana*; 1 *Rajshahi*; 4 LCP
MINE WARFARE • MINE COUNTERMEASURES
MHC 3 *Munsif* (FRA *Eridan*)
AMPHIBIOUS
LANDING CRAFT • UCAC 4 Griffon 2000
LOGISTICS AND SUPPORT 17
AGS 1 *Behr Paima*
AOL 2 *Madagar*
AORH 2:
  1 *Fuqing* with 1 *Phalanx* CIWS (capacity 1 SA319 *Alouette* III hel)
  1 *Moawin* with 1 *Phalanx* CIWS (capacity 1 *Sea King* Mk45 ASW hel)
AOT 3: 1 *Attock*; 2 *Gwadar*
AXS 1
YM 1 *Behr Kusha*
YTM 7

Marines ε3,200
FORCES BY ROLE
SPECIAL FORCES
  1 cdo gp
MANOEUVRE
  Amphibious
  3 mne bn
COMBAT SUPPORT
  1 AD bn

Naval Aviation
AIRCRAFT 10 combat capable
  ASW 10: 3 *Atlantic*; 7 P-3C *Orion*
  MP 6 F-27-200 MPA
  TPT 3: **Light** 2 ATR-72-500 (MP); **PAX** 1 Hawker 850XP
HELICOPTERS
  ASW 12: 5 *Sea King* Mk45; 7 Z-9C *Haitun*
  MRH 6 SA319B *Alouette* III
MSL • AShM AM-39 *Exocet*

Air Force 70,000
3 regional comds: Northern (Peshawar), Central (Sargodha), Southern (Masroor). The Composite Air Tpt Wg, Combat Cadres School and PAF Academy are Direct Reporting Units.
FORCES BY ROLE
FIGHTER
  2 sqn with F-7P/FT-7P *Skybolt*
  3 sqn with F-7PG/FT-7PG *Airguard*
  1 sqn with F-16A/B MLU *Fighting Falcon*
  1 sqn with F-16A/B ADF *Fighting Falcon*
  1 sqn with *Mirage* IIID/E (IIIOD/EP)
FIGHTER/GROUND ATTACK
  2 sqn with JF-17 *Thunder* (FC-1)
  1 sqn with F-16C/D Block 52 *Fighting Falcon*
  3 sqn with *Mirage* 5 (5PA)
ANTI SURFACE WARFARE
  1 sqn with *Mirage* 5PA2/5PA3 with AM-39 *Exocet* AShM
ELECTRONIC WARFARE/ELINT
  1 sqn with *Falcon* 20F
AIRBORNE EARLY WARNING & CONTROL
  1 sqn with Saab 2000; Saab 2000 *Erieye*
  1 sqn with ZDK-03
SEARCH & RESCUE
  1 sqn with Mi-171Sh (SAR/liaison)
  6 sqn with SA316 *Alouette* III
TANKER
  1 sqn with Il-78 *Midas*
TRANSPORT
  1 sqn with C-130B/E *Hercules*; CN-235M-220; L-100-20
  1 VIP sqn with B-707; Cessna 560XL *Citation Excel*; CN-235M-220; F-27-200 *Friendship*; *Falcon* 20E; Gulfstream IVSP
  1 (comms) sqn with EMB-500 *Phenom* 100; Y-12 (II)
TRAINING
  1 OCU sqn with F-7P/FT-7P *Skybolt*
  1 OCU sqn with *Mirage* III/*Mirage* 5
  1 OCU sqn with F-16A/B MLU *Fighting Falcon*
  2 sqn with K-8 *Karakorum**
  2 sqn with MFI-17
  2 sqn with T-37C *Tweet*
AIR DEFENCE
  1 bty with CSA-1 (SA-2 *Guideline*); 9K310 *Igla*-1 (SA-16 *Gimlet*)
  6 bty with *Crotale*
  10 bty with SPADA 2000
EQUIPMENT BY TYPE
AIRCRAFT 450 combat capable
  FTR 211: 50 F-7PG *Airguard*; 74 F-7P *Skybolt*; 24 F-16A MLU *Fighting Falcon*; 21 F-16B MLU *Fighting Falcon*; 9

F-16A ADF *Fighting Falcon*; 4 F-16B ADF *Fighting Falcon*; 21 FT-7; 6 FT-7PG; 2 *Mirage* IIIB
FGA 190: 12 F-16C Block 52 *Fighting Falcon*; 6 F-16D Block 52 *Fighting Falcon*; 49 JF-17 *Thunder* (FC-1); 7 *Mirage* IIID (*Mirage* IIIOD); 63 *Mirage* IIIE (IIIEP); 40 *Mirage* 5 (5PA)/5PA2; 3 *Mirage* 5D (5DPA)/5DPA2; 10 *Mirage* 5PA3 (ASuW)
ISR 10 *Mirage* IIIR* (*Mirage* IIIRP)
ELINT 2 *Falcon* 20F
AEW&C 3: 1 Saab 2000 *Erieye* (2 more non-op); 2 ZDK-03
TKR 4 Il-78 *Midas*
TPT 33: **Medium** 16: 5 C-130B *Hercules*; 10 C-130E *Hercules*; 1 L-100-20; **Light** 12: 1 Cessna 560XL *Citation Excel*; 4 CN-235M-220; 4 EMB-500 *Phenom* 100; 1 F-27-200 *Friendship*; 2 Y-12 (II); **PAX** 5: 1 B-707; 1 *Falcon* 20E; 2 Gulfstream IVSP; 1 Saab 2000
TRG 143: 39 K-8 *Karakorum**; 80 MFI-17B *Mushshak*; 24 T-37C *Tweet*
HELICOPTERS
  MRH 15 SA316 *Alouette* III
  TPT • **Medium** 4 Mi-171Sh
AD • **SAM** 190+
  TOWED 190: 6 CSA-1 (SA-2 *Guideline*); 144 *Crotale*; ε40 SPADA 2000
  MANPAD 9K310 *Igla*-1 (SA-16 *Gimlet*)
RADAR • **LAND** 6+: 6 AR-1 (AD radar low level); some *Condor* (AD radar high level); some FPS-89/100 (AD radar high level); MPDR 45/MPDR 60/MPDR 90 (AD radar low level); Type-514 (AD radar high level)
MSL
  ASM: AGM-65 *Maverick*; CM-400AKG (reported); *Raptor* II
  AShM AM-39 *Exocet*
  LACM *Ra'ad* (in test)
  ARM MAR-1
  AAM • **IR** AIM-9L/P *Sidewinder*; U-Darter; PL-5; **SARH** Super 530; **ARH** PL-12 (SD-10 – likely on order for the JF-17); AIM-120C AMRAAM

Paramilitary up to 304,000 active

Coast Guard
EQUIPMENT BY TYPE
PATROL AND COASTAL COMBATANTS 5
  PBF 4
  PB 1

Frontier Corps up to 65,000 (reported)
Ministry of Interior
FORCES BY ROLE
MANOEUVRE
  Reconnaissance
  1 armd recce sqn
  Other
  11 paramilitary regt (total: 40 paramilitary bn)
EQUIPMENT BY TYPE
APC (W) 45 UR-416

Maritime Security Agency ε2,000
EQUIPMENT BY TYPE
PRINCIPAL SURFACE COMBATANTS 1
  DESTROYERS • **DD** 1 *Nazim* (ex-US *Gearing*) with 2 triple 324mm ASTT, 1 twin 127mm gun
PATROL AND COASTAL COMBATANTS 15
  PCC 4 *Barkat*
  PBF 5
  PB 6: 2 *Subqat* (PRC *Shanghai* II); 1 *Sadaqat* (ex-PRC *Huangfen*); 3 *Guns*

National Guard 185,000
Incl Janbaz Force; Mujahid Force; National Cadet Corps; Women Guards

Northern Light Infantry ε12,000
FORCES BY ROLE
MANOEUVRE
  Other
  3 paramilitary bn

Pakistan Rangers up to 40,000
Ministry of Interior

DEPLOYMENT

CENTRAL AFRICAN REPUBLIC
UN • UNOCI 324; 1 inf bn(-)

CÔTE D'IVOIRE
UN • UNOCI 1,393; 12 obs; 1 inf bn; 1 engr coy; 1 tpt coy

DEMOCRATIC REPUBLIC OF THE CONGO
UN • MONUSCO 3,745; 38 obs; 3 mech inf bn; 1 inf bn; 1 hel sqn

LIBERIA
UN • UNMIL 908; 6 obs; 1 inf bn; 1 engr coy; 1 fd hospital

SUDAN
UN • UNAMID 1,301; 5 obs; 1 inf bn, 2 engr coy; 1 med pl

WESTERN SAHARA
UN • MINURSO 9 obs

FOREIGN FORCES
Figures represent total numbers for UNMOGIP mission in India and Pakistan
Chile 2 obs
Croatia 7 obs
Finland 6 obs
Ghana 1 obs
Italy 4 obs
Korea, Republic of 7 obs
Philippines 4 obs
Sweden 5 obs
Switzerland 3 obs
Thailand 3 obs
Uruguay 1 obs

Papua New Guinea PNG

Papua New Guinea Kina K		2013	2014	2015
GDP	K	34.6bn	39.8bn	
	US$	15.4bn	16.1bn	
per capita	US$	2,098	2,138	
Growth	%	5.5	5.8	
Inflation	%	5.0	5.3	
Def bdgt [a]	K	186m	246m	
	US$	83m	99m	
US$1=K		2.24	2.48	

[a] Includes defence allocations to the Public Sector Development Programme (PSDP), including funding to the Defence Division and the Defence Production Division.

Population	6,552,730					
Age	0–14	15–19	20–24	25–29	30–64	65 plus
Male	17.8%	5.3%	4.6%	4.0%	17.3%	2.1%
Female	17.2%	5.2%	4.5%	3.9%	16.2%	1.9%

Capabilities

In light of chronic funding problems, since 1999 the government has reduced the size of the Defence Force to its current strength of roughly 1,600 personnel. This compact force includes small air and naval elements and receives financial and training support from Australia and, to a lesser extent, China, France, Germany and New Zealand. Although it has engaged in internal security operations and minor regional deployments, the force would be stretched to provide comprehensive border security, let alone defend national territory, without substantial Australian support. In February 2013, the defence minister announced plans to increase personnel strength to 10,000. Though this ambition was widely criticised as unrealistic, the Defence White Paper of December 2013 confirmed this expansion as a long-term plan, to be achieved by 2030, with a force of 5,000 (including 1,000 reservists) planned for 2017. This substantial increase in strength will require an increase in defence spending from 1.4% in 2013 to 3% in 2017. However, the white paper also noted that the main external security challenges were 'non-traditional' rather than from other states, emphasising the particular need to improve capacity as a humanitarian-assistance and disaster-relief 'first responder'.

ACTIVE 1,900 (Army 1,600 Maritime Element 200 Air 100)

ORGANISATIONS BY SERVICE

Army ε1,600
FORCES BY ROLE
MANOEUVRE
  Light
  2 inf bn
COMBAT SUPPORT
  1 engr bn
  1 EOD unit
  1 sigs sqn
EQUIPMENT BY TYPE
ARTY • MOR 3+: 81mm; 120mm 3

Maritime Element ε200
1 HQ located at Port Moresby
EQUIPMENT BY TYPE
PATROL AND COASTAL COMBATANTS • PB 4 *Rabaul* (*Pacific*)
AMPHIBIOUS • LANDING SHIPS • LSM 2 *Salamaua* (ex-AUS *Balikpapan*)

Air Force ε100
FORCES BY ROLE
TRANSPORT
  1 sqn with CN-235M-100; IAI-201 *Arava*
TRANSPORT HELICOPTER
  1 sqn with Bell 205 (UH-1H *Iroquois*)†
EQUIPMENT BY TYPE
AIRCRAFT • TPT • Light 5: 2 CN-235M-100; 3 IAI-201 *Arava*
HELICOPTERS • TPT • Light 7: 4 Bell 205 (UH-1H *Iroquois*)†; 2 Bell 412 (leased); 1 Bell 212 (leased)

DEPLOYMENT

SOUTH SUDAN
UN • UNMISS 1 obs

FOREIGN FORCES

Australia 38; 1 trg unit; 1 LSD

Philippines PHL

Philippine Peso P		2013	2014	2015
GDP	P	11.5tr	12.7tr	
	US$	272bn	290bn	
per capita	US$	2,791	2,913	
Growth	%	7.2	6.2	
Inflation	%	2.9	4.5	
Def bdgt [a]	P	87.8bn	89.5bn	116bn
	US$	2.1bn	2.09bn	
FMA (US)	US$	27m	50m	40m
US$1=P		42.45	44.00	

[a] Excludes military pensions

Population	107,668,231					
Age	0–14	15–19	20–24	25–29	30–64	65 plus
Male	17.3%	5.1%	4.7%	4.3%	16.8%	1.9%
Female	16.7%	4.9%	4.5%	4.2%	17.2%	2.5%

Capabilities

The Philippines' armed forces, particularly the army and marines, are deployed extensively in an internal-security role in the face of continuing challenges from the Abu Sayyaf Group and other Muslim insurgents in the country's south, and across the country in a continuing, if low-key, counter-insurgency campaign against the communist New People's Army. Until the withdrawal of the US military presence in 1992, the Philippines had largely relied on Washington to provide external defence, and since then perennially low defence budgets have thwarted efforts to develop any significant capacity for conventional war fighting or deterrence. While the government has promised, since 2011, that it will defend its South China Sea claims more strongly in the face of Chinese pressure, military-modernisation budgets have consistently failed to provide the resources needed to fulfil procurement plans or to refurbish second-hand equipment, such as the F-16 combat aircraft that the air force has sought to procure. Though the armed forces have benefited from minor purchases of new equipment such as advanced jet trainers, as well as the transfer of surplus US helicopters and coast-guard cutters, it remains unlikely that the Philippines will be able to provide more than a token national capability to defend its maritime claims.

ACTIVE 125,000 (Army 86,000 Navy 24,000 Air 15,000) Paramilitary 40,500

RESERVE 131,000 (Army 100,000 Navy 15,000 Air 16,000) Paramilitary 50,000 (to age 49)

ORGANISATIONS BY SERVICE

Army 86,000
5 Area Unified Comd (joint service), 1 National Capital Region Comd
FORCES BY ROLE
SPECIAL FORCES
  1 spec ops comd (1 Scout Ranger regt, 1 SF regt, 1 lt reaction bn)
MANOEUVRE
  Mechanised
  1 lt armd div with (2 mech bde (total: 3 lt armd sqn; 7 armd cav tp; 4 mech inf bn; 1 cbt engr coy; 1 avn bn; 1 cbt engr coy, 1 sigs coy))
  Light
  10 div (each: 3 inf bde; 1 arty bn, 1 int bn, 1 sigs bn)
  Other
  1 (Presidential) gd gp
COMBAT SUPPORT
  1 arty regt HQ
  5 engr bde
EQUIPMENT BY TYPE
LT TK 7 *Scorpion*
AIFV 36: 2 YPR-765; 34 M113A1 FSV
APC 299
  APC (T) 76: 6 ACV300; 70 M113
  APC (W) 223: 77 LAV-150 *Commando*; 146 *Simba*

ARTY 254+
  TOWED 214: **105mm** 204 M101/M102/M-26/M-56 **155mm** 10 M114/M-68
  MOR 40+: **81mm** M-29; **107mm** 40 M-30
AT • RCL 75mm M20; **90mm** M67; **106mm** M40A1
AIRCRAFT
  TPT • Light 4: 1 Beech 80 *Queen Air*; 1 Cessna 170; 1 Cessna 172; 1 Cessna P206A
UAV • ISR • Medium *Blue Horizon*
ARV ACV-300; *Samson*; M578

Navy 24,000
EQUIPMENT BY TYPE
PRINCIPAL SURFACE COMBATANTS • FRIGATES
  FF 1 *Rajah Humabon* (ex-US *Cannon*) with 3 76mm gun
PATROL AND COASTAL COMBATANTS 68
  PSOH 2 *Gregorio del Pilar* (ex-US *Hamilton*) with 1 76mm gun, (capacity 1 Bo 105)
  PCF 1 *General Mariano Alvares* (ex-US *Cyclone*)
  PCO 11:
    3 *Emilio Jacinto* (ex-UK *Peacock*) with 1 76mm gun
    6 *Miguel Malvar* (ex-US) with 1 76mm gun
    2 *Rizal* (ex-US *Auk*) with 2 76mm gun
  PBF 16: 3 *Conrado Yap* (ex-ROK *Sea Hawk*); 7 *Tomas Batilo* (ex-ROK *Chamsuri*); 6 MPAC
  PB 32: 2 *Aguinaldo*; 22 *Jose Andrada*; 2 *Kagitingan*; 2 Point (ex-US); 4 *Swift* Mk3 (ex-US)
  PBR 6 Silver Ships
AMPHIBIOUS
  LANDING SHIPS • LST 5:
    2 *Bacolod City* (US *Besson*) with 1 hel landing platform (capacity 32 tanks; 150 troops)
    3 *Zamboanga del Sur* (capacity 16 tanks; 200 troops)
  LANDING CRAFT 30: 12 LCU; 2 LCVP; 16 LCM
LOGISTICS AND SUPPORT 18: **AFD** 4; **AK** 1; **AOL** 2; **AOT** 3; **AP** 1; **AR** 1; **AWT** 2; **YTL** 3; **YTM** 1

Naval Aviation
AIRCRAFT • TPT • Light 6: 4 BN-2A *Defender*; 2 Cessna 177 *Cardinal*
HELICOPTERS • TPT 11: **Medium** 4 Mi-171Sh; **Light** 7: 3 AW109; 4 Bo-105

Marines 8,300
FORCES BY ROLE
MANOEUVRE
  Amphibious
  4 mne bde (total: 12 mne bn)
COMBAT SUPPORT
  1 CSS bde (6 CSS bn)
EQUIPMENT BY TYPE
APC (W) 42: 19 LAV-150 *Commando*; 23 LAV-300
AAV 59: 4 LVTH-6†; 55 LVTP-7
ARTY 31+
  TOWED 105mm 31: 23 M101; 8 M-26
  MOR 107mm M-30

Air Force 15,000
FORCES BY ROLE
FIGHTER
  1 sqn with S-211*

GROUND ATTACK
1 sqn with OV-10A/C Bronco*
ISR
1 sqn with Turbo Commander 690A
SEARCH & RESCUE
4 (SAR/Comms) sqn with Bell 205 (UH-1M Iroquois); AUH-76
TRANSPORT
1 sqn with C-130B/H Hercules; L-100-20
1 sqn with N-22B Nomad; N-22SL Searchmaster
1 sqn with F-27-200 MPA; F-27-500 Friendship
1 VIP sqn with F-28 Fellowship
TRAINING
1 sqn with SF-260F/TP
1 sqn with T-41B/D/K Mescalero
ATTACK HELICOPTER
1 sqn with MD-520MG
TRANSPORT HELICOPTER
1 sqn with AUH-76
1 sqn with W-3 Sokol
4 sqn with Bell 205 (UH-1H Iroquois)
1 (VIP) sqn with Bell 412EP Twin Huey; S-70A Black Hawk (S-70A-5)
EQUIPMENT BY TYPE
AIRCRAFT 22 combat capable
MP 2: 1 F-27-200 MPA; 1 N-22SL Searchmaster
ISR 10 OV-10A/C Bronco*
TPT 9 Medium 5: 1 C-130B Hercules; 3 C-130H Hercules; 1 L-100-20; Light 3: 1 F-27-500 Friendship; 1 N-22B Nomad; 1 Turbo Commander 690A; PAX 1 F-28 Fellowship (VIP)
TRG 40: 12 S-211*; 8 SF-260F; 10 SF-260TP; 10 T-41B/D/K Mescalero
HELICOPTERS
MRH 27: 8 W-3 Sokol; 3 AUH-76; 3 Bell 412EP Twin Huey; 2 Bell 412HP Twin Huey; 11 MD-520MG
TPT 44: Medium 1 S-70A Black Hawk (S-70A-5); Light 43 Bell 205 (UH-1H Iroquois) (17 more due for delivery by end-2014)
UAV • ISR • Medium 2 Blue Horizon II

Paramilitary

Philippine National Police 40,500
Department of Interior and Local Government. 15 regional & 73 provincial comd. 62,000 auxiliaries.
EQUIPMENT BY TYPE
PATROL AND COASTAL COMBATANTS • PB 14 : 10 Rodman 101; 4 Rodman 38
AIRCRAFT
TPT • Light 5: 2 BN-2 Islander; 3 Lancair 320

Coast Guard
EQUIPMENT BY TYPE
PATROL AND COASTAL COMBATANTS 58
PCO 5: 4 San Juan; 1 Balsam
PCC 2 Tirad
PB 40: 3 De Haviland; 4 Ilocos Norte; 1 Palawan; 12 PCF 50 (US Swift Mk1/2); 10 PCF 46; 10 PCF 65 (US Swift Mk3)
PBR 11

AMPHIBIOUS • LANDING CRAFT 2
LCM 1
LCVP 1
LOGISTICS AND SUPPORT • ABU 3
HELICOPTERS 3 SAR

Citizen Armed Force Geographical Units
50,000 reservists
MANOEUVRE
Other
56 militia bn (part-time units which can be called up for extended periods)

DEPLOYMENT

CÔTE D'IVOIRE
UN • UNOCI 3; 3 obs

HAITI
UN • MINUSTAH 181; 1 HQ coy

INDIA/PAKISTAN
UN • UNMOGIP 4 obs

LIBERIA
UN • UNMIL 111; 2 obs; 1 inf coy

SUDAN
UN • UNISFA 1

FOREIGN FORCES
Brunei IMT 9
Indonesia IMT 9
Malaysia IMT 14
United States US Pacific Command: 320 (JSOTF-P)

Singapore SGP

Singapore Dollar S$		2013	2014	2015
GDP	S$	373bn	385bn	
	US$	298bn	307bn	
per capita	US$	55,182	56,113	
Growth	%	3.9	3.0	
Inflation	%	2.4	1.4	
Def bdgt	S$	12.2bn	12.6bn	
	US$	9.73bn	10bn	
US$1=S$		1.25	1.25	

Population 5,567,301
Ethnic groups: Chinese 76%; Malay 15%; Indian 6%

Age	0–14	15–19	20–24	25–29	30–64	65 plus
Male	6.9%	3.7%	5.1%	5.3%	24.3%	3.9%
Female	6.5%	3.6%	5.4%	5.7%	25.0%	4.6%

Capabilities

The Singaporean armed forces are the best equipped in Southeast Asia, and are organised essentially along Israeli lines; the air force and navy are staffed mainly by professional personnel while, apart from a small core of regulars, the much larger army is based on conscripts and reservists. The services have benefited since the late 1960s from steadily increasing defence spending and the gradual development of a substantial national defence industry capable of producing and modifying equipment for specific requirements. Training is routinely carried out overseas, notably in Australia, Brunei, Taiwan, Thailand and the United States. The armed forces also engage extensively in bilateral and multilateral exercises with regional and international partners, including through the Five Power Defence Arrangements. In lieu of a publicly available strategic outlook or military doctrine, it is widely presumed that the primary role of the armed forces is deterring attacks from within its immediate sub-region or interference with its vital interests. Since the 1990s, Singaporean forces have increasingly become involved in multinational peace-support operations. While these deployments have provided some operational experience, and training and operational readiness are high by international standards, the army's reliance on conscripts and reservists limits its capacity for sustained overseas operations.

ACTIVE 72,500 (Army 50,000 Navy 9,000 Air 13,500)
Paramilitary 75,100
Conscription liability 24 months

RESERVE 312,500 (Army 300,000 Navy 5,000 Air 7,500) **Paramilitary 44,000**
Annual trg to age of 40 for army other ranks, 50 for officers

ORGANISATIONS BY SERVICE

Army 15,000; 35,000 conscript (total 50,000)
FORCES BY ROLE
COMMAND
 3 (combined arms) div HQ
 1 (rapid reaction) div HQ
 3 armd bde HQ
 9 inf bde HQ
 1 air mob bde HQ
 1 amph bde HQ
SPECIAL FORCES
 1 cdo bn
MANOEUVRE
 Reconnaissance
 3 lt armd/recce bn
 Armoured
 1 armd bn
 Mechanised
 6 mech inf bn
 Light
 2 (gds) inf bn
 Other
 2 sy bn
COMBAT SUPPORT
 2 arty bn
 1 STA bn
 2 engr bn

 1 EOD bn
 1 ptn br bn
 1 int bn
 2 ISR bn
 1 CBRN bn
 3 sigs bn
COMBAT SERVICE SUPPORT
 3 med bn
 2 tpt bn
 3 spt bn

Reserves
Activated units form part of divisions and brigades listed above; 1 op reserve div with additional inf bde; People's Defence Force Comd (homeland defence) with 12 inf bn
FORCES BY ROLE
SPECIAL FORCES
 1 cdo bn
MANOEUVRE
 Reconnaissance
 6 lt armd/recce bn
 Mechanised
 6 mech inf bn
 Light
 ε56 inf bn
COMBAT SUPPORT
 ε12 arty bn
 ε8 engr bn
EQUIPMENT BY TYPE
MBT 96 *Leopard* 2SG; (80–100 *Tempest* (upgraded *Centurion*) reported in store)
LT TK ε350 AMX-13 SM1
RECCE 22 AMX-10 PAC 90
AIFV 707+: 22 AMX-10P; 135 AV-81 *Terrex*; 250 IFV-25 *Bionix*; 250 IFV-40/50 *Bionix*; 50+ M113A1/A2 (some with 40mm AGL, some with 25mm gun)
APC 1,395+
 APC (T) 1,100+: 700+ M113A1/A2; 400+ ATTC *Bronco*
 APC (W) 280: 250 LAV-150 *Commando*/V-200 *Commando*; 30 V-100 *Commando*
 PPV 15 *MaxxPro Dash*
ARTY 798+
 SP 155mm 54 SSPH-1 *Primus*
 TOWED 88: **105mm** (37 LG1 in store); **155mm** 88: 18 FH-2000; ε18 *Pegasus*; 52 FH-88
 MRL 227mm 18 M142 HIMARS
 MOR 638+
 SP 90+: **81mm**; **120mm** 90: 40 on *Bronco*; 50 on M113
 TOWED 548: **81mm** 500 **120mm** 36 M-65; **160mm** 12 M-58 *Tampella*
AT • MSL • MANPATS 60: 30 *Milan*; 30 *Spike* MR
 RCL 290: **84mm** ε200 *Carl Gustav*; **106mm** 90 M40A1
UAV • ISR • Light *Skylark*
RADAR • LAND AN/TPQ-36 *Firefinder*; AN/TPQ-37 *Firefinder* (arty, mor); 3 ARTHUR (arty)
AEV 80: 18 CET; 54 FV180; 8 M728
ARV *Bionix*; *Büffel*; LAV-150; LAV-300
VLB *Bionix*; LAB 30; *Leguan*; M2; M3; 12 M60
MW 910-MCV-2; *Trailblazer*

Navy 3,000; 1,000 conscript; ε5,000 active reservists (total 9,000)

EQUIPMENT BY TYPE
SUBMARINES • TACTICAL • SSK 6:
  3 *Challenger* (ex-SWE *Sjoormen*) with 4 single 533mm TT
  1 *Challenger* (ex-SWE *Sjoormen*; trg role) with 4 single 533mm TT
  2 *Archer* (ex-SWE *Västergötland*-class) (AIP fitted) with 6 single 533mm TT for WASS *Black Shark* HWT
PRINCIPAL SURFACE COMBATANTS 6:
  FRIGATES • FFGHM 6 *Formidable* with 2 quad lnchr with RGM-84 *Harpoon* AShM, 4 octuple VLS with *Aster* 15 SAM, 2 triple 324mm ASTT with A244 LWT, 1 76mm gun (capacity 1 S-70B *Sea Hawk* hel)
PATROL AND COASTAL COMBATANTS 35
  CORVETTES • FSGM 6 *Victory* with 2 quad Mk140 lnchr with RGM-84C *Harpoon* AShM, 2 octuple lnchr with *Barak* SAM, 2 triple 324mm ASTT with A244 LWT, 1 76mm gun
  PCO 11 *Fearless* with 2 sextuple *Sadral* lnchr with *Mistral* SAM, 1 76mm gun
  PBF 6
  PB 12
MINE WARFARE • MINE COUNTERMEASURES
  MHC 4 *Bedok*
AMPHIBIOUS
  PRINCIPAL AMPHIBIOUS SHIPS • LPD 4 *Endurance* with 2 twin lnchr with *Mistral* SAM, 1 76mm gun (capacity 2 hel; 4 LCVP; 18 MBT; 350 troops)
  LANDING CRAFT 34 LCU 100 **LCVP**
LOGISTICS AND SUPPORT 2
  ASR 1 *Swift Rescue*
  AX 1

Air Force 13,500 (incl 3,000 conscript)

5 comds
FORCES BY ROLE
FIGHTER/GROUND ATTACK
  1 sqn with F-5S/T *Tiger* II
  1 sqn with F-15SG *Eagle*
  3 sqn with F-16C/D *Fighting Falcon* (some used for ISR with pods)
MARITIME PATROL/TRANSPORT
  1 sqn with F-50
AIRBORNE EARLY WARNING & CONTROL
  1 sqn with G550-AEW
TANKER
  1 sqn with KC-135R *Stratotanker*
TANKER/TRANSPORT
  1 sqn with KC-130B/H *Hercules*; C-130H *Hercules*
TRAINING
  1 (FRA-based) sqn with M-346 *Master*
  4 (US-based) units with AH-64D *Apache*; CH-47D *Chinook*; F-15SG; F-16C/D
  1 (AUS-based) sqn with PC-21
ATTACK HELICOPTER
  1 sqn with AH-64D *Apache*
TRANSPORT HELICOPTER
  1 sqn with CH-47SD *Super D Chinook*
  2 sqn with AS332M *Super Puma*; AS532UL *Cougar*

ISR UAV
  2 sqn with *Searcher* MkII
  1 sqn with *Hermes* 450
AIR DEFENCE
  1 AD bn with *Mistral* opcon Army
  3 AD bn with RBS-70; 9K38 *Igla* (SA-18 *Grouse*) opcon Army
  1 ADA sqn with Oerlikon
  1 AD sqn with MIM-23 HAWK
  1 AD sqn with *Spyder*
  1 radar sqn with radar (mobile)
  1 radar sqn with LORADS
MANOEUVRE
  Other
  4 (field def) sy sqn
EQUIPMENT BY TYPE
AIRCRAFT 126 combat capable
  FTR 29: 20 F-5S *Tiger* II; 9 F-5T *Tiger* II
  FGA 92: 32 F-15SG *Eagle*; 20 F-16C *Fighting Falcon*; 40 F-16D *Fighting Falcon* (incl reserves)
  ATK (4 A-4SU *Super Skyhawk*; 10 TA-4SU *Super Skyhawk* in store)
  MP 5 F-50 *Maritime Enforcer**
  AEW&C 4 G550-AEW
  TKR 5: 1 KC-130H *Hercules*; 4 KC-135R *Stratotanker*
  TKR/TPT 4 KC-130B *Hercules*
  TPT 9: **Medium** 5 C-130H *Hercules* (2 ELINT); **PAX** 4 F-50
  TRG 31: 12 M-346 *Master*; 19 PC-21
HELICOPTERS
  ATK 19 AH-64D *Apache*
  ASW 6 S-70B *Seahawk*
  TPT 51: **Heavy** 16: 6 CH-47D *Chinook*; 10 CH-47SD *Super D Chinook*; **Medium** 30: 18 AS332M *Super Puma* (incl 5 SAR); 12 AS532UL *Cougar*; **Light** 5 EC120B *Colibri* (leased)
UAV • ISR • Medium 45: 5 *Hermes* 450; 40 *Searcher* MkII
AD
  SAM
    SP *Spyder*; *Mistral*; RBS-70; 9K38 *Igla* (SA-18 *Grouse*) (on V-200/M113)
    TOWED *Mistral*; RBS-70; MIM-23 HAWK
    MANPAD 9K38 *Igla* (SA-18 *Grouse*)
  GUNS 34
    SP 20mm GAI-C01
    TOWED 34 20mm GAI-C01; 35mm 34 GDF (with 25 *Super-Fledermaus* fire control radar)
MSL • TACTICAL
  ASM: AGM-65B/G *Maverick*; *Hellfire*
  AShM AGM-84 *Harpoon*; AM-39 *Exocet*
  ARM AGM-45 *Shrike*
  AAM • IR AIM-9N/P *Sidewinder*; *Python* 4 (reported); **IIR** AIM-9X *Sidewinder*; **SARH** AIM-7P *Sparrow*; **ARH** (AIM-120C AMRAAM in store in US)

Paramilitary 19,900 active

Civil Defence Force 5,600 (incl conscripts); 500 auxiliaries; (total 6,100)

Singapore Police Force (including Coast Guard) 8,500; 3,500 conscript (total 12,000)

EQUIPMENT BY TYPE
PATROL AND COASTAL COMBATANTS 99
PBF 78: 25 *Ray*; 11 *Sailfish*; 10 *Shark*; 32 other
PB 21: 19 *Amberjack*; 2 *Manta Ray*

Singapore Gurkha Contingent (under police) 1,800
FORCES BY ROLE
MANOEUVRE
Other
6 paramilitary coy

Cyber
The Singapore Ministry of Defence has long identified the potential damage that could be caused by cyber attacks, with this concern perhaps more acute following its adoption of the Integrated Knowledge-based Command-and-Control (IKC2) doctrine, designed to aid the transition of Singapore's Armed Forces to a 'third-generation' force. Meanwhile, Singapore established the Singapore Infocomm Technology Security Authority (SITSA) on 1 October 2009, as a division within the Internal Security Department of the Ministry of Home Affairs. Its main responsibilities will be dealing with cyber terrorism and cyber espionage, as well as operational IT security development.

DEPLOYMENT

AUSTRALIA
2 trg schools – 1 with 12 AS332 *Super Puma*/AS532 *Cougar* (flying trg) located at Oakey; 1 with PC-21 (flying trg) located at Pearce. Army: prepositioned AFVs and heavy equipment at Shoalwater Bay training area.

BRUNEI
1 trg camp with inf units on rotation; 1 hel det with AS332 *Super Puma*

FRANCE
200: 1 trg sqn with 12 M-346 *Master*

TAIWAN
3 trg camp (incl inf and arty)

THAILAND
1 trg camp (arty, cbt engr)

UNITED STATES
Trg units at Luke AFB (AZ) with F-16C/D; Mountain Home AFB (ID) with F-15SG; AH-64D *Apache* at Marana (AZ); 6+ CH-47D *Chinook* hel at Grand Prairie (TX)

FOREIGN FORCES
United States US Pacific Command: 180; 1 naval spt facility at Changi naval base; 1 USAF log spt sqn at Paya Lebar air base

Sri Lanka LKA

Sri Lankan Rupee Rs		2013	2014	2015
GDP	Rs	8.67tr	9.63tr	
	US$	66.7bn	71.6bn	
per capita	US$	3,204	3,414	
Growth	%	7.3	7.0	
Inflation	%	6.9	3.8	
Def bdgt	Rs	237bn	241bn	253bn
	US$	1.82bn	1.79bn	
FMA (US)	US$	0.5m	0.45m	
US$1=Rs		130.00	134.55	

[a] Includes all funds allocated to the Ministry of Defence & Urban Development except those disbursed to the following departments: Police, Immigration & Emigration, Registration of Persons, Coast Conservation and Civil Security.

Population 21,866,445

Age	0–14	15–19	20–24	25–29	30–64	65 plus
Male	12.6%	3.7%	3.8%	3.8%	21.2%	3.7%
Female	12.1%	3.6%	3.7%	3.7%	22.9%	5.0%

Capabilities
Internal security was the main focus for Sri Lanka's armed forces during the protracted campaign against the Tamil Tigers (LTTE), and as a result it remains limited in power-projection or symmetric capabilities. Since the defeat of the LTTE, the armed forces have been reorientating to a peace-time internal-security role, amid continuing allegations concerning the conduct of forces in the final push against the LTTE. The army is reducing in size, but overall plans are unclear. Sri Lanka has little capacity for force projection beyond national territory, however it has sent about 1,000 troops on a variety of UN missions. The navy has a littoral-protection capability and is equipped with fast-attack and patrol vessels. It also has experience gained from numerous if limited sea battles with LTTE naval commando units, and experience of coordinating with foreign navies in exercise scenarios. There appears to have been little spending on new equipment since the end of the war, although military support has been provided by China, in an indication of a growing military-to-military relationship.

ACTIVE 160,900 (Army 200,000 Navy 15,000 Air 28,000) **Paramilitary 62,200**

RESERVE 5,500 (Army 1,100 Navy 2,400 Air Force 2,000) **Paramilitary 30,400**

ORGANISATIONS BY SERVICE

Army 140,000; 60,00 active reservists (recalled) (total 200,000)

Regt are bn sized

FORCES BY ROLE
COMMAND
  7 region HQ
  22 div HQ

SPECIAL FORCES
1 indep SF bde
MANOEUVRE
Reconnaissance
3 armd recce regt
Armoured
1 armd bde (-)
Mechanised
1 mech inf bde
Light
65 inf bde
1 cdo bde
Air Manoeuvre
1 air mob bde
COMBAT SUPPORT
7 arty regt
1 MRL regt
8 engr regt
6 sigs regt
EQUIPMENT BY TYPE
MBT 62 T-55AM2/T-55A
RECCE 15 *Saladin*
AIFV 62: 13 BMP-1; 49 BMP-2
APC 211+
 APC (T) 30+: some Type-63; 30 Type-85; some Type-89
 APC (W) 181: 25 BTR-80/BTR-80A; 31 *Buffel*; 20 Type-92; 105 *Unicorn*
ARTY 908
 TOWED 96: **122mm** 20; **130mm** 30 Type-59-I; **152mm** 46 Type-66 (D-20)
 MRL **122mm** 28: 6 KRL-122; 22 RM-70 *Dana*
 MOR 784: **81mm** 520; **82mm** 209; **120mm** 55 M-43
AT • RCL 40: **105mm** ε10 M-65; **106mm** ε30 M40
GUNS **85mm** 8 Type-56 (D-44)
UAV • ISR • Medium 1 *Seeker*
RADAR • LAND 4 AN/TPQ-36 *Firefinder* (arty)
ARV 16 VT-55
VLB 2 MT-55

Navy 15,000 (incl 2,400 recalled reservists)
EQUIPMENT BY TYPE
PATROL AND COASTAL COMBATANTS 131
 PSOH 1 *Sayura* (IND *Vigraha*)
 PCG 2 *Nandimithra* (ISR *Sa'ar 4*) with 3 single lnchr with *Gabriel* II AShM, 1 76mm gun
 PCO 2: 1 *Samadura* (ex-US *Reliance*); 1 *Sagara* (IND *Vikram*)
 PCC 1 *Jayesagara*
 PBF 79: 26 *Colombo*; 2 *Dvora*; 3 *Killer* (ROK); 6 *Shaldag*; 10 *Super Dvora* MkII/III; 5 *Trinity Marine*; 27 *Wave Rider*
 PB 20: 4 *Cheverton*; 2 *Oshadi* (ex-AUS *Bay*); 2 *Prathapa* (PRC mod *Haizhui*); 3 *Ranajaya* (PRC *Haizhui*); 1 *Ranarisi* (PRC mod *Shanghai* II); 5 *Weeraya* (PRC *Shanghai* II); 3 (various)
 PBR 26
AMPHIBIOUS
 LANDING SHIPS • LSM 1 *Shakthi* (PRC *Yuhai*) (capacity 2 tanks; 250 troops)
 LANDING CRAFT 8
  LCM 2
  LCP 3 *Hansaya*
  LCU 2 *Yunnan*
 UCAC 1 M 10 (capacity 56 troops)
LOGISTICS AND SUPPORT 2: 1 **AP**; 1 **AX**

Air Force 28,000 (incl SLAF Regt)
FORCES BY ROLE
FIGHTER
 1 sqn with F-7BS/G; FT-7
FIGHTER/GROUND ATTACK
 1 sqn with MiG-23UB *Flogger* C; MiG-27M *Flogger* J2
 1 sqn with *Kfir* C-2/C-7/TC-2
 1 sqn with K-8 *Karakorum**
TRANSPORT
 1 sqn with An-32B *Cline*; C-130K *Hercules*; Cessna 421C *Golden Eagle*
 1 sqn with Beech B200 *King Air*; Y-12 (II)
TRAINING
 1 wg with PT-6, Cessna 150L
ATTACK HELICOPTER
 1 sqn with Mi-24V *Hind* E; Mi-35P *Hind*
TRANSPORT HELICOPTER
 1 sqn with Mi-17 *Hip* H; Mi-171Sh
 1 sqn with Bell 206A/B (incl basic trg), Bell 212
 1 (VIP) sqn with Bell 212; Bell 412 *Twin Huey*
ISR UAV
 1 sqn with *Blue Horizon*-2
 1 sqn with *Searcher* II
MANOEUVRE
 Other
 1 (SLAF) sy regt
EQUIPMENT BY TYPE
AIRCRAFT 30 combat capable
 FTR 8: 3 F-7BS; 4 F-7GS; 1 FT-7
 FGA 15: 4 *Kfir* C-2; 2 *Kfir* C-7; 2 *Kfir* TC-2; 6 MiG-27M *Flogger* J2; 1 MiG-23UB *Flogger* C (conversion trg)
 TPT 23: **Medium** 2 C-130K *Hercules*; **Light** 21: 5 An-32B *Cline*; 6 Cessna 150L; 1 Cessna 421C *Golden Eagle*; 7 Y-12 (II); 2 Y-12 (IV)
 TRG 14: 7 K-8 *Karakoram**; 7 PT-6
HELICOPTERS
 ATK 11: 6 Mi-24P *Hind*; 3 Mi-24V *Hind* E; 2 Mi-35V *Hind*
 MRH 18: 6 Bell 412 *Twin Huey* (VIP); 2 Bell 412EP (VIP); 10 Mi-17 *Hip* H
 TPT 16: **Medium** 4 Mi-171Sh; **Light** 12: 2 Bell 206A *Jet Ranger*; 2 Bell 206B *Jet Ranger*; 8 Bell 212
UAV • ISR • Medium 2+: some *Blue Horizon*-2; 2 *Searcher* II
AD • GUNS • TOWED 27: **40mm** 24 L/40; **94mm** 3 (3.7in)

Paramilitary ε62,200

Home Guard 13,000

National Guard ε15,000

Police Force 30,200; 1,000 (women) (total 31,200) 30,400 reservists

Ministry of Defence Special Task Force 3,000
Anti-guerrilla unit

Coast Guard n/k
EQUIPMENT BY TYPE
PATROL AND COASTAL COMBATANTS 11
 PBF 8: 1 *Dvora*; 4 *Super Dvora* MkI; 3 *Killer* (ROK)
 PB 2 Simonneau Type-508
 PBR 1

DEPLOYMENT

CENTRAL AFRICAN REPUBLIC
UN • MINUSCA 124; 1 hel sqn

DEMOCRATIC REPUBLIC OF THE CONGO
UN • MONUSCO 2 obs

HAITI
UN • MINUSTAH 861; 1 inf bn

LEBANON
UN • UNIFIL 151; 1 inf coy

SOUTH SUDAN
UN • UNMISS 89; 2 obs; 1 fd hospital

SUDAN
UN • UNISFA 1; 5 obs

WESTERN SAHARA
UN • MINURSO 3 obs

Taiwan (Republic of China) ROC

New Taiwan Dollar NT$		2013	2014	2015
GDP	NT$	14.6tr	15.2tr	
	US$	489bn	505bn	
per capita	US$	20,925	21,572	
Growth	%	2.1	3.5	
Inflation	%	0.8	1.4	
Def bdgt	NT$	307bn	304bn	319bn
	US$	10.3bn	10.1bn	
US$1=NT$		29.77	30.05	

Population 23,359,928
Ethnic groups: Taiwanese 84%; mainland Chinese 14%

Age	0–14	15–19	20–24	25–29	30–64	65 plus
Male	7.2%	3.4%	3.5%	3.6%	26.6%	5.6%
Female	6.7%	3.2%	3.3%	3.5%	26.9%	6.4%

Capabilities

Taiwan's security focus is its relationship with China and attempts to sustain a credible military capability in the light of Beijing's ongoing military recapitalisation. The armed forces are well trained and exercise regularly, though in some equipment areas a historic advantage over the PLA is being or has already been lost. Air and missile defence along with littoral maritime security are procurement drivers. Additional *Patriot* PAC-3 batteries are being acquired, while the air force's F-16A/B combat aircraft are to be upgraded. Efforts to acquire F-16C/Ds have so far been held up by the US. In the maritime domain the introduction of the UGM-84L *Harpoon* for its two diesel-electric submarines will provide a greater anti-ship capability. The fixed-wing ASW role has been transferred from the navy to the air force. The army continues to take delivery of the AH-64E *Apache* attack helicopter, 30 of which have so far been ordered. As part of force-reduction plans, Taiwan is to phase out conscription, though the end date for this has been put back to 2017.

ACTIVE 290,000 (Army 200,000 Navy 45,000 Air 45,000) **Paramilitary 17,000**
Conscript liability 12 months

RESERVE 1,657,000 (Army 1,500,000 Navy 67,000 Air Force 90,000)
Some obligation to age 30

ORGANISATIONS BY SERVICE

Space
EQUIPMENT BY TYPE
SATELLITES • ISR 1 Rocsat-2

Army ε200,000 (incl MP)
FORCES BY ROLE
COMMAND
 3 corps HQ
 5 defence comd HQ
SPECIAL FORCES/AVIATION
 1 SF/avn comd (2 spec ops gp, 2 avn bde)
MANOEUVRE
 Armoured
 4 armd bde
 Mechanised
 3 mech inf bde
 Light
 6 inf bde
COMBAT SUPPORT
 3 arty gp
 1 (coastal defence) AShM bn
 3 engr gp
 3 CBRN gp
 3 sigs gp

Reserves
FORCES BY ROLE
MANOEUVRE
 Light
 21 inf bde
EQUIPMENT BY TYPE
MBT 565: 200 M60A3; 100 M48A5; 265 M48H *Brave Tiger*
LT TK 625 M41/Type-64; (230 M24 *Chaffee* (90mm gun); in store)
RECCE 48+: BIDS (CBRN recce); 48 K216A1 (CBRN recce); KM453 (CBRN recce)
AIFV 225 CM-25 (M113 with 20–30mm cannon)
APC 1,058
 APC (T) 650 M113
 APC (W) 408: ε108 CM-32 *Yunpao*; 300 LAV-150 *Commando*

ARTY 2,254
  SP 492: **105mm** 100 M108; **155mm** 318: 225 M109A2/A5; 48 M44T; 45 T-69; **203mm** 70 M110; **240mm** 4
  TOWED 1,060+: **105mm** 650 T-64 (M101); **155mm** 340+: 90 M59; 250 T-65 (M114); M44; XT-69 **203mm** 70 M115
  COASTAL **127mm** ε50 US Mk32 (reported)
  MRL 330: **117mm** 120 *Kung Feng* VI; **126mm** 210: 60 *Kung Feng* III/*Kung Feng* IV; 150 RT 2000 *Thunder* (KF towed and SP)
  MOR 322+
    SP 162+: **81mm** 72+: M29; 72 M125; **107mm** 90 M106A2
    TOWED **81mm** 160 M29; T-75; **107mm** M30; **120mm** K5; XT-86
  AT • MSL
    SP TOW
    MANPATS *Javelin*; TOW
  RCL 500+: **90mm** M67; **106mm** 500+: 500 M40A1; Type-51
HELICOPTERS
  ATK 96: 67 AH-1W *Cobra*; 29 AH-64E *Apache*
  MRH 38 OH-58D *Kiowa Warrior*
  TPT 84: **Heavy** 8 CH-47SD *Super D Chinook*; **Light** 76 Bell 205 (UH-1H *Iroquois*)
  TRG 29 TH-67 *Creek*
UAV • ISR • **Light** *Mastiff* III
AD
  SAM
    SP 76: 74 FIM-92A *Avenger*; 2 M48 *Chaparral*
    MANPAD FIM-92A *Stinger*
  GUNS 400
    SP **40mm** M42
    TOWED 20: **35mm** 20 GDF-001 (30 systems with 20 guns) **40mm** L/70
MSL • AShM *Ching Feng*
RADAR 1 TPQ-37 *Firefinder*
AEV 18 M9
ARV CM-27/A1; 37 M88A1
VLB 22 M3; M48A5

Navy 45,000
3 district; 1 (ASW) HQ located at Hualien; 1 Fleet HQ located at Tsoying; 1 New East Coast Fleet
EQUIPMENT BY TYPE
SUBMARINES • TACTICAL • SSK 4:
  2 *Hai Lung* with 6 single 533mm TT with SUT HWT; UGM-84L *Harpoon* AShM
  2 *Hai Shih†* (ex-US *Guppy* II - trg role) with 10 single 533mm TT (6 fwd, 4aft) with SUT HWT
PRINCIPAL SURFACE COMBATANTS 26
  CRUISERS • CGHM 4 *Keelung* (ex-US *Kidd*) with 1 quad lnchr with RGM-84L *Harpoon* AShM, 2 twin Mk26 lnchr with SM-2MR SAM, 2 triple Mk32 324mm ASTT with Mk46 LWT, 2 *Phalanx* Block 1B CIWS, 2 127mm gun (capacity 1 S-70 ASW hel)
  FRIGATES 22
    FFGHM 20:
      8 *Cheng Kung* with 2 quad lnchr with *Hsiung Feng* II/III AShM, 1 Mk13 GMLS with SM-1MR SAM, 2 triple 324mm ASTT with Mk 46 LWT, 1 *Phalanx* Block 1B CIWS, 1 76mm gun (capacity 2 S-70C ASW hel)
      6 *Chin Yang* (ex-US *Knox*) with 1 octuple Mk112 lnchr with ASROC/RGM-84C *Harpoon* AShM, 2 triple lnchr with SM-1MR SAM, 2 twin lnchr with SM-1MR SAM, 2 twin 324mm ASTT with Mk 46 LWT, 1 *Phalanx* Block 1B CIWS, 1 127mm gun (capacity 1 MD-500 hel)
      6 *Kang Ding* with 2 quad lnchr with *Hsiung Feng* II AShM, 1 quad lnchr with *Sea Chaparral* SAM, 2 triple 324mm ASTT with Mk 46 LWT, 1 *Phalanx* Block 1B CIWS, 1 76mm gun (capacity 1 S-70C ASW hel)
    FFGH 2:
      2 *Chin Yang* (ex-US *Knox*) with 1 octuple Mk112 lnchr with ASROC/RGM-84C *Harpoon* AShM, 2 twin 324mm ASTT with Mk 46 LWT, 1 *Phalanx* Block 1B CIWS, 1 127mm gun (capacity 1 MD-500 hel)
PATROL AND COASTAL COMBATANTS 51
  PCG 12:
    10 *Jin Chiang* with 1 quad lnchr with *Hsiung Feng* II/III AShM
    2 *Jin Chiang* with 1 quad lnchr with *Hsiung Feng* III AShM, 1 76mm gun
  PBG 31 *Kwang Hua* with 2 twin lnchr with *Hsiung Feng* II AShM
  PBF 8 *Ning Hai*
MINE WARFARE • MINE COUNTERMEASURES 14
  MHC 2 *Yung Jin* (ex-US *Osprey*)
  MSC 8: 4 *Yung Chuan* (ex-US *Adjutant*); 4 *Yung Feng*
  MSO 4 *Yung Yang* (ex-US *Aggressive*)
COMMAND SHIPS • LCC 1 *Kao Hsiung*
AMPHIBIOUS
  PRINCIPAL AMPHIBIOUS SHIPS • LSD 1 *Shiu Hai* (ex-US *Anchorage*) with 2 *Phalanx* CIWS, 1 hel landing platform (capacity either 2 LCU or 18 LCM; 360 troops)
  LANDING SHIPS
    LST 12:
      10 *Chung Hai* (capacity 16 tanks; 200 troops)
      2 *Chung Ho* (ex-US *Newport*) with 1 *Phalanx* CIWS , 1 hel landing platform (capacity 3 LCVP, 400 troops)
  LANDING CRAFT 278: 8 LCU; 100 LCVP; 170 LCM
LOGISTICS AND SUPPORT 37
  AGOR 1 *Ta Kuan*
  AK 1 *Wu Kang* with 1 hel landing platform (capacity 1,400 troops)
  AOE 1 *Wu Yi* with 1 hel landing platform
  ARS 6
  YFD 6
  YTL 10
  YTM 12

Marines 15,000
FORCES BY ROLE
MANOEUVRE
  Amphibious
  3 mne bde
COMBAT SUPPORT
  Some cbt spt unit
EQUIPMENT BY TYPE
AAV 202: 52 AAV-7A1; 150 LVTP-5A1
ARTY • TOWED **105mm**; **155mm**
AT • RCL **106mm**
ARV 2 AAVR-7

Naval Aviation
FORCES BY ROLE
ANTI SUBMARINE WARFARE
3 sqn with S-70C *Seahawk* (S-70C *Defender*)
EQUIPMENT BY TYPE
HELICOPTERS • ASW 20 S-70C *Seahawk* (S-70C *Defender*)

Air Force 55,000
Flying hours   180 hrs/year
FORCES BY ROLE
FIGHTER
3 sqn with *Mirage* 2000-5E/D (2000-5EI/DI)
FIGHTER/GROUND ATTACK
3 sqn with F-5E/F *Tiger* II
6 sqn with F-16A/B *Fighting Falcon*
5 sqn with F-CK-1A/B *Ching Kuo*
ANTI SUBMARINE WARFARE
1 sqn with S-2T *Turbo Tracker*/P-3C *Orion*
ELECTRONIC WARFARE
1 sqn with C-130HE *Tien Gian*
ISR
1 sqn with RF-5E *Tigereye*
AIRBORNE EARLY WARNING & CONTROL
1 sqn with E-2T *Hawkeye*
SEARCH & RESCUE
1 sqn with EC225; S-70C *Black Hawk*
TRANSPORT
2 sqn with C-130H *Hercules*
1 (VIP) sqn with B-727-100; B-737-800; Beech 1900; F-50; S-70C *Black Hawk*
TRAINING
1 sqn with AT-3A/B *Tzu-Chung**
1 sqn with Beech 1900
1 (basic) sqn with T-34C *Turbo Mentor*
EQUIPMENT BY TYPE
AIRCRAFT 485 combat capable
  FTR 288: 87 F-5E/F *Tiger* II (some in store); 145 F-16A/B *Fighting Falcon*; 9 *Mirage* 2000-5D (2000-5DI); 47 *Mirage* 2000-5E (2000-5EI)
  FGA 128 F-CK-1A/B *Ching Kuo*
  ASW 15: 11 S-2T *Tracker*; 4 P-3C *Orion*
  EW 1 C-130HE *Tien Gian*
  ISR 7 RF-5E *Tigereye*
  AEW&C 6 E-2T *Hawkeye*
  TPT 34: **Medium** 20 C-130H *Hercules*; **Light** 10 Beech 1900; **PAX** 4: 1 B-737-800; 3 F-50
  TRG 98: 56 AT-3A/B *Tzu-Chung**; 42 T-34C *Turbo Mentor*
HELICOPTERS
  TPT • Medium 19: 3 EC225; 16 S-70C *Black Hawk*
MSL
  ASM AGM-65A *Maverick*
  AShM AGM-84 *Harpoon*
  ARM *Sky Sword* IIA
  AAM • IR AIM-9J/P *Sidewinder*; R-550 *Magic 2*; *Shafrir*; *Sky Sword* I; **IR/ARH** MICA; **ARH** AIM-120C AMRAAM; *Sky Sword* II
  AD • SAM *Antelope*

Missile Command
FORCES BY ROLE
COMBAT SUPPORT
3 SSM bty with *Hsiung Feng* IIE
AIR DEFENCE
2 AD/SAM gp (total: 13 bty with MIM-23 HAWK; 4 bty with *Patriot* PAC-3; 6 bty with Tien Kung I *Sky Bow*/Tien Kung II *Sky Bow*)
EQUIPMENT BY TYPE
MSL • LACM ε12 *Hsiung Feng* IIE
AD • SAM • TOWED 624+: 24+ *Patriot* PAC-3; 100 MIM-23 HAWK; ε500 *Tien Kung* I *Sky Bow*/*Tien Kung* II *Sky Bow*

Paramilitary 17,000

Coast Guard 17,000
EQUIPMENT BY TYPE
PATROL AND COASTAL COMBATANTS 138
  PSO 7: 2 *Ho Hsing*; 3 *Shun Hu 7*; 2 *Tainan*; 2 *Yilan* with 1 hel landing platform
  PCO 14: 1 *Teh Hsing*; 2 *Kinmen*; 2 *Mou Hsing*; 1 *Shun Hu 1*; 2 *Shun Hu 2/3*; 4 *Taichung*; 2 *Taipei*
  PBF 63 (various)
  PB 34: 1 *Shun Hu 5*; 1 *Shun Hu 6*; 52 (various)

Directorate General (Customs)
EQUIPMENT BY TYPE
PATROL AND COASTAL COMBATANTS 9
  PCO 1 *Yun Hsing*
  PB 8: 4 *Hai Cheng*; 4 *Hai Ying*

Cyber
Although Taiwan has a highly developed civilian IT sector, the Taiwanese government has been relatively slow to exploit this advantage for national-defence purposes. But for the past decade, Taipei has worked on its *Po Sheng* – Broad Victory – C4ISR programme, an all-hazards defence system with a significant defence component located in the Hengshan Command Center, which also houses the Tri-Service Command. The main focus of the military component of this programme is countering PLA IW and EW attacks. Responsible authorities for cyber activity include the National Security Bureau (NSB), the defence ministry, and the Research, Development and Evaluation Commission (RDEC). Among other projects, the Chungshan Institute of Science and Technology (a government R&D house) plans to invest in a project to 'display and confirm' Taiwan's latest 'cyber offensive system' between 2013 and 2015.

FOREIGN FORCES
Singapore 3 trg camp (incl inf and arty)

Thailand THA

Thai Baht b		2013	2014	
GDP	b	11.9tr	12.2tr	
	US$	387bn	380bn	
per capita	US$	5,676	5,550	
Growth	%	2.9	1.0	
Inflation	%	2.2	2.1	
Def bdgt [a]	b	180bn	183bn	193bn
	US$	5.88bn	5.69bn	
FMA (US)	US$	1.2m	1m	1m
US$1=b		30.73	32.19	

[a] Excludes military pensions

Population   67,741,401

Ethnic and religious groups: Thai 75%; Chinese 14%; Muslim 4%

Age	0–14	15–19	20–24	25–29	30–64	65 plus
Male	9.0%	3.8%	3.9%	3.6%	24.7%	4.2%
Female	8.6%	3.6%	3.8%	3.5%	26.0%	5.4%

Capabilities

Thailand's armed forces have benefited from substantially increased funding since reasserting their central political role in a 2006 coup, even under the 2011–14 democratically elected government. Despite increased resources, and other positive indicators such as involvement in multinational exercises and significant international deployments, the armed forces' entanglement in domestic politics has often overshadowed efforts to sustain and modernise operational capability. The May 2014 coup, led by the army commander-in-chief, reinforced the armed forces' political embroilment. Operations against insurgents in the three southernmost provinces continue, but ineffectively the low-intensity war there remains stalemated. Thailand's air force is one of the best equipped and trained in Southeast Asia, and benefits from regular exercises with its US, Australian and Singaporean counterparts. The induction into service of *Gripen* combat aircraft and Saab 340 AEW platforms, which will have data-links to ground-based air defences, naval vessels and army units under the air force's Network Centric plan (due for completion in 2014–15), promises to significantly boost the effectiveness of Thailand's air power.

ACTIVE 360,850 (Army 245,000 Navy 69,850 Air 46,000) **Paramilitary 92,700**
Conscription liability 2 years

RESERVE 200,000 Paramilitary 45,000

ORGANISATIONS BY SERVICE

Army 130,000; ε115,000 conscript (total 245,000)
FORCES BY ROLE
COMMAND
  4 (regional) army HQ
  3 corps HQ
SPECIAL FORCES
  1 SF div
  1 SF regt

MANOEUVRE
  Mechanised
  3 cav div
  1 mech inf div
  Light
  8 inf div
  1 Rapid Reaction force (1 bn per region forming)
  Aviation
  Some hel flt
COMBAT SUPPORT
  1 arty div
  1 ADA div (6 bn)
  1 engr div
COMBAT SERVICE SUPPORT
  4 economic development div
EQUIPMENT BY TYPE
MBT 288: 53 M60A1; 125 M60A3; (50 Type-69 in store); 105 M48A5; 5 T-84 *Oplot*
LT TK 194: 24 M41; 104 *Scorpion* (50 in store); 66 *Stingray*
RECCE 32+: 32 S52 Mk 3; M1114 HMMWV
AIFV 162 BTR-3E1 (incl variants)
APC 1,140
  APC (T) 880: *Bronco*; 430 M113A1/A3; 450 Type-85
  APC (W) 160: 18 *Condor*; 142 LAV-150 *Commando*
  PPV 100 *Reva*
ARTY 2,621
  SP 155mm 26: 6 CAESAR; 20 M109A5
  TOWED 617: **105mm** 340: 24 LG1 MkII; 12 M-56; 200 M101/-Mod; 12 M102; 32 M618A2; 60 L119; **155mm** 277: 90 GHN-45 A1; 48 M114; 118 M198; 21 M-71
  MRL 78: **130mm** 60 Type-85; **302mm** 18 DTI-1
  MOR 1,900+
    SP 33+: **81mm** 21 M125A3; **107mm** M106A3; **120mm** 12 M1064A3
    TOWED 1,867: **81mm**; **107mm**; **120mm**
AT
  MSL
    SP 18+ M901A5 (TOW); 6 BTR-3RK
    MANPATS M47 *Dragon*
  RCL 180: **75mm** 30 M20; **106mm** 150 M40
AIRCRAFT
  TPT • Light 19: 2 Beech 200 *King Air*; 2 Beech 1900C; 1 C-212 *Aviocar*; 10 Cessna A185E (U-17B); 2 ERJ-135LR; 2 *Jetstream* 41
  TRG 33: 11 MX-7-235 *Star Rocket*; 22 T-41B *Mescalero*
HELICOPTERS
  ATK 7 AH-1F *Cobra*
  MRH 13: 8 AS550 *Fennec*; 2 AW139; 3 Mi-17V-5 *Hip* H
  TPT 207: **Heavy** 5 CH-47D *Chinook*; **Medium** 12: 9 UH-60L *Black Hawk*; 3 UH-60M *Black Hawk*; **Light** 190: 94 Bell 205 (UH-1H *Iroquois*); 28 Bell 206 *Jet Ranger*; 52 Bell 212 (AB-212); 16 Enstrom 480B
  TRG 53 Hughes 300C
UAV • ISR • Medium *Searcher*; *Searcher* II
AD • SAM
  SP 8 *Starstreak*
  STATIC *Aspide*
  MANPAD 54 9K338 *Igla*-S (SA-24 *Grinch*)
GUNS 202+
  SP 54: **20mm** 24 M163 *Vulcan*; **40mm** 30 M1/M42 SP

TOWED 148+: **20mm** 24 M167 *Vulcan*; **37mm** 52 Type-74; **40mm** 48 L/70; **57mm** 24+: ε6 Type-59 (S-60); 18+ non-operational
RADAR • LAND AN/TPQ-36 *Firefinder* (arty, mor); RASIT (veh, arty)
ARV 48: 5 BTR-3BR; 22 M88A1; 6 M88A2; 10 M113; 5 Type-653; WZT-4
VLB Type-84
MW Bozena; *Giant Viper*

Reserves
FORCES BY ROLE
COMMAND
1 inf div HQ

Navy 44,000 (incl Naval Aviation, Marines, Coastal Defence); 25,850 conscript (total 69,850)
EQUIPMENT BY TYPE
PRINCIPAL SURFACE COMBATANTS 11
AIRCRAFT CARRIERS • CVH 1:
1 *Chakri Naruebet* with 2 sextuple *Sadral* lnchr with *Mistral* SAM (capacity 6 S-70B *Seahawk* ASW hel)
FRIGATES 10
FFGHM 2:
2 *Naresuan* with 2 quad Mk141 lnchr with RGM-84A *Harpoon* AShM, 1 8 cell Mk41 VLS with RIM-7M *Sea Sparrow* SAM (to be RIM-162 by 2015), 2 triple Mk32 324mm TT, 1 127mm gun (capacity 1 *Super Lynx* 300 hel)
FFGM 4:
2 *Chao Phraya* with 4 twin lnchr with C-802A AShM, 2 twin lnchr with HQ-61 (CSA-N-2) SAM (non-operational), 2 RBU 1200, 2 twin 100mm gun
2 *Kraburi* with 4 twin lnchr with C-802A AShM, 2 twin lnchr with HQ-61 (CSA-N-2) SAM, 2 RBU 1200, 1 twin 100mm gun, 1 hel landing platform
FFGH 2:
2 *Phuttha Yotfa Chulalok* (ex-US *Knox*, leased) with 1 octuple Mk112 lnchr with RGM-84C *Harpoon* AShM/ASROC, 2 twin 324mm ASTT with Mk 46 LWT, 1 *Phalanx* CIWS, 1 127mm gun (capacity 1 Bell 212 (AB-212) hel)
FF 2:
1 *Makut Rajakumarn* with 2 triple 324mm ASTT, 2 114mm gun
1 *Pin Klao* (trg role) with 6 single 324mm ASTT, 3 76mm gun
PATROL AND COASTAL COMBATANTS 83
CORVETTES 7
FSG 2 *Rattanakosin* with 2 quad Mk140 lnchr with RGM-84A *Harpoon* AShM, 1 octuple *Albatros* lnchr with *Aspide* SAM, 2 triple Mk32 324mm ASTT with *Stingray* LWT, 1 76mm gun
FS 5:
3 *Khamronsin* with 2 triple 324mm ASTT with *Stingray* LWT, 1 76mm gun
2 *Tapi* with 2 triple 324mm ASTT with Mk46 LWT, 1 76mm gun
PSO 1 *Krabi* (UK *River* mod) with 1 76mm gun
PCFG 6:
3 *Prabparapak* with 2 single lnchr with *Gabriel* I AShM, 1 triple lnchr with *Gabriel* I AShM, 1 57mm gun

3 *Ratcharit* with 2 twin lnchr with MM-38 *Exocet* AShM, 1 76mm gun
PCOH 2 *Pattani* with 1 76mm gun
PCO 3 *Hua Hin* with 1 76mm gun
PCC 9: 3 *Chon Buri* with 2 76mm gun; 6 *Sattahip* with 1 76mm gun
PBF 4
PB 51: 7 T-11; 4 *Swift*; 3 T-81; 9 T-91; 3 T-111; 3 T-210; 13 T-213; 3 T-227; 3 T-991; 3 T-994
MINE WARFARE • MINE COUNTERMEASURES 17
MCM SPT 1 *Thalang*
MCO 2 *Lat Ya*
MCC 2 *Bang Rachan*
MSR 12
AMPHIBIOUS
PRINCIPAL AMPHIBIOUS SHIPS 1
LPD 1 *Anthong* (SGP *Endurance*) with 1 76mm gun (capacity 2 hel; 19 MBT; 500 troops)
LANDING SHIPS 2
LST 2 *Sichang* with 2 hel landing platform (capacity 14 MBT; 300 troops)
LANDING CRAFT 56
LCU 13: 3 *Man Nok*; 6 *Mataphun* (capacity either 3–4 MBT or 250 troops); 4 *Thong Kaeo*
LCM 24
LCVP 12
LCA 4
LCAC 3 *Griffon* 1000TD
LOGISTICS AND SUPPORT 19
ABU 1
AGOR 1
AGS 2
AOL 6: 1 *Matra* with 1 hel landing platform; 4 *Prong*; 1 *Samui*
AOR 1 *Chula*
AORH 1 *Similan* (capacity 1 hel)
AWT 1
YTL 2
YTM 2
YTR 2

Naval Aviation 1,200
EQUIPMENT BY TYPE
AIRCRAFT 3 combat capable
ASW 2 P-3A *Orion* (P-3T)
ISR 9 *Sentry* O-2-337
MP 1 F-27-200 MPA*
TPT • **Light** 15: 7 Do-228-212*; 2 ERJ-135LR; 2 F-27-400M *Troopship*; 3 N-24A *Searchmaster*; 1 UP-3A *Orion* (UP-3T)
HELICOPTERS
ASW 8: 6 S-70B *Seahawk*; 2 *Super Lynx* 300
MRH 2 MH-60S *Knight Hawk*
TPT 13: **Medium** 2 Bell 214ST (AB-214ST); **Light** 11: 6 Bell 212 (AB-212); 5 S-76B
MSL • AShM AGM-84 *Harpoon*

Marines 23,000
FORCES BY ROLE
COMMAND
1 mne div HQ

MANOEUVRE
  Reconnaissance
  1 recce bn
  Light
  2 inf regt (total: 6 bn)
  Amphibious
  1 amph aslt bn
COMBAT SUPPORT
  1 arty regt (3 fd arty bn, 1 ADA bn)
EQUIPMENT BY TYPE
AIFV 14 BTR-3E1
APC (W) 24 LAV-150 *Commando*
AAV 33 LVTP-7
ARTY • TOWED 48: **105mm** 36 (reported); **155mm** 12 GC-45
AT • MSL 24+
  TOWED 24 HMMWV TOW
  MANPATS M47 *Dragon*; TOW
AD • GUNS 12.7mm 14
ARV 1 AAVR-7

Air Force ε46,000

4 air divs, one flying trg school

Flying hours 100 hrs/year

FORCES BY ROLE
FIGHTER
  2 sqn with F-5E/5F *Tiger II*
  3 sqn with F-16A/B *Fighting Falcon*
FIGHTER/GROUND ATTACK
  1 sqn with Gripen C/D
GROUND ATTACK
  1 sqn with *Alpha Jet**
  1 sqn with AU-23A *Peacemaker*
  1 sqn with L-39ZA *Albatros**
ELINT/ISR
  1 sqn with DA42 MPP *Guardian*; IAI-201 *Arava*
AIRBORNE EARLY WARNING & CONTROL
  1 sqn with Saab 340B; Saab 340 *Erieye*
TRANSPORT
  1 (Royal Flight) sqn with A310-324; A319CJ; B-737-800
  1 sqn with ATR-72; BAe-748
  1 sqn with BT-67; N-22B *Nomad*
  1 sqn with C-130H/H-30 *Hercules*
TRAINING
  1 sqn with L-39ZA *Albatros**
  1 sqn with CT-4A/B *Airtrainer*; T-41D *Mescalero*
  1 sqn with CT-4E *Airtrainer*
  1 sqn with PC-9
TRANSPORT HELICOPTER
  1 sqn with Bell 205 (UH-1H *Iroquois*)
  1 sqn with Bell 412 *Twin Huey*; S-92A
EQUIPMENT BY TYPE
AIRCRAFT 134 combat capable
  FTR 79: 1 F-5B *Freedom Fighter*; 21 F-5E *Tiger II*; 3 F-5F *Tiger II* (F-5E/F being upgraded); 39 F-16A *Fighting Falcon*; 15 F-16B *Fighting Falcon*
  FGA 12: 8 Gripen C; 4 Gripen D
  ATK 17 AU-23A *Peacemaker*
  EW 2 IAI-201TH *Arava*
  ISR 5 DA42 MPP *Guardian*
  AEW&C 2 Saab 340 *Erieye*
  TPT 49: **Medium** 14: 6 C-130H *Hercules*; 6 C-130H-30 *Hercules*; 2 Saab 340B; **Light** 25: 3 ATR-72; 3 Beech 200 *King Air*; 8 BT-67; 1 *Commander* 690; 6 DA42M; 4 N-22B *Nomad*; **PAX** 10: 1 A310-324; 1 A319CJ; 1 B-737-800; 5 BAe-748
  TRG 110: 16 *Alpha Jet**; 13 CT-4A *Airtrainer*; 6 CT-4B *Airtrainer*; 20 CT-4E *Airtrainer*; 27 L-39ZA *Albatros**; 21 PC-9; 7 T-41D *Mescalero*
HELICOPTERS
  MRH 11: 2 Bell 412 *Twin Huey*; 2 Bell 412SP *Twin Huey*; 1 Bell 412HP *Twin Huey*; 6 Bell 412EP *Twin Huey*
  TPT 20: **Medium** 3 S-92A *Super Hawk*; **Light** 17 Bell 205 (UH-1H *Iroquois*)
MSL
  AAM • IR AIM-9B/J *Sidewinder*; *Python* III; **ARH** AIM-120 AMRAAM
  ASM AGM-65 *Maverick*

Paramilitary ε92,700 active

Border Patrol Police 20,000

Marine Police 2,200
EQUIPMENT BY TYPE
PATROL AND COASTAL COMBATANTS 92
  PCO 1 *Srinakrin*
  PCC 2 *Hameln*
  PB 43: 2 *Chasanyabadee*; 3 *Cutlass*; 1 *Sriyanont*; 1 *Yokohama*; 36 (various)
  PBR 46

National Security Volunteer Corps 45,000 – Reserves

Police Aviation 500
EQUIPMENT BY TYPE
AIRCRAFT 6 combat capable
  ATK 6 AU-23A *Peacemaker*
  TPT 16: **Light** 15: 2 CN-235; 8 PC-6 *Turbo-Porter*; 3 SC-7 3M *Skyvan*; 2 Short 330UTT; **PAX** 1 F-50
HELICOPTERS
  MRH 6 Bell 412 *Twin Huey*
  TPT • Light 61: 27 Bell 205A; 14 Bell 206 *Jet Ranger*; 20 Bell 212 (AB-212)

Provincial Police 50,000 (incl est. 500 Special Action Force)

Thahan Phran (Hunter Soldiers) 21,000
Volunteer irregular force
FORCES BY ROLE
MANOEUVRE
  Other
  22 paramilitary regt (total: 275 paramilitary coy)

DEPLOYMENT

Legal provisions for foreign deployment:
Constitution: In addition to the below, government has to ensure no violation of Para. 1 and 2 of Provision 190 of the Constitution of the Kingdom of Thailand, BE 2550
Decision on deployment of troops abroad: Depends on operation. In case of PSO or HADR, cabinet resolution endors-

ing deployment and defence-council concurrence would constitute legislation. Legal provisions for foreign deployment generally under the Defence Act, BE 2551 (2008). Justification for overseas missions is in accordance with following sections of the Act: Provision 37, Art. 4: Minister of Defence has exclusive authority to arrange and deploy armed forces to areas considered appropriate; Provision 38, Art. 4: Employment of armed forces for peace operations shall be endorsed by council of ministers with concurrence of defence council. No terms of reference on 'the foreign deployment of forces for combat operations in [a] conventional war area are stipulated' in the Act, so deployment purpose and operation type should be clearly determined.

CÔTE D'IVOIRE
UN • UNOCI 1; 1 obs

INDIA/PAKISTAN
UN • UNMOGIP 3 obs

SUDAN
UN • UNAMID 6; 9 obs

FOREIGN FORCES
United States US Pacific Command: 300

Timor-Leste TLS

US$		2013	2014	2015
GDP	US$	4.94bn	4.51bn	
per capita	US$	4,142	3,664	
Growth	%	5.41	6.56	
Inflation	%	9.48	2.49	
Def bdgt	US$	67m	69m	72m
FMA (US)	US$		0.3m	0.3m

Population   1,201,542

Age	0–14	15–19	20–24	25–29	30–64	65 plus
Male	21.8%	5.4%	4.6%	3.4%	13.2%	1.8%
Female	20.6%	5.2%	4.6%	3.8%	13.8%	1.9%

Capabilities

The Timor-Leste Defence Force was formed in 2001 from the former Falintil insurgent army. However, it soon became clear that the new force suffered from poor morale and weak discipline. In 2006, these problems culminated in the dismissal of large numbers of personnel who had protested over poor conditions and alleged discrimination on regional lines, which precipitated the collapse of both the defence force and the national police. These circumstances forced the government to call for an international intervention, and a mainly Australian International Stabilisation Force remained in the country until early 2013. Meanwhile, the government has attempted to rebuild the defence force. Long-term plans outlined in the country's Force 2020 document, made public in 2006, call for an expanded defence force, conscription, the establishment of an air component and acquisition of modern weapons. However, these plans were widely criticised as over-ambitious and unrealistic. The Defence Force continues to depend heavily on foreign assistance and training, mainly from Australia, Portugal and Brazil.

ACTIVE 1,330 (Army 1,250 Naval Element 80)

ORGANISATIONS BY SERVICE

Army 1,250
Training began in January 2001 with the aim of deploying 1,500 full-time personnel and 1,500 reservists. Authorities are engaged in developing security structures with international assistance.

FORCES BY ROLE
MANOEUVRE
 Light
  2 inf bn
COMBAT SUPPORT
 1 MP pl
COMBAT SERVICE SUPPORT
 1 log spt coy

Naval Element 80
EQUIPMENT BY TYPE
PATROL AND COASTAL COMBATANTS 7
 PB 7: 2 *Albatros*; 2 *Dili* (ex-ROK); 2 *Shanghai II*; 1 *Kamenassa* (ex-ROK *Chamsuri*)

DEPLOYMENT

SOUTH SUDAN
UN • UNMISS 3 obs

Vietnam VNM

Vietnamese Dong d		2013	2014	2015
GDP	d	3,584tr	4,024tr	
	US$	171bn	188bn	
per capita	US$	1,902	2,073	
Growth	%	5.4	5.5	
Inflation	%	6.6	5.2	
Def bdgt	d	82.7tr	91tr	
	US$	4.03bn	4.26bn	
FMA (US)	US$	95m	10m	10m
US$1=d		21,014.05	21,421.57	

Population   93,421,835

Ethnic groups: Kinh 86%; Tay 2%; Thai 2%; Muang 1%; Khmei 1%; Mong 1%; Nung 1%; Hua 1%; Dao 1%; Other 4%

Age	0–14	15–19	20–24	25–29	30–64	65 plus
Male	12.8%	4.3%	4.9%	4.9%	21.0%	2.2%
Female	11.6%	4.0%	4.6%	4.6%	21.7%	3.5%

Capabilities

Communist Vietnam has a stronger military tradition and more operational experience than any of its Southeast-Asian counterparts. Its defence efforts and its conscript-based armed forces also have broad popular support, particularly in the context of current tensions with China. The end of the Cold War ended Soviet military aid and the armed forces suffered from much-reduced budgets and only limited procurement. With Vietnam's rapid economic growth over the last decade, however, defence spending has increased, and particular efforts have been made to re-equip the navy and air force, apparently with a view to deterring Chinese military pressure in the disputed Spratly Islands. While Vietnam cannot hope to balance China's power on its own, acquisition of a submarine capability during the present decade, with six *Kilo*-class boats ordered from Russia in 2009, may complicate Beijing's naval options, as might an order for more Su-30MK2 combat aircraft, due for delivery by 2015. In its efforts to enhance maritime and air capabilities, Vietnam is now turning to Western defence suppliers, and has ordered *Sigma*-class frigates from the Netherlands. The potential termination of a US arms embargo may also enable the acquisition of advanced maritime-patrol aircraft.

ACTIVE 482,000 (Army 412,000 Navy 40,000 Air 30,000) Paramilitary 40,000

Conscript liability 2 years army and air defence, 3 years air force and navy, specialists 3 years, some ethnic minorities 2 years

RESERVES 5,000,000

ORGANISATIONS BY SERVICE

Army ε412,000
8 Mil Regions (incl capital)
FORCES BY ROLE
COMMAND
    4 corps HQ
SPECIAL FORCES
    1 SF bde (1 AB bde, 1 demolition engr regt)
MANOEUVRE
    Armoured
    6 armd bde
    3 armd regt
    Mechanised
    2 mech inf div
    Light
    23 inf div
COMBAT SUPPORT
    13 arty bde
    1 arty regt
    11 AD bde
    10 engr bde
    1 engr regt
    1 EW unit
    3 sigs bde
    2 sigs regt
COMBAT SERVICE SUPPORT
    9 economic construction div
    1 log regt
    1 med unit
    1 trg regt

Reserve
MANOEUVRE
    Light
    9 inf div
EQUIPMENT BY TYPE
MBT 1,270: 70 T-62; 350 Type-59; 850 T-54/T-55; (45 T-34† in store)
LT TK 620: 300 PT-76; 320 Type-62/Type-63
RECCE 100 BRDM-1/BRDM-2
AIFV 300 BMP-1/BMP-2
APC 1,380
    APC (T) 280: 200 M113 (to be upgraded); 80 Type-63
    APC (W) 1,100 BTR-40/BTR-50/BTR-60/BTR-152
ARTY 3,040+
    SP 30+: **122mm** 2S1; **152mm** 30 2S3; **175mm** M107
    TOWED 2,300 **100mm** M-1944; **105mm** M101/M102; **122mm** D-30/Type-54 (M-1938)/Type-60 (D-74); **130mm** M-46; **152mm** D-20; **155mm** M114
    MRL 710+: **107mm** 360 Type-63; **122mm** 350 BM-21; **140mm** BM-14
    MOR 82mm; 120mm M-43; 160mm M-43
AT • MSL • MANPATS 9K11 *Malyutka* (AT-3 *Sagger*)
    RCL 75mm Type-56; **82mm** Type-65 (B-10); **87mm** Type-51
    GUNS
        SP 100mm SU-100; **122mm** SU-122
        TOWED 100mm T-12 (arty)
AD • SAM • MANPAD 9K32 *Strela-2* (SA-7 *Grail*)‡; 9K310 *Igla-1* (SA-16 *Gimlet*); 9K38 *Igla* (SA-18 *Grouse*)
    GUNS 12,000
        SP 23mm ZSU-23-4
        TOWED 14.5mm/30mm/37mm/57mm/85mm/100mm
MSL • SSM Scud-B/C

Navy ε40,000 (incl ε27,000 Naval Infantry)
EQUIPMENT BY TYPE
SUBMARINES • TACTICAL 4
    SSK 2 *Hanoi* (RUS *Varshavyanka*) with 6 533mm TT with TEST-71ME HWT
    SSI 2 *Yugo*† (DPRK)
PRINCIPAL SURFACE COMBATANTS 2
    FRIGATES • FFGM 2
        2 *Dinh Tien Hoang* (RUS *Gepard* mod) with 2 quad lnchr with Kh-35 *Uran* (SS-N-25 *Switchblade*), 1 Palma lnchr with *Sosna*-R SAM, 2 twin 533mm TT, 1 RBU 6000 *Smerch* 2; 2 AK630 CIWS, 1 76mm gun
PATROL AND COASTAL COMBATANTS 68
    CORVETTES • FSG 6:
        1 BPS-500 with 2 quad lnchr with 3M24 *Uran* (SS-N-25 *Switchblade*) AShM, 9K32 *Strela*-2M (SA-N-5 *Grail*) SAM (manually operated), 2 twin 533mm TT, 1 RBU-1600, 1 AK630 CIWS, 1 76mm gun
        3 *Petya* II (FSU) with 1 quintuple 406mm ASTT, 4 RBU 6000 *Smerch* 2, 2 twin 76mm gun
        2 *Petya* III (FSU) with 1 triple 533mm ASTT, 4 RBU 2500 *Smerch* 1, 2 twin 76mm gun
    PCFGM 8:
        4 *Tarantul* (FSU) with 2 twin lnchr with P-15 *Termit* (SS-N-2D *Styx*) AShM, 1 quad lnchr with 9K32 *Strela*-2M (SA-N-5 *Grail*) SAM (manually operated), 2 AK630 CIWS, 1 76mm gun

4 *Tarantul* V with 4 quad lnchr with 3M24 *Uran* (SS-N-25 *Switchblade*) AShM; 1 quad lnchr with 9K32 *Strela*-2M (SA-N-5 *Grail*) SAM (manually operated), 2 AK630 CIWS, 1 76mm gun
  PCC 9: 6 *Svetlyak* with 1 AK630 CIWS, 1 76mm gun; 3 TT-400TP with 2 AK630 CIWS, 1 76mm gun
  PBFG 8 *Osa* II with 4 single lnchr with P-15 *Termit* AShM
  PBFT 2 *Shershen*† (FSU) with 4 single 533mm TT
  PH 2 *Turya*† with 1 twin 57mm gun
  PHT 3 *Turya*† with 4 single 533mm TT, 1 twin 57mm gun
  PB 26: 2 *Poluchat* (FSU); 14 *Zhuk*†; 4 *Zhuk* (mod); 6 (various)
  PBR 4 *Stolkraft*
MINE WARFARE • MINE COUNTERMEASURES 13
  MSO 2 *Yurka*
  MSC 4 *Sonya*
  MHI 2 *Yevgenya*
  MSR 5 K-8
AMPHIBIOUS
  LANDING SHIPS 8
    LSM 5:
      1 *Polnochny* A† (capacity 6 MBT; 180 troops)
      2 *Polnochny* B† (capacity 6 MBT; 180 troops)
      2 *Nau Dinh*
    LST 3 LST-510-511 (US) (capacity 16 tanks; 200 troops)
  LANDING CRAFT 30: 15 **LCU**; 12 **LCM**; 3 **LCVP**
LOGISTICS AND SUPPORT 30
  AFD 2; **AGS** 1; **AGSH** 1; **AKSL** 18; **AP** 1; **AT** 2; **AWT** 1; **YDT** 2; **YTM** 2

Naval Infantry ε27,000

Navy Air Wing
FORCES BY ROLE
ASW/SAR
  1 regt with EC225; Ka-28 (Ka-27PL) *Helix* A; Ka-32 *Helix* C
EQUIPMENT BY TYPE
AIRCRAFT • TPT • Light 3 DHC-6-400 *Twin Otter*
HELICOPTERS
  ASW 10 Ka-28 *Helix* A
  TPT • Medium 4: 2 EC225; 2 Ka-32 *Helix* C

Air Force 30,000
3 air div, 1 tpt bde
FORCES BY ROLE
FIGHTER
  4 regt with MiG-21bis *Fishbed* L; MiG-21UM *Mongol* B
FIGHTER/GROUND ATTACK
  1 regt with Su-22M3/M4/UM *Fitter* (some ISR)
  1 regt with Su-27SK/Su-27UBK *Flanker*
  1 regt with Su-27SK/Su-27UBK *Flanker*; Su-30MK2
  1 regt with Su-30MK2
TRANSPORT
  2 regt with An-2 *Colt*; An-26 *Curl*; Bell 205 (UH-1H *Iroquois*); Mi-8 *Hip*; Mi-17 *Hip* H; M-28 *Bryza*
TRAINING
  1 regt with L-39 *Albatros*
  1 regt with Yak-52
ATTACK/TRANSPORT HELICOPTER
  2 regt with Mi-8 *Hip*; Mi-17 *Hip* H; Mi-171; Mi-24 *Hind*

AIR DEFENCE
  4 ADA bde
  Some (People's Regional) force (total: ε1,000 AD unit, 6 radar bde with 100 radar stn)
EQUIPMENT BY TYPE
AIRCRAFT 97 combat capable
  FGA 97: 25 MiG-21bis *Fishbed* L & N; 8 MiG-21UM *Mongol* B; 30 Su-22M3/M4/UM *Fitter* (some ISR); 6 Su-27SK *Flanker*; 5 Su-27UBK *Flanker*; 23 Su-30MK2 *Flanker*
  TPT • Light 19: 6 An-2 *Colt*; 12 An-26 *Curl*; 1 M-28 *Bryza*
  TRG 48: 18 L-39 *Albatros*; 30 Yak-52
HELICOPTERS
  ATK 26 Mi-24 *Hind*
  MRH 6 Mi-17 *Hip* H
  TPT 29: **Medium** 17: 14 Mi-8 *Hip*; 3 Mi-171; **Light** 12 Bell 205 (UH-1H *Iroquois*)
AD • SAM
  SP 12+: 2K12 *Kub* (SA-6 *Gainful*); 12 S-300PMU1 (SA-20 *Gargoyle*)
  TOWED S-75 *Dvina* (SA-2 *Guideline*); S-125 *Pechora* (SA-3 *Goa*)
  MANPAD 9K32 *Strela*-2 (SA-7 *Grail*)‡; 9K310 *Igla*-1 (SA-16 *Gimlet*)
  GUNS 37mm; 57mm; 85mm; 100mm; 130mm
MSL
  ASM Kh-29T/L (AS-14 *Kedge*); Kh-31A (AS-17B *Krypton*); Kh-59M (AS-18 *Kazoo*)
  ARM Kh-28 (AS-9 *Kyle*); Kh-31P (AS-17A *Krypton*)
  AAM • IR R-3 (AA-2 *Atoll*)‡; R-60 (AA-8 *Aphid*); R-73 (AA-11 *Archer*); **IR/SARH** R-27 (AA-10 *Alamo*)

Paramilitary 40,000+ active

Border Defence Corps ε40,000

Coast Guard
PATROL AND COASTAL COMBATANTS 37+
  PSO 1 Damen 9014 (1 more vessel awaiting commissioning; 2 more in build)
  PCO 2+: 1 *Mazinger* (ex-ROK) 1+ other
  PCC 4 TT-400TP
  PBF 2 *Shershen*
  PB 28: 2 *Hae Uri* (ex-ROK); 12 TT-200; 13 TT-120; 1 other
LOGISTICS AND SUPPORT • ATF 4
AIRCRAFT • MP 3 C-212-400 MPA

Fisheries Surveillance Force
PATROL AND COASTAL COMBATANTS 3
  PSOH 1
  PCO 2

Local Forces ε5,000,000 reservists
Incl People's Self-Defence Force (urban units), People's Militia (rural units); comprises static and mobile cbt units, log spt and village protection pl; some arty, mor and AD guns; acts as reserve.

DEPLOYMENT

SOUTH SUDAN
UN • UNMISS 2 obs

Table 6 Selected Arms Procurements and Deliveries, Asia

Designation	Type	Quantity	Contract Value (Current)	Supplier Country	Prime Contractor	Order Date	First Delivery Due	Notes
Afghanistan (AFG)								
C-130H *Hercules*	Med tpt ac	4	n.k.	US	Government surplus	2013	2013	Ex-USAF surplus. Third delivered late 2014. Fourth due by end of 2014
EMB-314 *Super Tucano*	Trg ac	20	US$427m	BRZ	Embraer	2013	2014	USAF Light Air Support (LAS) programme. First delivered to Moody AFB in Sep 2014 for pilot training. Final delivery due Apr 2015
MD530F	MRH hel	12	US$36.6m	US	MD Helicopters	2014	n.k.	Exercised option from 2011 contract. To be armed
Australia (AUS)								
Hobart-class	DDGHM	3	US$8bn	AUS/ESP	AWD Alliance	2007	2016	Air Warfare Destroyer (AWD). Delivery of first vessel delayed to Mar 2016. Option on fourth vessel. All to be *Aegis*-equipped
Canberra-class	LHD	2	A$3.1bn (US$2.8bn)	AUS/ESP	Navantia	2007	2014	To replace HMAS *Tobruk* and *Kanimbla*-class
F-35A *Lightning* II	FGA ac	2	n.k.	US	Lockheed Martin	2012	2014	First two test and trg ac ordered in LRIP 6. Rolled out Jul 2014
EA-18G *Growler*	EW ac	12	n.k.	US	Boeing	2013	n.k.	IOC planned for 2018. Training has begun at NAS Whidbey Island
P-8A *Poseidon*	ASW ac	8	A$4bn (US$3.6bn)	US	Boeing	2014	2017	All to be in service by 2021. Option on a further four ac
C-27J *Spartan*	Med tpt ac	10	A$1.4bn (US$1.4bn)	ITA	Finmeccanica (Alenia Aermacchi)	2012	2015	To replace DHC-4s. Contract price includes logistics support and training
MH-60R *Seahawk*	ASW hel	24	US$3bn+	US	UTC (Sikorsky)	2011	2013	To replace navy's S-70Bs. Four delivered as of mid-2014
NH90 NFH/TTH	ASW/Med tpt hel	47	A$2bn (US$1.47bn)	FRA/GER/ITA/NLD	NH Industries	2005	2007	First four built in Europe; remainder in AUS. Deliveries ongoing
CH-47F *Chinook*	Hvy tpt hel	7	A$755m (US$670m)	US	Boeing	2010	2015	All to be operational by 2017. To replace CH-47Ds
Bangladesh (BGD)								
NORA B-52	Arty (155mm SP)	18	n.k.	SER	Yugoimport	2011	2013	Deliveries ongoing
Yak-130	Trg ac	24	US$800m	RUS	UAC (Irkut)	2013	2015	Part of arms order financed by εUS$1bn loan from RUS
K-8W	Trg ac	9	n.k.	PRC	AVIC (Hongdu)	2013	2014	First four delivered Sep 2014
China (PRC)								
JL-2 (CSS-N-X-14)	SLBM	n.k.	n.k.	PRC	n.k.	1985	n.k.	Still in development; range 8,000km. Reportedly to equip Type-094 SSBN. ISD uncertain
Type-96A	MBT	n.k.	n.k.	PRC	NORINCO	n.k.	n.k.	Delivery in progress
Type-99A	MBT	n.k.	n.k.	PRC	NORINCO	n.k.	n.k.	In limited production
Type-05 (ZBD-05)	AIFV	n.k.	n.k.	PRC	NORINCO	n.k.	n.k.	Amphibious assault veh family. Issued to marine and army amph units
Type-04A (ZBD-04A)	AIFV	n.k.	n.k.	PRC	NORINCO	n.k.	2011	Infantry fighting vehicle family. Improved version of Type-04 with extra armour

Table 6 Selected Arms Procurements and Deliveries, Asia

Designation	Type	Quantity	Contract Value (Current)	Supplier Country	Prime Contractor	Order Date	First Delivery Due	Notes
Type-09 (ZBL-09)	AIFV	n.k.	n.k.	PRC	NORINCO	n.k.	n.k.	Infantry fighting vehicle family including aslt gun (ZTL-09) and 122mm SP how (PLL-09) variants
Type-07 (PLZ-07)	Arty (122mm SP)	n.k.	n.k.	PRC	n.k.	n.k.	n.k.	122mm tracked SP howitzer; first displayed in public at 2009 parade
Type-09 (PLC-09)	Arty (122mm SP)	n.k.	n.k.	PRC	n.k.	n.k.	n.k.	Truck-mounted 122mm howitzer. Also referred to as AH2
Type-05 (PLZ-05)	Arty (155mm SP)	n.k.	n.k.	PRC	n.k.	n.k.	n.k.	155mm tracked SP howitzer; first displayed in public at 2009 parade
Type-03 (PHL-03)	MRL (300mm SP)	n.k.	n.k.	PRC	n.k.	n.k.	n.k.	8x8 truck-mounted MRL; also referred to as AR2
Type-07 (PGZ-07)	AD	n.k.	n.k.	PRC	n.k.	n.k.	n.k.	Twin 35mm-armed tracked SPAAG
Jin-class (Type-094)	SSBN	5	n.k.	PRC	Huludao Shipyard	1985	2008	Commissioning status unclear; three vessels believed to be in service; at least one more awaiting commissioning
Shang II-class (Type-093 mod)	SSN	ε4	n.k.	PRC	Bohai Shipyard	n.k.	n.k.	First vessel launched early 2013
Yuan II-class (Type-039B)	SSK	5	n.k.	PRC	Wuchang Shipyard/ Jiangnan Shipyard	n.k.	2011	Follow-on to Type-039A *Yuan*-class.
Luyang II-class (Type-052C)	DDGHM	6	n.k.	PRC	Jiangnan Shipyard	2002	2004	Fifth vessel commissioned June 2014; sixth in sea trials, expected ISD early 2015
Luyang III-class (Type-052D)	DDGHM	5	n.k.	PRC	Jiangnan Shipyard	n.k.	2014	First vessel commissioned March 2014; fifth launched Aug 2014
Jiangkai II-class (Type-054A)	FFGHM	20	n.k.	PRC	Huangpu Shipyard/ Hudong Shipyard	2005	2008	16th vessel commissioned late 2013; four further vessels launched
Jiangdao-class (Type-056)	FSG	20	n.k.	PRC	Huangpu/ Hudong/ Wuchang/ Liaonan shipyards	n.k.	2013	Replacing *Hainan*-class PCCs. 15 commissioned by late 2014
J-10A/S	FGA ac	n.k.	n.k.	PRC	AVIC (Chengdu)	n.k.	2004	In service with PLAAF and PLANAF. Improved J-10B variant currently in flight test
J-11B/BS	FGA ac	n.k.	n.k.	PRC	AVIC (Shenyang)	n.k.	2007	Upgraded J-11; now fitted with indigenous WS-10 engines. In service with PLAAF and PLANAF
J-15/J-15S	FGA ac	n.k.	n.k.	PRC	AVIC (Shenyang)	n.k.	2012	For PLANAF. To operate from *Liaoning* CV
Y-9	Med tpt ac	n.k.	n.k.	PRC	AVIC (Shaanxi)	n.k.	2012	In production for transport and special missions.
Il-78	Tkr ac	3	US$44.7m	UKR	Government surplus	2011	2014	First delivered by Nov 2014
Z-10	Atk hel	n.k.	n.k.	PRC	AVIC (Harbin)	n.k.	2010	In service with eight army avn bde/regt
Z-19	Atk hel	n.k.	n.k.	PRC	AVIC (Harbin)	n.k.	n.k.	In service with five army avn bde/regt

Table 6 Selected Arms Procurements and Deliveries, Asia

Designation	Type	Quantity	Contract Value (Current)	Supplier Country	Prime Contractor	Order Date	First Delivery Due	Notes
HQ-16A	SAM	n.k.	n.k.	PRC	n.k.	n.k.	2011	First delivered to 39th Group Army in 2011
India (IND)								
Agni V	ICBM	n.k.	n.k.	IND	DRDO	n.k.	2012	In development. Est 5,500km range
Sagarika K-15	SLBM	n.k.	n.k.	IND	Bharat Dynamics	1991	n.k.	Test-firing programme under way. Est 700km range with 500kg+ payload
BrahMos Block II (Land Attack)	AShM/LACM	n.k.	US$1.73bn	IND/RUS	Brahmos Aerospace	2010	n.k.	To equip additional two regiments
Nirbhay	LACM	n.k.	n.k.	IND	DRDO	n.k.	n.k.	In development
T-90S Bhishma	MBT	236	n.k.	IND/RUS	Ordnance Factory Board	2013	n.k.	Deliveries under way
Arjun II	MBT	118	n.k.	IND	CVRDE	2014	2017	Upgraded variant. Currently in trials. To be delivered by 2017
BMP-2/2K	AIFV	362	US$293m	IND	Ordnance Factory Board	2014	n.k.	Approved by Defence Acquisitions Council
Arjun Catapult	Arty (130mm SP)	40	US$150m	IND	CVRDE	2014	n.k.	M-46 on Arjun chassis
Arihant-class	SSBN	5	n.k.	IND	DRDO	n.k.	2014	INS Arihant sea trials delayed. ISD now expected 2017
Scorpene-class (Project 75)	SSK	6	INR235.62bn (US$5.3bn)	FRA	DCNS	2005	2016	Built under license in IND. First delivery delayed again; now expected end of 2016. Option for a further six SSK
Vikrant-class (Project 71)	CV	1	US$730m	IND	Cochin Shipyard	2001	2015	Formerly known as Air Defence Ship (ADS). Launched Aug 2013. Expected ISD slipped to 2015. Second vessel of class anticipated
Improved Shivalik-class (Project 17A)	DDGHM	7	INR450bn (US$9.24bn)	IND	Mazagon Dock/GRSE	2009	2017	Follow-up to Project 17. Requires shipyard upgrade
Kolkata-class (Project 15A)	DDGHM	3	US$1.75bn	IND	Mazagon Dock	2000	2014	First of class, INS Kolkata, reported commissioned Aug 2014. Second under sea trials, expected ISD 2015
Project 15B	DDGHM	4	US$6.5bn	IND	Mazagon Dock	2011	2017	Follow-on from Kolkata-class. Keel of first vessel laid down 2014
Kamorta-class (Project 28)	FFGHM	4	INR70bn (US$1.5bn)	IND	GRSE	2003	2014	ASW role. First of class, INS Kamorta, commissioned Aug 2014
Su-30MKI	FGA ac	82	US$4.9bn	IND/RUS	HAL/UAC (Sukhoi)	2007	2008	2007 and 2011 contracts for 80 aircraft and two accident replacements. 15 Russian-built ac all delivered. Remaining ac being built in India. Deliveries ongoing
MiG-29K Fulcrum D	FGA ac	29	US$1.5bn	RUS	UAC (MiG)	2010	2012	21 ac due to be delivered by end of 2014. Remainder due 2015
Tejas	FGA ac	20	INR20bn (US$445m)	IND	HAL	2005	2011	Limited series production. To be delivered in initial op config. Option for a further 20 in full op config
P-8I Neptune	ASW ac	8	US$2.1bn	US	Boeing	2009	2013	Fifth ac delivered Sep 2014

Table 6 Selected Arms Procurements and Deliveries, Asia

Designation	Type	Quantity	Contract Value (Current)	Supplier Country	Prime Contractor	Order Date	First Delivery Due	Notes
EMB-145	AEW&C ac	3	US$210m	BRZ	Embraer	2008	2014	Part of an INR18bn (US$400m) AEW&C project. First two in trials; entry into service due by end of 2014
C-17A *Globemaster* III	Hvy tpt ac	10	US$4.1bn	US	Boeing	2011	2013	Eighth ac delivered Nov 2014
C-130J-30 *Hercules*	Med tpt ac	6	US$564.7m	US	Lockheed Martin	2014	n.k.	Follow-up to initial order for six. Will be based at Panagargh.
Hawk Mk132 Advanced Jet Trainer	Trg ac	57	US$780m	IND	HAL	2010	2013	40 for air force and 17 for navy. First four delivered late 2013. Final delivery due in 2016
Dhruv	MRH hel	191	n.k.	IND	HAL	2004	2004	Includes additional 32 ordered Jul 2014, to be split equally between navy and coast guard
Rudra	MRH hel	76	n.k.	IND	HAL	2012	2013	Armed version of *Dhruv* hel. Was *Dhruv*-WSI. 60 for army and 16 for air force
Mi-17V-5 *Hip*	MRH hel	139	IND144bn (US$2.7bn)	RUS	Russian Helicopters (Mil)	2008	2011	To be weaponised. Contract value includes 12 additional helicopters for the Ministry of Home Affairs. Final delivery due in 2015
Indonesia (IDN)								
Leopard 2A4/2 Revolution	MBT	103	See notes	GER	Rheinmetall	2012	2013	ex-Bundeswehr surplus. 42 2A4 and 61 2 Revolution. Part of US$280m deal including 42 *Marder* 1A3 AIFVs and 11 ARV/AEVs. 26 delivered by Aug 2014
Marder 1A3	AIFV	42	See notes	GER	Rheinmetall	2012	2013	ex-Bundeswehr surplus. Part of US$280m deal including 103 *Leopard* 2 MBTs and 11 ARV/AEVs. 30 delivered by Aug 2014
Anoa 6x6	APC (W)	31	Rp250bn (US$27m)	IDN	PT Pindad	2012	2014	First batch of 24 delivered in 2014
CAESAR	Arty (155mm SP)	37	€108m (US$139m)	FRA	Nexter	2012	2014	First four delivered 2014
ASTROS Mk6	MRL (127mm SP)	36	US$405m	BRZ	Avibras	2013	2014	First 13 delivered 2014
Type-209/1400	SSK	3	US$1.1bn	IDN/ROK	PT PAL/DSME	2012	2015	First to be built in ROK; second to be partially assembled in IDN and third to be largely built in IDN
SIGMA 10514	FFGHM	1	US$220m	NLD	Damen Schelde Naval Shipbuilding	2012	2016	Further acquisitions are expected, with technology transfers allowing greater proportions to be built in IDN. Keel laid in Apr 2014
Teluk Bintuni-class	LST	3	n.k.	IDN	PT Daya Radar Utama	2012	2014	First vessel delivered Sep 2014
F-16C/D *Fighting Falcon*	FGA ac	24	US$670m	US	Government surplus	2012	2014	19 F-16C and five F-16D. All ex-USAF ac. First three delivered Jul 2014
C-295M	Lt tpt ac	9	US$325m	Int'l	Airbus Group (Airbus Defence & Space)	2012	2012	Seven ESP-built ac delivered by late 2014. Final two IDN-built ac due by end of 2014
C-130H *Hercules*	Med tpt ac	9	Free transfer	AUS	Government surplus	2012	2013	AUS surplus aircraft. Two delivered by mid-2014

Table 6 Selected Arms Procurements and Deliveries, Asia

Designation	Type	Quantity	Contract Value (Current)	Supplier Country	Prime Contractor	Order Date	First Delivery Due	Notes
AH-64E *Apache Guardian*	Atk hel	8	US$500m	US	Boeing	2013	2014	Delivery due to commence by end of 2014
AS565Mbe *Panther*	ASW hel	11	n.k.	Int'l	Airbus Group (Airbus Helicopters)	2014	n.k.	For navy
EC725 *Super Cougar*	Hvy tpt hel	6	n.k.	Int'l	Airbus Group (Airbus Helicopters)	2012	2014	First delivered to PT Digrantara for modification Nov 2014
AS550 *Fennec*	MRH hel	12	n.k.	Int'l	Airbus Group (Airbus Helicopters)	n.k.	2014	First delivered Nov 2014
Japan (JPN)								
Type-10	MBT	68	JPY55.1bn (US$679m)	JPN	MHI	2010	2011	Deliveries ongoing
Soryu-class	SSK	9	n.k.	JPN	KHI/MHI	2004	2009	Seventh boat launched Oct 2014
Izumo-class	CVH	2	US$1.3bn	JPN	IHI Marine United	2010	2015	First vessel in sea trials; ISD expected 2015.
Improved *Akizuki*-class	DDGHM	2	JPY145.6bn (US$1.5bn)	JPN	MHI	2013	2017	25DD project
Kunigami-class	PSOH	10	JPY57bn (US$650m)	JPN	MHI	n.k.	2014	First two vessels commissioned Sep 2014, following two launched 2014
Enoshima-class	MSO	3	n.k.	JPN	Universal Shipbuilding Corporation	2008	2012	Improved *Hirashima*-class. Second vessel commissioned 2013. Third vessel launched 2013; ISD expected 2015
F-35A *Lightning II*	FGA ac	4	US$701m	US	Lockheed Martin	2012	2017	Planned orders for 38 more
Republic of Korea (ROK)								
K2	MBT	297	n.k.	ROK	Hyundai Rotem	2007	2014	Production delayed due to continuing problems with engine and transmission
K21	AIFV	ε500	n.k.	ROK	Doosan Infracore	2008	2009	Deliveries resumed after accident investigation
Son Won-il-class	SSK	6	εUS$3bn	ROK	DSME	2008	2014	Second batch of six KSS-II (with AIP). First boat launched Aug 2013; expected ISD by end of 2014
KSS-III	SSK	n.k.	n.k.	ROK	DSME/ Hyundai Heavy Industries	2007	2017	Design contract signed in 2007. No contract for build signed by late 2014. Expected to be fitted with VLS; cost concerns have delayed progress
Incheon-class	FFGHM	6	KRW1.7tr (US$1.8bn)	ROK	Hyundai Heavy Industries	2006	2013	To replace *Ulsan*-class FFG. Second vessel commissioned Nov 2014. Fourth and fifth vessels contracted to STX Marine
Gumdoksuri-class	FSG	18	n.k.	ROK	Hanjin Heavy Industries/ STX Offshore & Shipbuilding	2005	2008	15 commissioned by late 2014
Cheonwangbong-class	LPD	4	n.k.	ROK	Hanjin Heavy Industries	2011	2014	First vessel launched Sep 2013. Currently in trials
AW159 *Wildcat*	MRH hel	8	€270m (US$358m)	ITA	Finmeccanica (Agusta-Westland)	2013	2015	Part of US$560m contract including support and training. To be equipped with *Spike* NLOS missiles

Table 6 Selected Arms Procurements and Deliveries, Asia

Designation	Type	Quantity	Contract Value (Current)	Supplier Country	Prime Contractor	Order Date	First Delivery Due	Notes
FA-50 *Fighting Eagle*	FGA ac	ε60	US$1.6bn	ROK	KAI	2012	2013	To replace F-5E/F. Deliveries ongoing
AH-64E *Apache Guardian*	Atk hel	36	KRW1.8tr (US$1.6bn)	US	Boeing	2013	2016	Deliveries to commence late 2016
Malaysia (MYS)								
AV8 *Pars* 8x8	APC (W)	257	US$559m	TUR	FNSS	2010	2013	Letter of intent signed Apr 2010. To include 12 variants. Prototype delivered 2013
Second-Generation Patrol Vessel	FF	6	MYR9bn (US$2.8bn)	MYS	Boustead Naval Shipyard	2011	2017	License-built DCNS *Gowind* 100m design. First ISD expected to be 2019
A400M *Atlas*	Hvy tpt ac	4	MYR907m (US$246m)	Int'l	Airbus Group (Airbus Defence & Space)	2006	2016	In development. Official unit cost US$80m. First deliveries delayed until at least 2016
New Zealand (NZL)								
T-6C *Texan* II	Trg ac	11	n.k.	US	Textron	2014	2014	Deliveries ongoing
Pakistan (PAK)								
Hatf 8 (*Raad*)	ALCM	n.k.	n.k.	PAK	n.k.	n.k.	n.k.	In development. Successfully test-fired
Al Khalid I	MBT	ε110	n.k.	PAK/PRC	Heavy Industries Taxila/NORINCO	2012	2013	Version unclear
JF-17 *Thunder* (FC-1)	FGA ac	150	n.k.	PAK/PRC	PAC	2006	2008	150 currently on order; Block 2 in development
Philippines (PHL)								
OPV 270	PSO	1	See notes	FRA	OCEA	2012	2016	For coast guard. Part of €90m (US$116m) order including four FPB 72 MKII
Strategic Sealift Vessel	LPD	2	US$86.9m	IDN	PT PAL	2014	2015	Modified *Makassar*-class
FA-50 *Fighting Eagle*	FGA ac	12	US$420m	ROK	KAI	2014	2015	Final delivery due in 2018
C-295M	Lt tpt ac	3	US$118m	Int'l	Airbus Group (Airbus Defence & Space)	2014	n.k.	To replace Fokker F-27s
Singapore (SGP)								
Type-218SG	SSK	2	n.k.	GER	TKMS	2013	2020	To replace remaining *Challenger*-class SSKs
Littoral Mission Vessel	PCO	8	n.k.	SGP	ST Engineering	2013	2016	To replace *Fearless*-class PCOs. First keel laid Sep 2014
A330 MRTT	Tkr/Tpt ac	6	n.k.	Int'l	Airbus Group (Airbus Defence & Space)	2014	n.k.	To replace KC-135Rs
S-70B *Seahawk*	ASW hel	2	n.k.	US	UTC (Sikorsky)	2013	n.k.	For navy. Order confirmed 2014
Sri Lanka (LKA)								
OPV	PCO	2	n.k.	IND	Goa Shipyard	2013	2017	Delivery expected 2017 and 2018

Table 6 Selected Arms Procurements and Deliveries, Asia

Designation	Type	Quantity	Contract Value (Current)	Supplier Country	Prime Contractor	Order Date	First Delivery Due	Notes
Mi-171	Med tpt hel	12	n.k.	RUS	Russian Helicopters (Mil)	2012	2013	Part of order funded by US$300m Ten-year loan from RUS; order includes two Mi-171s for VIP use. First four delivered Jun 2013; status of further deliveries unclear
Taiwan (ROC)								
CM-32 *Yunpao*	APC (W)	up to 650	n.k.	ROC	Ordnance Readiness Development Centre	2010	2011	To replace existing M113s
Hsun Hai-class	FSG	1	n.k.	ROC	Lung Teh Shipbuilding	2011	2015	Prototype launched early 2014. Total requirement is for 12
Patriot PAC-3	SAM	24	US$6bn	US	Raytheon	2009	2013	Four batteries. Three existing batteries also being upgraded from PAC-2 to PAC-3. Upgrades ongoing
P-3C *Orion*	ASW ac	12	US$1.3bn	US	Lockheed Martin	2010	2013	Refurbished by Lockheed Martin. Four delivered by mid-2014
UH-60M *Black Hawk*	Med tpt hel	60	US$1.7bn	US	UTC (Sikorsky)	2010	2014	26 to be modified to ROC configuration. First delivery due Dec 2014
Hsiung Feng IIE	AShM	n.k.	n.k.	ROC	CSIST	2005	n.k.	In production
Hsiung Feng III	AShM	n.k.	n.k.	ROC	CSIST	n.k.	n.k.	In production
Thailand (THA)								
T-84 *Oplot*	MBT	54	THB7bn (US$241m)	UKR	KMP	2011	2013	First five delivered to THA May 2014
BTR-3E1 8x8	AIFV	121	US$140m	UKR	KMDB	2011	2013	Further deliveries delayed as a result of Ukraine conflict
DW3000H	FFGHM	1	KRW520bn (US$464m)	ROK	DSME	2013	2018	Order for second vessel anticipated. Based on KDX-1 derivative
EC725 *Super Cougar*	Hvy tpt hel	6	n.k.	Int'l	Airbus Group (Airbus Helicopters)	2012	2015	SAR configuration. For air force
Vietnam (VNM)								
Varshavyanka-class (*Kilo*)	SSK	6	US$1.8bn	RUS	Admiralty Shipyards	2009	2014	First two commissioned. Third due by end of 2014
Gepard	FFGM	2	n.k.	RUS	Zelenodolsk Shipyard	2014	n.k.	To be delivered by 2017
SIGMA 9814	FFGHM	2	n.k.	NLD	Damen Schelde Naval Shipbuilding	2013	n.k.	First two to be built in NLD. Option for two more to be built in VNM
Damen 9014	PSOH	4	n.k.	VNM	189 Shipbuilding Company/Son Thu Company/ Ha Long Shipbuilding	2011	2012	For marine police. CSB 8001 and 8002. First vessel (CSB 8001) delivered. Second launched Oct 2014
Su-30MK2	FGA ac	12	US$600m	RUS	UAC (Sukhoi)	2013	2014	First four due for delivery by end of 2014

Chapter Seven
Middle East and North Africa

As 2014 progressed, regional attention was focused not only on the ongoing Syrian civil war, but also on the rise of the jihadi-takfiri movement, the Islamic State of Iraq and al-Sham (ISIS). The severe threat posed to the region by ISIS triggered military engagement and political alignment by regional and international states that had not been seen for some time. The expansion of territory under its control – which effectively merged western Iraq and eastern and northeastern Syria – was followed, after the group's seizure of Mosul in June 2014, by its announcement of a caliphate. This compelled behavioural and policy changes among all actors engaged on the Syrian and Iraqi battlefields.

The Syrian war

In 2014, the position of President Bashar al-Assad's regime seemed stronger than at any point since 2012. The US decision to call off air-strikes in September 2013 in exchange for Damascus relinquishing its chemical arsenal, coupled with both continuing Western reluctance to back the armed rebellion and the rise of ISIS, offered the regime political and military space to engage in offensive operations, recover ground and frustrate the rebellion's efforts. As a result, regime forces relieved rebel pressure on the capital, reconquered most of Homs and squeezed rebel-held areas in Aleppo. This secured most of the central corridor linking Damascus to Aleppo and to the coastal regions.

The regime continued to demonstrate adaptability and maintain military superiority over the rebels. The Syrian conventional armed forces, supplemented by allied militias, became more adept at urban warfare and counter-insurgency tactics. Large units were broken into smaller, more deployable ones; junior commanders were promoted in lieu of the old cadre. Elite forces, notably the Presidential Guard and the 4th Division, remained loyal and battle-ready, and a robust cycle of air operations was maintained. As it handed its declared chemical arsenal to a UN-led mission, Damascus intensified its barrel- and chlorine-bomb campaign across the country. Steady Iranian and Russian supplies of weaponry for the regime contrasted with sporadic deliveries to the rebels. To break the will of rebels and civilians, the regime imposed harsh sieges on rebel-held areas.

To make up for personnel shortages, amid falling numbers of conscripts arriving for the draft, the Assad regime increasingly relied on militias as auxiliary forces. At times, this meant a weaker chain of command, operational breakdowns and tensions between the conventional army, local paramilitaries and foreign militias. For example, the local commander of the National Defense Force (NDF) in Homs opposed a UN-brokered ceasefire and evacuation plan, which required the intervention of a senior regime official. In the south, Druze members of the NDF resisted orders to deploy to a nearby province. Operational and command rifts between Alawite militias and the army led to the momentary loss of the town of Kessab in the province of Latakia. Foreign Shia militias significantly bolstered the war effort: Hizbullah led the battle against rebels in the Qalamoun region, on the Lebanese border, while evidence of Shia militiamen recruited and trained by Iran mounted. Iranian personnel also reportedly oversaw the siege of Aleppo.

Damascus maintained a de facto trade-off with ISIS throughout the first half of 2014. The existence of ISIS served to validate Assad's political narrative and forced the mainstream rebellion to fight on multiple fronts. However, this unspoken deal collapsed in the summer as ISIS sought to expand its territory and besieged military bases in Raqqa. Heavy losses there unsettled regime supporters, especially after well-publicised massacres of Alawite recruits by ISIS, and led to unprecedented demands for the resignation of the defence minister.

Meanwhile, fragmentation, military inferiority and the rise of ISIS impeded Syrian rebel performance, and while large alliances (notably the Islamic Front, and the Free Syrian Army (FSA)-aligned Syrian Revolutionaries Front and Harakat Hazm) might have emerged, this did not translate into substantive rebel gains. Tensions between foreign patrons, disarray within the FSA's Supreme Military Council, with General Salim Idriss replaced by General Abdul-Ilah Bashir, and American disappointment with FSA

Table 7 **Timeline: ISIS gains and coalition responses in 2014**

January	ISIS captures Fallujah	31 August	Iraqi security forces, Kurdish Peshmerga and Shia militias break ISIS's siege of Amerli, in Diyala Province.
February	al-Qaeda cuts ties with ISIS		
10 June	ISIS overruns Mosul	31 August	Germany announces weapons supplies to Peshmerga forces
11 June	ISIS seizes Tikrit; controls much of Nineveh Province		
23 June	Tal Afar falls to ISIS	7 September	US aircraft strike ISIS positions around Haditha Dam, in Anbar Province
29 June	ISIS declares an Islamic State		
2 August	ISIS gains control of Ain Zalah and Batma oil fields	9 September	UK announces weapons supplies to Peshmerga forces
5 August	ISIS beseiges Mount Sinjar where thousands of religious-minority Iraqis have fled.	15 September	US aircraft strike ISIS southwest of Baghdad and in Sinjar district, in Nineveh Province
7 August	US President Obama authorises limited air-strikes in Iraq	15 September	France begins military reconnaissance flights over Iraq
		22 September	Combat aircraft from Bahrain, Jordan, Qatar, Saudi Arabia, UAE and the US target ISIS in Syria
8 August	ISIS regains control of Mosul Dam from Peshmerga forces	30 September	UK RAF aircraft carry out their first strikes on ISIS targets in Iraq
8 August	First Iraqi supply of small-arms ammunition to Kurdish forces	2 October	Turkish parliament approves motion enabling cross-border military movement into Iraq and Syria
14 August	Siege of Mount Sinjar broken	6 October	US uses *Apache* attack helicopters against ISIS near Fallujah
15 August	EU to support the supply of weapons by member states to Peshmerga fighting ISIS in Iraq		
18 August	Peshmerga and Iraqi special forces retake Mosul Dam, with US air support	9 October	Australian aircraft undertake air-strikes in Iraq
		14 October	ISIS controls Hit, in Anbar Province
23 August	Iranian troops reportedly enter the Kurdish Autonomous Region to assist Peshmerga fighters	21 October	The governor of Kirkuk asks US-led coalition for air support against ISIS
26 August	US begins reconnaissance flights over Syria to track ISIS forces	22 October	The parliament of Iraqi Kurdistan agrees to send Peshmerga fighters to Kobane in Syria to help defend against ISIS

units compounded rebel woes. By late 2014, rebel forces held no major city in its entirety, having lost Raqqa to ISIS. In September, the entire top command of Ahrar al-Sham, the most powerful Islamist group in Syria, was killed by a car bomb.

Rebel forces maintained chaotic control over large parts of the south and the northeast, clashing with Kurdish militias, Jabhat al-Nusra and ISIS. Despite taking heavy casualties, starting in January 2014 rebel groups, including Salafi factions in the Islamic Front, were able to begin dislodging ISIS, thanks to local support. These gains were reversed when ISIS regrouped in the east and replenished its arsenal with arms captured in Iraq.

US policy on Syria remained ambivalent and non-committal in 2014. The US delivered arms, notably anti-tank weapons, to vetted rebel units in limited quantities to test the capabilities and reliability of these groups. In June, the US administration presented a US$500-million plan to train a small rebel force under Pentagon supervision. This plan, at first coolly welcomed in the US Congress, was boosted by the growing threat of ISIS and the international coalition's need to nurture local allies against the jihadi group. However, deep divisions between the US and its rebel allies remained: the former insisted on prioritising the fight against ISIS, while the latter saw Assad's forces as the main enemy.

ISIS: tactics, emergence and advance

ISIS evolved from al-Qaeda in Iraq and was formally established in 2013 (see *Strategic Survey 2014*, pp. 187–88). Several reasons explain its emergence and success. It thrived on the weakness and lack of legitimacy of central governments in Iraq and Syria, where the societal dislocation and disenfranchisement of Sunni communities provided fertile ground for local recruitment and the fostering of alliances with those seeking protection and order. In Iraq, a prime partner of ISIS was a Sunni group called the Army of the Men of the Naqshbandi Order, composed of former Ba'athists and headed by the Saddam Hussein regime's vice-president, Izzat Ibrahim al-Douri.

The hybrid, adaptable nature of ISIS – part-insurgency, part-light infantry and part-terrorist group – proved key to its advances. Having obtained the loyalty of Sunni tribes and insurgents, it was able to orchestrate complex operations and seize territory in mainly Sunni areas. Meanwhile, in areas it captured, it relied on a light, sophisticated bureaucratic structure as well as arrangements with local powers for administration, but also imposed repressive rule against residents, enforcing austere codes and eliminating any kind of dissent.

In both Iraq and Syria, ISIS – numbering up to 30,000–35,000 core and associated fighters – has been more effective than its opponents. About one-third of its personnel are foreign jihadis from over

80 countries, most notably Tunisia, Saudi Arabia and Jordan, and it has adopted a decentralised structure. Personnel are highly motivated and the group appears to have a cadre of effective military commanders. Some of these are former Sunni and al-Qaeda insurgents. In Iraq, others were drawn from Saddam's officer corps; and in Syria, from a mix of local and foreign commanders, including Chechens, Saudis and North Africans.

ISIS has employed bombings, assassinations and guerrilla-style attacks on Iraqi security forces and Sunni opponents, but it has also assembled more conventional forces, including effective 'flying columns' of fighters in pick-up trucks, armed with heavy machine guns and other direct-fire weapons. It uses mortars and artillery to bombard enemy positions for a day or more, undermining the morale of its opponents; small mobile units then deploy to swarm and seize bases and towns by capitalising on surprise and panic. Suicide bombers are used to breach obstacles and destroy checkpoints before close assault. These tactics have made ISIS able to disperse and regroup quickly, rendering it less vulnerable to Iraq's limited air capabilities and conventional counter-attacks.

The jihadi group also displays effective higher-level tactics. It appears to probe for weaknesses in enemy positions and subsequently exploits observed vulnerabilities by manoeuvring forces to outflank or unhinge enemy defences. Its campaigns in both Syria and Iraq have shown ISIS to be an adaptable organisation, demonstrated by an adjustment of tactics in autumn 2014 to reduce its vulnerability to coalition air power and intelligence, surveillance and reconnaissance (ISR) systems; this included, in some cases, abandoning larger, more visible weapons captured from state armed forces. It conducts a modern and sophisticated propaganda operation, mainly online, to garner international jihadi volunteers, financial donations and support from Syrian and Iraqi Sunnis. These are all integrated with economic activity such as smuggling, including oil, looting antiquities, and kidnapping for ransom, to generate revenue and sustain the populations it controls.

Further gains in 2014
In Iraq, ISIS dealt severe blows to the already weak security forces. Former Iraqi prime minister Nuri al-Maliki had centralised control of internal security by directly assuming ministerial authority for the armed forces, police and intelligence services. Experienced commanders were replaced by less capable, but politically loyal, proxies, which greatly reduced the effectiveness and impartiality of the security forces. Endemic corruption further reduced the effectiveness of the army and police, and eroded their logistic capability. As Maliki's oppression of Iraqi Sunnis increased, ISIS rebuilt its networks across Sunni communities in Western and Central Iraq, and other Sunni insurgent groups again took up arms against Baghdad. A key juncture was the April 2013 attack by Iraqi security forces on a Sunni protest camp at Hawija, west of Kirkuk.

In 2013 and 2014, ISIS gradually expanded its foothold in Anbar and Nineveh provinces, and conquered Fallujah. In June, it conducted a stealthy takeover of the city of Mosul. The precipitate self-evacuation of top Iraqi commanders from the city apparently triggered a widespread rout, resulting in the disintegration of the Iraqi second division and badly damaging three other divisions; several army bases containing vehicles and weaponry were captured. Hundreds of thousands of civilians were displaced, and ISIS announced that it would advance on Baghdad as well as the Shia shrines south of the capital. Over the summer, it approached the city of Kirkuk and the capital of Iraqi Kurdistan, Erbil. It also conducted a military and terror campaign to dislodge the Yazidi minority from the northeast, which culminated with the siege of thousands of fleeing Yazidis on Mount Sinjar. The US estimated that only about half of the 50 Iraqi brigades that it had assessed (see below) were combat capable, and the Pentagon announced that US troops would form a number of 'advise and assist' teams to partner Iraqi forces down to brigade level.

In Syria, after alienating rebel groups and local communities in late 2013, ISIS suffered setbacks and was pushed out of much of the north during the first half of 2014. It however preserved its stronghold of Raqqa and regrouped in towns bordering Iraq and along the Euphrates; it also benefited from a de facto quid pro quo with the Assad regime, which saw ISIS as a useful distraction that forced mainstream rebel groups to fight on two fronts. ISIS successes in Iraq created new momentum in Syria and its capture of Iraqi weaponry gave it military superiority over its poorly equipped rivals. It was able to expand its territorial hold throughout the second part of 2014, approaching Aleppo from the east, seizing important towns in the north and concentrating its attacks against the Kurdish militia, notably on and around the border town of Kobane. Perversely, ISIS successes attracted defectors from other armed groups, such as Liwa Dawood.

Coalition response

The rapid advance of ISIS in Iraq, coupled with the failure of the Iraqi army to halt the group, compelled international involvement. US ISR systems, both manned and unmanned, were deployed, and the US sent personnel to Iraq – including special forces – to assess the situation and establish joint-operations centres in Baghdad and Iraqi Kurdistan. In northern Iraq, the Kurdish Peshmerga served as the main fighting force; however, despite their fierce reputation, they had become less capable and, lacking supplies, required substantial foreign assistance. This was provided not only by the US, Germany and other European countries, but also by Iran. An ISIS threat to Baghdad and the south, meanwhile, triggered the mobilisation of Shia militias and, mid-year, the deployment of Iranian Revolutionary Guards. Yet more international action arose after ISIS attacked Yazidi and other minority communities in northern Iraq. Amid the scene of thousands of Yazidi refugees on the slopes of Mount Sinjar, the US conducted air-strikes against ISIS positions and – with UK support – began humanitarian airdrops. Kurdish forces, facing ISIS in the north after the Iraqi army there disintegrated, were hard pressed and running short of munitions. Air support from the newly emerging international coalition, as well as multiple pledges of ammunition, small arms, light anti-armour weapons and anti-tank guided weapons – and relevant training – bolstered their combat power and raised additional questions about the prospects for the newly resupplied and combat-tested Kurdish armed forces in the future Iraq, not least as they had in June expanded their footprint to include Kirkuk.

By mid-October, strategy was keeping pace with action on the ground. Statements by senior US leaders indicated Washington's military strategy, notably President Obama's 10 September speech: the first part of the campaign was to counter ISIS with a campaign of air-strikes in Iraq and, if necessary, Syria; there was to be increased support to Iraqi and Kurdish military forces, while Syrian opposition forces were to be trained and equipped; the US would look to coordinated counter-terrorism actions to prevent attacks, such as improving intelligence and tackling ISIS's funding streams; and humanitarian aid would be provided to displaced civilians. Some strands of this US policy took place concurrently. For instance, while the US-led air-strikes on ISIS positions in Iraq – with France, the UK, Australia, Canada and the Netherlands among a growing band of nations pledging offensive and surveillance assets – some nations were also involved in offensive operations against ISIS in Syria. The UK foreign secretary revealed on 16 October that: 'airstrikes are being carried out in Syria by the United States, Saudi Arabia, the UAE, Bahrain, and Jordan'. Though there seemed to be broad assent over air-strikes against ISIS, there was less consensus in the debate about how to train the Syrian opposition, which groups should benefit from this and whether the Assad regime would be targeted at a later stage. This latter uncertainty created tensions inside the coalition, which the Gulf states had joined in part to steer the US towards military action against Assad.

LIBYA: CONTINUING INSTABILITY

Libya continued its slide into a state of insecurity in 2014, abetted by the collapse of meaningful government and the increasing divisiveness of Libyan politics and security. In March, Prime Minister Ali Zeidan lost a no-confidence vote in the General National Congress (GNC) and was ousted by Islamist parliamentarians and their allies from Libya's third-largest city, Misrata. Defence Minister Abdullah al-Thinni assumed Zeidan's post until elections were held in June to replace the GNC with a House of Representatives. These elections only deepened the divisions in Libya by dealing a defeat to the Islamists, who then used low turnout to justify their non-acceptance of the results and a boycott of the new House.

To placate concerns that Libya's future governments would favour the western part of the country, the House convened in Libya's east, in Tobruk, home to tribes at odds with the Islamists, and not in Benghazi as originally planned. By September, Libya effectively had two parliaments and two governments: an elected parliament and an appointed government located in the east, with very limited power and far from its ministries; and a rump GNC parliament, with its own appointed government and access to ministries but no international and questionable local legitimacy.

This political crisis was accompanied by growing divisions between the major military and militia movements, none of whom respected the civilian-led government's authority. In March, renegade general Khalifa Haftar, who fought against Gadhafi forces during the revolution, announced a campaign intended to purge Libya of 'terrorism'. Despite ambitions to expand what was later dubbed *Operation Dignity* from Benghazi to Tripoli, Haftar made no appreciable gains other than uniting his opponents in a counter-operation called *Operation Dawn*. The two sides remained deadlocked throughout the summer, until Haftar's opponents in Tripoli – the well-armed brigades from Misrata and Islamist fighters from Tripoli – launched an extended battle for Tripoli International Airport, provoked, say analysts, by airstrikes against Islamist positions, reportedly carried out by Egypt and the United Arab Emirates.

The airport had been controlled by brigades from the eastern mountainous region of Zintan since 2012, who became allies of Haftar by virtue of their common opponents. The battle culminated in September with the near-destruction of the airport and the retreat of the Zintan brigades. Throughout this period, a campaign of assassinations and kidnappings continued to plague Benghazi, targeting military officers and civil-society activists on one side and Ansar al-Sharia and other Islamist militants on the other. Beyond the assassinations, direct confrontations between the rival factions have ebbed and flowed. The least deadly, and least effective, have involved stand-off weapons, including BM-21 *Grad* rockets as well as artillery; Haftar's loyalists have also conducted a few raids using Libya's small number of *Hind* attack helicopters and MiG combat aircraft. When engaged in direct combat, the rivals have relied on vehicle-mounted anti-aircraft guns and anti-tank missiles. The rival forces are relatively mobile due to their small size, partly accounting for occasional swift changes in the front line when an incident sparks a clash.

Attempts by the West to engineer an end to the violence have been unsuccessful and most embassies closed in July due to the violence. The United Nations Support Mission in Libya (UNSMIL) in September brokered a meeting between political representatives of the opposing factions. A follow-up session has not been scheduled and it remains unclear how much Libyan politicians can influence the loosely aligned militias, some of whom profit from ongoing violence and extortion activities. Plans to restructure the Libyan police and armed forces were developed by UNSMIL as early as 2012 but have generally been put on hold. The country's informal security organisations, formed during the revolution, have become increasingly intertwined with more formal state-security organs, particularly after they were legitimised by the government and began receiving higher payments than the regular military and police. This has resulted in a 'hybrid' security landscape, according to informed sources.

The formal armed forces remain top-heavy with mainly senior-ranking officers, few non-commissioned officers and little equipment; early attempts to provide more modern weaponry and vehicles mainly saw these diverted to the semi-official militias. Libya's Western allies have initiated some training programmes to address these problems, including a multinational effort to train a General Purpose Force intended to provide basic security

Regional extroversion

In the spring and summer of 2014, Egypt and the United Arab Emirates (UAE) allied to support the forces of Khalifa Haftar, a Libyan general seeking to confront both Islamist militias in Tripoli and Benghazi and rival warlords holding the city of Misrata and allegedly benefiting from Qatari sponsorship.

This took the form of military assistance and, most significantly, air-strikes carried out by Libyan aircraft with Egyptian and Emirati support. In August, US officials confirmed that the Emirati air force had flown missions from Egyptian air bases, without prior notification, to break the Islamist siege of Tripoli International Airport and destroy key Islamist-held facilities in the capital. This effort was in vain, and afterwards both Egypt and the UAE denied their role in the operations. The assertiveness of both countries and their decision to act, without US approval, marked a watershed in regional politics. It illustrated a readiness to use force despite US concerns, and the capacity to operate independently from Washington.

In comparison, the US was successful in enlisting the political and military support of key Arab states in the coalition to defeat the Islamic State of Iraq and al-Sham (ISIS). Gulf states calculated that ISIS was morphing into a severe ideological and security threat, as thousands of Gulf and North African youths flocked to jihad in Syria and Iraq. These Arab states also believed that their involvement was essential to shape US strategy in Syria and ensure that Iran could not emerge as the primary beneficiary of the campaign. Jordan, Saudi Arabia, Bahrain, the UAE and Qatar all contributed aircraft and other capabilities, and conducted air-strikes, with the UAE believed to have conducted the most air-strikes of all the Arab countries.

for Libya's key institutions. However, the fledgling defence ministry has not been able to provide sufficient numbers of prospective trainees, vetting mechanisms or an integration programme to incorporate troops into existing units when they complete their training. Furthermore, the international community is unlikely to make any headway in its efforts to rebuild the Libyan armed forces and police, and assist with an effective disarmament, demobilisation and reintegration programme, until there is a resolution to the governance crisis.

DEFENCE ECONOMICS

Regional macroeconomics

Escalating armed conflict continued to affect regional economic activity in 2014. Political and security uncertainties dampened business confidence – particularly in the non-oil economy – resulting in lower levels of private and foreign direct investment, and contributing to already high unemployment and low levels of competitiveness. This reduction in private-sector activity was partly offset by higher levels of public expenditure and investment, particularly since the Arab Spring began in 2011, as a number of countries embarked on or accelerated infrastructure and social-development projects. In oil-exporting states, increased public spending has been supported by high oil prices (generally above US$100 per barrel):

for example, fiscal break-even prices – the oil price at which state budgets are balanced – have been estimated at between US$65 per barrel and US$95 per barrel in Saudi Arabia, Qatar and the United Arab Emirates (UAE).

Non-oil-exporting states are consolidating expenditures after several years of sizeable fiscal deficits to support elevated governmental outlays, particularly on food and fuel subsidies: between 2010 and 2013, Egypt, Jordan and Lebanon all ran fiscal deficits averaging above 6% of GDP, and sometimes reaching around 12% of GDP. These states already have high debt-to-GDP ratios (above 90% of GDP), limiting the extent to which they can continue to rely on domestic debt issuance to fund outlays; public-debt service payments alone already amount to nearly a third of government spending in Lebanon. Consequently, they have had to rely on external sources to plug financing gaps – for example, Saudi Arabia and the UAE have contributed towards Egyptian economic and currency stabilisation (by providing some US$12 billion to boost central-bank foreign reserves, as well as fund infrastructure development in FY2013/14), while Jordan has agreed a US$2bn standby arrangement with the International Monetary Fund, as well as some US$5bn in external grants and concessional loans from Gulf Cooperation Council states.

Subsidy reforms have also been attempted in Morocco, Iran and Yemen. The latter two states are

Map 7 **Middle East and North Africa Regional Defence Spending**[1]

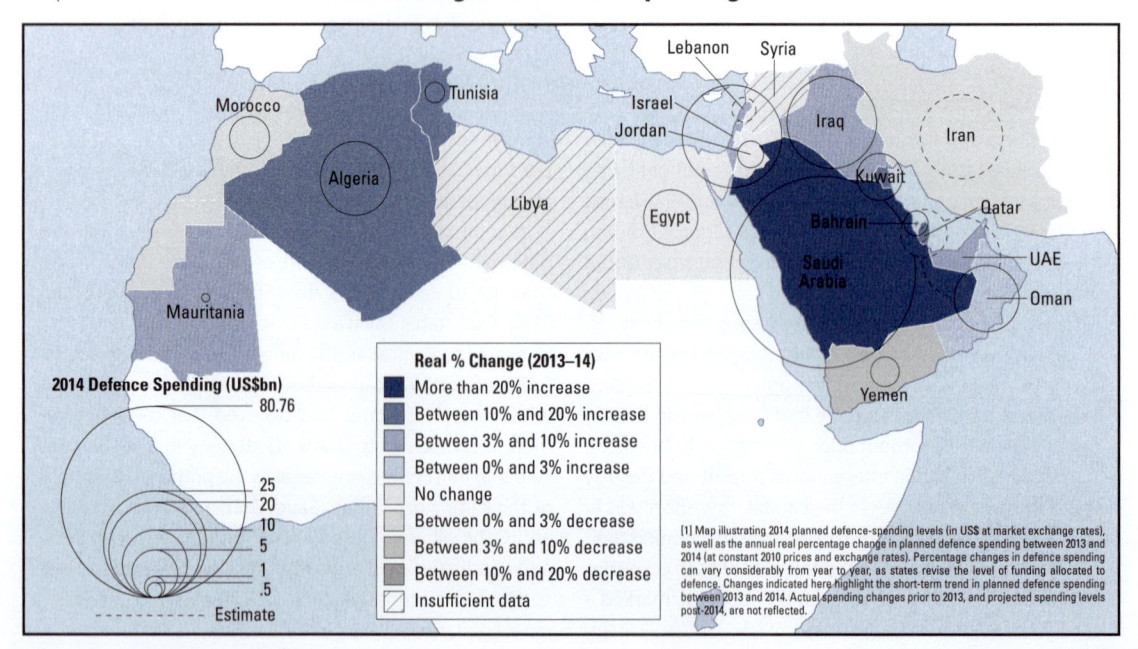

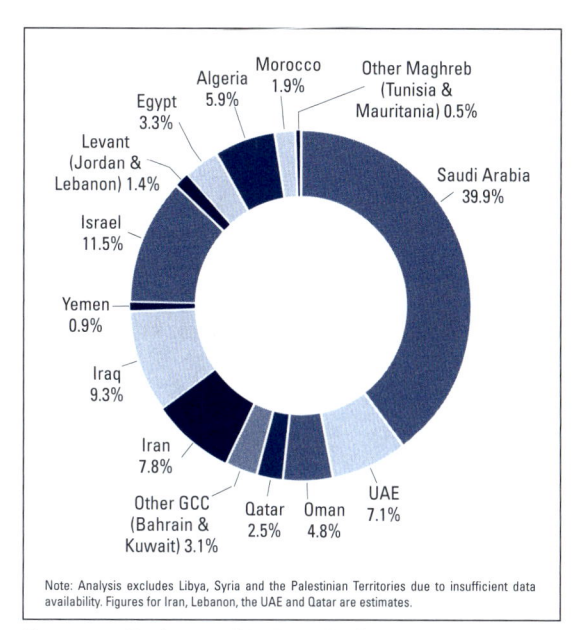

Figure 14 **Estimated MENA Defence Expenditure 2014: Sub-Regional Breakdown**

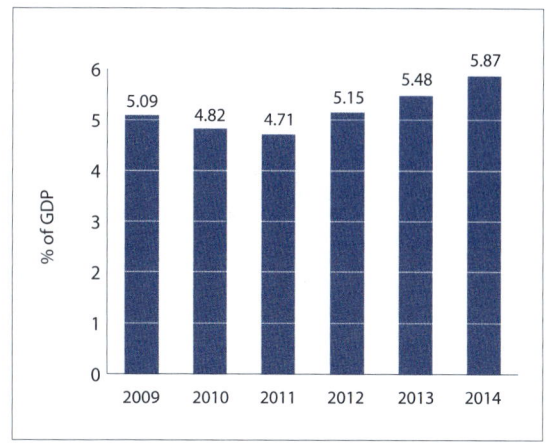

- Saudi Arabia 39.9%
- Israel 11.5%
- Iraq 9.3%
- Iran 7.8%
- UAE 7.1%
- Algeria 5.9%
- Oman 4.8%
- Egypt 3.3%
- Other GCC (Bahrain & Kuwait) 3.1%
- Qatar 2.5%
- Morocco 1.9%
- Levant (Jordan & Lebanon) 1.4%
- Yemen 0.9%
- Other Maghreb (Tunisia & Mauritania) 0.5%

Note: Analysis excludes Libya, Syria and the Palestinian Territories due to insufficient data availability. Figures for Iran, Lebanon, the UAE and Qatar are estimates.

Figure 15 **Middle East and North Africa Regional Defence Expenditure** as % of GDP

- 2009: 5.09
- 2010: 4.82
- 2011: 4.71
- 2012: 5.15
- 2013: 5.48
- 2014: 5.87

experiencing declining oil revenues due to international sanctions and sabotage of domestic pipelines respectively. Lower resource revenues in Iran and Yemen required them to run budget deficits in 2014 (around 6% of GDP in Yemen and an estimated 2.5% of GDP in Iran), while relatively high fiscal break-even oil prices in Algeria (around US$110 per barrel) and Bahrain (around US$120 per barrel) meant that both were on course to resort to deficit financing. In Israel, greater state expenditure than income – exacerbated by the Gaza conflict over the summer – has continued the budgetary pressures of recent years, with the government expected to run a budget shortfall equivalent to 3% of GDP in 2014.

Estimated defence-spending trends

Regional defence-budget transparency tends to be low, owing to a combination of bureaucratic opacity, limited legislative oversight and the use of off-budget funding in some states, such as Qatar and the UAE. War in Syria has made accurate estimates of military funding levels impossible to ascertain for several years now; and in 2014, clarity over allocated defence-budget levels was further reduced in Libya, Lebanon, Iraq and, to a lesser extent, Israel, due to political impasses that disrupted budgetary processes. Consequently, defence-spending trends for several states have to be estimated (see Map 7), and in some cases – Libya, Syria and the Palestinian Territories (PT) – omitted from analysis altogether.

In addition to increased investment and social expenditures, elevated defence-spending levels have made an appreciable contribution to the contraction in fiscal space (i.e. budgetary room for manoeuvre) in much of the region. Nominal regional defence spending is estimated to have risen by almost two-thirds since 2010 (a 65.4% increase, excluding changes in Libya, Syria and the PT), from US$122.4bn in 2010 to US$202.4bn in 2014. Factoring in exchange-rate and inflationary effects, this equates to a 40% increase in real defence outlays over the period, which have accelerated significantly since the onset of the Arab Spring: from a 3.5% real increase in 2011, real defence-spending increases in the three years between 2012 and 2014 trebled to an average of 10.7% per annum. Reflecting healthier fiscal balances, oil-exporting states have accounted for the vast majority of known and estimated real increases between those years (in excess of 90%), although this proportion is likely an overestimate due to the exclusion of Syria and Libya from analysis. Nonetheless, given that oil exporters account for the majority of regional GDP and defence spending (outstripping non-oil-exporting states by factors of 3:1 and more than 4:1 respectively), regional defence spending as a proportion of GDP has correspondingly risen from 4.7% of GDP in 2011 to 5.8% of GDP in 2014 (see Figure 15).

In part this reflects large increases by Saudi Arabia, which accounts for some 35–40% of the regional total. Riyadh has raised its annual defence and security budget by more than 10% in real terms since 2012, with real increments above 20% in 2013 and 2014.

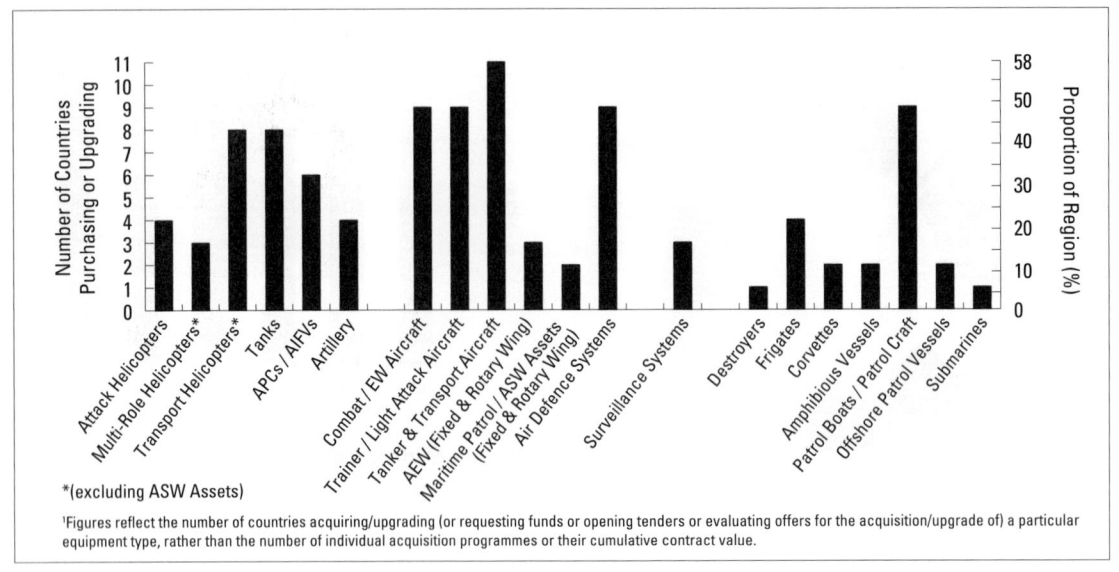

Figure 16 **Middle East & North Africa: Selected Procurement & Upgrade Priorities Since 2010**[1]

[1] Figures reflect the number of countries acquiring/upgrading (or requesting funds or opening tenders or evaluating offers for the acquisition/upgrade of) a particular equipment type, rather than the number of individual acquisition programmes or their cumulative contract value.

Neighbouring oil producer Oman saw real outlays rise by more than 40% in 2012 and 2013, and Iraq saw annual real-spending increases averaging 12% between 2012 and 2014. These increases partly reflect expanded equipment procurement (see *The Military Balance 2014*, pp. 304–6), although several states, including Saudi Arabia and Algeria, also raised military salaries in the wake of the Arab Spring. In 2014, Qatar placed some US$20bn in arms orders at the Doha International Maritime Defence Exhibition for items including tanker/transport and airborne early-warning-and-control aircraft, air-defence systems, attack helicopters and a variety of naval patrol vessels. By contrast, the need to consolidate the public finances of many non-oil-exporting states has limited the fiscal space to expand defence outlays: real spending either fell or remained stagnant in Egypt, Jordan, Iran and Yemen. Budgetary pressures in Israel would likely have caused real spending to fall in 2014, but the 50-day Gaza conflict – reportedly costing in excess of US$2.5bn – ended the long-running budgetary stand-off between the defence and finance ministries, and consequently Israeli real defence spending is assessed to have risen by 4.5% over 2013 levels.

ISRAEL: CHANGING SECURITY DYNAMICS

Israel's so-called 'security bubble' finally burst in 2014. Though insecurity and turmoil had rocked the Arab world for three years, Israel's citizens had been mostly insulated from direct threat. They remained largely unaffected by the collapse of Arab regimes and the rise of extremist organisations, the tension between Hamas and the new administration of President Abdel Fattah el-Sisi in Egypt, or even the growing arsenals of rockets obtained by regional guerrilla organisations. This had changed by summer 2014, after 50 days of fighting in the Gaza Strip between Israeli forces and Hamas.

The Israeli–Palestinian conflict once more became the focus of worldwide attention, as thousands of rockets were launched from Gaza (as well as some launched from the Syrian, Lebanese and Egyptian borders) and Israel launched a military offensive. The growing presence of jihadi groups along Israel's borders also escalated tensions on formerly quiet frontiers.

From the perspective of Israel's prime minister Benjamin Netanyahu, this new round of conflict served to strengthen his assessment of the regional security dynamic. The war with Hamas convinced the prime minister that he was correct in his assumption that the organisation was not a partner for peace, and that every concession made to the Palestinian Authority should be considered with utmost caution. The rocket threat, along with the progress of al-Qaeda-affiliated groups near Israel's border with Syria and fears for the internal stability of Jordan, served as further justification for Netanyahu's claim that Israel should maintain a long-term military presence along the River Jordan in order to prevent a more direct threat to its population centres.

Before 2014, the Israeli government felt that although it was surrounded by mostly hostile regimes, there usually remained a 'return address' in neighbouring countries for Israeli reprisals, in the case of attacks from the borders. This form of deterrence has been challenged as these surrounding states become more unstable. Within Israel's security establishment, a major concern after mid-2014 centred on the questions of who could be held responsible for the most recent attacks and, as a consequence, who needed to be deterred.

From the perspective of Israeli defence planners, the 2014 rocket attacks emphasised the need for a strong deterrence posture, which would rely on the capacity of the Israel Defense Forces (IDF) to deliver a swift military response. This emphasis also derived from the Israeli intelligence community's difficulty in estimating where rapid strategic changes might occur: intelligence branches had not foreseen, analysts said, either the 2014 conflict with Hamas or the rapid rise of the Islamic State of Iraq and al-Sham.

The IDF had been in the middle of a reorganisation before the war in Gaza, stemming from financial difficulties, as well as strategic changes in the region. Personnel were mandated to reduce by 4,500 career-officer and non-commissioned-officer posts by the end of 2015, and six reserve tank brigades (operating *Patton-Magach* 7 and *Merkava*-1 main battle tanks) and one unidentified air-force squadron were to be disbanded. Meanwhile, the IDF significantly increased spending on cyber warfare, intelligence and the air force. In light of growing instability in Syria, the new 210th Division was transferred to the Golan Heights to replace the 36th Armoured Division, which had held that ground for some years. The intention was that the 36th Armoured Division would then have more time to prepare for different operational scenarios. As part of a budget struggle, the IDF announced that it would cease ground- and air-force training at the beginning of June, although training resumed shortly before violence escalated in the West Bank and later in Gaza. Earlier, the Knesset approved a new recruitment law, which is expected to increase the enlistment of ultra-religious Jews (*Haredim*) in the armed forces. The law also includes a reduction from 36 to 32 months of the mandatory service term for men. This will take effect from August 2015 for new recruits.

Another war in Gaza

A total of 66 Israeli soldiers and six civilians were killed during the 2014 war in Gaza, while the United Nations estimated Palestinian deaths at over 2,000, many of them civilians. This latest round of fighting began as a stand-off conflict, with Palestinian groups launching rockets at Israel and the Israeli Air Force bombing targets in Gaza. However, after nine days of fighting, the Israeli cabinet ordered a limited ground operation. Called *Protective Edge* by the IDF, the operation focused on destroying Hamas's 'offensive tunnel' networks in Gaza, which had been excavated under the border towards Israeli territory. Of these tunnels, 32 were destroyed in two and a half weeks, though the fighting continued – on and off – for more than three. Though most tunnels were destroyed, and Hamas's rocket attacks proved unsuccessful in changing overall Israeli policy, the war also exposed the limits of a stand-off campaign: after all, Hamas had not surrendered. It continued to launch rockets until the last hours before the 26 August ceasefire took effect. Additionally, the IDF had needed to deploy ground forces in order to eliminate the tunnels, rather than relying on air power.

The war also showed the IDF's gaps in preparation for ground (and underground) warfare against terrorist and guerrilla organisations. Although military intelligence had extensive knowledge of the Gazan tunnels and senior officers had continually noted the threat these posed in the year leading up to *Protective Edge*, it was discovered that Israeli ground forces lacked the necessary doctrine, experience and equipment to quickly deal with the tunnels once an operation had been approved. Israel's defence minister, Moshe Ya'alon, assumed the operation to target tunnels would take about three days, but it took six times longer. Since the end of combat, the IDF has decided to purchase more equipment for underground warfare and will likely expand the units that deal with such threats. The IDF assumes that both Hamas and Hizbullah will continue to rely on tunnel warfare, as tunnels provide possible advantages in heavily populated urban areas. At the same time, Israel will be looking for a better technological solution to locate these tunnels.

The IDF's main problem, however, is more fundamental: most of its units train and prepare for large-scale armoured warfare – along the lines of the 1973 Yom Kippur War – against enemies that no longer exist. Defence planners are now considering the need to prepare Israel's armed forces specifically for conflicts with guerrilla organisations and, perhaps, additional structural changes. Analysts expect further procurement of systems used by the IDF during the

Figure 17 Equipment Analysis: Israel's *Merkava* IV Main Battle Tank

The latest Mark IV version of Israel's indigenous *Merkava* MBT family continues the series' strong emphasis on crew protection and survivability. Key to this is the **front-mounted engine** design, the first modern MBT to include this, increasing frontal protection and permitting a unique **rear hatch** for protected evacuation or embarkation without the reliance on – and exposure from – a top-mounted hatch. From the outset, the requirements for *Merkava* placed a strong emphasis on countering urban militia; Western armies' future designs may be influenced by the *Merkava* as well as lessons from their own recent conflicts. Advances in **modular composite armour** also enable easier replacement of damaged areas. From 2009, some featured the *Trophy* Heavy Vehicle (HV) Active Protection System (APS) – the first operational MBT to deploy an APS. This combination has been reportedly combat proven, including claimed successes during *Operation Protective Edge* in 2014. APS can theoretically reduce reliance on traditional armour, potentially allowing lighter, more mobile future MBTs, though this also depends on threat evolution.

- 7.62mm machine gun
- *Trophy* HV APS (total 4 radar antennas + 2 launchers)
- 12.7mm coaxial machine gun
- 7.62mm coaxial machine gun
- 120mm smoothbore main gun
- Front-mounted engine
- Advanced all-day/-night sights for target acquisition
- Modular turret armour
- Rear crew hatch
- 60mm internal mortar
- 2 x 6 smoke-grenade launchers
- Four crew members (commander, gunner, driver, loader)

Trophy Heavy Vehicle Active Protection System

1. Threat detection and tracking
- Onboard radar
- Track calculated
- Incoming projectile

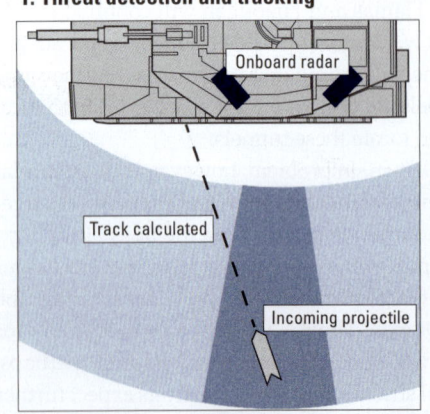

2. Hard Kill countermeasure
- Multiple Explosive Formed Penetrators activated

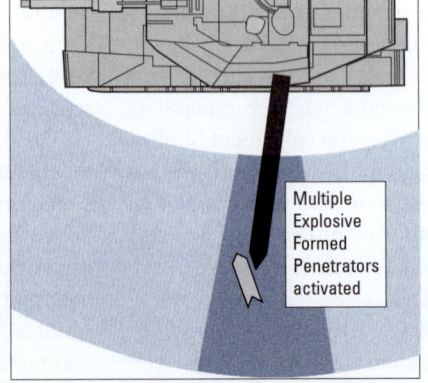

Trophy HV reportedly provides 360-degree azimuth and extensive elevation coverage against rocket-propelled grenades, anti-tank guided missiles and high-explosive anti-tank rounds. It is designed to only engage threats that are about to hit, reducing potential collateral damage including to nearby friendly troops, who are protected by predefined safe zones.

Photo: Michael Shvadron, IDF
© IISS

Hamas after the war in Gaza

Israel's security establishment estimated that Hamas and Palestinian Islamic Jihad possessed about 10,000 rockets before the 2014 war in Gaza, with between 2,000 and 3,000 remaining after (about 4,500 were used; others were destroyed in Israeli air-strikes). Some of these are probably capable of reaching the Tel Aviv area, in the heart of Israel. The capacity to produce new rockets has likely been degraded, however, since many manufacturing facilities were destroyed or damaged by Israeli forces.

Hamas did not publish an official record of its casualties as a proportion of the over 2,000 Palestinian dead. Israeli assessments of the number of dead who could be described as 'belonging to Palestinian military organisations' varied between 600 and 900, and Israeli analysts believe the lower number closer to reality. That still leaves over 1,000 non-combatant dead. According to the June–August 2014 *Humanitarian Bulletin* released by the UN's Office for the Coordination of Humanitarian Affairs (UNOCHA), 1,486 civilians, 146 of unknown affiliation and 557 'members of armed groups' died. However, the longer-term impact of the war remains significant, not least for the broader population in Gaza. UNOCHA pointed to the substantial damage to infrastructure resulting from the conflict: 'Around 13% of the housing stock in Gaza was destroyed or damaged ... and over 100,000 became homeless.' Meanwhile, Israeli authorities' wariness over the destination of building supplies entering the Strip (cement was a prime ingredient for the construction of both Hamas's offensive tunnels and those that may have carried everyday goods) has led to the continuation of restrictions on the supply of building materials, impeding rebuilding in Gaza.

Hamas could find some satisfaction in its ability to fight the Israel Defense Forces (IDF) for a period of 50 days. This is Israel's third large military campaign in Gaza in five and a half years, with no decisive victory achieved. The combination of heavily fortified defensive structures, the offensive tunnel network and a wide arsenal of rockets had been enough to deter the IDF from mounting large-scale manoeuvre operations in Gaza City. Hamas also managed to severely disrupt everyday life for southern Israelis and, to a lesser extent, those in central areas: for 36 hours, rocket fire even managed to force a near-complete closure of Israel's main international transport hub, Ben Gurion Airport.

Nevertheless, most of Hamas's offensive efforts ended in failure: the thousands of rockets launched had limited lethal effect; nearly all of its offensive tunnels were discovered and destroyed by the IDF; and most Hamas commando attacks were thwarted with no damage to the Israeli population. This would, analysts said, likely lead Hamas – and Hizbullah – to rethink their strategy against the Israeli home front. With the end result of the July–August war decisive for neither side, the question remained whether this could serve as an incentive for a new round of violence in the near future.

---

war in Gaza, including the *Trophy* point-defence system for armoured vehicles, *Keshet* self-propelled mortar systems and *Namer* armoured personnel carriers, plus equipment to enhance precision air-strikes and the IDF's intelligence apparatus.

The bombardment from Gaza also highlighted the importance of rocket- and missile-defence systems. During the war, the IDF was able to deploy nine *Iron Dome* batteries (it only officially had six batteries operating when the fighting began). These systems managed to intercept between 85% and 90% of rockets; these killed two Israelis, although 18, among them five civilians, were killed from short-range mortar fire. But the war demonstrated the need for at least four more *Iron Dome* and two *David's Sling* batteries (expected to arrive in 2015), as well as the *Arrow* 3 missile-defence system (expected within two years) for a better response to the rocket challenge. In addition, there could be a move to develop a more technological answer to mortar fire. The IDF leadership has identified, however, that in a possible future conflict with Hizbullah – which has a much larger and more capable rocket inventory than Hamas – even this bolstered defensive inventory may not be enough.

Compared to Israel's 2008–09 ground operation in Gaza (*Operation Cast Lead*), the 2014 mission was more substantial both in terms of deployed Israeli firepower and Palestinian resistance on the ground, although Israeli forces operated within a very narrow strip – about 2–3km deep into Palestinian territory. Israel also seemed less apprehensive about military casualties than in the past, though it remained very concerned about the possible abduction of soldiers. Nevertheless, the question remained about how willing Israel's authorities would be to incur substantial losses in full-scale urban combat operations of the order that might be required to fully destroy Hamas's military infrastructure in Gaza, or Hizbullah's military capabilities in southern Lebanon. While the

Israeli administration had shown some hesitation during *Operation Protective Edge*, it might accept greater casualty numbers if it believes it has no other alternative in a future confrontation.

The end of the fighting in August was accompanied, as usual, by internal budget battles. The defence ministry demanded US$5.5 billion both as compensation for expenses incurred during the war and for capability development over the next year and a half. In late September, Netanyahu agreed to add about US$4bn to the defence budget. However, the defence minister claimed that this was not enough; analysts believe that additional funds may be forthcoming during 2015.

UNITED ARAB EMIRATES

The United Arab Emirates (UAE) has in recent years displayed its developing security and military capabilities on regional operations, both locally and at range. Troops and equipment were sent to Afghanistan as part of the NATO-led ISAF mission – around 1,000 at the height of the deployment – while a small range of air-force assets engaged in offensive operations over Syria in late 2014 as part of the coalition of nations attempting to degrade the threat posed by the Islamic State of Iraq and al-Sham (ISIS).

These deployments owed much to the concern of the Emirates' rulers regarding the developing political and security situation in some regional states after the Arab Spring. However, since the UAE was federated in 1971, defence-policy considerations have generally related to the country's strategic location, placed between large, ideologically polarised regimes – the Kingdom of Saudi Arabia and the Islamic Republic of Iran. The UAE perceives asymmetric as well as conventional threats, from both state and non-state actors. The deteriorating security situation in key regional states has only exacerbated this concern.

Defence-policy developments

Since the creation of the Union, the UAE's armed forces have undergone three key rounds of modernisation. The first began after the foundation of the state in 1971; in the following five years, defence forces were developed and maintained on a national basis, with some of the Emirates maintaining individual forces to deter larger neighbours. National-level command structures were established, as were police forces, which still operate independently. The Abu Dhabi Defence Force, established in 1965, became the Western Command in 1976; the Dubai Defence force, established in 1971, became Central Command in 1996; and the Ras Al Khaimah mobile force, formed in 1969, became Northern Command in 1996, while the Sharjah National Guard, established in 1972, merged with the federal police in 1976.

The second modernisation round was spurred by the First Gulf War, when UAE policymakers took notice of their armed forces' limitations, especially in responding to comparatively larger neighbouring states. This led to the procurement of *Leclerc* main battle tanks (MBTs) and BMP-3 armoured infantry fighting vehicles, as well as an upgrade to the *Mirage* combat-aircraft fleet. The third period began at the turn of the millennium; since 2001, the UAE has procured a substantial F-16 *Fighting Falcon* fleet, modernised the navy and upgraded missile-defence capabilities.

Given the relatively recent establishment of the Emirati armed forces, and the incremental growth they have experienced, a key driver for military development has been the strategic imperative to strengthen military capabilities at the same time as developing the technical capacity of the UAE's workforce. Personnel limitations mean there is a drive to develop and place Emirati nationals into critical industrial sectors such as finance, oil and engineering, many of which have been supported by defence-offset agreements.

This industrial-development imperative for Emirati defence procurement has highlighted the attention that the UAE gives to the crucial personnel limitation. The UAE is a moderately sized nation with a population of nearly 9.3 million and official reports suggest there are around 3m people who are fit for military service (including non-nationals) – with about 51,000 reaching military age every year. Most personnel are positioned in the land forces, with the air force, navy and Presidential Guard (PG) possessing smaller numbers, but there is no reserve component. Some analysts believe that the introduction of national service in 2014 might, in time, lead to the creation of a reserve force. National service is also intended to significantly increase the number of Emirati nationals in the armed forces, which currently include a number of other nationalities.

Platforms and forces

Although the UAE ground forces have the largest number of troops, they remain relatively underfunded in comparison to the other services. For instance, the PG receives funding and training with the objective of mirroring the capabilities of the US Marine Corps (USMC), among other roles. They provide both a mechanised infantry brigade and a Special Operations Force, which is reflected in their training programme and mission status. The PG has taken part in training activities with the USMC, as well as the United Kingdom's Royal Marines and an array of special-forces units from around the world. The unit – in its current form – was only founded in 2010, which may account for its aggressive focus on training and development. International support for this developing capability was evidenced in the January 2014 US Defense Security Cooperation Agency announcement of a possible Foreign Military Sale deal for training valued at US$150m, to 'provide the continuation of [USMC] training of the UAE's Presidential Guard for counterterrorism, counter-piracy, critical infrastructure protection and national defense'. This is also perhaps a pointer to the wider roles envisaged for the Guard.

Despite underfunding, the ground-force inventory consists of nearly 400 French-made *Leclerc* MBTs, some in the PG; around 70 UK-manufactured *Scorpion* light tanks; and over 500 Russian-produced BMP-3s, the latter reportedly a favourite among land-forces personnel. There has been significant investment in armoured personnel carriers, with the latest fleet addition of around 750 Oshkosh Defense M-ATV mine-resistant ambush-protected vehicles arriving in 2013. The government has also ordered over 1,000 Emirati-made Nimr 4x4 and 6x6 vehicles.

The Emirati air force has undergone significant modernisation and remains the focus for investment. The UAE's air-superiority doctrine emphasises technology with multiplying effects. For instance, an unmanned aerial vehicle (UAV) capability is being pursued. Agreement was reached to procure *Predator XP* in early 2013, an export variant that addresses US concerns over range and payload for foreign customers. The UAE is also making headway in the development of indigenously produced UAVs, key examples being the *Yabhon* and *United 40*.

Manned combat air, however, is the most recently demonstrated element of Emirati air power, as evinced by combat missions against ISIS. The air fleet consists of over 70 F-16 Block 60s and just under 70 *Mirage* 2000s. An additional attrition purchase, coupled with an upgrade, dubbed the F-16 Block 61, was under discussion during 2014. Fleet modernisation – with an eye to the ageing *Mirage* airframes – has been much discussed in light of the failed negotiations in recent years to purchase Dassault's *Rafale* and BAE Systems' *Typhoon*. These foundered largely because the UAE was, in the case of France, unconvinced by the accompanying industrial packages; for *Typhoon*, some analysts believe pricing was the deciding factor. Another possibility is that the UAE might be waiting until an export version of the F-35 Joint Strike Fighter becomes available, though this could lead to a fleet comprised wholly of US-made aircraft. Furthermore, some analysts question whether the F-35 airframe is suitable for an air-superiority role, in addition to the time it would likely take for the aircraft to be released and enter service.

The air force also possesses three A330 MRTT tanker/transport aircraft that have allowed unprecedented capability to patrol home skies as well as deploy both aircraft and personnel further afield, adding to the lift capability of its C-130 and C-17 fleets. The Saab 340 *Erieye* currently fulfils the airborne early-warning-and-control requirement, though the UAE has been looking for a longer-term replacement in recent years. Most of the rotary-wing fleet has been separated out into the Joint Aviation Command (JAC), which now encompasses helicopters from the army, navy and air force, as well as special-mission fixed-wing aircraft, including Cessna 208B *Grand Caravan*. (The PG maintains its own rotary-wing fleet.) Air defence is also an air-force mission, and there has been some development in this area, with plans for a layered approach combining the UK *Rapier* with the US *Patriot* and Terminal High-Altitude Area Defense (THAAD) missile systems; the latter remain on order.

There has also been investment in air-force training. Fighter pilots have regularly taken part in the *Red Flag* exercises in the US since 2012, whilst also undertaking joint-training missions with a wide array of allies, including Australia's August 2014 *Pitch Black* exercise. The air force is prioritising joint operational capabilities in order to efficiently cooperate with NATO on multinational missions, and in 2013 opened a Mission to NATO, with an ambassador and military representation. (The UAE had already joined NATO's Istanbul Cooperation Initiative in 2004.)

There is limited maritime capability, with the UAE's principal vessels being six *Baynunah*-class corvettes, of which five were built in Abu Dhabi. There is also one *Abu Dhabi*-class corvette with the option – with Fincantieri's joint venture Etihad Ship Building – for two more. Maritime aerial reconnaissance is performed by the air force while surface patrols are conducted by a fleet of patrol craft, though local defence industry has started to test unmanned technology for some of these missions. The navy maintains close ties with its US, UK, Pakistani, French and Italian counterparts and is a long-time, active partner in the Combined Maritime Forces based in Bahrain. Junior officers and non-commissioned officers are often sent to the Pakistan Navy School while select personnel are sent to the Naval War College in the US and the UK's Britannia Royal Naval College. Ties with the French Indian Ocean base in Abu Dhabi have resulted in numerous training initiatives, as well as multinational exercise programmes.

International defence cooperation

Building on its existing defence contacts, the UAE has in the last decade strengthened relationships with the US, Australia, France and the UK, and developed relationships with South Africa and South Korea. Participation in NATO-led activities in Afghanistan and Libya has translated into training partnerships with some NATO member states. Industrial cooperation with the above countries has helped the UAE to diversify its economy, as well as build capabilities in related sectors.

The predominant drivers of this international cooperation are, firstly, the critical lack of personnel – which limits the current capabilities of the UAE armed forces – and, secondly, a drive to leverage defence technologies to further broader national industrial and economic advancement. The development of the PG can in some ways be seen as an outcome of these ties; so can the domestically produced *Yahsat* satellites and *Baynunah*-class corvettes.

Personnel shortages have led the UAE to absorb predominantly Pakistani, Jordanian and Comoran nationals into the armed forces; many have gained citizenship as a result. Although this trend has diminished, foreign nationals are still present in the armed services. These nationalities tend to occupy the lower ranks, while foreign nationals from Western countries hold higher ranks, either on secondment from host nations or in second careers after retirement. For instance, the PG is currently commanded by a retired Australian major-general, while the JAC is commanded by a retired American major-general. Foreign armed forces also maintain a presence at Emirati bases, notably al-Dhafra Air Base – at which US and French, as well as Emirati, air assets are located – and Jebel Ali Port.

Defence economics

As a result of its natural resources, principally related to energy, the UAE benefits from a very high GDP per capita, which has allowed it to substantially increase its estimated defence spend. However, while defence spending may have risen, the overall rise in GDP means that military expenditure as a percentage of GDP has in fact decreased.

With official data unavailable, analysts can only estimate UAE defence spending. However, official announcements at the International Defense Exhibition in Abu Dhabi indicated that procurement spending, while still strong, has fallen from US$4.9 billion in 2009 to US$3.95bn in 2011, and US$3.84bn in 2013. Ascertaining precise costs is additionally complicated, according to analysts, by the fact that the procurement of major systems, such as THAAD and a next-generation fighter aircraft, are not included in the budget. This derives in part from the Emirati view that spending on security should not be impeded, but also from the fact that the line between military and security budgets is somewhat blurred; there are many dual-use programmes that have undisclosed or opaque budgets. Furthermore, amid recruitment efforts and salary and pension increases – as well as the wish to transform and improve 'C4ISR' (command, control, communications, computers, intelligence, surveillance and reconnaissance) – considerable funds are being allocated to the security budget; this has led some analysts to conclude that military budgets are being substantially increased. In other words, there are military applications to elements of the security spend; but, because these are not registered as military expenditure, there needs to be careful examination of what line items are publicised by the UAE. Key examples are the *Yahsat* satellites and the establishment of the National Electronic Security Authority (NESA).

Growing local defence-industrial capacity
The UAE initiated a joint-logistics programme in 2011. With operations at home or overseas usually part of a joint effort or larger coalition, it was assessed that logistics provision should be both joint and coordinated. As part of this initiative, public–private partnerships are increasingly being explored for platform maintenance, repair and overhaul.

Advisory committees, or Centres of Excellence (CoE), were established to manage relationships between general headquarters and industry, both local and foreign. These CoEs are designed to help the UAE move away from transactional relationships toward a strategic-partnership model, which might reduce the number of deals but is intended to deliver longer-term relationships. This model will transfer some non-core capacities to industry and alleviate personnel weaknesses by greater involvement of the civilian sector in the day-to-day running of the armed forces. Key relationships with nations willing to transfer technology will remain; the US will retain influence in this regard because of perceptions of the advanced nature of its available technology. However, US International Traffic in Arms Regulations (ITAR) continue to be a stumbling block for US firms and this has resulted in strategic-industrial relationships being developed with new partners such as Yugoimport from Serbia and the Military Industrial Corporation of Belarus.

The name of the UAE Offset Program Bureau was changed to the Tawazun Economic Council (TEC) in 2012. This organisation is responsible for applying and managing offset-related deals and supervising the creation of joint ventures between the UAE and international contractors. UAE offset-obligation states that supply contracts valued at US$10m in any five-year period will have offset obligations applied. Contracts under US$10m in that period are not covered.

The TEC is a central part of the UAE's developing defence-industrial landscape, stemming from the role it plays in forging ties between international contractors and local defence industry. Additionally, the TEC is the strategic arm of state-owned defence industry, the Emirati defence conglomerate Tawazun. This conglomerate leads on most of the UAE's manufacturing capabilities and has seen substantial sales success in the vehicle programmes of its subsidiary Nimr Automotive. Other related companies include precision-guided munitions manufacturer Tawazun Dynamics – a joint venture with South Africa's Denel, and which locally assembles Denel's *Umbani* as the *Al-Tariq* weapons-guidance kit – small-arms manufacturer Caracal and Abu Dhabi Autonomous Systems Investments (ADASI).

However, Tawazun faces competition not just from international companies but also from other large, local defence concerns, including Mubadala, Emirates Advanced Investments, International Golden Group, Al Seer Marine and the UAV firm ADCOM Systems. This has led some analysts to consider whether the UAE might decide to merge some of these larger firms into an integrated defence organisation. This could be state-owned, with smaller companies remaining independent.

Part of the UAE's overall defence-industrial strategy is to broaden the technical capacities of the local workforce and engender a range of competencies that can be diffused through industry. Abu Dhabi Ship Building (ADSB), a subsidiary of Mubadala, in constructing five of the six *Baynunah*-class corvettes is a key example of the UAE's ambition to develop technical capabilities to alleviate previous reliance on foreign contractors. Caracal, a subsidiary of Tawazun, boasts a 100% Emirati workforce, emphasising the importance of the expansion in local technical capacity. Furthermore, when considering the ambitions of the joint-logistics programme, development of indigenous capabilities may be seen as a strategic imperative.

The UAE defence industry can boast major procurement deals with Libya, Algeria and Lebanon, and continues to compete for business with Gulf Cooperation Council states and abroad. The UAE and Algeria signed an agreement in 2012 to cooperatively manufacture Nimr vehicles and have produced over 1,000 so far, according to Tawazun. Additional vehicles have been sent to Libya, Lebanon and Jordan. ADSB hopes to sell the *Baynunah*-class corvette to Saudi Arabia and Kuwait, while Nimr Automotive is looking for more markets for its armoured vehicles. The Advanced Military Maintenance Repair and Overhaul Center, Global Aerospace Logistics and ADSB can all expect to gain more maintenance, repair and overhaul business in future, not least because they are able to offer financially attractive packages for platforms widely used in the region. Furthermore, ADCOM Systems is looking to export the *Yabhon* and *United 40* series UAVs; the latter is also reported to have undergone weapons testing.

While the UAE defence industry has yet to see significant commercial success, its contribution to diversifying the economy and successfully bringing UAE nationals into a strategically important industry is deemed a major success. However, international support has been pivotal, and in this regard the UAE has demonstrated considerable pragmatism, seeking assistance from a range of countries. Frustrated by ITAR regulations and other US restrictions, the UAE has sought partnerships with countries as far afield as Serbia, South Korea and South Africa. Coupling the expertise of these and other nations with the UAE's financial clout and ambition, the UAE's defence industry is growing at an unprecedented rate.

UAE-delivered platforms

The UAE has prioritised unmanned technology for indigenous production and is domestically developing armed UAVs through ADCOM Systems. The *Camcopter* S-100 UAV, meanwhile, has been co-developed locally as part of a joint programme between Austrian firm Schiebel and ADASI, a subsidiary of state-owned Mubadala. The resulting system, *Al-Sabr*, has been seen in UAE air-force colours. Aerostats have also been developed, though with limited commercial success. Al Seer Marine in Abu Dhabi has successfully constructed unmanned surface vessels to assist critical-infrastructure protection and increase general maritime-surveillance capacity. Unmanned systems have been, and will continue to be, at the forefront of industrial participation for the UAE's defence industry. Additionally, due to US ITAR restrictions – especially for unmanned systems – the UAE considers it a necessity to indigenously develop a range of platforms to ensure technical as well as construction expertise.

In the manned-systems domain, the standout products are those of Nimr Automotive, and the UAE has itself procured around 1,000 Nimr 4x4 and 6x6 vehicles. Other products include Jobaria Defense Systems' 122mm Multiple-Cradle Launcher (multiple-rocket launcher) system, created with assistance from Turkey's Roketsan. Within the maritime domain, the UAE is working to integrate the *Baynunah-* and *Abu Dhabi*-class corvettes into its wider naval force structure. It is unlikely the UAE Navy will procure any other major military assets given personnel restrictions. However, that the corvettes recently procured have, for the most part, been built in Abu Dhabi, clearly indicates the advances made in the local shipbuilding sector; as a result, the UAE has also gained some capability to maintain, repair and overhaul its vessels, and those of potential customers, without foreign assistance.

Another area of local industrial development concerns C4ISR systems. The UAE is looking to boost the capacities of its armed forces in this area, and has been procuring technology, knowledge and expertise that have been translated into indigenously manufactured products, notably the dual-use *Yahsat* Y1A and Y1B satellites currently in orbit. Locally made, these provide output to the UAE armed forces. The UAE has also been negotiating with the French government for two high-resolution *Pleiades*-type *Falcon Eye* military observation satellites. In addition, the UAE is developing its nascent cyber capabilities: in 2012 it created NESA to address online threats, protect networks and develop national policy on cyber security; in parallel, a military cyber command was established.

Algeria ALG

Algerian Dinar D		2013	2014	2015
GDP	D	16.9tr	18.2tr	
	US$	212bn	228bn	
per capita	US$	5,606	5,886	
Growth	%	2.8	3.8	
Inflation	%	3.3	3.2	
Def bdgt	D	826bn	956bn	
	US$	10.4bn	12bn	
US$1=D			79.37	79.69

Population 38,813,722

Age	0–14	15–19	20–24	25–29	30–64	65 plus
Male	14.5%	4.1%	4.8%	4.8%	20.0%	2.4%
Female	13.9%	3.9%	4.6%	4.6%	19.6%	2.8%

Capabilities

Defence planners remain concerned by the conflict in Mali, instability in Libya, regional terrorist activity and porous eastern and southern borders. These have motivated changing policy priorities, structures and deployments. New military regions and more garrisons in outlying areas have been established to protect border zones. In 2014, responsibility for borders passed to the defence ministry, and monitoring of the crossings with Mauritania, Mali, Niger and Libya was strengthened. As the strongest military force in the region, Algeria has been a leading proponent of combined training with neighbouring powers, partially to build counter-terrorist capacity in the Sahel and Maghreb regions. The armed forces have substantial counter-insurgency experience and took over the counter-narcotics-trafficking role in 2013. The army maintains a division-sized rapid-reaction force, although capability and deployment speed is hampered by the majority-conscript nature of the army. Mobility is enhanced by a large fleet of light armoured vehicles and helicopters and a modest power-projection capability is provided by transport and air-tanker fleets. Naval amphibious capability was enhanced in 2014 by the delivery of an LPD, and three Chinese-built corvettes destined for the navy were launched in mid-year.

ACTIVE 130,000 (Army 110,000 Navy 6,000 Air 14,000) **Paramilitary 187,200**

Conscript liability 18 months, only in the army (6 months basic, 12 months with regular army often involving civil projects)

RESERVE 150,000 (Army 150,000) to age 50

ORGANISATIONS BY SERVICE

Army 35,000; 75,000 conscript (total 110,000)
FORCES BY ROLE
6 Mil Regions; re-org into div structure on hold

MANOEUVRE
  Armoured
  2 (1st & 8th) armd div (3 tk regt; 1 mech regt, 1 arty gp)
  1 indep armd bde
  Mechanised
  2 (12th & 40th) mech div (1 tk regt; 3 mech regt, 1 arty gp)
  3 indep mech bde
  Light
  2 indep mot bde
  Air Manoeuvre
  1 AB div (4 para regt; 1 SF regt)
COMBAT SUPPORT
  2 arty bn
  7 AD bn
  4 engr bn

EQUIPMENT BY TYPE
MBT 1,195: 300 T-90S; 325 T-72; 300 T-62; 270 T-54/T-55
RECCE 134: 44 AML-60; 26 BRDM-2; 64 BRDM-2M with 9M133 *Kornet* (AT-14 *Spriggan*)
AIFV 1,089: 100 BMP-3; 304 BMP-2M with 9M133 *Kornet* (AT-14 *Spriggan*); 685 BMP-1
APC 731+
  APC (W) 729: 250 BTR-60; 150 BTR-80; 150 OT-64; 55 M3 Panhard; 24+ TPz-1 *Fuchs*; 100 *Fahd*
  PPV 2 *Marauder*
ARTY 1,091
  SP 224: **122mm** 140 2S1; **152mm** 30 2S3; **155mm** ε54 PLZ-45
  TOWED 393: **122mm** 345 160 D-30; 25 D-74; 100 M-1931/37; 60 M-30; **130mm** 10 M-46; **152mm** 20 ML-20 M-1937; **155mm** 18 Type-88 (PLL-01)
  MRL 144: **122mm** 48 BM-21; **140mm** 48 BM-14/16; **240mm** 30 BM-24; **300mm** 18 9A52 *Smerch*
  MOR 330: **82mm** 150 M-37; **120mm** 120 M-1943; **160mm** 60 M-1943
AT
  MSL • MANPATS *Milan*; 9K135 *Kornet*-E (AT-14 *Spriggan*); 9K115-2 *Metis*-M1 (AT-13 *Saxhorn*-2); 9K11 *Malyutka* (AT-3 *Sagger*); 9K111 *Fagot* (AT-4 *Spigot*); 9K113 *Konkurs* (AT-5 *Spandrel*)
  RCL 180: **107mm** 60 B-11; **82mm** 120 B-10
  GUNS 250: **57mm** 160 ZIS-2 M-1943; **85mm** 80 D-44; **100mm** 10 T-12
AD
  SAM 288+
    SP 132+: ε48 9K33M *Osa* (SA-8B *Gecko*); ε20 9K31 *Strela*-1 (SA-9 *Gaskin*); 96K6 *Pantsir*-S1 (SA-22 *Greyhound*)
    MANPAD 9K32 *Strela*-2 (SA-7A/B *Grail*)‡
  GUNS ε830
    SP ε225 ZSU-23-4
    TOWED ε605: **14.5mm** 100: 60 ZPU-2; 40 ZPU-4 **23mm** 100 ZU-23 **37mm** ε150 M-1939 **57mm** 75 S-60 **85mm** 20 M-1939 *KS-12* **100mm** 150 KS-19 **130mm** 10 KS-30

Navy ε6,000
EQUIPMENT BY TYPE
SUBMARINES • TACTICAL • SSK 4:
  2 *Kilo* (FSU *Paltus*) with 6 single 533mm TT with Test-71ME HWT/3M54 *Klub-S* (SS-N-27B) AShM

2 Improved *Kilo* (RUS *Varshavyanka*) with 6 single 533mm TT with Test-71ME HWT/3M54 *Klub*-S (SS-N-27B) AShM

PRINCIPAL SURFACE COMBATANTS 3
  FRIGATES • FF 3:
    3 *Mourad Rais* (FSU *Koni*) with 2 twin 533mm TT, 2 RBU 6000 *Smerch* 2, 2 twin 76mm gun

PATROL AND COASTAL COMBATANTS 24
  CORVETTES 6
    FSGM 3 *Rais Hamidou* (FSU *Nanuchka* II) with up to 4 twin lnchr with 3M24 *Uran* (SS-N-25 *Switchblade*) AShM, 1 twin lnchr with 9M33 *Osa*-M (SA-N-4 *Gecko*) SAM, 1 AK630 CIWS, 1 twin 57mm gun
    FSG 3 *Djebel Chenoua* with 2 twin lnchr with C-802 (CSS-N-8 *Saccade*) AShM, 1 AK630 CIWS, 1 76mm gun
    PBFG 9 *Osa* II (3†) with 4 single lnchr with P-15 *Termit* (SS-N-2B *Styx*) AShM
  PB 9 *Kebir* with 1 76mm gun

AMPHIBIOUS
  PRINCIPAL AMPHIBIOUS SHIPS • LPD 1 *Kalaat Beni Abbes* with 1 16-cell A50 VLS with *Aster*-15 SAM, 1 76mm gun (capacity 5 med hel; 15 MBT; 350 troops)
  LS 3:
    LSM 1 *Polnochny* B with 1 twin AK230 CIWS (capacity 6 MBT; 180 troops)
    LST 2 *Kalaat beni Hammad* (capacity 7 MBT; 240 troops) with 1 med hel landing platform

LOGISTICS AND SUPPORT 11
  AGS 1 *El Idrissi*
  AX 1 *Daxin* with 2 twin AK230 CIWS, 1 76mm gun, 1 hle landing platform
  YGS 2 *Ras Tara*
  YPT 1 *Poluchat* I (used for SAR)
  YTB 6: 1 *El Chadid*; 1 *Kader*; 4 *Mazafran*

Naval Aviation

EQUIPMENT BY TYPE
HELICOPTERS
  SAR 10: 6 AW101 SAR; 4 *Super Lynx* Mk130

Coast Guard ε500

EQUIPMENT BY TYPE
PATROL AND COASTAL COMBATANTS 55
  PBF 6 *Baglietto* 20
  PB 49: 6 *Baglietto Mangusta*; 12 *Jebel Antar*; 21 *Deneb*; 4 *El Mounkid*; 6 *Kebir* with 1 76mm gun
LOGISTICS AND SUPPORT 9
  ARL 1 *El Mourafek*
  ARS 3 *El Moundjid*
  AXL 5 *El Mouderrib* (PRC *Chui-E*) (2 more in reserve†)

Air Force 14,000

Flying hours 150 hrs/year

FORCES BY ROLE
FIGHTER
  1 sqn with MiG-25PDS/RU *Foxbat*
  4 sqn with MiG-29C/UB *Fulcrum*
FIGHTER/GROUND ATTACK
  2 sqn with Su-24M/MK *Fencer* D
  3 sqn with Su-30MKA *Flanker*
ELINT
  1 sqn with Beech 1900D
MARITIME PATROL
  2 sqn with Beech 200T/300 *King Air*
ISR
  1 sqn with Su-24MR *Fencer* E*; MiG-25RBSh *Foxbat* D*
TANKER
  1 sqn with Il-78 *Midas*
TRANSPORT
  1 sqn with C-130H/H-30 *Hercules*; L-100-30
  1 sqn with C-295M
  1 sqn with Gulfstream IV-SP; Gulfstream V
  1 sqn with Il-76MD/TD *Candid*
TRAINING
  2 sqn with Z-142
  1 sqn with Yak-130 *Mitten*
  2 sqn with L-39C/ZA *Albatros*
  1 hel sqn with PZL Mi-2 *Hoplite*
ATTACK HELICOPTER
  3 sqn with Mi-24 *Hind*
TRANSPORT HELICOPTER
  1 sqn with AS355 *Ecureuil*
  5 sqn with Mi-8 *Hip*; Mi-17 *Hip* H
  1 sqn with Ka-27PS *Helix* D; Ka-32T *Helix*
AIR DEFENCE
  3 ADA bde
  3 SAM regt with S-75 *Dvina* (SA-2 *Guideline*)/S-125 *Neva* (SA-3 *Goa*)/2K12 *Kub* (SA-6 *Gainful*); S-300PMU2 (SA-20 *Gargoyle*)

EQUIPMENT BY TYPE
AIRCRAFT 120 combat capable
  FTR 35: 12 MiG-25 *Foxbat*; 23 MiG-29C/UB *Fulcrum*
  FGA 77: 44 Su-30MKA; 33 Su-24M/MK *Fencer* D
  ISR 8: 4 MiG-25RBSh *Foxbat* D*; 4 Su-24MR *Fencer* E*
  TKR 6 Il-78 *Midas*
  TPT 67: **Heavy** 12: 3 Il-76MD *Candid* B; 9 Il-76TD *Candid*; **Medium** 17: 9 C-130H *Hercules*; 6 C-130H-30 *Hercules*; 2 L-100-30; **Light** 32: 3 Beech C90B *King Air*; 5 Beech 200T *King Air*; 6 Beech 300 *King Air*; 12 Beech 1900D (electronic surv); 5 C-295M; 1 F-27 *Friendship*; **PAX** 6: 1 A340; 4 Gulfstream IV-SP; 1 Gulfstream V
  TRG 99: 36 L-39ZA *Albatros*; 7 L-39C *Albatros*; 16 Yak-130 *Mitten*; 40 Z-142
HELICOPTERS
  ATK 32 Mi-24 *Hind*
  SAR 3 Ka-27PS *Helix* D
  MRH 3 Bell 412EP
  MRH/TPT 75 Mi-8 *Hip* (med tpt)/Mi-17 *Hip* H
  TPT 45: **Medium** 4 Ka-32T *Helix*; **Light** 41: 8 AS355 *Ecureuil*; 5 AW139 (SAR); 28 PZL Mi-2 *Hoplite*
UAV • ISR • Medium *Seeker* II
AD
  SAM S-75 *Dvina* (SA-2 *Guideline*); S-125 *Pechora*-M (SA-3 *Goa*); 2K12 *Kvadrat* (SA-6 *Gainful*); S-300PMU2 (SA-20 *Gargoyle*)
  GUNS 725 100mm/130mm/85mm
MSL
  ASM Kh-25 (AS-10 *Karen*); Kh-29 (AS-14 *Kedge*); Kh-23 (AS-7 *Kerry*); Kh-31P/A (AS-17A/B *Krypton*); Kh-59ME (AS-18 *Kazoo*): ZT-35 *Ingwe*

ARM Kh-25MP (AS-12 *Kegler*)
AAM • IR R-3 (AA-2 *Atoll*)‡; R-60 (AA-8 *Aphid*); R-73 (A-11 *Archer*); IR/SARH R-40/46 (AA-6 *Acrid*); R-23/24 (AA-7 *Apex*); R-27 (AA-10 *Alamo*); ARH R-77 (AA-12 *Adder*)

Paramilitary ε187,200

Gendarmerie 20,000
Ministry of Defence control; 6 regions
EQUIPMENT BY TYPE
RECCE AML-60
APC (W) 210: 100 *Fahd*; 110 M3 Panhard
HELICOPTERS • TPT • Light Some PZL Mi-2 *Hoplite*

National Security Forces 16,000
Directorate of National Security. Small arms

Republican Guard 1,200
EQUIPMENT BY TYPE
RECCE AML-60
APC (T) M3 half-track

Legitimate Defence Groups ε150,000
Self-defence militia, communal guards (60,000)

DEPLOYMENT

DEMOCRATIC REPUBLIC OF THE CONGO
UN • MONUSCO 5 obs

Bahrain BHR

Bahraini Dinar D		2013	2014	2015
GDP	D	12.3bn	12.8bn	
	US$	32.8bn	34bn	
per capita	US$	27,926	28,424	
Growth	%	5.3	3.9	
Inflation	%	3.3	2.5	
Def bdgt [a]	D	465m	502m	
	US$	1.24bn	1.33bn	
FMA (US)	US$	10m	10m	7.5m
US$1=D		0.38	0.38	

[a] Includes expenditure on National Guard in 2012. Excludes funds allocated to the Ministry of the Interior.

Population 1,314,089

Ethnic groups: Nationals 64%; Asian 13%; other Arab 10%; Iranian 8%; European 1%

Age	0–14	15–19	20–24	25–29	30–64	65 plus
Male	10.0%	3.9%	5.0%	6.5%	33.8%	1.3%
Female	9.7%	3.3%	3.7%	4.0%	17.3%	1.4%

Capabilities

Bahrain retains moderately well-trained and -equipped forces. Due to their limited size, the kingdom relies on the security umbrella offered by the Gulf Cooperation Council and the deterrent effect provided by the presence of a US naval HQ and base. Bahrain retains close alliances with the US and the UK, and participates in GCC military exercises. The armed forces' primary role is defence of the island from an amphibious invasion and/or aerial assault. While in general focused on the possibility of state-to-state conflict, their role in internal security has become more apparent since 2011. The domestic protests of 2011 saw the GCC's defence obligations invoked, when Saudi, Qatari and Emirati personnel were deployed as part of the Peninsula Shield force. Since then efforts have been made to modernise and improve police and internal-security capability. The primary procurement priority in the short term is likely to be replacement of the F-5E/F *Tiger* II, delivered in the 1980s; the Eurofighter *Typhoon* is a possible candidate. Bahrain is also introducing new patrol boats.

ACTIVE 8,200 (Army 6,000 Navy 700 Air 1,500)
Paramilitary 11,260

ORGANISATIONS BY SERVICE

Army 6,000
FORCES BY ROLE
SPECIAL FORCES
  1 SF bn
MANOEUVRE
  Armoured
  1 armd bde(-) (1 recce bn, 2 armd bn)
  Mechanised
  1 inf bde (2 mech bn, 1 mot bn)
  Light
  1 (Amiri) gd bn
COMBAT SUPPORT
  1 arty bde (1 hvy arty bty, 2 med arty bty, 1 lt arty bty, 1 MRL bty)
  1 AD bn (1 ADA bty, 2 SAM bty)
  1 engr coy
COMBAT SERVICE SUPPORT
  1 log coy
  1 tpt coy
  1 med coy
EQUIPMENT BY TYPE
MBT 180 M60A3
RECCE 22 AML-90
AIFV 25 YPR-765 (with 25mm)
APC • APC (T) 200 M113A2
ARTY 151
  SP 82: **155mm** 20 M109A5; **203mm** 62 M110A2
  TOWED 36: **105mm** 8 L118 Light Gun; **155mm** 28 M198
  MRL **227mm** 9 M270 MLRS (with 30 ATACMS)
  MOR 24: SP **120mm** 12 M113A2; **81mm** 12 L16
AT
  MSL
    SP HMMWV with BGM-71A TOW
    MANPATS *Javelin*; BGM-71A TOW
  RCL 31: **106mm** 25 M40A1; **120mm** 6 MOBAT
AD • SAM 91
  SP 7 *Crotale*
  TOWED 6 MIM-23B I-HAWK
  MANPAD FIM-92A *Stinger*; RBS-70

GUNS 24: **35mm** 12 Oerlikon; **40mm** 12 L/70
ARV 53 *Fahd* 240

Navy 700
EQUIPMENT BY TYPE
PRINCIPAL SURFACE COMBATANTS 1
   FRIGATES • FFGHM 1 *Sabha* (ex-US *Oliver Hazard Perry*) with 1 Mk13 GMLS with SM-1MR SAM/RGM-84C *Harpoon* AShM, 2 triple 324mm Mk32 ASTT with Mk46 LWT, 1 *Phalanx* Block 1B CIWS, 1 76mm gun, (capacity 1 Bo-105 hel)
PATROL AND COASTAL COMBATANTS 12
   CORVETTES • FSG 2 *Al Manama* (GER Lurssen 62m) with 2 twin lnchr with MM-40 *Exocet* AShM, 1 76mm gun, 1 hel landing platform
   PCFG 4 *Ahmed el Fateh* (GER Lurssen 45m) with 2 twin lnchr with MM-40 *Exocet* AShM, 1 76mm gun
   PB 4: 2 *Al Jarim* (US *Swift* FPB-20); 2 *Al Riffa* (GER Lurssen 38m)
   PBF 2 Mk V SOC
AMPHIBIOUS • LANDING CRAFT 9
   LCU 7: 1 *Loadmaster*; 4 *Mashtan*; 2 *Dinar* (ADSB 42m)
   LCVP 2 *Sea Keeper*
LOGISTICS AND SUPPORT 2
   YFL 1 *Tighatlib*
   YFU 1 *Ajeera*

Naval Aviation
EQUIPMENT BY TYPE
HELICOPTERS • TPT • Light 2 Bo-105

Air Force 1,500
FORCES BY ROLE
FIGHTER
   2 sqn with F-16C/D *Fighting Falcon*
FIGHTER/GROUND ATTACK
   1 sqn with F-5E/F *Tiger* II
TRANSPORT
   1 (Royal) flt with B-727; B-747; BAe-146; Gulfstream II; Gulfstream IV; Gulfstream 450; Gulfstream 550; S-92A
TRAINING
   1 sqn with *Hawk* Mk129*
   1 sqn with T-67M *Firefly*
ATTACK HELICOPTER
   2 sqn with AH-1E/F *Cobra*; TAH-1P *Cobra*
TRANSPORT HELICOPTER
   1 sqn with Bell 212 (AB-212)
   1 sqn with UH-60M *Black Hawk*
   1 (VIP) sqn with Bo-105; S-70A *Black Hawk*; UH-60L *Black Hawk*
EQUIPMENT BY TYPE
AIRCRAFT 39 combat capable
   FTR 12: 8 F-5E *Tiger* II; 4 F-5F *Tiger* II
   FGA 21: 17 F-16C *Fighting Falcon*; 4 F-16D *Fighting Falcon*
   TPT • PAX 10: 1 B-727; 2 B-747; 1 Gulfstream II; 1 Gulfstream IV; 1 Gulfstream 450; 1 Gulfstream 550; 3 BAe-146
   TRG 9: 6 *Hawk* Mk129*; 3 T-67M *Firefly*
HELICOPTERS
   ATK 28: 16 AH-1E *Cobra*; 12 AH-1F *Cobra*
   TPT 27: Medium 13: 3 S-70A *Black Hawk*; 1 S-92A (VIP); 1 UH-60L *Black Hawk*; 8 UH-60M *Black Hawk*; **Light** 14: 11 Bell 212 (AB-212); 3 Bo-105
   TRG 6 TAH-1P *Cobra*
MSL
   ASM AGM-65D/G *Maverick*
   AAM • IR AIM-9P *Sidewinder*; **SARH** AIM-7 *Sparrow*; **ARH** AIM-120 AMRAAM
AT • MSL some TOW

Paramilitary ε11,260

Police 9,000
Ministry of Interior
EQUIPMENT BY TYPE
RECCE 8 S52 *Shorland*
APC
   APC (W) Otokar ISV
   PPV *Cobra*
HELICOPTERS
   MRH 2 Bell 412 *Twin Huey*
   ISR 2 Hughes 500
   TPT • Light 1 Bo-105

National Guard ε2,000
FORCES BY ROLE
MANOEUVRE
   Other
   3 paramilitary bn
EQUIPMENT BY TYPE
APC
   APC (W) *Arma* 6x6
   PPV *Cobra*

Coast Guard ε260
Ministry of Interior
PATROL AND COASTAL COMBATANTS 52
   PBF 23: 2 *Ares* 18; 4 *Jaris*; 6 *Saham*; 6 *Fajr*; 5 *Jarach*
   PB 29: 6 *Haris*; 1 *Al Muharraq*; 10 *Deraa* (of which 4 *Halmatic* 20, 2 *Souter* 20, 4 *Rodman* 20); 10 *Saif* (of which 4 *Fairey Sword*, 6 *Halmatic* 160); 2 *Hawar*
AMPHIBIOUS • LANDING CRAFT • LCU 1 *Loadmaster* II
LOGISTICS AND SUPPORT • YAG 1 *Safra*

FOREIGN FORCES
Saudi Arabia GCC (SANG): Peninsula Shield ε1,000
United Kingdom Air Force 1 BAe-125 CC-3; 1 BAe-146 MKII
United States US Central Commmand: 3,250; 1 HQ (5th Fleet)

Egypt EGY

Egyptian Pound E£		2013	2014	2015
GDP	E£	1.75tr	1.99tr	
	US$	271bn	285bn	
per capita	US$	3,243	3,337	
Growth	%	2.1	2.2	
Inflation	%	6.9	10.1	
Def bdgt	E£	34.3bn	38bn	
	US$	5.31bn	5.45bn	
FMA (US)	US$	1.3bn	1.3bn	1.3bn
US$1=E£		6.46	6.97	

Population 86,895,099

Age	0–14	15–19	20–24	25–29	30–64	65 plus
Male	16.4%	4.6%	4.5%	4.6%	18.3%	2.2%
Female	15.7%	4.4%	4.3%	4.3%	18.0%	2.7%

Capabilities

In July 2013, the armed forces ousted the incumbent president, Muhammad Morsi, and in early 2014 former army chief Abdel Fatah al-Sisi was elected president. The military's already extensive domestic business and industrial interests are reported to have expanded. In recent years, instability in Sinai, increased Islamist activity and smuggling into Gaza has led to substantive troop deployments and military operations, whilst insurgent activity on Egypt's borders has led to closer security cooperation with Libya, Algeria and Tunisia, though state breakdown in Libya and smuggling across the border is of particular concern. While training is at a high standard for many within the armed forces, the large number of conscripts and reports of conscripts being employed in military-owned businesses makes effectiveness across the entire force hard to estimate. Egypt's relationship with the US came under strain after the ouster of Morsi. Soviet-era equipment had long been replaced with US systems, but a delivery of F-16 combat aircraft (part of an order for 20) was delayed and the *Bright Star* exercise cancelled. While broader supplies remained on hold, it was announced in April 2014 that ten *Apache* helicopters would be delivered to help combat terrorism, particularly in the Sinai.

ACTIVE 438,500 (Army 310,000 Navy 18,500 Air 30,000 Air Defence Command 80,000) **Paramilitary 397,000**

Conscription liability 12 months–3 years (followed by refresher training over a period of up to 9 years)

RESERVE 479,000 (Army 375,000 Navy 14,000 Air 20,000 Air Defence 70,000)

ORGANISATIONS BY SERVICE

Army 90,000–120,000; 190,000–220,000 conscript (total 310,000)

FORCES BY ROLE
SPECIAL FORCES
5 cdo gp
1 counter-terrorist unit
MANOEUVRE
Armoured
4 armd div (2 armd bde, 1 mech bde, 1 arty bde)
4 indep armd bde
1 Republican Guard bde
Mechanised
8 mech div (1 armd bde, 2 mech bde, 1 arty bde)
4 indep mech bde
Light
1 inf div
2 indep inf bde
Air Manoeuvre
2 air mob bde
1 para bde
COMBAT SUPPORT
15 arty bde
1 SSM bde with FROG-7
1 SSM bde with *Scud*-B
6 engr bde (3 engr bn)
2 spec ops engr bn
6 salvage engr bn
24 MP bn
18 sigs bn
COMBAT SERVICE SUPPORT
36 log bn
27 med bn

EQUIPMENT BY TYPE
MBT 2,540: 1,130 M1A1 *Abrams*; 300 M60A1; 850 M60A3; 260 *Ramses* II (mod T-54/55); (840 T-54/T-55 in store); (500 T-62 in store)
RECCE 412: 300 BRDM-2; 112 *Commando Scout*
AIFV 390 YPR-765 (with 25mm); (220 BMP-1 in store)
APC 4,060
  APC (T) 2,500: 2,000 M113A2/YPR-765 (incl variants); 500 BTR-50/OT-62
  APC (W) 1,560: 250 BMR-600P; 250 BTR-60S; 410 *Fahd*-30/TH 390 *Fahd*; 650 *Walid*
ARTY 4,468
  SP 492: **122mm** 124 SP 122; **155mm** 368: 164 M109A2; 204 M109A5
  TOWED 962: **122mm** 526: 190 D-30M; 36 M-1931/37; 300 M-30; **130mm** 420 M-46; **155mm** 16 GH-52
  MRL 450: **122mm** 356: 96 BM-11; 60 BM-21; 50 *Sakr*-10; 50 *Sakr*-18; 100 *Sakr*-36; **130mm** 36 *Kooryong*; **140mm** 32 BM-14; **227mm** 26 M270 MLRS; **240mm** (48 BM-24 in store)
  MOR 2,564
    SP 136: **107mm** 100: 65 M106A1; 35 M106A2 **120mm** 36 M1064A3
    81mm 50 M125A2; **82mm** 500; **120mm** 1,848: 1,800 M-1943; 48 Brandt; **160mm** 30 M160
AT • MSL
  SP 262: 52 M-901, 210 YPR 765 PRAT
  MANPATS 9K11 *Malyutka* (AT-3 *Sagger*) (incl BRDM-2); *Milan*; TOW-2
UAV • ISR • Medium R4E-50 *Skyeye*; ASN-204

AD
  SAM
    SP 96: 50 M998/M1097 *Avenger*; 26 M48 *Chaparral*; 20 9K31 *Strela-1* (SA-9 *Gaskin*)
    MANPAD *Ayn al-Saqr*/9K32 *Strela-2* (SA-7 *Grail*)‡; FIM-92A *Stinger*; 9K38 *Igla* (SA-18 *Grouse*)
  GUNS
    SP 355: **23mm** 165: 45 *Sinai-23*; 120 ZSU-23-4; **37mm** 150; **57mm** 40 ZSU-57-2
    TOWED 700: **14.5mm** 300 ZPU-4; **23mm** 200 ZU-23-2; **57mm** 200 S-60
  RADAR • LAND AN/TPQ-36 *Firefinder*; AN/TPQ-37 *Firefinder* (arty/mor)
  MSL • TACTICAL • SSM 42+: 9 FROG-7; 24 *Sakr-80*; 9 *Scud*-B
  ARV 355+: *Fahd* 240; GMR 3560.55; 220 M88A1; 90 M88A2; M113 ARV; 45 M578; T-54/55 ARV
  VLB KMM; MTU; MTU-20
  MW *Aardvark* JFSU Mk4

Navy ε8,500 (incl 2,000 Coast Guard); 10,000 conscript (total 18,500)

EQUIPMENT BY TYPE
SUBMARINES • TACTICAL • SSK 4 *Romeo*† (PRC Type-033) with 8 single 533mm TT with UGM-84C *Harpoon* AShM/Mk37 HWT
PRINCIPAL SURFACE COMBATANTS 8
  FRIGATES 8
    FFGHM 4 *Alexandria* (ex-US *Oliver Hazard Perry*) with 1 Mk13 GMLS with RGM-84C *Harpoon* AShM/SM-1MP SAM, 2 triple 324 mm ASTT with Mk 46 LWT, 1 *Phalanx* CIWS, 1 76mm gun (capacity 2 SH-2G *Super Seasprite* ASW hel)
    FFGH 2 *Damyat* (ex-US *Knox*) with 1 octuple Mk16 GMLS with RGM-84C *Harpoon* AShM/ASROC, 2 twin 324mm Mk 32 TT with Mk 46 LWT, 1 *Phalanx* CIWS, 1 127mm gun, (capacity 1 SH-2G *Super Seasprite* ASW hel)
    FFG 2 *Najim Al Zaffer* (PRC *Jianghu* I) with 2 twin lnchr with HY-2 (CSS-N-2 *Safflower*) AShM, 4 RBU 1200, 2 twin 57mm guns
PATROL AND COASTAL COMBATANTS 56
  CORVETTES • FSGM 2:
    2 *Abu Qir* (ESP *Descubierta* – 1†) with 2 quad Mk141 lnchr with RGM-84C *Harpoon* AShM, 1 octuple *Albatros* lnchr with *Aspide* SAM, 2 triple Mk32 324mm ASTT with *Sting Ray* LWT, 1 twin 375mm A/S mor, 1 76mm gun
  PCFG 13:
    2 *Ezzat* (US *Ambassador* IV) with 2 quad lnchr with RGM-84L *Harpoon* Block II AShM, 1 21-cell Mk49 lnchr with RAM Block 1A SAM, 1 Mk15 Mod 21 Block 1B *Phalanx* CIWS 1 76mm gun
    6 *Ramadan* with 4 single lnchr with *Otomat* MkII AShM, 1 76mm gun
    5 *Tiger* with 2 twin lnchr with MM-38 *Exocet* AShM, 1 76mm gun
  PCC 5:
    5 *Al-Nour* (ex-PRC *Hainan* – 3 more in reserve†) with 2 triple 324mm TT, 4 RBU 1200, 2 twin 57mm guns
  PBFG 17:
    4 *Hegu* (PRC – *Komar* type) with 2 single lnchr with SY-1 AShM (2 additional vessels in reserve)
    5 *October* (FSU *Komar* – 1†) with 2 single lnchr with *Otomat* MkII AShM (1 additional vessel in reserve)
    8 *Osa* I (ex-YUG – 3†) with 1 9K32 *Strela-2* (SA-N-5 *Grail*) SAM (manual aiming), 4 single lnchr with P-15 *Termit* (SS-N-2A *Styx*) AShM
  PBFM 4:
    4 *Shershen* (FSU) with 1 9K32 *Strela-2* (SA-N-5 *Grail*) SAM (manual aiming), 1 12-tube BM-24 MRL
  PBF 10:
    6 *Kaan 20* (TUR MRTP 20)
    4 *Osa* II (ex-FIN)
  PB 6:
    4 *Shanghai* II (PRC)
    2 *Shershen* (FSU – 1†) with 4 single 533mm TT, 1 8-tube BM-21 MRL
MINE WARFARE • MINE COUNTERMEASURES 14
  MHC 5: 2 *Al Siddiq* (ex-US *Osprey*); 3 *Dat Assawari* (US Swiftships)
  MSI 2 *Safaga* (US Swiftships)
  MSO 7: 3 *Assiout* (FSU T-43 class); 4 *Aswan* (FSU *Yurka*)
AMPHIBIOUS 12
  LANDING SHIPS • LSM 3 *Polnochny* A (FSU) (capacity 6 MBT; 180 troops)
  LANDING CRAFT • LCU 9 *Vydra* (FSU) (capacity either 3 AMX-30 MBT or 100 troops)
LOGISTICS AND SUPPORT 32
  AOT 7 *Ayeda* (FSU *Toplivo* – 1 additional in reserve)
  AE 1 *Halaib* (ex-GER *Westerwald*-class)
  AKR 3 *Al Hurreya*
  ARL 1 *Shaledin* (ex-GER *Luneberg*-class)
  ARS 2 *Al Areesh*
  ATA 5 *Al Maks*† (FSU *Okhtensky*)
  AX 5: 1 *El Fateh*† (ex-UK 'Z' class); 1 *El Horriya* (also used as the presidential yacht); 1 *Al Kousser*; 1 *Intishat*; 1 other
  YDT 2 *Nyryat* I (FSU Project 522)
  YPT 2 *Poluchat* I (FSU)
  YTL 4 *Galal Desouky* (Damen Stan 2208)

Coastal Defence
Army tps, Navy control
EQUIPMENT BY TYPE
ARTY • COASTAL 100mm; **130mm** SM-4-1; **152mm**
MSL • AShM 4K87 (SS-C-2B *Samlet*); *Otomat* MkII

Naval Aviation
All aircraft operated by Air Force
AIRCRAFT • TPT • Light 4 Beech 1900C (Maritime Surveillance)
HELICOPTERS
  ASW 10 SH-2G *Super Seasprite* with Mk 46 LWT
  MRH 5 SA342L *Gazelle*
UAV • ISR • Light 2 *Camcopter* 5.1

Coast Guard 2,000
PATROL AND COASTAL COMBATANTS 80
  PBF 15: 6 *Crestitalia*; 6 *Swift Protector*; 3 *Peterson*
  PB 65: 5 *Nisr*; 12 *Sea Spectre* MkIII; 15 Swiftships; 21 *Timsah*; 3 Type-83; 9 *Peterson*
LOGISTICS AND SUPPORT • YTL 4 *Khoufou*

Air Force 30,000 (incl 10,000 conscript)
FORCES BY ROLE
FIGHTER
 1 sqn with F-16A/B *Fighting Falcon*
 8 sqn with F-16C/D *Fighting Falcon*
 4 sqn with J-7/MiG-21 *Fishbed*/MiG-21U *Mongol* A
 2 sqn with *Mirage* 5D/E
 1 sqn with *Mirage* 2000B/C
FIGHTER/GROUND ATTACK
 2 sqn with F-4E *Phantom* II
 1 sqn with *Mirage* 5E2
ANTI-SUBMARINE WARFARE
 1 sqn with SH-2G *Super Seasprite*
MARITIME PATROL
 1 sqn with Beech 1900C
ELECTRONIC WARFARE
 1 sqn with Beech 1900 (ELINT); *Commando* Mk2E (ECM)
ELECTRONIC WARFARE/TRANSPORT
 1 sqn with C-130H/VC-130H *Hercules*
AIRBORNE EARLY WARNING
 1 sqn with E-2C *Hawkeye*
SEARCH & RESCUE
 1 unit with AW139
TRANSPORT
 1 sqn with An-74TK-200A
 1 sqn with C-130H/C-130H-30 *Hercules*
 1 sqn with C-295M
 1 sqn with DHC-5D *Buffalo*
 1 sqn with B-707-366C; B-737-100; Beech 200 *Super King Air*; *Falcon* 20; Gulfstream III; Gulfstream IV; Gulfstream IV-SP
TRAINING
 1 sqn with *Alpha Jet**
 1 sqn with DHC-5 *Buffalo*
 3 sqn with EMB-312 *Tucano*
 1 sqn with Grob 115EG
 ε6 sqn with K-8 *Karakorum**
 1 sqn with L-39 *Albatros*; L-59E *Albatros**
ATTACK HELICOPTER
 2 sqn with AH-64D *Apache*
 2 sqn with SA-342K *Gazelle* (with HOT)
 1 sqn with SA-342L *Gazelle*
TRANSPORT HELICOPTER
 1 sqn with CH-47C/D *Chinook*
 2 sqn with Mi-8 *Hip*
 1 sqn with S-70 *Black Hawk*; UH-60A/L *Black Hawk*
UAV
 Some sqn with R4E-50 *Skyeye*; Teledyne-Ryan 324 *Scarab*

EQUIPMENT BY TYPE
AIRCRAFT 569 combat capable
 FTR 62: 26 F-16A *Fighting Falcon*; 6 F-16B *Fighting Falcon*; ε30 J-7
 FGA 310: 29 F-4E *Phantom* II; 127 F-16C *Fighting Falcon*; 38 F-16D *Fighting Falcon*; 3 *Mirage* 2000B; 15 *Mirage* 2000C; 36 *Mirage* 5D/E; 12 *Mirage* 5E2; ε50 MiG-21 *Fishbed*/MiG-21U *Mongol* A
 ELINT 2 VC-130H *Hercules*
 ISR 6 *Mirage* 5R (5SDR)*
 AEW&C 7 E-2C *Hawkeye*
 TPT 64: **Medium** 24: 21 C-130H *Hercules*; 3 C-130H-30 *Hercules*; **Light** 29: 3 An-74TK-200A; 1 Beech 200 *King Air*; 4 Beech 1900 (ELINT); 4 Beech 1900C; 8 C-295M; 9 DHC-5D *Buffalo* **PAX** 11: 1 B-707-366C; 3 *Falcon* 20; 2 Gulfstream III; 1 Gulfstream IV; 4 Gulfstream IV-SP
 TRG 329: 36 *Alpha Jet**; 54 EMB-312 *Tucano*; 74 Grob 115EG; 120 K-8 *Karakorum**; 10 L-39 *Albatros*; 35 L-59E *Albatros**
HELICOPTERS
 ATK 35 AH-64D *Apache*
 ASW 10 SH-2G *Super Seasprite* (opcon Navy)
 ELINT 4 *Commando* Mk2E (ECM)
 MRH 72: 2 AW139 (SAR); 65 SA342K *Gazelle* (some with HOT); 5 SA342L *Gazelle* (opcon Navy)
 TPT 93: **Heavy** 19: 3 CH-47C *Chinook*; 16 CH-47D *Chinook*; **Medium** 74: 2 AS-61; 24 *Commando* (of which 3 VIP); 40 Mi-8 *Hip*; 4 S-70 *Black Hawk* (VIP); 4 UH-60L *Black Hawk* (VIP)
 TRG 17 UH-12E
UAV • ISR • Medium R4E-50 *Skyeye*; Teledyne-Ryan 324 *Scarab*
MSL
 ASM AGM-65A/D/F/G *Maverick*; AGM-114 *Hellfire*; AS-30L; HOT
 AShM AGM-84 *Harpoon*; AM-39 *Exocet*;
 ARM *Armat*; Kh-25MP (AS-12 *Kegler*)
 AAM • IR R-3 (AA-2 *Atoll*)‡; AIM-9FL/P *Sidewinder*; R-550 *Magic*; **SARH** AIM-7E/F/M *Sparrow*; R530

Air Defence Command 80,000 conscript; 70,000 reservists (total 150,000)
FORCES BY ROLE
AIR DEFENCE
 5 AD div (geographically based) (total: 12 SAM bty with M48 *Chaparral*, 12 radar bn, 12 ADA bde (total: 100 ADA bn), 12 SAM bty with MIM-23B I-HAWK, 14 SAM bty with *Crotale*, 18 SAM bn with *Skyguard*, 110 SAM bn with S-125 *Pechora*-M (SA-3A *Goa*); 2K12 *Kub* (SA-6 *Gainful*); S-75M *Volkhov* (SA-2 *Guideline*))

EQUIPMENT BY TYPE
AD
 SYSTEMS 72+: Some *Amoun* with RIM-7F *Sea Sparrow* SAM, 36+ quad SAM, *Skyguard* towed SAM, 36+ twin 35mm guns
 SAM 702+
  SP 130+: 24+ *Crotale*; 50+ M48 *Chaparral*; 56+ SA-6 *Gainful*
  TOWED 572+: 78+ MIM-23B I-HAWK; S-75M *Volkhov* (SA-2 *Guideline*) 282+ *Skyguard*; 212+ S-125 *Pechora*-M (SA-3A *Goa*)
 GUNS 1,566+
  SP • 23mm 266+: 36+ *Sinai*-23 (SPAAG) with *Ayn al-Saqr* MANPAD, Dassault 6SD-20S land; 230 ZSU-23-4
  TOWED 57mm 600 S-60; **85mm** 400 M-1939 *KS-12*; **100mm** 300 KS-19

Paramilitary ε397,000 active

Central Security Forces ε325,000
Ministry of Interior; Includes conscripts
APC (W) 100+: 100 *Hussar*; *Walid*

National Guard ε60,000
Lt wpns only
FORCES BY ROLE
MANOEUVRE
  Other
    8 paramilitary bde (cadre) (3 paramilitary bn)
EQUIPMENT BY TYPE
APC (W) 250 *Walid*

Border Guard Forces ε12,000
Ministry of Interior; lt wpns only
FORCES BY ROLE
MANOEUVRE
  Other
    18 Border Guard regt

DEPLOYMENT

CENTRAL AFRICAN REPUBLIC
UN • MINUSCA 2 obs

CÔTE D'IVOIRE
UN • UNOCI 176; 1 engr coy

DEMOCRATIC REPUBLIC OF THE CONGO
UN • MONUSCO 987; 18 obs; 1 SF coy; 1 mech inf bn

IRAQ
UN • UNAMI 1 obs

LIBERIA
UN • UNMIL 7 obs

MALI
UN • MINUSMA 9 obs

SOUTH SUDAN
UN • UNMISS 3 obs

SUDAN
UN • UNAMID 892; 23 obs; 1 inf bn; 1 tpt coy

WESTERN SAHARA
UN • MINURSO 20 obs

FOREIGN FORCES
Australia MFO (*Operation Mazurka*) 25
Canada MFO 28
Colombia MFO 354; 1 inf bn
Czech Republic MFO 13; 1 C-295M
Fiji MFO 338; 1 inf bn
France MFO 2
Hungary MFO 26; 1 MP unit
Italy MFO 79; 3 coastal ptl unit
Netherlands MFO 4
New Zealand MFO 28 1 trg unit; 1 tpt unit
Norway MFO 3
United States MFO 693; 1 inf bn; 1 spt bn (1 EOD coy, 1 medical coy, 1 hel coy)
Uruguay MFO 58 1 engr/tpt unit

Iran IRN

Iranian Rial r		2013	2014	2015
GDP	r	9,093tr	10,775tr	
	US$	367bn	403bn	
per capita	US$	4,769	5,165	
Growth	%	-1.9	1.5	
Inflation	%	34.7	19.8	
Def exp	r	ε366tr		
	US$	ε14.8bn		
US$1=r		24,770.02	26,755.83	

Population 80,840,713

Ethnic groups: Persian 51%; Azeri 24%; Gilaki/Mazandarani 8%; Kurdish 7%; Arab 3%; Lur 2%; Baloch 2%; Turkman 2%

Age	0–14	15–19	20–24	25–29	30–64	65 plus
Male	12.2%	4.1%	5.5%	5.8%	20.8%	2.4%
Female	11.6%	3.9%	5.2%	5.5%	20.4%	2.8%

Capabilities

The Iranian regular forces are large, but equipped with largely outdated equipment. The country's apparent strategic priority is the complementary independent Iranian Revolutionary Guard Corps, a capable organisation well versed in a variety of different operations. There has been some division of labour between the regular armed forces and the IRGC, with the IRGC Navy assuming greater responsibility for operations in the Persian Gulf and the navy assuming a greater extra-regional role. These is evidence of innovative and assymetric tactics; as such, Iran is able to present a challenge to most potential adversaries, especially its weaker neighbours. The air force's ageing fleets of combat aircraft are of limited value and many may already have been cannibalised. Effort has been put into the development of indigenous rockets, missiles, UAVs, submarines and radars. Although Tehran has attempted, with partial success, to invigorate its domestic defence industry, it relies on foreign-state support for high-tech equipment, including anti-ship missiles and advanced air-defence platforms. In 2012, Iran dispatched IRGC personnel to advise Syrian troops in urban and counter-insurgency warfare; in some cases it is believed they took part in the fighting. In 2014, Iran committed to support Iraqi efforts to counter the advances of ISIS. This included UAV flights, delivery of Su-25 aircraft and deployment of IRGC personnel.

ACTIVE 523,000 (Army 350,000 Iranian Revolutionary Guard Corps 125,000 Navy 18,000 Air 30,000) Paramilitary 40,000

Armed Forces General Staff coordinates two parallel organisations: the regular armed forces and the Revolutionary Guard Corps

RESERVE 350,000 (Army 350,000, ex-service volunteers)

TPT • **Light** 17: 5 Bell 205A (AB-205A); 2 Bell 206 *Jet Ranger* (AB-206); 10 Bell 212 (AB-212)

Air Force 30,000 (incl 12,000 Air Defence)
FORCES BY ROLE
Serviceability probably about 60% for US ac types and about 80% for PRC/Russian ac. Includes IRGC Air Force equipment.
FIGHTER
  1 sqn with F-7M *Airguard*; JJ-7*
  2 sqn with F-14 *Tomcat*
  2 sqn with MiG-29A/UB *Fulcrum*
FIGHTER/GROUND ATTACK
  1 sqn with *Mirage* F-1E; F-5E/F *Tiger* II
  1 sqn with Su-24MK *Fencer* D
  5 sqn with F-4D/E *Phantom* II
  3 sqn with F-5E/F *Tiger* II
MARITIME PATROL
  1 sqn with P-3MP *Orion**
ISR
  1 (det) sqn with RF-4E *Phantom* II*
SEARCH & RESCUE
  Some flt with Bell-214C (AB-214C)
TANKER/TRANSPORT
  1 sqn with B-707; B-747; B-747F
TRANSPORT
  1 sqn with B-707; *Falcon* 50; L-1329 *Jetstar*; Bell 412
  2 sqn with C-130E/H *Hercules*
  1 sqn with F-27 *Friendship*; *Falcon* 20
  1 sqn with Il-76 *Candid*; An-140 (Iran-140 *Faraz*)
TRAINING
  1 sqn with Beech F33A/C *Bonanza*
  1 sqn with F-5B *Freedom Fighter*
  1 sqn with PC-6
  1 sqn with PC-7 *Turbo Trainer*
  Some units with EMB-312 *Tucano*; MFI-17 *Mushshak*; TB-21 *Trinidad*; TB-200 *Tobago*
TRANSPORT HELICOPTER
  1 sqn with CH-47 *Chinook*
  Some units with Bell 206A *Jet Ranger* (AB-206A); *Shabaviz* 2-75; *Shabaviz* 2061
AIR DEFENCE
  16 bn with MIM-23B I-HAWK/*Shahin*
  5 sqn with FM-80 (*Crotale*); *Rapier*; *Tigercat*; S-75M *Volkhov* (SA-2 *Guideline*); S-200 *Angara* (SA-5 *Gammon*); FIM-92A *Stinger*; 9K32 *Strela*-2 (SA-7 *Grail*)‡; 9K331 *Tor*-M1 (SA-15 *Gauntlet*) (reported)

EQUIPMENT BY TYPE
AIRCRAFT 334 combat capable
  FTR 184+: 20 F-5B *Freedom Fighter*; 55+ F-5E/F *Tiger* II 24 F-7M *Airguard*; 43 F-14 *Tomcat*; 36 MiG-29A/U/UB *Fulcrum*; up to 6 *Azarakhsh* reported
  FGA 110: 64 F-4D/E *Phantom* II; 10 *Mirage* F-1E; 30 Su-24MK *Fencer* D; up to 6 *Saegheh* reported
  ATK 10: 7 Su-25K *Frogfoot*; 3 Su-25UBK *Frogfoot* (incl 4+ Su-25K/UBK deployed in Iraq; status unclear)
  ASW 5 P-3MP *Orion*
  ISR: 6+ RF-4E *Phantom* II*
  TKR/TPT 3: ε1 B-707; ε2 B-747

TPT 117: **Heavy** 12 Il-76 *Candid*; **Medium** ε19 C-130E/H *Hercules*; **Light** 75: 11 An-74TK-200; 5 An-140 (Iran-140 *Faraz*) (45 projected); 10 F-27 *Friendship*; 1 L-1329 *Jetstar*; 10 PC-6B *Turbo Porter*; 8 TB-21 *Trinidad*; 4 TB-200 *Tobago*; 3 *Turbo Commander* 680; 14 Y-7; 9 Y-12; **PAX** 11: 2 B-707; 1 B-747; 4 B-747F; 1 *Falcon* 20; 3 *Falcon* 50
TRG 151: 25 Beech F33A/C *Bonanza*; 15 EMB-312 *Tucano*; 15 JJ-7*; 25 MFI-17 *Mushshak*; 12 *Parastu*; 15 PC-6; 35 PC-7 *Turbo Trainer*; 9 T-33
HELICOPTERS
MRH 2 Bell 412
TPT 34+: **Heavy** 2+ CH-47 *Chinook*; **Medium** 30 Bell 214C (AB-214C); **Light** 2+: 2 Bell 206A *Jet Ranger* (AB-206A); some *Shabaviz* 2-75 (indigenous versions in production); some *Shabaviz* 2061
AD • **SAM** 529+: 250 FM-80 (*Crotale*); 30 *Rapier*; 15 *Tigercat*; 150+ MIM-23B I-HAWK/*Shahin*; 45 S-75 *Dvina* (SA-2 *Guideline*); 10 S-200 *Angara* (SA-5 *Gammon*); 29 9K331 *Tor*-M1 (SA-15 *Gauntlet*) (reported)
MANPAD FIM-92A *Stinger*; 9K32 *Strela*-2 (SA-7 *Grail*)‡
GUNS • **TOWED 23mm** ZU-23; **37mm** Oerlikon
MSL
  ASM AGM-65A *Maverick*; Kh-25 (AS-10 *Karen*); Kh-29 (AS-14 *Kedge*); C-801K AShM
  ARM Kh-58 (AS-11 *Kilter*)
  AAM • **IR** PL-2A‡; PL-7; R-60 (AA-8 *Aphid*); R-73 (AA-11 *Archer*); AIM-9 *Sidewinder*; **IR/SARH** R-27 (AA-10 *Alamo*) **SARH** AIM-54 *Phoenix*†; AIM-7 *Sparrow*

Air Defence Command
Established to coordinate army, air-force and IRGC air-defence assets. Precise composition unclear.

Paramilitary 40,000–60,000

Law-Enforcement Forces 40,000–60,000 (border and security troops); 450,000 on mobilisation (incl conscripts)
Part of armed forces in wartime
PATROL AND COASTAL COMBATANTS • **PB** ε90
AIRCRAFT • **TPT** • **Light** 2+: 2 An-140; some Cessna 185/Cessna 310
HELICOPTERS • **UTL** ε24 AB-205 (Bell 205)/AB-206 (Bell 206) *Jet Ranger*

Basij Resistance Force up to ε1,000,000 on mobilisation
Paramilitary militia, with claimed membership of 12.6 million; perhaps 1 million combat capable; in the process of closer integration with IRGC Ground Forces.
FORCES BY ROLE
MANOEUVRE
  Other
    2,500 militia bn (claimed, limited permanent membership)

Cyber
Iran has a developed capacity for cyber operations. The precise relationship of groups such as the 'Iranian Cyber Army' to regime and military organisations is unclear, but the former has launched hacking attacks against a

number of foreign organisations. In 2011/12, Tehran established a Joint Chiefs of Staff Cyber Command with emphasis on thwarting attacks against Iranian nuclear facilities, and it has also been reported that the IRGC has its own Cyber Defence Command; IRGC civilian business interests could aid its activities in this area. There are reports of university courses in cyber security. In June 2012, the head of the Civil Defence Organisation announced that plans to develop a cyber-defence strategy were under way.

DEPLOYMENT

GULF OF ADEN AND SOMALI BASIN
Navy: 1 FSG; 1 AORH

SUDAN
UN • UNAMID 2 obs

Iraq IRQ

Iraqi Dinar D		2013	2014	2015
GDP	D	267tr	271tr	
	US$	229bn	232bn	
per capita	US$	6,594	6,474	
Growth	%	4.2	-2.7	
Inflation	%	1.9	4.7	
Def bdgt [a]	D	19.7tr	22tr	
	US$	16.9bn	18.9bn	
US$1=D		1,166.00	1,166.00	

[a] Defence and security budget. Does not include US Overseas Contingency Operations Foreign Military Financing funding, the FY2015 request for which amounted to US$267m.

Population 32,585,692

Ethnic and religious groups: Arab 75–80% (of which Shia Muslim 55%, Sunni Muslim 45%); Kurdish 20–25%

Age	0–14	15–19	20–24	25–29	30–64	65 plus
Male	18.7%	5.3%	4.7%	4.5%	16.0%	1.5%
Female	18.0%	5.1%	4.5%	4.4%	15.6%	1.7%

Capabilities

The institutional problems that plagued the Iraqi defence establishment, traced in recent editions of *The Military Balance*, severely eroded military capability. In the first part of 2014, Iraqi forces in Anbar, Nineveh, Salahuddin and Diyala provinces were evicted by the forces of ISIS, with several Iraqi divisions effectively destroyed. ISIS gained a foothold in Iraq through a combination of discrimination, deliberate neglect and heavy-handed government repression of an increasingly disenfranchised Sunni minority. Kurdish Peshmerga forces in the north, bolstered by foreign military assistance, for a time constituted the main bulwark against ISIS expansion. By October, government forces had established a relatively strong defence of the Shia heartland, but failed to mount effective counter-offensives. Russia and Iran provided Su-25 ground-attack aircraft, but the Iraqi air force's capability remained extremely limited.

A coalition of foreign states launched air operations against ISIS targets in Iraq and Syria from the end of August, aimed at degrading its capability. The US deployed manned and unmanned ISR aircraft over Iraq and several hundred SOF as advisers, and at the end of the year announced a deployment of 1,500 troops as trainers. F-16 pilot training will continue, but in the US, and the enlarged US advise-and-assist mission will look to train nine Iraqi and three Peshmerga brigades. (See pp. 304–06.)

ACTIVE 177,600 (Army 100,000 Navy 3,600 Air 5,000 Air Defence 4,000 Support 65,000) Paramilitary n.k.

ORGANISATIONS BY SERVICE

Army ε100,000

Due to ongoing conflict with ISIS insurgents, there have been significant personnel and equipment losses in the Iraqi Army. Many formations are now under-strength. Military capability has been bolstered by the activity of Shia militia and Kurdish Peshmerga forces.

FORCES BY ROLE
SPECIAL FORCES
  2 SF bde
MANOEUVRE
  Armoured
  1 armd div (2 armd bde, 2 mech bde, 1 engr bn, 1 sigs regt, 1 log bde)
  Mechanised
  2 mech div (4 mech inf bde, 1 engr bn, 1 sigs regt, 1 log bde)
  1 mech div (3 mech inf bde, 1 engr bn, 1 sigs regt, 1 log bde)
  1 mech div (2 mech inf bde, 1 inf bde, 1 engr bn, 1 sigs regt, 1 log bde)
  Light
  1 mot div (1 mech bde, 3 mot inf bde, 2 inf bde, 1 engr bn, 1 sigs regt, 1 log bde)
  1 mot div (2 mot inf bde, 3 inf bde, 1 engr bn, 1 sigs regt, 1 log bde)
  1 inf div (4 lt inf bde, 1 engr bn, 1 sigs regt, 1 log bde)
  1 cdo div (5 lt inf bde, 1 engr bn, 1 sigs regt, 1 log bde)
  2 inf bde
  Aviation
  1 atk hel sqn (forming) with Mi-28NE *Havoc*
  1 atk hel sqn with Mi-35M *Hind*
  1 sqn with Bell 205 (UH-1H *Huey* II)
  3 atk hel sqn with Bell T407; EC635
  3 sqn with Mi-17 *Hip* H; Mi-171Sh
  1 ISR sqn with SA342M *Gazelle*
  2 trg sqn with Bell 206; OH-58C *Kiowa*

EQUIPMENT BY TYPE
MBT 270+: ε100 M1A1 *Abrams*; 120+ T-72; ε50 T-55;
RECCE 73: 18 BRDM 2; 35 EE-9 *Cascavel*; 20 *Fuchs* NBC
AIFV 240: ε80 BMP-1; ε60 BTR-4 (inc variants); 100 BTR-80A
APC 3,688+
  APC (T) 900: ε500 M113A2/*Talha*; ε400 MT-LB
  APC (W) 410: ε400 *Akrep/Scorpion*; 10 *Cobra*
  PPV 912+: 12 *Barracuda*; ε500 *Dzik*-3; ε400 ILAV *Cougar*; *Mamba*

ARTY 1,061+
SP 48+: **152mm** 18+ Type-83; **155mm** 30: 6 M109A1; 24 M109A5
TOWED 60+: **130mm** M-46/Type-59; **155mm** ε60 M198
MLRS 3+: **122mm** some BM-21; **220mm** 3+ TOS-1A
MOR 950+: **81mm** ε500 M252; **120mm** ε450 M120; **240mm** M-240
AT • MSL • MANPATS 9K135 *Kornet* (AT-14 *Spriggan*) (reported)
ARV 215+: 180 BREM; 35+ M88A1/2; T-54/55 ARV; Type-653; VT-55A
HELICOPTERS
ATK 13: 3 Mi-28NE *Havoc*; 10 Mi-35M *Hind*
MRH 4+ SA342 *Gazelle*
MRH/TPT ε21 Mi-17 *Hip* H/Mi-171Sh
ISR 10 OH-58C *Kiowa*
TPT • **Light** 46: 16 Bell 205 (UH-1H *Huey* II); 10 Bell 206B3 *Jet Ranger*; ε20 Bell T407; 24 EC635
MSL • ASM 9K114 *Shturm* (AT-6 *Spiral*)

Navy 3,600
EQUIPMENT BY TYPE
PATROL AND COASTAL COMBATANTS 32+
PCO 2 *Al Basra* (US *River Hawk*)
PCC 4 *Fateh* (ITA *Diciotti*)
PB 20: 12 Swiftships 35; 5 *Predator* (PRC-27m); 3 *Al Faw*
PBR 6: 2 Type-200; 4 Type-2010

Marines 1,500
FORCES BY ROLE
MANOEUVRE
Amphibious
2 mne bn

Air Force ε5,000
FORCES BY ROLE
GROUND ATTACK
1 sqn with Su-25/Su-25K/Su-25UBK *Frogfoot*
ISR
1 sqn with CH-2000 *Sama*; SB7L-360 *Seeker*
1 sqn with Cessna 208B *Grand Caravan*; Cessna AC-208B *Combat Caravan**
1 sqn with Beech 350 *King Air*
TRANSPORT
1 sqn with An-32B *Cline*
1 sqn with C-130E/J-30 *Hercules*
TRAINING
1 sqn with Cessna 172, Cessna 208B
1 sqn with *Lasta*-95
1 sqn with T-6A
EQUIPMENT BY TYPE
AIRCRAFT 11 combat capable
FGA 1 F-16D *Fighting Falcon* (still in US)
ATK 7+: 6+ Su-25/Su-25K *Frogfoot*; 1+ Su-25UBK *Frogfoot*
ISR 10: 3 Cessna AC-208B *Combat Caravan**; 2 SB7L-360 *Seeker*; 5 Beech 350ER *King Air*
TPT 32: **Medium;** 15: 3 C-130E *Hercules*; 6 C-130J-30 *Hercules*; 6 An-32B *Cline*; **Light** 17: 1 Beech 350 *King Air*; 8 Cessna 208B *Grand Caravan*; 8 Cessna 172
TRG 33+: 8 CH-2000 *Sama*; 10+ *Lasta*-95; 15 T-6A
MSL • ASM AGM-114 *Hellfire*

Air Defence Command ε4,000
FORCES BY ROLE
AIR DEFENCE
1 bn with 96K6 *Pantsir*-S1 (SA-22 *Greyhound*)
1 bn with M998/M1097 *Avenger*
1 bn with 9K338 *Igla*-S (SA-24 *Grinch*)
1 bn with ZPU-23
EQUIPMENT BY TYPE
AD
SAM
SP 3+: 3+ 96K6 *Pantsir*-S1 (SA-22 *Greyhound*); M998/M1097 *Avenger*
MANPAD 9K338 *Igla*-S (SA-24 *Grinch*)
GUNS • TOWED **23mm** ZU-23

Paramilitary n.k.

Iraqi Police Service n.k.

Iraqi Federal Police n.k.

Facilities Protection Service n.k.

Border Enforcement n.k.

Oil Police n.k.

FOREIGN FORCES
Canada *Operation Impact* 70 (trg team)
Egypt UNAMI 1 obs
Fiji UNAMI 192; 2 sy unit
India UNAMI 1 obs
Nepal UNAMI 77; 1 sy unit
United Kingdom *Operation Shader* 12 (trg team)
United States *Operation Inherent Resolve* 1,400; 1 inf div HQ; 1 mne coy; 1 atk hel coy; MQ-1B *Predator*

Israel ISR

New Israeli Shekel NS		2013	2014	2015
GDP	NS	1.05tr	1.09tr	
	US$	291bn	305bn	
per capita	US$	36,926	37,914	
Growth	%	3.2	2.5	
Inflation	%	1.5	0.8	
Def bdgt	NS	67.5bn	71.8bn [a]	
	US$	18.7bn	20.1bn	
FMA (US)	US$	3.08bn	3.1bn	3.1bn
US$1=NS		3.61	3.57	

[a] 2014 figure includes additional funds allocated to the MoD during the Gaza conflict

Population 7,821,850

Age	0–14	15–19	20–24	25–29	30–64	65 plus
Male	13.9%	4.1%	3.9%	3.7%	19.8%	4.7%
Female	13.2%	4.0%	3.7%	3.6%	19.4%	6.0%

Capabilities

The Israel Defense Forces remain the most capable force in the region, with the motivation, equipment and training to considerably overmatch the conventional capability of other regional armed forces. Currently able to contain but not destroy the threats posed by Hamas and Hizbullah, the IDF continues to launch frequent operations in Syria, Gaza and Lebanon to disarm, weaken and degrade the capabilities of these two organisations. The latest, a month-long offensive in Gaza, *Operation Protective Edge*, involved all three services and tested Israel's *Iron Dome* anti-rocket system. While there is a requirement to make significant budget savings and an apparent decline in the conventional threat posed by its neighbours, Israeli planners are aware that regional instability might also lead to asymmetric threats and difficulty in attributing responsibility for any future attacks. There is emphasis on maintaining Israel's technological superiority, especially in missile-defence, intelligence-gathering, precision-weapons and cyber capabilities. Budget cuts meant that ground and air training was halted at the beginning of June, though it restarted before violence escalated in the West Bank and Gaza later that month. There have been personnel cuts and reductions in air and naval platforms in recent years and army reductions include all M60 and *Merkava* I tanks. In 2014, a new division (210th) was transferred to the Golan Heights and the former (36th Armoured) division recalibrated training to prepare for different operational scenarios. Procurement programmes will continue for key systems, including *Dolphin*-class submarines and F-35A combat aircraft. (See pp. 310–14.)

ACTIVE 176,500 (Army 133,000 Navy 9,500 Air 34,000) **Paramilitary 8,000**
Conscript liability officers 48 months, other ranks 36 months, women 24 months (Jews and Druze only; Christians, Circassians and Muslims may volunteer)

RESERVE 465,000 (Army 400,000 Navy 10,000 Air 55,000)
Annual trg as cbt reservists to age 40 (some specialists to age 54) for male other ranks, 38 (or marriage/pregnancy) for women

ORGANISATIONS BY SERVICE

Strategic Forces
Israel is widely believed to have a nuclear capability – delivery means include ac, *Jericho* 1 SRBM and *Jericho* 2 IRBM, and, reportedly, *Dolphin*-class SSKs with LACM.
FORCES BY ROLE
MISSILE
 3 sqn with *Jericho* 1/2
EQUIPMENT BY TYPE
MSL • STRATEGIC
 IRBM: *Jericho* 2
 SRBM: *Jericho* 1

Strategic Defences
FORCES BY ROLE
AIR DEFENCE
 3 bty with *Arrow*/*Arrow* 2 ATBM with *Green Pine*/*Super Green Pine* radar and *Citrus Tree* command post.
 9 bty with *Iron Dome*
 17 bty with MIM-23B I-HAWK
 6 bty with MIM-104 *Patriot*

Space
SATELLITES 8
 COMMUNICATIONS 4 *Amos*
 ISR 5: 4 *Ofeq* (5, 7, 9 & 10); 1 TecSAR-1 (*Polaris*)

Army 26,000; 107,000 conscript; (total 133,000)
Organisation and structure of formations may vary according to op situations. Equipment includes that required for reserve forces on mobilisation.
FORCES BY ROLE
COMMAND
 3 (regional comd) corps HQ
 2 armd div HQ
 4 (territorial) inf div HQ
SPECIAL FORCES
 3 SF bn
MANOEUVRE
 Reconnaissance
 1 indep recce bn
 Armoured
 3 armd bde (1 armd recce coy, 3 armd bn, 1 AT coy, 1 cbt engr bn)
 Mechanised
 3 mech inf bde (3 mech inf bn, 1 cbt spt bn,1 sigs coy)
 1 mech inf bde (6 mech inf bn)
 1 indep mech inf bn
 Light
 1 indep inf bn
 Air Manoeuvre
 1 para bde (3 para bn,1 cbt spt bn. 1 sigs coy)
 Other
 1 armd trg bde (3 armd bn)
COMBAT SUPPORT
 3 arty bde
 3 engr bn
 1 EOD coy
 1 CBRN bn
 1 int bde (3 int bn)
 2 MP bn

Reserves 400,000+ on mobilisation
FORCES BY ROLE
COMMAND
 5 armd div HQ
 1 AB div HQ
MANOEUVRE
 Armoured
 10 armd bde
 Mechanised
 8 mech inf bde
 Light
 14 (territorial/regional) inf bde

Air Manoeuvre
4 para bde
Mountain
1 mtn inf bn
COMBAT SUPPORT
4 arty bde
COMBAT SERVICE SUPPORT
6 log unit
EQUIPMENT BY TYPE
MBT 500: ε120 *Merkava* MkII; ε160 *Merkava* MkIII; ε220 *Merkava* MkIV (ε330 *Merkava* MkII; ε270 *Merkava* MkIII; ε160 *Merkava* MkIV all in store)
RECCE 308: ε300 RBY-1 RAMTA; ε8 TPz-1 *Fuchs* NBC
APC 1,265
  APC (T) 1,165: ε65 *Namer*; ε200 *Achzarit* (modified T-55 chassis); 500 M113A2; ε400 *Nagmachon* (*Centurion* chassis); *Nakpadon* (5,000 M113A1/A2 in store)
  APC (W) 100 *Ze'ev*
ARTY 530
  SP 250: **155mm** 250 M109A5 (**155mm** 148 L-33; 30 M109A1; 50 M-50; **175mm** 36 M107; **203mm** 36 M110 all in store)
  TOWED (**122mm** 5 D-30; **130mm** 100 M-46; **155mm** 171: 40 M-46; 50 M-68/M-71; 81 M-839P/M-845P all in store)
  MRL 30: **227mm** 30 M270 MLRS (**122mm** 58 BM-21; **160mm** 50 LAR-160; **227mm** 30 M270 MLRS; **240mm** 36 BM-24; **290mm** 20 LAR-290 all in store)
  MOR 250: **81mm** 250 (**81mm** 1,100; **120mm** 650 **160mm** 18 Soltam M-66 all in store)
AT • MSL
  SP M113 with *Spike*; *Tamuz* (*Spike* NLOS); *Magach* mod with *Spike*
  MANPATS IMI MAPATS; *Spike* MR/LR/ER
AD • SAM
  SP 20 *Machbet*
  MANPAD FIM-92A *Stinger*
RADAR • LAND AN/PPS-15 (arty); AN/TPQ-37 *Firefinder* (arty); EL/M-2140 (veh)
MSL 100
  STRATEGIC ε100 *Jericho* 1 SRBM/*Jericho* 2 IRBM
  TACTICAL • SSM (7 *Lance* in store)
AEV D9R; *Puma*
ARV *Centurion* Mk2; *Eyal*; *Merkava*; M88A1; M113 ARV
VLB *Alligator* MAB; M48/60; MTU

Navy 7,000; 2,500 conscript (total 9,500)
EQUIPMENT BY TYPE
SUBMARINES
  TACTICAL
    SSK 3:
      3 *Dolphin* (GER Type-212 variant) with 6 single 533mm TT with UGM-84C *Harpoon* AShM/HWT, 4 single 650mm TT
      (1 *Tanin* (GER Type-212 variant with AIP) with 6 single 533mm TT with UGM-84C *Harpoon* AShM/HWT, 4 single 650mm TT (expected ISD 2015))
    SDV 20 *Alligator* (semi-submersible)
PATROL AND COASTAL COMBATANTS 55
  CORVETTES • FSGHM 3:
    2 *Eilat* (*Sa'ar* 5) with 2 quad Mk140 lnchr with RGM-84C *Harpoon* AShM, 2 32-cell VLS with *Barak*-1 SAM (being upgraded to *Barak*-8), 2 triple 324mm TT with Mk 46 LWT, 1 *Sea Vulcan* CIWS, 1 76mm gun (capacity either 1 AS565SA *Panther* ASW hel)
    1 *Eilat* (*Sa'ar* 5) with 2 quad Mk140 lnchr with RGM-84C *Harpoon* AShM, 2 32-cell VLS with *Barak*-8 SAM, 2 triple 324mm TT with Mk 46 LWT, 1 *Sea Vulcan* CIWS, 1 76mm gun (capacity either 1 AS565SA *Panther* ASW hel)
  PCGM 8 *Hetz* (*Sa'ar* 4.5) with 6 single lnchr with *Gabriel* II AShM, 2 twin Mk140 lnchr with RGM-84C *Harpoon* AShM, 1 16-32-cell Mk56 VLS with *Barak*-1 SAM, 1 *Vulcan* CIWS, 1 *Typhoon* CIWS, 1 76mm gun
  PCG 2 *Reshef* (*Sa'ar* 4) with 4–6 single lnchr with *Gabriel* II AShM, 1 twin or quad Mk140 lnchr with RGM-84C *Harpoon* AShM, 2 triple 324mm TT, 1 *Phalanx* CIWS
  PBF 18: 5 *Shaldag* with 1 *Typhoon* CIWS; 3 *Stingray*; 10 *Super Dvora* MK III (AShM & TT may be fitted)
  PBFT 13: 9 *Super Dvora* MkI with 2 single 324mm TT with Mk 46 LWT (AShM may also be fitted); 4 *Super Dvora* MkII with 2 single 324mm TT with Mk 46 LWT (AShM may also be fitted)
  PBT 11 *Dabur* with 2 single 324mm TT with Mk 46 LWT
AMPHIBIOUS • LANDING CRAFT • LCT 3: 1 *Ashdod*; 2 others
LOGISTICS AND SUPPORT 3
  AG 2 *Bat Yam* (ex German Type-745)
  AX 1 *Queshet*

Naval Commandos ε300

Air Force 34,000
Responsible for Air and Space Coordination
FORCES BY ROLE
FIGHTER & FIGHTER/GROUND ATTACK
  1 sqn with F-15A/B/D *Eagle*
  1 sqn with F-15B/C/D *Eagle*
  1 sqn with F-15I *Ra'am*
  6 sqn with F-16A/B/C/D *Fighting Falcon*
  4 sqn with F-16I *Sufa*
  (3 sqn with A-4N *Skyhawk*/F-4 *Phantom* II/*Kfir* C-7 in reserve)
ANTI-SUBMARINE WARFARE
  1 sqn with AS565SA *Panther* (missions flown by IAF but with non-rated aircrew)
MARITIME PATROL/TANKER/TRANSPORT
  1 sqn with IAI-1124 *Seascan*; KC-707
ELECTRONIC WARFARE
  2 sqn with RC-12D *Guardrail*; Beech A36 *Bonanza* (*Hofit*); Beech 200 *King Air*; Beech 200T *King Air*; Beech 200CT *King Air*
AIRBORNE EARLY WARNING & CONTROL
  1 sqn with Gulfstream G550 *Eitam*; Gulfstream G550 *Shavit*
TANKER/TRANSPORT
  1 sqn with C-130E/H *Hercules*; KC-130H *Hercules*
  1 sqn (forming) with C-130J-30 *Hercules*
TRAINING
  1 OPFOR sqn with F-16A/B *Fighting Falcon*
  1 sqn with A-4N/TA-4H/TA-4J *Skyhawk*
ATTACK HELICOPTER
  1 sqn with AH-64A *Apache*
  1 sqn with AH-64D *Apache*

TRANSPORT HELICOPTER
  2 sqn with CH-53D *Sea Stallion*
  2 sqn with S-70A *Black Hawk*; UH-60A *Black Hawk*
  1 medevac unit with CH-53D *Sea Stallion*
UAV
  1 ISR sqn with *Hermes* 450
  1 ISR sqn with *Searcher* MkII
  1 ISR sqn with *Heron* (*Shoval*); *Heron* TP (*Eitan*)
AIR DEFENCE
  3 bty with *Arrow*/*Arrow* 2
  6 bty with *Iron Dome*
  17 bty with MIM-23 I-HAWK
  6 bty with MIM-104 *Patriot*
EQUIPMENT BY TYPE
AIRCRAFT 440 combat capable
  FTR 143: 16 F-15A *Eagle*; 6 F-15B *Eagle*; 17 F-15C *Eagle*; 11 F-15D *Eagle*; 77 F-16A *Fighting Falcon*; 16 F-16B *Fighting Falcon*
  FGA 251: 25 F-15I *Ra'am*; 78 F-16C *Fighting Falcon*; 49 F-16D *Fighting Falcon*; 99 F-16I *Sufa*
  ATK 46: 20 A-4N *Skyhawk*; 10 TA-4H *Skyhawk*; 16 TA-4J *Skyhawk*
  FTR/FGA/ATK (200+ A-4N *Skyhawk*/F-4 *Phantom* II/F-15A *Eagle*/F-16A/B *Fighting Falcon*/*Kfir* C-7 in store)
  MP 3 IAI-1124 *Seascan*
  ISR 6 RC-12D *Guardrail*
  ELINT 4: 1 EC-707; 3 Gulfstream G550 *Shavit*
  AEW 4: 2 B-707 *Phalcon*; 2 Gulfstream G550 *Eitam* (1 more on order)
  TKR/TPT 11: 4 KC-130H *Hercules*; 7 KC-707
  TPT 59: **Medium** 12: 5 C-130E *Hercules*; 6 C-130H *Hercules*; 1 C-130J-30 *Hercules*; **Light** 47: 3 AT-802 *Air Tractor*; 9 Beech 200 *King Air*; 8 Beech 200T *King Air*; 5 Beech 200CT *King Air*; 22 Beech A36 *Bonanza* (*Hofit*)
  TRG 39: 17 Grob G-120; 2 M-346 *Lavi*; 20 T-6A
HELICOPTERS
  ATK 77: 33 AH-1E/F *Cobra*; 27 AH-64A *Apache*; 17 AH-64D *Apache* (*Sarat*)
  ASW 7 AS565SA *Panther* (missions flown by IAF but with non-rated aircrew)
  ISR 12 OH-58B *Kiowa*
  TPT 81: **Heavy** 26 CH-53D *Sea Stallion*; **Medium** 49: 39 S-70A *Black Hawk*; 10 UH-60A *Black Hawk*; **Light** 6 Bell 206 *Jet Ranger*
UAV • ISR 24+: **Heavy** 2+: *Heron* (*Shoval*); 3 *Heron* TP (*Eitan*); RQ-5A *Hunter*; **Medium** 22+: *Hermes* 450; *Hermes* 900; 22 *Searcher* MkII (22+ in store); **Light** *Harpy*
AD
  SAM 24+: 24 *Arrow*/*Arrow* 2; some *Iron Dome*; some MIM-104 *Patriot*; some MIM-23 I-HAWK
  GUNS 920
    SP 165: **20mm** 105 M163 *Machbet Vulcan*; **23mm** 60 ZSU-23-4
    TOWED 755: **23mm** 150 ZU-23; **20mm/37mm** 455 M167 *Vulcan* towed 20mm/M-1939 towed 37mm/TCM-20 towed 20mm; **40mm** 150 L/70
MSL
  ASM AGM-114 *Hellfire*; AGM-62B *Walleye*; AGM-65 *Maverick*; *Popeye* I/*Popeye* II; *Delilah* AL

  AAM • IR AIM-9 *Sidewinder*; *Python* 4; **IIR** *Python* 5; **ARH** *Derby*; AIM-120C AMRAAM
  BOMB • PGM • JDAM (GBU-31); *Spice, Lizard, Opher, Griffon*

Airfield Defence 3,000 active (15,000 reservists)

Paramilitary ε8,000

Border Police ε8,000

Cyber

Israel has substantial capacity for cyber operations. In early 2012, the Israel National Cyber Bureau (INCB) was created in the prime minister's office, to develop technology, human resources and international collaboration. In late October 2012, the INCB and the MoD's Directorate for Research and Development announced a dual cyber-security programme, called MASAD, 'to promote R&D projects that serve both civilian and defense goals at the national level'. Some reporting has highlighted a 'Unit 8200' believed responsible for ELINT, and reportedly cyber, operations. The IDF's Intelligence and C4I Corps are also concerned with cyber-related activity, with the C4I Corps having telecommunications and EW within its purview; specialist training courses exist, including the four-month 'Cyber Shield' activity. The IDF has, it says, 'been engaged in cyber activity consistently and relentlessly, gathering intelligence and defending its own cyber space. Additionally if necessary the cyber space will be used to execute attacks and intelligence operations.'

FOREIGN FORCES

UNTSO unless specified. UNTSO figures represent total numbers for mission in Israel, Syria & Lebanon
Argentina 3 obs
Australia 12 obs
Austria 5 obs
Belgium 2 obs
Canada 8 obs
Chile 3 obs
China 5 obs
Denmark 11 obs
Estonia 3 obs
Finland 18 obs
France 1 obs
Ireland 12 obs
Italy 6 obs
Nepal 4 obs
Netherlands 12 obs
New Zealand 7 obs
Norway 12 obs
Russia 4 obs
Serbia 1 obs
Slovakia 2 obs
Slovenia 3 obs

Sweden 7 obs
Switzerland 14 obs
United States 1 obs • US Strategic Command; 1 AN/TPY-2 X-band radar at Mount Keren

Jordan JOR

Jordanian Dinar D		2013	2014	2015
GDP	D	24bn	25.9bn	
	US$	33.9bn	36.6bn	
per capita	US$	5,174	5,460	
Growth	%	2.9	3.5	
Inflation	%	5.6	3.0	
Def bdgt [a]	D	862m	899m	924m
	US$	1.22bn	1.27bn	
FMA (US)	US$	300m	300m	300m
US$1=D		0.71	0.71	

[a] Excludes expenditure on public order and safety

Population   6,528,061

Ethnic groups: Palestinian ε50–60%

Age	0–14	15–19	20–24	25–29	30–64	65 plus
Male	17.7%	5.1%	4.9%	4.2%	16.2%	2.5%
Female	16.7%	4.9%	4.6%	4.1%	16.3%	2.7%

Capabilities

Jordan's armed forces benefit from a high level of defence spending relative to GDP and strong relationships with the US and the UK that have facilitated training. However, the size of the population and the lack of conventional threats mean the armed forces are relatively small and unable to compete directly with peers in the region. Security priorities remain the Israel–Palestine conflict but particularly in recent years the effect of overspill from the Syrian war, which is putting strain on the country and as a result border security has been boosted. The main roles of Jordan's fully professional armed forces are border and internal security, and the services are capable of combat and contributions to international expeditionary operations. Personnel are well trained, particularly aircrew and special forces, who are highly regarded and have served alongside ISAF forces in Afghanistan and participated in various UN missions. The country has developed a bespoke SF training centre, and regularly plays host to various SF contingents, affording its forces the opportunity to develop their own capability.

ACTIVE 100,500 (Army 74,000 Navy 500 Air 12,000 Special Operations 14,000) Paramilitary 15,000

RESERVE 65,000 (Army 60,000 Joint 5,000)

ORGANISATIONS BY SERVICE

Army 74,000

FORCES BY ROLE
MANOEUVRE
  Armoured
    1 (strategic reserve) armd div (3 armd bde, 1 arty bde, 1 AD bde)
    1 armd bde
  Mechanised
    5 mech bde
  Light
    3 lt inf bde
COMBAT SUPPORT
  3 arty bde
  3 AD bde
  1 MRL bn

EQUIPMENT BY TYPE
MBT 752: 390 CR1 *Challenger 1* (*Al Hussein*); 274 FV4030/2 *Khalid*; 88 M60 *Phoenix*; (292 *Tariq* Centurion; 115 M60A1A3; 23 M47/M48A5 in store)
LT TK (19 *Scorpion*; in store)
RECCE 153: 103 *Scimitar*; 50 *Ferret*
AIFV 452: 31 BMP-2; 321 *Ratel*-20; 100 YPR-765
APC 819+
  APC (T) 634+: 100 M113A1; 300 M113A2 Mk1J; some *Temsah*; 234 YPR-765
  PPV 185: 35 *Cougar*; 25 *Marauder*; 25 *Matador*; 100 *MaxxPro*
ARTY 1,441+
  SP 568: **105mm** 30 M52; **155mm** 390: 370 M109A1/A2; 20 M-44; **203mm** 148 M110A2
  TOWED 100: **105mm** 72: 54 M102; 18 MOBAT; **155mm** 28: 10 M1/M59; 18 M114; **203mm** (4 M115 in store)
  MRL 14+: **227mm** 12 HIMARS **273mm** 2+ WM-80
  MOR 759:
    SP **81mm** 50
    TOWED 709: **81mm** 359; **107mm** 50 M30; **120mm** 300 *Brandt*
AT • MSL 975
  SP 115: 70 M901; 45 YPR-765 with *Milan*
  MANPATS *Javelin*; M47 *Dragon*; TOW/TOW-2A; 9K135 *Kornet* (AT-14 *Spriggan*)
  RL **112mm** 2,300 APILAS
AD
  SAM 930+
    SP 140: 92 9K35 *Strela*-10 (SA-13 *Gopher*); 48 9K33 *Osa-M* (SA-8 *Gecko*)
    MANPAD FIM-43 *Redeye*; 9K32M *Strela*-2M (SA-7B *Grail*)‡; 9K36 *Strela*-3 (SA-14 *Gremlin*); 240 9K310 *Igla*-1 (SA-16 *Gimlet*); 9K38 *Igla* (SA-18 *Grouse*)
  GUNS • SP 356: **20mm** 100 M163 *Vulcan*; **23mm** 40 ZSU-23-4; **40mm** 216 M-42 (not all op)
RADAR • LAND 7 AN/TPQ-36 *Firefinder*/AN/TPQ-37 *Firefinder* (arty, mor)
ARV 137+: 55 *Al Monjed*; 55 *Chieftain* ARV; *Centurion* Mk2; 20 M47; 32 M88A1; 30 M578; YPR-806
MW 12 *Aardvark* Mk2

Navy ε500

EQUIPMENT BY TYPE
PATROL AND COASTAL COMBATANTS 7 (+ 12 patrol boats under 10 tonnes)

PB 7: 3 *Al Hussein* (UK Vosper 30m); 4 *Abdullah* (US *Dauntless*)

Air Force 12,000

Flying hours 180 hrs/year

FORCES BY ROLE
FIGHTER/GROUND ATTACK
  2 sqn with F-16AM/BM *Fighting Falcon*
FIGHTER/GROUND ATTACK/ISR
  1 sqn with F-5E/F *Tiger* II
TRANSPORT
  1 sqn with C-130E/H *Hercules*; CN-235; C-295M
  1 sqn with Cessna 208B; EC635
  1 unit with Il-76MF *Candid*
TRAINING
  1 OCU with F-5E/F *Tiger* II
  1 sqn with C-101 *Aviojet*
  1 sqn with T-67M *Firefly*
  1 hel sqn with AS350B3; Hughes 500
ATTACK HELICOPTER
  2 sqn with AH-1F *Cobra* (with TOW)
TRANSPORT HELICOPTER
  1 sqn with AS332M *Super Puma*
  1 sqn with Bell 205 (UH-1H *Iroquois*)
  1 (Royal) flt with S-70A *Black Hawk*; UH-60L/M *Black Hawk*
AIR DEFENCE
  1 comd (5–6 bty with PAC-2 *Patriot*; 5 bty with MIM-23B Phase III I-HAWK; 6 bty with *Skyguard/Aspide*)

EQUIPMENT BY TYPE
AIRCRAFT 75 combat capable
  FTR 29 F-5E/F *Tiger* II
  FGA 38 F-16AM/BM *Fighting Falcon*
  ATK 2 AC-235
  TPT 20: **Heavy** 2 Il-76MF *Candid*; **Medium** 7: 3 C-130E *Hercules*; 4 C-130H *Hercules*; **Light** 11: 6 AT802 *Air Tractor**; 5 Cessna 208B (2 C-295M in store being converted to gunships)
  TRG 25: 15 T-67M *Firefly*; 10 C-101 *Aviojet*
HELICOPTERS
  ATK 25 AH-1F *Cobra*
  MRH 13 EC635 (Tpt/SAR)
  TPT 70: **Medium** 20: 12 AS332M *Super Puma*; 3 S-70A *Black Hawk*; 3 UH-60L *Black Hawk*; 2 UH-60M *Black Hawk*; **Light** 50: 36 Bell 205 (UH-1H *Iroquois*); 8 Hughes 500D; 6 AS350B3
AD • SAM 64: 24 MIM-23B Phase III I-HAWK; 40 PAC-2 *Patriot*
MSL
  ASM AGM-65D *Maverick*; BGM-71 TOW
  AAM • IR AIM-9J/N/P *Sidewinder*; R-550 *Magic*; **SARH** AIM-7 *Sparrow*; R-530; **ARH** AIM-120C AMRAAM

Joint Special Operations Command 14,000

FORCES BY ROLE
SPECIAL FORCES
  1 spec ops bde (2 SF bn, 2 AB bn, 1 AB arty bn, 1 psyops unit)
  1 ranger bde (1 SF bn, 3 ranger bn)
MANOEUVRE
  Other
  1 (Royal Guard) sy bde (1 SF regt, 3 sy bn)

TRANSPORT
  1 sqn with An-32B
TRANSPORT HELICOPTER
  1 sqn with MD-530F
  1 sqn with UH-60L *Black Hawk*

EQUIPMENT BY TYPE
AIRCRAFT
  TPT Light 3 An-32B
HELICOPTERS
  MRH 6 MD-530F
  TPT • Medium 8 UH-60L *Black Hawk*

Paramilitary ε15,000 active

Gendarmerie ε15,000 active

3 regional comd

FORCES BY ROLE
SPECIAL FORCES
  2 SF unit
MANOEUVRE
  Other
  10 sy bn

EQUIPMENT BY TYPE
APC
  APC (W) 25+: AT105 *Saxon* (reported); 25+ EE-11 *Urutu*
  PPV AB-2 *Jawad*

Reserve Organisations ε35,000 reservists

Civil Militia 'People's Army' ε35,000 reservists
Men 16–65, women 16–45

DEPLOYMENT

AFGHANISTAN
NATO • ISAF 626; 1 mech inf bn

CÔTE D'IVOIRE
UN • UNOCI 549; 9 obs; 1 SF coy; 1 inf bn(-)

DEMOCRATIC REPUBLIC OF THE CONGO
UN • MONUSCO 169; 15 obs; 1 SF coy

HAITI
UN • MINUSTAH 8

LIBERIA
UN • UNMIL 5; 1 obs

SOUTH SUDAN
UN • UNMISS 3; 3 obs

SUDAN
UN • UNAMID 12; 15 obs

FOREIGN FORCES

Belgium 6 F-16AM *Fighting Falcon*
Netherlands 8 F-16AM *Fighting Falcon*
United States Central Command: *Operation Inherent Resolve* 1 FGA sqn with 12 F-16C *Fighting Falcon*

Kuwait KWT

Kuwaiti Dinar D		2013	2014	2015
GDP	D	49.9bn	50.6bn	
	US$	176bn	179bn	
per capita	US$	45,189	44,850	
Growth	%	-0.4	1.4	
Inflation	%	2.7	3.0	
Def bdgt	D	1.23bn	1.37bn	
	US$	4.34bn	4.84bn	
US$1=D		0.28	0.28	

Population   2,742,711

Ethnic groups: Nationals 35%; other Arab 35%; South Asian 9%; Iranian 4%; other 17%

Age	0–14	15–19	20–24	25–29	30–64	65 plus
Male	13.2%	3.3%	5.1%	7.5%	28.4%	1.1%
Female	12.2%	3.1%	3.8%	4.5%	16.6%	1.2%

Capabilities

Kuwait has a professional, relatively well-equipped, land-focused force, however it is too small to deter a major threat from its larger neighbours. It relies on its membership of the GCC and relationship with the US to guarantee its security. The US has afforded Kuwait access to high-tech weapons systems and combined training exercises and itself maintains substantial forces in the country. The navy has patrol boats capable of ensuring maritime security and defence against small flotillas. The air force regularly deploys aircraft to GCC air exercises and flew humanitarian flights during the 2011 Libya conflict. Its *Patriot* missile systems are to be increased and upgraded, while the two C-17 *Globemaster* IIIs and three KC-130J tanker transports that arrived in 2014 will boost airlift capabilities.

ACTIVE 15,500 (Army 11,000 Navy 2,000 Air 2,500)
Paramilitary 7,100

RESERVE 23,700 (Joint 23,700)
Reserve obligation to age 40; 1 month annual trg

ORGANISATIONS BY SERVICE

Army 11,000
FORCES BY ROLE
SPECIAL FORCES
  1 SF unit (forming)
MANOEUVRE
  Reconnaissance
  1 mech/recce bde
  Armoured
  3 armd bde
  Mechanised
  2 mech inf bde
  Light
  1 cdo bn

Other
  1 (Amiri) gd bde
COMBAT SUPPORT
  1 arty bde
  1 engr bde
  1 MP bn
COMBAT SERVICE SUPPORT
  1 log gp
  1 fd hospital

Reserve
FORCES BY ROLE
MANOEUVRE
  Mechanised
  1 bde
EQUIPMENT BY TYPE
MBT 293: 218 M1A2 *Abrams*; 75 M-84 (75 more in store)
RECCE 11 TPz-1 *Fuchs* NBC
AIFV 432: 76 BMP-2; 120 BMP-3; 236 *Desert Warrior*† (incl variants)
APC 260
  APC (T) 260: 230 M113A2; 30 M577
  APC (W) (40 TH 390 *Fahd* in store)
ARTY 218
  SP 155mm 106: 37 M109A3; 18 (AMX) Mk F3; 51 PLZ45; (18 AU-F-1 in store)
  MRL 300mm 27 9A52 *Smerch*
  MOR 78: 81mm 60; 107mm 6 M-30; 120mm ε12 RT-F1
AT • MSL 118+
  SP 74: 66 HMMWV TOW; 8 M901
  MANPATS TOW-2; M47 *Dragon*
  RCL 84mm ε200 *Carl Gustav*
AD • SAM 60+
  STATIC/SHELTER 12 *Aspide*
  MANPAD *Starburst*; *Stinger*
  GUNS • TOWED 35mm 12+ Oerlikon
ARV 24+: 24 M88A1/2; Type-653A; *Warrior*
MW *Aardvark* Mk2

Navy ε2,000 (incl 500 Coast Guard)
EQUIPMENT BY TYPE
PATROL AND COASTAL COMBATANTS 20
  PCFG 2:
    1 *Al Sanbouk* (GER Lurssen TNC-45) with 2 twin lnchr with MM-40 *Exocet* AShM, 1 76mm gun
    1 *Istiqlal* (GER Lurssen FPB-57) with 2 twin lnchr with MM-40 *Exocet* AShM, 1 76mm gun
  PBF 10 *Al Nokatha* (US Mk V *Pegasus*)
  PBG 8 *Um Almaradim* (FRA P-37 BRL) with 2 twin lnchr with *Sea Skua* AShM, 1 sextuple lnchr (lnchr only)
LOGISTICS AND SUPPORT • AG 1 *Sawahil* with 1 hel landing platform

Air Force 2,500
Flying hours   210 hrs/year

FORCES BY ROLE
FIGHTER/GROUND ATTACK
  2 sqn with F/A-18C/D *Hornet*
TRANSPORT
  1 sqn with C-17A *Globemaster*; KC-130J *Hercules*; L-100-30

TRAINING
1 unit with EMB-312 *Tucano* (*Tucano* Mk52)*; *Hawk* Mk64*
ATTACK HELICOPTER
1 sqn with AH-64D *Apache*
1 atk/trg sqn with SA342 *Gazelle* with HOT
TRANSPORT HELICOPTER
1 sqn with AS532 *Cougar*; SA330 *Puma*; S-92
AIR DEFENCE
1 comd (5–6 SAM bty with PAC-2 *Patriot*; 5 SAM bty with MIM-23B I-HAWK Phase III; 6 SAM bty with *Skyguard/Aspide*)
EQUIPMENT BY TYPE
AIRCRAFT 66 combat capable
  FGA 39: 31 F/A-18C *Hornet*; 8 F/A-18D *Hornet*
  TKR 3 KC-130J *Hercules*
  TPT 5: **Heavy** 2 C-17A *Globemaster*; **Medium** 3 L-100-30
  TRG 27: 11 *Hawk* Mk64*; 16 EMB-312 *Tucano* (*Tucano* Mk52)*
HELICOPTERS
  ATK 16 AH-64D *Apache*
  MRH 13 SA342 *Gazelle* with HOT
  TPT • **Medium** 13: 3 AS532 *Cougar*; 7 SA330 *Puma*; 3 S-92
MSL
  ASM AGM-65G *Maverick*; AGM-114K *Hellfire*
  AShM AGM-84A *Harpoon*
  AAM • **IR** AIM-9L *Sidewinder*; R-550 *Magic*; **SARH** AIM-7F *Sparrow*; **ARH** AIM-120C7 AMRAAM
AD • SAM 76: 40 PAC-2 *Patriot*; 24 MIM-23B I-HAWK Phase III; 12 *Skyguard/Aspide*

Paramilitary ε7,100 active

National Guard ε6,600 active
FORCES BY ROLE
SPECIAL FORCES
  1 SF bn
MANOEUVRE
  Reconnaissance
  1 armd car bn
  Other
  3 security bn
COMBAT SUPPORT
  1 MP bn
EQUIPMENT BY TYPE
RECCE 20 VBL
APC (W) 97+: 5+ *Desert Chameleon*; 70 *Pandur*; 22 S600 (incl variants)
ARV *Pandur*

Coast Guard 500
PATROL AND COASTAL COMBATANTS 32
  PBF 12 *Manta*
  PB 20: 3 *Al Shaheed*; 4 *Inttisar* (Austal 31.5m); 3 *Kassir* (Austal 22m); 10 *Subahi*
AMPHIBIOUS • LANDING CRAFT • LCU 4: 2 *Al Tahaddy*; 1 *Saffar*; 1 other
LOGISTICS AND SUPPORT • AG 1 *Sawahil*

FOREIGN FORCES

Canada *Operation Impact* 530: 6 F/A-18A *Hornet* (CF-18AM); 2 P-3 *Orion* (CP-140); 1 A310 MRTT (C-150T)
United Kingdom 40 • *Operation Shader* MQ-9A *Reaper*
United States Central Command: 13,000; 1 armd bde; 1 ARNG cbt avn bde; 1 ARNG spt bde; 2 AD bty with total of 16 *Patriot* PAC-3; 1 (APS) armd bde eqpt set; 1 (APS) inf bde eqpt set

Lebanon LBN

Lebanese Pound LP		2013	2014	2015
GDP	LP	67.9tr	71.6tr	
	US$	45bn	47.5bn	
per capita	US$	10,077	10,531	
Growth	%	1.5	1.8	
Inflation	%	3.2	3.5	
Def exp	LP	ε1.81tr		
	US$	ε1.2bn		
FMA (US)	US$	75m	75m	80m
US$1=LP		1,507.50	1,507.50	

Population   4,136,895

Ethnic and religious groups: Christian 30%; Druze 6%; Armenian 4%, excl ε300,000 Syrians and ε350,000 Palestinian refugees

Age	0–14	15–19	20–24	25–29	30–64	65 plus
Male	11.1%	4.1%	4.5%	4.5%	20.3%	4.4%
Female	10.6%	4.0%	4.4%	4.4%	22.5%	5.2%

Capabilities

Lebanon's armed forces are heavily dominated by the army and, despite some Western military assistance, reliant on outdated equipment. Surveillance requirements will be addressed to some degree by the recent arrival of C-208s, at least one armed with *Hellfire* missiles, though limited additional response capabilities will reduce effectiveness. Meanwhile, a reported agreement whereby French weapons sales would be financed by Saudi Arabia has the potential to boost platform capabilities. The armed forces play a key role in containing localised violence and mediating between rival groups across the country. A five-year plan to modernise capabilities was announced in September 2013, in the first attempt to draw a strategic plan for force requirements, including the potential incorporation of Hizbullah into the Lebanese Army. Given the fragilities of the armed forces, Hizbullah often plays a key role in domestic and international security. Since 2013, Hizbullah has provided advice and training to Syrian government forces as well as security to lines of communication and an expeditionary force of around 2,000 fighters. Inside Lebanon, it has sought to isolate Sunni towns in the Bekaa Valley and dismantle rebel support networks. The armed forces, meanwhile, were in 2014 engaged in combat with Nusra Front and ISIS fighters, after these groups threatened Lebanese border towns and killed some personnel.

ACTIVE 60,000 (Army 56,600 Navy 1,800 Air 1,600)
Paramilitary 20,000

ORGANISATIONS BY SERVICE

Army 56,600
FORCES BY ROLE
5 regional comd (Beirut, Bekaa Valley, Mount Lebanon, North, South)
SPECIAL FORCES
1 cdo regt
MANOEUVRE
Armoured
  2 armd regt
Mechanised
  11 mech inf bde
Air Manoeuvre
  1 AB regt
Amphibious
  1 mne cdo regt
Other
  1 Presidential Guard bde
  5 intervention regt
  2 border sy regt
COMBAT SUPPORT
2 arty regt
1 cbt spt bde (1 engr rgt, 1 AT regt, 1 sigs regt)
1 MP bde
COMBAT SERVICE SUPPORT
1 log bde
1 med regt
1 construction regt
EQUIPMENT BY TYPE
MBT 324: 92 M48A1/A5; 185 T-54; 47 T-55
RECCE 55 AML
AIFV 16 AIFV-B-C25
APC 1,330
  APC (T) 1,244 M113A1/A2 (incl variants)
  APC (W) 86 VAB VCT
ARTY 487
  TOWED 201: **105mm** 13 M101A1; **122mm** 35: 9 D-30; 26 M-30; **130mm** 15 M-46; **155mm** 138: 18 M114A1; 106 M198; 14 Model-50
  MRL **122mm** 11 BM-21
  MOR 275: **81mm** 134; **82mm** 112; **120mm** 29 Brandt
AT
  MSL • MANPATS 38: 26 *Milan*; 12 TOW
  RCL **106mm** 113 M40A1
  RL **73mm** 11 M-50; **90mm** 8 M-69
AD
  SAM • MANPAD 9K32 *Strela*-2/2M (SA-7A *Grail*/SA-7B *Grail*)‡
  GUNS • TOWED 77: **20mm** 20; **23mm** 57 ZU-23
ARV M113 ARV; T-54/55 ARV reported
VLB MTU-72 reported
MW Bozena
UAV • ISR • Medium 8 *Mohajer* 4

Navy 1,800
EQUIPMENT BY TYPE
In addition to the vessels listed, the Lebanese Navy operates a further 22 vessels with a full-load displacement below ten tonnes.

PATROL AND COASTAL COMBATANTS 13
  PCC 1 *Trablous*
  PB 11: 1 *Aamchit* (ex-GER *Bremen*); 1 *Al Kalamoun* (ex-FRA *Avel Gwarlarn*); 7 *Tripoli* (ex-UK *Attacker/Tracker Mk 2*); 1 *Naquora* (ex-GER *Bremen*); 1 *Tabarja* (ex-GER *Bergen*)
  PBF 1
AMPHIBIOUS • LANDING CRAFT • LCT 2 *Sour* (ex-FRA *Edic* – capacity 8 APC; 96 troops)

Air Force 1,600
4 air bases
FORCES BY ROLE
FIGHTER/GROUND ATTACK
  1 sqn with *Hunter* Mk6/Mk9/T66†; Cessna AC-208 *Combat Caravan**
ATTACK HELICOPTER
  1 sqn with SA342L *Gazelle*
TRANSPORT HELICOPTER
  4 sqn with Bell 205 (UH-1H)
  1 sqn with AS330/IAR330SM *Puma*
  1 trg sqn with R-44 *Raven* II
EQUIPMENT BY TYPE
AIRCRAFT 9 combat capable
  FGA 4: 3 *Hunter* Mk6/Mk9†; 1 *Hunter* T66†
  ISR 3 Cessna AC-208 *Combat Caravan**
  TRG 3 *Bulldog*
HELICOPTERS
  MRH 9: 1 AW139; 8 SA342L *Gazelle* (plus 5 unserviceable – could be refurbished); (5 SA316 *Alouette* III unserviceable – 3 could be refurbished); (1 SA318 *Alouette* II unserviceable – could be refurbished)
  TPT 29: **Medium** 13: 3 S-61N (fire fighting); 10 AS330/IAR330 *Puma*; **Light** 22: 18 Bell 205 (UH-1H *Huey*) (11 more unserviceable); 4 R-44 *Raven* II (basic trg); (7 Bell 212 unserviceable – 6 could be refurbished)

Paramilitary ε20,000 active

Internal Security Force ε20,000
Ministry of Interior
FORCES BY ROLE
Other Combat Forces
  1 (police) judicial unit
  1 regional sy coy
  1 (Beirut Gendarmerie) sy coy
EQUIPMENT BY TYPE
APC (W) 60 V-200 *Chaimite*

Customs
PATROL AND COASTAL COMBATANTS 7
  PB 7: 5 *Aztec*; 2 *Tracker*

FOREIGN FORCES
Unless specified, figures refer to UNTSO and represent total numbers for the mission in Israel, Syria & Lebanon.
Argentina 3 obs
Armenia UNIFIL 1

Australia 12 obs
Austria 5 obs • UNIFIL 171: 1 log coy
Bangladesh UNIFIL 326: 1 FFG; 1 FSG
Belarus UNIFIL 2
Belgium 2 obs • UNIFIL 99: 1 engr coy
Brazil UNIFIL 267: 1 FFGHM
Brunei UNIFIL 30
Cambodia UNIFIL 184: 1 engr coy
Canada 8 obs (*Op Jade*)
Chile 3 obs
China, People's Republic of 5 obs • UNIFIL 218: 1 engr coy; 1 fd hospital
Croatia UNIFIL 1
Cyprus UNIFIL 2
Denmark 11 obs
El Salvador UNIFIL 51: 1 inf pl
Estonia 3 obs
Finland 18 obs • UNIFIL 344; elm 1 mech inf bn
France 1 obs • UNIFIL 845: 1 inf BG; *Leclerc*; AMX-10P; PVP; VAB; CAESAR; AU-F1; *Mistral*
Germany UNIFIL 144: 1 FFGM
Ghana UNIFIL 871: 1 mech inf bn
Greece UNIFIL 48: 1 PB
Guatemala UNIFIL 2
Hungary UNIFIL 4
India UNIFIL 890: 1 mech inf bn; 1 fd hospital
Indonesia UNIFIL 1,287: 1 mech inf bn; 1 log b(-); 1 FFGM
Ireland 12 obs • UNIFIL 195: elm 1 mech inf bn
Italy 6 obs • UNIFIL 1,200: 1 mech bde HQ; 1 mech inf bn; 1 engr coy; 1 sigs coy; 1 CIMIC coy; 1 hel flt
Kenya UNIFIL 1
Korea, Republic of UNIFIL 321: 1 mech inf bn
Luxembourg UNIFIL 2
Macedonia, Former Yugoslav Republic of UNIFIL 1
Malaysia UNIFIL 828: 1 mech inf bn; 1 mech inf coy
Nepal 4 obs • UNIFIL 869: 1 inf bn
Netherlands 12 obs
New Zealand 7 obs
Nigeria UNIFIL 1
Norway 12 obs
Qatar UNIFIL 3
Russia 4 obs
Serbia 1 obs • UNIFIL 143; 1 inf coy
Sierra Leone UNIFIL 3
Slovakia 2 obs
Slovenia 3 obs • UNIFIL 14; 1 inf pl
Spain UNIFIL 589: 1 cav bde HQ; 1 lt armd cav BG
Sri Lanka UNIFIL 151: 1 inf coy
Sweden 7 obs
Switzerland 14 obs
Tanzania UNIFIL 158; 2 MP coy
Turkey UNIFIL 53: 1 FSGM
United States 1 obs

Libya LBY

Libyan Dinar D		2013	2014	2015
GDP	D	83.3bn	61.7bn	
	US$	65.5bn	49.3bn	
per capita	US$	10,702	7,942	
Growth	%	-13.6	-19.8	
Inflation	%	2.6	4.8	
Def exp	D	ε5.92bn		
	US$	ε4.66bn		
US$1=D		1.27	1.25	

Population 6,244,174

Age	0–14	15–19	20–24	25–29	30–64	65 plus
Male	13.8%	4.6%	4.8%	5.3%	21.4%	2.0%
Female	13.1%	4.3%	4.4%	4.7%	19.6%	2.0%

Capabilities

Civil war gripped Libya in June 2014, as a coalition of Islamist groups and Libyan Shield units took control of Tripoli, Benghazi and Misrata, and army bases were overrun. The central government fled to Tobruk, and assembled in a charted car ferry offshore. There was a breakdown in administration as militias took control of ministries in Tripoli, and army officers were assassinated in Benghazi. In response, air-strikes against Islamist militias were reportedly conducted by the UAE and Egypt. Attempts to incorporate militias into national institutions had proved difficult, with any meaningful authority over former rebels proving tenuous, and political, regional and tribal interests impeding security reform. The formal armed forces remain top-heavy with mainly senior-ranking officers, and plans for a 20,000-strong general-purpose force and restructuring the armed forces and police have been impeded by a lack of recruits and still-fledgling administrative mechanisms. Foreign states undertook to train troops as part of a 'General Purpose Force', but this proceeded haphazardly. Some Gadhafi-regime weapons were destroyed in 2011, but precise ownership of remaining equipment remains in doubt, as does serviceability. Until there is a resolution to the governance crisis, it will be difficult to proceed with an effective disarmament, demobilisation and reintegration programme. (See pp. 306–08.)

ACTIVE 7,000

ORGANISATIONS BY SERVICE

Army up to 7,000

FORCES BY ROLE
State military structures remain embryonic and personnel totals aspirational; training proceeds slowly while effective command-and-control remains questionable. Local control is often exercised by militia groups.
SPECIAL FORCES
1 SF bn

MANOEUVRE
    Armoured
    1 armd bn
    Light
    Some mot inf bn
    Other
    1 sy unit
COMBAT SUPPORT
    1+ AD bn
EQUIPMENT BY TYPE
Most of the equipment that survived the 2011 conflict in a salvageable condition is still awaiting reactivation.
MBT T-55; T-72
RECCE BRDM-2
AIFV BMP-1
APC
    APC (T) M113
    APC (W) BTR-60PB; Ratel; Puma
AT • MSL
    SP 9P122 Malyutka; 10 9P157-2 Khryzantema-S
    MANPATS 9K11 Malyutka (AT-3 Sagger); 9K11 Fagot (AT-4 Spigot); 9K113 Konkurs (AT-5 Spandrel); Milan
    RCL some: **106mm** M40A1; **84mm** Carl Gustav
AD
    SAM • SP: 9K338 Igla-S (SA-24 Grinch)
    GUNS
        SP **23mm** ZSU-23-4
        TOWED: **14.5mm** ZPU-2
MSL • TACTICAL • SSM Scud-B

Navy (incl Coast Guard) n.k.

The level of state control over remaining vessels is not clear
EQUIPMENT BY TYPE
SUBMARINES • TACTICAL • SSK 2 Khyber† (FSU Foxtrot) each with 10 533mm TT (6 fwd, 4 aft)
PRINCIPAL SURFACE COMBATANTS 1
    FRIGATES • FFGM 1 Al Hanit (FSU Koni) with 2 twin lnchr (with P-15 Termit-M (SS-N-2C Styx) AShM, 1 twin lnchr with 9K33 Osa-M (SA-N-4 Gecko) SAM, 2 twin 406mm ASTT with USET-95 Type-40 LWT, 1 RBU 6000 Smerch 2, 2 twin 76mm gun
PATROL AND COASTAL COMBATANTS 17
    PBFG 5:
        4 Al Zuara (FSU Osa II) with 4 single lnchr with P-15 Termit-M (SS-N-2C Styx) AShM
        1 Sharaba (FRA Combattante II) with 4 single lnchr with Otomat Mk2 AShM, 1 76mm gun (3 further vessels may be non-operational)
    PB: 11: 8 Burdi (Damen Stan 1605); 2 Ikrimah (FRA RPB20); 1 Hamelin
MINE WARFARE • MINE COUNTERMEASURES 4
    MSO 4 Ras al Gelais (FSU Natya) with 2 RBU 1200
AMPHIBIOUS
    LANDING SHIPS • LST 2 Ibn Harissa (capacity 1 hel; 11 MBT; 240 troops)
    LANDING CRAFT 5
        LCAC 2 Slingsby SAH 2200
        LCT 3† C107
LOGISTICS AND SUPPORT 11
    AFD 2

ARS 1 Al Munjed (YUG Spasilac)
YDT 1 Al Manoud (FSU Yelva)
YTB 7

Coastal Defence
EQUIPMENT BY TYPE
PBF 5 Bigliani
PB 6 PV30

Air Force n.k.
EQUIPMENT BY TYPE
A small number of aircraft inherited from the previous regime continue to be operated. Serviceability is an issue.
AIRCRAFT 8 combat capable
    FTR 1+ MiG-23MLD Flogger/MiG-23UB Flogger
    FGA 3+: 1+ MiG-21bis Fishbed; 2 MiG-21MF Fishbed; (Some Mirage F-1E(ED) in store)
    TPT 5: **Medium** 3: 2 C-130H Hercules; 1 L-100-30; **Light**: 2 An-26 Curl
    TRG 11: 4 G-2 Galeb; 3 L-39ZO Albatros; 4 SF-260WL Warrior*
HELICOPTERS
    ATK 3 Mi-25 Hind D
    TPT 9+: **Heavy** 2 CH-47C Chinook; **Medium** 5 Mi-8T Hip; **Light** 2+: 1+ Bell 206 Jet Ranger (AB-206); 1 PZL Mi-2 Hoplite
MSL
    ASM 9M17 (AT-2 Swatter)
    ARM Kh-58 (AS-11 Kilter)
    AAM • IR R-3 (AA-2 Atoll)‡; R-60 (AA-8 Aphid); R-550 Magic; **IR/SARH** R-23/24 (AA-7 Apex)

Mauritania MRT

Mauritanian Ouguiya OM		2013	2014	2015
GDP	OM	1.25tr	1.3tr	
	US$	4.19bn	4.29bn	
per capita	US$	1,128	1,127	
Growth	%	6.7	6.8	
Inflation	%	4.1	3.3	
Def exp	OM	ε44.5bn		
	US$	ε149m		
US$1=OM		298.77	303.03	

Population 3,516,806

Age	0–14	15–19	20–24	25–29	30–64	65 plus
Male	19.8%	5.2%	4.5%	3.8%	13.2%	1.5%
Female	19.7%	5.4%	4.8%	4.2%	15.7%	2.1%

Capabilities

The armed forces may be able to cope with some internal security contingencies, but force readiness appears low, there is little combat experience and much equipment is outdated. Patrol craft donated by the EU have enhanced the navy's littoral capabilities, and in mid-2014 the US gifted Mauritania two Cessna 208s, but limited airlift capacity means the armed forces lack mobility. Limited capability to secure territory and resources, combined with the perceived regional threat from Islamist groups and spillover from conflict in neighbouring Mali, has encouraged the US to provide training through the *Flintlock* Joint Combined Exchange Training programme and annual counter-terrorism exercise. Mauritania has pledged around 1,800 troops to the MINUSMA mission in Mali, but has stipulated that they should only be deployed on the border.

ACTIVE 15,850 (Army 15,000 Navy 600 Air 250)
Paramilitary 5,000
Conscript liability 24 months authorised

ORGANISATIONS BY SERVICE

Army 15,000
FORCES BY ROLE
6 mil regions
MANOEUVRE
 Reconnaissance
  1 armd recce sqn
 Armoured
  1 armd bn
 Light
  7 mot inf bn
  8 (garrison) inf bn
 Air Manoeuvre
  1 cdo/para bn
 Other
  2 (camel corps) bn
  1 gd bn
COMBAT SUPPORT
 3 arty bn
 4 ADA bty
 1 engr coy
EQUIPMENT BY TYPE
MBT 35 T-54/T-55
RECCE 70: 20 AML-60; 40 AML-90; 10 *Saladin*
APC
 APC (W) 25: 5 FV603 *Saracen*; ε20 M3 Panhard
ARTY 202
 TOWED 80: **105mm** 36 HM-2/M101A1; **122mm** 44: 20 D-30; 24 D-74
 MRL 8: **107mm** 4 Type-63; **122mm** 4 Type-81
 MOR 114: **60mm** 24; **81mm** 60; **120mm** 30 Brandt
AT • MSL • MANPATS *Milan*
RCL 114: **75mm** ε24 M20; **106mm** ε90 M40A1
AD • SAM
 SP ε4 SA-9 *Gaskin* (reported)
 MANPAD 9K32 *Strela*-2 (SA-7 *Grail*)‡
GUNS • TOWED 82: **14.5mm** 28: 16 ZPU-2; 12 ZPU-4; **23mm** 20 ZU-23-2; **37mm** 10 M-1939; **57mm** 12 S-60; **100mm** 12 KS-19
ARV T-54/55 ARV reported

Navy ε600
EQUIPMENT BY TYPE
PATROL AND COASTAL COMBATANTS 17
 PCO 1 *Voum-Legleita*
 PCC 5: 1 *Abourbekr Ben Amer* (FRA OPV 54); 1 *Arguin*; 2 *Conejera*; 1 *Limam El Hidran* (PRC *Huangpu*)
 PB 11: 1 *El Nasr*† (FRA *Patra*); 4 *Mandovi*; 2 Rodman 55M; 2 *Saeta*-12; 2 *Megsem Bakkar* (FRA RPB20 – for SAR duties)

Air Force 250
EQUIPMENT BY TYPE
AIRCRAFT 4 combat capable
 ISR 2 Cessna 208B *Grand Caravan*
 TPT 8: **Light** 7: 2 BN-2 *Defender*; 1 C-212; 2 PA-31T *Cheyenne* II; 2 Y-12(II); **PAX** 1 Basler BT-67 (with sensor turret)
 TRG 11: 3 EMB-312 *Tucano*; 4 EMB-314 *Super Tucano**; 4 SF-260E
HELICOPTERS
 MRH 3: 1 SA313B *Alouette* II; 2 Z-9

Paramilitary ε5,000 active

Gendarmerie ε3,000
Ministry of Interior
FORCES BY ROLE
MANOEUVRE
 Other
  6 regional sy coy

National Guard 2,000
Ministry of Interior

Customs
EQUIPMENT BY TYPE
PATROL AND COASTAL COMBATANTS • PB 2: 1 *Dah Ould Bah* (FRA *Amgram* 14); 1 *Yaboub Ould Rajel* (FRA RPB18)

DEPLOYMENT

CENTRAL AFRICAN REPUBLIC
UN • MINUSCA 1; 2 obs
MALI
UN • MINUSMA 6

Morocco MOR

Moroccan Dirham D		2013	2014	2015
GDP	D	873bn	920bn	
	US$	104bn	113bn	
per capita	US$	3,160	3,392	
Growth	%	4.4	3.5	
Inflation	%	1.9	1.1	
Def bdgt	D	31.3bn	31.5bn	
	US$	3.72bn	3.86bn	
FMA (US)	US$	8m	7m	5m
US$1=D		8.41	8.17	

Population 32,987,206

Age	0–14	15–19	20–24	25–29	30–64	65 plus
Male	13.6%	4.5%	4.3%	4.4%	19.5%	2.9%
Female	13.2%	4.5%	4.4%	4.6%	20.7%	3.5%

Capabilities

The armed forces are well trained and relatively mobile, relying on mechanised infantry supported by a modest fleet of medium-lift, fixed-wing transport aircraft and various transport helicopters. They have gained extensive experience in counter-insurgency operations in Western Sahara, where a large number of troops are based, which has given them expertise in desert warfare and combined air–land operations, although there is little capability to launch tri-service operations. While forces have taken part in many peacekeeping operations, there has been little experience in state-on-state warfare. Air-force equipment is ageing, with the bulk of the combat fleet procured in the 1970s and 1980s, although 24 F-16 combat aircraft were delivered in 2012. The navy has a moderately sized but ageing fleet of patrol and coastal craft that is incapable of preventing fast-boat smuggling across the Mediterranean. Nonetheless, more significant investment is now being seen in the fleet, with a FREMM destroyer on sea trials, which will provide improved sea-control capability.

ACTIVE 195,800 (Army 175,000 Navy 7,800 Air 13,000) Paramilitary 50,000

Conscript liability 18 months authorised; most enlisted personnel are volunteers

RESERVE 150,000 (Army 150,000)
Reserve obligation to age 50

ORGANISATIONS BY SERVICE

Army ε75,000; 100,000 conscript (total 175,000)
FORCES BY ROLE
2 comd (Northern Zone, Southern Zone)
MANOEUVRE
  Armoured
  12 armd bn
  Mechanised
  3 mech inf bde
  Mechanised/Light
  8 mech/mot inf regt (2–3 bn)
  Light
  1 lt sy bde
  3 (camel corps) mot inf bn
  35 lt inf bn
  4 cdo unit
  Air Manoeuvre
  2 para bde
  2 AB bn
  Mountain
  1 mtn inf bn
COMBAT SUPPORT
  11 arty bn
  7 engr bn
  1 AD bn

Royal Guard 1,500
FORCES BY ROLE
MANOEUVRE
  Other
  1 gd bn
  1 cav sqn

EQUIPMENT BY TYPE
MBT 434: 40 T-72, 220 M60A1; 120 M60A3; 54 Type-90-II (MBT-2000) (reported); (ε200 M48A5 in store)
LT TK 116: 5 AMX-13; 111 SK-105 *Kuerassier*
RECCE 384: 38 AML-60-7; 190 AML-90; 80 AMX-10RC; 40 EBR-75; 16 *Eland*; 20 M1114 HMMWV
AIFV 70: 10 AMX-10P; 30 *Ratel* Mk3-20; 30 *Ratel* Mk3-90
APC 851
  APC (T) 486: 400 M113A1/A2; 86 M577A2
  APC (W) 365: 45 VAB VCI; 320 VAB VTT
ARTY 2,141
  SP 282: **105mm** 5 Mk 61; **155mm** 217: 84 M109A1/A1B; 43 M109A2; 90 (AMX) Mk F3; **203mm** 60 M110
  TOWED 118: **105mm** 50: 30 L118 Light Gun; 20 M101; **130mm** 18 M-46; **155mm** 50: 30 FH-70; 20 M114
  MRL 35 BM-21
  MOR 1,706
    SP 56: **106mm** 32–36 M106A2; **120mm** 20 (VAB APC)
    TOWED 1,650: **81mm** 1,100 Expal model LN; **120mm** 550 Brandt
AT • MSL
  SP 80 M901
  MANPATS 9K11 *Malyutka* (AT-3 *Sagger*); M47 *Dragon*; *Milan*; TOW
RCL 106mm 350 M40A1
RL 89mm 200 M20
GUNS 36
  SP 100mm 8 SU-100
  TOWED 90mm 28 M-56
UAV • Heavy R4E-50 *Skyeye*
AD • SAM
  SP 49: 12 2K22M *Tunguska*-M (SA-19 *Grison*) SPAAGM; 37 M48 *Chaparral*
  MANPAD 9K32 *Strela*-2 (SA-7 *Grail*)‡
  GUNS 407
    SP 60 M163 *Vulcan*
    TOWED 347: **14.5mm** 200: 150–180 ZPU-2; 20 ZPU-4; **20mm** 40 M167 *Vulcan*; **23mm** 75–90 ZU-23-2; **100mm** 17 KS-19
RADAR • LAND: RASIT (veh, arty)
ARV 48+: 10 *Greif*; 18 M88A1; M578; 20 VAB-ECH

Navy 7,800 (incl 1,500 Marines)
EQUIPMENT BY TYPE
PRINCIPAL SURFACE COMBATANTS 6
  DESTROYERS 1
    DDGHM 1 *Mohammed VI*-class (FRA FREMM) with 2 quad lnchr with MM40 *Exocet* Block III AShM, 2 octuple A43 VLS with *Aster* 15 SAM, 2 triple B515 324mm ASTT with Mu-90 LWT, 1 76mm gun (capacity 1 AS565SA *Panther*)
  FRIGATES 5
    FFGHM 3 *Tarik ben Ziyad* (NLD SIGMA 9813/10513) with 4 single lnchr with MM-40 *Exocet* Block II/III AShM, 2 sextuple lnchr with MICA SAM, 2 triple 324 mm ASTT with Mu-90 LWT, 1 76mm gun (capacity 1 AS565SA *Panther*)
    FFGH 2 *Mohammed V* (FRA *Floreal*) with 2 single lnchr with MM-38 *Exocet* AShM, 1 76mm gun (can be fitted with *Simbad* SAM) (capacity 1 AS565SA *Panther*)

PATROL AND COASTAL COMBATANTS 50
  CORVETTES • FSGM 1
    1 *Lt Col Errhamani* (ESP *Descubierto*) with 2 twin lnchr with MM-38 *Exocet* AShM, 1 octuple *Albatros* lnchr with *Aspide* SAM, 2 triple 324mm ASTT with Mk46 LWT, 1 76mm gun
  PSO 1 *Bin an Zaran* (OPV 70) with 1 76mm gun
  PCG 4 *Cdt El Khattabi* (ESP *Lazaga* 58m) with 4 single lnchr with MM-38 *Exocet* AShM, 1 76mm gun
  PCO 5 *Rais Bargach* (under control of fisheries dept)
  PCC 12:
    4 *El Hahiq* (DNK *Osprey* 55, incl 2 with customs)
    6 *LV Rabhi* (ESP 58m B-200D)
    2 *Okba* (FRA PR-72) each with 1 76mm gun
  PB 27: 6 *El Wacil* (FRA P-32); 10 VCSM (RPB 20); 10 Rodman 101; 1 other (UK *Bird*)
AMPHIBIOUS 5
  LANDING SHIPS 4:
    LSM 3 *Ben Aicha* (FRA *Champlain* BATRAL) (capacity 7 tanks; 140 troops)
    LST 1 *Sidi Mohammed Ben Abdallah* (US *Newport*) (capacity 3 LCVP; 400 troops)
  LANDING CRAFT • LCM 1 CTM (FRA CTM-5)
LOGISTICS AND SUPPORT 9
  AGOR 1 *Abou Barakat Albarbari*† (ex-US *Robert D. Conrad*)
  AGS 1 Stan 1504
  AK 2
  AX 1 *Essaouira*
  AXS 2
  YDT 1
  YTB 1

Marines 1,500
FORCES BY ROLE
MANOEUVRE
  Amphibious
    2 naval inf bn

Naval Aviation
EQUIPMENT BY TYPE
HELICOPTERS • ASW/ASUW 3 AS565SA *Panther*

Air Force 13,000
Flying hours 100 hrs/year on *Mirage* F-1/F-5E/F *Tiger* II/F-16C/D *Fighting Falcon*

FORCES BY ROLE
FIGHTER/GROUND ATTACK
  2 sqn with F-5E/F-5F *Tiger* II
  3 sqn with F-16C/D *Fighting Falcon*
  1 sqn with *Mirage* F-1C (F-1CH)
  1 sqn with *Mirage* F-1E (F-1EH)
ELECTRONIC WARFARE
  1 sqn with EC-130H *Hercules*; *Falcon* 20 (ELINT)
MARITIME PATROL
  1 flt with Do-28
TANKER/TRANSPORT
  1 sqn with C-130/KC-130H *Hercules*
TRANSPORT
  1 sqn with CN-235
  1 VIP sqn with B-737BBJ; Beech 200/300 *King Air*; *Falcon* 50; Gulfstream II/III/V-SP
TRAINING
  1 sqn with *Alpha Jet**
  1 sqn T-6C
ATTACK HELICOPTER
  1 sqn with SA342L *Gazelle* (Some with HOT)
TRANSPORT HELICOPTER
  1 sqn with Bell 205A (AB-205A); Bell 206 *Jet Ranger* (AB-206); Bell 212 (AB-212)
  1 sqn with CH-47D *Chinook*
  1 sqn with SA330 *Puma*

EQUIPMENT BY TYPE
AIRCRAFT 92 combat capable
  FTR 22: 19 F-5E *Tiger* II; 3 F-5F *Tiger* II
  FGA 51: 16 F-16C *Fighting Falcon*; 8 F-16D *Fighting Falcon*; 16 *Mirage* F-1C (F-1CH); 11 *Mirage* F-1E (F-1EH)
  ELINT 1 EC-130H *Hercules*
  TKR/TPT 2 KC-130H *Hercules*
  TPT 47: **Medium** 17: 4 C-27J *Spartan*; 13 C-130H *Hercules*; **Light** 21: 4 Beech 100 *King Air*; 2 Beech 200 *King Air*; 1 Beech 200C *King Air*; 2 Beech 300 *King Air*; 3 Beech 350 *King Air*; 7 CN-235; 2 Do-28; **PAX** 9: 1 B-737BBJ; 2 *Falcon* 20; 2 *Falcon* 20 (ELINT); 1 *Falcon* 50 (VIP); 1 Gulfstream II (VIP); 1 Gulfstream III; 1 Gulfstream V-SP
  TRG 81: 12 AS-202 *Bravo*; 19 *Alpha Jet**; 2 CAP-10; 25 T-6C *Texan*; 9 T-34C *Turbo Mentor*; 14 T-37B *Tweet*
  FF 4 CL-415
HELICOPTERS
  MRH 19 SA342L *Gazelle* (7 with HOT, 12 with cannon)
  TPT 70: **Heavy** 7 CH-47D *Chinook*; **Medium** 24 SA330 *Puma*; **Light** 39: 25 Bell 205A (AB-205A); 11 Bell 206 *Jet Ranger* (AB-206); 3 Bell 212 (AB-212)
MSL
  AAM • IR AIM-9B/D/J *Sidewinder*; R-550 *Magic*; **IIR** (AIM-9X *Sidewinder* on order); **SARH** R-530; **ARH** (AIM-120 AMRAAM on order)
  ASM AASM (on order); AGM-62B *Walleye* (for F-5E); HOT

Paramilitary 50,000 active

Gendarmerie Royale 20,000
FORCES BY ROLE
MANOEUVRE
  Air Manoeuvre
    1 para sqn
  Other
    1 paramilitary bde
    4 (mobile) paramilitary gp
    1 coast guard unit
TRANSPORT HELICOPTER
  1 sqn

EQUIPMENT BY TYPE
PATROL AND COASTAL COMBATANTS • PB 15 Arcor 53
AIRCRAFT • TRG 2 R-235 *Guerrier*
HELICOPTERS
  MRH 14: 3 SA315B *Lama*; 2 S316 *Alouette* III; 3 SA318 *Alouette* II; 6 SA342K *Gazelle*
  TPT 8: **Medium** 6 SA330 *Puma*; **Light** 2 SA360 *Dauphin*

Force Auxiliaire 30,000 (incl 5,000 Mobile Intervention Corps)

Customs/Coast Guard
EQUIPMENT BY TYPE
PATROL AND COASTAL COMBATANTS • PB 36: 4 *Erraid*; 18 *Arcor* 46; 14 (other SAR craft)

DEPLOYMENT

CENTRAL AFRICAN REPUBLIC
UN • MINUSCA 749; 2 obs; 1 inf bn

CÔTE D'IVOIRE
UN • UNOCI 725; 1 inf bn

DEMOCRATIC REPUBLIC OF THE CONGO
UN • MONUSCO 840; 2 obs; 1 mech inf bn; 1 fd hospital

Oman OMN

Omani Rial R		2013	2014	2015
GDP	R	29.7bn	31bn	
	US$	77.1bn	80.5bn	
per capita	US$	21,456	21,688	
Growth	%	4.8	3.4	
Inflation	%	1.2	2.8	
Def bdgt	R	3.56bn	3.7bn	
	US$	9.25bn	9.62bn	
FMA (US)	US$	8m	8m	4m
US$1=R		0.38	0.38	

Population 3,219,775

Expatriates: 27%

Age	0–14	15–19	20–24	25–29	30–64	65 plus
Male	15.6%	5.0%	5.4%	6.1%	20.9%	1.7%
Female	14.8%	4.7%	4.8%	4.7%	14.8%	1.6%

Capabilities

Oman's armed forces, although small in comparison to regional neighbours, are well staffed, with a strong history of cooperation and training with UK armed forces. They retain an effective inventory managed by well-trained personnel, and maintain a good state of readiness. The armed forces remain well funded, ensuring a steady flow of new equipment, primarily from the UK and the US. Although focused on territorial defence, there is some amphibious capability, a relatively high proportion of airlift and modest sealift. The Royal Guard brigade, which reports directly to the Sultan, carries out internal security and ceremonial functions. Oman's Special Forces are well respected. The navy's third Khareef frigate arrived in 2014 and a range of other new equipment is on order, including *Typhoon* fighters, AIM-120C-7 air-to-air missiles, C-295 transports and NASAMS air-defence missiles. However, there are also capability gaps, such as in ASW, and greater training and equipment (particularly ISR systems) are required to cope more effectively with security issues such as smuggling across the Strait of Hormuz. Oman is a GCC member.

ACTIVE 42,600 (Army 25,000 Navy 4,200 Air 5,000 Foreign Forces 2,000 Royal Household 6,400) Paramilitary 4,400

ORGANISATIONS BY SERVICE

Army 25,000
FORCES BY ROLE
(Regt are bn size)
MANOEUVRE
  Armoured
  1 armd bde (2 armd regt, 1 recce regt)
  Light
  1 inf bde (5 inf regt, 1 arty regt, 1 fd engr regt, 1 engr regt, 1 sigs regt)
  1 inf bde (3 inf regt, 2 arty regt)
  1 indep inf coy (Musandam Security Force)
  Air Manoeuvre
  1 AB regt
COMBAT SUPPORT
  1 ADA regt (2 ADA bty)
COMBAT SERVICE SUPPORT
  1 tpt regt
EQUIPMENT BY TYPE
MBT 117: 38 CR2 *Challenger* 2; 6 M60A1; 73 M60A3
LT TK 37 *Scorpion*
RECCE 137: 13 *Sultan*; 124 VBL
APC 206
  APC (T) 16: 6 FV 103 *Spartan*; 10 FV4333 *Stormer*
  APC (W) 190: 175 *Piranha* (incl variants); 15 AT-105 *Saxon*
ARTY 233
  SP 155mm 24 G-6
  TOWED 108: **105mm** 42 ROF lt; **122mm** 30 D-30; **130mm** 24: 12 M-46; 12 Type-59-I; **155mm** 12 FH-70
  MOR 101: **81mm** 69; **107mm** 20 M-30; **120mm** 12 Brandt
AT • MSL 88
  SP 8 VBL (TOW)
  MANPATS 80: 30 *Javelin*; 32 *Milan*; 18 TOW/TOW-2A
AD • SAM
  SP 8 *Mistral* 2
  MANPAD *Javelin*; 9K32 *Strela*-2 (SA-7 *Grail*)‡
  GUNS 26: **23mm** 4 ZU-23-2; **35mm** 10 GDF-005 (with *Skyguard*); **40mm** 12 L/60 (Towed)
ARV 11: 4 *Challenger*; 2 M88A1; 2 *Piranha*; 3 *Samson*

Navy 4,200
EQUIPMENT BY TYPE
SUBMARINES • SDV 2 Mk 8
PRIMARY SURFACE COMBATANTS 3
  FFGHM 3 *Al-Shamikh* with 2 twin lnchr with MM-40 *Exocet* Block III AShM, 2 sextuple lnchr with VL MICA SAM, 2 DS 30M CIWS, 1 76mm gun

PATROL AND COASTAL COMBATANTS 13
  CORVETTES • FSGM 2:
    2 *Qahir Al Amwaj* with 2 quad lnchr with MM-40 *Exocet* AShM, 1 octuple lnchr with *Crotale* SAM, 1 76mm gun, 1 hel landing platform
  PCFG 4 *Dhofar* with 2 quad lnchr with MM-40 *Exocet* AShM, 1 76mm gun
  PCC 3 *Al Bushra* (FRA P-400) with 1 76mm gun
  PB 4 *Seeb* (UK Vosper 25m, under 100 tonnes)
AMPHIBIOUS 6
  LANDING SHIPS • LST 1 *Nasr el Bahr* (with hel deck) (capacity 7 tanks; 240 troops)
  LANDING CRAFT 5: 1 LCU; 3 LCM; 1 LCT
LOGISTICS AND SUPPORT 6
  AGSC 1 *Al Makhirah*
  AK 1 *Al Sultana*
  AP 2 *Shinas* (commercial tpt - auxiliary military role only) (capacity 56 veh; 200 tps)
  AX 1 *Al Mabrukah* (with hel deck, also used in OPV role)
  AXS 1 *Shabab Oman*

Air Force 5,000
FORCES BY ROLE
FIGHTER/GROUND ATTACK
  1 sqn with F-16C/D Block 50 *Fighting Falcon*
  1 sqn (forming) with F-16C/D Block 50 *Fighting Falcon*
  1 sqn with *Hawk* Mk103; *Hawk* Mk203
MARITIME PATROL
  1 sqn with SC.7 3M *Skyvan*
TRANSPORT
  1 sqn with C-130H/J/J-30 *Hercules*
  1 sqn (forming) with C-295M
TRAINING
  1 sqn with MFI-17B *Mushshak*; PC-9*; Bell 206 (AB-206) *Jet Ranger*
TRANSPORT HELICOPTER
  4 (med) sqn; Bell 212 (AB-212); NH-90; *Super Lynx* Mk300 (maritime/SAR)
AIR DEFENCE
  2 sqn with *Rapier*; *Blindfire*; S713 *Martello*
EQUIPMENT BY TYPE
AIRCRAFT 44 combat capable
  FGA 15: 10 F-16C Block 50 *Fighting Falcon*; 5 F-16D Block 50 *Fighting Falcon*
  TPT 17: **Medium** 6: 3 C-130H *Hercules*; 2 C-130J *Hercules*; 1 C-130J-30 *Hercules* (VIP); **Light** 9: 2 C-295M; 7 SC.7 3M *Skyvan* (radar-equipped, for MP); **PAX** 2 A320-300
  TRG 36: 4 *Hawk* Mk103*; 12 *Hawk* Mk203*; 8 MFI-17B *Mushshak*; 12 PC-9*
HELICOPTERS
  MRH 15 *Super Lynx* Mk300 (maritime/SAR)
  TPT 37+ **Medium** 12+ NH90 TTH; **Light** 25: 19 Bell 205 (possibly wfu); 3 Bell 206 (AB-206) *Jet Ranger*; 3 Bell 212 (AB-212)
AD • SAM 40 *Rapier*
RADAR • LAND 6+: 6 *Blindfire*; S713 *Martello*
MSL
  AAM • IR AIM-9N/M/P *Sidewinder*; **ARH** AIM-120C AMRAAM
  ASM AGM-65 *Maverick*
  AShM AGM-84D *Harpoon*

Royal Household 6,400
(incl HQ staff)
FORCES BY ROLE
SPECIAL FORCES
  2 SF regt

Royal Guard bde 5,000
FORCES BY ROLE
MANOEUVRE
  Light
  1 gd bde (2 gd regt, 1 armd sqn, 1 cbt spt bn)
EQUIPMENT BY TYPE
LT TK (9 VBC-90 in store)
RECCE 9 *Centauro* MGS
APC (W) 73: ε50 Type-92; 14 VAB VCI; 9 VAB VDAA
ARTY • MRL 122mm 6 Type-90A
AT • MSL • MANPATS *Milan*
AD • SAM • MANPAD 14 *Javelin*
GUNS • SP 9: **20mm** 9 VAB VDAA

Royal Yacht Squadron 150
EQUIPMENT BY TYPE
LOGISTICS AND SUPPORT 3
  AP 1 *Fulk Al Salamah* (also veh tpt) with up to 2 AS332 *Super Puma* hel
  YAC 2: 1 *Al Said*; 1 *Zinat Al Bihaar* (Royal Dhow)

Royal Flight 250
EQUIPMENT BY TYPE
AIRCRAFT • TPT • PAX 5: 2 B-747SP; 1 DC-8-73CF; 2 Gulfstream IV
HELICOPTERS • TPT • Medium 6: 3 SA330 (AS330) *Puma*; 2 AS332F *Super Puma*; 1 AS332L *Super Puma*

Paramilitary 4,400 active

Tribal Home Guard 4,000
org in teams of ε100

Police Coast Guard 400
EQUIPMENT BY TYPE
PATROL AND COASTAL COMBATANTS 33 (+20 *Cougar Enforcer* 33 PBF under 10 tonnes)
  PCO 2 *Haras*
  PBF 3 *Haras* (US Mk V *Pegasus*)
  PB 27: 3 Rodman 101; 1 *Haras* (SWE CG27); 3 *Haras* (SWE CG29); 14 Rodman 58; 1 D59116; 5 *Zahra*

Police Air Wing
EQUIPMENT BY TYPE
AIRCRAFT • TPT • Light 4: 1 BN-2T *Turbine Islander*; 2 CN-235M; 1 Do-228
HELICOPTERS • TPT • Light 5: 2 Bell 205A; 3 Bell 214ST (AB-214ST)

FOREIGN FORCES
United Kingdom 70: 1 *Sentinel*

Palestinian Territories PT

New Israeli Shekel NS	2011	2012	2013
GDP	US$		
per capita	US$		
Growth	%		
Inflation	%		

US$1=NS

*definitive economic data unavailable

Population 4,547,431

Age	0–14	15–19	20–24	25–29	30–64	65 plus
Male	19.2%	5.6%	5.3%	4.3%	15.1%	1.4%
Female	18.2%	5.3%	5.0%	4.1%	14.4%	1.9%

Capabilities

The Palestinian Authority's National Security Force (NSF) is a paramilitary organisation intended to provide internal-security support within Gaza and the West Bank. The NSF only has real authority within the West Bank, where it has generally proved capable of maintaining internal security. Since 2007, the Gaza Strip has been run by Hamas. The Izz ad-Din al-Qassam Brigades, Hamas's military wing, is seen by the organisation as its best-trained and most disciplined force. It has a strong, well-developed rocket-artillery capability, including manufacturing, development and testing, but this is increasingly countered by Israel's *Iron Dome* missile-defence system. The brigades also engage in innovative asymmetric attacks, utilising for the first time in 2014 a naval commando unit. Israel's military actions in recent years, including *Operation Protective Edge* in 2014, periodically degrade the command-and-control, as well as physical infrastructure, of Hamas forces and tunnels, but seemingly have little effect on the long-term ability of the brigades to produce, import, store and launch rockets. (See p. 313.)

ACTIVE 0 Paramilitary n.k.

Precise personnel strength figures for the various Palestinian groups are not known.

ORGANISATIONS BY SERVICE

There is little data available on the status of the organisations mentioned below. Following internal fighting in June 2007, Gaza is under the de facto control of Hamas, while the West Bank is controlled by the Palestinian Authority; both participate in a unity government.

Paramilitary

Palestinian Authority n.k.

Presidential Security ε3,000

Special Forces ε1,200

Police ε9,000

Preventative Security n.k.

Civil Defence ε1,000

The al-Aqsa Brigades n.k.

Profess loyalty to the Fatah group that dominates the Palestinian Authority.

Hamas n.k.

Izz al-Din al-Qassam Brigades ε15,000-20,000
FORCES BY ROLE
COMMAND
  6 bde HQ (regional)
MANOEUVRE
  Light
  1 cdo unit (Nukhba)
  27 bn
  100 cbt coy
COMBAT SUPPORT
  Some engr units
COMBAT SERVICE SUPPORT
  Some log units
EQUIPMENT BY TYPE
ARTY
  MRL • *Qassam* rockets (multiple calibres); **122mm** *Grad*
  MOR some (multiple calibres)
  AT • MSL • MANPATS 9K11 *Malyutka* (AT-3 *Sagger*) (reported)

Qatar QTR

Qatari Riyal R		2013	2014	2015
GDP	R	737bn	772bn	
	US$	202bn	212bn	
per capita	US$	98,986	94,744	
Growth	%	6.5	6.5	
Inflation	%	3.1	3.4	
Def exp	R	ε15.8bn		
	US$	ε4.35bn		
US$1=R		3.64	3.64	

Population 2,123,160

Ethnic groups: Nationals 25%; Expatriates 75% of which Indian 18%; Iranian 10%; Pakistani 18%

Age	0–14	15–19	20–24	25–29	30–64	65 plus
Male	6.3%	2.6%	7.2%	12.2%	48.2%	0.5%
Female	6.2%	1.5%	2.0%	3.0%	9.8%	0.3%

Capabilities

Qatar maintains small armed forces with increasingly modern capabilities. Its personnel are well trained and motivated. The introduction of conscription in 2014 will, though the terms of service are limited, lead to an increase in training among the general population and perhaps the creation of a military reserve. Qatar relies on its international alliances, primarily with the US and through the GCC, to guarantee its security. A high proportion of government spending goes on defence, and so, despite the forces' small size, adequate defence capability has been maintained. Some equipment, particularly MBTs and fast missile craft, are ageing, but guided weapons, such as *Exocet* anti-ship missiles, make these platforms capable of fulfilling their primary role of border and maritime security. The armed forces suffer from a number of capability gaps, particularly in air defence, and the age of some equipment may hamper its ability to perform in high-tempo operations. Adequate funding exists for an ambitious procurement programme, as shown by a US$11bn agreement to purchase *Apache* helicopters, *Patriot* and *Stinger* air-defence missiles and *Javelin* anti-tank missiles. Qatar is also purchasing Airbus A330 tankers and Boeing 737-based AWACS as well as signalling an intent to purchase modern fighters to replace its *Mirage* 2000s.

ACTIVE 11,800 (Army 8,500 Navy 1,800 Air 1,500)
Conscript liability 4 months National Service for those aged 18–35; reduced to 3 months for graduates. Reserve commitment for 10 years or to age 40.

ORGANISATIONS BY SERVICE

Army 8,500
FORCES BY ROLE
SPECIAL FORCES
  1 SF coy
MANOEUVRE
  Armoured
  1 armd bde (1 tk bn, 1 mech inf bn, 1 AT bn, 1 mor sqn)
  Mechanised
  3 mech inf bn
  Light
  1 (Royal Guard) bde (3 inf regt)
COMBAT SUPPORT
  1 fd arty bn
EQUIPMENT BY TYPE
MBT 30 AMX-30
RECCE 92: 12 AMX-10RC; 20 EE-9 *Cascavel*; 36 *Piranha* II 90mm; 8 V-150 *Chaimite*; 16 VBL
AIFV 40 AMX-10P
APC 190
  APC (T) 30 AMX-VCI
  APC (W) 160 VAB
ARTY 91+
  SP 155mm 28 (AMX) Mk F3
  TOWED 155mm 12 G-5
  MRL 6+: **122mm** 2+ (30-tube); **127mm** 4 ASTROS II Mk3
  MOR 45
    SP • 81mm 4 VAB VPM 81
    81mm 26 L16
    120mm 15 Brandt
AT • MSL 148
  SP 24 VAB VCAC HOT
  MANPATS *Milan*
  RCL 84mm ε40 *Carl Gustav*
ARV 3: 1 AMX-30D; 2 *Piranha*

Navy 1,800 (incl Coast Guard)
EQUIPMENT BY TYPE
PATROL AND COASTAL COMBATANTS 11

  PCFG 7:
    4 *Barzan* (UK *Vita*) with 2 quad lnchr with MM-40 *Exocet* Block III AShM, 1 sextuple lnchr with *Mistral* SAM, 1 *Goalkeeper* CIWS 1 76mm gun
    3 *Damsah* (FRA *Combattante* III) with 2 quad lnchr with MM-40 *Exocet* AShM, 1 76mm gun
  PBF 3 MRTP 16
  PB 1 MRTP 34
AMPHIBIOUS • LANDING CRAFT • LCT 1 *Rabha* (capacity 3 MBT; 110 troops)
LOGISTICS AND SUPPORT • YTB 2 *Al Jaroof* (Damen Stan 1907)

Coast Guard
EQUIPMENT BY TYPE
PATROL AND COASTAL COMBATANTS 12
  PBF 4 DV 15
  PB 8: 4 *Crestitalia* MV-45; 3 *Halmatic* M160; 1 other

Coastal Defence
FORCES BY ROLE
MISSILE
  1 bty with 3 quad lnchr with MM-40 *Exocet* AShM
EQUIPMENT BY TYPE
MSL • AShM 12 MM-40 *Exocet* AShM

Air Force 1,500
FORCES BY ROLE
FIGHTER/GROUND ATTACK
  1 sqn with *Alpha Jet**
  1 sqn with *Mirage* 2000ED; *Mirage* 2000D
TRANSPORT
  1 sqn with C-17A; C-130J-30
  1 sqn with A-340; B-707; B-727; *Falcon* 900
ATTACK HELICOPTER
  1 ASuW sqn with *Commando* Mk3 with *Exocet*
  1 sqn with SA341 *Gazelle*; SA342L *Gazelle* with HOT
TRANSPORT HELICOPTER
  1 sqn with *Commando* Mk2A; *Commando* Mk2C
  1 sqn with AW139
EQUIPMENT BY TYPE
AIRCRAFT 18 combat capable
  FGA 12: 9 *Mirage* 2000ED; 3 *Mirage* 2000D
  TPT 12: **Heavy** 2 C-17A *Globemaster*; **Medium** 4 C-130J-30 *Hercules*; **PAX** 6: 1 A340; 2 B-707; 1 B-727; 2 *Falcon* 900
  TRG 6 *Alpha Jet**
HELICOPTERS
  ASuW 8 *Commando* Mk3
  MRH 34: 21 AW139 (incl 3 for medevac); 2 SA341 *Gazelle*; 11 SA342L *Gazelle*
  TPT • Medium 4: 3 *Commando* Mk2A; 1 *Commando* Mk2C
AD • SAM 75: 24 *Mistral*
  SP 9 *Roland* II
  MANPAD *Blowpipe*; FIM-92A *Stinger*; 9K32 *Strela*-2 (SA-7 *Grail*)‡
MSL
  ASM AM-39 *Exocet*; *Apache*; HOT
  AAM • IR R-550 *Magic* 2; **ARH** *Mica*

DEPLOYMENT

LEBANON
UN • UNIFIL 3

FOREIGN FORCES

United Kingdom *Operation Shader* 1 RC-135V *Rivet Joint*
United States US Central Command: 8,000; USAF CAOC; 1 bbr sqn with 6 B-1B *Lancer*; 1 ISR sqn with 4 RC-135 *Rivet Joint*; 1 ISR sqn with 4 E-8C JSTARS; 1 tkr sqn with 24 KC-135R/T *Straotanker*; 1 tpt sqn with 4 C-17A *Globemaster*; 4 C-130H/J-30 *Hercules* • US Strategic Command: 1 AN/TPY-2 X-band radar

Saudi Arabia SAU

Saudi Riyal R		2013	2014	2015
GDP	R	2.81tr	2.92tr	
	US$	748bn	778bn	
per capita	US$	24,953	25,401	
Growth	%	4.0	4.6	
Inflation	%	3.5	2.9	
Def exp	R	251bn	303bn	
	US$	67bn	80.8bn	
US$1=R		3.75	3.75	

Population 27,345,986

Ethnic groups: Nationals 73% of which Bedouin up to 10%, Expatriates 27% of which Asians 20%, Arabs 6%, Africans 1%, Europeans <1%

Age	0–14	15–19	20–24	25–29	30–64	65 plus
Male	14.2%	4.8%	5.5%	6.0%	22.3%	1.6%
Female	13.5%	4.4%	4.6%	4.7%	16.8%	1.5%

Capabilities

Saudi Arabia has the best-equipped armed forces in the Gulf region, and is a GCC member, but it relies on overseas partners to ultimately guarantee its security and to assist its military development. The armed forces maintain a good relationship with overseas forces, in particular those of the US, the UK and France, which affords combined training possibilities as well as access to equipment. The army continues to acquire modern equipment while the navy has a reported interest in purchasing new submarines. Air-force priorities are air defence and deterrence. The country has an extensive air-defence network, and a good range of airlift, which enables a modest power-projection capability. In November 2012, Saudi Arabia requested the sale of 20 C-130Js and 5 KC-130J tankers, and has recently ordered the A330 MRTT. Public display of conventionally armed Chinese DF-3 MRBMs affirmed their deterrent role. The National Guard is an autonomous force, having both a conventional-defence and internal-security role under its own ministry (not the defence ministry). It is mainly a mechanised force, but includes a large, tribal-based militia. Modernisation plans include orders for AT missiles, wheeled AFVs and CAESAR artillery. It is forming its own air wing with confirmed orders for AH6i, *Apache* and *Black Hawk* helicopters.

ACTIVE 227,000 (Army 75,000 Navy 13,500 Air 20,000 Air Defence 16,000 Strategic Missile Forces 2,500 National Guard 100,000) Paramilitary 24,500

ORGANISATIONS BY SERVICE

Army 75,000

FORCES BY ROLE
MANOEUVRE
  Armoured
  4 armd bde (1 recce coy, 3 tk bn, 1 mech bn, 1 fd arty bn, 1 AD bn, 1 AT bn, 1 engr coy, 1 log bn, 1 maint coy, 1 med coy)
  Mechanised
  5 mech bde (1 recce coy, 1 tk bn, 3 mech bn, 1 fd arty bn, 1 AD bn, 1 AT bn, 1 engr coy, 1 log bn, 1 maint coy, 1 med coy)
  Light
  1 (Royal Guard) regt (3 lt inf bn)
  Air Manoeuvre
  1 AB bde (2 AB bn, 3 SF coy)
  Aviation
  1 comd (1 atk hel bde, 1 tpt hel bde)
COMBAT SUPPORT
  1 arty bde (5 fd arty bn, 2 MRL bn, 1 msl bn)

EQUIPMENT BY TYPE
MBT 600: 200 M1A2/A2S *Abrams* (173 more in store); 400 M60A3; (145 AMX-30 in store)
RECCE 300 AML-60/AML-90
AIFV 780: 380 AMX-10P; 400 M2A2 *Bradley*
APC 1,423
  APC (T) 1,200 M113A1/A2/A3 (incl variants)
  APC (W) 150 M3 Panhard; (ε40 AF-40-8-1 *Al-Fahd* in store)
PPV 73 *Aravis*
ARTY 771
  SP 155mm 224: 60 AU-F-1; 110 M109A1B/A2; 54 PLZ-45
  TOWED 50: **105mm** (100 M101/M102 in store); **155mm** 50 M114; (60 M198 in store); **203mm** (8 M115 in store)
  MRL 127mm 60 ASTROS II Mk3
  MOR 437
    SP 220: **81mm** 70; **107mm** 150 M30
    TOWED 217: **81mm/107mm** 70 incl M30 **120mm** 147: 110 Brandt; 37 M12-1535
AT
  MSL
    SP 290+: 90+ AMX-10P (HOT); 200 VCC-1 ITOW
    MANPATS M47 *Dragon*; TOW-2A
  RCL 84mm *Carl Gustav*; **106mm** M40A1; **90mm** M67
  RL 112mm APILAS
AD • SAM
  SP *Crotale*
  MANPAD FIM-43 *Redeye*; FIM-92A *Stinger*
RADAR • LAND AN/TPQ-36 *Firefinder*/AN/TPQ-37 *Firefinder* (arty, mor)
AEV 15 M728
ARV 283+: 8 ACV ARV; AMX-10EHC; 55 AMX-30D; *Leclerc* ARV; 130 M88A1; 90 M578

VLB 10 AMX-30
MW *Aardvark* Mk2
HELICOPTERS
  ATK 15: 12 AH-64D *Apache*; 3 AH-64E *Apache*
  MRH 21: 6 AS365N *Dauphin* 2 (medevac); 15 Bell 406CS *Combat Scout*
  TPT • Medium 58: 12 S-70A-1 *Desert Hawk*; 22 UH-60A *Black Hawk* (4 medevac); 24 UH-60L *Black Hawk*

Navy 13,500

Navy HQ at Riyadh; Eastern Fleet HQ at Jubail; Western Fleet HQ at Jeddah

EQUIPMENT BY TYPE
PRINCIPAL SURFACE COMBATANTS 7
  DESTROYERS • DDGHM 3 *Al Riyadh* (FRA *La Fayette* mod) with 2 quad lnchr with MM-40 *Exocet* Block II AShM, 2 8-cell A43 VLS with *Aster* 15 SAM, 4 single 533mm TT with F17P HWT, 1 76mm gun (capacity 1 AS365N *Dauphin* 2 hel)
  FRIGATES • FFGHM 4 *Madina* (FRA F-2000) with 2 quad lnchr with *Otomat* Mk2 AShM, 1 octuple lnchr with *Crotale* SAM, 4 single 533mm TT with F17P HWT, 1 100mm gun (capacity 1 AS365N *Dauphin* 2 hel)
PATROL AND COASTAL COMBATANTS 69
  CORVETTES • FSG 4 *Badr* (US *Tacoma*) with 2 quad Mk140 lnchr with RGM-84C *Harpoon* AShM, 2 triple 324mm ASTT with Mk 46 LWT, 1 *Phalanx* CIWS, 1 76mm gun
  PCFG 9 *Al Siddiq* (US 58m) with 2 twin Mk140 lnchr with RGM-84C *Harpoon* AShM, 1 *Phalanx* CIWS, 1 76mm gun
  PB 56: 17 (US *Halter Marine*); 39 *Simmoneau* 51
MINE WARFARE • MINE COUNTERMEASURES 7
  MCC 4 *Addriyah* (US MSC-322)
  MHC 3 *Al Jawf* (UK *Sandown*)
AMPHIBIOUS • LANDING CRAFT 8
  LCU 4 *Al Qiaq* (US LCU 1610) (capacity 120 troops)
  LCM 4 LCM 6 (capacity 80 troops)
LOGISTICS AND SUPPORT 17
  AORH 2 *Boraida* (mod FRA *Durance*) (capacity either 2 AS365F *Dauphin* 2 hel or 1 AS332C *Super Puma*)
  YAC 2
  YTB 2
  YTM 11 *Radhwa*

Naval Aviation
EQUIPMENT BY TYPE
HELICOPTERS
  MRH 34: 6 AS365N *Dauphin* 2; 15 AS565 with AS-15TT AShM; 13 Bell 406CS *Combat Scout*
  TPT • Medium 12 AS332B/F *Super Puma* with AM-39 *Exocet* AShM

Marines 3,000
FORCES BY ROLE
MANOEUVRE
  Amphibious
  1 inf regt with (2 inf bn)
EQUIPMENT BY TYPE
APC (W) 140 BMR-600P

Air Force 20,000

FORCES BY ROLE
FIGHTER
  1 sqn with F-15S *Eagle*
  4 sqn with F-15C/D *Eagle*
FIGHTER/GROUND ATTACK
  2 sqn with F-15S *Eagle*
  3 sqn with *Tornado* IDS; *Tornado* GR1A
  2 sqn with *Typhoon*
AIRBORNE EARLY WARNING & CONTROL
  1 sqn with E-3A *Sentry*; 2 Saab 2000 *Erieye*
ELINT
  1 sqn with RE-3A/B; Beech 350ER *King Air*
TANKER
  1 sqn with KE-3A
TANKER/TRANSPORT
  1 sqn with KC-130H *Hercules* (tkr/tpt)
  1 sqn (forming) with A330 MRTT
TRANSPORT
  3 sqn with C-130H *Hercules*; C-130H-30 *Hercules*; CN-235; L-100-30HS (hospital ac)
  2 sqn with Beech 350 *King Air* (forming)
TRAINING
  3 sqn with *Hawk* Mk65*; *Hawk* Mk65A*
  1 sqn with *Jetstream* Mk31
  1 sqn with Cessna 172; MFI-17 *Mushshak*
  2 sqn with PC-9
TRANSPORT HELICOPTER
  4 sqn with AS532 *Cougar* (CSAR); Bell 212 (AB-212); Bell 412 (AB-412) *Twin Huey* (SAR)
EQUIPMENT BY TYPE
AIRCRAFT 313 combat capable
  FTR 81: 56 F-15C *Eagle*; 25 F-15D *Eagle*
  FGA 180: 71 F-15S *Eagle*; 69 *Tornado* IDS; 40 *Typhoon*
  ISR 14+: 12 *Tornado* GR1A*; 2+ Beech 350ER *King Air*
  AEW&C 7: 5 E-3A *Sentry*; 2 Saab 2000 *Erieye*
  ELINT 2: 1 RE-3A; 1 RE-3B
  TKR/TPT 11: 4 A330 MRTT (2 more on order); 7 KC-130H *Hercules*
  TKR 7 KE-3A
  TPT 56+ **Medium** 36: 30 C-130H *Hercules*; 3 C-130H-30 *Hercules*; 3 L-100-30; **Light** 20+: 2+ Beech 350 *King Air*; 13 Cessna 172; 4 CN-235; 1 *Jetstream* Mk31
  TRG 100: 24 *Hawk* Mk65* (incl aerobatic team); 16 *Hawk* Mk65A*; 20 MFI-17 *Mushshak*; 40 PC-9
HELICOPTERS
  MRH 15 Bell 412 (AB-412) *Twin Huey* (SAR)
  TPT 30: **Medium** 10 AS532 *Cougar* (CSAR); **Light** 20 Bell 212 (AB-212)
MSL
  ASM AGM-65 *Maverick*
  AShM *Sea Eagle*
  LACM *Storm Shadow*
  ARM ALARM
  AAM • IR AIM-9P/L/X *Sidewinder*; **SARH** AIM-7 *Sparrow*; AIM-7M *Sparrow*; **ARH** AIM-120 AMRAAM

Royal Flt
EQUIPMENT BY TYPE
AIRCRAFT • TPT 24; **Medium** 8: 5 C-130H *Hercules*; 3 L-100-30; **Light** 3: 1 Cessna 310; 2 Learjet 35; **PAX** 13: 1

A340; 1 B-737-200; 2 B-737BBJ; 2 B-747SP; 4 BAe-125-800; 2 Gulfstream III; 1 Gulfstream IV
HELICOPTERS • TPT 3+; **Medium** 3: 2 AS-61; 1 S-70 *Black Hawk*; **Light** Some Bell 212 (AB-212)

Air Defence Forces 16,000

FORCES BY ROLE
AIR DEFENCE
16 bty with *Patriot* PAC-2; 17 bty with *Shahine*/AMX-30SA; 16 bty with MIM-23B I-HAWK; 73 units (static defence) with *Crotale*/*Shahine*

EQUIPMENT BY TYPE
AD • SAM 1,805
  SP 581: 40 *Crotale*; 400 M998/M1097 *Avenger*; 73 *Shahine*; 68 *Crotale*/*Shahine*
  TOWED 224: 128 MIM-23B I-HAWK; 96 *Patriot* PAC-2
  MANPAD FIM-43 *Redeye*
  NAVAL 500 *Mistral*
GUNS 1,070
  SP 942: **20mm** 92 M163 *Vulcan*; **30mm** 850 AMX-30SA
  TOWED 128: **35mm** 128 GDF Oerlikon; **40mm** (150 L/70 in store)
RADARS • AD RADAR 80: 17 AN/FPS-117; 28 AN/TPS-43; AN/TPS-59; 35 AN/TPS-63; AN/TPS-70

Strategic Missile Forces 2,500

EQUIPMENT BY TYPE
MSL • TACTICAL
  IRBM 10+ DF-3 (CSS-2) (40 msl)
  MRBM Some DF-21 (CSS-5 – variant unclear) (reported)

National Guard 75,000 active; 25,000 (tribal levies) (total 100,000)

FORCES BY ROLE
MANOEUVRE
  Mechanised
  4–5 mech bde (1 recce coy, 3 mech inf bn, 1 SP arty bn, 1 cbt engr coy, 1 sigs coy, 1 log bn)
  Light
  5 inf bde (3 combined arms bn, 1 arty bn, 1 log bn)
  Other
  2–3 (Special Security) sy bde (3 sy bn)
  1 (ceremonial) cav sqn
COMBAT SUPPORT
  1 MP bn

EQUIPMENT BY TYPE
RECCE 214 LAV-AG (90mm)
AIFV 648 LAV-25
APC • APC (W) 808: 119 LAV-A; 30 LAV-AC; 296 LAV-CC; 73 LAV-PC; 290 V-150 *Commando* (810 in store)
ARTY 359+
  SP 155mm 132 CAESAR
  TOWED 108: **105mm** 50 M102; **155mm** 58 M198
  MOR 119+ **81mm** some; **120mm** 119 LAV-M
AT
  MSL
    SP 183 LAV-AT
    MANPATS TOW-2A; M47 *Dragon*
  RCL • 106mm M40A1

AD • GUNS • TOWED 160: **20mm** 30 M167 *Vulcan*; **90mm** 130 M2
AEV 58 LAV-E
ARV 111 LAV-R; V-150 ARV

Paramilitary 24,500+ active

Border Guard 10,500

FORCES BY ROLE
Subordinate to Ministry of Interior. HQ in Riyadh. 9 subordinate regional commands
MANOEUVRE
  Other
  Some mobile def (long range patrol/spt) units
  2 border def (patrol) units
  12 infrastructure def units
  18 harbour def units
  Some coastal def units
COMBAT SUPPORT
  Some MP units

Coast Guard 4,500

EQUIPMENT BY TYPE
PATROL AND COASTAL COMBATANTS 14 (100+ small patrol boats are also in service)
  PBF 6: 4 *Al Jouf*; 2 *Sea Guard*
  PB 8: 6 *StanPatrol 2606*; 2 *Al Jubatel*
AMPHIBIOUS • LANDING CRAFT 8: 3 UCAC; 5 LCAC *Griffin 8000*
LOGISTICS AND SUPPORT 4: 1 AXL; 3 AO

Facilities Security Force 9,000+
Subordinate to Ministry of Interior

General Civil Defence Administration Units
EQUIPMENT BY TYPE
HELICOPTERS • TPT • Medium 10 Boeing Vertol 107

Special Security Force 500
EQUIPMENT BY TYPE
APC (W): UR-416

DEPLOYMENT

BAHRAIN
GCC • *Peninsula Shield* ε1,000 (National Guard)

FOREIGN FORCES

United States US Central Command: 350

Syria SYR

Syrian Pound S£		2013	2014	2015
GDP	S£			
	US$			
per capita	US$			
Growth	%			
Inflation	%			
Def exp	S£			
	US$			

US$1=S£

*definitive economic data unavailable

Population 22,597,531

Age	0–14	15–19	20–24	25–29	30–64	65 plus
Male	17.0%	5.4%	5.1%	4.8%	16.6%	1.8%
Female	16.2%	5.2%	4.9%	4.6%	16.3%	2.1%

Capabilities

The Syrian armed forces are currently engaged in a civil war that has demonstrated various weaknesses in command-and-control, armaments and the ability to engage in counter-insurgency operations. By late 2014, the most powerful non-state armed group in Syria had become ISIS, which undertook a rapid expansion in its territory in Iraq in mid-2014 and was therefore able to ferry arms and funding back into Syria. A variety of other groups and cells continued to exist. The regime continues to rely heavily on stand-off firepower, particularly from artillery and tanks, although Hizbullah fighters and other irregulars were able in 2013 and early 2014 to engage in close-quarters combat to a greater extent. Both the army and air force have faced significant losses of equipment and materiel, though there have been reports of improvments in rotary-wing capability. Indeed, the Assad regime's position seemed stronger in 2014 than at any point since 2012, as it had the political and military space to engage in offensive operations, recover ground and frustrate the rebellion's efforts. To make up for personnel shortages, amid falling numbers of conscripts arriving for the draft, the regime has increasingly relied on militias as auxiliary forces though this meant, at times, a weaker chain-of-command, operational breakdowns and tensions between the conventional army, local paramilitaries and foreign militias. Steady Iranian and Russian supplies of weaponry contrasted with intermittent deliveries to rebel forces; Russia maintains a naval facility in Tartus. (See pp. 303–04.)

ACTIVE 178,000 (Army 110,000 Navy 5,000 Air 17,500 Air Defence 30,000) **Paramilitary n.k.**

Conscript liability 30 months

RESERVE n.k.

ORGANISATIONS BY SERVICE

Army ε110,000 (plus ε100,000 auxiliaries)

FORCES BY ROLE
With the exception of the Republican Guard and 4th Armoured Division, remaining formations have abandoned pre-war doctrinal structures in all but name.
COMMAND
  3 corps HQ
SPECIAL FORCES
  2 SF div (total: 11 SF regt; 1 tk regt)
MANOEUVRE
  Armoured
  1 (4th) armd div (1 SF regt, 2 armd bde, 2 mech bde, 1 arty regt, 1 SSM bde (3 SSM bn with *Scud*-B/C))
  5 armd div (3 armd bde, 1 mech bde, 1 arty regt)
  2 armd bde
  Mechanised
  1 (Republican Guard) mech div (3 mech bde, 2 sy regt, 1 arty regt)
  3 mech div (1 armd bde, 3 mech bde, 1 arty regt)
  Light
  3+ indep inf bde
COMBAT SUPPORT
  3 arty regt
  1 SSM bde (3 SSM bn with FROG-7)
  1 SSM bde (3 SSM bn with SS-21)

EQUIPMENT BY TYPE
Ongoing attrition during the civil war has severely reduced equipment numbers for almost all types. It is unclear how much remains available for operations.
MBT T-55A; T-55AM; T-55AMV; T-62; T-72; T-72AV; T-72M1
RECCE BRDM-2
AIFV BMP-1; BMP-2
APC
  APC (T) BTR-50
  APC (W) BTR-152; BTR-60; BTR-70
ARTY
  SP 122mm 2S1; D-30 (mounted on T34/85 chassis); **130mm** M-46 (truck mounted); **152mm** 2S3
  TOWED 122mm D-30; M-30 (M1938); **130mm** M-46; **152mm** D-20/ML-20 M1937; **180mm** S23
  MRL 107mm Type-63; **122mm** BM-21 (*Grad*); **140mm** BM-14; **220mm** BM-27 *Uragan*; **300mm** BM-30 *Smerch* (reported); **330mm** some (reported)
  MOR 82mm some; **120mm** M-1943; **160mm** M-160; **240mm** M-240
AT • MSL
  SP 9P133 (BRDM-2 with AT-3 *Sagger*)
  MANPATS 9K111 Fagot (AT-4 *Spigot*); 9K113 Konkurs (AT-5 *Spandrel*); 9K115 Metis (AT-7 *Saxhorn*); 9K116-1 Bastion (AT-10 *Stabber*); 9K135 Kornet (AT-14 *Spriggan*); Milan
  RL 105mm RPG-29
AD
  SAM
    SP 9K33 *Osa* (SA-8 *Gecko*); 9K31 *Strela*-1 (SA-9 *Gaskin*); 9K37 *Buk* (SA-11 *Gadfly*); 9K35 *Strela*-10 (SA-13 *Gopher*); 96K6 *Pantsir*-S1 (SA-22 *Greyhound*); 9K317 *Buk*-M2 (SA-17 *Grizzly*)
    MANPAD 9K32 *Strela*-2 (SA-7 *Grail*)‡; 9K38 *Igla* (SA-18 *Grouse*); 9K36 *Strela*-3 (SA-14 *Gremlin*); 9K338 *Igla*-S (SA-24 *Grinch*)

GUNS
SP 23mm ZSU-23-4; 57mm ZSU-57
TOWED 23mm ZU-23; 37mm M-1939; 57mm S-60; 100mm KS-19
MSL • TACTICAL • SSM Scud-B/C/D; Scud look-a-like; FROG-7; Tochka (SS-21 Scarab)
ARV BREM-1 reported; T-54/55
MW UR-77
VLB MTU; MTU-20
UAV • ISR • Medium Mohajer 3/4; Light Ababil

Navy ε5,000

Some personnel are likely to have been drafted into other services.

EQUIPMENT BY TYPE
PATROL AND COASTAL COMBATANTS 32:
  CORVETTES • FS 2 Petya III (1†) with 1 triple 533mm ASTT with SAET-60 HWT, 4 RBU 2500 Smerch 1†, 2 twin 76mm gun
  PBFG 22:
    16 Osa I/II with 4 single lnchr with P-15M Termit-M (SS-N-2C Styx) AShM
    6 Tir with 2 single lnchr with C-802 (CSS-N-8 Saccade) AShM
  PB 8 Zhuk†
MINE WARFARE • MINE COUNTERMEASURES 7
  MHC 1 Sonya with 2 quad lnchr with 9K32 Strela-2 (SA-N-5 Grail)‡ SAM, 2 AK630 CIWS
  MSO 1 Natya with 2 quad lnchr with 9K32 Strela-2 (SA-N-5 Grail)‡ SAM
  MSI 5 Yevgenya
AMPHIBIOUS • LANDING SHIPS • LSM 3 Polnochny B (capacity 6 MBT; 180 troops)
LOGISTICS AND SUPPORT 2
  AX 1 Al Assad
  YDT 1 Palmyra

Coastal Defence

FORCES BY ROLE
COASTAL DEFENCE
  1 AShM bde with P-35 (SS-C-1B Sepal); P-15M Termit-R (SS-C-3 Styx); C-802; K-300P Bastion (SS-C-5 Stooge)

EQUIPMENT BY TYPE
MSL • AShM P-35 (SS-C-1B Sepal); P-15M Termit-R (SS-C-3 Styx); C-802; K-300P Bastion (SS-C-5 Stooge)

Naval Aviation

EQUIPMENT BY TYPE
HELICOPTER
  ASW 10: 4 Ka-28 Helix A (air force manned); 6 Mi-14 Haze

Air Force ε17,500

FORCES BY ROLE
FIGHTER
  2 sqn with MiG-23 MF/ML/UM Flogger
  2 sqn with MiG-29A/U Fulcrum
FIGHTER/GROUND ATTACK
  4 sqn with MiG-21MF/bis Fishbed; MiG-21U Mongol A
  2 sqn with MiG-23BN/UB Flogger
  4 sqn with Su-22 Fitter D
  1 sqn with Su-24 Fencer
TRANSPORT
  1 sqn with An-24 Coke; An-26 Curl; Il-76 Candid
  1 sqn with Falcon 20; Falcon 900
  1 sqn with Tu-134B-3
  1 sqn with Yak-40 Codling
TRAINING
  1 sqn with L-39 Albatros*
ATTACK HELICOPTER
  3 sqn with Mi-25 Hind D
  2 sqn with SA342L Gazelle
TRANSPORT HELICOPTER
  6 sqn with Mi-8 Hip/Mi-17 Hip H

EQUIPMENT BY TYPE
The level of readiness of a significant element of the air force's combat aircraft inventory is likely poor. Equipment numbers have significantly reduced during the civil war.
AIRCRAFT 277 combat capable
  FTR 75: 39 MiG-23MF/ML/UM Flogger; 6 MiG-25 Foxbat; 30 MiG-29A/SM/UB Fulcrum
  FGA 185: 70 MiG-21MF/bis Fishbed; 9 MiG-21U Mongol A; 41 MiG-23BN/UB Flogger; 36 Su-22 Fitter D; 19 Su-24 Fencer
  TPT 23: Heavy 3 Il-76 Candid; Light 13: 1 An-24 Coke; 6 An-26 Curl; 2 PA-31 Navajo; 4 Yak-40 Codling; PAX 7: 2 Falcon 20; 1 Falcon 900; 4 Tu-134B-3
  TRG 58: 17 L-39 Albatros*; 35 MBB-223 Flamingo (basic); 6 MFI-17 Mushshak
HELICOPTERS
  ATK 24 Mi-25 Hind D
  MRH 57: 27 Mi-17 Hip H; 30 SA342L Gazelle
  TPT • Medium 27 Mi-8 Hip
MSL
  AAM • IR R-3 (AA-2 Atoll)‡; R-60 (AA-8 Aphid); R-73 (AA-11 Archer); IR/SARH; R-23/24 (AA-7 Apex); R-27 (AA-10 Alamo)
  ASM Kh-25 (AS-7 Kerry); HOT
  ARM Kh-31P (AS-17A Krypton)

Air Defence Command ε30,000

FORCES BY ROLE
AIR DEFENCE
4 AD div (total: 25 AD bde with S-125 Pechora (SA-3 Goa); 2K12 Kub (SA-6 Gainful); S-75 Dvina (SA-2 Guideline))
3 AD regt with S-200 Angara (SA-5 Gammon)

EQUIPMENT BY TYPE
AD • SAM
  SP 2K12 Kub (SA-6 Gainful)
  TOWED S-75 Dvina (SA-2 Guideline); S-125 Pechora (SA-3 Goa)
  STATIC/SHELTER S-200 Angara (SA-5 Gammon)
  MANPAD 9K32 Strela-2/2M (SA-7A/B Grail)‡

Paramilitary n.k.

National Defence Force

Comprising pro-government militia groups. Have received training from Hizbullah and the Iranian Revolutionary Guard Corps.

Coast Guard

EQUIPMENT BY TYPE
PATROL AND COASTAL COMBATANTS 6
  PBF 2 *Mawani*
  PB 4

FOREIGN FORCES

UNTSO unless specified. UNTSO figures represent total numbers for mission in Israel, Syria and Lebanon.
Argentina 3 obs
Australia 12 obs
Austria 5 obs
Belgium 2 obs
Canada 8 obs
Chile 3 obs
China, People's Republic of 5 obs
Denmark 11 obs
Estonia 3 obs
Fiji UNDOF 445; 1 inf bn
Finland 18 obs
France 1 obs
India UNDOF 191; 1 log bn(-)
Ireland 12 obs • UNDOF 135; 1 inf coy
Italy 6 obs
Nepal 4 obs • UNDOF 153; 1 HQ coy
Netherlands 12 obs • UNDOF 2
New Zealand 7 obs
Norway 12 obs
Russia 4 obs • naval facility reportedly under renovation at Tartus
Serbia 1 obs
Slovakia 2 obs
Slovenia 3 obs
Sweden 7 obs
Switzerland 14 obs
United States 1 obs

Tunisia TUN

Tunisian Dinar D		2013	2014	2015
GDP	D	76.4bn	83bn	
	US$	47bn	49.1bn	
per capita	US$	4,317	4,467	
Growth	%	2.3	2.8	
Inflation	%	6.1	5.7	
Def bgt	D	1.23bn	1.54bn	
	US$	759m	911m	
FMA (US)	US$	17.5m	20m	25m
US$1=D		1.62	1.69	
Population	10,937,521			

Age	0–14	15–19	20–24	25–29	30–64	65 plus
Male	11.9%	3.9%	4.2%	4.2%	21.8%	3.9%
Female	11.1%	3.7%	4.2%	4.4%	22.7%	4.0%

Capabilities

Tunisia's armed forces rely on conscripts for personnel strength, and much equipment is ageing and, in some cases, approaching obsolescence. The armed forces have a limited internal-security role, with the National Guard taking the lead on domestic stability. During the Libyan uprising in 2011, the army and air force patrolled the borders relatively successfully and the navy competently dealt with migrant flows and search-and-rescue operations. The armed forces are well suited to these constabulary roles, but more traditional military roles, such as high-tempo war fighting, would likely prove a challenge. During 2014, the armed forces struggled with the Islamist spillover from neighbouring states through the porous borders with Algeria and Libya and there have been operations against insurgents in remote areas, with losses sustained on both sides. US–Tunisia relations have strengthened and in 2014 the armed forces received equipment for counter-terrorism units as well as patrol boats and night-vision equipment. Coordination with Algeria has also increased on common security threats.

ACTIVE 35,800 (Army 27,000 Navy 4,800 Air 4,000)
Paramilitary 12,000
Conscript liability 12 months selective

ORGANISATIONS BY SERVICE

Army 5,000; 22,000 conscript (total 27,000)
FORCES BY ROLE
SPECIAL FORCES
  1 SF bde
  1 (Sahara) SF bde
MANOEUVRE
  Reconnaissance
  1 recce regt
  Mechanised
  3 mech bde (1 armd regt, 2 mech inf regt, 1 arty regt, 1 AD regt, 1 engr regt, 1 sigs regt, 1 log gp)
COMBAT SUPPORT
  1 engr regt
EQUIPMENT BY TYPE
MBT 84: 30 M60A1; 54 M60A3
LT TK 48 SK-105 *Kuerassier*
RECCE 60: 40 AML-90; 20 *Saladin*
APC 270
  APC (T) 140 M113A1/A2
  APC (W) 110 Fiat 6614
  PPV ε20 *Kirpi*
ARTY 276
  TOWED 115: **105mm** 48 M101A1/A2; **155mm** 67: 12 M114A1; 55 M198
  MOR 161: **81mm** 95; **107mm** 48 (some SP); **120mm** 18 Brandt
AT • **MSL** 590
    SP 35 M901 ITV TOW
    MANPATS *Milan*; TOW
  RL 89mm 600: 300 LRAC; 300 M20

AD • SAM
  SP 26 M48 *Chaparral*
  MANPAD RBS-70
GUNS 127
  SP 40mm 12 M-42
  TOWED 115: 20mm 100 M-55; 37mm 15 Type-55 (M-1939)/Type-65
RADAR • LAND RASIT (veh, arty)
AEV 2 *Greif*
ARV 3 *Greif*; 6 M88A1

Navy ε4,800
EQUIPMENT BY TYPE
PATROL AND COASTAL COMBATANTS 26
  PCFG 3 *La Galite* (FRA *Combattante* III) with 2 quad Mk140 lnchr with MM-40 *Exocet* AShM, 1 76mm gun
  PCG 3 *Bizerte* (FRA P-48) with 8 SS 12M AShM
  PCF 6 *Albatros* (GER Type-143B) with 2 single 533mm TT, 2 76mm guns
  PB 14: 3 *Utique* (mod PRC *Haizhui* II); 5 *Joumhouria*; 6 V Series
LOGISTICS AND SUPPORT 10:
  ABU 3: 2 *Tabarka* (ex-US *White Sumac*); 1 *Sisi Bou Said*
  AGE 1 *Hannibal*
  AGS 1 *Khaireddine* (ex-US *Wilkes*)
  AWT 1 *Ain Zaghouan* (ex-ITA *Simeto*)
  AX 1 *Salambo* (ex-US *Conrad*, survey)
  YDT 2
  YTB 1 *Sidi Daoud* (ex-ITA *Porto d'Ischia*)

Air Force 4,000
FORCES BY ROLE
FIGHTER/GROUND ATTACK
  1 sqn with F-5E/F-5F *Tiger* II
TRANSPORT
  1 sqn with C-130B/H/J *Hercules*; G-222; L-410 *Turbolet*
  1 liaison unit with S-208A
TRAINING
  2 sqn with L-59 *Albatros**; MB-326B; SF-260
  1 sqn with MB-326K; MB-326L
TRANSPORT HELICOPTER
  2 sqn with AS350B *Ecureuil*; AS365 *Dauphin* 2; AB-205 (Bell 205); SA313; SA316 *Alouette* III; UH-1H *Iroquois*; UH-1N *Iroquois*
  1 sqn with HH-3E
EQUIPMENT BY TYPE
AIRCRAFT 24 combat capable
  FTR 12: 10 F-5E *Tiger* II; 2 F-5F *Tiger* II
  ATK 3 MB-326K
  TPT 18: Medium 13: 6 C-130B *Hercules*; 1 C-130H *Hercules*; 1 C-130J *Hercules*; 5 G-222; Light 5: 3 L-410 *Turbolet*; 2 S-208A
  TRG 30: 9 L-59 *Albatros**; 4 MB-326B; 3 MB-326L; 14 SF-260
HELICOPTERS
  MRH 10: 1 AS365 *Dauphin* 2; 6 SA313; 3 SA316 *Alouette* III
  SAR 11 HH-3 *Sea King*
  TPT • Light 33: 6 AS350B *Ecureuil*; 15 Bell 205 (AB-205); 10 Bell 205 (UH-1H *Iroquois*); 2 Bell 212 (UH-1N *Iroquois*)
MSL • AAM • IR AIM-9P *Sidewinder*

Paramilitary 12,000
National Guard 12,000
Ministry of Interior
EQUIPMENT BY TYPE
RECCE 2 EE-11 *Urutu* FSV
APC • APC (W) 16 EE-11 *Urutu* (Anti-Riot)
PATROL AND COASTAL COMBATANTS 24
  PCC 6 *Rais el Blais* (ex-GDR *Kondor* I)
  PBF 7: 4 *Gabes*; 3 *Patrouiller*
  PB 11: 5 *Breitla* (ex-GDR *Bremse*); 4 Rodman 38; 2 *Socomena*
HELICOPTERS • MRH 8 SA318 *Alouette* II/SA319 *Alouette* III

DEPLOYMENT

CÔTE D'IVOIRE
UN • UNOCI 3; 7 obs

DEMOCRATIC REPUBLIC OF THE CONGO
UN • MONUSCO 29 obs

United Arab Emirates UAE

Emirati Dirham D		2013	2014	2015
GDP	D	1.48tr	1.53tr	
	US$	402bn	416bn	
per capita	US$	44,552	44,771	
Growth	%	5.2	4.3	
Inflation	%	1.1	2.2	
Def bdgt	D	ε50.9bn		
	US$	ε13.9bn		
US$1=D		3.67	3.67	

Population 5,628,805

Ethnic groups: Nationals 24%; Expatriates 76% of which Indian 30%, Pakistani 20%; other Arab 12%; other Asian 10%; UK 2%; other European 1%

Age	0–14	15–19	20–24	25–29	30–64	65 plus
Male	10.6%	2.8%	5.3%	10.7%	38.6%	0.6%
Female	10.1%	2.3%	3.2%	4.0%	11.3%	0.4%

Capabilities

A GCC member, the UAE's seven separate emirates each retain influence within the overall armed-forces command structure through regional commands. Under the aegis of the federal Union Defence Force, this situation leads to greater autonomy and influence on procurement and organisation. Although comparatively small in number, the UAE's armed forces comprise a relatively large percentage of the population and maintain an extensive array of high-quality equipment. The introduction of conscription in 2014 should lead to an increase in training among the general population and perhaps the creation of a military reserve. The navy is undertaking a modernisation programme, including the recent delivery of six new corvettes.

The Presidential Guard is a fourth armed service and, as well as mechanised and marine forces, includes royal protection units, SOF and a dedicated aviation wing with helicopters and light-attack aircraft. The UAE has expanded its air-defence capabilities with purchases in recent years of *Patriot* missile systems and an order has been placed for THAAD batteries and missiles. The air force plans to upgrade its F-16 Block 60s. It is continuing to develop an indigenous defence industry, including armoured-vehicle, precision-munition and UAV capabilities. (See pp. 314–18.)

ACTIVE 63,000 (Army 44,000 Navy 2,500 Air 4,500 Presidential Guard 12,000)

Conscript liability 2 years National Service for men aged 18–30; reduced to 9 months for those completing secondary school. Voluntary 9 months service for women.

ORGANISATIONS BY SERVICE

Space
EQUIPMENT BY TYPE
SATELLITES • COMMUNICATIONS 2 *Yahsat*

Army 44,000
FORCES BY ROLE
MANOEUVRE
  Armoured
  2 armd bde
  Mechanised
  2 mech bde
  Light
  1 inf bde
COMBAT SUPPORT
  1 arty bde (3 SP arty regt)
  1 engr gp
EQUIPMENT BY TYPE
MBT 421: 340 *Leclerc*; 36 OF-40 Mk2 (*Lion*); 45 AMX-30
LT TK 76 *Scorpion*
RECCE 105: 49 AML-90; 24 VBL; 32 TPz-1 *Fuchs* NBC; (20 *Ferret* in store); (20 *Saladin* in store)
AIFV 405: 15 AMX-10P; 390 BMP-3
APC 1,552
  APC (T) 136 AAPC (incl 53 engr plus other variants)
  APC (W) 590: 120 EE-11 *Urutu*; 370 M3 Panhard; 80 VCR (incl variants); 20 VAB
  PPV 826: 750 M-ATV; 76 RG-31 *Nyala*
ARTY 579+
  SP 155mm 181: 78 G-6; 85 M109A3; 18 Mk F3
  TOWED 93: **105mm** 73 ROF lt; **130mm** 20 Type-59-I
  MRL 107+: **70mm** 18 LAU-97; **122mm** 63+: 48 Firos-25 (est 24 op); Type-90 (reported); **227mm** 20 HIMARS; **300mm** 6 9A52 *Smerch*
  MOR 213: **81mm** 134: 20 Brandt; 114 L16; **120mm** 79: 58 *Agrab* Mk2; 21 Brandt
AT
  MSL
    SP 20 HOT
    MANPATS Milan; TOW; (*Vigilant* in store)
  RCL 262: **84mm** 250 Carl Gustav; **106mm** 12 M40
AD
  SAM • MANPAD Blowpipe; Mistral

GUNS 62
  SP 20mm 42 M3 VDAA
  TOWED 30mm 20 GCF-BM2
MSL • TACTICAL • SSM 6 *Scud*-B (up to 20 msl)
AEV 53 ACV-AESV
ARV 143: 8 ACV-AESV Recovery; 4 AMX-30D; 85 BREM-L; 46 *Leclerc* ARV
UAV • ISR • Medium *Seeker* II

Navy 2,500
EQUIPMENT BY TYPE
SUBMARINES • SDV ε10
PATROL AND COASTAL COMBATANTS 29
  CORVETTES 8
    FSGHM 4:
      3 *Baynunah* with 2 quad lnchr with MM-40 *Exocet* Block III AShM, 1 8-cell Mk56 VLS with RIM-162 ESSM SAM, 1 21-cell Mk49 GMLS with RIM-116B SAM, 1 76mm gun (three additional vessels awaiting comissioning)
      1 *Abu Dhabi* with 2 twin lnchr with MM-40 *Exocet* Block III AShM, 1 76mm gun
    FSGM 4:
      2 *Muray Jib* (GER Lurssen 62m) with 2 quad lnchr with MM-40 *Exocet* Block II AShM, 1 octuple lnchr with *Crotale* SAM, 1 *Goalkeeper* CIWS, 1 76mm gun, 1 hel landing platform
      2 *Ganthoot* with 2 twin lnchr with MM-40 *Exocet* Block III AShM, 2 triple lnchr with VL *Mica* SAM, 1 76mm gun, 1 hel landing platform
  PCFGM 2 *Mubarraz* (GER Lurssen 45m) with 2 twin lnchr with MM-40 *Exocet* AShM, 1 sextuple lnchr with *Mistral* SAM, 1 76mm gun
  PCFG 6 *Ban Yas* (GER Lurssen TNC-45) with 2 twin lnchr with MM-40 *Exocet* Block III AShM, 1 76mm gun
  PBFG 7 *Al Bazam* (*Ghannatha* mod) with 4 single lncher with *Marte* Mk2/N AShM
  PB 6 *Ardhana* (UK Vosper 33m)
MINE WARFARE • MINE COUNTERMEASURES 2
  MHO 2 *Al Murjan* (ex-GER *Frankenthal*-class Type-332)
AMPHIBIOUS 29
  LANDING SHIPS • LS 1 *Sir Bunuer*
  LANDING CRAFT 28
    LCP 16: 12 *Ghannatha* (capacity 40 troops; currently undergoing modernisation to include weapons mounts); 4 Fast Supply Vessel (multi-purpose)
    LCU 5: 3 *Al Feyi* (capacity 56 troops); 2 (capacity 40 troops and additional vehicles)
    LCT 7
LOGISTICS AND SUPPORT 5: 1 **AKL**; 1 **YDT**; 1 **YTB**; 2 **YTM**

Air Force 4,500
Flying hours 110 hrs/year
FORCES BY ROLE
FIGHTER/GROUND ATTACK
  3 sqn with F-16E/F Block 60 *Fighting Falcon*
  3 sqn with *Mirage* 2000-9DAD/EAD/RAD
AIRBORNE EARLY WARNING AND CONTROL
  1 flt with Saab 340 *Erieye*

SEARCH & RESCUE
  2 flt with AW109K2; AW139
TANKER
  1 flt with A330 MRTT
TRANSPORT
  1 sqn with C-17A *Globemaster*
  1 sqn with C-130H/H-30 *Hercules*; L-100-30
  1 sqn with CN-235M-100
TRAINING
  1 sqn with Grob 115TA
  1 sqn with *Hawk* Mk102*
  1 sqn with PC-7 *Turbo Trainer*
  1 sqn with PC-21
TRANSPORT HELICOPTER
  1 sqn with Bell 412 *Twin Huey*
EQUIPMENT BY TYPE
AIRCRAFT 157 combat capable
  FGA 138: 54 F-16E Block 60 *Fighting Falcon* (*Desert Eagle*); 24 F-16F Block 60 *Fighting Falcon* (13 to remain in US for trg); 16 *Mirage* 2000-9DAD; 44 *Mirage* 2000-9EAD
  ISR 7 *Mirage* 2000 RAD*
  AEW&C 2 Saab 340 *Erieye*
  TPT/TKR 3 A330 MRTT
  TPT 16; **Heavy** 6 C-17 *Globemaster*; **Medium** 6: 3 C-130H *Hercules*; 1 C-130H-30 *Hercules*; 2 L-100-30; **Light** 4 DHC-8 *Dash* 8 (MP)
  TRG 79: 12 Grob 115TA; 12 *Hawk* Mk102*; 30 PC-7 *Turbo Trainer*; 25 PC-21
HELICOPTERS
  MRH 15: 6 AW139; 9 Bell 412 *Twin Huey*
  TPT • **Light** 4: 3 AW109K2; 1 Bell 407
MSL
  AAM • IR AIM-9L *Sidewinder*; R-550 *Magic*; IIR/ARH *Mica*; ARH AIM-120 AMRAAM
  ASM AGM-65G *Maverick*; *Hakeem* 1/2/3 (A/B)
  ARM AGM-88 HARM
  LACM *Black Shaheen* (*Storm Shadow*/SCALP EG variant)

Air Defence
FORCES BY ROLE
AIR DEFENCE
  2 AD bde (3 bn with MIM-23B I-HAWK; *Patriot* PAC-3)
  3 (short range) AD bn with *Crotale*; *Mistral*; *Rapier*; RB-70; *Javelin*; 9K38 *Igla* (SA-18 *Grouse*); *Pantsir*-S1
EQUIPMENT BY TYPE
AD • SAM
  SP 50+: *Crotale*; RB-70; 50 *Pantsir*-S1
  TOWED MIM-23B I-HAWK; *Patriot* PAC-3; *Rapier*
  MANPAD *Javelin*; 9K38 *Igla* (SA-18 *Grouse*)
  NAVAL *Mistral*

Presidential Guard Command 12,000
FORCES BY ROLE
MANOEUVRE
  Reconaissance
  1 recce sqn
  Mechanised
  1 mech bde (1 tk bn, 4 mech inf bn, 1 AT coy, 1 cbt engr coy, 1 CSS bn

  Amphibious
  1 mne bn
EQUIPMENT BY TYPE
MBT 50 *Leclerc*
AIFV 200 BMP-3
APC • APC (W) 90 BTR-3U *Guardian*
AT • MSL • SP HMMWV with 9M133 *Kornet*

Joint Aviation Command
FORCES BY ROLE
GROUND ATTACK
  1 sqn with AT802 *Air Tractor*
ANTI SURFACE/ANTI SUBMARINE WARFARE
  1 sqn with AS332F *Super Puma*; AS565 *Panther*
TRANSPORT
  1 (Spec Ops) gp with AS365F *Dauphin* 2; AS550C3 *Fennec*; AW139; Bell 407MRH; Cessna 208B *Grand Caravan*; CH-47C/F *Chinook*; DHC-6-300/400 *Twin Otter*; UH-60L/M *Black Hawk*
ATTACK HELICOPTER
  1 gp with AH-64D *Apache*
EQUIPMENT BY TYPE
AIRCRAFT 18 combat capable
  TPT • **Light** 33: 2 Beech 350 *King Air*; 8 Cessna 208B *Grand Caravan*; 1 DHC-6-300 *Twin Otter*; 4 DHC-6-400 *Twin Otter*; 18 AT802 *Air Tractor**
HELICOPTERS
  ATK 30 AH-64D *Apache*
  ASW 7 AS332F *Super Puma* (5 in ASuW role)
  MRH 37: 4 AS365F *Dauphin* 2 (VIP); 18 AS550C3 *Fennec*; 7 AS565 *Panther*; 2 AW139 (VIP); 2 Bell 407MRH; 4 SA316 *Alouette* III
  TPT 63+: **Heavy** 22: 12 CH-47C *Chinook* (SF); 10 CH-47F *Chinook*; **Medium** 41+: 11 UH-60L *Black Hawk*; 30+ UH-60M *Black Hawk*
MSL
  ASM AGM-114 *Hellfire*; *Hydra*-70; HOT
  AShM AS-15TT; AM-39 *Exocet*

Paramilitary
Coast Guard
Ministry of Interior
EQUIPMENT BY TYPE
PATROL AND COASTAL COMBATANTS 112
  PSO 1 *Al Watid*
  PBF 58: 6 *Baglietto* GC23; 3 *Baglietto* 59; 15 DV-15; 34 MRTP 16
  PB 53: 2 *Protector*; 16 (US Camcraft 65); 5 (US Camcraft 77); 6 *Watercraft* 45; 12 *Halmatic Work*; 12 *Al Saber*

DEPLOYMENT
AFGHANISTAN
NATO • ISAF 35

FOREIGN FORCES
Australia 800; 1 FGA det with 8 F/A-18F *Super Hornet*; 1 B-737-700 *Wedgetail* (E-7A); 1 A330 MRTT (KC-30A); 1 tpt det with 3 C-130 *Hercules*; 1 MP det with 2 AP-3C *Orion*

France 750: 1 (Foreign Legion) BG (2 recce sqn, 2 inf sqn, 1 aty bty, 1 engr coy); 9 *Rafale*, 1 *Atlantique* 2; 1 KC-135F
Korea, Republic of: 150 (trg activities at UAE Spec Ops School)
United Kingdom 1 tkr/tpt flt with C-17A *Globemaster*; C-130J *Hercules*; A330 MRTT *Voyager*
United States: 5,000; 1 ftr sqn with 6 F-22A *Raptor*; 1 ftr sqn with 12 F-15C *Eagle*; 1 FGA sqn with 12 F-15E *Strike Eagle*; 1 ISR sqn with 4 U-2; 1 AEW&C sqn with 4 E-3 *Sentry*; 1 tkr sqn with 12 KC-10A; 1 ISR UAV sqn with RQ-4 *Global Hawk*; 2 AD bty with MIM-104 *Patriot*

Yemen, Republic of YEM

Yemeni Rial R		2013	2014	2015
GDP	R	8.68tr	9.77tr	
	US$	40.4bn	45.5bn	
per capita	US$	1,516	1,655	
Growth	%	4.8	1.9	
Inflation	%	11.0	9.0	
Def bdgt	R	397bn	405bn	413bn
	US$	1.85bn	1.89bn	
FMA (US)	US$	20m	20m	25m
US$1=R		214.89	214.89	

Population 26,052,966

Ethnic groups: Majority Arab; some African and South Asian

Age	0–14	15–19	20–24	25–29	30–64	65 plus
Male	21.2%	5.7%	5.0%	4.4%	13.1%	1.2%
Female	20.5%	5.6%	4.8%	4.2%	12.8%	1.4%

Capabilities

Yemen's armed forces are under-equipped and of variable training standards. Given internal military and political conflict, and continuing struggles with Houthi militia in the north and tensions with southern secessionists, maintaining force cohesion and morale will be a challenge. Houthi militia entered Sana'a in late 2014 and, though there was a subsequent agreement with the government, tensions persist and parallel military structures (militia/government) are now reported to operate in some parts. Former president Ali Abdullah Saleh was reportedly allied with the Houthi militia. Despite a relatively high level of defence spending compared to GDP, the country's underdeveloped economic status and political instability means that the state is unable to exercise full control over internal security. The importance of tribal ties combined with the reintroduction of conscription in 2007 has created difficulties in encouraging loyalty to the armed forces. The air force and navy are unable to fulfil their core roles of defending territorial sovereignty, with insufficient equipment and training. Whilst the air force is to receive some US ISR aircraft, airlift is almost non-existent, leading to internal mobility problems. The country's forces have mounted a number of offensives against insurgents, supported by Yemeni air-strikes and missile attacks by US UAVs.

ACTIVE 66,700 (Army 60,000 Navy 1,700 Air Force 3,000, Air Defence 2,000) **Paramilitary 71,200**
Conscript liability 2 years

ORGANISATIONS BY SERVICE

Army 60,000 (incl conscripts)
7 regional comd
FORCES BY ROLE
SPECIAL FORCES
  1 SF bde
MANOEUVRE
  Armoured
  12 armd bde
  Mechanised
  11 mech bde
  Light
  22 inf bde
  Air Manoeuvre
  3 cdo/AB bde
  Mountain
  5 mtn inf bde
  Other
  1 (Presidential Protection) gd force (2 armd bde, 2 sy bde)
  3 (border gd) sy bde
COMBAT SUPPORT
  3 arty bde
  1 SSM bde
  2 AD bn
EQUIPMENT BY TYPE
MBT 880: 50 M60A1; 70 T-72; 80 T-80; 200 T-62; 450 T-54/T-55; 30 T-34
RECCE 130+: 80 AML-90; 50 BRDM-2; *Ratel*
AIFV 200: 100 BMP-1; 100 BMP-2
APC 258
  APC (T) 60 M113A2
  APC (W) 180: 60 BTR-40; 100 BTR-60; 20 BTR-152; (470 BTR-40/BTR-60/BTR-152 in store)
  PPV 18 YLAV *Cougar*
ARTY 1,307
  SP 122mm 25 2S1
  TOWED 310: **105mm** 25 M101A1; **122mm** 200: 130 D-30; 30 M-1931/37; 40 M-30 M-1938; **130mm** 60 M-46; **152mm** 10 D-20; **155mm** 15 M114
  COASTAL 130mm 36 SM-4-1
  MRL 294: **122mm** 280 BM-21 (150 op); **140mm** 14 BM-14
  MOR 642: **81mm** 250; **82mm** 144 M-43; **107mm** 12; **120mm** 136; **160mm** ε100
AT
  MSL • MANPATS 9K11 *Malyutka* (AT-3 *Sagger*); M47 *Dragon*; TOW
  RCL 75mm M-20; **82mm** B-10; **107mm** B-11
  GUNS 50+
    SP 100mm 30 SU-100
    TOWED 20+: **85mm** D-44; **100mm** 20 M-1944
AD
  SAM ε800
    SP 9K31 *Strela*-1 (SA-9 *Gaskin*); 9K35 *Strela*-10 (SA-13 *Gopher*)

MANPAD 9K32 *Strela*-2 (SA-7 *Grail*)‡; 9K36 *Strela*-3 (SA-14 *Gremlin*)
GUNS 530
SP 70: **20mm** 20 M163 *Vulcan*; **23mm** 50 ZSU-23-4
TOWED 460: **20mm** 50 M167 *Vulcan*; **23mm** 100 ZU-23-2; **37mm** 150 M-1939; **57mm** 120 S-60; **85mm** 40 M-1939 KS-12
MSL • TACTICAL • SSM 28: 12 FROG-7; 10 SS-21 *Scarab* (*Tochka*); 6 *Scud*-B (ε33 msl)
ARV T-54/55 reported
VLB MTU reported

Navy 1,700
EQUIPMENT BY TYPE
PATROL AND COASTAL COMBATANTS 22
  PCO 1 *Tarantul*† with 2 twin lnchr (fitted for P-15 *Termit*-M (SS-N-2C *Styx*) AShM), 1 quad lnchr (manual aiming) with 9K32 *Strela*-2 (SA-N-5 *Grail*) SAM, 2 AK630 CIWS, 1 76mm gun
  PBF 6 *Baklan*
  PB 15: 3 *Hounan*† with 4 single lnchr (fitted for C-801 (CSS-N-4 *Sardine*) AShM), 2 twin AK230 CIWS; 10 P-1000 (Austal 37.5m); 2 *Zhuk* (FSU *Osa* II) (1†)
MINE WARFARE • MINE COUNTERMEASURES 1:
  MSO 1 *Natya* (FSU) with 2 RBU 1200
AMPHIBIOUS 4:
  LANDING SHIPS • LSM 1 *Bilqis* (POL NS-722) (capacity 5 MBT; 110 troops)
  LANDING CRAFT • LCU 3 *Deba* (POL NS-717)
LOGISTICS AND SUPPORT 2: 1 AFD; 1 AGS

Air Force 3,000
FORCES BY ROLE
FIGHTER
  3 sqn with F-5E *Tiger* II; MiG-21 *Fishbed*; MiG-29SM/MiG-29UB *Fulcrum*
FIGHTER/GROUND ATTACK
  1 sqn with Su-22 *Fitter* D/Su-22UMS *Fitter* G
MARITIME PATROL
  1 unit with DHC-8 MPA
ISR
  1 unit with Cessna 208B (forming)
TRANSPORT
  1 sqn with An-12 *Cub*; An-26 *Curl*; C-130H *Hercules*; Il-76 *Candid*
ATTACK/TRANSPORT HELICOPTER
  3 sqn with Bell 205 (UH-1H); Bell 212; Ka-27; Mi-8 *Hip*; Mi-17 *Hip* H; Mi14PS; Mi-35 *Hind*
EQUIPMENT BY TYPE
AIRCRAFT 75 combat capable
  FTR 10 F-5E *Tiger* II
  FGA 65: 15 MiG-21 *Fishbed*; 3 MiG-21U *Mongol* A*; 15 MiG-29SM *Fulcrum*; 1 MiG-29UB *Fulcrum*; 27 Su-22 *Fitter* D; 4 Su-22UM3 *Fitter* G
  MP 2 DHC-8 MPA
  TPT 13: **Heavy** 3 Il-76 *Candid*; **Medium** 5: 2 An-12 *Cub*; 2 C-130H *Hercules*; 1 CN-235-300 **Light** 5: 3 An-26 *Curl*; 2 Cessna 208B

TRG 36: 24 L-39C; 12 Z-242
HELICOPTERS
  ATK 8 Mi-35 *Hind*
  ASW 1 Ka-27 (tpt role)
  MRH 10 Mi-17 *Hip* H
  TPT 14: **Medium** 8 Mi-8 *Hip*; **Light** 6: 2 Bell 212; 4 Bell 205 (UH-1H)
MSL
  AAM • IR R-3 (AA-2 *Atoll*)‡; R-60 (AA-8 *Aphid*); AIM-9 *Sidewinder*; IR/SARH R-27 (AA-10 *Alamo*)
  ARM Kh-31P (AS-17A *Krypton*)

Air Defence 2,000
EQUIPMENT BY TYPE
AD • SAM:
  SP 2K12 *Kub* (SA-6 *Gainful*); 9K31 *Strela*-1 (SA-9 *Gaskin*); 9K35 *Strela*-10 (SA-13 *Gopher*)
  TOWED S-75 *Dvina* (SA-2 *Guideline*); S-125 *Pechora* (SA-3 *Goa*)
  MANPAD 9K32 *Strela*-2 (SA-7 *Grail*)‡; 9K36 *Strela*-3 (SA-14 *Gremlin*)

Paramilitary 71,200+

Ministry of the Interior Forces 50,000

Tribal Levies 20,000+

Yemeni Coast Guard Authority ε1,200
EQUIPMENT BY TYPE
PATROL AND COASTAL COMBATANTS 17
  PBF 4 *Archangel* (US)
  PB 13: 2 *Marine Patrol*; 11 various

DEPLOYMENT

CENTRAL AFRICAN REPUBLIC
UN • MINUSCA 1 obs

CÔTE D'IVOIRE
UN • UNOCI 1; 9 obs

DEMOCRATIC REPUBLIC OF THE CONGO
UN • MONUSCO 4 obs

LIBERIA
UN • UNMIL 1

MALI
UN • MINUSMA 4

SOUTH SUDAN
UN • UNMISS 3; 7 obs

SUDAN
UN • UNAMID 12; 49 obs
UN • UNISFA 2; 3 obs

WESTERN SAHARA
UN • MINURSO 11 obs

Table 8 Selected Arms Procurements and Deliveries, Middle East and North Africa

Designation	Type	Quantity (Current)	Contract Value	Prime Nationality	Prime Contractor	Order Date	First Delivery Due	Notes
Algeria (ALG)								
Fuchs 2	APC (W)	54	n.k.	GER	Rheinmetall	2011	2013	First 24 delivered 2013
Varshavyanka-class (*Kilo*)	SSK	2	US$1.2bn	RUS	Admiralty Shipyards	2014	2018	To be delivered by 2018
MEKO A200	FFGHM	2	See notes	GER	TKMS	2012	2016	Part of US$3.3bn (€2.5bn) deal including six *Super Lynx* 300 hel
C28A	FFGHM	3	n.k.	PRC	Hudong-Zhonghua Shipbuilding	2012	2015	First vessel launched in PRC in Aug 2014
Mi-28NE *Havoc*	Atk hel	42	n.k.	RUS	Russian Helicopters (Rostvertol)	2013	n.k.	Contract signed Dec 2013
Super Lynx 300	MRH hel	6	See notes	ITA	Finmeccanica	2012	n.k.	Part of US$3.3bn (€2.5bn) deal including two MEKO A200 FFGHM. First in test Oct 2014
Mi-26T2 *Halo*	Hvy tpt hel	6	n.k.	RUS	Russian Helicopters (Rostvertol)	2013	n.k.	Contract signed Jun 2013
S-300PMU-2 *Favorite* (SA-20B)	SAM	32	US$1bn	RUS	Almaz-Antey	2006	2008	Eight bty. First bty delivered 2008. Deliveries resumed in 2011 after suspension
96K6 *Pantsir*-S1	AD	38	US$500m	RUS	KBP Instrument Design Bureau	2006	2010	Deliveries ongoing
Egypt (EGY)								
Gowind-class	FSGM	4	€1bn (US$1.4bn)	FRA	DCNS	2014	2017	First to be built in FRA; remainder in EGY
F-16C/D *Fighting Falcon*	FGA ac	20	n.k.	US	Lockheed Martin	2010	2013	16 F-16C and four F-16D. First eight ac delivered by mid-2013. Further deliveries put on hold
C-295M	Lt tpt ac	14	n.k.	Int'l	Airbus Group (Airbus Defence & Space)	2013	2014	Third and fourth orders; delivery suspended in Aug 2013, but later resumed
AH-64D *Apache*	Atk hel	10	n.k.	US	Boeing	2012	2014	Delivery suspension lifted Apr 2014
S-300VM	SAM	n.k.	US$500m	RUS	Almaz-Antey	2014	n.k.	Production under way 2014
Iran (IRN)								
Mowj-class	FSGM	5	n.k.	IRN	IRIN	2004	2010	Second vessel in sea trials at Bandar Anzali 2014. Third launched at Bandar Abbas
Iraq (IRQ)								
F-16C/D *Fighting Falcon*	FGA ac	36	n.k.	US	Lockheed Martin	2011	2014	24 C and 12 D models. First ac handed over Jun 2014, but remains in US
FA-50	FGA ac	24	US$1.1bn	ROK	KAI	2013	2016	Deliveries to occur 2016–17
Mi-28NE *Havoc*	Atk hel	15	n.k.	RUS	Russian Helicopters (Rostvertol)	2012	2014	First batch of three delivered Oct 2014
Mi-35M *Hind*	Atk hel	28	n.k.	RUS	Russian Helicopters (Rostvertol)	2013	2013	Third batch of four delivered Sep 2014
96K6 *Pantsir*-S1	AD	n.k.	n.k.	RUS	KBP Instrument Design Bureau	2012	2014	Total number on order unclear. Deliveries under way

Table 8 **Selected Arms Procurements and Deliveries, Middle East and North Africa**

Designation	Type	Quantity (Current)	Contract Value	Prime Nationality	Prime Contractor	Order Date	First Delivery Due	Notes
Israel (ISR)								
Merkava Mk IV	MBT	Up to 400	n.k.	ISR	MANTAK	2001	2003	Deliveries ongoing
Dolphin-class (Type-800)	SSK	2	€1bn (US$1.21bn)	GER	TKMS	2006	2014	With Air-Independent Propulsion (AIP) system. First boat, INS Tanin, delivered Sep 2014
F-35A Lightning II	FGA ac	2	US$2.75bn	US	Lockheed Martin	2010	2016	LRIP 8 includes first two F-35A for ISR
C-130J-30 Hercules	Med tpt ac	3	US$215.7m	US	Lockheed Martin	2011	2014	First arrived in ISR Apr 2014
M-346 Lavi	Trg ac	30	US$1bn	ITA	Finmeccanica (Alenia Aermacchi)	2012	2014	First two ac delivered Jul 2014
Arrow 2	SAM	n.k.	Undisclosed	ISR/US	IAI	2008	n.k.	Number and cost undisclosed
Jordan (JOR)								
Mbombe	APC (W)	50	n.k.	JOR/RSA	ADI	2014	n.k.	To be built in JOR as part of KADDB/Paramount Group joint venture
Gepard	AD	60	€21m (US$29m)	NLD	Government surplus	2013	2014	ex-NLD surplus vehicles
Kuwait (KWT)								
Patriot PAC-3	SAM Upgrade	72	US$263m	US	Lockheed Martin	2013	2015	Upgrade of existing PAC-2 launchers
Lebanon (LBN)								
VAB	APC (W)	Up to 100	See notes	FRA	Renault Trucks Defense/Government surplus	2014	2015	Part of package paid for by US$3bn SAU grant. Either ex-FRA or new build
CAESAR	Arty (155mm SP)	Up to 30	See notes	FRA	Nexter	2014	2015	Part of package paid for by US$3bn SAU grant
VBL with Mistral	SAM (SP)	n.k.	See notes	FRA	Renault Trucks Defense/MBDA	2014	2015	Part of package paid for by US$3bn SAU grant
Combattante FS56	PCFM	3 to 4	See notes	FRA	Abu Dhabi Mar (CMN)	2014	2015	Part of package paid for by US$3bn SAU grant
SA342 Gazelle	MRH hel	n.k.	See notes	FRA	Government surplus	2014	2015	Part of package paid for by US$3bn SAU grant
AS532 Cougar	Med tpt hel	n.k.	See notes	FRA	Airbus Group (Airbus Helicopters)/Government surplus	2014	2015	Part of package paid for by US$3bn SAU grant. Either ex-FRA or new build
Oman (OMN)								
Al-Ofouq-class	PCO	4	US$880m	SGP	ST Engineering	2012	2015	First three vessels launched 2014; awaiting commissioning
F-16C/D Fighting Falcon	FGA ac	12	n.k.	US	Lockheed Martin	2011	2014	First four delivered Jul 2014
NH90 TTH	Med tpt hel	20	n.k.	FRA/GER/ITA/NLD	NH Industries	2004	2010	Deliveries ongoing
Eurofighter Typhoon	FGA ac	12	See notes	GER/ITA/ESP/UK	Eurofighter GmbH (BAE Systems)	2013	2017	Part of UK£2.5bn (US$4bn) deal including eight Hawk Mk128. Nine single-seat and three twin-seat
C-295M	Lt tpt ac	8	n.k.	Int'l	Airbus Group (Airbus Defence & Space)	2012	2013	For air force. Five in tpt and three in MP configuration. First delivered 2013

Table 8 Selected Arms Procurements and Deliveries, Middle East and North Africa

Designation	Type	Quantity (Current)	Contract Value	Prime Nationality	Prime Contractor	Order Date	First Delivery Due	Notes
Qatar (QTR)								
Leopard 2A7	MBT	62	See notes	GER	KMW	2013	2015	Part of €1.89bn (US$2.47bn) contract incl 24 PzH 2000
PzH 2000	Arty (155mm SP)	24	See notes	GER	KMW	2013	2015	Part of €1.89bn (US$2.47bn) contract incl 62 Leopard 2A7
B-737 AEW	AEW&C ac	3	R6.6bn (US$1.8bn)	US	Boeing	2014	n.k.	Part of US$23bn package
A330 MRTT	Tkr/Tpt ac	2	See notes	Int'l	Airbus Group (Airbus Defence & Space)	2014	n.k.	Part of US$23bn package
AH-64E Apache Guardian	Atk hel	24	R8.9bn (US$2.4bn)	US	Boeing	2014	n.k.	Part of US$23bn package
Patriot PAC-3	SAM	n.k.	n.k.	US	Raytheon	2014	n.k.	Part of US$23bn package
Saudi Arabia (SAU)								
Patriot PAC-3	SAM upgrade	n.k.	US$1.7bn	US	Raytheon	2011	n.k.	Incl ground systems, training package and support equipment
Eurofighter Typhoon	FGA ac	72	GB£4.43bn (US$8.9bn)	GER/ITA/ESP/UK	Eurofighter GmbH (BAE Systems)	2005	2008	Project Salam. Original plan to final assemble remaining 48 in SAU dropped
F-15E Strike Eagle	FGA ac	84	US$11.4bn	US	Boeing	2012	2015	F-15SA variant. Part of a package including F-15S upgrades, AH-64 and AH-6i helicopters that could total US$24bn
A330 MRTT	Tkr/Tpt ac	6	US$600m	FRA	Airbus Group (Airbus Defence & Space)	2008	2011	Includes additional three ac ordered July 2009; fourth ac delivered Apr 2014
KC-130J Hercules	Tkr ac	2	US$180m	US	Lockheed Martin	2013	n.k.	Initial two ac pending agreement of larger order
AH-64E Apache Guardian	Atk hel	48	US$450m	US	Boeing	2013	2014	36 for RSLF and 12 for national guard. First three delivered to RSLF Oct 2014
AH-6i Little Bird	MRH hel	24	n.k.	US	Boeing	2014	n.k.	For national guard
Syria (SYR)								
MiG-29M2 Fulcrum	Ftr ac	12	n.k.	RUS	UAC (MiG)	2007	2016	Delivery delayed by Syrian conflict
Yak-130	Trg ac	36	US$550m	RUS	UAC (Irkut)	2012	2014	Delivery to begin by late 2014
United Arab Emirates (UAE)								
Falcon Eye	ISR Satellite	2	€800m (US$1.1bn)	Int'l	Airbus Group/Thales	2013	2017	First satellite due to launch in 2017; second 2018
Agrab Mk2 (Scorpion) MMS	Arty (120mm SP Mor)	72	US$214m	RSA/SGP/UAE/UK	IGG	2011	2014	Deliveries ongoing
Baynunah-class	FSGHM	6	AED3bn (US$820m)	FRA/UAE	ADSB	2003	2006	First of class built in FRA, others in UAE. Third vessel commissioned Dec 2013. Sixth vessel launched Feb 2014
Terminal High Altitude Area Defense (THAAD)	SAM	12	n.k.	US	Lockheed Martin	2011	2015	Two batteries
Patriot PAC-3	SAM	42	US$3.3bn	US	Raytheon	2008	2012	To replace HAWK. First bty delivered 2012

Chapter Eight
Latin America and the Caribbean

Combating organised crime

The use of Latin American armed forces to combat drug trafficking and other organised crime continued in 2014. New agencies combining police and military structures were created, while equipment acquisitions were often tailored to law-enforcement capabilities. Brazil and Mexico, which have the two largest economies in the region, carried out new internal military deployments amid continuing drug-related violence. Countries that have experienced increased drug trafficking in recent years, especially in the Andean region and Central America, took steps to increase their monitoring and air-interception capabilities, conforming to a regional trend towards increasing air mobility. As regional security threats have often been multidimensional in nature, and transnational in their origin and impact, there have been some recent attempts at cooperative dialogue between regional security agencies and armed forces. For example, in the first half of 2014 the Central American Integration System (SICA) announced equipment donations for Honduran, Guatemalan and Salvadoran border-security authorities, as well as their integration into the database of Ameripol, the hemispheric police-cooperation mechanism.

Central America

Honduras, Guatemala and El Salvador, which comprise the 'northern triangle' of Central America, have some of the highest homicide rates in the world. All have taken steps to increase the range of military tools available to fight criminal groups, although budgetary constraints have meant that recent acquisitions, despite constituting a capability improvement in national terms, remain modest in the face of well-armed and adaptable transnational criminal groups. El Salvador acquired ten used Cessna A-37B *Dragonfly* fighter/ground-attack aircraft from Chile in 2014, opting for this model rather than the Embraer EMB-314 *Super Tucano* (see *The Military Balance 2014*, p. 356). These additional A-37s were demonstrated at El Salvador's Soldiers' Day parade in May 2014, and added to the number of ageing A-37s in Central American air forces. However, the arrival of additional A-37s in El Salvador raised some concern in neighbouring Honduras about the effect on the region's military balance. In response, Salvadoran authorities said that the aircraft would be used primarily in the fight against criminal groups.

The new Honduran president, Juan Orlando Hernández, announced in April that a number of EMB-312 *Tucanos* would be repaired and overhauled, after an offer of support from the Brazilian government. Honduras reportedly considered the purchase of a small number of EMB-314 *Super Tucano* ground-attack aircraft. It also received three radars for detecting the light aircraft commonly used in the transport of illicit narcotics. The radars will be crucial for Honduran authorities implementing a 'shoot-down' law passed in January 2014 (Ley de Protección de la Espacio Aéreo, or the Aerospace Protection Law), which allows for the interception of aircraft they believe to be carrying drugs.

Merging police with military capabilities and responses

Honduras stood up in 2014 two new security agencies dedicated to the fight against criminal groups. Both had been approved by congress the previous year. According to the United Nations, the country had the highest homicide rate in the world in 2012; the president's promise to put 'a soldier on every corner' received popular support, despite the concerns of civil-society organisations and opposition lawmakers about the excessive involvement of the armed forces in law enforcement. The decision led to the deployment of 2,000 members of the new Public Order Military Police (PMOP). The group is under military control but roled as a special law-enforcement unit capable of deploying to areas with high levels of criminality and violence. The second new security force, the Intelligence Troops and Special Security Response Teams (Tropa de Inteligencia y Grupos de Respuesta Especial de Seguridad, or TIGRES), is under the command of the Ministry of Security (which is also responsible for the civilian police) and is being trained in both police and military tactics. The two new forces are designed to counter criminal groups, which often possess greater firepower than the police. Neighbouring Guatemala has since 2012 launched 11 joint police–military task forces to tackle security in areas with high levels of criminality. The country has also established two new rural task forces, during December 2013 and July 2014, in a bid to better protect its borders with Mexico and Honduras.

Mexico has taken a similar approach with its Gendarmería Nacional (National Gendarmerie). This paramilitary internal-security force was first proposed during President Enrique Peña Nieto's presidential campaign in 2012. It had been postponed several times since, and little was said about its composition and role until 2014. Finally launched in August, the force was composed of new recruits rather than transferees from other units, although its commanders previously served in the federal police. According to the head of Mexico's National Security Council, Monte Alejandro Rubido, the new body has an 'army outlook' in its discipline and training, but also incorporates policing tactics, especially in its approach to patrols and its interaction with the population. The stated purpose of the Gendarmería Nacional is to protect supply chains and economic activity (such as agriculture, mining and tourism) in areas threatened by criminal groups. Launched in August 2014, the initial force of 5,000 personnel was first deployed to Valle de Bravo, an area near the capital with a high homicide rate, but alongside the gendarmerie; the established strategy of emergency deployments of both military and federal-police forces to such areas continued. Federal police and military reinforcements were sent during 2014 to the states of Michoacán and Tamaulipas, in the southwest and the northeast respectively. The latter state also received reinforcements from the Gendarmería Nacional, raising questions about how much the new force would differ from those used in existing joint military and federal-police deployments.

Equipment acquisitions and plans

Like some of its southern neighbours, Mexico is modernising its air capabilities, principally to bolster its ability to combat criminal groups. It announced in August 2014 the purchase of more than 20 new aircraft, including 14 Bell 407GX light helicopters, mainly to eradicate narcotics plantations, and an unspecified number of Beechcraft *King Air* 350ERs, for surveillance and reconnaissance. The navy increased its coastal capabilities with the delivery of two new *Tenochtitlan*-class patrol vessels. It also announced that it would build four 1,680-tonne ocean-patrol vessels at its shipyards in Tampico, Tamaulipas State and Salina Cruz, Oaxaca State, with delivery scheduled for 2016.

Some of the acquisitions in Central America and Mexico are supported by Washington, under the Mérida Initiative in the latter and as part of broader US support for SICA in the former. Between late 2013 and mid-2014, the US government donated 74 light-armoured 4x4s to two Guatemalan task forces: Task Force Tecún Uman, which was established in April 2013 and has operated in San Marcos, on the border with Mexico; and Task Force Chortí, deployed in July 2014 along the border with Honduras. This was part of a renewed push to strengthen the capacities of the United States' southern neighbours.

Countries in the Andean region – located at what is the start of international cocaine-trafficking networks – also took steps to build surveillance and air capabilities against organised-crime and guerrilla groups operating in remote, often border, areas. Bolivia is, analysts believe, increasingly used as a transit point for groups moving cocaine from Peru to Brazil and Paraguay. In a bid to bolster capacity in the face of this threat, the arrival in early August of the first of six AS332 *Super Puma* helicopters, ordered in January from Airbus, moderately improved La Paz's rotary-lift capabilities. These were further boosted in mid-September by the arrival of six H425 (Z-9) helicopters from China. Like Honduras, Bolivia enacted a law permitting its air force to shoot down aircraft suspected of carrying drugs. President Evo Morales promoted the legislation as a way of enforcing national sovereignty, which has been threatened by a variety of small criminal groups operating in dense jungle areas along the country's northern and eastern borders.

Confronted with similar topographical challenges to its security forces, Peru also seeks to acquire new monitoring systems and helicopters. The country faces a serious threat from the remnants of the Shining Path guerrilla movement, which is well armed and trained, and in recent years has carried out persistent low-level attacks in the Apurímac, Ene and Mantaro River Valleys Region. A plan for a major coca-eradication drive in areas of Shining Path activity in the south was cancelled by the government in May over fears that the initiative might alienate the local population. In response to guerrilla activity, Peru is increasing its rotary-wing fleet with the acquisition of 24 Mi-171Sh helicopters from Russia.

Peru's economy, one of the fastest-growing in Latin America, has provided Lima with the revenue to move ahead with the National and Amazonian Monitoring System (SIVAN). This extensive monitoring-and-surveillance network, first mooted in the mid-2000s, is the Peruvian equivalent of Brazil's more ambitious 'System for the Vigilance of the Amazon' (SIVAM) border-monitoring system, which is already in its initial implementation phase. The Peruvian plan includes several air- and land-based systems designed to monitor sparsely inhabited jungle areas for signs of illegal mining and cocaine production and trafficking, the main sources of funding for Shining Path and smaller groups. Peru's defence ministry moved closer to implementation in 2014 by buying four land-based air-surveillance radars and awarding, in April, a €150-million (US$203m) contract to Airbus to build the country's first Earth observation satellite, which will form the centrepiece of SIVAN. The satellite is scheduled for launch in 2016.

The system originated from a 'strategic-alliance' agreement signed by Peru and Brazil in 2003. The SIVAN system typifies Brazil's participation in regional security initiatives and capacity-building; these are, according to analysts, often conducted without much publicity. The 'strategic alliance' led to a Bi-National Working Group Agreement to build Peru's surveillance capacity, which was signed on 9 November 2006. This led to Peru's gradual inclusion in technical meetings, including those on Brazil's SIVAM system.

SIVAN is also reflective of a perceived requirement to build surveillance capacity on the Peruvian side of the shared frontier. The importance of this security concern is reflected in Brazil's 2011 agreements with Peru and Paraguay to conduct cross-border raids against criminal groups. Faced with an increasing flow of drugs from Peru and Bolivia, Brazil began in 2014 a project with Colombia to develop a new river-patrol vessel designed for operations on the Amazon. The initiative was developed under a bilateral defence-cooperation agreement signed in 2008, which included a contract with Colombia's COTECMAR to produce four LPR-40 river-patrol boats for Brazil (the last of which was delivered in early 2014).

However, Brazil's most visible regional defence project is not primarily focused on countering criminality. In 2014 construction began on the prototype of the KC-390 medium airlifter at Embraer's plant in São Paulo State. This is the largest aircraft ever constructed by Embraer and its main regional partner in the project, Fábrica Argentina de Aviones. Embraer has received letters of intent to purchase from several Latin American countries, as well as from the Czech Republic and Portugal. International commitments amount to orders for 32 aircraft, in addition to the 28 being constructed for the Brazilian Air Force.

REGIONAL DEFENCE ECONOMICS

Macroeconomics

Regional economic activity has slowed, with average growth rates falling from 4.2% in 2011 to a projected 2.6% in 2014, the lowest since 2009. Many states are grappling with the challenge of stimulating economic growth following the stagnation of global commodity prices and domestic supply-side constraints. Policy uncertainties and a lack of structural reform in many states have led to deteriorating business confidence and lower levels of capital investment. Slowing productivity increases and rising inflation have started to dampen consumer spending, adversely affecting aggregate demand. These factors were most evident in Brazil, where the economy was projected to grow by just 0.3% in 2014. The country experienced a technical recession in the first half of the year, with two consecutive quarters of economic contraction. Meanwhile, room for policy action was limited by rising inflation, which in September 2014 reached 6.5%, the upper limit of the central bank's target range. To address this, interest rates were increased by 375 basis points in the year to April 2014. This raised government debt-service costs, reduced private-sector investment and limited household-

Figure 18 **Latin America and the Caribbean Regional Defence Expenditure** as % of GDP

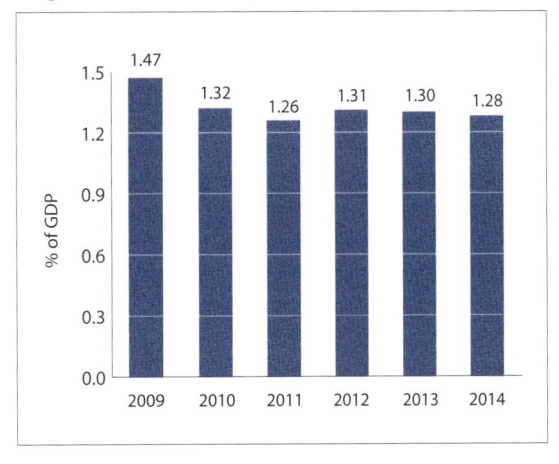

Year	% of GDP
2009	1.47
2010	1.32
2011	1.26
2012	1.31
2013	1.30
2014	1.28

Extra-budgetary sources of defence financing

A number of Latin American states utilise extra-budgetary funding for military operations and/or acquisitions. Some have done so for historical reasons (for example, to allow the armed forces a greater degree of autonomy from political processes in states undergoing democratic transitions), while for others the establishment of additional funding streams provides a convenient means of tapping into newly developed revenue sources, such as commodity-export earnings. A few states also utilise off-budget sources in order to bypass budgetary processes and minimise legislative oversight of military activities, reducing transparency and accountability.

The oldest of these mechanisms is Chile's 1958 'copper law' (Ley Reservada del Cobre, or Copper Reserve Law). After several modifications, it now allocates 10% of the proceeds from exports by state-owned copper producer Codelco to purchases of military equipment. Although no precise figures have been published, Chilean newspaper *El Mercurio* has estimated that income accrued under the copper law and spent by the armed forces amounted to US$6.4bn between 2004 and 2014. The volatility of copper prices makes multi-year acquisition timetables difficult to plan and finance using the copper law, and since 2011 there have been increased calls for greater budgetary transparency and the replacement of the law with a dedicated multi-year equipment budget, as well as a Strategic Contingency Fund in case of security emergencies or natural disasters.

Established in January 2005, Peru's National Defence Fund equally distributes part of the proceeds from natural-gas extraction (particularly those generated by specified plots of the Camisea Gas Project in central Peru) between the army, air force, navy and national police. In 2007 the government proposed that additional resources from mineral exports be allocated to the armed forces, but before a vote could be taken the proposal was blocked by the finance ministry, which argued that defence and security budgets had recently been increased.

In the last few years, governments in some of Latin America's poorest states have increased their reliance on extra-budgetary resources to combat rising criminal violence. In August 2014, Bolivia announced plans to create a defence fund using income from an existing tax on hydrocarbon extraction (Impuesto Directo a los Hidrocarburos). In 2011 Honduras introduced a security-tax bill that raised revenue by targeting certain financial transactions, including bank deposits, certain types of money transfers and some credit cards. On average, the scheme has collected 96.7m lempiras (around US$4.8m) per month, totalling 1.9bn lempiras (US$95m) between May 2012 and December 2013. The head of the technical committee overseeing the disbursement of tax revenues stated that these had been used to acquire three radars, which were installed in 2014 to aid the fight against drug trafficking. Proceeds of the tax have also been allocated to the military police and the TIGRES special-operations unit. An amendment to the bill has delayed its expiry until 2021.

Venezuela purchased military equipment with resources from two little-known development funds. The larger of these is El Fondo Nacional para el Desarrollo Nacional (FONDEN), a state investment vehicle that receives a proportion of national oil revenues, and the Joint Chinese–Venezuelan Fund, which largely comprises loans granted by Beijing in exchange for regular supplies of oil. The allocation of resources from these funds is highly secretive, with little oversight from congress. In November 2012, however, the finance ministry provided information about FONDEN, highlighting the military dimension of its allocation of funds. Between January 2005 and September 2012, FONDEN assigned more funds to defence-project acquisitions and maintenance than to the construction of houses, one of the flagship social programmes of former president Hugo Chávez. A total of US$6bn was spent on assets such as an ammunition factory, aircraft and hangars for the air force, as well as helicopter repairs. In February 2014, the defence ministry announced an order of 12 patrol vessels from the Netherlands' Damen Shipyards, to be funded by FONDEN.

---

credit growth, all of which restrained economic activity. Sharp slowdowns were also seen in Peru and Chile during 2014, with both countries affected by lower global commodity prices (principally, lower metals prices), as well as reduced domestic investment and consumption. However, well-anchored inflation expectations in both states permitted monetary easing in support of economic activity, while low public-debt-to-GDP ratios also provided the opportunity to implement counter-cyclical fiscal policies (i.e. fiscal expansion during cyclical downturns), with Peru announcing stimulus measures in both July and September.

Economic volatility in Argentina and Venezuela worsened in 2014. In Venezuela, substantial increases in the money supply over recent years (up by almost 75% in the first half of 2014 alone) resulted in currency depreciation and spiralling inflation, which

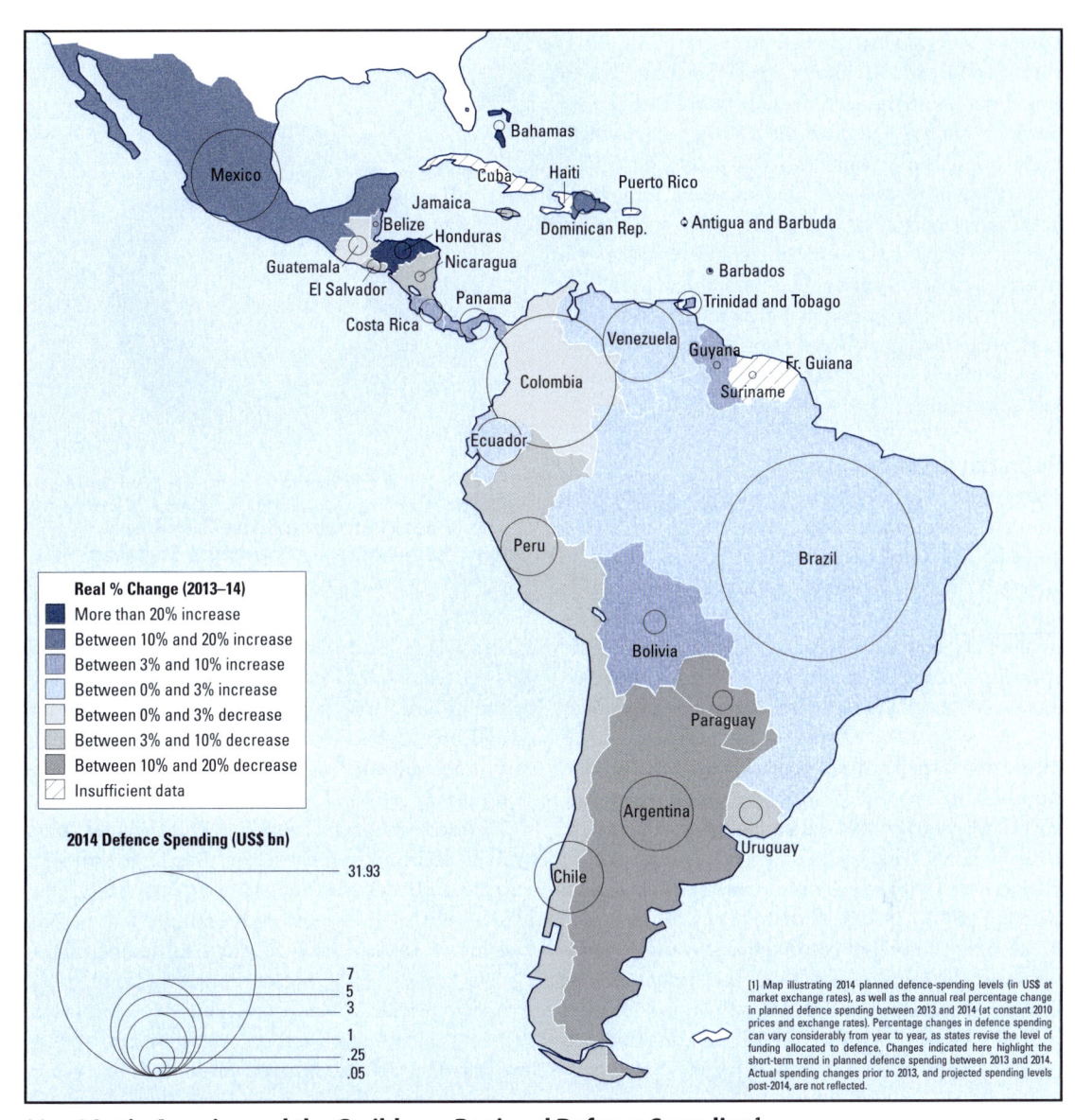

Map 8 **Latin America and the Caribbean Regional Defence Spending**[1]

rose from around 40% in 2013 to more than 60% in 2014, despite the imposition of price controls. Capital flight was stemmed only by the imposition of capital and exchange controls, which resulted in reduced imports and shortages of food, consumer goods and even medical supplies. Venezuela's economy was projected to contract by 3% in 2014, with production and investment deterred by high inflation. State revenues were eroded by this decline in domestic output, as well as falling oil prices, and the government resorted to further currency devaluations and the adoption of a three-tiered exchange-rate system to help finance budget deficits. Argentina's economy was also projected to shrink in 2014, by 1.7%. Buenos Aires found it increasingly difficult to borrow internationally due to its sovereign default in August 2014, and resorted to monetising its fiscal deficit and lowering interest rates the following month, despite already high inflation (of around 35–40%), in an effort to support demand. Continued expansionary policies in 2014 led to sustained currency devaluation; the government responded by imposing increasingly strict foreign-exchange controls.

In contrast to much of South America, Colombia and Mexico experienced greater economic growth (4.8% and 2.4% respectively), with both states buoyed by improved construction activity. Central American countries broadly maintained their healthy growth trajectories, with the 4.2% overall growth rate of 2013 declining slightly to a projected 3.8% in 2014. Growth in the Caribbean was anticipated to accelerate to 3.8% in 2014 (up from 3.2% the previous year). Yet relative economic buoyancy in Mexico, Colombia and Central American states was insufficient to offset major weaknesses elsewhere, leading the International Monetary Fund to cut its 2014 regional-growth forecast by 1.2 percentage points between April and October, to 1.3%, a reflection of weakening economic fundamentals across much of Latin America.

Regional defence spending

The general slowdown in economic activity also affected defence spending. After rising by 13.4% between 2010 and 2013 (from US$66.2 billion to US$75bn), nominal defence spending in the region fell by 1.9% (to US$73.4bn) in 2014. After adjusting for inflationary and exchange-rate effects, real defence spending remained flat relative to 2013, with an increase of only 0.2%. Although total regional outlays in 2014 were still 8.9% higher, in real terms, than those in 2010, real defence-spending growth declined from 6.2% in 2012 to 3.1% in 2013. As rates of defence-spending growth have fallen below GDP growth rates, regional defence spending as a proportion of GDP has also declined slightly, from 1.31% of GDP in 2012 to 1.28% in 2014 (see Figure 18).

In 2014 sub-regional defence-spending variations closely mirrored economic performance. The largest absolute and percentage reductions occurred in South America, where total real spending declined by 1.2%, with Argentina and Paraguay both registering double-digit reductions. In Argentina, this was mainly the result of high inflation eroding the 15% nominal increase in the defence budget. In Paraguay, however, the country's defence capital budget was halved after two years of high outlays, as the armed forces' modernisation programme was scaled back. The reduction came amid a broader effort at fiscal consolidation in the year, although it was proposed in September 2014 that the procurement programme be re-assigned to a funding vehicle separate from the annual defence budget. Sizeable real reductions were also seen in Chile (-6.7%), Peru (-5.3%) and Uruguay (-5.7%), where a combination of lower commodity prices, subdued economic activity, public-finance reforms and other fiscal priorities all affected real defence spending.

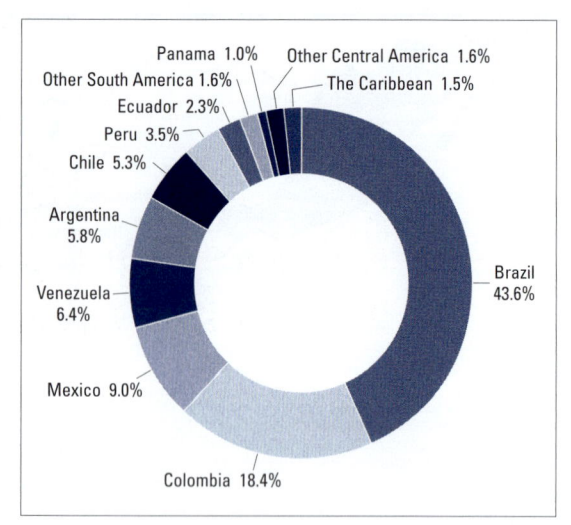

Figure 19 **Latin America & the Caribbean Defence Spending by Country & Sub-Region**

Small real increases in defence spending were seen in Brazil (2%) and Venezuela (2.2%). In Venezuela, this reflected salary increases of between 45% and 60% for officers and enlisted personnel, as well as the issuance of large-scale domestic debt to fund military procurement. The result was that, despite inflation rates in excess of 60%, Venezuela still registered a small increase in real funding in 2014. In keeping with its decisions in recent years, Brazil's government cut the 2014 defence budget from previously allocated levels, as it targeted an overall primary budget surplus of 1.9% of GDP in order to dampen inflationary pressures and bolster its credibility in global financial markets. Mandatory outlays on salaries, pensions and benefits account for around 70–80% of the Brazilian defence budget. These have been ring-fenced, so reductions were primarily imposed on the annual discretionary expenditures on capital items. For example, acquisition funds for army, navy and air-force equipment were, respectively, 56%, 29% and 45% below the levels service chiefs claimed necessary. In the case of the air force, the defence ministry said that shortfalls would not affect its purchase of 36 *Gripen* combat aircraft.

Mexico and many Central American states increased defence spending in 2014, with total sub-regional spending rising by 9.2% in real terms. This continued the trend, seen since 2011, of accelerating real sub-regional outlays, which had previously risen by 6.3% in 2012 and 8.9% in 2013. Overall, real sub-regional spending was more than one-quarter higher (27.8%) than 2010 levels. In 2014 there were double-

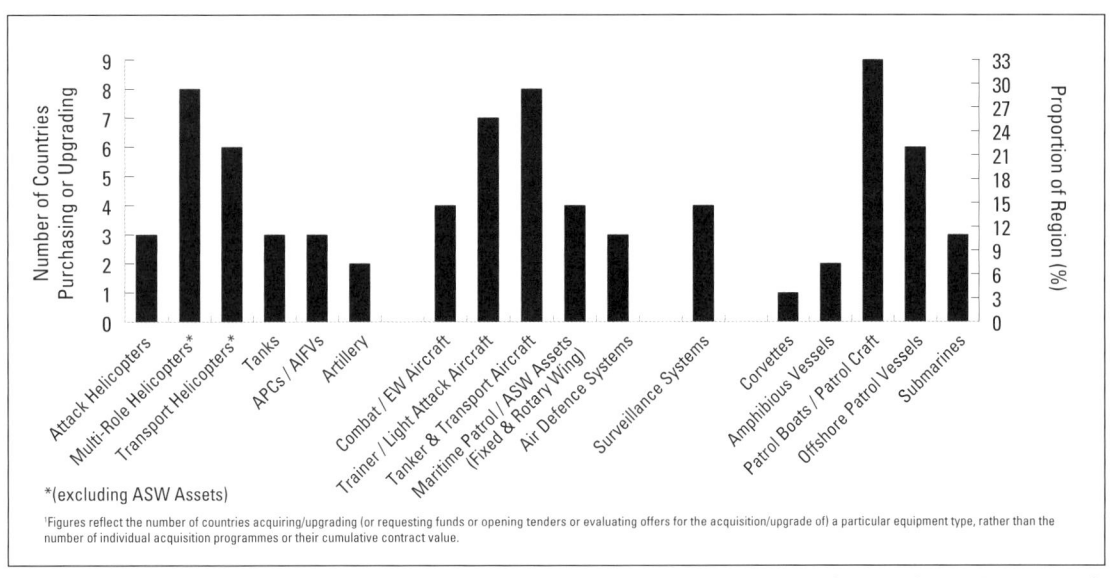

Figure 20 **Latin America & the Caribbean: Selected Procurement & Upgrade Priorities Since 2010**[1]

¹Figures reflect the number of countries acquiring/upgrading (or requesting funds or opening tenders or evaluating offers for the acquisition/upgrade of) a particular equipment type, rather than the number of individual acquisition programmes or their cumulative contract value.

digit real-percentage increases in Mexico (10.1%) and Honduras (20.8%) – with both states increasing procurement, particularly of aviation assets – which offset real declines elsewhere in the sub-region, especially those in El Salvador (-3.9%), Nicaragua (-3.3%) and Guatemala (-2.5%).

BRAZIL

Internal security priorities

Brazil's armed forces continued their internal law-enforcement efforts, exemplified by the March 2014 deployment to reinforce operations in Rio de Janeiro. The army sent 2,050 soldiers to the Maré *favela* complex as part of a wider 'pacification' programme that aimed to enforce state control over slums with high levels of criminality. The mission was due to end by 31 July, but increased attacks led the government to postpone withdrawal. The criminal response was more intense in Maré than in previous operations, and there was a spate of hit-and-run attacks on troops. Five police officers lost their lives in pacification operations during 2014, the highest annual death toll since the programme began in 2007.

Operation *Ágata* 8, the latest in a series of deployments to western border areas, involved 30,000 troops and led to the seizure, in May, of a record 40 tonnes of narcotics in 11 days. But it is unclear what, if any, strategic impact these temporary deployments have had, given Brazil's increased importance as a route for drugs transiting from the Andes region to West Africa. *Ágata* 8 was also shorter than previous operations, perhaps due to the deployment of 59,500 troops to 12 cities in June and July as part of the security operation for the FIFA World Cup. To boost security prior to the tournament, the army acquired RBS 70 man-portable air-defence systems from Saab Dynamics.

The growing role of the armed forces in internal security has caused tension. Residents of Maré protested following a clash with military forces, one week after the start of the deployment. Another crisis erupted when the head of the government's Secretariat for Security of Large Events resigned less than two months before the World Cup was due to begin, in protest at the level of military involvement in the security operation. Despite this, no significant incidents were reported during the tournament, and Minister of Defence Celso Amorim stated afterwards that the main legacy of the event for Brazil's security forces was an improvement in their cooperation with civilian agencies.

Brazil's broader military doctrine and platform capabilities remain geared towards deterring conventional forces. The ongoing programme to build four conventional and one nuclear-powered submarine (PROSUB) is an example of this, as are efforts to develop advanced air capabilities. However, a number of current procurements have been conceived with a view to their potential utility in the fight against organised crime. In March 2014, the first batch of Iveco VBTP-MR *Guarani* armoured personnel carriers delivered to the army was deployed as part of the Maré mission. The navy, meanwhile, received four LPR-40 Mk2 riverine fast patrol boats, built by Colombia's COTECMAR for operations in the western Amazon border region.

Despite new emergency budgetary restrictions in 2014 – including R$3.5bn (US$1.53bn) for the defence ministry – the navy and air force's most ambitious procurements continued (see *The Military Balance 2014*, p. 363). The first boat under the PROSUB programme was scheduled for delivery in 2017, and the navy received the first EC-725 multi-role military helicopter assembled entirely in Brazil, which was developed by Airbus in partnership with Helibras. Although part of the air-force budget allocated to Embraer's KC-390 medium airlifter was withheld during the first half of 2014, some of the withheld funds for the programme were later gradually released. The delay was caused by the defence ministry's efforts to comply with the emergency budgetary restrictions.

Decision reached on FX-2

In December 2013, after several false starts, Brazil finally ended its two-decade-long 'FX-2' requirement for a new multi-role combat aircraft, when the Swedish *Gripen* E/F was chosen over the Boeing F/A-18E/F *Super Hornet* and the Dassault *Rafale*. Following initial evaluations, it was reported that this was the choice of the Brazilian Air Force (FAB), irrespective of announcements by Brazil's politicians – including one by then-president Luiz Inácio Lula da Silva in 2009 – that the *Rafale* was to be selected.

A SEK39.3bn (US$5.9bn, or R$13.4bn) contract for 36 *Gripen* E/Fs was signed on 27 October; the first of these are due to arrive in 2019. With its *Mirage* 2000s already retired, the air force remains interested in an interim combat-aircraft capability, with discussions focused on the provision of around a squadron's-worth of *Gripen* C/Ds in the near term.

The broader implications of the sale are significant for both Sweden and Brazil. It secures the first export customer for the mid-life upgrade of the *Gripen* – the single-seat E and two-seat F models – while also building a closer industrial relationship between Saab and Brazil's Embraer; the bulk of the design work for the *Gripen* F is to be carried out by Embraer in-country. There is also the possibility that more than 36 aircraft will be procured, and that the FAB will buy one or two more batches, eventually holding up to 100 of the type in its inventory. The FAB will be the first air force in the region to field a fighter with an active electronically scanned array radar.

Embraer is broadening its business base in the defence-aerospace market. Alongside the planned *Gripen* assembly, the company is also working towards the first flight of its KC-390 medium airlifter by the end of 2014. A derivative of the *Gripen* E known as *Sea Gripen* could be offered to replace the navy's ageing A-4M *Skyhawks*, while Saab and Embraer are also discussing marketing the upgraded *Gripen* for export.

Gripen will also provide a platform for Brazil's national guided-weapons company, Mectron, which is now part of the country's Odebrecht Group. Brazil is also the first export customer for South Africa's *A-Darter* imaging infrared-guided air-to-air missile, which is jointly funded by the two countries. Production of the missile is due to begin in 2015/16. There are ambitions to follow the development of *A-Darter* with a medium-range active radar-guided missile sometimes referred to as *Marlin*.

COLOMBIA

Defence-policy drivers

Colombia's policymakers face a complex strategic environment characterised by internal security threats and potential external sources of instability. Domestically, the country contends with a combination of threats from guerrilla groups and organised crime, both supported by illegal economies associated with drug trafficking and illegal mining; internationally, it is involved in disputes with Venezuela and Nicaragua regarding land and maritime borders respectively. The political opposition of these neighbouring states to the traditional Bogotá–Washington security alliance also has the potential to complicate their bilateral relationships with Colombia. Internal and external security threats combine in Colombia's border zones, which have been destabilised by the presence of guerrilla groups, organised crime, drug trafficking and smuggling, as well as episodic diplomatic tension with neighbouring states.

Over the past 15 years, Colombia has developed a security policy that has proven successful in reducing internal threats and substantially lowering levels of violence. President Juan Manuel Santos has accelerated efforts to weaken guerrilla groups – including FARC and the National Liberation Army (ELN) – and to disrupt large criminal gangs (*bandas criminales*, or *bacrim*). The government launched the *Operacion Troya* series in 2011, combining activities by the National Police, armed forces and the general prosecutor's office to counter *bacrim*. This helped reduce the number of large criminal groups from seven to three between 2010 and 2014. In parallel, the 'Sword of Honour' plan, launched in 2012, resulted in the death, capture or demobilisation of more than 50 guerrilla leaders, as well as a 20% reduction in FARC troops. Furthermore, efforts continued to dismantle the illicit economies that fed much of the violence. There was a crackdown on illegal mining and, according to the UN, the land occupied by coca fell from 618 square kilometres to 481sq km between 2010 and 2013. This was the strategic environment in which the government announced talks with FARC, in November 2012, to try and reach a demobilisation agreement.

Meanwhile, relations with neighbouring countries have improved. This reduces the likelihood of a security crisis similar to that which occurred in 2008, when Colombian troops entered Ecuador to attack a FARC camp. Bogotá has renewed cooperation with Quito on border security, and maintains a political dialogue with Caracas. Venezuela has even become one of the guarantor countries in the talks with guerrilla groups, but the possibility of a regional security crisis has not disappeared. A 2012 International Court of Justice decision that gave Nicaragua more than 75,000sq km of maritime territory, which Colombia claims as its own, revived the countries' dormant dispute over the area. The political and economic crisis in Venezuela has also created growing instability on the border with Colombia. This has led to an increase in terrorism and criminal activity, including drug trafficking and corruption, which could make the border zone more volatile.

In response to this range of security concerns, Colombia's armed forces have developed structures enabling them to undertake both external-defence and internal-security missions. The post-1990s expansion in resources to combat low-level and asymmetric threats, at the expense of forces and equipment for conventional warfare, has caused Colombia's defence apparatus to grow unevenly – to the point where the armed forces could be considered largely focused on internal-security operations, with a smaller capacity for external-defence tasks. However, such distinctions are sometimes arbitrary. In practice, the army, navy and air force have learnt to use capabilities originally intended for conventional roles in counter-insurgency and anti-drug-trafficking operations: navy frigates support drug interdiction and fighter aircraft conduct close air-support missions against guerrillas. Indeed, the use of conventional capabilities in low-level operations has made it easier to maintain a minimal conventional-deterrent capability without duplication or excessive financial cost.

Armed forces

The army is the largest branch of Colombia's armed forces. Conscripts on a mandatory year of service are assigned to units responsible for territorial control and the protection of economic infrastructure, but offensive capability resides with the professional soldiers grouped into 'mobile brigades'. These light-infantry formations are designed primarily for counter-insurgency operations. A special-forces brigade and a number of commando battalions carry out operations against guerrilla groups and criminal networks, with air mobility provided by the helicopters of the Air Assault Division. As part of an effort to update external defence capabilities, a number of procurement decisions aimed at the conventionally orientated (battalion-sized) cavalry groups and artillery battalions have introduced, among other systems, 155mm howitzers, LAV III armoured personnel carriers and *Guardian* M1117 armoured vehicles. These are deployed to small detachments, providing fire support and protection to light-infantry units in counter-insurgency operations.

Although the navy and the air force are smaller services, their capability for low-level operations and conventional warfare is more balanced. The navy possesses two key organisations for counter-insurgency and counter-narcotics: the Coast Guard, which carries out some maritime-interdiction tasks, and the Marine Corps, which has acquired a broad range of riverine capabilities by sidelining the traditional amphibious-assault role. As a part of the effort to counter drug trafficking by sea, in February 2012 a Naval Task Force was created in Nariño Department, which borders the Pacific Ocean and Ecuador. Meanwhile, a small, conventionally focused navy has at its core four German-made *Almirante Padilla*-class frigates, two *Pijao*-class submarines (German Type-209/1200) and two *Intrepido*-class submarines (German Type-206A), with the fleet boosted by the arrival, in October 2014, of a *Pohang*-class vessel from South Korea, renamed ARC *Nariño*.

The air force maintains a force mix characterised by the need for conventional deterrence as well as the capability to prosecute low-intensity operations.

It fields 21 Israeli-made *Kfir* fighters and a range of assets that provide close air support, including EMB-314 *Super Tucano*s and AH-60L *Arpia* helicopters – a gunship version of the UH-60 *Blackhawk* developed by Colombia. In the medium term, the air force intends to develop conventional capabilities principally by acquiring an integrated air-defence system and a new fighter type. However, these plans are contingent upon the budget.

Bogotá has also shown interest in increasing its unmanned aerial vehicle (UAV) and cyber-defence capabilities. Significant purchases of surveillance-and-reconnaissance UAVs have been reported, including the US-made RQ-11B *Raven* and *Scan Eagle*, and the Israeli *Hermes*-450 and -900. Colombia is building cyber capabilities focused on critical-infrastructure protection. As part of this effort, a Joint Command for Cyber Operations will be set up. This will work alongside the existing Cyber Emergency Response Group of Colombia (COLCERT), which reports to the defence ministry and the National Police's Cyber Center.

While Bogotá maintains a close alliance with Washington, in recent years the US has reduced its military assistance as a result of domestic budgetary restrictions and Colombia's improving security situation. Nonetheless, the US still provides important support in areas such as equipment supply, training and intelligence cooperation. Similarly, the United Kingdom has an active, albeit more discreet, security relationship with Colombia. Beyond such traditional defence partnerships, Colombia has made a systematic effort to internationalise its experience in fighting terrorism and drug trafficking by establishing cooperation agreements that provide training and advice to governments facing similar threats, such as those of Mexico and Paraguay. Likewise, there has been progress in talks with the UN and NATO that might enable the Colombian armed forces and the National Police to take part in international peacekeeping missions.

The future of the Colombian security apparatus will be significantly influenced by the results of the talks with FARC. In principle, the orientation of Colombia's security policy is not covered in the talks. But if an agreement is reached that leads to FARC's demobilisation, the strategic environment will change so fundamentally that a transformation of the security and defence apparatus could be almost unavoidable. With this possibility in mind, there have been discussions over the creation of a new Ministry of Citizen Security, to which the National Police would be transferred. This would have major implications. The defence ministry's control of the National Police is a characteristic of the current Colombian security model that has helped in the development of a unified defence and security strategy, and the rationalisation of defence expenditure, but has nonetheless received some criticism. Another issue to be considered is the possibility of a 'peace dividend': whether an end to the internal conflict might lead to pressure to reduce the defence budget. However, scenarios such as this depend on the progress of talks with the guerrilla groups; the outcome of these remains uncertain.

DEFENCE ECONOMICS

Defence spending

Colombia allocates a higher proportion of national income to defence than any other Latin American state: between 2009 and 2013, this spending ranged between 3.3% and 3.8% of GDP, more than three times the regional average. Defence spending also accounts for a significant share of government expenditure, in 2013 representing 14.3% of total government outlays, more than those for the ministries of education (13.8%) or health (7.7%). However, the official defence budget includes disbursements to the National Police, as well as funds to meet the pension liabilities of the entire security sector (including the armed forces and the National Police). The inclusion of the National Police's funding in the defence-ministry budget is particularly significant, given that its budget exceeds that of the armed services: in 2014, the police received 26.5% of the defence budget (around 1% of GDP), higher than allocations to the army (25.7%), navy (6.7%) or air force (6.3%). Security-sector pensions comprise a significant share of the defence budget, with spending in this area rising rapidly in recent years – by more than 50% between 2008 and 2013 – to around 0.5% of GDP. This upward trend is likely to continue, as an increasing number of personnel are projected to retire in the near future.

In common with much of the region, spending on military personnel accounts for the largest segment of the defence budget, in 2013 representing nearly half (47.1%) of total expenditure. If the part of the budget allocated to pensions (18.6%) is included, total personnel-related expenditure rises to nearly two-thirds (65.7%) of defence outlays. In comparison, military and police operational expenditure accounted for 17.5% of outlays, while expenditure on

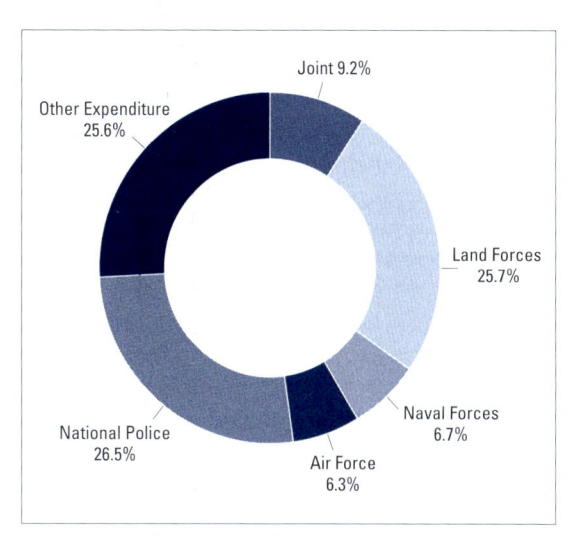

Figure 21 **Colombia Defence Budget Breakdown 2014 (%)**

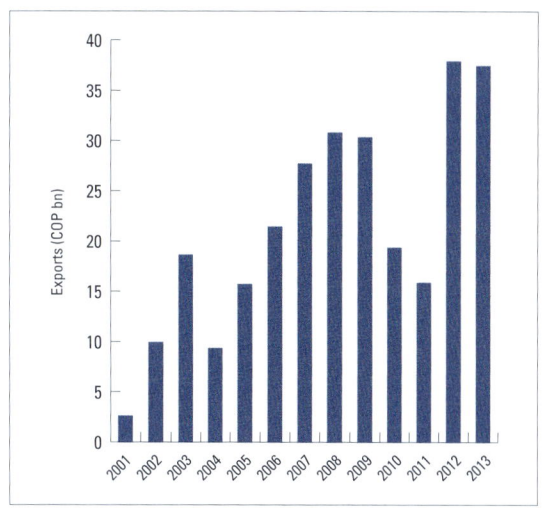

Figure 22 **COTECMAR Defence Exports 2001–13 (COP bn)**

defence-equipment investment was just 9.7%. While these figures reflect a security model that has traditionally relied more on the use of personnel than on technological and materiel investments to confront internal threats, they also point to potential budgetary risks faced by the Colombian defence apparatus. Given current legal limitations on reducing personnel spending, if fiscal difficulties force a reduction in the defence budget, cuts will have to be disproportionately allocated to already-limited levels of investment and operational funding. Such a scenario could lead to a rapid deterioration in military and police capabilities, although robust growth forecasts for the Colombian economy over the next few years militate against this outcome.

Defence industry

Colombia's defence industry has traditionally focused on producing limited numbers of products of low-to-medium complexity. Over the last decade, however, the defence sector has expanded considerably, in terms of both the quality and variety of systems produced. This process of industrial growth has had two key pillars. The first of these is the defence ministry's policy of sourcing equipment domestically (provided that it meets service requirements) before turning to international suppliers, which has supported the development of the national technological base. The second is diversification to civilian economic activity by some defence-equipment companies, which has enabled them to better balance their finances, and to generate additional revenue streams that help sustain investments to develop new military systems.

The defence sector is mainly state-owned, and comprises four key companies. INDUMIL, the oldest and largest defence firm, was created to ensure that Colombia maintained a degree of autonomy in armament production; its military businesses mainly produce light weapons, ammunition and aviation munitions. It also manufactures large volumes of explosives for civilian purposes, such as mining and public-works projects. The second-largest, and most technologically advanced, state company is COTECMAR, which mainly focuses on the design, construction, maintenance and repair of different types of naval vessels, such as the Heavy Riverine Patrol Craft and the *July 20th*-class Ocean Patrol Vessel 80. Through the implementation of the Orion Plan (which involved the upgrade of the country's frigates and submarines), the company augmented its expertise in naval-modernisation programmes. The third key defence firm is CIAC, which specialises in the production and upgrade of military-aviation and related systems. Although small, it has gradually transitioned from basic maintenance and upgrade work to production, constructing aircraft such as the T-90 *Calima*, which is designed for basic training. CIAC also operates a centre for training helicopter pilots that includes a Sikorsky-built simulator for the UH-60 *Blackhawk*. Lastly, newly created firm CODALTEC undertakes military-electronics projects; for example, in 2013 it produced a SIMART UAV flight simulator, and in 2014 a MARKAB armoured-vehicle simulator.

As its domestic defence sector grows in capacity and technological sophistication, Colombia has begun to export some military equipment. INDUMIL and COTECMAR have a larger international presence than other Colombian firms, with the former exporting products worth COP$14.58bn (US$8.1m) in 2012 and just over COP$10bn (US$5.4m) in 2013, while the latter registered its highest level of exports ever (COP$37.93bn, or US$21.1m) in 2012. COTECMAR has also launched a series of international-cooperation initiatives, including projects to develop light coastal-patrol vessels with South Korea's STX and construct riverine-patrol craft with Brazil's EMGEPRON.

The continued expansion of Colombia's defence industry will depend on how well it manages to resolve three key challenges. Firstly, management structures need to be reformed in companies that have grown in size and therefore require stronger institutional arrangements. Secondly, boosting innovation and achieving technological advances will require the creation of favourable conditions for the entry of private domestic, as well as foreign, capital into the sector. Finally, state firms must diversify their sales away from sole reliance on the Colombian armed forces and police for orders, to ensure that any reduction in the defence budget does not also severely weaken the industry.

Antigua and Barbuda ATG

East Caribbean Dollar EC$		2013	2014	2015
GDP	EC$	3.24bn	3.34bn	
	US$	1.2bn	1.24bn	
per capita	US$	13,734	13,994	
Growth	%	1.8	1.9	
Inflation	%	1.1	1.1	
Def bdgt [a]	EC$	70m	74m	
	US$	26m	27m	
US$1=EC$		2.70	2.70	

[a] Budget for the Ministry of National Security & Labour. Includes funds for labour, immigration, passport and citizenship departments, in addition to the prison service, police and Barbuda Defence Force.

Population   91,295

Age	0–14	15–19	20–24	25–29	30–64	65 plus
Male	12.4%	4.5%	3.8%	3.4%	20.1%	3.2%
Female	12.0%	4.5%	4.0%	3.9%	24.2%	4.2%

Capabilities

Internal security and counter-narcotics operations are the main focus for the state's small armed forces. A US Air Force station, operated under a lease agreement between the two governments, provides an extra layer of security, although the C-band radar that was stationed there is relocating to Australia. The armed forces have contributed personnel to peacekeeping operations. The country is a regular host nation for the *Tradewinds* exercise series, including the 2014 iteration, providing training for counter-narcotics, peacekeeping and disaster-response operations.

ACTIVE 180 (Army 130 Navy 50)
(all services form combined Antigua and Barbuda Defence Force)
RESERVE 80 (Joint 80)

ORGANISATIONS BY SERVICE

Army 130

Navy 50
EQUIPMENT BY TYPE
PATROL AND COASTAL COMBATANTS • PB 2: 1 *Dauntless*; 1 *Swift*

Argentina ARG

Argentine Peso P		2013	2014	2015
GDP	P	3.34tr	4.41tr	
	US$	610bn	536bn	
per capita	US$	14,709	12,778	
Growth	%	2.9	-1.7	
Inflation	%	10.6	n/a	
Def bdgt [a]	P	30.5bn	35.1bn	50.3bn
	US$	5.58bn	4.26bn	
US$1=P		5.48	8.23	

[a] Excludes funds allocated to the Ministry of Security.

Population   43,024,374

Age	0–14	15–19	20–24	25–29	30–64	65 plus
Male	12.8%	4.0%	4.0%	3.8%	20.0%	4.7%
Female	12.2%	3.8%	3.8%	3.8%	20.4%	6.7%

Capabilities

Argentina's armed forces remain configured towards conventional state-on-state warfare, though there has also been increased attention to counter-narcotics tasks. A programme to restructure and re-equip the services is under way, though funding has so far been limited. Equipment is ageing and increasingly difficult and expensive to maintain, leading to low availability and often low levels of operational readiness. The air force's *Dagger* fighter aircraft have been in service for over 40 years, though the type has seen limited system upgrades in past decades, however current negotiations with Brazil over a potential deal for 24 *Gripen* NG would, if carried through, provide a significant capability upgrade. Both the air force and army have aspirations to acquire UAVs, while the army wishes to upgrade its armour. Delivery of new logistics vehicles has begun, and the Brazilian *Guarani* is a candidate for some of the light armoured-vehicle requirement. The navy struggles with maintenance, with both its surface fleet and its air component suffering, however a submarine-upgrade programme is in progress. The armed forces have limited capability for power projection, although infantry and rotary-wing units have contributed to UN peacekeeping missions.

ACTIVE 74,400 (Army 42,800 Navy 19,000 Air 12,600) **Paramilitary 31,250**

ORGANISATIONS BY SERVICE

Army 42,800; 7,000 civilian
Regt and gp are usually bn-sized
FORCES BY ROLE
SPECIAL FORCES
  1 SF gp
MANOEUVRE
  Mechanised
  1 (1st) div (1 armd bde (4 tk regt, 1 mech inf regt, 1 SP arty gp, 1 cbt engr bn, 1 int coy, 1 sigs coy, 1 log coy),

1 jungle bde (3 jungle inf regt, 1 arty gp, 1 engr bn, 1 int coy, 1 sigs coy, 1 log coy, 1 med coy), 2 engr bn, 1 sigs bn, 1 log coy)

1 (3rd) div (1 mech bde (1 armd recce regt, 1 tk regt, 2 mech inf regt, 1 SP arty gp, 1 cbt engr bn, 1 int coy, 1 sigs coy, 1 log coy), 1 mech bde (1 armd recce tp, 1 tk regt, 2 mech inf regt, 1 SP arty gp, 1 cbt engr bn, 1 int coy, 1 sigs coy, 1 log coy), 1 int bn, 1 sigs bn, 1 log coy)

1 (Rapid Deployment) force (1 armd bde (1 recce sqn, 3 tk regt, 1 mech inf regt, 1 SP arty gp, 1 cbt engr coy, 1 int coy, 1 sigs coy, 1 log coy), 1 mech bde (1 armd recce regt, 3 mech inf regt, 1 arty gp, 1 cbt engr coy, 1 int coy, 1 sigs coy, 1 log coy), 1 AB bde (1 recce tp, 2 para regt, 1 arty gp, 1 cbt engr coy, 1 sigs coy, 1 log coy), 1 AD gp (2 AD bn))

Light
1 mot cav regt (presidential escort)

Air Manoeuvre
1 air aslt regt

Mountain
1 (2nd) div (2 mtn inf bde (1 armd recce regt, 3 mtn inf regt, 2 arty gp, 1 cbt engr bn, 1 sigs coy, 1 log coy), 1 mtn inf bde (1 armd recce bn, 2 mtn inf regt, 1 jungle inf regt, 2 arty gp, 1 cbt engr bn, 1 sigs coy, 1 construction coy, 1 log coy), 1 AD gp, 1 sigs bn)

Aviation
1 avn gp (bde) (1 avn bn, 1 hel bn)

COMBAT SUPPORT
1 arty gp (bn)
1 engr bn
1 sigs gp (1 EW bn, 1 sigs bn, 1 maint bn)
1 sigs bn
1 sigs coy

COMBAT SERVICE SUPPORT
5 maint bn

EQUIPMENT BY TYPE
MBT 213: 207 TAM, 6 TAM S21
LT TK 123: 112 SK-105A1 *Kuerassier*; 6 SK-105A2 *Kuerassier*; 5 *Patagón*
RECCE 81: 47 AML-90; 34 M1025A2 HMMWV
AIFV 377: 263 VCTP (incl variants); 114 M113A2 (20mm cannon)
APC (T) 294: 70 M113A1-ACAV; 224 M113A2
ARTY 1,117
  SP 155mm 37: 20 Mk F3; 17 VCA 155 *Palmaria*
  TOWED 189: **105mm** 80 M-56 (Oto Melara); **155mm** 109: 25 CITEFA M-77/CITEFA M-81; 84 SOFMA L-33
  MRL 8: **105mm** 4 SLAM *Pampero*; **127mm** 4 CP-30
  MOR 883: **81mm** 492; **120mm** 353 Brandt
    SP 38: 25 M106A2; 13 TAM-VCTM
AT
  MSL • SP 3 HMMWV with TOW-2A
  RCL 150 M-1968
  RL 78mm MARA
AIRCRAFT
  TPT • Light 15: 1 Beech 80 *Queen Air*; 1 C-212-200 *Aviocar*; 3 Cessna 207 *Stationair*; 1 Cessna 500 *Citation* (survey); 2 DHC-6 *Twin Otter*; 3 SA-226 *Merlin* IIIA; 3 SA-226AT *Merlin* IVA; 1 *Sabreliner* 75A (*Gaviao* 75A)
  TRG 5 T-41 *Mescalero*

HELICOPTERS
  MRH 5: 4 SA315B *Lama*; 1 Z-11
  TPT 47: **Medium** 3 AS332B *Super Puma*; **Light** 44: 1 Bell 212; 25 Bell 205 (UH-1H *Iroquois* – 6 armed); 5 Bell 206B3; 13 UH-1H-II *Huey* II
AD
  SAM 6 RBS-70
  GUNS • TOWED 411: **20mm** 230 GAI-B01; **30mm** 21 HS L81; **35mm** 12 GDF Oerlikon (*Skyguard* fire control); **40mm** 148: 24 L/60 training, 40 in store; 76 L/60; 8 L/70
  RADAR • AD RADAR 11: 5 Cardion AN/TPS-44; 6 *Skyguard*
  LAND 18+: M113A1GE *Green Archer* (mor); 18 RATRAS (veh, arty)
ARV Greif

Navy 19,000; 7,200 civilian

Commands: Surface Fleet, Submarines, Naval Avn, Marines

EQUIPMENT BY TYPE
SUBMARINES • TACTICAL • SSK 3:
  1 *Salta* (GER T-209/1200) with 8 single 533mm TT with Mk 37/SST-4 HWT
  2 *Santa Cruz* (GER TR-1700) with 6 single 533mm TT with SST-4 HWT (one undergoing MLU)
PRINCIPAL SURFACE COMBATANTS 11
  DESTROYERS 5
    DDGHM 4 *Almirante Brown* (GER MEKO 360) with 2 quad lnchr with MM-40 *Exocet* AShM, 1 octuple *Albatros* lnchr with *Aspide* SAM, 2 triple B515 ILAS-3 324mm TT with A244 LWT, 1 127mm gun (capacity 1 AS555 *Fennec*/SA316B *Alouette* III hel)
    DDH 1 *Hercules* (UK Type-42 – utilised as a fast troop transport ship), with 1 114mm gun (capacity 1 SH-3H *Sea King* hel)
  FRIGATES • FFGHM 6:
    6 *Espora* (GER MEKO 140) with 2 twin lnchr with MM-38 *Exocet* AShM, 2 triple B515 ILAS-3 324mm ASTT with A244 LWT, 1 76mm gun (capacity either 1 SA319 *Alouette* III hel or 1 AS555 *Fennec* hel)
PATROL AND COASTAL COMBATANTS 17
  CORVETTES • FSG 3 *Drummond* (FRA A-69) with 2 twin lnchr with MM-38 *Exocet* AShM, 2 triple Mk32 324mm ASTT with A244 LWT, 1 100mm gun
  PSO 3:
    2 *Irigoyen* (ex-US *Cherokee*)
    1 *Teniente Olivieri* (ex-US oilfield tug)
  PCO 3:
    2 *Murature* (ex-US *King* – trg/river patrol role) with 3 105mm gun
    1 *Sobral* (ex-US *Sotoyomo*)
  PCGT 1 *Intrepida* (GER Lurssen 45m) with 2 single lnchr with MM-38 *Exocet* AShM, 2 single 533mm TT with SST-4 HWT, 1 76mm gun

PCC 1 *Intrepida* (GER Lurssen 45m) with 1 76mm gun
PB 6: 4 *Baradero* (*Dabur*); 2 *Point*
AMPHIBIOUS 18 **LCVP**
LOGISTICS AND SUPPORT 26
  ABU 3 *Red*
  AFD 1
  AGB 1 *Almirante Irizar* (damaged by fire in 2007; now expected to return to service in 2015)
  AGE 2
  AGHS 1 *Puerto Deseado* (ice-breaking capability, used for polar research)
  AGOR 1 *Commodoro Rivadavia*
  AK 3 *Costa Sur*
  AOR 1 *Patagonia* (FRA *Durance*) with 1 hel platform
  AORL 1 *Ingeniero Julio Krause*
  AXS 1 *Libertad*
  YTB 11

Naval Aviation 2,000
AIRCRAFT 23 combat capable
  FGA 2 *Super Etendard* (9 more in store)
  ATK 1 AU-23 *Turbo Porter*
  ASW 10: 4 S-2T *Tracker*; 6 P-3B *Orion*
  TPT 9: **Light** 7 Beech 200F/M *King Air*; **PAX** 2 F-28 *Fellowship*
  TRG 10 T-34C *Turbo Mentor**
HELICOPTERS
  ASW 6 SH-3H (ASH-3H) *Sea King*
  MRH 4 AS555 *Fennec*
  TPT • **Medium** 4 UH-3H *Sea King*
MSL
  AAM • **IR** R-550 *Magic*
  ASM AS-25K CITEFA *Martin Pescador*‡
  AShM AM-39 *Exocet*

Marines 2,500
FORCES BY ROLE
MANOEUVRE
  Amphibious
  1 (fleet) force (1 cdo gp, 1 (AAV) amph bn, 1 mne bn, 1 arty bn, 1 ADA bn)
  1 (fleet) force (2 mne bn, 2 navy det)
  1 force (1 mne bn)
EQUIPMENT BY TYPE
  RECCE 52: 12 ERC-90F *Sagaie*; 40 M1097 HMMWV
  APC (W) 24 Panhard VCR
  AAV 17: 10 LARC-5; 7 LVTP-7
  ARTY 100
    TOWED 105mm 18: 6 M101; 12 Model 56 pack howitzer
    MOR 82: 70 **81mm**; 12 **120mm**
  AT
    MSL • **MANPATS** 50 *Cobra*/RB-53 *Bantam*
    RCL **105mm** 30 M-1974 FMK-1
    RL **89mm** 60 M-20
  AD
    SAM 6 RBS-70
    GUNS **30mm** 10 HS-816; **35mm** GDF-001
  ARV AAVR 7

Air Force 12,600; 6,900 civilian
4 Major Comds – Air Operations, Personnel, Air Regions, Logistics, 8 air bde

Air Operations Command
FORCES BY ROLE
FIGHTER/GROUND ATTACK
  1 sqn with *Mirage* IIID/E (*Mirage* IIIDA/EA)
  1 sqn with *Nesher* S/T (*Dagger* A/B)
GROUND ATTACK
  2 sqn with A-4/OA-4 (A-4AR/OA-4AR) *Skyhawk*
  2 (tac air) sqn with IA-58 *Pucara*; EMB-312 *Tucano* (on loan for border surv/interdiction)
ISR
  1 sqn with Learjet 35A
SEARCH & RESCUE/TRANSPORT HELICOPTER
  2 sqn with Bell 212; Bell 212 (UH-1N); Mi-171, SA-315B *Lama*
TANKER/TRANSPORT
  1 sqn with C-130B/E/H *Hercules*; KC-130H *Hercules*; L-100-30
TRANSPORT
  1 sqn with B-707
  1 sqn with DHC-6 *Twin Otter*; Saab 340
  1 sqn with F-27 *Friendship*
  1 sqn with F-28 *Fellowship*; Learjet 60
  1 (Pres) flt with B-757-23ER; S-70A *Black Hawk*, S-76B
TRAINING
  1 sqn with AT-63 *Pampa*
  1 sqn with EMB-312 *Tucano*
  1 sqn with Grob 120TP
  1 hel sqn with Hughes 369; SA-315B *Lama*
TRANSPORT HELICOPTER
  1 sqn with Hughes 369; MD-500; MD500D
EQUIPMENT BY TYPE
AIRCRAFT 100 combat capable
  FGA 18: 8 *Mirage* IIID/E (*Mirage* IIIDA/EA); 7 *Nesher* S (*Dagger* A), 3 *Nesher* T (*Dagger* B)
  ATK 62: 30 A-4 (A-4AR) *Skyhawk*; 2 OA-4 (OA-4AR) *Skyhawk*; 21 IA-58 *Pucara*; 9 IA-58M *Pucara*
  ELINT 1 Cessna 210
  TKR 2 KC-130H *Hercules*
  TPT 37: **Medium** 7: 1 C-130B *Hercules*; 1 C-130E *Hercules*; 4 C-130H *Hercules*; 1 L-100-30; **Light** 22: 1 Cessna 310; 8 DHC-6 *Twin Otter*; 4 F-27 *Friendship*; 4 Learjet 35A (test and calibration); 1 Learjet 60; 4 Saab 340; **PAX** 8: 1 B-757-23ER; 7 F-28 *Fellowship*
  TRG 43: 20 AT-63 *Pampa** (LIFT); 19 EMB-312 *Tucano*; 4 Grob 120TP
HELICOPTERS
  MRH 26: 1 Bell 412EP; 15 Hughes 369; 3 MD-500; 4 MD-500D; 3 SA315B *Lama*
  TPT 11 **Medium** 3: 2 Mi-171E; 1 S-70A *Black Hawk*; **Light** 8: 7 Bell 212; 1 S-76B
MSL
  AAM • **IR** AIM-9L *Sidewinder*; R-550 *Magic*; *Shafrir* II‡
AD
  GUNS 88: **20mm**: 86 Oerlikon/Rh-202 with 9 Elta EL/M-2106 radar; **35mm**: 2 Oerlikon GDF-001 with *Skyguard* radar
  RADAR 6: 5 AN/TPS-43; 1 BPS-1000

Paramilitary 31,250

Gendarmerie 18,000
Ministry of Security
FORCES BY ROLE
COMMAND
  5 regional comd
MANOEUVRE
  Other
  16 paramilitary bn
EQUIPMENT BY TYPE
RECCE S52 *Shorland*
APC (W) 87: 47 *Grenadier*; 40 UR-416
ARTY • MOR 81mm
AIRCRAFT
  TPT • **Light** 12: 3 Cessna 152; 3 Cessna 206; 1 Cessna 336; 1 PA-28 *Cherokee*; 2 PC-6B *Turbo Porter*; 2 PC-12
HELICOPTERS
  MRH 2 MD-500C
  TPT • **Light** 16: 5 Bell 205 (UH-1H *Iroquois*); 7 AS350 *Ecureuil*; 1 EC135; 3 R-44 *Raven* II
  TRG 1 S-300C

Prefectura Naval (Coast Guard) 13,250
Ministry of Security
PATROL AND COASTAL COMBATANTS 67
PCO 6: 1 *Delfin*; 5 *Mantilla* (F30 *Halcón* – undergoing modernisation)
PCC 2: 1 *Mandubi*; 1 *Mariano Moreno*
PBF 1 *Surel*
PB 57: 1 *Dorado*; 25 *Estrellemar*; 2 *Lynch* (US *Cape*); 18 *Mar del Plata* (Z-28); 8 Damen Stan 2200; 3 Stan Tender 1750
PBR 1 *Tonina*
LOGISTICS & SUPPORT 19
  AG 2
  ARS 3
  AX 4
  YTL 10
AIRCRAFT
  MP 1 Beech 350ER *King Air*
  TPT • **Light** 6: 5 C-212 *Aviocar*; 1 Beech 350ER *King Air*
  TRG 2 Piper PA-28 *Archer* III
HELICOPTERS
  SAR 3 AS565MA *Panther*
  MRH 1 AS365 *Dauphin 2*
  TPT 4: **Medium** 2 SA330L (AS330L) *Puma*; **Light** 2 AS355 *Ecureuil* II
  TRG 4 S-300C

DEPLOYMENT

CYPRUS
UN • UNFICYP 268; 2 inf coy; 1 hel flt; 2 Bell 212

HAITI
UN • MINUSTAH 555; 1 inf bn; 1 spt coy; 1 fd hospital; 1 hel sqn

MIDDLE EAST
UN • UNTSO 3 obs

WESTERN SAHARA
UN • MINURSO 3 obs

Bahamas BHS

Bahamian Dollar B$		2013	2014	2015
GDP	B$	8.42bn	8.65bn	
	US$	8.42bn	8.65bn	
per capita	US$	23,639	24,014	
Growth	%	0.7	1.2	
Inflation	%	0.4	1.4	
Def exp	B$	64m		
	US$	64m		
Def bdgt	B$	64m	87m	102m
	US$	64m	87m	
US$1=B$		1.00	1.00	

Population 321,834

Age	0–14	15–19	20–24	25–29	30–64	65 plus
Male	11.8%	4.4%	4.5%	3.8%	21.9%	2.7%
Female	11.5%	4.2%	4.3%	3.7%	23.0%	4.3%

Capabilities

The country's defence tasks are focused principally on maritime security, resource protection and counter-narcotics. The Bahamas Defence Force priorities are reflected in the ongoing 'Sandy Bottom' fleet upgrade and expansion project. As part of this, the first of four 42-metre-class vessels was commissioned in June 2014, while four 30-metre-class vessels and a 56m roll-on/roll-off landing craft are also on order. The programme includes naval-infrastructure upgrades. The landing craft will add to the forces' limited amphibious capability, which is supported by an infantry battalion. The country is a regular participant in the *Tradewinds* exercise series.

ACTIVE 1,300

ORGANISATIONS BY SERVICE

Royal Bahamian Defence Force 1,300
FORCES BY ROLE
MANOEUVRE
  Amphibious
  1 mne coy (incl marines with internal and base security duties)
EQUIPMENT BY TYPE
PATROL AND COASTAL COMBATANTS 19 (additional 7+ patrol boats under 10 tonnes)
  PCC 2 *Bahamas*
  PBF 6 *Nor-Tech*
  PB 11: 3 *Arthur Dion Hanna*; 2 *Dauntless*; 1 *Eleuthera*; 1 *Protector*; 2 Sea Ark 12m; 2 Sea Ark 15m
AIRCRAFT • **TPT** • **Light** 3: 1 Beech A350 *King Air*; 1 Cessna 208 *Caravan*; 1 P-68 *Observer*

FOREIGN FORCES

Guyana Navy: Base located at New Providence Island

Barbados BRB

Barbados Dollar B$		2013	2014	2015
GDP	B$	8.46bn	8.56bn	
	US$	4.23bn	4.28bn	
per capita	US$	15,173	15,311	
Growth	%	-0.3	-0.6	
Inflation	%	1.8	1.7	
Def bdgt [a]	B$	70m	67m	
	US$	35m	33m	
US$1=B$		2.00	2.00	

[a] Defence & security expenditure

Population   289,680

Age	0–14	15–19	20–24	25–29	30–64	65 plus
Male	9.2%	3.2%	3.6%	3.5%	24.7%	4.2%
Female	9.2%	3.2%	3.6%	3.5%	25.8%	6.3%

Capabilities

Maritime security and resource protection are key roles for the Barbados Defence Force, the country's coast guard and constabulary-style force. It also has limited ability to participate in regional peacekeeping and disaster relief. The country takes part in the *Tradewinds* exercise series.

ACTIVE 610 (Army 500 Navy 110)

RESERVE 430 (Joint 430)

ORGANISATIONS BY SERVICE

Army 500
FORCES BY ROLE
MANOEUVRE
  Light
  1 inf bn (cadre)

Navy 110
HQ located at HMBS Pelican, Spring Garden
EQUIPMENT BY TYPE
PATROL AND COASTAL COMBATANTS • PB 6:
1 *Dauntless*; 2 *Enterprise* (Damen Stan 1204); 3 *Trident* (Damen Stan 4207)
LOGISTICS & SUPPORT • AX 1

Belize BLZ

Belize Dollar BZ$		2013	2014	2015
GDP	BZ$	3.23bn	3.33bn	
	US$	1.62bn	1.67bn	
per capita	US$	4,619	4,670	
Growth	%	0.7	2.0	
Inflation	%	0.5	1.8	
Def bdgt [a]	BZ$	34m	35m	37m
	US$	17m	18m	
FMA (US)	US$	0.2m	1m	0.8m
US$1=BZ$		2.00	2.00	

[a] Excludes funds allocated to Coast Guard and Police Service

Population   340,844

Age	0–14	15–19	20–24	25–29	30–64	65 plus
Male	18.0%	5.5%	5.1%	4.5%	15.6%	1.7%
Female	17.3%	5.3%	5.0%	4.4%	15.5%	1.9%

Capabilities

Belize has small armed forces, largely built around under-equipped infantry battalions; there is very limited capability to project power. The principal role of the Belize Defence Force is countering narcotics smuggling, although its ability to do so is hampered by insufficient maritime-patrol or aerial-surveillance capacity. Other tasks include territorial defence and support to civil authorities. Maritime operations are based around two interdiction teams, but there is only limited maritime-domain awareness. Although well trained in jungle operations, the relatively small size of the BDF means that its capabilities are limited to countering relatively minor threats.

ACTIVE ε1,050 (Army ε1,050)

RESERVE 700 (Joint 700)

ORGANISATIONS BY SERVICE

Army ε1,050
FORCES BY ROLE
MANOEUVRE
  Light
  3 inf bn (each 3 inf coy)
COMBAT SERVICE SUPPORT
  1 spt gp
EQUIPMENT BY TYPE
MOR 81mm 6
RCL 84mm 8 *Carl Gustav*

Air Wing
EQUIPMENT BY TYPE
AIRCRAFT
  TPT • **Light** 3: 1 BN-2A *Defender*; 1 BN-2B *Defender*; 1 Cessna 182 *Skylane*
  TRG 1 T-67M-200 *Firefly*

Reserve
FORCES BY ROLE
MANOEUVRE
　Light
　　3 inf coy

Paramilitary 150

Coast Guard 150
EQUIPMENT BY TYPE
Approx 20 small craft under 10 tonnes

FOREIGN FORCES
United Kingdom Army 10

Bolivia BOL

Bolivian Boliviano B		2013	2014	2015
GDP	B	211bn	234bn	
	US$	30.8bn	34.1bn	
per capita	US$	2,793	3,031	
Growth	%	6.8	5.2	
Inflation	%	5.7	6.0	
Def bdgt	B	2.56bn	2.78bn	
	US$	373m	405m	
US$1=B			6.86	6.86

Population 10,631,486

Age	0–14	15–19	20–24	25–29	30–64	65 plus
Male	17.0%	5.1%	4.9%	4.5%	15.8%	2.2%
Female	16.3%	5.0%	4.8%	4.5%	17.2%	2.8%

Capabilities

Counter-narcotics and internal and border security are the main tasks of the armed forces, and modest procurement programmes are intended to improve the services' ability to undertake these roles. Though forces have taken part in recent UN peacekeeping missions, there is only limited independent power-projection capacity. The government plans a 30% increase in military personnel to over 38,000, with the army component to help increase the military presence in the provinces. The defence budget is to increase and new infrastructure is to be funded by a hydrocarbon tax. The army and air force are receiving new or upgraded equipment, though in small numbers, with deliveries of some EC145, H425 and *Super Puma* helicopters made in 2014. Tactical airlift is provided by a variety of aircraft, including a handful of C-130 *Hercules*.

ACTIVE 46,100 (Army 34,800 Navy 4,800 Air 6,500)
Paramilitary 37,100
Conscript liability 12 months (18–22 years of age)

ORGANISATIONS BY SERVICE

Army 9,800; 25,000 conscript (total 34,800)

FORCES BY ROLE
COMMAND
　6 mil region HQ
　10 div HQ
SPECIAL FORCES
　3 SF regt
MANOEUVRE
　Reconnaissance
　1 mot cav gp
　Armoured
　1 armd bn
　Mechanised
　1 mech cav regt
　2 mech inf regt
　Light
　1 (aslt) cav gp
　5 (horsed) cav gp
　3 mot inf regt
　21 inf regt
　1 (Presidential Guard) inf regt
　Air Manoeuvre
　2 AB regt (bn)
　Aviation
　2 avn coy
COMBAT SUPPORT
　6 arty regt (bn)
　1 ADA regt
　6 engr bn
　1 int coy
　1 MP bn
　1 sigs bn
COMBAT SERVICE SUPPORT
　2 log bn

EQUIPMENT BY TYPE
LT TK 54: 36 SK-105A1 *Kuerassier*; 18 SK-105A2 *Kuerassier*
RECCE 24 EE-9 *Cascavel*
APC 152+
　APC (T) 87+: 50+ M113, 37 M9 half-track
　APC (W) 61: 24 EE-11 *Urutu*; 22 MOWAG *Roland*; 15 V-100 *Commando*
ARTY 311+
　TOWED 61: **105mm** 25 M101A1; **122mm** 36 M-30 (M-1938)
　MOR 250+: **81mm** 250 M29; Type-W87; **107mm** M30; **120mm** M120
AT
　MSL
　　SP 2 *Koyak* with HJ-8
　　MANPATS HJ-8
　RCL **106mm** M40A1; **90mm** M67
　RL **89mm** 200+ M20
AIRCRAFT
　TPT • Light 4: 1 Fokker F-27-200; 1 Beech 90 *King Air*; 1 C-212 *Aviocar*; 1 Cessna 210 *Centurion*
HELICOPTERS
　MRH 6 H425
　TRG 1 Robinson R55
AD • GUNS • TOWED **37mm** 18 Type-65
ARV 4 4K-4FA-SB20 *Greif*; M578

Navy 4,800

Organised into six naval districts with HQ located at Puerto Guayaramerín.

EQUIPMENT BY TYPE
PATROL AND COASTAL COMBATANTS • PBR 3: 1 *Santa Cruz*; 2 others (additional five patrol boats and 30–40 small craft under 10 tonnes)
LOGISTICS AND SUPPORT 27
  AG 1
  AH 2
  YFL 10 (river transports)
  YTL 14

Marines 1,700 (incl 1,000 Naval Military Police)

FORCES BY ROLE
MANOEUVRE
  Mechanised
    1 mech inf bn
  Amphibious
    6 mne bn (1 in each Naval District)
COMBAT SUPPORT
  4 (naval) MP bn

Air Force 6,500 (incl conscripts)

FORCES BY ROLE
GROUND ATTACK
  2 sqn with AT-33AN *Shooting Star*
  1 sqn with K-8WB *Karakorum*
ISR
  1 sqn with Cessna 206; Cessna 402; Learjet 25B/25D (secondary VIP role)
SEARCH & RESCUE
  1 sqn with AS332B *Super Puma*; AS350B3 *Ecureuil*; EC145
TRANSPORT
  1 sqn with BAe-146-100; CV-580; MA60
  1 (TAB) sqn with C-130A *Hercules*; MD-10-30F
  1 sqn with C-130B/H *Hercules*
  1 sqn with F-27-400M *Troopship*
  1 (VIP) sqn with Beech 90 *King Air*; Beech 200 *King Air*; Beech 1900; *Falcon* 900EX; *Sabreliner* 60
  6 sqn with Cessna 152/206; IAI-201 *Arava*; PA-32 *Saratoga*; PA-34 *Seneca*
TRAINING
  1 sqn with DA40; T-25
  1 sqn with Cessna 152/172
  1 sqn with PC-7 *Turbo Trainer*
  1 hel sqn with R-44 *Raven* II
TRANSPORT HELICOPTER
  1 (anti-drug) sqn with Bell 205 (UH-1H *Iroquois*)
AIR DEFENCE
  1 regt with Oerlikon; Type-65
EQUIPMENT BY TYPE
AIRCRAFT 38 combat capable
  ATK 15 AT-33AN *Shooting Star*
  TPT 85: **Heavy** 1 MD-10-30F; **Medium** 4: 1 C-130A *Hercules*; 2 C-130B *Hercules*; 1 C-130H *Hercules*; **Light** 70: 1 *Aero Commander* 690; 3 Beech 90 *King Air*; 2 Beech 200 *King Air*; 1 Beech 1900; 5 C-212-100; 10 Cessna 152; 2 Cessna 172; 19 Cessna 206; 1 Cessna 402; 1 CV-580; 9 DA40; 3 F-27-400M *Troopship*; 4 IAI-201 *Arava*; 2 Learjet 25B/D; 2 MA60; 1 PA-32 *Saratoga*; 3 PA-34 *Seneca*; 1 *Sabreliner* 60; **PAX** 10: 1 B-727; 3 B-737-200; 5 BAe-146-100; 1 *Falcon* 900EX (VIP)
  TRG 29: 6 K-8W *Karakorum**; 6 T-25; 17 PC-7 *Turbo Trainer**
HELICOPTERS
  MRH 1 SA316 *Alouette* III
  TPT 30 **Medium** 1 AS332B *Super Puma*; **Light** 29: 2 AS350B3 *Ecureuil*; 19 Bell 205 (UH-1H *Iroquois*); 2 EC145; 6 R-44 *Raven* II
AD • GUNS 18+: **20mm** Oerlikon; **37mm** 18 Type-65

Paramilitary 37,100+

National Police 31,100+
FORCES BY ROLE
MANOEUVRE
  Other
    27 frontier sy unit
    9 paramilitary bde
    2 (rapid action) paramilitary regt

Narcotics Police 6,000+
FOE (700) – Special Operations Forces

DEPLOYMENT

CENTRAL AFRICAN REPUBLIC
UN • MINUSCA 3 obs

CÔTE D'IVOIRE
UN • UNOCI 3 obs

DEMOCRATIC REPUBLIC OF THE CONGO
UN • MONUSCO 1; 8 obs

HAITI
UN • MINUSTAH 209; 1 mech inf coy

LIBERIA
UN • UNMIL 1; 2 obs

SOUTH SUDAN
UN • UNMISS 3 obs

SUDAN
UN • UNAMID 2 obs

Brazil BRZ

Brazilian Real R		2013	2014	2015
GDP	R	4.84tr	5.12tr	
	US$	2.25tr	2.24tr	
per capita	US$	11,173	11,067	
Growth	%	2.5	0.3	
Inflation	%	6.2	6.3	
Def bdgt [a]	R	67.8bn	72.9bn	
	US$	31.4bn	31.9bn	
US$1=R		2.16	2.28	

[a] Includes military pensions

Population 202,656,788

Age	0–14	15–19	20–24	25–29	30–64	65 plus
Male	12.1%	4.2%	4.1%	4.3%	21.4%	3.2%
Female	11.6%	4.1%	4.0%	4.2%	22.3%	4.3%

Capabilities

Brazil has the largest defence budget in South America, and is the region's most capable military power. Brasilia continues to develop its armed forces, with ambitions to enhance power-projection capabilities in line with government aspirations to take a more global role, commensurate with Brazil's developing economic strength. Moves to develop its industrial base continue, with additional research and technology funding allocated to the defence-aerospace sector. While internal law and order deployments continue, security of the Amazon region and coastal waters, and assuring territorial integrity, remains a priority. The country's SIVAM border-monitoring system is also now past its initial implementation stage. Substantial recapitalisation of the equipment inventory is required to fully support the ambitions of the National Defence Strategy. Procurement, however, remains patchwork. Brazil purchased *Hermes* UAVs and short-range air-defence systems, in part to meet security requirements for the 2014 World Cup and the 2016 Olympics. The air forces' ageing fighter fleet is to be upgraded with the purchase of 36 *Gripen* fighters, contracted in October 2014, which fulfils the 'FX-2' requirement. Airlift capabilities will be enhanced with the delivery of the KC-390 medium airlifter from domestic manufacturer Embraer. The country's PROSUB submarine-development programme is emblematic of the navy's long-term blue-water ambition. The armed forces participate in domestic and international exercises, and lead the UN peacekeeping mission in Haiti. Brazil is actively developing its cyber-defence capabilities for which the armed forces have the lead. (See pp. 369–70.)

ACTIVE 318,500 (Army 190,000 Navy 59,000 Air 69,500) **Paramilitary 395,000**

Conscript liability 12 months (can go to 18; often waived)

RESERVE 1,340,000

ORGANISATIONS BY SERVICE

Army 120,000; 70,000 conscript (total 190,000)

FORCES BY ROLE
COMMAND
 8 mil comd HQ
 12 mil region HQ
 7 div HQ (2 with regional HQ)
SPECIAL FORCES
 1 SF bde (1 SF bn, 1 cdo bn)
 1 SF coy
MANOEUVRE
 Reconnaissance
 3 mech cav regt
 Armoured
 1 (5th) armd bde (1 mech cav sqn, 2 armd bn, 2 armd inf bn, 1 SP arty bn, 1 engr bn, 1 sigs coy, 1 log bn)
 1 (6th) armd bde (1 mech cav sqn, 2 armd bn, 2 armd inf bn, 1 SP arty bn, 1 AD bty, 1 engr bn, 1 sigs coy, 1 log bn)
 Mechanised
 3 (1st, 2nd & 4th) mech cav bde (1 armd cav bn, 3 mech cav bn, 1 arty bn, 1 engr coy, 1 sigs coy, 1 log bn)
 1 (3rd) mech cav bde (1 armd cav bn, 2 mech cav bn, 1 arty bn, 1 engr coy, 1 sigs coy, 1 log bn)
 1 (15th) mech inf bde (3 mech inf bn, 1 arty bn, 1 engr coy, 1 log bn)
 Light
 1 (3rd) mot inf bde (1 mech cav sqn, 2 mot inf bn, 1 inf bn, 1 arty bn, 1 engr coy, 1 sigs coy, 1 log bn)
 1 (4th) mot inf bde (1 mech cav sqn, 1 mot inf bn, 1 inf bn, 1 mtn inf bn, 1 arty bn, 1 sigs coy, 1 log bn)
 1 (7th) mot inf bde (3 mot inf bn, 1 arty bn)
 1 (8th) mot inf bde (1 mech cav sqn, 3 mot inf bn, 1 arty bn, 1 log bn)
 1 (10th) mot inf bde (1 mech cav sqn, 4 mot inf bn, 1 inf coy, 1 arty bn, 1 engr coy, 1 sigs coy)
 1 (13th) mot inf bde (1 mot inf bn, 2 inf bn, 1 inf coy, 1 arty bn)
 1 (14th) mot inf bde (1 mech cav sqn, 3 inf bn, 1 arty bn)
 1 (11th) lt inf bde (1 mech cav regt, 3 inf bn, 1 arty bn, 1 engr coy, 1 sigs coy, 1 MP coy, 1 log bn)
 11 inf bn
 Air Manoeuvre
 1 AB bde (1 cav sqn, 3 AB bn, 1 arty bn, 1 engr coy, 1 sigs coy, 1 log bn)
 1 (12th) air mob bde (1 cav sqn, 3 air mob bn, 1 arty bn, 1 engr coy, 1 sigs coy, 1 log bn)
 Jungle
 1 (1st) jungle inf bde (1 mech cav sqn, 2 jungle inf bn, 1 arty bn)
 3 (2nd, 16th & 17th) jungle inf bde (3 jungle inf bn)
 1 (23rd) jungle inf bde (1 cav sqn, 4 jungle inf bn, 1 arty bn, 1 sigs coy, 1 log bn)
 2 jungle inf bn
 Other
 1 (9th) mot trg bde (3 mot inf bn, 1 arty bn, 1 log bn)
 1 (18th) sy bde (2 sy bn, 2 sy coy)
 1 sy bn
 7 sy coy

3 gd cav regt
1 gd inf bn
Aviation
1 avn bde (3 hel bn, 1 maint bn)
1 hel bn
COMBAT SUPPORT
3 SP arty bn
6 fd arty bn
1 MRL bn
1 ADA bde (5 ADA bn)
6 engr bn
1 EW coy
1 int coy
6 MP bn
3 MP coy
4 sigs bn
2 sigs coy
COMBAT SERVICE SUPPORT
1 engr gp (1 engr bn, 4 construction bn)
1 engr gp (4 construction bn, 1 construction coy)
2 construction bn
5 log bn
1 tpt bn
4 spt bn
EQUIPMENT BY TYPE
MBT 393: 128 *Leopard* 1A1BE; 220 *Leopard* 1A5BR; 45 M60A3/TTS
LT TK 152 M41B/C
RECCE 408 EE-9 *Cascavel*
APC 907
  APC (T) 584 M113
  APC (W) 323: 223 EE-11 *Urutu*; 100 VBTP-MR *Guarani*
ARTY 1,811
  SP 109: **105mm** 72 M7/108; **155mm** 37 M109A3
  TOWED 431
    105mm 336: 233 M101/M102; 40 L-118 Light Gun; 63 Model 56 pack howitzer
    155mm 95 M114
  MRL **127mm** 26: 20 ASTROS II Mk3; 6 ASTROS II Mk6
  MOR 1,245: **81mm** 1,168: 453 Royal Ordnance L-16, 715 M936 AGR; **120mm** 77 M2
AT
  MSL • MANPATS *Eryx*; *Milan*; MSS-1.2 AC
  RCL 343: **106mm** 194 M40A1; **84mm** 149 *Carl Gustav*
HELICOPTERS
  MRH 49: 32 AS565 *Panther* (HM-1); 17 AS550U2 *Fennec* (HA-1 – armed)
  TPT 31: **Heavy** 4 EC725 *Super Cougar* (HM-4); **Medium** 12: 8 AS532 *Cougar* (HM-3); 4 S-70A-36 *Black Hawk* (HM-2); **Light** 15 AS350L1 *Ecureuil* (HA-1)
AD
  SAM • MANPAD 9K38 *Igla* (SA-18 *Grouse*)
  GUNS 76:
    SP **35mm** 10 *Gepard* 1A2
    TOWED 66 **35mm** 39 GDF-001 towed (some with *Super Fledermaus* radar); **40mm** 27 L/70 (some with BOFI)
RADAR: 5 SABER M60
AEV 4+: *Greif*; HART; 4+ *Leopard* 1; M578
ARV *Leopard* 1
VLB 4+: XLP-10; 4 *Leopard* 1

Navy 59,000
FORCES BY ROLE
Organised into 9 districts with HQ I Rio de Janeiro, HQ II Salvador, HQ III Natal, HQ IV Belém, HQ V Rio Grande, HQ VI Ladario, HQ VII Brasilia, HQ VIII Sao Paulo, HQ IX Manaus.
EQUIPMENT BY TYPE
SUBMARINES • TACTICAL • SSK 5:
  4 *Tupi* (GER T-209/1400) with 8 single 533mm TT with Mk48 HWT
  1 *Tikuna* with 8 single 533mm TT with Mk48 HWT
PRINCIPAL SURFACE COMBATANTS 15
  AIRCRAFT CARRIERS • CV 1:
    1 *Sao Paulo* (FRA *Clemenceau*) with 2 sextuple *Sadral* lnchr with *Mistral* SAM (capacity 15–18 A-4 *Skyhawk* atk ac; 4–6 SH-3D/A *Sea King*/S-70B *Seahawk* ASW hel; 3 AS355/AS350 *Ecureuil* hel; 2 AS532 *Cougar* hel)
  DESTROYERS • DDGHM 3:
    3 *Greenhalgh* (UK *Broadsword*, 1 low readiness) with 4 single lnchr with MM-40 *Exocet* Block II AShM, 2 sextuple lnchr with *Sea Wolf* SAM, 6 single STWS Mk2 324mm ASTT with Mk 46 LWT (capacity 2 *Super Lynx* Mk21A hel)
  FRIGATES 11
    FFGHM 6 *Niteroi* with 2 twin lnchr with MM-40 *Exocet* Block II AShM, 1 octuple *Albatros* lnchr with *Aspide* SAM, 2 triple Mk32 324mm ASTT with Mk 46 LWT, 1 twin 375mm A/S mor, 2 *Sea Trinity* Mk3 CIWS, 1 115mm gun (capacity 1 *Super Lynx* Mk21A hel)
    FFGH 5:
      4 *Inhauma* with 2 twin lnchr with MM-40 *Exocet* Block II AShM, 2 triple Mk32 324mm ASTT with Mk 46 LWT, 1 115mm gun (1 *Super Lynx* Mk21A hel)
      1 *Barroso* with 2 twin lnchr with MM-40 *Exocet* Block II AShM, 2 triple 324mm ASTT with Mk 46 LWT, 1 *Sea Trinity* CIWS, 1 115mm gun (capacity 1 *Super Lynx* Mk21A hel)
PATROL AND COASTAL COMBATANTS 50
  PSO 3 *Amazonas*
  PCO 7: 4 *Bracui* (UK *River*); 2 *Imperial Marinheiro* with 1 76mm gun; 1 *Parnaiba* with 1 hel landing platform
  PCC 3 *Macaé*
  PCR 5: 2 *Pedro Teixeira*; 3 *Roraima*
  PB 28: 12 *Grajau*; 6 *Marlim*; 6 *Piratini* (US PGM); 4 *Tracker* (Marine Police)
  PBR 4 LPR-40
MINE WARFARE • MINE COUNTERMEASURES •
MSC 6 *Aratu* (GER *Schutze*)
AMPHIBIOUS
  PRINCIPAL AMPHIBIOUS SHIPS • LSD 1:
    1 *Ceara* (US *Thomaston*) with 3 twin 76mm guns (capacity either 21 LCM or 6 LCU; 345 troops)
  LANDING SHIPS 3
    LST 1 *Mattoso Maia* (US *Newport*) with 1 *Phalanx* CIWS (capacity 3 LCVP; 1 LCPL; 400 troops)
    LSLH 2: 1 *Garcia D'Avila* (UK *Sir Galahad*) (capacity 1 hel; 16 MBT; 340 troops); 1 *Almirante Saboia* (UK *Sir Bedivere*) (capacity 1 med hel; 18 MBT; 340 troops)
  LANDING CRAFT 32: 3 **LCU**; 8 **LCVP**; 21 **LCM**

LOGISTICS AND SUPPORT 97+
   ABU 35+: 4 *Comandante Varella*; 1 *Faroleiro Mario Seixas*; 30+ others
   ABUH 1 *Almirante Graca Aranah* (lighthouse tender)
   AFD 4
   AG 1 *Potengi*
   AGHS 4 *Rio Tocantin*
   AGOB 2: 1 *Ary Rongel* with 1 hel landing platform; 1 *Almirante Maximiano* (capacity 2 AS350/AS355 *Ecureuil* hel)
   AGS 6: 1 *Aspirante Moura*; 1 *Cruzeiro do Sul*; 1 *Antares*; 3 *Amorim Do Valle* (ex-UK *Rover*)
   AGSC 4
   AGSH 1 *Sirius*
   AH 5: 2 *Oswaldo Cruz* with 1 hel landing platform; 1 *Dr Montenegro*; 1 *Tenente Maximianol* with 1 hel landing platform; 1 *Soares de Meirelles*
   AK 5
   AOR 2: 1 *Gastao Motta*; 1 *Marajo*
   AP 7: 1 *Paraguassu*; 1 *Piraim*; 1 *Para* (all river transports); 4 *Rio Pardo*
   ASR 1 *Felinto Perry* (NOR *Wildrake*) with 1 hel landing platform
   ATF 5: 3 *Tritao*; 2 *Almirante Guihem*
   AX 1 *Brasil* with 1 hel landing platform
   AXL 3 *Nascimento*
   AXS 1 *Cisne Barco*
   YTB 8
   YPT 1

Naval Aviation 2,500
FORCES BY ROLE
GROUND ATTACK
   1 sqn with A-4/4M (AF-1) *Skyhawk*; TA-4/4M (AF-1A) *Skyhawk*
ANTI SURFACE WARFARE
   1 sqn with *Super Lynx* Mk21A
ANTI SUBMARINE WARFARE
   1 sqn with SH-3G/H *Sea King*; S-70B *Seahawk* (MH-16)
TRAINING
   1 sqn with Bell 206B3 *Jet Ranger* III
TRANSPORT HELICOPTER
   1 sqn with AS332 *Super Puma*; AS532 *Cougar*
   4 sqn with AS350 *Ecureuil* (armed); AS355 *Ecureuil* II (armed)
EQUIPMENT BY TYPE
AIRCRAFT 12 combat capable
   ATK 12: 9 A-4/4M (AF-1/1B) *Skyhawk*; 3 TA-4/4M (AF-1A) *Skyhawk*
HELICOPTERS
   ASW 20: 12 *Super Lynx* Mk21A; 4 SH-3G/H *Sea King* (being withdrawn); 4 S-70B *Seahawk* (MH-16)
   TPT 49: **Heavy** 4 EC725 *Super Cougar* (UH-15); **Medium** 7: 5 AS332 *Super Puma*; 2 AS532 *Cougar* (UH-14); **Light** 38: 15 AS350 *Ecureuil* (armed); 8 AS355 *Ecureuil* II (armed); 15 Bell 206B3 *Jet Ranger* III (IH-6B)
MSL • AShM: AM-39 *Exocet*; *Sea Skua*; AGM-119 *Penguin* (on order)

Marines 15,000
FORCES BY ROLE
SPECIAL FORCES
   1 SF bn
MANOEUVRE
   Amphibious
   1 amph div (1 lt armd bn, 3 mne bn, 1 arty bn)
   1 amph aslt bn
   7 (regional) mne gp
   1 rvn bn
COMBAT SUPPORT
   1 engr bn
COMBAT SERVICE SUPPORT
   1 log bn
EQUIPMENT BY TYPE
LT TK 18 SK-105 *Kuerassier*
APC 60
   APC (T) 30 M113A1 (incl variants)
   APC (W) 30 *Piranha* IIIC
AAV 25: 13 AAV-7A1; 12 LVTP-7
ARTY 59
   TOWED 41: **105mm** 33: 18 L118 Light Gun; 15 M101; **155mm** 8 M114
   MOR 81mm 18 M29
AT
   MSL • MANPATS RB-56 *Bill*; MSS-1.2 AC
   RL 89mm M20
AD • GUNS 40mm 6 L/70 (with BOFI)
AEV 1 AAVR7

Air Force 69,500
Brazilian air space is divided into 7 air regions, each of which is responsible for its designated air bases. Air assets are divided among four designated air forces (I, II, III & V) for operations (IV Air Force temporarily deactivated).
FORCES BY ROLE
FIGHTER
   4 sqn with F-5EM/FM *Tiger* II
FIGHTER/GROUND ATTACK
   2 sqn with AMX (A-1A/B)
GROUND ATTACK/ISR
   4 sqn with EMB-314 *Super Tucano* (A-29A/B)*
MARITIME PATROL
   1 sqn with P-3AM *Orion*
   2 sqn with EMB-111 (P-95A/P-95B)
ISR
   1 sqn with AMX-R (RA-1)*
   1 sqn with Learjet 35 (R-35A); EMB-110B (R-95)
AIRBORNE EARLY WARNING & CONTROL
   1 sqn with EMB-145RS (R-99); EMB-145SA (E-99)
TANKER/TRANSPORT
   1 sqn with C-130H/KC-130H *Hercules*
TRANSPORT
   1 VIP sqn with A319 (VC-1A); EMB-190 (VC-2); AS332M *Super Puma* (VH-34); AS355 *Ecureuil* II (VH-55); EC635 (VH-35)
   1 VIP sqn with EMB-135BJ (VC-99B); ERJ-135LR (VC-99C); ERJ-145LR (VC-99A); Learjet 35A (VU-35); Learjet 55C (VU-55C)

2 sqn with C-130E/H *Hercules*
2 sqn with C-295M (C-105A)
7 (regional) sqn with Cessna 208/208B (C-98); Cessna 208-G1000 (C-98A); EMB-110 (C-95); EMB-120 (C-97)
1 sqn with ERJ-145 (C-99A)
1 sqn with EMB-120RT (VC-97), EMB-121 (VU-9)

TRAINING
1 sqn with EMB-110 (C-95)
2 sqn with EMB-312 *Tucano* (T-27) (incl 1 air show sqn)
1 sqn with T-25A/C

ATTACK HELICOPTER
1 sqn with Mi-35M *Hind* (AH-2)

TRANSPORT HELICOPTER
1 sqn with AS332M *Super Puma* (H-34)
1 sqn with AS350B *Ecureuil* (H-50); AS355 *Ecureuil* II (H-55)
1 sqn with Bell 205 (H-1H); EC725 *Super Cougar* (H-36)
2 sqn with UH-60L *Black Hawk* (H-60L)

ISR UAV
1 sqn with *Hermes* 450/900

EQUIPMENT BY TYPE
AIRCRAFT 221 combat aircraft
FTR 57: 6 F-5E *Tiger* II; 51 F-5EM/FM *Tiger* II
FGA 49: 38 AMX (A-1); 11 AMX-T (A-1B)
ASW 9 P-3AM *Orion*
MP 19: 10 EMB-111 (P-95A *Bandeirulha*)*; 9 EMB-111 (P-95B *Bandeirulha*)*
ISR: 8: 4 AMX-R (RA-1)*; 4 EMB-110B (R-95)
ELINT 6: 3 EMB-145RS (R-99); 3 Learjet 35A (R-35A)
AEW&C 5 EMB-145SA (E-99)
SAR 5: 4 EMB-110 (SC-95B), 1 SC-130E *Hercules*
TKR/TPT 2 KC-130H
TPT 200: **Medium** 20: 4 C-130E *Hercules*; 16 C-130H *Hercules*; **Light** 172: 12 C-295M (C-105A); 7 Cessna 208 (C-98); 9 Cessna 208B (C-98); 13 Cessna 208-G1000 (C-98A); 53 EMB-110 (C-95A/B/C/M); 16 EMB-120 (C-97); 4 EMB-120RT (VC-97); 5 EMB-121 (VU-9); 7 EMB-135BJ (VC-99B); 3 EMB-201R *Ipanema* (G-19); 2 EMB-202A *Ipanema* (G-19A); 2 ERJ-135LR (VC-99C); 7 ERJ-145 (C-99A); 1 ERJ-145LR (VC-99A); 9 Learjet 35A (VU-35); 1 Learjet 55C (VU-55); 9 PA-34 *Seneca* (U-7); 12 U-42 *Regente*; **PAX** 8: 1 A319 (VC-1A); 3 EMB-190 (VC-2); 4 Hawker 800XP (EU-93A – calibration)
TRG 265: 101 EMB-312 *Tucano* (T-27); 39 EMB-314 *Super Tucano* (A-29A)*; 44 EMB-314 *Super Tucano* (A-29B)*; 81 T-25A/C

HELICOPTERS
ATK 9 Mi-35M *Hind* (AH-2)
TPT 86: **Heavy** 6 EC725 *Super Cougar* (4 H-36 & 2 VH-36); **Medium** 26: 10 AS332M *Super Puma* (H-34/VH-34); 16 UH-60L *Black Hawk* (H-60L); **Light** 54: 24 AS350B *Ecureuil* (H-50); 4 AS355 *Ecureuil* II (H-55/VH-55); 24 Bell 205 (H-1H); 2 EC635 (VH-35)
UAV • ISR • **Medium** 5: 4 *Hermes* 450; 1 *Hermes* 900
MSL • AAM • IR MAA-1 *Piranha*; *Magic* 2; *Python* III; IIR *Python* IV; SARH Super 530F; ARH *Derby*
ARM MAR-1 (in development)

Paramilitary 395,000 opcon Army

Public Security Forces 395,000

State police organisation technically under army control. However, military control is reducing, with authority reverting to individual states.

EQUIPMENT BY TYPE
UAV • ISR • **Heavy** 3 *Heron* (deployed by Federal Police for Amazon and border patrols)

Cyber

Cyber was a key component of the 2008 National Defence Strategy and the July 2012 Defence White Paper. The Federal Police, focused on internal law enforcement, has opened a 24-hour cyber-crime monitoring centre. In 2011, the army inaugurated Brazil's cyber-defence centre (CDCiber) to coordinate the existing activities of the army, navy and air force. In February 2012, Brazil's military cyber chief said that the country only had a 'minimum' level of preparedness to defend against theft and large-scale cyber attacks, such as a large cyber attack on government websites in June 2011, but he hoped a new anti-virus system and cyber-attack simulator, bought in January 2012, would improve readiness. A late 2013 contract for a strategic-communications satellite intended to enhance government communications security was, analysts believed, driven by recent allegations of cyber exploitation of Brazilian systems.

DEPLOYMENT

CÔTE D'IVOIRE
UN • UNOCI 3; 4 obs

CYPRUS
UN • UNFICYP 1

DEMOCRATIC REPUBLIC OF THE CONGO
UN • MONUSCO 7; 1 obs

HAITI
UN • MINUSTAH 1,359; 1 inf bn; 1 engr coy

LEBANON
UN • UNIFIL 267; 1 FFGHM

LIBERIA
UN • UNMIL 2; 2 obs

SOUTH SUDAN
UN • UNMISS 3; 4 obs

SUDAN
UN • UNISFA 2; 2 obs

WESTERN SAHARA
UN • MINURSO 8 obs

Chile CHL

Chilean Peso pCh		2013	2014	2015
GDP	pCh	137tr	147tr	
	US$	277bn	264bn	
per capita	US$	15,776	14,911	
Growth	%	4.2	2.0	
Inflation	%	1.8	4.4	
Def bdgt [a]	pCh	2.2tr	2.16tr	
	US$	4.44bn	3.88bn	
US$1=pCh		495.31	556.53	

[a] Includes military pensions

Population   17,363,894

Age	0–14	15–19	20–24	25–29	30–64	65 plus
Male	10.6%	4.0%	4.3%	4.0%	22.1%	4.2%
Female	10.1%	3.8%	4.1%	3.9%	23.0%	5.8%

Capabilities

Assuring sovereignty, territorial integrity and internal security are core roles for the armed forces though the services also have an important disaster-relief role. The army has shifted to a brigade structure with an increased emphasis on mobility. Its heavy-armour inventory is unusual in regional armed forces. This includes second-hand *Leopard* 2 tanks and *Marder* IFVs. The country has an amphibious-assault capability built around its marine corps. Second-hand purchases have also been used to revamp the navy's frigate inventory over the past ten years, and new offshore-patrol vessels and maritime-patrol aircraft are being procured to bolster littoral and blue-water surveillance capabilities. Though the air force has a modest tactical-airlift fleet, its operational reach has been improved by the acquisition of three KC-135 tanker aircraft. A mix of surplus and new-build F-16s has been acquired since 2005 to improve the air force's combat-aircraft fleet, and in 2013 tenders were opened for attack and transport helicopters. Replacing the air force's ageing jet trainers is also increasingly pressing. Slower economic growth, however, will likely affect the progress of some plans. The armed forces train regularly on a national basis, and also participate routinely in exercises with international and regional partners. The country also has a significant interest in Antarctic security.

ACTIVE 61,400 (Army 34,650 Navy 18,700 Air 8,050)
Paramilitary 44,700
Conscript liability Army 1 year; Navy 21 months; Air Force 18 months. Legally, conscription can last for 2 years

RESERVE 40,000 (Army 40,000)

ORGANISATIONS BY SERVICE

Space
EQUIPMENT BY TYPE
SATELLITES
  ISR 1 SSOT (Sistema Satelital del la Observación del la Tierra)

Army 34,650
6 military administrative regions.
FORCES BY ROLE
Currently being reorganised into 4 armd, 2 mot, 2 mtn and 1 SF brigade. Standard regt/gp are single bn strength, reinforced regt comprise multiple bn.
COMMAND
  6 div HQ
SPECIAL FORCES
  1 SF bde (1 SF bn, 1 (mtn) SF gp, 1 para bn, 1 cdo coy, 1 log coy)
  2 cdo coy
MANOEUVRE
  Reconnaissance
  1 armd recce pl
  3 cav sqn
  4 recce pl
  Armoured
  3 (1st, 2nd & 3rd) armd bde (1 armd recce pl, 1 armd cav gp, 1 mech inf bn, 1 arty gp, 1 AT coy, 1 engr coy, 1 sigs coy)
  1 (4th) armd bde (1 armd recce pl, 1 armd cav gp, 1 mech inf bn, 1 arty gp, 1 engr coy)
  Mechanised
  1 (1st) mech inf regt
  Light
  1 (1st) reinforced regt (1 mot inf bn, 1 arty gp, 2 AT coy, 1 engr bn)
  1 (4th) reinforced regt (1 mot inf bn, 1 MRL gp, 1 mor coy, 1 AT coy, 1 engr bn)
  1 (5th) reinforced regt (1 armd cav gp, 1 mech inf coy, 1 arty gp, 1 engr coy)
  1 (7th) reinforced regt (1 mot inf bn, 1 arty gp, 1 sigs coy)
  1 (10th) reinforced regt (1 mot inf bn, 1 AT coy, 1 engr bn, 1 sigs bn)
  2 (11th & 24th) reinforced mot inf regt (1 mot inf bn, 1 arty gp, 1 AT coy)
  1 (14th) reinforced mot inf regt (1 mot inf bn, 1 sigs coy, 1 AT coy)
  7 mot inf regt
  Mountain
  1 (3rd) reinforced mtn regt (1 mtn inf bn, 1 arty gp, 1 engr coy)
  1 (9th) reinforced mtn regt (1 mtn inf bn, 1 engr bn)
  1 (17th) reinforced mtn regt (1 mtn inf bn, 1 engr coy)
  2 mtn inf regt
  Aviation
  1 avn bde (1 tpt avn bn, 1 hel bn, 1 maint bn, 1 spt bn, 1 log coy)
COMBAT SUPPORT
  3 arty regt
  1 engr regt
  2 sigs regt
  1 int regt
  1 MP bn
COMBAT SERVICE SUPPORT
  1 log div (2 log regt)
  4 log regt
  6 log coy
  1 maint div (1 maint regt)

EQUIPMENT BY TYPE
MBT 245: 114 *Leopard* 1; 131 *Leopard* 2A4
AIFV 191: 173 *Marder*; 18 YPR-765
APC 538
  APC (T) 359 M113A1/A2
  APC (W) 179 Cardoen *Piranha*
ARTY 1,379
  SP 155mm 36: 24 M109A3; 12 M109A5+
  TOWED 233: 105mm 193: 89 M101; 104 Mod 56; 155mm 40 M-68
  MRL 160mm 12 LAR-160
  MOR 1,098:
    81mm 744: 303 ECIA L65/81; 175 FAMAE; 266 Soltam;
    120mm 282: 173 ECIA L65/120; 16 FAMAE; 93 Soltam M-65
    SP 120mm 72: 36 FAMAE (on *Piranha* 6x6); 36 Soltam (on M113A2)
AT
  MSL • MANPATS *Spike*
  RCL 84mm *Carl Gustav*; 106mm M40A1
AIRCRAFT
  TPT 10: Light 8: 2 C-212-300 *Aviocar*; 3 Cessna 208 *Caravan*; 3 CN-235; PAX 2: 1 Cessna 680 *Sovereign*; 1 Cessna 650 *Citation* III
HELICOPTERS
  ISR 9 MD-530F *Lifter* (armed)
  TPT 18: Medium 13: 8 AS532AL *Cougar*; 1 AS532ALe *Cougar*; 4 SA330 *Puma*; Light 5: 4 AS350B3 *Ecureuil*; 1 AS355F *Ecureuil* II
AD
  SAM • MANPAD *Mistral*
  GUNS 41:
    SP 20mm 16 *Piranha*/TCM-20
    TOWED 20mm 25 M167 *Vulcan*
AEV 8 *Leopard* 1
ARV 21 *Leopard* 1
VLB 13 *Leopard* 1
MW 3 *Leopard* 1

Navy 18,700

5 Naval Zones; 1st Naval Zone and main HQ at Valparaiso; 2nd Naval Zone at Talcahuano; 3rd Naval Zone at Punta Arenas; 4th Naval Zone at Iquique; 5th Naval Zone at Puerto Montt.

EQUIPMENT BY TYPE
SUBMARINES • TACTICAL • SSK 4:
  2 *O'Higgins* (*Scorpene*) with 6 single 533mm TT with A-184 *Black Shark* HWT/SUT HWT/SM-39 *Exocet* Block II AShM (1 currently in repair)
  2 *Thompson* (GER T-209/1300) with 8 single 533mm TT A-184 *Black Shark* HWT/SUT HWT/SM-39 *Exocet* Block II AShM
PRINCIPAL SURFACE COMBATANTS 8
  DESTROYERS • DDGHM 1 *Almirante Williams* (UK Type-22) with 2 quad Mk141 lnchr with RGM-84 *Harpoon* AShM, 2 octuple VLS with *Barak* SAM; 2 triple 324mm ASTT with Mk46 LWT, 1 76mm gun (capacity 1 AS-532SC *Cougar*)

FRIGATES 7:
  FFGHM 5:
    3 *Almirante Cochrane* (UK *Duke*-class Type-23) with 2 quad Mk141 lnchr with RGM-84C *Harpoon* AShM, 1 32-cell VLS with *Sea Wolf* SAM, 2 twin 324mm ASTT with Mk46 Mod 2 LWT, 1 114mm gun (capacity 1 AS-532SC *Cougar*)
    2 *Almirante Riveros* (NLD *Karel Doorman*-class) with 2 twin lnchr with RGM-84 *Harpoon* AShM, 1 octuple Mk48 lnchr with RIM-7P *Sea Sparrow* SAM, 4 single Mk32 Mod 9 324mm ASTT with Mk46 Mod 5 HWT, 1 76mm gun (capacity 1 AS532SC *Cougar*)
  FFGM 2:
    2 *Almirante Lattore* (NLD *Jacob Van Heemskerck*-class) with 2 twin Mk141 lnchr with RGM-84 *Harpoon* AShM, 1 Mk13 GMLS with SM-1MR SAM, 1 octuple Mk48 lnchr with RIM-7P *Sea Sparrow* SAM, 2 twin Mk32 324mm ASTT with Mk46 LWT, 1 *Goalkeeper* CIWS
PATROL AND COASTAL COMBATANTS 11
  PCG 5:
    3 *Casma* (ISR *Sa'ar* 4) with 4 GI *Gabriel* I AShM, 2 76mm guns
    2 *Tiger* (GER Type-148) with 4 single lnchr with MM-38 *Exocet* AShM, 1 76mm gun
  PCO 6 *Micalvi*
AMPHIBIOUS
  PRINCIPAL AMPHIBIOUS SHIPS
    LPD 1 *Sargento Aldea* (FRA *Foudre*) with 3 twin *Simbad* lnchr with *Mistral* SAM
  LANDING SHIPS 3
    LSM 1 *Elicura*
    LST 2 *Maipo* (FRA *Batral* – capacity 7 tanks; 140 troops)
  LANDING CRAFT 3
    LCT 1 CDIC (for use in *Sargento Aldea*)
    LCM 2 (for use in *Sargento Aldea*)
LOGISTICS AND SUPPORT 18
  ABU 1 *George Slight Marshall* with 1 hel landing platform
  AFD 3
  AGOR 1 *Cabo de Hornos*
  AGP 1 *Almirante Jose Toribio Merino Castro* (also used as general spt ship) with 1 hel landing platform
  AGS 1 Type-1200 (ice-strengthened hull, ex-CAN) with 1 hel landing platform
  AOR 2: 1 *Almirante Montt* with 1 hel landing platform; 1 *Araucano*
  AP 1 *Aguiles* (1 hel landing platform)
  ATF 2 *Veritas*
  AXS 1 *Esmeralda*
  YFB 2
  YTB 3
MSL • AShM MM-38 *Exocet*

Naval Aviation 600

EQUIPMENT BY TYPE
AIRCRAFT 17 combat capable
  ASW 4: 2 C-295ASW *Persuader*; 2 P-3ACH *Orion*
  MP 4: 1 C-295MPA *Persuader*; 3 EMB-111 *Bandeirante**
  ISR 2 Cessna O-2A *Skymaster**
  TRG 7 PC-7 *Turbo Trainer**

HELICOPTERS
ASW 5 AS532SC *Cougar*
MRH 8 AS365 *Dauphin*
TPT • Light 7: 3 Bell 206 *Jet Ranger*; 4 Bo-105S
MSL • AShM AM-39 *Exocet*

Marines 3,600
FORCES BY ROLE
MANOEUVRE
Amphibious
1 amph bde (2 mne bn, 1 cbt spt bn, 1 log bn)
2 coastal def unit
EQUIPMENT BY TYPE
LT TK 15 *Scorpion*
APC (W) 25 MOWAG *Roland*
ARTY 39
TOWED 23: **105mm** 7 KH-178; **155mm** 16 Soltam M-71
MOR 81mm 16
AShM MM-38 *Exocet*
AD • SAM • SP 14: 4 M998 *Avenger*; 10 M1097 *Avenger*

Coast Guard
Integral part of the Navy
EQUIPMENT BY TYPE
PATROL AND COASTAL COMBATANTS 57
PSOH 2 *Piloto Pardo* (1 additional vessel in build)
PBF 26 *Archangel*
PB 29: 18 *Alacalufe* (*Protector*-class); 4 *Grumete Diaz* (*Dabor*-class); 6 *Pelluhue*; 1 *Ona*

Air Force 8,050
Flying hours   100 hrs/year
FORCES BY ROLE
FIGHTER
1 sqn with F-5E/F *Tiger* III+
2 sqn with F-16AM/BM *Fighting Falcon*
FIGHTER/GROUND ATTACK
1 sqn with F-16C/D Block 50 *Fighting Falcon* (*Puma*)
ISR
1 (photo) flt with; DHC-6-300 *Twin Otter*; Learjet 35A
AIRBORNE EARLY WARNING
1 flt with B-707 *Phalcon*
TANKER/TRANSPORT
1 sqn with B-737-300; C-130B/H *Hercules*; KC-135
TRANSPORT
3 sqn with Bell 205 (UH-1H *Iroquois*); C-212-200/300 *Aviocar*; Cessna O-2A; Cessna 525 *Citation* CJ1; DHC-6-100/300 *Twin Otter*; PA-28-236 *Dakota*; Bell 205 (UH-1H *Iroquois*)
1 VIP flt with B-737-500 (VIP); Gulfstream IV
TRAINING
1 sqn with EMB-314 *Super Tucano**
1 sqn with PA-28-236 *Dakota*; T-35A/B *Pillan*
TRANSPORT HELICOPTER
1 sqn with Bell 205 (UH-1H *Iroquois*); Bell 206B (trg); Bell 412 *Twin Huey*; Bo-105CBS-4; S-70A *Black Hawk*
AIR DEFENCE
1 AD regt (5 AD sqn) with *Crotale*; *Mistral*; M163/M167 *Vulcan*; Oerlikon GDF-005

EQUIPMENT BY TYPE
AIRCRAFT 79 combat capable
FTR 48: 10 F-5E *Tigre* III+; 2 F-5F *Tigre* III+; 29 F-16AM *Fighting Falcon*; 7 F-16BM *Fighting Falcon*
FGA 10: 6 F-16C Block 50 *Fighting Falcon*; 4 F-16D Block 50 *Fighting Falcon*
ATK 9 C-101CC *Aviojet* (A-36 *Halcón*)
ISR 2 Cessna O-2A
AEW&C 1 B-707 *Phalcon*
TKR 3 KC-135
TPT 37: **Medium** 3: 1 C-130B *Hercules*; 2 C-130H *Hercules*; **Light** 30: 2 C-212-200 *Aviocar*; 1 C-212-300 *Aviocar*; 4 Cessna 525 *Citation* CJ1; 3 DHC-6-100 *Twin Otter*; 7 DHC-6-300 *Twin Otter*; 2 Learjet 35A; 11 PA-28-236 *Dakota*; **PAX** 4: 1 B-737-300; 1 B-737-500; 1 B-767-300ER; 1 Gulfstream IV
TRG 42: 12 EMB-314 *Super Tucano**; 30 T-35A/B *Pillan*
HELICOPTERS
MRH 12 Bell 412EP *Twin Huey*
TPT 22: **Medium** 1 S-70A *Black Hawk*; **Light** 21: 13 Bell 205 (UH-1H *Iroquois*); 5 Bell 206B (trg); 2 BK-117; 1 Bo-105CBS-4
UAV • ISR Medium 3 *Hermes* 900
AD
SAM
SP 5 *Crotale*; *Mistral* (*Aspic*)
MANPAD *Mistral*
SYSTEMS *Mygale*
GUNS • TOWED **20mm** M163/M167 *Vulcan*; **35mm** Oerlikon GDF-005
MSL
AAM • IR AIM-9J/M *Sidewinder*; *Python* III; *Python* IV; *Shafrir*‡; ARH AIM-120C AMRAAM; *Derby*
ASM AGM-65G *Maverick*
BOMBS
INS/GPS guided JDAM
Laser-guided *Paveway* II

Paramilitary 44,700

Carabineros 44,700
Ministry of Interior; 15 zones, 36 districts, 179 *comisaria*
EQUIPMENT BY TYPE
APC (W) 20 MOWAG *Roland*
ARTY • MOR **60mm**; **81mm**
AIRCRAFT
TPT • Light 4: 1 Beech 200 *King Air*; 1 Cessna 208; 1 Cessna 550 *Citation* V; 1 PA-31T *Cheyenne* II
HELICOPTERS • TPT • Light 15: 5 AW109E *Power*; 1 Bell 206 *Jet Ranger*; 2 BK 117; 5 Bo-105; 2 EC135

Cyber
The Joint Staff coordinates cyber-security policies for the Ministry of Defense and the Armed Forces. Each service has a cyber-security organisation within their security structure. The Ministry of Interior and Public Security (Internal Affairs) is the national coordination authority for cyber security and is currently developing a National Cyber Security Strategy.

DEPLOYMENT

Legal provisions for foreign deployment:
Constitution: Constitution (1980, since amended)
Decision on deployment of troops abroad: Article 63, number 13 of the Constitution, concerning matters of law, states that the procedures for foreign deployment are a matter that must be established by law by Congress. Law Number 19.067 regulates matters concerning the foreign deployment of Chilean troops and deployment of foreign troops in Chile. It states that the government needs to request congressional approval.

BOSNIA-HERZEGOVINA
EU • EUFOR • *Operation Althea* 15

CYPRUS
UN • UNFICYP 13

HAITI
UN • MINUSTAH 412; 1 mech inf bn; elm 1 engr coy; 1 hel sqn

INDIA/PAKISTAN
UN • UNMOGIP 2 obs

MIDDLE EAST
UN • UNTSO 3 obs

Colombia COL

Colombian Peso pC		2013	2014	2015
GDP	pC	707tr	775tr	
	US$	378bn	400bn	
per capita	US$	8,031	8,394	
Growth	%	4.7	4.8	
Inflation	%	2.0	2.8	
Def exp	pC	25.1bn		
	US$	13m		
Def bdgt [a]	pC	25.3tr	26.1tr	
	US$	13.6bn	13.4bn	
FMA (US)	US$	40m	28.5m	25m
US$1=pC		1,868.79	1,936.96	

[a] Includes decentralised expenditures & expenditure on National Police

Population 46,245,297

Age	0–14	15–19	20–24	25–29	30–64	65 plus
Male	13.0%	4.6%	4.6%	4.2%	20.2%	2.8%
Female	12.4%	4.4%	4.4%	4.1%	21.3%	3.9%

Capabilities

While Colombia's security and defence requirements continue to be dominated by counter-insurgency and counter-narcotics operations, recent successes in both are slowly beginning to enable the armed forces to consider moving towards more conventional military structures and inventories. An eventual end to the hostilities with FARC would likely see a modest shift in procurement to support a more general force structure. To bolster its counter-narcotics effort, Bogotá enjoys US support for training and equipment provision, although this has lessened in recent years due to Colombia's improving security situation. The air force operates a large fleet of US helicopter types to provide tactical mobility for the army. Training ties with the US continue, and the air force in 2014 hosted US personnel and aircraft for the joint *Relampago* 2014 exercise. The navy has upgraded its frigates and submarines through the Orion Plan, is developing a new river-patrol vessel with Brazil and has increased its offshore-patrol capabilities by acquiring a new corvette and patrol boats. (See pp. 370–74.)

ACTIVE 296,750 (Army 237,000, Navy 46,150 Air 13,600) Paramilitary 159,000

RESERVE 34,950 (Army 25,050 Navy 6,500 Air 3,400)

ORGANISATIONS BY SERVICE

Army 237,000
FORCES BY ROLE
SPECIAL FORCES
  1 anti-terrorist SF bn
MANOEUVRE
  Mechanised
  1 (1st) div (1 (2nd) mech bde (2 mech inf bn, 1 mtn inf bn, 1 engr bn, 1 MP bn, 1 cbt spt bn, 1 log bn, 1 Gaula anti-kidnap gp); 1 (10th) mech bde (1 (med) tk bn, 1 mech cav bn, 1 mech inf bn, 1 mtn inf bn, 2 sy bn, 2 arty bn, 1 engr bn, 1 cbt spt bn, 2 Gaula anti-kidnap gp); 2 sy bn; 1 log bn)
  Light
  1 (2nd) div (1 (5th) lt inf bde (3 lt inf bn, 1 jungle inf bn, 1 sy bn, 1 arty bn, 1 AD bn, 1 engr bn, 1 cbt spt bn, 1 Gaula anti-kidnap gp); 1 (30th) lt inf bde (1 cav recce bn, 2 lt inf bn, 1 sy bn, 1 arty bn, 1 engr bn, 1 cbt spt bn, 1 log bn); 1 rapid reaction force (3 mobile sy bde, 1 fixed sy bde))
  1 (3rd) div (1 (3rd) lt inf bde (2 lt inf bn, 1 mtn inf bn, 1 COIN bn, 1 arty bn, 1 engr bn, 1 cbt spt bn, 1 MP bn, 1 log bn, 1 Gaula anti-kidnap gp); 1 (23rd) lt inf bde (1 cav gp, 1 lt inf bn, 1 jungle inf bn, 1 cbt spt bn, 1 log bn); 1 (29th) mtn bde (1 mtn inf bn, 1 lt inf bn, 2 COIN bn, 1 cbt spt bn, 1 log bn); 2 rapid reaction force (total: 7 mobile sy bde))
  1 (4th) div (1 (7th) air mob bde (2 air mob inf bn, 1 lt inf bn, 1 COIN bn, 1 engr bn, 1 cbt spt bn, 1 log bn, 1 Gaula anti-kidnap gp); 1 (22nd) jungle bde (1 air mob inf bn, 1 lt inf bn, 1 jungle inf bn, 1 COIN bn, 1 cbt spt bn, 1 log bn); 1 (31st) jungle bde (1 lt inf bn, 1 jungle inf bn))
  1 (5th) div (1 (6th) lt inf bde (2 lt inf bn,1 mtn inf bn, 2 COIN bn, 1 cbt spt bn, 1 log bn, 1 Gaula anti-kidnap gp); 1 (8th) lt inf bde (1 lt inf bn, 1 mtn inf bn, 1 arty bn, 1 engr bn, 1 cbt spt bn, 1 Gaula anti-kidnap gp); 1 (9th) lt inf bde (1 SF bn, 2 lt inf bn, 1 arty bn, 1 COIN bn, 1 cbt spt bn, 1 sy bn, 1 log bn, 1 Gaula anti-kidnap gp); 1 (13th) lt inf bde (2 cav recce bn, 1 airmob inf

bn, 3 lt inf bn, 1 COIN bn, 1 arty bn, 1 engr bn, 1 cbt spt bn, 2 MP bn, 1 log bn, 2 Gaula anti-kidnap gp); 1 rapid reaction force (3 mobile sy bde))

1 (6th) div (1 (12th) lt inf bde (2 lt inf bn, 2 jungle inf bn, 1 COIN bn, 1 engr bn, 1 cbt spt bn, 1 Gaula anti-kidnap gp); 1 (13th) mobile sy bde (4 COIN bn); 1 (26th) jungle bde (1 lt jungle inf bn, 1 COIN bn, 1 cbt spt bn); 1 (27th) lt inf bde (2 lt inf bn, 1 jungle inf bn, 1 sy bn, 1 arty bn, 1 cbt spt bn, 1 log bn))

1 (7th) div (1 (4th) lt inf bde (1 cav recce bn, 3 lt inf bn, 1 sy bn, 1 arty bn, 1 engr bn, 1 MP bn, 1 cbt spt bn, 1 log bn); 1 (11th) lt inf bde (2 lt inf bn, 1 sy bn, 1 engr bn, 1 cbt spt bn); 1 (14th) lt inf bde (2 lt inf bn, 1 sy bn, 1 engr bn, 1 cbt spt bn, 1 log bn); 1 (15th) jungle bde (1 lt inf bn, 1 COIN bn, 1 engr bn, 1 log bn); 1 (17th) lt inf bde (2 lt inf bn, 1 COIN bn, 1 engr bn, 1 cbt spt bn, 1 log bn); 1 rapid reaction force (1 (11th) mobile sy bde (3 COIN bn)))

1 (8th) div (1 (16th) lt inf bde (1 mech cav recce bn, 1 lt inf bn, 1 log bn, 1 Gaula anti-kidnap gp); 1 (18th) lt inf bde (1 air mob gp, 1 sy bn, 1 arty bn, 1 engr bn, 1 cbt spt bn, 1 log bn); 1 (28th) jungle bde (2 inf, 2 COIN, 1 cbt spt bn); 1 rapid reaction force (1 (5th) mobile sy bde (3 COIN bn); 1 (31st) mobile sy bde (5 COIN bn)))

3 COIN mobile bde (each: 4 COIN bn, 1 cbt spt bn)

Other

1 indep rapid reaction force (1 SF bde, 3 mobile sy bde)

Aviation

1 air aslt div (1 SF bde (2 SF bn); 1 counter-narcotics bde (3 counter-narcotics bn, 1 spt bn); 1 (25th) avn bde (4 hel bn; 5 avn bn; 1 avn log bn); 1 (32nd) avn bde (1 avn bn, 2 maint bn, 1 trg bn, 1 spt bn); 1 SF avn bn)

COMBAT SUPPORT

1 cbt engr bde (1 SF engr bn, 1 (emergency response) engr bn, 1 EOD bn, 1 construction bn, 1 demining bn, 1 maint bn)

1 int bde (2 SIGINT bn, 1 kog bn, 1 maint bn)

COMBAT SERVICE SUPPORT

2 spt/log bde (each: 1 spt bn, 1 maint bn, 1 supply bn, 1 tpt bn, 1 medical bn, 1 log bn)

EQUIPMENT BY TYPE

RECCE 216: 121 EE-9 *Cascavel*; 39 M1117 *Guardian*; 56 VCL

AIFV 52: 28 *Commando Advanced*; 24 LAV III

APC 114

APC (T) 54: 28 M113A1 (TPM-113A1); 26 M113A2 (TPM-113A2)

APC (W) 56 EE-11 *Urutu*

PPV 4 RG-31 *Nyala*

ARTY 1,603

TOWED 121: **105mm** 108: 20 LG1 MkIII; 88 M101; **155mm** 13 155/52 APU SBT-1

MOR 1,482: **81mm** 1,374; **120mm** 108

AT

MSL • SP 77 *Nimrod*

MANPATS TOW; *Spike*-ER; APILAS

RCL 106mm 73 M40A1

RL 90mm 121 C-90C

AD • GUNS • TOWED 40mm 4 M1A1

AIRCRAFT

ELINT 3: 2 Beech B200 *King Air*; 1 Beech 350 *King Air*

TPT • Light 21: 2 An-32B; 2 Beech B200 *King Air*; 2 Beech 350 *King Air*; 2 Beech 200 *King Air* (Medevac); 1 Beech C90 *King Air*; 2 C-212 *Aviocar* (Medevac); 8 Cessna 208B *Grand Caravan*; 4 Turbo Commander 695A

HELICOPTERS

MRH 21: 8 Mi-17-1V *Hip*; 8 Mi-17MD; 5 Mi-17V-5 *Hip*

TPT 99: **Medium** 59: 52 UH-60L *Black Hawk*; 7 S-70i *Black Hawk*; **Light** 40: 24 Bell 205 (UH-1H *Iroquois*); 16 Bell 212 (UH-1N *Twin Huey*)

Navy 46,150 (incl 12,100 conscript)

HQ (Tri-Service Unified Eastern Command HQ) located at Puerto Carreño.

EQUIPMENT BY TYPE

SUBMARINES • TACTICAL • SSK 4:

2 *Pijao* (GER T-209/1200) each with 8 single 533mm TT each with HWT

2 *Intrepido* (GER T-206A) each with 8 single 533mm TT each with HWT

PRINCIPAL SURFACE COMBATANTS 4

FRIGATES • FFG 4 *Almirante Padilla* with 2 twin lnchr with MM-40 *Exocet* AShM, 2 twin *Simbad* lnchr with *Mistral* SAM, 2 triple B515 ILAS-3 324mm ASTT each with A244 LWT, 1 76mm gun (capacity 1 Bo-105/AS555SN *Fennec* hel)

PATROL AND COASTAL COMBATANTS 51

CORVETTES • FS 1 *Narino* (ex-ROK *Dong Hae*) with 2 triple 324mm ASTT with Mk46 LWT, 1 76mm gun

PSOH 2 *20 de Julio*

PCO 2: 1 *Valle del Cauca Durable* (ex-US *Reliance*) with 1 hel landing platform; 1 *San Andres* (ex-US *Balsam*)

PCR 10: 2 *Arauca* with 2 76mm guns; 8 *Nodriza* (PAF-II) with hel landing platform

PBF 1 *Quitasueño* (US *Asheville*) with 1 76mm gun

PB 12: 1 *11 de Noviembre* (CPV-40) with 1 *Typhoon* CIWS; 2 *Castillo Y Rada* (*Swiftships* 105); 2 *Jaime Gomez*; 1 *José Maria Palas* (*Swiftships* 110); 4 *Point*; 2 *Toledo*

PBR 23: 6 *Diligente*; 3 LPR-40; 3 *Swiftships*; 9 *Tenerife*; 2 PAF-L

AMPHIBIOUS 19

LCAC 8 Griffon 2000TD

LCM 3 LCM-8 (there are more than 200 small assault RHIBs also in service)

LCU 8: 1 *Golfo de Tribuga*; 7 *Morrosquillo* (LCU 1466)

LOGISTICS AND SUPPORT 20

ABU 1 *Quindio*

AG 2 *Luneburg* (ex-GER, depot ship for patrol vessels)

AGOR 2 *Providencia*

AGP 1 *Inirida*

AGS 1 *Gorgona*

AXS 1 *Gloria*

YTL 12

Naval Aviation 150

AIRCRAFT

MP 3 CN-235 MPA *Persuader*

ISR 1 PA-31 *Navajo* (upgraded for ISR)

TPT • Light 11: 1 C-212 (Medevac); 4 Cessna 206; 3 Cessna 208 *Caravan*; 1 PA-31 *Navajo*; 1 PA-34 *Seneca*; 1 Beech 350 *King Air*

HELICOPTERS
MRH 7: 2 AS555SN *Fennec*; 5 Bell 412 *Twin Huey*
TPT • **Light** 10: 1 Bell 212; 6 Bell 212 (UH-1N); 1 BK-117; 2 Bo-105

Marines 25,600
FORCES BY ROLE
SPECIAL FORCES
1 SF bde (4 SF bn)
MANOEUVRE
Amphibious
1 mne bde (1 SF (Gaula) bn, 5 mne bn, 2 rvn bn, 1 spt bn)
1 mne bde (1 SF bn, 2 mne bn, 2 rvn bn, 1 spt bn)
1 rvn bde (1 SF bn, 1 mne bn, 2 rvn bn, 1 spt bn)
1 rvn bde (4 rvn bn)
1 rvn bn (3 rvn bn)
COMBAT SERVICE SUPPORT
1 log bde (6 spt bn)
1 trg bde (7 trg bn, 1 spt bn)
EQUIPMENT BY TYPE
ARTY • MOR 82: **81mm** 74; **120mm** 8

Air Force 13,600
6 Combat Air Commands (CACOM) plus CACOM 7 (former Oriental Air Group) responsible for air ops in specific geographic area. Flts can be deployed or 'loaned' to a different CACOM.
FORCES BY ROLE
FIGHTER GROUND ATTACK
1 sqn with *Kfir* C-10/C-12/TC-12
GROUND ATTACK/ISR
1 sqn with A-37B/OA-37B *Dragonfly*
1 sqn with AC-47T; Hughes 369
1 sqn with EMB-312 *Tucano**
2 sqn with EMB-314 *Super Tucano** (A-29)
1 Sqn with OV-10A *Bronco*
EW/ELINT
2 sqn with Beech 350 *King Air*; Cessna 208; Cessna 560; C-26B *Metroliner*; SA 2-37
MARITIME PATROL/SEARCH & RESCUE
1 sqn with Bell 212, EMB-110P1 (C-95)
TRANSPORT
1 (Presidential) sqn with B-707 Tkr; B-727; B-737BBJ; EMB-600 *Legacy*; KC-767; Bell 212; Bell 412EP; F-28 *Fellowship*
1 sqn with C-130B/H *Hercules*; C-295M
1 sqn with Beech C90 *King Air*; C-212; CN-235M; Do-328; IAI *Arava*
TRAINING
1 (primary trg) sqn with Bell 205 (UH-1H *Iroquois*); PA-42 *Cheyenne*
1 (basic trg) sqn with Lancair *Synergy* (T-90 *Calima*)
1 sqn with T-37B
2 hel sqn with Bell 206B3
HELICOPTER
1 sqn with AH-60L *Arpia* III
1 sqn with UH-60L *Black Hawk* (CSAR)
1 sqn with MD500; Bell 205 (UH-1H)
1 sqn with Hughes 369
1 sqn with Bell 205 (UH-1H); Hughes 369
1 sqn with Bell 206B3; Hughes 369
EQUIPMENT BY TYPE
AIRCRAFT 86 combat capable
FGA 20: 10 *Kfir* C-10; 9 *Kfir* C-12; 1 *Kfir* TC-12
ATK 18: 7 A-37B/OA-37B *Dragonfly*; 6 AC-47T *Spooky* (*Fantasma*); 5 OV-10A *Bronco*
ISR 13: 1 C-26B *Metroliner*; 5 Cessna 560 *Citation* V; 6 SA 2-37; 1 Beech C90 *King Air*
ELINT 12: 4 Beech 350 *King Air*; 6 Cessna 208 *Grand Caravan*; 2 Cessna 337G
TKR/TPT 2: 1 B-707 Tkr; 1 KC-767
TPT 63: **Medium** 8: 4 C-130B *Hercules* (3 more in store); 3 C-130H *Hercules*; 1 B-737F; **Light** 47: 5 ATR-42; 2 ATR-72; 2 Beech 300 *King Air*; 2 Beech 350C *King Air*; 4 Beech C90 *King Air*; 4 C-212; 6 C-295M; 1 Cessna 182R; 12 Cessna 208B (medevac); 1 Cessna 550; 3 CN-235M; 2 EMB-110P1 (C-95); 1 EMB-170-100LR; 1 IAI-201 *Arava*; 1 Turbo Commander 695; **PAX** 8: 2 B-727; 1 B-737-400 1 B-737BBJ; 1 EMB-600 *Legacy*; 1 F-28-1000 *Fellowship*; 1 F-28-3000 *Fellowship*; 1 Learjet 60
TRG 80: 14 EMB-312 *Tucano**; 24 EMB-314 *Super Tucano* (A-29)*; 25 Lancair *Synergy* (T-90 *Calima*); 17 T-37B
HELICOPTERS
ISR 22 OH-58 *Kiowa*
MRH 18: 14 AH-60L *Arpia* III; 2 Bell 412EP *Twin Huey* VIP tpt); 2 Hughes 500M
TPT 47: **Medium** 12 UH-60L *Black Hawk* (incl 1 VIP hel); **Light** 35: 12 Bell 205 (UH-1H *Iroquois*); 12 Bell 206B3 *Jet Ranger* III; 11 Bell 212
UAV • ISR **Medium** 2 *Hermes* 450
MSL • IR *Python* III; IIR *Python* IV ARH *Derby*

Paramilitary 159,000

National Police Force 159,000
AIRCRAFT
ELINT 3 C-26B *Metroliner*
TPT • **Light** 42: 2 ATR-42; 3 Beech 200 *King Air*; 3 Beech 300 *King Air*; 2 Beech 1900; 1 Beech C99; 4 BT-67; 4 C-26 *Metroliner*; 3 Cessna 152; 3 Cessna 172; 9 Cessna 206; 2 Cessna 208 *Caravan*; 2 DHC 6 *Twin Otter*; 1 DHC-8; 3 PA-31 *Navajo*
HELICOPTERS
MRH 3: 1 Bell 412EP; 2 MD-500D
TPT 67: **Medium** 10 UH-60L *Black Hawk*; **Light** 57: 35 Bell 205 (UH-1H-II *Huey II*); 3 Bell 206B; 6 Bell 206L/L3/L4 *Long Ranger*; 8 Bell 212; 5 Bell 407

DEPLOYMENT

EGYPT
MFO 354; 1 inf bn

FOREIGN FORCES
United States US Southern Command: 50

Costa Rica CRI

Costa Rican Colon C		2013	2014	2015
GDP	C	24.8tr	27.2tr	
	US$	49.6bn	50.5bn	
per capita	US$	10,528	10,568	
Growth	%	3.5	3.6	
Inflation	%	5.2	3.4	
Sy Bdgt [a]	C	201bn	227bn	
	US$	402m	420m	
FMA (US)	US$	0.82m	1.4m	1.2m
US$1=C		499.77	540.00	

[a] No armed forces. Paramilitary budget

Population 4,755,234

Age	0–14	15–19	20–24	25–29	30–64	65 plus
Male	12.0%	4.3%	4.6%	4.6%	21.4%	3.2%
Female	11.5%	4.2%	4.4%	4.5%	21.5%	3.8%

Capabilities

Armed forces were constitutionally abolished in 1949, and Costa Rica relies on a series of moderately sized paramilitary-style organisations for internal security and participation in regional peacekeeping operations. Some elements, such as the special-operations unit, have received training from non-regional states, including the US. The coast-guard unit has benefited from a series of US donations and the air wing is relatively well equipped with light aircraft.

Paramilitary 9,800

ORGANISATIONS BY SERVICE

Paramilitary 9,800

Special Intervention Unit
FORCES BY ROLE
SPECIAL FORCES
  1 spec ops unit

Public Force 9,000
FORCES BY ROLE
MANOEUVRE
  Other
    1 (tac) police *comisaria*
    6 (provincial) paramilitary *comisaria*
    7 (urban) paramilitary *comisaria*
    2 (border) sy comd (8 *comisaria*)
    8 paramilitary comd

Coast Guard Unit 400
EQUIPMENT BY TYPE
PATROL AND COASTAL COMBATANTS 8:
  PB 8: 2 *Cabo Blanco* (US *Swift* 65); 1 *Isla del Coco* (US *Swift* 105); 3 *Point*; 1 *Primera Dama* (US *Swift* 42); 1 *Puerto Quebos* (US *Swift* 36)

Air Surveillance Unit 400
AIRCRAFT • TPT • Light 15: 4 Cessna T210 *Centurion*; 4 Cessna U206G *Stationair*; 1 DHC-7 *Caribou*; 2 PA-31 *Navajo*; 2 PA-34 *Seneca*; 1 Piper PA-23 *Aztec*; 1 Cessna 182RG
HELICOPTERS • MRH : 3 2 MD-500E; 1 MD 600N

Cuba CUB

Cuban Peso P		2013	2014	2015
GDP	P			
	US$			
per capita	US$			
Growth	%			
Inflation	%			
Def bdgt	P			
	US$			
US$1=P				

*definitive economic data unavailable

Population 11,047,251

Age	0–14	15–19	20–24	25–29	30–64	65 plus
Male	8.4%	3.3%	3.6%	3.8%	24.9%	5.7%
Female	7.9%	3.2%	3.5%	3.6%	25.2%	7.0%

Capabilities

Though numerically significant, the Cuban armed forces are hampered by an ageing and predominantly Soviet-era equipment inventory. It is also unlikely that Cuba will be in a position to finance significant equipment recapitalisation in the near term. The military focus now is on protecting territorial integrity along with sustaining ties to some regional military partners such as Venezuela. There is also the potential of increased military ties with Russia and during the course of 2014 there were reports that Moscow was looking to re-establish a signals-intelligence capability on the island. A security-cooperation agreement was signed with Russia in May 2014, although no official details were released.

ACTIVE 49,000 (Army 38,000 Navy 3,000 Air 8,000)
Paramilitary 26,500
Conscript liability 2 years

RESERVE 39,000 (Army 39,000) **Paramilitary 1,120,000**
Ready Reserves (serve 45 days per year) to fill out Active and Reserve units; see also Paramilitary.

ORGANISATIONS BY SERVICE

Army ε38,000
FORCES BY ROLE
COMMAND
  3 regional comd HQ
  3 army comd HQ

MANOEUVRE
Armoured
up to 5 armd bde
Mechanised
9 mech inf bde (1 armd regt, 3 mech inf regt, 1 arty regt, 1 ADA regt)
Light
1 (frontier) bde
Air Manoeuvre
1 AB bde
COMBAT SUPPORT
1 ADA regt
1 SAM bde

Reserves 39,000
FORCES BY ROLE
MANOEUVRE
Light
14 inf bde
EQUIPMENT BY TYPE†
MBT ε900 T-34/T-54/T-55/T-62
LT TK PT-76
RECCE BRDM-2; BTR-60 100mm
AIFV ε50 BMP-1/1P
APC ε500 BTR-152/BTR-50/BTR-60
ARTY 1,715+
SP 40+: 100mm AAPMP-100; CATAP-100; 122mm 2S1; AAP-T-122; AAP-BMP-122; *Jupiter* III; *Jupiter* IV; 130mm AAP-T-130; *Jupiter* V; 152mm 2S3
TOWED 500: 122mm D-30; M-30; 130mm M-46; 152mm D-1; M-1937
MRL • SP 175: 122mm BM-21 140mm BM-14
MOR 1,000: 82mm M-41; 82mm M-43; 120mm M-43; 120mm M-38
AT
MSL • MANPATS 2K16 *Shmel* (AT-1 *Snapper*); 9K11 *Malyutka* (AT-3 *Sagger*)
GUNS 600+: 57mm 600 M-1943; 85mm D-44
AD • SAM
SP 200+: 200 9K35 *Strela*-10 (SA-13 *Gopher*); 2K12 *Kub* (SA-6 *Gainful*); 9K33 *Osa* (SA-8 *Gecko*); 9K31 *Strela*-1 (SA-9 *Gaskin*)
MANPAD 9K36 *Strela*-3 (SA-14 *Gremlin*); 9K310 *Igla*-1 (SA-16 *Gimlet*); 9K32 *Strela*-2 (SA-7 *Grail*)‡
GUNS 400
SP 23mm ZSU-23-4; 30mm BTR-60P SP; 57mm ZSU-57-2
TOWED 100mm KS-19/M-1939/85mm KS-12/57mm S-60/37mm M-1939/30mm M-53/23mm ZU-23

Navy ε3,000
Western Comd HQ at Cabanas; Eastern Comd HQ at Holquin.
EQUIPMENT BY TYPE
PATROL AND COASTAL COMBATANTS 8
PSO 1 *Rio Damuji* with two single P-15M *Termit* (SS-N-2C *Styx*) AShM, 2 57mm guns, 1 hel landing platform
PCM 1 *Pauk* II† (FSU) with 1 quad lnchr (manual aiming) with 9K32 *Strela*-2 (SA-N-5 *Grail*) SAM, 4 single ASTT, 2 RBU 1200, 1 76mm gun
PBF 6 *Osa* II† (FSU) each with 4 single lnchr (for P-15 *Termit* (SS-N-2B *Styx*) AShM – missiles removed to coastal defence units)
MINE WARFARE AND MINE COUNTERMEASURES 5
MHI 3 *Yevgenya*† (FSU)
MSC 2 *Sonya*† (FSU)
LOGISTICS AND SUPPORT 5
ABU 1
AX 1
YTL 3

Coastal Defence
ARTY • TOWED 122mm M-1931/37; 130mm M-46; 152mm M-1937
MSL• AShM 4+: *Bandera* IV (reported); 4 4K51 *Rubezh* (SS-C-3 *Styx*)

Naval Infantry 550+
FORCES BY ROLE
MANOEUVRE
Amphibious
2 amph aslt bn

Anti-aircraft Defence and Revolutionary Air Force ε8,000 (incl conscripts)
Air assets divided between Western Air Zone and Eastern Air Zone.

Flying hours 50 hrs/year

FORCES BY ROLE
FIGHTER/GROUND ATTACK
3 sqn with MiG-21ML *Fishbed*; MiG-23ML/MF/UM *Flogger*; MiG-29A/UB *Fulcrum*
TRANSPORT
1 (VIP) tpt sqn with An-24 *Coke*; Mi-8P *Hip*; Yak-40
ATTACK HELICOPTER
2 sqn with Mi-17 *Hip H*; Mi-35 *Hind*
TRAINING
2 (tac trg) sqn with L-39C *Albatros* (basic); Z-142 (primary)
EQUIPMENT BY TYPE
AIRCRAFT 45 combat capable
FTR 33: 16 MiG-23ML *Flogger*; 4 MiG-23MF *Flogger*; 4 MiG-23U *Flogger*; 4 MiG-23UM *Flogger*; 2 MiG-29A *Fulcrum*; 3 MiG-29UB *Fulcrum* (6 MiG-15UTI *Midget*; 4+ MiG-17 *Fresco*; 4 MiG-23MF *Flogger*; 6 MiG-23ML *Flogger*; 2 MiG-23UM *Flogger*; 2 MiG-29 *Fulcrum* in store)
FGA 12: 4 MiG-21ML *Fishbed*; 8 MiG-21U *Mongol* A (up to 70 MiG-21bis *Fishbed*; 30 MiG-21F *Fishbed*; 28 MiG-21PFM *Fishbed*; 7 MiG-21UM *Fishbed*; 20 MiG-23BN *Flogger* in store)
ISR 1 An-30 *Clank*
TPT 11: Heavy 2 Il-76 *Candid*; Light 9: 1 An-2 *Colt*; 3 An-24 *Coke*; 2 An-32 *Cline*; 3 Yak-40 (8 An-2 *Colt*; 18 An-26 *Curl* in store)
TRG 45: 25 L-39 *Albatros*; 20 Z-326 *Trener Master*
HELICOPTERS
ATK 4 Mi-35 *Hind* (8 more in store)
ASW (5 Mi-14 in store)
MRH 8 Mi-17 *Hip* H (12 more in store)
TPT • Medium 2 Mi-8P *Hip*

AD • SAM
SP S-75 *Dvina* mod (SA-2 *Guideline* – on T-55 chassis); S-125 *Pechora* mod (SA-3 *Goa* – on T-55 chassis)
TOWED S-75 *Dvina* (SA-2 *Guideline*); S-125 *Pechora* (SA-3 *Goa*)
MSL
AAM • IR R-3‡ (AA-2 *Atoll*); R-60 (AA-8 *Aphid*); R-73 (AA-11 *Archer*); **IR/SARH** R-23/24‡ (AA-7 *Apex*); R-27 (AA-10 *Alamo*)
ASM Kh-23‡ (AS-7 *Kerry*)

Paramilitary 26,500 active

State Security 20,000
Ministry of Interior

Border Guards 6,500
Ministry of Interior
PATROL AND COASTAL COMBATANTS 20
  PCC: 2 *Stenka*
  PB 18 *Zhuk*

Youth Labour Army 70,000 reservists

Civil Defence Force 50,000 reservists

Territorial Militia ε1,000,000 reservists

FOREIGN FORCES
United States US Southern Command: 750 (JTF-GTMO) at Guantánamo Bay

Dominican Republic DOM

Dominican Peso pRD		2013	2014	2015
GDP	pRD	2.56tr	2.73tr	
	US$	61.3bn	62.5bn	
per capita	US$	5,882	5,894	
Growth	%	4.6	5.3	
Inflation	%	4.8	3.6	
Def exp	pRD	11.3bn		
	US$	270m		
Def bdgt	pRD	15.5bn	17.4bn	
	US$	371m	397m	
US$1=pRD		41.74	43.66	

Population 10,349,741

Age	0–14	15–19	20–24	25–29	30–64	65 plus
Male	14.2%	4.8%	4.6%	4.2%	19.5%	3.3%
Female	13.8%	4.7%	4.4%	4.0%	18.8%	3.8%

Capabilities

Internal and border security, along with counter-narcotics operations, are the main tasks of the country's armed forces. The shared border with Haiti continues to be a focus of attention; a military operation was launched to apprehend Haitian prison inmates who broke out in August 2014 and then crossed the border. The armed forces exercise regularly and during the course of 2014 took part in training operations with the US and France. In recent years, the small air force has benefited from investment in aircraft and equipment to allow it to better conduct counter-narcotics surveillance and interdiction. Legislation drafted in 2013 aims to further civilianise and professionalise the armed forces, introducing mandatory retirement for generals after ten years of service, new senior-officer-to-enlisted-personnel ratios and renaming the Armed Forces Ministry the Ministry of Defence.

ACTIVE 46,000 (Army 26,000 Navy 10,000 Air 10,000) Paramilitary 15,000

ORGANISATIONS BY SERVICE

Army 26,000
5 Defence Zones
FORCES BY ROLE
SPECIAL FORCES
  3 SF bn
MANOEUVRE
  Mechanised
  1 armd bn
  Light
  1 (2nd) inf bde (4 inf bn, 1 mtn inf bn)
  2 (1st & 3rd) inf bde (3 inf bn)
  2 (4th & 5th) inf bde (2 inf bn)
  1 (6th) inf bde (1 inf bn)
  Air Manoeuvre
  1 air cav bde (1 cdo bn, 1 (6th) mtn regt, 1 hel sqn with Bell 205 (op by Air Force); OH-58 *Kiowa*; R-22; R-44 *Raven* II)
  Other
  1 (Presidential Guard) gd regt
  1 (MoD) sy bn
COMBAT SUPPORT
  2 arty bn
  1 engr bn
EQUIPMENT BY TYPE
LT TK 12 M41B (76mm)
APC (W) 8 LAV-150 *Commando*
ARTY 104
  TOWED 105mm 16: 4 M101; 12 *Reinosa* 105/26
  MOR 88: **81mm** 60 M1; **107mm** 4 M-30; **120mm** 24 Expal Model L
AT
  RCL 106mm 20 M40A1
  GUNS 37mm 20 M3
HELICOPTERS
  ISR 8: 4 OH-58A *Kiowa*; 4 OH-58C *Kiowa*
  TPT • Light 6: 4 R-22; 2 R-44 *Raven* II

Navy 10,000
HQ located at Santo Domingo
FORCES BY ROLE
SPECIAL FORCES
  1 (SEAL) SF unit

MANOEUVRE
  Amphibious
  1 mne sy unit
EQUIPMENT BY TYPE
PATROL AND COASTAL COMBATANTS 17
  PCO 1 *Almirante Didiez Burgos* (ex-US *Balsam*)
  PCC 2 *Tortuguero* (ex-US *White Sumac*)
  PB 14: 2 *Altair* (Swiftships 35m); 4 *Bellatrix* (US Sewart Seacraft); 2 *Canopus* (Swiftships 101); 3 *Hamal* (Damen Stan 1505); 3 *Point*
AMPHIBIOUS 1 *Neyba* (ex-US LCU 1675)
LOGISTICS AND SUPPORT 13
  AG 8
  YFD 1
  YTL 4

Air Force 10,000

Flying hours   60 hrs/year
FORCES BY ROLE
GROUND ATTACK
  1 sqn with EMB-314 *Super Tucano**
SEARCH & RESCUE
  1 sqn with Bell 205 (UH-1H *Huey II*); Bell 205 (UH-1H *Iroquois*); Bell 430 (VIP); OH-58 *Kiowa* (CH-136); S-333
TRANSPORT
  1 sqn with C-212-400 *Aviocar*; PA-31 *Navajo*
TRAINING
  1 sqn with T-35B *Pillan*
AIR DEFENCE
  1 ADA bn with 20mm guns
EQUIPMENT BY TYPE
AIRCRAFT 8 combat capable
  ISR 1 AMT-200 *Super Ximango*
  TPT • Light 12: 3 C-212-400 *Aviocar*; 1 Cessna 172; 1 Cessna 182; 1 Cessna 206; 1 Cessna 207; 1 *Commander* 690; 3 EA-100; 1 PA-31 *Navajo*
  TRG 13: 8 EMB-314 *Super Tucano**; 5 T-35B *Pillan*
HELICOPTERS
  ISR 9 OH-58 *Kiowa* (CH-136)
  TPT • Light 16: 8 Bell 205 (UH-1H *Huey* II); 5 Bell 205 (UH-1H *Iroquois*); 1 EC155 (VIP); 2 S-333
AD • GUNS 20mm 4

Paramilitary 15,000

National Police 15,000

DEPLOYMENT

MALI
UN • MINUSMA 2

Ecuador ECU

United States Dollar $ [a]		2013	2014	2015
GDP	US$	93.7bn	100bn	
per capita	US$	5,943	6,270	
Growth	%	4.5	4.0	
Inflation	%	2.7	3.1	
Def bdgt	US$	1.62bn	1.7bn	
FMA (US)	US$	0.45m	0.45m	

[a] The US dollar was adopted as the official currency in 2000

Population   15,654,411

Age	0–14	15–19	20–24	25–29	30–64	65 plus
Male	14.5%	4.9%	4.5%	4.2%	18.2%	3.3%
Female	14.0%	4.7%	4.5%	4.2%	19.3%	3.6%

Capabilities

Defence policy is aimed at guaranteeing sovereignty and territorial integrity, and also allows the armed forces to participate in international peacekeeping operations. Border security has long been a priority and a source of friction, most recently tension with Colombia over their shared border and the impact of the conflict with FARC. The armed forces have little capacity for sustained power projection beyond national borders. There has been a growing emphasis on maritime security, with a number of potential acquisitions intended to improve surveillance and patrol capabilities. A modernisation programme announced in 2014 is intended to reduce bases and units, and reduce personnel numbers by 2025. The armed forces' role is to expand from border security to include law-enforcement support. Much of the inventory is ageing, with acquisitions often second-hand. The air force purchased additional C-295 transport aircraft and the coast guard is acquiring additional patrol boats. All three services have acquired Israeli UAVs to counter oil smuggling and drug trafficking, and Ecuador is collaborating with Belarus on UAV development. The services take part in regular domestic exercises, with the army and navy also participating in exercises with international partners.

ACTIVE 58,000 (Army 46,500 Navy 7,300 Air 4,200)
Paramilitary 500
Conscript liability 1 year, selective

RESERVE 118,000 (Joint 118,000)
Ages 18–55

ORGANISATIONS BY SERVICE

Army 46,500
FORCES BY ROLE
gp are bn sized.
COMMAND
  4 div HQ
SPECIAL FORCES
  1 (9th) SF bde (3 SF gp, 1 SF sqn, 1 para bn, 1 sigs sqn, 1 log comd)

MANOEUVRE
Mechanised
1 (11th) armd cav bde (3 armd cav gp, 1 mech inf bn, 1 SP arty gp, 1 engr gp)
1 (5th) inf bde (1 SF sqn, 2 mech cav gp, 2 inf bn, 1 cbt engr coy, 1 sigs coy, 1 log coy)
Light
1 (1st) inf bde (1 SF sqn, 1 armd cav gp, 1 armd recce sqn, 3 inf bn, 1 med coy)
1 (3rd) inf bde (1 SF gp, 1 mech cav gp, 1 inf bn, 1 arty gp, 1 hvy mor coy, 1 cbt engr coy, 1 sigs coy, 1 log coy)
1 (7th) inf bde (1 SF sqn, 1 armd recce sqn, 1 mech cav gp, 3 inf bn, 1 jungle bn, 1 arty gp, 1 cbt engr coy, 1 sigs coy, 1 log coy, 1 med coy)
1 (13th) inf bde (1 SF sqn, 1 armd recce sqn, 1 mot cav gp, 3 inf bn, 1 arty gp, 1 hvy mor coy, 1 cbt engr coy, 1sigs coy, 1 log coy)
Jungle
2 (17th & 21st) jungle bde (3 jungle bn, 1 cbt engr coy, 1 sigs coy, 1 log coy)
1 (19th) jungle bde (3 jungle bn, 1 jungle trg bn, 1 cbt engr coy, 1 sigs coy, 1 log coy)
Aviation
1 (15th) avn bde (2 tpt avn gp, 2 hel gp, 1 mixed avn gp)
COMBAT SUPPORT
1 (27th) arty bde (1 SP arty gp, 1 MRL gp, 1 ADA gp, 1 cbt engr coy, 1 sigs coy, 1 log coy)
1 ADA gp
1 (23rd) engr bde (3 engr bn)
2 indep MP coy
1 indep sigs coy
COMBAT SERVICE SUPPORT
1 (25th) log bde
2 log bn
2 indep med coy
EQUIPMENT BY TYPE
LT TK 24 AMX-13
RECCE 67: 25 AML-90; 10 EE-3 *Jararaca*; 32 EE-9 *Cascavel*
APC 123
  APC (T) 95: 80 AMX-VCI; 15 M113
  APC (W) 28: 18 EE-11 *Urutu*; 10 UR-416
ARTY 541+
  SP 155mm 5 (AMX) Mk F3
  TOWED 100: **105mm** 78: 30 M101; 24 M2A2; 24 Model 56 pack howitzer; **155mm** 22: 12 M114; 10 M198
  MRL 122mm 24: 18 BM-21; 6 RM-70
  MOR 412+: **81mm** 400 M-29; **107mm** M-30 (4.2in); **160mm** 12 M-66 Soltam
AT
  RCL 404: **106mm** 24 M40A1; **90mm** 380 M67
AIRCRAFT
  TPT • Light 15: 1 Beech 200 *King Air*; 2 C-212; 1 CN-235; 4 Cessna 172; 2 Cessna 206; 1 Cessna 500 *Citation* I; 4 IAI-201 *Arava*
  TRG 6: 2 MX-7-235 *Star Rocket*; 2 T-41D *Mescalero*; 2 CJ-6A
HELICOPTERS
  MRH 29: 2 AS550C3 *Fennec*; 6 Mi-17-1V *Hip*; 3 SA315B *Lama*; 18 SA342L *Gazelle* (13 with HOT for anti-armour role)
  TPT 11: **Medium** 7: 5 AS332B *Super Puma*; 2 Mi-171E; (3 SA330 *Puma* in store); **Light** 4: 2 AS350B *Ecureuil*; 2 AS350B2 *Ecureuil*
AD
  SAM • MANPAD Blowpipe; 9K32 *Strela-2* (SA-7 *Grail*)‡; 9K38 *Igla* (SA-18 *Grouse*)
  GUNS 240
    SP 44 M163 *Vulcan*
    TOWED 196: **14.5mm** 128 ZPU-1/-2; **20mm** 38: 28 M-1935, 10 M167 *Vulcan*; **40mm** 30 L/70/M1A1

Navy 7,300 (incl Naval Aviation, Marines and Coast Guard)
EQUIPMENT BY TYPE
SUBMARINES • TACTICAL • SSK 2:
  2 *Shyri* (GER T-209/1300, 1 undergoing refit in Chile) each with 8 single 533mm TT each with SUT HWT
PRINCIPAL SURFACE COMBATANTS 2
  FRIGATES 2
    FFGHM 1 *Moran Valverde*† (ex-UK *Leander* batch II) with 4 single lnchr with MM-40 *Exocet* AShM, 3 twin lnchr with *Mistral* SAM, 1 *Phalanx* CIWS, 1 twin 114mm gun (capacity 1 Bell 206B *Jet Ranger* II hel)
    FFGH 1 *Presidente Alfaro* (mod UK *Leander*) with 4 single lnchr with MM-40 *Exocet* AShM, 2 triple 324mm ASTT with Mk 46 LWT, 1 *Phalanx* CIWS, 1 twin 114mm gun (capacity 1 Bell 206B *Jet Ranger* II hel)
PATROL AND COASTAL COMBATANTS 9
  CORVETTES • FSGM 6 *Esmeraldas* (3†) with 2 triple lnchr with MM-40 *Exocet* AShM, 1 quad *Albatros* lnchr with *Aspide* SAM, 2 triple B515 ILAS-3 324mm ASTT with A244 LWT (removed from two vessels), 1 76mm gun, 1 hel landing platform (upgrade programme ongoing)
  PCFG 3 *Quito* (GER Lurssen TNC-45 45m) with 4 single lnchr with MM-38 *Exocet* AShM, 1 76mm gun (upgrade programme ongoing)
LOGISTICS AND SUPPORT 15
  AE 1 *Calicuchima*
  AGOS 1 *Orion* with 1 hel landing platform
  AGSC 1 *Sirius*
  AK 1 *Galapagos*
  ATF 1
  AWT 2: 1 *Quisquis*; 1 *Atahualpa*
  AXS 1 *Guayas*
  YFD 2 *Rio Napo* (US ARD 12)
  YTL 5

Naval Aviation 380
AIRCRAFT
  MP 1 CN-235-300M
  ISR 3: 2 Beech 200T *King Air*; 1 Beech 300 *Catpass King Air*
  TPT • Light 3: 1 Beech 200 *King Air*; 1 Beech 300 *King Air*; 1 CN-235-100
  TRG 6: 2 T-34C *Turbo Mentor*; 4 T-35B *Pillan*
HELICOPTERS
  TPT • Light 9: 3 Bell 206A; 3 Bell 206B; 1 Bell 230; 2 Bell 430
UAV • ISR 5: **Heavy** 2 *Heron*; **Medium** 3 *Searcher* Mk.II

Marines 2,150

FORCES BY ROLE
SPECIAL FORCES
 1 cdo unit
MANOEUVRE
 Amphibious
 5 mne bn (on garrison duties)
EQUIPMENT BY TYPE
ARTY • MOR 32+ 60mm/81mm/120mm
AD • SAM • MANPAD Mistral; 9K38 Igla (SA-18 Grouse)

Air Force 4,200

Operational Command

FORCES BY ROLE
FIGHTER
 1 sqn with Cheetah C/D
FIGHTER/GROUND ATTACK
 2 sqn with EMB-314 Super Tucano*
 1 sqn with Kfir C-10 (CE); Kfir C-2; Kfir TC-2

Military Air Transport Group

FORCES BY ROLE
SEARCH & RESCUE/TRANSPORT HELICOPTER
 1 sqn with Bell 206B Jet Ranger II
 1 sqn with Dhruv; PA-34 Seneca
TRANSPORT
 1 sqn with C-130/H Hercules; L-100-30
 1 sqn with HS-748
 1 sqn with DHC-6-300 Twin Otter
 1 sqn with B-727; EMB-135BJ Legacy 600; F-28 Fellowship; Sabreliner 40/60
TRAINING
 1 sqn with Cessna 150/206; DA20-C1; MXP-650; T-34C Turbo Mentor
EQUIPMENT BY TYPE
AIRCRAFT 42 combat capable
 FGA 25: 10 Cheetah C; 2 Cheetah D; 4 Kfir C-2; 7 Kfir C-10 (CE); 2 Kfir TC-2
 TPT 36: **Medium** 4: 2 C-130B Hercules; 1 C-130H Hercules; 1 L-100-30; **Light** 22: 1 Beech E90 King Air; 1 C-295M; 7 Cessna 150; 1 Cessna 206; 3 DHC-6 Twin Otter; 1 EMB-135BJ Legacy 600; 2 EMB-170; 2 EMB-190; 1 MXP-650; 2 Sabreliner 40; 1 PA-34 Seneca; **PAX** 10: 2 A320; 2 B-727; 6 HS-748
 TRG 40: 11 DA20-C1; 17 EMB-314 Super Tucano*; 12 T-34C Turbo Mentor
HELICOPTERS
 MRH 5 Dhruv
 TPT • **Light** 7 Bell 206B Jet Ranger II
MSL • AAM • IR Python III; Python IV; R-550 Magic; Shafrir‡; SARH Super 530
AD
 MSL
  SP 13: 6 9K33 Osa (SA-8 Gecko); 7 M48 Chaparral
  MANPAD Blowpipe; 9K32 Strela-2 (SA-7 Grail)‡; 9K310 Igla-1 (SA-16 Gimlet); 9K38 Igla (SA-18 Grouse)
 GUNS
  SP **20mm** 28 M35
  TOWED 64: **23mm** 34 ZU-23; **35mm** 30 GDF-002 (twin)
 RADAR: 2 CFTC gap fillers; 2 CETC 2D

Paramilitary

All police forces; 39,500

Police Air Service

EQUIPMENT BY TYPE
HELICOPTERS
 ISR 3 MD530F
 TPT • **Light** 6: 2 AS350B Ecureuil; 1 Bell 206B Jet Ranger; 3 R-44

Coast Guard 500

EQUIPMENT BY TYPE
PATROL AND COASTAL COMBATANTS 20
 PCC 3 Isla Fernandina (Vigilante)
 PB 14: 1 10 de Agosto; 2 Espada; 1 Isla Isabela; 2 Manta (GER Lurssen 36m); 1 Point; 4 Rio Coca; 3 Isla Santa Cruz (Damen Stan 2606)
 PBR 3: 2 Rio Esmeraldas; 1 Rio Puyango

DEPLOYMENT

CÔTE D'IVOIRE
UN • UNOCI 2 obs

HAITI
UN • MINUSTAH 53; elm 1 engr coy

LIBERIA
UN • UNMIL 1; 2 obs

SUDAN
UN • UNAMID 1; 1 obs
UN • UNISFA 1; 1 obs

El Salvador SLV

El Salvador Colon C		2013	2014	2015
GDP	C	24.3bn	25.1bn	
	US$	24.3bn	25.1bn	
per capita	US$	3,835	3,958	
Growth	%	1.7	1.7	
Inflation	%	0.8	1.2	
Def bdgt	C	1.37bn	1.33bn	
	US$	154m	150m	
FMA (US)	US$	1.25m	1.8m	1.6m
US$1=C		1.00	1.00	

Population	6,125,512					
Age	0–14	15–19	20–24	25–29	30–64	65 plus
Male	14.4%	5.5%	4.9%	4.0%	16.2%	3.1%
Female	13.7%	5.4%	5.0%	4.3%	19.7%	3.8%

Capabilities

El Salvador's armed forces are generally focused on land-based security tasks and the main manoeuvre units are light infantry. The air wing is reasonably well equipped with transport and multi-role fixed- and rotary-wing aircraft, and in 2014 acquired a further ten second-hand Cessna A-37B fighter/ground-attack aircraft from Chile. The navy retains a small patrol and amphibious capability. Despite these limitations, El Salvador was able to deploy small forces to both Iraq and Afghanistan. Current challenges include boosting professionalisation – conscription accounts for a little under half of recruits – and tackling organised crime and narcotics trafficking. In 2009, high crime rates led the government to deploy the army in support of the police, as well as to secure prisons and border crossings.

ACTIVE 15,300 (Army 13,850 Navy 700 Air 750)
Paramilitary 17,000
Conscript liability 18 months voluntary

RESERVE 9,900 (Joint 9,900)

ORGANISATIONS BY SERVICE

Army 9,850; 4,000 conscript (total 13,850)
FORCES BY ROLE
SPECIAL FORCES
  1 spec ops gp (1 SF coy, 1 para bn, 1 (naval inf) coy)
MANOEUVRE
  Reconnaissance
    1 armd cav regt (2 armd cav bn)
  Light
    6 inf bde (3 inf bn)
  Other
    1 (special) sy bde (2 border gd bn, 2 MP bn)
COMBAT SUPPORT
  1 arty bde (2 fd arty bn, 1 AD bn)
  1 engr comd (2 engr bn)
EQUIPMENT BY TYPE
RECCE 5 AML-90; (4 more in store)
APC (W) 38: 30 M37B1 *Cashuat* (mod); 8 UR-416
ARTY 217+
  TOWED 105mm 54: 36 M102; 18 M-56 (FRY)
  MOR 163+: **81mm** 151 M29; **120mm** 12+: (M-74 in store); 12 UBM 52
AT
  RCL 399: **106mm** 20 M40A1 (incl 16 SP); **90mm** 379 M67
AD • GUNS 35: **20mm** 31 M-55; 4 TCM-20

Navy 700 (incl some 90 Naval Inf and SF)
EQUIPMENT BY TYPE
PATROL AND COASTAL COMBATANTS 10
  PB 10: 3 *Camcraft* (30m); 1 *Point*; 1 *Swiftships* 77; 1 *Swiftships* 65; 4 Type-44 (ex-USCG)
AMPHIBIOUS • LANDING CRAFT
  LCM 4

Naval Inf (SF Commandos) 90
FORCES BY ROLE
SPECIAL FORCES
  1 SF coy

Air Force 750 (incl 200 Air Defence)
Flying hours 90 hrs/year on A-37 *Dragonfly*
FORCES BY ROLE
FIGHTER/GROUND ATTACK/ISR
  1 sqn with A-37B/OA-37B *Dragonfly*; O-2A/B *Skymaster*
TRANSPORT
  1 sqn with BT-67; Cessna 210 *Centurion*; Cessna 337G; *Commander* 114; IAI-202 *Arava*; SA-226T *Merlin* IIIB
TRAINING
  1 sqn with R-235GT *Guerrier*; T-35 *Pillan*; T-41D *Mescalero*; TH-300
TRANSPORT HELICOPTER
  1 sqn with Bell 205 (UH-1H *Iroquois*); Bell 407; Bell 412EP *Twin Huey*; MD-500E; UH-1M *Iroquois*
EQUIPMENT BY TYPE
AIRCRAFT 25 combat capable
  ATK 14 A-37B *Dragonfly*
  ISR 11: 6 O-2A/B *Skymaster**; 5 OA-37B *Dragonfly**
  TPT • Light 10: 2 BT-67; 2 Cessna 210 *Centurion*; 1 Cessna 337G *Skymaster*; 1 *Commander* 114; 3 IAI-201 *Arava*; 1 SA-226T *Merlin* IIIB
  TRG 11: 5 R-235GT *Guerrier*; 5 T-35 *Pillan*; 1 T-41D *Mescalero*
HELICOPTERS
  MRH 14: 4 Bell 412EP *Twin Huey*; 8 MD-500E; 2 UH-1M *Iroquois*
  TPT• Light 19: 18 Bell 205 (UH-1H *Iroquois*) (incl 4 SAR); 1 Bell 407 (VIP tpt, govt owned)
  TRG 5 TH-300
MSL • AAM • IR *Shafrir*‡

Paramilitary 17,000

National Civilian Police 17,000
Ministry of Public Security
AIRCRAFT
  ISR 1 O-2A *Skymaster*
  TPT • Light 1 Cessna 310
HELICOPTERS
  MRH 2 MD-520N
  TPT • Light 3: 1 Bell 205 (UH-1H *Iroquois*); 2 R-44 *Raven* II

DEPLOYMENT

CÔTE D'IVOIRE
UN • UNOCI 3 obs

HAITI
UN • MINUSTAH 35

LEBANON
UN • UNIFIL 51; 1 inf pl

SOUTH SUDAN
UN • UNMISS 2 obs

SUDAN
UN • UNISFA 1 obs

WESTERN SAHARA
UN • MINURSO 3 obs

FOREIGN FORCES

United States US Southern Command: 1 Forward Operating Location (Military, DEA, USCG and Customs personnel)

Guatemala GUA

Guatemalan Quetzal q		2013	2014	2015
GDP	q	423bn	460bn	
	US$	53.8bn	58.3bn	
per capita	US$	3,475	3,674	
Growth	%	3.7	3.4	
Inflation	%	4.3	3.5	
Def bdgt	q	2.04bn	2.08bn	
	US$	259m	264m	
FMA (US)	US$	0.5m	1.7m	1m
US$1=q		7.86	7.89	

Population 14,647,083

Age	0–14	15–19	20–24	25–29	30–64	65 plus
Male	18.4%	5.8%	5.3%	4.3%	13.5%	2.0%
Female	17.7%	5.7%	5.3%	4.5%	15.2%	2.3%

Capabilities

Guatemala's armed forces retain a limited capability to participate in international operations and disaster-relief tasks. Rising levels of organised crime and narcotics trafficking have resulted in proposals to increase the defence budget, linked to new procurement and recruitment drives. In 2013, new brigades were established to assist with coastal and border security. Equipment requirements include aerial-surveillance radars and coastal-patrol craft to monitor littoral waters. In the first half of 2014, the Central American Integration System announced equipment donations to the Guatemalan border-security authorities, and in late 2013 and mid-2014 the US government donated 74 light-armoured 4x4s to two new border-protection task forces. An order for six *Super Tucano* aircraft, however, was put on hold. Given the transnational nature of organised criminality in Central America, there is close cooperation with counterparts from Mexico, El Salvador and Honduras.

ACTIVE 17,300 (Army 15,550 Navy 900 Air 850)
Paramilitary 25,000

RESERVE 63,850 (Navy 650 Air 900 Armed Forces 62,300)

(National Armed Forces are combined; the army provides log spt for navy and air force)

ORGANISATIONS BY SERVICE

Army 15,550
15 Military Zones
FORCES BY ROLE
SPECIAL FORCES
  1 SF bde (1 SF bn, 1 trg bn)
  1 SF bde (1 SF coy, 1 ranger bn)
  1 SF mtn bde
MANOEUVRE
  Light
  1 (strategic reserve) mech bde (1 inf bn, 1 cav regt, 1 log coy)
  6 inf bde (1 inf bn)
  Air Manoeuvre
  1 AB bde with (2 AB bn)
  Amphibious
  1 mne bde
  Other
  1 (Presidential) gd bde (1 gd bn, 1 MP bn, 1 CSS coy)
COMBAT SUPPORT
  1 engr comd (1 engr bn, 1 construction bn)
  2 MP bde with (1 MP bn)

Reserves
FORCES BY ROLE
MANOEUVRE
  Light
  ε19 inf bn
EQUIPMENT BY TYPE
RECCE (7 M8 in store)
APC 47
  APC (T) 10 M113 (5 more in store)
  APC (W) 37: 30 *Armadillo*; 7 V-100 *Commando*
ARTY 149
  TOWED 105mm 76: 12 M101; 8 M102; 56 M-56
  MOR 73: **81mm** 55 M1; **107mm** (12 M-30 in store); **120mm** 18 ECIA
AT
  RCL 120+: **105mm** 64 M-1974 FMK-1 (ARG); **106mm** 56 M40A1; **75mm** M20
AD • GUNS • TOWED 32: **20mm** 16 GAI-D01; 16 M-55

Navy 900
EQUIPMENT BY TYPE
PATROL AND COASTAL COMBATANTS 10
  PB 10: 6 *Cutlass*; 1 *Dauntless*; 1 *Kukulkan* (US Broadsword 32m); 2 *Utatlan* (US Sewart)
AMPHIBIOUS • LANDING CRAFT • LCP 2 *Machete*
LOGISTICS AND SUPPORT • AXS 3

Marines 650 reservists
FORCES BY ROLE
MANOEUVRE
  Amphibious
  2 mne bn (-)

Air Force 850

2 air comd

FORCES BY ROLE
FIGHTER/GROUND ATTACK/ISR
1 sqn with A-37B *Dragonfly*
1 sqn with PC-7 *Turbo Trainer**
TRANSPORT
1 sqn with BT-67; Beech 90/100/200/300 *King Air*; IAI-201 *Arava*
1 (tactical support) sqn with Cessna 206; PA-31 *Navajo*
TRAINING
1 sqn with Cessna R172K *Hawk* XP; T-35B *Pillan*
TRANSPORT HELICOPTER
1 sqn with Bell 206 *Jet Ranger*; Bell 212 (armed); Bell 412 *Twin Huey* (armed); UH-1H *Iroquois*

EQUIPMENT BY TYPE
Serviceability of ac is less than 50%
AIRCRAFT 9 combat capable
ATK 2 A-37B *Dragonfly*
TPT • Light 27: 5 Beech 90 *King Air*; 1 Beech 100 *King Air*; 2 Beech 200 *King Air*; 2 Beech 300 *King Air*; 4 BT-67; 2 Cessna 206; 1 Cessna 208B; 5 Cessna R172K *Hawk* XP; 4 IAI-201 *Arava*; 1 PA-31 *Navajo*
TRG 11: 7 PC-7 *Turbo Trainer**; 4 T-35B *Pillan*
HELICOPTERS
MRH 2 Bell 412 *Twin Huey* (armed)
TPT • Light 17: 2 Bell 205 (UH-1H *Iroquois*); 8 Bell 206 *Jet Ranger*; 7 Bell 212 (armed)

Tactical Security Group
Air Military Police

Paramilitary 25,000 active

National Civil Police 25,000
FORCES BY ROLE
SPECIAL FORCES
1 SF bn
MANOEUVRE
Other
1 (integrated task force) paramilitary unit (incl mil and treasury police)

DEPLOYMENT

CÔTE D'IVOIRE
UN • UNOCI 5 obs

DEMOCRATIC REPUBLIC OF THE CONGO
UN • MONUSCO 152; 1 obs; 1 SF coy

HAITI
UN • MINUSTAH 138; 1 MP coy

LEBANON
UN • UNIFIL 2

SOUTH SUDAN
UN • UNMISS 3; 2 obs

SUDAN
UN • UNISFA 1; 2 obs

Guyana GUY

Guyanese Dollar G$		2013	2014	2015
GDP	G$	614bn	670bn	
	US$	2.99bn	3.14bn	
per capita	US$	3,755	3,945	
Growth	%	5.2	3.3	
Inflation	%	2.2	2.6	
Def bdgt	G$	7.24bn	7.93bn	
	US$	35m	37m	
US$1=G$		205.39	213.31	

Population 735,554

Age	0–14	15–19	20–24	25–29	30–64	65 plus
Male	14.8%	5.8%	5.0%	3.9%	18.8%	2.2%
Female	14.2%	5.6%	4.6%	3.5%	18.5%	3.1%

Capabilities

The country has a limited military capability based on the Guyana Defence Force, which also undertakes paramilitary and policing tasks. The GDF's main tasks are territorial integrity, assisting the civil power and contributing to economic development. Border issues with Venezuela and Suriname have, in the past, been the focus of security concerns. Brazil is increasingly supportive of the country's modest defence needs, providing officer training in Brazil, instructors for jungle- and amphibious-warfare training in Guyana and funds for infrastructure projects. Additionally, it was reported that Guyana signed a US$8.4m military-aid package with China in 2014.

ACTIVE 1,100 (Army 900 Navy 100 Air 100)
Active numbers combined Guyana Defence Force

RESERVE 670 (Army 500 Navy 170)

ORGANISATIONS BY SERVICE

Army 900
FORCES BY ROLE
SPECIAL FORCES
1 SF coy
MANOEUVRE
Light
1 inf bn
Other
1 (Presidential) gd bn
COMBAT SUPPORT
1 arty coy
1 (spt wpn) cbt spt coy
1 engr coy

EQUIPMENT BY TYPE
RECCE 9: 6 EE-9 *Cascavel* (reported); 3 S52 *Shorland*
ARTY 54
TOWED 130mm 6 M-46†
MOR 48: **81mm** 12 L16A1; **82mm** 18 M-43; **120mm** 18 M-43

Navy 100

EQUIPMENT BY TYPE
PATROL AND COASTAL COMBATANTS 5
 PCO 1 *Essequibo* (ex-UK *River*)
 PB 4 *Barracuda* (ex-US Type-44)

Air Force 100

FORCES BY ROLE
TRANSPORT
 1 unit with Bell 206; Cessna 206; Y-12 (II)

EQUIPMENT BY TYPE
AIRCRAFT • TPT • Light 2: 1 Cessna 206; 1 Y-12 (II)
HELICOPTERS
 MRH 1 Bell 412 *Twin Huey*†
 TPT • Light 2 Bell 206

Haiti HTI

Haitian Gourde G			2013	2014	2015
GDP		G		365bn	398bn
		US$		8.46bn	8.92bn
per capita		US$		820	853
Growth		%		4.3	3.8
Inflation		%		6.8	4.0
FMA (US)		US$			1.5m	0.8m
US$1=G				43.13	44.66

Population 9,996,731

Age	0–14	15–19	20–24	25–29	30–64	65 plus
Male	17.0%	5.7%	5.1%	4.4%	15.6%	1.8%
Female	16.9%	5.7%	5.1%	4.4%	15.9%	2.3%

Capabilities

Haiti now has embryonic armed forces, reflecting presidential ambitions to create a small army. The army was abolished in 1995, while since 2004 the country has played host to the United Nations Multinational Stabilisation Mission (MINUSTAH). Training of recruits to re-establish the armed forces began in 2013 with support provided by Ecuador. When the first planned elements of the army were activated in February 2014, to support infrastructure development, it was envisaged that they would not be used for routine internal-security tasks, which would remain the purview of the police. However, a future border-security role has been identified.

ACTIVE 70 (Army 70) **Paramilitary 50**

ORGANISATIONS BY SERVICE

Army 70

Paramilitary 50

 Coast Guard ε50
 EQUIPMENT BY TYPE
 PATROL AND COASTAL COMBATANTS • PB 8: 5
  Dauntless; 3 3812-VCF

FOREIGN FORCES

Argentina 555; 1 inf bn; 1 spt coy; 1 fd hospital; 1 hel sqn
Bolivia 209; 1 mech inf coy
Brazil 1,359; 1 inf bn; 1 engr coy
Canada 7
Chile 412; 1 mech inf bn; elm 1 engr coy; 1 hel sqn
Ecuador 53; elm 1 engr coy
El Salvador 35
Guatemala 138; 1 MP coy
Honduras 38
Indonesia 2
Jordan 8
Korea, Republic of 2
Nepal 13
Paraguay 114; 1 engr coy
Peru 373; 1 inf coy
Philippines 181; 1 HQ coy
Sri Lanka 861; 1 inf bn
United States 9
Uruguay 606; 1 inf bn

Honduras HND

Honduran Lempira L		2013	2014	2015
GDP	L	378bn	408bn	
	US$	18.5bn	19.4bn	
per capita	US$	2,283	2,344	
Growth	%	2.6	3.0	
Inflation	%	5.2	6.1	
Def bdgt [a]	L	3.65bn	4.55bn	
	US$	179m	216m	
FMA (US)	US$	1m	4.5m	3.1m
US$1=L		20.42	21.08	

[a] Defence & national security budget

Population 8,598,561

Age	0–14	15–19	20–24	25–29	30–64	65 plus
Male	17.8%	5.7%	5.1%	4.5%	15.4%	1.8%
Female	17.0%	5.4%	4.9%	4.4%	15.6%	2.3%

Capabilities

Honduras retains a broad range of capabilities, though in many cases its equipment is ageing, with serviceability in doubt. Before the 2009 coup, the administration appeared to have achieved some success in improving the conditions, morale and professionalism of the armed forces. Although recruitment levels improved, the declared target of 15,000 troops was not achieved. Equipment maintenance and procurement still accounts for a small proportion of the defence budget. In 2011, the armed forces began to deploy in a paramilitary role, in conjunction with the police, to combat organised crime and narcotics trafficking. A new maritime special-forces unit was established in 2012 to assist in this task, and in 2014 two new security agencies – the Public Order Military Police and the TIGRES – were stood up. Also in 2014, Honduras received three aerial-surveillance radars for the tracking and interception of drug traffickers. The US maintains a small military presence at Soto Cano air base.

ACTIVE 12,000 (Army 8,300 Navy 1,400 Air 2,300) Paramilitary 8,000

RESERVE 60,000 (Joint 60,000; Ex-servicemen registered)

ORGANISATIONS BY SERVICE

Army 8,300
6 military zones
FORCES BY ROLE
SPECIAL FORCES
1 (special tac) SF gp (1 SF bn, 1 inf/AB bn)
MANOEUVRE
Mechanised
1 armd cav regt (1 recce sqn, 1 lt tk sqn, 2 mech bn, 1 arty bty, 1 ADA bty)
Light
3 inf bde (3 inf bn, 1 arty bn)
1 inf bde (3 inf bn)
Other
1 (Presidential) gd coy
COMBAT SUPPORT
1 engr bn

Reserves
FORCES BY ROLE
MANOEUVRE
Light
1 inf bde
EQUIPMENT BY TYPE
LT TK 12 *Scorpion*
RECCE 57: 13 RBY-1; 40 *Saladin*; 3 *Scimitar*; 1 *Sultan*
ARTY 118+
TOWED 28: **105mm:** 24 M102; **155mm:** 4 M198
MOR 90+: **81mm**; **120mm** 60 FMK-2; **160mm** 30 M-66
AT • RCL 170: **106mm** 50 M40A1; **84mm** 120 *Carl Gustav*
AD • GUNS **20mm** 48: 24 M55A2; 24 TCM-20

Navy 1,400
EQUIPMENT BY TYPE
PATROL AND COASTAL COMBATANTS 17
PB 17: 2 *Lempira* (Damen Stan 4207 – leased); 1 *Chamelecon* (Swiftships 85); 1 *Tegucilgalpa* (US *Guardian* 32m); 4 *Guanaja* (ex-US Type-44); 3 *Guaymuras* (Swiftships 105); 5 *Nacaome* (Swiftships 65); 1 *Rio Coco* (US PB Mk III)
AMPHIBIOUS • LANDING CRAFT 3
LCU 1 *Punta Caxinas*
LCM 2

Marines 830
FORCES BY ROLE
MANOEUVRE
Amphibious
1 mne bn

Air Force 2,300
FORCES BY ROLE
FIGHTER/GROUND ATTACK
1 sqn with A-37B *Dragonfly*
1 sqn with F-5E/F *Tiger* II
GROUND ATTACK/ISR/TRAINING
1 unit with Cessna 182 *Skylane*; EMB-312 *Tucano*; MXT-7-180 *Star Rocket*
TRANSPORT
1 sqn with Beech 200 *King Air*; C-130A *Hercules*; Cessna 185/210; IAI-201 *Arava*; PA-42 *Cheyenne*; Turbo Commander 690
1 VIP flt with PA-31 *Navajo*; Bell 412SP *Twin Huey*
TRANSPORT HELICOPTER
1 sqn with Bell 205 (UH-1H *Iroquois*); Bell 412SP *Twin Huey*
EQUIPMENT BY TYPE
AIRCRAFT 17 combat capable
FTR 11: 9 F-5E *Tiger* II†; 2 F-5F *Tiger* II†
ATK 6 A-37B *Dragonfly*
TPT 11: **Medium** 1 C-130A *Hercules*; **Light** 10: 1 Beech 200 *King Air*; 2 Cessna 182 *Skylane*; 1 Cessna 185; 2 Cessna 210; 1 IAI-201 *Arava*; 1 PA-31 *Navajo*; 1 PA-42 *Cheyenne*; 1 Turbo Commander 690
TRG 16: 9 EMB-312 *Tucano*; 7 MXT-7-180 *Star Rocket*
HELICOPTERS
MRH 7: 5 Bell 412SP *Twin Huey*; 2 Hughes 500
TPT • **Light** 3: 2 Bell 205 (UH-1H *Iroquois*); 1 AS350 *Ecureuil*
MSL • AAM • IR *Shafrir*‡

Paramilitary 8,000

Public Security Forces 8,000
Ministry of Public Security and Defence; 11 regional comd

DEPLOYMENT

HAITI
UN • MINUSTAH 38

WESTERN SAHARA
UN • MINURSO 12 obs

FOREIGN FORCES
United States US Southern Command: 370; 1 avn bn with CH-47 *Chinook*; UH-60 *Black Hawk*

Jamaica JAM

Jamaican Dollar J$		2013	2014	2015
GDP	J$	1.43tr	1.56tr	
	US$	14.2bn	13.9bn	
per capita	US$	5,100	4,974	
Growth	%	0.2	1.1	
Inflation	%	9.4	8.8	
Def bdgt	J$	13.1bn	13.4bn	
	US$	130m	120m	
US$1=J$		100.76	111.89	

Population   2,930,050

Age	0–14	15–19	20–24	25–29	30–64	65 plus
Male	14.5%	5.5%	5.4%	4.5%	16.1%	3.5%
Female	14.0%	5.4%	5.4%	4.7%	16.7%	4.3%

Capabilities

Regionally amongst the most capable armed forces, they nonetheless have very limited airlift capacity and no ability to deploy independently overseas. Internal and maritime security, along with disaster relief, are key tasks, and on occasion the armed forces have been used to support police operations against organised crime. Jamaica's forces train with larger and more capable armed services from the likes of the UK and Canada.

ACTIVE 2,830 (Army 2,500 Coast Guard 190 Air 140) (combined Jamaican Defence Force)

RESERVE 980 (Army 900 Navy 60 Air 20)

ORGANISATIONS BY SERVICE

Army 2,500
FORCES BY ROLE
MANOEUVRE
  Light
    2 inf bn
COMBAT SUPPORT
  1 engr regt (4 engr sqn)
COMBAT SERVICE SUPPORT
  1 spt bn (1 MP coy, 1 med coy, 1 log coy, 1 tpt coy)
EQUIPMENT BY TYPE
APC (W) 4 LAV-150 *Commando*
MOR 81mm 12 L16A1

Reserves
FORCES BY ROLE
MANOEUVRE
  Light
    1 inf bn

Coast Guard 190
EQUIPMENT BY TYPE
PATROL AND COASTAL COMBATANTS 11

PBF 3
PB 8: 3 *Cornwall* (Damen Stan 4207); 4 *Dauntless*; 1 *Paul Bogle* (US 31m)

Air Wing 140
Plus National Reserve
FORCES BY ROLE
MARITIME PATROL/TRANSPORT
  1 flt with BN-2A *Defender*; Cessna 210M *Centurion*
SEARCH & RESCUE/TRANSPORT HELICOPTER
  1 flt with Bell 407
  1 flt with Bell 412EP
TRAINING
  1 unit with Bell 206B3; DA40-180FP *Diamond Star*
EQUIPMENT BY TYPE
AIRCRAFT
TPT • Light 4: 1 BN-2A *Defender*; 1 Cessna 210M *Centurion*; 2 DA40-180FP *Diamond Star*
HELICOPTERS
MRH 2 Bell 412EP
TPT • Light 5: 2 Bell 206B3 *Jet Ranger*; 3 Bell 407

Mexico MEX

Mexican Peso NP		2013	2014	2015
GDP	NP	16.1tr	17.2tr	
	US$	1.26tr	1.3tr	
per capita	US$	10,650	10,837	
Growth	%	1.1	2.4	
Inflation	%	3.8	3.9	
Def exp [a]	NP	60.8bn		
	US$	4.76bn		
Def bdgt [a]	NP	75.7bn	86.7bn	98.3bn
	US$	5.93bn	6.55bn	
FMA (US)	US$	7m	7m	5m
US$1=NP		12.77	13.24	

[a] National security expenditure

Population   120,286,655

Age	0–14	15–19	20–24	25–29	30–64	65 plus
Male	14.3%	4.7%	4.5%	4.2%	18.5%	3.0%
Female	13.7%	4.5%	4.4%	4.2%	20.5%	3.6%

Capabilities

Mexico has the most capable armed forces in Central America. They are constitutionally disbarred from international deployment except in wartime, but have been involved in disaster-relief operations. As well as these, main tasks for the armed forces include defending state sovereignty and territorial integrity, internal security and extending aid to civil authorities. The navy retains well-equipped frigates, but the majority of its forces and primary roles are dedicated to maritime security. Under the Calderón administration operations against drug cartels became the army's primary activity, involving about a quarter of its active strength at any given time, while the navy and air force both prioritised procurement of ISR and transport platforms. In 2014, the purchase of light helicopters to destroy narcotics plantations was announced, as well as *King Air* surveillance aircraft. A new National Gendarmerie was activated in August 2014, although plans for an initial establishment of 10,000 were subsequently reduced to 5,000. A continuing problem with desertion has prompted efforts to improve benefits, training and conditions for serving personnel. There exists a significant air- and sea-lift capability that would allow for regional deployments if necessary.

ACTIVE 266,550 (Army 204,950 Navy 53,600 Air 8,000) **Paramilitary 58,900**

RESERVE 87,350 (National Military Service)

ORGANISATIONS BY SERVICE

Space
SATELLITES • COMMUNICATIONS 1 *Mexsat*

Army 204,950
12 regions (total: 46 army zones)
FORCES BY ROLE
SPECIAL FORCES
  3 SF bde (12 SF bn)
  1 amph SF bde (5 SF bn)
MANOEUVRE
  Reconnaissance
  3 armd bde (2 armd recce bn, 2 lt armd recce bn, 1 (Canon) AT gp)
  3 armd recce regt
  2 lt armd recce regt
  25 mot recce regt
  Light
  1 (1st) armd corps (1 armd bde (2 armd recce bn, 2 lt armd recce bn, 1 (Canon) AT gp), 3 inf/rapid reaction bde (each: 3 inf bn, 1 arty regt, 1 (Canon) AT gp), 1 cbt engr bde (3 engr bn))
  3 indep lt inf bde (2 lt inf bn, 1 (Canon) AT gp)
  106 indep inf bn
  25 indep inf coy
  Air Manoeuvre
  1 para bde with (1 (GAFE) SF gp, 3 bn, 1 (Canon) AT gp)
  Other
  1 (Presidential) gd corps (1 SF gp, 1 mech inf bde (2 inf bn, 1 aslt bn), 1 mne bn (Navy), 1 cbt engr bn, 1 MP bde (3 bn, 1 special ops anti-riot coy))
COMBAT SUPPORT
  6 indep arty regt
  2 MP bde (3 MP bn)
EQUIPMENT BY TYPE
RECCE 237: 124 ERC-90F1 *Lynx* (4 trg); 40 M8; 41 MAC-1; 32 VBL
APC 706
  APC (T) 472: 398 DNC-1 (mod AMX-VCI); 40 HWK-11; 34 M5A1 half-track

  APC (W) 234: 95 BDX; 25 DN-4; 19 DN-5 *Toro*; 26 LAV-150 ST; 25 MOWAG *Roland*; 44 VCR (3 amb; 5 cmd post)
ARTY 1,390
  TOWED 123: **105mm** 123: 40 M101; 40 M-56; 16 M2A1, 14 M3; 13 NORINCO M-90
  MOR 1,267: **81mm** 1,100: 400 M1; 400 Brandt; 300 SB **120mm** 167: 75 Brandt; 60 M-65; 32 RT61
AT
  MSL • SP 8 *Milan* (VBL)
  RCL 1,187+
    SP 106mm M40A1
    106mm M40A1
  GUNS 37mm 30 M3
AD
  GUNS 80
    TOWED 12.7mm 40 M55; **20mm** 40 GAI-B01
  ARV 3 M32 *Recovery Sherman*

Navy 53,600
Two Fleet Commands: Gulf (6 zones), Pacific (11 zones)
EQUIPMENT BY TYPE
PRINCIPAL SURFACE COMBATANTS 6
  FRIGATES 6
    FFGHM 4 *Allende* (US *Knox*) with 1 octuple Mk16 lnchr with ASROC/RGM-84C *Harpoon* AShM, 1 Mk25 GMLS with RIM-7 *Sea Sparrow* SAM, 2 twin Mk32 324mm ASTT with Mk46 LWT, 1 127mm gun (capacity 1 MD-902 hel)
    FF 2 *Bravo* (US *Bronstein*) with 1 octuple Mk112 lnchr with ASROC†, 2 triple Mk32 324mm ASTT with Mk46 LWT, 1 twin 76mm gun, 1 hel landing platform
PATROL AND COASTAL COMBATANTS 122
  PSOH 4 *Oaxaca* with 1 76mm gun (capacity 1 AS565MB *Panther* hel)
  PCOH 16:
    4 *Durango* with 1 57mm gun (capacity 1 Bo-105 hel)
    4 *Holzinger* (capacity 1 MD-902 *Explorer*)
    3 *Sierra* with 1 57mm gun (capacity 1 MD-902 *Explorer*)
    5 *Uribe* (ESP *Halcon*) (capacity 1 Bo-105 hel)
  PCO 10 *Leandro Valle* (US *Auk* MSF) with 1 76mm gun
  PCG 2 *Huracan* (ISR *Aliya*) with 4 single lnchr with *Gabriel* II AShM, 1 *Phalanx* CIWS
  PCC 2 *Democrata*
  PBF 73: 6 *Acuario*; 2 *Acuario B*; 48 *Polaris* (SWE CB90); 17 *Polaris* II (SWE IC 16M)
  PB 15: 8 *Azteca*; 3 *Cabo* (US *Cape Higgon*); 2 *Punta* (US *Point*); 2 *Tenochtitlan* (Damen Stan 4207)
AMPHIBIOUS • LS • LST 2 *Papaloapan* (US *Newport*) with 4 76mm guns, 1 hel landing platform
LOGISTICS AND SUPPORT 53
  AFD 5
  AG 2
  AGOR 3: 2 *Altair* (ex-US *Robert D. Conrad*); 1 *Humboldt*
  AGS 8: 4 *Arrecife*; 1 *Onjuku*; 1 *Rio Hondo*; 1 *Rio Tuxpan*; 1 *Moctezuma* II (also used as AXS)
  AK 4: 1 *Tarasco*; 1 *Rio Suchiate*; 2 *Montes Azules* (can also be used as landing ship) with 1 hel landing platform
  ATF 4 *Otomi* with 1 76mm gun
  AX 3: 1 *Manuel Azuela* with 3 76mm guns; 2 *Huasteco* (also serve as troop transport, supply and hospital ships)

AXS 1 *Cuauhtemoc* with 2 65mm saluting guns
YTL 6
YM 17

Naval Aviation 1,250
FORCES BY ROLE
MARITIME PATROL
  5 sqn with Cessna 404 *Titan*; MX-7 *Star Rocket*; Lancair IV-P
  1 sqn with C-212PM *Aviocar**; CN-235-300 MPA *Persuader*
  1 sqn with L-90 *Redigo*
TRANSPORT
  1 sqn with An-32B *Cline*
  1 (VIP) sqn with DHC-8 *Dash 8*; Learjet 24; *Turbo Commander* 1000
TRANSPORT HELICOPTER
  2 sqn with AS555 *Fennec*; AS-565MB *Panther*; MD-902; PZL Mi-2 *Hoplite*
  2 sqn with Bo-105 CBS-5
  5 sqn with Mi-17-1V/V-5 *Hip*
EQUIPMENT BY TYPE
AIRCRAFT 7 combat capable
  MP 6 CN-235-300 MPA *Persuader*
  ISR 7 C-212PM *Aviocar**
  TPT • **Light** 23: 1 An-32B *Cline*; 2 Beech 350ER *King Air*; 4 C-295M; 1 Cessna 404 *Titan*; 1 DHC-8 *Dash 8*; 6 Lancair IV-P; 3 Learjet 24; 5 *Turbo Commander* 1000
  TRG 26: 3 L-90TP *Redigo*; 4 MX-7 *Star Rocket*; 2 T-6C+ *Texan* II; 17 Z-242L
HELICOPTERS
  MRH 30: 2 AS555 *Fennec*; 4 MD-500E; 20 Mi-17-1V *Hip*; 4 Mi-17V-5 *Hip*
  SAR 4 AS565MB *Panther*
  TPT 25: **Heavy** 3 EC725 *Cougar*; **Medium** 3 UH-60M *Black Hawk*; **Light** 19: 11 Bo-105 CBS-5; 5 MD-902 (SAR role); 2 PZL Mi-2 *Hoplite*; 1 R-44

Marines 21,500 (Expanding to 26,560)
FORCES BY ROLE
SPECIAL FORCES
  3 SF unit
MANOEUVRE
  Light
    32 inf bn(-)
  Air Manoeuvre
    1 AB bn
  Amphibious
    2 amph bde
  Other
    1 (Presidential) gd bn (included in army above)
COMBAT SERVICE SUPPORT
  2 CSS bn
EQUIPMENT BY TYPE
APC (W) 29: 3 BTR-60 (APC-60); 26 BTR-70 (APC-70)
ARTY 122
  TOWED **105mm** 16 M-56
  MRL **122mm** 6 Firos-25
  MOR 100 **60mm/81mm**

AT • **RCL 106mm** M40A1
AD • **SAM** • **MANPAD** 5+ 9K38 *Igla* (SA-18 *Grouse*)

Air Force 8,000
FORCES BY ROLE
FIGHTER
  1 sqn with F-5E/F *Tiger* II
GROUND ATTACK/ISR
  4 sqn with PC-7*
  1 sqn with PC-7*/PC-9M
ISR/AEW
  1 sqn with EMB-145AEW *Erieye*; EMB-145RS; SA-2-37B; SA-227-BC *Metro* III (C-26B)
TRANSPORT
  1 sqn with IAI-201 *Arava*; C-295M; PC-6B
  1 squadron with B-727; Beech 90
  1 sqn with C-27J *Spartan*; C-130E/K *Hercules*; L-100-30
  6 (liaison) sqn with Cessna 182/206
  1 (anti-narcotic spraying) sqn with Bell 206; Cessna T206H;
  1 (Presidential) gp with AS332L *Super Puma*; B-737; B-757; EC225; Gulfstream III; Learjet 35A; Learjet 36A; *Turbo Commander* 680
  1 (VIP) gp with B-737; Beech 200 *King Air*; Cessna 500 *Citation*; L-1329 *Jetstar* 8; S-70A-24
TRAINING
  1 sqn with Cessna 182
  1 sqn with PC-7*
  1 sqn with SF-260EU
  1 unit with T-6C *Texan* II
TRANSPORT HELICOPTER
  1 sqn with Bell 206B; Bell 212; S-65 *Yas'ur* 2000
  3 sqn with Bell 206B; Bell 212
  1 sqn with MD-530MF/MG
  1 sqn with Mi-8T; Mi-17; Mi-26T
  1 sqn with EC725 *Super Cougar*; Bell 412EP *Twin Huey*; S-70A-24 *Black Hawk*
ISR UAV
  1 unit with *Hermes* 450
EQUIPMENT BY TYPE
AIRCRAFT 74 combat capable
  FTR 8: 6 F-5E *Tiger* II; 2 F-5F *Tiger* II
  ISR 6: 2 SA-2-37A; 4 SA-227-BC *Metro* III (C-26B)
  ELINT 2 EMB-145RS
  AEW&C 1 EMB-145AEW *Erieye*
  TPT 110: **Medium** 12: 4 C-27J *Spartan*; 3 C-130E *Hercules*; 2 C-130K *Hercules*; 2 C-130K-30 *Hercules*; 1 L-100-30; **Light** 89: 2 Beech 90 *King Air*; 1 Beech 200 *King Air*; 6 C-295M; 59 Cessna 182; 3 Cessna 206; 8 Cessna T206H; 1 Cessna 500 *Citation*; 1 L-1329 *Jetstar* 8; 2 Learjet 35A; 1 Learjet 36; 1 Learjet 45XP; 3 PC-6B; 1 *Turbo Commander* 680; **PAX** 9: 4 B-727; 2 B-737; 1 B-757; 2 Gulfstream III
  TRG 114: 4 Beech F33C *Bonanza*; 64 PC-7*; 2 PC-9M*; 7 PT-17; 25 SF-260EU; 12 T-6C *Texan* II
HELICOPTERS
  MRH 32: 12 Bell 412EP *Twin Huey*; 20 Mi-17 *Hip* H
  ISR 14: 5 MD-530MF; 9 MD-530MG
  TPT 104: **Heavy** 12: 8 EC725 *Super Cougar*; 4 S-65C *Yas'ur* 2000; **Medium** 13: 3 AS332L *Super Puma*; 2 EC225 (VIP); 2 Mi-8T *Hip*; 6 S-70A-24 *Black Hawk*; **Light** 79: 45 Bell 206; 13 Bell 206B *Jet Ranger* II; 7 Bell 206L; 14 Bell 212

UAV • ISR 8: **Medium** 3 *Hermes* 450; **Light** 5 S4 *Ehécatl*
MSL • AAM • IR AIM-9J *Sidewinder*

Paramilitary 62,900

Federal Police 41,000 (Incl 5,000 Gendarmerie)
Public Security Secretariat
AIRCRAFT
  TPT 13: **Light** 7: 2 CN-235M; 2 Cessna 182 *Skylane*; 1 Cessna 500 *Citation*; 2 Turbo Commander 695; **PAX** 6: 4 B-727; 1 *Falcon* 20; 1 Gulfstream II
HELICOPTERS
  MRH 3 Mi-17 *Hip* H
  TPT 24: **Medium** 10: 1 SA330J *Puma*; 6 UH-60L *Black Hawk*; 3 UH-60M *Black Hawk*; **Light** 14: 2 AS350B *Ecureuil*; 1 AS355 *Ecureuil* II; 6 Bell 206B; 5 EC-120
UAV • ISR • **Light** 10 S4 *Ehécatl*

Federal Ministerial Police 4,500
EQUIPMENT BY TYPE
HELICOPTERS
  TPT • **Light** 35: 18 Bell 205 (UH-1H); 7 Bell 212; 10 Schweizer 333

Rural Defense Militia 17,400
FORCES BY ROLE
  MANOEUVRE Light
  13 inf unit
  13 (horsed) cav unit

Cyber

It was announced that a Cyberspace Operations Centre would be created by 2018, to address this 'fourth dimension of military operations' and better coordinate defence work on cyber security and in cyberspace. Key documentation includes the 2013–18 National Defence Sector Programme, the 2013–18 National Development Programme and the 2014–18 National Security Programme.

Nicaragua NIC

Nicaraguan Gold Córdoba Co		2013	2014	2015
GDP	Co	278bn	308bn	
	US$	11.3bn	11.8bn	
per capita	US$	1,831	1,904	
Growth	%	4.6	4.0	
Inflation	%	7.1	6.3	
Def bdgt	Co	2.1bn	2.15bn	
	US$	85m	83m	
FMA (US)	US$			0.39m
US$1=Co		24.72	25.96	
Population	5,848,641			

Age	0–14	15–19	20–24	25–29	30–64	65 plus
Male	14.9%	5.6%	5.6%	4.4%	16.1%	2.2%
Female	14.4%	5.5%	5.6%	4.6%	18.3%	2.7%

Capabilities

Nicaragua's armed forces are postured to provide assistance to border- and internal-security operations, with a central reserve focused on a single mechanised brigade. Specialised units focusing on disaster relief, coastal security and combatting illegal logging were added in 2010, 2011 and 2012 respectively. Other new units are under discussion, including new marine and land-force contingents to tackle drug traffickers. Most equipment is of Cold War vintage, and although there has been some recent modernisation and refurbishment there has been little in the way of procurement. Current requirements are fixed- and rotary-wing aircraft and coastal-patrol vessels. While the armed forces retain a sufficient airlift capacity to provide mobility within the country, it is insufficient to deploy overseas independently.

ACTIVE 12,000 (Army 10,000 Navy 800 Air 1,200)

ORGANISATIONS BY SERVICE

Army ε10,000
FORCES BY ROLE
SPECIAL FORCES
  1 SF bde (2 SF bn)
MANOEUVRE
  Mechanised
  1 mech inf bde (1 armd recce bn, 1 tk bn, 1 mech inf bn, 1 arty bn, 1 MRL bn, 1 AT coy)
  Light
  1 regional comd (3 lt inf bn)
  4 regional comd (2 lt inf bn)
  2 indep lt inf bn
  Other
  1 comd regt (1 inf bn, 1 sy bn, 1 int unit, 1 sigs bn)
COMBAT SUPPORT
  1 engr bn
COMBAT SERVICE SUPPORT
  1 med bn
  1 tpt regt
EQUIPMENT BY TYPE
MBT 62 T-55 (65 more in store)
LT TK (10 PT-76 in store)
RECCE 20 BRDM-2
AIFV BMP-1
APC (W) 86+: 41 BTR-152 (61 more in store); 45 BTR-60 (15 more in store); Some BTR-70M
ARTY 766
  TOWED 12: **122mm** 12 D-30; (**152mm** 30 D-20 in store)
  MRL 151: **107mm** 33 Type-63: **122mm** 118: 18 BM-21; 100 GRAD 1P (BM-21P) (single-tube rocket launcher, man portable)
  MOR 603: **82mm** 579; **120mm** 24 M-43; (**160mm** 4 M-160 in store)
AT
  MSL
    SP 12 BRDM-2 with 9K11 *Malyutka* (AT-3 *Sagger*)
    MANPATS 9K11 *Malyutka* (AT-3 *Sagger*)
  RCL 82mm B-10
  GUNS 281: **57mm** 174 ZIS-2; (90 more in store); **76mm** 83 ZIS-3; **100mm** 24 M-1944

AD • SAM • MANPAD 9K36 *Strela-3* (SA-14 *Gremlin*); 9K310 *Igla-1* (SA-16 *Gimlet*); 9K32 *Strela-2* (SA-7 *Grail*)‡
AEV T-54/T-55
VLB TMM-3

Navy ε800
EQUIPMENT BY TYPE
PATROL AND COASTAL COMBATANTS • PB 8: 3 *Dabur*; 4 Rodman 101, 1 *Zhuk*

Marines
FORCES BY ROLE
MANOEUVRE
Amphibious
1 mne bn

Air Force 1,200
FORCES BY ROLE
TRANSPORT
1 sqn with An-26 *Curl*; Beech 90 *King Air*; Cessna U206; Cessna 404 *Titan* (VIP)
TRAINING
1 unit with Cessna 172; PA-18 *Super Cub*; PA-28 *Cherokee*
TRANSPORT HELICOPTER
1 sqn with Mi-17 *Hip* H (armed)
AIR DEFENCE
1 gp with ZU-23
EQUIPMENT BY TYPE
AIRCRAFT
TPT • Light 9: 3 An-26 *Curl*; 1 Beech 90 *King Air*; 1 Cessna 172; 1 Cessna U206; 1 Cessna 404 *Titan* (VIP); 2 PA-28 *Cherokee*
TRG 2 PA-18 *Super Cub*
HELICOPTERS
MRH 7 Mi-17 *Hip* H (armed)†
TPT • Medium 2 Mi-171E
AD • GUNS 18 ZU-23
MSL • ASM 9M17 *Skorpion* (AT-2 *Swatter*)

Panama PAN

Panamanian Balboa B		2013	2014	2015
GDP	B	40.5bn	44.7bn	
	US$	40.5bn	44.7bn	
per capita	US$	10,876	11,800	
Growth	%	8.4	6.6	
Inflation	%	4.0	3.2	
Def bdgt [a]	B	637m	717m	
	US$	637m	717m	
FMA (US)	US$	2.34m	1.8m	1.8m
US$1=B		1.00	1.00	

[a] Public security expenditure

Population   3,608,431

Age	0–14	15–19	20–24	25–29	30–64	65 plus
Male	14.0%	4.6%	4.2%	4.1%	19.9%	3.6%
Female	13.4%	4.4%	4.1%	3.9%	19.7%	4.2%

Capabilities

Panama's armed forces were abolished in 1990. A police force and an air/naval coast-guard organisation were retained for low-level security activities. This is focused on transport aircraft and small patrol craft, with some interceptor vessels for interdiction operations.

Paramilitary 12,000

ORGANISATIONS BY SERVICE

Paramilitary 12,000

National Police Force 11,000
No hvy mil eqpt, small arms only
FORCES BY ROLE
SPECIAL FORCES
1 SF unit (reported)
MANOEUVRE
Other
1 (presidential) gd bn (-)
8 paramilitary coy
18 police coy
COMBAT SUPPORT
1 MP bn

National Aeronaval Service ε1,000
FORCES BY ROLE
TRANSPORT
1 sqn with C-212M *Aviocar*; Cessna 210; PA-31 *Navajo*; PA-34 *Seneca*
1 (Presidential) flt with ERJ-135BJ; S-76C
TRAINING
1 unit with Cessna 152; Cessna 172; T-35D *Pillan*
TRANSPORT HELICOPTER
1 sqn with AW139; Bell 205; Bell 205 (UH-1H *Iroquois*); Bell 212; Bell 407; Bell 412EP; EC145; MD-500E
EQUIPMENT BY TYPE
PATROL AND COASTAL COMBATANTS 22
PCO 1 *Independencia* (ex-US *Balsam*)
PCC 2 *Saettia*
PB 19: 3 *Chiriqui* (ex-US PB MkIV); 1 *Escudo de Veraguas*; 1 *Naos*; 2 *Panama*; 2 *Panquiaco* (UK Vosper 31.5m); 5 3 *De Noviembre* (ex-US *Point*), 1 *Taboga*; 4 Type-200
AMPHIBIOUS • LANDING CRAFT • LCU 1 *General Estaban Huertas*
LOGISTICS AND SUPPORT • AG 2
AIRCRAFT
TPT • Light 12: 5 C-212M *Aviocar*; 1 Cessna 152, 1 Cessna 172; 1 Cessna 210; 1 ERJ-135BJ; 1 PA-31 *Navajo*; 2 PA-34 *Seneca*
TRG 6 T-35D *Pillan*
HELICOPTERS
MRH 8: 6 AW139; 1 Bell 412EP; 1 MD-500E
TPT • Light 21: 2 Bell 205; 13 Bell 205 (UH-1H *Iroquois*); 2 Bell 212; 2 Bell 407; 1 EC145; 1 S-76C

Paraguay PRY

Paraguayan Guaraní Pg		2013	2014	2015
GDP	Pg	129tr	140tr	
	US$	29.1bn	31.3bn	
per capita	US$	4,281	4,536	
Growth	%	13.6	4.0	
Inflation	%	2.7	4.8	
Def bdgt	Pg	1.54tr	1.4tr	
	US$	347m	313m	
FMA (US)	US$	0.35m		
US$1=Pg		4,436.90	4,483.59	
Population	6,703,860			

Age	0–14	15–19	20–24	25–29	30–64	65 plus
Male	13.3%	5.2%	5.1%	4.4%	19.0%	3.1%
Female	12.9%	5.2%	5.0%	4.5%	18.8%	3.5%

Capabilities

The armed forces have limited capacity for power projection, however the potential re-emergence of a territorial dispute with Bolivia is a security concern. This is contributing to increased interest in renewing elements of the equipment inventory, much of which is obsolete. The army continues to use very old land systems, some from the late 1940s, while the air force has a small number of light counter-insurgency aircraft and a variety of utility and tactical transport aircraft. Though landlocked, the country supports a naval force of mainly river-patrol craft, reflecting the importance of its river systems. There are aspirations to acquire turboprop combat-capable aircraft, UAVs and additional air-defence radars to combat drug trafficking. The services train regularly and participate in UN peacekeeping missions on a limited scale.

ACTIVE 10,650 (Army 7,600 Navy 1,950 Air 1,100)
Paramilitary 14,800
Conscript liability 12 months, Navy 2 years

RESERVE 164,500 (Joint 164,500)

ORGANISATIONS BY SERVICE

Army 6,100; 1,500 conscript (total 7,600)

Much of the Paraguayan army is maintained in a cadre state during peacetime; the nominal inf and cav divs are effectively only at coy strength. Active gp/regt are usually coy sized.

FORCES BY ROLE
MANOEUVRE
  Reconnaissance
  1 armd cav sqn
  Light
  3 inf corps (total: 6 inf div (-), 3 cav div (-), 6 arty bty)
  Other
  1 (Presidential) gd regt (1 SF bn, 1 inf bn, 1 sy bn, 1 log gp)

COMBAT SUPPORT
  1 arty bde with (2 arty gp, 1 ADA gp)
  1 engr bde with (1 engr regt, 3 construction regt)
  1 sigs bn

Reserves
MANOEUVRE
  Light
  14 inf regt (cadre)
  4 cav regt (cadre)

EQUIPMENT BY TYPE
MBT 3 M4A3 Sherman
LT TK 12 M3A1 Stuart (6‡)
RECCE 28 EE-9 Cascavel
APC (T) 20 M9 half-track
APC (W) 12 EE-11 Urutu
ARTY 94
  TOWED 105mm 14 M101
  MOR 81mm 80
AT
  RCL 75mm M20
AD • GUNS 19:
  SP 20mm 3 M9
  TOWED 16: 40mm 10 M1A1, 6 L/60

Navy 1,100; 850 conscript (total 1,950)

EQUIPMENT BY TYPE
PATROL AND COASTAL COMBATANTS 22
  PCR 3: 1 Itaipú; 1 Nanawa‡; 1 Paraguay‡ with 2 twin 120mm gun, 3 76mm gun
  PBR 19: 1 Capitan Cabral; 2 Capitan Ortiz (ROC Hai Ou); 2 Novatec; 6 Type-701; 3 Croq 15; 5 others
AMPHIBIOUS • LANDING CRAFT • LCVP 3
LOGISTICS AND SUPPORT 5
  YAC 1
  YGS 1
  YTL 3

Naval Aviation 100

FORCES BY ROLE
TRANSPORT
  1 (liaison) sqn with Cessna 150; Cessna 210 Centurion; Cessna 310; Cessna 401
TRANSPORT HELICOPTER
  1 sqn with AS350 Ecureuil (HB350 Esquilo); Bell 47 (OH-13 Sioux)

EQUIPMENT BY TYPE
AIRCRAFT • TPT • Light 6: 2 Cessna 150; 1 Cessna 210 Centurion; 2 Cessna 310; 1 Cessna 401
HELICOPTERS • TPT • Light 2 AS350 Ecureuil (HB350 Esquilo)

Marines 700; 200 conscript (total 900)

FORCES BY ROLE
MANOEUVRE
  Amphibious
  3 mne bn(-)

Air Force 900; 200 conscript (total 1,100)

FORCES BY ROLE

GROUND ATTACK/ISR
1 sqn with EMB-312 *Tucano**

TRANSPORT
1 gp with B-707; C-212-200/400 *Aviocar*; DHC-6 *Twin Otter*

1 VIP gp with Beech 58 *Baron*; Bell 427; Cessna U206 *Stationair*; Cessna 208B *Grand Caravan*; Cessna 210 *Centurion*; Cessna 402B; PA-32R *Saratoga* (EMB-721C *Sertanejo*); PZL-104 *Wilga* 80

TRAINING
1 sqn with T-25 *Universal*; T-35A/B *Pillan*

TRANSPORT HELICOPTER
1 gp with AS350 *Ecureuil* (HB350 *Esquilo*); Bell 205 (UH-1H *Iroquois*)

EQUIPMENT BY TYPE

AIRCRAFT 6 combat capable
TPT • **Light** 19: 1 Beech 58 *Baron*; 4 C-212-200 *Aviocar*; 2 C-212-400 *Aviocar*; 2 Cessna 208B *Grand Caravan*; 1 Cessna 210 *Centurion*; 1 Cessna 310; 2 Cessna 402B; 2 Cessna U206 *Stationair*; 1 DHC-6 *Twin Otter*; 1 PA-32R *Saratoga* (EMB-721C *Sertanejo*); 2 PZL-104 *Wilga* 80
TRG 22: 6 EMB-312 *Tucano**; 6 T-25 *Universal*; 7 T-35A *Pillan*; 3 T-35B *Pillan*
HELICOPTERS • TPT • **Light** 10: 3 AS350 *Ecureuil* (HB350 *Esquilo*); 6 Bell 205 (UH-1H *Iroquois*); 1 Bell 427 (VIP)

Paramilitary 14,800

Special Police Service 10,800; 4,000 conscript (total 14,800)

DEPLOYMENT

CÔTE D'IVOIRE
UN • UNOCI 2; 7 obs

CYPRUS
UN • UNFICYP 14

DEMOCRATIC REPUBLIC OF THE CONGO
UN • MONUSCO 13 obs

HAITI
UN • MINUSTAH 114; 1 engr coy

LIBERIA
UN • UNMIL 1; 2 obs

SOUTH SUDAN
UN • UNMISS 3 obs

WESTERN SAHARA
UN • MINURSO 5 obs

Peru PER

Peruvian Nuevo Sol NS		2013	2014	2015
GDP	NS	547bn	582bn	
	US$	202bn	208bn	
per capita	US$	6,541	6,625	
Growth	%	5.8	3.6	
Inflation	%	2.8	3.2	
Def exp	NS	8bn		
	US$	2.96bn		
Def bdgt	NS	7.44bn	7.24bn	7.61bn
	US$	2.75bn	2.59bn	
FMA (US)	US$	1.98m	2.5m	1.8m
US$1=NS		2.70	2.80	

Population 30,147,935

Age	0–14	15–19	20–24	25–29	30–64	65 plus
Male	13.9%	4.8%	4.8%	4.1%	18.4%	3.3%
Female	13.4%	4.8%	4.8%	4.3%	19.9%	3.6%

Capabilities

The armed forces have been involved in a decades-long conflict with Shining Path leftist guerrillas, and narcotics producers and traffickers. This has strongly influenced the focus of the services, in particular the army, for which internal security remains the primary role. This focus is reflected by the age of much of its conventional equipment, however additional bases are being considered as part of a counter-narcotics effort and the SIVAN monitoring-and-surveillance system is now moving ahead. Territorial disputes have, in the past, also led to clashes, most notably with Ecuador in 1995. A military-modernisation programme is under way, intended to shape the forces to better meet its perceived future security requirements. The air force is well equipped by regional standards, and continues to upgrade some of its primary platforms, including the MiG-29 fleet and possibly the *Mirage* 2000. The air force also has an adequate tactical-airlift capability, enhanced by the purchase of new C-27J transports and Mi-171Sh helicopters. The navy plans to acquire additional amphibious and patrol vessels and AAVs, and has purchased a replenishment ship. It is expanding its shipyards accordingly. All three services train regularly, and participate in multinational exercises.

ACTIVE 115,000 (Army 74,000 Navy 24,000 Air 17,000) **Paramilitary 77,000**

RESERVE 188,000 (Army 188,000)

ORGANISATIONS BY SERVICE

Army 74,000
4 mil region

FORCES BY ROLE
SPECIAL FORCES
1 (1st) SF bde (4 cdo bn, 1 airmob arty gp, 1 MP Coy, 1 cbt spt bn)
1 (3rd) SF bde (3 cdo bn, 1 airmob arty gp, 1 MP coy)
1 SF gp (regional troops)
MANOEUVRE
Armoured
1 (3rd) armd bde (2 tk bn, 1 armd inf bn, 1 arty gp, 1 AT coy, 1 AD gp, 1 engr bn, 1 cbt spt bn)
1 (9th) armd bde (forming - 1 tk bn)
Mechanised
1 (3rd) armd cav bde (3 mech cav bn, 1 mot inf bn, 1 arty gp, 1 AD gp, 1 engr bn, 1 cbt spt bn)
1 (1st) cav bde (4 mech cav bn, 1 MP coy, 1 cbt spt bn)
Light
2 (2nd & 31st) mot inf bde (3 mot inf bn, 1 arty gp, 1 MP coy, 1 log bn)
3 (1st, 7th & 32nd) inf bde (3 inf bn, 1 MP coy, 1 cbt spt bn)
Mountain
1 (4th) mtn bde (1 armd regt, 3 mot inf bn, 1 arty gp, 1 MP coy, 1 cbt spt bn)
1 (5th) mtn bde (1 armd regt, 2 mot inf bn, 3 jungle coy, 1 arty gp, 1 MP coy, 1 cbt spt bn)
Jungle
1 (5th) jungle inf bde (1 SF gp, 3 jungle bn, 3 jungle coy, 1 jungle arty gp, 1 AT coy, 1 AD gp, 1 jungle engr bn)
1 (6th) jungle inf bde (4 jungle bn, 1 engr bn, 1 MP coy, 1 cbt spt bn)
Other
1 (18th) armd trg bde (1 mech cav regt, 1 armd regt, 2 tk bn, 1 armd inf bn, 1 engr bn, 1 MP coy, 1 cbt spt bn)
Aviation
1 (1st) avn bde (1 atk hel/recce hel bn, 1 avn bn, 2 aslt hel/tpt hel bn)
COMBAT SUPPORT
1 (1st) arty bde (4 arty gp, 2 AD gp, 1 sigs gp)
1 (3rd) arty bde (4 arty gp, 1 AD gp, 1 sigs gp)
1 AD gp (regional troops)
1 (22nd) engr bde (3 engr bn, 1 demining coy)
EQUIPMENT BY TYPE
MBT 165 T-55; (75† in store)
LT TK 96 AMX-13
RECCE 95: 30 BRDM-2; 15 Fiat 6616; 50 M9A1
APC 299
  APC (T) 120 M113A1
  APC (W) 179: 150 UR-416; 25 Fiat 6614; 4 *Repontec*
ARTY 998
  SP • 155mm 12 M109A2
  TOWED 290
    105mm 152: 44 M101; 24 M2A1; 60 M-56; 24 Model 56 pack howitzer; **122mm**; 36 D-30; **130mm** 36 M-46; **155mm** 66: 36 M114, 30 Model 50
  MRL • 122mm 22 BM-21 *Grad*
  MOR 674+
    SP 107mm 24 M106A1
    TOWED 650+ **81mm/107mm** 350; **120mm** 300+ Brandt/Expal Model L

AT
  MSL
    SP 22 M1165A2 HMMWV with 9K135 *Kornet* E (AT-14 *Spriggan*)
    MANPATS 9K11 *Malyutka* (AT-3 *Sagger*); HJ-73C; 9K135 *Kornet* E (AT-14 *Spriggan*); *Spike*-ER
  RCL 106mm M40A1
AIRCRAFT
  TPT • Light 16: 2 An-28 *Cash*; 3 An-32B *Cline*; 1 Beech 350 *King Air*; 1 Beech 1900D; 4 Cessna 152; 1 Cessna 208 *Caravan* I; 2 Cessna U206 *Stationair*; 1 PA-31T *Cheyenne* II; 1 PA-34 *Seneca*
  TRG 4 IL-103
HELICOPTERS
  MRH 8 Mi-17 *Hip* H
  TPT 19: **Heavy** (3 Mi-26T *Halo* in store); **Medium** 6 Mi-171Sh; **Light** 13: 2 AW109K2; 9 PZL Mi-2 *Hoplite*; 2 R-44
  TRG 5 F-28F
AD
  SAM • MANPAD 9K36 *Strela*-3 (SA-14 *Gremlin*); 9K310 *Igla*-1 (SA-16 *Gimlet*); 9K32 *Strela*-2 (SA-7 *Grail*)‡
  GUNS 165
    SP 23mm 35 ZSU-23-4
    TOWED 23mm 130: 80 ZU-23-2; 50 ZU-23
ARV M578

Navy 24,000 (incl 1,000 Coast Guard)

Commands: Pacific, Lake Titicaca, Amazon River
EQUIPMENT BY TYPE
SUBMARINES • TACTICAL • SSK 6:
  6 *Angamos* (GER T-209/1200 – 2 in refit/reserve) with 8 single 533mm TT with A-185 HWT
PRINCIPAL SURFACE COMBATANTS 8
  CRUISERS • CG 1 *Almirante Grau* (NLD *De Ruyter*) with 8 single lnchr with *Otomat* Mk2 AShM, 4 twin 152mm guns
  FRIGATES • FFGHM 7:
    4 *Aguirre* (ITA *Lupo*) with 8 single lnchr with *Otomat* Mk2 AShM (undergoing upgrade to MM-40 *Exocet* Block III AShM from 2014), 1 octuple Mk29 lnchr with RIM-7P *Sea Sparrow* SAM, 2 triple 324mm ASTT with A244 LWT, 1 127mm gun (capacity 1 Bell 212 (AB-212)/SH-3D *Sea King*)
    3 *Carvajal* (mod ITA *Lupo*) with 8 single lnchr with *Otomat* Mk2 AShM, 1 octuple *Albatros* lnchr with *Aspide* SAM, 2 triple 324mm ASTT with A244 LWT, 1 127mm gun (capacity 1 Bell 212 (AB-212)/SH-3D *Sea King*)
PATROL AND COASTAL COMBATANTS 14
  CORVETTES • FSG 6 *Velarde* (FRA PR-72 64m) with 4 single lnchr with MM-38 *Exocet* AShM, 1 76mm gun
  PCR 5:
    2 *Amazonas* with 1 76mm gun
    1 *Manuel Clavero* (1 additional vessel undergoing acceptance trials)
    2 *Marañon* with 2 76mm guns
  PBR 3 *Punta Malpelo*
AMPHIBIOUS
  LANDING SHIPS • LST 2 *Paita* (capacity 395 troops) (US *Terrebonne Parish*)

LANDING CRAFT • LCAC 7 Griffon 2000TD (capacity 22 troops)
LOGISTICS AND SUPPORT 33
AFD 3
AG 1 *Rio Napo*
AGOR 1 *Humboldt*
AGSC 5: 1 *Carrasco*; 2 *Van Straelen*; 1 *La Macha*, 1 *Stiglich* (river survey vessel for the upper Amazon)
AH 4 (river hospital craft)
AO 2 *Noguera*
AOR 1 *Mollendo*
AOT 2 *Bayovar*
ATF 1
AW 1 *Caloyeras*
AXS 1 *Marte*
YPT 1 *San Lorenzo*
YTL 10

Naval Aviation ε800
FORCES BY ROLE
MARITIME PATROL
1 sqn with Beech 200T; Bell 212 ASW (AB-212 ASW); F-27 *Friendship*; F-60; SH-3D *Sea King*
TRANSPORT
1 flt with An-32B *Cline*; Cessna 206
TRAINING
1 sqn with F-28F; T-34C *Turbo Mentor*
TRANSPORT HELICOPTER
1 (liaison) sqn with Bell 206B *Jet Ranger II*; Mi-8 *Hip*
EQUIPMENT BY TYPE
AIRCRAFT
MP 8: 4 Beech 200T; 4 F-60
ELINT 1 F-27 *Friendship*
TPT • **Light** 4: 3 An-32B *Cline*; 1 Cessna 206
TRG 5 T-34C *Turbo Mentor*
HELICOPTERS
ASW 5: 2 Bell 212 ASW (AB-212 ASW); 3 SH-3D *Sea King*
TPT 11: **Medium** 8: 2 Mi-8 *Hip*; 6 UH-3H *Sea King*; **Light** 3 Bell 206B *Jet Ranger* II
TRG 5 F-28F
MSL • AShM AM-39 *Exocet*

Marines 4,000
FORCES BY ROLE
SPECIAL FORCES
1 cdo gp
MANOEUVRE
Light
2 inf bn
1 inf gp
Amphibious
1 mne bde (1 SF gp, 1 recce bn, 2 inf bn, 1 amph bn, 1 arty gp)
Jungle
1 jungle inf bn
EQUIPMENT BY TYPE
APC (W) 35+: 20 BMR-600; V-100 *Commando*; 15 V-200 *Chaimite*

ARTY 18+
TOWED 122mm D-30
MOR 18+: 81mm; 120mm ε18
RCL 84mm *Carl Gustav*; 106mm M40A1
AD • GUNS 20mm SP (twin)

Air Force 17,000
Divided into five regions – North, Lima, South, Central and Amazon.
FORCES BY ROLE
FIGHTER
1 sqn with MiG-29S/SE *Fulcrum* C; MiG-29UB *Fulcrum* B
FIGHTER/GROUND ATTACK
1 sqn with *Mirage* 2000E/ED (2000P/DP)
2 sqn with A-37B *Dragonfly*
1 sqn with Su-25A *Frogfoot* A†; Su-25UB *Frogfoot* B†
ISR
1 (photo-survey) sqn with *Commander* 690; Learjet 36A; SA-227-BC *Metro* III (C-26B)
TRANSPORT
1 sqn with B-737; An-32 *Cline*
1 sqn with DHC-6 *Twin Otter*; DHC-6-400 *Twin Otter*; PC-6 *Turbo Porter*
1 sqn with L-100-20
TRAINING
2 (drug interdiction) sqn with EMB-312 *Tucano*
1 sqn with MB-339A*
1 sqn with Z-242
1 hel sqn with Schweizer 300C
ATTACK HELICOPTER
1 sqn with Mi-25/Mi-35P *Hind*
TRANSPORT HELICOPTER
1 sqn with Mi-17 *Hip* H
1 sqn with Bell 206 *Jet Ranger*; Bell 212 (AB-212); Bell 412 *Twin Huey*
1 sqn with Bo-105C/LS
AIR DEFENCE
6 bn with S-125 *Pechora* (SA-3 *Goa*)
EQUIPMENT BY TYPE
AIRCRAFT 78 combat capable
FTR 20: 15 MiG-29S *Fulcrum* C; 3 MiG-29SE *Fulcrum* C (8 upgraded to SMP standard by end of 2012); 2 MiG-29UB *Fulcrum* B
FGA 12: 2 *Mirage* 2000ED (2000DP); 10 *Mirage* 2000E (2000P) (some†)
ATK 36: 18 A-37B *Dragonfly*; 10 Su-25A *Frogfoot* A†; 8 Su-25UB *Frogfoot* B†
ISR 6: 2 Learjet 36A; 4 SA-227-BC *Metro* III (C-26B)
TPT 24: **Medium** 2 L-100-20; **Light** 18: 4 An-32 *Cline*; 1 *Commander* 690; 3 DHC-6 *Twin Otter*; 9 DHC-6-400 *Twin Otter* (further 3 on order); 1 PC-6 *Turbo-Porter*; **PAX** 4 B-737
TRG 49: 19 EMB-312 *Tucano*; 10 MB-339A*; 6 T-41A/D *Mescalero*; 14 Z-242
HELICOPTERS
ATK 18: 16 Mi-25 *Hind* D; 2 Mi-35P *Hind* E
MRH 21: 2 Bell 412 *Twin Huey*; 19 Mi-17 *Hip* H
TPT • **Light** 21: 8 Bell 206 *Jet Ranger*; 6 Bell 212 (AB-212); 1 Bo-105C; 6 Bo-105LS
TRG 4 Schweizer 300C

AD • SAM
  TOWED S-125 *Pechora* (SA-3 *Goa*);
  MANPAD *Javelin*
MSL
  AAM • IR R-3 (AA-2 *Atoll*)‡; R-60 (AA-8 *Aphid*)‡; R-73 (AA-11 *Archer*); R-550 *Magic*; IR/SARH R-27 (AA-10 *Alamo*); ARH R-77 (AA-12 *Adder*)
  ASM AS-30; Kh-29L (AS-14A *Kedge*)
  ARM Kh-58 (AS-11 *Kilter*)

Paramilitary 77,000

National Police 77,000 (100,000 reported)
EQUIPMENT BY TYPE
APC (W) 100 MOWAG *Roland*

General Police 43,000

Security Police 21,000

Technical Police 13,000

Coast Guard 1,000
Personnel included as part of Navy
EQUIPMENT BY TYPE
PATROL AND COASTAL COMBATANTS 36
  PSOH 1 *Carvajal* (mod ITA *Lupo*) with 1 127mm gun (capacity 1 Bell 212 (AB-212)/SH-3D *Sea King*)
  PCC 5 *Rio Nepena*
  PB 10: 6 *Chicama* (US *Dauntless*); 1 *Río Chira*; 3 *Río Santa*
  PBR 20: 1 *Río Viru*; 8 *Parachique*; 10 *Zorritos*; 1 other
LOGISTICS AND SUPPORT • AH 1 *Puno*
AIRCRAFT
  TPT • Light 3: 1 DHC-6 *Twin Otter*; 2 F-27 *Friendship*

Rondas Campesinas
Peasant self-defence force. Perhaps 7,000 rondas 'gp', up to pl strength, some with small arms. Deployed mainly in emergency zone.

DEPLOYMENT

CÔTE D'IVOIRE
UN • UNOCI 2 obs

DEMOCRATIC REPUBLIC OF THE CONGO
UN • MONUSCO 2; 12 obs

HAITI
UN • MINUSTAH 373; 1 inf coy

LIBERIA
UN • UNMIL 2; 2 obs

SOUTH SUDAN
UN • UNMISS 2 obs

SUDAN
UN • UNAMID 4 obs
UN • UNISFA 2

Suriname SUR

Suriname Dollar srd		2013	2014	2015
GDP	srd	16.6bn	17.4bn	
	US$	5.04bn	5.27bn	
per capita	US$	9,206	9,539	
Growth	%	4.1	3.3	
Inflation	%	1.9	2.6	
Def bdgt	srd	ε134m		
	US$	ε41m		
US$1=srd		3.30	3.30	

Population 573,311

Age	0–14	15–19	20–24	25–29	30–64	65 plus
Male	13.4%	4.6%	4.3%	4.6%	21.0%	2.4%
Female	12.9%	4.4%	4.2%	4.4%	20.6%	3.2%

Capabilities

The fundamental role of the nation's small armed forces is assuring sovereignty and territorial integrity, however they would struggle to fulfil this were they ever to face a concerted attack. The army is the largest of the three services, with naval and air units having very limited capability. Defence ties with Brazil have been growing with the upgrade and supply of a small number of armoured vehicles. Further defence cooperation is being pursued, with a view to Brazil assisting the development of a national maritime capability.

ACTIVE 1,840 (Army 1,400 Navy 240 Air 200)
Paramilitary 100
(All services form part of the army)

ORGANISATIONS BY SERVICE

Army 1,400
FORCES BY ROLE
MANOEUVRE
  Mechanised
    1 mech cav sqn
  Light
    1 inf bn (4 coy)
COMBAT SUPPORT
  1 MP bn (coy)
EQUIPMENT BY TYPE
RECCE 6 EE-9 *Cascavel*
APC (W) 15 EE-11 *Urutu*
ARTY • MOR 81mm 6
AT • RCL 106mm: M40A1

Navy ε240
EQUIPMENT BY TYPE
PATROL AND COASTAL COMBATANTS 10
  PB 5: 3 Rodman 101†; 2 others
  PBR 5 Rodman 55

Air Force ε200
EQUIPMENT BY TYPE
AIRCRAFT 3 combat capable

MP 1 C-212-400 *Aviocar**
TPT • Light 2: 1 BN-2 *Defender**; 1 Cessna 182
TRG 1 PC-7 *Turbo Trainer**

Paramilitary ε100

Coast Guard ε100
Formed in November 2013; 3 Coast Guard stations to be formed; HQ at Paramaribo
EQUIPMENT BY TYPE
PATROL AND COASTAL COMBATANTS • PB 3: 1 OCEA FPB 98; 2 OCEA FPB 72 MkII

Trinidad and Tobago TTO

Trinidad and Tobago Dollar TT$		2013	2014	2015
GDP	TT$	179bn	191bn	
	US$	27.7bn	29.6bn	
per capita	US$	20,622	21,934	
Growth	%	1.6	2.3	
Inflation	%	5.2	4.7	
Def exp		2.59bn		
		402m		
Def bdgt	TT$	2.55bn	2.81bn	3.12bn
	US$	395m	436m	
US$1=TT$			6.44	6.44

Population 1,223,916

Age	0–14	15–19	20–24	25–29	30–64	65 plus
Male	9.9%	3.2%	3.6%	4.7%	25.1%	4.1%
Female	9.5%	2.9%	3.4%	4.4%	23.7%	5.4%

Capabilities

The Trinidad and Tobago Defence Force faces no external threats, with border and maritime security and counter-narcotics as its primary roles. Narcotics and light-weapons trafficking on the western coastline is an issue. It has in terms of personnel the largest coast guard in the Caribbean. Vessels are being upgraded while additional utility and coastal-patrol vessels are planned, although an earlier proposal to purchase three offshore-patrol vessels was shelved in 2010. The Defence Forces also want to acquire helicopters and unmanned aerial vehicles. Trinidad and Tobago is also exploring the possibility of receiving increased training from the United States and support from US SOUTHCOM.

ACTIVE 4,050 (Army 3,000 Coast Guard 1,050)
(All services form the Trinidad and Tobago Defence Force)

ORGANISATIONS BY SERVICE

Army ε3,000
FORCES BY ROLE
SPECIAL FORCES
 1 SF unit
MANOEUVRE
 Light
 2 inf bn

COMBAT SUPPORT
 1 engr bn
COMBAT SERVICE SUPPORT
 1 log bn
EQUIPMENT BY TYPE
MOR 6: **81mm** L16A1
AT
 RCL **84mm** ε24 *Carl Gustav*

Coast Guard 1,050
FORCES BY ROLE
COMMAND
 1 mne HQ
EQUIPMENT BY TYPE
PATROL AND COASTAL COMBATANTS 20
 PCO 1 *Nelson* (UK *Island*)
 PB 19: 2 *Gasper Grande*; 1 *Matelot*; 4 *Plymouth*; 4 *Point*; 6 *Scarlet Ibis* (Austal 30m); 2 *Wasp*; (1 *Cascadura* (SWE *Karlskrona* 40m) non-operational)

Air Wing 50
AIRCRAFT
 TPT • Light 2 SA-227 *Metro* III (C-26)
HELICOPTERS
 MRH 2 AW139
 TPT • Light 1 S-76

Uruguay URY

Uruguayan Peso pU		2013	2014	2015
GDP	pU	1.14tr	1.27tr	
	US$	55.7bn	55.6bn	
per capita	US$	16,421	16,332	
Growth	%	4.4	2.8	
Inflation	%	8.6	8.8	
Def bdgt	pU	9.55bn	9.75bn	
	US$	466m	427m	
US$1=pU		20.48	22.85	

Population 3,332,972

Age	0–14	15–19	20–24	25–29	30–64	65 plus
Male	10.7%	4.1%	4.0%	3.6%	20.3%	5.6%
Female	10.3%	4.0%	3.9%	3.6%	21.5%	8.4%

Capabilities

Along with the basic aim of assuring sovereignty and territorial integrity, the armed forces have in recent years taken on peacekeeping missions, most notably in Haiti. In regional terms, the services provide a competent force, though much of their equipment inventory is second-hand and there is little capacity for independent power projection. The air force is focused on a counter-insurgency role, with a limited tactical-airlift capacity augmented by the recent purchase of two C-212 transports. Air-force ambitions to purchase a light fighter aircraft continue to be stymied by a lack of funds. The army is receiving additional utility vehicles, tactical radars and M41 light tanks donated by Brazil. Two offshore-patrol vessels are to be procured by the navy. An indigenous light UAV is used for peacekeeping and internal-security operations. The military trains regularly, and on a joint basis, as well as participating in multinational exercises.

ACTIVE 24,650 (Army 16,250 Navy 5,400 Air 3,000)
Paramilitary 800

ORGANISATIONS BY SERVICE

Army 16,250

Uruguayan units are sub-standard size, mostly around 30%. Div are at most bde size, while bn are of reinforced coy strength. Regts are also coy size, some bn size, with the largest formation being the 2nd armd cav regt.

FORCES BY ROLE
COMMAND
  4 mil region/div HQ
MANOEUVRE
  Mechanised
  2 armd regt
  1 armd cav regt
  5 mech cav regt
  8 mech inf regt
  Light
  1 mot inf bn
  5 inf bn
  Air Manoeuvre
  1 para bn
COMBAT SUPPORT
  1 (strategic reserve) arty regt
  5 fd arty gp
  1 AD gp
  1 (1st) engr bde (2 engr bn)
  4 cbt engr bn
EQUIPMENT BY TYPE
MBT 15 *Tiran-5*
LT TK 38: 16 M24 *Chaffee*; 22 M41A1UR
RECCE 110: 15 EE-9 *Cascavel*; 48 GAZ-39371 *Vodnik*; 47 OT-93;
AIFV 18 BMP-1
APC 283
  APC (T) 29: 24 M113A1UR; 3 M-93 (MT-LB); 2 PTS
  APC (W) 254: 54 *Condor*; 53 OT-64; 147 MOWAG *Piranha*
ARTY 185
  SP 122mm 6 2S1
  TOWED 44: **105mm** 36: 28 M101A1; 8 M102; **155mm** 8 M114A1
  MOR 135: **81mm** 91: 35 M1, 56 LN; **120mm** 44 SL
AT
  MSL • MANPATS *Milan*
  RCL 69: **106mm** 69 M40A1
UAV • ISR • Light 1 *Charrua*
AD • GUNS • TOWED 14: **20mm** 14: 6 M167 *Vulcan*; 8 TCM-20 (w/Elta M-2016 radar)
AEV MT-LB

Navy 5,400 (incl 1,800 Prefectura Naval Coast Guard)

HQ at Montevideo

EQUIPMENT BY TYPE
PRINCIPAL SURFACE COMBATANTS • FRIGATES 2
  FF 2 *Uruguay* (PRT *Joao Belo*) with 2 triple Mk32 324mm ASTT with Mk46 LWT, 2 100mm gun
PATROL AND COASTAL COMBATANTS 15
  PB 15: 2 *Colonia* (US *Cape*); 1 *Paysandu*; 9 Type-44 (coast guard); 3 PS (coast guard)
MINE WARFARE • MINE COUNTERMEASURES 3
  MSO 3 *Temerario* (*Kondor* II)
AMPHIBIOUS 3: 2 LCVP; 1 LCM
LOGISTICS AND SUPPORT 10
  ABU 2
  AG 2: 1 *Artigas* (GER *Freiburg*, general spt ship with replenishment capabilities); 1 *Maldonado* (also used as patrol craft)
  AGS 1 *Helgoland*
  AGSC 1 *Trieste*
  ARS 1 *Vanguardia*
  AXS 2: 1 *Capitan Miranda*; 1 *Bonanza*
  YTB 1

Naval Aviation 210

FORCES BY ROLE
ANTI-SUBMARINE WARFARE
  1 flt with Beech 200T*; *Jetstream* Mk2
SEARCH & RESCUE/TRANSPORT HELICOPTER
  1 sqn with AS350B2 *Ecureuil* (*Esquilo*); Bo-105M
TRANSPORT/TRAINING
  1 flt with T-34C *Turbo Mentor*
EQUIPMENT BY TYPE
AIRCRAFT 2 combat capable
  MP 2 *Jetstream* Mk2
  ISR 2 Beech 200T*
  TRG 2 T-34C *Turbo Mentor*
HELICOPTERS
  MRH 6 Bo-105M
  TPT • Light 1 AS350B2 *Ecureuil* (*Esquilo*)

Naval Infantry 450

FORCES BY ROLE
MANOEUVRE
  Amphibious
  1 mne bn(-)

Air Force 3,000

Flying hours 120 hrs/year

FORCES BY ROLE
FIGHTER/GROUND ATTACK
  1 sqn with A-37B *Dragonfly*
  1 sqn with IA-58B *Pucará*
ISR
  1 flt with EMB-110 *Bandeirante*
TRANSPORT
  1 sqn with C-130B *Hercules*; C-212 *Aviocar*; EMB–110C *Bandeirante*; EMB-120 *Brasilia*
  1 (liaison) sqn with Cessna 206H; T-41D
  1 (liaison) flt with Cessna 206H
TRAINING
  1 sqn with PC-7U *Turbo Trainer*
  1 sqn with Beech 58 *Baron* (UB-58); SF-260EU

TRANSPORT HELICOPTER
1 sqn with AS365 *Dauphin*; Bell 205 (UH–1H *Iroquois*); Bell 212

EQUIPMENT BY TYPE
AIRCRAFT 15 combat capable
  ATK 15: 10 A-37B *Dragonfly*; 5 IA-58B *Pucará*
  ISR 1 EMB-110 *Bandeirante*
  TPT 20: **Medium** 2 C-130B *Hercules*; **Light** 18: 2 Beech 58 *Baron* (UB-58); 4 C-212 *Aviocar*; 9 Cessna 206H; 2 EMB-110C *Bandeirante*; 1 EMB-120 *Brasilia*
  TRG 21: 5 PC-7U *Turbo Trainer*; 12 SF-260EU; 4 T-41D *Mescalero*
HELICOPTERS
  MRH 2 AS365N2 *Dauphin* II
  TPT • **Light** 10: 6 Bell 205 (UH–1H *Iroquois*); 4 Bell 212

Paramilitary 800

Guardia de Coraceros 350 (under Interior Ministry)

Guardia de Granaderos 450

DEPLOYMENT

CÔTE D'IVOIRE
UN • UNOCI 2 obs

DEMOCRATIC REPUBLIC OF THE CONGO
UN • MONUC 1,181; 8 obs; 1 inf bn; 1 mne coy; 1 hel flt

EGYPT
MFO 58; 1 engr/tpt unit

HAITI
UN • MINUSTAH 606; 1 inf bn

INDIA/PAKISTAN
UN • UNMOGIP 1 obs

Venezuela VEN

Venezuelan Bolivar Fuerte Bs		2013	2014	2015
GDP	Bs	2.21tr	3.25tr	
	US$	227bn	209bn	
per capita	US$	7,576	6,870	
Growth	%	1.3	-3.0	
Inflation	%	40.6	64.3	
Def bdgt [a]	Bs	32.1bn	72.2bn	
	US$	3.3bn	4.65bn	
US$1=Bs		9.74	15.52	

[a] US dollar conversions should be treated with caution due to effects of currency revaluation and wide differentials between official and parallel exchange rates

Population   28,868,486

Age	0–14	15–19	20–24	25–29	30–64	65 plus
Male	14.4%	4.8%	4.6%	4.0%	19.0%	2.6%
Female	13.8%	4.7%	4.6%	4.0%	20.1%	3.3%

Capabilities

The armed forces are tasked with protecting the sovereignty of the state, assuring territorial integrity and assisting with internal security and counter-narcotic operations. President Nicolas Maduro made several changes to senior military positions after the death of Hugo Chávez and is focused on improving domestic security, including using the army to suppress anti-government protests. A small increase in defence spending was recorded in 2014, and there was a significant uplift for military salaries. The country's Russian Su-30MKV fighters and S-300VM, *Pechora* 2M and *Buk*-M2E surface-to-air missile systems provide one of the region's most capable air defences. The marine corps is re-equipping with new Chinese armoured vehicles. Delivery of offshore-patrol vessels is complete, providing further coastal-patrol capabilities, and more patrol and logistic vessels are on order. The armed forces train regularly and there is an increasing focus on joint training.

ACTIVE 115,000 (Army 63,000 Navy 17,500 Air 11,500 National Guard 23,000)
Conscript liability 30 months selective, varies by region for all services

RESERVE 8,000 (Army 8,000)

ORGANISATIONS BY SERVICE

Army ε63,000
FORCES BY ROLE
MANOEUVRE
  Armoured
    1 (4th) armd div (1 armd bde, 1 lt armd bde, 1 AB bde, 1 arty bde)
  Mechanised
    1 (9th) mot cav div (1 mot cav bde, 1 ranger bde, 1 sy bde)
  Light
    1 (1st) inf div (1 SF bn, 1 armd bde, 1 mech inf bde, 1 ranger bde, 1 inf bde, 1 arty unit, 1 spt unit)
    1 (2nd) inf div (1 mech inf bde, 1 inf bde, 1 mtn inf bde)
    1 (3rd) inf div (1 inf bde, 1 ranger bde, 1 sigs bde, 1 MP bde)
  Jungle
    1 (5th) inf div (1 SF bn, 1 cav sqn, 2 jungle inf bde, 1 engr bn)
  Aviation
    1 avn comd (1 tpt avn bn, 1 atk hel bn, 1 ISR avn bn)
COMBAT SUPPORT
  1 cbt engr corps (3 engr regt)
COMBAT SERVICE SUPPORT
  1 log comd (2 log regt)

Reserve Organisations 8,000
FORCES BY ROLE
MANOEUVRE
  Armoured
    1 armd bn
  Light
    4 inf bn
    1 ranger bn

COMBAT SUPPORT
1 arty bn
2 engr regt
EQUIPMENT BY TYPE
MBT 173: 81 AMX-30V; 92 T-72B1
LT TK 109: 31 AMX-13; 78 *Scorpion* 90
RECCE 441: 42 *Dragoon* 300 LFV2; 10 TPz-1 *Fuchs* (CBRN); 79 V-100/-150; 310 UR-53AR50 *Tiuna*
AIFV 237: 123 BMP-3 (incl variants); 114 BTR-80A (incl variants)
APC 81
  APC (T) 45: 25 AMX-VCI; 12 VCI-PC; 8 VACI-TB
  APC (W) 36 *Dragoon* 300
ARTY 515+
  SP 60: **152mm** 48 2S19 (replacing Mk F3s); **155mm** 12 (AMX) Mk F3
  TOWED 92: **105mm** 80: 40 M101A1; 40 Model 56 pack howitzer; **155mm** 12 M114A1
  MRL 56: **122mm** 24 BM-21; **160mm** 20 LAR SP (LAR-160); **300mm** 12 9A52 *Smerch*
  GUN/MOR 120mm 13 2S23 NONA-SVK
  MOR 294+: **81mm** 165; **120mm** 108: 60 Brandt; 48 2S12
    SP 21+: **81mm** 21 *Dragoon* 300PM; AMX-VTT
AT
  MSL • MANPATS IMI MAPATS
  RCL 106mm 175 M40A1
  GUNS 76mm 75 M18 *Hellcat*
RADAR • LAND RASIT (veh, arty)
AIRCRAFT
  TPT • Light 28: 1 Beech 90 *King Air*; 1 Beech 200 *King Air*; 1 Beech 300 *King Air*; 1 Cessna 172; 6 Cessna 182 *Skylane*; 2 Cessna 206; 2 Cessna 207 *Stationair*; 1 IAI-201 *Arava*; 2 IAI-202 *Arava*; 11 M-28 *Skytruck*
HELICOPTERS
  ATK 10 Mi-35M2 *Hind*
  MRH 33: 10 Bell 412EP; 2 Bell 412SP; 21 Mi-17V-5 *Hip* H
  TPT 9: **Heavy** 3 Mi-26T2 *Halo*; **Medium** 2 AS-61D; **Light** 4: 3 Bell 206B *Jet Ranger*, 1 Bell 206L3 *Long Ranger* II
ARV 5: 3 AMX-30D; 2 *Dragoon* 300RV; *Samson*
VLB *Leguan*

Navy ε14,300; ε3,200 conscript (total ε17,500)
EQUIPMENT BY TYPE
SUBMARINES • TACTICAL • SSK 2:
  2 *Sabalo* (GER T-209/1300) with 8 single 533mm TT with SST-4 HWT
PRINCIPAL SURFACE COMBATANTS • FRIGATES 6
  FFGHM 6 *Mariscal Sucre* (ITA mod *Lupo*) with 8 single lnchr with *Otomat* Mk2 AShM, 1 octuple *Albatros* lnchr with *Aspide* SAM, 2 triple 324mm ASTT with A244 LWT, 1 127mm gun (capacity 1 Bell 212 (AB-212) hel)
PATROL AND COASTAL COMBATANTS 10
  PSOH 4 *Guaiqueri* with 1 *Millennium* CIWS, 1 76mm gun
  PBG 3 *Federación* (UK Vosper 37m) with 2 single lnchr with *Otomat* Mk2 AShM
  PB 3 *Constitucion* (UK Vosper 37m) with 1 76mm gun; 1 *Fernando Gomez de Saa* (Damen 4207)
AMPHIBIOUS
  LANDING SHIPS • LST 4 *Capana* (capacity 12 tanks; 200 troops) (FSU *Alligator*)

LANDING CRAFT 3:
  LCU 2 *Margarita* (river comd)
  LCAC 1 Griffon 2000TD
LOGISTICS AND SUPPORT 10
  AGOR 1 *Punta Brava*
  AGS 2
  AK 4 *Los Frailes*
  AORH 1 *Ciudad Bolivar*
  ATF 1
  AXS 1 *Simon Bolivar*

Naval Aviation 500
FORCES BY ROLE
ANTI-SUBMARINE WARFARE
  1 sqn with Bell 212 (AB-212)
MARITIME PATROL
  1 flt with C-212-200 MPA
TRANSPORT
  1 sqn with Beech 200 *King Air*; C-212 *Aviocar*; Turbo Commander 980C
TRAINING
  1 hel sqn with Bell 206B *Jet Ranger* II; TH-57A *Sea Ranger*
TRANSPORT HELICOPTER
  1 sqn with Bell 412EP *Twin Huey*; Mi-17V-5 *Hip* H
EQUIPMENT BY TYPE
AIRCRAFT 3 combat capable
  MP 3 C-212-200 MPA*
  TPT • Light 7: 1 Beech C90 *King Air*; 1 Beech 200 *King Air*; 4 C-212 *Aviocar*; 1 Turbo Commander 980C
HELICOPTERS
  ASW 5 Bell 212 ASW (AB-212 ASW)
  MRH 12: 6 Bell 412EP *Twin Huey*; 6 Mi-17V-5 *Hip*
  TPT • Light 1 Bell 206B *Jet Ranger* II (trg)
  TRG 1 TH-57A *Sea Ranger*

Marines ε7,000
FORCES BY ROLE
COMMAND
  1 div HQ
SPECIAL FORCES
  1 spec ops bde
MANOEUVRE
  Amphibious
  1 (rvn) mne bde
  2 (landing) mne bde
COMBAT SUPPORT
  1 arty gp (3 arty bty, 1 AD bn)
  1 cbt engr bn
  1 MP bde
  1 sigs bn
COMBAT SERVICE SUPPORT
  1 log bn
EQUIPMENT BY TYPE
APC (W) 37 EE-11 *Urutu*
AAV 11 LVTP-7
ARTY 30
  TOWED 105mm 18 M-56
  MOR 120mm 12 Brandt
AT • RCL 84mm M3 *Carl Gustav*; **106mm** M40A1

AEV 1 AAVR7
AMPHIBIOUS • LANDING CRAFT • 1 LCM; 1 LCU; 12 **LCVP**
PATROL AND COASTAL COMBATANTS • PBR 23: 18 *Constancia*; 2 *Manaure*; 3 *Terepaima* (*Cougar*)

Coast Guard 1,000

EQUIPMENT BY TYPE
PATROL AND COASTAL COMBATANTS 22
   PSOH 3 *Guaicamacuto* with 1 *Millennium* CIWS, 1 76 mm gun (capacity 1 Bell 212 (AB-212) hel) (1 additional vessel in build)
   PB 19: 12 *Gavion*; 1 *Pagalo* (Damen Stan 2606); 4 *Petrel* (US Point); 2 *Protector*
LOGISTICS AND SUPPORT 5
   AG 2 *Los Tanques* (salvage ship)
   AKSL 1
   AP 2

Air Force 11,500

Flying hours 155 hrs/year

FORCES BY ROLE
FIGHTER/GROUND ATTACK
   1 sqn with F-5 *Freedom Fighter* (VF-5)
   2 sqn with F-16A/B *Fighting Falcon*
   4 sqn with Su-30MKV
   1 sqn with K-8W *Karakorum**
GROUND ATTACK/ISR
   1 sqn with K-8W *Karakorum**
   1 sqn with EMB-312 *Tucano**; OV-10A *Bronco*
ELECTRONIC WARFARE
   1 sqn with *Falcon* 20DC; SA-227 *Metro* III (C-26B)
TRANSPORT
   1 sqn with Y-8; C-130H *Hercules*; KC-137
   1 sqn with A319CJ; B-737
   4 sqn with Cessna T206H; Cessna 750
   1 sqn with Cessna 500/550/551; *Falcon* 20F; *Falcon* 900
   1 sqn with G-222; Short 360 *Sherpa*
TRAINING
   1 sqn with Cessna 182N; SF-260E
   1 sqn with EMB-312 *Tucano**
TRANSPORT HELICOPTER
   1 VIP sqn with AS532UL *Cougar*; Mi-172
   3 sqn with AS332B *Super Puma*; AS532 *Cougar*
   2 sqn with Mi-17 *Hip* H

EQUIPMENT BY TYPE
AIRCRAFT 95 combat capable
   FTR 31: 5 F-5 *Freedom Fighter* (VF-5), 4 F-5B *Freedom Fighter* (NF-5B); 1 CF-5D *Freedom Fighter* (VF-5D); 17 F-16A *Fighting Falcon*; 4 F-16B *Fighting Falcon*
   FGA 24 Su-30MKV
   ATK 7 OV-10A *Bronco*
   EW 4: 2 *Falcon* 20DC; 2 SA-227 *Metro* III (C-26B)
   TKR 1 KC-137
   TPT 74: **Medium** 14: 5 C-130H *Hercules* (some in store); 1 G-222; 8 Y-8; **Light** 55: 6 Beech 200 *King Air*; 2 Beech 350 *King Air*; 10 Cessna 182N *Skylane*; 12 Cessna 206 *Stationair*; 4 Cessna 208B *Caravan*; 1 Cessna 500 *Citation* I; 3 Cessna 550 *Citation* II; 1 Cessna 551; 1 Cessna 750 *Citation* X; 2 Do-228-212; 11 Quad City *Challenger* II; 2 Short 360 *Sherpa*;

   PAX 5: 1 A319CJ; 1 B-737; 1 *Falcon* 20F; 2 *Falcon* 900
   TRG 46: 1 DA40NG; 18 EMB-312 *Tucano**; 15 K-8W *Karakorum** ; 12 SF-260E
HELICOPTERS
   MRH 8 Mi-17 (Mi-17VS) *Hip* H
   TPT • Medium 15: 3 AS332B *Super Puma*; 8 AS532 *Cougar*; 2 AS532UL *Cougar*; 2 Mi-172 (VIP)
MSL
   AAM • IR AIM-9L/P *Sidewinder;* R-73 (AA-11 *Archer*); PL-5E; *Python* 4; R-27T/ET (AA-10B/D *Alamo*); **SARH** R-27R/ER (AA-10A/C *Alamo*); **ARH** R-77 (AA-12 *Adder*)
   ASM Kh-29L/T (AS-14A/B *Kedge*); Kh-31A (AS-17B *Krypton*); Kh-59M (AS-18 *Kazoo*)
   AShM AM-39 *Exocet*
   ARM Kh-31P (AS-17A *Krypton*)

Air Defence Command (CODAI)

Joint service command with personnel drawn from other services

FORCES BY ROLE
COMBAT SERVICE SUPPORT
   1 log bde (5 log gp)
AIR DEFENCE
   5 AD bde

EQUIPMENT BY TYPE
AD
   SAM
      SP S-300VM; *Buk*-M2E (SA-17 *Grizzly*)
      TOWED S-125 *Pechora*-2M (SA-3 *Goa*)
      MANPAD 9K338 *Igla*-S (SA-24 *Grinch*); ADAMS; *Mistral*; RBS-70
   GUNS 440+
      SP 212+: **23mm** ε200 ZSU-23-2 **40mm** 12+: 6+ AMX-13 *Rafaga*; 6 M-42
      TOWED 228+: **20mm**: 114 TCM-20; **35mm**; **40mm** 114+: 114+ L/70; Some M1
RADARS • LAND *Flycatcher*

National Guard (Fuerzas Armadas de Cooperacion) 23,000

(Internal sy, customs) 9 regional comd

EQUIPMENT BY TYPE
APC (W) 44: 24 Fiat 6614; 20 UR-416
ARTY • MOR 50 **81mm**
PATROL AND COASTAL COMBATANTS • PB 34: 12 *Protector*; 12 *Punta*; 10 *Rio Orinoco* II
AIRCRAFT
   TPT • Light 34: 1 Beech 55 *Baron*; 1 Beech 80 *Queen Air*; 1 Beech 90 *King Air*; 1 Beech 200C *Super King Air*; 3 Cessna 152 *Aerobat*; 2 Cessna 172; 2 Cessna 402C; 4 Cessna U206 *Stationair*; 6 DA42 MPP; 1 IAI-201 *Arava*; 12 M-28 *Skytruck*
   TRG 3: 1 PZL 106 *Kruk*; 2 PLZ M2-6 *Isquierka*
HELICOPTERS
   MRH 13: 8 Bell 412EP; 5 Mi-17V-5 *Hip* H
   TPT • Light 20: 9 AS355F *Ecureuil* II; 4 AW109; 6 Bell 206B/L *Jet Ranger/Long Ranger*; 1 Bell 212 (AB 212);
   TRG 5 F-280C

Table 9 Selected Arms Procurements and Deliveries, Latin America and the Caribbean

Designation	Type	Quantity (Current)	Contract Value	Prime Nationality	Prime Contractor	Order Date	First Delivery Due	Notes
Argentina (ARG)								
M-56	Arty (105mm Towed)	24	n.k.	ITA	Oto Melara	2013	2014	Ten delivered in 2014
IA-63 *Pampa* III	Trg ac	18	n.k.	ARG	FAdeA	2010	n.k.	Production halted due to economic dislocation
Bahamas (BHS)								
Arthur Dion Hanna-class	PCC	4	See notes	NLD	Damen Schelde Naval Shipbuilding	2014	2014	Part of a US$228m order including four Damen 3007 and one Damen 5612. First of class commissioned 2014
Bolivia (BOL)								
AS332 *Super Puma*	Med tpt hel	6	n.k.	Int'l	Airbus Group (Airbus Helicopters)	2014	2014	First delivered May 2014
Brazil (BRZ)								
SGDC	Comms Sat	1	n.k.	FRA/ITA	Thales Alenia Space	2013	2016	Geostationary Defense and Strategic Communications Satellite
VBTP-MR *Guarani*	APC (W)	Up to 2044	R6bn (€2.5bn) (US$3bn)	BRZ/ITA	IVECO Latin America	2009	2012	To replace EE-9 *Cascavel* and EE-11 *Urutu*. Final delivery due in 2030
ASTROS Mk6	MRL (127mm SP)	30	R246m (US$126m)	BRZ	Avibras	2012	2014	For army and marines; first six delivered Jun 2014
SN-BR (Submarino Nuclear Brasileiro)	SSN	1	See notes	BRZ	DCNS	2009	2025	Part of €6.7bn (US$8.3bn) naval programme. Contract covers work on the non-nuclear sections of the submarine
Scorpene-class	SSK	4	See notes	FRA	DCNS	2009	2017	Part of €6.7bn (US$8.3bn) naval programme. To be built by Itaguaí Construções Navais (JV between DCNS and Odebrecht). Final delivery due in 2022
Gripen E/F	FGA ac	36	US$5.43bn	SWE	Saab	2014	2019	28 E variants to be built in SWE and eight F variants in BRZ
C-295M (SC-105)	SAR ac	3	n.k.	Int'l	Airbus Group (Airbus Defence & Space)	2014	2014	SAR configuration. First delivery due by end of 2014
KC-390	Tkr/Tpt ac	28	US$3.25bn	BRZ	Embraer	2014	2016	First ac rolled out Oct 2014
A-*Darter*	AAM	n.k.	ZAR1bn (US$143m)	BRZ/RSA	Denel	2007	2019	Progamme schedule has slipped; to be integrated onto *Gripen* FGA from 2019
Mi-35M *Hind* (AH-2 *Sabre*)	Atk hel	12	US$150–300m	RUS	Russian Helicopters (Rostvertol)	2008	2010	Contract value incl spares and trg. Nine delivered by mid-2012; remaining three now due by end of 2014
EC725 *Super Cougar*	Hvy tpt hel	50	US$2bn	Int'l	Airbus Group (Airbus Helicopters)	2008	2010	First three built in FRA. Remainder being manufactured in BRZ by Helibras. 14 delivered as of late 2014
AS365K *Panther*	MRH hel	34	R376m (US$215m)	Int'l	Airbus Group (Airbus Helicopters)	2009	2011	To be manufactured in BRZ by Helibras. Final delivery due 2021
Gepard 1A2	AD	34	€37m (US$48.5m)	GER	Government surplus	2013	2013	34 plus three more used for spares. Deliveries under way

Table 9 **Selected Arms Procurements and Deliveries, Latin America and the Caribbean**

Designation	Type	Quantity (Current)	Contract Value	Prime Nationality	Prime Contractor	Order Date	First Delivery Due	Notes
Chile (CHL)								
Piloto Pardo-class	PSO	4	See notes	CHL/GER	ASMAR	2005	2008	Fassmer OPV 80 design. First two in service with coast guard. Third vessel launched Apr 2014
Colombia (COL)								
CPV-46	PCC	3	KRW34bn (US$31m)	ROK	STX Offshore & Shipbuilding	2013	2014	Two built in ROK to be delivered before end of 2014. First COL-built vessel was launched end of Oct 2014
Bell 412	MRH hel	4	n.k.	US	Textron (Bell)	2013	2014	For navy. First two delivered Jan 2014
Ecuador (ECU)								
Damen Stan 5009	PCC	2	n.k.	NLD	Damen Schelde Naval Shipbuilding	2014	n.k.	For coast guard
C-295M	Lt tpt ac	3	n.k.	Int'l	Airbus Group (Airbus Defence & Space)	2014	2014	First delivered Jun 2014
Jamaica (JAM)								
Bushmaster	PPV	12	n.k.	FRA	Thales	2013	2015	All APC variants
Mexico (MEX)								
MEXSAT	Comms Sat	3	US$1bn	US	Boeing	2010	2012	First satellite launched Dec 2012
Beech 350ER *King Air*	Lt tpt ac	4	n.k.	US	Textron (Textron Aviation)	n.k.	2014	For navy. Two ac delivered 2014. Remaining ac to be delivered in 2015.
EC725 *Super Cougar*	Hvy tpt hel	6	n.k.	Int'l	Airbus Group (Airbus Helicopters)	2010	2013	Follow-on from order signed in 2009. First delivered by Jun 2013
UH-60M *Black Hawk*	Med tpt hel	18	US$203.5m	US	UTC (Sikorsky)	2014	n.k.	For air force
Peru (PER)								
LAV II	APC (W)	32	US$67m	US	General Dynamics (GDLS Canada)	2014	2015	For marines. To replace the BMR-600s being transferred to the National Police
Makassar-class	LPD	2	n.k.	ROK	Dae Sun Shipbuilding & Engineering	2012	2015	Construction of first vessel commenced Jul 2013
Amsterdam-class	AOR	1	n.k.	NLD	Government surplus	2014	2015	Delivery expected in 2015
DHC-6-400 *Twin Otter*	Lt tpt ac	12	n.k.	CAN	Viking Air	2010	2011	Seven delivered by mid-2014
C-27J *Spartan*	Med tpt ac	2	€100m (US$122m)	ITA	Finmeccanica (Alenia Aermacchi)	2013	2015	In build as of late 2014
KT-1	Trg ac	20	US$200m	ROK	KAI	2012	2014	Ten KT-1 and ten KA-1 variants. First four manufactured in ROK, remainder in PER

Table 9 **Selected Arms Procurements and Deliveries, Latin America and the Caribbean**

Designation	Type	Quantity (Current)	Contract Value	Prime Nationality	Prime Contractor	Order Date	First Delivery Due	Notes
Mi-171Sh	Med tpt hel	24	US$407m	RUS	Russian Helicopters (Ulan-Ude)	2013	2014	First eight to be delivered in late 2014
SH-2G *Super Seasprite*	ASW hel	5	US$80m	NZL	Government surplus	2014	n.k.	For navy. Ex-RNZAF SH-2Gs to be refurbished and modified in CAN
Uruguay (URY)								
C-212-300MP	MP ac	2	n.k.	PRT	Government surplus	2014	n.k.	PRT surplus ac. For air force
Venezuela (VEN)								
VN16	Lt tk	n.k.	n.k.	PRC	NORINCO	2012	n.k.	Export version of Type-05 (ZTD-09). For marines
VN1	AIFV	n.k.	n.k.	PRC	NORINCO	2012	n.k.	Export version of Type-09 (ZBL-09). For marines
VN18	AIFV	n.k.	n.k.	PRC	NORINCO	2012	n.k.	Export version of Type-05 (ZBD-05). For marines
Guaicamacuto-class	PSOH	4	n.k.	ESP	Navantia	2005	2010	Three in service. Fourth vessel, *Comandante Eterno Hugo Chávez*, launched Jul 2014
Do-228	Lt tpt ac	10	n.k.	CHE	RUAG	2013	2014	Eight Do-228NG and two second-hand Do-228-212
DA40NG	Trg ac	30	n.k.	AUT	Diamond Aircraft	2013	2014	First delivered Jul 2014. Arrived in VEN Nov 2014
L-15	Trg ac	24	n.k.	PRC	AVIC (Hongdu)	2014	n.k.	Contract reportedly signed in 2014
S-300VM	SAM	n.k.	n.k.	RUS	n.k.	n.k.	2013	Deliveries ongoing

Chapter Nine
Sub-Saharan Africa

The complexity of threats to stability and security in Africa was exemplified by the developing crisis over Ebola in West Africa in 2014. It tested the governance capacity of regional states, was called a threat to international peace and security by the United Nations and led to another large Africa-focused international military mobilisation. At the same time, insecurity and conflict still bedevilled progress towards more stable and sustainable development in the region.

New crises emerged early in the year, including in the world's newest state, South Sudan, while lingering flashpoints re-ignited elsewhere. On occasion, these provoked both African and broader military intervention, and by France in particular. Motivated by the continuing confluence of problems in the broader Sahel region, France has wholly reshaped its continental anti-terrorism posture and deployments. Conflict in Africa has, in many cases, an increasingly transnational dimension. One manifestation of this is the attention focused on these conflicts by non-regional governments; another is the increasingly cross-border impact of conflict. Refugee flows place increasing demands on some countries, while many of the region's criminal, insurgent and terrorist groups have demonstrated the ability to operate across borders.

This is apparent in the activities of the Somali militant Islamist group al-Shabaab, which has mounted terror attacks in Kenya and Uganda, two of the countries that contribute forces to the African Union (AU) Mission in Somalia (AMISOM). It is also visible in the activities of Boko Haram, against which Nigeria continues to struggle in its northeast. The group's activities have highlighted not only its propensity for violence and its adaptability, but also the relative freedom of action that it has so far enjoyed. Attacks on schools continued, with the kidnap of over 200 schoolgirls in Chibok in April prompting protests in Nigeria and an international outcry. The response from Abuja was criticised, and the United States, the United Kingdom, France, China and Israel, among others, offered support in the form of advisers, surveillance aircraft and intelligence sharing. Boko Haram also expanded its attacks on military facilities; its campaign has illustrated the difficulties that governments face in using primarily military instruments to address broad security challenges. Additionally, the group prompted military deployments by neighbouring Cameroon, which during the year moved from reconnaissance flights over the area bordering Nigeria's Borno State to ground operations against militants who had crossed the border.

This transnational dimension is particularly noticeable in the Sahel, where the effective collapse of border controls in recent years has enabled armed groups to operate within substantial ungoverned space. Arguably, this has been enabled by wider problems of governance in some countries, where a lack of institutional capacity means authorities have been unable to extend their authority fully across the state. In Mali, although there was a democratic transition of power, state authority was fragile and dependent on foreign assistance. The crisis there did not cause state institutions to collapse; though severely stressed, security-force structures remained generally intact and foreign training teams had at least some local counterparts with whom they could deal on arrival.

The situation was worse in the Central African Republic (CAR), where a descent into ethnic and sectarian conflict prompted, in late 2013, France's second military intervention in sub-Saharan Africa within a year. Already weak state institutions were faced not just with the tasks of rebuilding capacity, restoring security and enabling development, but also with rebuilding severely eroded inter-communal trust. Indeed, the absence of state security institutions in the CAR led the UN to authorise what it called 'urgent temporary measures' to address issues relating to the rule of law when the AU-led mission transferred authority to the UN in September, and a new peacekeeping mission began. Entry into this fragile environment meant that the UN was again engaging in a peacekeeping mission in Africa when there was doubt over whether there was actually any peace to keep.

The 'capacity deficit' seen in the CAR is a common problem in Africa; it impels and abets fragility. The Somali authorities have with AMISOM assistance made substantial gains against al-Shabaab in recent years, but state authority and institutions remain weak, as shown by the Islamist group's attacks against landmark targets, such as the presidential palace. These attacks have two purposes: to kill and to demonstrate the government's vulnerability. They show that the organisation retains considerable capability. Developing durable security and robust economic activity is also vital to address piracy emanating from Somalia and in the Gulf of Guinea.

Instability and continuing conflict have also impeded economic and social progress, and not just in countries where conflict originates. Ebola has added another dimension to this; given how the virus has spread, and the impact it has had on countries with outbreaks, the broader region and internationally, policymakers will have to consider adding public-health capacity to the factors considered as potential drivers of insecurity in sub-Saharan Africa.

Developing greater continental security capacity, principally through the African Standby Force (ASF) concept, continues to be an aspiration, but progress remains limited. As noted in last year's *Military Balance*, the crisis in Mali spurred action towards developing African rapid-response capabilities. This had always been an objective of the African Peace and Security Architecture, principally through the ASF, and in 2013 an African Capacity for Immediate Response to Crises was proposed and gained traction. Regional state contributions to ad hoc responses, for example in the CAR, Somalia and the Democratic Republic of the Congo, have acted as a test bed not just for force capabilities, but also for regional institutions' appetite for such interventions. Examples include the AU's increasing engagement across the continent and the Intergovernmental Authority on Development's negotiation role over the conflict in South Sudan. Nonetheless, external support remains critical, with the EU and UN particularly important partners for funding and logistical support.

The Ebola crisis

The damaging impact of state capacity deficits was exemplified by West Africa's Ebola crisis. By the end of October 2014, the World Health Organization had reported a cumulative total of 13,567 cases registered in eight affected countries, with 4,591 registered deaths. There was also 'intense transmission' in Guinea (1,667 cases, 1,018 deaths), Liberia (6,535 cases, 2,413 deaths) and Sierra Leone (5,338 cases, 1,510 deaths). Ebola became a security crisis, and one with international dimensions; health-care personnel returning to home countries received particular attention, and screening also began on air travellers from affected areas. Early on in the outbreak, states in West Africa found themselves unable to cope with the effects of the virus. Isolation rooms, already limited, quickly filled and health-care capacity buckled. The limited number of local medical personnel able to handle such complex cases also came under pressure, with some prominent local experts themselves dying through inadvertent exposure to patients. Ebola also had a direct impact on populations who could no longer bring goods to market and, in many cases, no longer bury their own dead owing to the risk of potential further transmission.

In a bid to stop further transmission of the virus across borders and within states, some international borders were closed, and the armed forces and police were deployed in some states to stop the movement of goods and people. This had a serious social and economic impact on communities and West African states. The government of Sierra Leone reportedly revised agricultural output down by 30%, while the IMF noted that the 'outlook for those [Ebola hit] countries … has worsened with large financing needs likely for 2015'.

The UN initiated its first emergency health mission, the UN Mission for Ebola Emergency Response, and a range of other international agencies – including the World Bank and the IMF – and governments offered assistance. Responses were framed in terms of development, health-care and economic assistance, but countries also deployed military assistance consisting of medical, logistics (including airlift) and engineers, as well as force-protection detachments. This military support was aimed at rapidly improving capacity to test and treat patients. The UN reported that, at the end of October, a 'US Navy Ebola testing lab in Liberia [was] giving those who might be infected their results within hours rather than days'. While this showcases the impressive planning and response capacities of those armed forces deploying assets, it also highlights the lack of capacity within local states; as part of the response and broader assistance, building enduring local capabilities will be central to prevent future crises having similar effects on regional states.

DEFENCE ECONOMICS

Sub-Saharan African economies emerged relatively unscathed from the 2008 financial crisis, in part due to their low levels of integration with global financial markets. The region has seen steady rates of economic expansion between 2009 and 2013 (averaging 4.7% per year), reflecting only a minor slowdown from the high-growth patterns observed during the mid-2000s (when growth averaged 6.4% between 2004 and 2008). Rising real incomes, along with sustained public and private investment, have led to strong domestic demand in many states. Higher commodity prices and a reorientation of trade towards East Asian and Latin American economies have also contributed to regional economic buoyancy, improved trade balances and the accumulation of foreign reserves. This broad-based economic resilience has allowed public debt-to-GDP ratios to decline across the region (gross debt fell from an average of 119% of GDP in 2001 to an average of just 41% of GDP in 2013), while healthy fiscal balances have enabled several states – particularly the more globally integrated middle-income countries such as South Africa – to enact counter-cyclical policies against the contagion effects of the 2008 financial crash. However, for other states in the region, growth remains elusive and reliant on fragile political, development and security dynamics. The Ebola epidemic in West Africa highlights this, with the IMF noting that the region's more positive outlook 'co-exists with the dire situation in Guinea, Liberia and Sierra Leone, where … the Ebola outbreak is exacting a heavy economic toll, with economic spillovers starting to materialise in some neighbouring countries'.

The region's three largest economies – Angola, South Africa and Nigeria – tend to dominate regional defence outlays: collectively, these three states accounted for 56.4% of total regional defence spending, or some US$13 billion, in 2013. Although this was nearly the same fraction of regional GDP accounted for by these states (56.9%), the distribution

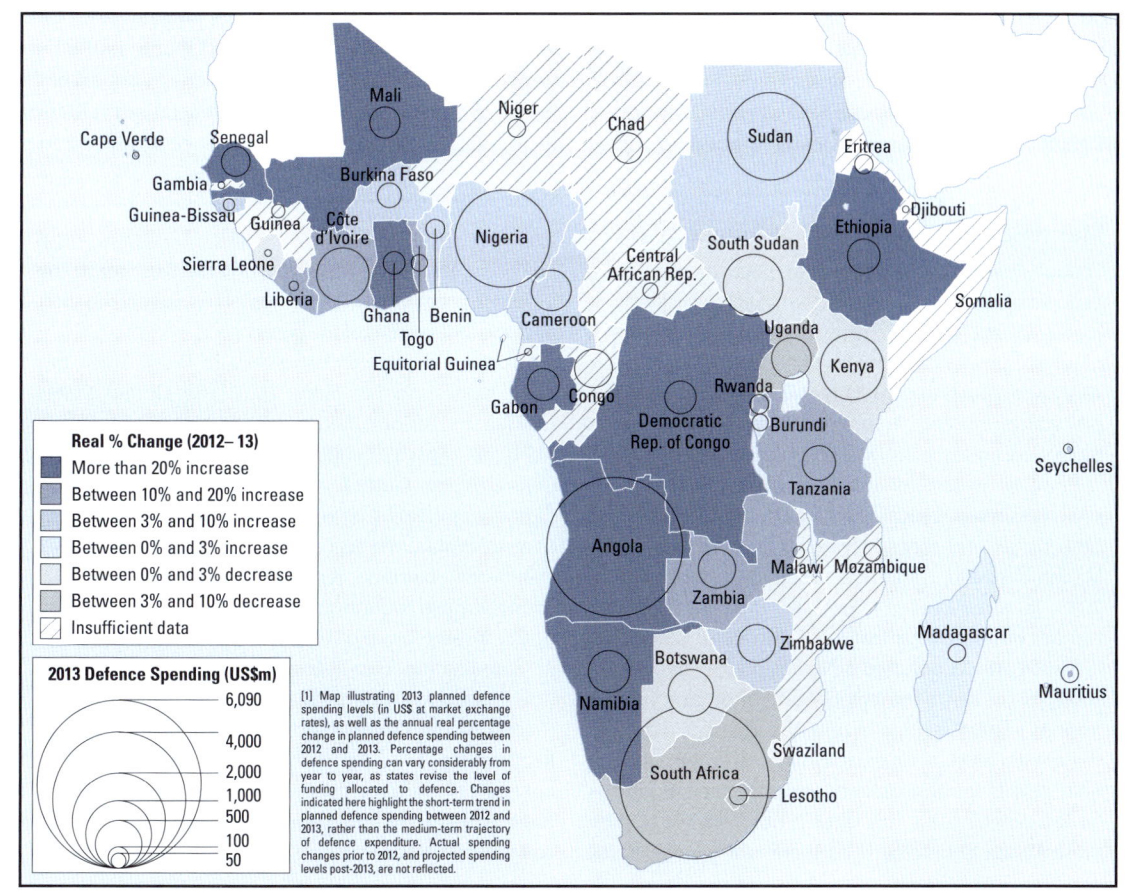

Map 9 **Sub-Saharan Africa Regional Defence Spending**[1]

of defence spending between them did not reflect the relative sizes of their economies. For example, although Nigeria accounted for some 20.6% of sub-Saharan African GDP (before the near-doubling of Nigerian GDP in 2014 due to a statistical rebasing exercise), it only accounted for around 9.3% of regional defence spending, with corruption, high levels of oil theft and pipeline damage all limiting government revenues and the country's ability to fund defence outlays (despite oil prices in excess of US$100 per barrel). By contrast, Angola accounted for only around 9.1% of regional GDP, but constituted some 26.1% of regional defence spending. The country had increased military spending in 2013 to fund its ambitious procurement plans, which include purchases of main battle tanks, multi-role combat aircraft and transport helicopters. Meanwhile, several years of underfunding caused South African defence outlays to lag relative to its economic power – it accounted for around 27.2% of regional GDP but only 21% of regional defence outlays. This trend continued in 2014, with a defence-budget increase that only just maintained real-spending levels, despite widespread acknowledgement that funding levels would be insufficient to implement the country's recent Defence Review.

A number of procurement trends continued in 2014. Gulf of Guinea states continued to invest heavily in maritime security, acquiring capabilities for anti-piracy activities and resource protection, among others, reflecting the growth of maritime piracy in that area. Equatorial Guinea, Côte d'Ivoire, Nigeria and Cameroon were among those states adding maritime capabilities, ranging from patrol boats to rigid-hulled inflatables and, in the case of Equatorial Guinea, a frigate. Ghana looked to improve its maritime-domain awareness, as part of its 'Smart Strategy' of investing in coastal-surveillance technology within its exclusive economic zone.

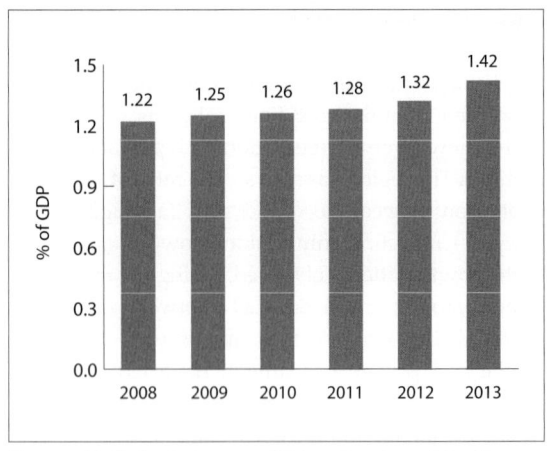

Figure 23 **Sub-Saharan Africa Regional Defence Expenditure** as % of GDP

Year	% of GDP
2008	1.22
2009	1.25
2010	1.26
2011	1.28
2012	1.32
2013	1.42

Maritime piracy in the Gulf of Guinea

Though international attention has, since the mid-2000s, been focused on piracy off the coast of Somalia, attacks in that region are reducing. This owes much to multinational naval and private maritime-security deployments, better security measures aboard ships and investment in judicial procedures on land. According to the EU Naval Force, there were no successful attacks in either 2013 or 2014.

However, waters off the west coast of Africa have seen continued pirate attacks, with developments in both tactics and scope. According to the International Maritime Bureau, 51 attacks occurred in the region in 2013. In recent years, large-scale theft of oil-related cargoes has become a feature of west-coast piracy. The first such attacks occurred off Benin in 2010 and quickly spread to the rest of the region. West African piracy differs from its eastern relation in both the methods used and the greater level of violence. While pirates were able to hold vessels for an indefinite period of time along the lawless Somali coast, this tactic is not available to their West African counterparts as there is a greater, if still imperfect, level of governance along the west coast. The incentive is not ransom of the vessel but mainly the theft of cargo and ransom of the crew.

Coordination to combat piracy in West Africa has been limited so far. Since 2007, the United States has led its African Partnership Station, engaging in maritime capacity-building and training in West and Central Africa. Further, an Inter-regional Coordination Centre was created, as well as a Regional Coordination Centre for Maritime Security in Central Africa. However, significant barriers remain to effective regional cooperation in counter-piracy, including a lack of shared goals, rivalry among regional states and difficulty in coordinating two relevant regional organisations (the Economic Community of West African States and the Economic Community of Central African States). Regional maritime capabilities are limited and there is only partial maritime-domain awareness, meaning that there is relatively little capability to develop effective counter-piracy forces.

It also channelled resources towards a new naval special-forces unit for interdiction and hostage-rescue operations. Further south, Angola and South Africa are also investing in naval capabilities, with Angola agreeing a memorandum of understanding with Brazil for seven new *Macae*–class patrol boats, while South Africa in February approved its long-delayed Project Biro to acquire offshore-patrol vessels to boost its capacity to protect its sea lines of communication.

KENYA

Kenyan defence policy has traditionally looked outward, bypassing the region, and engaging Western partners (principally the United States and the United Kingdom, but now with other European and Asian states) and participating in United Nations peacekeeping operations, both in Africa and more widely. In light of renewed Western and East African interest in resolving the security situation in Somalia, Kenya has looked closer to home to address regional challenges. The conferences in Kenya in 2004 that led to the formation of the Transitional Federal Government (TFG) in Somalia were the first sign of this change in policy. Some analysts and media reports have also alleged this increasing engagement of regional and wider African states was possibly related to a desire to engender African support in light of the ICC case against President Uhuru Kenyatta and Vice President William Ruto.

The Kenya Defence Force (KDF) has traditionally been accustomed to non-operational roles and little scrutiny of its activities. Until 2011, the KDF was effectively a peacetime army, exhibiting some of the issues that develop with many years of training but no operations on which to test capability. Following the kidnapping of three Westerners from Kenya in late 2011, approximately 5,000 Kenyan troops from the army, air force and navy moved across the Somali land and sea borders as part of *Operation Linda Nchi*. The timing of this intervention – shortly before the seasonal rains, which make military movement in southern Somalia and Jubaland extremely difficult – was driven by al-Shabaab activity in Somalia and Kenya. Although it initially found operations in Somalia challenging, the KDF developed and learned lessons that are now, after three years of operations, being incorporated into doctrine and taught at its well-established training schools, which are largely based on the British model. The combat units that have rotated through Somalia now have a higher level of confidence and capability, which is reflected in the Kenyan contribution to UN peacekeeping missions. However, the lessons of external operations in Somalia are not all applicable to the internal-security role in Kenya, and the revision and production of internal-security doctrine will have to be conducted carefully so as to enable the KDF to better adjust to lower-level operations within Kenya.

Regularising the operations in Somalia, transitioning from a mission that had, for some Western observers, been of questionable legitimacy into a legitimate operation – particularly given the TFG's mixed messages regarding prior consultation and lack of authorisation – required engagement with the African Union (AU) and through it with the UN and European Union. Subsequent responses by al-Shabaab – bringing the campaign back into Kenya with bomb attacks – heightened the need for Kenya to work with and through its neighbours, particularly Ethiopia and Uganda, and to focus on regional issues.

The African Standby Force (ASF) and the East African Standby Force (EASF) have offered the KDF a setting in which to deal with its larger neighbours on a more equal basis. This is one of the principal reasons that Kenya has so wholeheartedly participated in, and indeed led, the development of the EASF, largely through the activity of the International Peace Support Training Centre in Nairobi.

The Standby Force developments suit Kenya's well-trained, doctrinally mature, Western-orientated armed forces; however, its leading role in the EASF has irritated some partners. As a result, Kenya is working with its East African Community (EAC) neighbours (Burundi, Rwanda, Tanzania and Uganda), supported by the US through the Combined Joint Task Force–Horn of Africa, to develop similar capabilities to the EASF but within this smaller grouping, in which Kenya has a larger voice. While not formally integrated into the ASF, the EAC contributes to the development of integrated military and disaster-response capabilities in the region. The conflict in South Sudan has illustrated that if the region is to respond militarily to such events it must be able to do so in an integrated fashion, but regional EAC activities have been a distraction to the development of the AU-integrated EASF in this regard. Given the KDF's enhanced leadership role in the EAC, which would be diluted in the larger EASF, such activity is likely to continue.

Defence economics

Until the new Kenyan Defence Forces Act came into being in 2012 – subsequent to the Kenyan troop movement into Somalia – there was no explicit defence policy on which Kenya could base its procurement decisions. The size and shape of the army reflected the defence budget, which was generally determined using comparisons with the defence-spending levels (as a percentage of GDP) of neighbouring countries. The intention was to maintain, at a minimum, parity. The modernisation of Kenya's newly operational defence forces is now at least partially guided by the Act, but also by lessons learned during operations in Somalia, the internal-security situation within Kenya itself and by the requirements of the African Standby Force.

As part of the modernisation effort, Kenya aims to acquire advanced defence equipment, including new helicopters, armoured vehicles, unmanned aerial vehicles and border-surveillance and monitoring equipment. In June 2014, the government announced plans to spend US$1 billion on military and security capabilities in support of both internal security and operations in Somalia, which are now inextricably linked. US$205.6 million has been allocated for ten new military helicopters and for the refurbishment of three Mi-17 *Hip* medium multi-role helicopters, which are currently grounded. A further US$11.4m has been allocated for a helicopter leasing contract, while US$171.3m was earmarked for the development of a new Integrated Public Safety Communication and Surveillance System. This system will link the ten main towns in Kenya with an integrated CCTV and radio network. It is backed by an additional US$33.8m for 10,000 new police officers.

With the relatively small defence and police forces now challenged to provide security amid both internal and external challenges – and with almost 20% of the armed forces deployed in neighbouring Somalia – Kenya is turning to technology to address its internal-security problem, following the lead of many Western nations. This stands in contrast to other nations in the region (Uganda and Ethiopia, for example), which have chosen to implement more personnel-intensive, less technological solutions to the same problem. Kenya is taking a bold step, and placing great trust in its defence forces' ability to use and integrate these technologies. Even sophisticated Western armed forces find this transition challenging, and Kenya could experience similar difficulties.

In addition, alleged corruption poses a significant challenge for the Kenyan security establishment, as it diminishes the efficiency of military outlays and results in sub-optimal procurement outcomes. For example, in October 2010, KDF officers were allegedly linked to corrupt practices relating to the purchase of armoured personnel carriers from a South African firm; other allegations of corruption included concerns about soldier-recruitment procedures. If corruption concerns remain unaddressed, security operations could potentially be hampered.

Defence industry

Kenya's defence-industrial base is limited and currently has little capacity to fulfil the armed forces' growing equipment requirements. There is only one indigenous defence company, the Kenya Ordnance Factories Corporation, established in 1997, which is limited to low-level mechanical assembly work and the production of 7.62mm, 5.56mm and 9mm live and blank ammunition. Despite this, Kenya has the most sophisticated ordnance arsenal, albeit numerically limited, of any of the East and Horn of Africa states, and is also surrounded by a number of armed UN missions in Somalia, Sudan, South Sudan, Central African Republic and Democratic Republic of the Congo.

This combination of limited indigenous industrial capacity, sophisticated equipment requirements and potential access to a wider UN market presents an opportunity for international arms companies looking to invest in frontier defence markets. With Kenya's reputation as a place in which Western companies can do business, several have either established a presence in Kenya or are preparing to do so, both to meet local supply requirements as well as to tap into the wider regional market, particularly as some analysts project overall African defence-investment outlays of up to US$20bn across the continent over the next decade.

In January 2014, Italian shipbuilder Fincantieri said that it would soon establish its first African shipyard to build and provide maintenance, repair and overhaul facilities in Mombasa, to serve both the Kenyan and regional (including Somali) markets. In February, Eurocopter Southern Africa Limited announced plans to establish a permanent base at Wilson Airport, Nairobi. This would fulfil the needs of the defence forces, as well as police and wildlife services. In addition, a number of firms – including BAE Systems and Osprea Logistics – have looked at establishing an assembly and fourth-line repair and maintenance facility for the hundreds of armoured personnel carriers involved in UN and AU operations in the region. This would allow maintenance to be carried out in commercial factories where complete overhaul is possible, rather than in military facilities with limited industrial capacity.

Russian helicopter manufacturer Oboronprom is also looking to establish itself in Kenya, following the state's recent allocation of funds for additional helicopter purchases, as well as the refurbishment of the three grounded Mi-17 *Hip* helicopters. The Aviation Industry Corporation of China is involved in the reconstruction of Nairobi's Jomo Kenyatta International Airport and the Kenya Air Force operates the Chinese Harbin Z-9W attack helicopter alongside the US Hughes MD 500 light reconnaissance/attack helicopters used by army cavalry units. These are operating regularly in Somalia. The signing of a memorandum of understanding on aviation cooperation between the Kenyan and Chinese governments in May 2014 could lead to further Chinese involvement in Kenyan military aviation, including perhaps in air-force infrastructure developments.

THE SOMALI NATIONAL ARMY: STRUCTURAL AND OPERATIONAL DEVELOPMENTS

The developing Somali National Army (SNA), in 2014 numbering just under 11,000, is intended to grow into a 22,000-strong force. However, some analysts argue that amid ongoing operations not enough attention is being devoted to the long-term purpose, functions and structure of the SNA in a stable and secure post-war Somalia. This scenario carries some risk. Once peace is established, international interest and resources could move elsewhere. In turn, this increases the pressure to generate optimum structures and strategies at the first attempt. One factor that has been highlighted is the imbalance in size between the planned SNA and the police force, which is projected to number just 12,000 personnel.

In an attempt to build the necessary institutions to underpin the SNA, effort has been concentrated on intelligence, logistics and medical and training functions. Under the chief of staff of the army there are deputies for operations, plans and support, and below them the standard J1–J8 branches (J1 – personnel; J2 – intelligence; J3 – operations, etc.). The Somali national intelligence service has existed in some form for at least the past four years and SNA J2, although not yet functional, builds on that. The limited authority given to the UN Support Office for the African Union Mission in Somalia (AMISOM) under UN Security Council Resolution 2124 ('to provide – as exceptional support – food, water, fuel, transport, tents and "in-theatre" medical evacuation to front-line units of the SNA, the funding for which would be provided from an appropriate United Nations trust fund') has meant that targeted, non-lethal support has been provided in the areas of logistics, medicine and training. The UN Support Office for AMISOM (UNSOA) now provides medical and limited casualty-evacuation support to the SNA, an important factor in the development of morale. Training support had been given to approximately 4,000 of the 10,900 extant SNA troops by the beginning of *Operation Indian Ocean* in late 2014.

In addition to Somali ground forces, the armed forces' structure has included both a navy and an air force for at least two years. Given the nature of current operations in Somalia, neither of these organisations is yet mature, with the air force showing strength of a little over 100 and the navy about 350 personnel. Neither has the equipment to conduct viable operations, but there is international interest in supporting the navy and coast guard. The EU maritime capacity-building mission EUCAP NESTOR has Somali maritime capability on its 'to engage' list but has not yet done so in any practical way. Maritime surveillance – particularly in support of a fisheries-licensing system – is a likely future role for the Somali air force.

Structural development within the SNA remains at such an early stage that it is difficult yet to identify precisely what capabilities it may need in future and, therefore, what gaps are most important to fill and in what order. Given the imperative of current operations, with AMISOM about 15,000 troops short of the strength believed required for concurrent operations to clear Somalia of al-Shabaab (according to AMISOM Force Commander Andrew Guti in 2010), effort is being concentrated on the development of immediate fighting capabilities. The provision of weapons and ammunition is a key problem area, with so much of the support to AMISOM – and particularly the EU Africa Peace Facility – coming from development money, with the limitations on military spending traditionally associated with support from the Development Assistance Committee and Official Development Assistance. This problem was

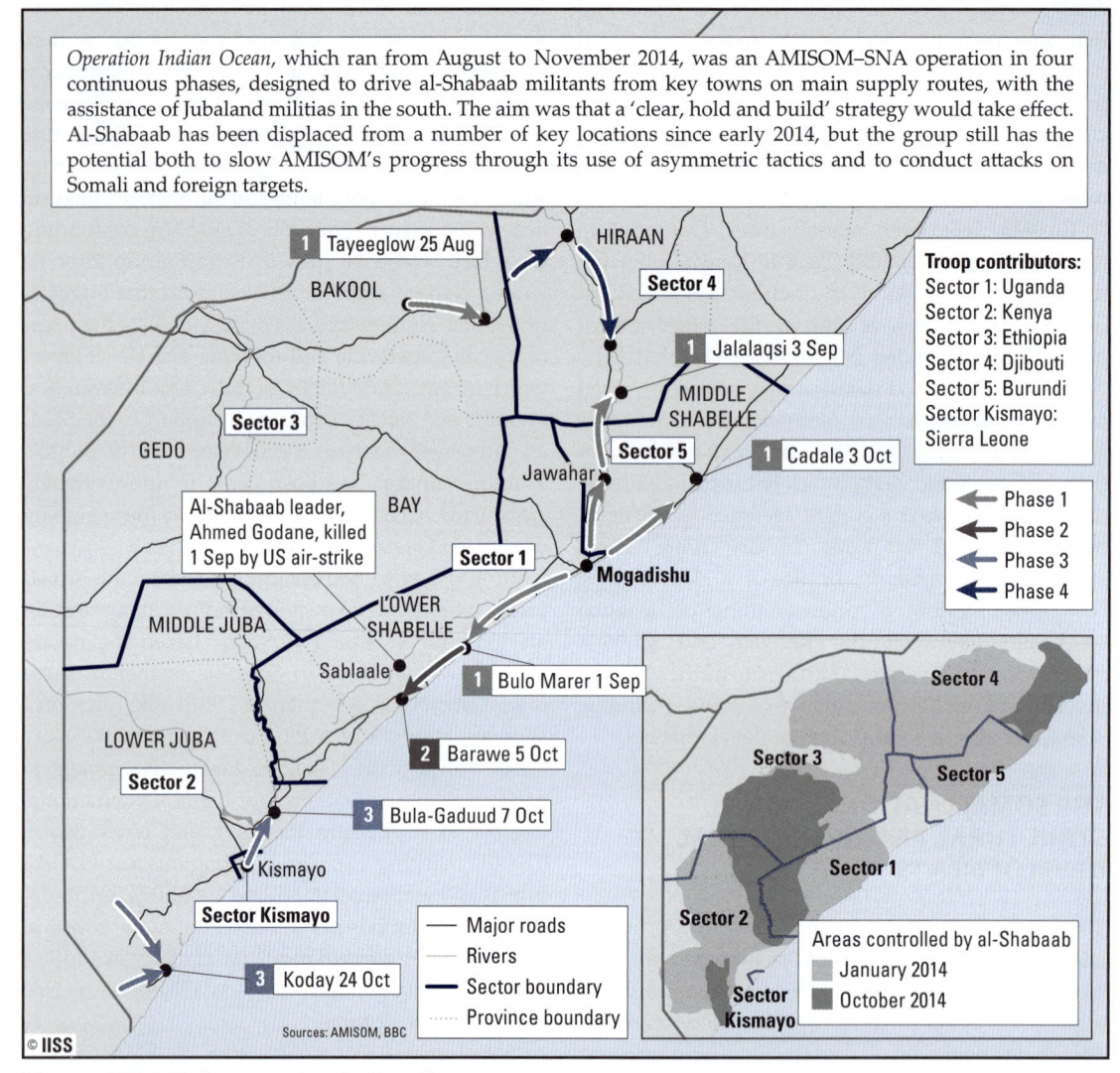

Map 10 **AMISOM's *Operation Indian Ocean***

Operation Indian Ocean, which ran from August to November 2014, was an AMISOM–SNA operation in four continuous phases, designed to drive al-Shabaab militants from key towns on main supply routes, with the assistance of Jubaland militias in the south. The aim was that a 'clear, hold and build' strategy would take effect. Al-Shabaab has been displaced from a number of key locations since early 2014, but the group still has the potential both to slow AMISOM's progress through its use of asymmetric tactics and to conduct attacks on Somali and foreign targets.

well illustrated by the UN request to Ethiopia, after it had joined AMISOM, to provide 200 4x4 vehicles to the SNA in AMISOM Sectors 3 and 4 – a request that Ethiopia was only partially able to fulfil owing to its own commitments in Somalia and elsewhere. The problem is further exacerbated by the alleged diversion of weapons intended for the SNA to other parties, resulting in international reluctance to donate. Only the establishment of an effective SNA quartermastering system will solve this issue, such that the force can obtain, manage and disburse its own supplies.

Operations and tactics

SNA operations are largely undertaken within the framework of the AMISOM strategic plan, agreed in early 2014. Two distinct phases of operations, *Operation Eagle* in early 2014 and *Operation Indian Ocean* in late 2014, depended upon SNA forces supporting AMISOM personnel, and in many cases leading the move into al-Shabaab-held areas. The need for the SNA to operate in compatible units to those of AMISOM (brigades, battalions, companies and platoons) has driven its development – through the National Security and Stabilisation Plan adopted in August 2012 – towards the structures and organisations of modern armed forces.

Several versions of an order of battle (ORBAT) have circulated. The latest iteration, from early 2014, shows the SNA operationally mirroring the AMISOM deployment, with forces assigned to each of the

AMISOM sectors. This ORBAT, for a force of 22,000 soldiers divided into 12 brigades and 33 battalions, gives an appearance of strength but the total figure is as yet aspirational.

The nature of operations in Somalia has meant that the SNA is infantry-heavy but support- and logistics-light. This dichotomy has created tensions between the optimal system for Somalis operating in Somalia – a clan-based, lightly armed, agile militia – and the most compatible force type to fight alongside, and eventually replace, AMISOM: ordered, structured battalions with all of the essential prerequisites of combat support, logistics support, transport, communications and medical and finance organisations.

The need to fight as a conventional army – receiving, giving and disseminating orders and supplies – has raised difficult requirements. Once in a fight, SNA forces are able to use the same small-unit tactics as when operating as a militia, but when out of contact they are on unfamiliar ground in terms of sustainment and organisation.

International training support

International training programmes between 2007 and 2014 have concentrated on soldier skills and sub-unit tactics. This has been effective in improving the fighting capability of individuals but has done little to close the gap between militia-type organisation and a standard military force such as AMISOM. This has been recognised and, increasingly, international effort is being channelled into inter-operability and unit tactics. The Ethiopian National Defence Forces, after joining AMISOM in January 2014, conducted two-week inter-operability and operational rehearsal packages for up to four SNA battalions in their sectors in the immediate run-up to the AMISOM offensive in March–May 2014 (*Operation Eagle*). The EU Training Mission, having moved from Uganda in 2013, is continuing to provide limited training support to the SNA in the AMISOM Jazeera camp in Mogadishu. The constraining factor is insecurity and this is illustrated by an overarching paradox for all support provided to the SNA: until the areas within which the SNA operates are secure it is difficult or impossible to provide effective international support, but in order to secure these areas international support is required.

AMISOM also has its difficulties. Some analysts have speculated whether international patience and the ability to fund the considerable cost of the mission – possibly in the region of US$50 million per month – may be running out. (The EU contributes approximately US$1.1m per month per thousand men, and the UNSOA logistic-support bill may be as high as US$30m per month.) In searching for an exit strategy for AMISOM, the UN and AU have identified that the development of an SNA capable of largely taking over combat operations is a prerequisite. This comes with a further bill for the international community of an estimated US$160m over three years, a figure that is only likely to rise. The implication of this AMISOM exit strategy is that its planners may be considering handing over operations to the SNA and drawing down its troops before peace, stability and security have been fully established, which could be a high-risk strategy.

Angola ANG

New Angolan Kwanza AOA		2013	2014	2015
GDP	AOA	12tr	12.9tr	
	US$	124bn	131bn	
per capita	US$	5,964	6,128	
Growth	%	6.8	3.9	
Inflation	%	8.8	7.3	
Def bdgt	AOA	588bn	673bn	
	US$	6.09bn	6.85bn	
USD1=AOA		96.5	98.3	

Population 19,088,106

Ethnic groups: Ovimbundu 37%; Kimbundu 25%; Bakongo 13%

Age	0–14	15–19	20–24	25–29	30–64	65 plus
Male	22.0%	5.8%	4.6%	3.8%	12.9%	1.4%
Female	21.2%	5.6%	4.5%	3.7%	12.9%	1.6%

Capabilities

The armed forces' role is to ensure sovereignty and territorial integrity, though the continuing activity of secessionist groups in the northern province of Cabinda is a continuing challenge. On paper the army and air force constitute a considerable regional force, but equipment availability and serviceability remains questionable. Force health and education have been investment priorities, and although growing defence ties with China might result in equipment recapitalisation, Angola's equipment inventory is largely of Soviet or Russian origin, acquired during the conflict with UNITA, which ended in 2002. To increase land-force manoeuvre, *Casspir* APCs have been ordered from South Africa and there are reports of possible orders of Russian AFVs. The air force has ordered Su-30 *Flanker* fighters and Mi-17 helicopters from Russia. It retains a tactical-airlift capability and also has a limited capacity for longer-range transport missions. To counter maritime-security threats, and enable better control of its littoral waters, the navy is to purchase Brazilian patrol vessels, signing an MoU in September 2014 as part of its PRONAVAL modernisation strategy. The armed forces train regularly, and participate in multinational exercises.

ACTIVE 107,000 (Army 100,000 Navy 1,000 Air 6,000) Paramilitary 10,000

ORGANISATIONS BY SERVICE

Army 100,000

FORCES BY ROLE
MANOEUVRE
  Armoured
    1 tk bde
  Light
    1 SF bde
    1 (1st) div (1 mot inf bde, 2 inf bde)
    1 (2nd) div (3 mot inf bde, 3 inf bde, 1 arty regt)
    1 (3rd) div (2 mot inf bde, 3 inf bde)
    1 (4th) div (1 tk regt, 5 mot inf bde, 2 inf bde, 1 engr bde)
    1 (5th) div (2 inf bde)
    1 (6th) div (3 inf bde, 1 engr bde)
COMBAT SUPPORT
  Some engr units
COMBAT SERVICE SUPPORT
  Some log units

EQUIPMENT BY TYPE†
MBT 300: ε200 T-54/T-55; 50 T-62; 50 T-72
LT TK 10 PT-76
RECCE 600 BRDM-2
AIFV 250+: 250 BMP-1/BMP-2; BMD-3
APC (W) ε170 BTR-152/BTR-60/BTR-80
ARTY 1,408+
  SP 16+: **122mm** 2S1; **152mm** 4 2S3; **203mm** 12 2S7
  TOWED 552: **122mm** 500 D-30; **130mm** 48 M-46; **152mm** 4 D-20
  MRL 90+: **122mm** 90: 50 BM-21; 40 RM-70 *Dana*; **240mm** BM-24
  MOR 750: **82mm** 250; **120mm** 500
AT • MSL • MANPATS 9K11 (AT-3 *Sagger*)
  RCL 500: 400 **82mm** B-10/**107mm** B-11 †; **106mm** 100†
  GUNS • SP **100mm** SU-100†
AD • SAM • MANPAD 500 9K32 *Strela*-2 (SA-7 *Grail*)‡;
  9K36 *Strela*-3 (SA-14 *Gremlin*); 9K310 *Igla*-1 (SA-16 *Gimlet*)
  GUNS • TOWED 450+: **14.5mm** ZPU-4; **23mm** ZU-23-2; **37mm** M-1939; **57mm** S-60
ARV T-54/T-55
MW Bozena

Navy ε1,000

EQUIPMENT BY TYPE
PATROL AND COASTAL COMBATANTS 22
  PCO 2 *Ngola Kiluange* with 1 hel landing platform (Ministry of Fisheries)
  PCC 5 *Rei Bula Matadi* (Ministry of Fisheries)
  PBF 5 PVC-170
  PB 10: 4 *Mandume*; 5 *Comandante Imperial Santana* (Ministry of Fisheries); 1 Damen 2810 (Ministry of Fisheries)

Coastal Defence

EQUIPMENT BY TYPE
MSL • AShM 4K44 *Utyos* (SS-C-1B *Sepal* - at Luanda)

Air Force/Air Defence 6,000

FORCES BY ROLE
FIGHTER
  1 sqn with MiG-21bis/MF *Fishbed*
  1 sqn with Su-27/Su-27UB *Flanker*
FIGHTER/GROUND ATTACK
  1 sqn with MiG-23BN/ML/UB *Flogger*
  1 sqn with Su-22 *Fitter* D
  1 sqn with Su-25 *Frogfoot*
MARITIME PATROL
  1 sqn with F-27-200 MPA; C-212 *Aviocar*
TRANSPORT
  3 sqn with An-12 *Cub*; An-26 *Curl*; An-32 *Cline*; An-72 *Coaler*; BN-2A *Islander*; C-212 *Aviocar*; Do-28D

Skyservant; EMB-135BJ *Legacy* 600 (VIP); Il-76TD *Candid*
TRAINING
  1 sqn with Cessna 172K/R
  1 sqn with EMB-312 *Tucano*
  1 sqn with L-29 *Delfin*; L-39 *Albatros*
  1 sqn with PC-7 *Turbo Trainer*; PC-9*
  1 sqn with Z-142
ATTACK HELICOPTER
  2 sqn with Mi-24/Mi-35 *Hind*; SA342M *Gazelle* (with HOT)
TRANSPORT HELICOPTER
  2 sqn with AS565; SA316 *Alouette* III (IAR-316) (trg)
  1 sqn with Bell 212
  1 sqn with Mi-8 *Hip*; Mi-17 *Hip* H
AIR DEFENCE
  5 bn/10 bty with S-125 *Pechora* (SA-3 *Goa*); 9K35 *Strela*-10 (SA-13 *Gopher*)†; 2K12 *Kub* (SA-6 *Gainful*); 9K33 *Osa* (SA-8 *Gecko*); 9K31 *Strela*-1 (SA-9 *Gaskin*); S-75M *Volkhov* (SA-2 *Guideline*)

EQUIPMENT BY TYPE†
AIRCRAFT 83 combat capable
  FTR 24: 6 Su-27/Su-27UB *Flanker*; 18 MiG-23ML *Flogger*
  FGA 42+: 20 MiG-21bis/MF *Fishbed*; 8 MiG-23BN/UB *Flogger*; 13 Su-22 *Fitter* D; 1+ Su-24 *Fencer*
  ATK 10: 8 Su-25 *Frogfoot*; 2 Su-25UB *Frogfoot*
  ELINT 1 B-707
  TPT 62: **Heavy** 4 Il-76TD *Candid*; **Medium** 6 An-12 *Cub*; **Light** 52: 12 An-26 *Curl*; 3 An-32 *Cline*; 8 An-72 *Coaler*; 8 BN-2A *Islander*; 3 C-212-200 *Aviocar*; 4 C-212-300M *Aviocar*; 5 Cessna 172K; 6 Cessna 172R; 1 Do-28D *Skyservant*; 1 EMB-135BJ *Legacy* 600 (VIP); 1 Yak-40
  TRG 39: 13 EMB-312 *Tucano*; 3 EMB-314 *Super Tucano** (3 more on order); 6 L-29 *Delfin*; 2 L-39C *Albatros*; 5 PC-7 *Turbo Trainer*; 4 PC-9*; 6 Z-142
HELICOPTERS
  ATK 44: 22 Mi-24 *Hind*; 22 Mi-35 *Hind*
  MRH 26: 8 AS565 *Panther*; 10 SA316 *Alouette* III (IAR-316) (incl trg); 8 SA342M *Gazelle*
  MRH/TPT 27 Mi-8 *Hip*/Mi-17 *Hip* H
  TPT • Light 8 Bell 212
AD • SAM 122
  SP 70: 10 9K35 *Strela*-10 (SA-13 *Gopher*)†; 25 2K12 *Kub* (SA-6 *Gainful*); 15 9K33 *Osa* (SA-8 *Gecko*); 20 9K31 *Strela*-1 (SA-9 *Gaskin*)
  TOWED 52: 40 S-75M *Volkhov* (SA-2 *Guideline*)‡; 12 S-125 *Pechora* (SA-3 *Goa*)
MSL
  ASM AT-2 *Swatter*; HOT
  ARM Kh-28 (AS-9 *Kyle*)
  AAM • IR R-3 (AA-2 *Atoll*)‡; R-60 (AA-8 *Aphid*); R-73 (AA-11 *Archer*); **IR/SARH** R-23/24 (AA-7 *Apex*)‡; R-27 (AA-10 *Alamo*)

Paramilitary 10,000

Rapid-Reaction Police 10,000

Benin BEN

CFA Franc BCEAO fr		2013	2014	2015
GDP	fr	4.1tr	4.4tr	
	US$	8.31bn	9.24bn	
per capita	US$	805	872.055	
Growth	%	5.65	5.481	
Inflation	%	0.97	1.651	
Def bdgt	fr	42.5bn		
	US$	86m		
US$1=fr		493.89	476.78	

Population 10,160,556

Age	0–14	15–19	20–24	25–29	30–64	65 plus
Male	22.3%	5.6%	4.6%	3.9%	12.7%	1.1%
Female	21.4%	5.4%	4.5%	3.8%	13.1%	1.7%

Capabilities

The country's small armed forces are mainly focused on border and internal security, reflected in the army's emphasis on light infantry. However, maritime security remains an area of concern, with incidents of piracy rising in the Gulf of Guinea. Benin's small navy has been trying to bolster its anti-piracy capability by acquiring further high-speed craft. The air force has a limited number of light transport aircraft and helicopters for intra-theatre airlift, and is also developing a surveillance role. The army, numerically the largest of the three services, has also been the recipient of US AFRICOM training.

ACTIVE 6,950 (Army 6,500 Navy 200 Air 250)
Paramilitary 2,500
Conscript liability 18 months (selective)

ORGANISATIONS BY SERVICE

Army 6,500
FORCES BY ROLE
MANOEUVRE
  Armoured
    2 armd sqn
  Light
    1 (rapid reaction) mot inf bn
    8 inf bn
  Air Manoeuvre
    1 AB bn
COMBAT SUPPORT
  1 arty bn
  1 engr bn
  1 sigs bn
COMBAT SERVICE SUPPORT
  1 log bn
  1 spt bn
EQUIPMENT BY TYPE
LT TK 18 PT-76†
RECCE 31: 14 BRDM-2; 7 M8; 10 VBL

APC (T) 22 M113
ARTY 16+
TOWED 105mm 16: 12 L118 Light Gun; 4 M101
MOR 81mm
AT • RL 89mm LRAC

Navy ε200
EQUIPMENT BY TYPE
PATROL AND COASTAL COMBATANTS
PB 5: 2 *Matelot Brice Kpomasse* (ex-PRC); 3 FPB 98

Air Force 250
AIRCRAFT
TPT 4: Light 1 DHC-6 *Twin Otter*†; PAX 3: 2 B-727; 1 HS-748†
TRG 2 LH-10 *Ellipse*
HELICOPTERS
TPT • Light 5: 4 AW109BA; 1 AS350B *Ecureuil*†

Paramilitary 2,500

Gendarmerie 2,500
FORCES BY ROLE
MANOEUVRE
  OTHER
    4 (mobile) paramilitary coy

DEPLOYMENT

CÔTE D'IVOIRE
UN • UNOCI 383; 8 obs; 1 inf bn(-)

DEMOCRATIC REPUBLIC OF THE CONGO
UN • MONUSCO 454; 9 obs; 1 inf bn(-)

LIBERIA
UN • UNMIL 1; 1 obs

MALI
UN • MINUSMA 253; 1 mech inf coy

SUDAN
UN • UNISFA 1; 1 obs

Botswana BWA

Botswana Pula P		2013	2014	2015
GDP	P	124bn	140bn	
	US$	14.8bn	16.3bn	
per capita	US$	7,120	7,750	
Growth	%	5.9	4.4	
Inflation	%	5.8	4.8	
Def bdgt [a]	P	2.65bn	2.96bn	
	US$	316m	346m	
FMA (US)	US$	0.2m	0.2m	
US$1=P		8.39	8.56	

[a] Defence, Justice and Security Budget

Population   2,155,784

Age	0–14	15–19	20–24	25–29	30–64	65 plus
Male	16.8%	5.5%	5.3%	5.0%	16.6%	1.6%
Female	16.1%	5.4%	5.5%	5.1%	14.8%	2.4%

Capabilities

The armed forces are land-dominated, with a small air contingent. Their main task is to ensure territorial integrity, coupled with domestic tasks such as anti-poaching, and there is a history of involvement in peacekeeping operations. The army is also developing a limited mechanised capability. Air-combat capacity is provided by the F-5 *Freedom Fighter* which, though aged, is adequate for the roles it is tasked with. The air force, whose training was boosted by PC-7 MkII arrivals in 2013, also provides tactical airlift. The forces train regularly and also participate in regional military exercises. The operations centre for the SADC Standby Force is located in Gaborone.

ACTIVE 9,000 (Army 8,500 Air 500) **Paramilitary 1,500**

ORGANISATIONS BY SERVICE

Army 8,500
FORCES BY ROLE
MANOEUVRE
  Armoured
    1 armd bde(-)
  Light
    2 inf bde (1 armd recce regt, 4 inf bn, 1 cdo unit, 2 ADA regt, 1 engr regt, 1 log bn)
COMBAT SUPPORT
  1 arty bde
  1 AD bde(-)
  1 engr coy
  1 sigs coy
COMBAT SERVICE SUPPORT
  1 log gp
EQUIPMENT BY TYPE
LT TK 55: ε30 SK-105 *Kuerassier*; 25 *Scorpion*
RECCE 72+: RAM-V-1; ε8 RAM-V-2; 64 VBL

APC 156
  APC (T) 6 FV 103 *Spartan*
  APC (W) 150: 50 BTR-60; 50 LAV-150 *Commando* (some with 90mm gun); 50 MOWAG *Piranha* III
ARTY 78
  TOWED 30: **105mm** 18: 12 L-118 Light Gun; 6 Model 56 pack howitzer; **155mm** 12 Soltam
  MRL **122mm** 20 APRA-40
  MOR 28: **81mm** 22; **120mm** 6 M-43
AT
  MSL
    SP V-150 TOW
    MANPATS TOW
  RCL **84mm** *Carl Gustav*
AD
  SAM • MANPAD *Javelin*; 9K310 *Igla-1 (SA-16 Gimlet)*; 9K32 *Strela-2 (SA-7 Grail)*‡
  GUNS • TOWED **20mm** 7 M167 *Vulcan*
ARV *Greif*; M578

Air Wing 500
FORCES BY ROLE
FIGHTER/GROUND ATTACK
  1 sqn with F-5A *Freedom Fighter*; F-5D *Tiger* II
ISR
  1 sqn with O-2 *Skymaster*
TRANSPORT
  2 sqn with BD-700 *Global Express*; BN-2A/B *Defender**; Beech 200 *Super King Air* (VIP); C-130B *Hercules*; C-212-300 *Aviocar*; CN-235M-100; Do-328-110 (VIP)
TRAINING
  1 sqn with PC-7 MkII *Turbo Trainer**
TRANSPORT HELICOPTER
  1 sqn with AS350B *Ecureuil*; Bell 412EP/SP *Twin Huey*
EQUIPMENT BY TYPE
AIRCRAFT 33 combat capable
  FTR 14: 9 F-5A *Freedom Fighter*; 5 F-5D *Tiger* II
  ISR 5 O-2 *Skymaster*
  TPT 20: **Medium** 3 C-130B *Hercules*; **Light** 16: 4 BN-2 *Defender**; 6 BN-2B *Defender**; 1 Beech 200 *King Air* (VIP); 2 C-212-300 *Aviocar*; 2 CN-235M-100; 1 Do-328-110 (VIP); **PAX** 1 BD700 *Global Express*
  TRG 5 PC-7 MkII *Turbo Trainer**
HELICOPTERS
  MRH 7: 2 Bell 412EP *Twin Huey*; 5 Bell 412SP *Twin Huey*
  TPT • **Light** 8 AS350B *Ecureuil*

Paramilitary 1,500

Police Mobile Unit 1,500 (org in territorial coy)

Burkina Faso BFA

CFA Franc BCEAO fr		2013	2014	2015
GDP	fr	5.95tr	6.41tr	
	US$	12bn	13.4bn	
per capita	US$	711	768	
Growth	%	6.6	6.7	
Inflation	%	0.5	1.5	
Def bdgt	fr	75.9bn	78.4bn	
	US$	154m	164m	
US$1=fr		493.90	479.21	

Population 18,365,123

Age	0–14	15–19	20–24	25–29	30–64	65 plus
Male	22.7%	5.5%	4.6%	3.8%	12.2%	0.9%
Female	22.6%	5.4%	4.6%	3.7%	12.4%	1.5%

Capabilities

Burkino Faso in February 2014 was one of the five founder members of the 'G5 Sahel' (along with Chad, Mali, Mauritania and Niger) intended to support regional security and development. The G5 Sahel partners the French-led *Opération Barkhane*, aimed at countering Islamist armed groups in the region. The country's armed forces struggle with a lack of funding – in part a cause of unrest within the armed forces in 2011 – and this is reflected in its equipment inventory. The army is structured around light-infantry units, while the air force has a small number of fixed-wing aircraft and helicopters suitable for counter-insurgency operations. The army has provided personnel for a range of UN peacekeeping operations, including in Mali. Training and support is provided by the US and France.

ACTIVE 11,200 (Army 6,400 Air 600 Gendarmerie 4,200) Paramilitary 250

ORGANISATIONS BY SERVICE

Army 6,400
Three military regions. In 2011, several regiments were disbanded and merged into other formations, including the new 24th and 34th *régiments interarmes*.
FORCES BY ROLE
MANOEUVRE
  Mechanised
  1 cbd arms regt
  Light
  1 cbd arms regt
  6 inf regt
  Air Manoeuvre
  1 AB regt (1 CT coy)
COMBAT SUPPORT
  1 arty bn (2 arty tp)
  1 engr bn

EQUIPMENT BY TYPE
RECCE 83: 19 AML-60/AML-90; 24 EE-9 *Cascavel*; 30 *Ferret*; 2 M20; 8 M8
APC 21+
    APC (W) 13 M3 Panhard
    PPV 8+ *Bastion Patsas*
ARTY 50+
    TOWED 14: **105mm** 8 M101; **122mm** 6
    MRL 9: **107mm** ε4 Type-63; **122mm** 5 APRA-40
    MOR 27+: **81mm** Brandt; **82mm** 15; **120mm** 12
AT
    RCL 75mm Type-52 (M20); **84mm** *Carl Gustav*
    RL 89mm LRAC; M20
AD • SAM • MANPAD 9K32 *Strela-2 (SA-7 Grail)*‡
    GUNS • TOWED 42: **14.5mm** 30 ZPU; **20mm** 12 TCM-20

Air Force 600
FORCES BY ROLE
GROUND ATTACK/TRAINING
    1 sqn with SF-260WL *Warrior**; Embraer EMB-314 *Super Tucano**
TRANSPORT
    1 sqn with AT-802 *Air Tractor*; B-727 (VIP); Beech 200 *King Air*; CN-235-220; PA-34 *Seneca*
ATTACK/TRANSPORT HELICOPTER
    1 sqn with AS350 *Ecureuil*; Mi-8 *Hip*; Mi-17 *Hip* H; Mi-35 *Hind*
EQUIPMENT BY TYPE
AIRCRAFT 5 combat capable
    ISR 1 DA42M (reported)
    TPT 9: **Light** 8: 1 AT-802 *Air Tractor*; 2 Beech 200 *King Air*; 1 CN-235-220; 1 PA-34 *Seneca*; 3 *Tetras*; **PAX** 1 B-727 (VIP)
    TRG 5: 3 EMB-314 *Super Tucano**; 2 SF-260WL *Warrior**
HELICOPTERS
    ATK 2 Mi-35 *Hind*
    MRH 2 Mi-17 *Hip* H
    TPT 2 **Medium** 1 Mi-8 *Hip*; **Light** 1 AS350 *Ecureuil*

Gendarmerie 4,200

Paramilitary 250

People's Militia (R) 45,000 reservists (trained)

Security Company 250

DEPLOYMENT
CENTRAL AFRICAN REPUBLIC
UN • MINUSCA 2
DEMOCRATIC REPUBLIC OF THE CONGO
UN • MONUSCO 4 obs
MALI
UN • MINUSMA 860; 1 inf bn
SUDAN
UN • UNAMID 807; 10 obs; 1 inf bn
UN • UNISFA 1 obs

Burundi BDI

Burundi Franc fr		2013	2014	2015
GDP	fr	4.23tr	4.79tr	
	US$	2.72bn	3.04bn	
per capita	US$	303	330	
Growth	%	4.5	4.7	
Inflation	%	9.0	7.0	
Def bdgt	fr	102bn	96.2bn	
	US$	66m	61m	
US$1=fr		1,552.29	1,575.64	

Population 10,395,931

Ethnic groups: Hutu 85%; Tutsi 14%

Age	0–14	15–19	20–24	25–29	30–64	65 plus
Male	22.9%	5.2%	4.4%	3.8%	12.3%	1.1%
Female	22.7%	5.2%	4.4%	3.8%	12.6%	1.4%

Capabilities

The armed forces consist predominantly of infantry, supported by some light armour, and are able to engage in internal-security operations. There is a notional air unit with a handful of light aircraft and helicopters. In recent years, the country has deployed both military and police personnel to the UN mission in the Central African Republic and to AMISOM's mission in Somalia, where they have gained valuable combat experience and specialist military skills. To prepare for operational deployment to AMISOM, exercises with US troops taught patrolling skills, IED detection and EOD capabilities.

ACTIVE 20,000 (Army 20,000) **Paramilitary 31,000**
DDR efforts continue, while activities directed at professionalising the security forces have taken place, some sponsored by BNUB, the UN mission.

ORGANISATIONS BY SERVICE

Army 20,000
FORCES BY ROLE
MANOEUVRE
    Mechanised
    2 lt armd bn (sqn)
    Light
    7 inf bn
    Some indep inf coy
COMBAT SUPPORT
    1 arty bn
    1 AD bn 1 engr bn

Reserves
FORCES BY ROLE
MANOEUVRE
    Light
    10 inf bn (reported)

EQUIPMENT BY TYPE
RECCE 55: 6 AML-60; 12 AML-90; 30 BRDM-2; 7 S52 *Shorland*
APC 72:
    APC (W) 60: 20 BTR-40; 10 BTR-80; 9 M3 Panhard; 15 Type-92; 6 *Walid*
    PPV 12 RG-31 *Nyala*
ARTY 120
    TOWED 122mm 18 D-30
    MRL 122mm 12 BM-21
    MOR 90: 82mm 15 M-43; 120mm ε75
AT
    MSL • MANPATS *Milan* (reported)
    RCL 75mm Type-52 (M-20)
    RL 83mm RL-83 *Blindicide*
AD
    SAM • MANPAD 9K32 *Strela*-2 (SA-7 *Grail*)‡
    GUNS • TOWED 150+: 14.5mm 15 ZPU-4; 135+ 23mm ZU-23/37mm Type-55 (M-1939)

Naval detachment 50
EQUIPMENT BY TYPE
AMPHIBIOUS • LCT 2
LOGISTICS AND SUPPORT • AG 2

Air Wing 200
EQUIPMENT BY TYPE
AIRCRAFT 1 combat capable
    TPT 4: Light 2 Cessna 150L†; PAX 2 DC-3
    TRG 1 SF-260W *Warrior**
HELICOPTERS
    ATK 2 Mi-24 *Hind*
    MRH 2 SA342L *Gazelle*
    TPT • Medium (2 Mi-8 *Hip* non-op)

Paramilitary ε31,000

General Administration of State Security ε1,000

Local Defence Militia ε30,000

DEPLOYMENT

CENTRAL AFRICAN REPUBLIC
UN • MINUSCA 853; 4 obs; 1 inf bn

SOMALIA
AU • AMISOM 5,432; 6 inf bn

SUDAN
UN • UNAMID 2; 7 obs
UN • UNISFA 1 obs

Cameroon CMR

CFA Franc BEAC fr		2013	2014	2015
GDP	fr	14.5tr	15.6tr	
	US$	29.3bn	32.2bn	
per capita	US$	1,331	1,427	
Growth	%	5.5	5.1	
Inflation	%	2.1	3.2	
Def bdgt	fr	194bn	199bn	
	US$	393m	410m	
US$1=fr		493.88	484.28	

Population 23,130,708

Age	0–14	15–19	20–24	25–29	30–64	65 plus
Male	21.6%	5.3%	4.6%	4.1%	13.1%	1.5%
Female	21.3%	5.2%	4.6%	4.0%	13.1%	1.7%

Capabilities

The armed forces' immediate concerns are the actions of Boko Haram and piracy. During 2014 there were repeated clashes with Boko Haram fighters in the northern area of the country bordering Nigeria. The far north of the country was also being used as an arms conduit for the group. The army is by far the largest of the three services and consists mostly of light infantry. While significant elements of its equipment inventory are ageing, it has in recent years acquired infantry fighting vehicles and other armour from China. The air force's airlift capacity was bolstered in 2013 with the delivery of a CN-235; two Mi-17 medium helicopters were ordered in the same year. Two large patrol craft for the navy were under construction in China in 2014, intended to support anti-piracy efforts in the Gulf of Guinea. The army has contributed personnel to UN peacekeeping operations. Exercises conducted during 2014 included *Central Accord 2014*, with five other African nations, the US and the Netherlands, part of which was a joint airborne exercise with US and Cameroonian paratroopers.

ACTIVE 14,200 (Army 12,500 Navy 1,300 Air 400)
Paramilitary 9,000

ORGANISATIONS BY SERVICE

Army 12,500
3 Mil Regions
FORCES BY ROLE
MANOEUVRE
    Light
    1 rapid reaction bde (1 armd recce bn, 1 AB bn, 1 amph bn)
    3 mot inf bde (3 mot inf bn, 1 spt bn)
    1 mot inf bde (2 mot inf bn, 1 spt bn)
    3 (rapid reaction) inf bn
    Air Manoeuvre
    1 cdo/AB bn
    Other
    1 (Presidential Guard) gd bn

COMBAT SUPPORT
1 arty regt (5 arty bty)
1 AD regt (6 AD bty)
3 engr regt

EQUIPMENT BY TYPE
RECCE 70: 31 AML-90; 6 AMX-10RC; 15 *Ferret*; 8 M8; 5 RAM-2000; 5 VBL
AIFV 30: 8 LAV-150 *Commando* with 20mm gun; 14 LAV-150 *Commando* with 90mm gun; ε8 Type-07P
APC 33
  APC (T) 12 M3 half-track
  APC (W) 21 LAV-150 *Commando*
ARTY 108+
  SP 155mm 18 ATMOS 2000
  TOWED 52: **105mm** 20 M101; **130mm** 24: 12 Model 1982 gun 82 (reported); 12 Type-59 (M-46); **155mm** 8 I1
  MRL 122mm 20 BM-21
  MOR 16+: **81mm** (some SP); **120mm** 16 Brandt
AT
  MSL 49
    SP 24 TOW (on Jeeps)
    MANPATS 25 *Milan*
  RCL 53: **106mm** 40 M40A2; **75mm** 13 Type-52 (M-20)
  RL 89mm LRAC
  GUNS • SP 105mm ε12 PTL-02 mod (Cara 105)
AD • GUNS • TOWED 54: **14.5mm** 18 Type-58 (ZPU-2); **35mm** 18 GDF-002; **37mm** 18 Type-63

Navy ε1,300
HQ located at Douala

EQUIPMENT BY TYPE
PATROL AND COASTAL COMBATANTS 13
  PCC 2: 1 *Bakassi* (FRA P-48); 1 *Dipikar* (FRA *Flamant*)
  PB 9: 2 Aresa 2400; 2 Rodman 101; 4 Rodman 46; 1 *Quartier Maître Alfred Motto*
  PBR 2 Swift-38
AMPHIBIOUS • LANDING CRAFT 2
  LCM 1 Aresa 2300
  LCU 2 *Yunnan*

Fusiliers Marin
FORCES BY ROLE
MANOEUVRE
  Amphbious
  3 mne bn

Air Force 300–400
FORCES BY ROLE
FIGHTER/GROUND ATTACK
  1 sqn with MB-326K; *Alpha Jet*†
TRANSPORT
  1 sqn with C-130H/H-30 *Hercules*; DHC-4 *Caribou*; DHC-5D *Buffalo*; IAI-201 *Arava*; PA-23 *Aztec*
  1 VIP unit with AS332 *Super Puma*; AS365 *Dauphin* 2; Bell 206B *Jet Ranger*; Gulfstream III
TRAINING
  1 unit with *Tetras*
ATTACK HELICOPTER
  1 sqn with SA342 *Gazelle* (with HOT)
TRANSPORT HELICOPTER
  1 sqn with Bell 206L-3; Bell 412; SA319 *Alouette* III

EQUIPMENT BY TYPE
AIRCRAFT 9 combat capable
  ATK 5: 1 MB-326K *Impala* I; 4 MB-326K *Impala* II
  TPT 20: **Medium** 3: 2 C-130H *Hercules*; 1 C-130H-30 *Hercules*; **Light** 16: 1 CN-235; 1 DHC-4 *Caribou*; 1 DHC-5D *Buffalo*; 1 IAI-201 *Arava*; 2 J.300 *Joker*; 1 MA60; 2 PA-23 *Aztec*; 7 *Tetras*; **PAX** 1 Gulfstream III
  TRG 4 *Alpha Jet*†
HELICOPTERS
  MRH 8: 1 AS365 *Dauphin* 2; 1 Bell 412 *Twin Huey*; 2 SA319 *Alouette* III; 4 SA342 *Gazelle* (with HOT)
  TPT 7: **Medium** 4: 2 AS332 *Super Puma*; 2 SA330J *Puma*; **Light** 3: 2 Bell 206B *Jet Ranger*; 1 Bell 206L3 *Long Ranger*

Fusiliers de l'Air
FORCES BY ROLE
MANOEUVRE
  Other
  1 sy bn

Paramilitary 9,000

Gendarmerie 9,000
FORCES BY ROLE
MANOEUVRE
  Reconnaissance
  3 (regional spt) paramilitary gp

DEPLOYMENT

CENTRAL AFRICAN REPUBLIC
UN • MINUSCA 979; 1 inf bn

CÔTE D'IVOIRE
UN • UNOCI 1 obs

DEMOCRATIC REPUBLIC OF THE CONGO
UN • MONUSCO 6 obs

Cape Verde CPV

Cape Verde Escudo E		2013	2014	2015
GDP	E	154bn	159bn	
	US$	1.86bn	1.98bn	
per capita	US$	3,633	3,810	
Growth	%	0.5	1.0	
Inflation	%	1.5	0.8	
Def bdgt	E	855m	992m	885m
	US$	10m	12m	
US$1=E		83.00	80.58	

Population 538,535

Age	0–14	15–19	20–24	25–29	30–64	65 plus
Male	15.4%	5.4%	5.3%	4.7%	15.7%	1.9%
Female	15.2%	5.4%	5.3%	4.8%	17.6%	3.2%

Capabilities

Maritime security, counter-narcotics operations and patrolling the littoral waters of the archipelago are the main tasks of Cape Verde's small armed forces.

ACTIVE 1,200 (Army 1,000 Coast Guard 100 Air 100)
Conscript liability Selective conscription

ORGANISATIONS BY SERVICE

Army 1,000
FORCES BY ROLE
MANOEUVRE
  Light
  2 inf bn (gp)
COMBAT SUPPORT
  1 engr bn
EQUIPMENT BY TYPE
RECCE 10 BRDM-2
ARTY • MOR 18: **82mm** 12; **120mm** 6 M-1943
AT • RL **89mm** (3.5in)
AD
  SAM • MANPAD 9K32 *Strela* (SA-7 *Grail*)‡
  GUNS • TOWED 30: **14.5mm** 18 ZPU-1; **23mm** 12 ZU-23

Coast Guard ε100
EQUIPMENT BY TYPE
PATROL AND COASTAL COMBATANTS 5
  PCC 2: 1 *Guardião*; 1 *Kondor I*
  PB 2: 1 *Espadarte*; 1 *Tainha* (PRC-27m)
  PBF 1 *Archangel*

Air Force up to 100
FORCES BY ROLE
MARITIME PATROL
  1 sqn with C-212 *Aviocar*; Do-228
EQUIPMENT BY TYPE
AIRCRAFT • TPT • Light 5: 1 C-212 *Aviocar*; 1 Do-228; 3 An-26 *Curl*†

Central African Republic CAR

CFA Franc BEAC fr		2013	2014	2015
GDP	fr	760bn	829bn	
	US$	1.54bn	1.73bn	
per capita	US$	334	368	
Growth	%	-36.0	1.0	
Inflation	%	6.6	7.4	
Def bdgt	fr	n.k.	n.k.	
	US$	n.k.	n.k.	
US$1=fr		493.96	479.18	

Population 5,277,959

Age	0–14	15–19	20–24	25–29	30–64	65 plus
Male	20.4%	5.3%	4.8%	4.2%	13.4%	1.4%
Female	20.2%	5.3%	4.8%	4.2%	13.9%	2.2%

Capabilities

Effective military and security organisations have largely disintegrated in the wake of the violence that has wracked the country since 2013, though a small core of personnel remain in Bangui; some equipment remains, but inventory numbers are difficult to verify, while looting of barracks during fighting might have led to some equipment dispersing to non-state actors. A UNDP-supported registration process has assessed available personnel numbers for the armed forces, and a UNDP project is working towards rebuilding police, gendarmerie and justice capacity; this will be a long task, given the fractures that have developed throughout society. In December 2013, the Economic Community of Central African States' MICOPAX mission transitioned to an African-led International Support Mission and in April 2014 the UN Multidimensional Integrated Stabilisation Mission in CAR (MINUSCA) began. This in turn transitioned to a UN mission, MINUSCA, in September 2014. An EU military mission continues, as does the French *Opération Sangaris* deployment. For the foreseeable future, security will be provided by multinational forces, until durable local structures can be reconstructed.

ACTIVE 7,150 (Army 7,000 Air 150) Paramilitary 1,000
Conscript liability Selective conscription 2 years; reserve obligation thereafter, term n.k.

ORGANISATIONS BY SERVICE

Army ε7,000
EQUIPMENT BY TYPE
MBT 3 T-55†
RECCE 9: 8 *Ferret*†; 1 BRDM-2
AIFV 18 *Ratel*
APC (W) 39+: 4 BTR-152†; 25+ TPK 4.20 VSC ACMAT†; 10+ VAB†
ARTY • MOR 12+: **81mm**†; **120mm** 12 M-1943†
AT • RCL **106mm** 14 M40†
  RL **89mm** LRAC†
PATROL AND COASTAL COMBATANTS 9 PBR†

Air Force 150
EQUIPMENT BY TYPE
AIRCRAFT • TPT 7: **Medium** 1 C-130A *Hercules*; **Light** 6: 3 BN-2 *Islander*; 1 Cessna 172RJ *Skyhawk*; 2 J.300 *Joker*
HELICOPTERS
  TPT • Light 1 AS350 *Ecureuil*

FOREIGN FORCES

MINUSCA unless stated
Austria EUFOR RCA 6
Bangladesh 332; 1 inf bn(-)
Bhutan 2
Bolivia 3 obs
Burkina Faso 2
Burundi 853; 4 obs; 1 inf bn

Cameroon 979; 1 inf bn
Congo 793; 1 inf bn
Czech Republic 2 obs
Democratic Republic of the Congo 837; 1 inf bn
Egypt 2 obs
Finland EUFOR RCA 30; 1 CIMIC unit; 1 EOD unit
France 8 • Operation Sangaris 2,000; 2 inf BG; 1 spt det; 1 hel det with 2 SA342 *Gazelle*; 1 hel det with 2 AS555 *Fennec*; 1 SAR/tpt det with 3 SA300 *Puma* • EUFOR RCA 250; 1 inf coy
Gabon 513; 1 inf bn
Georgia EUFOR RCA 140; 1 inf coy
Germany EUFOR RCA 4
Italy EUFOR RCA 49; 1 engr pl
Latvia EUFOR RCA 40
Lithuania EUFOR RCA 1
Luxembourg EUFOR RCA 1
Madagascar 1
Mali 1
Mauritania 1; 2 obs
Morocco 749; 2 obs; 1 inf bn
Nepal 1
Netherlands EUFOR RCA 1
Niger 2 obs
Pakistan 324; 1 inf bn(-)
Poland EUFOR RCA 50
Rwanda 858; 4 obs; 1 mech inf bn
Serbia EUFOR RCA 6
Senegal 2; 1 obs
Spain EUFOR RCA 99; 1 SF unit
Sri Lanka 124; 1 hel sqn
Tanzania 1
Yemen 1 obs
Zambia 2; 3 mil obs

Chad CHA

CFA Franc BEAC fr		2013	2014	2015
GDP	fr	6.62tr	7.59tr	
	US$	13.4bn	15.8bn	
per capita	US$	1,218	1,404	
Growth	%	3.9	9.6	
Inflation	%	0.2	2.8	
Def exp	fr	ε103bn		
	US$	ε209m		
FMA (US)	US$	0.2m	0.2m	
US$1=fr		493.87	479.19	

Population 11,412,107

Age	0–14	15–19	20–24	25–29	30–64	65 plus
Male	22.7%	5.7%	4.4%	3.6%	10.6%	1.2%
Female	22.0%	5.8%	4.8%	4.2%	13.2%	1.7%

Capabilities

Chad's two most pressing security concerns are instability in Western Africa and the Sahel and counter-insurgency operations against Boko Haram. Chad withdrew its contingent from the CAR in early 2014, though it remains concerned by instability in that country. The country is part of the 'G5 Sahel' nations, and has encouraged African armed forces to take ownership of regional security. The French-led *Opération Barkhane* has a base in the Chadian capital, N'Djamena. The capability of the country's small air force was strengthened by the acquisition of second-hand Su-25 *Frogfoot* aircraft from Ukraine and it has also ordered a handful of MiG-29 *Fulcrum*s, the first of which was test-flown in 2014. Intra-theatre airlift has also been improved with the purchase of two C-27J *Spartan*s, both of which were in flight-test by mid-2014.

ACTIVE 25,350 (Army 17,000–20,000 Air 350 Republican Guard 5,000) **Paramilitary 9,500**
Conscript liability Conscription authorised

ORGANISATIONS BY SERVICE

Army ε17,000–20,000 (being reorganised)
7 Mil Regions
FORCES BY ROLE
MANOEUVRE
  Armoured
    1 armd bn
  Light
    7 inf bn
COMBAT SUPPORT
  1 arty bn
  1 engr bn
  1 sigs bn
COMBAT SERVICE SUPPORT
  1 log gp
EQUIPMENT BY TYPE
MBT 60 T-55
RECCE 309+: 132 AML-60/AML-90; 22 *Bastion Patsas*; ε100 BRDM-2; 20 EE-9 *Cascavel*; 4 ERC-90F *Sagaie*; 31+ RAM-2000
AIFV 92: 83 BMP-1; 9 LAV-150 *Commando* (with 90mm gun)
APC (W) 85: 24 BTR-80; 8 BTR-3E; ε20 BTR-60; 25 VAB-VTT; 8 WZ-523
ARTY 25+
  SP 122mm 10 2S1
  TOWED 105mm 5 M2
  MRL 122mm 10: 4 APRA-40; 6 BM-21 *Grad*
  MOR 81mm some; **120mm** AM-50
AT
  MSL • MANPATS *Eryx*; *Milan*
  RCL 106mm M40A1
  RL 112mm APILAS; **89mm** LRAC
  GUN • SP 105mm 30 PTL-02 *Assaulter*
AD
  SAM
    SP 2K12 *Kub* (SA-6 *Gainful*)

MANPAD 9K310 *Igla*-1 (SA-16 *Gimlet*)
GUNS • TOWED 14.5mm ZPU-1/ZPU-2/ZPU-4; **23mm** ZU-23

Air Force 350

FORCES BY ROLE
GROUND ATTACK
  1 unit with PC-7; PC-9*; SF-260WL *Warrior**; Su-25 *Frogfoot*
TRANSPORT
  1 sqn with An-26 *Curl*; C-130H-30 *Hercules*; Mi-17 *Hip* H; Mi-171
  1 (Presidential) Flt with B-737BBJ; Beech 1900; DC-9-87; Gulfstream II
ATTACK HELICOPTER
  1 sqn with AS550C *Fennec*; Mi-24V *Hind*; SA316 *Alouette* III

EQUIPMENT BY TYPE
AIRCRAFT 14 combat capable
  FTR 1 MiG-29 *Fulcrum*
  ATK 10: 8 Su-25 *Frogfoot*; 2 Su-25UB *Frogfoot* B
  TPT 8: **Medium** 1 C-130H-30 *Hercules*; **Light** 4: 3 An-26 *Curl*; 1 Beech 1900; **PAX** 3: 1 B-737BBJ; 1 DC-9-87; 1 Gulfstream II
  TRG 4: 2 PC-7 (only 1*); 1 PC-9 *Turbo Trainer**; 1 SF-260WL *Warrior**
HELICOPTERS
  ATK 3 Mi-24V *Hind*
  MRH 11: 6 AS550C *Fennec*; 3 Mi-17 *Hip* H; 2 SA316 *Alouette* III
  TPT • **Medium** 2 Mi-171

Paramilitary 9,500 active

Republican Guard 5,000

Gendarmerie 4,500

DEPLOYMENT

CÔTE D'IVOIRE
UN • UNOCI 1; 4 obs

MALI
UN • MINUSMA 1,046; 1 SF coy; 1 inf bn; 2 inf coy

FOREIGN FORCES

France *Operation Barkhane* 1,250; 1 recce BG; 1 air unit with 3 *Rafale* F3; 1 C-130H *Hercules*; 1 C-160 *Transall*; 1 C-135FR; 1 hel det with 4 SA330 *Puma*

Republic of Congo COG

CFA Franc BEAC fr		2013	2014	2015
GDP	fr	6.66tr	6.83tr	
	US$	13.5bn	14.1bn	
per capita	US$	3,223	3,302	
Growth	%	3.3	6.0	
Inflation	%	4.6	2.2	
Def bdgt	fr	181bn	349bn	
	US$	367m	720m	
US$1=fr		493.89	484.27	

Population 4,662,446

Age	0–14	15–19	20–24	25–29	30–64	65 plus
Male	20.7%	4.6%	4.2%	3.6%	15.6%	1.3%
Female	20.4%	4.6%	4.3%	4.1%	14.8%	1.7%

Capabilities

Congo's armed forces are small, utilise aged equipment, and have low levels of training and limited overall capability. They have struggled to recover from the brief but devastating civil war in the late 1990s. Training levels are low and equipment serviceability is also a challenge, particularly given the age of much equipment. This is despite a defence budget that fares relatively well in comparison to immediate neighbours. The air force is effectively grounded for lack of spares and serviceable equipment, and the navy is little more than a riverine force despite the need for maritime security on the country's small coastline. However, the country was able to host and manage the CEEAC Standby Force exercise *Loango 2014*, which ended in October 2014.

ACTIVE 10,000 (Army 8,000 Navy 800 Air 1,200)
Paramilitary 2,000

ORGANISATIONS BY SERVICE

Army 8,000
FORCES BY ROLE
MANOEUVRE
  Armoured
  2 armd bn
  Light
  2 inf bn (gp) each with (1 lt tk tp, 1 arty bty)
  1 inf bn
  Air Manoeuvre
  1 cdo/AB bn
COMBAT SUPPORT
  1 arty gp (with MRL)
  1 engr bn

EQUIPMENT BY TYPE†
MBT 40: 25 T-54/T-55; 15 Type-59; (some T-34 in store)
LT TK 13: 3 PT-76; 10 Type-62
RECCE 25 BRDM-1/BRDM-2
APC 120+

APC (W) 68+: 20 BTR-152; 30 BTR-60; 18 *Mamba*; M3 Panhard
PPV 52: 15 *Fox*; 37 *Marauder*
ARTY 66+
 SP 122mm 3 2S1
 TOWED 25+: 100mm 10 M-1944; 122mm 10 D-30; 130mm 5 M-46; 152mm D-20
 MRL 10+: 122mm 10 BM-21; 122mm BM-14; 140mm BM-16
 MOR 28+: 82mm; 120mm 28 M-43
AT • RCL 57mm M18
 GUNS 57mm 5 ZIS-2 *M-1943*
AD • GUNS 28+
 SP 23mm ZSU-23-4
 TOWED 14.5mm ZPU-2/ZPU-4; 37mm 28 M-1939; 57mm S-60; 100mm KS-19

Navy ε800
EQUIPMENT BY TYPE
PATROL AND COASTAL COMBATANTS 8
 PCC 4 *Février*
 PBR 4

Air Force 1,200
FORCES BY ROLE
FIGHTER/GROUND ATTACK
 1 sqn with *Mirage* F-1AZ
TRANSPORT
 1 sqn with An-24 *Coke*; An-32 *Cline*; CN-235M-100
ATTACK/TRANSPORT HELICOPTER
 1 sqn with Mi-8 *Hip*; Mi-35P *Hind*
EQUIPMENT BY TYPE†
AIRCRAFT
 FGA 2 *Mirage* F-1AZ
 TPT • Light 4: 1 An-24 *Coke*; 2 An-32 *Cline*; 1 CN-235M-100
HELICOPTERS†
 ATK (2 Mi-35P *Hind* in store)
 TPT • Medium (3 Mi-8 *Hip* in store)
MSL • AAM • IR R-3 (AA-2 *Atoll*)‡

Paramilitary 2,000 active
Gendarmerie 2,000
FORCES BY ROLE
MANOEUVRE
 Other
  20 paramilitary coy

Presidential Guard some
FORCES BY ROLE
MANOEUVRE
 Other
  1 paramilitary bn

DEPLOYMENT
CENTRAL AFRICAN REPUBLIC
UN • MINUSCA 793; 1 inf bn

Côte D'Ivoire CIV

CFA Franc BCEAO fr		2013	2014	2015
GDP	fr	15.3tr	16.7tr	
	US$	32.1bn	34bn	
per capita	US$	1,332	1,370	
Growth	%	8.7	8.5	
Inflation	%	2.6	0.6	
Def bdgt [a]	fr	371bn	400bn	
	US$	775m	812m	
FMA (US)	US$	0.3m	0.3m	
US$1=fr		478.65	492.61	

[a] Defence, order and security expenses.

Population 22,848,945

Age	0–14	15–19	20–24	25–29	30–64	65 plus
Male	19.8%	5.5%	5.1%	4.3%	14.4%	1.5%
Female	19.5%	5.5%	5.0%	4.2%	13.6%	1.6%

Capabilities

The army comprises personnel from both sides of the previous conflict. The air force has no combat capability and a very limited capacity for transport, and there remain questions as to serviceability. The latter is also an issue for the small naval unit. Internal and border-security incidents – on the country's border with Liberia – flared up in the first half of 2014, with the army deployed in response. The government has attempted to tackle the use of illegal checkpoints. The country remains the subject of a UN arms embargo until at least April 2015, although restrictions on the supply of non-lethal equipment have eased.

ACTIVE ε40,000 target

RESERVE n.k.

Moves to restructure and reform the armed forces continue.

ORGANISATIONS BY SERVICE

Army n.k.
FORCES BY ROLE
MANOEUVRE
 Armoured
  1 armd bn
 Light
  4 inf bn
 Air Manoeuvre
  1 cdo/AB bn
COMBAT SUPPORT
 1 arty bn
 1 AD bn
 1 engr bn
COMBAT SERVICE SUPPORT
 1 log bn

EQUIPMENT BY TYPE
MBT 10 T-55†
LT TK 5 AMX-13
RECCE 34: 15 AML-60/AML-90; 13 BRDM-2; 6 ERC-90F4 *Sagaie*
AIFV 10 BMP-1/BMP-2†
APC (W) 31: 12 M3 Panhard; 13 VAB; 6 BTR-80
ARTY 36+
  TOWED 4+: **105mm** 4 M-1950; **122mm** (reported)
  MRL 122mm 6 BM-21
  MOR 26+: **81mm**; **82mm** 10 M-37; **120mm** 16 AM-50
AT • MSL • MANPATS 9K113 *Konkurs* (AT-5 *Spandrel*) (reported); 9K135 *Kornet* (AT-14 *Spriggan*) (reported)
  RCL 106mm ε12 M40A1
  RL 89mm LRAC
AD • SAM • MANPAD 9K32 *Strela*-2 (SA-7 *Grail*)‡ (reported)
  GUNS 21+
    SP 20mm 6 M3 VDAA
    TOWED 15+: **20mm** 10; **23mm** ZU-23-2; **40mm** 5 L/60
VLB MTU
AIRCRAFT • TPT • Medium 1 An-12 *Cub*†

Navy ε900
EQUIPMENT BY TYPE
PATROL AND COASTAL COMBATANTS 4
  PB 2: 1 *L'Emergence*; 1 *Intrepide* † (FRA *Patra*)
  PBR 2 Rodman (fishery protection duties)
AMPHIBIOUS
  LCM 2 *Aby* †
LOGISTICS AND SUPPORT
  YT 2

Air Force n.k.
EQUIPMENT BY TYPE†
AIRCRAFT
  TPT • PAX 1 B-727
HELICOPTERS
  ATK 1 Mi-24 (reported)
  TPT • Medium 3 SA330L *Puma* (IAR-330L)

Paramilitary n.k.

Republican Guard unk
APC (W) 4 *Mamba*

Gendarmerie n.k.
APC (W) some VAB
PATROL AND COASTAL COMBATANTS • PB 1 *Bian*

Militia n.k.

DEPLOYMENT
DEMOCRATIC REPUBLIC OF THE CONGO
UN • MONUSCO 1

MALI
UN • MINUSMA 121; 1 tpt coy

FOREIGN FORCES
All forces part of UNOCI unless otherwise stated.
Bangladesh 1,694; 12 obs; 2 mech inf bn; 1 engr coy; 1 sigs coy; 1 fd hospital; 1 avn coy
Benin 383; 8 obs; 1 inf bn(-)
Bolivia 3 obs
Brazil 3; 4 obs
Cameroon 1 obs
Chad 1; 4 obs
China, People's Republic of 4 obs
Ecuador 2 obs
Egypt 176; 1 engr coy
El Salvador 3 obs
Ethiopia 2 obs
France 6 • *Operation Licorne* 450; 1 armd BG; 1 hel unit with 1 C-160 *Transall*; 1 AS555 *Fennec*
Gambia 3 obs
Ghana 156; 6 obs; 1 hel sqn; 1 fd hospital
Guatemala 5 obs
Guinea 3 obs
India 9 obs
Ireland 2 obs
Jordan 549; 9 obs; 1 SF coy; 1 inf bn(-)
Korea, Republic of 2 obs
Malawi 2; 3 obs
Moldova 4 obs
Morocco 725; 1 inf bn
Namibia 2 obs
Nepal 1; 3 obs
Niger 871; 5 obs; 1 inf bn
Nigeria 3 obs
Pakistan 1,393; 12 obs; 1 inf bn; 1 engr coy; 1 tpt coy
Paraguay 2; 7 obs
Peru 2 obs
Philippines 3; 3 obs
Poland 2 obs
Romania 6 obs
Russia 11 obs
Senegal 463; 5 obs; 1 inf bn
Serbia 3 obs
Spain 1
Tanzania 1; 1 obs
Togo 469; 6 obs; 1 inf bn
Tunisia 3; 7 obs
Uganda 2; 3 obs
Ukraine 40; 1 hel flt
Uruguay 2 obs
Yemen, Republic of 1; 9 obs
Zambia 2 obs
Zimbabwe 3 obs

Democratic Republic of the Congo DRC

Congolese Franc fr		2013	2014	2015
GDP	fr	27.5tr	30.6tr	
	US$	29.9bn	32.7bn	
per capita	US$	388	412	
Growth	%	8.5	8.6	
Inflation	%	0.8	2.4	
Def bdgt	fr	393bn	426bn	684bn
	US$	427m	456m	
US$1=fr		919.49	935.32	

Population 77,433,744

Age	0–14	15–19	20–24	25–29	30–64	65 plus
Male	21.7%	5.8%	4.9%	3.9%	12.4%	1.1%
Female	21.4%	5.8%	4.9%	3.9%	12.7%	1.5%

Capabilities

The DRC ostensibly retains the largest armed forces in Central Africa. However, given the country's size and the poor level of training, morale and equipment, the DRC armed forces (FARDC) are unable to provide security throughout the country. The DRC has suffered the most protracted war in the post-Cold War era. For this reason, much military equipment is in a poor state of repair and the armed forces, which have since incorporated a number of non-state armed groups, struggle with a variety of loyalties. Rebellion by former FARDC troops, dubbed M23, was only ended in December 2013 after an offensive by the FARDC, supported by the UN's Intervention Brigade. Nonetheless, eastern DRC remains an area of poor governance and further action by the UN MONUSCO mission was mooted in late 2014, this time against the ADF rebel group, accused of massacres in the east. FARDC is heavily dominated by land forces; the air force retains a limited combat capability of mostly Soviet-origin aircraft; and the navy acts as a riverine force.

ACTIVE ε134,250 (Central Staffs ε14,000, Army 103,000 Republican Guard 8,000 Navy 6,700 Air 2,550)

ORGANISATIONS BY SERVICE

Army (Forces du Terre) ε103,000

The DRC has eleven Military Regions. In 2011, all brigades in North and South Kivu provinces were consolidated into 27 new regiments, the latest in a sequence of reorganisations designed to integrate non-state armed groups. The actual combat effectiveness of many formations is doubtful.

FORCES BY ROLE
MANOEUVRE
  Light
  6 (integrated) inf bde
  ε3 inf bde (non-integrated)
  27+ inf regt
COMBAT SUPPORT
  1 arty regt
  1 MP bn

EQUIPMENT BY TYPE†
(includes Republican Guard eqpt)
MBT 149: 12–17 Type-59 †; 32 T-55; 100 T-72AV
LT TK 40: 10 PT-76; 30 Type-62† (reportedly being refurbished)
RECCE up to 52: up to 17 AML-60; 14 AML-90; 19 EE-9 *Cascavel*; 2 RAM-V-2
AIFV 20 BMP-1
APC 144:
  APC (T) 9: 3 BTR-50; 6 MT-LB
  APC (W) 135: 30-70 BTR-60PB; 58 M3 Panhard†; 7 TH 390 *Fahd*
ARTY 720+
  SP 16: **122mm** 6 2S1; **152mm** 10 2S3
  TOWED 119: **122mm** 77 (M-30) M-1938/D-30/Type-60; **130mm** 42 Type-59 (M-46)/Type-59 I
  MRL 57+: **107mm** 12 Type-63; **122mm** 24+: 24 BM-21; some RM-70; **128mm** 6 M-51; **130mm** 3 Type-82; **132mm** 12
  MOR 528+: **81mm** 100; **82mm** 400; **107mm** M-30; **120mm** 28: 18; 10 Brandt
AT
  RCL 57mm M18; **73mm**; **75mm** M20; **106mm** M40A1
  GUNS 85mm 10 Type-56 (D-44)
AD
  SAM • MANPAD 9K32 *Strela*-2 (SA-7 *Grail*)‡
  GUNS • TOWED 114: **14.5mm** 12 ZPU-4; **37mm** 52 M-1939; **40mm** ε50 L/60† (probably out of service)

Republican Guard 8,000

FORCES BY ROLE
MANOEUVRE
  Armoured
  1 armd regt
  Light
  3 gd bde
COMBAT SUPPORT
  1 arty regt

Navy 6,700 (incl infantry and marines)

EQUIPMENT BY TYPE
PATROL AND COASTAL COMBATANTS 16
  PB 16: 1 *Shanghai* II; ε15 various (all under 50ft)

Air Force 2,550

EQUIPMENT BY TYPE
AIRCRAFT 6 combat capable
  FTR 2: 1 MiG-23MS *Flogger*; 1 MiG-23UB *Flogger* C
  ATK 4 Su-25 *Frogfoot*
  TPT 6: **Medium** 1 C-130H *Hercules*; **Light** 3 An-26 *Curl*; **PAX** 2 B-727
HELICOPTERS
  ATK 9: 4 Mi-24 *Hind*; 5 Mi-24V *Hind*
  TPT 3: **Heavy** (1 Mi-26 *Halo* non-operational); **Medium** 3: 1 AS332L *Super Puma*; 2 Mi-8 *Hip*

Paramilitary

National Police Force
incl Rapid Intervention Police (National and Provincial forces)

People's Defence Force

DEPLOYMENT

CENTRAL AFRICAN REPUBLIC

UN • MINUSCA 837; 1 inf bn

FOREIGN FORCES

All part of MONUSCO unless otherwise specified.
Algeria 5 obs
Bangladesh 2,550; 20 obs; 2 mech inf bn; 2 engr coy; 1 avn coy; 2 hel coy
Belgium 2
Benin 454; 9 obs; 1 inf bn(-)
Bolivia 1; 8 obs
Bosnia and Herzegovina 5 obs
Brazil 7; 1 obs
Burkina Faso 4 obs
Cameroon 6 obs
Canada (*Operation Crocodile*) 8
China, People's Republic of 221; 12 obs; 1 engr coy; 1 fd hospital
Cote d'Ivoire 1
Czech Republic 3 obs
Egypt 987; 18 obs; 1 SF coy; 1 mech inf bn
France 4
Ghana 465; 22 obs; 1 mech inf bn(-)
Guatemala 152; 1 obs; 1 SF coy
Guinea 1 obs
India 3,720; 38 obs; 3 mech inf bn; 1 inf bn; 1 hel coy; 1 fd hospital
Indonesia 175; 14 obs; 1 engr coy
Ireland 4
Jordan 169; 15 obs; 1 SF coy
Kenya 6; 18 obs
Malawi 857; 8 obs; 1 inf bn
Malaysia 9; 4 obs
Mali 6 obs
Mongolia 2 obs
Morocco 840; 2 obs; 1 mech inf bn; 1 fd hospital
Nepal 1,031; 18 obs; 1 inf bn; 1 engr coy
Niger 4; 8 obs
Nigeria 5; 12 obs
Pakistan 3,745; 38 obs; 3 mech inf bn; 1 inf bn; 1 hel sqn
Paraguay 13 obs
Peru 2; 12 obs
Poland 3 obs
Romania 21 obs
Russia 28 obs
Senegal 19; 6 obs
Serbia 8
South Africa (*Operation Mistral*) 1,343; 4 obs; 1 inf bn; 1 atk hel coy; 1 hel coy; 1 engr coy
Sri Lanka 2 obs
Sweden 5 obs
Switzerland 4
Tanzania 1,264; 1 SF coy; 1 inf bn; 1 arty coy
Tunisia 29 obs
Ukraine 254: 10 obs; 2 atk hel sqn; 1 hel sqn
United Kingdom 6
United States 3
Uruguay 1,181; 8 obs; 1 inf bn; 1 mne coy; 1 hel flt
Yemen, Republic of 4 obs
Zambia 2; 18 obs

Djibouti DJB

Djiboutian Franc fr		2013	2014	2015
GDP	fr	259bn	281bn	
	US$	1.46bn	1.58bn	
per capita	US$	1,593	1,684	
Growth	%	5.0	5.5	
Inflation	%	2.4	3.2	
Def bdgt	fr	ε1.72bn		
	US$	ε10m		
FMA (US)	US$	1.5m	1.5m	0.7m
US$1=fr		177.77	177.67	

Population   810,179

Ethnic groups: Somali 60%; Afar 35%

Age	0–14	15–19	20–24	25–29	30–64	65 plus
Male	16.5%	5.3%	5.0%	4.1%	13.4%	1.6%
Female	16.4%	5.6%	6.0%	5.4%	18.6%	1.9%

The small armed forces are almost entirely dominated by the army, which has concentrated on mobility and artillery in its recent equipment purchases. However, it lacks armoured-warfare capability, and it is also unclear whether the armed forces have the capacity to self-sustain on operations. Djibouti is the lead nation in AMISOM's Sector 4. It has also pledged a company-level element and special police units to the East Africa Standby Force. Training and external security is bolstered by the presence of the US Combined Joint Task Force–Horn of Africa at Camp Lemonnier, as well as a French base with air-combat and transport assets. Other states base forces in Djibouti to participate in counter-piracy missions and Japan opened its first overseas base there in 2010. A growing relationship exists with China, exemplified by a strategic-defence partnership agreed in February 2014 and the delivery of a MA60 transport aircraft in June 2014.

ACTIVE 10,450 (Army 8,000 Navy 200 Air 250 Gendarmerie 2,000) **National Security Force 2,500**

ORGANISATIONS BY SERVICE

Army ε8,000
FORCES BY ROLE
4 military districts (Tadjourah, Dikhil, Ali-Sabieh and Obock)
MANOEUVRE
  Mechanised
  1 armd regt (1 recce sqn, 3 armd sqn, 1 (anti-smuggling) sy coy)
  Light
  4 inf regt (3-4 inf coy, 1 spt coy)
  1 rapid reaction regt (4 inf coy, 1 spt coy)
  Other
  1 (Republican Guard) gd regt (1 sy sqn, 1 (close protection) sy sqn, 1 cbt spt sqn (1 recce pl, 1 armd pl, 1 arty pl), 1 spt sqn)
COMBAT SUPPORT
  1 arty regt
  1 demining coy
  1 sigs regt
  1 CIS sect
COMBAT SERVICE SUPPORT
  1 log regt
  1 maint coy
EQUIPMENT BY TYPE
RECCE 56: 4 AML-60†; 17 AML-90; 15 VBL; 16-20 *Ratel*
AIFV 8 BTR-80A
APC 30
  APC (W) 18: 12 BTR-60†; 6 *Puma*
  PPV 12 *Cougar* 4×4
ARTY 69
  SP 155mm 10 M109L
  TOWED 122mm 6 D-30
  MRL 122mm 8: 6 (6-tube Toyota Land Cruiser 70 series); 2 (30-tube Iveco 110-16)
  MOR 45: 81mm 25; 120mm 20 Brandt
AT
  RCL 106mm 16 M40A1
  RL 89mm LRAC
AD • GUNS 15+
  SP 20mm 5 M693
  TOWED 10: 23mm 5 ZU-23; 40mm 5 L/70

Navy ε200
EQUIPMENT BY TYPE
PATROL AND COASTAL COMBATANTS 12
  PBF 2 Battalion-17
  PB 10: 1 *Plascoa*†; 2 Sea Ark 1739; 1 *Swari*†; 6 others
AMPHIBIOUS • LCT 1 EDIC 700

Air Force 250
EQUIPMENT BY TYPE
AIRCRAFT
  TPT • Light 4: 1 Cessna U206G *Stationair*; 1 Cessna 208 *Caravan*; 1 L-410UVP *Turbolet*; 1 MA60
HELICOPTERS
  ATK 2 Mi-35 *Hind* in store
  MRH 1 Mi-17 *Hip* H
  TPT 3: Medium 1 Mi-8T *Hip*; Light 2 AS355F *Ecureuil* II

Gendarmerie 2,000+
Ministry of Defence
FORCES BY ROLE
MANOEUVRE
  Other
  1 paramilitary bn
EQUIPMENT BY TYPE
PATROL AND COASTAL COMBATANTS 1 PB

Paramilitary ε2,500

National Security Force ε2,500
Ministry of Interior

Coast Guard 145
EQUIPMENT BY TYPE
PATROL AND COASTAL COMBATANTS 9 PB

DEPLOYMENT

SOMALIA
AU • AMISOM 960; 1 inf bn

WESTERN SAHARA
UN • MINURSO 1 obs

FOREIGN FORCES

France 2,000: 1 (Marine) combined arms regt (2 recce sqn, 2 inf coy, 1 arty bty, 1 engr coy); 1 hel det with 4 SA330 *Puma*; 2 SA342 *Gazelle*; 1 LCM; 1 *Falcon* 50MI; 1 air sqn with 7 *Mirage* 2000C/D; 1 C-160 *Transall*; 2 SA330 *Puma*; 1 AS555 *Fennec*
Germany Operation Atalanta 1 AP-3C *Orion*
Japan 180; 2 P-3C *Orion*
New Zealand 1 P-3K2 *Orion*
Spain Operation Atalanta 1 P-3A *Orion*
United States US Africa Command: 1,200; 1 tpt sqn with C-130H/J-30 *Hercules*; 1 spec ops sqn with MC-130H; PC-12 (U-28A); 1 CSAR sqn with HH-60G *Pave Hawk*; 1 naval air base

Equatorial Guinea EQG

CFA Franc BEAC fr		2013	2014	2015
GDP	fr	7.71tr	7.46tr	
	US$	15.6bn	15.4bn	
per capita	US$	20,605	19,788	
Growth	%	-4.8	-2.5	
Inflation	%	3.2	3.9	
Def exp	fr	ε3.8bn		
	US$	ε8m		
US$1=fr		494.04	484.28	

Population 722,254

Age	0–14	15–19	20–24	25–29	30–64	65 plus
Male	20.7%	5.3%	4.6%	3.9%	13.6%	1.7%
Female	20.0%	5.1%	4.4%	3.8%	14.5%	2.3%

Capabilities

The country's armed forces are dominated by the army, with smaller naval and air components. The army's primary role is internal security, and there is only limited ability for power projection. There has been significant navy investment in recent years, including both equipment and onshore infrastructure at Malabo and Bata. Most equipment is of Soviet or Russian origin, and some fixed- and rotary-wing aircraft may be operated by contractors. Maritime-security concerns in the Gulf of Guinea have resulted in increased emphasis on bolstering a limited coastal-patrol capacity, with new commissions of Bulgarian-built, Ukrainian-designed offshore-patrol vessels.

ACTIVE 1,320 (Army 1,100 Navy 120 Air 100)

ORGANISATIONS BY SERVICE

Army 1,100
FORCES BY ROLE
MANOEUVRE
  Light
    3 inf bn(-)
EQUIPMENT BY TYPE
MBT 3 T-55
RECCE 6 BRDM-2
AIFV 20 BMP-1
APC (W) 10 BTR-152

Navy ε120
EQUIPMENT BY TYPE
PATROL AND COASTAL COMBATANTS 11
  PSO 2:
    1 *Bata* with 1 76mm gun, 1 hel landing platform
    1 *Wele Nzas* with 2 AK630M 30mm CIWS, 2 76mm gun, 1 hel landing platform
  PCC 2 OPV 62
  PBF 2 *Shaldag* II
  PB 5: 1 *Daphne*; 2 *Estuario de Muni*; 2 *Zhuk*
LOGISTICS AND SUPPORT
  AKRH 1 *Capitan David Eyama Angue Osa* with 1 76 mm gun

Air Force 100
EQUIPMENT BY TYPE
AIRCRAFT 4 combat capable
  ATK 4: 2 Su-25 *Frogfoot*; 2 Su-25UB *Frogfoot* B
  TPT 4: **Light** 3: 1 An-32B *Cline*; 2 An-72 *Coaler*; **PAX** 1 *Falcon* 900 (VIP)
  TRG 2 L-39C *Albatros*
HELICOPTERS
  ATK 5 Mi-24P/V *Hind*
  MRH 1 Mi-17 *Hip* H
  TPT 4: **Heavy** 1 Mi-26 *Halo*; **Medium** 1 Ka-29 *Helix*; **Light** 2 Enstrom 480

Paramilitary

Guardia Civil
FORCES BY ROLE
MANOEUVRE
  Other
    2 paramilitary coy

Coast Guard
PATROL AND COASTAL COMBATANTS • PB 1†

Eritrea ERI

Eritrean Nakfa ERN		2013	2014	2015
GDP	ERN	53bn	59.5bn	
	US$	3.44bn	3.87bn	
per capita	US$	544	592	
Growth	%	1.3	2.0	
Inflation	%	12.3	12.3	
Def exp	ERN	ε1.2bn		
	US$	ε78m		
USD1=ERN		15.38	15.37	

Population 6,380,803

Ethnic groups: Tigrinya 50%; Tigre and Kunama 40%; Afar 4%; Saho 3%

Age	0–14	15–19	20–24	25–29	30–64	65 plus
Male	20.5%	5.5%	4.6%	3.8%	13.4%	1.6%
Female	20.3%	5.5%	4.6%	3.9%	14.2%	2.1%

Capabilities

Eritrea maintains a large standing army (mostly conscripted), the primary focus of which is defence of the border with Ethiopia; many troops are also used for civilian development and construction tasks. A UN arms embargo and age will have affected an inventory dominated by outdated but numerous weapons platforms, and it is likely that many platforms will be slowly cannibalised for parts. The armed forces appear to have been relatively successful in adapting from an insurgent army – in the 1980s – to standing armed forces. However, lines of command and organisation are still only slowly forming. There has been some investment in the nascent air force to produce a regionally comparable fighter wing, though this lacks experienced and trained pilots, while the navy remains capable of only limited coastal-patrol and interception operations.

ACTIVE 201,750 (Army 200,000 Navy 1,400 Air 350)
Conscript liability 16 months (4 months mil trg)

RESERVE 120,000 (Army ε120,000)

ORGANISATIONS BY SERVICE

Army ε200,000
Heavily cadreised

FORCES BY ROLE
COMMAND
  4 corps HQ
MANOEUVRE
  Mechanised
  1 mech bde
  Light
  19 inf div
  1 cdo div

Reserve ε120,000

FORCES BY ROLE
MANOEUVRE
  Light
  1 inf div
EQUIPMENT BY TYPE
MBT 270 T-54/T-55
RECCE 40 BRDM-1/BRDM-2
AIFV 15 BMP-1
APC 35
  APC (T) 10 MT-LB†
  APC (W) 25 BTR-152/BTR-60
ARTY 208+
  SP 45: **122mm** 32 2S1; **152mm** 13 2S5
  TOWED 19+: **122mm** D-30; **130mm** 19 M-46
  MRL 44: **122mm** 35 BM-21; **220mm** 9 BM-27/9P140 *Uragan*
  MOR 120mm/160mm 100+
AT
  MSL • MANPATS 9K11 *Malyutka* (AT-3 *Sagger*); 9K113 *Konkurs* (AT-5 *Spandrel*)
  GUNS 85mm D-44
AD
  SAM • MANPAD 9K32 *Strela-2* (SA-7 *Grail*)‡
  GUNS 70+
    SP 23mm ZSU-23-4
    TOWED 23mm ZU-23
ARV T-54/T-55 reported
VLB MTU reported

Navy 1,400

EQUIPMENT BY TYPE
PATROL AND COASTAL COMBATANTS 12
  PBF 9: 5 Battalion-17; 4 *Super Dvora*
  PB 3 Swiftships
AMPHIBIOUS 3
  LS • LST 2: 1 *Chamo*† (Ministry of Transport); 1 *Ashdod*†
  LC • LCU 1 T-4† (in harbour service)

Air Force ε350

FORCES BY ROLE
FIGHTER/GROUND ATTACK
  1 sqn with MiG-29/MiG-29SMT/MiG-29UB *Fulcrum*
  1 sqn with Su-27/Su-27UBK *Flanker*
TRANSPORT
  1 sqn with Y-12(II)
TRAINING
  1 sqn with L-90 *Redigo*
  1 sqn with MB-339CE*

TRANSPORT HELICOPTER
  1 sqn with Bell 412 *Twin Huey*
  1 sqn with Mi-17 *Hip H*
EQUIPMENT BY TYPE
AIRCRAFT 20 combat capable
  FTR 6: 4 MiG-29 *Fulcrum*; 2 MiG-29UB *Fulcrum*;
  FGA 10: 2 MiG-29SMT *Fulcrum*; 5 Su-27 *Flanker*; 3 Su-27UBK *Flanker*
  TPT • Light 5: 1 Beech 200 *King Air*; 4 Y-12(II)
  TRG 12: 8 L-90 *Redigo*; 4 MB-339CE*
HELICOPTERS
  MRH 8: 4 Bell 412 *Twin Huey* (AB-412); 4 Mi-17 *Hip* H
MSL
  AAM • IR R-60 (AA-8 *Aphid*); R-73 (AA-11 *Archer*); **IR/SARH** R-27 (AA-10 *Alamo*)

Ethiopia ETH

Ethiopian Birr EB		2013	2014	2015
GDP	EB	853bn	998bn	
	US$	46bn	49.9bn	
per capita	US$	518	548	
Growth	%	9.7	8.2	
Inflation	%	8.1	7.7	
Def bdgt	EB	6.5bn	7.5bn	8bn
	US$	351m	375m	
FMA (US)	US$	0.84m	0.84m	0.7m
US$1=EB		18.54	20.01	

Population 96,633,458

Ethnic groups: Oromo 40%; Amhara and Tigrean 32%; Sidamo 9%; Shankella 6%; Somali 6%; Afar 4%

Age	0–14	15–19	20–24	25–29	30–64	65 plus
Male	22.1%	5.4%	4.5%	3.8%	12.6%	1.3%
Female	22.1%	5.5%	4.6%	3.8%	12.8%	1.6%

Capabilities

Ethiopia maintains one of the region's most effective armed forces, which have become battle-hardened and experienced following a history of conflict. Ethiopia is still engaged in a ten-year (2005–15) modernisation plan, designed to create flexible armed forces able to respond to regional contingencies. The country has enough deployable capability to make significant contributions to UN missions in Darfur and South Sudan, as well as the AMISOM mission in Somalia, though these – and standing deployments on the Eritrean border – mean it has to try and transform while on operations. The country's arsenal remains focused on Soviet-era equipment, but there is increasing procurement of Chinese systems, particularly armoured vehicles and artillery. The air force maintains only modest airlift capacity, which limits deployment within Ethiopia and overseas.

ACTIVE 138,000 (Army 135,000 Air 3,000)

ORGANISATIONS BY SERVICE

Army 135,000
4 Mil Regional Commands (Northern, Western, Central, and Eastern) each acting as corps HQ

FORCES BY ROLE
MANOEUVRE
Light
1 (Agazi Cdo) SF comd
1 (Northern) corps (1 mech div, 4 inf div)
1 (Western) corps (1 mech div, 3 inf div)
1 (Central) corps (1 mech div, 5 inf div)
1 (Eastern) corps (1 mech div, 5 inf div)

EQUIPMENT BY TYPE
MBT 446+: 246+ T-54/T-55/T-62; 200 T-72
RECCE/AIFV/APC (W) ε450 BRDM/BMP/BTR-60/BTR-152/Type-89/Type-92/*Ze'ev*
ARTY 524+
　SP 10+: **122mm** 2S1; **152mm** 10 2S19
　TOWED 464+: **122mm** 464 D-30/M-1938 (M-30); **130mm** M-46; **155mm** AH2
　MRL 122mm ε50 BM-21
　MOR 81mm M1/M29; **82mm** M-1937; **120mm** M-1944
AT
　MSL • MANPATS 9K11 *Malyutka* (AT-3 *Sagger*); 9K111 *Fagot* (AT-4 *Spigot*); 9K135 *Kornet-E* (AT-14 *Spriggan*)
　RCL 82mm B-10; **107mm** B-11
　GUNS 85mm εD-44
AD • SAM ε370
　TOWED S-75 *Dvina* (SA-2 *Guideline*); S-125 *Pechora* (SA-3 *Goa*)
　MANPAD 9K32 *Strela*-2 (SA-7 *Grail*)‡
　GUNS
　　SP 23mm ZSU-23-4
　　TOWED 23mm ZU-23; **37mm** M-1939; **57mm** S-60
ARV T-54/T-55 reported
VLB MTU reported
MW Bozena

Air Force 3,000

FORCES BY ROLE
FIGHTER/GROUND ATTACK
　1 sqn with MiG-21MF *Fishbed* J†; MiG-21UM *Mongol* B†
　1 sqn with Su-27/Su-27UB *Flanker*
TRANSPORT
　1 sqn with An-12 *Cub*; An-26 *Curl*; An-32 *Cline*; C-130B *Hercules*; DHC-6 *Twin Otter*; L-100-30; Yak-40 *Codling* (VIP)
TRAINING
　1 sqn with L-39 *Albatros*
　1 sqn with SF-260
ATTACK/TRANSPORT HELICOPTER
　2 sqn with Mi-24/Mi-35 *Hind*; Mi-8 *Hip*; Mi-17 *Hip* H; SA316 *Alouette* III

EQUIPMENT BY TYPE
AIRCRAFT 26 combat capable
　FGA 26: 15 MiG-21MF *Fishbed* J/MiG-21UM *Mongol* B†; 8 Su-27 *Flanker*; 3 Su-27UB *Flanker*
　TPT 12: **Medium** 8: 3 An-12 *Cub*; 2 C-130B *Hercules*; 1 C-130E *Hercules*; 2 L-100-30; **Light** 4: 1 An-26 *Curl*; 1 An-32 *Cline*; 1 DHC-6 *Twin Otter*; 1 Yak-40 *Codling* (VIP)
　TRG 16: 12 L-39 *Albatros*; 4 SF-260
HELICOPTERS
　ATK 18: 15 Mi-24 *Hind*; 3 Mi-35 *Hind*
　MRH 7: 1 AW139; 6 SA316 *Alouette* III
　MRH/TPT 12 Mi-8 *Hip*/Mi-17 *Hip* H
　MSL
　　AAM • IR R-3 (AA-2 *Atoll*)‡; R-60 (AA-8 *Aphid*); R-73 (AA-11 *Archer*); **IR/SARH** R-23/R-24 (AA-7 *Apex*); R-27 (AA-10 *Alamo*)

DEPLOYMENT

CÔTE D'IVOIRE
UN • UNOCI 2 obs

LIBERIA
UN • UNMIL 3; 6 obs

SOMALIA
AU • AMISOM 4,395; 4 inf bn

SOUTH SUDAN
UN • UNMISS 1,250; 3 inf bn(-)

SUDAN
UN • UNAMID 2,537; 16 obs; 3 inf bn
UN • UNISFA 3,887; 74 obs; 1 recce coy; 1 armd coy; 1 mech inf bn; 2 inf bn; 1 hel sqn; 2 arty coy; 1 engr coy; 1 sigs coy; 1 fd hospital

FOREIGN FORCES
United States some MQ-9 *Reaper*

Gabon GAB

CFA Franc BEAC fr		2013	2014	2015
GDP	fr	9.52tr	9.91tr	
	US$	19.3bn	20.7bn	
per capita	US$	12,326	13,039	
Growth	%	5.6	5.1	
Inflation	%	0.5	4.7	
Def bdgt [a]	fr	139bn	87.6bn	
	US$	282m	183m	
US$1=fr		493.88	479.20	

[a] Includes funds allocated to Republican Guard

Population	1,672,597					
Age	0–14	15–19	20–24	25–29	30–64	65 plus
Male	21.2%	5.4%	4.7%	4.1%	12.7%	1.6%
Female	21.0%	5.4%	4.7%	4.1%	12.9%	2.2%

Capabilities

Gabon's small armed forces are reasonably well equipped for their size, and there is sufficient airlift to ensure mobility within the country and even a limited capability to project power into its near abroad both by sea and air. The country has benefited from the long-term presence of French troops acting as a security guarantor, while oil revenues have allowed the government to support, in regional terms, capable armed forces. The army is reasonably well equipped, while the navy has a coastal-patrol and fishery-protection role. There is regular training with international partners. Military medicine is well regarded, and Gabon contributed a field hospital to the CEEAC *Loango 2014* exercise. The air force's combat capability was increased with the acquisition of six ex-South African Air Force *Mirage* F1s.

ACTIVE 4,700 (Army 3,200 Navy 500 Air 1,000)
Paramilitary 2,000

ORGANISATIONS BY SERVICE

Army 3,200
Republican Guard under direct presidential control
FORCES BY ROLE
MANOEUVRE
  Light
  1 (Republican Guard) gd gp (bn)
    (1 armd/recce coy, 3 inf coy, 1 arty bty, 1 ADA bty)
  8 inf coy
  Air Manoeuvre
  1 cdo/AB coy
COMBAT SUPPORT
  1 engr coy
EQUIPMENT BY TYPE
RECCE 70: 24 AML-60/AML-90; 12 EE-3 *Jararaca*; 14 EE-9 *Cascavel*; 6 ERC-90F4 *Sagaie*; 14 VBL
AIFV 12 EE-11 *Urutu* (with 20mm gun)
APC 62+
  APC (W) 28+: 9 LAV-150 *Commando*; 6 Type-92 (reported); 12 VXB-170; M3 Panhard; 1 *Pandur* (Testing)
  PPV 34 *Matador*
ARTY 51
  TOWED 105mm 4 M101
  MRL 140mm 8 *Teruel*
  MOR 39: **81mm** 35; **120mm** 4 Brandt
AT • MSL • MANPATS 4 *Milan*
  RCL 106mm M40A1
  RL 89mm LRAC
AD • GUNS 41
  SP 20mm 4 ERC-20
  TOWED 37: **23mm** 24 ZU-23-2; **37mm** 10 M-1939; **40mm** 3 L/70

Navy ε500
HQ located at Port Gentil
EQUIPMENT BY TYPE
PATROL AND COASTAL COMBATANTS 11
  PCC 2 *General Ba'Oumar* (FRA P-400) with 1 57 mm gun
  PBG 1 *Patra* with 4 SS 12M AShM
  PB 8: 4 *Port Gentil* (FRA VCSM); 4 Rodman 66

AMPHIBIOUS 14
  LANDING SHIPS • LST 1 *President Omar Bongo* (FRA *Batral*) (capacity 1 LCVP; 7 MBT; 140 troops) with 1 hel landing platform
  LANDING CRAFT 13
    LCU 1 Mk 9 (ex-UK)
    LCVP 12

Air Force 1,000
FORCES BY ROLE
FIGHTER/GROUND ATTACK
  1 sqn with *Mirage* F-1AZ
TRANSPORT
  1 (Republican Guard) sqn with AS332 *Super Puma*; ATR-42F; *Falcon* 900; Gulfstream IV-SP
  1 sqn with C-130H *Hercules*; CN-235M-100
TRAINING
  1 (Republican Guard) sqn with T-34 *Turbo Mentor*
ATTACK/TRANSPORT HELICOPTER
  1 sqn with Bell 412 *Twin Huey* (AB-412); SA330C/H *Puma*; SA342M *Gazelle*
EQUIPMENT BY TYPE
AIRCRAFT 6 combat capable
  FGA 6 *Mirage* F-1AZ
  MP (1 EMB-111* in store)
  TPT 5: **Medium** 1 C-130H *Hercules*; (1 L-100-30 in store); **Light** 2: 1 ATR-42F; 1 CN-235M-100; **PAX** 2: 1 *Falcon* 900; 1 Gulfstream IV-SP
  TRG 3 T-34 *Turbo Mentor*; (4 CM-170 *Magister* in store)
HELICOPTERS
  MRH 2: 1 Bell 412 *Twin Huey* (AB-412); 1 SA342M *Gazelle*; (2 SA342L *Gazelle* in store)
  TPT 5: **Medium** 4: 1 AS332 *Super Puma*; 3 SA330C/H *Puma*; **Light** 1 EC135

Paramilitary 2,000

Gendarmerie 2,000
FORCES BY ROLE
MANOEUVRE
  Armoured
  2 armd sqn
  Other
  3 paramilitary bde
  11 paramilitary coy
  Aviation
  1 unit with AS350 *Ecureuil*; AS355 *Ecureuil* II
EQUIPMENT BY TYPE
  HELICOPTERS • TPT • Light 4: 2 AS350 *Ecureuil*; 2 AS355 *Ecureuil* II

DEPLOYMENT

CENTRAL AFRICAN REPUBLIC
UN • MINUSCA 513; 1 obs; 1 inf bn

FOREIGN FORCES

France 450; 1 SAR/tpt sqn with 1 CN-235M; 1 SA330 *Puma*

Gambia GAM

Gambian Dalasi D		2013	2014	2015
GDP	D	32.7bn	36.9bn	
	US$	850m	918m	
per capita	US$	453	476	
Growth	%	6.3	7.4	
Inflation	%	5.2	5.3	
Def exp	D	ε189m		
	US$	ε5m		
US$1=D		38.44	40.16	

Population 1,925,527

Age	0–14	15–19	20–24	25–29	30–64	65 plus
Male	19.4%	5.4%	5.0%	4.3%	13.8%	1.5%
Female	19.3%	5.5%	5.1%	4.5%	14.5%	1.7%

Capabilities

The country has a small army supported by air and marine units. In 2013 the country signed a cooperation agreement for Turkey to provide logistics support. Its forces have been deployed in support of UN missions, and have received training assistance from the US.

ACTIVE 800 (Army 800)

ORGANISATIONS BY SERVICE

Gambian National Army 800

FORCES BY ROLE
MANOEUVRE
  Light
   2 inf bn
  Other
   1 (Presidential Guard) gd coy
COMBAT SUPPORT
  1 engr sqn

Marine Unit ε70
EQUIPMENT BY TYPE
PATROL AND COASTAL COMBATANTS 9
  PBF 4: 2 Rodman 55; 2 *Fatimah* I
  PB 5: 1 *Bolong Kanta*†; 4 *Taipei* (ROC *Hai Ou*) (of which one damaged and in reserve)

Air Wing
EQUIPMENT BY TYPE
AIRCRAFT
  TPT 5: **Light** 2 AT-802A *Air Tractor*; **PAX** 3: 1 B-727; 1 CL-601; 1 Il-62M *Classic* (VIP)

DEPLOYMENT

CÔTE D'IVOIRE
UN • UNOCI 3 obs

LIBERIA
UN • UNMIL 2 obs

MALI
UN • MINUSMA 2

SUDAN
UN • UNAMID 215; 1 inf coy

Ghana GHA

Ghanaian New Cedi C		2013	2014	2015
GDP	C	93.5bn	117bn	
	US$	47.8bn	35.5bn	
per capita	US$	1,871	1,353	
Growth	%	7.1	4.5	
Inflation	%	11.7	15.7	
Def bdgt	C	576m	914m	1.15bn
	US$	295m	277m	
FMA (US)	US$	0.35m	0.35m	0.3m
US$1=C		1.95	3.30	

Population 25,758,108

Age	0–14	15–19	20–24	25–29	30–64	65 plus
Male	19.4%	5.0%	4.4%	3.9%	14.8%	1.9%
Female	19.2%	5.0%	4.5%	4.1%	15.7%	2.2%

Capabilities

The Ghanaian armed forces are some of the most capable regionally, with a long-term development plan covering both this and the next decade. Internal and maritime security are central roles, along with participation in peacekeeping missions. The air force is building its light- and medium-lift capacity, although a British RAF C-17 heavy airlifter was used for troop and vehicle deployments to Mali in 2013. The ability to control its maritime EEZ is of increasing importance because of growing piracy and resource exploitation, and this underpins the navy's expansion ambitions. The army is a regular contributor to UN peacekeeping missions.

ACTIVE 15,500 (Army 11,500 Navy 2,000 Air 2,000)

ORGANISATIONS BY SERVICE

Army 11,500
FORCES BY ROLE
COMMAND
  2 comd HQ
MANOEUVRE
  Reconnaissance
   1 armd recce regt (3 recce sqn)
  Light
   1 (rapid reaction) mot inf bn
   6 inf bn
  Air Manoeuvre
   2 AB coy
COMBAT SUPPORT
  1 arty regt (1 arty bty, 2 mor bty)

1 fd engr regt (bn)
1 sigs regt
1 sigs sqn
COMBAT SERVICE SUPPORT
1 log gp
1 tpt coy
2 maint coy
1 med coy
1 trg bn
EQUIPMENT BY TYPE
RECCE 3 EE-9 *Cascavel*
AIFV 39: 24 *Ratel*-90; 15 *Ratel*-20
APC (W) 56: 50 *Piranha*; 6 Type-05P
ARTY 87+
  TOWED 122mm 6 D-30
  MRL 3+: **107mm** Type-63; **122mm** 3 Type-81
  MOR 78: 81mm 50; **120mm** 28 *Tampella*
AT • RCL 84mm 50 *Carl Gustav*
AD • SAM • MANPAD 9K32 *Strela*-2 (SA-7 *Grail*)‡
  GUNS • TOWED 8+: **14.5mm** 4+: 4 ZPU-2; ZPU-4; **23mm** 4 ZU-23-2
ARV *Piranha* reported

Navy 2,000
Naval HQ located at Accra; Western HQ located at Sekondi; Eastern HQ located at Tema
EQUIPMENT BY TYPE
PATROL AND COASTAL COMBATANTS 14
  PCO 2 *Anzone* (US)
  PCC 10: 2 *Achimota* (GER Lurssen 57m) with 1 76 mm gun; 2 *Dzata* (GER Lurssen 45m); 2 *Warrior* (GER Gepard); 4 *Snake* (PRC 47m)
  PBF 1 *Stephen Otu* (ROK *Sea Dolphin*)
  PB 1 *David Hansen* (US)

Air Force 2,000
FORCES BY ROLE
GROUND ATTACK
  1 sqn with K-8 *Karakorum**; L-39ZO*: MB-326K; MB-339A*
ISR
  1 unit with DA-42
TRANSPORT
  1 sqn with BN-2 *Defender*; Cessna 172; F-27 *Friendship*; F-28 *Fellowship* (VIP)
TRANSPORT HELICOPTER
  1 sqn with AW109A; Bell 412SP *Twin Huey*; Mi-17V-5 *Hip* H; SA319 *Alouette* III
EQUIPMENT BY TYPE†
AIRCRAFT 11 combat capable
  ATK 3 MB-326K
  TPT 14: Light 13: 1 BN-2 *Defender*; 2 C-295; 3 Cessna 172; 3 DA-42; 4 F-27 *Friendship*; **PAX** 1 F-28 *Fellowship* (VIP)
  TRG 8: 4 K-8 *Karakorum**; 2 L-39ZO*; 2 MB-339A*
HELICOPTERS
  MRH 6: 1 Bell 412SP *Twin Huey*; 3 Mi-17V-5 *Hip* H; 2 SA319 *Alouette* III
  TPT 6: **Medium** 4 Mi-171Sh; **Light** 2 AW109A

DEPLOYMENT

CENTRAL AFRICAN REPUBLIC
UN • MINUSCA 3 obs

CÔTE D'IVOIRE
UN • UNOCI 156; 6 obs; 1 hel sqn; 1 fd hospital

DEMOCRATIC REPUBLIC OF THE CONGO
UN • MONUSCO 465; 22 obs; 1 mech inf bn(-)

INDIA/PAKISTAN
UN • UNMOGIP 1 obs

LEBANON
UN • UNIFIL 871; 1 inf bn

LIBERIA
UN • UNMIL 707; 8 obs; 1 inf bn

MALI
UN • MINUSMA 160; 1 engr coy;1 fd hospital

SOUTH SUDAN
UN • UNMISS 304; 6 obs; 1 inf bn(-)

SUDAN
UN • UNAMID 18; 8 obs
UN • UNISFA 2; 3 obs

WESTERN SAHARA
UN • MINURSO 6; 8 obs

Guinea GUI

Guinean Franc fr		2013	2014	2015
GDP	fr	43tr	47.4tr	
	US$	6.23bn	6.77bn	
per capita	US$	560	594	
Growth	%	2.3	2.5	
Inflation	%	11.9	10.1	
Def exp	fr	ε275bn		
	US$	ε40m		
FMA (US)	US$	0.4m	0.4m	
US$1=fr		6,909.82	6,999.66	

Population 11,474,383

Age	0–14	15–19	20–24	25–29	30–64	65 plus
Male	21.2%	5.4%	4.5%	3.8%	13.6%	1.6%
Female	20.8%	5.3%	4.4%	3.8%	13.7%	2.0%

Capabilities

Much of the country's military equipment is ageing and of Soviet-era vintage; serviceability will be questionable for some types. The professionalism of the armed forces has in the past proved suspect, with some reports suggesting gaps in institutional cohesiveness and accountability. There is no fixed-wing airlift capacity and very limited rotary-wing airlift.

ACTIVE 9,700 (Army 8,500 Navy 400 Air 800)
Paramilitary 2,600
Conscript liability 2 years

ORGANISATIONS BY SERVICE

Army 8,500
FORCES BY ROLE
MANOEUVRE
  Armoured
  1 armd bn
  Light
  1 SF bn
  5 inf bn
  1 ranger bn
  1 cdo bn
  Air Manoeuvre
  1 air mob bn
  Other
  1 (Presidential Guard) gd bn
COMBAT SUPPORT
  1 arty bn
  1 AD bn
  1 engr bn
EQUIPMENT BY TYPE
MBT 38: 8 T-54; 30 T-34
LT TK 15 PT-76
RECCE 27: 2 AML-90; 25 BRDM-1/BRDM-2
AIFV 2 BMP-1
APC 50
  APC (T) 10 BTR-50
  APC (W) 30: 16 BTR-40; 8 BTR-60; 6 BTR-152
  PPV 10 *Mamba*†
ARTY 47+
  TOWED 24: **122mm** 12 M-1931/37; **130mm** 12 M-46
  MRL 220mm 3 BM-27/9P140 *Uragan*
  MOR 20+: **82mm** M-43; **120mm** 20 M-1943/M-38
AT
  MSL • MANPATS 9K11 *Malyutka* (AT-3 *Sagger*); 9K113 *Konkurs* (AT-5 *Spandrel*)
  RCL 82mm B-10
  GUNS 6+: **57mm** ZIS-2 *M-1943*; **85mm** 6 D-44
AD • SAM • MANPAD 9K32 *Strela*-2 (SA-7 *Grail*)‡
  GUNS • TOWED 24+: **30mm** M-53 (twin); **37mm** 8 M-1939; **57mm** 12 Type-59 (S-60); **100mm** 4 KS-19
ARV T-54/T-55 reported

Navy ε400
EQUIPMENT BY TYPE
PATROL AND COASTAL COMBATANTS • PB 4: 1 Swiftships†; 3 RPB 20

Air Force 800
EQUIPMENT BY TYPE†
AIRCRAFT
  FGA (3 MiG-21 *Fishbed* non-op)
  TPT • Light 2 An-2 *Colt*
HELICOPTERS
  ATK 4 Mi-24 *Hind*

  MRH 5: 2 MD-500MD; 2 Mi-17-1V *Hip* H; 1 SA342K *Gazelle*
  TPT 2: **Medium** 1 SA330 *Puma*; **Light** 1 AS350B *Ecureuil*
MSL
  AAM • IR R-3 (AA-2 *Atoll*)‡

Paramilitary 2,600 active

Gendarmerie 1,000

Republican Guard 1,600

People's Militia 7,000 reservists

DEPLOYMENT

CÔTE D'IVOIRE
UN • UNOCI 3 obs

DEMOCRATIC REPUBLIC OF THE CONGO
UN • MONUSCO 1 obs

MALI
UN • MINUSMA 215 1 inf coy

SOUTH SUDAN
UN • UNMISS 2 obs

SUDAN
UN • UNISFA 1 obs

WESTERN SAHARA
UN • MINURSO 5 obs

Guinea Bissau GNB

CFA Franc BCEAO fr		2013	2014	2015
GDP	fr	476bn	504bn	
	US$	964m	1.04bn	
per capita	US$	567	599	
Growth	%	0.3	2.6	
Inflation	%	0.8	-1.3	
Def exp	fr	ε13bn		
	US$	ε26m		
US$1=fr		493.72	484.40	

Population 1,693,398

Age	0–14	15–19	20–24	25–29	30–64	65 plus
Male	19.8%	5.3%	4.7%	4.1%	13.6%	1.3%
Female	19.9%	5.4%	4.8%	4.1%	14.9%	2.0%

Capabilities

The armed forces have often played a direct role in politics, by mounting military coups. However, elections in May 2014 replaced the transitional administration – in power since the most recent military takeover in 2012 – with an elected president. Narcotics trafficking remains a substantial problem that the armed forces have so far been unable to tackle. The parlous state of the economy limits any ability to replace its ageing inventory of mainly Soviet-era equipment. Previous attempts at SSR have largely been unsuccessful, and long-term international support will be necessary for a new attempt to gain traction.

ACTIVE 4,450 (Army 4,000 Navy 350 Air 100)
Gendarmerie 2,000
Conscript liability Selective conscription
Manpower and eqpt totals should be treated with caution. A number of draft laws to restructure the armed services and police have been produced.

ORGANISATIONS BY SERVICE

Army ε4,000 (numbers reducing)
FORCES BY ROLE
MANOEUVRE
  Reconnaissance
    1 recce coy
  Armoured
    1 armd bn (sqn)
  Light
    5 inf bn
COMBAT SUPPORT
  1 arty bn
  1 engr coy
EQUIPMENT BY TYPE
MBT 10 T-34
LT TK 15 PT-76
RECCE 10 BRDM-2
APC (W) 55: 35 BTR-40/BTR-60; 20 Type-56 (BTR-152)
ARTY 26+
  TOWED 122mm 18 D-30/*M-1938*
  MOR 8+: 82mm M-43; **120mm** 8 M-1943
AT
  RCL 75mm Type-52 (M20); **82mm** B-10
  RL 89mm M20
  GUNS 85mm 8 D-44
AD • SAM • MANPAD 9K32 *Strela*-2 (SA-7 *Grail*)‡
  GUNS • TOWED 34: **23mm** 18 ZU-23; **37mm** 6 M-1939; **57mm** 10 S-60

Navy ε350
EQUIPMENT BY TYPE
PATROL AND COASTAL COMBATANTS • PB 2
Alfeite†

Air Force 100
EQUIPMENT BY TYPE
HELICOPTERS • MRH 1 SA319 *Alouette* III†

Paramilitary 2,000 active
  Gendarmerie 2,000

DEPLOYMENT
MALI
UN • MINUSMA 1

FOREIGN FORCES
Nigeria ECOMIB 160
Senegal ECOMIB 200

Kenya KEN

Kenyan Shilling sh		2013	2014	2015
GDP	sh	4.74tr	5.38tr	
	US$	55bn	62.7bn	
per capita	US$	1,316	1,461	
Growth	%	4.6	5.3	
Inflation	%	5.7	7.3	
Def bdgt [a]	sh	83.5bn	89.4bn	90.7bn
	US$	970m	1.04bn	
FMA (US)	US$	1.5m	1.5m	1.2m
US$1=sh		86.12	85.80	

[a] Excludes allocations for internal security operations.

Population 45,010,056
Ethnic groups: Kikuyu ε22–32%

Age	0–14	15–19	20–24	25–29	30–64	65 plus
Male	21.1%	4.8%	4.5%	4.3%	13.9%	1.2%
Female	21.0%	4.8%	4.5%	4.3%	13.9%	1.6%

Capabilities

Kenya's armed forces are a leading element of the East African Standby Force and AMISOM in Somalia, where they have been at the vanguard of operations against al-Shabaab militants since late 2011. Combat units that have rotated through Somalia have a higher level of confidence and capability, which is also reflected in Kenya's contribution to UN peacekeeping missions. In tandem with the police, the armed forces have been involved in internal-security tasks in the wake of al-Shabaab terrorist attacks in recent years. Operations are personnel-intensive, and it is estimated that around 20% of forces are deployed in Somalia. Kenya is looking to technology, such as an integrated CCTV network, to help in internal-security tasks. After the Kenya Defence Forces Act in 2012, there is a defence-policy guide on which to base procurement decisions. Modernisation is focused on helicopters, armoured vehicles, UAVs and border-surveillance equipment. The navy undertakes coast-guard and counter-piracy roles, and supported the seaborne attack on al-Shabaab at Kismayu. The country has the ability to project power beyond its own territory, on a limited basis, via the air force's tactical support and airlift. The armed forces regularly join UK troops training in Kenya and take part in international exercises in Africa. (See pp. 425–27.)

ACTIVE 24,120 (Army 20,000 Navy 1,600 Air 2,500)
Paramilitary 5,000
(incl HQ staff)

ORGANISATIONS BY SERVICE

Army 20,000
FORCES BY ROLE
MANOEUVRE
  Armoured
  1 armd bde (1 armd recce bn, 2 armd bn)
  Light
  1 spec ops bn
  1 ranger bn
  1 inf bde (3 inf bn)
  1 inf bde (2 inf bn)
  1 indep inf bn
  Air Manoeuvre
  1 air cav bn
  1 AB bn
COMBAT SUPPORT
  1 arty bde (2 arty bn, 1 mor bty)
  1 ADA bn
  1 engr bde (2 engr bn)
EQUIPMENT BY TYPE
MBT 78 Vickers Mk 3
RECCE 92: 72 AML-60/AML-90; 12 Ferret; 8 S52 Shorland
APC 189
  APC (W) 84: 52 UR-416; 32 Type-92; (10 M3 Panhard in store)
  PPV 105 Puma M26-15
ARTY 110
  TOWED 105mm 48: 8 Model 56 pack howitzer; 40 L-118 Light Gun
  MOR 62: 81mm 50; 120mm 12 Brandt
AT • MSL • MANPATS Milan; Swingfire
  RCL 84mm 80 Carl Gustav
AD • GUNS • TOWED 94: 20mm 81: 11 Oerlikon; ε70 TCM-20; 40mm 13 L/70
ARV 7 Vickers ARV
MW Bozena
HELICOPTERS
  MRH 37: 2 Hughes 500D†; 12 Hughes 500M†; 10 Hughes 500MD Scout Defender† (with TOW); 10 Hughes 500ME†; 3 Z-9W

Navy 1,600 (incl 120 marines)
EQUIPMENT BY TYPE
PATROL AND COASTAL COMBATANTS 7
  PCO 1 Jasiri (to be fitted with 1 76 mm gun)
  PCFG 2 Nyayo
  PCC 3: 1 Harambee (FRA P400); 2 Shujaa with 1 76mm gun
  PBF 1 Archangel
AMPHIBIOUS • LCM 2 Galana
LOGISTICS AND SUPPORT • AP 2

Air Force 2,500
FORCES BY ROLE
FIGHTER/GROUND ATTACK
  2 sqn with F-5E/F Tiger II
TRANSPORT
  Some sqn with DHC-5D Buffalo†; DHC-8†; F-70† (VIP); Y-12(II)†
TRAINING
  Some sqn with Bulldog 103/Bulldog 127†; EMB-312 Tucano†*; Hawk Mk52†*; Hughes 500D†
TRANSPORT HELICOPTER
  1 sqn with SA330 Puma†
EQUIPMENT BY TYPE†
AIRCRAFT 38 combat capable
  FTR 22: 18 F-5E Tiger II; 4 F-5F Tiger II
  TPT 17 Light 16: 4 DHC-5D Buffalo†; 3 DHC-8†; 9 Y-12(II)†; (6 Do-28D-2† in store); PAX 1 F-70 (VIP)
  TRG 30: 8 Bulldog 103/127†; 11 EMB-312 Tucano†*; 6 Grob 120A; 5 Hawk Mk52†*
HELICOPTERS
  TPT • Medium 13: 2 Mi-171; 11 SA330 Puma†
MSL
  AAM • IR AIM-9 Sidewinder
  ASM AGM-65 Maverick; TOW

Paramilitary 5,000

Police General Service Unit 5,000
PATROL AND COASTAL COMBATANTS • PB 5 (2 on Lake Victoria)

Air Wing
AIRCRAFT • TPT 7 Cessna
HELICOPTERS
  TPT • Light 1 Bell 206L Long Ranger
  TRG 2 Bell 47G

DEPLOYMENT

DEMOCRATIC REPUBLIC OF THE CONGO
UN • MONUSCO 6; 12 obs

LEBANON
UN • UNIFIL 1

LIBERIA
UN • UNMIL 2

MALI
UN • MINUSMA 1

SOMALIA
AU • AMISOM 3,664: 3 inf bn

SOUTH SUDAN
UN • UNMISS 694; 6 obs; 1 inf bn

SUDAN
UN • UNAMID 111; 6 obs; 1 MP coy

FOREIGN FORCES
United Kingdom Army 170

Lesotho LSO

Lesotho Loti M		2013	2014	2015
GDP	M	21.9bn	24.2bn	
	US$	2.27bn	2.46bn	
per capita	US$	1,190	1,286	
Growth	%	5.7	4.3	
Inflation	%	5.3	6.5	
Def bdgt	M	466m	535m	
	US$	48m	54m	
US$1=M		9.65	9.85	

Population   1,942,008

Age	0–14	15–19	20–24	25–29	30–64	65 plus
Male	16.5%	4.8%	4.7%	4.7%	15.9%	2.7%
Female	16.4%	5.1%	5.4%	5.5%	15.6%	2.7%

Capabilities

Lesotho's small armed forces are charged with protecting territorial integrity and sovereignty, although an alleged military coup was attempted in September 2014. South Africa, in effect, acts as a security guarantor. Infantry units constitute the majority of personnel, and are supported by light vehicles. The forces possess a small number of tactical transport aircraft and utility helicopters, including a new Eurocopter EC135, delivered in late 2013.

ACTIVE 2,000 (Army 2,000)

ORGANISATIONS BY SERVICE

Army ε2,000

FORCES BY ROLE
MANOEUVRE
  Reconnaissance
    1 recce coy
  Light
    7 inf coy
  Aviation
    1 sqn
COMBAT SUPPORT
  1 arty bty(-)
  1 spt coy (with mor)

EQUIPMENT BY TYPE
MBT 1 T-55
RECCE 30: 4 AML-90; 2 BRDM-2†; 6 RAM-2000; 10 RBY-1; 8 S52 *Shorland*
ARTY 12
  TOWED 105mm 2
  MOR 81mm 10
AT • RCL 106mm 6 M40

Air Wing 110
AIRCRAFT
  TPT • Light 3: 2 C-212-300 *Aviocar*; 1 GA-8 *Airvan*
HELICOPTERS
  MRH 3: 1 Bell 412 *Twin Huey*; 2 Bell 412EP *Twin Huey*
  TPT • Light 2: 1 Bell 206 *Jet Ranger*; 1 Bo-105LSA-3

DEPLOYMENT

SUDAN
UN • UNAMID 2 obs

Liberia LBR

Liberian Dollar L$		2013	2014	2015
GDP	L$	1.96bn	2.07bn	
	US$	1.96bn	2.07bn	
per capita	US$	479	495	
Growth	%	8.7	2.5	
Inflation	%	7.6	11.4	
Def bdgt	L$	27m	24m	
	US$	27m	24m	
FMA (US)	US$	6.5m	6.5m	2.5m
US$1=L$		1.00	1.00	

Population   4,092,310
Ethnic groups: Americo-Liberians 5%

Age	0–14	15–19	20–24	25–29	30–64	65 plus
Male	21.8%	5.2%	3.5%	4.2%	13.7%	1.5%
Female	21.4%	5.4%	3.8%	4.2%	13.8%	1.6%

Capabilities

The development of the Liberian armed forces has been underpinned by US support for almost the past decade, although the UN's UNMIL mission is still required as a stabilisation force 11 years after it was established. In 2014 a Liberian was appointed as chief of staff of the armed forces, the first since the end of the civil war in 2003. US aid in 2014 included two 33ft fast patrol craft for the coast guard to help with maritime security. There is no domestic lift capacity; this will have hindered attempts to respond to the 2014 Ebola outbreak, which constituted a major challenge for the developing local security forces and led to a substantial international response. The US focused its response on Liberia, despatching around 4,000 troops to build healthcare facilities and train local medical staff.

ACTIVE 2,050 (Army 2,000, Coast Guard 50)

ORGANISATIONS BY SERVICE

Army 2,000
FORCES BY ROLE
MANOEUVRE
  Light
    1 (23rd) inf bde with (2 inf bn, 1 engr coy, 1 MP coy)
COMBAT SERVICE SUPPORT
  1 trg unit (forming)

Coast Guard 50
10 craft (8 *Zodiac* and 2 *Defender*) under 10t FLD

DEPLOYMENT

MALI
UN • MINUSMA 49; 1 inf pl

FOREIGN FORCES

All under UNMIL comd unless otherwise specified
Bangladesh 515; 12 obs; 2 engr coy; 1 log pl; 1 fd hospital
Benin 1; 1 obs
Bolivia 1; 2 obs
Brazil 2; 2 obs
Bulgaria 1 obs
China, People's Republic of 563; 2 obs; 1 engr coy; 1 tpt coy; 1 fd hospital
Croatia 1
Denmark 2; 3 obs
Ecuador 1; 2 obs
Egypt 7 obs
Ethiopia 3; 6 obs
Finland 3; 1 obs
Gambia 2 obs
Ghana 707; 8 obs; 1 inf bn; 1 log pl
Indonesia 1 obs
Jordan 5; 1 obs
Korea, Republic of 1; 1 obs
Kyrgyzstan 3 obs
Malaysia 4 obs
Moldova 2 obs
Montenegro 2 obs
Namibia 3
Nepal 18; 2 obs
Niger 1 obs
Nigeria 1,401; 8 obs; 2 inf bn
Pakistan 908; 6 obs; 2 inf bn; 2 engr coy; 1 fd hospital
Paraguay 1; 2 obs
Philippines 111; 2 obs; 1 log coy
Poland 1 obs
Romania 2 obs
Russia 3 obs
Senegal 1
Serbia 4 obs
Togo 1; 2 obs
Ukraine 177; 2 obs; 1 hel sqn
United States 5; 4 obs • 2,000; *Operation United Assistance* 1 air aslt div HQ; 1 mne recce coy; 1 engr bde
Yemen, Republic of 1
Zambia 3 obs
Zimbabwe 1 obs

Madagascar MDG

Malagsy Ariary fr		2013	2014	2015
GDP	fr	23.5tr	26tr	
	US$	10.6bn	11.2bn	
per capita	US$	463	475	
Growth	%	2.4	3.0	
Inflation	%	5.8	7.3	
Def bdgt	fr	163bn	173bn	207bn
	US$	74m	74m	
US$1=fr		2,206.99	2,323.58	

Population 23,201,926

Age	0–14	15–19	20–24	25–29	30–64	65 plus
Male	20.5%	5.5%	4.8%	4.0%	13.7%	1.4%
Female	20.2%	5.5%	4.8%	4.0%	13.9%	1.7%

Capabilities

The armed forces have played a significant role in the island's recent political instability. Elements were involved in the ousting of former president Marc Ravalomanana in 2009, an abortive coup attempt in 2010 and a mutiny in 2012. The army is the dominant force; neither of the small air or naval units has substantive combat capacity, and the state has no power-projection capability.

ACTIVE 13,500 (Army 12,500 Navy 500 Air 500)
Paramilitary 8,100
Conscript liability 18 months (incl for civil purposes)

ORGANISATIONS BY SERVICE

Army 12,500+
FORCES BY ROLE
MANOEUVRE
  Light
  2 (intervention) inf regt
  10 (regional) inf regt
COMBAT SUPPORT
  1 arty regt
  1 ADA regt
  3 engr regt
  1 sigs regt
COMBAT SERVICE SUPPORT
  1 log regt
EQUIPMENT BY TYPE
LT TK 12 PT-76
RECCE 73: ε35 BRDM-2; 10 *Ferret*; ε20 M3A1; 8 M8
APC (T) ε30 M3A1 half-track
ARTY 25+
  TOWED 17: **105mm** 5 M101; **122mm** 12 D-30
  MOR 8+: **82mm** M-37; **120mm** 8 M-43
AT • RCL 106mm M40A1
  RL 89mm LRAC
AD • GUNS • TOWED 70: **14.5mm** 50 ZPU-4; **37mm** 20 Type-55 (M-1939)

Navy 500 (incl some 100 Marines)
EQUIPMENT BY TYPE
PATROL AND COASTAL COMBATANTS 7
  PCC 1 *Chamois*
  PB 7: 6 (ex-US); 1 *Daikannon Maru* (fishery protection)
AMPHIBIOUS • LCT 1 (FRA *Edic*)
LOGISTICS AND SUPPORT 3
  YT 2 *Aigrette*
  YTB 1 *Trozona*

Air Force 500
FORCES BY ROLE
TRANSPORT
  1 sqn with An-26 *Curl*; Yak-40 *Codling* (VIP)
  1 (liaison) sqn with Cessna 310; Cessna 337 *Skymaster*; PA-23 *Aztec*
TRAINING
  1 sqn with Cessna 172; J.300 *Joker*; *Tetras*
TRANSPORT HELICOPTER
  1 sqn with SA318C *Alouette* II
EQUIPMENT BY TYPE
AIRCRAFT • TPT 16: **Light** 14: 1 An-26 *Curl*; 4 Cessna 172; 1 Cessna 310; 2 Cessna 337 *Skymaster*; 2 J.300 *Joker*; 1 PA-23 *Aztec*; 1 *Tetras*; 2 Yak-40 *Codling* (VIP); **PAX** 2 B-737
HELICOPTERS • MRH 4 SA318C *Alouette* II

Paramilitary 8,100

Gendarmerie 8,100
EQUIPMENT BY TYPE
PATROL AND COASTAL COMBATANTS • 5 PB

DEPLOYMENT

CENTRAL AFRICAN REPUBLIC
UN • MINUSCA 1

Malawi MWI

Malawian Kwacha K		2013	2014	2015
GDP	K	1.42tr	1.79tr	
	US$	3.82bn	4.41bn	
per capita	US$	223	250	
Growth	%	5.2	5.7	
Inflation	%	28.3	19.6	
Def bdgt	K	8.75bn	17bn	
	US$	24m	42m	
US$1=K		370.18	405.70	

Population 17,241,754

Age	0–14	15–19	20–24	25–29	30–64	65 plus
Male	22.3%	5.6%	4.7%	4.0%	12.1%	1.2%
Female	22.2%	5.6%	4.7%	4.1%	12.1%	1.6%

Capabilities

The armed forces' role is to ensure the sovereignty and territorial integrity of the state, but there is only limited capacity for power projection. The army is the largest force, consisting mainly of infantry units supported by light armoured vehicles. The air wing and the naval unit are much smaller, supporting services. Counter-trafficking is one role of the latter, which has recently taken delivery of new RHIBs. A contract for the supply of South African patrol boats, to provide greater capability in this area, was cancelled in September 2014. The army exercises regularly, participates in multinational exercises, is involved in supporting UN missions and has received some non-combat training from AFRICOM.

ACTIVE 5,300 (Army 5,300) Paramilitary 1,500

ORGANISATIONS BY SERVICE

Army 5,300
FORCES BY ROLE
COMMAND
  2 bde HQ
MANOEUVRE
  Light
    5 inf bn
  Air Manoeuvre
    1 para bn
COMBAT SUPPORT
  1 (general) bn (1+ mne coy, 1 armd recce sqn, 2 lt arty bty, 1 engr unit)
COMBAT SERVICE SUPPORT
  8 log coy
EQUIPMENT BY TYPE
Less than 20% serviceability
RECCE 41: 13 *Eland*; 20 FV721 *Fox*; 8 *Ferret*
APC • PPV 10 *Puma* M26-15
ARTY 17
  TOWED 105mm 9 lt
  MOR 81mm 8 L16
AD • SAM • MANPAD 15 *Blowpipe*
GUNS • TOWED 14.5mm 40 ZPU-4

Navy 220
EQUIPMENT BY TYPE
PATROL AND COASTAL COMBATANTS • PB 1 *Kasungu*†

Air Wing 200
EQUIPMENT BY TYPE
AIRCRAFT • TPT • **Light** 1 Do-228
HELICOPTERS • TPT 3 **Medium** 2: 1 AS532UL *Cougar*; 1 SA330H *Puma*; **Light** 1 AS350L *Ecureuil*

Paramilitary 1,500

Mobile Police Force 1,500
RECCE 8 S52 *Shorland*
AIRCRAFT
  TPT • **Light** 4: 3 BN-2T *Defender* (border patrol); 1 SC.7 3M *Skyvan*
HELICOPTERS • MRH 2 AS365 *Dauphin* 2

DEPLOYMENT

CÔTE D'IVOIRE
UN • UNOCI 2; 3 obs

DEMOCRATIC REPUBLIC OF THE CONGO
UN • MONUSCO 857; 8 obs; 1 inf bn

WESTERN SAHARA
UN • MINURSO 3 obs

Mali MLI

CFA Franc BCEAO fr		2013	2014	2015
GDP	fr	5.37tr	5.77tr	
	US$	10.9bn	12bn	
per capita	US$	646	693	
Growth	%	1.7	5.9	
Inflation	%	-0.6	1.5	
Def bdgt	fr	149bn	175bn	202bn
	US$	302m	365m	
US$1=fr		493.91	479.32	

Population 16,455,903

Ethnic groups: Tuareg 6–10%

Age	0–14	15–19	20–24	25–29	30–64	65 plus
Male	23.9%	5.1%	3.9%	3.1%	11.2%	1.5%
Female	23.7%	5.4%	4.5%	3.8%	12.3%	1.5%

Capabilities

In January 2013, the shortcomings of the Malian armed forces were exposed by its inability to deal with Islamist and Tuareg insurgents; this later led to French military intervention. A peace deal was in the process of being negotiated with two Tuareg rebel groups in the latter half of 2014, while tranches of the reconstituted armed forces were being trained by an EU Training Mission (EUTM). Originally due to end in 2014, the mission was extended to May 2016 and includes 200 instructors. A UN stabilisation mission (MINUSMA) took over from an African-led support mission in July 2013. The army received ACMAT Light Tactical Vehicles from France to equip the new combined-arms battle groups being trained by the EUTM.

ACTIVE 4,000 (Army 4,000) Paramilitary 7,800

ORGANISATIONS BY SERVICE

Army ε4,000
FORCES BY ROLE
The remanants of the pre-war Malian army are being reformed into new combined-arms battle groups, each of which comprise one lt mech coy, three mot inf coy, one arty bty and additional recce, cdo and cbt spt elms.
MANOEUVRE
 Light
  4 mot inf BG

EQUIPMENT BY TYPE
RECCE BRDM-2†
APC (W) 19+: 10+ BTR-60PB; 9 BTR-70
ARTY • MRL 122mm 30+ BM-21

Navy
EQUIPMENT BY TYPE
PATROL AND COASTAL COMBATANTS 3 PBR†

Air Force
FORCES BY ROLE
FIGHTER
 1 sqn with MiG-21MF *Fishbed*; MiG-21UM *Mongol* B
TRANSPORT
 1 sqn with An-24 *Coke*; An-26 *Curl*; BN-2 *Islander*; BT-67
TRAINING
 1 sqn with L-29 *Delfin*; SF-260WL *Warrior**; *Tetras*
TRANSPORT HELICOPTER
 1 sqn with Mi-8 *Hip*; Mi-24D *Hind*; Z-9

EQUIPMENT BY TYPE
AIRCRAFT 4 combat capable
 FGA 2: 1 MiG-21MF *Fishbed*†; 1 MiG-21UM *Mongol* B†
 TPT • Light 10: 1 An-24 *Coke*; 2 An-26 *Curl*; 1 BT-67; 2 BN-2 *Islander*; 4 *Tetras*
 TRG 8: 6 L-29 *Delfin*†; 2 SF-260WL *Warrior**
HELICOPTERS
 ATK 2 Mi-24D *Hind*
 MRH 1 Z-9
 TPT 1 **Medium** 1 Mi-8 *Hip*; **Light** (1 AS350 *Ecureuil* in store)

Paramilitary 7,800 active

Gendarmerie 1,800
FORCES BY ROLE
MANOEUVRE
 Other
  8 paramilitary coy

Republican Guard 2,000

National Police 1,000

Militia 3,000

DEPLOYMENT

CENTRAL AFRICAN REPUBLIC
UN • MINUSCA 1

DEMOCRATIC REPUBLIC OF THE CONGO
UN • MONUSCO 6 obs

SOUTH SUDAN
UN • UNMISS 3 obs

SUDAN
UN • UNAMID 6 obs
UN • UNISFA 1

FOREIGN FORCES

All under MINUSMA comd unless otherwise specified

Austria EUTM Mali 8
Bangladesh 1,471; 1 inf bn; 1 engr coy; 1 rvn coy; 2 sigs coy; 1 tpt coy
Belgium EUTM Mali 82
Benin 253; 1 mech inf coy
Burkina Faso 860; 1 inf bn
Cambodia 306; 1 engr coy; 1 EOD coy
Chad 1,046; 1 SF coy; 1 inf bn; 2 inf coy
China 402; 1 sy coy; 1 engr coy; 1 fd hospital
Côte d'Ivoire 121; 1 tpt coy
Czech Republic EUTM Mali 38
Denmark 10
Dominican Republic 2
Egypt 9
Estonia 2 • EUTM Mali 8
Finland 6 • EUTM Mali 12
France 20 • *Operation Barkhane* 1,450; 1 inf BG; 1 log bn; 1 hel unit with 3 EC665 *Tiger*; 2 NH90 TTH; 6 SA330 *Puma*; 6 SA342 *Gazelle* • EUTM Mali 70
Gambia 2
Germany 6 • EUTM Mali 146
Ghana 160; 1 engr coy; 1 hel sqn
Guinea 215; 1 inf coy
Guinea-Bissau 1
Hungary EUTM Mali 13
Ireland EUTM Mali 8
Italy 2 • EUTM Mali 15
Kenya 1
Latvia EUTM 7
Liberia 49; 1 inf pl
Lithuania EUTM Mali 3
Luxembourg EUTM Mali 1
Mauritania 6
Nepal 145; 1 EOD coy
Netherlands 544; 1 SF coy; 1 atk hel sqn; 1 engr coy • EUTM Mali 1
Niger 861; 1 inf bn
Nigeria 179; 1 sigs coy; 1 fd hospital
Norway 19
Poland EUTM Mali 20
Portugal 47 • EUTM Mali 7
Romania EUTM Mali 1
Senegal 473; 1 inf bn HQ; 1 inf coy; 1 arty coy; 1 engr coy
Sierra Leone 4
Slovenia EUTM Mali 3
Spain EUTM Mali 114
Sweden 26 • EUTM Mali 10
Switzerland 1
Togo 933; 1 inf bn
United Kingdom 2 • EUTM Mali 37
United States 10
Yemen 4

Mauritius MUS

Mauritian Rupee R		2013	2014	2015
GDP	R	366bn	392bn	
	US$	11.9bn	12.7bn	
per capita	US$	9,165	9,715	
Growth	%	3.2	3.3	
Inflation	%	3.5	3.7	
Def bdgt [a]	R	2.59bn	2.58bn	
	US$	84m	84m	
US$1=R		30.70	30.80	

[a] Defence and Home Affairs Budget

Population 1,331,155

Age	0–14	15–19	20–24	25–29	30–64	65 plus
Male	10.7%	3.7%	4.1%	3.6%	23.6%	3.4%
Female	10.3%	3.7%	4.0%	3.5%	24.3%	5.0%

Capabilities

The country has no standing armed forces, but the Special Mobile Force (part of the police force) is tasked with providing internal and external security. The coast guard operates a number of patrol craft, including one blue-water patrol ship. An OPV for the coast guard was launched in India in 2013, and New Delhi has also provided credit for the purchase of 12 fast patrol craft.

ACTIVE NIL Paramilitary 2,500

ORGANISATIONS BY SERVICE

Paramilitary 2,500

Special Mobile Force ε1,750

FORCES BY ROLE
MANOEUVRE
 Reconnaissance
  2 recce coy
 Light
  5 (rifle) mot inf coy
COMBAT SUPPORT
 1 engr sqn
COMBAT SERVICE SUPPORT
 1 spt pl
EQUIPMENT BY TYPE
RECCE 4 *Shorland*
AIFV 2 VAB (with 20mm gun)
APC (W) 16: 7 *Tactica*; 9 VAB
ARTY • MOR 81mm 2
AT • RL 89mm 4 LRAC

Coast Guard ε800

EQUIPMENT BY TYPE
PATROL AND COASTAL COMBATANTS 5
 PSOH 1 *Vigilant*† (1 hel landing platform) (vessel has been laid up since 2006 and is for sale)
 PB 4: 1 P-2000; 1 SDB-Mk3; 2 *Zhuk* (FSU)

LOGISTICS AND SUPPORT
  AGS 1 *Pathfinder*
  AIRCRAFT • TPT • Light 3: 1 BN-2T *Defender*; 2 Do-228-101

Police Air Wing
EQUIPMENT BY TYPE
HELICOPTERS
  MRH 5: 1 *Dhruv*; 4 SA316 *Alouette* III
  TPT • Light 1 AS355 *Ecureuil* II

Mozambique MOZ

Mozambique New Metical M		2013	2014	2015
GDP	M	461bn	528bn	
	US$	15.3bn	16.6bn	
per capita	US$	593	626	
Growth	%	7.1	8.3	
Inflation	%	4.2	4.6	
Def bdgt	M	1.01bn	1.11bn	
	US$	33m	35m	
US$1=M			30.12	31.80

Population 24,692,144

Age	0–14	15–19	20–24	25–29	30–64	65 plus
Male	22.8%	5.8%	4.6%	3.2%	11.1%	1.3%
Female	22.5%	5.9%	5.0%	3.8%	12.4%	1.6%

Capabilities

The armed forces are tasked with combating maritime piracy and people-trafficking, assuring the country's territorial integrity and internal security. In general, levels of equipment serviceability remain open to question, but cooperative anti-piracy patrols with South Africa have provided Mozambique's forces with experience. Budget constraints have limited the ability to address areas of weakness, leaving the armed forces dependent on cascaded defence equipment from other nations. However, it has funded the reconditioning of its MiG-21 *Fishbed* fighters, with this completed in mid-2014. Rising revenues from hydrocarbon exploitation will likely help overall budgets, and it is possible that the need to protect the growing maritime energy infrastructure could drive procurements. There are growing defence ties with China and with Italy, including the provision of naval training.

ACTIVE 11,200 (Army 10,000 Navy 200 Air 1,000)
Conscript liability 2 years

ORGANISATIONS BY SERVICE

Army ε9,000–10,000
FORCES BY ROLE
SPECIAL FORCES
  3 SF bn
MANOEUVRE
Light
  7 inf bn

COMBAT SUPPORT
  2-3 arty bn
  2 engr bn
COMBAT SERVICE SUPPORT
  1 log bn
EQUIPMENT BY TYPE†
Equipment at estimated 10% or less serviceability
MBT 60+ T-54
RECCE 30 BRDM-1/BRDM-2
AIFV 40 BMP-1
APC 426
  APC (T) 30 FV430
  APC (W) 285: 160 BTR-60; 100 BTR-152; 25 *Saxon*
  PPV 11 *Casspir*
ARTY 126
  TOWED 62: **100mm** 20 M-1944; **105mm** 12 M101; **122mm** 12 D-30; **130mm** 6 M-46; **152mm** 12 D-1
  MRL **122mm** 12 BM-21
  MOR 52: **82mm** 40 M-43; **120mm** 12 M-43
AT
  MSL • MANPATS 9K11 *Malyutka* (AT-3 *Sagger*); 9K111 *Fagot* (AT-4 *Spigot*)
  RCL **75mm**; **82mm** B-10; **107mm** 24 B-12
  GUNS **85mm** 18: 6 D-48; 12 Type-56 (D-44)
AD • SAM • MANPAD 9K32 *Strela*-2 (SA-7 *Grail*)‡
  GUNS 290+
    SP **57mm** 20 ZSU-57-2
    TOWED 270+: **20mm** M-55; **23mm** 120 ZU-23-2; **37mm** 90 M-1939; (10 M-1939 in store); **57mm** 60 S-60; (30 S-60 in store)

Navy ε200
EQUIPMENT BY TYPE
PATROL AND COASTAL COMBATANTS • PB 1
  Pebane (ex-ESP *Conejera*-class)

Air Force 1,000
FORCES BY ROLE
FIGHTER/GROUND ATTACK
  1 sqn with MiG-21bis *Fishbed*; MiG-21UM *Mongol* B
TRANSPORT
  1 sqn with An-26 *Curl*; FTB-337G *Milirole*
ATTACK/TRANSPORT HELICOPTER
  1 sqn with Mi-24 *Hind*†
AIR DEFENCE
  Some bty with S-75 *Dvina* (SA-2 *Guideline*)†‡
EQUIPMENT BY TYPE
AIRCRAFT
  FGA 8: 6 MiG-21bis *Fishbed*; 2 MiG-21UM *Mongol* B
  ISR 2 FTB-337G *Milirole*
  TPT 3: **Light** 2 An-26 *Curl*; (4 PA-32 *Cherokee* non-op);
  PAX 1 Hawker 850XP
HELICOPTERS
  ATK 2 Mi-24 *Hind*†
  TPT • **Medium** (2 Mi-8 *Hip* non-op)
AD • SAM • TOWED: S-75 *Dvina* (SA-2 *Guideline*)† ‡; (10+ S-125 *Pechora* SA-3 *Goa* non-op‡)

DEPLOYMENT

SUDAN
UN • UNISFA 1 obs

Namibia NAM

Namibian Dollar N$		2013	2014	2015
GDP	N$	118bn	131bn	
	US$	12.3bn	12bn	
per capita	US$	5,636	5,467	
Growth	%	4.3	4.3	
Inflation	%	5.6	5.9	
Def bdgt	N$	3.96bn	4.47bn	4.8bn
	US$	411m	410m	
US$1=N$		9.65	10.90	

Population 2,198,406

Age	0–14	15–19	20–24	25–29	30–64	65 plus
Male	16.0%	6.0%	5.7%	5.2%	15.7%	1.9%
Female	15.7%	5.9%	5.5%	5.0%	14.9%	2.5%

Capabilities

The armed forces support territorial integrity and civil authorities, and participate in peace-support operations. They also take part in multinational exercises and have been involved in United Nations and African Union deployments, though there is only limited ability for independent power projection beyond national territory. Improving mobility remains a priority in terms of both land vehicles and air transport. The army has also ordered a package of weapons from Russia, including *Kornet* ATGW, whereas the air force has turned to China as its main source of combat aircraft and received helicopters from both China and India. The navy, by contrast, has a long-standing equipment and training relationship with Brazil.

ACTIVE 9,200 (Army 9,000 Navy 200) **Paramilitary 6,000**

ORGANISATIONS BY SERVICE

Army 9,000
FORCES BY ROLE
MANOEUVRE
  Reconniassance
    1 recce regt
  Light
    3 inf bde (total: 6 inf bn)
  Other
    1 (Presidential Guard) gd bn
COMBAT SUPPORT
  1 arty bde with (1 arty regt)
  1 AT regt
  1 AD regt
  1 engr regt
  1 sigs regt

COMBAT SERVICE SUPPORT
  1 log bn
EQUIPMENT BY TYPE
MBT T-54/T-55†; T-34†
RECCE 12 BRDM-2
APC 68
  APC (W) 48: 10 BTR-60; 8 Type-05P; 30 *Wolf Turbo 2*
  PPV 20 *Casspir*
ARTY 69
  TOWED 140mm 24 G2
  MRL 122mm 5 BM-21
  MOR 40: **81mm**; **82mm**
AT • RCL 82mm B-10
  GUNS 12+: **57mm**; **76mm** 12 ZIS-3
AD • SAM • MANPAD 9K32 *Strela*-2 (SA-7 *Grail*)‡
  GUNS 65
    SP 23mm 15 *Zumlac*
    TOWED 14.5mm 50 ZPU-4
ARV T-54/T-55 reported

Navy ε200
EQUIPMENT BY TYPE
PATROL AND COASTAL COMBATANTS 5
  PSO 1 *Elephant*
  PCC 1 *Oryx*
  PB 3: 1 *Brendan Simbwaye*; 2 *Marlim*
AIRCRAFT • TPT • Light 1 F406 *Caravan II*
HELICOPTERS • TPT • Medium 1 S-61L

Air Force
FORCES BY ROLE
FIGHTER/GROUND ATTACK
  1 sqn with F-7 (F-7NM); FT-7 (FT-7NG)
ISR
  1 sqn with O-2A *Skymaster*
TRANSPORT
  Some sqn with An-26 *Curl*; Falcon 900; Learjet 36; Y-12
TRAINING
  1 sqn with K-8 *Karakorum**
ATTACK/TRANSPORT HELICOPTER
  1 sqn with H425; Mi-8 *Hip*; Mi-25 *Hind* D; SA315 *Lama* (*Cheetah*); SA316B *Alouette* III (*Chetak*)
EQUIPMENT BY TYPE
AIRCRAFT 12 combat capable
  FTR 8: 6 F-7 (F-7NM); 2 FT-7 (FT-7NG)
  ISR 5 O-2A *Skymaster*
  TPT 6: **Light** 5: 2 An-26 *Curl*; 1 Learjet 36; 2 Y-12; **PAX** 1 *Falcon* 900
  TRG 4+ K-8 *Karakorum**
HELICOPTERS
  ATK 2 Mi-25 *Hind* D
  MRH 5: 1 H425; 1 SA315 *Lama* (*Cheetah*); 3 SA316B *Alouette* III (*Chetak*)
  TPT • Medium 1 Mi-8 *Hip*

Paramilitary 6,000

Police Force • Special Field Force 6,000 (incl Border Guard and Special Reserve Force)

Ministry of Fisheries
EQUIPMENT BY TYPE
PATROL AND COASTAL COMBATANTS • PCO 3: 2 *Nathanael Maxwilili*; 1 *Tobias Hainyenko*
LOGISTICS AND SUPPORT 5
  AGE 1 *Mirabilis*
  AGOR 4

DEPLOYMENT

CÔTE D'IVOIRE
UN • UNOCI 2 obs

LIBERIA
UN • UNMIL 3

SOUTH SUDAN
UN • UNMISS 2 obs

SUDAN
UN • UNAMID 2; 9 obs
UN • UNISFA 1; 3 obs

Niger NER

CFA Franc BCEAO fr		2013	2014	2015
GDP	fr	3.66tr	3.95tr	
	US$	7.41bn	8.29bn	
per capita	US$	447	484	
Growth	%	4.1	6.3	
Inflation	%	2.3	-1.1	
Def exp	fr	ε35.6bn		
	US$	ε72m		
FMA (US)	US$		0.4m	
US$1=fr		493.89	476.73	

Population 17,466,172
Ethnic groups: Tuareg 8–10%

Age	0–14	15–19	20–24	25–29	30–64	65 plus
Male	25.1%	5.2%	3.9%	3.2%	11.4%	1.3%
Female	24.7%	5.2%	4.1%	3.3%	11.2%	1.3%

Capabilities

Internal and border security are key roles for the armed forces, in light of the regional threat from Islamist groups. The country is a member of the 'G5 Sahel' aimed at improving the ability to counter jihadists in the region. However, the armed forces remain under-equipped and resourced to fully meet these challenges. In March 2014 the country hosted Exercise *Flintlock*, a US-led Special Operations Forces exercise. It also provides UAV basing for the US, the first at Niamey (which also has a French presence), while the second US site is planned at Agadez. Both countries have been providing equipment for surveillance tasks, including Cessna 208Bs from the US and *Gazelle* light helicopters from France. Niger also acquired two Su-25 *Frogfoot* aircraft from Ukraine in 2013.

ACTIVE 5,300 (Army 5,200 Air 100) Paramilitary 5,400
Conscript liability Selective conscription, 2 years

ORGANISATIONS BY SERVICE

Army 5,200
3 Mil Districts
FORCES BY ROLE
MANOEUVRE
  Reconnaissance
  4 armd recce sqn
  Light
  7 inf coy
  Air Manoeuvre
  2 AB coy
COMBAT SUPPORT
  1 AD coy
  1 engr coy
COMBAT SERVICE SUPPORT
  1 log gp
EQUIPMENT BY TYPE
RECCE 132: 35 AML-20/AML-60; 90 AML-90; 7 VBL
APC (W) 24: 22 M3 Panhard; 2 WZ-523
ARTY • MOR 40: **81mm** 19 Brandt; **82mm** 17; **120mm** 4 Brandt
AT • RCL 14: **75mm** 6 M20; **106mm** 8 M40
  RL **89mm** 36 LRAC
AD • GUNS 39
  SP **20mm** 10 M3 VDAA
  TOWED **20mm** 29

Air Force 100
EQUIPMENT BY TYPE
AIRCRAFT 2 combat capable
  ATK 2 Su-25 *Frogfoot*
  ISR 2 DA42 MPP *Twin Star*
  TPT 7: **Medium** 1 C-130H *Hercules*; **Light** 3: 1 An-26 *Curl*; 2 Cessna 208 *Caravan*; 1 Do-28; 1 Do-228-201; PAX 1 B-737-700 (VIP)
HELICOPTERS
  MRH 5: 2 Mi-17 *Hip*; 3 SA342 *Gazelle*

Paramilitary 5,400

Gendarmerie 1,400

Republican Guard 2,500

National Police 1,500

DEPLOYMENT

CENTRAL AFRICAN REPUBLIC
UN • MINUSCA 2 obs

CÔTE D'IVOIRE
UN • UNOCI 871; 5 obs; 1 inf bn

DEMOCRATIC REPUBLIC OF THE CONGO
UN • MONUSCO 4; 8 obs

LIBERIA
UN • UNMIL 1 obs

MALI
UN • MINUSMA 861; 1 inf bn

FOREIGN FORCES
France *Opération Barkhane* 300; 1 FGA det with 3 *Mirage* 2000D; 1 hel det with 4 *Harfang*; 2 MQ-9A *Reaper*

Nigeria NGA

Nigerian Naira N		2013	2014	2015
GDP	N	81tr	92.2tr	
	US$	522bn	594bn	
per capita	US$	3,082	3,416	
Growth	%	5.4	7.0	
Inflation	%	8.5	8.3	
Def bdgt	N	364bn	350bn	
	US$	2.35bn	2.25bn	
FMA (US)	US$	1m	1m	0.6m
US$1=N		155.25	155.22	

Population 177,155,754

Ethnic groups: North (Hausa and Fulani), Southwest (Yoruba), Southeast (Ibo); these tribes make up ε65% of population

Age	0–14	15–19	20–24	25–29	30–64	65 plus
Male	22.1%	5.3%	4.6%	3.9%	13.6%	1.5%
Female	21.1%	5.1%	4.4%	3.8%	13.1%	1.6%

Capabilities
Internal security is the central concern for the comparatively well-equipped and trained armed forces, with border and maritime security also vital tasks. There have been repeated clashes with Boko Haram in Borno State in the north of the country with reports that the difficulty in defeating the insurgents was adversely affecting morale, despite training support from the US and other countries. The armed forces have been attempting to adopt COIN tactics, looking to establish forward-operating bases and quick-reaction groups. However, the threat from IEDs remained during 2014. In response to the continuing insurgency, items have been brought out of storage and into service, including transport aircraft and light fighters. Equipment maintenance and serviceability has been a long-standing issue. Piracy remains a problem in western waters and in the Niger Delta, with renewed activity in early 2014. To increase anti-piracy capabilities, the navy received a second *Hamilton*-class cutter from the US Coast Guard in May 2014.

ACTIVE 80,000 (Army 62,000 Navy 8,000 Air 10,000)
Paramilitary 82,000
Reserves planned, none org

ORGANISATIONS BY SERVICE

Army 62,000
FORCES BY ROLE
MANOEUVRE
  Armoured
  1 (3rd) armd div (1 armd bde, 1 arty bde)
  Mechanised
  2 (1st) mech div (1 recce bn, 1 mech bde, 1 mot inf bde, 1 arty bde, 1 engr regt)
  1 (2nd) mech div (1 recce bn, 2 armd bde, 1 arty bde, 1 engr regt)
  1 (81st) composite div (1 recce bn, 1 mech bde, 1 arty bde, 1 engr regt)
  Light
  1 (7th) inf div (1 recce bn, 1 armd bde, 1 inf bde, 1 arty bde, 1 engr regt)
  1 (82nd) composite div (1 recce bn, 1 mech bde, 2 mot inf bde, 1 amph bde, 1 AB bn, 1 arty bde, 1 engr regt)
  Other
  1 (Presidential Guard) gd bde with (4 gd bn)
COMBAT SUPPORT
  1 AD regt
EQUIPMENT BY TYPE
MBT 276: 176 Vickers Mk 3; 100 T-55†
LT TK 157 *Scorpion*
RECCE 452: 90 AML-60; 40 AML-90; 70 EE-9 *Cascavel*; 50 FV721 *Fox*; 20 *Saladin* Mk2; 72 VBL; 110 *Cobra*
APC 484+
  APC (T) 317: 250 4K-7FA *Steyr*; 67 MT-LB
  APC (W) 167+: 10 FV603 *Saracen*; 110 AVGP *Grizzly* mod/*Piranha* I 6x6; 47 BTR-3U; EE-11 *Urutu* (reported)
ARTY 482+
  SP 155mm 39 VCA 155 *Palmaria*
  TOWED 88: **105mm** 50 M-56; **122mm** 31 D-30/D-74; **130mm** 7 M-46; (**155mm** 24 FH-77B in store)
  MRL 122mm 25 APR-21
  MOR 330+: **81mm** 200; **82mm** 100; **120mm** 30+
AT • MSL • MANPATS *Swingfire*
  RCL 84mm *Carl Gustav*; **106mm** M40A1
AD • SAM 164
  SP 16 *Roland*
  MANPAD *Blowpipe*; 9K32 *Strela*-2 (SA-7 *Grail*)‡
GUNS 90+
  SP 30 ZSU-23-4
  TOWED 60+: **20mm** 60+; **23mm** ZU-23; **40mm** L/70
RADAR • LAND: some RASIT (veh, arty)
ARV 17+: AVGP *Husky*; 2 *Greif*; 15 Vickers ARV
VLB MTU-20; VAB

Navy 8,000 (incl Coast Guard)
Western Comd HQ located at Apapa; Eastern Comd HQ located at Calabar;
EQUIPMENT BY TYPE
PRINCIPAL SURFACE COMBATANTS 1
  FRIGATES • FFGHM 1 *Aradu* (GER MEKO 360) with 8 single lnchr with *Otomat* AShM, 1 octuple *Albatros* lnchr with *Aspide* SAM, 2 triple STWS 1B 324mm ASTT with A244 LWT, 1 127mm gun, (capacity 1 *Lynx* Mk89 hel)

PATROL AND COASTAL COMBATANTS 113
  CORVETTES • FSM 1 *Enymiri* (UK Vosper Mk 9) with 1 triple lnchr with *Seacat* SAM, 1 twin 375mm A/S mor, 1 76mm gun
  PSOH 2 *Thunder* (US *Hamilton*) with 1 76 mm gun
  PCFG 1 *Ayam* (FRA *Combattante*) with 2 twin lnchr with MM-38 *Exocet* AShM, 1 76mm gun (additional 2 vessels† - 1 used as spares; 1 non-operational; both without *Exocet* AShM)
  PCO 4 *Balsam* (buoy tenders (US))
  PCC 3 *Ekpe*† (GER Lurssen 57m) with 1 76mm gun
  PBF 30: 21 *Manta* (Suncraft 17m); 4 *Manta* MkII; 3 *Shaldag* II; 2 *Torie*
  PB 72: 1 *Andoni*; 1 *Dorina*; 3 *Okpoku* (FPB 98 MkII); 4 Swiftships; 2 *Sea Eagle* (Suncraft 38m); 2 *Sentinel* (Nautic 17m); 15 *Stingray* (Suncraft 16m); 40 Suncraft 12m; 2 *Town* (of which one laid up); 2 *Yola*; (a further 150 small patrol craft under 10 tonnes FLD may be in operation)
MINE WARFARE • MINE COUNTERMEASURES 2:
  MCC 2 *Ohue* (mod ITA *Lerici*)
AMPHIBIOUS 5
  LS • LST 1 *Ambe*† (capacity 5 tanks; 220 troops) (GER)
  LC • LCVP 4 *Stingray* 20
LOGISTICS AND SUPPORT 9
  AGHS 1
  YFL 2 (ex-GER Damen Stan 1905)
  YTB 2 (ex-GER Damen Stan 2909/2608)
  YTL 4

Naval Aviation
EQUIPMENT BY TYPE
HELICOPTERS
  MRH 2 AW139 (AB-139)
  TPT • Light 3 AW109E *Power*†

Air Force 10,000
FORCES BY ROLE
Very limited op capability
FIGHTER/GROUND ATTACK
  1 sqn with F-7 (F-7NI); FT-7 (FT-7NI)
MARITIME PATROL
  1 sqn with ATR-42-500 MP; Do-128D-6 *Turbo SkyServant*; Do-228-100/200
TRANSPORT
  2 sqn with C-130H *Hercules*; C-130H-30 *Hercules*; G-222
  1 (Presidential) gp with B-727; B-737BBJ; BAe-125-800; Beech 350 *King Air*; Do-228-200; *Falcon* 7X; *Falcon* 900; Gulfstream IV/V
TRAINING
  1 unit with *Air Beetle*†;
  1 unit with *Alpha Jet**
  1 unit with L-39 *Albatros*†*; MB-339A*
  1 hel unit with Mi-34 *Hermit* (trg);
ATTACK/TRANSPORT HELICOPTER
  2 sqn with AW109LUH; Mi-24/Mi-35 *Hind*†
EQUIPMENT BY TYPE†
AIRCRAFT 53 combat capable
  FTR 15: 12 F-7 (F-7NI); 3 FT-7 (FT-7NI)
  ELINT 2 ATR-42-500 MP

TPT 33: **Medium** 5: 1 C-130H *Hercules* (4 more in store†); 1 C-130H-30 *Hercules* (2 more in store); 3 G-222† (2 more in store†); **Light** 19: 3 Beech 350 *King Air*; 1 Cessna 550 *Citation*; 8 Do-128D-6 *Turbo SkyServant*; 1 Do-228-100; 6 Do-228-200 (incl 2 VIP); **PAX** 9: 1 B-727; 1 B-737BBJ; 1 BAe 125-800; 2 *Falcon* 7X; 2 *Falcon* 900; 1 Gulfstream IV; 1 Gulfstream V
  TRG 106: 58 *Air Beetle*† (up to 20 awaiting repair); 13 *Alpha Jet**; 23 L-39 *Albatros*†*; 12 MB-339AN* (all being upgraded)
HELICOPTERS
  ATK 8: 2 Mi-24P *Hind*; 2 Mi-24V *Hind*; 4 Mi-35 *Hind*
  MRH 6 AW109LUH
  TPT 3: **Medium** 2 AS332 *Super Puma* (4 more in store); **Light** 1 AW109
UAV • ISR • Medium (9 *Aerostar* non-operational)
MSL • AAM • IR R-3 (AA-2 *Atoll*)‡; PL-9C

Paramilitary ε82,000

Nigerian Police

Port Authority Police ε2,000
PATROL AND COASTAL COMBATANTS • MISC BOATS/CRAFT 60+ boats
AMPHIBIOUS 5+ ACV

Security and Civil Defence Corps • Police 80,000
EQUIPMENT BY TYPE
APC (W) 74+: 70+ AT105 *Saxon*†; 4 BTR-3U; UR-416
AIRCRAFT • TPT • Light 4: 1 Cessna 500 *Citation* I; 2 PA-31 *Navajo*; 1 PA-31-350 *Navajo Chieftain*
HELICOPTERS • TPT • Light 4: 2 Bell 212 (AB-212); 2 Bell 222 (AB-222)

DEPLOYMENT

CÔTE D'IVOIRE
UN • UNOCI 3 obs

DEMOCRATIC REPUBLIC OF THE CONGO
UN • MONUSCO 5; 12 obs

GUINEA-BISSAU
ECOWAS • ECOMIB 160

LEBANON
UN • UNIFIL 1

LIBERIA
UN • UNMIL 1,401; 8 obs; 2 inf bn

MALI
UN • MINUSMA 179; 1 sigs coy; 1 fd hospital

SOUTH SUDAN
UN • UNMISS 1; 4 obs

SUDAN
UN • UNAMID 937; 10 obs; 1 inf bn
UN • UNISFA 3; 3 obs

WESTERN SAHARA
UN • MINURSO 3 obs

Rwanda RWA

Rwandan Franc fr		2013	2014	2015
GDP	fr	4.92tr	5.44tr	
	US$	7.6bn	8bn	
per capita	US$	704	721	
Growth	%	4.7	6.0	
Inflation	%	4.2	2.6	
Def bdgt	fr	54.1bn	55.1bn	
	US$	84m	81m	
FMA (US)	US$		0.2m	
US$1=fr		646.63	680.16	

Population 12,337,138

Ethnic groups: Hutu 80%; Tutsi 19%

Age	0–14	15–19	20–24	25–29	30–64	65 plus
Male	21.2%	5.1%	4.4%	4.3%	13.9%	1.0%
Female	20.9%	5.1%	4.4%	4.3%	14.0%	1.5%

Capabilities

The main tasks for the armed forces are to defend territorial integrity and national sovereignty. The country fields a comparatively large army, but units are lightly equipped, with little mechanisation. The land forces have been involved in combat operations in the DRC as recently as 2009, when a joint operation was conducted to combat rebels. The army regularly takes part in multinational exercises and is a key contributor to the East Africa Standby Force, having pledged a motorised infantry battalion. A small number of helicopters constitute the air force and the lack of fixed-wing aircraft limits the armed forces' ability to deploy independently overseas. US forces transported 800 Rwandan personnel, plus equipment, on deployment to the CAR in January 2014.

ACTIVE 33,000 (Army 32,000 Air 1,000) Paramilitary 2,000

ORGANISATIONS BY SERVICE

Army 32,000
FORCES BY ROLE
MANOEUVRE
  Light
   2 cdo bn
   4 inf div (3 inf bde)
COMBAT SUPPORT
   1 arty bde
EQUIPMENT BY TYPE
MBT 34: 24 T-54/T-55; 10 *Tiran*-5
RECCE 106: ε90 AML-60/AML-90/AML-245; 16 VBL
AIFV 35+: BMP; 15 *Ratel*-90; 20 *Ratel*-60
APC 56+
  APC (W) 20+: BTR; *Buffalo* (M3 Panhard); 20 Type-92 (reported)
  PPV 36 RG-31 *Nyala*

ARTY 160+
  TOWED 35+: **105mm** 29 Type-54 (D-1); **122mm** 6 D-30; **152mm**†
  MRL 10: **122mm** 5 RM-70; **160mm** 5 LAR-160
  MOR 115: **81mm**; **82mm**; **120mm**
AD • SAM • MANPAD 9K32 *Strela*-2 (SA-7 *Grail*)‡
  GUNS ε150: **14.5mm**; **23mm**; **37mm**
ARV T-54/T-55 reported

Air Force ε1,000
FORCES BY ROLE
ATTACK/TRANSPORT HELICOPTER
  1 sqn with Mi-17/Mi-17MD/Mi-17V-5/Mi-17-1V *Hip* H; Mi-24P/V *Hind*
EQUIPMENT BY TYPE
HELICOPTERS
  ATK 5: 2 Mi-24V *Hind* E; 3 Mi-24P *Hind*
  MRH 10: 1 AW139; 4 Mi-17 *Hip* H; 1 Mi-17MD *Hip* H; 1 Mi-17V-5 *Hip* H; 3 Mi-17-1V *Hip* H
  TPT • Light 1 AW109S

Paramilitary
Local Defence Forces ε2,000

DEPLOYMENT

CENTRAL AFRICAN REPUBLIC
UN • MINUSCA 858; 4 obs; 1 mech inf bn

MALI
UN • MINUSMA 6

SOUTH SUDAN
UN • UNMISS 1,777; 3 obs; 2 inf bn

SUDAN
UN • UNAMID 2,449; 9 obs; 3 inf bn
UN • UNISFA 1; 2 obs

Senegal SEN

CFA Franc BCEAO fr		2013	2014	2015
GDP	fr	7.31tr	7.69tr	
	US$	14.8bn	15.9bn	
per capita	US$	1,048	1,092	
Growth	%	3.5	4.5	
Inflation	%	0.7	-0.5	
Def bdgt	fr	123bn	123bn	
	US$	248m	254m	
FMA (US)	US$	0.325m	0.325m	0.3m
US$1=fr		493.89	484.28	

Population 13,635,927

Ethnic groups: Wolof 36%; Fulani 17%; Serer 17%; Toucouleur 9%; Man-dingo 9%; Diola 9% (of which 30–60% in Casamance)

Age	0–14	15–19	20–24	25–29	30–64	65 plus
Male	21.3%	5.5%	4.7%	3.9%	11.7%	1.3%
Female	21.1%	5.5%	4.8%	4.2%	14.5%	1.6%

Capabilities

The armed forces' priorities are internal and border security, including countering an insurgency in the country's south and Islamist activity in neighbouring states, and combating narcotics trafficking. Peace talks with the separatist movement in Casamance Province to end the three-decade-long insurrection were under way as of the third quarter of 2014. The armed forces have a limited capability only to address national-security requirements, while France retains a military presence in the country and provides training support. China's PLAN made a port visit to Senegal for the first time in May 2014.

ACTIVE 13,600 (Army 11,900 Navy 950 Air 750)
Paramilitary 5,000

Conscript liability Selective conscription, 2 years

ORGANISATIONS BY SERVICE

Army 11,900 (incl conscripts)
7 Mil Zone HQ
FORCES BY ROLE
MANOEUVRE
  Reconnaissance
  4 armd recce bn
  Light
  1 cdo bn
  6 inf bn
  Air Manoeuvre
  1 AB bn
  Other
  1 (Presidential Guard) horse cav bn
COMBAT SUPPORT
  1 arty bn
  1 engr bn
  1 sigs bn
COMBAT SERVICE SUPPORT
  3 construction coy
  1 log bn
  1 med bn
  1 trg bn
EQUIPMENT BY TYPE
RECCE 124: 30 AML-60; 74 AML-90; 10 M8; 4 M20; 6+ RAM-2000
AIFV 26 *Ratel-20*
APC 36
  APC (T) 12 M3 half-track
  APC (W) 16 M3 Panhard
  PPV 8 *Casspir*
ARTY 36
  TOWED 20: **105mm** 6 HM-2/M101; **155mm** 14: ε6 Model-50; 8 TR-F1
  MOR 16: **81mm** 8 Brandt; **120mm** 8 Brandt
AT • MSL • MANPATS 4 *Milan*
  RL 89mm 31 LRAC
AD • GUNS • TOWED 33: **20mm** 21 M-693; **40mm** 12 L/60

Navy (incl Coast Guard) 950
EQUIPMENT BY TYPE
PATROL AND COASTAL COMBATANTS 11
  PCC 4: 1 *Fouta* (DNK *Osprey*); 1 *Njambour* (FRA SFCN 59m) with 2 76mm gun; 2 *Saint Louis†* (PR-48)
  PBF 1 *Ferlo* (RPB 33)
  PB 6: 2 *Alioune Samb*; 2 *Alphonse Faye* (operated by Fisheries Protection Directorate); 1 *Conejera*; 1 *Senegal II*
AMPHIBIOUS • LANDING CRAFT 5
  LCT 2 *Edic 700*
  LCM 3
LOGISTICS AND SUPPORT 3
  AG 1
  YAG 1 *Archangel*
  YTM 1

Air Force 750
FORCES BY ROLE
MARITIME PATROL/SEARCH & RESCUE
  1 sqn with C-212 *Aviocar*; CN-235; Bell 205 (UH-1H *Iroquois*)
ISR
  1 unit with BN-2T *Islander* (anti-smuggling patrols)
TRANSPORT
  1 sqn with B-727-200 (VIP); F-27-400M *Troopship*
TRAINING
  1 sqn with R-235 *Guerrier**; TB-30 *Epsilon*
ATTACK/TRANSPORT HELICOPTER
  1 sqn with AS355F *Ecureuil II*; Bell 206; Mi-35P *Hind*; Mi-171Sh
EQUIPMENT BY TYPE
AIRCRAFT 1 combat capable
  TPT 11: **Light** 9: 1 BN-2T *Islander* (govt owned, mil op); 1 C-212-100 *Aviocar*; 2 CN-235; 2 Beech B200 *King Air*; 3 F-27-400M *Troopship* (3 more in store); **PAX** 2: 1 A319; 1 B-727-200 (VIP)
  TRG 3: 1 R-235 *Guerrier**; 2 TB-30 *Epsilon*
HELICOPTERS
  ATK 2 Mi-35P *Hind*
  MRH 1 AW139
  TPT 8: **Medium** 2 Mi-171Sh; **Light** 6: 1 AS355F *Ecureuil II*; 1 Bell 205 (UH-1H *Iroquois*); 2 Bell 206; 2 Mi-2 *Hoplite*

Paramilitary 5,000

Gendarmerie 5,000
APC (W) 24: 12 *Gila*; 12 VXB-170

Customs
PATROL AND COASTAL COMBATANTS • PB 2 VCSM

DEPLOYMENT

CENTRAL AFRICAN REPUBLIC
UN • MINUSCA 2; 1 obs

CÔTE D'IVOIRE
UN • UNOCI 463; 5 obs; 1 inf bn

DEMOCRATIC REPUBLIC OF THE CONGO
UN • MONUSCO 19; 6 obs

GUINEA-BISSAU
ECOWAS • ECOMIB 200

LIBERIA
UN • UNMIL 1

MALI
UN • MINUSMA 473; 1 inf bn HQ; 1 inf coy; 1 arty coy; 1 engr coy

SOUTH SUDAN
UN • UNMISS 3; 3 obs

SUDAN
UN • UNAMID 803; 4 obs; 1 inf bn

FOREIGN FORCES
France 350; 1 *Falcon* 50MI; 1 C-160 *Transall*

Seychelles SYC

Seychelles Rupee SR		2013	2014	2015
GDP	SR	16.7bn	18.1bn	
	US$	1.39bn	1.47bn	
per capita	US$	14,918	15,674	
Growth	%	3.5	3.7	
Inflation	%	4.3	3.6	
Def bdgt	SR	ε155m		
	US$	ε13m		
US$1=SR		12.07	12.27	

Population 91,650

Age	0–14	15–19	20–24	25–29	30–64	65 plus
Male	10.7%	3.5%	3.9%	4.3%	25.9%	2.8%
Female	10.2%	3.3%	3.5%	3.8%	23.5%	4.5%

Capabilities
Piracy is a primary concern for the small People's Defence Forces, with the coast guard and the air force engaged in anti-piracy activities.

ACTIVE 420 (Land Forces 200; Coast Guard 200; Air Force 20)

ORGANISATIONS BY SERVICE

People's Defence Force

Land Forces 200
FORCES BY ROLE
SPECIAL FORCES
  1 SF unit
MANOEUVRE
  Light
    1 inf coy

Other
  1 sy unit
COMBAT SUPPORT
  1 MP unit
EQUIPMENT BY TYPE†
RECCE 6 BRDM-2†
ARTY• MOR 82mm 6 M-43†
AD • SAM • MANPAD 10 9K32 *Strela*-2 (SA-7 *Grail*) ‡
GUNS • TOWED 14.5mm ZPU-2†; ZPU-4†; **37mm** M-1939†

Coast Guard 200 (incl 80 Marines)
EQUIPMENT BY TYPE
PATROL AND COASTAL COMBATANTS 9
  PCC 2: 1 *Andromache* (ITA *Pichiotti* 42m); 1 *Topaz*
  PB 7: 2 *Aries*; 1 *Junon*; 2 Rodman 101; 1 *Shanghai* II; 1 *Fortune* (UK *Tyne*)

Air Force 20
EQUIPMENT BY TYPE
AIRCRAFT
TPT • Light 5: 3 DHC-6-320 *Twin Otter*; 2 Y-12

FOREIGN FORCES
United States US Africa Command: some MQ-9 *Reaper* UAV

Sierra Leone SLE

Sierra Leonean Leone L		2013	2014	2015
GDP	L	21.4tr	24tr	
	US$	4.92bn	5.41bn	
per capita	US$	805	868	
Growth	%	20.1	8.0	
Inflation	%	9.8	8.8	
Def bdgt	L	65.3bn	67.6bn	68.2bn
	US$	15m	15m	
US$1=L		4,345.03	4,435.98	

Population 5,743,725

Age	0–14	15–19	20–24	25–29	30–64	65 plus
Male	20.9%	4.8%	4.3%	3.8%	13.1%	1.6%
Female	21.0%	5.1%	4.6%	4.1%	14.5%	2.1%

Capabilities
The armed forces' primary task is internal security, and there has been much focus on institutional development of the armed forces, with international support. The improved overall internal security environment was reflected by the end of the UN's 15-year-long peacekeeping mission in early 2014. The army has also been used to try to quarantine areas affected by the outbreak of the Ebola virus in 2014. Training has been provided by the US and the UK, and the army takes part in peacekeeping operations, most notably through its deployment of a battalion to AMISOM in Somalia.

ACTIVE 10,500 (Joint 10,500)

ORGANISATIONS BY SERVICE

Armed Forces 10,500
FORCES BY ROLE
MANOEUVRE
  Light
  3 inf bde (total: 12 inf bn)
EQUIPMENT BY TYPE
ARTY • MOR 31: 81mm ε27; 82mm 2; 120mm 2
AT • RCL 84mm *Carl Gustav*
HELICOPTERS • MRH/TPT 2 Mi-17 *Hip* H/Mi-8 *Hip*† AD • GUNS 7: 12.7mm 4; 14.5mm 3

Navy ε200
EQUIPMENT BY TYPE
PATROL AND COASTAL COMBATANTS • PB 2: 1 *Shanghai* III; 1 *Isle of Man*

DEPLOYMENT

LEBANON
UN • UNIFIL 3

MALI
UN • MINUSMA 4

SOMALIA
AU • AMISOM 850; 1 inf bn

SUDAN
UN • UNAMID 6; 9 obs
UN • UNISFA 1 obs

FOREIGN FORCES
United Kingdom 750; 1 AG; 3 AW101 ASW *Merlin* HM2

Somalia SOM

Somali Shilling sh		2012	2013	2014
GDP	US$			
per capita	US$			

*Definitive economic data unavailable
US$1=sh

Population 10,428,043

Age	0–14	15–19	20–24	25–29	30–64	65 plus
Male	22.0%	5.1%	4.4%	3.8%	14.1%	0.9%
Female	22.0%	5.1%	4.2%	3.7%	13.3%	1.4%

Capabilities

Somalia's armed forces are only developing, and the authorities are still reliant on international support to tackle the principal threat to national stability emanating from al-Shabaab jihadists. Until two major AMISOM operations in 2014, al-Shabaab controlled substantial territory; it still remains capable of mounting terrorist attacks. An internationally backed attempt to forge a Somali National Army has produced a force trained by AMISOM, the EU and private security companies. The SNA is infantry-heavy but support- and logistics-light, meaning that there are challenges in terms of conventional-force sustainment and organisation. With the decline in Somalia-based piracy, international focus on developing the SNA could sharpen (an EU objective is to boost integration of various clan-based militias into the SNA) but it remains unclear how long AMISOM will stay. In some cases, government forces have been accompanied on operations by allied militias. Somaliland and Puntland have their own militias, while a privately funded Puntland Maritime Police Force operates a small number of rigid inflatable boats and small aircraft. (See pp. 427–29.)

ACTIVE 11,000 (Army 11,000)

ORGANISATIONS BY SERVICE

Army ε11,000 (plus ε10,000 militias)
FORCES BY ROLE
COMMAND
  1 (21st) div HQ
MANOEUVRE
  Light
  Some cdo unit
  6 inf bde (total: ε18 inf bn)

FOREIGN FORCES
Burundi AMISOM 5,432; 6 inf bn
Djibouti AMISOM 960; 1 inf bn
Ethiopia AMISOM 4,395; 4 inf bn
Kenya AMISOM 3,664; 3 inf bn
Sierra Leone AMISOM 850; 1 inf bn
Uganda AMISOM 6,223; 7 inf bn

TERRITORY WHERE THE RECOGNISED AUTHORITY (SNG) DOES NOT EXERCISE EFFECTIVE CONTROL

Data presented here represents the de facto situation. This does not imply international recognition as a sovereign state.

Somaliland
Population 3.5m

Militia unit strengths are not known. Equipment numbers are generalised assessments; most of this equipment is in poor repair or inoperable.

ORGANISATIONS BY SERVICE

Army ε15,000
FORCES BY ROLE
MANOEUVRE
  Armoured
  2 armd bde

Mechanised
1 mech inf bde
Light
14 inf bde
COMBAT SUPPORT
2 arty bde
COMBAT SERVICE SUPPORT
1 spt bn
EQUIPMENT BY TYPE†
MBT 33: M47; T54/55
RECCE AML-90; BRDM-2
APC
  APC (T) BTR-50
  APC(W) 15-20 Fiat 6614
ARTY 69
  TOWED 122mm 12 D-30
  MRL: 8-12 BM-21 *Grad*
  MOR 45: 81mm; 120mm
AT • RCL 106mm 16 M40A1
AD • GUNS • TOWED 20mm; some 23mm ZU-23

Coast Guard 600

Ministry of the Interior
EQUIPMENT BY TYPE
PATROL AND COASTAL COMBATANTS 26
  PB 7 *Dolphin* 26
  PBR 19

Puntland

Armed Forces ε5,000–10,000; coast guard

South Africa RSA

South African Rand R		2013	2014	2015
GDP	R	3.39tr	3.65tr	
	US$	351bn	341bn	
per capita	US$	6,621	6,354	
Growth	%	1.9	1.4	
Inflation	%	5.8	6.3	
Def bdgt	R	40.7bn	42.8bn	45.3bn
	US$	4.21bn	4.01bn	
FMA (US)	US$	0.7m	0.7m	0.45m
US$1=R		9.65	10.69	

Population   48,375,645

Age	0–14	15–19	20–24	25–29	30–64	65 plus
Male	14.2%	4.9%	5.3%	5.3%	17.5%	2.5%
Female	14.1%	4.9%	5.2%	5.0%	17.5%	3.8%

Capabilities

The National Defence Force remains on paper the most capable force in the region, despite financial and structural problems, which have eroded capacity in many areas. There is some capacity for power projection, limited by the four C-130s available, lack of military sealift and by the impact of funding constraints. Maritime security is a growing concern, illustrated by an ongoing counter-piracy mission in the Mozambique Channel. The March 2014 defence review highlighted the SANDF's troubles, and contained a prioritisation plan to rebuild capability. The defence budget was assessed to be 24% short of the necessary funding. It is to increase by 6% over the next two years, but some analysts assess that this will be insufficient to reverse this decline. Equipment recapitalisation efforts in all services have been delayed by funding problems, although Germany's Rheinmetall has been contracted to upgrade air defences and new OPVs have been funded. The armed forces still deploy regularly on peacekeeping missions and participate in multinational exercises; together with the demand from operations this can cause overstretch, particularly in the army. Historically South African forces have also played a significant role in training and supporting other regional forces. They are a key contributor to the UN's intervention brigade in eastern DRC and plan to offer a combined-arms battalion to the African Capacity for Immediate Response to Crises, set up in 2013.

ACTIVE 62,100 (Army 37,150 Navy 6,250 Air 10,650 South African Military Health Service 8,050)

RESERVE 15,050 (Army 12,250 Navy 850 Air 850 South African Military Health Service Reserve 1,100)

ORGANISATIONS BY SERVICE

Army 37,150
FORCES BY ROLE
Formations under direct command and control of SANDF Chief of Joint Operations: 9 Joint Operational Tactical HQs, troops are provided when necessary by permanent and reserve force units from all services and SF Bde. A new army structure is planned with 2 divisions (1 mechanised, 1 motorised) with 10 bdes (1 armd, 1 mech, 7 motorised and 1 rapid reaction). Training, Support and Land Commands are also planned, while Divisional HQ is to be re-established.
COMMAND
2 bde HQ
SPECIAL FORCES
1 SF bde (2 SF bn(-))
MANOEUVRE
  Reconnaissance
  1 armd recce bn
  Armoured
  1 tk bn
  Mechanised
  2 mech inf bn
  Light
  10 mot inf bn (1 bn roles as AB, 1 as amph)
COMBAT SUPPORT
1 arty bn
1 ADA bn
1 engr regt

COMBAT SERVICE SUPPORT
2 maint units
1 construction bn

Reserve 12,250 reservists (under strength)
FORCES BY ROLE
MANOEUVRE
  Reconnaissance
  2 armd recce bn
  1 recce bn
  Armoured
  3 tk bn
  Mechanised
  6 mech inf bn
  Light
  16 mot inf bn (1 bn roles as AB, 1 as amph)
  3 lt inf bn (converting to mot inf)
  Air Manoeuvre
  1 AB bn
COMBAT SUPPORT
  7 arty regt
  4 AD regt
  2 engr regt
EQUIPMENT BY TYPE
MBT 34 *Olifant* 1A (133 *Olifant* 1B in store)
RECCE 82 *Rooikat-76* (94 in store)
AIFV 534 *Ratel-20/Ratel-60/Ratel-90*
PPV 810: 370 *Casspir*; 440 *Mamba*
ARTY 1,255
  SP 155mm 2 G-6 (41 in store)
  TOWED 140mm (75 G-2 in store); **155mm** 6 G-5 (66 in store)
  MRL 127mm 21: (26 *Valkiri* Mk I in store) (24 tube)); 21 *Valkiri* Mk II MARS *Bateleur* (40 tube); (4 in store (40 tube))
  MOR 1,226: **81mm** 1,190 (incl some SP); **120mm** 36
AT
  MSL • MANPATS ZT-3 *Swift*; Milan ADT/ER
  RCL 106mm M40A1 (some SP)
  RL 92mm FT-5
AD • GUNS 76
  SP 23mm 36 *Zumlan*
  TOWED 35mm 40 GDF-002
RADAR • LAND ESR 220 *Kameelperd*; 2 Thales *Page*
ARV *Gemsbok*
VLB *Leguan*
UAV • ISR • Light up to 4 *Vulture*

Navy 6,250
Fleet HQ and Naval base located at Simon's Town; Naval stations located at Durban and Port Elizabeth
EQUIPMENT BY TYPE
SUBMARINES • TACTICAL • SSK 3 *Heroine* (Type-209) with 8 533mm TT with AEW SUT 264 HWT (of which one cyclically in reserve/refit)
PRINCIPAL SURFACE COMBATANTS • FRIGATES 4:
  FFGHM 4 *Valour* (MEKO A200) with 2 quad lnchr with MM-40 *Exocet* AShM (upgrade to Block III planned); 2 16-cell VLS with *Umkhonto*-IR SAM, 1 76mm gun (capacity 1 *Super Lynx* 300 hel)

PATROL AND COASTAL COMBATANTS 6
  PCC 3 *Warrior* (ISR *Reshef*) with 2 76mm gun
  PB 3 *Tobie*
MINE WARFARE • MINE COUNTERMEASURES 2
  MHC 2 *River* (GER *Navors*) (Limited operational roles; training and dive support); (additional vessel in reserve)
AMPHIBIOUS • LCU 6 *Lima*
LOGISTICS AND SUPPORT 7
  AORH 1 *Drakensberg* (capacity 4 LCU; 100 troops)
  AGHS 1 *Protea* (UK *Hecla*)
  YTM 5

Air Force 10,650
Air Force office, Pretoria, and 4 op gps
Command & Control: 2 Airspace Control Sectors, 1 Mobile Deployment Wg, 1 Air Force Command Post
FORCES BY ROLE
FIGHTER/GROUND ATTACK
  1 sqn with *Gripen* C/D (JAS-39C/D)
TRANSPORT
  1 (VIP) sqn with B-737 BBJ; Cessna 550 *Citation* II; *Falcon* 50; *Falcon* 900;
  1 sqn with BT-67 (C-47TP)
  2 sqn with C-130B/BZ *Hercules*; C-212; Cessna 185; CN-235
  9 (AF Reserve) sqn with ε130 private lt tpt ac
TRAINING
  1 (Lead-in Ftr Trg) sqn with *Hawk* Mk120*
ATTACK HELICOPTER
  1 (cbt spt) sqn with AH-2 *Rooivalk*
TRANSPORT HELICOPTER
  4 (mixed) sqn with AW109; BK-117; *Oryx*
EQUIPMENT BY TYPE
AIRCRAFT 50 combat capable
  FGA 26: 17 *Gripen* C (JAS-39C); 9 *Gripen* D (JAS-39D)
  TPT 34: **Medium** 7 C-130B/BZ *Hercules*; **Light** 23: 3 Beech 200C *King Air*; 1 Beech 300 *King Air*; 3 BT-67 (C-47TP - maritime); 2 C-212-200 *Aviocar*; 1 C-212-300 *Aviocar*; 10 Cessna 208 *Caravan*; 2 Cessna 550 *Citation* II; 1 PC-12; **PAX** 4: 1 B-737BBJ; 2 *Falcon* 50; 1 *Falcon* 900
  TRG 74: 24 *Hawk* Mk120*; 50 PC-7 Mk II *Astra*
HELICOPTERS
  ATK 11 AH-2 *Rooivalk* (Only 5 in service as of late 2012)
  MRH 4 *Super Lynx* 300
  TPT 75: **Medium** 39 *Oryx*; **Light** 36: 28 AW109; 8 BK-117
UAV • ISR • Medium *Seeker* II
MSL • AAM • IR V3C *Darter*; **IIR** IRIS-T

Ground Defence
FORCES BY ROLE
MANOEUVRE
  Other
  12 sy sqn (SAAF regt)
EQUIPMENT BY TYPE
2 Radar (static) located at Ellisras and Mariepskop; 2 (mobile long-range); 4 (tactical mobile). Radar air control sectors located at Pretoria, Hoedspruit

South African Military Health Service 8,050; ε1,100 reservists (total 9,150)

Department of Agriculture, Fisheries and Forestry

EQUIPMENT BY TYPE
PATROL AND COASTAL COMBATANTS 4
 PSO 1 *Sarah Baartman*
 PBO 3 *Lilian Nyogi*
LOGISTICS AND SUPPORT • AGE 2: 1 *Africana*; 1 *Ellen Khuzmayo*

Department of Environmental Affairs

EQUIPMENT BY TYPE
LOGISTICS AND SUPPORT • AGOS 1 *S A Agulhas* II (used for Antarctic survey)

DEPLOYMENT

DEMOCRATIC REPUBLIC OF THE CONGO
UN • MONUSCO • *Operation Mistral* 1,343; 4 obs; 1 inf bn; 1 atk hel coy; 1 hel coy; 1 engr coy

MOZAMBIQUE CHANNEL
Navy • 1 FFGHM

SUDAN
UN • UNAMID • *Operation Cordite* 809; 15 obs; 1 inf bn

South Sudan SSD

South Sudanese Pound d		2013	2014	2015
GDP	ssp	41.4bn	35.1bn	
	US$	14bn	11.9bn	
per capita	US$	1,289	1,045	
Growth	%	27.1	-12.3	
Inflation	%	-0.0	0.2	
Def bdgt [a]	ssp	2.54bn	3.08bn	3.97bn
	US$	862m	1.04bn	
FMA (US)	US$			0.2m
US$1=ssp		2.95	2.95	

[a] Security and law enforcement spending.

Population 11,562,695

Age	0–14	15–19	20–24	25–29	30–64	65 plus
Male	23.3%	5.9%	4.6%	3.7%	12.1%	1.2%
Female	22.4%	5.2%	4.2%	3.6%	12.9%	0.9%

Capabilities

Security concerns are dominated by continuing friction with Sudan and political and ethnic factionalism, highlighted in late 2013 and 2014 when military units from the Sudan People's Liberation Army defected to support the dissident former vice-president Riek Machar. While President Salva Kiir has attempted to consolidate his control over the armed forces, there remains disaffection and a significant rebel faction that resists a ceasefire agreement. Three divisions split, with some formed units and equipment going to rebel forces. However, as both sides originated in the national army, they share the same basic equipment and tactics, though the government side enjoys wider tactical and logistic options. Ukraine and China have been sources of new equipment, and prior to the recent conflict there was international assistance in establishing the foundations of a security structure, such as NCO academies. DDR and SSR are on hold pending the resolution of the fighting and after the SPLA's internal breakdown subsequent reform initiatives are unlikely to be solely focused on defence transformation and capability development; developing institutional capacity and accountability will likely also become a key task.

ACTIVE 185,000 (Army 185,000)

ORGANISATIONS BY SERVICE

Army ε185,000
FORCES BY ROLE
3 military comd
MANOEUVRE
 Light
 8 inf div
COMBAT SUPPORT
 1 engr corps
EQUIPMENT BY TYPE
MBT 80+: some T-55†; 80 T-72AV†
APC (W) Streit *Typhoon*; Streit *Cougar*; *Mamba*
ARTY 69+
 SP 122mm 2S1; **152mm** 2S3
 TOWED 130mm Some M-46
 MRL 122mm BM-21; **107mm** Type-63
 MOR 82mm; **120mm** Type-55 look-alike
AT
 MSL • MANPATS HJ-73; 9K115 *Metis* (AT-5 *Saxhorn*)
 RCL 73mm SPG-9 (with SSLA)
AD
 SAM • MANPAD 9K32 *Strela*-2 (SA-7 *Grail*)‡; 9K310 *Igla*-1 (SA-16 *Gimlet*)
 GUNS 14.5mm ZPU-4; **23mm** ZU-23-2; **37mm** Type-65/74

Air Force
EQUIPMENT BY TYPE
AIRCRAFT • TPT • Light 1 Beech 1900
HELICOPTERS
 MRH 9 Mi-17 *Hip* H
 TPT 3: **Medium** 1 Mi-172 (VIP); **Light** 2 AW109 (civ livery)

FOREIGN FORCES

All UNMISS, unless otherwise indicated
Australia 18; 4 obs
Bangladesh 275; 4 obs; 1 engr coy
Belarus 4 obs
Bolivia 3 obs
Brazil 3; 4 obs

Cambodia 145; 3 obs; 1 fd hospital
Canada 5; 5 obs
China, People's Republic of 347; 3 obs; 1 engr coy; 1 fd hospital
Denmark 13; 2 obs
Egypt 3 obs
El Salvador 2 obs
Ethiopia 1,250; 3 inf bn(-)
Fiji 4; 2 obs
Germany 7; 7 obs
Ghana 304; 6 obs; 1 inf bn(-)
Guatemala 3; 2 obs
Guinea 2 obs
India 2,250; 5 obs; 2 inf bn; 1 engr coy; 1 fd hospital
Indonesia 3 obs
Japan 271; 1 engr coy
Jordan 3; 3 obs
Kenya 694; 6 obs; 1 inf bn
Korea, Republic of 273; 2 obs; 1 engr coy
Kyrgyzstan 2 obs
Mali 3 obs
Moldova 1
Mongolia 856; 2 obs; 1 inf bn
Namibia 2 obs
Nepal 1,710; 4 obs; 2 inf bn
Netherlands 6; 2 obs
New Zealand 1; 2 obs
Nigeria 1; 4 obs
Norway 10; 3 obs
Papua New Guinea 1 obs
Paraguay 3 obs
Peru 2 obs
Poland 2 obs
Romania 2; 5 obs
Russia 3; 2 obs
Rwanda 1,777; 3 obs; 2 inf bn
Sri Lanka 89; 2 obs; 1 fd hospital
Sweden 2; 3 obs
Switzerland 1; 2 obs
Tanzania 4; 2 obs
Timor-Leste 3 obs
Togo 1
Uganda 2
Ukraine 1; 3 obs
United Kingdom 4
United States 5
Vietnam 2 obs
Yemen 3; 7 obs
Zambia 4; 3 obs
Zimbabwe 2 obs

Sudan SDN

Sudanese Pound sdg		2013	2014	2015
GDP	sdg	318bn	435bn	
	US$	66.7bn	70bn	
per capita	US$	1,941	1,985	
Growth	%	3.3	3.0	
Inflation	%	36.5	38.0	
Def bdgt	sdg	ε9bn		
	US$	ε1.89bn		
US$1=sdg			4.76	6.21

Population 35,482,233

Ethnic and religious groups: Muslim 70% mainly in North; Christian 10% mainly in South; Arab 39% mainly in North

Age	0–14	15–19	20–24	25–29	30–64	65 plus
Male	20.7%	5.7%	4.7%	3.9%	13.6%	1.8%
Female	20.1%	5.3%	4.5%	3.9%	14.3%	1.5%

Capabilities

Sudan retains large armed forces with significant holdings of ageing and at times obsolete equipment, although in regional terms the services are reasonably well equipped. The country likely has limited regional power-projection capabilities, with a significant fixed- and rotary-wing airlift capacity, though the primary focus remains ongoing tensions with South Sudan and counter-insurgency. The armed forces are also involved in clashes with rebels in the south of the country, in the Blue Nile and South Kordofan provinces. A mixture of Russian and Chinese equipment is operated, although the indigenous Military Industry Corporation is able to manufacture ammunition, small arms and light vehicles. The air force, though small, fields several comparatively modern combat-aircraft types, including the MiG-29 *Fulcrum* and Su-25 *Frogfoot*. Tactical airlift is provided by a variety of transport aircraft. The navy is limited to littoral and river patrols.

ACTIVE 244,300 (Army 240,000 Navy 1,300 Air 3,000) **Paramilitary 20,000**
Conscript liability 2 years for males aged 18–30

RESERVE NIL Paramilitary 85,000

ORGANISATIONS BY SERVICE

Army ε240,000
FORCES BY ROLE
SPECIAL FORCES
  5 SF coy
MANOEUVRE
  Reconnaissance
  1 indep recce bde
  Armoured
  1 armd div

Mechanised
1 mech inf div
1 indep mech inf bde
Light
11+ inf div
6 indep inf bde
Air Manoeuvre
1 AB div
Other
1 (Border Guard) sy bde
COMBAT SUPPORT
3 indep arty bde
1 engr div (9 engr bn)
EQUIPMENT BY TYPE
MBT 465: 20 M60A3; 60 Type-59/Type-59D; 305 T-54/T-55; 70 T-72M1; 10 *Al-Bashier* (Type-85-IIM)
LT TK 115: 70 Type-62; 45 Type-63
RECCE 248: 6 AML-90; 70 BRDM-1/2; 50–80 *Ferret*; 42 M1114 HMMWV; 30–50 *Saladin*
AIFV 152: 135 BMP-1/2; 10 BTR-3; 7 BTR-80A
APC 412
  APC (T) 66: 20-30 BTR-50; 36 M113
  APC (W) 346: 10 BTR 70; 50–80 BTR-152; 20 OT-62; 50 OT-64; 10 Type-92 (reported); 55-80 V-150 *Commando*; 96 *Walid*
ARTY 860+
  SP 66: **122mm** 56 2S1; **155mm** 10 (AMX) Mk F3
  TOWED 128+ **105mm** 20 M101; **122mm** 21+: 21 D-30; D-74; M-30; **130mm** 87: 75 M-46/Type-59-I; 12 M114A1
  MRL 666+: **107mm** 477 Type-63; **122mm** 188: 120 BM-21; 50 *Saqr*; 18 Type-81; **302mm** 1+ WS-1
  MOR 81mm; **82mm**; **120mm** AM-49; M-43
AT • MSL • MANPATS *Swingfire*; 9K11 *Malyutka* (AT-3 *Sagger*)
  RCL 106mm 40 M40A1
  GUNS 40+: 40 **76mm** ZIS-3/**100mm** M-1944; **85mm** D-44
AD • SAM • MANPAD 9K32 *Strela*-2 (SA-7 *Grail*)‡
  GUNS 996+
  SP 20: **20mm** 8 M163 *Vulcan*; 12 M3 VDAA
  TOWED 946+: 740+ **14.5mm** ZPU-2/**14.5mm** ZPU-4/**37mm** Type-63/**57mm** S-60/**85mm** M-1944; **20mm** 16 M167 *Vulcan*; **23mm** 50 ZU-23-2; **37mm** 80 M-1939; (30 M-1939 unserviceable); **40mm** 60
RADAR • LAND RASIT (veh, arty)

Navy 1,300
EQUIPMENT BY TYPE
PATROL AND COASTAL COMBATANTS 4
  PBR 4 *Kurmuk*
AMPHIBIOUS • LANDING CRAFT 7
  LCT 2 *Sobat*
  LCVP 5
LOGISTICS AND SUPPORT 2
  AG 1
  AWT 1 *Baraka*

Air Force 3,000
FORCES BY ROLE
FIGHTER
2 sqn with MiG-29SE/UB *Fulcrum*

GROUND ATTACK
1 sqn with A-5 *Fantan*
1 sqn with Su-25/Su-25UB *Frogfoot*
TRANSPORT
Some sqn with An-26 *Curl** (modified for bombing); An-30 *Clank*; An-32 *Cline*; An-72 *Coaler*; An-74TK-200/300; C-130H *Hercules*; Il-76 *Candid*; Y-8
1 VIP unit with *Falcon* 20F; *Falcon* 50; *Falcon* 900; F-27; Il-62M *Classic*
TRAINING
1 sqn with K-8 *Karakorum**
ATTACK HELICOPTER
2 sqn with Mi-24/Mi-24P/Mi-24V/Mi-35P *Hind*
TRANSPORT HELICOPTER
2 sqn with Mi-8 *Hip*; Mi-17 *Hip* H; Mi-171
AIR DEFENCE
5 bty with S-75 *Dvina* (SA-2 *Guideline*)‡
EQUIPMENT BY TYPE
AIRCRAFT 63 combat capable
  FTR 22: 20 MiG-29SE *Fulcrum*; 2 MiG-29UB *Fulcrum*
  ATK 29+: 15 A-5 *Fantan*; 3+ Su-24 *Fencer*; 9 Su-25 *Frogfoot*; 2 Su-25UB *Frogfoot* B
  ISR 2 An-30 *Clank*
  TPT 23: **Heavy** 1 Il-76 *Candid*; **Medium** 6: 4 C-130H *Hercules*; 2 Y-8; **Light** 12: 1 An-26 *Curl** (modified for bombing); 2 An-32 *Cline*; 2 An-72 *Coaler*; 4 An-74TK-200; 2 An-74TK-300; 1 F-27 (VIP); **PAX** 4: 1 *Falcon* 20F (VIP); 1 *Falcon* 50 (VIP); 1 Falcon 900; 1 Il-62M *Classic*
  TRG 15: 12 K-8 *Karakorum**; 3 UTVA-75
HELICOPTERS
  ATK 40: 25 Mi-24 *Hind*; 2 Mi-24P *Hind*; 7 Mi-24V *Hind* E; 6 Mi-35P *Hind*
  MRH ε5 Mi-17 *Hip* H
  TPT 24: **Medium** 23: 21 Mi-8 *Hip*; 2 Mi-171; **Light** 1 Bell 205
AD • SAM • TOWED: 90 S-75 *Dvina* (SA-2 *Guideline*)‡
MSL • AAM • IR R-3 (AA-2 *Atoll*)‡; R-60 (AA-8 *Aphid*); R-73 (AA-11 *Archer*); **IR/SARH** R-23/24 (AA-7 *Apex*); **ARH** R-77 (AA-12 *Adder*)

Paramilitary 20,000

Popular Defence Force 20,000 (org in bn 1,000); 85,000 reservists (total 102,500)
mil wing of National Islamic Front

FOREIGN FORCES
All UNAMID, unless otherwise indicated
Bangladesh 220; 15 obs; 1 inf coy
Benin UNISFA 1; 1 obs
Bolivia 2
Brazil UNISFA 2; 2 obs
Burkina Faso 807; 10 obs; 1 inf bn • UNISFA 1 obs
Burundi 2; 7 obs • UNISFA 1 obs
Cambodia 3 • UNISFA 3 obs
China, People's Republic of 233; 1 engr coy
Ecuador 1; 1 obs; • UNISFA 1; 1 obs
Egypt 892; 23 obs; 1 inf bn; 1 tpt coy
El Salvador UNISFA 1 obs

Ethiopia 2,537; 16 obs; 3 inf bn • UNISFA 3,887; 74 obs; 1 recce coy; 1 armd coy; 1 mech inf bn; 2 inf bn; 1 hel sqn; 2 arty coy; 1 engr coy; 1 sigs coy; 1 fd hospital
Gambia 215; 1 inf coy
Germany 10
Ghana 18; 8 obs • UNISFA 2; 3 obs
Guatemala UNISFA 1; 2 obs
Guinea UNISFA 1 obs
India UNISFA 2
Indonesia 1; 3 obs • UNISFA 2; 2 obs
Iran 2 obs
Jordan 12; 15 obs
Kenya 111; 6 obs; 1 MP coy
Korea, Republic of 2
Kyrgyzstan 2 • UNISFA 1 obs
Lesotho 2 obs
Malaysia 13; 3 obs • UNISFA 1 obs
Mali 6 obs • UNISFA 1
Mongolia 70; 1 fd hospital • UNISFA 2 obs
Mozambique UNISFA 1 obs
Namibia 2; 9 obs • UNISFA 1; 3 obs
Nepal 364; 15 obs; 1 SF coy; 1 inf coy
Nigeria 937; 10 obs; 1 inf bn • UNISFA 3; 3 obs
Pakistan 1,301; 5 obs; 1 inf bn; 2 engr coy; 1 med pl
Palau 1; 1 obs
Peru 4 • UNISFA 2
Russia UNISFA 1 obs
Rwanda 3,236; 10 obs; 4 inf bn • UNISFA 1; 2 obs
Senegal 812; 17 obs; 1 inf bn
Sierra Leone 6; 9 obs • UNISFA 1 obs
South Africa 809; 15 obs; 1 inf bn
Sri Lanka UNISFA 1; 5 obs
Tanzania 815; 20 obs; 1 inf bn • UNISFA 1 obs
Thailand 6; 9 obs
Togo 6 obs
Ukraine UNISFA 2; 4 obs
Yemen, Republic of 12; 41 obs • UNISFA 2; 3 obs
Zambia 5; 13 obs • UNISFA 1; 2 obs
Zimbabwe 2; 5 obs • UNISFA 1; 2 obs

Tanzania TZA

Tanzanian Shilling sh		2013	2014	2015
GDP	sh	53.2tr	60.1tr	
	US$	33.3bn	36.6bn	
per capita	US$	719	768	
Growth	%	7.0	7.2	
Inflation	%	7.9	5.9	
Def exp	sh	621bn		
	US$	389m		
Def bdgt [a]	sh	531bn	651bn	
	US$	333m	396m	
FMA (US)	US$	0.2m	0.2m	
US$1=sh		1,597.56	1,641.97	

[a] Excludes expenditure on Ministry of Defence administration and National Service

Population 49,639,138

Age	0–14	15–19	20–24	25–29	30–64	65 plus
Male	22.5%	5.3%	4.4%	3.9%	12.4%	1.3%
Female	22.1%	5.3%	4.5%	3.9%	12.8%	1.7%

Capabilities

Tanzania's ability to revamp an ageing equipment inventory is hampered by a limited budget. This reflects a relatively benign security environment, although there remain concerns about instability in the DRC, piracy and internal stability. A buoyant relationship with the country's main trading partner, China, has led to a series of procurement programmes, including fighter and jet-trainer aircraft, armoured vehicles and multiple-rocket launchers, as well as training contacts. In September 2014, authorities claimed that a modernisation programme would lead to a reduction in personnel numbers and more equipment procurement, although no details were released. A small tactical-transport fleet provides some intra-theatre mobility but otherwise there is limited ability to project power independently beyond its own territory. In recent years, Tanzania has regularly taken part in multinational exercises in Africa and provided some training assistance to other African forces. Its contribution to the UN's Force Intervention Brigade in the eastern DRC, notably its special forces, will have provided many lessons for force development.

ACTIVE 27,000 (Army 23,000 Navy 1,000 Air 3,000)
Paramilitary 1,400
Conscript liability National service reintroduced in 2012 for those aged 18–23. Three months basic military training combined with social service.

RESERVE 80,000 (Joint 80,000)

ORGANISATIONS BY SERVICE

Army ε23,000

FORCES BY ROLE
SPECIAL FORCES
  1 SF unit
MANOEUVRE
  Armoured
  1 tk bde
  Light
  5 inf bde
COMBAT SUPPORT
  4 arty bn
  1 mor bn
  2 AT bn
  2 ADA bn
  1 engr regt (bn)
COMBAT SERVICE SUPPORT
  1 log gp
EQUIPMENT BY TYPE†
MBT 45: 30 T-54/T-55; 15 Type-59G
LT TK 57+: 30 *Scorpion*; 25 Type-62; 2+ Type-63A
RECCE 10 BRDM-2
APC (W) 14: ε10 BTR-40/BTR-152; 4 Type-92
ARTY 384+
  TOWED 170: **76mm** ε40 ZIS-3; **122mm** 100: 20 D-30; 80 Type-54-1 (M-30); **130mm** 30 Type-59-I
  GUN/MOR **120mm** 3+ Type-07PA
  MRL 61+: **122mm** 58 BM-21; **300mm** 3+ A100
  MOR 150: **82mm** 100 M-43; **120mm** 50 M-43
AT • RCL **75mm** Type-52 (M-20)
  GUNS **85mm** 75 Type-56 (D-44)

Navy ε1,000

EQUIPMENT BY TYPE
PATROL AND COASTAL COMBATANTS 8
  PHT 2 *Huchuan* each with 2 533mm ASTT
  PB 6: 2 *Ngunguri*; 2 *Shanghai* II (PRC); 2 VT 23m
AMPHIBIOUS 3
  LCU 2 *Yuchin*
  LCT 1 *Kasa*

Air Defence Command ε3,000

FORCES BY ROLE
FIGHTER
  3 sqn with F-7/FT-7; FT-5; K-8 *Karakorum**
TRANSPORT
  1 sqn with Cessna 404 *Titan*; DHC-5D *Buffalo*; F-28 *Fellowship*; F-50; Gulfstream G550; Y-12 (II)
TRANSPORT HELICOPTER
  1 sqn with Bell 205 (AB-205); Bell 412EP *Twin Huey*
EQUIPMENT BY TYPE†
AIRCRAFT 18 combat capable
  FTR 12: 10 F-7TN; 2 FT-7TN
  TPT 12: **Medium** 2 Y-8; **Light** 7: 2 Cessna 404 *Titan*; 3 DHC-5D *Buffalo*; 2 Y-12(II); **PAX** 3: 1 F-28 *Fellowship*; 1 F-50; 1 Gulfstream G550
  TRG 9: 3 FT-5 (JJ-5); 6 K-8 *Karakorum**
HELICOPTERS
  MRH 1 Bell 412EP *Twin Huey*
  TPT • **Light** 1 Bell 205 (AB-205)

AD
  SAM 160:
    SP 40: 20 2K12 *Kub* (SA-6 *Gainful*)†; 20 S-125 *Pechora* (SA-3 *Goa*)†
    MANPAD 9K32 *Strela*-2 (SA-7 *Grail*)‡
  GUNS 200
    TOWED **14.5mm** 40 ZPU-2/ZPU-4†; **23mm** 40 ZU-23; **37mm** 120 M-1939

Paramilitary 1,400 active

Police Field Force 1,400

18 sub-units incl Police Marine Unit

Air Wing

AIRCRAFT • TPT • **Light** 1 Cessna U206 *Stationair*
HELICOPTERS
  TPT • **Light** 4: 2 Bell 206A *Jet Ranger* (AB-206A); 2 Bell 206L *Long Ranger*
  TRG 2 Bell 47G (AB-47G)/Bell 47G2

Marine Unit 100

PATROL AND COASTAL COMBATANTS • MISC BOATS/CRAFT some boats

DEPLOYMENT

CENTRAL AFRICAN REPUBLIC
UN • MINUSCA 1

CÔTE D'IVOIRE
UN • UNOCI 2; 1 obs

DEMOCRATIC REPUBLIC OF THE CONGO
UN • MONUSCO 1,264; 1 SF coy; 1 inf bn; 1 arty coy

LEBANON
UN • UNIFIL 158; 2 MP coy

SOUTH SUDAN
UN • UNMISS 4; 2 obs

SUDAN
UN • UNAMID 815; 20 obs; 1 inf bn
UN • UNISFA 1 obs

Togo TGO

CFA Franc BCEAO fr		2013	2014	2015
GDP	fr	2.14tr	2.32tr	
	US$	4.34bn	4.84bn	
per capita	US$	637	691	
Growth	%	5.1	5.6	
Inflation	%	1.8	1.5	
Def bdgt	fr	35.5bn	42.5bn	
	US$	72m	89m	
US$1=fr		493.88	479.35	

Population 7,351,374

Age	0–14	15–19	20–24	25–29	30–64	65 plus
Male	20.4%	5.2%	4.8%	4.2%	13.6%	1.4%
Female	20.3%	5.2%	4.8%	4.2%	14.0%	1.8%

Capabilities

The Togolese armed forces are adequate for the internal-security roles for which they might be used and equipment, though limited, is generally well maintained and serviceable.

ACTIVE 8,550 (Army 8,100 Navy 200 Air 250)
Paramilitary 750
Conscript liability Selective conscription, 2 years

ORGANISATIONS BY SERVICE

Army 8,100+
FORCES BY ROLE
MANOEUVRE
  Reconnaissance
  1 armd recce regt
  Light
  2 cbd arms regt
  2 inf regt
  1 rapid reaction force
  Air Manoeuvre
  1 cdo/para regt (3 cdo/para coy)
  Other
  1 (Presidential Guard) gd regt (1 gd bn, 1 cdo bn, 2 indep gd coy)
COMBAT SUPPORT
  1 spt regt (1 fd arty bty, 2 ADA bty, 1 engr/log/tpt bn)
EQUIPMENT BY TYPE
MBT 2 T-54/T-55
LT TK 9 *Scorpion*
RECCE 61: 3 AML-60; 7 AML-90; 36 EE-9 *Cascavel*; 4 M3A1; 6 M8; 3 M20; 2 VBL
AIFV 20 BMP-2
APC (W) 30 UR-416
ARTY 30
  SP 122mm 6
  TOWED 105mm 4 HM-2
  MOR 82mm 20 M-43
AT • RCL 75mm Type-52 (M-20)/Type-56; **82mm** Type-65 (B-10)
  GUNS 57mm 5 ZIS-2
AD • GUNS • TOWED 43 **14.5mm** 38 ZPU-4; **37mm** 5 M-1939

Navy ε200 (incl Marine Infantry unit)
EQUIPMENT BY TYPE
PATROL AND COASTAL COMBATANTS 3
  PBF 1 RPB 33
  PB 2 *Kara* (FRA *Esterel*)

Air Force 250
FORCES BY ROLE
FIGHTER/GROUND ATTACK
  1 sqn with *Alpha Jet**; EMB-326G*
TRANSPORT
  1 sqn with Beech 200 *King Air*
  1 VIP unit with DC-8; F-28-1000
TRAINING
  1 sqn with TB-30 *Epsilon**
TRANSPORT HELICOPTER
  1 sqn with SA315 *Lama*; SA316 *Alouette* III; SA319 *Alouette* III
EQUIPMENT BY TYPE†
AIRCRAFT 10 combat capable
  TPT 5: **Light** 2 Beech 200 *King Air*; **PAX** 3: 1 DC-8; 2 F-28-1000 (VIP)
  TRG 10: 3 *Alpha Jet**; 4 EMB-326G *; 3 TB-30 *Epsilon**
HELICOPTERS
  MRH 4: 2 SA315 *Lama*; 1 SA316 *Alouette* III; 1 SA319 *Alouette* III
  TPT • Medium (1 SA330 *Puma* in store)

Paramilitary 750

Gendarmerie 750
Ministry of Interior
FORCES BY ROLE
2 reg sections
MANOEUVRE
  Other
  1 (mobile) paramilitary sqn

DEPLOYMENT

CÔTE D'IVOIRE
UN • UNOCI 469; 6 obs; 1 inf bn

LIBERIA
UN • UNMIL 1; 2 obs

MALI
UN • MINUSMA 933; 1 inf bn; 1 fd hospital

SOUTH SUDAN
UN • UNMISS 1

SUDAN
UN • UNAMID 6 obs

WESTERN SAHARA
UN • MINURSO 1 obs

Uganda UGA

Ugandan Shilling Ush		2013	2014	2015
GDP	Ush	59.3tr	67.4tr	
	US$	22.9bn	26.1bn	
per capita	US$	623	686	
Growth	%	5.8	5.9	
Inflation	%	5.0	5.5	
Def bdgt	Ush	945bn	1.05tr	1.08tr
	US$	365m	405m	
FMA (US)	US$	0.2m	0.2m	0.2m
US$1=Ush		2,586.93	2,583.69	

Population 35,918,915

Age	0–14	15–19	20–24	25–29	30–64	65 plus
Male	24.4%	5.8%	4.8%	3.7%	10.1%	0.9%
Female	24.5%	5.8%	4.8%	3.7%	10.2%	1.2%

Capabilities

Uganda's armed forces are relatively large and well equipped. They have, in recent years, seen some advanced capability acquisitions, boosting military capacity, particularly in the air force. Forces have deployed to Somalia as part of AMISOM since 2007, and in that time will have gained valuable combat experience in terms of planning and tactics, such as in counter-IED and urban patrolling on foot and with armour. A number of years combating the Lord's Resistance Army has also ensured experience in more rural counter-insurgency tactics, while an intervention in South Sudan in 2014 reflected the force's relative regional capability and willingness to engage in stabilisation missions. Uganda is one of the largest contributors to the East Africa Standby Force, having pledged a motorised infantry battalion and special police units. The armed forces have a good standard of training, and the country has a number of training facilities that are used by international partners as well as Ugandan troops.

ACTIVE 45,000 (Ugandan People's Defence Force 45,000) Paramilitary 1,800

RESERVE 10,000

ORGANISATIONS BY SERVICE

Ugandan People's Defence Force ε40,000–45,000

FORCES BY ROLE
MANOEUVRE
  Armoured
    1 armd bde
  Light
    1 cdo bn
    5 inf div (total: 16 inf bde)
  Other
    1 (Presidential Guard) mot bde

COMBAT SUPPORT
  1 arty bde
  2 AD bn

EQUIPMENT BY TYPE†
MBT 239: 185 T-54/T-55; 10 T-72; 44 T-90S
LT TK ε20 PT-76
RECCE 46: 40 *Eland*; 6 *Ferret*
AIFV 31 BMP-2
APC 121
  APC (W) 19: 15 BTR-60; 4 OT-64
  PPV 102: 20 *Buffel*; 42 *Casspir*; 40 *Mamba*
ARTY 333+
  SP 155mm 6 ATMOS 2000
  TOWED 243+: **122mm** M-30; **130mm** 221; **155mm** 22: 4 G-5; 18 M-839
  MRL 6+: **107mm** (12-tube); **122mm** 6+: BM-21; 6 RM-70
  MOR 78+: **81mm** L16; **82mm** M-43; **120mm** 78 *Soltam*
AD
  SAM
    TOWED 4 S-125 *Pechora* (SA-3 *Goa*)
    MANPAD 9K32 *Strela*-2 (SA-7 *Grail*)‡; 9K310 *Igla*-1 (SA-16 *Gimlet*)
  GUNS • TOWED 20+: **14.5mm** ZPU-1/ZPU-2/ZPU-4; **37mm** 20 M-1939
ARV T-54/T-55 reported
VLB MTU reported
MW *Chubby*

Air Wing

FORCES BY ROLE
FIGHTER/GROUND ATTACK
  1 sqn with MiG-21bis *Fishbed*; MiG-21U/UM *Mongol A/B*; Su-30MK2
TRANSPORT
  1 unit with Y-12
  1 VIP unit with Gulfstream 550; L-100-30
TRAINING
  1 unit with L-39 *Albatros*†*
ATTACK/TRANSPORT HELICOPTER
  1 sqn with Bell 206 *Jet Ranger*; Bell 412 *Twin Huey*; Mi-17 *Hip* H; Mi-24 *Hind*; Mi-172 (VIP)

EQUIPMENT BY TYPE
AIRCRAFT 16 combat capable
  FGA 13: 5 MiG-21bis *Fishbed*; 1 MiG-21U *Mongol* A; 1 MiG-21UM *Mongol* B; 6 Su-30MK2
  TPT 4: **Medium** 1 L-100-30; **Light** 2 Y-12; **PAX** 1 Gulfstream 550
  TRG 3 L-39 *Albatros*†*
HELICOPTERS
  ATK 1 Mi-24 *Hind* (2 more non-op)
  MRH 5: 2 Bell 412 *Twin Huey*; 3 Mi-17 *Hip* H (1 more non-op)
  TPT 3: **Medium** 1 Mi-172 (VIP); **Light** 2 Bell 206A *Jet Ranger*
MSL
  AAM • IR R-73 (AA-11 *Archer*); **SARH** R-27 (AA-10 *Alamo*); **ARH** R-77 (AA-12 *Adder*) (reported)
  ARM Kh-31P (AS-17A *Krypton*) (reported)

Paramilitary ε1,800 active

Border Defence Unit ε600
Equipped with small arms only

Police Air Wing ε800
EQUIPMENT BY TYPE
HELICOPTERS • TPT • Light 1 Bell 206 *Jet Ranger*

Marines ε400
EQUIPMENT BY TYPE
PATROL AND COASTAL COMBATANTS 8 PBR

Local Militia Forces

Amuka Group ε3,000; ε7,000 (reported under trg) (total 10,000)

DEPLOYMENT

CÔTE D'IVOIRE
UN • UNOCI 2; 3 obs

SOMALIA
AU • AMISOM 6,223; 7 inf bn

SOUTH SUDAN
UN • UNMISS 2

FOREIGN FORCES
(all EUTM, unless otherwise indicated)
Belgium 5
Finland 10
Germany 6
Hungary 4
Italy 78
Netherlands 8
Portugal 5
Serbia 5
Spain 14
Sweden 8
UK 5

Zambia ZMB

Zambian Kwacha K		2013	2014	2015
GDP	K	145bn	166bn	
	US$	26.8bn	25.6bn	
per capita	US$	1,845	1,705	
Growth	%	6.7	6.5	
Inflation	%	7.0	8.0	
Def bdgt [a]	K	2.04bn	2.74bn	3.25bn
	US$	377m	422m	
US$1=K		5.40	6.50	

[a] Excludes allocations for public order and safety

Population 14,638,505

Age	0–14	15–19	20–24	25–29	30–64	65 plus
Male	23.2%	5.5%	4.5%	3.9%	11.9%	1.0%
Female	23.0%	5.5%	4.6%	3.9%	11.8%	1.4%

Capabilities

Ensuring territorial integrity and border security, and a commitment to international peacekeeping operations, are key tasks of the armed forces. In common with many of the continent's armed forces, Zambia's struggle with ageing equipment, limited funding and the challenges of maintaining ageing weapons systems. As a landlocked nation, there is no navy, but a small number of light patrol craft are retained for riverine duties. The air force has a very limited tactical air-transport capability, but the armed forces have no independent capacity for power projection. The services have been occasional participants in international exercises.

ACTIVE 15,100 (Army 13,500 Air 1,600) **Paramilitary 1,400**

RESERVE 3,000 (Army 3,000)

ORGANISATIONS BY SERVICE

Army 13,500
FORCES BY ROLE
COMMAND
 3 bde HQ
SPECIAL FORCES
 1 cdo bn
MANOEUVRE
 Armoured
 1 armd regt (1 tk bn, 1 armd recce regt)
 Light
 6 inf bn
COMBAT SUPPORT
 1 arty regt (2 fd arty bn, 1 MRL bn)
 1 engr regt
EQUIPMENT BY TYPE
Some equipment†
MBT 30: 20 Type-59; 10 T-55
LT TK 30 PT-76
RECCE 70 BRDM-1/BRDM-2 (ε30 serviceable)
AIFV 23 *Ratel*-20
APC (W) 33: 13 BTR-60; 20 BTR-70
ARTY 182
 TOWED 61: **105mm** 18 Model 56 pack howitzer; **122mm** 25 D-30; **130mm** 18 M-46
 MRL 122mm 30 BM-21 (ε12 serviceable)
 MOR 91: **81mm** 55; **82mm** 24; **120mm** 12
AT • MSL • MANPATS 9K11 *Malyutka* (AT-3 *Sagger*)
 RCL 12+: **57mm** 12 M18; **75mm** M20; **84mm** *Carl Gustav*
AD • SAM • MANPAD 9K32 *Strela*-2 (SA-7 *Grail*)‡
 GUNS • TOWED 136: **20mm** 50 M-55 (triple); **37mm** 40 M-1939; **57mm** ε30 S-60; **85mm** 16 M-1939 *KS-12*
ARV T-54/T-55 reported

Reserve 3,000
FORCES BY ROLE
MANOEUVRE
 Light
 3 inf bn

Air Force 1,600

FORCES BY ROLE
FIGHTER/GROUND ATTACK
  1 sqn with K-8 *Karakorum**
  1 sqn with MiG-21MF *Fishbed* J†; MiG-21U *Mongol* A
TRANSPORT
  1 sqn with MA60; Y-12(II); Y-12(IV); Y-12E
  1 (VIP) unit with AW139; CL-604; HS-748
  1 (liaison) sqn with Do-28
TRAINING
  2 sqn with MB-326GB; MFI-15 *Safari*
TRANSPORT HELICOPTER
  1 sqn with Mi-17 *Hip* H
  1 (liaison) sqn with Bell 47G; Bell 205 (UH-1H *Iroquois*/AB-205)
AIR DEFENCE
  3 bty with S-125 *Pechora* (SA-3 *Goa*)

EQUIPMENT BY TYPE†
Very low serviceability.
AIRCRAFT 25 combat capable
  FGA 10: 8 MiG-21MF *Fishbed* J; 2 MiG-21U *Mongol* A
  TPT 23: Light 21: 5 Do-28; 2 MA60; 4 Y-12(II); 5 Y-12(IV); 5 Y-12E; PAX 2: 1 CL-604; 1 HS-748
  TRG 41: 15 K-8 *Karakourm**; 10 MB-326GB; 8 MFI-15 *Safari*; 6 SF-260TW
HELICOPTERS
  MRH 5: 1 AW139; 4 Mi-17 *Hip* H
  TPT • Light 13: 10 Bell 205 (UH-1H *Iroquois*/AB-205); 3 Bell 212
  TRG 5 Bell 47G
AD • SAM S-125 *Pechora* (SA-3 *Goa*)
MSL
  ASM 9K11 *Malyutka* (AT-3 *Sagger*)
  AAM • IR R-3 (AA-2 *Atoll*)‡; PL-2; *Python* 3

Paramilitary 1,400

Police Mobile Unit 700
FORCES BY ROLE
MANOEUVRE
  Other
    1 police bn (4 police coy)

Police Paramilitary Unit 700
FORCES BY ROLE
MANOEUVRE
  Other
    1 paramilitary bn (3 paramilitary coy)

DEPLOYMENT

CENTRAL AFRICAN REPUBLIC
UN • MINUSCA 2; 3 obs

CÔTE D'IVOIRE
UN • UNOCI 2 obs

DEMOCRATIC REPUBLIC OF THE CONGO
UN • MONUSCO 2; 18 obs

LIBERIA
UN • UNMIL 3 obs

SOUTH SUDAN
UN • UNMISS 4; 3 obs

SUDAN
UN • UNAMID 5; 13 obs
UN • UNISFA 1; 2 obs

Zimbabwe ZWE

Zimbabwe Dollar Z$ [a]		2013	2014	2015
GDP	US$	13.2bn	13.7bn	
per capita	US$	1,007	1,036	
Growth	%	3.3	3.1	
Inflation	%	1.6	0.3	
Def bdgt	US$	356m	368m	389m
US$1=Z$		1.00	1.00	1.00

[a] Zimbabwe dollar no longer in active use

Population   13,771,721

Age	0–14	15–19	20–24	25–29	30–64	65 plus
Male	19.9%	5.9%	5.3%	4.8%	12.1%	1.5%
Female	19.5%	5.8%	5.5%	5.4%	12.3%	2.2%

Capabilities

The armed forces' role is to defend the nation's independence, sovereignty and territorial integrity. However, the erosion of the country's already limited military capabilities, due to economic problems, suggests that these tasks would likely be unachievable in the face of a committed aggressor. An international deployment on the scale of the c.10,000 personnel deployed to the DRC between 1998 and 2002 would now be extremely difficult to replicate. China has been the only source of defence equipment for the country's limited number of procurements. A proposed donation of ex-South African *Alouette* III helicopters, ostensibly for spare parts, was blocked by a South African court in early 2013. Both the EU and the US have arms embargoes in place, which the Zimbabwean air-force commander acknowledges have reduced air-force readiness. The armed forces have taken part intermittently in multinational training exercises with regional states.

ACTIVE 29,000 (Army 25,000 Air 4,000) **Paramilitary 21,800**

ORGANISATIONS BY SERVICE

Army ε25,000
FORCES BY ROLE
COMMAND
  1 SF bde HQ
  1 mech bde HQ
  5 inf bde HQ

SPECIAL FORCES
  1 SF regt
MANOEUVRE
  Armoured
  1 armd sqn
  Mechanised
  1 mech inf bn
  Light
  15 inf bn
  1 cdo bn
  Air Manoeuvre
  1 para bn
  Other
  3 gd bn
  1 (Presidential Guard) gd gp
COMBAT SUPPORT
  1 arty bde
  1 fd arty regt
  1 AD regt
  2 engr regt

EQUIPMENT BY TYPE
MBT 40: 30 Type-59†; 10 Type-69†
RECCE 115: 20 *Eland*; 15 *Ferret*†; 80 EE-9 *Cascavel* (90mm)
APC 85
  APC (T) 30: 8 Type-63; 22 VTT-323
  APC (W) 55 TPK 4.20 VSC ACMAT
ARTY 254
  SP 122mm 12 2S1
  TOWED 122mm 20: 4 D-30; 16 Type-60 (D-74)
  MRL 76: 107mm 16 Type-63; 122mm 60 RM-70 *Dana*
  MOR 146: 81mm/82mm ε140; 120mm 6 M-43
AD
  SAM • MANPAD 9K32 *Strela*-2 (SA-7 *Grail*)‡
  GUNS • TOWED 116: 14.5mm 36 ZPU-1/ZPU-2/ZPU-4; 23mm 45 ZU-23; 37mm 35 M-1939
ARV T-54/T-55 reported
VLB MTU reported

Air Force 4,000

Flying hours   100 hrs/year

FORCES BY ROLE
FIGHTER
  1 sqn with F-7 II†; FT-7†
FIGHTER/GROUND ATTACK
  1 sqn with K-8 *Karakorum**
  (1 sqn Hawker *Hunter* in store)
GROUND ATTACK/ISR
  1 sqn with Cessna 337/O-2A *Skymaster**
ISR/TRAINING
  1 sqn with SF-260F/M; SF-260TP*; SF-260W *Warrior**
TRANSPORT
  1 sqn with BN-2 *Islander*; CASA 212-200 *Aviocar* (VIP)
ATTACK/TRANSPORT HELICOPTER
  1 sqn with Mi-35 *Hind*; Mi-35P *Hind* (liaison); SA316 *Alouette* III; AS532UL *Cougar* (VIP)
  1 trg sqn with Bell 412 *Twin Huey*, SA316 *Alouette* III

AIR DEFENCE
  1 sqn

EQUIPMENT BY TYPE
AIRCRAFT 46 combat capable
  FTR 9: 7 F-7 II†; 2 FT-7†
  FGA (12 Hawker *Hunter* in store)
  ISR 2 O-2A *Skymaster*
  TPT • Light 26: 5 BN-2 *Islander*; 8 C-212-200 *Aviocar* (VIP - 2 more in store); 13 Cessna 337 *Skymaster**; (10 C-47 *Skytrain* in store)
  TRG 34: 11 K-8 *Karakorum**; 5 SF-260M; 8 SF-260TP*; 5 SF-260W *Warrior**; 5 SF-260F
HELICOPTERS
  ATK 6: 4 Mi-35 *Hind*; 2 Mi-35P *Hind*
  MRH 10: 8 Bell 412 *Twin Huey*; 2 SA316 *Alouette* III
  TPT • Medium 2 AS532UL *Cougar* (VIP)
MSL • AAM • IR PL-2; PL-5
AD • GUNS 100mm (not deployed); 37mm (not deployed); 57mm (not deployed)

Paramilitary 21,800

Zimbabwe Republic Police Force 19,500
incl air wg

Police Support Unit 2,300
PATROL AND COASTAL COMBATANTS • PB 5: 3 Rodman 38; 2 Rodman 46 (five Rodman 790 are also operated, under 10 tonnes FLD)

DEPLOYMENT

CÔTE D'IVOIRE
UN • UNOCI 3 obs

LIBERIA
UN • UNMIL 1 obs

SOUTH SUDAN
UN • UNMISS 2 obs

SUDAN
UN • UNAMID 2; 5 obs
UN • UNISFA 1; 2 obs

DEPLOYMENT

CÔTE D'IVOIRE
UN • UNOCI 3 obs

LIBERIA
UN • UNMIL 2 obs

SUDAN
UN • UNAMID 2; 7 obs
UN • UNISFA 1

Table 10 **Selected Arms Procurements and Deliveries, Sub-Saharan Africa**

Designation	Type	Quantity	Contract Value (Current)	Prime Nationality	Prime Contractor	Order Date	First Delivery Due	Notes
Angola (ANG)								
Casspir NG	PPV	45	n.k.	RSA	Denel	2013	2014	Delivery status unclear
Macaé-class (NAPA 500)	PCC	7	n.k.	BRZ	Empresa Gerencial de Projetos Navais	2014	n.k.	Four will be built in BRZ, three at a new shipyard in ANG
Su-30K/MK	FGA ac	12	n.k.	RUS	Government surplus	2013	2015	Ex-IND Air Force ac. Under test
Chad (CHA)								
MiG-29 *Fulcrum*	FGA ac	n.k.	n.k.	UKR	Ukroboron-prom	n.k.	2013	First ac delivered in 2014
C-27J *Spartan*	Med tpt ac	2	€100m (US$133m)	ITA	Finmeccanica (Alenia Aermacchi)	2013	n.k.	Both ac currently in tests
Djibouti (DJB)								
n.k.	PB	2	n.k.	JPN	n.k.	2014	2015	For coast guard; JPN-funded project for two 20m patrol boats
Gabon (GAB)								
P400	PCC	1	n.k.	FRA	Piriou	2014	2015	Ex-FRA P691. Being refitted
OPV50	PCC	1	n.k.	FRA	Kership	2014	2016	Delivery due mid-2016
Mauritius (MUS)								
Barracuda-class	PCO	1	US$58.5m	IND	GRSE	2012	2014	Commissioning delayed until end of 2014
Mozambique (MOZ)								
HIS 32	PCC	3	See notes	UAE	Abu Dhabi MAR (CMN)	2013	2016	Part of €200m (US$266m) order inculding three 42m patrol craft
Ocean Eagle 43	PCC	3	See notes	UAE	Abu Dhabi MAR (CMN)	2013	2016	Part of €200m (US$266m) order including three 42m patrol craft; first hull delivered Sep 2014
Nigeria (NGA)								
Centenary-class	PSOH	2	US$42m	PRC	CSIC	2012	2015	First launched in PRC in Jan 2014; half of second to be built in NGA
n.k.	PSOH	2	US$200–250m	IND	Pipavav Defence and Offshore Engineering	2012	2015	To be delivered by early 2015. Option for a further two vessels. First vessel reported to have completed sea trials by Nov 2014
Mi-35M *Hind*	Atk hel	6	n.k	RUS	Russian Helicopters	2014	2015	First delivery expected 2015
Mi-171Sh	Med tpt hel	6	n.k.	RUS	Russian Helicopters	2014	2015	First delivery expected 2015
AW101 *Merlin*	Med tpt hel	2	n.k.	ITA (UK)	Finmeccanica (Agusta-Westland)	2014	n.k.	VIP config. Part of order originally intended to fill IND's VVIP requirement. First hel in test
South Africa (RSA)								
Badger (AMV 8x8)	APC (W)	238	ZAR9bn (US$900m)	FIN/RSA	Patria/Denel	2013	2013	Five variants. Five pre-production vehicles delivered by late 2014
A-Darter	AAM	n.k.	n.k.	RSA	Denel	2007	2016	Programme schedule has slipped; ISD 2016

Chapter Ten
Country comparisons – commitments, force levels and economics

Table 11 **Selected Training Activity 2014**	482
Table 12 **International Comparisons of Defence Expenditure and Military Personnel**	484
Selected Non-State Armed Groups: Observed Equipment Holdings	491

Table 11 Selected Training Activity 2014

Date	Title	Location	Aim	Principal Participants
North America (US and Canada)				
17–26 Feb 2014	COPE NORTH 2014	US (Guam)	FTX	AUS, JPN, US
03 Mar–14 Mar 2014	RED FLAG 14–2	US	Air cbt ex	BEL, DNK, JPN, NATO, SAU, US
16 May–02 Jun 2014	MAPLE FLAG 47	CAN	Air cbt ex	CAN, CHI, FRA, US (obs BEL, COL, GER, NL)
26 Jun–01 Aug 2014	RIMPAC 2014	US (Hawaii)	NAVEX	AUS, BRN, CAN, CHL, COL, FRA, IDN, IND, JPN, MYS (pl), MEX, NLD, NZL, NOR, PRC, PER, PHL (staff), ROK, SGP, Tonga (pl), UK, US (obs BNG, BRZ, DNK, GER, ITA, PNG)
14–23 Jul 2014	RED FLAG 14–3	US	Air cbt ex	FRA, SGP, US
07–22 Aug 2014	RED FLAG ALASKA 14–3	US	Air cbt ex	AUS, NZL, JPN, US
17–24 Sep 2014	REGIONAL COOPERATION 2014	US	CPX	AFG, MNG, TJK (obs PAK, KAZ)
Europe				
21 Mar–04 Apr 2014	SABER GUARDIAN	BUL	CPX	ARM, AZE, BEL, BUL, GEO, MOL, NATO, POL, ROM, SER, TUR, UKR, US
31 Mar–11 Apr 2014	FRISIAN FLAG 14	NLD	Air cbt ex	BEL, DAN, ESP, FIN, GER, ITA, NATO, NLD, NOR, POR
12–23 May 2014	STEADFAST COBALT 2014	LTU	CIS Interop ex	BUL, CAN, CRO, CZE, DNK, ESP, EST, FRA, GER, GRE, ITA, LTU, NLD, POL, TUR, UK, US
21–22 May 2014	LOCKED SHIELDS 2014	EST (Europe-wide)	Cyber defence ex	AUT, CZE, ESP, EST, FIN, FRA, GER, HUN, ITA, LAT, LTU, NLD, POL, SVK, TUR, NATO
06–21 Jun 2014	BALTOPS 2014	Baltic	NAVEX/MCM/MSO	DNK, EST, FIN, FRA, GEO, GER, LTU, LVA, NLD, POL, SWE, UK, US
09–20 Jun 2014	ANATOLIAN EAGLE	TUR	Air cbt ex	ESP, JOR, QTR, TUR, UK
09–20 Jun 2014	SABER STRIKE 2014	EST, LTU, LVA	Interop CPX/FTX	CAN, DNK, EST, FIN, LTU, LVA, NOR, POL, UK, US
29 Aug–12 Sep 2014	NORTHERN COASTS 2014	Baltic Sea	NAVEX	BEL, DNK, EST, FIN, GER, LTU, LVA, NLD, SWE, TUR, UK, US
30 Sep–01 Oct 2014	BRTE (BALTIC REGION TRAINING EVENT)	Baltic states	Air cbt ex	GER, EST, FIN, LTU, LVA, POR, SWE, US
05–16 Oct 2014	JOINT WARRIOR 14–2	UK	NAVEX	BEL, DEN, ESP, EST, FRA, GER, LTU, LVA, POL, UK, US
Nov 2014	SREM–2014	SER	CT ex	RUS, SER
08–17 Nov 2014	TRIDENT JUNCTURE	EST (and EUR)	CPX/FTX	NATO member states
Russia and Eurasia				
26 Feb–03 Mar 2014	n.k.	RUS	FTX	Snap exercise – Western and Central MD
21–25 May 2014	AVIADARTS	RUS	Air cbt ex	BLR, PRC, RUS
21–28 Jun 2014	n.k.	RUS	FTX	Snap exercise – Central MD
29 Jul–01 Aug 2014	PEACEKEEPING TRAINING 2014	RUS	HADR ex	CSTO states
18–22 Aug 2014	INTERACTION 2014	KAZ	CSTO (KSOR) FTX	ARM, BLR, KAZ, KGZ, RUS, TAJ
11–18 Sep 2014	n.k.	RUS	FTX	Snap exercise – Eastern MD
15–26 Sep 2014	RAPID TRIDENT	UKR	FTX	AZE, BLG, CAN, ESP, GEO, GER, LAT, LTU, MOL, NOR, POL, ROM, UK, US
19–25 Sep 2014	VOSTOK 2014	RUS	FTX	Large-scale ex in Eastern MD
23 Sep–02 Oct 2014	INDRA 2014	RUS	CT ex	IND, RUS
Asia				
11–21 Feb 2014	COBRA GOLD 14	THA	PSO/HADR ex	IDN, JPN, MAL, PRC, ROK, SGP, THA, US
23–25 Apr 2014	MARITIME COOPERATION	PRC	NAVEX	BGD, BRN, IDN, IND, MYS, PAK, PRC, SGP
18–29 Aug 2014	FOAL EAGLE	ROK	FTX	ROK, US
10–21 Mar 2014	COPE TIGER	THA	Air cbt ex	SGP, THA, US

Table 11 Selected Training Activity 2014

Date	Title	Location	Aim	Principal Participants
05–16 May 2014	BALIKATAN 14	PHL	Interop/HADR ex	PHL, US
06–27 May 2014	SHAHEEN III	PAK	Air ex	PAK, PRC
22 May–04 Jun 2014	BERSAMA SHIELD 14	MAL & SGP	FPDA NAVEX	AUS, MYS, NZL, SGP, UK
20–26 May 2014	JOINT SEA 2014	PRC	NAVEX	PRC, RUS
24 June–01 Jul 2014	KHAAN QUEST	MNG	PSO ex	AUS, BAN, BLR, CAN, CZE, FRA, GER, HUN, IDN, IND, JPN, MON, NPL, PAK, POL, PRC, ROK, RUS, SGP, TAJ, THA, TUR, UK, US
24–30 July 2014	MALABAR 2014	IND	Interop ex	IND, JPN, US
01–22 Aug 2014	PITCH BLACK	AUS	Air cbt ex	AUS, FRA, NZL, SGP, THA, UAE, US
24–29 Aug 2014	PEACE MISSION 2014	PRC	Interop ex	KAZ, KGZ, PRC, RUS, TJK
13–22 Oct 2014	BERSAMA LIMA 14	MAL & SGP	CPX/FTX	AUS, MYS, NZL, SGP, UK (FPDA)
08–19 Nov 2014	KEEN SWORD	JPN	FTX	JPN, US

Middle East and North Africa

Date	Title	Location	Aim	Principal Participants
Feb 2014	FALCON DEFENDER	Gulf waters	NAVEX	BAH, UK, US
26 Mar–03 Apr 2014	AFRICAN LION	MOR	CPX/FTX	MOR, US
11 May 2014	EAGER TIGER	JOR	Air cbt & CT FTX	JOR, US
01–16 Apr 2014	FRIENDSHIP/ IRONHAWK 3	SAU	CBT trg ex	SAU, US
19–23 May 2014	JUNIPER COBRA	ISR	BMD ex	ISR, US
25 May–08 Jun 2014	EAGER LION	JOR	AD/HADR ex	BHR, CAN, EGY, FRA, IRQ, ITA, JOR, KWT, LBN, PAK, POL, QTR, SAU, TUR, UAE, UK, US
27 Oct–13 Nov 2014	IMCMEX 14		MCM ex	BHR, CAN , FRA, GER, IRQ, ITA, JPN, KWT, NLD, NOR, OMN, PAK, QTR, SAU, UAE, UK, US

Latin America and the Caribbean

Date	Title	Location	Aim	Principal Participants
Apr–Jun 2014	BEYOND THE HORIZON/ NEW HORIZONS 2014	BLZ, DOM GUA	HADR ex	BLZ, PAN, SLV, US
23 Apr–01 May 2014	COOPERACION III	PER	HADR ex	ARG, BZL, CAN, CHI, COL, PER, URU (obs: DOM, GUA, PAR, MEX)
01–25 Jun 2014	TRADEWINDS 14	Caribbean Sea	NAVEX	ATG, BHS, Grenada, GUY, HTI, ST Kitts & Nevis, St Vincent & Grenadines, TTO, SUR, US
08–14 Aug 2014	PANAMAX 14	PAN, US	Infrastructure protection ex	ARG, BEL, BRZ, CAN, CHL, COL, CRI, DOM, ECU, FRA, GUA, HND, MEX, NIC, PAN, PER, PRY, SLV
Aug 2014	VIEKAREN XIV	Beagle Channel	NAVEX/SAR ex	ARG, CHL
12–26 Sep 2014	UNITAS 14	COL	NAVEX	ARG, BZL, CHL, COL, DOM, HON, ITA, MEX, NZL, PAN, PER, UK, US

Sub-Saharan Africa

Date	Title	Location	Aim	Principal Participants
19 Feb–12 Mar 2014	FLINTLOCK 2014	NER	CT ex	ALG, BFA, CAN, CHA, ESP, MLI, MRT, NLD, NER, NGA, RSA, SEN, TUN, US
11–21 Mar 2014	CENTRAL ACCORD 2014	CMR	Interop/HADR ex	BDI, CAM, CHA, COG, GAB, NGA, NLD, US
16–23 April 2014	OBANGAME EXPRESS 2014	Gulf of Guinea	NAVEX	ANG, BEL, BEN, BRZ, CAM, CIV, COG, ESP, EQG, FRA, GAB, GER, GHA, NGA, NLD, PRT, STP, TGO, TUR, US
06–13 Mar 2014	SAHARAN EXPRESS 2014	SEN	NAVEX/Interop ex	CPV, FRA, LBR, MOR, MRT, SEN, POR, ESP, NLD, UK, US
16–30 June 2014	WESTERN ACCORD 14	SEN	CPX/FTX	ECOWAS, FRA, NLD, US
19–29 Oct 2014	LOANGO 2014	COG	Interop/HADR ex	CEEAC
13–22 Nov 2014	MASHARIKI SALAM 2014	ETH	CPX (planning and C2)	EASF states

Table 12 **International Comparisons of Defence Expenditure and Military Personnel**

	Defence Spending current US$ m 2012	2013	2014	Defence Spending per capita (current US$) 2012	2013	2014	Defence Spending % of GDP 2012	2013	2014	Number in Armed Forces (000) 2015	Estimated Reservists (000) 2015	Paramilitary (000) 2015
North America												
Canada	18,445	16,166	15,925	538	468	457	1.01	0.88	0.89	66	31	0
United States	645,000	578,000	581,000	2,055	1,827	1,822	3.99	3.45	3.34	1,433	855	0
Total	663,445	594,166	596,925	1,905	1,693	1,688	3.69	3.20	3.11	1,499	886	0
Europe												
Albania	187	185	166	62	62	55	1.47	1.38	1.19	8	0	1
Austria	3,189	3,230	3,325	388	393	404	0.80	0.76	0.77	23	162	0
Belgium	5,264	4,985	5,038	504	477	482	1.09	0.98	0.97	31	0	7
Bosnia-Herzegovina	231	n.k.	227	60	n.k.	59	1.33	n.k.	1.15	11	0	0
Bulgaria	659	750	736	94	107	106	1.29	1.38	1.31	31	303	16
Croatia	818	799	774	183	179	173	1.43	1.33	1.24	17	0	3
Cyprus	450	460	432	395	398	368	1.96	2.11	2.01	12	50	1
Czech Republic	2,221	2,149	2,089	210	203	197	1.13	1.06	1.01	21	0	3
Denmark	4,422	4,553	4,811	798	819	864	1.41	1.39	1.45	17	54	0
Estonia	437	480	520	343	379	413	2.00	1.99	2.05	6	30	0
Finland	3,625	3,812	3,725	689	724	707	1.45	1.44	1.36	22	354	3
France	50,258	52,317	53,080	766	793	801	1.93	1.91	1.90	215	28	103
Germany	40,974	44,172	43,934	504	544	542	1.20	1.23	1.20	182	45	0
Greece	6,676	5,898	5,639	620	548	523	2.68	2.42	2.33	145	217	4
Hungary	1,196	1,103	1,004	120	111	101	0.94	0.83	0.72	27	44	12
Iceland	33	38	39	105	121	122	0.24	0.26	0.25	0	0	0
Ireland	1,148	1,202	1,217	243	252	252	0.55	0.54	0.53	9	5	0
Italy	23,993	25,212	24,274	392	410	394	1.19	1.21	1.16	176	18	184
Latvia	180	210	n.k.	82	97	n.k.	0.63	0.68	n.k.	5	8	0
Lithuania	317	359	436	90	102	124	0.75	0.78	0.90	11	7	11
Luxembourg	267	249	255	524	484	491	0.47	0.41	0.41	1	0	1
Macedonia (FYROM)	129	n.k.	131	62	n.k.	62	1.33	n.k.	1.19	8	5	0
Malta	50	60	61	122	145	148	0.57	0.64	0.64	2	0	0
Montenegro	52	65	80	79	99	123	1.21	1.42	1.70	2	0	10

Table 12 International Comparisons of Defence Expenditure and Military Personnel

	Defence Spending current US$ m 2012	2013	2014	Defence Spending per capita (current US$) 2012	2013	2014	Defence Spending % of GDP 2012	2013	2014	Number in Armed Forces (000) 2015	Estimated Reservists (000) 2015	Paramilitary (000) 2015
Netherlands, The	10,335	10,344	10,683	618	616	633	1.34	1.28	1.30	37	3	6
Norway	6,974	7,236	6,977	1,389	1,423	1,355	1.39	1.35	1.28	26	46	0
Poland	8,552	8,942	10,380	223	233	271	1.75	1.74	1.91	99	0	73
Portugal	2,639	2,772	2,633	245	257	243	1.24	1.27	1.19	35	212	45
Romania	2,211	2,423	2,875	101	111	132	1.31	1.30	1.49	71	45	80
Serbia	841	689	711	116	95	99	2.25	1.61	1.58	28	50	0
Slovakia	881	994	1,063	161	181	193	0.96	1.01	1.04	16	0	0
Slovenia	509	466	455	255	234	229	1.12	1.00	0.96	8	2	6
Spain	15,826	14,622	15,070	336	309	316	1.17	1.05	1.07	133	14	81
Sweden	6,170	6,494	6,688	644	673	725	1.17	1.13	1.17	15	0	1
Switzerland	4,831	5,054	5,260	610	632	652	0.76	0.78	0.80	21	155	0
Turkey	10,166	10,692	10,047	127	132	123	1.28	1.26	1.14	511	379	102
United Kingdom	61,274	58,075	61,818	972	916	970	2.51	2.40	2.47	159	79	0
Total**	**277,983**	**281,454**	**286,922**	**449**	**453**	**461**	**1.49**	**1.45**	**1.44**	**2,140**	**2,312**	**752**
Russia and Eurasia												
Armenia	396	458	470	129	150	154	3.98	4.39	4.23	45	210	4
Azerbaijan	1,759	1,948	2,108	185	203	218	2.56	2.65	2.71	67	300	15
Belarus*	552	n.k.	n.k.	57	n.k.	n.k.	0.87	n.k.	n.k.	48	290	110
Georgia	394	397	393	80	80	80	2.49	2.46	2.44	21	0	12
Kazakhstan	2,280	2,290	2,030	130	129	113	1.12	0.99	0.90	39	0	32
Kyrgyzstan	105	101	95	19	18	17	1.59	1.40	1.24	11	0	10
Moldova	22	24	25	6	7	7	0.31	0.30	0.33	5	58	2
Russia	58,765	66,073	70,048	412	464	492	2.91	3.15	3.40	771	2,000	489
Tajikistan	170	194	186	22	24	23	2.24	2.28	2.03	9	0	8
Turkmenistan*	539	n.k.	n.k.	107	n.k.	n.k.	1.53	n.k.	n.k.	22	0	0
Ukraine	2,050	2,414	3,587	46	54	81	1.16	1.35	2.66	122	1,000	n.k.
Uzbekistan*	1,455	n.k.	n.k.	51	n.k.	n.k.	2.84	n.k.	n.k.	48	0	20
Total**	**68,488**	**76,784**	**81,604**	**243**	**271**	**288**	**2.57**	**2.74**	**2.98**	**1,207**	**3,857**	**701**

Table 12 International Comparisons of Defence Expenditure and Military Personnel

	Defence Spending current US$ m 2012	2013	2014	Defence Spending per capita (current US$) 2012	2013	2014	Defence Spending % of GDP 2012	2013	2014	Number in Armed Forces (000) 2015	Estimated Reservists (000) 2015	Paramilitary (000) 2015
Asia												
Afghanistan	2,077	2,751	3,286	68	88	103	10.43	13.11	14.55	179	0	152
Australia	27,099	24,535	22,512	1,231	1,102	1,000	1.76	1.54	1.38	57	23	0
Bangladesh	1,537	1,713	1,956	10	10	12	1.25	1.27	1.34	157	0	64
Brunei	411	413	573	1,005	993	1,356	2.47	2.51	3.40	7	1	2
Cambodia	348	399	445	23	26	29	2.44	2.55	2.57	124	0	67
China	102,643	115,844	129,408	76	85	95	1.25	1.28	1.30	2,333	510	660
Fiji	63	58	50	71	65	55	1.57	1.40	1.15	4	6	0
India	40,986	41,896	45,212	34	34	37	2.25	2.12	2.12	1,346	1,155	1,404
Indonesia	6,531	7,834	7,076	26	31	28	0.74	0.83	0.69	396	400	281
Japan	59,077	48,709	47,685	464	383	375	0.99	0.95	0.90	247	56	13
Korea, DPR of	n.k.	n.k.	n.k.	n.k.	n.k.	n.k.	n.k.	n.k.	n.k.	1,190	600	189
Korea, Republic of	29,257	31,506	34,438	599	644	702	2.53	2.50	2.58	655	4,500	5
Laos	20	22	24	3	3	4	0.22	0.21	0.22	29	0	100
Malaysia	4,440	4,840	5,031	152	163	167	1.46	1.48	1.42	109	52	25
Mongolia	115	114	105	40	39	36	1.12	0.94	0.75	10	137	8
Myanmar	2,188	2,179	2,433	40	40	44	4.12	3.79	3.91	406	0	107
Nepal	235	233	311	8	8	10	1.21	1.14	1.40	96	0	62
New Zealand	2,207	2,605	3,186	510	597	724	1.30	1.42	1.69	9	2	0
Pakistan	5,814	5,926	6,006	31	31	31	2.51	2.48	2.44	644	0	304
Papua New Guinea	78	83	99	12	13	15	0.49	0.48	0.52	2	0	0
Philippines	1,761	2,069	2,035	17	20	19	0.70	0.73	0.65	125	131	41
Singapore	9,843	9,730	10,015	1,839	1,782	1,799	3.56	3.39	3.38	73	313	75
Sri Lanka	1,533	1,821	1,789	71	84	82	2.58	2.79	2.54	161	6	62
Taiwan	10,452	10,321	10,126	450	443	433	2.21	2.09	1.92	290	1,657	17
Thailand	5,426	5,874	5,685	81	87	84	1.48	1.38	1.22	361	200	93
Timor-Leste	64	67	69	56	57	58	1.54	1.57	1.59	1	0	0
Vietnam	3,355	3,938	4,248	37	43	45	2.43	2.52	2.49	482	5,000	40
Total	317,562	325,482	343,804	82	83	87	1.43	1.43	1.41	9,490	14,748	3,769

Table 12 International Comparisons of Defence Expenditure and Military Personnel

	Defence Spending current US$ m 2012	2013	2014	Defence Spending per capita (current US$) 2012	2013	2014	Defence Spending % of GDP 2012	2013	2014	Number in Armed Forces (000) 2015	Estimated Reservists (000) 2015	Paramilitary (000) 2015
Middle East and North Africa												
Algeria	9,324	10,405	11,996	250	273	309	4.49	4.90	5.27	130	150	187
Bahrain	1,018	1,236	1,335	816	965	1,016	3.32	3.77	3.92	8	0	11
Egypt	4,578	5,310	5,449	55	62	63	1.75	1.96	1.91	439	479	397
Iran*	18,137	14,786	15,705	230	185	194	4.56	4.03	3.90	523	350	40
Iraq	14,727	16,897	18,868	473	530	579	6.82	7.37	8.13	178	0	n.k.
Israel	16,855	18,703	20,139	2,220	2,427	2,575	6.55	6.43	6.60	177	465	8
Jordan	1,520	1,216	1,268	234	188	194	4.91	3.59	3.47	101	65	15
Kuwait	4,728	4,338	4,841	1,787	1,609	1,765	2.72	2.47	2.70	16	24	7
Lebanon*	1,148	n.k.	n.k.	277	n.k.	n.k.	2.67	n.k.	n.k.	60	0	20
Libya	2,988	4,656	n.k.	532	776	n.k.	3.65	7.11	n.k.	7	n.k.	n.k.
Mauritania	112	149	n.k.	33	43	n.k.	2.82	3.56	n.k.	16	0	5
Morocco	3,403	3,723	3,859	105	114	117	3.55	3.59	3.43	196	150	50
Oman	6,723	9,246	9,623	2,176	2,931	2,989	8.91	11.99	11.95	43	0	4
Palestinian Territories	n.k.	n.k.	n.k.	n.k.	n.k.	n.k.	n.k.	n.k.	n.k.	0	0	n.k.
Qatar*	3,728	n.k.	n.k.	1,910	n.k.	n.k.	1.96	n.k.	n.k.	12	0	0
Saudi Arabia	56,724	67,020	80,762	2,138	2,488	2,953	7.73	8.95	10.38	227	0	25
Syrian Arab Republic	n.k.	n.k.	n.k.	n.k.	n.k.	n.k.	n.k.	n.k.	n.k.	178	n.k.	n.k.
Tunisia	670	759	911	62	70	83	1.48	1.62	1.85	36	0	12
UAE*	13,433	n.k.	n.k.	2,528	n.k.	n.k.	3.61	n.k.	n.k.	63	0	0
Yemen	1,634	1,849	1,885	66	73	72	4.62	4.57	4.15	67	0	71
Total**	**158,463**	**175,083**	**197,585**	**439**	**477**	**529**	**5.00**	**5.33**	**5.73**	**2,473**	**1,683**	**853**
Latin America and the Caribbean												
Antigua and Barbuda	28	26	27	317	286	301	2.34	2.14	2.22	0	0	0
Argentina	4,858	5,578	4,265	115	131	99	0.81	0.91	0.80	74	0	31
Bahamas, The	57	64	87	179	201	271	0.69	0.76	1.01	1	0	0
Barbados	33	35	33	113	121	115	0.77	0.83	0.78	1	0	0
Belize	16	17	18	48	52	52	0.99	1.07	1.06	1	1	0
Bolivia	336	373	405	33	36	38	1.23	1.21	1.19	46	0	37

Table 12 International Comparisons of Defence Expenditure and Military Personnel

	Defence Spending current US$ m 2012	2013	2014	Defence Spending per capita (current US$) 2012	2013	2014	Defence Spending % of GDP 2012	2013	2014	Number in Armed Forces (000) 2015	Estimated Reservists (000) 2015	Paramilitary (000) 2015
Brazil	33,163	31,441	31,930	166	156	158	1.48	1.40	1.42	318	1,340	395
Chile	4,274	4,444	3,877	250	258	223	1.60	1.60	1.47	61	40	45
Colombia	12,682	13,551	13,444	280	296	291	3.43	3.58	3.36	297	35	159
Costa Rica	348	402	420	75	86	88	0.77	0.81	0.83	0	0	10
Cuba	n.k.	n.k.	n.k.	n.k.	n.k.	n.k.	n.k.	n.k.	n.k.	49	39	27
Dominican Republic	362	371	397	36	36	38	0.60	0.61	0.64	46	0	15
Ecuador	1,508	n.k.	1,702	99	n.k.	109	1.72	n.k.	1.69	58	118	1
El Salvador	144	154	150	24	25	24	0.60	0.63	0.59	15	10	17
Guatemala	211	259	264	15	18	18	0.42	0.48	0.45	17	64	25
Guyana	33	35	37	45	48	51	1.16	1.18	1.18	1	1	0
Haiti	n.a.	n.a.	n.a.	n.a.	n.a.	n.a.	n.a.	n.a.	n.a.	0	0	0
Honduras	150	179	216	18	21	25	0.81	0.97	1.11	12	60	8
Jamaica	138	130	120	48	45	41	0.94	0.91	0.86	3	1	0
Mexico	5,230	5,927	6,548	45	50	54	0.44	0.47	0.51	267	87	59
Nicaragua	66	85	83	11	15	14	0.62	0.76	0.70	12	0	0
Panama	548	637	717	156	179	199	1.53	1.57	1.60	0	0	12
Paraguay	336	347	313	51	52	47	1.35	1.20	1.00	11	165	15
Peru	2,653	2,752	2,588	90	92	86	1.38	1.36	1.24	115	188	77
Suriname*	49	n.k.	n.k.	87	n.k.	n.k.	1.01	n.k.	n.k.	2	0	0
Trinidad and Tobago	442	395	436	360	323	356	1.67	1.43	1.47	4	0	0
Uruguay	460	466	427	139	140	128	0.92	0.84	0.77	25	0	1
Venezuela	3,886	3,300	4,655	139	116	161	1.30	1.45	2.22	115	8	0
Total**	72,111	72,736	73,297	121	121	121	1.27	1.27	1.28	1,552	2,156	933
Sub-Saharan Africa												
Angola	4,145	6,091	6,846	230	328	359	3.59	4.91	5.21	107	0	10
Benin	78	86	89	8	9	9	1.04	1.04	0.96	7	0	3
Botswana	332	316	346	158	149	161	2.28	2.14	2.12	9	0	2
Burkina Faso	137	154	164	8	9	9	1.24	1.28	1.22	11	0	0
Burundi	62	66	61	6	7	6	2.47	2.41	2.01	20	0	31

Table 12 International Comparisons of Defence Expenditure and Military Personnel

	Defence Spending current US$ m 2012	2013	2014	Defence Spending per capita (current US$) 2012	2013	2014	Defence Spending % of GDP 2012	2013	2014	Number in Armed Forces (000) 2015	Estimated Reservists (000) 2015	Paramilitary (000) 2015
Cameroon	355	393	410	16	17	18	1.34	1.34	1.27	14	0	9
Cape Verde	10	10	12	20	19	23	0.59	0.55	0.62	1	0	0
Central African Rep*	50	n.k.	n.k.	10	n.k.	n.k.	2.31	n.k.	n.k.	7	0	1
Chad*	202	n.k.	n.k.	18	n.k.	n.k.	1.63	n.k.	n.k.	25	0	10
Congo, Republic of*	324	n.k.	720	72	n.k.	154	2.37	n.k.	5.10	10	0	2
Cote d'Ivoire	647	775	812	29	35	36	2.34	2.42	2.39	n.k.	n.k.	n.k.
Dem Republic of the Congo	232	427	456	3	6	6	0.84	1.43	1.39	134	0	0
Djibouti*	10	n.k.	n.k.	13	n.k.	n.k.	0.72	n.k.	n.k.	10	0	3
Equatorial Guinea*	7	n.k.	n.k.	11	n.k.	n.k.	0.05	n.k.	n.k.	1	0	0
Eritrea*	78	n.k.	n.k.	13	n.k.	n.k.	2.52	n.k.	n.k.	202	120	0
Ethiopia	254	351	375	3	4	4	0.60	0.76	0.75	138	0	0
Gabon	225	282	183	140	172	109	1.26	1.47	0.88	5	0	2
Gambia*	6	n.k.	n.k.	3	n.k.	n.k.	0.65	n.k.	n.k.	1	0	0
Ghana	112	295	277	5	12	11	0.27	0.62	0.78	16	0	0
Guinea*	39	n.k.	n.k.	4	n.k.	n.k.	0.69	n.k.	n.k.	10	0	3
Guinea Bissau*	26	n.k.	n.k.	16	n.k.	n.k.	2.66	n.k.	n.k.	4	0	2
Kenya	930	970	1,042	22	22	23	1.85	1.76	1.66	24	0	5
Lesotho	55	48	54	29	25	28	2.33	2.13	2.21	2	0	0
Liberia	23	n.k.	n.k.	6	n.k.	n.k.	1.32	n.k.	n.k.	2	0	0
Madagascar	69	74	74	3	3	3	0.69	0.70	0.66	14	0	8
Malawi	31	24	42	2	1	2	0.75	0.62	0.95	5	0	2
Mali	213	302	365	14	19	22	2.08	2.78	3.03	4	0	8
Mauritius	71	84	84	54	64	63	0.62	0.71	0.66	0	0	3
Mozambique	33	33	35	1	1	1	0.23	0.22	0.21	11	0	0
Namibia	381	411	410	176	188	186	2.91	3.35	3.42	9	0	6
Niger*	70	n.k.	n.k.	4	n.k.	n.k.	1.04	n.k.	n.k.	5	0	5
Nigeria	2,100	2,347	2,253	12	14	13	0.45	0.45	0.38	80	0	82
Rwanda	76	84	81	6	7	7	1.04	1.10	1.01	33	0	2
Senegal	192	248	254	15	19	19	1.37	1.68	1.60	14	0	5

Table 12 International Comparisons of Defence Expenditure and Military Manpower

	Defence Spending current US$ m 2012	2013	2014	Defence Spending per capita (current US$) 2012	2013	2014	Defence Spending % of GDP 2012	2013	2014	Number in Armed Forces (000) 2015	Estimated Reservists (000) 2015	Paramilitary (000) 2015
Seychelles	10	13	n.k.	110	141	n.k.	0.88	0.93	n.k.	0	0	0
Sierra Leone	14	15	15	3	3	3	0.37	0.31	0.28	11	0	0
Somalia	n.k.	n.k.	n.k.	n.k.	n.k.	n.k.	n.k.	n.k.	n.k.	11	0	0
South Africa	5,069	4,213	4,005	104	87	83	1.33	1.20	1.17	62	0	15
South Sudan	819	862	1,044	77	78	90	8.01	6.14	8.78	185	0	0
Sudan	n.k.	1,892	n.k.	n.k.	54	n.k.	n.k.	2.83	n.k.	244	0	20
Tanzania	264	333	396	6	7	8	0.93	1.00	1.08	27	80	1
Togo	62	72	89	9	10	12	1.58	1.65	1.83	9	0	1
Uganda	375	365	405	11	11	11	1.76	1.59	1.55	45	10	2
Zambia	320	377	422	23	27	29	1.28	1.41	1.65	15	3	1
Zimbabwe	318	356	368	25	27	27	2.55	2.70	2.68	29	0	22
Total**	**20,519**	**23,262**	**24,184**	**23**	**25**	**26**	**1.32**	**1.42**	**1.39**	**1,574**	**213**	**264**
Summary												
North America	663,445	594,166	596,925	1,905	1,693	1,688	3.69	3.20	3.11	1,499	886	0
Europe	277,983	281,454	286,922	449	453	461	1.49	1.45	1.44	2,140	2,312	752
Russia and Eurasia	68,488	76,784	81,604	243	271	288	2.57	2.74	2.98	1,207	3,857	701
Asia	317,562	325,482	343,804	82	83	87	1.43	1.43	1.41	9,490	14,748	3,769
Middle East and North Africa	158,463	175,083	197,585	439	477	529	5.00	5.33	5.73	2,473	1,683	853
Latin America and the Carribean	72,111	72,736	73,297	121	121	121	1.27	1.27	1.28	1,552	2,156	933
Sub-Saharan Africa	20,519	23,262	24,184	23	25	26	1.32	1.42	1.39	1,574	213	264
Global totals	**1,578,570**	**1,548,967**	**1,604,322**	**226**	**220**	**225**	**2.20**	**2.09**	**2.08**	**19,936**	**25,856**	**7,271**

* Estimates
** Totals include defence spending estimates for states where insufficient official information is available, in order to enable approximate comparisons of regional defence spending between years.

Selected Non-State Armed Groups: Observed Equipment Holdings

The Military Balance details below information about the observed capacities of selected non-state groups. It is intended to complement the assessments carried within the written and data sections of *The Military Balance*, as well as other IISS products such as the Armed Conflict Database and the *Armed Conflict Survey*. This 'observed equipment', which should not be taken as an exhaustive list of equipment in each inventory, has been assessed by the IISS as being present within a particular area of operations. While in many cases it is possible to attribute the equipment operator, in other cases it has proven difficult to ascertain precise ownership.

The Military Balance does not detail in its country inventories vehicles commonly called 'technicals' **(tch)**, but for some non-state groups these – often modified civilian vehicles – can constitute a principal manoeuvre capability and as such are relevant to informed assessments of inventory holdings.

EASTERN UKRAINE SEPARATIST FORCES

It has proven problematic to apportion ownership to either of the main separatist entities in the Donetsk and Luhansk oblasts, and as such this list reflects equipment that has been generally observed as employed in support of the separatist cause in eastern Ukraine.

EQUIPMENT BY TYPE
MBT T-64BV; T-64B; T-64BM†; T-72B1; T-72BA[a]; T-72B3[a]
RECCE BDRM-2
AIFV BMD-1, BMD-2; BMP-2; BTR-4; BTR-82A[a]
APC
　APC (W) BTR-60; BTR-70; BTR-80
　APC (T) MT-LB; BTR-D GT-MU; PTS-2
ARTY
　SP 2S1; 2S3; 2S19†
　TOWED 122mm D30 **152mm** 2A65
　GUN/MOR • 120mm • SP 2S9 **TOWED:** 2B16 *Nona-K*
　MRL BM-21
　MOR 120mm 2B11 **82mm** 2B14
AT
　MSL 9K115 *Metis* (AT-7 *Saxhorn*); 9K135 *Kornet* (AT-14 *Spriggan*)
　RCL SPG-9
　GUNS 100mm MT-12
AD
　SAM • SP 9K37 *Buk* (SA-11 *Gadfly*) (reported); 9K35 *Strela*-10 (SA-13 *Gopher*); 9K33 *Osa* (SA-8 *Gecko*)
　MANPAD 9K32M *Strela*-2M (SA-7B *Grail*); 9K38 *Igla* (SA-18 *Grouse*); GROM
　GUNS:
　　SP 30mm 2S6; **23mm** ZU-23-2 (tch/on MT-LB)
　　TOWED 14.5mm ZPU-2; **57mm** ε400 S-60
AIRCRAFT
　TRG 3+ *Yak*-52 (status unclear)

[a] observed advanced equipment variants of clearer Russian origin within eastern Ukraine (operator/ownership unknown, but in support of separatist cause).

NAGORNO-KARABAKH

The equipment displayed below for forces in Nagorno-Karabakh is a reflection of military equipment observed by IISS analysts. Based on IISS observations, it is probable that the equipment seen in Nagorno-Karabakh includes some equipment originally procured for Armenian forces.

EQUIPMENT BY TYPE
MBT T-72
AIFV BMP-1; BMP-2
ARTY 232
　SP 122mm 2S1; **152mm** 2S3
　TOWED 122mm D-30; **152mm** 2A36
　MRL 122mm BM-21; **273mm** WM-80
AT • MSL
　SP 9P148 *Konkurs*; 9P149 MT-LB *Spiral*
AD
　SAM
　　SP 2K11 *Krug* (SA-4 *Ganef*); 2K12 *Kub* (SA-6 *Gainful*); 9K33 *Osa* (SA-8 *Gecko*)
　　TOWED S-75 *Dvina* (SA-2 *Guideline*); S-125 *Pechora* (SA-3 *Goa*)
　　MANPAD 9K310 *Igla*-1 (SA-16 *Gimlet*); 9K38 *Igla* (SA-18 *Grouse*)
　GUNS
　　SP ZSU-23-4
　　TOWED 23mm ZU-23-2
MSL • TACTICAL • SSM 9K72 *Elbrus* (SS-1C *Scud B*)

Air and Air Defence Aviation Forces

EQUIPMENT BY TYPE
HELICOPTERS
　ATK 5 Mi-24 *Hind*
　MRH 5 Mi-8MT *Hip*

PESHMERGA (including Zeravani)

The equipment displayed below for Peshmerga forces operating in northern Iraq includes that of the Zeravani police units of the Kurdistan Regional Government. It reflects some of the equipment that began to be delivered during 2014 as international military assistance arrived to bolster Kurdish forces fighting ISIS in northern Iraq.

EQUIPMENT BY TYPE
MBT T-54; T-55; T-62
RECCE EE-9 *Cascavel*
AIFV 2+ EE-11 *Urutu*
APC
　APC (T) MT-LB; YW-701 (Type-63)
　APC (W) M1117 ASV
　PPV HMMWV; M1114 (up-armoured HMMWV); ILAV *Cougar* 6x6; Otokar APV; *Reva*; 5 *Dingo*

ARTY
   SP 122mm 2S1
   TOWED 87.6mm 1+ 25 pdr; 122mm 6+ D-30
   MRL 107mm Type 63 (Tch); 122mm BM-21 (inc mod); HM20 (reported)
   MOR 60mm M224; 81mm M252; 120mm M120; 130mm M-46/Type-59; 152mm D-20
AT
   MSL • MANPATS Milan
   RCL 73mm SPG-9; 84mm Carl Gustav; 105mm M40
   RL 110mm Panzerfaust 3
AD
   GUNS
      SP 14.5mm ZPU-1 (tch); ZPU-2 (tch); ZPU-4 (tch) 20mm 53T2 Tarasque (tch); 23mm ZU-23-2 (tch/on MT-LB); 57mm ZSU-57; S-60 (tch)
      TOWED 14.5mm ZPU-1; ZPU-2; ZPU-4; 20mm 53T2 Tarasque; 57mm S-60
ARV 1+ T-55

ISIS IN IRAQ

The equipment displayed below for forces of the Islamic State of Iraq and al-Sham reflects that observed and assessed in Iraq, and does not include equipment that these forces may have displayed in Syria. ISIS forces will not necessarily have the training, spare parts or ammunition to operate this equipment on a routine basis.

EQUIPMENT BY TYPE
MBT T-54/55; T-72†; M1 Abrams†
AIFV BTR4†
APC
   APC (T) M113; MT-LB
   APC (W) M1117 ASV
   PPV HMMWV; M1114 (up-armoured HMMWV); ILAV Cougar Dzik-3;
ARTY • TOWED 130mm M46/Type 59; 150mm M198
   MOR 120mm M120
AT
   MSL • MANPATS 9K135 Kornet (AT-14 Spriggan) (reported)
   RCL 73mm SPG-9; 105mm M40; 90mm M79 Osa (reported)

AD
   SAM • MANPAD (reported)
GUNS
SP 57mm S-60 (tch); 14.5mm ZPU (tch); 23mm ZSU-23 (tch)

BOKO HARAM

The equipment displayed below should not be considered exhaustive given changes in the group's operational locations, the fluid nature of ongoing combat with Nigeria's armed forces, and also the flexible and devolved nature of Boko Haram itself, which has a number of factions and splinter groups.

EQUIPMENT BY TYPE
MBT T-55
RECCE ECR-90 (reported)
APC
   APC (T) 4K-7FA Steyr
   APC (W) AVGP Cougar (mod)
   PPV Otokar Cobra; Streit Spartan
AD • SP 14.5mm ZPU-2 (tch); 23mm ZU-23-2 (tch)

SUDAN PEOPLE'S LIBERATION ARMY (SPLA) – IN OPPOSITION (SOUTH SUDAN)

The equipment displayed below for SPLA–IO forces is a reflection of the shared heritage with government armed forces, the SPLA. Both sides originated in the national army, and so share the same basic equipment and tactics: large-scale infantry equipped with heterogeneous small arms; vehicle-mounted anti-aircraft guns; and simple anti-armour and artillery weapons.

EQUIPMENT BY TYPE
MBT T-55
APC (W) Typhoon
ARTY
   TOWED 122mm M30 (M1938)
   MRL 122mm BM-21; 107mm Type-63
   MOR 120mm Type 55 look-a-like
AT
   RCL 73mm SPG-9
AD
   GUNS 23mm ZU-23-2 (tch)

PART TWO
Explanatory Notes

The Military Balance provides an assessment of the armed forces and defence expenditures of 171 countries and territories. Each edition contributes to the provision of a unique compilation of data and information, enabling the reader to discern trends by studying editions as far back as 1959. The data in the current edition is accurate according to IISS assessments as at November 2014, unless specified. Inclusion of a territory, country or state in *The Military Balance* does not imply legal recognition or indicate support for any government.

GENERAL ARRANGEMENT AND CONTENTS

The introduction is an assessment of global defence developments and key themes in the 2015 edition. Next, three analytical essays focus on trends in conflict, defence technology and defence industry. A graphical section follows, analysing comparative defence statistics by domain, as well as key trends in defence economics.

Regional chapters begin with an assessment of key military issues facing each area and regional defence economics; they now also include graphical analysis of selected equipment. These are followed by country-specific analysis of defence policy and capability issues, and defence economics. These are followed by military-capability and defence-economics data for regional countries, in alphabetical order. Selected Arms Procurements and Deliveries tables complete each region.

The book closes with comparative and reference sections containing data on military exercises, comparisons of expenditure and personnel statistics and, this year, assessments of observed military equipments for a selection of non-state armed groups.

THE MILITARY BALANCE WALL CHART

The theme for *The Military Balance 2015* wall chart is Russia's armed forces. The display is intended to show generalised force dispositions, as well as text analyses of key elements of the military-reform process. The Chart of Conflict, hitherto carried in *The Military Balance*, will in future appear with the IISS *Armed Conflict Survey*.

USING THE MILITARY BALANCE

The country entries assess personnel strengths, organisation and equipment holdings of the world's armed forces.

Abbreviations And Definitions

Qualifier	
'At least'	Total is no less than the number given
'Up to'	Total is at most the number given, but could be lower
'About'	Total could be higher than given
'Some'	Precise inventory is unavailable at time of press
'In store'	Equipment held away from front-line units; readiness and maintenance varies
Billion (bn)	1,000 million (m)
Trillion (tr)	1,000 billion
$	US dollars unless otherwise stated
ε	Estimated
*	Aircraft counted by the IISS as combat capable
-	Part of a unit is detached/less than
+	Unit reinforced/more than
†	IISS assesses that the serviceability of equipment is in doubt[a]
‡	Equipment judged obsolete (weapons whose basic design is more than four decades old and which have not been significantly upgraded within the past decade)[a]

[a] Not to be taken to imply that such equipment cannot be used

Force-strength and equipment-inventory data are based on the most accurate data available, or on the best estimate that can be made. In estimating a country's total capabilities, old equipment may be counted where it is considered that it may still be deployable.

The data presented reflects judgements based on information available to the IISS at the time the book is compiled. Where information differs from previous editions, this is mainly because of changes in national forces, but it is sometimes because the IISS has reassessed the evidence supporting past entries. Given this, care must be taken in constructing time-series comparisons from information given in successive editions.

COUNTRY ENTRIES

Information on each country is shown in a standard format, although the differing availability of information and differences in nomenclature result in some variations. Country entries include economic, demographic and military data. Population figures are based on demographic statistics taken from the US Census Bureau. Data on ethnic and religious minorities is also provided in some country entries. Military data includes manpower, length of conscript service where relevant, outline organisation, number of formations and units, and an inventory of the major equipment of each service. Details of national forces stationed abroad and of foreign forces stationed within the given country are also provided.

ARMS PROCUREMENTS AND DELIVERIES

Tables at the end of the regional texts show selected arms procurements (contracts and, in selected cases, major development programmes that may not yet be at contract stage) and deliveries listed by country buyer, together with additional information including, if known, the country supplier, cost, prime contractor and the date on which the first delivery was due to be made. While every effort has been made to ensure accuracy, some transactions may not be fulfilled or may differ – for instance in quantity – from those reported. The information is arranged in the following order: strategic systems; land; sea; air.

DEFENCE ECONOMICS

Country entries include defence expenditures, selected economic-performance indicators and demographic aggregates. All country entries are subject to revision each year as new information, particularly regarding defence expenditure, becomes available. The information is necessarily selective. In the 'country comparisons' section on p. 484–90, there are also international comparisons of defence expenditure and military personnel, giving expenditure figures for the past three years in per capita terms and as a % of GDP. The aim is to provide an accurate measure of military expenditure and the allocation of economic resources to defence.

Individual country entries show economic performance over the past two years and current demographic data. Where this data is unavailable, information from the last available year is provided. Where possible, official defence budgets for the current and previous two years are shown, as well as an estimate of actual defence expenditures for those countries where true defence expenditure is thought to be higher than official budget figures suggest. Estimates of actual defence expenditure, however, are only made for those countries where there is sufficient data to justify such a measurement. Therefore, there will be several countries listed in *The Military Balance* for which only an official defence-budget figure is provided but where, in reality, true defence-related expenditure is almost certainly higher.

All financial data in the country entries is shown both in national currency and US dollars at current year – not constant – prices. US-dollar conversions are generally, but not invariably, calculated from the exchange rates listed in the entry. In some cases a US-dollar purchasing-power parity (PPP) rate is used in preference to official or market exchange rates and this is indicated in each case.

Definitions of terms

Despite efforts by NATO and the UN to develop a standardised definition of military expenditure, many countries prefer to use their own definitions (which are often not made public). In order to present a comprehensive picture, *The Military Balance* lists three different measures of military-related spending data.

- For most countries, an official defence-budget figure is provided.
- For those countries where other military-related outlays, over and above the defence budget, are known or can be reasonably estimated, an additional measurement referred to as defence expenditure is also provided. Defence-expenditure figures will naturally be higher than official budget figures, depending on the range of additional factors included.
- For NATO countries, an official defence-budget figure as well as a measure of defence expenditure (calculated using NATO's definition) is quoted.

NATO's military-expenditure definition (the most comprehensive) is cash outlays of central or federal governments to meet the costs of national armed forces. The term 'armed forces' includes strategic, land, naval, air, command, administration and support forces. It also includes other forces if these forces are trained, structured and equipped to support defence forces and are realistically deployable. Defence expenditures are reported in four categories: Operating Costs, Procurement and Construction, Research and Development (R&D) and Other Expenditure. Operating Costs include salaries and pensions for military and civilian personnel; the cost of maintaining and training units, service organisations, headquarters and support elements; and the cost of servicing and repairing military equipment and infrastructure. Procurement and Construction expenditure covers national equipment and infrastructure spending, as well as common infrastructure programmes. R&D is defence expenditure up to the point at which new equipment can be put in service, regardless of whether new equipment is actually procured. Foreign Military Aid (FMA) contributions are also noted.

For many non-NATO countries the issue of transparency in reporting military budgets is fundamental. Not every UN member state reports defence-budget data (even fewer report real defence expenditures) to their electorates, the UN, the IMF or other multinational organisations. In the case of governments with a proven record of transparency, official figures generally conform to the standardised definition of defence budgeting, as adopted by the UN, and consistency problems are not usually a major issue. The IISS cites official defence budgets as reported by either national governments, the UN, the OSCE or the IMF.

For those countries where the official defence-budget figure is considered to be an incomplete measure of total military-related spending, and appropriate additional data is available, the IISS will use data from a variety of sources to arrive at a more accurate estimate of true defence expenditure. The most frequent instances of budgetary manipulation or falsification typically involve equipment procurement, R&D, defence-industrial investment, covert weapons programmes, pensions for retired military and civilian personnel, paramilitary forces and non-budgetary sources of revenue for the military arising from ownership of industrial, property and land assets.

Percentage changes in defence spending are referred to in either nominal or real terms. Nominal terms relate to the percentage change in numerical spending figures, and do not account for the impact of price changes (i.e. inflation) on defence spending. By contrast, real terms account for inflationary effects, and may therefore be considered a more accurate representation of change over time.

The principal sources for national economic statistics cited in the country entries are the IMF, the Organisation for Economic Cooperation and Development, the World Bank and three regional banks (the Inter-American, Asian and African Development banks). For some countries, basic economic data is difficult to obtain. Gross Domestic Product (GDP) figures are nominal (current) values at market prices. GDP growth is real, not nominal, growth, and inflation is the year-on-year change in consumer prices.

Calculating exchange rates

Typically, but not invariably, the exchange rates shown in the country entries are also used to calculate GDP and defence-budget and -expenditure dollar conversions. Where they are not used, it is because the use of exchange-rate dollar conversions can misrepresent both GDP and defence expenditure. For some countries, PPP rather than market exchange rates are sometimes used for dollar conversions of both GDP and defence expenditures. Where PPP is used, it is annotated accordingly.

The arguments for using PPP are strongest for Russia and China. Both the UN and IMF have issued caveats concerning the reliability of official economic statistics on transitional economies, particularly those of Russia, and some Eastern European and Central Asian countries. Non-reporting, lags in the publication of current statistics and frequent revisions of recent data (not always accompanied by timely revision of previously published figures in the same series) pose transparency and consistency problems. Another problem arises with certain transitional economies whose productive capabilities are similar to those of developed economies, but where cost and price structures are often much lower than world levels. No specific PPP rate exists for the military sector, and its use for this purpose should be treated with caution. Furthermore, there is no definitive guide as to which elements of military spending should be calculated using the limited PPP rates available. The figures presented here are only intended to illustrate a range of possible outcomes depending on which input variables are used.

GENERAL DEFENCE DATA

Personnel

The 'Active' total comprises all servicemen and women on full-time duty (including conscripts and long-term assignments from the Reserves). When a gendarmerie or equivalent is under control of the defence ministry, they may be included in the active total. Only the length of conscript liability is shown; where service is voluntary there is no entry. 'Reserve' describes formations and units not fully manned or operational in peacetime, but which can be mobilised by recalling reservists in an emergency. Some countries have more than one category of reserves, often kept at varying degrees of readiness. Where possible, these differences are denoted using the national descriptive title, but always under the heading of 'Reserves' to distinguish them from full-time active forces. All personnel figures are rounded to the nearest 50, except for organisations with under 500 personnel, where figures are rounded to the nearest ten.

Other forces

Many countries maintain forces whose training, organisation, equipment and control suggest they may be used to support or replace regular military forces; these are called 'paramilitary'. They include some forces that may have a constabulary role. These are detailed after the military forces of each country, but their manpower is not normally included in the totals at the start of each entry.

Non-state armed groups

The Military Balance includes some detail on selected non-state groups that are militarily significant armed actors, this year detailing observed military equipments for some of these groups. Some may be aligned with national or

Units and formation strength	
Company	100–200
Battalion	500–1,000
Brigade	3,000–5,000
Division	15,000–20,000
Corps or Army	50,000–100,000

regional governments or religious or ethnic groups. They may pose a threat to state integrity or to international stability. For more information, see the IISS Armed Conflict Database (*http://acd.iiss.org*) or the *Armed Conflict Survey*.

Cyber

The Military Balance includes detail on selected national cyber capacities, particularly those under the control of, or designed to fulfil the requirements of, defence organisations. Capabilities are not assessed quantitatively. Rather, national organisations, legislation, national security strategies etc. are noted, where appropriate, to indicate the level of effort states are devoting to this area. Generally, civil organisations are not traced here, though in some cases these organisations could have dual civil–military roles.

Forces by role and equipment by type

Quantities are shown by function (according to each nation's employment) and type, and represent what are believed to be total holdings, including active and reserve operational and training units. Inventory totals for missile systems relate to launchers and not to missiles. Equipment held 'in store' is not counted in the main inventory totals.

Deployments

The Military Balance mainly lists permanent bases and operational deployments, including peacekeeping operations, which are often discussed in the text for each regional section. Information in the country-data files details, first, deployments of troops and, second, military observers and, where available, the role and equipment of deployed units.

Training activity

Selected exercises, which involve two or more states and are designed to improve inter-operability or test new doctrine, forces or equipment, are detailed in tables on p. 482–83. (Exceptions may be made for particularly important exercises held by single states that indicate important capability or equipment developments.)

LAND FORCES

To make international comparison easier and more consistent, *The Military Balance* categorises forces by role and translates national military terminology for unit and formation sizes. Typical personnel strength, equipment holdings and organisation of formations such as brigades and divisions vary from country to country. In addition some unit terms, such as 'regiment', 'squadron', 'battery' and 'troop' can refer to significantly different unit sizes in different countries. Unless otherwise stated these terms should be assumed to reflect standard British usage where they occur.

NAVAL FORCES

Classifying naval vessels according to role is complex. A post-war consensus on primary surface combatants revolved around a distinction between independently operating cruisers, air-defence escorts (destroyers) and anti-submarine-warfare escorts (frigates). However, new ships are increasingly performing a range of roles. For this reason, *The Military Balance* has drawn up a classification system based on full-load displacement (FLD) rather than a role classification system. These definitions will not necessarily conform to national designations.

AIR FORCES

Aircraft listed as combat capable are assessed as being equipped to deliver air-to-air or air-to-surface ordnance. The definition includes aircraft designated by type as bomber, fighter, fighter ground attack, ground attack, and anti-submarine warfare. Other aircraft considered to be combat capable are marked with an asterisk (*). Operational groupings of air forces are shown where known. Typical squadron aircraft strengths can vary both between aircraft types and from country to country.

When assessing missile ranges, *The Military Balance* uses the following range indicators: Short-Range Ballistic Missile (SRBM): less than 1,000km; Medium-Range Ballistic Missile (MRBM): 1,000–3,000km; Intermediate-Range Ballistic Missile (IRBM): 3,000–5,000km; Intercontinental Ballistic Missile (ICBM): over 5,000km.

ATTRIBUTION AND ACKNOWLEDGEMENTS

The International Institute for Strategic Studies owes no allegiance to any government, group of governments, or any political or other organisation. Its assessments are its own, based on the material available to it from a wide variety of sources. The cooperation of governments of all listed countries has been sought and, in many cases, received. However, some data in *The Military Balance* is estimated. Care is taken to ensure that this data is as accurate and free from bias as possible. The Institute owes a considerable debt to a number of its own members, consultants and all those who help compile and check material. The Director-General and Chief Executive and staff of the Institute assume full responsibility for the data and judgements in this book. Comments and suggestions on the data and textual material contained within the book, as well as on the style and presentation of data, are welcomed and should be communicated to the Editor of *The Military Balance* at: IISS, 13–15 Arundel Street, London WC2R 3DX, UK, email: *milbal@iiss.org*. Copyright on all information in *The Military Balance* belongs strictly to the IISS. Application to reproduce limited amounts of data may be made to the publisher: Taylor & Francis, 4 Park Square, Milton Park, Abingdon, Oxon, OX14 4RN. Email: *society.permissions@tandf.co.uk*. Unauthorised use of data from *The Military Balance* will be subject to legal action.

Principal Land Definitions

Forces by role

Command: free-standing, deployable formation headquarters (HQs).

Special Forces (SF): elite units specially trained and equipped for unconventional warfare and operations in enemy-controlled territory. Many are employed in counter-terrorist roles.

Manoeuvre: combat units and formations capable of manoeuvring include:

Reconnaissance: combat units and formations whose primary purpose is to gain information.

Armoured: armoured formations are principally equipped with main battle tanks (MBTs) and heavy armoured infantry fighting vehicles (AIFVs) to provide mounted close-combat capability.

Mechanised: mechanised formations use lighter armoured vehicles than armoured formations, and fewer, if any, tanks. They have less mounted firepower and protection, but can usually deploy more infantry than armoured formations.

Light: light formations may have few, if any, organic armoured vehicles. Some may be motorised and equipped with soft-skinned vehicles. Dismounted infantry constitute a primary capability.

Air Manoeuvre: formations and units trained and equipped for delivery by transport aircraft and/or helicopters. Some may have integral aviation assets.

Aviation: army units and formations organically equipped with helicopters and/or fixed-wing aircraft.

Amphibious: amphibious forces are trained and equipped to project force from the sea.

Mountain: formations and units trained and equipped to operate in mountainous terrain.

Other Forces: specifically trained and equipped 'jungle' or 'counter-insurgency' brigades and security units such as Presidential Guards, or formations permanently employed in training or demonstration tasks.

Combat Support (CS): includes artillery, engineers, air defence, intelligence, EOD and other CS not integral to manoeuvre formations. They support combat units and formations to enable them to fight and manoeuvre.

Combat Service Support (CSS): includes construction, logistics, maintenance, medical, supply and transport formations and units.

Equipment by type

Light Weapons: include all small arms, machine guns, grenades and grenade launchers and unguided man-portable anti-armour and support weapons. These weapons have proliferated so much and are sufficiently easy to manufacture or copy that listing them would be impractical.

Crew-Served Weapons: crew-served recoilless rifles, man-portable ATGW, MANPAD and mortars of greater than 80mm calibre are listed, but the high degree of proliferation and local manufacture of many of these weapons means that estimates of numbers held may not be reliable.

Armoured Fighting Vehicles (AFVs):

Main Battle Tank (MBT): armoured, tracked combat vehicles, armed with a turret-mounted gun of at least 75mm calibre and weighing at least 25 metric tonnes unladen. Lighter vehicles that meet the first three criteria are considered light tanks.

Reconnaissance: combat vehicles designed and equipped to enable reconnaissance tasks.

Armoured Infantry Fighting Vehicle (AIFV): armoured combat vehicles designed and equipped to transport an infantry squad and armed with a cannon of at least 20mm calibre.

Armoured Personnel Carrier (APC): lightly armoured combat vehicles designed and equipped to transport an infantry squad but either unarmed or armed with a cannon of less than 20mm calibre.

Protected Patrol Vehicle (PPV): role-specific armoured vehicles designed to protect troops from small arms, RPGs and roadside-bomb threats. Most have little or no cross-country mobility and are not designed for combined-arms manoeuvre.

Artillery: weapons (including guns, howitzers, gun/howitzers, multiple-rocket launchers, mortars and gun/mortars) with a calibre greater than 100mm for artillery pieces and 80mm and above for mortars, capable of engaging ground targets with indirect fire.

Anti-Tank (AT): guns, guided weapons and recoilless rifles designed to engage armoured vehicles and battle-field hardened targets.

Air Defence (AD): guns and missiles designed to engage fixed-wing, rotary-wing and unmanned aircraft.

Combat Support and Combat Service Support Equipment: includes assault bridging, engineer tanks, armoured recovery vehicles and armoured ambulances. Civilian equipment is excluded.

Principal Naval Definitions

To aid comparison between fleets, the following definitions, which do not conform to national definitions, are used:

Submarines: all vessels designed to operate primarily under water. Submarines with a dived displacement below 250 tonnes are classified as midget submarines; those below 500 tonnes are coastal submarines.

Principal surface combatants: all surface ships designed for combat operations on the high seas, with an FLD above 1,500 tonnes. Aircraft carriers, including helicopter carriers, are vessels with a flat deck primarily designed to carry fixed- and/or rotary-wing aircraft, without amphibious capability. Other principal surface combatants include cruisers (with an FLD above 9,750 tonnes), destroyers (with an FLD above 4,500 tonnes) and frigates (with an FLD above 1,500 tonnes).

Patrol and coastal combatants: surface vessels designed for coastal or inshore operations. These include corvettes, which usually have an FLD between 500 and 1,500 tonnes and are distinguished from other patrol vessels by their heavier armaments. Also included in this category are offshore-patrol ships, with an FLD greater than 1,500 tonnes; patrol craft, which have an FLD between 250 and 1,500 tonnes; and patrol boats with an FLD between ten and 250 tonnes. Vessels with a top speed greater than 35 knots are designated as 'fast'.

Mine warfare vessels: all surface vessels configured primarily for mine laying or countermeasures. Countermeasures vessels are either: sweepers, which are designed to locate and destroy mines in an area; hunters, which are designed to locate and destroy individual mines; or countermeasures vessels, which combine both roles.

Amphibious vessels: vessels designed to transport personnel and/or equipment onto shore. These include landing helicopter assault vessels, which can embark fixed- and/or rotary-wing air assets as well as landing craft; landing helicopter docks, which can embark rotary-wing or VTOL assets and have a well dock; landing platform helicopters, which have a primary role of launch and recovery platform for rotary-wing or VTOL assets with a dock to store equipment/personnel for amphibious operations; and landing platform docks, which do not have a through deck but do have a well dock. Landing ships are amphibious vessels capable of ocean passage and landing craft are smaller vessels designed to transport personnel and equipment from a larger vessel to land or across small stretches of water. Landing ships have a hold; landing craft are open vessels.

Auxiliary vessels: ocean-going surface vessels performing an auxiliary military role, supporting combat ships or operations. These generally fulfil five roles: under-way replenishment (such as tankers and oilers); logistics (such as cargo ships); maintenance (such as cable-repair ships or buoy tenders); research (such as survey ships); and special purpose (such as intelligence-collection ships and ocean-going tugs).

Yard craft/miscellaneous vessels: surface vessels performing a support role in coastal waters or to ships not in service. These vessels often have harbour roles, such as tugs and tenders. Other miscellaneous craft, such as royal yachts, are also included.

Weapons systems: weapons are listed in the following order: land-attack missiles, anti-ship missiles, surface-to-air missiles, torpedo tubes, anti-submarine weapons, CIWS, guns and aircraft. Missiles with a range less than 5km and guns with a calibre less than 57mm are generally not included.

Organisations: naval groupings such as fleets and squadrons frequently change and are shown only where doing so would aid qualitative judgements.

Principal Aviation Definitions

Bomber (Bbr): comparatively large platforms intended for the delivery of air-to-surface ordnance. Bbr units are units equipped with bomber aircraft for the air-to-surface role.

Fighter (Ftr): aircraft designed primarily for air-to-air combat, which may also have a limited air-to-surface capability. Ftr units are equipped with aircraft intended to provide air superiority, which may have a secondary and limited air-to-surface capability.

Fighter/Ground Attack (FGA): multi-role fighter-size platforms with significant air-to-surface capability, potentially including maritime attack, and at least some air-to-air capacity. FGA units are multi-role units equipped with aircraft capable of air-to-air and air-to-surface attack.

Ground Attack (Atk): aircraft designed solely for the air-to-surface task, with limited or no air-to-air capability. Atk units are equipped with fixed-wing aircraft.

Attack Helicopter (Atk Hel): rotary-wing platforms designed for delivery of air-to-surface weapons, and fitted with an integrated fire-control system.

Anti-Submarine Warfare (ASW): fixed- and rotary-wing platforms designed to locate and engage submarines, many with a secondary anti-surface-warfare capacity. ASW units are equipped with fixed- or rotary-wing aircraft.

Anti-Surface Warfare (ASuW): ASuW units are equipped with fixed- or rotary-wing aircraft intended for anti-surface-warfare missions.

Maritime Patrol (MP): fixed-wing aircraft and unmanned aerial vehicles (UAVs) intended for maritime surface surveillance, which may possess an anti-surface-warfare capability. MP units are equipped with fixed-wing aircraft or UAVs.

Electronic Warfare (EW): fixed- and rotary-wing aircraft and UAVs intended for electronic countermeasures. EW units are equipped with fixed- or rotary-wing aircraft or UAVs.

Intelligence/Surveillance/Reconnaissance (ISR): fixed- and rotary-wing aircraft and UAVs intended to provide radar, visible light or infrared imagery, or a mix thereof. ISR units are equipped with fixed- or rotary-wing aircraft or UAVs.

Combat/Intelligence/Surveillance/Reconnaissance (CISR): aircraft and UAVs that have the capability to deliver air-to-surface weapons, as well as undertake ISR tasks. CISR units are equipped with armed aircraft and/or UAVs for ISR and air-to-surface missions.

COMINT/ELINT/SIGINT: fixed- and rotary-wing platforms and UAVs capable of gathering electronic (ELINT), communication (COMINT) or signals intelligence (SIGINT). COMINT units are equipped with fixed- or rotary-wing aircraft or UAVs intended for the communications-intelligence task. ELINT units are equipped with fixed- or rotary-wing aircraft or UAVs used for gathering electronic intelligence. SIGINT units are equipped with fixed- or rotary-wing aircraft or UAVs used to collect signals intelligence.

Airborne Early Warning (& Control) (AEW (&C)): fixed- and rotary-wing platforms capable of providing airborne early warning, with a varying degree of onboard command-and-control depending on the platform. AEW(&C) units are equipped with fixed- or rotary-wing aircraft.

Search and Rescue (SAR): units are equipped with fixed- or rotary-wing aircraft used to recover military personnel or civilians.

Combat Search and Rescue (CSAR): units are equipped with armed fixed- or rotary-wing aircraft for recovery of personnel from hostile territory.

Tanker (Tkr): fixed- and rotary-wing aircraft designed for air-to-air refuelling. Tkr units are equipped with fixed- or rotary-wing aircraft used for air-to-air refuelling.

Tanker Transport (Tkr/Tpt): platforms capable of both air-to-air refuelling and military airlift.

Transport (Tpt): fixed- and rotary-wing aircraft intended for military airlift. Light transport aircraft are categorised as having a maximum payload of up to 11,340kg, medium up to 27,215kg and heavy above 27,215kg. Medium transport helicopters have an internal payload of up to 4,535kg; heavy transport helicopters greater than 4,535kg. PAX aircraft are platforms generally unsuited for transporting cargo on the main deck. Tpt units are equipped with fixed- or rotary-wing platforms to transport personnel or cargo.

Trainer (Trg): a fixed- and rotary-wing aircraft designed primarily for the training role, some also have the capacity to carry light to medium ordnance. Trg units are equipped with fixed- or rotary-wing training aircraft intended for pilot or other aircrew training.

Multi-role helicopter (MRH): rotary-wing platforms designed to carry out a variety of military tasks including light transport, armed reconnaissance and battlefield support.

Unmanned Aerial Vehicles (UAVs): remotely piloted or controlled unmanned fixed- or rotary-wing systems. Light UAVs are those weighing 20–150kg; medium: 150–600kg; and large: more than 600kg.

Reference

Table 13 **List of Abbreviations for Data Sections**

AAA anti-aircraft artillery
AAM air-to-air missile
AAV amphibious assault vehicle
AB airborne
ABM anti-ballistic missile
ABU sea-going buoy tender
ac aircraft
ACP airborne command post
ACV air cushion vehicle/armoured combat vehicle
AD air defence
ADA air defence artillery
adj adjusted
AE auxiliary, ammunition carrier
AEV armoured engineer vehicle
AEW airborne early warning
AFDL auxiliary floating dry dock small
AFS logistics ship
AG misc auxiliary
AGB icebreaker
AGE experimental auxiliary ship
AGF command ship
AGHS hydrographic survey vessel
AGI intelligence collection vessel
AGOR oceanographic research vessel
AGOS oceanographic surveillance vessel
AGS survey ship
AH hospital ship
AIFV armoured infantry fighting vehicle
AK cargo ship
aka also known as
AKEH dry cargo/ammunition ship
AKL cargo ship (light)
AKR roll-on/roll-off cargo ship
AKSL stores ship (light)
ALCM air-launched cruise missile
amph amphibious/amphibian
AO oiler
AOE fast combat support ship
AOR fleet replenishment oiler with RAS capability
AORH oiler with hel capacity
AORL replenishment oiler (light)
AORLH oiler light with hel deck
AOT oiler transport
AP armour-piercing/anti-personnel/transport
APB barracks ship
APC armoured personnel carrier
AR repair ship
ARC cable repair ship
ARD auxiliary repair dry dock
ARG amphibious ready group
ARH active radar homing
ARL airborne reconnaissance low
ARM anti-radiation missile

armd armoured
ARS rescue and salvage ship
arty artillery
ARV armoured recovery vehicle
AS anti-submarine/submarine tender
ASCM anti-ship cruise missile
AShM anti-ship missile
aslt assault
ASM air-to-surface missile
ASR submarine rescue craft
ASTT anti-submarine torpedo tube
ASW anti-submarine warfare
ASuW anti-surface warfare
AT tug/anti-tank
ATBM anti-tactical ballistic missile
ATF tug, ocean going
ATGW anti-tank guided weapon
ATK attack/ground attack
AVB aviation logistic support ship
avn aviation
AWT water tanker
AX training craft
AXL training craft (light)
AXS training craft (sail)
BA budget authority (US)
Bbr bomber
BCT brigade combat team
bde brigade
bdgt budget
BG battle group
BMD ballistic missile defence
BMEWS ballistic missile early warning system
bn battalion/billion
bty battery
C2 command and control
casevac casualty evacuation
cav cavalry
cbt combat
CBRN chemical, biological, radiological, nuclear, explosive
cdo commando
C/G/H/M/N/L cruiser/guided missile/with hangar/with missile/nuclear-powered/light
CISR Combat ISR
CIMIC civil–military cooperation
CIWS close-in weapons system
COIN counter-insurgency
comb combined/combination
comd command
COMINT communications intelligence
comms communications
coy company
CPX command post exercise
CS combat support
CSAR combat search and rescue

CSS combat service support
CT counter-terrorism
CV/H/L/N/S aircraft carrier/helicopter/light/nuclear powered/VSTOL
CW chemical warfare/weapons
DD/G/H/M destroyer/with AShM/with hangar/with SAM
DDS dry deck shelter
def defence
det detachment
div division
ECM electronic countermeasures
ELINT electronic intelligence
elm element/s
engr engineer
EOD explosive ordnance disposal
eqpt equipment
ESM electronic support measures
est estimate(d)
EW electronic warfare
excl excludes/excluding
exp expenditure
FAC forward air control
fd field
FF/G/H/M fire-fighting/frigate/with AShM/with hangar/with SAM
FGA fighter ground attack
FLD full-load displacement
flt flight
FMA Foreign Military Assistance
FS/G/H/M corvette/with AShM/with hangar/with SAM
FSSG force service support group
Ftr fighter
FTX field training exercise
FW fixed-wing
FY fiscal year
GBU guided bomb unit
gd guard
GDP gross domestic product
GNP gross national product
gp group
HA/DR humanitarian assistance/disaster relief
hel helicopter
HMTV high-mobility tactical vehicle
how howitzer
HQ headquarters
HUMINT human intelligence
HWT heavyweight torpedo
hy heavy
IBU inshore boat unit
ICBM intercontinental ballistic missile
IMINT imagery intelligence
imp improved
incl includes/including

indep independent
inf infantry
INS inertial navigation system
int intelligence
IR infrared
IIR imaging infrared
IRBM intermediate-range ballistic missile
ISD in-service date
ISR intelligence, surveillance and reconnaissance
ISTAR intelligence, surveillance, target acquisition and reconnaissance
LACV light armoured combat vehicle
LACM land-attack cruise missile
LC/A/AC/D/H/M/PA/PL/T/U/VP landing craft/assault/air cushion/dock/heavy/medium/personnel air cushion/personnel large/tank/utility/vehicles and personnel
LCC amphibious command ship
LFV light forces vehicles
LGB laser-guided bomb
LHA landing ship assault
LHD amphibious assault ship
LIFT lead-in ftr trainer
LKA amphibious cargo ship
lnchr launcher
log logistic
LP/D/H landing platform/dock/helicopter
LS/D/L/LH/M/T landing ship/dock/logistic/logistic helicopter/medium/tank
Lt light
LWT lightweight torpedo
maint maintenance
MANPAD man-portable air-defence system
MANPATS man-portable anti-tank system
MBT main battle tank
MC/C/I/O mine countermeasure coastal/inshore/ocean
MCD mine countermeasure diving support
MCM mine countermeasures
MCMV mine countermeasures vessel
MD military district
MDT mine diving tender
mech mechanised
med medium/medical
medevac medical evacuation
MGA machine gun artillery
MH/C/D/I/O mine hunter/coastal/drone/inshore/ocean
mil military
MIRV multiple independently targetable re-entry vehicle
MIUW mobile inshore undersea warfare
mk mark (model number)
ML minelayer
MLU mid-life update
mne marine
mob mobilisation/mobile
mod modified/modification
mor mortar
mot motorised/motor
MP maritime patrol/military police
MR maritime reconnaissance/motor rifle
MRBM medium-range ballistic missile
MRH multi-role helicopter
MRL multiple rocket launcher

MS/A/C/D/I/O/R mine sweeper/auxiliary/coastal/drone/inshore/ocean
msl missile
Mtn mountain
MW mine warfare
n.a. not applicable
n.k. not known
NBC nuclear biological chemical
NCO non-commissioned officer
nm nautical mile
nuc nuclear
O & M operations and maintenance
obs observation/observer
OCU operational conversion unit
op/ops operational/operations
OPFOR opposition training force
org organised/organisation
para paratroop/parachute
PAX passenger/passenger transport aircraft
PB/C/F/I/R patrol boat/coastal/fast/inshore/riverine
PC/C/F/G/H/I/M/O/R/T patrol craft/coastal with AShM/fast/guided missile/with hangar/inshore/with CIWS missile or SAM/offshore/riverine/torpedo
pdr pounder
pers personnel
PG/G/GF/H patrol gunboat/guided missile/fast attack craft/hydrofoil
PGM precision-guided munitions
PH/G/M/T patrol hydrofoil/with AShM/missile/torpedo
pl platoon
PKO peacekeeping operations
PPP purchasing-power parity
PPV protected patrol vehicle
PRH passive radar-homing
prepo pre-positioned
PSO/H peace support operations/offshore patrol vessel over 1,500 tonnes/with hangar
ptn pontoon bridging
qd quadrillion
quad quadruple
R&D research and development
RCL recoilless launcher/ramped craft logistic
recce reconnaissance
regt regiment
RIB rigid inflatable boat
RL rocket launcher
ro-ro roll-on, roll-off
RRC/F/U rapid-reaction corps/force/unit
RV re-entry vehicle
rvn riverine
SAM surface-to-air missile
SAR search and rescue
SARH semi-active radar homing
sat satellite
SDV swimmer delivery vehicles
SEAD suppression of enemy air defence
SF special forces
SHORAD short-range air defence
SIGINT signals intelligence
sigs signals
SLBM submarine-launched ballistic missile
SLCM submarine-launched cruise missile
SLEP service life extension programme
SP self-propelled

Spec Ops special operations
SPAAGM self-propelled anti-aircraft gun and missile system
spt support
sqn squadron
SRBM short-range ballistic missile
SS submarine
SSA submersible auxiliary support vessel
SSAN submersible auxiliary support vessel (nuclear)
SSBN nuclear-powered ballistic-missile submarine
SSC coastal submarine
SSG guided-missile submarine
SSGN nuclear-powered guided-missile submarine
SSK attack submarine with ASW capability (hunter-killer)
SSM surface-to-surface missile
SSN nuclear-powered attack submarine
SSP attack submarine with air-independent propulsion
SSW midget submarine
str strength
Surv surveillance
sy security
t tonnes
tac tactical
temp temporary
tk tank
tkr tanker
TMD theatre missile defence
torp torpedo
tpt transport
tr trillion
trg training
TRV torpedo recovery vehicle
TT torpedo tube
UAV unmanned aerial vehicle
UCAV unmanned combat air vehicle
utl utility
UUV unmanned undersea vehicle
veh vehicle
VLB vehicle launched bridge
VLS vertical launch system
VSHORAD very short-range air defence
wfu withdrawn from use
wg wing
WLIC inland construction tenders
WMD weapon(s) of mass destruction
WTGB US Coast Guard Icebreaker tugs
YAC royal yacht
YAG yard craft, miscellaneous
YDG degaussing
YDT diving tender
YFB ferry boat
YFL launch
YFRT range support tenders
YP yard patrol craft
YPT torpedo recovery vessel
YTB harbour tug
YTL light harbour tug
YTM medium harbour tug
YTR firefighting vessel
YTT torpedo trials craft
YY general yard craft

Table 14 Index of Country/Territory Abbreviations

AFG	Afghanistan	
ALB	Albania	
ALG	Algeria	
ANG	Angola	
ARG	Argentina	
ARM	Armenia	
ATG	Antigua and Barbuda	
AUS	Australia	
AUT	Austria	
AZE	Azerbaijan	
BDI	Burundi	
BEL	Belgium	
BEN	Benin	
BFA	Burkina Faso	
BGD	Bangladesh	
BHR	Bahrain	
BHS	Bahamas	
BIH	Bosnia-Herzegovina	
BIOT	British Indian Ocean Territory	
BLG	Bulgaria	
BLR	Belarus	
BLZ	Belize	
BOL	Bolivia	
BRB	Barbados	
BRN	Brunei	
BRZ	Brazil	
BWA	Botswana	
CAM	Cambodia	
CAN	Canada	
CAR	Central African Republic	
CHA	Chad	
CHE	Switzerland	
CHL	Chile	
CIV	Côte d'Ivoire	
CMR	Cameroon	
COG	Republic of Congo	
COL	Colombia	
CPV	Cape Verde	
CRI	Costa Rica	
CRO	Croatia	
CUB	Cuba	
CYP	Cyprus	
CZE	Czech Republic	
DJB	Djibouti	
DNK	Denmark	
DOM	Dominican Republic	
DPRK	Korea, Democratic People's Republic of	
DRC	Democratic Republic of the Congo	
ECU	Ecuador	
EGY	Egypt	
EQG	Equitorial Guinea	
ERI	Eritrea	
ESP	Spain	
EST	Estonia	
ETH	Ethiopia	
FIN	Finland	
FJI	Fiji	
FLK	Falkland Islands	
FRA	France	
FYROM	Macedonia, Former Yugoslav Republic	
GAB	Gabon	
GAM	Gambia	
GEO	Georgia	
GER	Germany	
GF	French Guiana	
GHA	Ghana	
GIB	Gibraltar	
GNB	Guinea-Bissau	
GRC	Greece	
GRL	Greenland	
GUA	Guatemala	
GUI	Guinea	
GUY	Guyana	
HND	Honduras	
HTI	Haiti	
HUN	Hungary	
IDN	Indonesia	
IND	India	
IRL	Ireland	
IRN	Iran	
IRQ	Iraq	
ISL	Iceland	
ISR	Israel	
ITA	Italy	
JAM	Jamaica	
JOR	Jordan	
JPN	Japan	
KAZ	Kazakhstan	
KEN	Kenya	
KGZ	Kyrgyzstan	
KWT	Kuwait	
LAO	Laos	
LBN	Lebanon	
LBR	Liberia	
LBY	Libya	
LKA	Sri Lanka	
LSO	Lesotho	
LTU	Lithuania	
LUX	Luxembourg	
LVA	Latvia	
MDA	Moldova	
MDG	Madagascar	
MEX	Mexico	
MHL	Marshall Islands	
MLI	Mali	
MLT	Malta	
MMR	Myanmar	
MNE	Montenegro	
MNG	Mongolia	
MOR	Morocco	
MOZ	Mozambique	
MRT	Mauritania	
MUS	Mauritius	
MWI	Malawi	
MYS	Malaysia	
NAM	Namibia	
NCL	New Caledonia	
NER	Niger	
NGA	Nigeria	
NIC	Nicaragua	
NLD	Netherlands	
NOR	Norway	
NPL	Nepal	
NZL	New Zealand	
OMN	Oman	
PT	Palestinian Territories	
PAN	Panama	
PAK	Pakistan	
PER	Peru	
PHL	Philippines	
POL	Poland	
PNG	Papua New Guinea	
PRC	China, People's Republic of	
PRT	Portugal	
PRY	Paraguay	
PYF	French Polynesia	
QTR	Qatar	
ROC	Taiwan (Republic of China)	
ROK	Korea, Republic of	
ROM	Romania	
RSA	South Africa	
RUS	Russia	
RWA	Rwanda	
SAU	Saudi Arabia	
SDN	Sudan	
SEN	Senegal	
SER	Serbia	
SGP	Singapore	
SLB	Solomon Islands	
SLE	Sierra Leone	
SLV	El Salvador	
SOM	Somalia	
SSD	South Sudan	
STP	São Tomé and Príncipe	
SUR	Suriname	
SVK	Slovakia	
SVN	Slovenia	
SWE	Sweden	
SYC	Seychelles	
SYR	Syria	
TGO	Togo	
THA	Thailand	
TJK	Tajikistan	
TKM	Turkmenistan	
TLS	Timor-Leste	
TTO	Trinidad and Tobago	
TUN	Tunisia	
TUR	Turkey	
TZA	Tanzania	
UAE	United Arab Emirates	
UGA	Uganda	
UK	United Kingdom	
UKR	Ukraine	
URY	Uruguay	
US	United States	
UZB	Uzbekistan	
VEN	Venezuela	
VNM	Vietnam	
YEM	Yemen, Republic of	
ZMB	Zambia	
ZWE	Zimbabwe	

Table 15 Index of Countries and Territories

Country	Code	Page	Country	Code	Page	Country	Code	Page
Afghanistan	AFG	228	Georgia	GEO	179	Niger	NER	461
Albania	ALB	72	Germany	GER	96	Nigeria	NGA	462
Algeria	ALG	319	Ghana	GHA	449	Norway	NOR	121
Angola	ANG	430	Greece	GRC	100	Oman	OMN	345
Antigua and Barbuda	ATG	375	Guatemala	GUA	399	Pakistan	PAK	276
Argentina	ARG	375	Guinea Bissau	GNB	451	Palestinian Territories	PT	347
Armenia	ARM	174	Guinea	GUI	450	Panama	PAN	407
Australia	AUS	229	Guyana	GUY	400	Papua New Guinea	PNG	280
Austria	AUT	73	Haiti	HTI	401	Paraguay	PRY	408
Azerbaijan	AZE	175	Honduras	HND	401	Peru	PER	409
Bahamas	BHS	378	Hungary	HUN	103	Philippines	PHL	280
Bahrain	BHR	321	Iceland	ISL	104	Poland	POL	123
Bangladesh	BGD	232	India	IND	247	Portugal	PRT	126
Barbados	BRB	379	Indonesia	IDN	253	Qatar	QTR	347
Belarus	BLR	177	Iran	IRN	326	Romania	ROM	128
Belgium	BEL	74	Iraq	IRQ	330	Russia	RUS	184
Belize	BLZ	379	Ireland	IRL	105	Rwanda	RWA	464
Benin	BEN	431	Israel	ISR	331	Saudi Arabia	SAU	349
Bolivia	BOL	380	Italy	ITA	106	Senegal	SEN	464
Bosnia-Herzegovina	BIH	76	Jamaica	JAM	403	Serbia	SER	130
Botswana	BWA	432	Japan	JPN	257	Seychelles	SYC	466
Brazil	BRZ	382	Jordan	JOR	335	Sierra Leone	SLE	466
Brunei	BRN	234	Kazakhstan	KAZ	180	Singapore	SGP	282
Bulgaria	BLG	77	Kenya	KEN	452	Slovakia	SVK	133
Burkina Faso	BFA	433	Korea, Democratic People's Republic of DPRK		261	Slovenia	SVN	134
Burundi	BDI	434				Somalia	SOM	467
Cambodia	CAM	235	Korea, Republic of	ROK	264	South Africa	RSA	468
Cameroon	CMR	435	Kuwait	KWT	337	South Sudan	SSD	470
Canada	CAN	37	Kyrgyzstan	KGZ	182	Spain	ESP	135
Cape Verde	CPV	436	Laos	LAO	267	Sri Lanka	LKA	285
Central African Republic	CAR	437	Latvia	LVA	111	Sudan	SDN	471
Chad	CHA	438	Lebanon	LBN	338	Suriname	SUR	412
Chile	CHL	386	Lesotho	LSO	454	Sweden	SWE	139
China, People's Republic of	PRC	237	Liberia	LBR	454	Switzerland	CHE	142
Colombia	COL	389	Libya	LBY	340	Syria	SYR	352
Congo, Republic of	COG	439	Lithuania	LTU	112	Taiwan (Republic of China)	ROC	287
Costa Rica	CRI	392	Luxembourg	LUX	114	Tajikistan	TJK	198
Côte D'Ivoire	CIV	440	Macedonia, Former Yugoslav Republic FYROM		114	Tanzania	TZA	473
Croatia	CRO	79				Thailand	THA	290
Cuba	CUB	392	Madagascar	MDG	455	Timor-Leste	TLS	293
Cyprus	CYP	81	Malawi	MWI	456	Togo	TGO	475
Czech Republic	CZE	83	Malaysia	MYS	268	Trinidad and Tobago	TTO	413
Democratic Republic of the Congo	DRC	442	Mali	MLI	457	Tunisia	TUN	354
			Malta	MLT	116	Turkey	TUR	144
Denmark	DNK	85	Mauritania	MRT	341	Turkmenistan	TKM	199
Djibouti	DJB	443	Mauritius	MUS	458	Uganda	UGA	476
Dominican Republic	DOM	394	Mexico	MEX	403	Ukraine	UKR	200
Ecuador	ECU	395	Moldova	MDA	183	United Arab Emirates	UAE	355
Egypt	EGY	323	Mongolia	MNG	271	United Kingdom	UK	147
El Salvador	SLV	397	Montenegro	MNE	117	United States	US	40
Equatorial Guinea	EQG	444	Morocco	MOR	342	Uruguay	URY	413
Eritrea	ERI	445	Mozambique	MOZ	459	Uzbekistan	UZB	203
Estonia	EST	87	Multinational Organisations		118	Venezuela	VEN	415
Ethiopia	ETH	446	Myanmar	MMR	272	Vietnam	VNM	293
Fiji	FJI	246	Namibia	NAM	460	Yemen, Republic of	YEM	358
Finland	FIN	88	Nepal	NPL	274	Zambia	ZMB	477
France	FRA	90	Netherlands	NLD	118	Zimbabwe	ZWE	478
Gabon	GAB	447	New Zealand	NZL	275			
Gambia	GAM	449	Nicaragua	NIC	406			